John Kenneth Galbraith

JOHN KENNETH GALBRAITH

His Life, His Politics,

His Economics

Richard Parker

FARRAR, STRAUS AND GIROUX

NEW YORK

Farrar, Straus and Giroux
19 Union Square West, New York 10003

All the photographs included here are reprinted with
the kind permission of John Kenneth and Catherine Galbraith,
from whose personal collection they come. Additional grateful acknowledgment is made to
the following for permission to reprint the following photographs: JKG with Gloria Steinem:
© Burt Glinn, Magnum; JKG on motorcycle: © Bernard Charlon; JKG strolling in Paris
park: © Bernard Charlon; JKG with Schlesinger: © Jim Hamilton; JKG with Greenspan,
Moynihan: © Ron Edmunds, AP Laserphoto; JKG with Streisand: © Martha Stewart; JKG
and Kitty in Vermont: © John Goodman.

Library of Congress Cataloging-in-Publication Data
Parker, Richard, 1946–
    John Kenneth Galbraith : his life, his politics, his economics / Richard Parker.
        p.   cm.
    Includes bibliographical references and index.
    ISBN-13: 978-0-374-28168-7
    ISBN-10: 0-374-28168-8 (alk. paper)
    1. Galbraith, John Kenneth, 1908–   2. Economists—United States—
Biography.   I. Title.

HB119.G33P37 2005
330'.092—dc22

                                                                2004057595

Designed by Debbie Glasserman

www.fsgbooks.com

1   3   5   7   9   10   8   6   4   2

*To my wife, Robin, whose love made this book possible
and to whom my debt is boundless*

We shall not succeed in banishing what besets us—the sense of being born too late for a great political era—unless we understand how to become the forerunner of a greater one.

— MAX WEBER

CONTENTS

John Kenneth Galbraith

INTRODUCTION

On First Coming to Cambridge

THE SUMMER SUN had risen shortly after five that early September morning, and by seven the sky already promised both faint warmth and a fine New England day. Out in Cape Cod Bay, the S.S. *Acadia*, a coastal steamer of the old Merchant & Miners line, was cutting northward through calm waters on her regular two-day run from Baltimore to Boston. She was due to dock in less than three hours, and at the rail of her upper deck a lanky young passenger was peering carefully westward at the low Massachusetts coastline off her port side.

He'd been up since dawn, as the ship passed through the Cape Cod Canal; now he watched as the gray rocky shore slid by, its beaches backed with green pine and oak, the treeline broken here and there by occasional houses and compact little villages and towns. A crew member had paused momentarily to point out Plymouth, where the Pilgrims had landed three centuries earlier and he'd thanked the man politely, then continued to watch as fishing boats made their way out from small harbors in search of the day's catch in the quiet bay. He noticed that a few other of the *Acadia*'s passengers were up now, too, strolling the decks, ready to start their own day.

Several of his fellow passengers, as they passed, took note of the young man, as they had casually ever since they sailed: at six feet eight inches, after all, he quickly and naturally stood out among them. At dinner the night before, he'd chatted pleasantly with his table companions and, in response to their questions, told something about himself.

He was an economist, they'd discovered, with a freshly minted Ph.D. from the University of California, awarded that June. Just twenty-five years old, he'd been in Washington for the summer, working for one of President Roosevelt's new "alphabet agencies," something called the Agricultural Adjustment Administration. His listeners, all East Coast city dwellers, weren't quite sure what the year-old "Triple A" did exactly, but they understood that now, in 1934, with America mired deep in the Depression, the one out of three Americans who still farmed were in desperate need of help—and were a priority for the New Deal.

He'd worked, they'd learned, on the question of abandoned, tax-delinquent farmlands—a "very large problem," he assured them, involving millions of acres across the country. At issue, he said—and here a couple of his Republican tablemates had winced—was the possibility of their takeover by the federal government. His companions seemed calmed and duly impressed, however, when the young man explained that he was now sailing to Boston to begin teaching at Harvard University. Harvard, they must have felt, would surely shield him from further exposure to the dangerous and radical currents then flowing in Washington.

Something about the young man would have struck them, though. He was very confident, clearly intelligent, and over the course of their leisurely evening meal, able to range across a wide variety of topics having to do with the country's immense economic crisis. His tan summer suit, slicked-back chestnut hair, horn-rimmed glasses, and polished brown shoes all bespoke attentiveness to the academic style of the day. Handsomely attractive in a rugged way, with strongly drawn features, he projected great vitality and ambition, making him appear the sort of man Harvard valued. There was this troublesome issue of his working for Roosevelt, and his obvious admiration for the new President and his policies, but Harvard would no doubt smooth that out with time, settle him down, point him in the right direction.

As they finished their coffees and made their good nights, several at the table might even have guessed that this young fellow would be "going places," someone who with good luck and time would leave a mark.

CELEBRITY, IN MODERN AMERICAN LIFE, is a transient, ephemeral thing, bestowed almost randomly nowadays by the media, especially the omnivorous cyclops lens of television. Sitcom stars, popular singers, athletes, accident victims, lottery winners, successful (or disgraced) politicians all race past us in an unending cavalcade, forgotten the next week or next year, displaced by whatever new face has been chosen to replace them.

True fame is something different. The ancient Greeks understood it to reflect character, and mere celebrity had nothing to do with it. To them, character was a tapestry woven of innate abilities and virtues, imprinted with the stamp of experience and with destiny. Unlike celebrity, it rightly marked only a few and endured much longer.

Today—seventy years after that voyage, and more than a half century since his writing first won him widespread acclaim—the Harvard professor John Kenneth Galbraith remains the world's most famous living economist. The author of four dozen books and more than eleven hundred articles, recipient of nearly fifty honorary degrees, former president of the American Economic Association as well as a former ambassador and presidential adviser, he has continued writing, traveling, and lecturing into his nineties. And as his dinner-mates instinctively understood that night aboard the *Acadia*, he has in innumerable ways left his mark upon his times.

In the late summer of 1934, though, striding down the gangplank of the *Acadia* after she docked at Boston's Commonwealth Pier, Ken Galbraith (as he has always preferred to be known) was just a young, unknown university instructor. To be sure, he was going to be teaching at America's premier university, but he was one of several hundred young men like him, just then pouring into Cambridge as others like them had for years, young men full of promise but still untested for real achievement. Yet as we look back at the scene now, seven decades later, we can see that three defining influences on Galbraith's later, mature character were already evident, influences that would mark his subsequent Harvard career, his relation to the larger world of economics, and his ultimate fame.

The first revealed itself in the way he got to Cambridge. Unlike most of the other faculty and students arriving to begin their fall classes, Galbraith's choice of the *Acadia* set him apart. Choosing to come by ship wasn't happenstance; the Baltimore & Ohio Raid Road's overnight train from Washington would have been faster and cheaper, hence more efficient, a notion almost sacred to most economists then as now. But to this young economist, efficiency alone was already only one criterion among many worth considering, and he had wanted something distinctive to mark his first coming to Cambridge as memorable. Because he'd never seen the Atlantic Ocean, the choice of ship's travel had thus been an easy one. The leisurely voyage, for which he paid $18 (berth and meals included), offered plenty of time for contemplation of expansive sea vistas and, not surprisingly, had filled his mind with a sense of life's vast possibilities. Harvard itself, he realized even then, promised to be the start of a future rich with opportunity.[1]

The choice of a sea voyage revealed a second important characteristic: it was the latest twist and turn in a career path that already showed signs of being distinctively circuitous and often challenging. He'd been born in 1908 into an Ontario farm family, and his early academic experience hardly seemed to prepare him for a Harvard faculty appointment. Unlike so many of the other young men around him, there had been no prep-school training, no trips to Europe for "polish," no Ivy League education. Instead he'd grown up in tiny Iona Station, a farming hamlet just north of Lake Erie with only twenty-five or thirty inhabitants then, and been educated at Willey's School, the local one-room schoolhouse, with a dozen or so other students, and then at the high school in nearby Dutton Township.[2] From Iona Station, he'd graduated to the singularly undistinguished Ontario Agricultural College, where he'd taken five years to earn a bachelor's degree.

What's more, although now he was about to join the economics department of America's most distinguished university, at OAC he hadn't even majored in economics, but in animal husbandry. Shorthorns and Herefords were what he'd studied, not cost curves or maximizing equations. Indeed, only after jour-

neying nearly twenty-five hundred miles west to California had he been introduced to the issues and methods of modern professional economics. As he recalled years later, not until he went to graduate school at the University of
California at Berkeley did he discover such prominent economic figures as "Alfred Marshall or Thorstein Veblen, or learn much about Marx, apart from what
one read in the papers."[3]

Galbraith's arrival in Cambridge also revealed a third characteristic factor:
Harvard's distinguished faculty, its senior economists included, barely took
notice of him that day, or in the weeks or months thereafter. Under the circumstances, this in itself was not unusual. Galbraith was only another new
instructor appointed for a one-year term. Moreover, his specialty, agricultural
economics, was hardly going to capture the attention of either the university's
urbane faculty or its well-groomed and privileged student body.

These three partly innate, partly imposed attributes—a cultivated and self-
conscious singularity of thought and style, a certain circuitousness of career,
and a marked distancing on the part of cautious or conservative colleagues—
have helped to define much of what is distinctive in John Kenneth Galbraith's
life, and in his work in economics. By now, of course, the early promise of his
character has been maturely realized, and few admirers or critics could argue
that his life has been without influence or effect. By the time he retired in
1975 as Paul M. Warburg Professor of Economics at Harvard, he'd been
elected president of the American Economic Association, and after, he was
made president of the American Academy of Arts and Letters, a double honor
no one else has shared and a measure of his intellectual range. He'd served as
adviser to three American presidents, ambassador to India, an editor of *Fortune*, and, during World War II, "tsar" of consumer price controls. His writing
on economics, not least the seven million copies of his books that have been
published in nearly three dozen languages, had made him the most widely
known American economist of the twentieth century. His distinctive voice and
imagination added a lengthy list of memorable phrases to economic argument
and the English language—"the affluent society," "the conventional wisdom,"
"countervailing power," "the technostructure," to name only a few.

Yet for all his successes, Ken Galbraith remains a disputed figure in American economics and public life. His unabashedly, eloquently liberal political
views have in recent years (as in other times past) been out of step with dominant trends. His economics, deeply entwined with his politics, has brought
discomfort, criticism, and even occasional scorn from a vocal coterie of colleagues, who sometimes label his notions as perhaps interesting but finally
marginal contributions to what they think of as the mathematically sophisticated "mainstream" of contemporary economic thought. The MIT economist
(and Nobel laureate) Paul Samuelson, for example, no doubt spoke for many
lesser-known colleagues when he dryly described Galbraith as "America's foremost economist for non-economists."

But is this description of his work, and its contributions to how we think
about economics and its relationship to politics and power, fair or, more impor-

tant, accurate? To be sure, there is no "Galbraithian" school per se as, say, there have been "Keynesian" or "Marshallian" schools in modern economics. Yet Galbraith's persistent critiques of the mainstream's dominant assumptions and research methods have had much more effect than Samuelson's slighting words might suggest.

Consider a survey of economists published in 1979 by the *American Economic Review* that measured consensus about key theoretical points within the profession. Among the thirty questions asked, only one mentioned a specific economist by name—the often-dissident Galbraith. The question concerned his famously corrosive assault on "the corporate state," the centerpiece of perhaps his most controversial major work, *The New Industrial State*. Asked whether his critique "accurately depicted the context and structure of the U.S. economy"— even though it eschewed mathematical models and flew in the face of mainstream notions like "market efficiency" and hence the very foundations of economic orthodoxy itself—52 percent said they *agreed* with Galbraith.[4] Hearing the news, Galbraith declared himself satisfied that 48 percent disagreed.[5]

BUT IN SEPTEMBER 1934, this young economist, fresh off the *Acadia* and staring up at Boston's modest skyline, could hardly anticipate the career or achievements that lay ahead, or the complicated, sometimes contradictory, turns modern economics itself would take. For the moment, he could satisfy himself that he was now a member of America's most highly regarded economics department, at the country's most prestigious university, and leave the rest while he attended to the mundane matters of beginning a new life.

From Boston Harbor, Galbraith rode over to Cambridge by subway, crossing the Charles River in the early afternoon's heat to Harvard Square. By arrangement, his luggage was meanwhile forwarded directly to the simple lodgings he had booked in the home of two elderly Yankee ladies named Bradford, a short walk from Harvard Yard.

Leaving the subway station, he gazed on the red-brick outer walls of Harvard Yard, the center of the university's life and its home since 1636. Around him, traffic coursed noisily up and down Massachusetts Avenue, and pedestrians crowded the sidewalks. The Harvard students stood out: confident young men distinguished by the coats and ties that were then still customary undergraduate dress, who carried bags toward their lodgings or books freshly purchased from the Harvard Cooperative Society across the Square.

Later that day, after paying his first call on the economics department, Galbraith was shown to his own office—a "large, gloomy room," he still glumly recalls, on the top floor of Widener Library, some distance from the main economics faculty. Here he would begin his Harvard career.

That evening, the young instructor, perhaps hoping to create a positive first impression, shared with his new landladies, the Misses Bradford, an account of his just-finished heady summer's foray into the New Deal and the AAA. Whatever he intended, the tales of Rooseveltian activism apparently caused the two old Yankee Republicans to take umbrage, because the next morning they invited him to leave. At first taken aback, Galbraith soon found lodgings on Irving Terrace, nearby. His new landlady was "an Irish woman of ferocious aspect" who "tolerated me for the academic year," he warmly remembers, "and the Boston Irish have ever since been deep in my affection."[6]

But if his first few hours in Cambridge brought rather sudden change to the young Canadian's new life, it was small compared to the momentous change then sweeping not just the department and university he was joining, but the economics profession as well, and, most important, the United States itself. As part of a textile workers strike stretching from Maine to Georgia, 20,000 militant workers in nearby Lowell, Lawrence, and New Bedford had clashed that same day with state police armed with truncheons, outside darkened mills protected by barbed wire and wooden barricades. In Maine, Rhode Island, and Connecticut, governors had called out the National Guard to deal with more than 150,000 strikers, and the Boston papers were reporting "a looming insurrection" in the South. Nearly a dozen strikers had been killed, riots had occurred in several cities, and the White House was being beseiged by calls to use troops to quell them.[7]

Franklin Roosevelt had been in office barely eighteen months, and for the new President this strike was only the latest, and by no means largest, crisis he'd faced. In March 1933, he had come down from his Albany governorship into the midst of the worst collapse American capitalism had yet—or has since—known. An estimated 13 million Americans, one quarter of the U.S. workforce, were out of work (though some put the real number closer to 20 million); national income had fallen by well over half in the previous four years, foreign trade by two thirds.[8] During the same period, annual auto production had dropped from 2.7 million new cars to just 600,000, while agricultural prices had plummeted 40 percent, and the New York Stock Exchange, where the average share price had fallen from $90 to just $17, now bore, as one journalist caustically remarked, striking resemblance to Flanders Field.[9]

Roosevelt's Republican predecessor, the ill-starred Herbert Hoover, had presided over this unprecedented collapse, and until too late he had failed to grasp the magnitude of the crisis. In June 1930, for example, to reassure a delegation of frightened business leaders who had come to the White House seeking federal action, he had blithely announced, "Gentlemen, you have come sixty days too late. The depression is over."[10] Speaking at the very moment when, as the economist Joseph Schumpeter later wrote, "people felt the ground give way beneath their feet,"[11] President Hoover's flawed sense of timing was impeccable: it was, of course, just the beginning. (Hoover's aides didn't help his popularity with the electorate. After initially insisting there was "no cause for worry" and that stocks were "cheap at current prices," his millionaire Secretary of the Treasury, Andrew Mellon, came around to believing there was only one solution to the crisis: "Liquidate labor, liquidate stocks," he declared, "liquidate the farmers, liquidate real estate."[12]) In reward, Hoover had been swept from office after one term in a landslide defeat without precedent in American history.

In his inaugural address, FDR clearly sought to reassure his frightened countrymen in the depths of their nightmare, especially when he promised that "the only thing we have to fear is fear itself." But even Roosevelt was unprepared for the response his words evoked. During the next few days, more than half a million letters flooded the White House mailroom. The overwhelming majority declared their support for the new President, but among them were thousands that carried simpler and more direct messages: "Mr. President, can you get me a job?"; "Mr. Roosevelt, please save my farm"; "Dear Mr. President, I can't feed my family. Please help." After seven decades of mostly Republican political domination, with the once-booming economy lying shattered and in ruins, the country was ready not only for Democrats in the White House and Congress, but for dramatic change. But what exactly needed to be done? And what risks did such change entail?

Eleanor Roosevelt later recalled Inauguration Day as "very, very solemn, and a little terrifying." It was terrifying most of all, she wrote in her diary that night, "because when Franklin got to that part of his speech where he said it might become necessary for him to assume powers ordinarily granted to a President in war time, he received his biggest demonstration." Adolf Hitler had become the new Reich Chancellor a month earlier, and with Stalin and Mussolini in power, what could this possibly mean for the future of American democracy? "One has a feeling of going it blindly," she wrote in anguish that night, "because we're in a tremendous stream, and none of us knows where we're going to land."[13]

Mrs. Roosevelt wasn't alone in her fears. Several years later, and still pledging them to secrecy, the President told some of his aides of his own feelings during his first moments in the Oval Office. The morning after the inaugural, one of them later recounted, Roosevelt said he awakened

> with a pressing sense of work to be done, ate an early breakfast and had himself wheeled over to his new office. There, seated for the first time in the presidential chair, he found himself suddenly alone in the empty room. The desk was empty, the drawers were empty, the President could not even find pencil and pad to make a note. He looked for buzzers on the desk, but found no button to push, no way to signal the outside world. He sat for a moment, the great chamber echoing and silent, the center of action cut off from the nation at the moment of crisis. At last he bestirred himself and gave a mighty shout, which brought [his aides] Missy LeHand and Marvin McIntyre running from adjacent rooms.[14]

Fortunately for the rest of the country, only a trusted few would hear that story until after "The Boss" was dead. But realizing that the President himself felt adrift that first morning in office only underscores why his wife spoke of those early days as "terrifying."

As Roosevelt began to face not just the burdens but the dangers of his office, throughout much of the country many of his own supporters and nominal allies were engaged in ferocious debates. What should the new administration do? What were its programs? What were its goals, its visions? And was Roosevelt in fact the man for the job?

"The fashion of the liberal left in the election of 1932, it is now forgotten, was to dismiss Roosevelt and Hoover as equally hopeless," Galbraith still vividly recalls. "People of perception supported [the Socialist Party candidate] Norman Thomas, and the intellectually uncompromising were for the Communists or else they disdained involvement." The country's conservative and established citizens meanwhile predictably greeted such views with unalloyed alarm, and in some cases with the darkest fears, in their own minds quickly linking Roosevelt to his Socialist and Communist challengers.

To Galbraith, who closely followed these debates (even though, as a Canadian citizen, he was ineligible to vote), support for either the Socialists and Communists or their conservative opponents (not all of them Republicans) seemed unimaginable. "As a youngster in Canada, I had a different instruction. There were two parties and you chose, or more likely were born to, one or the other. Every family was known for its party as it was known for its church."[15]

Birthright (or birth duty) for Galbraith was augmented by his own father's active work as a Liberal Party figure of some note back in Ontario. From the age of nine or ten, Ken had regularly accompanied his father to local electoral events for tutelage in the arts of political persuasion. Years later he still loves to recall his father's lesson about humor's power by telling how Galbraith senior once mounted a manure pile at a farm rally to address the audience—and then proceeded to apologize for speaking from the Tory platform.[16]

Though FDR's taking office was marked by an initial momentary uncertainty, the President moved swiftly to overcome this sense of dazed paralysis. Within days, his aides were furiously working to draft a series of extraordinarily bold acts and declarations designed, in the clichéd words of every can-do politician since, to "get the country moving again." Vigor and swift action set the tone, even when the legislation and proclamations, on later, more sober reflection, left much for the measure.

Now enshrined in our history as "the Hundred Days," those first few months of the Roosevelt administration have formed the benchmark for activist government ever since, whether liberal or conservative—a measure of presidents as keenly understood by Ronald Reagan as by John F. Kennedy or Lyndon Johnson. What Roosevelt himself recognized was that, more than a consistent program, the country hungered for consistent action, for a sense that something was being done in Washington to make things better, or at least not make them worse.

The historian Arthur Schlesinger, Jr., has captured the breathtaking output of America's new leader:

> In the three months after Roosevelt's inauguration, Congress and the country were subjected to a presidential barrage of ideas and programs unlike any-

thing known to American history . . . In this period Franklin Roosevelt sent fifteen messages to Congress, guided fifteen major laws to enactment, delivered ten speeches, held press conferences and cabinet meetings twice a week, conducted talks with foreign heads of state, sponsored an international conference, made all the major decisions in domestic and foreign policy, and never displayed fright or panic and rarely even bad temper. His mastery astonished many who thought that they had long since taken his measure. [White House aide] Norman Davis, encountering [his colleague] Raymond Fosdick outside the presidential office, expressed the incredulity of those who had worked with him during the Wilson administration: "Ray, that fellow in there is not the fellow we used to know. There's been a miracle here."[17]

Roosevelt's activism inspired his admirers, and worried—in some cases terrified—his detractors. Republican congressmen and the Hearst newspapers, which had stridently supported his Republican opponent in 1932, began talking darkly of the President's "communistic" policies; among the wealthy, he was famously reviled as "a traitor to his class." In one telling sign of just how heated such conservative fears were, in March 1934 several newspapers (including *The New York Times*, on its front page) reported allegations that plans for an imminent coup were being secretly drawn up by some of the President's own aides. Based on purported conversations with members of FDR's "Brains Trust," the papers claimed that Roosevelt himself was personally unaware of the plans and would be replaced by an unnamed "American Stalin."[18]

Opposition to Roosevelt's programs, and their thrust toward an activist government's deep involvement in America's capitalist economy in order to save it, wasn't solely the province of the President's radical left or conservative critics. Among America's then-small fraternity of professional economists, the direction in which FDR seemed to be heading was a cause for alarm.

Debates over economics and public policy were hardly new to America, of course. In the late 1760s, hatred of Britain's Stamp Act, for example, which had been intended to regulate America's colonial trade in the mercantilist tradition, had fueled calls for the American Revolution. The early republic had found itself repeatedly embroiled in contentious struggles over issues such as government land policy, tariffs, monetary and banking questions, and of course most violently over free labor versus slavery. Even though the Civil War brutally settled the slavery issue, other questions endured as the Industrial Revolution took root, and were joined by new debates over unions, railroad and utility regulation, immigration, monopoly, stock market fraud, wages and working conditions, and the manifold problems of America's burgeoning new cities.

But economics as an academically trained *profession* was something much newer. Harvard awarded the nation's first Ph.D. in economics only in the late 1870s, and as late as 1900 there were no more than a hundred or so U.S.-trained Ph.D. economists in the country. On the eve of the Depression that number still probably exceeded no more than 2,000 to 2,500, in a population of 120 million.[19] Guided by the model of the natural sciences that had emerged in the nineteenth century, the dominant group among these new "scientific" economists still struggled to present themselves as "value-free," dispassionate, neutral analysts. In this, they were aided immeasurably by publication of Alfred Marshall's *Principles of Economics* (1890), an eight-hundred-page work that set forth the field's fundamental ideas and methods. As the foundation of what is called "neoclassical" economics, this book still broadly guides the profession today, and by the 1920s was the principal introduction to the field for students (Galbraith at Berkeley included).

To most of those who embraced Marshall's views, the ideas embodied in the New Deal were anathema, because they represented an overt interference by government in the otherwise efficient workings of markets. To be sure, Marshall himself had recognized that markets might fluctuate and thereby produce, on occasion, troubling recession or inflation, but left alone they were self-correcting and would return to an "equilibrium" that fully and efficiently utilized capital, workers, and natural resources. To Marshall's followers, this was the inviolate and core axiom of "scientific economics" itself.[20]

But the reputation of these economists, with their calculus- and geometry-based mathematical proofs that "markets know best," had suffered at the start of the Great Depression. Irving Fisher of Yale, perhaps the best-known of them, had, for example, after careful study, confidently assured investors that "stock prices have reached what looks like a permanently high plateau." Unfortunately, he spoke just weeks before the Great Crash in October 1929. Yale's finest was not alone in his error. Joseph Stagg Lawrence of Princeton, in a similarly mistimed statement that achieved minor notoriety, insisted that "stocks are not at present over-valued," even though price/earnings ratios in some industries had by then soared above 50 (much as Internet stocks did in the 1990s), five times the market's long-run average.

A month *after* the Great Crash, not to be outdone, Harvard economists ventured their own "scientific" appraisal of the situation through the Harvard Economic Society, one of America's first ventures in academic forecasting for private clients. Although it had been mildly bearish in early 1929, the society now, with the wreckage of the New York exchanges in plain view, reassured its wealthy patrons that "a severe depression like that of 1920–21 is outside the range of probability. We are not facing protracted liquidation." The society kept reiterating this view until it was itself liquidated not long thereafter.[21]

Their predictive errors notwithstanding, the election of Franklin Roosevelt in November 1932 brought new cause for alarm to many of these men. If Roosevelt carried through on the assumptions behind the torrent of legislation passed in "the Hundred Days," there was more than a problem of prediction; it was a matter of fundamental policies that threatened the very theories on which Marshall's economics had until then operated and, they feared, the "free market" structure of the American economy itself.

In late 1933, in a hastily published volume entitled *The Economics of the Recovery Program*, a group of Harvard economists struck hard at the President's early New Deal policies. Because the book denounced the government's various interventions in the markets virtually across the board and did so from an ostensibly "scientific," not political, point of view (and because it came from *Harvard*, no less), it earned widespread attention from the press and for a time threatened to precipitate an authentic political crisis in Washington. The crisis eventually passed, but the book was a clear sign of the mood not just among professional economists but specifically at Harvard. It underscores even today the currents roiling the young profession, millions of people in the economy itself, and America's dramatically shifting views about the proper interconnection between the private and public sectors in national life.

Through the accident of luck, timing, and circumstance, then, Galbraith began his work at what would turn out to be perhaps the twentieth century's single most important juncture, not just for modern economics but for the American economy and government. As surely as the Great War had overturned vast swaths of Europe's ancient monarchies and empires, here now America was about to overthrow many of the patterns and convictions that had governed it since the Revolution. And in this, the new profession of academic economics not only was going to lead the way, but would find itself transformed.

It has recently become common—indeed fashionable—to talk about the end of the New Deal legacy that was born in 1934. In this view, Franklin Roosevelt's idea of activist government, and the kind of economic theory eventually (if somewhat inaccurately) labeled "Keynesian"—activist, interventionist, and liberally purposive—with which Galbraith is associated, has come to a close. Replacing it, we are told, is our "new" era; the Information Age has replaced the Industrial Age; computers, fiber optics, and biotechnology are the new iron and steel of American economic power; and with them is coming a new way not just of doing things, but of living itself. We're told we'll be "set free" to change our jobs (and careers) repeatedly, to manage our health care, investments, and retirement on our own, to compete globally, and thereby to win (if we compete successfully) an unprecedented new prosperity alongside our new freedom.

But how new is all this? And what can we learn from reexamining the origins of, and reasons for, that world we are now said to be leaving? Americans notoriously are given to constant reinvention of themselves, their assumptions, and their dreams. But that was true in 1934, too, when both leaders like Roosevelt and young men like Galbraith set out to reinvent the world *they* had inherited.

What issues were they facing? What divisions of belief, habit, prejudice— let alone class, religion, race, and background—explain how their generation arrived at their crossroads? In 1934, the United States was living through its worst economic crisis. The economic crises of the recent past—oil-price hikes, stagflation, the savings-and-loan debacle, Third World debt and Asian, Russian, or Mexican collapse, Social Security's presumed perils, the country's widening wealth and income gaps, to note but a few—all pale compared to the crisis of the 1930s.

The United States survived, and it did so in the context and as a result of the material and intellectual world that was being reborn and slowly rebuilt out of the disaster. For our own sake, then, we should consider what that generation did, where it came from, and how it created the world we were born into.

To be sure, market capitalism's greatest political challenge is now gone, swept away with the rubble of the Berlin Wall. And so, too, new technologies abound that promise to reshape the way we live. On this we can agree. But those realities alone don't have guaranteed outcomes. The revolutions in science and technology of the early twentieth century—the airplane, automobile, radio, motion picture, phonograph, the stunning advances in physics and chemistry and medicine—were as important as the Internet and the personal computer, cellular phones, satellites and optic fibers, and advances in genetics that we rush to celebrate today. Yet they did not guarantee unending peace and prosperity. Likewise, with the Middle East unstable, China and Russia immense question marks, and much of the Third World in worse economic straits than it was twenty-five years ago, who can say for certain what the new century holds for us?

What John Kenneth Galbraith's life gives us is more than the chance to see the prodigious career of a single man. It is the opportunity to revisit not only his own views about how modern economies (and governments) should operate, but the larger world of transformed, and still transforming, economic theories of which they are a part and with which they sometimes clash, to gauge the economies they seek to guide, and thus to understand something larger about where we are all now going.

1

Growing Up in Special Places

IN THE FALL of 1934, a twenty-five-year-old Canadian economist freshly arrived at Harvard stood at a crossroads. How had he gotten there? What forces had propelled him, and what had brought his world to such a juncture? We need to turn back a quarter century to 1908, which for many today feels like a simpler time, to answer those questions.

On October 15 of that year, John Kenneth Galbraith was born into one of the world's quieter and more remote corners, the hamlet of Iona Station, Ontario, Canada. He was delivered, at home, as most children were in those days, in the back upstairs bedroom of his family's two-story, white clapboard farmhouse. Several days later, the local weekly, *The Dutton Advance*, duly noted the baby's healthy arrival, the third child born to William Archibald Galbraith and his wife, Sarah Catherine Kendall Galbraith.

Archie and Kate, as his parents were known, owned not one but two modest farms totaling a comfortable 150 acres. Archie had inherited much of the original farm from his father in the mid-1890s, and then built a home on it for his new bride, adding a second nearby property shortly after. Painted white with green trim and wrapped by a wide veranda, the Galbraiths' four-bedroom house stood along a two-lane gravel road, surrounded by oak, maple, apple, and pear trees; a large garden in back supplied much of the family's produce, and several green frame outbuildings included a large barn and a garage for their Model T Ford.

Like neighboring farms along Hogg Street, as the road was known, the Galbraith property gave off an air of a modestly comfortable and secure prosperity. Although farm equipment and livestock shared the various structures scattered across the large yard, the neighborhood itself felt quietly genteel by rural standards. (According to local legend, boosters had added the second *g* to "Hogg" Street to betoken the gentility.[1])

It is easy now to imagine such a setting untouched by the momentous forces even then forging our "modern world"—and in many respects Iona Station was just that. Galbraith has recalled the quality with slightly mixed affection:

> I remember it . . . as having a breathtaking loveliness . . . On a dozen winter
> mornings the snow was deep over the fields and fences and sat in great
> patches on the evergreens in the yard. The purity of color was matched by
> equal purity of line. Even the steep roofs of the houses disappeared under a
> white mantle, with somewhat of the architecture of an English thatch curving
> gently out from the eave . . . [and] a full moon turned everything into a shim-
> mering fairyland. On such nights we went skating at Gow's gravel pit and
> came home in subdued wonder at what we saw.
>
> [T]here were other moments—one of them when the apple trees blos-
> somed and the grass was rich and green against the newly seeded land . . .
> [T]he spring brought thick patches of violets and forget-me-nots and a little
> later of wild phlox . . . Every three or four years circumstances favored black-
> berries and one picked them for hours under a bright green and red canopy of
> sumac, encountering at intervals one's neighbors similarly engaged.

Yet Galbraith is quick to poke holes in his own recollections, lest a modern urban reader view them solely as pastoral reverie:

> Other children of which one read had streams to patrol and mountains to
> climb and some natural curiosities such as caves or springs. We had none of
> these. A spring was only a muddy hole where the cattle watered. One brook
> ran in a dull way from the end of a tile drain just beyond our farm to the lake
> five or six miles to the south. It had water in it for only a few weeks in the
> spring and after especially heavy rains . . . The only available hill could be
> climbed in a matter of four or five minutes.[2]

But however pastoral and remote, this rural countryside was far from untouched by the outside world. Iona Station is located about as far south as a Canadian town can be, set low in the province of Ontario just a few miles above Lake Erie's northern shore. Cleveland lies only sixty miles south, across the lake; Detroit is a hundred miles west and Buffalo only a bit farther east. Regularly each morning, the big-city newspapers would arrive from Toronto, Ottawa, and Windsor, pitched along with the mailbag onto the local station platform from a passing express train.

Each evening, the local farmers would pause after dinner and final chores to read from those papers, typically from the *Toronto Globe*, known locally as "the Bible" for its stalwart Liberal Party support and progressive views, and the faith these Scots-Canadians placed in it.[3] Some read by kerosene light, others (including the Galbraiths) by their recently installed electric lamps. Most checked the grain and livestock prices in Chicago or Toronto first, then the car-loadings of wheat in Minneapolis or Winnipeg or the tons of flour processed by mills in nearby Buffalo. After that, some readers—though not all—turned back to the front pages, to learn about broader matters, including affairs in Ottawa and Washington and the events and larger forces that shaped them.

The world those papers described in 1908 often appeared to their readers as convulsive as it would seem in 1934. It was one of those historical moments when on a dozen fronts simultaneously, an entire age seemed to be giving way to the next. That year in Detroit, the first Model T went on sale, and the first oil well was drilled in the Middle East. The Grand Canyon became a national park, and the FBI was formed; both J. C. Penney and the first exhibit of Cubist paintings opened to the public. Mother's Day was inaugurated and the first international meeting of psychiatrists convened; the Geiger counter was invented, and the Austro-Hungarian Empire annexed Bosnia and Herzegovina. The Geiger counter's significance wasn't fully understood until 1945, but the effects of Vienna's actions came quickly.

By 1914, the bloodiest and most extensive war the world had ever seen would unfold from an assassin's bullet in the Balkans. Within a decade, the United States would start to displace Britain as the world's dominant political and financial power. In both Europe and Asia, empires that had survived centuries of turmoil came crashing down, and the specter of Marxist revolution triumphed in Russia after a long struggle over the rights and powers of industrial workers.

Since prehistoric times agriculture had employed most men and women, but it was now in a downward employment spiral on both sides of the Atlantic, as farmers everywhere well knew. In 1908, farming and farm-related work still occupied a majority of Canadians and Americans, but just barely. (By 1911, Canada's rural population outnumbered city dwellers by about 1 million out of a 7 million total, though in Ontario, a slight majority was by then urban.[4]) The direction of change toward cities, factories, shops, and services was irreversible.

Technology's vast modern sweep—electricity, the automobile, the telephone, the airplane, even common household appliances now taken for granted—was the source of endless wonder, discussion, and excitement. Since the mid-nineteenth century, the custom of organizing "world's fairs" had become popular in Europe, and it transferred easily to North America, especially after the success of the Philadelphia Centennial Exposition, in 1876. These celebrations of technology's wonders, with their glass palaces and iron towers, immense networks of electrical lighting, mechanical amusements, and the latest machinery, transfixed those who came to see them, or who heard of them from neighbors or relatives lucky enough to attend, as was the case in Iona Station. In the public imagination, these great pageants captured the benign promise that science and technology held out for humankind.

Politically and economically, the world of 1908 was also in change, and here the change felt less benign, for industrialism's advances had created new poverty and suffering. South of Iona Station, in the United States, politics by 1908 was in the midst of the Progressive Era, when an alarmed middle class sought to stem the sufferings the new capitalist order imposed on its workers, and simultaneously to secure a new, "scientific" kind of state and social order that placed public rationality, nonviolent but far-reaching reform, and extensive new democratic structures at the heart of public life. Theodore Roosevelt, the Rough Rider whose sharp attacks on "malefactors of great wealth" and "trust-busting" assaults on corporate power made him a new kind of Republican, was President. Muckraking journalists like Ida Tarbell, Lincoln Steffens, and Ray Stannard Baker were at the apogee of their influence, detailing how the power of Rockefeller, Morgan, Carnegie, and other titans threatened America's ideals of freedom and equality of opportunity. Unions, suffragettes, prohibitionists, a dozen strains of socialists and radical social reformers, all preached redemption through even further-reaching changes.[5]

Canada was scarcely immune to the same forces and debates—indeed, the country's official centenary history refers to the period as the time of Canada's "Great Transformation."[6] During the tenure of Sir Wilfrid Laurier and his Liberal Party, between his first election in 1896 and his narrow defeat fifteen years later, Canada's small population grew by nearly 50 percent, heavily augmented by immigrant growth, much of it from non-English-speaking countries. Industrialization redefined the balance between the city and countryside and, because many new factories were U.S.-owned, between Canada and its powerful southern neighbor. The western provinces acquired new power vis-à-vis Ontario and Quebec. New sources of mineral wealth and energy were opened in the north, and wheat became Canada's signature export.

As in the United States, much of this dramatic change was welcomed and embraced. As one history puts it,

> For the majority, optimism was the ruling passion, even after signs of collapse had begun to appear in the Edwardian world. Material expansion became, for most, the measure of national and moral progress. The potential for Canada seemed unlimited. The vast, empty spaces of the land would welcome millions of settlers that would challenge the United States and surpass Great Britain. That population would exploit the untold resources of the country, providing a standard of living envied by the rest of the world. The twentieth century would belong to Canada.[7]

But the optimism was shadowed with doubts, resistance, and conflict. Canada's cities, like those in the United States, were all too typically, as one historian described them, "a place of violent contrasts, a home for the very rich and the very poor, for the rural immigrant from a neighbouring county or a far distant land, and the native urbanite, for respectable church-goers and for prostitutes, a place of conspicuous consumption and forced destitution."[8] One government study of Toronto's housing conditions, published shortly before

Galbraith's birth, found, for example, that "there is scarcely a vacant house fit to live in that is not inhabited, and in many cases by numerous families; in fact . . . respectable people have had to live in stables, tents, old cars, sheds (others in damp cellars), where we would not place a valued animal, let alone a human being."[9] And on Canada's farms, conditions were often equally harsh, since farmers faced falling prices for farm goods as acreage and productivity grew, rising prices for manufactured and consumer goods, high freight rates, processor monopolies, protective tariffs, and rural depopulation. They were becoming restive and, frequently, radical.*

During Laurier's administration, the restiveness of Canada's farmers spurred new forms of rural organization. More important politically, often radical new "farmers' unions" also appeared, especially in the west, where wheat harvests multiplied a stunning tenfold in the Laurier years. These new "unions," redolent with the same Populist sympathies that had sparked William Jennings Bryan's 1896 campaign in the United States, swiftly displaced their politically quieter predecessors, like the Grange.

In Ontario, this new impulse for agrarian organizing led to formation of the United Farmers of Ontario a year before Galbraith's birth.[10] Mostly contained in their agitation during the Laurier years by the shrewd prime minister's delicately balanced policies, by 1921 the UFO, with Galbraith's father Archie active in it, would not just overthrow the provincial government but permanently reshape the nation's traditional two-party system. In a stunning political stroke, which in many ways succeeded where Bryan's 1896 Populist campaign in the United States had failed, it ushered in a new era in Canadian politics.

But in 1908, although farmers across Canada were restive, in Elgin County, Ontario, support still inclined strongly and steadily, as it had for many years, to Laurier and the Liberals. This was not because places like Iona Station escaped the economic pressures bearing down on all farmers then, but because local farmers had several particular advantages. First, they practiced a mixed agriculture of crops and livestock, never depending solely on a single crop such as wheat for their incomes, as did so many in western Canada. Second, time and again, they proved themselves adept at shifting the mix when market conditions changed. Third, they had the railroad.

Besides being blessed with a temperate climate (the weather's extremes moderated by nearby Lake Erie), Iona Station was bisected by the major rail line connecting Buffalo to Detroit. Indeed, Iona Station owed its existence to the line and the entrepreneurs who'd built it in the 1870s. Originally intended to transport settlers and goods west to Michigan farmlands, within a few years it was bringing their products (and eventually, the industrial outpourings of Detroit and other Michigan cities) to eastern markets.[11] When the railmen en-

---

*Agricultural prices in the late nineteenth century had fallen relative to manufacturing and consumer prices, and in absolute terms. After 1900, thanks to rising urban demand and exports, as well as the political pressures exerted by farmers, prices rose, creating a twenty-year-long "Golden Age."

countered important farm roads crossing their right-of-way, they would build a small terminal of sorts to service the surrounding economy; hence "Iona Station," the name chosen in recognition of the local Scottish majority who had long ago named the adjoining hamlet Iona.

The rail line—originally owned by the Canadian Southern, in Galbraith's youth by the Michigan Central, and later the New York Central—had two important effects locally: it guaranteed that city goods, as well as city newspapers carrying the latest ideas and fashions, flowed easily into towns like Iona Station and the surrounding Dunwich Township;* more directly important to economic security, the higher wages paid by big-city assembly plants, steel works, and construction projects became powerful magnets that drew local farm youth to the cities. (It also meant for local people there that the distinction imposed by Canadian or U.S. citizenship exercised only a modest, sometimes irrelevant pull. "Movement back and forth across the Detroit River was commonplace," Galbraith has said, "and based on the secure knowledge that no immigration or customs official could tell a Canadian from an American by inspection alone."†)

Yet while the Michigan Central linked the land of Galbraith's youth to larger urban worlds and allowed for easy passage of people and goods between them, Iona Station itself remained deeply rural. Throughout Elgin County and much of the surrounding peninsula, farmers were the dominant caste, and among them the Scots (or "Scotch," as Galbraith calls them, respecting local custom) predominated. Surrounded by the McKillops, McPhails, Camerons, McFarlands, McKellers, Grahams, as well as the extensive Galbraith clan, the boy grew up with a steadfast sense of belonging to a people and a place with a history.

The Galbraiths' own family history in southern Ontario dates back to the early nineteenth century and perhaps the late eighteenth—family records aren't clear. Galbraith has written that his first Canadian ancestor was born in the 1770s in western Scotland, but never mentions when he reached Canada. Other family members date that arrival around 1820.[12] Back in Britain, the lines are clearer. The Galbraith clan traces its ancestry deep into Scottish history—"Galbraith" is an adaptation of the Celtic "Gael Breaton," or "strange Briton," suggesting an earlier, forgotten migration from the south. The clan's chiefs dominated much of the territory to the south and west of Loch Lomond, and the earliest land records, for a Gellespick Galbrait (the *h* was added sometime later), appear in about A.D. 1210.

During the fifteenth century, the powerful MacDonald clan came to domi-

---

*Four hamlets—Iona Station, Iona, Dutton, and Wallacetown—made up Dunwich Township, in Elgin County. (The *w* in "Dunwich" is silent, the *g* in "Elgin" is hard.)

†The relaxed atmosphere surrounding citizenship also introduced him to equally inexact political values. Thus, he recalls, "After the crops were harvested in Canada and the seasonal migration to the assembly lines had begun . . . a man could vote in Canada in the summer and, by courtesy of the Detroit Democratic organization that assigned registered names, possibly from the local funeral directors, in Michigan in the autumn. No thought of corruption was involved. Men wished to have the best people in office in both countries" (Galbraith, *A Life*, 5).

nate the Galbraiths and several other clans in western Scotland, and the Galbraiths took to wearing the MacDonald tartan. Along with the MacDonalds, many of them apparently soon also took up the profitable occupation of piracy against English trading vessels that plied the area's coastal waters. This practice ended only when Queen Elizabeth's army succeeded in routing the MacDonalds and their allies in 1592, as part of her bloody subjugation of Scotland, a process that included the famous execution of her rival, Mary, and that put an end to Scottish claims to independence. Following their defeat by Elizabeth's troops (and subsequent English occupation of their lands), parts of the Galbraith clan migrated to the north of Ireland, while others settled farther south in Scotland, in Argyllshire. It is from this Argyllshire branch of the clan that Ken Galbraith descends.

In the mid-eighteenth century a second wave of Galbraith (and Scottish) migration occurred, following parliamentary acts in 1744 and 1746. The ruthlessly enforced acts, meant to suppress a still-resistant Scottish nationalism, prohibited the wearing of clan tartans or the taking of clan oaths. While succeeding in their immediate goal, the laws set off a massive exodus from Scotland to overseas British colonies. Hundreds of thousands of Scots left their homeland, by one estimate 120,000 alone in the seven years prior to the American Revolution.[13] Resentful of aristocracy and wealthy landlords, the Scottish emigrants to North America pioneered independent communities in a broad swath across northern New England, western New York, and greater "Quebec," an area that then encompassed most of present-day Ontario, including Iona Station. With them came an abiding sense of Scottish identity, history, and dissent from reigning authority. (As late as World War I, Galbraith's father, manifesting the region's feelings toward the British Crown, volunteered to head the local draft board, and then promptly exempted all who saw no reason for serving in "England's bloody slaughter."[14])

A third wave of Scottish emigration ensued at the end of the eighteenth century, fed by a complex wellspring of motives. One source was excitement throughout Europe inspired first by the American, then the French revolutions. When Tom Paine's *The Rights of Man* was published in 1791, his insurrectionary defense of the French Revolution sold more than 50,000 copies in England and Scotland in the first few weeks. Given that most adults were barely literate at the time, the number was extraordinary. Over the decade, Paine's work is said to have sold an even more unheard-of total of more than 1.5 million copies. Nowhere was the pamphlet's impact more prominent than in Scotland. Early on, one Edinburgh bookseller reported selling 750 copies in a single week. Deeply alarming to the Crown in London, these sales levels earned Paine new celebrity in the form of a royal proclamation that denounced his "divers wicked and seditious writings" and brought booksellers themselves a series of arrests and celebrated state trials.[15]

The popular hunger for greater political liberty and independence, born of England's repression and felt most bitterly and strongly in Scotland and Ireland, was fed by the punishing economic realities of life during Britain's early

Industrial Revolution. It was the time of the Enclosures, when wealthy land-owners fenced off their tenants' traditional farmlands and common grazing lands and turned them into private pasturage for sheep. For these big landown-ers, supplying wool for the immense new mechanized textile industry was vastly more profitable than their rents from traditional farming. But for the na-tion's small-holders and tenant farmers, the resulting evictions were often an unmitigated disaster. Millions of families throughout Great Britain were peremptorily, often brutally, forced from their lands. In Scotland, the evictions fueled further mass exodus to the cities and colonies, and left a deep, festering scar on the land and its people.

For decades thereafter, Britain's industrialization brought no relief to the re-maining rural inhabitants in Scotland. As late as the 1850s, for example, a Gal-braith cousin whose family had doggedly stayed in the Highlands awkwardly and painfully wrote to his uncle (Ken's grandfather) in Ontario about the bitter conditions during this time when Britain was at the height of Victorian power and self-confidence:

> Dear Uncle you wish us to go to that country [Canada], that we would be better off than here. Undoubtly that is true, if I had the means of going there. But my brother and me has nothing but our daily work and very poorly paid for the same, hardly what will support the body, when a man works all day for 1/shilling and 2 pence, and of that small sum keep himself and family. I leave yourself to judge how that man can be but poor . . .
>
> If you wish us to go, which we fain wish ourselves, if you would assist us in immigrating there, I am of the opinion that we would be able to pay you back but to ask us to go there without support is quite impossible. It would be enough for any of us to pay our passage to Glasgow. Time is very hard in this part of the world and poor wadges [wages] and since the potatoes is en-tirely gone in this place, there is nothing to be got without the money and the money you cannot get . . . every day it is getting worse and I am much afraid it is not at its height yet.[16]

The letter closes somberly, "I remain, Dear Uncle, yours truly, Nephew till Death, John Galbraith"—and a poignant postscript adds: "I forgot to let you know about my Brother Neill. We do not no [know] whether he is leaving [liv-ing] or not. We did not hear of him the last two years. We do not know what ship he is with or what has come over him."

By contrast, for those Galbraiths who had chosen emigration to Canada, the family records show that life by then seemed constantly to improve. Gal-braith's Canadian ancestors descend directly from an earlier Archibald Gal-braith and his wife, Mary Campbell Galbraith (both born in Argyllshire, he in 1771, she eight years later). This first Archie Galbraith and his wife appear to have arrived as homesteaders in Canada in 1819 (possibly 1818) aboard a small passenger ship laden with several dozen like-minded Scottish families.[17]

With them, the couple brought four of their six children (the other two had died in Scotland as infants).

Like most of those aboard the ship, the Galbraiths had been persuaded by land agents in Scotland to begin their new lives on what was called "the Talbot Settlement," an immense, supposedly fertile tract of southern Ontario purchased in 1803 by Colonel Thomas Talbot, a minor figure of the English-installed Anglo-Irish nobility. Already approaching middle age, Archie and Mary had not made the decision lightly, but they had seen no future in Argyllshire.[18]

The passengers quickly discovered on their arrival at tiny Port Talbot on Lake Erie's north shore that the Talbot Tract, far from being the prime farmland the colonel's agents had described, was heavily wooded, with soil of uneven quality, loamy in some parts, sandy in others, and sparsely populated. Like their fellow settlers, the Galbraiths consequently would spend years working the land into first-rate condition. The fifty-acre plot they chose (not far from where Ken Galbraith was later born), and the work they put into it proved beneficent in one respect, though: having arrived when he was nearly fifty, Archie lived to be 103, his wife Mary, to 79.

Longevity, however, was not passed on to their children, including the youngest, John, who was a teenager when he arrived at the Talbot Settlement. Like his older brother, the sturdy young man took up farming on his own, near his parents' homestead. Once his land was cleared, he soon married, and with his wife, Christina McCallum Galbraith, John had eight children, the second of whom they also named John. The family prospered as both parents and children (how many survived infancy isn't clear) toiled steadily to improve their land. Then, without warning, John the father died in 1849 after a fall from a tree, when his son was just fourteen.

The family, now headed by his widow, kept working, aided by sympathetic neighbors when time allowed. But as the children grew, like their father before them, they struck out on their own. Young John cleared his own farm nearby when he was in his early twenties, on land then formally incorporated as Dunwich Township, Elgin County, Ontario. Even so, for several years, he returned as often as possible to work his mother's farm, as she struggled to raise the remaining children. Then, having established himself, he married a neighbor's daughter, Sarah Black. John and Sarah had four sons, two of whom survived infancy: the elder, born in 1865, whom they named John like his father and grandfather before him, and William Archibald, born three years later.

John and Sarah proved to be not only successful farmers but, like their forebears, well liked and respected in the surrounding Scottish community. By the 1870s, in a sign of this respect and popularity, John was chosen the "reeve," or mayor, of Dunwich Township, a special honor considering he was then only in his late thirties. A photograph of the Elgin County Council from the time shows a very tall, handsome man, in tweed suit and vest, with bow tie, leather boots, a full beard, and neatly parted hair—sandy-red, according to family letters—solemnly posed and staring firmly back at the camera with his elected peers. (Height even then ran prominently in the Galbraith line.)

But sorrow haunted the family, as it did so many in the nineteenth century, when life was hard and medical care so primitive. And death came unexpectedly as it had with his father: just forty-seven, his wife, Sarah, died suddenly after a short illness. The loss was hard and the memory lingered on for her husband, and for her two boys. For her younger son, the tall but quiet William Archibald, nicknamed "Archie," who had been lovingly indulged and much favored by his mother, as the youngest often are, her unexpected passing was especially powerful and harsh; he was barely seventeen.

After Sarah's passing, her husband lived on without remarrying, a much quieter, more somber man, relatives remember. With the help of his two sons, though, his farm prospered, enough so that he was able to expand its acreage considerably. Successful as a farmer, the father clearly wanted to offer his sons wider options. Uncommonly for the time, he made sure that Archie and his older brother completed school through twelfth grade, even as they helped their father work the farm.

Archie over the years proved the better student, and with his father's blessing and support continued his education at a nearby teachers' college after high school. His older brother stayed on the farm; then, setting his own course, left to try over time several occupations with only moderate success, eventually drifting into selling farm implements out West. When their father died in 1898, the two boys divided his property, located five miles above Lake Erie, with John inheriting the house, outbuildings, and a smaller portion of the land. Archie, who by then had been teaching school locally for several years, decided to go back to farming and made it thereafter his principal (though by no means sole) occupation. The reason for his return to farming was uncomplicated: a year before his father died, the young schoolteacher had married, and raising a family on a teacher's salary was barely possible.

His new wife, Sarah Catherine Kendall, was a local girl. The Kendalls were farmers, too, and like the Galbraiths generally well regarded in the community (although a few more suspicious neighbors considered them a trifle "too English," it is said, apparently because Kate's grandfather had once served as an officer in the British Army). A tall, very attractive young woman, with dark brown hair and deep brown eyes, Kate Kendall had been adventuresome enough to move after high school to Niagara Falls, where she worked in a dry-goods store until marrying Archie in 1897. She was then twenty-three, and Archie was twenty-nine, and they used part of his inheritance the next year to have a house built on his portion of the land. There, on Hogg Street, in Iona Station, they began their life together.

BY THE TIME of Ken Galbraith's birth in October 1908, the Scots had turned much of the vast old Talbot Tract into a prosperous patchwork of family farms. The loamy soil that had once intermingled with sandy, ill-drained lands, had been transformed through effort and skill over several generations into rich fields of corn, beans, oats, hay, and pasturage for fat herds of cattle and sheep. The cattle, especially the purebred Shorthorns which the Galbraith family raised, were the community's pride.

As a boy, young Ken looked forward eagerly each fall to the nearby Wallacetown Fair, and competition with Duncan Brown, a neighboring farmer, to decide whose family had raised the best Shorthorns. One year the Browns would take first place, and the Galbraiths second; the next year the order would be reversed. But the competition was neighborly, and the two families regularly divided the prize money, forty or fifty dollars between them. "My pets were really those cattle. I was always quite involved with them and gave them a lot of attention," Galbraith says.[19]

Farm life easily and naturally formed the early center of his life, and it imbued him with habits that endured throughout his life. Foremost was his capacity for hard work, despite an often laconic posture that suggested to some an easygoing country gentleman. "A long day following a plodding, increasingly reluctant team behind a harrow endlessly back and forth over the uninspiring Ontario terrain persuaded one," he wrote, "that all other work was easy."[20]

His work habits were reinforced by his relations with his younger brother Bill, who proved as inattentive to family chores as Ken was diligent. Two years younger, Bill was the family charmer, "gregarious, good-looking, feckless, exceedingly popular with the boys and girls of the neighborhood, carefree, and lazy," as one acquaintance put it—and, like his father and brother, unusually tall.[21] Bill was also the natural athlete of the family, while Ken's sporting interests were desultory at best.

As their sister Catherine remembers it, Bill was always willing to wriggle out of his chores at a moment's notice to play ball or go swimming with pals; Ken would then do his own chores and Bill's as well.[22] In later years, the brothers weren't close—as Ken's career prospered, Bill's turned in smaller, familiar circles, always around the family farm and nearby employments of no particular distinction. Galbraith has said about his brother (who died in 1998), "I had no real relationship with him."[23]

With his two sisters, Alice, four years older, and Catherine, five years younger, things were different.* Alice, who never married, grew up to become a teacher like her father, working for many years with retarded children; much beloved by family, friends, and students, she died in 1974. Catherine (who also became a teacher) and Ken were the closest, bound together from childhood until her death in 2002 by a love of reading and words. In a sign of that love, during their childhood he read stories to her constantly, changing the words when he grew bored—much to her consternation, because the stories then weren't the same (though, she remembered her brother always improved them). Both separately recalled, as a landmark in their young lives, the day the Dutton Library amended its policy of lending just two books every two weeks, to allow unlimited borrowing.[24]

---

*A third sister, Helen, born in January 1907, died of whooping cough the same year.

Galbraith's parents were much adored by all four children, and in the latter's common retelling of childhood tales, both figure prominently. Early on, though, tragedy struck: in October 1923, their mother, Kate, died suddenly. Ken had turned fifteen just three days earlier.

Galbraith, despite his prolific writing, has never described either the circumstances or emotions surrounding his mother's death. In his memoirs more than five hundred pages long, there is only one austere sentence about her: "My mother, a beautiful, affectionate, and decidedly firm woman, died when her children—my brother, my two sisters, and I—were not yet all in their teens." Nothing more, among the thousands of pages written in his life, exists.[25]

His unwillingness to discuss his mother's death belies the depth of its effect on the family. The previous spring, according to her daughter, she had gone into hospital for a hysterectomy and throughout the summer had never really recovered. Complicating matters, she had been bothered for several years by a weak heart, and in the fall her health started to fail. When she returned to the hospital, her doctors nonetheless predicted an early recovery. Two days later, barely fifty, she was dead.

"Ken was out in the yard when the news came," his sister recalled. "He'd just ridden his bicycle home from somewhere, and was kneeling down working on it. I wanted to tell him, but I couldn't summon up the words. Finally, I went out. He was kneeling as I told him, and he didn't say a word. He just got up, dropped his bicycle, and ran in to the house."[26]

Kate Galbraith's funeral was attended by hundreds of neighbors and relatives, the largest funeral in years, according to the local paper, which eulogized her for her work with the schools and the local women's institute.[27] Devastated by Kate's death, her husband seemed lost for almost two years afterward. Christmas that first winter was an especially somber time for the family. Accustomed to the gaiety, music, food, and presents that had always marked the house at Christmastime, the children found no tree that year, no presents, no celebration. Archie was haunted by the memory that his own beloved mother had died under similarly abrupt circumstances when he was only seventeen, and one can only try to guess what he lived through in those first months.

But the children, too, were in pain, and Ken's high-school work suffered visibly. By the end of his senior year two years later, "I had a couple of courses to make up," he wrote obliquely in his memoirs, "which either I hadn't taken at all or my grades weren't good enough. I don't remember."[28]

Archie Galbraith never remarried. For a time, the eldest daughter, Alice, took on many of the duties of the absent mother. When she left for teacher's college (she was eighteen at the time of her mother's death), a young relative named Gladys McCallum was hired to help keep house. The children and their father shared in the household chores and did their best to entertain one another with reading and conversation, while keeping up the inevitable farm work. Gradually, as he recovered emotionally, Archie returned to the extensive community affairs to which he was dedicated and which he loved.

· · ·

FOR KEN ESPECIALLY, his father's public involvements proved not only consoling but an avenue into the larger world of politics and public debate. Among the Scots of Elgin County, Archie Galbraith was well known and highly regarded. In addition to being a successful farmer who kept up with the latest methods and technologies, he always found time for community involvement. He helped establish the local telephone exchange and a cooperative insurance company, and for many years was a township and county official, supervising the auditing of local finances.

Archie Galbraith was also a man of decided opinions. A life-long activist in Laurier's Liberal Party, an allegiance to which the Scots of southern Ontario generally adhered, he was a prominent public speaker on behalf of candidates and causes alike. Six feet, nine inches tall, with reddish-brown hair, a thick mustache, and the large, rough-hewn handsome features he passed on to his son, Archie was constantly sought out by neighbors and clansmen for his opinions on many matters, from proper farming methods to whom to support for prime minister or MP in upcoming elections. "If Archie approved, one was safe to go ahead," one friend recalled, "but if the project was faulty, he had the gift of seeing straight through to the hidden weakness, and with his disapproval the scheme was condemned." Another acquaintance said simply of him that in Elgin County, Archie Galbraith's "word was as good as a Dominion of Canada bond."[29]

In matters of religion, the family was moderate by the Calvinist standards of many of their neighbors. Archie had been raised an austere Old School Baptist by his parents, but was relaxed about the practice of his faith. Once a month, the family attended local services, where along with the rest of the congregation they heard the lurid details of hell and eternal damnation recounted by Elder Reston (the little church, in denominational custom, had no paid minister). "Father," said Ken's sister, "never could get it quite straightened out what God and church were all about."[30]

Sunday afternoons at the Galbraith farm were a gayer time, certainly while Kate was alive, then gradually again after her death.[31] Friends and allies would gather in the house (or yard, weather permitting) to discuss the issues of the day. Often there would be music and—with the carpets rolled up and furniture pushed back in the big formal living room—even dancing (though no drinking: the Galbraiths were steadfast teetotalers).

Ken never took to the dancing, his sister remembered. Instead he watched and listened actively, absorbing not only the issues being debated but the tone in which they were discussed. When his father went to speak at local meetings or rallies, Ken was often an eager companion, and he says he learned from his father the importance of humor in making a telling point.

Ken's proud awareness of his father's active community work also taught him important lessons about the structure and hierarchy of the world he grew up in. Although these self-employed Scots farmers were spared the stark divisions of urban wealth and poverty, they nonetheless inhabited a universe carefully prescribed by a well-understood and stable division of class and clan.

Rank, however, was less a matter of a man's financial position than the more loosely defined one of "standing." (Income and wealth, as Galbraith notes, were not issues of disinterest among the Scots; to the contrary, they would have been of considerable interest had they been known, but were considered to "be a secret between a man and his wife.") "Standing" among the Scots in turn was ranked broadly in terms of three social "classes":

> At the bottom were those who, although by all outward signs they were treated like everyone else, did not enjoy full citizenship. Their views did not command respect; no one would think of quoting them except possibly as an example of error.

In the middle was the largest group,

> whose views determined the position of the others . . . A man's farming methods, marketing decisions, livestock purchases, machinery acquisitions, wife, family, relatives, temperament, drinking, stomach complaints, tumors, personal expenditures, physical appearance and his political, social and economic views were dwelt upon in detail by his neighbors. Out of this discussion came the consensus as to his place . . . And while the Scotch did not quickly change their minds about those to whom they had accorded positions of honor or had excluded from membership, they kept their people subject to constant scrutiny.

Standing above both these groups in turn were "men of standing."

> They were so described and, except in rare instances, were also aware of their position. Others sought their views and in some measure accepted them, especially on matters removed from the common knowledge of the community.[32]

Archie Galbraith's place as a "man of standing" was unquestionable, and not just for an admiring son. He had been appointed Elgin County auditor in the early 1890s while still in his mid-twenties, and continued to serve in various public positions until his death in the late 1930s, by which time he was so widely and warmly regarded that seven hundred people turned out for his funeral in a raging midwinter snowstorm. According to the local paper, when one friend's car stalled on the snow-clogged roads on the way to the funeral, the man hired a sleigh and team of horses to carry him and his car seven miles over the fields in order to reach the service.[33]

ARCHIE'S POLITICAL BELIEFS were as influential on his son as his public service. Canadian politics had been safely divided since the 1860s between the Liberals and Conservatives, with the Liberals under Laurier after 1896 the dominant force until his narrow loss of power to the Conservatives in 1911.[34] But

World War I created a crisis in what had been a durable two-party system. The issue that triggered it was simple: conscription, the draft of Canadians to serve as Allied troops in Europe's Great War.

In 1914, Canada had entered the war alongside Britain in a patriotic and bipartisan mood of support among its middle and upper classes (though less so among its urban workers and the French Québecois). Canadians' support for the war had waned dramatically by 1916, though, as the cost in men and materiel grew horrific. (Sixty-eight thousand of the 242,000 soldiers from Ontario alone were dead, wounded or missing by war's end.)[35] Volunteers for the armed forces plummeted, and the Conservative government, under pressure from Britain, decided that it would have to implement conscription.

This created an enormous and bitter division within the Liberal Party, and in 1917 the party openly split, with one wing (including the now aged Laurier) entering a coalition "Union" government with the Conservatives, and the other wing restively searching for alternatives that would sustain their opposition to the draft. Conscription and the Unionists narrowly won in the passionately fought December 1917 election; but this "bitterest campaign in Canadian history" left deep, gaping wounds throughout the country.[36]

Yet Archie's service on the county draft board and his willing deferment of local boys grew from more than what his son has described as residual Scottish distrust of their English overlords. It was at the heart of a bitter and fundamental national political battle. In 1917 hundreds of thousands of angry Canadians, including the Galbraiths, abandoned the Liberal Party and the once beloved Laurier in favor of the rebellious party wing that opposed conscription and its Union Government supporters.[37] Within months of the war's end in November 1918, the opponents of the now-hated Unionists struck back. Out on the Canadian prairie, anger burst forth in the fabled and brutally fought Winnipeg general strike, just one of so many strikes throughout the country in 1919 that a record was set for Canadian labor strife.

Ontario farmers like Archie Galbraith, who'd broken with their Liberal Unionist colleagues, now presented the government with an unprecedented challenge. Hundreds of thousands of them bolted the provincial Liberal Party for a new third party that had suddenly appeared, the United Farmers of Ontario. Having begun twelve years earlier as a reforming farm movement, by the end of 1919 the UFO shocked the country by sweeping Ontario's elections; rural counties like Elgin formed the heart of its support.

The new party was led by E. C. Drury, a politically gifted forty-six-year-old farmer who had been a well-known, well-liked figure in the prewar Liberal Party. A head of the National Grange (and son of the province's first Minister of Agriculture), Drury now almost overnight found himself premier of Ontario after successfully forging a coalition with the Labour Party, which had been marginal until 1919 but now spoke for thousands of angry urban workers. His new government horrified the Canadian political establishment, with the Crown-appointed lieutenant governor of Ontario, Sir John Hendrie, declaring it as "a move away from party representation toward class or factional representation."

Some leaders took an even darker view, wildly identifying the United Farmers with Bolshevism and even with the Irish nationalist Sinn Fein.[38]

Canadian farmers were not Leninists or Irish nationalists, but they were nonetheless in a revolutionary mood. As Drury assured his supporters,

> [T]he United Farmers of Ontario form the nucleus of a new party which is going to sweep the two old parties into a single organization, which they really are, a new party that will stand for wisdom, justice and honesty in public affairs; a party untainted by campaign funds contributed by selfish interests, that will cleanse the whole of public life of Canada.[39]

The party's inspiration was an unadulterated agrarian populism, deeply fused with the language of the Christian Social Gospel movement—precisely the kind that William Jennings Bryan had spoken for in the United States in 1896 and that Governor Robert La Follette of Wisconsin would champion in 1924. W. C. Good, one of the UFO's early leaders, put it simply: "God made the country, Man made the town." Men like Good believed that Canadian public policy had for too long favored the city and industry over farmers, and he made clear the cost:

> Our future destiny, and *national* character depend on the quality of life that we can maintain in our rural districts . . . Now when the flower of our manhood has been sacrificed for the purpose of preserving Liberty and Democracy . . . at last we can make an honest effort to establish in this, our native land, a Kingdom of Righteousness.[40]

Once in office, the new Farmer-Labour government moved swiftly. "In our first two sessions," Drury later wrote, "we enacted such a program of social legislation as Ontario and indeed all Canada and North America had never seen, or perhaps thought possible."[41]

He did not exaggerate: minimum wage laws for women, expanded welfare for widows and orphans, civil service pensions, workers' compensation reforms, education overhaul, new taxes on corporations and utilities, new public savings banks, new credits for farmers and cooperatives, rural road and rail construction, giant public hydroelectric projects, even the critical funding for medical research that led to the discovery of insulin—all these now poured forth from the Drury government.[42]

Despite these early legislative achievements, however, the rebellion didn't last. Unlike the New Deal, the Farmer-Labour government, and with it the United Farmers, collapsed within four years of Drury's taking office. In retrospect, its failure seems inevitable: tensions between farmers and workers over wage reforms, between the countryside and cities over tariff policy (with farmers devoutly in favor of free trade), and, perhaps most important, divisions over alcohol had torn at the young coalition from the start.

The farmers were temperance men, and their newly enfranchised wives were even dryer; workers and the cities, by and large, weren't. But Drury's government had chosen to support provincial prohibition, and as the 1923 elections approached, it became the party's divisive sword, just as conscription had been for the Liberals in 1917. In a light turnout, the government fell to the Conservatives, whose campaign slogan, "business methods in administration," firmly echoed the new Republican era in the United States.

With Drury back on his farm, the United Farmers of Ontario spiraled downward into oblivion, as Archie Galbraith and thousands of others drifted back to the Liberal Party. But the fabled Laurier had died in 1919 at the age of seventy-eight, and a new generation had taken over with a newly conservative message that meant that in Ontario, the Liberals were to be shut out of power for more than a decade.

Ken Galbraith was only eleven when Drury was elected and fourteen when the Farmer-Labour government failed, and one can easily imagine him listening to his father discuss politics on those Sunday afternoons, absorbing lessons that would reappear years later in a parallel to his father's own political journey. In the mid-1960s, Galbraith became a vocal, vehement opponent of America's war in Vietnam, a leader of the "Dump Johnson" movement, and floor manager for the insurgent Senator Eugene McCarthy at the 1968 Democratic Convention. As happened with his father, his disaffection grew out of wartime policies, not least the draft, and a steadfast belief that certain core values took precedence over party loyalties. McCarthy lost the Democratic nomination to Vice President Hubert Humphrey, and Humphrey then lost to the Republican Richard Nixon. But like his father before him, Galbraith refused to abandon politics. Four years later, he helped lead the successful fight to nominate Senator George McGovern on the Democratic ticket, a man who in many important respects resembled Drury, and whose insurgent campaign similarly shared the qualities and spirit that had once characterized the UFO.

FOR THE TEENAGED GALBRAITH, the loss of his beloved mother in 1923, then his father's heartbroken withdrawal after her death (and the collapse of the UFO the same year) had inevitable effects, although throughout his life he remained oblique about what they were. He acknowledged that he struggled with school over the next two years after his mother's death, but blamed his troubles on "foot problems." (His sister recalled only that he had flat feet.) But even before then, high school hadn't been easy; he'd entered it at age twelve, hadn't been well prepared by his one-room Willey's School experience, and found the atmosphere, under what he describes as a tyrannical principal, repellent. Because the Galbraith children traveled the six miles to school by horse and buggy, they were frequently late, which resulted in routine punishment. Moreover, all the boys in the school were required to participate in the school's cadet corps, a holdover from World War I. The close-order drills twice a week were a nightmare for the gangly Ken, and he was humiliatingly assigned to the "Awkward Squad" and forced to write repetitively "My left foot is not my right" in further punishment.[43] On the advice of his teachers,

Archie arranged for his son to repeat his senior year somewhere other than Dutton.

So after spending a fifth year attending nearby St. Thomas High School, Ken graduated in June 1926 and three months later set off for college in Guelph, Ontario. A month shy of turning eighteen, he must have found Guelph attractively far away from the traumatic pains he associated with home. The two-and-a-half-hour train ride that carried him and two other local boys there marked the start of a fresh life and the chance for distracting new adventures. It was the farthest he'd ever been from home.[44]

Adventure for college freshmen is always relative, and in this Galbraith was no exception. Guelph, only eighty miles northeast of Iona Station, hardly qualified even as a provincial metropolis, but it was home to Ontario Agricultural College, the "farm school" branch of the much more distinguished University of Toronto. OAC wasn't young Ken's first choice; indeed, he hadn't made a choice about where (or even whether) to attend college. That had been his father's decision, announced perfunctorily the previous fall, near the end of a hard day that the two had spent cleaning and repairing the family's granary. Archie—without pausing or even looking up from his work—had simply remarked quietly, "I think you'd better decide to go on to college at Guelph." It never occurred to Ken to protest the decision.

OAC was a practical choice, though. Tuition fees were nominal (twenty dollars annually for the first two years, fifty dollars thereafter, with room and board an additional five to six dollars per week), and the entrance requirements undemanding. To enroll, one had to be eighteen, show evidence of "moral character and physical ability," and produce a certificate affirming that one had spent at least a year on a farm, and thereby acquired "a practical knowledge of ordinary farm operations, such as harnessing and driving horses, plowing, harrowing, drilling, etc." A high school diploma was not listed among the school's entrance requirements.

Galbraith years later created a furor at his alma mater by referring to it in a *Time* interview as in his youth "not only the cheapest but probably the worst college in the English-speaking world." There was much angry talk in Guelph about rescinding the honorary degree he'd been given as "OAC's greatest living alumnus," and dozens of outraged alumni wrote to denounce him. Galbraith eventually backtracked, but only slightly, claiming that his comment applied to OAC in his undergraduate years and that he would allow that Arkansas A&M was no doubt worse, although there was some question whether English was spoken there.

Yet by the standards of the times OAC offered a decently advanced curriculum in farm management practices, if not much else. The college's thirty full-time professors included three Ph.D.s, and classes in the humanities, social sciences, and natural sciences, beyond nominal introductory offerings, were considered best reserved for Toronto's main campus and its more urbane student body.[45] Still, as he walked onto the school's grounds for the first time, Ken recalled, "it was a lovely autumn day, the campus was extremely beautiful, the football team was practicing. I was shown to my room—and I felt I had arrived."

Galbraith spent five years at OAC, the fifth year necessitated by health problems ("an incipient tuberculosis") and his weak high-school preparation. His major was animal husbandry, and he seems to have done quite well, mastering degree requirements in field husbandry, poultry husbandry, horticulture, soil management, forestry, veterinary principles, and apiculture with relative ease; he graduated with distinction. This he credits, however, less to the excellence of his teachers than to the practices he'd learned from his father and their neighbors. (He likes to recall that among the profound insights of his dairy husbandry professor was the gravely offered observation that "the dairy cow is the foster mother of the human race."[46])

Campus sports were only a desultory outlet for his youthful energies. As a freshman, he tried a bit of intramural football and track, and played hockey without distinction; at one match he accidentally knocked the puck into his own goal, a feat noted in his class yearbook. The school's basketball coach, who was also his entomology teacher, was delighted to have a six-foot-eight-inch freshman on campus and encouraged him to try out for the team, but this too proved a mismatch. "I was awkward. A fellow a foot shorter than I would take the ball away from me at center. My coordination was extremely poor, and the crowd would react with contempt at my playing."[47]

For this young, ungainly, but very bright farmboy, the awkwardness that came with his upbringing, especially when faced with the relative "sophistication" of his more citified classmates, was overcome finally through his discovery of writing. Among the otherwise mediocre faculty, Galbraith found two English teachers, O. J. Stevenson and E. C. McLean, who were "well known Canadian literary figures, of the secondary sort," but demanding enough. Students wrote weekly compositions that were corrected and evaluated meticulously, and Galbraith soon became one of their favorites. "That was where I first became involved in writing." Building on his new-found abilities, he helped found a college newspaper, *The OACIS*, which he mischievously claims he edited with enough independence that it "gave maximum offense to the faculty" (elsewhere he has said that in truth "I kept well to the side of safety"[48]).

With the paper came a degree of campus celebrity and a self-ascribed nickname, "Spike" Galbraith. If the moniker suggests the Damon Runyonesque reputation of journalists in those days, Galbraith says that he also chose it in hopes that his high-school nickname, "Soupy," would remain undiscovered as his campus reputation grew. (At Dutton High, thanks to the various harassments and embarrassments he endured, he'd had several teary public outbursts, which had earned him the cruel nickname.) "Spike" sounded rugged and brave to him, and he'd had it printed on a sweatshirt which he wore regularly on the OAC campus until the name caught hold. Seeking a wider audience, "Spike" started freelancing a few pieces on contemporary agricultural issues for two small western Ontario papers, the St. Thomas *Times Journal* and the Stratford *Beacon Herald*. This led in turn to the offer of a weekly column, for which he was paid the munificent fee of five dollars per column. It was "an enormous sum," he proudly remembered, which "paid for all my forms of recreation."

Recreational opportunities were, however, limited. Among its other deficiencies, OAC enrolled few women, and of those, none—at least in Galbraith's recollection—was interesting to or interested in him. OAC did, however, allow him to travel, including a trip his senior year all the way to Chicago for the 1930 International Livestock Exhibition, an expedition he still considers "the greatest triumph of my college days." The trip included stopovers to view agricultural facilities at Michigan State, Purdue, and the University of Illinois, and it opened entirely new vistas in his life.[49]

But as the Depression fatefully began to descend across North America, a return to farm life and Iona Station, however informed by modern animal husbandry, no longer seemed to be his certain future. Something more challenging, something broader, seemed to be calling. But what that new future would be was hazy at best. As he admits,

> I didn't have any long-range view and neither did my colleagues. We all lived in the present. But there were various possibilities. If you were good you might be taken on as a county agent, advising farmers on how to improve their agriculture. That was a very attractive job. Or there were other quite good "escapes." Some of the boys went on to take a year at the University of Toronto School of Education and then to teach agriculture in high school. Others got good jobs grading livestock in the stock yards of Toronto, or being hog graders.[50]

Hog grading wasn't quite at the high frontier of his now-stirring ambitions. In the summer of 1930, a research job interviewing more than a hundred tenant farmers and their families underscored for Galbraith the poignant suffering the Depression was inflicting on the province's once-prosperous (and still ingenious and hardworking) rural population, and it led him to conclude that something was terribly wrong with the way agricultural markets worked. Farming was as close to neoclassical textbook perfection as existed, a world generally of small producers and small buyers (there were certainly exceptions) who competed sedulously, adopted new technologies, improvised new marketing strategies, sought out new customers—all the things that in the modern equilibrium-based conception of free markets should guarantee success. And yet they didn't. Galbraith, entering his last year at OAC, decided to find out why—and so he enrolled in a course on agricultural economics. His interest was not purely abstract: if he "could there come to understand the real problem [behind the Depression] . . . that understanding might also help me get a job."[51]

Realizing the intellectual and occupational promises of academic economics, even agricultural economics, was not easy at OAC. The school offered no major in the field, and the half dozen courses available were stronger on simple and practical application than on theory. (OAC's pedagogical approach offered "so wide ranging an education," Galbraith dryly remarked in his memoirs, that it "involved some sacrifice of depth."[52]) Still, the classes hinted at a world more challenging than life on the farm or, more exaltedly, as a county agent.

The moment he truly committed himself to economics came that same autumn, when he happened upon a poster tacked to the bulletin board at the campus post office. It advertised graduate research fellowships being offered by the Giannini Foundation of Agricultural Economics at the University of California.* The annual stipend was $720, a princely sum—and the lure of California, an exotic place by comparison to Guelph, was strong. He applied shortly afterward, and some months later received notice that he'd been accepted.

AND SO, IN LATE JULY 1931, after several weeks spent back on the family farm, Ken Galbraith departed his life in Canada never to return, save for short visits. From Iona Station his father drove him to nearby Port Stanley, where he boarded the Lake Erie steamer that ran daily across the lake to Cleveland. By prearrangement, he rendezvoused after landing with the nephew of a family acquaintance, the town's local jeweler and oculist, who was going out to Berkeley to study astronomy. The young man had bought a well-used 1926 Oakland sedan to make the journey, and the two had agreed to share what they assumed would be the modest costs for the trip. But the car guzzled gas and leaked oil from the start and then threw a rod in rural Iowa, turning the heady adventure of a cross-country drive in the days before the route to California was fully paved into a minor financial disaster. Galbraith had borrowed five hundred dollars from an aunt to supplement his promised fellowship for the coming year—and by the time he reached Berkeley eleven days after leaving home, much of it was gone.[53]

Yet their arrival in Berkeley, after a tiring day-long drive over the Sierra and then across the hot plains of California's Central Valley, produced a magical moment in young Ken's life.

> It was about six o'clock on a bright summer evening when we got to Berkeley and drove up Bancroft Way to the International House. The hills behind were very bleached and sere but the low sun glistened on the live oaks and the green lawns and the masses of pink geraniums which elsewhere are only geraniums but in Berkeley are the glory of the whole city. The sun also lit up a vast yellow-buff facade of the International House with the large Spanish arches of the portico below. We passed into the great hall, then gleaming new, and combining the best mission style with the finest in Moorish revival. I thought it a place of unimaginable splendor . . . Never before had I been so happy.[54]

---

*A. P. Giannini, a poor Italian immigrant, had transformed the tiny San Francisco–based Bank of Italy into the powerful Bank of America, already then the largest bank west of the Mississippi, through a surprisingly progressive policy of lending to fellow immigrants, to an aspiring middle class, and to farmers and small businessmen who were often shunned by established financial institutions. The bank was an especially heavy lender to California agriculture, and the purpose of the Giannini Foundation (endowed by a $1.5 million gift from its namesake) was to spur technological and managerial innovations, a subject in which the bank was not disinterested.

Berkeley was more than an aesthetic delight. In contrast to his stolid professors at OAC—who had solemnly passed on conventional truths even when, at least to some students, those truths seemed wildly at odds with the facts—his new teachers "knew their subjects and paradoxically, invited debate on what they knew." To his delight, "I first discovered at Berkeley . . . that a professor might like to be informed on some subject by a graduate student—not just polite but pleased." Yet he also learned soon enough that there was a well-established hierarchy of knowledge among these California scholars, just as there had been, at a lower level, at OAC.

The Gianinni Foundation operated (and was housed) apart from the university's economics department, a more than geographical separation, as Galbraith acknowledges.

> We agricultural economists were second-class citizens. Our concern was with the prices of cling peaches, which were then appalling, and the financial condition of the Merced irrigation district which was equally bad and the prune industry which was chronically indigent, and other such useful subjects. I earned my research stipend by tramping the streets of Los Angeles and also Oakland and San Jose to ascertain the differing preferences as to package and flavor—sage, orange blossom, clover—of Mexican, Japanese, Negro, and (as we then thought of them) ordinary white Americans, for honey. No differences emerged. This kind of work was not well regarded by the non-agricultural or pure economists.[55]

To compensate for his inferior status, and determined to expand his horizons lest he fall backward into the narrower life his OAC education held out for him, Galbraith quickly enrolled in graduate courses in the economics department itself, a privilege accorded at no additional cost to the Giannini fellows. There he studied "Economic Theory, Advanced Economic Theory, Research Methods (in Social Sciences), Economics of Agricultural Production, Agricultural Policy, Marketing, Money and Banking, Farm Management, History of Economic Thought, Economic History, Agricultural Credit, and Land Economics," and audited courses in "Public Finance, Political Science, and others."[56] In all of them he did quite well—a surprise, given his lack of preparation. Years later, FBI agents investigating his fitness for government service reported that his Berkeley transcript and interview showed he'd been an "outstanding student." Galbraith was hitting his stride.

His new professors left lasting impressions at a time when the department included some of the best teachers (if not scholars) in economics. A good many of them, moreover, shared with colleagues at Wisconsin, Minnesota, Texas, and other prominent public land-grant colleges a more progressive approach to economics and policy than those who taught at their older, more prestigious, and wealthier private competitors in the East. Marshall and conventional neoclassical theory was certainly a mainstay at Berkeley, but the liberal influences of Progressive-Era pioneers such as Richard Ely, John R.

Commons, Wesley Mitchell, and Thorstein Veblen were more noticeable than at Harvard or Yale.* The arrival of Franklin Roosevelt in the White House in 1933 would not be greeted by most of Berkeley's economists, as it was by Harvard's, with a shudder of fear and trepidation.

Leo Rogin, among the most progressive of Galbraith's teachers, introduced him to the works of Smith, Ricardo, Marx, and the German figures such as Schmoller, Knies, and Roscher in nineteenth-century economics, as well as to those of John Maynard Keynes (although these were the somewhat more restricted and cautious ideas of his pre–*General Theory* period). In agricultural policy, Galbraith was taught by Henry Erdman and Howard Tolley, both important figures in modernizing American farm policy. Tolley had held major policy posts in the Department of Agriculture before joining the Giannini faculty, and in the soon-to-arrive New Deal he was to return to Washington, where he eventually headed the Agricultural Adjustment Administration. Paul Taylor, then a young faculty member—although Galbraith never took a course from him—was admired for his compassionate, reformist involvement in the plight of California's farmworkers, a plight soon made world famous by his friend John Steinbeck in *The Grapes of Wrath*.

Somewhat less progressive, but no less useful in imparting basic economic theory, were men such as Ewald Grether, M. M. Knight, and Carl Plehn. "I learned Alfred Marshall from Ewald Grether," Galbraith has written, "who taught with a drillmaster's precision for which I have ever since been grateful. Marshall is the quintessence of classical economics and much of what he says is wrong. But no one can know what is wrong if he does not understand it first." By comparison, Knight—brother of the more distinguished Frank Knight, a totemic conservative figure at the University of Chicago and later a godfather to postwar Chicago stars such as Milton Friedman and George Stigler—produced a less positive memory: his seminar in economic history was "a gifted exercise in irrelevancy."[57]

At the end of his first year, Galbraith was able to renew his fellowship and begin work on his doctorate. Although restricted finances forced him to move out of International House into cheaper private lodgings nearby, he found time for a more active student life. Berkeley in those days hadn't quite established the reputation for turbulence it acquired in the 1960s, but the mood among its graduate students ranged, as Galbraith and others have described it, "from liberal to revolutionary." He noted proudly:

> The graduate students with whom I associated in the thirties were uniformly radical, and the most distinguished were communists. I listened to them eagerly and would like to have joined both the conversation and the Party but here my agricultural background was a real handicap. It meant that, as a mat-

---

*Ely's textbook—which explained economics in institutional and historical terms, and unabashedly argued for greater equality and reform—outsold Marshall's *Principles* at land grant colleges and universities in the early decades of the twentieth century.

ter of formal Marxian doctrine, I was politically immature. Among the merits of capitalism to Marx was the fact that it rescued men from the idiocy of rural life. I had only very recently been retrieved. I sensed this bar and I knew also that my pride would be deeply hurt by rejection. So I kept outside.

To this he added, with a touch of chagrin, "There was possibly one other factor. Although I recognized that the system could not and should not survive, I was enjoying it so much that, secretly, I was a little sorry."[58]

Gregory Silvermaster, somewhat older than Galbraith, was among the department's more "mature" graduate students whom Galbraith came to admire. (Silvermaster later joined the New Deal in Washington, where his radicalism apparently carried him into the much darker world of spying for the Soviet Union.[59]) Robert Merriman, a talented teaching fellow, was another. Merriman eventually won a traveling fellowship to Europe, and in due course this led him to Spain, then in the midst of its tragic civil war. Ardently antifascist, he used the skills he'd acquired as an undergraduate member of ROTC to become commander of the Abraham Lincoln Brigade, the battalion of American volunteers who fought alongside Spanish Republicans against General Franco and his Falangists. Killed in Aragon during the retreat from Belchite in 1938, he was immortalized by his friend Ernest Hemingway as Robert Jordan in *For Whom the Bell Tolls*. Of Merriman Galbraith has written simply, "I think of him with admiration."[60]

Among the thinkers and ideas passionately discussed among the radical students, Marx and Marxism were less attractive to Galbraith than Thorstein Veblen. Veblen, who'd taught for several years at nearby Stanford (before being dismissed for serial philandering), had died in 1929, but his reputation was still large—and still controversial.

Veblen had first won celebrity in 1899, when his brilliant but turgid *The Theory of the Leisure Class* was published. The book had become an instant national success even though it was a peculiar, even perplexing hybrid of competing disciplines, and so densely written as to be almost impenetrable. Indeed its fame proved to be as surprising to its author as to his critics, who swiftly became legion. Its unusual popularity owed much to the times in which it appeared and the haunting questions it posed.

The United States' once-primitive industrial sector had soared so quickly in the years 1840–1900 that a young, rural, agrarian nation had become the world's largest economy. A wave of immigrants had flooded in with industrialization, and American cities had grown crowded with vast slums that teemed in sharp contrast to the tiny islands of extraordinary opulence that floated uneasily in their midst. Veblen's book captured the unease about this—and gave seeming academic and scientific justification to it—even as it belittled the academy's pretensions. At one level it was a coruscating satirical indictment of the fabulous new wealth that industrialism and the Gilded Age had brought to a few (Veblen's new "leisure class"). It was also a devastating critique of the then-new neoclassical economic theory of Alfred Marshall, which defended the logic of industrial capitalism. Part economics, part sociology, part history, part cultural anthropology, *The Theory of the Leisure Class* was far from accessible or enjoyable, and yet it struck a chord among the tens of thousands who read it, persuading them that the new world of industrial brutality, widespread poverty, and conspicuous display of vulgar wealth was not scientifically defensible as the logical and systemic consequence of progressive human evolution, which the new "scientific economics" claimed.

Veblen, the son of immigrant Norwegian parents who'd been raised on farms in Wisconsin and Minnesota, seemed an unlikely bearer of such a message. But he had studied under distinguished scholars and couldn't be easily dismissed as an ignorant populist or scrofulous socialist rabble-rouser or pamphleteer. John Bates Clark, one of neoclassical economics' most distinguished American pioneers, had been his professor, C. S. Pierce had taught him philosophy at Johns Hopkins, and at Yale he had earned his doctorate under the august and redoubtable William Graham Sumner, the country's reigning apostle of Social Darwinism.

Veblen's rough-hewn manners, however, his outspoken skepticism about religion and conventional mores, his unkempt appearance, and his bohemian attraction to other men's wives left him unemployed for seven years after finishing his doctorate, and back on his family's isolated farm. It wasn't until 1892, at the age of thirty-five, that he landed his first real teaching job, at the newly established University of Chicago. There, his career finally prospered and he eventually completed *The Theory of the Leisure Class*.* Galbraith admitted fifty years after discovering him at Berkeley that Veblen's rural upbringing, thirst for academic knowledge, awkward failure to "fit in," and skeptical distrust of established authority (the Norwegians' attitude toward Swedes, from whom they'd won national independence only recently, resembled that of the Scots toward the English) were "perhaps dangerously attractive to someone of my background."

> He was not a constructive figure; no alternative economic system and no penetrating reforms are associated with his name. There was danger here. Veblen was a skeptic and an enemy of pretense. Those who drank too deeply could be in doubt about everything and everybody; they could believe that all effort at reform was humbug. I've thought to resist this tendency, but in other respects Veblen's influence on me has lasted long.[61]

---

*The political scientist Harold Lasswell, trying to define Veblen's influence, wrote, "When I was a freshman at the University of Chicago I ran smack into a small chapel of Veblenians who burned a frantic candle of admiration in perpetual recognition of the master. I met the hero occasionally as he journeyed from one place of exile or retirement to the next. He was rarely of any sparkle when he spoke. But there was a very special aura of potentiality about his every mannerism. At first he struck you as a rumpled and crumpled Van Dyke . . . [yet] his permissive irreverence chimed with the mood of the twenties, and gave everyone with any claim to brightness the obligation to be smart . . . [He] avoided the political implications of a responsible Marxism, and contributed to the undertone of disapproval and alienation that characterized the posture of the well-turned-out intellectual in this country whenever our leading economic, political and social institutions were referred to" (Lasswell quoted in David Riesman, *Thorstein Veblen* [New York: Scribner's, 1953], 1).

Campus political life and the heated debate over political and economic ideas weren't the only interest Galbraith discovered. He found time to explore the delights of San Francisco (then still connected by ferries rather than a bridge to the East Bay) and the soaring beauty of the Sierra, and to indulge in a modest amount of student carousing, fueled (this was when Prohibition was still in force) by alcohol purloined from the university's chemistry labs and cut with grapefruit juice.

For a brief time, he even carried on his first real courtship, as he likes to tell, a distant twinkle in his eye, "with a slim, boyish-looking girl who, improbably in light of her build, claimed to have been in Texas Guinan's chorus before turning to the higher learning. More recently she had been in Tahiti and then in Bora Bora where she had gone native and had as proof a comprehensive suntan." She (he claims to have forgotten her name) was studying anthropology, and "I fell deeply in love with her." But on their second or third date, she peremptorily demanded to know whether he, as an economist, thought it right to be wasting her and his time with his pursuit. "Nothing in my Canadian and Calvinist background had prepared me for such a personal concept of efficiency." Shortly afterward, following an all-night party at which he thought there might be hope for them after all, she insisted on being driven straight to the train station. "She had just remembered that, on the day following, she was scheduled to marry a banker in New Mexico." (Galbraith ran into her many years later in New York. This time she was just back from Haiti and without a husband but preparing to marry a Pan Am pilot. She was working on her memoirs, she said, encouraged allegedly by the conservative columnist Westbrook Pegler. At first Galbraith felt a trace of fear about how he might be portrayed therein; only later, he says, did he regret that the book never appeared.[62])

By the fall of 1933, the start of his third and final year at Berkeley, the neophyte economist was hard at work on his doctoral thesis, a public-finance study of county expenditures in California. (The choice of this nonagrarian subject is a measure of the scholarly latitude the university offered to "second-rate" agricultural economists, for which he was grateful.) By then, he was also teaching at Berkeley's own "farm school" at Davis, a small rural town located between Berkeley and Sacramento. In the 1930s, the tiny Davis campus, such as it was, functioned as a slightly more sophisticated version of OAC, where Galbraith found rather dismayingly that he'd been put "in charge of teaching in economics, agricultural economics, farm management and accounting and, apart from the assistance of an elderly dean, provided all the instruction in these fields." Yet the $1,800 stipend for his commute was very welcome: it helped finance his own expenses and allowed him to extend a loan to his sister Catherine for her own education. With the prospect of graduation just ahead, Galbraith was also by then taking sober account of his alternatives. Jobs were scarcer than ever; a quarter of the U.S. labor force was out of work that year.

During the Christmas holidays, Galbraith returned to see his family for the first time since leaving Canada, and then went on to Philadelphia to attend the annual meeting of the American Economic Association, where he hoped to cultivate connections that might lead to a job that coming June. In Iona Station, he and his father talked at length—about his future, about politics, about the family, and about the straitened circumstances the Depression had brought to the farm. Ken had maintained an almost weekly correspondence with his father since his first year at OAC, and continued it throughout his years at Berkeley. Those letters have been lost, but a few surviving ones sent to his sisters Alice and Catherine show him to be a conscientious, earnest young man, warmly tied to his father and sisters. One, written to Alice in May 1933 near the end of his second academic year at Berkeley, discussed at length his application for a Royal Society of Canada fellowship that would pay for postgraduate work at Harvard—the first sign of where and how high he was now setting his sights. But he had not won the fellowship, he reported, and was now in a quandary, without solid immediate prospects. He regretted, he told his older sister, not his own situation, but his uncertainty about how to help pay for Catherine to attend college the following year, as Alice was then helping on her own meager salary to pay for his education at Berkeley.[63]

A month later he wrote Catherine directly, in a letter full of the affection and solicitude older brothers often show for younger sisters. She was by then thinking she, too, might go to OAC or possibly to MacDonald, an adjacent Ontario college. He carefully parsed for her his opinion of her options—and then sensitively reviewed the basic fact that, given the family's finances, there was a risk she might not be able to attend college at all, let alone a first-rate institution. But he promised he would find funds to help her.

WHAT THE MANY letters he and his father exchanged during his college and graduate years might have shown, had they survived, one cannot say, but they were undoubtedly full of lively, opinionated discussion of contemporary political affairs as well as life in the family. There would have been plenty of news about the U.S. presidential campaign and Roosevelt's landslide election, in 1932; the rise of Hitler to power in Germany; and the extraordinary measures of the New Deal's first hundred days, with their revolutionary implications for agriculture. And Archie would undoubtedly have kept his son abreast of goings-on in Canadian and provincial politics. Catherine has said that during Ken's OAC years, their father finally fully recovered from the tragedy of 1923 and resumed his position as a "man of standing" in Elgin County, including his active involvement in local and provincial politics once again in the Liberal Party. But, she added, Archie often chafed at the party's new conservative cast and minority status. His great hope for the Liberals' renewal in the late 1920s became a promising young political figure named Mitchell Hepburn.[64]

Hepburn was a local Elgin County boy whom Archie made into a protégé, first helping him win a provincial legislative seat, then sending him on to the national parliament in Ottawa. By the time Ken moved to Berkeley, Mitchell Hepburn had become the head of the Liberal Party in Ontario and was rising in national prominence and influence.

Hepburn was, by all accounts, a charismatic, witty, and brilliant character, a natural politician—and, as Archie well knew, had started his career as "a Drury man" in the UFO. During the late 1920s, he became known as a Liberal Party "reformer," campaigning to renew the old-fashioned progressive liberalism of Laurier along with newer populist ideas drawn from Drury. The Depression had reignited a hunger among the country's voters for just such a man, and by the spring of 1934 as elections loomed, Hepburn—by now an accomplished and passionate orator—was being celebrated, as one Canadian historian put it, as "the very voice of the cresting rage of the depression . . . [who] professed to be storming the walls of privilege on behalf of the locked-out." For the first time in almost two decades, it seemed the Liberal Party would be restored to power.

Ken Galbraith, meanwhile, was campaigning himself that spring, once again hoping to get a position at Harvard a year after failing to win the Royal Society fellowship. At the AEA meeting in Philadelphia, he made several connections he thought might help. As luck would have it, the Harvard economics department was looking for a junior researcher in agricultural economics, and the young Canadian's résumé and supporting letters of recommendation (submitted for his Royal Society fellowship) caught the eye of the department's senior agricultural economist. Letters went back and forth between Harvard and Berkeley about Ken's qualifications. Galbraith, even so, knew he was not certain of getting the job; he was one of several eager and qualified applicants for this minor one-year posting. As winter turned into spring and no final word came from Cambridge, he worriedly began to think that his only practical option was to stay on at Berkeley after receiving his degree in June, and to support himself by teaching at Davis.

Back in Canada, the election, too, was coming down to the wire, with Hepburn sure to become Ontario's premier if the Liberal Party won. Archie was confident: Hepburn was being favorably compared to FDR, and Roosevelt's first two years in office were admired among Ontario's Liberal Party voters, including the Scots. But opinion polls did not exist, and one could not be sure of the outcome.

Early that June, Archie rose before dawn on election day, and after a few necessary chores set aside his farm work to make sure that his voters turned out. He stayed up late into the night, listening to the radio as the results came in. The outcome, as it turned out, wasn't even close. The Liberal Party, under Hepburn's leadership, after its long exile surged back to power that night in a landslide, winning an overwhelming 66 out of 90 seats in the provincial House. Mitchell Hepburn became Ontario's new premier. Archie, as he prepared for bed that evening, was well pleased.[65]

The victory wasn't his only reason for delight: there had been a phone call earlier that evening from Berkeley. His son would be getting his doctorate from the University of California in two weeks, making him the family's first Ph.D.—and was going to start teaching at Harvard University that fall.

2

Harvard in the 1930s

HARVARD IN THE FALL OF 1934 was fast approaching its three-hundredth anniversary, in 1936, as America's epicenter of higher learning, and it was in
the midst of visible and profound change. James Bryant Conant, a quiet but
distinguished Yankee chemist, had been installed just a year earlier as its
twenty-third president, succeeding the redoubtable A. Lawrence Lowell, a
quintessential Brahmin who in 1909 had followed in turn the legendary
Charles Eliot, perhaps Harvard's greatest president. Over a forty-year tenure
that began shortly after the Civil War, Eliot had lifted the once sleepy New
England college to its undisputed rank as the nation's foremost university.

Eliot had turned Harvard away from its ossified function as educator of
young New England Brahmins by following the then-revolutionary German
model of "scientific scholarship." Dropping requirements in Greek and Latin
(as well as mandatory daily chapel), he had vastly expanded the faculty's
research and teaching in natural sciences and the new social sciences. Committed to strengthening graduate education, he also introduced the elective-
course system and the seminar, with its intimate give-and-take, and did away
with rote-based teaching and learning-by-memorization. In the fledgling social
sciences especially—nowhere more so than in economics—he encouraged
dramatic innovation. Under Eliot, Harvard in 1871 appointed the country's
first full-time professor of political economy (as economics was then called),
five years later granted the first economics Ph.D., and then in 1886 launched
the first academic journal of economics in the English-speaking world, the
Quarterly Journal of Economics.[1]

A. Lawrence Lowell, an august and very conservative man, could hardly
hope to equal these achievements, and so instead sought to burnish Eliot's
legacy, in part by discouraging abrupt change, in part by expanding Harvard's
architectural glories—over its intellectual vitality, some claimed. Initially he
tightened and deepened academic standards by introducing Oxbridge-style tu-
torials, comprehensive final exams, and concentration requirements for under-

graduates, but by the late 1920s, Lowell's tenure was increasingly controversial. He sought to set a quota on Jewish admissions, kept the few black freshmen admitted out of Harvard dorms, chaired the state review commission that affirmed the death penalty for Sacco and Vanzetti, and refused Marie Curie an honorary doctorate because she was a woman. When an aged professor's homosexuality was discovered, Lowell not only demanded the man's immediate resignation but told him to get a gun and "destroy himself."[2]

With Lowell's retirement and Conant's succession in 1933, accumulated demands for academic change cascaded forth. The deceptively soft-spoken Conant, forty years old, was liberal by comparison to Lowell, having voted for FDR in 1932 (and even, he later said, for the Progressive Party candidate, Robert La Follette, in 1924). He was descended from settlers who'd arrived in the Massachusetts Bay Colony in 1623, but his father was a mere photoengraver from unfashionable Dorchester. As Conant put it, he was a "native" Bostonian but not a "proper" one, a distinction Lowell underscored when the freshly appointed Conant diffidently asked what his salary should be. The Brahmin coldly shot back that he of course had no idea, since he had always returned his to Harvard.

After his first six months in office, *The New York Times* approvingly described Conant as devoted to a "new Harvard," in which he was "not to be builder but operator; to see the best material and the best workmanship go into the educational product."[3] But to achieve a "new Harvard," not least of the issues Conant faced was the need for new faculty. Many of Harvard's senior professors owed their appointments not to Lowell but to Eliot—nowhere more noticeably than in the Economics Department.[4]

The department's faculty roster told the tale, for six of the department's ten full professors in 1934 suddenly began to depart. Of these, Frank Taussig was both the most senior and, after fifty-two years of teaching at Harvard, still the most influential. As one colleague explained,

> It was in Taussig's advanced course in economic theory that [he] had his greatest effect on the teaching of economics at Harvard in the twentieth century. Economics 11 was required of all graduate students, and it was from these students that Harvard recruited its host of tutors, instructors, and section men from whom—in turn—Harvard selected most of its senior faculty.[5]

To his colleague Joseph Schumpeter, he was, simply put, "The American [Alfred] Marshall."

Taussig, the son of a wealthy German-Jewish industrialist from St. Louis (though his own sense of being Jewish, it was said, was all but invisible), had studied economics and history at Harvard, served as Eliot's personal secretary, and then been appointed to the Department of Political Economy in 1883, as its third faculty member. Although he'd hesitated to join the American Economic Association because of its early "radicalism," he was twice elected its head, in 1904 and 1905. During World War I, he served as a government adviser on trade and tariff policy, and helped to draft the tariff sections of the Versailles Treaty. A moderate conservative for the times, Taussig opposed the minimum wage and unemployment insurance, while blaming labor unrest on the lack of paternal leadership among the wealthy. Though still vigorous and a daunting figure to the younger men, by the time Galbraith arrived the thickset, powerfully built Taussig was due to retire the next spring, at the age of seventy-five.[6]

C. J. Bullock, appointed in 1902, had founded the Harvard Economic Service, the 1920s business forecasting unit that in 1929 so disastrously denied the coming of the Depression. By all accounts the department's most antediluvian member in outlook, Bullock likewise was shortly to step down.

Thomas Nixon Carver, who joined the department in 1900 and taught agricultural economics, economic history, and sociology as well as economic theory, had already left two years earlier, in 1932. A devout Social Darwinist, Carver in his prime was a large, broad-shouldered man (he rowed crew for many years) who in his teaching held with powerful certainty to a limited range of views. Even Lowell thought Carver a trifle too conservative, once remarking of him that he "sees things clearly but through a very small keyhole." (Carver was also a figure of idiosyncratic caution. Advised by President Eliot, when offered his appointment, that "none of us here uses either liquor or tobacco. . . . If either of these is necessary for comfort, you will probably not care to consider this position," Carver refrained from using either throughout his life. To students inclined to smoke, he recommended whittling as an alternative.)

Edwin Gay, who started teaching at Harvard in 1902 and whose preoccupation was discovering historical cycles underlying economic change, was now leaving as well. An active, energetic figure with a bristling black mustache that he allegedly dyed in later years, he was a demanding supervisor of graduate students who never wrote a book of his own. Gay's fixation on historical cycles led him to spend nearly three decades reading every available work on Europe's economic development between 1600 and 1730 for his never-finished masterpiece, and now he was departing for a quiet research position at the Huntington Library in California.*[7]

O.M.W. Sprague, another professor appointed in the 1890s (after studying under and then serving as assistant to Taussig), had left for the Harvard Business School. And William Z. Ripley, who started teaching in 1901 and for many years championed the biological superiority of Anglo-Saxons as reason for the United States' and England's economic success, had recently been forced to resign because of ill health. Thus, just as Galbraith arrived in Cam-

---

*To be fair, Gay was equally a man of affairs; he was first dean of the Harvard Business School, then editor of the *New York Evening Post*, later first president of the National Bureau of Economic Research and cofounder of the Council on Foreign Relations. Still, a festschrift volume for him captured his essence: "A scholar who might have been a scholar, an administrator who might have been an administrator, an editor who might have been an editor, if circumstances had conspired in his favor; a variety of tasks that he has not fully accomplished—that is really the situation."

bridge, most of the men who had assured Harvard of its first rank among American economics departments were gone.*

To offset these losses, the university was now drawing heavily on two rather unaccustomed sources: Continental Europe and the American Midwest. Until then, Harvard had most often been content to promote from within: from 1903 to 1919, no one had gotten a full-time departmental appointment without earning his Ph.D. at Harvard. But with so many senior men departing, new Ph.D.s were too young, inexperienced, and few in number. (Harvard in those days awarded only five to ten doctorates in economics annually.)

From the Continent came perhaps the more celebrated replacements, the most notable being the Austrian Joseph Aloïs Schumpeter, who remained Harvard's most outstanding conservative economist until his death in 1950. Given to the manners and dress of a European aristocrat and always colorfully arrogant (as a young man, he'd once hired an elegant carriage and a pair of prostitutes to promenade along the streets of Vienna), he'd also served briefly as minister of finance in postwar Austria. Privately, Schumpeter was given to dark lamentations about the vulgarity of modern life, the excessive influence of Jews, and the heresies of Keynes and Roosevelt. But he was a more complex figure than this suggests. He was liked by his students (many of them Jewish), who called him "Schumpy" and eagerly gathered in the afternoons at The Merle, a now long-gone coffee shop across the street from Widener Library, where they raptly listened to him opine about economics and contemporary life, his remarks leavened by a singular sense of humor. He liked, for example, to claim that he had set out as a young man to be his generation's greatest scholar, greatest lover, and greatest horseman—and had failed only in the last, owing to the collapse of the Austro-Hungarian cavalry in the Great War. He also liked to insist that a good servant was worth a thousand gadgets and that until he came to America, he'd not known what a mailbox was; until then, he claimed, he had always placed his outgoing letters on a silver tray in the hallway and found them gone the next morning.[8] Hired as a theorist of business cycles, Schumpeter, among his many contributions, introduced serious mathematical economics and even an early version of econometrics to the department for the first time in its history.

Gottfried Haberler was a fellow Austrian (though a grayer figure) who had earned his degree under Ludwig von Mises, been a visiting lecturer in 1931, and shortly thereafter became a regular member of the department. The German-born Sumner Slichter, another specialist in business-cycle theory, started at the Harvard Business School, then transferred across the Charles River to the Economics Department. And Wassily Leontief, a brilliant Russian émigré, later to win a Nobel Prize for developing input-output analysis, was also hired in this period.

---

*As a measure of their importance not just to the department but to the profession itself, four of the six—Taussig on two occasions, plus Carver, Gay, and Ripley—had served as president of the American Economic Association.

From the Midwest, Harvard's best-known addition was Alvin Hansen. Hansen was a South Dakotan who had been educated at the University of Wisconsin and was teaching at the University of Minnesota when Harvard approached him.[9] Having written several important works on long-term stagnation that made him skeptical of capitalism's self-equilibrating tendencies, he was counterweight to the department's conservative Austrians.

Another Minnesota transplant and Wisconsin graduate, John D. Black, was not only by then one of America's leading agricultural economists but a key figure in New Deal agricultural policies and Galbraith's first important mentor. Edward Chamberlin, trained at Iowa State College before earning his Harvard doctorate, was already renowned in professional circles, despite his youth, for his *Theory of Oligopolistic Capitalism* (1933), an important qualification on the mainstream's orthodox views about competition.

The Harvard economics department was also filled with a bright array of younger talent from new sources. The prolific Seymour Harris, its second Jewish member (who became Galbraith's closest friend in the department), was already publishing the first of what would be more than fifty scholarly works.[10] Paul Samuelson, also Jewish and fresh from the University of Chicago, starred among the graduate students and young instructors who included Paul Sweezy, Lloyd Meltzer, Robert Roosa, Richard Goodwin, Gabriel Hauge, and Sidney Alexander.[11]

For the young men at Harvard in 1934, the shift in departmental personnel posed both an opportunity and a challenge. Unlike their elders, many of the younger instructors and graduate students were inspired by Roosevelt and by his willingness to abandon orthodoxies in search of what worked. Most of these young men, faced with the Great Depression, believed that capitalism's collapse meant that economists must change some of their most cherished and fundamental beliefs. But what sort of change was called for? The Soviet Union represented one model, Nazi Germany and Fascist Italy another. Along the spectrum of choices in between lay an array of ideas, some more thought out than others, some better established; but how to choose?

In today's introductory economics textbooks, the 1930s has about it a monolithic simplicity as the decade that inaugurated "the Age of Keynes." In this simplified view, it was a time when economists and public leaders accepted the inescapable influence of the state in shaping market economies. But in the fall of 1934, for Galbraith and most American economists the revolutionary ideas of Keynes's *General Theory of Employment, Interest, and Money* (1936) lay in the future. Of more pressing concern were the debates over what had brought Americans to their anguished and suffering state and what lay ahead. Those arguments, their implications and likely outcomes, lacked Keynesian cohesion and indeed often pressed off in several directions at once. Nowhere was the road so clear, the path so sure, as the apostles of the elegant Lord Keynes later made it seem.

Roosevelt may have won in a landslide in 1932, but at Harvard he and his policies were hardly popular, to say the least. In a *Crimson* straw poll taken days before his election, Harvard students had chosen Hoover by a three-to-one margin. (So unpopular was Roosevelt that even Norman Thomas, the Socialist Party candidate, outpolled him in five of Harvard's seven undergraduate houses.[12]) And Harvard's students weren't the only ones critical of Roosevelt and his policies. The Great Crash—and then the New Deal—had struck Harvard's economists a hard blow. Hardly immune to human suffering, they could not help but be moved by the appalling conditions around them; but for many what struck with nearly equal (in some cases, greater) force was the seeming possibility that theories on which they had built their careers and lives were collapsing too. These orthodox men believed in markets with a faith bordering on religion, and they viewed talk of government intervention, let alone socialism, with only the darkest emotions.

Carver, for example, had for some years taught a course on social reform which attracted, as one student recalled, "every kind of radical the student body could furnish" and in which, like a temperance preacher in a saloon, he "battled valiantly for the souls of the unenlightened." The journalist Heywood Broun, who never tired of telling how he became a socialist at Harvard, captured the mood in Carver's class. According to Broun, the spring-term course would start with Carver inviting visiting socialists to state their case during February and March; he would then spend April and May on slashing rebuttal. Broun claimed that baseball saved him from Carver's attempts at capitalist redemption—Boston's two teams, the Red Sox and Braves, opened their seasons in April, and took precedence over socialism's refutation.[13]

C. J. Bullock was even more wounded by the Depression and its New Deal aftermath. Neolithicly conservative, he taught a course on the history of economic thought popularly known to students as "From Adam to Adam Smith." Class lectures would frequently veer from their established order, one student recalled, as "Bullock suddenly remembered some Bolshevist aberration, as he saw it, of Herbert Hoover. He did not denounce Roosevelt; Roosevelt was beyond the pale."[14]

William Crum, a statistical expert, likewise had little good to say of the New Deal, though on the eve of Roosevelt's landslide reelection in 1936, he fell afoul of his prejudices. When the *Literary Digest* mailed out trial ballots to its readers, seeking "scientifically" to predict the electoral outcome, the results indicated that the Republican, Alfred Landon, would beat Roosevelt handily. Crum then proceeded to "correct" these results for sampling error, thereby enlarging Landon's expected winning margin. When Roosevelt won 61 percent of the vote and carried forty-six of the forty-eight states, this statistician duly retired back to dustier work.*

Taussig at least took a milder view of Washington's forays into economic *dirigisme*—perhaps the result of his age or the fact that President Hoover himself had favored public-works spending. Even before Roosevelt took office,

---

*Crum wasn't alone at Harvard in foreseeing FDR's defeat in 1936: a *Crimson* poll found that Harvard students, having favored Hoover 3 to 1 in 1932, supported Landon, though this time by a smaller margin.

Taussig had thus given qualified endorsement to the idea that this might be needed to free the country from stagnation. Though many of his colleagues were alarmed, he took comfort from the fact that a number of leading Republicans and business leaders shared his views, saving him the ignominy of standing entirely outside the pale.

Taussig's feelings were not shared by his successor as the department chairman, however. Harold Hitching Burbank, personally one of the most gracious of men, took a dim view of not just the New Deal but virtually all forms of "alien" influence—among which he included Roosevelt and his Brains Trusters, Jews, Bolsheviks, and anyone else not thoroughly "American." Perhaps because "Burbie" (as colleagues unaffectionately called him behind his back) felt Canadians the least "foreign" of foreigners, Galbraith somehow escaped opprobrium, though not close examination. Years later, on receiving his FBI file, Galbraith found that J. Edgar Hoover's agents had interviewed Burbank in the late 1930s about Galbraith's "loyalties." He had advised the agents that

> Galbraith was an excellent teacher; that he gave a commanding appearance due to his height of 5' 6" [*sic*—Galbraith was 6' 8"] and his dignified bearing. It was [Burbank's] emphatic statement that Galbraith was absolutely loyal and patriotic. He said that though the subject leaned as far to the left as President Roosevelt, he was completely in sympathy with a democratic form of government.[15]

For Galbraith and the other young men of the economics department, salvation lay in the fact that these men (Burbank excepted) were at or near the end of their careers. As a consequence, at least a few among the junior faculty could express a slightly wider range of opinions, including some their elders had (or would have) found heretical. It was an advantage that lowly instructors such as Galbraith and the brighter graduate students eventually put to great advantage, both in their careers and in remaking American economics. First, though, they learned the reasons for caution.

The lesson came in two parts: the first concerned the publication of a book by some of the department's leading figures, and its fallout on younger men who chose to disagree; the second came in a complicated tenure fight that drew national attention to Harvard's reputation for academic freedom. During the 1930s, the powerful light of orthodoxy among Harvard's established economists never shined more brightly than in a little book coauthored by seven of them, published in the winter of 1934. Entitled *The Economics of the Recovery Program*, it took direct aim at the New Deal's nascent recovery efforts, and fired away.[16] Schumpeter set the book's overall tone in a review of the nineteenth century's experience with widespread economic collapse. In every case recovery had come by itself, he concluded, "the only action of government being the maintenance of a sound fiscal policy working under an undisturbed capitalist system." Any government interference, he ominously warned, "leaves part of the work of depressions undone and adds to an undigested remnant of maladjustment."

Rooseveltian programs were thus to be opposed, not on "political" but on "scientific" grounds. Trust-busting and market regulation would be ineffectual, another professor wrote, because "elimination of unfair competition is not likely to constitute an important step toward recovery." Government efforts to raise wages, according to yet another, were doomed because "an increase in the rate of wages means an increase in the costs of production." From that he concluded, "An increase in costs leads to lower profits and, if profits are small or negligible, to bankruptcy, or to higher prices."

The government's monetary policy was called "unfriendly toward capital," threatening "a wild orgy of inflation," and should instead consist of dollar stabilization and a quick return to the gold standard. The farm program was seen as built on "uneconomic principles" that merely favored the farmer over the consumer. Public works "provide no panacea for recovery" and threatened to be "merely a political football and drain upon harassed treasuries."

The group's conclusions were harsh, even incendiary—and widely publicized by *The New York Times* and dozens of other papers.[17] Republican opponents of Roosevelt rushed to praise the book for its "neutral" and "scientific" judgment, and in the White House, it was taken as a major political blow. A month later, however, the President released to reporters a letter he had just received from Cambridge. In it, six other Harvard economists wrote of their strong support for the New Deal's efforts:

> In view of the amount of adverse criticism that has been directed against the policies of your administration by professional economists, we feel it incumbent upon us to express to you our sincere admiration both of your general objectives and the statesmanship with which you have sought to attain these objectives . . . Our support extends broadly to all the major efforts of your administration.[18]

For Roosevelt, it was just what the political moment called for. The public brouhaha over condemnation of his programs by "scientific economics" now swiftly dissolved into a dispute among professors.

For the six signers of the letter, though, things ended less pleasantly. Unlike the authors of *The Economics of the Recovery Program*, the letter writers were all young, untenured instructors, and they soon found themselves no longer needed in Cambridge. Their abilities weren't so much at issue: when Harvard swiftly released one of the signers, a young Canadian named Lauchlin Currie, the prominent economist Jacob Viner derisively declared that he had been "too good" for Harvard. Currie's academic career was ended, but he was quickly hired by the New Deal, and by the late 1930s he served as Roosevelt's personal economic adviser, a position he used to help implant Keynesianism in Washington. Let go at the same time, Currie's friend Harry Dexter White went on to a senior position at the Treasury, and became coarchitect with Keynes of the Bretton Woods agreement.[19]

Two of the signers, Raymond Walsh and Alan Sweezy, soon found their dismissal from Harvard at the center of a national firestorm over academic freedom. After President Conant refused to renew their teaching contracts, the "Walsh-Sweezy Affair" became a consuming and prolonged battle that pitted some of Harvard's most eminent professors against Conant and Harvard's governing Board of Overseers over the alleged relations between politics and Harvard's tenure policy. It was the most famous of many such fights in the 1930s.

For Galbraith, meanwhile, 1934–35 turned out to be surprisingly productive. "Walsh-Sweezy" was still in the future, and he arrived too late to be touched by Currie's and White's forced departures. Assigned to teach a section of introductory economics and a seminar in agricultural issues, he still found time most Fridays to board the B. & O.'s overnight Federal Express train to Washington, where he retained a minor consulting position with the Agriculture Department, courtesy of one of his former professors at Berkeley. On a one-year contract, Galbraith also soon began to master the status elements of Harvard's teaching system, the better to renew his instructorship for the coming year. By embroidering a bit on his "Washington contacts" among the younger fellows, he was able to develop a network of companionable acquaintances who saw in the lanky Canadian a man worth cultivating.

The favorable impressions created by talk of "great things" (and the dropping of a few choice New Deal names here and there) had no visible effects on his first formal Harvard teaching assignment, however. Only three students appeared for his agricultural economics seminar—one a Japanese student who spoke almost no English, the second a young man who fell asleep as soon as Galbraith began to speak, the third at least modestly talented. "It was a horrifying experience," Galbraith recalled, and not likely to encourage the department's renewal of his contract.[20]

Galbraith fortunately hadn't been hired merely to teach. Professor Black had picked Galbraith from among several candidates on the basis of recommendations about his research and writing abilities. Black, whose own boundless energies made him what today would be described as an academic entrepreneur, had other ways to keep his young colleague busy.

Little remembered now, Black was a towering figure in agricultural economics in the 1930s, whose presence at Harvard made urbane Cambridge, incongruously, one of the nation's preeminent centers in the field. (In the 1930s, Harvard was the second largest source of doctorates in agricultural economics, trailing only the predictable Cornell.[21]) Black accomplished this by tirelessly recruiting graduate students from around the world, and then persuading governments and foundations to support their tuition and research. "Black's people" came from Canada, Australia, Latin America, and Europe as well as the United States to study agricultural economics, and all the complexities of rapidly changing rural life, on the banks of the Charles River. Galbraith wrote of his mentor with deep affection and respect years after their first encounter:

> Fifty-one when I met him, solid but not quite stout, John D., as he was called, viewed everyone with an expression of infinite benignity and kindness.* With notable exceptions, Joseph Schumpeter whom he disliked being one, it was the way he really felt. He was one of a family of ten born on a small Wisconsin farm and one of seven who survived to adulthood. (One brother was killed leading a charge against the Germans in 1918.) Of the seven, five had achieved college or beyond. Black had taught rhetoric, as it was called, to engineers at the Michigan College of Mines on the Upper Peninsula, financed his own work in economics at the University of Wisconsin in the heyday of LaFollette liberalism, and had gone on to a professorship and department chairmanship in agricultural economics at the University of Minnesota. He has a substantial claim to being called the father of the subject.
>
> Preeminently he was a teacher. Though he had never been known to prepare a lecture, his students listened with rapt attention to personal reminiscences, the rights and wrongs in the struggle for agricultural legislation, the personality and thoughts of the other agricultural economists and to his injunctions never, under any circumstances, to sacrifice what you perceived as the public interest to personal ambition or pecuniary interest. His office door was always open to his students from shortly after dawn to dusk, and he had never been known to terminate a conversation. He assumed responsibility for his students' careers for life, and they brought him their intended wives for review. Their achievements were his. In later years, when I acquired a certain distinction in economics, he was, if possible, more pleased than I.[22]

In Black, Galbraith had come upon that critical figure so many talented young people seek (and need) at the beginnings of their careers: teacher, patron, mentor, protector. Unlike so many of the other senior men in the department, Black had no antipathy to Roosevelt or to the New Deal idea that government was needed to shape capitalism's powers productively and equitably. He also had a background much like Galbraith's: he had been raised on a farm, he had earned his doctorate at a land-grant college, and like Galbraith's father, he had a practical engagement in the larger world and a strong vision of liberal social justice.

From the beginning of their relationship Black took a keen interest in Galbraith's work and career. Galbraith owed to Black not only his first appointment to Harvard but the subsequent renewal of his contract there for the next several years. Then, when Galbraith won a fellowship that allowed him to study at Cambridge University, where John Maynard Keynes and others were

---

*He sometimes acted differently, notably when defending his ideas and beliefs to bureaucrats and politicians. Galbraith has reported that Black was known in Washington as the "insulting economist."

formulating what was to become economics' new reigning doctrine, we see Black's hand behind the award. In 1939, when the "Walsh-Sweezy" controversy led to Harvard's release of Galbraith, we discover Black helping him find new employment; and in the late 1940s, it is Black we find engineering Galbraith's return to Harvard.

Perhaps the single most important push Black gave to Galbraith's nascent career was at the beginning, in the spring of 1935, when he asked him to co-author "The Quantitative Position of Marketing in the United States."[23] Galbraith had already written some academic articles that had been published while he was at Berkeley, but they had focused on safely agrarian topics such as branch banking's role in farm lending, honey marketing, and the theory of marginally productive farmland. Black now put Galbraith to work on a broader project about business marketing in general.

"The Quantitative Position of Marketing in the United States" showed no signs of the later Galbraithian style; it lacked both wit and noticeable erudition, but intellectually it was significant, for it was Galbraith's debut in Harvard's prestigious *Quarterly Journal of Economics*. And because the article was coauthored with Black, senior economists took notice of a promising (and approved) young talent in their midst.

The paper's core is an analysis of U.S. government data on business employment and the costs for marketing manufactured goods. The data themselves were sometimes preliminary (one important census series was new in 1930) and, as the authors cautioned, error-prone. But to Galbraith and Black, they were valuable to a significant argument in the Depression-era debate over paths to recovery. Business's manufacturing costs as a percentage of both wholesale and retail goods prices had been steadily declining for thirty years—so much, the authors showed, that aggregate marketing costs now nearly equaled manufacturing costs.

Although both manufacturing output and sales were deeply depressed in the 1930s, most economists who worried about economic recovery preferred to focus on the problems of manufacturing and its productivity rather than on sales. Better-quality data for manufacturing was one reason, but for Black and Galbraith, it wasn't enough. Should productivity be measured by manufacturing cost or by the final selling price of the goods? Galbraith and Black's point was that the former, which showed constant improvement, was in a sense offset by the latter; if one neglected the effects of marketing on the overall shape of the economy, one failed to explain "why much of our gains in industrial and agricultural efficiency have been offset by the additional efforts expended" in selling. One resulting question, of importance to the measurement of total business productivity, was whether "some considerable part of our economized industrial effort has not merely involved the substitution of increased commercial activity."

What did marketing's massive new significance in the American economy imply? Summarizing the sector's employment figures and its share in national income (by the 1930s second only to manufacturing itself, and surpassing agriculture), Galbraith and Black came down firmly on the side of the New Dealers' arguments for stimulating *consumer* demand.

Here was a challenge to the orthodox view that further wage and job cuts were a good means to restore "business confidence"—the view vividly expressed by Schumpeter and his Harvard coauthors in *The Economics of the Recovery Program* a year earlier. But if, Galbraith and Black tartly observed, their own thesis was correct, with so much of the economy now tied to *consumer* confidence, "nothing more need be said of the part played by consumer demand for conveniences or services . . . in the national economy." Business confidence per se, and public acceptance of further economic contraction in order to reestablish "equilibrium," should no longer be the focal element for recovering from the Depression. Rather, restoring consumer confidence was paramount, and this—although Galbraith and Black left the matter unexplored—would require the intervention of government.[24]

Keynes was shortly to make the issue of consumer demand versus business confidence a central feature of his *General Theory*, arguing that business and investor confidence can sometimes plunge so low that the economy enters a "liquidity trap" from which only government's deficit spending can ensure its recovery. Although the Galbraith-Black article did not explicitly go so far and did not have Keynes's theoretical rigor, its authors nonetheless showed a temperament and cast of mind that would welcome Keynes's revolutionary new focus on aggregate consumption.

Perhaps most important for the short term, the paper satisfied Black, who arranged renewal of Galbraith's contract at Harvard for a second year. Over the next few years, Black assigned Galbraith several important research projects (notably a Brookings Institution study that Black himself directed), which brought the young man in even closer contact with New Deal programs and new ways of thinking about the function of government in the economy.

Galbraith thus not only survived his first year at Harvard, but by its end seemed launched on what could become a tenure track at the nation's leading university. Although most of the Economics Department's professors showed no inclination to favor the intellectual directions in which Galbraith would now travel, in Black he had found someone who would. For the young animal husbandry major from rural Ontario, it was a promising beginning.

3

American Agriculture and the New Deal

IF KEN GALBRAITH had counted on his teaching abilities alone, his budding Harvard career might well have ended after nine months. Instead, by plunging into a new research field with the help of his new mentor and quickly publishing the results, he learned a crucial lesson about academic initiative—and got an intriguing introduction to economics off the farm. But agriculture was still Galbraith's specialty, and he did not abandon it.

The New Deal response to the agonies farmers were enduring in the Depression deeply influenced Galbraith's thinking about all economics and shaped his most influential works, such as *American Capitalism*, *The Affluent Society*, and *The New Industrial State*, even though none of them more than mentions agriculture per se. Though he eventually stopped doing agricultural economics, it served him as an intellectual crucible and shaped his understanding of the relations between blackboard economics and the real-world applications of policy.

Nowadays, the significance of New Deal agriculture policies is easily overlooked or misunderstood. Apart from a sentimental attachment to "the family farm" or recurring concerns about too much dietary fat or pesticides, most Americans know little of rural life or its complex history. But in the 1930s, more than half of all Americans still lived on farms or in the small towns near them, and in the bigger towns and cities, millions more were sons or daughters of farmers who still remembered what it meant to draw a living from the soil.* Moreover, agriculture was a cornerstone of New Deal reform. Just twelve days after taking office, Roosevelt introduced the landmark Agricultural Adjustment Act, a bill that the journalist Walter Lippmann aptly described at the time as "the most daring economic experiment ever seriously proposed in the United States." As the historian Arthur J. Schlesinger, Jr., put it: "The fight to save the

---

*Officially, the United States was more urban than rural by the 1930s, but the Census Bureau counted as urban anyone living in a town of more than 2,500.

banking system opened the Hundred Days; the fight to save the farmers opened the New Deal proper."[1] And the Roosevelt administration then went on to create dozens of programs for the American farmer, involving billions of dollars and thousands of federal workers annually—of which some of the most prominent were the Farm Credit Administration, the Federal Emergency Relief Administration, the Soil Conservation Service, the Resettlement Administration, and the Rural Electrification Agency, each one of them a dramatic break both with historic attitudes about government and with the conventional wisdom of academic economics.

In fact, in many ways agriculture came to serve as the New Deal's largest laboratory in social and economic experimentation. In part, this was due to the then much greater importance of agriculture's output and population, but it was also due to the unprecedented array of talent—and the distinctive approach to public economic intervention and planning—that the Roosevelt administration used to address the question of rural life. American leaders, including Roosevelt himself, and the public still placed great store in rural ideals and values, and when it came to farmers they were willing and ready to experiment with alternatives to the traditional theory and practice of market economics.

As one measure of farming's importance in New Deal thinking, one recent study concludes that in the 1930s the Department of Agriculture was "among the—if not *the*—most prestigious of all federal government agencies of cabinet rank."[2] Another recent history credits the department with maintaining "the best established group" of economists in Washington.[3] It even ran its own degree-granting graduate school, with course offerings that covered the latest in statistical and theoretical advances in economics and social sciences. Thus we can see at work the intricate web of New Deal approaches to economic theory, policy, and practice, along with the legacy of older debates from which they grew. We can also see that powerful divisions among economic theorists belied the later notion that there was a long-running "mainstream" continuity, and better understand how the ground was laid for the imminent Keynesian revolution and Galbraith's part in it.

Starting in the summer of 1935, Black assigned Galbraith a series of research projects that grew out of a five-year study that the Brookings Institution had commissioned from him. The earliest of the Washington policy think tanks, Brookings was interested in analyzing and documenting independently the policies of the Roosevelt administration, even though it was often critically at odds with them.[4] Thus Galbraith got to see the workings of the New Deal's extraordinary experimentalism close up. He wrote five long papers on New Deal farm policies, most of them published in nonagrarian journals (anticipating his later habit of always seeking the broader audience), including the *Harvard Business Review*, the *Journal of Political Economy*, and the *American Economic Review*.[5] His principal focus was on the federal financing mechanisms that the New Deal established to stabilize and enhance farmers' income and security.

If the subject sounds esoteric and technical today, the underlying problem was not: by 1933, half of all farm mortgages were in default, and large parts of rural America hovered on the edge of open insurrection. Tens of thousands of farms were being abandoned, hundreds of thousands of acres of crops were being plowed under, and livestock was being slaughtered by the millions, the farmers unable to bring their animals to market, even as authorities around the country reported pervasive rural malnutrition and sometimes starvation. As just one example of the prevalent mood, in one Iowa town a judge sitting in a farm foreclosure case was hauled down from his bench by a mob of five hundred angry farmers and driven down a country road, where the crowd threw a noose over a nearby telephone pole. Someone put a hubcap on his head and told him to start praying; only at the last moment did cooler heads prevail. The same week, another crowd of farmers attacked deputies trying to foreclose another farm. The governor of Iowa, in response, sent National Guard troops into six counties. Watching the armed soldiers marching through the spring mud, a farmer told a *New York Times* reporter, "I guess this is Russia now." But these confrontations were hardly confined to Iowa, which was better off than states in the South or in the Dust Bowl then enveloping the southern Great Plains. Citing similar examples of vigilantism in more than twenty states, the head of the American Farm Bureau openly warned a congressional committee that "unless something is done for the farmers, we will have a revolution in the countryside in less than twelve months."[6] It was a warning many took seriously.

Yet government intervention in agriculture was wildly controversial, even though its precedent in many ways had long been established, and in terms of federal land-use policy could be traced back to the days of the Northwest Ordinance and George Washington.[7] In 1929, President Hoover had dramatically broken with fellow conservatives by creating the Federal Farm Board to deal with the spreading collapse well before it peaked; he then allocated the immense sum of $500 million (the federal budget was less than $4 billion) to rescue failing farms. But the effort was to no avail: after three years of operation, the FFB lost 70 percent of its appropriation. Black, as the board's chief economist, had seen its failures close up, and thus when Galbraith set to work analyzing the functioning of the Farm Credit Administration—a New Deal agency that consolidated the work of the older and loosely coordinated federal land banks, federal intermediate credit banks, banks for cooperatives, and the production credit corporations and associations—he knew he was entering a political and economic minefield.

He later recalled both the subject's complexity and his aptitude for it with wry self-deprecation:

> Everything there was to know . . . could have been learned in a couple of months and reported on in literate and detailed fashion in a couple more. But then, as now, any such dispatch would have been considered a grave defect in scholarly behavior and performance. A quickly completed job, regardless of quality, is bad. A lifetime work, not quite finished at death, is superb.[8]

Nonetheless (and still on renewable one-year contracts, which undoubtedly focused his attention), Galbraith applied himself with steadfast diligence. Quickly mastering essentials not just of the subject but of academic style, he energetically cross-referenced the articles, thereby lending to each subsequent piece a conspicuous sense of his efflorescing body of work. He also used the research to travel well beyond academic circles, making frequent visits to Washington as well as to the Midwest and the South, where he could learn about actual conditions first-hand.

What unifies the articles, apart from their roughly common (and rather eso-teric) subject, is the young author's repeated willingness to go beyond formal and neutral analysis, not only to show that the New Deal remedies (unlike Hoover's Federal Farm Board) were actually working, but to suggest creative new functions for the credit agencies that favored the farmer as borrower. Gal-braith here was affirming Black's own separate research conclusions (they wrote two of the papers together), and establishing two hallmarks of his work that set him apart from many of his colleagues.

First, none of the papers used any of the profession's preferred evaluative apparatus: calculus, algebra, geometry, or even simple regression analysis. In-stead Galbraith examined the empirical data, which he organized in clear ta-bles, and used logical reasoning expressed in an English that noneconomists could easily follow. Galbraith's reasoning followed the accepted conventions of neoclassical economics—marginal pricing, profit maximization, and so on—but he was quick to highlight real-world economic behavior that might violate the axiomatic canons, because the real world, especially in the Depression, was proving more complex than abstract axioms or modeling permitted.

Second, Galbraith did not insist on a rigorous "value-neutrality," whose im-portance was being reaffirmed by many mainstream economists at just this time, most famously by the conservative British economist Lionel Robbins.[9] Galbraith's audience might be economists, but his constituency was the Amer-ican farmer. Implied throughout (when not explicitly stated) is the belief that stable incomes and reasonable profits for farmers and an ongoing central obli-gation of government to assure decent incomes and profits (not just when mar-kets fail) should be agreed on. The papers were not intended simply and neutrally to assess the technical merits or liabilities of hypothetical commodity or credit markets so much as to use empirical economic data and widely acces-sible reasoning to get on with practical improvements in rural life.

In one article, for example, Galbraith detailed the enormous expansion of federal agricultural credit: by 1935 the U.S. government was the world's largest holder of farm mortgages.[10] Noting that Washington agencies, after swiftly deploying almost $3 billion in emergency funding, held nearly 40 per-cent of the country's farm mortgages, he argued that it was incumbent on gov-ernment to use its newfound power to smooth out fluctuations in farm family income henceforth. As examples, he offered several practical ways to do so: by damping down lending during recoveries, then stimulating it during recession;

by making mortgage-payment amounts similarly dependent on farm business cycles; and by using land-sales policy to modulate price, selling during price rises and holding during price drops.

In another article, he offered an ingenious array of farm-mortgage repayment plans likewise meant to stabilize farm income across business cycles.[11] Throughout the 1920s and 1930s (indeed, until the late 1940s) commercial banks offered farm mortgages only with down payments of 25 to 35 percent of a property's value and generally for periods of five years or less. Galbraith described variable payment schedules, mortgage lengths, and the merits of automatic versus contractual adjustment, and he showed how to measure farmers' net income in order to set shifting rates and repayment periods, emphasizing not only the need to experiment with these alternatives but also the fact that federal ownership of so many mortgages could facilitate experimentation.

In a third article (notable because it appeared in the *Harvard Business Review*), Galbraith wanted his audience to understand what had changed for the American farmer during FDR's first term. Despite the presumably laissez-faire predilections (and indifference to farmers generally) of *HBR* readers, he made no apology for the New Deal's ongoing intervention in farm-credit markets. He detailed the Farm Credit Administration's scope and successes, its precedents, and its likely future, concluding, "[That the agency] is permanent no one can doubt." It had technical and political problems to work out, but nonetheless had "gained the complete acceptance of the farmers; and there is at least a reasonable likelihood that it will again be a refuge for distressed debtors in future depressions. Any question of its discontinuance is purely academic."[12]

Perhaps the most telling of Galbraith's articles (written with Black) was "The Maintenance of Agricultural Production During the Depression," a summary overview of what he and Black believed had been learned about the farm economy in depression, and, by implication, what activist positions government should now take. The central question was why agriculture, unlike industry, had failed to show "rational" economic responses to depression or recession. From the late 1920s to the mid-1930s, the volume of industrial production had fallen 40 percent while agricultural production had dropped only 4 percent. Why didn't agricultural output fall dramatically when prices fell, if indeed the "rationality" of economic actors was, as neoclassical theory stipulated, true for all? They argued that the answer lay in the specific "rationality" of the individual farmer's behavior, and explained how that individual rationality produced the collective irrationality of overproduction. In so doing, they advanced a notion at odds with the fundamental tenets of conventional economic thought; it anticipated Keynes's more generalized critique of capitalism's capacity for crisis—and the need for government intervention to solve it.

Part of the explanation, the authors observed, lay (ironically) in the very fact that agriculture, compared to industry, more accurately matches the theoretical world of "perfect competition" so central to conventional economics. Many farmers producing a relatively homogenous product (wheat, or cotton, or corn) for many consumers is the paradigm of the Marshallian model, unlike the possibility of combination represented by monopoly or oligopoly in industry, where one or a few firms dominate and "sticky" prices resist decline.

But there was more: the smoothly functioning Marshallian textbook and blackboard models assume easily substituted production factors that are both mobile and divisible. But agriculture is a world full of "lumpy" supply costs: farmers face fixed elements (such as mortgages and equipment payments) whose costs don't simply fall when prices fall, and "ancillary" expenses (field maintenance, spraying, and so on) that must be incurred before the final selling prices are known. Farming is also hampered by the sheer difficulty of rationally forecasting its final real output, let alone the demand or ultimate selling price, given its long time horizons and uncontrollable factors such as weather. Moreover, the very disparity between sharply falling farm prices and stubbornly "sticky" industry prices meant that the store-bought consumer goods that farmers needed to live also drove them to resist production cuts.

Galbraith and Black made their concluding point clear:

> We fear that our attempt to analyze our problem in the language of current economics has given altogether too much of an appearance of rationality to the conduct of agricultural producers. No doubt the production decisions of the majority of farmers are made without any reasoned considerations of maximized return. If these respond to economic change in a "rational" direction they are likely to do it as a matter of submission to economic pressures; or perhaps in imitation of their more successful neighbors. It is a commonly observed phenomena [sic] that large numbers of farmers fail to respond at all at times indicated by the conjunctures of economic change; or, if they do respond, they turn in directions adverse to their individual fortunes.[13]

In short, while over the long term market economics "worked" (and farmers in the aggregate gradually did adjust their production in the 1930s, although not enough to become profitable without government help), Galbraith and Black wanted their readers to realize how visibly and durably real-world practices could diverge from economic theory—and with what disastrous results.

Throughout his major works, Galbraith again and again returned to this central issue of economic structure—of real-world relations in tension with, even in opposition to, the blackboard models of economists. In *American Capitalism*, he rationalized the "countervailing power" struggles of large institutions such as retailers against manufacturers, which resulted in a rough "equilibrium" quite different from the one predicted by theory. In *The New Industrial State*, it was key to his description of the "technostructure" that, he argued, dominates and sets the rhythms of America's largest corporations. Critics see aspects of Keynesian influence or even of the so-called Institutionalist school in his focus; but the 1930s articles show that much of his theoretical worldview grew out of his early research in agricultural and marketing economics and was then carried into his later work, however distant from its origins.

The very factors that Galbraith highlighted in agricultural economics, factors that cause it to deviate from the Marshallian model, are clearly explained in game theory, a development in economic thought that did not become influential for another thirty years, as well as in behavioral economics, which didn't appear until the 1980s. As we shall see, both game-theoretic terms and behavioralist models represent a quantum leap in economists' efforts to describe actual economic behavior. They also reveal serious underlying problems in the neoclassical model itself—but this takes us ahead of our story.

IF ECONOMIC STRUCTURE early on emerged as a key component in Galbraith's thought, a second factor was economic and political power and its effect on the actions of public and private actors. Mainstream economists have never been comfortable with "power" as a concept, save for the abstract "power" of "the market" itself to enforce competitive equilibrium and discipline on participants. Even today, the word almost never appears in textbooks or standard dictionaries of economic terms. (When, in a famous exception, Mancur Olson set out to describe "the logic of collective action" to fellow economists in the 1960s, he began by admitting that his colleagues had for the most part neglected the subject—and then himself avoided using the term, relying heavily on sociologists and political scientists to address the problem-that-cannot-be-named.[14]) But Galbraith's major works never lacked attention to power, and his small book *The Anatomy of Power* (1983) showed his ideas on the importance of the subject for economics.[15] Where did his attentiveness to power come from?

The most obvious initial source was his first-hand exposure to the way farm politics, economics, and policy collided the summer before he began teaching at Harvard. By then, among his young Berkeley colleagues,

> word [had] . . . reached the university that a nearly unlimited number of jobs were open for economists at unbelievably high pay in the federal government. Students who had been resisting for years the completion of theses and the resulting unemployment now finished them up in weeks. Some did not stop even to do that. So a new gold rush began, back across the American River, up by Calaveras County, over the crest of the Sierras and on across the Rockies and the Plains to the Potomac.[16]

Although he already had notice of his Harvard appointment for the fall, Galbraith (like so many before and after) had accumulated substantial debts financing his education. And so he, too, headed to Washington. After a cross-country drive from Berkeley (with a stopover, he still recalls with a twinkle, to see the fan-dancer Sally Rand perform at the Chicago World's Fair), he arrived in the capital, where he promptly called Howard Tolley, one of his old Berkeley professors who had recently become chief of the planning division of the Agricultural Adjustment Administration.

Tolley hired the young Canadian on the spot, offering him a temporary sum-

mer assignment at what seemed to Galbraith the incredible salary of nearly
$300 a month (this was more than the annual $2,400 Harvard was offering,
and Galbraith used it to pay off a $500 school loan from his sister). But before
he could start the job, it was explained that he needed to introduce himself to
a representative of Postmaster General James Farley, the "custodian," as he
genteelly put it, "of Democratic patronage." Galbraith, who claims he was surprised that the official cared more that he was a New Deal supporter than that
he was a U.S. citizen, plunged into work the next day.

The project to which Tolley assigned him concerned options for the disposition of millions of acres of tax-delinquent farmland, including the possibility
of a federal takeover of a large portion of them.[17] Even today, one can easily
forget how immense the United States' public landholdings are: more than
750 million acres, nearly a third of the nation's total land mass. And farming's
collapse in the Depression suddenly opened up the possibility of a vast, if
painful, potential addition to this patrimonial store. Most of the millions of
tax-delinquent acres had been abandoned by their owners by then. Half of
Florida's farmlands were subject to seizure, for example, while throughout the
South; in northern Michigan, Wisconsin, Minnesota; and across the Dust
Bowl states Galbraith found that farmers' tax delinquency was "not the exception, but the rule."[18]

In his memoirs, he says he came to favor government takeover of much of
the lands, but as a new, summertime employee who found little support from
his superiors, he soon abandoned his advocacy. "I was surrounded by sensible
men, who thought the whole idea irresponsible. I did not fight very hard, for I
was concerned to show that, although young, I was a very responsible chap."[19]
He suggests that this was only a minor footnote in Washington policy history.
But in the fractious laboratory of social experimentation that was the AAA, the
issue of tax-delinquent lands—and government control of farmland generally—was spawning near-open warfare, part of a larger war among those trying
to shape the New Deal's agricultural agenda.

Barely a year old, the AAA had been a house divided from its birth. On the
one hand there were "the Old Reformers," the cautious men (epitomized by
sixty-year-old George Peek, the first director of AAA) most of whom had
started their careers as Progressives but by 1934 were barely reformers at all.
Roosevelt had chosen Peek—described by one colleague as "bandy-legged,
red-faced, and blunt . . . a little stupid, but shrewd, like an English squire"—
on the recommendation of the financier Bernard Baruch and officials at the
stolidly mainline American Farm Bureau, in order to mollify conservative critics who FDR knew would bedevil the agency.[20] Not incidentally, both Peek
and his senior staff were men who, as Schlesinger noted, "had very substantial
upper-middle- or upper-class ties, with strong roots in the commercial, financial, and agricultural communities."[21] The former head of a big agricultural-
implements company, Peek was troubled by the enormous power AAA in
theory now held over American agriculture, and was determined not to let it
fall into the "wrong hands."

Those "wrong hands" were easy to identify: they belonged to Jerome Frank and Rexford Tugwell (whom Peek derisively called "boys with their hair ablaze"). Frank, a Yale Law professor and former corporate lawyer turned zealous reformer, was the AAA's new general counsel; his friend Tugwell, a member of Roosevelt's original "Brains Trust" and a former Columbia Law professor, was the new Undersecretary of Agriculture. Along with several dozen others in the department's legal and consumer affairs offices, Frank and Tugwell represented the "Urban Liberals."* The idea that city dwellers, liberal or conservative, were players in New Deal agricultural policy may seem implausible. Yet these "Urban Liberals" were among the most visionary of the people working on rural and farm policy, the most sensitive to the issue of poverty and minorities, the most interested not just in restoring farm prices but in pushing American agriculture toward a more radical, ultimately Jeffersonian, ideal (opponents claimed to see more Marx than Monticello in the mix).

A third, middle faction comprised agricultural academics, farm journalists, and veteran department officials who, publicly at least, were closely identified with FDR's new secretary of agriculture, Henry Wallace. They have been called the agency's "Agricultural Pragmatists," but in their own ways they were as disposed to dramatic change as the "Urban Liberals," though they came from different experiences and represented a different constituency. Drawn heavily from Midwestern or Western farm families and trained at land grant colleges, these men took deep pride in their extensive practical knowledge of American farming. Born when farmers and their families were still the nation's majority, they saw the long march toward urbanization as leading to a world that would in no way be intrinsically superior to life on the farm. Most of all, these "Pragmatists" wanted to restore prosperity to the middle-sized farms as they had once known them, to see all farmers enjoy the same respect and legislative treatment as business, and to have them reap the benefits of modernity—from electricity, mechanization, and modern plant genetics—without losing their character and way of life. The key "Pragmatists" included M. L. Wilson, Mordecai Ezekiel, Chester Davis, Albert Black, Paul Appleby (Secretary Wallace's personal assistant), and Howard Tolley.[22] Every one of these men was a longtime ally (and most were close friends) of John D. Black, who had helped Wilson and Ezekiel draft the original Agricultural Adjustment Act, and who had taught both Ezekiel and Albert Black.

At the moment Galbraith arrived in Washington, the agency was in the midst of a defining power struggle among these three groups. George Peek had

---

*These included some remarkable young men, with Thurman Arnold, Abraham Fortas, Adlai Stevenson, George Ball, and Paul Porter among the most prominent. But there also proved to be a dozen or two young Communists and party sympathizers, including Lee Pressman, John Abt, Nathan Witt, Harold Ware, and Alger Hiss. It was not illegal for Communists to work in government in the 1930s, but most of them were discreet about their affiliations, knowing Frank and Tugwell were hostile to it. The fact that many of them were Jewish, intellectual Ivy Leaguers, and knew almost nothing about farming didn't help. Pressman in a staff meeting belligerently demanded to know what the AAA intended to do about macaroni growers—a story that "Old Reformers" like Peek loved to retell.

just noisily resigned over a policy dispute with Jerome Frank, while Rexford Tugwell was fresh on the job, having prevailed in a contentious Senate confirmation fight only a few days before Galbraith called Tolley. Meanwhile, the agency faced the issue of how—even whether—it should aid American agriculture's most vulnerable members, the South's sharecroppers and tenant farmers.

Tenant farmers and sharecroppers, heavily (but not exclusively) concentrated in the South, form a deeply bitter and moving part of American history. Their poverty was the stuff of legend—and a passionate *cause célèbre* for liberal and radical reformers. Steinbeck's *The Grapes of Wrath*, James Agee's *Let Us Now Praise Famous Men*, and the photography of Walker Evans and Dorothea Lange are only the most famous of the literary and artistic works that shamed the nation over the extraordinary poverty and suffering of these men and women. For Tugwell, Frank, and the other "Urban Liberals," the sharecropper issue was a litmus test of the AAA's willingness to engage in far-reaching social reform.

Ironically, the fight over what to do pivoted around unforeseen consequences of the Agricultural Adjustment Act itself, and its pathbreaking and progressive attempt first to restore and then to stabilize farm incomes through a system of "domestic allotments." In effect, under the new system the government promised to pay farmers not to raise crops. If they withdrew land from cultivation, the farmers would be paid from taxes imposed on processors and handlers of the commodities. The actual prices paid for not planting would be determined by a "parity" formula, based on earlier price ratios between agricultural and industrial products. The "parity" provision was intended to restore not just the income farmers had been losing in the Depression, but the much greater and longer-running comparative loss of their purchasing power vis-à-vis city dwellers. It promised to be the largest single redistribution of income ever attempted by the American government—and it had been crafted in no small part by John D. Black.[23]

Far from deserving the "Stalinist planning" epithets that critics threw at it, the domestic allotment program was designed to be democratic and decentralized. Most farmers growing a specific crop had to agree to the plan before curtailment went into effect, and actual operations were structured to emphasize county-by-county decision making, controlled by the farmers themselves. For good reason, Secretary Wallace called it "a contrivance as new in the field of social relations as the first gasoline engine was new in the field of mechanics."[24]

For the thousands of typical Midwestern or Western middle-sized farmers who grew wheat, corn, and other crops, "domestic allotments" worked well from the beginning and were quickly embraced. But to the alarm of men like Tugwell and Frank, nowhere were domestic allotments more quickly adopted than in the Southern cotton belt, where large-scale plantations predominated and land ownership was concentrated in a small number of wealthy hands. More than 10 million acres of cotton were withdrawn in the first year of the act's operation, for which Washington paid $100 million. And with the government paying big Southern growers to reduce production, the growers in turn found themselves with too many now-unemployed sharecroppers and tenants on their land. The threat to these already brutally impoverished men and women was outright disaster, made all the more bitter because it was the result of ostensibly progressive government policy. Needless to say, given who so many of those sharecroppers were, it touched on the incendiary issue of race.

At the point when Galbraith started working for Howard Tolley, the fate of several million very poor white and black rural Americans hinged on an obscure paragraph in section 7 of the Cotton Acreage Reduction Contract of 1934–35. The issue was how allotment payments should be divided between a landlord and his tenant and whether, with his acreage reduced, the landlord could evict tenants as he pleased. The position of the large cotton growers was straightforward: they wanted the government's money but would brook no interference in these matters. The AAA's reformers believed otherwise: they thought tenants should receive part of the government's payments and shouldn't be evicted.

One young AAA lawyer recalled what happened when Senator Ellison Du-Rant Smith of South Carolina discovered the AAA had begun sending allotment checks to the sharecroppers. First elected to the Senate in 1908, "Cotton Ed" was chairman of the powerful Agriculture Committee and a major cotton grower himself. Massively rotund, with thinning gray hair and a walrus mustache stained by a lifetime habit of chewing tobacco,

> Senator Smith came to my office when he heard that the [allotment] checks were going out to the tenants. A senator coming to see a young bureaucrat shows how things were turned upside down by the New Deal . . . He said, "Young fella, you can't do this to my niggers, paying checks to them. They don't know what to do with the money. The money should come to me. I'll take care of them. They're mine." That attitude, much less kindly expressed, was widespread.[25]

The debate spread outside the AAA that summer, to the front pages of the nation's newspapers and continued into the fall and winter of 1934. By the end of Galbraith's first semester at Harvard (and while he was still making weekly trips to AAA), tensions had reached a boiling point. Roosevelt, with his entire legislative agenda suddenly at risk through defection by Southern Democrats who controlled the Agriculture, Appropriations, and Rules committees, ordered Secretary Wallace and the AAA to surrender.

The aftermath was harsh: Jerome Frank was fired, Rexford Tugwell was sent off on a tour of European agriculture, and half a dozen other "Urban Liberals" were either dismissed or pushed out. Section 7 was "reinterpreted" so that no more allotment checks would go to sharecroppers directly, and the planters were left with what was deemed a "moral obligation" not to evict their tenants. Over the next year, the growers acted on that moral obligation by evicting more than 700,000 Southern tenant farmers and their families, with many ending up homeless and on general relief.[26] "Cotton Ed" himself won national attention again the following year by walking out of the 1936 Democratic National Convention when a black minister gave the invocation.[27]

The section 7 debacle was a watershed moment for the AAA, and an embittering, embarrassing one for Black, Tolley, and the other "Pragmatists" who had been responsible for creating the AAA and domestic allotments. Caught between the "Urban Liberals" and reactionaries like Senator Smith, they had followed the President's lead, first equivocating and then searching for compromise, only to lose abjectly—and in the process losing some of the agency's most talented figures.

Tolley later admitted that the fight and its aftermath took a terrible toll on the AAA and the Pragmatists. When the New Dealers entered office, there had been "new blood, new ideas, new thoughts . . . the desire . . . [by] government to do things that it never would face before." But after the purge, the difference was palpable: "Any organization, any agency—public or private—tends to ossify, get hardening of the arteries, settle down, not want to do anything new." This happened "with surprising rapidity . . . in the AAA."[28]

The battle over cotton allotments in 1934–35 and its outcome represented the convergence of several lessons about power and practice, and not just for Ken Galbraith. The first lesson, which concerned the New Deal and its putative "radicalism," was that early on in Roosevelt's first term, the "radicals" (at least in agriculture) were forced from center stage to the edges of power at best. Second, the conflict was defined, even within the administration, not as between "conservatives" and "liberals," but between complex strains of liberalism, progressivism, reformism, and "pragmatism," nourished by very different wellsprings of experience and temperament.

On the one hand, the "Pragmatists" thought of themselves as drawing on America's rural traditions yet as being fully committed to far-reaching changes in how farmers operated and how government could help them. But they also felt they understood what most farmers would be willing to accept—not to mention what was possible, given the powerful farm establishment composed of associations such as the Farm Bureau, the Agriculture Department's bureaucracy, and Congress's Southern-dominated committee system. Their long, persistent battle, dating back to the late nineteenth century, had been to right the imbalance between cities and farms, to give middle-income farm families the prospect of decent and stable incomes, and to escape what they saw as the de facto Social Darwinism of the conservative urban intelligentsia, which included most Marshallian economists. They shared European Protestant backgrounds and deep roots in the soil of the Midwest and West, and, when they allowed themselves the freedom, they thought their efforts were important and heroic. They deplored the conditions of tenants and sharecroppers, yet also realized that for Midwestern and Western farmers to survive, compromise (however distasteful) with the plantation system of the South and the congressional power it controlled was inescapable. On the other hand, the "Urban Liberals" thought that agricultural reform required social justice for the poorest farmer as well, and should be part of a massive reorganization of American life (not just farming) that would require a much larger degree of planning and direction from Washington.

In truth, the "Pragmatists" and "Urban Liberals" agreed on many issues, but they differed on matters of execution, timing, and personality. Little wonder that Galbraith (like Black in his writing) chose to pass over this early lesson in how power affects economics and the economic lives of so many.* It had grown out of the very system of "domestic allotments" that Black had been so central in creating—and it had resulted in a bitter triage.

Yet the compelling fact about the AAA and domestic allotments is that they worked, the battle over tenants and sharecroppers notwithstanding. Virtually overnight, the AAA sprang from an idea into an agency with more than 6,000 employees, and it moved decisively to cut back production and thereby to raise prices, just as Black, Wilson, and Ezekiel had hoped. By mid-1935, Black and his allies could feel vindicated: farm prices showed a marked improvement. Wheat prices had sharply risen after harvests that year fell nearly 40 percent (although probably due more to weather than to the AAA), and the United States was suddenly even importing significant quantities of the grain. In Iowa, Senator Louis Murphy buoyantly wrote FDR that "corn is 70 cents on the farm . . . [t]wo years ago it was 10 cents. Top hogs sold at Iowa plants yesterday at $7.40, or $4.50 to $5.00 better than a year ago. Farmers are very happy and convinced of the virtues of planning. Secretary Wallace can have whatever he wants from Iowa farmers." By 1936, gross farm income rose 50 percent from its nadir four years earlier, and the aggregate cash receipts of farmers, including government payments, nearly doubled.[29]

Galbraith never forgot the battle over the Southern tenants and sharecroppers. Hereafter, power—a concept so uncomfortable to conventional economists because it disrupts the very workings of economic theory—was a central and defining idea for him.

---

*Galbraith's 1930s academic articles on farming never mentioned the AAA's fight over tenants and sharecroppers, and his memoirs, published in 1981, make only this oblique reference: "Franklin D. Roosevelt won the affection and support of northern blacks because he gave them jobs. He did nothing that would disturb the great southern baronage in the Senate . . . for these men gave the President his prime congressional base. . . . The New Deal remembered the forgotten man but not the truly forgotten. Looking back, I am astonished how little we were concerned" (Galbraith, *A Life*, 41–42).

4

Getting Ready for Keynes

I believe myself to be writing a book on economic theory which will largely revolutionize—not, I suppose, at once but in the course of the next ten years—the way the world thinks about economic problems.
　　　　　　　　　　　　—John Maynard Keynes,
　　　　　　　　　　　　writing to George Bernard Shaw, 1935

GALBRAITH BEGAN TO settle in at Harvard in 1935–36, his second year. Thanks to the publicity and controversies swirling around New Deal farm policies, as well as cultivation of younger colleagues who recommended him to their own students, enrollment in his seminar burgeoned from three to forty. Apparently concerned, however, lest this place too much authority over young minds in junior and inexperienced hands, department elders arranged for Black to take charge of the much-enlarged course with Galbraith as his assistant.

Galbraith now altered his living arrangements as well, moving onto campus as a tutor at Winthrop House, one of the seven new neo-Georgian "river houses" President Lowell had ordered built in his final years as on-campus quarters for Harvard's undergraduates.* "After my Irving Street lodgings," he remembers, "these accommodations—living room, fireplace, bedroom, bathroom, respectable furniture—were a great luxury. I even had a telephone."[1] With all this, and free meals in Winthrop's dining hall, too, in exchange for a few hours each week counseling bewildered undergraduates on the challenges of introductory economics, it seemed a satisfactory bargain.

Galbraith also found time to audit several graduate courses and to widen his reading beyond agricultural economics. His broadening conversations with

---

*Until the river houses' construction, most students were scattered in apartments and rooming houses throughout Cambridge and nearby towns, a situation Lowell viewed as detrimental to full realization of what he deemed "the Harvard experience."

other instructors and graduate students led him to new issues, foremost among them the ideas of Edward Chamberlin, one of the new generation in the Economics Department, concerning a new view of industrial concentration which he called "monopolistic competition." Chamberlin's theory (which was simultaneously being developed by Joan Robinson at Cambridge University in England*), represented a major challenge to the received wisdom of Marshallian economics.

The widely observed tendency of late-nineteenth-century capitalism had been away from competition and toward monopoly, though this was contrary to most economists' comfortable assumptions. In American parlance, this development concerned "the trusts" of Rockefeller, Carnegie, and other titans that President Theodore Roosevelt and Progressive leaders strongly opposed. The power of these early trusts immensely influenced thinking about industry, government, and democracy itself. American government was thrust into its first great regulatory effort of the industrial era, initially via the Sherman Antitrust Act in 1890 (used at first, ironically, against unions more often than corporations) and then, during the Progressive Era, through the Clayton Antitrust Act, the Interstate Commerce Commission, and the Federal Trade Commission.

Because of their repeated and corrupt influence-buying of politicians, the trusts and big business generally drew Americans into various campaigns for "clean government," including those to create a permanent civil service to replace patronage, direct election of U.S. senators, referendum campaigns as a form of direct citizen governance, and various prohibitions on lobbying and influence peddling that tried to limit the corporations' once unbridled power over democratic institutions. And not least, the trusts' often brutal treatment of their employees advanced the cause of labor unions as a source of countervailing power. These measures, taken during the Progressive Era, were considered for some time to be sufficient prophylactic against the evils of industrial combinations, at least among conventional economists. But during the 1920s more progressive colleagues began to argue that the measures hadn't achieved their purpose. Between 1919 and 1930, nearly 12,000 large manufacturing, utility, banking, and mining companies were merged or acquired, five times the number that had so alarmed earlier Progressives. Unions were withering, meanwhile, as was government oversight of business generally under three successive Republican administrations.[2]

Economists by the 1930s were thus sharply divided on what if anything to do about the new level of business concentration. The more conservative among them thought, as so often, that nothing much was needed, that the "invisible hand" would in due time obviate the problem, if indeed there was any. But New Dealers thought this was manifestly at odds with the facts. The more radically inclined among them felt that, at a minimum, more "trust busting"

---

*Chamberlin suspected that Robinson had somehow learned of his own work as he was developing it and had effectively plagiarized him. No such evidence ever appeared, however, and the charge is wildly improbable. Robinson, unlike Chamberlin, soon gave up on "imperfect competition," as she called it, in favor of her own version of Keynesianism. Over the years, she became a close and enduring friend of Galbraith's.

was required, while others suggested various forms of national planning and public ownership, control, or regulation. (Socialists and Communists, of course, had even more drastic prescriptions.)

Enter "monopoly competition" theory. Between the assumed Marshallian textbook norm of a competition among many sellers and buyers and the recognized "exception" of outright monopoly, Chamberlin and Robinson postulated an entire world of intermediate possibilities. They saw that a seller might use advertising (expenditures for which had quadrupled on a per capita basis in the years after the Great War), brand names, patents, copyrights, resale price restrictions, a product's strength in certain regions or among a range of similar goods, and so on to exercise an important, if not absolute, ability to control price, and hence profit. The innovation in the Chamberlin-Robinson model was that it didn't require the existence of outright monopoly—a single firm that exercised dominance of an entire industry, like Rockefeller's Standard Oil—but rather only the congenial coexistence of a few large firms that together acted in similar, mutually cooperative ways.

In this world of "oligopoly" (the term for a market with few sellers and many buyers), Chamberlin showed that the oligopolists' effective pricing practices would differ only modestly from the simpler "exception" of monopoly—that is, that their price and profits would settle at a level above the competitive neoclassical ideal. And because it was obvious that many basic American industries could be classified as "oligopolistic"—steel, autos, tires, machine tools, and farm equipment for example—the very presumption of pure competition as the normal state of capitalism was cast in doubt. This difficulty was enormously fascinating to—and fiercely debated by—economists, for it affected the very underpinnings of their theory. Although "monopolistic competition" theory was soon overshadowed by Keynes and his ideas, in the early 1930s it quickly captured the attention of economists trying to explain the empirical realities of their time. Its "most revolutionary feature," the distinguished Yale economist Robert Triffin noted later, was "the unprecedented pace" at which it "conquered" its audience.[3]

Galbraith's article written with Black about modern marketing practices had primed him for just such a theory, and now caused him to stray from his focus on agricultural credit. Black seems not to have objected, and the result was Galbraith's second article (and first on his own) on a nonfarm subject: "Monopoly Power and Price Rigidities," which was published even as he toiled away under Black on farmers' credit problems.

Galbraith's article shows him beginning to wrestle with seminal assumptions that grew robustly in his major works. He was eager to have readers see that this "new idea of monopoly power," by which he means not classic Marshallian monopoly, but the type of monopoly competition identified by Chamberlin and Robinson, must explain not just its operation in "normal" economic times but the reasons why holders of such power in the "abnormal" conditions of the Depression were apparently willing to forego the short-term profits they would gain by lowering their prices even when faced with falling demand.

Galbraith's answer was to argue that the Depression had changed the structure of demand itself, which explained why oligopolists' response to it didn't match Marshall's theory. He concluded that in periods of sharply falling demand, what economists call the "elasticity of demand" also falls, but unevenly. That is, looking past "aggregate demand" for a product or products to demand among different income groups, we see several simultaneous patterns. The one quarter of Americans who were unemployed of course were effectively removed from the demand curve. Apart from whatever savings, borrowing, or government relief allowed them to sustain the purchase of food and shelter, they no longer were buyers. But among the remaining majority who were still employed, there were sharp divergences in behavior, based not least on each group's class position and employment characteristics, including its members' sense of job security and future prospects.

"People with decreased money incomes and increased concern for their economic security," Galbraith noted, tend to save rather than consume, make do with what they have, not add to their store of goods, and thus are "less rather than more responsive to lower prices." In consequence, the market divides between "very able" and "very needy" buyers, between the affluently secure on the one hand and most worker-consumers on the other. The result is that even though there is demand for a smaller volume of goods by fewer buyers, the affluent and their ongoing purchases relieve some of the downward pressure on price. In such a situation, perfect competition would nonetheless predict lowered prices as producers tried to restore the market's original size. But with competition far from actually perfect, Galbraith argued, oligopolists fear sharp price reductions—and favor cuts in production instead of competitive "price warfare," which might lead to the collapse of stable oligopolistic relations.

Galbraith also significantly imputed price rigidities to customs and practices within business. Contrary to what conventional theory maintained, he noted that businessmen prefer to use average, rather than marginal, cost figures in their accounting to determine selling prices. They are also swayed by habits of simple inertia, even in recession: "No decision on a matter of price is so simple," he coolly remarked, "as the decision to let it stay where it is."[4]

Here are core characteristics of Galbraithian reasoning already at work. Critical of the inherited wisdom, he draws on novel and still controversial theories as a starting point. Combining them with his agricultural training, he stresses the actualities of the day: farm prices (because they most closely approached "pure competition") had collapsed while retail and industrial prices remained stubbornly high (contrary to conventional theory), exacerbating conditions for farmers and workers—and thereby worsening the chances for a general recovery. He extended the Chamberlin-Robinson model by showing not only how real-world practice produced a counter-theoretical empirical result (in this case, sharply falling demand that led to no, or only slowly falling, price changes), but also how real-world business practice and custom observably ignored theory, operating by a rhythm and logic of its own.

Equally striking, Galbraith did not conclude that more "trust busting" was needed, even though the Great Depression eventually produced three times more prosecutions under the Sherman Antitrust Act than had occurred in its previous fifty years combined. He instead accepted the reality of business concentration as an inescapable given. "Anti-trust legislation will be of little avail as an instrument" of public policy, he warned; to the contrary, it "is quite useless and possibly worse." Instead he worried about restoring the smooth functioning of the overall economic system, its oligopolistic characteristics notwithstanding. "No longer is public policy concerned merely with fair prices or prices which prevent exploitation of the public. It is also concerned with the problem of *harmonious* prices and *harmonious* price changes; the problem of prices which do not intensify and prolong fluctuations in the economy."[5]

To this end he recommended that in lieu of antitrust the government consider extending some of business's monopoly-competitive power to other sectors of the economy while "smoothing" the system's functioning with "a revised attitude toward copyrights, patents on 'distinctions' and brand advertising, and a positive program for extending consumer standards." In a premonition of his mature sardonic style, he also inserted a jibe at businessmen, suggesting they needed "training" on the "proper" use of cost accounting and analysis in pricing. "So far the Government has deemed it necessary to educate the farmer, consumer, laborer, even the banker," he dryly observed. "But the American business man has been credited with an omniscience which places him above the need for such attention. This assumption may warrant reexamination."

Six years later, Galbraith's rulings at the Office of Price Administration exhibited the same sort of pragmatism, and the same attention to the louche foibles of the business community. And later, in *American Capitalism*, *The Affluent Society*, and *The New Industrial State*, he returned to themes compactly covered in these early articles.

NEW THEORIES ABOUT monopolistic competition weren't the only influence on Galbraith. Another was *The Modern Corporation and Private Property*, written by Adolf Berle and Gardiner Means and published in 1932. Berle and Means had reached two compelling conclusions, one in effect quantitative, the second qualitative. The first was that American business was by the early 1930s dominated by a handful of firms: the two hundred top companies out of several million collectively controlled half of total U.S. corporate assets. Here, in clear numerical terms, was what Progressives had been worrying about for nearly fifty years. Second, and more dramatic (several studies had already highlighted the concentration issue), Berle and Means argued that in most of these giant enterprises, control had passed from their shareholder owners to the companies' senior managers, seemingly irretrievably.

The two points were the more challenging because they came from what seemed quite unlikely critics. The arrogant, dapper Adolf Berle was unquestionably brilliant (he'd entered Harvard at the age of fourteen and become, at twenty-one, the Harvard Law School's youngest graduate ever). He was also a figure of notable contradictions, who combined a lucrative legal practice specializing in Wall Street finance and marriage into an aristocratic family with a zeal for far-reaching liberal reform that matched what he had inherited from his Presbyterian minister father.* He and Means, a young self-effacing Columbia University economist, neither of them inclined to radicalism by 1930s standards, combined solid legal research and empirical statistical data to indict the very structure of management and ownership of America's major companies.

The modern corporation, they argued, no longer resembled the firm of Marshallian theory. Instead it had to be understood "not in terms of business enterprise but in terms of social organization":

> On the one hand, it involves a concentration of power in the economic field comparable to the concentration of religious power in the medieval church or the political power in the national state. On the other hand, it involves the interrelation of a wide diversity of economic interest—those of the "owners" who supply capital, those of the workers who "create," those of the consumers who give value to the products of the enterprise, and above all those in control who wield power.[6]

Power was the book's true subject—and Berle in particular, with his Wall Street experience, passionately believed that just as the nascent business and middle classes had once usurped the power of kings and clergy, so now the United States was seeing giant corporations usurp the power of citizens and their government. They represented not just an economic problem of decreased competition, but a political challenge in the form of a private oligarchy. "A Machiavelli writing today would have very little interest in princes, and every interest in the Standard Oil Company of Indiana," he declared. "And he would be right; because the prince of today is the president or dominant interest in a great corporation."[7] Americans needed to turn not just to courts and legislatures but to new models of business and government to redress this dangerous imbalance.

As alternatives, the authors hardly inclined to either Soviet-style state socialism or the socialism of worker control. In truth, they were seeking what in recent years has been called "the stakeholder society." As a corporate lawyer, Berle repeatedly stressed that the corporation is a legal entity whose form, rights, and obligations have always been subject to change and modification. The law had once given certain individuals the right to own others as property, or had dictated that an individual's estate could pass only to the first-born son, or had denied women ownership rights of their own; by the 1930s, the laws (and underlying beliefs) governing these matters had changed dramatically. So

---

*A measure of Berle's sense of self-importance is that during one heady period in the 1930s he confided to his wife that his "real ambition in life is to be the American Karl Marx—a social prophet." His biographer, slightly more sardonically, called him "The Marx of the shareholder class" (Schwarz, *Liberal*, 62). Means, like Berle, was a Harvard graduate (B.A. and Ph.D.) and a minister's son (his father and grandfather were Congregationalists).

too, Berle and Means believed, the time had come for the laws and regulations regarding corporate governance, ownership, and responsibilities to change.

> Should the corporate leaders, for example, set forth a program comprising fair wages, security to employees, reasonable service to their public, and stabilization of business, all of which would divert a portion of the profits from the owners of passive property, and should the community generally accept such a scheme as a logical humane solution of industrial difficulties, the interests of the passive property owners would have to give way.[8]

In true Rooseveltian fashion, the two made clear they had come not to destroy capitalism but to save it:

> It is conceivable—indeed it seems almost essential if the corporate system is to survive—that the "control" of the great corporations should develop into a purely neutral technocracy, balancing a variety of claims by various groups in the community and assigning to each a portion of the income stream on the basis of public policy rather than private cupidity.[9]

But Berle and Means could be maddeningly vague, as Roosevelt himself was, as to how such a transfer of authority would occur, or how power would devolve through broadened share ownership to check the managers' dominance and the self-interested cupidity of their "purely neutral" technocrats. Berle puckishly suggested that a committee composed of a banker, a manufacturer, and a corporate lawyer could solve the problem, but the idea's utter improbability only underscored the book's prescriptive weakness.

Yet *The Modern Corporation and Private Property* almost overnight became a national sensation. This was due partly to its controversial thesis but also to the fact that Berle was a member of Roosevelt's Brains Trust (striking in itself, since he was a reforming Mugwump Republican, not a Democrat). On the front page of the *New York Herald Tribune*'s book review, the economic historian Charles Beard called the book "a masterly achievement," perhaps "the most important work . . . on American statecraft" since *The Federalist Papers*. *Time* called it "the economic Bible of the Roosevelt administration," and *The New Republic* judged it the most significant book of 1932. Within two months, Justice Louis Brandeis drew on Berle and Means in an opinion in a landmark Supreme Court corporations case, the first of what would become hundreds of such citations by federal courts.[10]

Conservatives on the Harvard faculty were alarmed by the book's effect. W. C. Crum, the department's leading statistician, launched a running battle with Means in the *American Economic Review* over the book's use of data, a debate that quickly took on more than the usual edge of scholarly disagreement. Schumpeter and Bullock, too, were aghast, and vocally criticized the book (even though Schumpeter himself had earlier expressed similar concerns about the era's change in corporate governance and control).[11]

Galbraith vividly remembered the effect of *The Modern Corporation and Private Property* on his own thinking, and that of his peers:

> Here was subversion indeed. Given this concentration, not competition but oligopoly was the norm. The trend thereto, as foreseen by Marx, had obviously been proceeding in a relentless fashion. But there was worse yet to conclude. Not Marx's capitalists but the professional managers were now extensively in control. There now existed power without property. The corporate bureaucrat, not the greatly celebrated entrepreneur. Bureaucracy, not entrepreneurship.

Moreover, as Galbraith recognized, this idea of a shift to "managerial" control was far more challenging to traditional theory than Chamberlin's and Robinson's model of monopolistic competition. In their model, at least "the capitalist or entrepreneur still ruled and profits were still maximized—or such was the effort. The results were not socially optimal, but they could be accommodated to classical thought. The views of Berle and Means could not."[12]

In short, what Berle and Means seemed to demonstrate empirically was what Chamberlain and Robinson had accomplished theoretically: they showed that large firms could powerfully direct and shape the markets they operated in, and that their own individual performance was less and less subject to influence by the capital markets in which their shares were traded. If Berle and Means were correct, and managers were now in charge and shareholders merely passive dividend-recipients, then two cornerstones of economics' traditional theory of the firm were washed away.

THE INFLUENCE ON Galbraith of both monopolistic competition theory and Berle and Means's theory of managerial control quickly found application in the spring of 1936, thanks, ironically, to a millionaire American businessman. Henry Dennison was the Harvard-educated scion of an old New England family whose company even today produces the distinctive red-rimmed gummed labels sold in most stationery stores. Thirty years older than Galbraith, he was already well known as a progressive reformer and author as well as a successful businessman. Short and compactly built, the bald-headed Dennison was an immensely energetic man who was an accomplished violinist and pianist, a naturalist and inventor, as well as deeply involved in the scientific and progressive management issues of the day. Fascinated by the pioneering time-management studies of Frederick Taylor, for example, he had served as president of the Taylor Society for the Advancement of Management and of the International Management Institute. At the same time, he implemented employee stock ownership and profit-sharing plans in his own company.

As was true of a number of far-sighted businessmen of the time, Dennison had concerns about the erratic instabilities of capitalism and its widespread social inequalities that gradually drew him to hope for a new kind of market economy yoking private entrepreneurial energies to national public direction.

He foresaw an enlightened technocratic class of engineers and managers who would press the United States toward greater equality and efficiency simultaneously.[13]

In the late 1920s, Dennison joined a small coterie of talented and diverse businessmen who shared his sense of responsibility and mission. The brothers Lincoln and Edward Filene were using their Boston department store fortune for a host of activist causes. (Edward founded the Twentieth Century Fund to advance progressive social science research.) Morris Leeds was a manufacturer from Philadelphia as well as a Quaker of great conscience, and Ralph Flanders was a successful Vermont machine-tool manufacturer who later became a U.S. senator (and courageous scourge of Senator Joseph McCarthy). As a group, they spoke often in support of the New Deal and Roosevelt and served on his influential Business Advisory Council.[14]

In early 1936, these men decided to write a book defending their support of the New Deal, and outlining what they saw as a larger strategy for renewing the American economy. But they were all busy, and none was an economist, so Dennison inquired of friends at Harvard who might assist them. Galbraith's name was mentioned, and after brief negotiations, Dennison hired him for the summer to help draft the manuscript, and then generously invited him to live at Juniper Hill, the Dennison home, to expedite their cooperation. As Galbraith later wrote, his new lodgings represented an almost magical introduction to a world far from his modest upbringing:

> The Dennison house, a large, low-slung structure with deep sleeping porches, stood on a high wooded hill a few miles from Framingham. Surrounded by forest and with a view all the way to Boston and the Bay, it was the most civilized place of abode in all New England . . . I was lodged back of one of the porches in a room I continued to occupy at intervals for several years. My working space was in Dennison's excellent library, although he considered the word pretentious and called it the bookroom. My instruction took place under a pine tree just west of the house. It was frequently interrupted as Dennison shifted suddenly to some other topic, and I tried to discern meaning without the help of subjects or sometimes verbs. Soon a major difficulty arose.[15]

The "difficulty" was the collision of two equally well entrenched intellects. The now twenty-seven-year-old Galbraith—tutored in Marshallian orthodoxy and struggling to synthesize and articulate the new prescriptions drawn from both "monopoly competition" and Berle and Means—saw the Depression as a failure of competition: too much money was wasted on advertising and salesmanship. He insisted to Dennison that "the remedy was more competition," and says he wrote a now-lost lengthy paper "explaining and affirming this revelation."[16] Dennison, at fifty-nine, with several decades of business experience and a good deal of practical thought behind him, saw the matter quite differently. In a manner that reminds us that many elements anticipating "Keynesian" thought had evolved autonomously, Dennison saw the economy in terms of separate spending and savings streams. Depression, he believed, was caused by the nonspending of income in the savings stream—in concrete terms, by the behavior of the affluent and of business enterprises.

To remedy this, a fiscal solution was needed that shifted taxation onto non-spending elements and off consumption—for example, by drawing public revenue away from sales taxes and onto sharply progressive corporate and personal income taxes. As Galbraith recalls, "to anyone properly learned in economics, it would be hard to imagine a more horrifying thought."[17]

The two might have remained at loggerheads had not Galbraith then taken up John Maynard Keynes's just-published *The General Theory of Employment, Interest, and Money*, intrigued by the commotion surrounding it. Poring over its pages while drafting his manuscript for Dennison, Galbraith began to realize that Dennison's heretical view was shared by the British economist:

> His explanation of oversavings was much more sophisticated than Dennison's but in practical consequences precisely the same. There could be unspent savings; when they appeared, prices did not adjust smoothly down to ensure that the same volume of goods would be bought by the reduced (after-saving) purchasing power. Instead output and employment fell until reduced profits, increased losses and the need to spend from past savings ensured that all income from current production or its equivalent was spent. A new economic equilibrium was thus established, one with a lot of people out of work—the underemployment equilibrium. I was shaken.[18]

After several weeks of careful reconsideration, Galbraith had to tell Dennison of Keynes's effect on him. Over drinks one evening at Juniper Hill, he acknowledged that the Englishman's new work clearly supported Dennison, not himself. Dennison gave the admission careful pause, then "replied that he was not surprised; Keynes had always made more sense than most economists."[19]

Their newfound agreement notwithstanding, this left open the question of how to shape the manuscript that Galbraith had been contracted to cowrite. Laboring now simultaneously under his rather conventional Marshallian training, the heterodox effects of Chamberlin and Berle and Means, and the fresh impact of Keynes and Dennison, Galbraith produced a draft of what became *Modern Competition and Business Policy*.

Galbraith later dismissively claimed that it "is a bad book that should never have been printed; I have not ventured to look inside it for nearly forty years."[20] But reviewers of the time were less harsh, and the book offers several insights. Most important, it suggests that if, as Galbraith later claimed, Keynes was now "revolutionizing" his conceptual world, the influence remained still largely private. *Modern Competition and Business Policy* is far from "Keynesian"; its analysis is affected most by monopoly competition theory and its prescriptions by the "national planning" debates then embodied in the wing of the New Deal most influenced by Berle and Means.

The first part of this short book criticized the various theories and policies that claimed to restore pure competition to the economy. As one reviewer rightly noted, *Modern Competition* was in these chapters essentially "a popularized version of the Chamberlin monopolistic-competition analysis and a selection of familiar indictments of business organization and practices." But the second half is a fascinating *tour d'horizon* of the reform proposals floating around at the time, covering issues from corporate organization and finance to dissemination of business and economic data, and, finally, national industrial organization. It shows that Galbraith was still less Keynesian in outlook than he later claimed, or in fact later became.

To be sure, he would undoubtedly have alarmed the National Association of Manufacturers or the members of certain private gentlemen's clubs in America's big cities, but most of what he proposed was already on the New Deal agenda.* Galbraith and Dennison put great stock in public disclosure of corporate information about profits, assets, prices, and share ownership, for example. Today these are routinely and readily available in any large corporation's annual report or SEC filings. They also believed in the need for a federal minimum-wage law, greater regulation of utilities, and basic consumer protection legislation—all now commonplace facets of American economic life but either quite new or still unachieved when they wrote.

Only on the question of national industrial organization did Galbraith and Dennison break with prevailing New Deal views, and then more in degree than in substance. They suggested that a federal commission be equipped with extraordinary powers to initiate, investigate, and enforce a host of reform policies; it should be built around an industry-based "code" system, an idea that echoed elements of the National Recovery Administration, Roosevelt's aborted experiment in semicooperative public regulation of business. But its powers were to be carefully drawn so as to avoid the NRA's fate—invalidation by the Supreme Court, although how to do this was left remarkably vague.

What exactly was the commission to do? Galbraith and Dennison proposed that it should have a mandate over wages, prices, earnings, production, and labor conditions; to promote economic recovery, it could modify tariffs, grant federal subsidies, establish yardstick competition, even prescribe taxes for industries that fell below certain norms in wages, profits or working conditions. (Given the Supreme Court's almost certain hostility, such a proposal was unlikely to escape the NRA's fate—if indeed, it could even pass Congress. The political plan for it was never clear.)

So the authors were supremely unspecific as to the commission's purposes or criteria; but they believed that this inexactness was necessary under the circumstances (an echo of Berle and Means's defense against the charge of prescriptive vagueness). Pointing backward to the country's forty-year-long experiment with business regulation since the Sherman Antitrust Act, they

---

*To Galbraith's amusement, when he visited China in 1972, he found that *Modern Competition* was the only one of his books in the University of Beijing's library.

judged it "a misdirection of legislative emphasis" because of its focus on trust busting and its underlying faith in the workability of pure competition.

> For a business structure as varied and complex as that of the United States there can be no simple formula, no easy rule which can be laid down for all . . . The device we recommend is not regulation *per se*, but exploration of the art or technique of regulation . . . The objectives of . . . regulation itself, are, of course, enlarged and regularized output and the maintenance of such price policies, labor standards, and earnings as would place the industry in the best relation to the welfare of the community. But even these are not matters to which we would care to give *a priori* definition. A major task in the development of the art of regulation is the appraisal of specific industrial policies in their relation to the general welfare.[21]

Anathema to conservatives as well as most economists then and now, the Galbraith-Dennison "commission" is a measure of how widely liberals in Roosevelt's second term—even business liberals like Dennison—were willing to search for programs that would end the Depression.

In retrospect, Galbraith is right: *Modern Competition and Business Policy* is "a bad book," but in fairness one should remember the circumstances when it was composed and published. By the time it appeared, the country was in the grip of recession—the so-called "Little Depression" of 1937—which threatened to destroy much of the fragile recovery that had begun during Roosevelt's first term. Unemployment, which had dropped from 25 percent to 14 percent of the workforce in those first four years, rose again to 19 percent; Gross National Product, which had grown from $55 billion in 1933 to $90 billion, fell sharply as well. Conservatives could offer no apparent solution other than to abandon government intervention and return to market forces—not an option the country was ready to accept, to judge by FDR's reelection margin in 1936, when he carried all but two states. But Roosevelt himself seemed uncertain as to where the New Deal should turn. After his landslide reelection, he briefly returned to conventional fiscal policy, persuaded by Treasury Secretary Henry Morgenthau to seek a balanced budget and to end his first-term deficit-based "pump-priming." In retrospect, many economists believe Morgenthau's conservative advice was a central factor in precipitating the 1937 recession.[22]

How should the New Deal restore recovery? With Morgenthau's fiscal conservatism discredited, one major contender for policy leadership was the old Progressive-Era model of trust busting, still advocated by younger New Dealers such as Thomas Corcoran and Benjamin Cohen (who had studied under Felix Frankfurter at the Harvard Law School) or, most famously, Thurman Arnold, who headed the Justice Department's antitrust division.

Galbraith and Dennison, adamantly opposed to restoration of "trust busting," drew on the alternative "planning" strategies of Berle, Rexford Tugwell, and Raymond Moley. And leaving aside the NRA, they had plenty of models to point to: apart from the government's extensive intervention in the farm economy, there were new federal regulations governing banking and the securities industry, the Wagner Act's National Labor Relations Board, the Federal Power Commission's oversight of utilities, the Robinson-Patman Act's limitation on preferential price discounting to large retailers, not to mention industry-specific arrangements covering coal, trucking, railroads, and airlines, for example. In short, the commission proposed by Galbraith and Dennison represented as much a consolidation and coordination of disparate existing programs as a dramatically new expansion of government's power over the economy. In fact, the proposals seemed so reasonable for the times that even the normally orthodox *American Economic Review* welcomed them as "a provocative addition to the literature," and recommended that they "be regarded highly as an outline of some major implications of monopoly competition."[23]

When Galbraith returned to teaching and research in Cambridge in the fall of 1936, he had reason to think that his career at Harvard would now move along smartly—perhaps even toward a tenured position in the department. His research work in farm credit was going well, he'd written several well-received professional articles, and he had just finished his first book, with a prominent (albeit nonacademic) coauthor. His colleagues noticed the change. Paul Samuelson, already recognized as the department's star graduate student, says that "when he started at Harvard there were two Kens": one an agricultural economist "from a jerkwater college" (Samuelson was a University of Chicago graduate) who came East as "John D. Black's boy. But the first sign of the new Ken was when he teamed up with Dennison and wrote that book."[24] Black was pleased and arranged a promotion to faculty instructor, a $350 raise, and, most important, a three-year renewal of Galbraith's appointment.

In Black's mind, his young protégé's star was quickly rising in agricultural economics, and promised an important future. With a revolution now taking place in the relationship between government and farmers, thanks not least to Black's pioneering efforts, the field offered rich opportunities. Yet what was in Galbraith's mind? Agriculture had defined his upbringing and professional training, and agricultural economics had brought him to Harvard. But new interests now tugged at him, awakened by his readings of Chamberlin and Robinson, Berle and Means, and, not least, Keynes. Both Black and Galbraith well understood that agriculture would never again have an all-encompassing position in American life. The twentieth century was about the machine, about cities, about new issues and horizons. Although the country was still locked in the Depression, they also understood that the slump would eventually end and prosperity would be restored. But in what kind of world? What would its reigning values be? And what would economists do in it?

Something about Keynes, and about *The General Theory*, struck Galbraith as pointing toward answers to those questions. He hadn't grasped what it was clearly or quickly enough to incorporate it in his first book, despite his conversations with Dennison and Dennison's "premature Keynesian" ideas. But back at Harvard, Galbraith discovered not just that all the bright young men were talking about Keynes, but that sometimes it seemed that no one could talk of anything else. Here was truly path-breaking economic theory, and concepts more important than "monopoly competition" or "managerial control." Keynes's book was also complicated in argument and bolstered by unfamiliar concepts, so even its critics weren't sure they had grasped its arguments. Still, they sensed their own discomfort with its implications for both traditional economics and public policy.

Galbraith understood that Black was pleased with him, and that logically continuing on the path of agricultural economics was the safest and surest means to career advancement. Surely it was what he knew best. But Keynes—and the conversations and controversies he provoked—gnawed at Galbraith, excited him, kept pushing him to confront an entire new world of economics, and a bold new theory that might possibly provoke change in the real world itself, not just among cosseted academics.

What to do? Follow the safe path or break out onto a new and risky one? And how could Galbraith even answer that question, how could he make the change even if he decided he wanted to? What were his credentials, his expertise not just in Keynesian thought (no one save Keynes and a handful around him could claim "expertise" in the new theory yet) but in nonfarm economics? A couple of articles? No classroom experience? No book, save one published with a businessman? Would Black continue to be his mentor and sponsor? Would Harvard want him, or agree to keep him?

MOST OF GALBRAITH'S young colleagues were no more certain than he how to proceed after reading *The General Theory*, yet the book was, in Galbraith's words, like "a tidal force" sweeping across all their assumptions about economic theory. Paul Samuelson, displaying a capacity for genteel literary allusion rare among economists, compared his own reaction on first reading Keynes's magnum opus that year to the poet John Keats's excitement on first looking into Chapman's Homer.[25] The reaction among most of the department's other graduate students and young instructors was similar.

But not everyone in economics was energetically or poetically losing himself to Keynes. Joseph Schumpeter and several other senior men at Harvard found themselves in almost instant disagreement, just as they had with the first New Deal policies four years earlier. Hearing that some of his own graduate students had placed a bulk order for *The General Theory* in the summer of 1936, hoping to hasten its arrival from England, Schumpeter reported to a colleague, "The majority of our very best young people are almost fanatically for Mr. Keynes." He was dismayed, to say the least.

Schumpeter's antagonism toward *The General Theory* never wavered: near the end of World War II he still insisted that "perhaps the majority" of his colleagues were, like him, "opposed to the ideas of Keynes." Schumpeter sourly greeted news of Keynes's death in 1946 with an acid-tinged essay, and his biographer candidly admits that the Austrian's resentment was fed by his prideful sense of being wrongly upstaged. (The only work by Keynes that Schumpeter ever admitted admiring was his *Essays in Biography*.[26])

Alvin Hansen, soon to arrive at Harvard, was among Keynes's early critics, and like Schumpeter he wrote a hostile initial review of *The General Theory*. But within less than two years, after further consideration and much debate, Hansen became Keynes's chief American apostle. His conversion, as we shall see, was crucial to the academic acceptance of Keynes in the late 1930s—and also to the evolution of a particular style, or school, of Keynesianism, in which Galbraith eventually located his own unique thought.

But why was *The General Theory* greeted with such excitement (and hostility) when it appeared, and why did it so dramatically redefine economic theory and policy? What *was* Keynes's theory, and why did it stand in "revolutionary" contrast, as he himself believed, to the Marshallian economics preceding it?

HOWEVER NEW HIS theory might have been, Keynes himself was a familiar figure to millions of Americans, thanks especially to his devastating critique of the Versailles Treaty, *The Economic Consequences of the Peace*, written immediately after the conference that "settled" the Great War. In that slender 1919 volume, he'd warned of the destabilizing effects that the Allies' harsh terms would have on Germany, effects that subsequently destroyed the Weimar Republic's hopes for democracy. Keynes had gone on in the 1920s to become a figure of stature in England's postwar Liberal Party, while his excoriating opinions of Conservative, Liberal, and Labour policies were much discussed and debated. A prolific writer for Britain's leading newspapers and opinion magazines, by the 1930s he also sent his work to American publications as divergent as *The New York Times*, *The New Republic*, and the *Saturday Evening Post*. Shortly after Roosevelt took office, Keynes wrote the new President an "open letter" that appeared in the *Times*, in which he foreshadowed elements of *The General Theory* and called on FDR to leave both economic orthodoxy and revolution behind and instead use "new and bolder methods [to] date the first chapter of a new economic era from your accession to office."*

Given his pedigree and prominence, Keynes had also long been well known to American economists. Maynard, as he was universally known to his friends, was the son of John Neville Keynes, a turn-of-the-century Cambridge University economist and administrator who'd been an early protégé of Alfred Marshall's. He had shown great promise in mathematics and logic at King's College, Cambridge, and after a brief stint in the India Office, where his views on economic matters such as the gold standard had been both insightful and orthodox, he won appointment as an economics lecturer in Cambridge, largely through Marshall's influence. At the tender age of twenty-eight he became editor of *The Economic Journal*, and over the next two decades wrote many arti-

---

*The open letter, plus the admiration of Labor Secretary Frances Perkins and other senior New Dealers, earned him a private meeting with Roosevelt soon after. But the meeting didn't go well: Keynes afterward coolly told Perkins that he had "supposed the President was more literate, economically speaking." FDR, for his part, jauntily told Felix Frankfurter that "I had a grand talk with Keynes and liked him immensely," but to Perkins admitted less happily, "I saw your friend Keynes. He left a whole rigmarole of figures. He must be a mathematician rather than a political economist."

cles and texts, most important his *Treatise on Money*, which in the early 1930s garnered broad professional acclaim (though Keynes would soon disavow much of it).

Maynard Keynes's life, however, was hardly confined to economics and politics. As a Cambridge undergraduate, he'd been elected to The Apostles, the secret society then under the sway of the philosopher G. E. Moore; Moore's concern for the moral and the beautiful suffused all of what Keynes thought or wrote. While a student the handsome Maynard also discovered his homosexual nature and became a close friend of his fellow Apostle Lytton Strachey, who introduced him to the Bloomsbury world of painters, poets, and novelists, including most famously Virginia Woolf. Here Keynes cultivated his love of the theater and dance, a lifelong passion that also—to the surprise of many of his friends—eventually led him to fall in love with and then to marry Lydia Lopokova, a Russian ballerina, and with her to establish a marriage that by all accounts happily defined his life after forty. (Nothing about Keynes's complex sexual choices, it should be noted, was known during his lifetime except to a close and discreet circle of friends and acquaintances, and was punctiliously overlooked by his first major biographer, his friend the Oxford economist Sir Roy Harrod.) Adding to all these complexities, Keynes also turned out to be a first-class businessman and investor, who accumulated a fortune for himself (and later for King's College, which he served as treasurer, among his many duties).

However fascinating and modern his biography, the dominant and undeniable fact about John Maynard Keynes was his genius, a genius recognized by Marshall early on, and by almost all who came in contact with him thereafter. Tall, slender, always well tailored and well spoken, Keynes, with his gentle, deeply intelligent eyes, full lips, and thick brigadier's mustache, attracted the admiration of an extraordinary range of brilliant men and women in the arts, politics, business, and economics. The philosopher Bertrand Russell, a genius in his own field who was parsimonious in bestowing that title on most others (his friend Ludwig Wittgenstein was one of the few exceptions), wrote unabashedly: "Keynes's intellect was the sharpest and clearest that I have ever known. When I argued with him, I felt that I took my life in my hands, and I seldom emerged without feeling something of a fool. I was sometimes inclined to feel that so much cleverness must be incompatible with depth, but I do not think this feeling was justified."[27]

In *The General Theory*, Keynes captured intellectually the crisis not only of his times but of the system that defined it, and he offered what seemed a plausible solution in a way that no one else had before. He began by focusing on the short run, not the long, because, as he declared in a pungent well-known phrase, "in the long run we are all dead." His point was that to focus on the market's ability to achieve long-term equilibrium was to treat the short run inadequately (by the short run Keynes meant several years, possibly even decades), in which actual economies might suffer horrifying bouts of unemployment or inflation with devastating consequence. Keynes believed that people living in the midst of the Depression, with U.S. unemployment still hovering at 17 percent seven years after the Great Crash, were right to ignore orthodox economics. Too many conventional economists, as he dryly put it, were "trying to solve unemployment with a theory which is based on the assumption that there is no unemployment."[28]

He set out to show that, contrary to the standard view that economic equilibrium entailed full employment, capitalist economies, left to their own devices, could in fact sustain high levels of unemployment for long periods of time, for more powerful forces were at play than worker resistance to the wage cuts that were the Marshallians' remedy for unemployment. To be sure, workers sturdily resisted cuts in their money incomes, as one could easily see from observation not only of trade unions but of workers when they voted. (This also was a reminder that economies are functionally dependent on governments and are only conceptually autonomous.)

These realities were of much greater relevance than they had been in the late nineteenth century, when Marshall wrote, and Keynes elevated his observation about "wage rigidity" to a theoretical tenet; this allowed him to attack a second proposition underpinning older equilibrium views: Say's Law. Say's Law asserts, as a general proposition for all market exchanges, that supply always equals (that is, creates) demand. Assuming Say's Law, there is no such thing as excess production, because wages paid in production will assure the product's final consumption. Yet this "law," formulated in Napoleonic France in 1803, seemed to people in the 1930s, with the decade's glut of excess productive capacity in idled stores and factories and its daunting unemployment, manifestly at odds with reality.

Keynes then offered his own alternative explanation for the Depression. Unemployment and employment needed at any given moment to be examined from the viewpoint of aggregate, or economy-wide, demand, he argued.* Inadequate demand meant inadequate production meant inadequate employment. For theoretical purposes, Keynes used a radically simplified model of the economy that focused on domestic markets and excluded both government spending and foreign trade. In such a model, he explained, aggregate demand is effectively composed of two parts, current consumption and the purchase of new investment goods (for example, machine tools or new factories). The first varies as a fairly stable function of aggregate income (with savings the difference between the two), but purchase of new investment goods was anything but stable; it depended weakly on the prevailing interest rate and mainly on the volatile, ever-changing sense that businessmen had about the future and about whether the risk of investment would be rewarded.

Consumers as a group were largely responsible for savings, whereas busi-

---

*Keynes's economy-wide or "aggregate" viewpoint soon came to be called "macroeconomics," versus the "micro-economic" viewpoint of neoclassical economists, who began with assumptions about individuals and firms and then built upward to the economy as a whole.

nesses made the actual decisions to invest, but the two were linked by the prevailing aggregate level of income. For example, if consumers increased their savings but businessmen failed to match this with increased new investment (fearing it wouldn't pay off), the aggregate income level would fall until the two matched, creating a new equilibrium. But without a clear, consistent way to match savings and investment decisions, there was no guarantee that this would be a full-employment equilibrium. Contrary to Marshallian belief, "equilibrium" could settle at any number of levels well below full employment.

Up to that point, Keynes developed his model in what economists call "real" terms, excluding the function of money (and banking). In Marshall's system, money, and in particular the interest rate, matched the banks' horde of savings of consumers to the business community's willingness to borrow in order to invest; when savings increased faster than investment, interest rates would fall, making it cheaper to borrow. It was this "natural" adjustment of interest rates, the Marshallians said, that solved the riddle of "mismatched" financial behavior because it encouraged investment at a lower cost to business.

Keynes, however, reconceived the function of money and interest and its relation to his "real"-term model. To Keynes, earning interest was for consumers an alternative to holding cash; it was the reward, in effect, for allowing banks to lend in order to make new investment rather than hoarding what wealth one already had. But in a depression, an investor might well find it preferable to hold onto his own cash rather than to risk making an investment that might never be repaid, and not borrow from a bank, a phenomenon Keynes called investors' "liquidity preference." In such a situation, the prevailing interest rate was a minor influence on investment, since the promise of interest to be earned on a loan that might never be repaid is obviously not an incentive to invest.

But if interest rates weren't the mechanism to equilibrate the supply of money (in other words, savings) with demand for it (new investment), as Marshall and his followers thought, money and interest lacked the power they ascribed to them. The willingness of entrepreneurs to invest—not interest rates or the quantity of money—was the key to new investment. And how could one persuade investors to invest? To Keynes, the answer was clear: in order to induce an increase in investment, one had to raise the level of aggregate income and thus consumption, not simply lower interest rates.

But how could the level of aggregate income be raised when private investors wouldn't undertake sufficient new investment? Enter the government. Government, Keynes said, would have to take on the job of matching savings and investment—not by taking over the private economy, as socialists argued, but by adjusting aggregate income through its own investment. In times when unemployment was high, public deficit spending—public projects financed with borrowed money—would be required; when the economy raced ahead and inflation threatened, fiscal restraint (and monetary restraint, though much less than Marshallians posited) was called for.

In this Keynesian scheme, property ownership and investment decisions remained private. Socialism wasn't the answer. Government instead should focus on assuring a level of aggregate income that produced full employment and thus full utilization of all private-sector resources, capital's and labor's alike. Moreover, in recessionary times (even extreme ones such as the Great Depression) government spending would produce a several-fold increase—through what Keynes called "the multiplier effect"—in ultimate aggregate income, because the initial recipients of higher incomes would spend their new resources on goods and services whose providers then would spend out of *their* new incomes, leading to further rounds of increased consumption. Given this multiplier effect, government borrowing to finance its stimulative deficit would not rise to the level where it crowded out the private borrowing needed for new investment.

In the barest of terms, *this* was "Keynesianism." Set out in often dense passages over more than five hundred pages, the argument Keynes was making seemed to offer an entirely new way out of the Depression, because one no longer needed to choose between a socialist overthrow of capitalism or an endless wait, through round after round of plant closings, firings, and stock-market falls, for the economy to reestablish its "normal" full-employment equilibrium. Nor did one have to decide about the immediate consequences of Chamberlin's and Robinson's problem of "monopoly competition," or settle whether Berle and Means were right and extensive "trust busting" was called for, or elect perhaps some vaguely defined "national planning" system (as Galbraith and Dennison had proposed in their little book).

In other words, Keynes placed the rationale for government spending on a new footing. Economists and public officials had long recognized that spending on public works, for example, helped to mop up unemployment during a recession. Under Keynes, this was no longer an isolated, partial, or interim ad hoc step but part of a larger conceptual scheme. And it no longer carried a moral rationale about "helping the poor"; it was now integrated into a system of economic logic aimed at raising aggregate income, which aided everyone. Little wonder then that as *The General Theory*'s argument seemed to grow clearer and clearer, men like Galbraith or Samuelson or Hansen could talk of "tidal forces" or "revolution," and then reach out ("fanatically," as Schumpeter would have it) in support of the elegant Englishman's complex structure of ideas. Problems that had haunted conventional economic theories—about the function of government in economies, about equity versus efficiency, about defending the advantages of markets while addressing equally clear problems that markets did not solve—now seemed fully capable of resolution. And Keynes was giving the profession a new intellectual project: to flesh out his model with rapidly advancing mathematical skills and a wealth of new economic data.

One can't overlook an even more basic reason why Keynesianism dominated an entire generation of economists: *It gave them a purpose.* Years later Paul Samuelson underscored vividly the psychological effects the Depression had on his colleagues, who before *The General Theory* felt they could offer little more than their elders' stale orthodox thinking or a jumbled analysis jury-rigged out of contemporary critiques of that orthodoxy.

> Events of the years following 1929 destroyed the previous economic synthesis. The economists' belief in the orthodox synthesis was not overthrown, but had simply atrophied; it was not as though one's soul had faced a showdown as to the existence of the deity and that faith was unthroned . . . [R]ather it was realized . . . that one no longer had faith, that one had been living without faith for a long time, and that what, after all, was the difference?[29]

Samuelson's analysis was of course not shared by those who saw the Depression as opportunity for radical change or proof of capitalism's necessary failure, or for those on the other hand who never doubted that Marshall would always and everywhere be true. But for Samuelson as for so many others, *The General Theory* was a lifeboat in a turbulent sea, an opportunity to advance a clear theoretical project and to find practical application, and practical work, that would advance the well-being of the nation, even the world. On this promise alone, Keynes had scored undeniable victory.

YET IN LATE 1936 and early 1937 what precisely Keynes's work would yield remained unknown and in the future. But with days taken up teaching agricultural economics and researching the Farm Credit Administration, he had plenty on his plate. Harvard offered little to advance his newfound allegiances apart from late-night discussions with other young instructors and graduate students. There were no classes in Keynesian thought, no textbook but *The General Theory* itself, and despite the numerous review articles, no consensus on how to begin interpreting the book. John Hicks's decisively influential article, "Mr. Keynes and the 'Classics,' " in which Hicks reformulated Keynes into the durable terms of what became known as "the IS-LM model,"* appeared in 1937, but in a British journal with a limited circulation—at a time when photocopying, let alone scanning and e-mail, were nonexistent—so its effects were delayed.[30]

Several graduate students ingeniously tried to remedy this by having Keynes invited to Harvard. They ambitiously petitioned the university to give Keynes an honorary doctorate as part of its Tercentennial Celebration, set for Septem-

---

*The IS-LM model, still taught today, seeks to relate the markets for money and real goods to one another. It is presented to the student graphically on an X-Y Cartesian axis, with the vertical line measuring interest rates and the horizontal showing the output of real goods. The IS line ("investment equals savings") slopes downward from left to right, signifying a rise in planned investment as interest rates fall; simultaneously, the LM line ("liquidity-money" means the idea that the demand for money, or "liquidity preference," equals the fixed supply of money) slopes upward from left to right. At the point where the two lines cross, an equilibrium is said to be reached between the money and goods markets. By adjusting the lines left or right and up and down, one can see what different mixes of fiscal and monetary policy will do to both markets.

As an expository device, the IS-LM model has merit, but whether it accurately reflects Keynes's own ideas is a matter of some real controversy. Hicks long believed it did, and so for many years did most macroeconomists. But by the 1970s, Hicks himself had come to believe that IS-LM failed to give serious attention to what Keynes considered the irremediable uncertainty of markets.

ber 1936. But a Harvard degree *honorus causus* was given that year to a Cambridge University economist, Dennis Robinson, a now largely forgotten figure who was, to his credit in Harvard's eyes, a stout Keynesian critic.*

Amidst this period of fertile uncertainty, with Keynes ignored by official Harvard, Galbraith concocted in remedy his own adventuresome plan. In the late fall of 1936, he decided that *he* would go to England to study with Keynes. The realization of this ingenious idea lacked only such minor features as the funds by which to do so, the permission of his department, and, not least, the approval of Black, who had him hard at work on matters far distant from the realms of Keynesian theory.

But that third year, Keynes wasn't the only thing pressing on Galbraith's mind. He'd met a young woman.

CATHERINE ATWATER was a graduate student at Radcliffe working on a doctorate in comparative literature. After finishing Smith College in 1934, where she'd been a junior-year Phi Beta Kappa, she'd taken a year abroad to study in Munich (she'd earlier spent her junior year at the Sorbonne). In Cambridge, she had chosen to room with Madeleine Rowse, a friend from Smith days who was also working on a doctorate, in German. By 1936, Kitty Atwater had begun research for her thesis, whose topic was the influence of the German Romantic poet Novalis on French writers.

Kitty and Madeleine were having lunch one day early that fall at the Hayes Bickford, a cafeteria in Harvard Square that for years was much beloved by students not only for its low prices but also because it stayed open all night. They were talking when Madeleine looked up to say hello to someone standing behind her lunchmate. When Kitty turned in her chair to be introduced, she says all she could do at first was "look up and up and up!"

Ken Galbraith and Madeleine Rowse had met on the banks of the Charles River the previous spring. Ken, apparently indulging a taste for the full "Harvard experience," had decided to take up rowing on the Charles. Assigned first to an old wherry, rowing's version of a bike with training wheels, he had somehow managed to tip over the supposedly untippable boat and plunge himself, oars, arms, legs, and all, into the river. Madeleine, who'd been reading quietly on the riverbank, had watched as Ken emerged, sodden and embarrassed, and had asked him if he was all right. He was, save for his wounded pride, and as the conversation progressed to mutual laughter, he'd overcome his chagrin enough to ask her out. She'd accepted, but their chemistry yielded a friendship, not a romance.

*Keynes wasn't the only one snubbed by the Tercentenary's planners. President Roosevelt, class of '08, rather naturally expected he'd be invited to speak. But Harvard's president emeritus Lowell, in charge of the ceremonies and intensely hostile to the New Deal and to FDR, at first tried to discourage him even from attending. After Felix Frankfurter castigated him over the obvious insult, Lowell grudgingly invited Roosevelt to speak: "I suppose you will want to say something about what Harvard has meant to the nation," he wrote FDR, but told the President he must keep his remarks to no more than 10 to 15 minutes at most. Roosevelt came and gave a brilliant, self-deprecating, short address. Even so, one of his more moderate classmates reported being stunned at "the rancorous and almost hysterical" reaction displayed by many of the alumni. "I was amazed and disgusted to hear the way men talked of him . . ." (John Bethell, "Frank Roosevelt at Harvard," 49).

Now several months later, as Ken, Madeleine, and Kitty chatted at the Hayes Bickford, Ken was taken with Madeleine Rowse's shy, pretty roommate. Before long he called to arrange an evening with Madeleine and suggested that perhaps Kitty might like to come along. On the appointed evening, the two women met Ken, with Kitty accompanied by a Winthrop House tutor she'd brought along (Ken says it was Fred Skinner, soon better known as Harvard's famed behavioral psychologist B. F. Skinner, but Kitty vehemently denies this. "Fred asked me out three times, but I never went out with him.") Surprised but not deterred, Ken spent most of the evening chatting up—and charming—Kitty.

They saw each other increasingly after that. Sixty-five years later, Galbraith insisted that, from their first evening together, "I was never in doubt." Kitty, too, seemed quickly convinced of her feelings, although she wasn't sure where her commitments would take her. She was determined to finish her doctorate and to teach. "She wasn't at all sure she wanted to get married," her husband remembered, "but still she was certain she wanted us to stick together."

Kitty was the eldest of three children and the only daughter of a successful New York lawyer and his wife. As she grew up in Plandome, a little village on the North Shore of Long Island, her parents had encouraged her intellect and her independence. She graduated from high school at sixteen, and the fact that she twice traveled to Europe for year-long stays on her own bespoke a determination and independence in her that might not find marriage to a young instructor, however promising, the way to realize her carefully nurtured dreams. She found Ken "very supportive and very amusing," but "I wasn't at all sure I wanted to marry him."

But Ken was immune to her doubts. He was far from experienced in serious matters of the heart, though. There had been the usual crush or two in childhood, his fling at Berkeley, and some casual dates in Cambridge.* Courting Kitty Atwater was in truth his first serious love affair, and he was determined to win this woman as his bride.

Courtship and career plans came together in the midwinter of 1937 when Galbraith realized he could advance both at once: he wanted to study with Keynes, and he was in love with a young woman who loved to travel abroad, as he had never done. Hastily, he put together an application to the Rockefeller-funded Social Science Research Council for a traveling fellowship to Europe for the next academic year. When the SSRC notified him that spring that he had been awarded one of their fellowships, he was delighted, and now turned to Kitty. He was able "to tighten the vise on his sometimes elusive bride-to-be," a friend observed, "by convincing her that he would be too much an innocent

---

*Galbraith occasionally likes to allude to slightly more amorous experience (or would-be experience) than is likely true. One story he recounts involves his late high-school days in Iona Station. One summer, he and an attractive young neighbor were leaning against a fence near his home, passing the afternoon in desultory conversation. Out in the pasture, a handsome bull approached a cow and mounted her. The two teenagers watched, and Ken thought his companion might be doing so with rising interest. Looking down at the ground, he said—stammered, more likely—"I think it would be fun to try that."

The girl didn't miss a beat. "Well, go ahead. It's your cow."

abroad without her knowledge of foreign lands and tongues, her supply of Baedeker guidebooks, and her inexhaustible commitment to seeing every cathedral, museum, castle, ruin, monument, stately home, and historical site in every country he promised to visit with her."[31] Armed with the fellowship, and knowing they might not see each other for more than a year, he decided to propose.

Kitty, after some considerable and, to Ken, anxiety-producing hesitation, said yes. She admits the allure of a third year in Europe had its attraction, though it was never the deciding factor. Love of travel was, at the same time, never far from her mind. As she told her Smith class at their fifty-fifth reunion, "He promised me that though we were married we would not settle down, and on that part he kept his word." The Galbraiths' nuptial voyage was the start of a lifelong habit of global travel.*[32]

The two spent the summer of 1937 working in Washington, he on farm-credit issues, she in the cataloging department of the Library of Congress. On weekends, in a sort of dress rehearsal for the year that lay ahead, they'd take his Model A coupe out for drives in the Virginia countryside. There, with Ken behind the wheel and Kitty carefully directing, they'd navigate from one recommended site to another, stopping for visits at Monticello, Charlottesville, and Civil War battlefields, each stop meticulously noted and checked off in Kitty's guidebooks.

They were married on September 17, 1937, at the Reformed Church in North Hempstead, Long Island, with the reception held at Kitty's parents' house. Three days earlier, Ken had become an American citizen. The *Times* reported the ceremony the next day in a brief wedding announcement, noting the couple's travel plans, and the fact that Kitty's father was consul general for Siam.[33] The day was, by all accounts, a complete success—full of joy, merriment, and mutual affection. The Atwaters welcomed with unalloyed pleasure Ken's father and sisters, who had driven down from Ontario, and the Galbraiths reciprocated. Archie Galbraith was especially taken by Kitty's beauty, kindness, and generosity, and when he got home to Canada, for a time he talked of nothing else, according to his daughter.

Ken himself loved Kitty's family almost as much as his bride. Her mother he found "young and vital, entertaining and kind—a wonderfully attractive person." Her father was an equal pleasure—progressive, intellectually enthusiastic, a Harvard Law School graduate who loved engaging his talented, opinionated son-in-law in discussion of politics, economics, and world affairs.

There was also Kitty's grandfather, a chemistry professor at Wesleyan who'd made several significant contributions to the new science of human nutrition and had been one of three founders of the Department of Agriculture. When Galbraith visited Secretary Henry Wallace's offices in Washington, he proudly noted a portrait of Professor Atwater hanging in the secretary's anteroom.

---

*Once, when Galbraith failed to show up for a routine faculty meeting, as he frequently did, someone peevishly demanded to know where he was, and a colleague replied, "At a meeting in Rhode Island." Someone else, who obviously knew him better, coolly broke in: "Ken doesn't go to meetings in Rhode Island. He must be on the Island of Rhodes."

The day after the wedding, Ken and Kitty Galbraith drove his convertible into Manhattan, pulling to a stop at one of the Hudson River piers. There, along with several hundred others, they walked up the gangplank of the S.S. *Britannic*, bound for Southampton. Virtually the entire wedding party came to see them off, laughing and waving festively from the dock as tugs nudged the big liner out into the river. Pictures taken then show a slender, petite, spirited young woman with her husband proudly towering over her, smiling genially, bespectacled in horn-rimmed glasses, and dressed in what even then defined Harvard's tweedy academic style. On board, tucked in the ship's hold, their secondhand Ford sailed with them.

The young couple was leaving behind a country still gripped by the Depression but poised on the brink of dramatic change. As they sailed, the United States was in the grips of the "little Depression" of 1937, when the economy reversed once again, as production fell and unemployment rose. At his rain-streaked second inaugural six months earlier, Roosevelt had spoken of the millions of Americans "denied education, recreation, and the opportunity to better their lot and that of their children. I see millions lacking the means to buy the products of farm and factory and by their poverty denying work and productiveness to many other millions. I see one third of a nation ill-housed, ill-clad, ill-nourished." But FDR had then let Henry Morgenthau, his Secretary of the Treasury, persuade him that balancing the budget was more important than using government deficits to prime the economic pump. Keynes was aghast at the news and wrote a chiding article about the President's error in English papers, as well as sending a private letter to Roosevelt himself, pleading for reversal of his balanced-budget plans.* To no avail. Roosevelt followed Morgenthau, and then was stunned as the economy slipped further backward.

If Keynes's ideas were capturing "the very best of our young people" at Harvard, as Schumpeter feared, it was clear that in Washington the Englishman's message was making perilously little headway, at least at the levels that really mattered. Perhaps after all it was an ideal time for a young man like Galbraith to sail for England. In America, for the moment, there seemed little to do—and in England, much to learn.

---

*In the letter, Keynes criticized the New Deal for not spending enough to end the Depression and encouraged more of the massive public works Galbraith was analyzing for the NPRB, advising Roosevelt to put "most of the eggs in the housing basket," and recommended a public takeover of utilities and railroads (though he knew political opposition might make this impossible).

The "little Depression" of 1937–38, he maintained, was partly psychological in orgin, and he offered Roosevelt his own memorable reading of the business mind. "Businessmen have a different set of delusions from politicians and need, therefore, different handling. They are, however, much milder than politicians, at the same time allured and terrified by the glare of publicity, easily persuaded to be 'patriots,' perplexed, bemused, indeed terrified, yet only too anxious to take a cheerful view, vain perhaps but very unsure of themselves, pathetically responsive to a kind word. You could do anything you want to them if you would treat them (even the big ones) not as wolves or tigers, but as domestic animals by nature, even though they have been badly brought up and not trained as you would wish. It is a mistake to think that they are more immoral than politicians. If you work them into the surly, obstinate, terrified mood, of which domestic animals, wrongly handled, are so capable, the nation's burdens will not get carried to market; and in the end public opinion will veer their way" (Keynes to FDR, February 1, 1938, quoted in Hession, Keynes, 305–306).

5

Going to the Temple

THE TRANSATLANTIC CROSSING on the *Britannic*, Galbraith has written discreetly about the start of his honeymoon, "combined the ecstasy of travel on a great ocean liner with the more routine rewards of love and marriage."[1] He and Kitty spent most of their time strolling the deck, reading, and refining plans for their year abroad. A week after their wedding, the two cleared customs on the Southampton docks and began motoring up to Cambridge, only to receive the disturbing news that John Maynard Keynes wouldn't be available in Cambridge for some time. He had suffered a heart attack and was recuperating and would be unavailable throughout the Galbraiths' stay in England.

Actually, Keynes's attack had occurred several months earlier, late in the spring. Although the diagnosis was a "thrombosis of a coronary artery," his uncle, a chest specialist, thought the problem was pseudo-angina, and advised Keynes's mother, "[t]he treatment is that of the underlying neurosis and the prognosis is a good one, sudden death not occurring." Keynes repaired to a castle in Wales for several months to convalesce and didn't make a public appearance until February 1938; yet while recuperating he kept up a lively stream of articles and correspondence, and even took time to arrange production of a new play by W. H. Auden and Christopher Isherwood, in which his wife, Lydia, appeared. His old friend, the Cambridge economist A. C. Pigou, wrote him that fall, "You're a marvel. How the devil do you continue to be so intelligent when you're so unfit?"[2]

Keynes's absence might have given a lesser man pause, but Galbraith was not to be deterred. "I had resolved to go to the temple," he insisted in his memoirs.[3] If the master wasn't available, Keynes's acolytes, friends, and students were—the star-studded galaxy of talent that in the 1930s gave Cambridge University economists such extraordinary influence over their profession, just as Marshall and his followers had done a generation earlier.

At the temple's center was the little circle known in Cambridge as "the Circus"—an intimate group consisting of Richard Kahn, Joan Robinson and her husband, Austin, James Meade, Piero Sraffa, and a few others who had worked since the early 1930s helping Keynes refine the ideas presented in *The General Theory*. The members of the Circus were all in residence that year, and they "were as deeply into the ideas of the master as Keynes was himself. Indeed, they discussed little else, and neither, in the months ahead, did I."[4]

There is a curious lapse in Galbraith's story of going "to the temple," however. Although his fascination with Keynes was hardly in doubt, why had the Social Science Research Council thought *Galbraith* would make an ideal student for Keynes? After all, he was a young agricultural economist whose published work had a clear agrarian focus. There was little to suggest a background suited for sending this particular man to England for study. At Harvard alone any number of other young men were doing work more directly affected by Keynes's new theories.

The SSRC's records offer a revealing explanation for how Galbraith got to Cambridge. The SSRC had several subdivisions, each governed by its own board; one board covered agricultural economics, and for many years its chairman had been John D. Black. (As it happened, Black wasn't chairman when Galbraith applied for his fellowship; but, like Howard Tolley, he was still on the board.) In fact, Galbraith wasn't appointed to a year's work under Keynes at all; rather, as one of six postdoctoral fellows that year, he was funded "for study in Great Britain, Italy and Germany of current developments in the theory of money and banking in relation to agricultural investment and the stability of agricultural enterprise."[5] Conceivably, Galbraith knew that Keynes kept a farm at Tilton, Sussex, and took pride in his knowledge of farming. (Later, during a wartime visit, Keynes called on Galbraith at the Office of Price Administration to discuss hog production, and was, Galbraith remembered, quite knowledgeable.) But it is not likely. Showing early promise as an academic entrepreneur, it seems Ken simply converted his SSRC grant into a year at Cambridge.

By October 1937, the Galbraiths were living on the north edge of Cambridge in a neighborhood of small, unattractive semidetached homes (his fellowship paid $200 per month plus expenses). To help manage, the Galbraiths shared their lodgings with John Dunlop, another young American economist, and his wife, Dorothy. The slightly younger Dunlop, who like Galbraith had gone to Berkeley but was still doing his doctoral research, earned Galbraith's admiration by correcting Keynes on an important technical matter in *The General Theory* involving the relative movements of money and wages. "Keynes not only conceded his error but thanked Dunlop for the correction. One thought of a graduate student in physics who successfully amended Einstein."*[6]

Galbraith filled his days at Cambridge with lectures, seminars, and extensive reading, especially the works of Keynes and of the members of the Circus,

---

*Galbraith was so impressed that he wrote to Harvard recommending Dunlop as an instructor.[7] The economics department hired him, and Dunlop went on to become a highly regarded Harvard labor economist (as well as department chairman, faculty dean, the head of Nixon's Cost of Living Council, and Secretary of Labor under Gerald Ford).

as well as the teas, sherry parties, and high-table meals where he got to know Sraffa, Kahn, the Robinsons, and others now less remembered in the Keynes circle. He also decided that once a week he would go to London to attend lectures given by Keynes's opponents at the London School of Economics, "the better to sharpen my grasp" of his new hero. Although LSE had been founded in 1895 by Sidney and Beatrice Webb as a Fabian Socialist institution that would offer an alternative to the establishment orthodoxies purveyed by Oxford and Cambridge, by the 1930s it harbored some of the most conservative economists in Britain, figures such as Lionel Robbins and Friedrich von Hayek. Both were deeply committed to their particular variants of neoclassical economics and were profoundly critical of Keynes and the "radical" tendencies that abounded at Cambridge.

LSE seminars, an especially lively part of Galbraith's stay in England, often had fifty to seventy-five participants, many of them talented exiles from Germany or Eastern Europe who never hesitated to interrupt or challenge a professor. At one such gathering, Hayek entered a packed classroom, took his seat, and genteelly began, "Now gentlemen, as I proposed to you at our last meeting, we will on this evening discuss the rate of interest." A student stopped him before he could go further, insisting, "Professor Hayek, I really must beg to disagree." The student was Nicholas Kaldor, a brilliant young economist from Hungary, who went on to a distinguished career at Cambridge and friendship with Galbraith.

Kitty was less happy, however; frustrated in her own work, she hated the damp cold and was tired of all the talk about economics (which she'd never studied) and melancholy in her isolation.[8] She even considered leaving her new husband, "except I had no money and couldn't." Ken saved the moment— and his marriage—by taking Kitty to London for a weekend, where they checked into "one of those places where you have room and bath and breakfast included," she has recalled. "We spent the weekend taking hot baths."[9]

Even without Keynes's active presence at Cambridge to press the ideas in *The General Theory* forward, they were by then starting to exert visible influence. Journals of economics in 1934 had carried just twenty articles discussing Keynes, but in the years 1936–40 the number rose to 269.[10] And the book's impact was hardly confined to university economists. In Washington it was greeted with special warmth by Lauchlin Currie, one of the six dissident supporters of the New Deal who had left Harvard in 1934; he was now working at the Federal Reserve Bank under the chairmanship of the exceptional Utah banker Marriner Eccles. Not unlike Henry Dennison, Currie and Eccles had independently arrived at "Keynesian" views on their own, and both welcomed *The General Theory* as a formal exposition of what they had already intuited.[11] This recognition came at a strategic moment: given the apparent contribution of Morgenthau's balanced budget to the little Depression of 1937, Roosevelt and his senior aides were open to a different approach.

Eccles and Currie had already by then fought a major battle for their own version of Keynesianism and learned a crucial lesson thereby. In pressing for passage of the Banking Act of 1935, the two men had tried to curb the power of the big New York banks and to consolidate control of the Fed's open-market operations, rather than leaving power dispersed among the regional Federal Reserve banks. Though monetary policy was secondary to fiscal policy in Keynes's thinking, opponents of the Banking Act had labeled it derisively "Curried Keynes," and the Banking Act passed only very narrowly. Currie realized how woefully understaffed the Keynesian camp was in the administration compared to the trust-busting and national-planning camps. Serious recruitment and careful placement of sympathetic allies in key Washington offices became an imperative.

By the spring of 1938, Roosevelt brought Currie to the White House as his personal economic adviser, where he used his new position to great effect. For example, when half a dozen young economists from Harvard and Tufts wrote a set of quasi-Keynesian articles and got them published as *An Economic Program for American Democracy*, Currie wasted no time getting it to Roosevelt.[12] The President was so impressed by the little volume that he began recommending it to intimate advisers as an excellent summary of New Deal economic philosophy—which it wasn't yet.[13] Sensing opportunity, Currie got hold of the book's authors. Two years later, nearly every contributor was working in the federal government, part of Currie's rapidly expanding network.[14]

CURRIE'S EMBRACE OF Keynes underscores a feature of Keynesianism that was central to its triumph: it was being absorbed as policy while it was being absorbed as theory. Many academic economists presume that sound economic policy and practice should *emerge* from sound theory, but in the case of early Keynesianism, the two evolved almost simultaneously, with policy applications serving to refine and expand the theory itself.

Keynes himself welcomed this process. Even while recovering from his heart attack, he kept up a steady output of magazine and newspaper articles, as well as correspondence, meant to advance his views. Early in 1938, for example, he wrote to Roosevelt, chiding him for listening to Morgenthau and pressing him to adopt new policies to recover not just from the "little Depression" but from the larger crisis:

> I am terrified lest progressive causes in all the democratic countries should suffer injury, because you have taken too lightly the risk to their prestige which would result from a failure measured in terms of immediate prosperity. There *need* be no failure. But the maintenance of prosperity in the modern world is extremely *difficult*, and it is so easy to lose precious time.[15]

This spirit of pragmatism—seeing that economics needed to cycle back and forth constantly between theory and policy, as well as the real-world politics underpinning policy—was profoundly influential with Galbraith. Agricultural economics had firmly established the precedent—Black's work and influence on Ken as well as Ken's own early writings make that clear. But Keynes's example affirmed Galbraith's confidence in maintaining this outlook in the broader realms of macroeconomics. And beyond the theoretical content of *The General Theory* he was absorbing several lessons from Keynes that would guide him throughout his life and career.

First, Keynes presented a model of the economist as an engaged and politically purposive intellectual. Black was already such a model, but Keynes strode on a wider stage, and he was at least as concerned to reach a large audience as he was to persuade professional colleagues. Galbraith has been endlessly sniped at by economists who have treated his work as mere popularizing, unbecoming to academic dignity and theoretical advance. In fact, Keynes himself was Galbraith's model. By one estimate, he wrote more than three hundred magazine and newspaper articles for popular publications, and his first really influential work was not a theoretical one but *The Economic Consequences of the Peace*, written for a large general audience.[16] During the 1920s, Keynes had kept up his steady use of the press to attack government economic policies (most important, Britain's return to the gold standard under Winston Churchill), and during the Depression, he poured out a steady stream of newspaper and magazine articles criticizing American and British policies. The appearance of his masterpiece in 1936 did nothing to alter these practices. Indeed, after war broke out in Europe in 1939, his articles in *The Times* of London on "How to Pay for the War" were crucial in setting Britain's wartime economic policies—and not inconsequentially gave Keynesians a pragmatic demonstration of how the ideas of *The General Theory* could be successfully adapted to conditions of high employment and potentially rapid inflation.[17]

Keynes also gave Galbraith a model of how elite social and political networks shape acceptance of economists' theories, a matter seldom formally or openly discussed. Keynes's childhood upbringing in the heart of a late-Victorian academic aristocracy, as well as his Bloomsbury friendships, allowed him throughout his life to move suavely through a world that encompassed scholarship, journalism, the arts, investment, corporate management, and Liberal Party politics. For Galbraith, the Canadian farm boy still not quite certain of his own social standing or direction, this particular aspect of Keynes's life— even with Keynes absent—was especially instructive. Still in many respects unchanged since Keynes's Edwardian-era youth, Cambridge far more than Harvard affected Galbraith's decisions on how to proceed in the social world.

> Life in the Oxford and Cambridge colleges between the wars retained virtually all of its [pre-twentieth-century] style. Servants still attended to the needs of students, although Cambridge had weakened to the point of allowing women to serve. Proctors in their gowns and their assisting bulldogs in full regalia patrolled the streets to keep order and enforce the curfew. The menu at the better High Tables was far above the British average, as also the wine, and especially so at the numerous feasts. Much store was set by the quality of the after-dinner conversation among Fellows and guests in the Combination Rooms.[18]

Galbraith's talent for making friends with wealthy and powerful people largely began while he was in England. David Rockefeller, grandson of the Standard Oil titan, was the first in a long line. Rockefeller, a young Harvard economics graduate who met Galbraith for the first time at LSE, was charmed enough to visit the Galbraiths in Cambridge. After a congenial dinner, the two men spent a relaxed evening playing poker, though Galbraith (wisely calculating the situation) persuaded Rockefeller to play for matchsticks. The encounter left an enduring impression on Rockefeller, enough so that David and his brother Nelson actively pursued Ken eight years later, hoping he'd direct a new global economic research program for them, as well as help manage the family's fortune.

Though Galbraith was still far from being the urbane raconteur he later became, being basically quite serious and focused on his work and career, he grew comfortable not just with the likes of Rockefellers but with the brilliant scholars at Cambridge. His contact with Joan Robinson, for example, formed the basis of a close and mutually respectful affection that endured until her death a half century later;* similarly, Piero Sraffa, Richard Kahn, Michal Kalecki, and Nicholas Kaldor all became friends.

Keynes was also a model for Galbraith inasmuch as he had a clear preference for expressing economics arguments in English rather than in mathematical models or equations. Keynes was hardly alone in this practice, since most economists then did not frequently use advanced mathematical expression. The journal *Econometrica*, ever since a showcase for the most advanced uses of mathematics in economics, was new then, as was econometrics itself, and the famed Cowles Commission, dedicated to advancing the use of mathematics in economics, was likewise new. Graduate students like Paul Samuelson, who in many ways officiated at the postwar marriage of Keynesian theory with sophisticated mathematical techniques, have testified that Harvard in the late 1930s was devoid of serious mathematical training; even in the 1940s, when Robert Solow studied economics there, he "discovered" probability and statistics almost on his own, because it was "a subject not taught to economists at Harvard then . . . [T]he courses in statistics that were taught were really dreadful; it was a scandal. So I took courses in the mathematics department."[19]

This general absence of advanced mathematical reasoning in economics was not unique to Harvard. Keynes himself generally relied on verbal argument and confined mathematical reasoning and presentation to footnotes or rare insertions in the text itself. It wasn't due to a lack of understanding of mathematics (which he had studied as an undergraduate, earning his degree with highest honors), but rather to an entrenched pedagogic tradition in Cambridge. After World War II, this absence of advanced mathematical forms was often taken as a sign of intellectual weakness—a curious judgment, given the

---

*In England two decades after their first meeting, Galbraith casually asked Robinson who the bright new economists were. Robinson, who famously deplored the directions of postwar mainstream economics, looked at him quite sternly and said, "Kenneth, we were the last good generation" (Galbraith, interview with author).

theoretical accomplishments of Marshall, Pigou, Hayek, von Mises, Hicks, Schumpeter, and Knight, not to mention Keynes. Their works lack even the mathematical expressions now taught to advanced undergraduates, yet they produced theories that still form the foundations for economics today. It is a central issue to which we shall return.

GALBRAITH'S WORK DURING and after his year at Cambridge shows that he quickly became a full-fledged Keynesian, a process best seen in a measured and rather elegant defense of Keynesian ideas that he wrote for the *Harvard Business Review* after his return to the United States, titled "Fiscal Policy and the Employment-Investment Controversy." The issue was government expenditure and its relation to unemployment. Orthodox economic theory, so often automatically beloved in the business community, had said that reducing wages was crucial to overcoming the Depression, with the resulting lowered "equilibrium" the key to restoring full employment and growth. But, Galbraith explained, Keynes had shown why equilibrium could last for a long time without full employment, why this meant underutilized capacity, and so why both business leaders and policymakers had to focus on the restoration of aggregate income through government deficit spending.

Galbraith summarized *The General Theory*'s analysis of the employment-equilibrium debate and the related savings-investment one quite clearly and succinctly. Neither lowering wages nor manipulating interest rates would restore an optimally efficient (that is, full-employment) equilibrium. But he was also at pains to show his own differences with the book. He stressed, for example, that he disagreed with Keynes's focus on aggregate income reduction as leading to an unemployment equilibrium. To Galbraith, the argument "always seemed to me a bit roundabout." For him, the emphasis should be on the unevenness of wage reductions among various sectors and their effects not on the money supply but on profit levels. "Rather than producing lower costs relative to prices, [unevenly distributed wage cuts] may lower costs and at the same time produce a corresponding diminution in demand. The result is that profits *as a whole* are not improved and things are not changed for the better."[20]

Here is a motif that Galbraith was to return to again and again. In stressing that wages and income fall unevenly across different groups during an economic downturn, he refined the economic and political implications of Keynes's argument about the behavior of aggregate income in the absence of government spending and more closely captured what he saw as the empirical reality. The effect was to underscore the significance of income inequality in periods of rapid change, as individual companies or industries (or groups of them) responded to recession relative to others. He stressed to his business audience the adverse effects of such shifts of income inequality on profits, but he was also implicitly focusing on the role of occupation and social class as well.

Mainstream Keynesians after World War II would focus on full-employment growth, and mostly ignore the structure of income and wealth inequality, simply preferring to believe, as President Kennedy put it, that "a ris-ing tide lifts all boats." Galbraith would not, because he believed that the structure of inequality itself directly gave shape to different levels of aggregate income, and thus implied very different government remedies for achieving optimal economic performance. He most famously revisited this argument during the Kennedy administration's debates over how to spur economic growth, arguing then, as he did in the 1930s, that targeted deficit spending should be chosen over across-the-board tax cuts because of its distributive, along with its efficiency, effects.

Galbraith also addressed Alvin Hansen's views on stagnation as part of an extended crisis in the business cycle. Hansen—who had been recruited to Harvard largely because of his own pre-Keynesian theory of business cycles, which overlapped Keynesian views in some important ways but differed markedly in others—had for many years concentrated on the long-term slow-down in investment returns with arguments that bore a vague resemblance to Marxist critiques, although he and most business-cycle theorists were hardly Marxists. Galbraith shrewdly stressed that although Hansen's argument might have a certain "empirical attractiveness" regarding past performance, it inade-quately demonstrated its validity for the future—and the country's subsequent economic growth affirmed his instinct here.

None of these caveats and exceptions diminished Galbraith's support for the central Keynesian message. Since full-employment equilibrium is but one of many possible economic equilibria characterizing capitalist society, and since high unemployment characterized the current period, Galbraith urged his business executive audience to weigh the consequences of unemployment against the principal arguments against state intervention. First, "as a commu-nity, we have the choice between considering new action which will employ workers . . . or accepting idleness"; second, "if we choose to employ idle men . . . it is a government responsibility to bring about this end. The government cannot logically place upon private enterprise the responsibility for [solving] unemployment if full employment is not the normal achievement of private enterprise."

The government must then itself choose between two lines of action: "indi-rect action," which centered on manipulating interest rates and lowering wage rates; and "direct action," consisting of deficit-based public investment and straightforward government employment. Galbraith dealt swiftly with the indi-rect alternative, for interest-rate adjustments had already produced little employment and the merits of reducing wages seemed "wholly academic": "The policy of workers is against wage reductions and is likely to remain so. This means, in a democratic state, that wage reductions as an instrument of economic policy may not exist. In my judgment this is, in fact, no important handicap."

It is to "direct action" that Americans must turn to end the Depression. "Public subsidy to private investment is an old and established policy," Gal-braith reminded his audience, long applied to railroads, canals, roads, new land development, and natural resources. As for public employment, he emphasized that with the "multiplier effect" (drawing directly on Keynes), the number of workers the government must employ would be far less than the total unemployed, and hence less expensive than businessmen might at first fear.

Even so, if the government must go into debt to finance such direct actions, so be it. "Debt and capitalism," he remarked flatly, "are indissoluble partners." Businessmen and conservative politicians might wring their hands about public debt "choking off" private investment, but they simply didn't understand that, at levels so far below full employment, idle capacity and investment opportunities would continue to abound. And even approaching full employment one shouldn't shy away from public deficits too abruptly, for

> it is investment and debt-creation which produce the income that keeps the debt from becoming burdensome . . . The ideal economic state for those who fear debt would be full employment, optimum output, and no debt creation of any kind. We have never lived in such an ideal economy, so there is little hesitation over accepting the debt which private enterprise must necessarily create in order to provide full employment and, incidentally, liquidate its past borrowing. If we are so far from the ideal that not even private investment is sufficient to maintain employment and income, then it is probable that we should not worry too much about . . . public investment directed toward the same end.[21]

Keynes, reading those words, would have had no difficulty recognizing a disciple.

Still, the article bears early signs of a distinctly Galbraithian style. His exceptions to Keynes, for example, were based on a reasoning process that tried to avoid what he calls "academic" and "roundabout" argument. For both relevance and for criteria of importance, he looked to empirical facts and institutional relations rather than to deductive constructs or mathematical formulae. And the arguments themselves went beyond conventional economic boundaries, concerned as they were with the political effect of the American economy on American democracy and the need to formulate public policy that didn't weaken the latter while strengthening the former.

One can't know what most business executive readers thought, but the *Harvard Business Review* article earned Galbraith quite positive reaction in a few well-placed nonbusiness circles. Alvin Hansen, for one, graciously congratulated him for "a remarkably clear and compressed statement applying the whole range of modern economic thinking to a very difficult problem," and then asked Galbraith for permission to use the piece in his famous Fiscal Policy Seminar, where much American thought about Keynesian economics began—a powerful compliment.[22]

GALBRAITH WAS EQUALLY active on two other fronts during the 1937–38 academic year, immersing himself in Europe's culture and doing research on its agricultural conditions (which, after all, was why the SSRC had sent him to Europe in the first place).

The Galbraiths began their Continental travels during the month-long 1937 Christmas break, when they crossed the Channel by ferry and drove along snow- and ice-covered roads in one of Europe's worst winters from Ostend to Bruges, then Ghent, Brussels, Lièges, Aachen, Cologne, Göttingen, Hamburg, Flensburg, and finally Copenhagen, where they spent Christmas Eve. On Christmas Day they visited Elsinore, then went by ferry to Sweden. The itinerary was fundamentally Kitty's, set by Baedeker and her fluency in languages. "A castle an hour" was the regimen, her bemused husband claims, even though "the roads almost everywhere were covered in ice, and sometimes, as in the Harz mountains, the snow was high beside the roads." The roadster itself was cause for discomfort, since for much of the trip, the Galbraiths shared it with two American friends from Cambridge. Given the weather, use of the car's rumble seat was impossible, so Kitty, "being the smallest, was forced to curl up on the shelf behind the front seat. She had to be told of the view. We had time to stop and see whatever was to be seen, and my wife placed a neat check mark against each monument, birthplace, museum, church and castle listed in the Baedeker. She would not willingly abandon a town while any sight remained unmarked."[23]

On this hurried and rather cramped approximation of a Grand Tour, Galbraith was able to find time for economics and to make new acquaintances. In Sweden, for example, he was introduced to Bertil Ohlin, later a Nobel laureate and longtime leader of the Liberal Party; a young Dag Hammarskjöld; the prominent economist Gustav Cassel; and Gunnar and Alva Myrdal, a couple who became lifelong friends. (The Myrdals eventually won two Nobel Prizes, he in economics, she for peace.)

Myrdal, at their first meeting, mentioned that the Carnegie Corporation had just invited him to come to the United States in order to examine what was then called "the Negro question." The Swede was flattered but said he was disinclined to make the journey. "My reaction was rather different," Galbraith remembered. "No one, I believed, should turn down free money and travel from a foundation," and he encouraged Myrdal to accept the invitation. The result was *The American Dilemma*, perhaps the most influential study of American race relations of the time.[24]

In May 1938, the Galbraiths headed off again, this time via France to Rome, where Ken was to attend a conference of the International Institute of Agriculture (courtesy of Professor Black). Once again, Kitty's gifts for history and culture assured that no straight lines were followed: a Paris stop was obligatory, not only to visit the city but to see friends Kitty had made while studying at the Sorbonne. To that were added Chartres and Compiègne, an excursion north to Amiens, Rheims, and Verdun, then travel through Burgundy and Provence, with a side trip to Geneva, a stately procession along the Riviera, stopovers in Genoa, Pisa, and Siena, and then finally Rome.

Officially Galbraith was part of the U.S. delegation, headed by the Undersecretary of Agriculture, at this international conference. But with Europe drifting slowly yet inexorably to war, there was little for the delegates to decide; it was endless papers, panels, and speeches. Galbraith found almost nothing worthwhile to do—"I attended the opening and closing sessions, and, after a brief exposure to other parts of the program, went only to the receptions and dinners in between." At the conference's end, he and Kitty extended their tour. With her Baedeker firmly in hand, they proceeded to Naples, Florence, Ravenna, Venice, and then, moving circuitously north, to Vienna, Prague, Munich, Berlin, and then to East Prussia to visit the great Junker estates. In his written recollections, Galbraith commented on the pleasures of the journey— and the fact that Prussia was one area of Germany where Kitty had not previously spent any time. But it was, in fact, a time for industrious study of what nowadays seems a most peculiar topic: agricultural land policies under the Third Reich.[25]

Having spent much of his year at Cambridge advancing his understanding of Keynesianism, the original purpose of Galbraith's SSRC fellowship now intruded. The fellowship required a report, and Galbraith plunged into a whirlwind of research. First he met academic and bureaucratic specialists in Berlin to discuss the obscurities of Third Reich land policies (Kitty was his part-time translator), then conscientiously traveled among Prussian estates, talking to landowners and regional officials about the effect of current policies designed to prevent the breakup of traditional farmlands, and these policies' effect on agricultural production. After two trips into Hitler's Reich in less than a year, Galbraith's choice of topics seems odd to say the least. It was, after all, a momentous and ominous time. German policies were pitching Europe painfully toward murderous conflict, and war commenced barely a year after the Galbraiths' return to the United States. Ken and Kitty had seen what was happening at first hand—watching Nazi troops goose-step down boulevards in Berlin and Mussolini's black shirts throng in Rome; they had arrived in Vienna just nine days after Germany's annexation of Austria.

One might imagine that Galbraith was filled with repugnance and horror at what he saw. But in fact he had no outspoken reaction at the time. Like most Americans in the late 1930s, he was inclined to neutrality in Europe's conflicts, convinced they were part of a murderous history in which Americans should play no part. Though he "was eloquently adverse," as he put it, "in my views of Hitler and National Socialism, passionately with the Loyalists in Spain . . . there seemed little against spending a few weeks in Germany, ostensibly on academic studies."[26] In any case, Galbraith applied himself with great energy to completing his research on German land policy, and by the end of the summer, he was ready to report to the SSRC's field representative in Paris on his progress.[27] As he described his travels—no doubt playing down Kitty's shaping of much of them—the representative grew exhausted and advised him to take a good vacation after so much work.

The Galbraiths sailed from Rotterdam aboard the S.S. *Statendam* ten days later. Kitty, shrewdly citing the SSRC man's advice, had persuaded Galbraith that they should go from Paris to Holland via the Loire Valley, Mont-Saint-Michel, and the Brittany coast. Now heading back to America—and the final year of Ken's three-year Harvard contract—they began to think of the future. During his year in England, Ken had kept up a steady correspondence with both Professor Black and the department chairman, Harold Burbank, reporting on his research and discreetly pursuing the matter of tenure. He had carefully avoided mention of his newfound Keynesian allegiances, rightly sensing that neither man, for quite different reasons, would be entirely pleased.

He also had not mentioned—nor has he ever since spoken of—the tragedy that scarred all the pleasures and excitement of his life in Europe. In mid-January, on Kitty's birthday, a telegram arrived from Canada. Thinking her father-in-law had rather extravagantly wired her birthday wishes, Kitty opened it, intending to add it to the cards other friends and family members had sent. But the telegram announced that Ken's father was dead, killed the day before in a gruesome automobile accident. Archie had been riding in a friend's car as it pulled up to an unmarked railroad crossing near home. Two cars before them had paused briefly, then crossed the track. It was near dark and with a fading winter sun in the driver's face, neither man saw the eastbound freight train bearing down. The locomotive struck the car at nearly forty miles an hour, and carried it almost half a mile before stopping. Both men were killed instantly.[28]

Ken Galbraith had last seen his father just four months earlier, at the pier in New York the day after his wedding. Archie had waved good-bye, proud of his son, delighted by his new daughter-in-law, as full of joy in that moment as the two newlyweds.

6

Moving On—Toward War

BY THE FALL of 1938 and the start of the last year of Galbraith's three-year appointment at Harvard, it was time, in the well-worn academic tradition, for "up or out." He turned thirty that October, he was married, and he and his wife were thinking about starting a family. Galbraith earned $2,750 as a faculty instructor, but, thanks to Harvard's rules in such matters, because he was now married he and Kitty couldn't take up his subsidized living quarters at Winthrop House. To offset this loss of free room and board, Galbraith agreed to teach introductory economics to Radcliffe students, who were not yet allowed to attend Harvard classes (the presence of young women—again the antiquarian rules—was thought to be a learning impediment for young men). To supplement their income, Kitty took a job at Widener Library, juggling this with work on her dissertation. Stretched financially, they decided to make do until the elders of the Economics Department could settle on the matter of an assistant professorship.

A number of signs pointed in Galbraith's favor. Black strongly supported him. His book with Henry Dennison had received positive reviews, and his articles had appeared in well-regarded academic venues. The SSRC fellowship had been prestigious, and he could list modestly important service in Washington at the Agricultural Adjustment Administration and the Brookings Institution. Galbraith wrote in his memoirs that he foresaw little difficulty in moving forward toward tenure. This was a painful—and career-altering—misjudgment.[1]

Harvard at the time was locked in a raging academic controversy unmatched in celebrity or ferocity until the student revolts of the 1960s. The controversy revolved around Raymond Walsh and Alan Sweezy, just ahead of Galbraith in the Economics Department's promotion ranks and active in progressive campus politics.

Walsh, who'd done his undergraduate and doctoral work at Harvard, was the department's only labor economist. His commitment to labor, however, was not merely academic: he openly supported the newly formed Congress of In-dustrial Organizations and was president of the Cambridge Union of Univer-sity Teachers, a short-lived attempt to unionize Harvard and MIT faculty. A popular teacher, highly regarded by students and colleagues (even the conser-vative Harold Hitchings Burbank called him "the most brilliant teacher" in the department, possibly in the College), Walsh had also won a certain campus notoriety for daring to criticize publicly former President Lowell's opposition to a statewide ban on child labor.

Sweezy, Harvard-educated like Walsh, was the son of a New York banker (and the older brother of Paul Sweezy, who was then completing his doctoral thesis under Joseph Schumpeter). Like Walsh, he was an active member of the teachers' union and a popular, effective teacher. (Walsh taught the introduc-tory economics course Econ A, which regularly drew five to six hundred stu-dents; Sweezy's course in economic theory was so well liked that students petitioned the department to expand it from one to two semesters.) In April 1937, the two men, both in line for tenure, had instead been singled out by President Conant for termination.

When news of this broke, it almost instantly became a national *cause célèbre*. Convinced that fundamental issues of academic freedom were at stake, Harvard students and faculty signed petitions, organized protest gather-ings, and began marching in public demonstrations, while off-campus the American Federation of Labor, the American Federation of Teachers, the American Civil Liberties Union, and forty-two Rhodes Scholars at Oxford weighed in against the ruling. Soon more than a third of Harvard's faculty, in-cluding Galbraith, signed an unprecedented open letter calling for reversal of the decision. (Galbraith was the only economist among the letter's handful of organizers, though he was in distinguished company, with W. V. Quine, F. O. Matthiessen, and Crane Brinton.[2])

President Conant said initially that he had ordered the dismissals "solely on the grounds" of the two men's "teaching capacity" and "scholarly ability." But when supporters pointed out that the Economics Department had unani-mously voted them three-year reappointments during which time it "might wish to recommend their advancement," Conant found himself in an embar-rassing bind. Threatened with libel action by the Cambridge Union of Uni-versity Teachers, he backtracked, claiming that because of its straitened finances, Harvard could not afford so many instructors. Few were convinced by this new explanation, even though it was of a piece with Conant's intention, proclaimed in 1935, to trim the size of the junior faculty. Yet Harvard hadn't until then noticeably curtailed its number of instructors; in fact, the size of the faculty actually had grown during the 1930s. Realizing that the outcry wouldn't die down, Conant retreated again, issued a letter of apology for im-pugning the men's abilities, and agreed to appoint a senior faculty committee to review his decision.[3]

The Committee of Eight—which included Arthur Schlesinger, Sr., Felix Frankfurter, and Samuel Eliot Morison—spent months interviewing witnesses and poring over departmental and university records, then issued its report in the late spring of 1938. Conant had made the hard, but wise, choice, it said: there were too many worthy candidates for too few slots, and despite an "appearance" of political prejudice, there had been "no departure whatsoever from Harvard's tradition of tolerance and untrammeled scientific inquiry." The committee acknowledged that two other economists had been promoted over Walsh and Sweezy, but that they held more temperate political views and were more restrained in the expression of them was simply "an accident." (Galbraith, who knew all the parties, was among the doubters. If this was "an accident," he dryly observed years later, "it was the kind of accident to which universities are prone."*[4]) But the committee also suggested in its report that Walsh's and Sweezy's cases should be reconsidered.

Conant's refusal to heed this recommendation quickly set off a second round of petitions, demonstrations, and embarrassing national news coverage. The Committee of Eight was asked for a second report, and the review dragged on for another year. Walsh and Sweezy resigned, but not before Conant and Harvard had been subjected to excoriating criticism and more protests—and Conant had dismissed ten more men, again claiming budget problems. (Even today Harvard does not allow full review of its internal Walsh-Sweezy records.[5])

Conant's victory didn't come easily: it almost cost him his own job. Several members of the Committee of Eight were in fact privately furious with him; Felix Frankfurter said that Harvard's future was "very ominous indeed" if Conant were to prevail, citing "great danger" that "authoritarian rule" would overtake the campus. Kenneth Murdock began plotting with others to force Conant's resignation, and some of the committee's members thought of quitting. Of the turmoil Conant wrote to a friend, "I feel quite as though war had come to Cambridge!" His "unpopularity can hardly be exaggerated in that era," Conant's provost Paul Buck later wrote. "The faculty meetings were terrible experiences." Conant prevailed in the end, but "two years of academic warfare had left deep wounds on all sides," his biographer concluded.[6]

The prolonged imbroglio created, for Galbraith, his own unpleasant career crisis. He had been on campus in the spring of 1937 when the affair first broke, and the letters he sent back from England that winter clearly indicated—contrary to his memoirs—that he knew it boded ill for him. Shortly be-

---

*It's worth noting that Harvard's Department of Economics—the nation's first—had been born through a not dissimilar presidential "accident." In the late 1860s, a group of Boston businessmen (several of them Overseers) approached President Eliot and "made it clear that Harvard should teach political economy and teach it correctly." The university's one teacher in the field, Francis Bowen, was an advocate of protective tariffs and thought that the nation's Civil War debts should be repaid at a discount. These Boston merchants were angered by such heresy and initially funded an annual lecture series on economics, "to be filled only by men known for their sound money views." Sensing that wouldn't be enough to correct Harvard's "errors," they then persuaded Eliot to reassign Bowen to a course on Christian ethics, and to appoint in his place Charles Dunbar. "Dunbar's only qualification for the chair," noted a frank study produced by Harvard Provost Paul Buck a century later, "appears to have been the economic orthodoxy of the editorials he had written while editor of the Boston *Daily Advertiser*" (see Robert Church, "Economists Study Society," in Paul Buck, ed., *Social Sciences at Harvard*, 24–5).

fore Christmas 1937, Black had warned him that prospects for renewal, let alone advancement, were cloudy at best, and hinged on the outcome of Walsh-Sweezy. By the spring of 1938, with the Committee of Eight backing Conant's decision even though calling for the two men's reinstatement, Galbraith suggested to Black that he'd be willing to remain at Harvard—at least for a while—on a non-tenure-track basis.

> I have never objected to the competition at Harvard for the higher posts—in fact I have rather enjoyed it. But I do not feel inclined to stay in the game if there is prospect of a permanent ban on the prize money. I am not able to satisfy myself as to the future from Professor Burbank's letter and I should very much like your best estimate of what I should count on.[7]

Black's answer soon after, however, made clear that the Walsh-Sweezy controversy had poisoned the well. Back at Harvard by the fall of 1938, Galbraith realized that it was time to look for new work. Harvard wasn't going to keep him, let alone promote him.

Jobs, including academic jobs, were at a premium in the late Depression, and to a young instructor, the prospect of unemployment was a real and unpleasant possibility. Galbraith had by then gotten several initial offers since coming to Harvard, apart from Theodore Schultz's, to come to Iowa State.* But with his Harvard post secure, he had politely declined all of them, at first content to be working with Black, then aware that his future work lay in new fields. Now things were different—and several anxious months ensued.

By winter break, rather surprisingly, an offer came from Princeton, hardly a well-known center for agricultural economists. At least it was an assistant professorship. Galbraith, with newfound expertise in Keynesian ideas, grudgingly thought it might be minimally acceptable. In his memoirs, he curtly titled the chapter covering his Princeton experience "Interlude," and wrote that the prospect of teaching there gave him no real excitement. Given Princeton's commitment to pre-Keynesian orthodoxy, it would mean being "one dissonant voice in an otherwise harmonious choir," and he claimed that he pursued the offer only in order to provoke a competitive counteroffer from Harvard.[8]

But Harvard didn't budge. Galbraith was dining with the chairman of Princeton's Economics Department when the bad news arrived:

> I was handed a telegram from Harold Hitchings Burbank. He had just come from a meeting with James Bryant Conant, and he advised me to take any post that was offered at Princeton. My Harvard prospects, the wire said, were very slim. My bargaining position went into a severe slump as did my morale. I recall that evening with distaste.[9]

---

*Schultz, whose later work led to a Nobel Prize, is remembered by economists for a second, unique distinction: he is the only department chair known to have offered jobs to both Galbraith and (after Schultz moved to the University of Chicago) Milton Friedman.

Galbraith wasn't the only disappointed Harvard economist that spring. Six of the department's seven instructors who had chances for tenure when the Walsh-Sweezy affair began were gone two years later. Reflecting on the exodus, senior economics professors chose to note the affair's effect on President Conant, who "undoubtedly had more difficulties of this sort with the Economics Department than with any other, and there is some evidence that these difficulties tended to sour his view of the Department."[10] Galbraith and the others who were sent packing had their own views of Conant's suffering.

Yet Galbraith had powerful admirers, two in particular whose energies and extensive contacts now kept his career moving forward. Henry Dennison and John D. Black saw Galbraith as destined for greater things, and both men set out to help him. In the fall of 1938, just as he started his job search, he got an unexpected phone call from Charles Eliot II, the son of Harvard's legendary president. Eliot was now director of FDR's National Resources Planning Board, and he wanted Galbraith to head up a major (though temporary) review of the New Deal's public-works spending that would include making recommendations to the President on its future. Eliot's offer was a plum assignment, and Dennison, one of two chief advisers to Eliot and the NRPB's executive committee, had brought it about.[11] The executive committee was headed by the President's uncle, Frederic A. Delano, and it reported directly to the White House.*

Keynes's theory that public deficit spending could stimulate consumption, investment, and hence growth rested heavily on "the multiplier effect." Here was an ideal opportunity to evaluate and measure it—and publicly validate, at a single stroke, both Keynesian policy and a new rationale for New Deal practice. Roosevelt had just abandoned Morgenthau's balanced-budget strategy and was now committed to what, one historian rightly observes, was "the first outright recommendation" ever made by any American president that government explicitly use fiscal policy and deficit spending as the principal tools for economic recovery.[12] Calling for an unprecedented and massive increase in relief and public works spending (and, in a foreshadowing of what was to come, military expenditures), Roosevelt had just persuaded Congress to authorize an extraordinary *sixfold* rise in the deficit in the second half of 1938. An economic history of the time recounts,

> This was not the pump priming that had been tried before 1938 when it had been believed that a relatively small expenditure of public monies would stimulate private investment and bring the economy to full employment. Now it was recognized that large and persistent public spending would be necessary.[13]

---

*Galbraith's first meeting with FDR occurred one day in 1939, when the board met to review his study. A call came for the group to come to the White House. "We filed into the Oval Office," Galbraith recalls, "and were greeted each in turn by FDR. Thus encouraged in our efforts, we were discharged without recourse to any substantive business. It was my first meeting with the President; thereafter I was able to advert to him in personal terms."

For the small but rapidly growing band of American Keynesians, it seemed a moment of unalloyed triumph, remarkable not least in the swiftness with which it had come about.

But those closest to Roosevelt also sensed that it was a fragile victory and open to reversal. That November—just two years after Roosevelt had carried forty-six of forty-eight states in his reelection—voters cut badly into the Democrats' congressional majorities, a sign not only of their concerns and frustrations about economic recovery but of their fear that America under Roosevelt might be drawn, for the second time in just twenty years, into a European war.

THE 1938 ELECTION only affirmed what Roosevelt already understood: he now needed to operate with the utmost political delicacy, even as he pressed for a deficit-driven recovery at home and began to prepare for what seemed an inevitable war in Europe. For many of those around him, not least his new economic adviser Lauchlin Currie, it was a moment to consolidate and expand Keynesian policy footholds in the administration. The job Charles Eliot offered Galbraith thus had symbolic and strategic importance, although it was not permanent.

Today, Galbraith's completed study, published as *The Economic Effects of the Federal Public Works Expenditures, 1933–1938*, reads at one level as a succinct overview of the New Deal's experience with public works. At another, it is implicitly intended to persuade skeptical officials and congressmen to do what Roosevelt had sought to do when he ordered the study: "promote wider understanding of the part which the wise choice and timing of public works can play toward increasing national income."[14] The document also shows at a glance the extraordinary dimensions that public-works spending had taken on in the Depression, and why Keynesians thought they were so important. In the 1920s, public works—mostly state and local, not federal—had accounted for less than 20 percent of all construction jobs in the United States; by the late 1930s, they accounted for nearly 80 percent. In dollar terms, federal public-works spending made up as much as 40 percent of all national purchases of cast-iron pipes, cement, and structural steel, and state and local spending rivaled federal spending levels.

Galbraith faced the practical challenge of pressing his newfound Keynesianism forward among competing currents in the ongoing debate about federal spending policies. Knowing that Keynesian thinking had not yet won the day, despite its fresh victories, he carefully distanced himself from Keynes on issues of modest technical importance while deftly serving up the main lines of the Keynesian argument. He thus divided the arguments about public-works spending into four broad camps, three of which were dominating the debate at the time. Most conservative economists and business leaders saw no need for massive public-works investment, because they thought that economic contractions, even one as terrible as the Depression, were self-correcting. A second camp held to the positive effects of a modest works program; this had essentially been President Hoover's position and that of many orthodox economists. The third view was that a large but temporary and ad hoc public-works program was needed to lift the economy back to full employment; broadly speaking, this was the New Deal position in FDR's first term. All three positions were now under strong attack from different quarters, for often quite contradictory reasons.

Acutely aware that, thanks to the "little Depression" then still under way, New Dealers' attitudes toward Keynes's *General Theory* were at a turning point, Galbraith's fourth view of public works built on Washington's wary new openness to Keynesian thinking. In his words, it "abandons the idea of the business cycle as the central source of unemployment and makes the unemployed men and materials the normal or equilibrium situation in the modern economy." This places public works in an entirely new light: "It is no longer something to be planned in relation to periodic slumps in private employment; it is something (along with other public activity) to be placed in relation to a continuing low level of private employment."

As Galbraith explained, the country must now finally, economically and politically, adjust to two new notions: to even out periodic swings in private investment, the federal government would have to use public investment, not just public works, countercyclically; and to combat the tendency of modern capitalism toward underemployment equilibrium, it would have to expand such spending vastly and *permanently*. What were the expenditure implications of these new assumptions? The prevailing orthodox theory claimed that because capital markets were finite, federal borrowing to finance deficit spending tended to displace or "crowd out" private borrowing and private investment. But Galbraith argued that in periods of underemployment not only was this not so, but, more important, financing public spending through an increase in public debt was of minor concern so long as the works produced real gains in productivity and growth. He took a positive attitude toward the entire issue of debt creation, both public and private, noting that in American history the times of most rapid economic growth always coincided with an increase in total indebtedness.

> Active private financing means an addition to the funds which are spent and respent; and from the income so created, private companies can meet with greater ease higher interest charges on bonds and bank loans. Public financing, though we have usually seen it on a smaller scale, means the expenditure and reexpenditure of additional funds, and to the extent that profits and personal incomes are enhanced, tax payments even though larger are less burdensome.

Galbraith outlined this position on the theory of public finance in detail, then carefully made the case for the "multiplier effect" of such public expenditures, financed through public debt, on private-sector employment.

Nowhere in the discussion did the name "Keynes" ever appear. Of course, to those who had read *The General Theory* or were current with the academic and press debates, the references were clear. But even within New Deal ranks, it was tactically shrewder for Galbraith to unfold his arguments free of reference to the still-unsettled judgments about their original sources.

Galbraith acknowledged his awareness of the policy divisions in New Deal ranks in his memoirs. He aimed the study, he said, at

> the cautious men from the Departments of Labor and Commerce who had been given a watching brief to counter any serious unsoundness of views. As is frequently the case, these were not conservatives but liberals who were impressed by the extreme political danger in their own faith and who were willing, accordingly, to become conservatives to avoid controversy . . . Liberals especially yearn to show they are not above pragmatic concession. American conservatives are much firmer in their faith.[15]

What Galbraith did not say, however, was that his study took sides in a more important debate then raging between the early Keynesians (led by Alvin Hansen) and the so-called liberal structuralists (specifically Gardiner Means), an American debate which nonetheless surprisingly came to involve Keynes personally.

Several months before Charles Eliot called Galbraith, the NRPB in early 1938 had launched a major research project directed by Means, who had been working for the board since 1935. Means envisaged the resulting work, *The Structure of the American Economy*, as a comprehensive analysis that would update the research he and Berle had done in the early 1930s, and solidify his argument that "administered prices" by the giant corporations were a key impediment to escape from the Depression.[16] By the time it appeared, however, Keynes's *General Theory* was having its explosive effect on theory and policy, and Means was also eager to connect the two issues, believing that although Keynes had made an enormous contribution to the analysis of the "underemployment equilibrium," his own theory of price and wage inflexibility was broader and that Keynes's ideas could be subsumed under his.

On one level, here was a classic illustration of how adherents of older theories attempt to reduce the novelty of a new challenger and maintain intellectual continuity (a process made famous by Thomas Kuhn's *The Structure of Scientific Revolutions* thirty years later). It was also, of course, a clash of egos between two influential figures over who would dominate their discipline, and its real-world effects.

Means had eagerly recruited Alvin Hansen to join the study, confident that Hansen would support his position against Keynes's. But to Means's surprise, Hansen was just then abandoning his own views about long-term "secular stagnation" and by that summer was starting to take on his new role as Keynes's chief American apostle. Both men swiftly understood that while *The General Theory* was transforming modern economics, they couldn't agree on its impact—which led to a protracted dispute that soon drew in Ed Mason, Gottfried Haberler, Alan Sweezy, John Blair, and Gerhard Colm; and, ultimately,

Keynes himself. The question at issue was a profound one: did Keynes's model of less-than-full-employment equilibrium depend on the inflexibility of wages and prices? If so, to Means, it means that *The General Theory* was an extension of the "administered prices" argument he and Berle had advanced four years earlier. To Hansen, Means's argument was reversed: it was the latter's "administered price" model that was a special case to which *The General Theory* applied. Tinkering with prices would not solve the Depression; only through government intervention in the investment cycle would recovery come.

As the disagreement heated up, Means began a correspondence with Keynes in 1938, hoping to overcome his disagreements with Hansen by having Keynes show Hansen why he was wrong. As his NRPB study got under way, the two continued exchanging letters, finally deciding to meet in England in July 1939 to discuss the issue in person.[17] In their initial correspondence, Means had tried to argue that he and Keynes had "reached the same conclusion" but "on different grounds."

But were those different grounds, one of Means's letters asked, in fact really different? To Means's chagrin, Keynes replied with an emphatic "yes." At their London meeting, he insisted that *The General Theory* was "not at all" dependent on inflexible wages or prices; Means's work on inflexibility had validity, he said, but was a "similar but less general theory" than his own, "because it is applicable to . . . degrees of flexibility and inflexibility of wages and prices" alike. Structuralism and Keynesianism, in short, could not be reconciled—and economists would have to choose between them.

Galbraith's participation in this pivotal moment of Keynesian ascendency was in one respect modest. He was much younger and far less known than Keynes, Means, or Hansen. Yet in other respects it wasn't: he grasped the debate's importance, and provided in his NRPB study compelling data and arguments for Hansen's views—even while soft-pedaling his rejections of Means's.[18] Galbraith was right when he observed retrospectively that his study was "perhaps the first unambiguous commitment to Keynesian policy by an official arm of the United States government"—an opinion his Keynesian New Deal colleagues shared.[19] Yet he admitted that the study "attracted none of the attention for which I hoped and none of the outrage that my censors so greatly feared."

Although completed months earlier, the study wasn't issued until November 1940 thanks largely to all this internal wrangling. By then, Europe had been at war for more than a year, France had fallen five months earlier, and the Germans were bombing London nightly. That month FDR was elected to an unprecedented third term and the Roosevelt administration had a strong new interest in "public works," but not of the peacetime sort: ships, not roads; tanks, not dams; Lend-Lease, not the WPA were the new order of the day. In England, Keynes and Keynesianism were meanwhile being put to a new test: designing a wartime economy capable of victory.

With the NRPB's study, Galbraith had established himself in Washington among the small but rapidly growing circle of Keynesian initiates. No longer was he primarily an agricultural economist, to be consulted for an analysis of farm credit or commodity marketing; he was, in the watchful eyes of men like Lauchlin Currie, "one of us."

But we are slightly ahead of our story.

IN THE FALL of 1939, Ken and Kitty moved into a comfortable new apartment in Palmer Square, in the center of Princeton. New York was nearby, and he was making regular trips to Washington, but he had a sense of being caught "in one of the great cul-de-sacs of history." Princeton's Economics Department, unlike Harvard's, had been untouched by the winds blowing from England, and the students were generally indifferent; those who weren't "risked being thought eccentric."[20] Increasingly Galbraith was thinking of himself as an economist specializing in industrial organization. (The term "macroeconomist," denoting Keynesian attention to aggregate economic relations—national income, investment, and the like—wasn't yet in common use.) And since he maintained an ongoing expertise and interest in agricultural economics, even though Princeton offered no courses in that subject, he was working to reconcile those interests in his career.

After a semester, he began to look for ways out, certain there was no useful future for him in New Jersey—"I frankly doubt if I will be here very long," he wrote to a Berkeley friend. Partly the problem was Princeton itself. Although the salary was decent and he had indications of prompt promotion, the Economics Department "has no research tradition, . . . is strongly biased in the direction of teaching (and textbooks) and the facilities are lousy." But the larger issue was the shift of his own interests. "I should no longer like to work entirely in agriculture. (I am still very much interested in the field but as part of the general problem of industrial structure and policy.)" Referring to a mutual acquaintance who had recently made the same shift, he called it, melodramatically, "crossing the Rubicon."

> You ask me how closely I am tied to Princeton. At the moment the thread is not so strong!
>
> In the face of almost any alternatives, I could be induced to catch a train to San Francisco. The inducement: congenial course work in the general area of industrial organization and policy including, perhaps, something in agricultural structure or a little theory; a little time for research in the same fields particularly as approached from the more theoretical side; a salary consistent with the fact of a change but implying no exhorbitant [sic] notion of the price to be put on my services.[21]

His work for the National Resources Planning Board pressed Galbraith further in the direction of his newfound Keynesian interests, and he conscientiously furthered his ambitions by circulating his *Harvard Business Review* article, with its outline of his interpretation of Keynes, among people he thought would recognize and somehow appreciate, in career terms, his new identity.

But the pull of agriculture was still strong. Even as he worked on the NRPB study, he drafted a detailed memorandum for Secretary of Agriculture Henry Wallace, outlining his thoughts on directions for New Deal farm credit policy, which he likewise carefully circulated. The memorandum showed little of the broadening effect of Galbraith's year in England, and nowhere did he allude to Keynesian concepts or even mention Keynes; instead he relied on the Farm Credit Administration research he had started before going abroad. Galbraith wanted the Department of Agriculture to distinguish between "banking policy" and "public policy" when allocating farm credit. "Public" policy should measure the macro-consequences on farm incomes and the farm sector as a whole; this, he argued, was preferable to adhering strictly to "bankerly" concerns about interest rates, repayment schedules, and so on.[22]

Galbraith shared a copy of his memorandum to Wallace with Professor Black, who was reminded once again just how gifted his protégé was—and what a contribution he could still make in farm economics. Though Black was clear-eyed about Galbraith's increasing loyalties to Keynes, in his own determined mind, he believed that Galbraith should come back to Harvard once the wounds left by Walsh-Sweezy had healed.

He also knew how unhappy Galbraith was at Princeton (though he wasn't quite so clear about Ken's desire to leave farm economics entirely). But if Princeton wasn't going to work out, and there were still no open positions at Harvard, what could Black do to keep him focused on agricultural economics? The answer, it turned out, was going to come from Europe, and the ruthless act of a madman.

IN SEPTEMBER 1939, Adolf Hitler invaded Poland, and Europe plunged into a second immense conflict only twenty years after the conclusion of the Great War. Yet to most Americans, the unfolding slaughter in Europe seemed far away. Even as the Wehrmacht swept across the Polish plains, Americans were far from inclined to support the idea of the United States entering the war. The country was still preoccupied with recovering from the Depression and still isolationist, as Galbraith knew well.

In Congress, conservative Republican leaders like Robert Taft and Arthur Vandenberg were as vocally opposed to U.S. involvement as old-line progressives such as Hiram Johnson and Burton Wheeler. The leading isolationist group America First claimed nearly a million members, and war opponents ranged from figures such as the famous radio broadcaster Father Charles Coughlin and the *Chicago Tribune* publisher Colonel Robert McCormack on the right to the Socialist Party's Norman Thomas and the former *Nation* editor Oswald Garrison Villard on the left. When a Gallup poll not long before the war began asked whether, if one nation attacked another, the United States should with others intervene to stop the war, only 29 percent said yes.[23]

But Americans also knew that the war would deeply affect the United States whether it joined the conflict or not. Economically, the Great War had brought a surging demand for American manufactured goods and food supplies in Europe that created a domestic boom. And the collapse of demand in 1918, Americans also remembered, had brought on a severe recession, with soaring unemployment, falling wages and prices, and widespread labor unrest. Among America's producers, none had been more affected than the farmers. During the war, production, prices, and farm profits had all soared, as Washington patriotically exhorted farmers to "plow to the fences." But the 1920s recession was one from which farmers had never really escaped. To much of rural America, the Depression hadn't marked a fall from prosperity but only the latest and worst in an ongoing string of calamities and failures.

With the outbreak of war, American farmers anxiously began to debate how to avoid a repetition of what had happened in 1914–19. Ed O'Neal, president of the American Farm Bureau, was looking for a talented economist to help formulate and present a new set of agricultural policies. John D. Black was among the first he turned to for advice, and Black now played the role that Henry Dennison had with Charles Eliot II and the NRPB earlier the same year. He told O'Neal he had the ideal candidate, a young fellow teaching at Princeton. The Farm Bureau president was impressed but unpersuaded; he thought someone older and more experienced would be better, and sought the advice of Theodore Schultz, at Iowa State, and Howard Tolley. Tolley, who had taught Galbraith at Berkeley and hired him to work for the Agricultural Adjustment Administration in the summer of 1934, was now head of the Agriculture Department's Bureau of Agricultural Economics. Both likewise recommended the same man; O'Neal now knew whom he wanted.

In February 1940, Black forewarned Galbraith that an important job offer from the Farm Bureau would be coming his way shortly. Black artfully emphasized that the job wasn't just researching agricultural economic issues; Ed O'Neal, he said, was "looking for someone to analyze some of the political questions which arise and prepare reports on them and discuss them with the head men of the organization . . . He is particularly concerned with getting someone who sees the problems of agriculture in the larger setting."[24] And he also stressed that the job was in no way a permanent shift out of academic life. Hinting again that opportunity might arise at Harvard once the memories of Walsh-Sweezy had faded, he urged Galbraith to take the Farm Bureau job for a couple of years and arrange a leave of absence with Princeton—and then see what happened.

Black, here as elsewhere, showed that he was a shrewd judge of character and situation: in stepping backward, in career terms, Galbraith might better be able to step forward. Although it meant moving to Chicago, where the Farm Bureau had its headquarters, there would be plenty of trips to Washington and talks with fellow economists; and with war in Europe, agriculture was certain to have great prominence and influence.

Still, the American Farm Bureau was a strange turnabout. A year before,

Galbraith had been dining with Keynes's apostles at Cambridge high tablés and enjoying the pleasures of Paris and Rome, whereas the Bureau's constituency represented "an American culture little encountered in Cambridge or Princeton":

> The Farm Bureau wives were solemn, functional of form and deeply religious and seemed always to be expecting a challenge to some profoundly held belief. In their presence I usually felt the impulse to explain that I was neither an adulterer nor an anti-Christ. The men were not so ostentatiously devout. They were also open to argument as long as it did not involve the divine rights of agriculture, the sanctity of property or any need to change their minds.[25]

Galbraith wrote this with forty years' hindsight. But in early 1940 he discovered that the Bureau wasn't as simply conservative or as opposed to the New Deal as his later description suggests. True, the Farm Bureau often spoke for the most powerful and conservative farmers, who were deeply suspicious of FDR, Henry Wallace, and urban reformers. But New Deal policies, especially its domestic allotment and price-support programs, had won over the Bureau's members in often tangled ways:

> [D]ivided between North and South, corn and cotton, the Farm Bureau was similarly divided in its politics. The southerners were Democrats and cosmopolitan, secular and generally liberal in outlook. All were firm supporters of Roosevelt and the New Deal. However, the liberalism did not extend to civil rights for their black field hands and tenants; such thoughts in those days did not even fleetingly arise. The midwestern Bureau members were Republicans, parochial, isolationist and (those from Ohio and Missouri apart) conservative. They accepted F.D.R. and the New Deal reluctantly and with a sense of self-abasement. As a practical matter, they could not afford the luxury of their ancient Republican faith; that might mean forgoing government benefits and price supports. But they did not cease to be sorry.[26]

Black, Tolley, and Schultz, who knew the intricacies of Bureau politics, might have preferred working with the Grange or the Farmers' Union. But the Grange, although older, was weak, and the Farmers' Union was too radical—popular among younger farmers (and among those old enough to remember voting for William Jennings Bryan) but hated by congressional committee chairmen. The American Farm Bureau was the best platform from which to advance their reforming views on agricultural policy and a necessary battleground—an ideal place to have one of their own on the inside.

For Galbraith personally, there was an additional attraction: when O'Neal called, he offered Ken a $7,500 salary, more than double his assistant professor's pay. And in truth, the prospect of working with O'Neal himself was enticing after the dour solemnity of Princeton. The Farm Bureau president was a well-to-do Alabamian of antebellum aspect: gracious, well educated, well traveled, a connoisseur of food and wine. To cover his ample frame he ordered his suits from Savile Row and told his constituents he thought every farmer should earn enough to do the same. He was also colorfully profane, a worrisome figure on any live radio broadcast. Galbraith seems to have hesitated only as long as decorous reflection in negotiation required. Princeton readily granted him a leave of absence—a bit too readily, perhaps, Galbraith might have noticed, had he not been so busy packing. Leaving Kitty to finish the job and his students to mail in their take-home exams, he set off by train for Chicago in early May 1940.

BY LATE JUNE, Galbraith had been in Chicago only a few weeks and was just settling into his new work—still waiting—a bit worriedly, it seems—for Kitty to arrive. (With family and friends on the East Coast to visit, and still piqued that he'd left her with their belongings to box up, his wife had decided there would be time enough over the summer for her to get settled into their new Midwestern life.) Then suddenly news came that, under a lightning German advance France had fallen. The Galbraiths, like millions of Americans, had been watching the onslaught with a sense of foreboding: 90,000 troops had just died in less than two weeks of fighting, and 350,000 retreating soldiers of the British Expeditionary Force trapped at Dunkirk had just barely escaped capture.

Paris's surrender was a terrible shock. Galbraith walked down State Street on an errand from the Farm Bureau's offices. Hearing newsboys shouting "Extra! Extra!" he was stunned by the oversized headlines that told of the French collapse: "It was the last in the terrible sequence, the invasion and fall of Poland, the invasion of Denmark and Norway, then of Holland, Belgium and France, the evacuation at Dunkirk and now the end." Despite the doubts he shared with other Americans about Europe's great powers and their wars, he believed that the United States could no longer stay neutral. "I was one of the many who, for those years, put their pacifism away."[27]

But what did giving up neutrality mean? Even then Americans weren't sure—in fact, they were deeply confused. In the fall of 1939, 40 percent of the country had expected that the United States would be dragged into the war no matter what; after the fall of France, perhaps sensing that the collapse of Great Britain might be next and that the Nazis would then control Europe, the percentage dropped to only 8.[28] What stood starkly unanswered was how the United States would respond to such a *fait accompli*.

Three days after France's surrender, Galbraith's secretary announced a call from the White House. Lauchlin Currie wanted to know whether Galbraith would come to Washington: the newly created National Defense Advisory Commission required his attention and skills.* If the United States was headed toward war, extensive economic planning and controls would be

---

*How Currie came to know about Galbraith is not clear: he had little relation to agriculture and had left Harvard before Galbraith arrived. Alvin Hansen is one possibility; another is Henry Dennison, whom Currie knew from the National Resources Planning Board. And since Currie was also involved in public-works legislation, he may have seen Galbraith's NRPB study in draft.

needed, as the years 1916–18 had taught. Now was the time to design those plans and controls, Currie said, not after America had entered the conflict. Wartime demands could set off dangerous inflation, hoarding, and black markets, and might put the war effort itself at risk.

"I was excited and my excitement deepened when Currie told me my presence in Washington . . . was essential," Galbraith says. He immediately agreed, then realized after hanging up that he needed to talk with Ed O'Neal first.[29] O'Neal was taken aback but nonetheless granted his newest staff member a temporary leave of absence, on two conditions: that Galbraith would return to the Farm Bureau, and that he would keep O'Neal intimately informed of whatever NDAC was considering about agriculture. Galbraith quickly agreed to both. Now on leave from not one but two jobs, the next evening he boarded the B. & O.'s sleek *Capitol Limited* for the overnight trip to Washington.

When Galbraith showed up late the next morning at Currie's cluttered office in the Executive Office Building, next to the White House, Currie told him he would be working for Leon Henderson, one of the most senior and colorful figures in the New Deal. The news momentarily surprised Galbraith (it hadn't been discussed in their phone call) but pleased him. From the press, Galbraith knew that Henderson, an economics major at Swarthmore and graduate of the Wharton School, had started his Washington career in 1933 as director of research and planning for the National Recovery Administration, then had gone on to various tasks that used his talents for both economics and politics. By 1940, he was a Securities and Exchange commissioner and a trusted White House insider; FDR had in fact personally made sure Henderson was put in charge of the National Defense Advisory Commission. Sent off by Currie to meet his new boss that same afternoon, Galbraith left his meeting an hour later convinced that he was starting not just a job but a grand adventure.

Henderson at forty-five was a man in the Hemingway mold, given to heavy drinking, all-night poker games, the unadorned vernacular, and a love of racehorses and beautiful women. When not in Washington, he could often be found at the legendary Stork Club in New York. Stout, of medium height, and always indifferently dressed, Henderson had a face, Galbraith says, that constantly alternated "between an expression of unconvincing belligerence and one of shocked, unbelieving innocence, and sometimes he affected both at the same time. Mostly, however, he favored the belligerent expression, and this he sought to reinforce with a sharply jutting cigar that he rolled in his mouth but rarely smoked."[30] Henderson never shied away from a good brawl, especially political brawls with politicians or businessmen who dared question the purposes or motives of the New Deal and its leader. Henderson, as the journalist David Brinkley recalls, simply "was not one of the boys. He was never known to have slapped a back at a Rotary Club luncheon." At the same time, he was "a brilliant public servant who took nothing for himself."[31]

Roosevelt had transferred Henderson to NDAC from his post as research director for the infamously controversial Temporary National Economic Committee, where he had spent two grueling years investigating concentration in the business community while under relentless attack from conservatives in Congress and the press. Tasked originally with the goal of proposing "reforms" to ensure greater business competition, the TNEC heard more than 500 witnesses, compiled 20,000 pages of records and 3,300 technical exhibits, and sponsored 43 monographs. The committee's voluminous final report was a stark indictment of business structure and practices, and momentarily seemed to press the administration into an all-out confrontation with big business itself. But FDR, after his losing 1937 battle to reshape the Supreme Court and the setbacks in the 1938 midterm elections, chose to ignore the TNEC's findings. With war drawing closer, he realized that he now needed big business's cooperation, not its antagonism. To some in the administration, however, that made the President's selection of Henderson a challenge. They worried that Henderson was still associated with issues of concentration and oligopoly, and would send the wrong signals. Meanwhile, the growing fraternity of Keynesians, including Currie, who saw macromanagement of the economy as requiring more subtle talents, feared that Henderson's perceived preference for the cudgel of antitrust might jeopardize their own goals. Currie made it clear to Galbraith that his job as Henderson's deputy was "to keep policy in line with a rational Keynesian faith. I agreed wholly as to the need."[32]

Galbraith pardonably had left his meeting with Currie with a certain jaunty step. Three years earlier, after all, he hadn't even been an American citizen. But after talking to Henderson, he intuited that the grand adventure faced a disconcerting problem: "There was absolutely nothing for anyone to do." Apart from a few aides, Henderson had no staff, and the aides had no desks.[33] Moreover, the prices they were meant to watch and, if need be, control were stable. This produced a baleful reaction in Galbraith:

> After death and dismemberment, idleness was the nightmare of World War II and much the greater threat in Washington. Men and an occasional woman received the call to serve their government, bade farewell to coworkers, friends and relatives, heard themselves congratulated for the service they were to perform, sensed joyously the envy of those left behind and arrived in the capital to find themselves unexpected, often unwanted and with little whatever to occupy their time.[34]

Although this is cast in the third-person plural, the feelings expressed have an individual, personal ring. Excited but uncertain where his government service would lead, Galbraith prudently made sure both Princeton and the Farm Bureau considered his Washington work temporary. To his Princeton dean he soothingly wrote, "I have every intention of coming back to Princeton next September [1941] and have so informed [NDAC]. Academic work is my life and I might say that I look forward to getting back to it with more anticipation than you can guess."[35] And to O'Neal he kept up a stream of letters describing

NDAC actions he thought might affect agriculture—from defense-plant sitings in rural areas to price supports and military plans for farm surpluses, all issues critically important to the Bureau's constituents—and clearly designed to keep Chicago open as an alternative place for retreat.[36]

Galbraith was not alone in feeling adrift and hedging his bets in the summer of 1940. Germany by then ruled Western Europe from the Baltic to the Mediterranean, but Pearl Harbor was still a year and a half away. Roosevelt was maneuvering to ready the country for war, but he was facing unenviable political, economic, and military tasks. The political problem was the most obvious: 1940 was an election year, and only at the very last moment had FDR publicly decided to seek an unprecedented third term. In much of the country, enthusiasm for the New Deal was waning, and the Republican candidate, Wendell Wilkie, an Indianan who'd become a rich utility executive in New York, was going to be the most formidable Roosevelt had yet faced.

The military problem was no less daunting. In late May, only weeks after the German invasion of France, Roosevelt had called on a special joint session of Congress to authorize a massive American buildup—he'd said 50,000 planes a year were needed—matched by spending that would dwarf any of the New Deal's domestic programs. He'd been answered with tremendous applause from both sides of the aisle, and then gotten a good deal less than he'd hoped. After the British army escaped from Dunkirk, leaving their weapons behind, Winston Churchill's newly installed government, fearful of imminent Nazi invasion, begged the White House for help. But the Neutrality Act of 1937, which forbade sale of U.S. arms to active combatants in foreign wars, prohibited Roosevelt's support.

To evade the law, he ordered the War Department to sell more than a million rifles and machine guns, ammunition, and heavier equipment to U.S. Steel under the fiction that these were "surplus" arms. By prior agreement, U.S. Steel then immediately resold them to Britain. But at the last minute, FDR's own Secretary of War, backed by the Army's and Navy's top brass, tried to halt the release, so fearful were they concerning America's own lack of preparedness. With a dozen British ships secretly tied up at American docks, a direct order from the President was required to reverse the situation.

FDR's subterfuge was only one indication of the complicated task he was facing, because in striking ways those who opposed him on domestic matters supported him on war, whereas some of his closest domestic allies and aides openly feared what the war would do to the New Deal agenda. As Galbraith gradually learned that summer, the National Defense Advisory Commission itself epitomized the President's dilemmas. Knowing he needed corporate cooperation, and not mere grudging assent, to ready the country for war, he'd chosen three millionaire businessmen to sit on the seven-member board, including the heads of General Motors and U.S. Steel. But this olive branch to business had required a separate offering to New Deal loyalists, and so Roosevelt had chosen Sidney Hillman, John L. Lewis's top deputy at the Congress of Industrial Organizations, and Leon Henderson to reassure his closest supporters. (To round out the board, he named two "moderates," university dean Harriet Elliott to represent consumers, and the agricultural veteran Chester Davis to speak for farmers.)

From the start, the National Defense Advisory Commission pleased almost no one. Businessmen loathed the idea of government controls over production, and many were suspicious that Roosevelt would use war preparations to create a left-wing "dictatorship." Few of them had forgotten that this was the President who in his 1936 campaign had told supporters, "I should like to have it said of my first Administration that in it the forces of selfishness and of lust for power met their match. I should like to have it said of my second Administration that in it these forces met their master."[37] With Hillman and Henderson on the NDAC board, who could doubt where Roosevelt's antibusiness attitudes would go?*

But Roosevelt's choice of William Knudsen, the $350,000-a-year boss of General Motors, and Edward Stettinius, Jr., head of U.S. Steel, as commissioners, left liberals no less alarmed. When the conservative press soon began demanding that Knudsen be given executive authority over the board as "tsar" of America's preparedness effort, the liberal weekly *The New Republic* spoke for many of Roosevelt's supporters: "The cry for a czar sprang from the desire of big business to take full control of defense and to use defense for its own purposes," it warned. "If the lack of a chairman becomes a real problem, [Leon Henderson] would be the excellent choice."[38]

THE CLASS ANTAGONISMS behind this conflict had long stalked the debates over the New Deal's domestic agenda. Now, with war imminent, liberals and conservatives were once again forced to rethink the relationship of government to the economy.

For devoted New Dealers, the Depression had shown conclusively that the laissez-faire economics favored by Republicans (and not a few Democrats) was a disaster and that once the Depression was over government would still need to maintain a strong visible hand in the economy, not only to prevent another collapse but to assure fair and equitable lives for all Americans. By themselves, these opinions were hardly unique: they were traceable to the Progressive Era, and had been heard repeatedly in one form or another in campaigns against the robber barons in the 1880s, in the fight by Radical Republicans during Reconstruction, in the 1830s struggle by Democrats for Jacksonian democracy, and even in the American Revolution itself.

But key figures in FDR's administration were subtly changing their views by 1939–40. For eight years, the New Deal had been an experiment in how to achieve their ideals. They had frankly cobbled together the government's programs, drawing on disparate inspirations—sometimes from the Progressive Era, sometimes from Hoover's dream of cooperative "associationism," sometimes even from unprecedented *de novo* experiments. But now, with New Dealers more accustomed to governing, a new sense of the purposes, function,

---

*A month before Pearl Harbor, a *Fortune* survey found that three quarters of business executives still feared that Roosevelt would use the war to push through "undesirable" reforms.

and extent of government was emerging from the welter of conflicting programs and beliefs. In a seminal essay, "The Idea of the State," the historian Alan Brinkley has described this evolution:

> The New Dealers of the late 1930s used many different labels to describe their political ideals: "antimonopoly," "regulation," "planning." But while once those words had seemed to represent quite distinct concepts of reform, they described now a common vision of government—a vision of capable, committed administrators who would seize command of state institutions, invigorate them, expand their powers when necessary, and make them permanent forces in the workings of the marketplace.
>
> Increasing the regulatory functions of the federal government was not, of course, an idea new to the 1930s. Curbing corporate power, attacking monopoly, imposing order on a disordered economic world—those had been the dreams of generations of reformers since the advent of large-scale industrialization. But the concept of an administrative state that was gaining favor in the late New Deal, while rhetorically familiar, was substantively different from the visions that had attracted reformers even five years earlier . . .
>
> For decades, American reformers had dreamed of creating a harmonious industrial economy, a system that could flourish without extensive state interference and produce enough wealth to solve the nation's most serious social problems. There had been widely varying ideas about how to create such an economy, from the associational visions of creating a smoothly functioning, organic whole out of the clashing parts of modern capitalism to the antimonopolist yearning for a small-scale decentralized economy freed of the nefarious influence of large combinations. But the larger dream—the dream of somehow actually "solving" the problems of modern capitalism—had been one of the most evocative of all reform hopes and the goal of most progressives and liberals who advocated an expanded state role in the economy.
>
> By the end of the 1930s, faith in such broad solutions was in retreat . . . The state could not, liberals were coming to believe, in any fundamental way "solve" the problems of the economy. The industrial economy was too large, too complex, too diverse; no single economic plan could encompass it all. Americans would have to accept the inevitability of conflict and instability in their economic lives. And they would have to learn to rely on the state to regulate that conflict and instability.[39]

By 1940, then, the appeal of Keynes's *General Theory* was not least that it bypassed older attempts at detailed microsupervision of industries and eschewed outright the passion for trust busting. In their place, it offered government a new macroeconomic function: fostering aggregate growth through ongoing, effective regulation of the business cycle. If Keynesians failed to promise an elusive economic harmony or resolution of America's class tensions, they nonetheless offered the prospect of growth that would mean an exit from a decade of depression—and a much more stable and secure future.

Eight years of hard and practical experience had tempered progressive thought, and its adherents now foresaw Keynesianism as a "bargain" that business, labor, farmers, and consumers might be persuaded to accept.

But the prospect of a massive war on an unprecedented scale still haunted all liberals. Who could foretell the bargains war might force on a liberal administration still hated by business? The Great War in 1914–18 had put an end to the progressive reforms of Woodrow Wilson and to the Progressive Era itself, after all, and had ushered in three successive Republican presidents. If war came to the United States again, how would liberal domestic programs—let alone a still-nascent Keynesian agenda—survive, given the demands the armed forces would inevitably place on limited resources? How would voters who had clearly benefited from those programs and who supported Roosevelt react? And how would the New Deal deal with big business—which alone had the capability of turning out the needed arms and materiel—without losing what many considered the heart and soul of Rooseveltian reforms? It "is not a mark of barren isolationism," *The New Republic* declared, "to believe with all one's heart and soul that the best contribution Americans can make to the future of humanity is to fulfill democracy in the United States."[40]

ROOSEVELT HIMSELF SAW the challenges war preparations posed for his peacetime programs and understood his New Dealers' doubts, even if personally he didn't count himself a Keynesian. But should war come, he intended to pursue it unconditionally, even if it meant sacrificing beloved domestic programs. Once the war effort shifted into high gear, he was to tell the country, in a famous phrase, that the time had come to "put away Dr. New Deal" in favor of "Dr. Win-the-War." But in the summer and fall of 1940, Roosevelt was still maneuvering between his desire for a more aggressive, interventionist foreign policy and the difficult matter of a reluctant public and his reelection.

When Wendell Willkie, whose foreign policy views at least were similar to Roosevelt's, attacked FDR for promoting policies that would lead to war "within six months," Roosevelt told a cheering crowd in Boston, an isolationist city, given Irish animosity toward the British, "I have said this before, but I shall say it again and again and again; your boys are not going to be sent into any foreign wars."[41] This was of course not true, and Roosevelt knew it. But the exigencies of reelection—and the deep ambivalence of the American public—required such a statement. As one historian shrewdly observed, Roosevelt's rhetoric wasn't simply hypocritical but was "a necessary feature of the odd dialectic between President and people, in which FDR gave assurances he did not mean, and they pretended to believe him."[42] (Lincoln found himself in much the same predicament during the Civil War. "The fact is," he admitted in 1862, "that the people have not yet made up their minds that we are at war.")

Yet Roosevelt had nonetheless matched his often evasive or misleading words with acts of striking political courage throughout 1940. In June, as noted, he used a legal fiction to force shipment of vital military supplies to England over the virulent objections of his own Secretary of War and the Joint

Chiefs of Staff. Relying on an equally tenuous interpretation of American laws, three months later he openly transferred fifty destroyers to Britain. Then, just three weeks before the election, showing remarkable political boldness, he ordered 16 million American men to register for the draft.

Nor did Roosevelt hesitate to ask Congress that year for an unprecedented $4.5 billion military budget, and his call for producing 50,000 warplanes annually came at a time when the Army Air Corps had only 160 pursuit planes and when General George Marshall told him the army probably couldn't field a single battle-ready division. (As Roosevelt and Marshall both knew, the U.S. Army in 1940 had 250,000 men, making it the world's nineteenth largest—smaller than Belgium's, just larger than Bulgaria's. Germany had invaded Poland with 1.5 million troops in 1939 and then attacked France with nearly 2 million troops in May 1940.[43])

But if Roosevelt sometimes acted with courage and foresight, the paralysis Galbraith discovered at NDAC showed that he had been much less aggressive in readying the government and the economy for war. Although the government's administrative reorganization would be vital in prosecuting the coming war, after failing with fitful half-measures in 1939, FDR had dallied until May 1940 before taking his first real steps toward a "war-ready" restructuring. After their attempts to block his arms transfer to Britain, he dismissed his Secretary of War and accepted his Navy Secretary's resignation and then appointed two prominent Republicans, the Wall Street lawyer Henry Stimson and the Chicago newspaper publisher Frank Knox, to the posts. Stimson had been Secretary of War under William Howard Taft and Secretary of State under Hoover. Knox, who had been a Rough Rider with Teddy Roosevelt in Cuba, was publisher of the Chicago *Daily News* and had been the Republican vice-presidential candidate in 1936. Roosevelt next had ordered the recalcitrant Joint Chiefs of Staff into offices adjoining the White House (the Pentagon did not yet exist) and then set up the National Defense Advisory Council.

The trouble was that, following these lightning strikes in late spring, for the next several months there was nothing but confusion. Galbraith's recollection of arriving in Washington to disorganization and "nothing to do" matches the conclusion of many historians about the NDAC's overall contribution, as well as the overall preparedness effort prior to Pearl Harbor.

Why Roosevelt hesitated to force order out of that confusion remains a source of debate. Part of the reason was the President's unwillingness to delegate power, and his pattern of deliberately allowing competing agencies—even competing officials within agencies—to battle to a standstill, then turn to him for a decision.* There was also his authentic reluctance to go to war until the very last possible moment, knowing the price Americans would have to pay in blood and suffering. Also, he knew that the New Deal itself would inevitably be set aside. Yet as lawyers for the War Department drafted legislation that

---

*When Donald Knudsen asked FDR who NDAC's "boss" would be (clearly hoping for the job), the President replied, "I am."

would allow new "cost-plus-fixed-fee" contracts, accelerated tax depreciation on new plants and nearly free government financing for businesses that undertook war production, FDR promised Americans in one of his "fireside chats" that he would make sure

> in all that we do that there [would] be no breakdown or cancellation of any of the great social gains which we have made in these past years. We have carried on an offensive on a broad front against social and economic inequalities, against abuses which had made our society weaker. That offensive should not now be broken down by the pincer movements of those who would use the present needs of physical military defense to destroy it.[44]

Ultimately, Roosevelt's reasons for slow and haphazard preparation for war don't matter. They were far from unique: none of the other Allies were truly "prepared" for war when it came. For that matter, Germany never fully mobilized its economy, not even after 1941, when both the Soviet Union and the United States were arrayed against it. In fact, among the principal combatants only Japan, with a disciplined quasi-feudal society and scarce domestic resources, and the totalitarian Soviet Union, which suffered half of the war's 40 million casualties, came close to full mobilization.

For Galbraith, though, his new job at NDAC swiftly let him see how even a policy so vital to the nation's very existence—the President's determination to begin preparations for war—first had to pass a gauntlet of selfish and competing political and economic interests. That experience became a subject to which he returned throughout his life, in a series of cautionary tales about the applications of clean-cut theory to the realities of economic life.

In late July Galbraith got a call from Paul Porter, a talented young Kentucky-born lawyer.* He, too, was working in NDAC, as deputy to the agricultural veteran Chester Davis. Porter said his group desperately needed an economist—and for a moment Galbraith thought his career was about to turn back to the farm for the second time that year. But no: Porter explained that Davis had been given authority—in classic haphazard fashion—to review proposed locations for dozens of new government-sponsored explosives, ammunition, and ordnance factories, for reasons obscure to everyone. Would Ken, Porter asked, come over and help them site the plants?

Galbraith leapt at the offer, and with Henderson's permission, gratefully abandoned issues of (nonexistent) price controls. The job of analyzing locations for new munitions factories wasn't what he'd come to Washington to do, and he was no expert, yet it at least offered the prospect of something to do, and Davis agreed to match his Farm Bureau salary. (Munitions plants weren't the only thing Ken ended up analyzing in NDAC's farm offices. His files show that under Davis he also got involved, in the ever-mysterious ways of bureau-

---

*Porter went on after the war to cofound Arnold & Porter, one of Washington's quintessential "insider" law firms.

cracy, in studying supply problems related to "woolen drawers and under-shirts," as well as corresponding with a certain Colonel Twaddle about milk supplies for Army bases. Such were the disparate demands of the prewar pre-paredness effort.[45])

Once in his new post, Galbraith quickly found himself in a cross fire. The Army-Navy Munitions Board had sent Davis a list of four dozen proposed plant sites, most of them along the Eastern Seaboard and in the industrial Northeast. Wilmington, Pittsburgh, and Cleveland led the favored cities. To the military men, as to any conventional economist or policy planner, the choices seemed self-evident and compelling. These were the places where ex-isting plants were located and where start-ups could proceed most easily. Workers and managers, shipping facilities and infrastructure, the ability and willingness to build quickly were all in place. (There were other attractions, Galbraith quickly discovered. "Neighbors, schools, golf courses, and a power-ful homing instinct, I was to learn, are a significant factor in plant location."[46])

In time-honored tradition, a Washington ritual, the Baptism of Public Works, began. "I received congressional delegations and representatives of chambers of commerce; they praised Davis's and my enlightened policy and my own public personality with a warmth I have only rarely experienced."[47] But neither he nor Davis was inclined to go along. Both men were troubled by the strate-gic implications of following this well-worn path. If the Germans invaded, Eastern Seaboard plants would be among the first to be captured or de-stroyed. Besides, in the previous war, the concentration of industry in the Northeast and the demands put on port and rail facilities there had created terrible bottlenecks that impeded the war effort. And after the war, investiga-tions into profiteering by these plants' owners (including celebrated hearings by Senator Nye) had led to infamous charges against industrialists and bankers such as Alfred DuPont and J. P. Morgan that they were—the phrase still echoes—"merchants of death" who had placed profit interests ahead of the lives of valiant doughboys.

As Davis and Galbraith well knew, there were plenty of alternative locations, where land and labor were cheap, where new plants and new jobs could perhaps spark economic development and disperse it more equitably. No doubt both men were affected by the peacetime values of the New Deal; but they were equally influenced by upbringing and experience. Galbraith the Ontario farm boy, like Davis the Montana rancher, was long attuned to the imbalance in development between rural and urban regions, between the industrial East and the agricul-tural Midwest and South, and his just-completed study of public works for the NRPB had sharpened his sense of unemployment differences among regions.[48] No, the men decided, the plants should go to new sites. Galbraith quickly for-mulated their guidelines into a memorandum. Henceforth plant locations would, wherever possible, favor the South and other regions with high unemployment; suburban areas, for plants requiring skilled industrial labor; the interior over coastal areas; and a deconcentration of industry.[49] The issue then became how to make their new ad hoc social policy work. Davis, "had an unparalleled capacity for making his way through the bureaucratic thickets. He now instructed me in the art of getting one's way in Washington."[50]

Galbraith, sent round to Henderson, Hillman, and other liberal members of the NDAC board, got them to agree to veto the next plant proposed for a traditional industrial location. The group did so forthwith, and to immediate effect. "That same afternoon representatives of the Army-Navy Munitions Board, the operative agency of the War Department, came to *my* office to discuss a new list of locations, all in admirably bucolic settings. They reported that teams were being dispatched to assess other similarly remote precincts."[51]

Galbraith continued to add to his store of knowledge about Washington folkways throughout the summer and fall of 1940. Location of a munitions plant in Alabama led to acquaintance with Joe Starnes, an antediluvian conservative congressman from Gadsden, Alabama, who was a ranking Democrat on what later became the House Un-American Activities Committee; he was even-handedly hostile to equal rights for blacks and the idea of organized labor. When tire manufacturers had expanded their operations southward in the mid-1930s after rubber workers in Akron, Ohio, formed a union, Starnes had benefited by having several new plants built in his district, but the United Rubber Workers had then sent its organizers into town, in pursuit, and a series of fierce battles had ensued. At one point, a crowd led by Goodyear foremen, supervisors, and "flying squadron" members trapped eleven union members, including the Rubber Workers' president, in an office building, whereupon the mob "smashed down the door and beat the unarmed men," resulting in the prolonged hospitalization of several of them.[52] Congressman Starnes successfully avoided exhibiting public alarm over this fracas.

So it was no surprise that when his district was proposed as a site for the new munitions plant, Galbraith found Sidney Hillman, the NDAC's labor representative, in profound opposition. Galbraith hoped to convince Starnes that perhaps a more favorable view of labor might have some bearing on the decision to put the plant in his district.

> The conversation remains in my mind:
> "Doctor, how many people did y'all say that mill would be hiring?"
> "It's very big, Congressman. Ten, twenty thousand, maybe."
> "Well, Doctor, with something like that at stake, a man jest can't ever stand on principle."
> The Gadsden fathers convened at Joe's behest and passed a resolution promising complete safety and freedom of speech and action to all persons coming to Gadsden, although it is quite possible that the concept of civil liberty was not then fully understood there. They added as an effusive touch that Sidney Hillman, if he visited Gadsden, would be treated with true Southern hospitality.[53]

The plant went to Gadsden despite Hillman's lingering misgivings. Four years later, in the 1944 election, the town was solidly pro-FDR and Starnes was soundly defeated—proof, as Galbraith dryly put it, that "a public man should stand on principle."

Alabama gave Galbraith a second powerful lesson in the art of applied economic policy. This time it involved the Tennessee Valley Authority and Muscle Shoals; it was, Galbraith recalls, "the first public controversy in which I had a major, even decisive, role."[54]

The Tennessee Valley Authority, the nation's first federal electric utility, had been one of the New Deal's most controversial undertakings. When first proposed in 1933, it had been greeted among conservatives as nothing less than the first step toward FDR's encompassing public takeover of the free-enterprise system, and proof positive that Roosevelt was the socialist they feared. The fact that nothing untoward happened and that the TVA's cheap public power, along with its maze of dams and flood-control systems, spawned economic growth in a hitherto deeply poor region quieted the critics only slightly. Muscle Shoals was a matter of equal controversy and longer duration.

During the Great War, the government had built two gigantic nitrate plants in this small Alabama town to produce explosives. Because the nitrate produced was as valuable in making fertilizer as it was for munitions, a coalition of farmers and reformers called on the government to keep operating the plants for this redirected purpose at the end of the war. There was much debate at the time about the so-called "fertilizer trust," which controlled production; both farmers and reformers thought that Muscle Shoals could teach a lesson in the public limits on private power. Needless to say, the chemical and fertilizer companies, their lobbyists, and their allies in the Congress viewed the matter differently. For fifteen years, until 1933, the debate over Muscle Shoals raged on, a matter of practical uses so deeply entrenched in politics, values, and symbols that it became a lightning rod of allegiances: "A liberal in the 1920s and early 1930s," Galbraith noted, "was one who wished to have the government operate Muscle Shoals. Conservatives were as easily identified by their antipathy."[55] After the Depression swept the Republicans from office in 1932, the liberals acted. Led by Senator George Norris of Nebraska, a legendary old-school Progressive, the Muscle Shoals plants became the heart of the whole enormous Tennessee Valley Authority, a fate that Galbraith cheerfully noted was "far more devastating than the most ardent defender of free enterprise could ever have imagined."[56]

By 1940, the Muscle Shoals plants, now run by the TVA, were technically obsolete for the production of fertilizer but still quite serviceable to the munitions process. To the Army, this suggested a ready use which the TVA was delighted to embrace and which overnight caused its old opponents to rise from the grave. A classic debate ensued over some of the New Deal's hardest-fought values. Once again, Galbraith, Davis, and their New Deal allies on the NDAC board eventually carried the day, over the strident objections of William Knudsen, Edward Stettinius, and their backers in the affected industries, particularly DuPont and Allied Chemical. But the battle caused the young economist anguish about the difficulties created by this "war within a war," for the job of preparedness was a second front that continued right through to 1945.

Galbraith's dismay has been echoed by virtually every historian who has examined the labyrinth that Washington became during World War II. The period from Hitler's attack on Poland in September 1939 until the attack on Pearl Harbor in December 1941 are considered "lost years" for the most part so far as American military preparedness is concerned, just as the government's military production and domestic economic operations during the war years themselves are derided as "the administration of anarchy." The terms are Eliot Janeway's but similar (sometimes harsher) characterizations can be found in dozens of other chronicles of the American home front. Indeed, if one focuses on Washington, it is sometimes easy to wonder how in fact America and her allies ever won. The many commissions with overlapping and contradictory authorities, uncertain powers, constantly changing leaders, and a constant barrage of congressional and public criticism, business and labor distrust, and unpopular policy missteps make the headquarters of the United States as the great "arsenal of democracy" seem closer to a real-life *Marx Brothers Go to War*.

Yet the haphazard, disorganized, and deeply inefficient way in which the nation first prepared for war, and then fought it, resulted in victory. And even Janeway, for all his criticism, shrewdly saw in Roosevelt's seemingly erratic carelessness—a style for which the President was excoriated at the time—a deeper importance and meaning:

> Roosevelt's critics have said—and say—that he mobilized the Washington echelon of the home front on a basis that he better than any knew would not work; . . . that he reorganized and reorganized wartime Washington into a comptroller's hell, into a jungle of confusion and duplication and self-contradiction in which even he ended by feeling lost.
>
> They are right. He did. And yet this irresponsibility—so disastrous on the face of it—did not culminate in disaster. To Roosevelt, as the crisis deepened . . . the important question was the participation of the nation as a whole in its own defense, not the administrative planning for this participation . . . His administrative performance was indeed amateurish.
>
> But the message he meant to make clear got through to the people in the end and in time: industrial mobilization for defense was necessary, and if war came only America's industrial mobilization could win it . . . He expected to win the war on the home front, but he expected to win it at the cost of the Battle of Washington . . . For Roosevelt was gambling that the home front would win the war as fast as the war could set it in motion; and this is exactly what happened . . .
>
> So long as the home front was big at the base, Roosevelt was willing to bet that he could afford to let it be confused at the top—and he and he alone had

the power, the genius, the dramatic instinct and, above all, the daring to make it as big outside Washington and as amorphous inside Washington as he pleased.[57]

As in all wars, whether fought on blood-stained ground or in marbled corridors, there remain challenges and prizes for those bold enough to act. For young men such as Galbraith, the unexpected virtue of the country's confused preparations for war was opportunity to learn and to advance.* Eight years of the New Deal had swelled the number of talented young people willing to hitch their careers to a new concept of government and public service. As war drew closer, those ranks swelled with new arrivals eager to seize opportunity and make their mark on the times. (The NDAC, for example, multiplied from a handful when Galbraith arrived in June to nearly five hundred by December.[58]) In this impending war as in most others, age and experience counted for less amidst such a cacophony than in peacetime. The demand was for energy, brains, and unbending confidence that things would get done.

AS 1940 DREW to a close, remarkable signs could be seen that the country was finally heading in the direction toward which Roosevelt had been cautiously but steadily compassing it. Sluggish at the wheel, heeling only slowly against the winds, and still manned by a crew made raucous by doubters and noisome opponents, nonetheless the United States was moving steadily toward war.

Despite the weaknesses and divisions in the NDAC, much had been accomplished in the seven months since France's collapse. By the narrowest of margins—a single vote in the House—Congress had authorized a draft. By Christmas 16 million young men had registered and several hundred thousand had reported for training—the first in a stream that would grow over the next four years into the most powerful military force the world has ever seen. To equip them, the government authorized more than $10 billion in multiyear contracts for military supplies and support—a vast sum in the dollars of the time, and twice the size of federal revenues that year—including more than $3 billion for new ships, $1.5 billion for new planes, and another $1.5 billion for new plants and defense-related housing. Although spending under the contracts was spread over the next two years and was a pittance compared to the $100 billion authorized in the six months after Pearl Harbor, it was a beginning. And the contracts called for an awe-inspiring buildup: 50,000 aircraft; 130,000 engines; 65,000 artillery pieces (and 33 million shells); 50,000 trucks; more than 2 million rifles, plus ammunition; 380 new Navy vessels; 200 merchantmen; 40 government arsenals; 210 military camps; 80,000 miles of road construction and repair; and, not least, clothing and equipment for 1.2 million men. For the armed forces, the scope of enlargement was breathtaking.[59]

---

*It also forged his later views about peacetime policy making and economists' overreliance on detailed econometric analyses of policy options. Leadership and bold visions can create great policies by inspiring courage and generosity among the citizens of a democracy, a theme he returned to again and again.

For the economy as a whole, the effect was no less noticeable. In the last two months of 1940, with 8 million Americans still unemployed and the employed workforce no larger than it had been in 1929, a million new jobs opened up and more than 5 million people registered with the government as available for defense work. Among those businessmen who had survived the Depression, though the economy had still not recovered the heights it had reached in 1929, the words "war boom" could be heard with increasing frequency.

This "war boom" talk raised alarms, however. War has always justified extraordinary measures, including the recognition that "the markets" cannot be left to supply the needed men and materiel. National survival trumps the invisible hand, and then economists are called upon to balance the visible effort with the invisible forces. The haphazard yet rapid buildup of military power in 1940 was already straining the fragile structure of the American economy at crucial points.

It was also exacting a toll on those who would be called upon to direct the war effort. Roosevelt had won an unprecedented third term in November, and chose to read his reelection as affirmation of his new war-related policies, but he also complained of the fatigue he felt and the unlimited difficulties that lay ahead. And even Galbraith, thirty years younger than the President, was experiencing exhaustion after six months at the NDAC. Checking into the Johns Hopkins Hospital shortly before Christmas, he was diagnosed as suffering from massive fatigue. In his memoirs, he devotes one sentence to the matter. But at the time his wife, Kitty, who was expecting their first child, knew that it raised vast and unspoken fears about what war might do to their family.[60] Embellishing a doctor's orders to get away from work, Galbraith rebounded from his hospital stay by taking Kitty first to Chicago for the Farm Bureau's annual convention, then to New Orleans for the American Economic Association's convention, with a side trip to visit a potential defense-plant site, and from there on to Mexico for a short vacation with the English economic historian Eric Roll and his wife, Freda.

The break restored his energy, and on the trip back to Washington, he and Kitty talked about what life would be like as parents. Galbraith also wondered about his future with NDAC, about where it was headed, whether its chaotic organization could be put in order, and how Roosevelt would continue to prepare the country for war. Germany now controlled the Continent, and beleaguered Britain would not stand alone forever.

7

Now Comes War

BY THE SPRING of 1941, Roosevelt was telling his key associates he expected that war would come to the United States through a Japanese, not a German, attack, though he didn't say where. He cut off shipments of scrap metal to Japan and soon cut off sales of petroleum, too. He also froze U.S. assets in countries that Germany had invaded in order to keep them from falling into Nazi hands. In March 1941, after two months of tense debate, Congress passed the Lend-Lease Act, finally allowing the President legally to ship $7 billion worth of arms and supplies to embattled Britain.

German U-boats, meanwhile, began shifting public opinion toward the President's implicit policy by sinking not only U.S. merchantmen bound for Britain but several U.S. Navy vessels on North Atlantic patrol. Germany's leaders understood FDR's goals despite his continued protestations of American noninvolvement. "The U.S.A. is preparing to make the leap to war," Joseph Goebbels, Hitler's propaganda minister, wrote in his diary that spring. "If Roosevelt were not so chary of public opinion, he would have declared war on us long ago."[1]

Yet Americans had little right in 1941 to real military confidence about the outcome of the war. The German and Japanese military vastly outnumbered the still weak and disorganized U.S. forces. Yet ultimately America's strength was economic, built upon its people and resources. The key would lie in the President's mobilization and management of those American strengths.

Galbraith was among the few who had recognized all this from the very outbreak of war in Europe in 1939—and anticipated what lay beyond, in the aftermath of war. In stark contrast, men such as Joseph Kennedy, then Roosevelt's ambassador to Britain, the Republican Senate leader, Robert Taft, and the celebrated aviator Charles Lindbergh had all said they believed England could not survive and had publicly predicted a complete Nazi victory on the Continent.[2] Yet in December 1939, while still at Princeton, Galbraith had written a long letter to the English biologist Julian Huxley that touched on this issue.

The grandson of the great Darwinist T. H. Huxley (and brother of the novelist Aldous Huxley and the Nobel Prize–winning scientist Andrew Huxley), Julian Huxley was a radical social reformer and prominent biologist,[3] whom Galbraith had met at a dinner party in Washington. At the dinner, Huxley had talked about his vision for a great "European federation" that would end the Continent's nationalist rivalries, if only fascism could be defeated. Galbraith took sharp exception to some of his views, and his letter shows how he foresaw the course of the war and its consequences for the future of the United States.

The defeat of Hitler, Mussolini, and Japan should, first of all, simply be presumed, he boldly told Huxley. The pressing issue was how "the *economic* machinery of a postwar Europe is to function and be regulated," which Huxley had neglected in his talk about a postwar *political* federation.

> Broadly speaking the choice for the postwar organization lies somewhere between two poles. At the one pole is a market regulated economy where, as until comparatively recent times, major reliance is placed upon individual and corporate profit-seeking within the framework of a price system . . .
>
> At the other pole we have a large degree of responsibility on the part of the central authority for the proper function of the economy. While the forms of the market mechanism remain . . . the central authority assumes responsibility for the level and character of the employment provided and brings to bear a variety of weapons—its fiscal, monetary, and regulatory powers—to these ends. So far as individual comfort, health, recreational opportunities and the like are not forthcoming otherwise, the central authority provides them as a matter of course.

Between these two alternatives Galbraith proposed a Rooseveltian, and Keynesian, middle course.

> It seems perfectly plain to me that we cannot have all the virtues and none of the vices of both systems. One cannot regulate without impairing the freedom of contract and the control over private property for private property is nothing more nor less than the privileges which are associated with private ownership. One cannot have perfect individual freedom and at the same time a greater effort to regulate relations between individuals in the community interest. But most important of all, and here the question is more one of choice than of compromise, a decision must be reached as to whether central reliance is to be placed upon the central authority or upon the market in the maintenance of full employment.

A pragmatic balance between the opposing ideological ideals lay at the heart of Galbraith's reasoning. The market has value, but so does the state when it acts in the democratic interest. This is the core of the Galbraithian approach to economics.

Huxley, by contrast, had more utopian views; his allegiances had been shaped by arguments among England's academic aristocrats in the interwar years, and like many of them, he had expressed deep admiration for Soviet Russia in the early 1930s. Huxley's position in late 1939 seemed to Galbraith still deeply flawed, and earned the sort of rebuke one might expect from a Scotsman who hereditarily questioned English judgment:

> From reading your memorandum I have the feeling that you are asking for all the freedom and individualism associated with a market controlled economy and all of the stability, productivity, and freedom for welfare measures associated with totalitarian organization and control. You are, I think, asking for the moon! . . .
>
> If I am correct in assuming that, wherever one's personal preference may lie, we are in for a long period of public control then any discussion of [political] federation is meaningless unless the central government of the Federation is equipped with requisite powers for accepting its responsibilities in economic welfare . . .
>
> There are controls and controls; the economy can be guided by harsh and repressive means or by equally effective but far less restrictive devices. (There is a great difference between ordering a man to produce and buying his willingness to do so with a publicly financed purchase.)[4]

To make sure that his own allegiances were completely clear, Galbraith concluded, "I must say that the recent tradition in English economic thought, particularly that of Mr. Keynes," was the model Huxley should be following.

Galbraith's letter neatly summarizes both the reasons why the New Deal's leaders were so confident as war grew nearer and the hopes its liberals (especially the Keynesians) had for a fundamentally reordered outcome that would leave laissez-faire and socialism behind.

GALBRAITH'S LONG-TERM CONFIDENCE about the world was not, however, matched by short-term confidence about his own situation. In early January 1941 Roosevelt announced he was dissolving the National Defense Advisory Commission. For Galbraith, the President's decision couldn't have come at a more awkward moment. A month earlier, counting on NDAC's continuation, he had resigned his post with the American Farm Bureau, ending the fiction that he was merely on leave.[5] Returning to Princeton remained an option but an unpleasant one—and besides, the university didn't expect him back until the fall. Galbraith was about to become one of America's 9 million unemployed, and Kitty was four months pregnant.

What should he do? Since arriving in Washington, he'd kept up a steady stream of contacts with Harvard, including both letters and trips to Cambridge to lecture at various Economics Department seminars about the goings-on in Washington.[6] In February, he wrote to Alvin Hansen about his thoughts on fiscal policy and inflation. His letter and the accompanying memorandum proved a turning point in his career.

Hansen by now was John Maynard Keynes's leading American apostle, and the legendary Fiscal Policy Seminar he ran for select Harvard graduate students and faculty was *the* academic sounding board for the new Keynesian thinking in the United States. Hansen knew Galbraith and had been impressed by his work, so when Galbraith's letter arrived at his offices, he opened it promptly, curious to know its contents. Galbraith, he found, had a serious argument to take up with him.

Hansen had just published an important article in *The Review of Economic Statistics*, "Defense Financing and Inflation Potentialities,"[7] which reflected the growing concern among leading economists about the pressure that Roosevelt's haphazard military buildup was placing on prices. Inflation was widely and often bitterly remembered by all Americans who had lived through the last world war, when wholesale prices had more than doubled and retail prices had largely followed suit (although government price fixing had held down the cost of many consumer essentials).[8] Hansen assumed that war was inevitable, and in his article he tried to estimate its economic costs and impact. Extrapolating from the big increases FDR had already won for military spending he estimated that a war with Germany and Japan would last until 1945 and consume $40 billion. He was right on the timing but not on the costs: the United States ultimately spent $250 billion.

Of course, Hansen realized that his estimates were guesses at best. His real concern was to sketch out economic policies that would meet the nation's military and consumer needs, and prevent both wartime inflation and postwar collapse. This, he believed, meant using the new idea of Keynesian aggregates to devise an appropriate mix of fiscal and monetary policies. In his view, this required first using heavy government borrowing from banks to reduce monetary liquidity, then selling bonds, and then levying both payroll deductions and "value-added" consumer taxes—a sequence that, if managed well, would both finance the war effort and prevent inflation when defense production pressed the economy to its full employment limits. He also urged planners to address early on the kind of plant and supply bottlenecks that had hindered the country in 1916–18.

Among the ever-growing circle of Keynesians in Cambridge and Washington, Hansen's thinking was bound to have a significant impact, and for Galbraith, this was alarming, because he thought Hansen's theoretically correct recommendations nonetheless misjudged the actual conditions of the American economy. Based on his experience at NDAC, he did not believe that the economy would respond as Hansen expected it would, a conclusion that separated him painfully not only from Hansen but from other Keynesians he respected and with whom he was eager to associate. Some might have kept such doubts private, for fear of posing an intellectual and career risk, yet to his credit, Galbraith hardly hesitated. Reading Hansen's article after six months inside Washington's halting mobilization machinery, he felt compelled to share his experiences—and their implications—in his detailed memo.[9] It's also clear that Hansen was impressed, because, although Galbraith's arguments clashed directly with his own, he quickly arranged for its publication in the next issue of *The Review of Economics and Statistics.*[10]

Galbraith offered two litmus tests in using fiscal policy for containing expected inflationary pressures: "(1) that it not inhibit expansion in the economy during periods of heavy defense expenditures; (2) that the measures do not leave us in some future period with a heavy burden of consumer taxes and a consequent relation between a savings and investment propensity as bad or worse than that of the 1930s." Then, in a long passage that displayed both his intellectual independence and a young man's self-confidence (and perhaps a wee bit of academic hubris, because the passage was deleted from the *Review* version), he warned:

> I am inclined to believe that the development of the concept of full employment in recent years has given us a rather warped technical apparatus for dealing with this problem. Keynes, Mrs. Robinson, Harrod, and the rest have talked glibly about full employment as a flat ceiling which is approached uniformly by all sectors of the economy—they have assumed that the production functions for different industries are similarly shaped and, at any time, the rate of utilization is uniform. Nothing, of course, could be farther from the truth.

Galbraith quite rightly then pointed to the profound structural effects that a decade of depression had had on the American economy: consumer preferences were distorted, plants and equipment had decayed unevenly, and the degree of competition among economic sectors and industries varied widely. With war on the horizon, growth would be channeled into heavy industry, chemicals, and machine tools and not spread evenly throughout the economy. The very real danger was that

> half of the economy may show extreme bottlenecks while the other half shows wide unemployment of resources . . . A uniform reduction of consumer purchasing power with curtailment of investment under such circumstances would serve only to remove the pressure from that part of the economy which was bottlenecked while leaving unemployment elsewhere. This, over a period of time, could be a serious handicap to the defense program.

Galbraith was urging Hansen to take the issue of bottlenecks more seriously and to see them in a partly political, rather than purely economic, light. The idea of bottlenecks as a technical one of plant capacity and worker training was insufficient. "The real limiting factors are the institutional and technical ones," by which he meant the resistance of owners and workers to conversion from consumer to defense production. Overcoming this would require political will on the part of government leaders, which Hansen had completely ignored.

Much more than Hansen, he was also eager to see the role of progressive taxes on income and profits put front and center, as much for political and fairness reasons as for revenue raising. He was acutely aware that workers would resist both payroll tax deductions and appeals for voluntary bond purchases if they thought that the wealthy and the large corporations were benefiting unfairly. And although both men were inclined to support Keynes's proposal for some sort of payroll deduction system that channelled the wages removed into savings that could be released at war's end to prevent recession, Galbraith did not agree with Hansen's proposals for "value-added" consumption taxes as an additional source of revenue and mechanism for restraining inflation. Again, the disagreement came at the juncture of academic theory, political reality, and postwar goals. If Hansen's recommendations on consumption taxes were adopted by Washington, Galbraith shrewdly warned that

> after the [war], the old battle between rational fiscal policy and orthodoxy will have to be fought all over again to get rid of the taxes. The critical period will be one of declining revenue and there will be the old difficulty or impossibility of getting the taxes lifted since the budget will be thrown more and more out of balance. While we have learned a little about a rational expenditure policy in recent years, the record does not show any important progress in the development of a rational revenue policy.

Although that last sentence seems almost timeless, in early 1941 it touched profoundly on what still-undecided strategy Washington would adopt to pay for fighting the war. In the pageant of history from Marathon through Agincourt to Waterloo, wars were popularly understood as battlefield affairs, their outcomes determined by the strategy, tactics, and courage of soldiers. But by the twentieth century wars were at least as importantly economic affairs, with the home front management of real and financial resources as critical to victory as the warriors' daring. For Galbraith, winning the war required economic policies that met both battlefield and home-front needs and carefully husbanded political and economic resources, so that after military victory was assured, the vision and energy unleashed by Roosevelt and the New Deal would be sustained and, with luck, extended. This meant, first, understanding that control of inflation did "not consist of any single measure but of a series of measures designed to fit different stages of our progress toward full employment." The timing and selection of controls was paramount. Aggregate inflation by itself was not the chief danger; misallocation through premature aggregate anti-inflation policies was. As a practical matter Washington first had to focus on price controls and rationing, well before addressing Hansen's vital but more abstract concerns about inflation under conditions of full employment, or his proposed general tax levy.

Second, before the economy reached overall capacity limits, government action would be needed to reduce consumer or investment spending that flowed toward the "bottlenecked industries": for example, Galbraith argued, there would need to be a cap on consumer credit or licensing of certain types of investment—say, for office-building construction or new plants and machinery for non-defense-related goods—because both measures would cut down consumer demand for products like cars or refrigerators that competed with the military's need for steel, rubber, aluminum, and so on.

But all questions of wartime finance, Galbraith repeatedly underscored, needed to be addressed in light of postwar consequences and postwar goals. Though Roosevelt had just won handily against Wilkie, Republicans and Southern Democrats were growing bolder and stronger, and public support for the impending war was not secure. Planning for war meant planning for peace, and for the political values that would govern that peace. The relevance of Keynesian theory to situations other than depression was only just then becoming visible, and winning its application after the war was more than a matter of getting the new theory "right" in academic terms. Voters as well as economists needed to be won to the Keynesian approach with policies that were equitable as well as optimally efficient.

WHILE GALBRAITH AND HANSEN debated the intricacies of managing a wartime economy (and its postwar consequences), those charged with readying the United States for war still faced inertia and chaos. By the spring of 1941, FDR finally seemed determined to move the economy toward a realistic war footing, but to anyone who understood Washington's inner workings, he seemed equally determined to become his own worst enemy. Having abolished NDAC, he now replaced it with an even messier structure of command—"a monstrosity," in the words of one historian. To manage military production needs, he created the Office of Production Management and installed as its "codirectors" two former NDAC commissioners—the former GM boss, William Knudsen, and the CIO's Sidney Hillman, whose backgrounds and allegiances guaranteed antagonism. At the same time, he ordered the Office of Price Administration and Civilian Supply, OPACS, into existence and put Leon Henderson in charge of it. OPACS was, in theory, supposed to ensure adequate supplies of civilian essentials, to curtail nonessentials, and to keep prices stable, but the language of the executive order that created it was indicatively and colorfully redundant: "to take all lawful steps necessary or appropriate in order to prevent price spiralling, rising cost of living, profiteering and inflation."

But faced with pressure from farm-state congressmen, FDR exempted agriculture from these controls, a mistake he then compounded by refusing to give Henderson or anyone else control over wages—even though controlling prices but not wages was by itself a recipe for disaster. To complicate matters, he put his new vice president, Henry Wallace, who had spent eight years as Secretary of Agriculture but knew little about industrial production, in charge of something called the Economic Defense Board; meanwhile he delegated his top White House aide, Harry Hopkins, to oversee, as one historian put it, "whatever Roosevelt was most interested in at the moment."[11]

As if all these overlapping directorates weren't enough, they were barely four months old when, in June, Hitler turned his military fury against his former Soviet ally. FDR, realizing that Russia as well as Britain now required U.S.

aid, responded by creating the Supplies Priorities and Allocations Board, SPAB, meant to set priorities for the Office of Production Management. The resulting lines of authority over what amounted to life-and-death priorities for millions now resembled a Rube Goldberg contraption or—though there was nothing comic about it—a Keystone Cops folly. One historian vividly describes the leadership dimension of its problems:

> FDR . . . chose [OPM executive Donald] Nelson to be the Executive Director of SPAB without relieving him of his post with OPM. Thus, Nelson remained Knudsen's subordinate as chief of purchasing for OPM, while becoming his superior as head of SPAB. Roosevelt also appointed [Leon] Henderson to SPAB, while at the same time he split Henderson's agency [the newly created OPACS] into two parts, an Office of Price Administration and a Division of Civilian Supply. OPA remained independent while DCS became a unit of the Office of Production Management, and therefore subject to the policies laid down by SPAB.
>
> This meant that Henderson was subordinate to Knudsen in his capacity as a division head in OPM, but his equal as a member of SPAB. It also made Henderson his own superior, for on SPAB he was one of those issuing directives which as a division chief of the OPM he had to implement.[12]

Surveying the "monstrosity" the President had created, the Wall Street financier Bernard Baruch, who had led the American mobilization effort in the previous war, curtly told reporters that it was at best "a faltering step forward." Privately, Baruch told friends the reality was much, much worse.[13]

Leon Henderson, with a veteran Washington insider's instinct for seizing opportunity amidst confusion, moved swiftly to give shape to OPACS. He needed an economist to take charge of prices, and Galbraith quickly became a leading candidate. (An aide had given Henderson a copy of Galbraith's memo to Hansen.) Late in April, Henderson summoned Galbraith to Blaine Mansion, a dark, undistinguished red-brick building near Dupont Circle where OPACS was temporarily quartered. Henderson asked him,

> Would I be in charge of the control of prices in the United States? It was an admirably casual offer of the most powerful civilian post in the management of the wartime economy (as it would soon be called) . . .
>
> I accepted. I was not the first choice; Henderson told me he would have preferred Isador Lubin, a more senior figure in the New Deal pantheon . . . It was my good fortune that Lube, my friend from those years until his death in 1978, was not available. I have always felt grateful to him.[14]

Galbraith's first act after leaving Henderson's office was to go into the former bedroom that was now to be his office and call his wife. Her response was to burst into tears. "You promised me you'd help me move!" Kitty sobbed. "There are so many books to pack up!"

"Most wives," Galbraith remarked wistfully, "would have been proud of their husbands."

"I *was* proud," she recalled. "But I was also seven months pregnant, and we were just about to move to Virginia for the summer."[15]

IN LATER YEARS, Galbraith would often describe his OPA job with titles like "price tsar" and terms like "most powerful post in the civilian economy," which suggest a grant of sweeping and unchallengeable authority. But in 1941 in reality his work was hemmed in from the start, and not just by Roosevelt's organizational chaos.[16]

Big business was far from sure whether it really wanted war, for starters. To be sure, it welcomed the armed forces' new "cost-plus" contracts with their guaranteed profits, Washington's cheap loans, and generous tax breaks for new plant and equipment.[17] Yet the auto industry, for example, even as it signed contracts for tanks, trucks, and planes worth billions of dollars refused to cut production of new cars. (In fact it boosted its 1941 output goals by 20 percent over the 1940 level.) And Detroit automobiles were consuming 80 percent of all rubber, nearly 50 percent of sheet steel, and 34 percent of lead. The companies' preoccupation with peacetime profits meant that production of warplanes by mid-1941 was 30 percent behind schedule. Leon Henderson was irate. "It took Hitler more than five years to get ready for this war," he fulminated. "We've got months, not years . . . You can't have 500 bombers a month *and* business as usual."[18] He and others eventually rolled back most of the 20 percent increase Detroit had planned for car production in 1942, but even the 1941 levels were unconscionably high.

But business wasn't the only problem: labor was a challenge, too. In 1940, strikes had reached a Depression-era low, but then in 1941 they just as suddenly hit a new high, with more workers going out on strike than at any time since 1919. In Detroit, the Ford Motor Company, flush with hundreds of millions of dollars in new military contracts, kept up its bitter, often brutal decades-long fight against unionization. Three months after the Supreme Court found Ford in open violation of the Wagner Act, it defiantly fired key union organizers in its plants (this was just days before Galbraith took up his "price tsar" position). Thousands of workers went out on strike, although 2,000 black workers, loyal to Henry Ford, refused to join them and remained in the plants.

The situation soon grew bitterly worse. When peaceful picketers approached Ford's main plant, hundreds of the black workers hurled metal buckets at them, and more than 200 more, armed with steel bars and crudely fashioned swords, rushed other picketers at the main gate. With a race war threatening as well as collapse of the company's war production, Edsel Ford pleaded with his elderly father at least to allow a union election; though convinced he would win, Henry Ford stubbornly resisted for weeks. When the election was finally held the unions won overwhelmingly—just 2.6 percent of Ford workers voted not to join. Henry Ford was personally devastated, but union leaders meanwhile proclaimed the Ford strike the greatest victory of their generation.

Labor-management battles hardly ended there. Strikes now hit the aircraft industry, especially on the West Coast, where companies had fought a bitter rearguard action against unionization for years. In June, sensing that the strikes threatened not just the country's military buildup but public support for his leadership, Roosevelt ordered 2,500 federal troops into an aircraft plant in Los Angeles to compel the workers to return.[19]

Congress at times was no less difficult. Republicans never tired of fearing FDR's covert designs as war neared, and the idea of price controls over free-market capitalism stirred the deepest of those fears; "The New Dealers," Senator Taft darkly declared, "are determined to make the country over under the cover of war if they can."[20]

Resistance to FDR's mobilization plans crossed party lines as lobbyists and hometown leaders whispered to key congressmen about the dangers price controls posed for affected industries. Passage of price-control legislation consequently dragged on for nearly eight months; the marathon hearings on the bill lasted from early August until the end of October. Henderson and Galbraith spent precious autumn weeks journeying up to Capitol Hill to cajole members, brief staff, and deal with price control's armada of opponents.

The scale and ferocity of this opposition richly validated Galbraith's warning to Hansen that the nature of "bottlenecks" in the economy was far from "technical." But winning the theoretical argument offered Galbraith little relief from the day-to-day pressures of his job.

Though both he and Henderson realized that opposition was unavoidable, neither had anticipated how vehement it would be. Their opponents went to extraordinary lengths: when they discovered that one of Galbraith's staff had written a book published in England by the Left Book Club, the charge of "Communist infiltration" arose. Then they learned that Henderson himself four years earlier had chaired the Washington Friends of Spanish Democracy, a group that supported Republican Spain fighting against the fascist forces of General Franco. Because the United States had been neutral in Spain's tragic civil war and Henderson was a government official at the time, this led to new charges hinting of possible sedition. Henderson rescued the moment by reading to his congressional accusers the speech he'd given when accepting the group's chairmanship. In it, he had correctly predicted the dangers of ignoring Hitler's and Mussolini's support for Franco and had warned of a wider war in Europe that might engulf the United States. Afterward, a chastened committee member demurely observed that Henderson had "exercised a little foresight there that some of the rest of us did not exercise." The danger passed.[21]

Communist leanings weren't the only charge thrown up to block price controls. During one hearing, Georgia's Commissioner of Agriculture testified that the controls were a Jewish plot, and that Henderson was secretly Jewish himself, under the influence of "Baruch, Morgenthau, Straus, Ginsburg and the

Guggenheim interests." Galbraith dryly observed that the man would have liked Hitler's Nuremberg Laws "had he heard of them."

FINALLY, IN LATE NOVEMBER 1941, the new Office of Price Administration cleared Congress, and its mandate became law. Galbraith exaggerated only slightly when he wrote that the fight to create it was, "by a wide margin, the most discussed and the most controversial of World War II. There was a sharp debate over renewing the draft [at the same time], but the draft involved only the life and liberty of the subject. Price control involved money and property and thus had to be taken more seriously."[22]

The initial task for Galbraith's staff was to gather information, but they needed a plan.

> On my first Sunday in office I went to the Blaine Mansion and sat down by myself with the Census classification of American industry. From this I derived the subdivisions of my office—nonferrous metals; fuel; steel and iron and steel products; textiles, leather and apparel; and so forth. It seemed almost too simple.[23]

It *was* too simple. As the complexity of their task and the requisite bureaucracy grew, so did the intricacy of these divisions. Soon under textiles and apparel came clothing; under clothing, footwear; under footwear, a section for soles and another for (reclaimed) rubber heels. For the soles-and-heels people at OPA to estimate quality and grade accurately, they recruited Washington postmen and carefully measured the wear-and-tear on their footwear. (Galbraith himself fell prey to the obsession over detail; one memo to Henderson somberly begins, "A big move is coming very soon on the sardine and pilchard situation . . ."[24])

That such a labyrinthine system could function at all owed much to the quality of the people Galbraith recruited, many of them young scholars like him. Faced with both internal and external challenges at every step, there were times when Galbraith wondered whether they'd ever be ready, but the answer to that question came soon enough.

At three o'clock on Sunday afternoon, December 7, the phone rang in the hallway of the Galbraiths' rented Georgetown home. Richard Gilbert, an OPA senior staff member, was on the line. "Something has happened in Hawaii," Gilbert said simply. "Turn on the radio." Galbraith hung up and shook himself out of the nap that on Sundays helped him recover from his 70-to-80-hour workweeks at OPA. As he and Kitty listened to the news that Japanese planes had attacked Pearl Harbor, a second call came in, this one ordering him to an emergency meeting of senior defense officials within the hour. Dressing quickly, Galbraith paused to peek in at the bedroom where Alan, his five-month-old son, lay sleeping in his crib. He touched his child's forehead, careful not to wake him, then rushed out to his car, briefcase and overcoat in hand.

A mile away, at the White House, President Roosevelt had learned of the

Japanese attack only ninety minutes earlier. He'd been sitting in his study with Harry Hopkins when Navy Secretary Frank Knox called. As it quickly became clear that the United States' Pacific Fleet now lay in smoking ruins, Eleanor Roosevelt noted that the President took the news with "deadly calm." After staff people rushed in with more news—"each report more terrible than the last"—Roosevelt and Hopkins began to discuss how to resist a Japanese invasion on the West Coast, and whether the United States could fully mobilize before Japanese armies reached Chicago.

When Prime Minister Churchill telephoned the White House around two that afternoon to ask if the news of the Japanese attack was true, Roosevelt replied, "It's quite true. They have attacked us at Pearl Harbor. We are all in the same boat now." Churchill, though he didn't say so, was elated: "To have the United States at our side to me was the greatest joy," he wrote later. After fifteen months of lonely fighting, he could now foresee the war's outcome. "Silly people—and there were many—might discount the force of the United States," he mused, but America was like "a gigantic boiler. Once the fire is lighted under it there is no limit to the power it can generate."

Shortly before five, Roosevelt called his secretary, Grace Tully, into his study. "Sit down, Grace," he said quietly. "I'm going before Congress tomorrow. I'd like to dictate my message. It will be short." Then in the same slow, steady voice he used to dictate his mail, he began, "Yesterday comma December seventh comma 1941 dash a day which will live in infamy . . ."[25]

As FDR spoke, a few blocks away Ken Galbraith and a dozen other officials were sitting in OPM director William Knudsen's offices. It was the moment they had all been preparing for, and Galbraith had arrived "with a sense of awe. The war had come, and of all the people in the land, I was one of the chosen" who would now lead the nation into war. But the meeting conveyed none of the steely resolve with which their President was going about his task. No one seemed to know what to say or do in the presence of the others, all drawn from the different—often competing—branches of Roosevelt's mobilization "monstrosity." Yet the meeting's haphazard quality was typical of the way the country itself now unexpectedly plunged into war:

> [Participants] that late afternoon assembled irregularly. Men arrived when they heard the news or got the summons. Some were in tennis shoes, golf pants, pullovers, other athletic or casual garb . . . It was soon evident that the gathering would be a major disaster.
>
> That was because there was nothing to decide, and, in any case, so important were the people attending that none could speak firmly about a needed course of action lest it be a decision. So there was a reference only to the news, and of this no one had heard more than was on the radio.[26]

As America began its fabled "rendezvous with destiny," Galbraith realized someone in the group had started reviewing alphabetically various supply needs, and was bogged down over the issue of kapok and its availability for sleeping bags. To break the logjam, someone else asked Knudsen, "Bill, what are the marching orders for tomorrow?" to which Knudsen, who'd arrived late and was sitting on a couch with his hat still on, distractedly replied, "I expect we will be worrying about copper shortages just as we are today." At this, Galbraith's reaction was straightforward. "On that greatest of all evenings, I decided to go home." (In fact, he went to see Henry Dennison, who'd just been hospitalized after a heart attack, and then to a second meeting with Henderson and other OPA officials that lasted until well after midnight, and only then returned to Georgetown.[27])

Knudsen's response, like the meeting itself, remained in Galbraith's memory over the years because it came to illustrate one of his core tenets about power generally, especially the curious way in which decisions are often reached by bureaucratic elites in moments of crisis. In one of his most enduring works, *The Great Crash, 1929*, he put it this way:

> Meetings are held because men seek companionship or, at a minimum, wish to escape the tedium of solitary duties. They yearn for the prestige which accrues to the man who presides over meetings, and this leads them to convoke assemblages over which they can preside. Finally, there is the meeting which is called not because there is business to be done, but because it is necessary to create the impression that business is being done. Such meetings are more than a substitute for action. They are widely regarded as action.[28]

However common Galbraith's experience of December 7 was for many in Washington, the next day dawned with far more foreboding. "Monday was almost worse than Sunday," the journalist Marquis Childs remembered, because "a merciful kind of shock prevailed under the first impact and now as that wore off the truth was inescapable." Throughout the capital, frank talk of unpreparedness "hovered like a low-hanging gas, spreading the panic that seemed to infect" almost everyone.[29]

But Galbraith felt no panic on December 8. Reaching his office shortly before dawn, he quickly and practically plotted out the most urgent tasks he faced. When the regional commodity exchanges opened in a few hours, prices would start spiraling upward almost immediately, so he arranged for cables to be sent to the exchanges—most important, the one in Chicago—to place limits on the daily increases in wheat, soybeans, butter, eggs, and other products. He then ordered aides to wire or call executives at major companies, and place limits on the prices of dozens of other products that would face immediate speculative pressures.

His obviously necessary actions nonetheless brought howls from Congress within hours of its voting for war that afternoon. Patriotism and the willingness to sacrifice were now the order of the day for millions of ordinary Americans, but not for their elected representatives, at least when it risked even modest sacrifice on the part of Congress's most powerful backers. Cottonseed oil, and hence cottonseed, were among the list of OPA's controlled goods. On Tuesday Henderson and Galbraith were ordered up to Capitol Hill where at a hastily called meeting with a dozen or so senators and congressmen, it was made abundantly clear that OPA ought not to "open up hostilities against both the Japanese Empire and the cotton kingdom at the same time." Similar meetings, and dozens of demanding calls and cables, soon followed. Henderson executed a retreat on cottonseed but was able to hold the line on most other products. By week's end, OPA's quick action had throttled a price surge, and the agency settled down to working on the longer-term matter of blunting a more gradual and broader price rise.[30]

How to go about this latter job, though, was still the subject of sharp and substantial debate within the government. Galbraith had warned Henderson three weeks before Pearl Harbor that difficulties were approaching, even without war. The few price schedules issued in 1941, mainly for raw materials, had worked reasonably well mainly because they covered industries with excess capacity or inventory. Now that war had come, the surge in demand from the armed forces and from consumers, fueled in the latter case by rising wages and a tightening labor market, would remove that excess.

> What made our schedules or some of them work before will not make them work in the future. In these circumstances if we are to do our job, we must have in addition to price fixing powers two other powers: the power to control supply and the power to ration . . . It has been thought that rationing is in some way tied in with priorities-allocation setup [of the military]. Actually the two have little to do with each other.[31]

As the new year of 1942 began, the United States was reeling militarily. U.S. troops were holding out in the Philippines but were encircled on Bataan and Corregidor and would soon surrender. In a matter of weeks Japan seized control of more than a million square miles of territory, a hundred million people, and natural resources that included rubber. In the Atlantic, German submarine packs were sinking U.S. ships faster than Americans could build them.

On the home front, Galbraith had by late January won the administrative battle to link control of rationing with his price-control duties, but only through sheer audacity. Two days after Pearl Harbor, he had imposed a nationwide freeze on the sale of new tires and then hastily put in place a rationing scheme to make sure that the precious commodity—now that foreign sources of rubber were in enemy hands—would flow first to military priorities.

Doing so had required an exercise in bureaucratic duplicity to overcome Washington's initial inertia. When the war began, tires hadn't been part of OPA's responsibility because, in Roosevelt's mobilization monstrosity, they fell under the Rubber Branch of the Office of Production Management. But OPM, fearful of the political consequences, wasn't inclined to issue a tough rationing rule. So Galbraith had drafted the initial freeze order himself; then, without identifying himself as an OPA staffer he had spent an afternoon going round to various OPM bureaucrats to get their signatures on it. "They, apparently accustomed to signing documents without reading them, all signed up." Back at his office by seven that evening, he became rightly worried that his order would be reversed once his ruse was discovered. So he phoned CBS Radio in New York, where a friend worked. He persuaded the network to begin broadcasting the freeze order nationwide that night and to get the nation's other radio networks to do likewise. To be doubly sure his order wasn't reversed the next morning, he hit upon "another happy though somewhat unconstitutional idea." Via Western Union, he had an identical telegram sent to thousands of city mayors ordering them to make sure local police halted all tire sales immediately. "I went home toward midnight" that evening, he says, "feeling reasonably certain that tires would not be sold the next morning."*[32]

Thus began the experience of rationing in wartime America. Limits on tires were quickly followed by rationing of gasoline and a host of consumer products, from butter, cigarettes, and sugar to nylon, shoes, canned vegetables, and fruit—all maintained by a nationwide network of 70,000 salaried bureaucrats, 5,000 ration boards, nearly 500 rent-control boards—and eventually by nearly 500,000 local volunteers, who monitored stores for potential violations; in the process the agency's annual budget swelled from $25 million to $130 million.[33] (One of the thousands of OPA's Washington staffers was a young California lawyer, Richard M. Nixon, whose duties including writing letters on Galbraith's behalf to service-station owners regarding the details of tire rationing. He'd come to Washington hoping for a job with the FBI, which rejected him, and went unnoticed by Galbraith among his myriad of subordinates. After years trying to conceal the fact that he'd worked at OPA, President Nixon ended up imposing America's only peacetime wage-and-price controls.[34])

The system itself turned on ration cards, which allowed citizens a choice among restricted items up to a fixed limit. Heavy fines and prison sentences were prescribed for violations, though few during the war actually went to jail. Overall, the system met with overwhelming success, given public support for the war effort, and despite ongoing attacks by congressional and media conservatives. After Roosevelt gave a "fireside chat" to the nation on the importance of conserving rubber in June 1942, for example, Americans during the next two weeks donated more than 800,000 pounds of scrap rubber—from garden hoses to girdles. Nothing escaped the nation's new patriotic fervor: a club in Reading, Pennsylvania, even turned in more than a hundred thousand rubber bands bound into a seventy-pound ball.[35] By war's end, the initial contribution of scrap rubber had grown a thousandfold to more than 450,000 *tons*.[36]

---

*Although the initial freeze worked well, setting up the rules to govern who could eventually purchase tires was a daunting task. When Galbraith a few weeks later issued an order defining "priority occupations"—such as doctors, war workers, civil defense officials—entitled to buy new tires, he got back a note of personal rebuke from the White House because he'd omitted ministers. "F.D.R. was outraged that anyone should be so casual about both fundamentalist religion and the fundamentals of American politics. Ministers were promptly proclaimed essential" to the war effort.

Most ordinary citizens seemed willing to embrace the necessity of rationing and price control, but big business continued to resist not just price controls but conversion to military production. In the first six months of 1942, $100 billion in military contracts were placed; even so, it took an executive order to stop Detroit from continuing after Pearl Harbor to tie up its production lines with passenger cars. (The automakers showed their continued recalcitrance by wheedling an extra two months of car-making "to use up inventories." Irate, Henderson took revenge by appropriating the 200,000 vehicles produced for government service.) And Detroit was far from alone in such behavior. In a *Fortune* poll of business executives, three out of four suspected "darker designs" behind the government's plans for rationing and price controls, an attitude Galbraith encountered with full force when he flew to California to talk with oil industry representatives.

> A spectacular meeting [convened] in San Francisco on the prices of California crude, following a request [by OPA] to the Standard of California that they roll back their buying price of crude petroleum . . .
> Along with some thirty invited guests, about fifty uninvited and extremely militant ones (mostly smaller producers) turned up.

What happened next epitomized the animus many in business felt toward any kind of government interference, even when war required it.

> The meeting was not artistically conducted. When it concluded with a request that the price be returned to the levels prior to the recent increase, a near riot occurred. While the press had been excluded from the meeting, they were able adequately to cover it from the hall outside.
> So violent and strenuous was the objection that at a high strategy meeting in Henderson's office a day or so later the request to Standard of California was withdrawn.[37]

The meeting with oil producers was just one of hundreds of such meetings that took place almost weekly with OPA price executives as the United States tooled up for war. They were tempered by a wry sense of humor, though, as illustrated by one of Galbraith's oft-told stories. When business executives or their lobbyists pleaded for one form or another of special relief, the listening OPA staffers would wiggle their forefingers discreetly at certain junctures in the presentation. This was a reference to the behavior of a queen ant in an ant colony that one day discovers a large pile of horse manure nearby, enough to feed the colony for weeks. The worker ants begin maneuvering it toward the colony in pieces. Then a large chunk breaks off and rolls downhill toward the colony, threatening to destroy it. The ants' queen rushes forward, wriggling her antennae furiously to the workers, signaling them to "Stop the shit!" Listening to the business pleadings, OPA's harried executives were silently repeating her message.

From a handful of products under government supervision in mid-1941, the list burgeoned: 132 price schedules covered thousands of products by February 1942, and more were added every day.* To cut off inflation, price rollbacks were ordered on dozens of items from antifreeze to glass, copper, aluminum scrap, even secondhand typewriters (desperately in demand for government and military clerks).[38] Resistance from business was matched at every step by the logistical problems of managing an immense new bureaucracy, the sheer number of people to be hired, trained, and assigned to positions equaled by the inevitable Washington issue of power and responsibility.

Just thirty-two years old when Henderson gave him the job in April 1941, and with barely a dozen aides at first, within months after Pearl Harbor Galbraith was in direct charge of more than 1,300 employees in Washington and another 2,300 in dozens of field offices around the country—tracking, evaluating, and supervising the prices of thousands of goods produced or sold by 8 million to 10 million manufacturers, wholesalers, and retailers.[39] His team was making five or six major decisions every week and issuing thirty to thirty-five amendments or adjustments. His responsibilities kept growing as rents, retail food prices, and dual military-civilian goods (such as clothing) were put in his charge. Years later, when President Kennedy made him ambassador to India, Galbraith chuckled when friends commented on the post's tremendous burdens. "By comparison with the regimen of a price-fixer," he noted, "it was a life of appalling idleness."[40]

With OPA in charge of an estimated 80 percent of all civilian goods and services (but still without responsibility for wages or farm prices), the internal and external conflicts were many, and well summarized by this confidential 1942 memo from Galbraith to Henderson:

> On two or three occasions during the past month I have attempted to draw your attention to the alarming state of affairs in the OPA organization. Things have now reached the point where there is little hope of recovery. Our prestige and with it our effectiveness are disappearing so rapidly that steps which a month ago might have been effective will no longer suffice.[41]

In six terse, single-spaced pages, Galbraith outlined the OPA's failings. He concluded by warning Henderson that he and his staff might well quit en masse if matters weren't resolved. "They will not stay . . . associated with a policy and a prospect of failure about which they can do nothing. They will fight the war where they feel they are really being effective."[42] Henderson's reply hasn't survived, but Galbraith and his price executives remained on the job.

As his duties and staff numbers mushroomed, Galbraith realized that the OPA's category-by-category approach to rationing and price controls wasn't working well enough. Under the patchwork system, overall consumer prices in early 1942 were still rising at 1 percent a month, and wholesale prices even

---

*OPA even briefly weighed regulating the prices charged by prostitutes, deeming it a service fee rather than a wage. The War Department, however, quickly vetoed the proposal.

faster. Clearly, a far more comprehensive attack was needed. Galbraith and Alvin Hansen had discussed the idea of a general price freeze in early 1941, and Bernard Baruch had raised it even earlier. Galbraith had concluded that such a freeze was economically and politically premature, with America still at peace. But within a month of Pearl Harbor, the idea resurfaced, and Henderson put Galbraith in charge of a committee to explore the option and draft the necessary implementation plans.

By late April, the United States had been at war for barely five months, and the armed forces had yet to go on the offensive. On April 18, Lieutenant Colonel Jimmy Doolittle led sixteen B-25 bombers on a strategically meaningless, yet thrilling and morale-boosting raid over Tokyo, but the crucial naval battle of Midway was still two months away, and the Allied invasion of North Africa was only on the drawing boards, not scheduled until November. On the home front, however, Galbraith and the OPA now launched their own major offensive. On April 27, President Roosevelt went on the radio to announce a sweeping new program—the General Maximum Price Regulation, based on the work of Galbraith's committee. Swiftly dubbed "General Max," the new regulation rolled back prices across the board to their levels a month earlier and then froze them—ostensibly for the duration of the war. Elegantly simple in its premise, General Max was presented to the public not merely as a means for fighting inflation, but as dispersing sacrifice on an equitable basis. All now would share in the economic forbearance the war required.

But for Galbraith and his price controllers, the seeming simplicity of General Max multiplied the complexity of their task. In the first ninety days following its proclamation, more than six hundred formal complaints were filed, and OPA's offices were flooded with thousands of letters, telegrams, and individuals protesting the regulation's effects.[43]

The OPA had to establish price schedules as quickly as possible, industry by industry, product by product. "Where necessary," Galbraith remembered, "these prices would . . . be tied to objective grades and standards"—often with excruciating precision, lest they be abused. "The ratio of peas to water would otherwise be gradually but infinitely widened against the peas and in favor of the water. The association of prices with specific grades and standards, including a reliable ratio of peas to water, would be our most controversial action."[44]

The sheer complexity of price controls made for never-ending internal wrangling over the division of authority between OPA's economists and its lawyers, between its Washington headquarters and the field offices, between OPA and other agencies. Application and enforcement of rules were equally problematical, with each new decision generating new questions and conflicts. For example, because so many "civilian" goods were also consumed by the military, one large question to be answered was when OPA's controls applied—and when not. "Price control on finished battleships had a novelty about it which, however, did not appeal to the Navy Department," Galbraith wryly remarked.[45]

The welter of bureaucratic problems was soon overshadowed by the political ramifications. General Max reignited the fires of opposition to Roosevelt and the New Deal. Republicans, sensing they couldn't attack the war effort directly, focused instead on the home front. Overlooking their own steadfast resistance to mobilization earlier, they blamed the OPA, and government's management of the economy generally, for every possible sin, from corruption to incompetence to directly impeding the war effort. Even more than price controls, though, they hated Roosevelt for the "victory tax" he imposed by executive order in October. Through it, FDR intended to tax the wealthiest two to three thousand Americans (who were profiting monumentally from the war boom) at steep rates on earnings above $67,000 a year. At the time the average annual family income was less than $2,000.

The public supported the tax on the superrich by a nearly two-to-one ratio in polls, but Republican campaign coffers suddenly swelled in the weeks before November's congressional elections. With millions either away at war or transplanted to new defense jobs where they hadn't registered to vote, the race produced the lightest turnout in years—just half the record 50 million two years earlier, and the lowest since 1930. The Democrats would undoubtedly have been helped by news of the Allied invasion of North Africa, but General Eisenhower delayed the invasion until four days after the election, citing weather and logistical problems. In the event, Republicans picked up forty-six seats in the House and ten in the Senate, many by razor-thin margins. Democrats still controlled the Congress, but by the narrowest of leads since Roosevelt took office. In reality, a working alliance between Republicans and conservative Democrats meant that the New Deal was effectively dead.

After the elections, conservative congressmen and editorial writers, knowing they couldn't hit at the commander in chief while the invasion of North Africa was under way, instead singled out Leon Henderson and the OPA for attack. Acutely aware of Roosevelt's larger dilemma—the need to put away "Dr. New Deal" in favor of "Dr. Win-the-War"—and facing a congressional coalition threatening to cut off OPA's funding unless he was replaced, Henderson chose to submit his resignation shortly before Christmas. After more than a decade in public service, he declined the alternative posts Roosevelt offered him, fearing he would continue to serve as a lightning rod for the President's enemies. "Different times require different types of men. I hope I have been suited to the battling formative period," he wrote FDR. "I am now decidedly not adjustable to the requirements of the future as it now begins to disclose its outline."[46]

Liberal New Dealers were distraught. "We have lost one of the bravest and best of the generals that we possessed," *The New Republic* wrote.

> If there was one high ranking leader in government who was right on policy all the way through it was Leon Henderson. He was right on the battle for expansion; he was right on the steel construction program; right in demanding a year before it was accomplished, right in foreseeing, early, the necessity for adequate price and cost control.[47]

In *The Nation*, I. F. Stone called the resignation the most important setback on the home front since the war began.[48] After his resignation, Galbraith noted, Henderson "was never completely happy again. The public interest had been his mistress, his true love, and now he was cut off from that love. Divorced from public concerns, he did not wholly exist."[49]

Despite the loss of Henderson, OPA and the price controls and rationing that he and Galbraith had devised actually worked remarkably well—and, according to wartime polls, enjoyed remarkably strong support. The overall consumer-price index during the war years barely budged, thanks to the system they created out of extraordinary chaos and against often even more extraordinary opposition. Between October 1942 (when most farm prices were finally included in the system) and the war's end three years later, inflation rose a little more than 2 percent annually; unemployment meanwhile was nearly zero, industrial production rose 250 percent, and federal spending soared from a tenth to nearly half of gross domestic product.

But in 1943, none of this mattered to the political opponents of the President and of OPA. Henderson was replaced in January by Prentiss Brown, a one-term senator from Michigan who had been among those defeated in November. Brown understood little about OPA and desired to understand even less; management he left to his deputy, Lou Maxon, a former advertising man. Galbraith, as a consequence, now drew the full force of venomous ire that once had been directed toward Henderson.[50]

In the press, Cissy Patterson's *Washington Times-Herald*, the *Chicago Tribune* (owned by Patterson's cousin, the eternally Roosevelt-hating Colonel McCormack), and right-wing radio commentators such as Fulton Lewis, Jr., all went on the attack. One business trade journal headlined its monthly bulletin: "GALBRAITH MUST GO." Conservative congressmen and senators joined in—not least Senator "Cotton Ed" Smith, who in 1935 had cut off the Agricultural Adjustment Administration's payments to black sharecroppers. A Republican congressman meanwhile told the FBI that an operative of the Republican National Committee had assured him that Galbraith was not merely a Communist but a dangerously "doctrinaire" one. Somehow, the FBI agent mistranscribed this as "Doctor Ware," and—as Galbraith learned years later, when he obtained his FBI files under the Freedom of Information Act—he was suspected for some years thereafter of being under the control of a nefarious but unlocatable Soviet spy code-named Dr. Ware.

For five months after Henderson's departure, the embattled Galbraith was implacable in his resistance to his attackers, and by late spring his struggles were getting almost daily coverage in *The New York Times*, *The Washington Post*, and dozens of other papers around the country. OPA reeled when its general counsel, David Ginsburg, resigned, followed by John Hamm, another top official—both close colleagues of Galbraith's. A dozen midlevel officials soon joined the walkout, but conservatives in Congress, led by Congressman Everett Dirksen of Illinois, insisted they wouldn't be satisfied until Galbraith himself was gone.

The infighting by the end of May seemed to threaten chaos and possible collapse for the OPA. In congressional hearings on May 28, business leaders from the food, textile, and dry goods industries took turns denouncing Galbraith's "communistic tendencies," and Congressman Dirksen called for major cuts in OPA's budget as well as new rules requiring that all senior OPA officials have at least five years' experience working in business. Then on May 31, Prentiss Brown called Galbraith into his offices and told him he was being let go. A job had been arranged for him with Lend-Lease, and Brown offered Galbraith the chance to cite "health reasons" for his "resignation." Galbraith refused the fig leaf. The next day, amid stories recounting the Allies' victory in North Africa and word of the outbreak of race riots in Alabama shipyards—riots that would soon burst forth nationwide and leave hundreds dead—*The Washington Post* carried the news of Galbraith's forced departure on its front page.[51]

A day later, he suddenly collapsed on the floor of his living room. "It was awful," Kitty recalled with a shudder. "I don't think I've ever been more frightened. Emily [Wilson, their housekeeper] and I tried to lift him up on to the couch and loosen his collar. We managed to get a doctor to come; he said Kenneth's [blood] pressure was terribly low and we just had to get him out of town to some place he could get a complete rest."

Kitty had given birth to the Galbraiths' second son, Douglas, only two weeks earlier, and she wasn't "in that great shape either." But when the doctor offered to arrange a special gasoline ration card so they could get away for a rest, Galbraith lifted himself up slightly on the couch and steadfastly refused. He wouldn't seek any special favors from the OPA, he said, no matter what his condition.[52]

For the next several days, Kitty frantically sought some way to get her family out of town, away from the reporters, away from the stress and gloom of her husband's forced departure. Finally, she arranged train tickets to her family's home on Long Island, and from there, several days later, on to a quiet inn in Connecticut. The inn was restful, but the papers kept bringing bleak news about OPA from Washington. There were more resignations, and Dirksen's bills cutting OPA's budget and imposing a business background for OPA staff both passed in the newly conservative Congress. There was one consolation though: Lou Maxon, Galbraith's OPA nemesis, was forced to resign in disgrace over private abuse of ration cards. It was not consolation enough.

8

Luce, Keynes, and "The American Century"

My debt to Harry Luce and Fortune . . . *is not slight . . . Harry Luce's instruction in writing was a lifetime gift. And there was another professional dividend. The early* Fortune . . . *saw the modern large corporation as a primary economic and social force . . . From those years came a lasting immunity to the mythology of the neoclassical textbook economics and its image of competitive firms.*

—John Kenneth Galbraith

I taught Kenneth Galbraith to write. And I can tell you I've certainly regretted it ever since.

—Henry Luce to President Kennedy

KEN GALBRAITH, THIRTY-FOUR, unemployed, with a wife and two little children, had every reason to wonder where his life would head next. There was the quite real possibility that his career was about to plummet downward. And yet it did not, thanks to a most improbable savior—a man whom one might think of as Galbraith's perfect antithesis. For his own reasons, this quite peculiar man propelled not just John Kenneth Galbraith, but the equally controversial ideas of John Maynard Keynes, onto an entirely new stage in American life. He decided to make Galbraith into a journalist.

Henry Robinson Luce, a missionary's son reared in China, a loyal Yale graduate (and Skull and Bonesman) and almost genetically Republican, was by 1943 arguably America's most powerful publisher. He was just forty-three when the war began, but the three magazines he had founded—*Time*, *Life*, and *Fortune*—already dominated their fields. In 1941, the newsweekly *Time* had a circulation approaching the million mark; *Life*, Luce's experiment in photo-journalism, sold well over 3 million and was rapidly overtaking the venerable *Saturday Evening Post* as America's most popular weekly; and *Fortune*, the smallest of the three, at 160,000, was influential well beyond its numbers because it was read by most of America's top business executives. In addition, Luce produced *The March of Time*, a filmed newscast that was shown in 13,000 American movie theaters. All told, more than 2,500 men and women worked in Luce's organization and the journalism they produced reached an audience that totaled in the tens of millions.[1]

Luce was an authentic genius, a self-taught publisher and editor who at the age of twenty-four had launched *Time* with a Yale classmate on a near shoe-string. (In the early days, he frequently rewrote *New York Times* overseas dispatches in colorful "*Time*-ese" because he couldn't afford his own foreign correspondents.) A slender man of medium height, with heavy eyebrows, strong features, and restless, searching eyes, he had unparalleled energy and curiosity, and he involved himself in every aspect of his publications from editing and printing to delivery and advertising.

Luce was also a man of decided beliefs and sometimes gargantuan prejudices, whose Presbyterian upbringing in Asia had given him a deep Christian faith that mixed, often uneasily, with his business decisions and various zealous "campaigns." Central to his politics was a profound dislike for Franklin Roosevelt personally and for the New Deal in general, which Roosevelt and the New Dealers reciprocated. Whenever they reported on FDR or his administration, Luce's writers navigated a perilous line between a decent respect for objective journalism and their chief's powerfully held prejudices. The enmity between Luce and Roosevelt reached a nadir of sorts in 1940, when Luce and other powerful men virtually invented Wendell Willkie as a candidate to oppose FDR's bid for a third term. Luce's support didn't stop with frequent and fulsome coverage of Willkie in his magazines; for good measure, he sent Russell Davenport, one of his top editors, to run Willkie's campaign. FDR returned the favor by frequently attacking Luce's power, in one instance even publicly accusing *Time* of spreading rumors that were making "a notable contribution to Nazi propaganda."[2]

When Japan struck Pearl Harbor, however, Luce immediately rallied to the President. Though his views of what America stood for differed profoundly from FDR's, an attack on their country required a higher patriotism. A month before Pearl Harbor, Luce and his editors had decided to honor Henry Ford as *Time*'s "Man of the Year," but on December 8, the already-written Ford cover story was torn up and the honor passed to Roosevelt. A few days later, Luce wrote the President a private note that concluded, "The drubbing you handed out to *Time*—before Dec. 7—was as tough a wallop as I ever had to take. If it will help you any to win the war, I can take worse ones. Go to it! And God bless you." Obviously touched, Roosevelt replied: "I like your letter . . . because it combines honest patriotism with genuine sportsmanship . . . The waters of Pearl Harbor have closed over many differences which formerly bulked big."[3]

Hawaii's blood-stained waters closed over their differences only briefly. Within weeks of Pearl Harbor, when Roosevelt established the Office of Censorship, Luce's editors fired a warning shot across the White House's bow. In a box on its lead news page, *Time* proclaimed its independence:

> In wartime to disclose secret military information which might be of value to the enemy is not only illegal but unpatriotic . . . But *Time* does pledge itself 1) to report, as soon as its disclosure will do no harm, any military information that may be temporarily withheld, 2) to have the courage to send its editors to jail rather than connive at the concealment of any significant facts of a non-military nature.[4]

It wasn't long before FDR was once again fulminating against Luce. In a note to his press secretary, Stephen Early, Roosevelt wrote, "Honestly, I think that something has got to be done about Luce and his papers." When Early deliberately leaked the note to *Time* editors, hoping to subdue their coverage, the response was swift. *Time's* managing editor memoed his colleagues, "I do not see that we have any choice—difficult as that choice many be in wartime—other than to tell F.D.R. to go jump in the Potomac . . . To hell with sedate language." Luce himself declared that "it may be *Time's* duty to evoke from dear Franklin considerable [*sic*] more fireworks than a peevish blowoff to his confidential secretary."[5]

Censorship wasn't the real source of wartime disagreement between Luce and Roosevelt, though; it was the conduct of the war itself and, more important, America's aims for a postwar world. In a famous *Life* article entitled "The American Century," published early in 1941, Luce had set forth a vision of a postwar world benignly dominated by the United States in which Americans would lead others to a better age of freedom, justice, and prosperity.[6] He followed this a year later with "America's War and America's Peace," in which he firmly declared, "Because America alone among the nations of the earth was founded on ideas and ideals which transcend class and caste and racial and occupational differences, America alone can provide the pattern for the future."[7]

No one who knew Luce doubted his sincerity. These words weren't so much those of a power-hungry press magnate as of a devout missionary's son who had grown up amid the rubble and suffering of a collapsing Chinese empire. But his words gave off an air of Kiplingesque imperialism, of valiant gentlemen going off to save benighted savages from themselves. Among New Dealers, this rankled, and Vice President Henry Wallace made a point of attacking Luce directly: "Some have spoken of the 'American Century,'" he told a cheering crowd. "I say that the century into which we are entering—the century which will come out of this war—can be and must be the century of the common man." Luce's wife, the colorful and combative Clare Boothe Luce, responded by calling the Wallace speech "globaloney." The head of the National Association of Manufacturers fulminated, "I am not fighting for a quart of milk every day for every Hottentot, nor a TVA on the Danube."[8]

New Dealers weren't alone in their attacks on "the American Century."

Yale's *Literary Magazine,* on whose board Luce had once served, called it "insulting" and "jingoistic jargon." The theologian Reinhold Niebuhr, whom Luce deeply admired, likewise attacked it as "egoistic corruption" and compared it to Russia's desire for "a communist world society." Luce claimed that Niebuhr's criticisms helped him see "the pitfalls and heresies" of his vision, but he never bothered to recant them.

It might seem strange that Harry Luce of all people invited Ken Galbraith to join the ranks of Time, Incorporated, let alone that he helped Galbraith make the company his working home for five years. But Luce never let his beliefs interfere in the hiring of talented writers and editors. He admittedly favored Ivy Leaguers, especially if they hailed from his beloved Yale or (with only a hint of suspicion) Harvard, but although several of his editors and writers actively supported the Republican Party, in truth a larger number (probably a majority) were Democrats, and most of them were strong believers in the New Deal.

Galbraith thought that Luce's acceptance of dissidence among his writers was partly pragmatics: "It had been Harry Luce's reluctant discovery that, with rare exceptions, good writers on business were either liberals or socialists. To this he was reconciled. Better someone with questionable ideas who wrote interesting and readable English than a man of sound view who could not be read at all."[9] Notoriously, though, some were even unrepentant socialists, such as *Fortune* editor Dwight Macdonald, and a few others even ex-Communists.* The mix often made for uncomfortable office politics and assured a steady stream of office rows, with memos flying back and forth between Luce and his subordinates over the pitch or slant of any article that touched on what one staffer called Luce's "Big Beliefs—Christ and Capitalism." Galbraith observed that the tension between the writers' beliefs and what appeared in Luce's publications was resolved in three ways:

> One group accommodated their writing but not their convictions to what would appear in the magazine . . . They were assisted by the ample pay, and, on the whole, they found contentment in their work. A second group tried to believe what they felt they needed to write. Their life was much more difficult, and alcohol and psychiatry were regularly required to facilitate the adjustment. A third, yet small number believed what they wrote, and their adjustment was excellent . . . What they wrote was frequently a bore, and they were poorly regarded by their colleagues.[10]

Even among those who disagreed with him politically, Harry Luce the man, and the energies he brought to his fractious empire, evoked respect. The once-Trotskyite Dwight Macdonald, for example, confessed that he thought of Luce as "a hero" to his writers:

*Whittaker Chambers became the most infamous in this last group; others avoided following Chambers to the far anti-Communist ends of the political spectrum.

Even if his style was closer to Shakespeare's "beef-witted" Ajax than wily Ulysses, the man of many counsels, a hero he was.

Luce had the Stalingrad Spirit, with which he infected us all, for prudential rather than principled reasons: jobs were scarce [when Macdonald was first hired by *Fortune*, fresh out of Yale] and, to a man, nearly all his writers, headed by the wily and prestigious Archie MacLeish, were ardent liberals, and, when F.D.R. came in, New Dealers.

This made for a rich, interesting mulligan stew to begin with—a never-say-die conservative commander struggling with a mutinous crew of liberals. But as I say, we all caught the Stalingrad Spirit from Luce and it was a heroic, slightly mad period.[11]

Macdonald himself had left *Fortune* before the war in a row over a series of articles he wrote on U.S. Steel (the last of which he wanted to open with Lenin's epigraph, "Monopoly is the final stage of capitalism"), but Luce continued to hire men he knew were equally independent.

Like his hiring practices, Luce's editorial conservatism—unlike that of so many of his advertisers and most devout readers—was dynamic and constantly in search of new ideas. That meant, in the early 1940s, that Luce had become interested in Keynesianism.

To be sure, his interest lacked Galbraith's or Hansen's passion and never embraced Keynesianism's most progressive aspects. But magnetically drawn to big ideas, ideas that matched the thrust and power of his own personality, Luce saw in Keynes something he believed American conservatives couldn't oppose or ignore. Given his otherwise absolute faith in free markets, the reasons for his fascination grew out of the same impulses that had led him to declare "the American Century." Watching the Depression, and the ever-so-slow, always seemingly incomplete recovery from it, he somehow understood viscerally that capitalism in its laissez-faire version was the past, not the future.

Some of his understanding derived no doubt from his work as a publisher who depended on the aggregate performance of the economy to assure advertising revenues, who never identified himself with a particular industry, and who thought constantly not merely about production but consumption as well and how to enlarge both. Luce's view of the country's future and his grand design for its postwar global obligations, required something in economics that would not only complete American economic recovery but complement the scale of his political hopes for continuing expansion and for a grand, America-led world.

Some months before Pearl Harbor, Luce had set up a special little working group at Time, Inc., headquarters that he initially called the "Q Department," naming it after the World War I warships known as Q-boats that, disguised as merchantmen, were used first to lure and then to destroy the Germans' predacious U-boats. Concealing the group's activities from all but his top aides, he told them that "while there is nothing 'secret' about it, we do not wish any publicity." Its purpose and the reason for confidentiality, he said, was to stimulate thinking among his senior men that would then—through his magazines—"educate" the rest of the country about the postwar world, how it should be organized, and to what ends.[12] (Some of his closest aides also felt that because the Q Department had access to secret government documents through leaks to enterprising reporters, secrecy was well advised, since there was a risk of foreign spies at the magazines, as well as loose lips.) Over the course of the war, many of the Q Department's ideas filtered into articles in Luce's magazines. (According to Luce himself, half a million Americans had read one or more of *Fortune*'s essays on the postwar world by early 1943, a number he then vastly expanded by reworking the essays for *Time* and *Life* and by creating a "postwar curriculum," which was ultimately adopted by hundreds of colleges and universities.[13])

One Q Department working paper, a fifty-page memo read only by the company's senior executives and editors, turned out to be especially powerful.[14] In it, the company's vice president and treasurer, Charles Stillman, undertook to outline the new economics of John Maynard Keynes and oft-repeated Alvin Hansen. This was indeed a sensitive topic, since most businessmen, including the company's advertisers, were just beginning to enjoy war-era profits and looked upon Keynes as an upper-class proselyte for socialism or worse.

Stillman, as Time, Inc.'s, chief financial officer, was in some sense an odd choice to analyze—let alone recommend—Keynes to Luce. Yet though "hired to be a figure-man," as a perceptive colleague put it, Stillman "understood a much wider world than figures." It was Stillman's wider understanding that convinced him (and ultimately Luce)

> that compensatory fiscal policies were not only compatible with the free enterprise system but essential to full employment and an expanding economy. Luce, who was never an economist and who never pretended to have a special knowledge in the field, did have a puritan's prejudice in favor of a balanced budget. But Stillman's fifty-page memorandum convinced him that Keynes's doctrine was not inconsistent with fiscal morality and brought about a considerable change in the editorial attitudes of Time, Inc. publications.[15]

Thus Harry Luce—ardent Republican, millionaire publisher, visceral opponent of FDR—came to embrace the teachings of *The General Theory of Employment, Interest, and Money*. He knew that trying to persuade his advertisers and the corporate world generally of Keynes's merits would require the utmost delicacy. The immediate questions were how to begin the process and who should carry it out.

But Luce, as it turned out, had an even greater general theory of his own, whose outlines came into focus after he read Stillman's memorandum. In the spring of 1943, Luce produced his own memorandum for Q Department discussion. Modestly titled "The Reorganization of the World," it laid out in exquisite detail what he felt needed to be done in the years after the war. Luce foresaw no mere Keynesian reconstruction of the American economy—that scale was too narrow—but quite literally what the paper's title avowed, the reorganization of the world. In that world, the U.S. must be stronger than "any two nations combined," and willing to spend billions first for the reconstruction of Europe. A United States of Europe would then be created, sponsored by Britain, the United States, and the Soviet Union. The Soviets should be helped to "develop a prosperous and noble" society; China, with U.S. aid and tutelage, would experience the "renaissance of a great Chinese civilization" once Mao Tse-tung and his allies were quelled. Freed of British domination, a new United States of India would appear, while Britain, no longer burdened with colonies, would become America's partner in creating "a capitalist orderly trading system for the world."[16]

IN HIS MEMOIRS, Galbraith insists that his shift into journalism in the summer of 1943 was entirely serendipitous, not at all intended. Several months before losing his OPA job, he says, he attended a dinner with several *Fortune* editors to talk about price controls; afterward, he was surprised when Ralph "Del" Paine, *Fortune's* brilliant young editor, suggested that he think about joining the magazine if he ever decided to leave government. Galbraith says he declined at the time but, after being pushed out of OPA, went up to New York to see Paine, "and accepted his offer. It is possible that he had forgotten making it."[17]

The Time, Inc., archives, however, reveal a lengthier chronology, at key moments a definitely actively interested Galbraith, and the reasons why *Fortune* pursued him. First, the dinner Galbraith mentions in his memoirs took place not in 1943, but in September 1941, during a *Fortune* roundtable discussion on "demobilizing after the war," which included about thirty participants, including Luce himself. The fact that Luce convened such a discussion three months *before* Pearl Harbor helps date the scope of his own strategic thinking. After this meeting he formed the Q Department. He must have been enough impressed by Galbraith as was Del Paine, so that Paine indeed made the job offer, which Galbraith declined because he was caught up in pushing the legislation creating OPA through Congress.

Six months later, though, Galbraith seems to have had second thoughts. In March 1942, four months after Pearl Harbor and in the midst of the OPA debate over "General Max," Ed Lockett, in the *Time* Washington bureau, wrote Paine that "there are two guys here in Washington who would make swell *Fortune* men, in my opinion, one of whom has talked to me innumerable times about the likelihood [*sic*] of being hired." The "two guys" were Galbraith and Bruce Catton, who went on to become the famous historian of the Civil War; the one who talked "innumerable times" about working at *Fortune* was clearly Galbraith.

> Ken's major attribute, as you know—you had him up to one of Fortune's round table meetings—is ideas. He modestly avers that he can write better than almost anybody you or I ever saw, and although he obviously can't back up that statement, he's pretty good . . . He asked me flatly whether I knew if

he could get a job on Fortune, saying he was getting a little tired of running the price control setup.[18]

Lockett, writing this, apparently didn't know that Paine had already made Galbraith a job offer. But Paine now made a second offer: come to work for us by July, write about economic issues, and we'll pay you $12,000 a year. He also assured Galbraith that Luce was personally eager to bring him on board.[19]

Yet once again the timing was wrong: Galbraith initially replied saying that he'd take the job, then several weeks later backed out, citing his duties under the newly announced "General Max" regulations.[20] Dismayed, Paine wrote in August renewing the offer a third time, and once again Galbraith declined, telling Paine he just couldn't leave OPA at that point.[21]

There matters rested until mid-June 1943. Galbraith had left OPA on May 31 and suddenly collapsed. After recuperating, he'd grudgingly accepted a job with Lend-Lease but was bored with his minor duties: being assigned to watch over trade with South Africa was a clear demotion, and at the height of the war, Washington suddenly looked like a dead end. It was time to get out of town.

But where to go? Teaching seemed a nonstarter: most universities were hovering on the edge of bankruptcy, thanks to the draft's effect on enrollments, and weren't looking for new faculty. Having turned down *Fortune* three times, it seemed unlikely that journalism was still a viable option.

There was only one way to find out. This time, it was Galbraith's turn to write, and he did so in the most direct possible fashion:

> Dear Paine,
>
> Several months ago you addressed me what you described as a blunt query about going to work for FORTUNE . . . I have now joined the column of former price-fixers. My own "blunt query" is do you still want me. I offer you smart economics, a cosmic knowledge of the folkways of American business, and qualifications as a journalist which, although they undoubtedly will involve me in certain personal risks, are better than my profession normally has to offer.[22]

Del Paine at first hesitated—understandably, after three rejections.[23] But several weeks later, and after likely consultation with Luce, he brought Galbraith on board. *Fortune*'s board of editors needed a strong economist, he still believed, and Galbraith had practical wartime economic management experience and, more important, the Keynesian worldview he knew Luce was looking for. After several weeks of back-and-forth negotiations, a deal was sealed. In late August, Galbraith notified Ed Stettinius, the former U.S. Steel chairman who was now running Lend-Lease, that he'd be leaving on October 1.[24]

With his new $12,000 salary, Ken and Kitty chose a large, comfortable apartment on New York's Riverside Drive as the family's new living quarters. With spacious views of the Hudson River and with Riverside Park to the west, it was a special treat for his two young sons, Alan and Douglas; Alan loved to watch the wartime convoys assembling in the river below before sailing for Europe.

At *Fortune*, Paine assigned Galbraith the general project of directing the magazine's coverage of the economy's gradual demobilization and transition to a postwar world. (The war's outcome was now becoming clear, though it would take two more long and terrible years to bring it to conclusion.) But he judiciously never mentioned anything about the Q Department, Stillman's fifty-page memo on Keynes, or Luce's plan to reorganize the world.

Quickly getting down to work, Galbraith completed his first 7,000-word piece in late November 1943—a debut article that by all accounts was an immediate success. After reading it, Paine "came down to my stark office, manuscript in hand, to tell me that it was the best thing of the year."[25] It was more than flattering encouragement for a new and untested writer: the editor then tore up plans for the January 1944 issue in order to make it *Fortune's* lead piece. In modest celebration of his triumphant inauguration into professional journalism, Kitty and Ken went out to an inexpensive little Mexican restaurant and then on to a twenty-five-cent movie. "We did enjoy that evening so," she says.[26]

Paine gave Ken's article what even now seems a peculiar title: "Transition to Peace: Business in A.D. 194Q".[27] What, readers—let alone Galbraith—must have wondered, was "194Q"? Why not "194X," for example? Or simply "Business After the War"? To Luce, Stillman, and the company's other top insiders, Paine's choice was almost certainly a private wink to the Q Department and to Stillman's confidential argument for promoting Keynes. And perhaps the inclusion of "A.D."—*anno Domini*, "year of our Lord"—was a sly second wink by Paine at Luce's piety or even at his exalted status within the company. In any case, here finally was the article that Luce—unknown to Galbraith—had been looking for.

Given the audience it was meant to persuade, the article itself began judiciously not by describing Keynesian economics but by using Commerce Department data, based on the new national income accounts developed by the economist Simon Kuznets, to project the American economy's likely performance after the war. Casting it in the sturdily uplifting tone Luce always loved—"The U.S. isn't going back to 1939 because 1939 wasn't good enough"—and carefully avoiding any mention of Keynes by name, Galbraith established why big business itself should want a Keynesian-style activist government.

His first argument was straightforward in its appeal to a pair of classic emotions: his readers' fear and greed. Unlike the period after World War I, he promised, the economy this time needn't collapse; accumulated savings and deferred consumption at war's end would fuel a boom, including fat business profits—enough to "make a Midas ill with envy." (This confidence, it should be noted, was not shared by all economists. Paul Samuelson, for one, feared a major postwar recession, if not another depression. "All our findings," he wrote in a 1943 study, "lead to the conclusion that there is serious danger of underestimating the magnitude of the problem of maintaining continuing full employment in the postwar period." Samuelson repeated his warning two years later in a *New Republic* article entitled bluntly "Unemployment Ahead.")[28]

To assure a postwar boom would require business's assent to government leadership, however, which Galbraith knew much of his audience stoutly resisted, war profits or not. To sweeten the message, he called this a new kind of leadership, a "kind of public regulation (management might be a better word) that makes it unqualifiedly attractive for men and women by their own decision to work, invest, invent and plan." His argument then shifted from fear and greed to an analogy drawn from business experience: business needed to accept that the nation's economy, like a large corporation, cannot thrive without conscious planning and direction.

After the war, he soothed, wartime production regulations would of course go, as would price controls and rationing, and taxes would be substantially reduced. But businessmen could not dream of complete extirpation of their New Deal nemesis, he warned. Corporate taxes would be sharply cut, but progressive income taxes would drop less, and government would have to take a direct hand in investment in such areas as housing. There would be a deficit for a time (for reasons of wartime debt repayment, Galbraith cagily averred, not macroeconomic stimulation). Prewar regulation of securities and commodity markets, transportation, utilities, and banking would all remain, though programs developed to reduce Depression-era poverty—the Works Project Administration, the Civilian Conservation Corps, and the like—which had been ended by the war, would not return. Maintaining "strong"—but not necessarily "full"—employment and strong private investment would be encouraged, and so would public spending, although it would be sharply curtailed from its wartime high. In concrete terms, he projected 8 percent unemployment as initially "transitional," without mentioning what percentage would thereafter be the government's long-term goal.

This article, with its predictions about not just the performance but the size and shape of America's postwar economy, is mildly disconcerting if one expects something overtly "Keynesian" or "Galbraithian." But it should be read as a Keynesian's diplomatic overture to those whom Galbraith once told Paine he thought of as "well-cushioned heathens." Its tone about postwar life closely approached Luce's rather than Galbraith's (or Keynes's) more liberal personal views. Keynes was never mentioned, the concepts of full employment and strategic deficit spending weren't rigorously advanced, and, Galbraith promised, government activity would consume "only" one fifth of the GDP. (He carefully failed to remind his readers that federal spending had been only 2.6 percent of GDP at the start of the Depression.) Nonetheless, government was not to be rolled back or simply opposed out of old ideological habits. The "new" businessman could and must work with this new kind of government, which should no longer be seen as the enemy of business.

Galbraith's article ignited several strong protests. Inside the Luce empire, Paine had to quell the objections that a group he called "the Irreconcilables" raised over *Fortune's* publishing such heresies, written by a former New Deal official now on the company payroll. In an interoffice memo, he met Galbraith's opponents head-on:

TO THE IRRECONCILABLES:
1. Yes, Mr. Galbraith is on the staff.
2. We are very glad he is.
3. He is, in our opinion, an exceptionally able individual, a man of good judgment and well-balanced opinions.
4. He has had unusual experience which is of great value to us in reporting on government.
5. He is, in our opinion, a man of honesty and integrity.
6. What the hell more do you want?[29]

Never mentioning Luce's support or the Q Department, Paine's reply—and the protest itself—show how tightly compartmentalized Luce kept the Q Department's work from most of his staff. (Luce by contrast was so pleased with the article that he had Galbraith reprise its arguments, appropriately popularized, for *Life* that spring.)

GALBRAITH'S "194Q" ARTICLE tells a great deal about where the United States was headed by 1944, and about the changing powers and attitudes of the forces that had been contending so vehemently since Roosevelt took office. It covertly advanced a formulation of Keynesianism that Galbraith hoped big business might accept, while simultaneously it symbolized the decline of older New Deal forces and alliances and the rising power of big business and the armed forces, the alliance that President Eisenhower later warned of as America's "military-industrial complex."

Roosevelt was reelected again in November 1944, but politically the war had not been kind to liberal Democrats. Republicans made substantial gains in Congress as they had in 1942. (*Life*, after the 1942 election, had joyfully if prematurely reported that "the U.S. is now a Republican country . . . [T]he Republicans are now the majority party."[30]) An increasingly conservative (though nominally still Democratic) Congress and the President skirmished repeatedly about controlling inflation, about spreading the cost of the war equitably, and about the shape of the country's postwar economy.

In 1943, for example, the National Resources Planning Board (for which Galbraith had written his public works study and to which Alvin Hansen was then chief advisor) had released *Security, Work and Relief Policies*, a bold study that redefined the idea of "social security" with such breadth and ambition that it became known as the "American Beveridge Report," after the contemporaneous British study that led to the creation of Britain's postwar welfare state.

President Roosevelt had endorsed it, but Congress, with its working majority of Republicans and conservative Democrats, responded by abolishing the NRPB.

In January 1944, Roosevelt tried to rally the old New Deal forces in his State of the Union address. He called for a "second Bill of Rights" that would guarantee the right to a decent job, adequate housing, medical care, education, and a secure retirement to every American. Liberals were thrilled—Dr. New Deal was alive after all alongside Dr. Win-the-War. But when, as a down payment on ensuring such rights, Roosevelt tried to increase taxes on upper-class incomes, corporations, and estates that were swelling with wartime profits, Congress filled the President's bill with special-interest loopholes and voted only a fraction of the request. Furious, FDR vetoed the congressional version, and—in an echo of his second-term denunciations of concentrated wealth—called it a "tax relief bill . . . not for the needy but the greedy." But Congress then promptly overrode FDR's veto—the only time tax legislation had passed over a presidential veto in American history. To many, the old New Deal now seemed truly dead.[31]

Supremely adept at maneuvering, and aware that he was actually trailing in the polls, Roosevelt privately took a new tack. His frustration with conservatives in his own party by then was at the boiling point, and he resolved on an unprecedented strategy to be rid of them. He decided to approach Wendell Willkie—the Republican he'd defeated four years earlier—to see whether together they could create a new liberal party made up of progressive Democrats and Republicans and shorn of the antediluvian elements in the South. "We ought to have two real parties," FDR told his aide Samuel Rosenman, "one liberal and the other conservative." When Rosenman, on FDR's instructions, broached the idea to Willkie at a secret meeting in New York, the Republican responded instantly. "You tell the President that I'm ready to devote almost full time to this," he said. "A sound liberal government in the U.S. is absolutely essential." But the news of their plan then leaked out, and both men, greatly embarrassed, were forced to back off, though they secretly agreed to take up the issue immediately after the November elections. American politics for a brief moment seemed poised to head in a remarkable direction, but then Willkie suddenly died in the fall of 1944 and Roosevelt himself was gone the following spring.[32]

Having failed to break with his party's conservatives, at the Democratic National Convention that summer, Roosevelt was entrapped by them. Party chieftains could see that his health was failing and presumed he wouldn't survive a fourth term. Horrified that the liberal-left vice president, Henry Wallace, would succeed to the White House, party bosses set out to have him replaced. Aware of what they wanted, the President tried to fend them off by playing a cat-and-mouse game. That July, at a White House meeting with three of them—Democratic National Committee Chairman Robert Hannegan, Frank Walker, and Ed Flynn—FDR reviewed the options. Warned that conservatives would stage a damaging convention fight over Wallace's renomination, Roosevelt proposed Supreme Court Justice William O. Douglas; too liberal, said the bosses, who suggested James Byrnes, a former senator and justice. But Byrnes, a lapsed Catholic and Southern segregationist, would alienate Catholics, Negroes, and liberals, the President countered. What about Truman? replied the bosses. FDR was ambivalent—he hardly knew the Missouri senator—but reluctantly said he would support Douglas or Truman, in that order. The party bosses, elated that they'd picked off Wallace, put FDR under intense pressure to sign a short letter naming Douglas and Truman on the eve of the convention, as they formulated a plan to rid themselves of Douglas as well.

As the President's secretary was typing the note, Hannegan rushed in and told her it should read "Harry Truman and Bill Douglas," leaving the clear impression that Truman was the President's first choice. The maneuver was of course a success.[33]

Throughout the 1944 presidential campaign, the Republicans were in high dudgeon, sensing the chance to turn the hated Roosevelt out at last, and they were not to be restrained after nominating the New York prosecutor Thomas Dewey as their standard-bearer. "The Republican campaign," as one historian put it, "began by being dull. It moved on to become scurrilous. When it coasted to a halt, it was running on pure venom." It was, in fact, a campaign full of hateful conservative attacks, including the sort of red-baiting later associated with Senator Joseph McCarthy. Dewey unhesitatingly and repeatedly portrayed Roosevelt as a captive of Communists. Earl Browder, head of the U.S. Communist Party, who had been imprisoned during the early part of the war as a subversive, "had been released from prison to organize Roosevelt's campaign," according to Dewey. The Congress of Industrial Organizations' new political action committee was helpfully described by *Life* as "a foreign object," an instrument of class warfare, something appropriate to totalitarian states. Senator Harry Truman of Missouri, FDR's running mate, was whispered to be a former member of the Ku Klux Klan.[34]

But new congressional alignments and a resurgent Republican Party weren't the only reason for the new conservative tides. During the war, the architecture and alliances of the New Deal had shifted, and along with them the rationales for supporting Roosevelt. Many New Deal relief agencies—WPA, CCC, and so on—had naturally disappeared as unemployment fell below 2 percent and total employment had soared. More alarmingly to old-school liberals, antitrust enforcement, a major feature of Roosevelt's second term, had also fallen by the wayside, as the government chose to overlook business consolidation in favor of increased production. Organized labor, whose struggles to unionize the New Deal had favored, found itself chastened for its strikes and wage demands.[35]

The management of the war itself had also brought unwelcome change—not least, new managers with new ideas of whom government was to serve. (The "dollar-a-year" men brought in from business frequently returned their government salaries and benefits, knowing their financial "sacrifice" was temporary, with their old jobs awaiting them.) Roosevelt's divided and often chaotic organizational structure offered no clear models on which to advance old New Deal optimism about the state as a liberal force. As the historian Alan Brinkley describes it,

> For many liberals, [Roosevelt's War Production Board] served not as an inspiration but as an alarming indication of what government management of the economy could become: a mechanism by which members of the corporate world could take over the regulatory process and turn it to their own advantage . . . Corporate "capture" of state institutions had been a lament of many liberals for years; that the war not only failed to reverse that tendency, but seemed to advance it, raised questions about whether traditional forms of regulation were workable at all.[36]

This was doubly alarming to liberals, because they had acceded to setting aside New Deal aims in order to win the war. David Lilienthal, head of the Tennessee Valley Authority, spoke for many when he declared in 1942, "Progressives should understand that programs which do not forward the war must be given up or drastically curtailed. Where a social service doesn't help to beat Hitler, it may have to be sacrificed. This may sound tough—but we have to be tough."[37] But by 1944, it seemed that the actual heart of the New Deal government apparatus was being sacrificed to victory, victory, victory. Social engineering was out, production engineering was in. Where the old New Dealers remained, their influence waned. Many more left government service, some for the armed forces, others as sacrificial offerings to congressional committees, still others because they and their hopes were exhausted. In their place the "dollar-a-year" businessmen solely focused—or so it seemed to those they replaced—on output and profit, to the benefit of the nation's biggest corporations. "The New Dealers are a vanishing tribe," the liberal journalist James Weschler observed of wartime Washington's daily life, "and the money changers who were driven from the temple are now quietly established in government offices."[38] The abandonment of Henry Wallace for Harry Truman at the party's 1944 convention was final proof for many.

Yet if the "old" New Deal was dying, Galbraith also optimistically believed something new was being born—the outlines of a Keynesian economy that could in powerful ways transcend the limits of old, often fruitless New Deal strategies of antitrust and ill-defined national planning.[39] He saw his job at *Fortune* as persuading the country's business leaders to accept—or at least not attack—the merits of that Keynesianism. A month after "194Q," he wrote "Public Regulation Is No Dilemma," *Fortune*'s lead editorial on business-government relations.[40] Still not mentioning Keynes by name, he advanced arguments for postwar Keynesian-style macroeconomic controls—and defended the maintenance of New Deal advances in labor, farm, securities, and utility regulation. (He even offered support for limited antitrust action, which he usually denigrated on the ground that it impeded innovation in industry.) A month later came an article on the impact on business of the Pentagon's demobilization, stressing the government's importance in managing the transition and the postwar economy as a whole.[41]

BY MAY 1944, a month before D-Day in Europe, *Fortune* and Galbraith seemed finally ready to introduce the magazine's readers directly to the dangerous Keynes himself. In a stunningly flattering feature article, the magazine extolled Keynes's brilliance—of a caliber, it said, that would have "delighted" the greatest of American leaders such as Jefferson, Hamilton, Jay, and Madison.[42] "Now that the U.S. is launching out on wider world responsibility it perhaps needs more such statesmen" as Keynes. Readers who found him a dangerous, even revolutionary, figure were simply mistaken: in *The General Theory*, "Keynes' great contribution was to clothe common sense in rigorous analytical form and to show that the economic system is by no means automatically self-adjusting."

> Keynes himself . . . is far from an enemy of free enterprise, and even further from being a theoretical socialist. Indeed, his thesis is that stimulation, both private and public, by government may in certain circumstances prove the one way of avoiding the destruction of economic forms in their entirety.

Fortune went on to applaud Keynes's proposals for postwar coordination of monetary affairs and development, proposals the magazine knew he was about to present to a major international conference at Bretton Woods, New Hampshire. There, in negotiation with U.S. Treasury officials, Keynes would in fact create the architecture of the postwar international economic system—including GATT, the World Bank, and the International Monetary Fund.

Interestingly enough, Galbraith wasn't the author of this article; the task had been assigned to John Davenport, one of *Fortune*'s most conservative editors. But Galbraith's hand wasn't absent; Paine had by then put him in charge of economic feature articles, and he oversaw Davenport's work from creation to final form.

Two decades later, in 1965, *Time* put John Maynard Keynes on its cover, the first time it had so honored a nonliving person, and declared America's postwar affluence to be the consequence of its choosing to live in "the Keynesian era." It even quoted the conservative economist Milton Friedman as saying, "We're all Keynesians now"—a stunning admission for someone who supported Barry Goldwater (exceeded only by President Richard Nixon's announcement a few years later that "now I am a Keynesian").[43]

Time's 1965 encomium traced the development of Keynes's ideas through the 1930s and stressed the importance of America's successful wartime management of the economy as central to acceptance of Keynesianism. It highlighted Alvin Hansen's leadership in convincing academic economists of the validity of Keynesian arguments, and the effectiveness of New Deal figures such as Lauchlin Currie. Ironically, *Time* never mentioned *Fortune*'s work—or

Galbraith's, let alone that of the Q Department—in persuading America's business executives at the height of the war to embrace, or at least accede to, the new Keynesian era, even though in practical political terms, it was as vital as what Hansen and Currie had accomplished.

To be sure, Keynesianism was a theoretical enterprise at one level, the exposition of a model of capitalism that transformed the ways in which the profession addressed its concerns. But it was, equally, an applied model of public policy, entailing an idea of government that was at odds with the most fundamental tenets of American business and American conservatism.

Fortune wasn't alone in its Keynesian work, though it was far and away the most prominent voice in business journalism. *The Wall Street Journal*, *Nation's Business*, *BusinessWeek*, and *Forbes*, its four chief competitors, were far more hostile to the idea of a Keynesian-led postwar America during the war (and would be for many years after). The *Journal*, for example, ran more than one hundred war-time articles and editorials on various aspects of Keynesianism, and looked on his Bretton Woods proposals with especial disfavor, denouncing them as "bunk" and certain to generate "the wildest spiral of inflation in history."[44] But *Fortune*'s efforts were paralleled and aided by an important new voice in the business community: the Committee for Economic Development. Based in Chicago, with its research work directed from 1942 until 1967 by three consecutive University of Chicago–trained economists, the CED, with 50,000 business-executive members, asserted, intriguingly, that major corporations had to adopt a broadly Keynesian outlook toward government and the economy. Herbert Stein (who later was President Nixon's chairman of the Council of Economic Advisors), for example, assigned great prominence to the CED in its efforts to advance "both the spirit and the substance of the postwar consensus." Similarly, President Kennedy's CEA chairman, Walter Heller, observed that any review of the CED's policies was identical to "a review of the dominant theme in postwar fiscal-policy thinking."[45] Histories of the CED make clear that, especially during the war it was a vital counterweight to the older National Association of Manufacturers, which viewed any expansion of the postwar government with the deepest suspicion.[46]

The CED's voice was amplified when in 1944 its vice chairman became head of the U.S. Chamber of Commerce and gradually moved the much larger Chamber away from its devoutly anti-Keynesian views (though not its anti-Rooseveltian ones).[47] And the CED brought into its own leadership circle men who later helped to shape the United States' postwar economic policies: Truman's Federal Reserve chairman, the heads of the New York and Boston Federal Reserve banks, two Republican secretaries of the treasury, several U.S. senators, the staff director of the congressional Joint Economic Committee, the head of the Marshall Plan in Europe; even Dwight Eisenhower (then president of Columbia University).

Three features about CED's rapid rise to influence link it to *Fortune* and Galbraith, although he was never personally active in CED. First, the CED originated in the Department of Commerce's Business Advisory Council, a group of liberal executives once headed by Henry Dennison that was led during the war by Dennison's close friend Ralph Flanders, one of the trio who in 1937 had hired Galbraith to work on the book with Dennison. Second, Henry Luce was, not surprisingly, among the very first men whom the CED had approached upon its formation. He assured them of his company's active support and commitment to disseminate the group's work—not only through the magazines but by providing a string of senior executives as CED leaders. Third was the CED's publication of *A Postwar Federal Tax Plan for High Employment* in 1944. Although it was, "by all odds, the most difficult" challenge the group undertook during the war years, eighteen months in preparation and requiring more than a dozen major drafts, it became the blueprint for American postwar fiscal architecture—and it debuted to a national audience in *Fortune* in December 1944, thanks to Ken Galbraith.*[48]

The concerted influence of *Fortune*, the CED, and others can be traced through *Fortune*'s own polls of management attitudes. A month before Pearl Harbor three out of four top executives insisted that Roosevelt's war preparations concealed darker ambitions for extensive government controls over business. By October 1943 (the month Galbraith began working for *Fortune*), those views hadn't changed, with 74 percent of senior business executives maintaining that after the war, "reasonably full employment can be maintained by private business" alone. Keynesian-style deficit spending for any reason meanwhile remained anathema: 86 percent wanted balanced budgets as soon as the war ended, agreeing that "otherwise possible ruin follows." And if a new depression came after the war (as many feared), only 1.3 percent believed that greater government regulation of business would aid recovery; the correct remedy, two thirds said, was to cut government spending and corporate taxes. Even as late as May 1944 (ironically in the same issue that heaped such fulsome praise on Keynes), *Fortune* still found 66 percent of business leaders insisting that it was not the "function of government today to maintain substantially full employment." "The overwhelming response," observed Elmo Roper, who directed *Fortune*'s polling, "indicates widespread business mistrust of the philosophy of Keynes in England and Hansen in the United States."[49]

Yet by 1945, after more than a year of steady celebration of Keynesian-style government leadership in more than two dozen *Fortune* articles, when the executives were asked whether "full employment is something that will require government action as well as planning by industry," Roper found that 64 percent *agreed*, and only 27 percent still thought it was the job of private enterprise alone.[50] In short, between late 1943 and early 1945 the attitudes of

---

*In September, William Benton, CED's cochair, had written Galbraith at the suggestion of Flanders, outlining the new plan. Benton was cofounder (with Chester Bowles) of the legendary advertising agency Benton & Bowles; after the war he was an Assistant Secretary of State under Truman and then was elected senator from Connecticut. Galbraith immediately grasped the importance of the CED plan and arranged to make it the lead feature article in the December issue, titled "Taxes After the War." He also arranged to publish, a month earlier, Benton's policy declaration "The Economics of a Free Society," setting the larger context for the article that appeared in December.

America's senior business executives shifted away from a position that had been steadfast for decades—opposing deficit spending and government actions to ensure high levels of employment—to the very opposite.

It is, of course, too much to claim that *Fortune*'s editorial policies alone caused this phenomenal change. By 1945, all Americans were looking forward to peace—and most were expecting economic difficulties when it came. Lucrative government contracts were being curtailed, and fear of massive unemployment and even depression were in the air. But still, with Roosevelt's original agendas exhausted by 1944 or restructured by the imperatives of war, the recruitment of the country's business leaders to Keynesian views was truly important. And since there was little chance of re-creating the New Deal after the war, given the Republican gains in the Congress, the trust busters, old-style "national" planners, and Currie's Keynesian policy-makers faced a grim future. But in helping to convert many of the nation's most powerful business leaders to a new way of thinking, Galbraith, Luce, and *Fortune* laid the groundwork for a new liberalism in economic policy. As one historian of public policy has described it,

> The older ideal of national planning . . . was amorphous as an intellectual concept and, to many people, deeply unsettling in practice . . . Keynesian techniques had an appeal that planning did not. They were grounded in theory, and they suggested certain limits to governmental intervention. Rather than focusing on the performance of particular economic sectors, with the cumbersome idea of adjusting production in each industry . . . postwar economic policymakers would use the broader tools of federal spending, interest rates, and (on occasion) tax policy to stimulate or restrict aggregate demand.

The shift in approach helped to redefine the function of expertise in government and the qualifications that would be most valuable:

> The Keynesian approach also determined the main kinds of expertise (training in macroeconomics) and the sorts of analysis (aggregate economic analysis) that would be given the most weight in public policy debates. Postwar policymakers defined a much narrower economic role for the federal government than advocates of national planning had foreseen in the 1930s, but the effect was to create a much more secure place for economists in the government and to justify their advisory role not in terms of generalized knowledge, but as a consequence of specific professional skills.

Now, finally, unlike in preceding decades, "the economist's theory and analytic techniques were directly linked to policy measures that required the ongoing presence of economists in the government. For the first time, intellectual consensus on a social science theory of how the economy functioned had yielded broad agreement on its policy implications."[51]

The conversion of business leaders to Keynesian views became a triumph with complications, however. The policies that emerged after the war and continued through the 1950s eventually came to be labeled "commercial" or "military Keynesianism," and were roundly derided by many of Keynes's liberal followers as a heretical misuse of *The General Theory*. Others (including some of Keynes's closest colleagues) viewed the so-called Neoclassical Synthesis that was offered in the 1950s as a "refinement" of Keynes through the application of advanced mathematical techniques as a loss of Keynes's most original insights. But all these disputes lay in the future, and for now a thirty-six-year-old farm economist, who had changed jobs five times in five years, could feel that what he had done at OPA and *Fortune*, all things considered, was a not immodest achievement. But what would come next?

9

Surveying the Consequences of War

AT NOON ON THURSDAY, April 12, 1945, Franklin Roosevelt was sitting in the living room of his Warm Springs, Georgia, retreat. Wearing a double-breasted gray suit and crimson tie, he looked in "exceptionally good color," according to the painter Elizabeth Shoumatoff, who was at her easel nearby, finishing a portrait. As she worked, she chatted casually with a handful of others in the room, while FDR went through a thick stack of letters and documents, among them a letter from the State Department. Roosevelt read it, she remembered later, then laughed. "A typical State Department letter," he chuckled. "It says nothing at all."

At one o'clock, the butler came in to set up a table for lunch. The President, glancing at his watch, told Shoumatoff, "We've got just fifteen minutes more." Then, she recalled, "he raised his right hand and passed it over his forehead several times in a strange jerky way." Daisy Suckley, FDR's cousin, who was sitting nearby, thought perhaps he had dropped his cigarette. She got up and went over to him; he looked up and tried to smile at her, she recalled, but his face seemed furrowed in agony. "I have a terrific pain," he said softly, "in the back of my head." Then he collapsed.

The President's unconscious body was carried to his bedroom and his physician summoned; after a quick preliminary exam, the doctor realized there was little to do. Yet the unconscious Roosevelt kept fighting to remain alive—with "deep, steady, long gasps," an aide recalled. "His eyes were closed, mouth open—the awful breathing . . . [B]ut the Greek nose and the noble forehead were grand as ever."[1] Shortly after 3:30 p.m., the longest-serving President in American history—the only one ever elected to four terms in office, the man who had led the country through its greatest economic nightmare and to what would shortly be its greatest military victory—died. He was sixty-three.

In Washington, White House aides raced to find Mrs. Roosevelt and Vice President Truman. The First Lady was attending a piano recital at the Sulgrave Club when word reached her that she was "urgently" needed at the White House.

Harry Truman, meanwhile, presiding at the Senate, was discreetly scrawling a letter to his wife and daughter. "Dear Mama & Mary," he had begun on a white legal pad, "I am trying to write you a letter today . . . while a windy Senator . . . is making a speech on a subject with which he is no way familiar . . ."

Reaching the White House and told that her husband was dead, Mrs. Roosevelt sat quietly at first, then gathered herself and insisted on dictating a brief telegram to the couple's four sons, all on active duty overseas. "DARLINGS PA SLEPT AWAY THIS AFTERNOON. HE DID HIS JOB TO THE END AS HE WOULD WANT YOU TO DO. BLESS YOU. ALL OUR LOVE, MOTHER." By the time Truman arrived at the White House, not knowing why he'd been called, Mrs. Roosevelt had already changed into a black dress. She stepped forward to greet him, and placed her hand on his shoulder. "Harry," she said simply, "the President is dead." Truman found himself momentarily unable to speak.

At 5:47, the White House switchboard alerted the Associated Press, United Press, and the International News Service to get ready for an important conference call. The President's press secretary came on a moment later, waited briefly to be sure all three wire services were on the line, then slowly spoke: "This is Steve Early. I have a flash for you. The President died suddenly this afternoon at—" The INS didn't wait for Early to finish, and went on the wire first with just four words: "FLASH. WASHN—FDR DEAD." UP followed thirty seconds later, AP ninety seconds after that.[2]

In New York, Ken Galbraith was at his apartment on Riverside Drive when radio stations started breaking into their regular programming. He had left *Fortune*'s Rockefeller Center offices earlier than usual that afternoon, because he was leaving for Europe the next day on special duty. He'd been called back unexpectedly into government service a month earlier—just two years after leaving the Office of Price Administration—and was about to begin a then classified overseas assignment, and he needed to pack.[3] He and Kitty had decided to give a little good-bye party, and both were dressing for the evening when a friend called with the news.

Some of the party-goers hadn't yet heard of the President's death when they arrived at the Galbraiths', and their faces instantly turned from smiles to shock, then grief, and in some cases tears, as they were told what had happened. The evening went forward, but it was now more a solemn wake than a celebration. The guests stared pensively out on the dark Hudson River, or slowly turned to talk quietly, to reminisce and then gradually to speculate on what Roosevelt's death meant for the war, the country, and the world.[4]

In London, word of Roosevelt's death reached Churchill shortly after midnight. "I felt as if I had been struck a physical blow," he recalled later. Joseph Stalin, awakened at 3 a.m. by the U.S. ambassador, Averell Harriman, who'd rushed to the Kremlin to tell him personally of the news, held the envoy's hand silently for half a minute. After Harriman described the circumstances of Roosevelt's death, Stalin pressed him for assurances that an autopsy would be performed to determine whether the President had been poisoned.[5]

In Berlin, Joseph Goebbels rushed to Hitler's bunker to awaken his leader. Even as Russian artillery shells fell outside, Goebbels exclaimed triumphantly, "My Führer! I congratulate you! Roosevelt is dead! It is written in the stars that the second half of April will be the turning point for us. This is Friday 13 April. It *is* the turning point."[6]

Goebbels was right: it *was* a turning point—but not as he expected. Hitler's death was announced less than three weeks later, on May 1; Berlin fell to the Red Army the next day; on May 8, the remnants of what the Führer had promised the world would be a "thousand-year" Reich formally surrendered, 988 years sooner than planned.

Galbraith was in London when word came first of Hitler's death and then of V-E Day. The morning after Roosevelt's death, as the President's coffin was being loaded aboard a special train to begin its journey to Washington, he had himself boarded a train for the nation's capital. Then before dawn on April 15—while the Roosevelt train was making its way into Virginia past little stations and towns that even in the darkness were filled with mourners hoping to glimpse the passing cortège—he flew from the Naval Air Station in Patuxent, Maryland, on a military transport plane and, after nearly twenty-two hours of travel, arrived in London to take up his post as division head of what turned out to be a kind of autopsy. The subject of the "autopsy" was not a person but, rather, the German war effort, and also the effect that an entirely new factor in war had had upon its defeat.

For three years, the combined air forces of the United States and Great Britain had carried out a systematic bombing of the Nazi homeland, with American planes alone dropping nearly 1.4 million tons of high explosives on German factories, refineries, munitions plants, airfields, cities, rail lines, and roads.[7] The devastation in many cases had been extraordinary: the most celebrated target, the beautiful city of Dresden, had been literally incinerated, with losses greater, by some estimates, than those that would shortly be inflicted on Hiroshima or Nagasaki.

These air raids had been controversial for several reasons. One concerned the morality of targeting German cities and civilian populations.[8] A more technical, but no less important, issue was whether the bombing had worked. Simply put, had the enormous amounts of men, money, and materiel that had been poured into the bombing of Germany impaired the Nazi war machine and hastened the end of the war?

To answer this question, the War Department appointed a blue-ribbon, civilian-led investigative commission, the United States Strategic Bombing Survey, or USSBS.* The decisions to undertake such an investigation and also to place it in civilian hands hadn't been made lightly; in fact, they were the re-

---

*The USSBS confined itself to examining the impact of *American* bombing efforts. A combined Anglo-American survey was briefly considered but rejected, because it would then also require the inclusion of the Soviet Union as a partner and, worse, would assess the RAF's deliberate policy of bombing German cities, which was controversial. Most important, a joint study would draw attention away from finding an implicit justification for an independent U.S. Air Force based on the success of strategic bombing.

sult of a bitter division within the armed services and reflected deep mutual distrust.[9]

Assistant Secretary of War for Air Robert Lovett was crucial not only to the creation of the USSBS. A well-connected Wall Street investment banker at Brown Brothers, Harriman (and the son of the president of the Harrimans' Union Pacific railroad), Lovett had been a Navy combat pilot in World War I. He had taken part in early, primitive bombing attacks against German submarine pens in 1918 and firmly believed in strategic air power. Lovett wrote for FDR's signature the letter authorizing the formation of the Bombing Survey, and recruited its first director and top deputy directors. Lovett always knew what conclusions he wanted the Bombing Survey to reach.

Before and during the war, the Navy had adamantly opposed expansion of American strategic air power, which it considered a diversion of scarce budget resources and its own loss. Within the Army, the debate between advocates of traditional ground forces, who had accounted before the war for more than 90 percent of Army personnel, and the fledgling Army Air Corps was often no less controversial.[10]

In 1940, when Roosevelt had called for the United States swiftly to build 50,000 warplanes as part of its rearmament for "national defense," largely at Lovett's urging, he had come out heavily in favor of the tiny Army Air Corps, and intended three quarters of those 50,000 planes for it—a far cry from the 1,700 mostly obsolete aircraft the Corps had at the time.[11] But Lovett had then cut a deal with army chief General George Marshall—much to the consternation of the Army Air Corps—to block any further moves for an independent air force until the war's end, in exchange for greater operational autonomy for the airmen during the war. By September 1941, two months before Pearl Harbor, the renamed and now rapidly expanding Army Air Force had issued staff plans calling for an even greater buildup to more than 60,000 planes and 2.1 million airmen. In declaration of its faith in the power of "strategic bombing," the AAF's staff plans called for the bomber-based destruction of the German economy as its primary mission.[12] Lovett was a prime mover in support of round-the-clock bombing of Germany, and explicitly argued for attacks on civilian centers as a way to break German morale.

But shortly after the United States entered the war, doubts had emerged about the effectiveness of strategic bombing. The Luftwaffe had tried it in daylight during the Battle of Britain in 1940, but unsustainable losses had forced the Germans into nighttime raids, with a striking loss of accuracy and impact. The Royal Air Force had also tried strategic bombing but halted its operations in November 1941 after losing a fifth of its planes per raid and discovering that only one in four air crews that claimed to have hit their targets had actually dropped their bombs within five miles of them.[13]

The Americans didn't carry out their own first strategic raid until August 1942—against a rail yard near Rouen, in Nazi-occupied France. By then, the British had shifted RAF policy from "strategic" to "area" bombing, a decision behind which lay a grim and heated War Cabinet debate on whether to concentrate on inherently military targets or on the wholesale destruction of German cities and civilians. By the end of the war, RAF "area" bombing, to which Britain devoted a third of its entire war spending, had killed more than 400,000 unarmed German noncombatants. The cost of the policy to the British themselves was, however, not immaterial: more than 55,000 RAF airmen died in the war. (By one estimate, out of every one hundred RAF crewmen sent up against German targets, sixty died and only twenty-four escaped death, serious injury, or capture.[14]) The RAF Commander, Air Marshal Arthur Harris, whom an adoring British press dubbed "Bomber" Harris, among his own men carried a different and darker nickname: "Butch," for butcher.[15]

The Americans began bombing raids against Germany in June 1943 and elected, unlike the British by then, a "strategic" policy concentrated on Nazi war-fighting and war-making capacities. In making this choice, American military leaders expressed less a moral repugnance against attacking civilians* than a confidence that their heavily armored and armed B-17s and B-24s, flying in massive formations, could do greater damage in raids against Nazi factories and rail yards. Thus, by mutual agreement the British were left free to bomb cities at night, while the Americans concentrated on factories and other strategic targets most often by day.

Almost from the start, the American plan showed major flaws. General H. H. "Hap" Arnold, the Army Air Force chief—like his civilian boss, Secretary Lovett—was passionately eager to prove the worth of strategic bombing, and exerted enormous pressure on U.S. commanders in England "to get the ball rolling." But with their flight crews and command staff still green, the lumbering B-17s and B-24s sent over Germany without fighter escorts (which until 1944 lacked fuel range for the task) took enormous losses. A fifth of the bombers ordered to attack ball-bearing plants at Schweinfurt and Regensburg in August and October 1943 never returned, and many of those that did had to be scrapped because they were so heavily damaged. At the height of this first phase of the American air war, one Army medical study found that 60 percent of airmen sent up were killed, wounded, or missing in action; only one in four completed a twenty-five-flight tour of duty.[16] The Americans called a halt and began to regroup, even though Arnold and Lovett were worried less about the casualties than about the weakening of faith in strategic bombing. Arnold had actually expected much higher casualties.[17]

In early 1944, with new or redesigned long-range fighter escorts at their side, and new tactics devised by a rising Army Air Force star, a cigar-chomping young bulldog of a colonel named Curtis LeMay, the bombers of the Eighth and Fifteenth Air Forces were once again sent aloft to attack German aircraft and ball-bearing plants. This time the raids lost many fewer men and machines, and were a success in a second sense: the Luftwaffe lost control of the skies over Germany; more than 600 German fighter planes and nearly 300 of

---

*Later in the war, the United States attacked Japanese cities with phosphorous-laden "fire bombs," inflicting massive civilian casualties.

its pilots were eliminated. By early spring, the Americans were carrying out their bombing raids virtually unimpeded by enemy air attacks.[18]

But now a new problem emerged: General Eisenhower, reviewing the effectiveness of both British "area" and American "strategic" bombing as D-Day approached, found that little of Germany's crucial war-making capacities had actually been destroyed. A fierce senior staff battle over targeting priorities ensued (and continued even after the ground invasion of France began). The Americans favored "the Oil Plan," which focused on eliminating German sources and supplies of petroleum, whereas the British pushed "the Transportation Plan," which concentrated on German rail and road systems. In classic wartime fashion both plans were eventually pursued, along with a third, for the destruction of German airbases and aircraft plants, right to the war's end.[19]

Despite their divided and often conflicting priorities, to both RAF and U.S. Army Air Force commanders there seemed reason for great satisfaction by then, given the initially poor showing that aerial bombing had made. By the time Germany surrendered, Allied intelligence reports claimed that four fifths of Nazi refinery and synthetic-oil plants had been rendered inoperable and that U.S. and British bombers had hit virtually all key rail lines and yards, bridges, and roads. The German Air Force meanwhile—once the most powerful in Europe—appeared to be in ruins. Having commenced an almost entirely new and unproven era in modern warfare with what seemed at times a string of near disasters, strategic air power by early 1945 had become an overwhelming success.

Or had it?

THAT WAS THE question that Ken Galbraith, as one of the civilian chiefs of the U.S. Strategic Bombing Survey, came to London to answer. (Technically, he wasn't a civilian, having been given a temporary commission as a colonel in the Army Air Force; the status and uniform proved invaluable at opening military doors.) The USSBS was officially a presidential commission, charged with determining whether the Army Air Force's primary strategic mission, established before Pearl Harbor, had been achieved, and at what cost. It also had to address a second, hugely controversial issue—controversial, not least, within the U.S. military command and the huge weapons industry that had grown up almost overnight around it.

Army airmen had chafed for nearly three decades under the control of "ground men": the United States, alone among the major powers fighting in the war, did not have a separate air force. Its commanders had won a measure of independence for the AAF, but given its size, budget, and separate strategic priorities, what they wanted most was a real and final break with the foot soldiers. A U.S. Air Force with power, prestige, and standing equal to the Army and Navy was the goal. If strategic bombing was judged a success, that goal could be theirs.

Initially conceived as a job for "a small committee" of air force officers, by the time the USSBS went into full operation in early 1945, more than

700 civilian and 500 military personnel were at work, allocated among a dozen separate duties that roughly conformed to the AAF's target categories: transportation, oil, utilities, munitions, and German civil defense and civilian morale.[20]

As a sign of the significance they gave the group, Harvard President James Conant had been Secretary Lovett's and General Arnold's first choice to head the Survey. But Conant's wartime "boss," Vannevar Bush, who was in charge of all military-related U.S. science, refused to release him from his top-secret work with the Manhattan Project.[21] Lovett and Arnold eventually settled on Franklin D'Olier, the affable, elderly chairman of Prudential Insurance, who'd been the American Legion's first national commander. Operationally, however, they made sure the USSBS was run not by D'Olier but by Henry Alexander, a tall, elegant, and handsome young Southerner who was both a Yale-trained lawyer and senior partner at J. P. Morgan.* Under Alexander, a secretariat of three Boston lawyers (including Charles Cabot of *the* Boston Cabots) had the job of summarizing the Bombing Survey's findings.[22] The trio was hardly a representative cross-section of the American population and gave off every sign of producing preordained conclusions.

Of the eleven division directors under D'Olier and Alexander, Galbraith had perhaps the most difficult and sensitive task: to evaluate the "Overall Economic Effects" of American bombing. The team he quickly assembled for the job included some of the most important and influential young economists of the time, among them Nicholas Kaldor, Tibor Scitovsky, Paul Baran, and Edward Dennison.[23] Working initially out of offices in London's Grosvenor Square, the USSBS soon redeployed most of its personnel (including Galbraith) into occupied Germany, to the little spa town of Bad Nauheim, just

---

*Alexander knew the American and European arms industry. At the New York law firm of Davis, Polk, he'd been the lawyer for J. P. Morgan, Jr., during the Nye Committee investigations in 1936—the infamous "merchant of death" hearings in the U.S. Senate. Senator Nye, a Midwestern populist and isolationist, fearing U.S. involvement in a second world war, had wanted to show in detail what J. P. Morgan & Co. and other Wall Street firms had done in engineering America's entry into the war in 1916. He strongly suspected the bankers had acted out of concern for their massive loans to Britain, Russia, and France and for their heavy financing of U.S. arms manufacturers such as Winchester, Remington, and DuPont. Almost all of what he suspected turned out to be true: shortly after war broke out in 1914, the three European powers had quietly appointed Morgan as their U.S. financial representative (quietly, because the job was illegal under U.S. neutrality laws), and Britain had used Morgan to buy (also illegally) more than $3 billion in military supplies. As a result of those purchases, for a time the bank owned on London's behalf three quarters of all U.S. copper supplies. Morgan even served as an industrial spy for Britain, at one point blocking the buyout of Bethlehem Steel by German investors; the bank also served as a stock agent for Whitehall, selling into the New York markets $3 billion of English-owned shares in U.S. companies, with the proceeds used to finance the British war effort.

Testifying before the Nye Committee, Morgan (guided by Alexander) had played down the bank's pecuniary interests, instead emphasizing its loyalty to Britain and displaying a naive innocence concerning the popular indignation this aroused.

Nye's hearings were meant to keep the United States out of a second world war, but by 1944, none of this was of any interest to the Army Air Force or to Alexander's friend Lovett. Meanwhile, it should be noted, the Morgan partner in charge of Britain's massive illegal U.S. arms buying in 1916–18 had been Edward Stettinius, and it was his son, Edward junior, who did the same for Britain in 1940, when Roosevelt sold millions of dollars of "surplus" government arms "scrap" to U.S. Steel, the company Stettinius chaired, which then promptly resold the scrap to London.

north of Frankfurt. There he and George Ball comfortably shared a small private hotel, while the other men were billeted at a somewhat larger spa resort nearby, with its own German staff of seven; here the Bombing Survey's offices were also established.* As the Allied troops advanced, there was a race to capture key Nazi documents and personnel that were at risk of destruction or dispersal by Germans, by invading troops, and by the hordes of refugees wandering across Europe. With the Russian Army in control of eastern Germany (including Berlin), there was the additional issue of getting material before the Soviets did. Two of Galbraith's men sneaked into the Soviet-guarded former Nazi Air Ministry in Berlin one night to crack a safe containing the Germans' crucial top-secret evaluation of the Allied bombing's effects before the Russians came upon it.[24]

As the Survey teams pored over the immense caches of documents they managed to recover, and interrogated German officials who had managed war production, a startling picture emerged. Despite the steady and ever-increasing Anglo-American bombing, the Nazis' production of vital armaments had *increased*, not decreased. For example, the manufacture of tanks, self-propelled guns, and assault guns averaged 136 per month in 1940; 316 in 1941; and 516 in 1942. When Allied bombing began in earnest in 1943, production didn't fall but rose to 1,005, and then again in 1944 to 1,583; in the last months of the war, in 1945, output had been only slightly below the previous year's peak.[25]

Similarly, German plants kept increasing the production of combat aircraft throughout the war despite the Allies' massive and ever-escalating air attacks. In February 1944, every known air-frame plant in Germany had come under severe and coordinated assault, with heavy American bomber losses despite significant fighter escorts. Yet Luftwaffe fighter and bomber production *rose* by more than 10 percent between January and March that year, to more than 2,200 planes a month; by September, output was nearly double what it had been before the attacks.[26] Even the special targeting of oil and rail facilities after D-Day did little more than slow the German army and air force, rather than cripple them. Troop movements were sometimes delayed but never halted, and gasoline was harder to find but never in amounts that hindered a major campaign.

Overall, Galbraith and his staff discovered, German war production had increased massively throughout the war, tripling between early 1942 and late

---

*Ball appreciated the relative safety of Germany. In London not long before the move, he'd been bathing. "Just when I was well covered with soap, the sky fell in. My bathroom had a casement window I had left ajar; it was blown wide open with an explosive thud that seriously strained my ear drums. Seconds later, as the debris that had been blown skyward began to crash, I heard people running compulsively up and down the hall, shouting and laughing idiotically. My first thought was of an air burst, but when I opened the bathroom door, the floor, the bed, the entire living room were covered with shattered glass, while the casement windows hung limply like Daliesque watches, swinging slowly back and forth.

"A V-2 had fallen a hundred yards away within a few feet of the Marble Arch. Had I not altered course while dressing, I would have formed part (or parts) of the debris blown wildly into the air—as, indeed, happened to one poor fellow, various pieces of whose anatomy decorated surrounding trees and bushes" (Ball, *The Past Has Another Pattern*, 48–49).

1944 and remaining at high levels until just before the final surrender.[27] If indeed the primary mission of the Army Air Force had been to destroy Germany's war-making capacities, this was disconcerting news: by Galbraith's estimate, only 5 percent of the damage inflicted by the Allies had been by the AAF.

These troubling conclusions emerged not just from the captured documents, which at times could be faulted for incompleteness, having been scattered or damaged, but also from interviews with German officials, including Albert Speer.[28] A tall, handsome figure of supreme confidence, Speer, an architect by profession, according to Galbraith was "charming, cultivated, and intelligent." Appointed by Hitler as head of German armaments and war production in 1942, by all accounts he'd done a spectacular job for the Third Reich. Much trusted by the Nazi leader, Speer was among the handful who celebrated Hitler's birthday in his Berlin bunker days before the war's end. In the confusing final days of the war Speer had joined the caretaker government of Admiral Karl Dönitz in a small resort town fifty miles north of Hamburg. He had taken refuge in Schloss Glücksburg, an immense, luxurious (and undamaged) sixteenth-century castle overlooking the Baltic Sea near the Danish border that came complete with a moat, turrets, and a drawbridge. There he was surrounded by well-armed Nazi soldiers, and no one had yet bothered to detain him. Galbraith, alerted by Ball on May 19 of Speer's whereabouts and fearful he might flee, rushed along with Ball and Paul Nitze to interrogate him.[29]

The next few days proved to be a singular adventure from beginning to end. As Ball later wrote of their colorful arrival, as their plane touched down,

> Flensburg airport was crowded with Luftwaffe planes in various stages of disrepair and with Luftwaffe officers still quite intact. Soldiers with swastikas on their caps were pursuing a busy routine as though Germany had never surrendered, while . . . the handful of Allied troops at the field seemed uncertain whether they were conquerors or guests. They were trying hard to avoid diplomatic *gaffes* but had only the vaguest of instructions . . .
>
> We stood about awkwardly, blinking in the cold morning air. An RAF squadron leader approached with two men in gray uniforms and we shook hands all around; only when the two men responded in German gutterals did we note the insignia on their caps . . .
>
> [Suddenly] a caravan wound slowly toward our plane. It consisted of four conscripted cars with German drivers led by a curious kind of gypsy wagon, which I recognized as [a U.S.] major's jeep, long a legend in the area. In his movements throughout the Twenty-First Army Group, the major carried a fantastic inventory of merchandise that he turned over with a velocity to put Macy's and Gimbel's in awe. Those trade goods, constantly replenished, were contained in four captured ammunition cases welded on the sides and back of the jeep. It was the least military-looking vehicle in the theater . . .
>
> After lunch we set out for Glucksburg . . . Our vehicle was an oversized Mercedes-Benz, on which no one had yet bothered to paint an American

Army identification; it was driven by a young Jewish lieutenant . . . Without advance notice, he introduced me to a game he had invented: he would bear down on the barricades at fifty miles an hour, put his head out of the front window, and shout in angry German, "Out of the way, you swine." The SS guards would raise their Sten guns and advance toward the middle of the road, while I speculated in a detached way whether we would crash into the gates before the bullets crashed into us. But, with the implausible timing of a . . . movie serial, the guards would recognize our American uniforms just in time to leap to the side and jerk up the gates as our car scraped under.[30]

Arriving at the castle, the men presented themselves to a butler, who went solemnly off in search of Speer. Several minutes passed before the butler returned to lead them to him. Speer, surprised by the men's arrival, greeted them in the castle's Great Hall dressed in a brown Wehrmacht uniform. "I'm glad you've come," he said. "I was afraid I've been forgotten." After hearing why the men had come, and that they had no immediate plans to arrest him, he quickly decided to cooperate, and agreed to describe in detail the wartime German economy's performance. (Galbraith remarked to Ball that Speer, only forty years old, looked like a young college professor and "like any professor, he enjoyed an audience.") That afternoon and evening, and then over the next several days, as Speer talked, it became apparent that Germany, far from being highly mobilized in the early war years, had operated well below its economic capacities. Few factories had ever run a night shift, nor was the workweek even significantly lengthened (he said aircraft manufacturers hadn't gone to a second shift until 1944). Nor had women been recruited for war production; there had been no Nazi version of "Rosie the Riveter." (This, Galbraith noted, was due to the availability of slave labor and imported foreign workers, voluntary and otherwise, a point on which Speer did not dwell.) Even domestic servants had remained in ample supply throughout the war—1.5 million of them, only a slight reduction from prewar levels.

When Allied bombing intensified in 1944, Speer proudly continued, the Germans showed great energy and resourcefulness in dispersing, reorganizing, and repairing their damaged plants. As Galbraith observed, they often pulled machinery "out from under the rubble, and then got it going again in neighborhood schools, halls, churches or wherever space was available." At the peak of Allied attacks, 350,000 men were engaged in repair of Germany's huge synthetic oil plants, in their dispersal, and in construction of immense underground storage facilities impervious to air attack.[31]

By the summer, the Survey's staff had pored over hundreds of thousands of pages of captured documents, visited hundreds of wartime plants and factories, and interviewed several thousand German officials, from Speer down to plant shift managers. The conclusion they were gradually coming to was disquieting: strategic bombing of Germany hadn't in fact succeeded in destroying—or even in seriously hindering—the Germans' war production capacities.

Senior Army Air Force officers and civilian officials were deeply alarmed.

They had been initially in favor of a dispassionate analysis by independent experts; now they decided to rush out their own evaluation. Working overtime, AAF intelligence units produced "The Contribution of Air Power to the Defeat of Germany."* It admiringly described the operational struggle to gain air supremacy over Germany and the tactical and ground support efforts that the AAF had carried out in addition to its strategic bombing mission. Circulated in mimeographed form to senior military and civilian officials in Europe and Washington, the slender work was meant to blunt what the Air Force feared would be the implications of the Bombing Survey's much more detailed research.[32]

Appalled by this preemption of their own work, the directors of the Bombing Survey found themselves in June in a second struggle they were unprepared for: over the final bombing of Japan. Unaware that the top-secret Manhattan Project was by then rushing to complete the world's first nuclear bomb, several of the Survey directors (though not Galbraith) were flown back to Washington. In a Pentagon meeting with sixty or so military officers, then with General Marshall and the secretaries of war and the navy, they were closely interrogated on what targeting priorities should be set for the showdown with Japan. At first, they hedged their answers, not only because their own work was still unfinished but because they knew Japan's war industries were differently organized and located than Germany's. But they quickly abandoned circumspection when they realized that the prevailing wisdom in Washington favored continuation of the massive incendiary raids by giant B-29s already under way on Japanese cities that were filled with defenseless civilians.† Fresh from scenes of horrendous destruction in Germany, the Survey's directors spoke out as strongly as they dared for a focus not on cities but on transportation—rail lines and coastal shipping—followed by oil and chemical plants and national electrical grids.

The facts they presented on strategic bombing's failure in Germany were irrefutable, but they were heavily resisted. After several weeks of intense arguments with Pentagon planners, the directors thought they'd succeeded in getting their goals incorporated into new orders the Pentagon sent to the Pacific Theater's air commanders. But the victory was pyrrhic: the orders reached Pacific headquarters too late to halt the massive incendiary attacks that killed more Japanese civilians in the closing months of the war than the combined nuclear attacks on Hiroshima and Nagasaki.[33]

As the war with Japan rushed toward its inexorable conclusion—Hiroshima

---

*This intelligence document was known inside the AAF as "The Coffin Report," after its author, a Lieutenant Colonel Coffin. The military's obliviousness to the irony of the title, Galbraith later remarked, was greater than usual.

†The AAF's Japanese campaign was designed and directed by (now) General LeMay. After the war, he directed the fabled Berlin Airlift in 1948–49, then created the Strategic Air Command. Under President Kennedy, he was Air Force chief of staff, and advocated with frightening frequency the use of nuclear weapons in Vietnam, Laos, and Cuba. Retired from the Air Force, in the 1968 presidential race he was George Wallace's running mate. His notoriety allegedly made him the model for Buck Turgeson, the nuclear-trigger-happy general in Stanley Kubrick's film *Dr. Strangelove*.

was struck on August 6; Nagasaki, three days later—the Bombing Survey rushed to complete its massive work, a ten-volume study more than 3,000 pages long.[34] While Galbraith and his team labored in Europe to finish the "Overall Economic Effects" section, in Washington Charles Cabot and his fellow lawyers were separately preparing their own "summary report." Galbraith and George Ball were both stunned when they saw a draft of it: carefully composed to give an overall positive evaluation of the Army Air Force's achievements in Germany, it fundamentally contradicted the painstaking conclusions the full report would show. They appealed to Henry Alexander for a chance to return to Washington and redraft the summary. Alexander—who, according to Galbraith, was upset less with the summary's conclusions than with its "abysmal level of literacy"—somewhat reluctantly agreed, and so over the next several days, holed up in the Cosmos Club, Galbraith with Ball's help labored on the rewrite. "By giving way on the nonessentials, we kept the basic case . . . Strategic bombing had not won the war. At most, it had eased somewhat the task of the ground troops who did."

The battle over conclusions didn't end with their redraft of the summary; instead it moved into high gear. Cabot and the other lawyers counterattacked, disputing Galbraith sentence by sentence, and they were joined by General Orvil Anderson, deputy chief of the Army Air Force in Europe. At times, the debates grew bitter; years later Galbraith recalled telling Anderson at one point, "General, this is just a matter of intellectual honesty," to which Anderson replied, "Goddamn it, Ken, you carry intellectual honesty to extremes."[35]

In the end, Galbraith claims to have (mostly) prevailed, though the final overall summary was not as critical as he'd hoped. Nonetheless, it made what he felt were the key points:

> German war production had, indeed, expanded under the bombing. The greatly heralded efforts, those on the ball-bearing and aircraft plants for example, emerged as costly failures. Other operations, those against oil and the railroads, did have military effect.
>
> But strategic bombing had not won the war. At most, it had eased somewhat the task of the ground troops who did. The aircraft, manpower and bombs used in the campaign had cost the American economy far more in output than they had cost Germany. However, our economy being much larger, we could afford it. A final paragraph or two written by Henry Alexander somewhat overstated the contribution of air power to the outcome without altering the basic facts. The purposes of both history and future policy would have been served by a more dramatic finding of failure, for this would have better prepared us for the costly ineffectiveness of the bombers in Korea and Vietnam, and we might have been spared the reproach of civilized opinion. Still, no essential information was concealed or seriously compromised.

Whether in fact the "Overall Effects Summary" was as clear as Galbraith says is debatable. It *does* make his key points, but it also makes Cabot's and

Anderson's, leaving an unwary reader with a more affirmative impression of air power than Galbraith claims. It requires reading the long-term effects study that Galbraith himself had directed, "which made all the basic points, [and] was published without censorship of any kind, to grasp fully just how limited the impact of bombing had been."[36]

IN EARLY SEPTEMBER 1945, word of the still-secret and still-uncompleted Bombing Survey study began leaking out to the press. Hanson Baldwin of *The New York Times* noted obliquely that it was already being greeted "with astonishment and some concern by some of the older and conservative officers in both the War and Navy Departments," who feared the precedent might lead to "similar reviews and critiques of ground and naval campaigns." The study, he said, might not in fact be declassified.[37] But Baldwin's article—and a column by Drew Pearson that suggested that several American businessmen assigned to the USSBS had stolen German patents and plant designs for use by their own companies*—got lost amid much larger news. The very day Baldwin's article appeared, the Japanese surrendered in Tokyo Bay on the decks of the U.S.S. *Missouri*.

By late October, a copy of a USSBS introductory report (not the Galbraith summary) fell into the hands of another journalist, who quite accurately conveyed its conclusions, which were generally Galbraith's and Ball's views, not Cabot's and Anderson's. Alarmed Air Force officials pressed to contain what they feared would be ever-spreading damage. A hastily organized Pentagon press conference was convened, where Henry Alexander, contrary to the detailed findings of his own men and clearly under pressure, told reporters that "Allied air power" had "brought the [German] economy which sustained the enemy's armed forces to virtual collapse. . . . It brought home to the German people the full impact of modern war with all its horror and suffering. Its imprint on the German nation will be lasting." Alexander's meticulous choice of words was artful layering at its best: he did not actually claim this was the result of "strategic bombing" or of "American" efforts, and spoke only of "Allied" efforts and "air power" broadly, strategic and tactical alike. General Anderson, standing a few feet away, fully grasped Alexander's qualifications, and feared lest the newsmen might catch on as well.

But in the exuberance following V-J Day, reporters and editors never even noticed. Headline writers instead rushed to celebrate the victory of the U.S. Army Air Force and its strategic-bombing doctrine. The next morning, the *New York Herald Tribune* declared "Strategic Bombing Is Termed Decisive in Victory"; *The Philadelphia Inquirer*'s headline read "Air Power Beats Reich, D'Olier Survey Finds"; the *Washington Times-Herald* announced "Bombers Beat Germany Civilian Survey Finds."[38] Despite Galbraith's and Ball's efforts

---

*When Galbraith testified as a defense witness for Daniel Ellsberg in the Pentagon Papers Trial in 1973, discussing "leaks," he admitted he had been the source of the Pearson column.

honestly to cast the summary report to express the true conclusions of the immense research they had done, the journalists mostly relied on Alexander's oral summary. "Sound-bite" journalism triumphed over sound research.

Had Galbraith been at the Pentagon briefing, there's a solid likelihood that a different story might have emerged. But he was in Tokyo, where he'd been suddenly ordered to work on a second round of the USSBS, rushing to evaluate the effect of strategic bombing on Japan's defeat. Ten thousand miles from Washington, Galbraith faced what he called a scene of "unspeakable gloom." Here Alexander's press conference seemed eerily even more distant than it was. Germany had presented sights of unimaginable devastation, but they paled by comparison to Japan.

Although only a tenth of the bomb tonnage that struck Germany had rained down on its Asian ally, the work had been done by the giant new B-29 Superfortresses, carrying new and highly explosive incendiary weapons developed during the war by Harvard scientists. Ninety percent of Japanese homeland targets—sixty of the sixty-six cities the B-29s struck—had been attacked only in the last three months of the war. And, in an operational and moral reversal of America's reluctance to use "area bombing" in Europe, barely a fifth of the bombs the Americans dropped were targeted on industrial sites of any military importance.[39]

In one night of bombing alone, for example, American Superfortresses had laid waste to Tokyo. Coming in at low levels to assure accuracy, wave after wave of B-29s had poured down their payloads, creating a firestorm that swept through sixteen square miles of the Japanese capital; 250,000 homes and buildings were destroyed, 125,000 Japanese killed or wounded, and 1 million more left homeless.* "The most devastating single air attack in history," as one historian put it, "it exceeded all expectations." Eighty percent of Tokyo's industrial area, however, remained untouched by the attack.[40] Two months later 800 B-29s burned a two-mile-wide swath that ran twenty-one miles from Tokyo to Yokohama.

The USSBS Japan team quickly discovered that the airborne destruction of Japan's war-making capacities had been even less significant than in Germany. Japan lacked the resources to sustain its war-fighting capacity and had drawn its rubber, petroleum, bauxite, and iron ore mainly from captured nations and colonies in Southeast Asia. As the Navy, Army, and Marines had fought their way north toward Japan, they had cut off those territories; combined with the Navy's assault on Japanese shipping (especially by submarine), this had

---

*U.S. commanders, including General Arnold, understood exactly what they were doing by shifting to the bombing of Japanese cities—and its consequences for civilians. At Elgin Field in Florida, the AAF had carefully tested materials and construction techniques used for the housing of Japanese workers, then staged a series of mock bombing raids. First, the rate at which the resulting fires spread was measured. Then firefighters were sent in at staged intervals to quench the fires. Eventually an optimal mix of high explosives and incendiaries was discovered that would make Japanese fire-fighting impossible, leaving the blaze unchecked and out of control. The AAF set its bombing routines accordingly (see Futrell, *Ideas, Concepts, Doctrines*, 84, and Schaeffer, *Wings of Judgement*, 114–16).

stripped Japan of its war-making ability. The firebombing of Japanese cities in the last months of the war helped to induce surrender, but that was hardly the same as "destroying the Japanese economy," let alone "winning the war."

The Survey's study of Japan opened with a blunt warning:

> Blockade [especially by submarines] and bombing together deprived Japanese forces of about four months' munitions production. That production could have made a substantial difference in Japan's ability to cause us losses had we invaded but could not have affected the outcome of the war . . . The outcome of the war was decided in the waters of the Pacific and on the landing beaches of invaded islands.[41]

On the question of whether bombing—including atomic bombing—had induced Japan's surrender, the Survey was no less forthright:

> Based on a detailed investigation of all the facts, and supported by testimony of the surviving Japanese leaders involved, it is the Survey's opinion that certainly prior to 31 December 1945, and in all probability prior to 1 November 1945, Japan would have surrendered even if the atomic bombs had not been dropped, even if Russia had not entered the war, and even if no invasion had been planned or contemplated.[42]

In an early draft of the Survey's "economic effects" findings, Galbraith tried to strengthen these already stunning evaluations. In one sentence summarizing the "conclusions to be derived from this miserable business," there is a hand-drawn line through the word "miserable" and, penciled in above, the word "appalling." But none of this appeared in the final report.[43]

General Anderson, who had followed Galbraith to Tokyo to represent the Army Air Force's interests in the Survey, took bitter exception even to much of what did appear, and insisted he and his staff be allowed to include a separate summary report. In it, he insisted:

> Airpower was the dominant combat force of the war against Japan and was decisive in that—
> Airpower dominated its own element.
> Airpower dominated naval warfare.
> Airpower dominated ground warfare.
> Airpower possessed powerful and independent logistical capabilities.
> Airpower established effective area interdiction by occupation over an objective area.
> Airpower was capable of forcing the capitulation of an enemy without surface invasion.[44]

The Army and Navy, needless to say, were irate over this subordination of their own work, not to mention the mendacious and undifferentiated inclusion of the Navy's carrier-based planes and the Army's and Marine's tactical fighters and fighter-bombers in Anderson's sweeping victory declaration for "air power."

The Survey's work in Japan enormously pleased Army Air Force commanders in one regard: its "Recommendations" for the future. The key one was precisely what the commanders had hoped for: "Within a department of common defense which provides unity of command and is itself oriented toward air and new weapons, the Survey believes that, in addition to the Army and Navy, there should be an equal and coordinate position for a third establishment."[45] "Reading these words," an Air Force historian later remarked, "one can see them all—[AAF commanders] Arnold, Spaatz, Eaker, Fairchild, Kuter, Anderson, joined by many of their colleagues and the ghost of Billy Mitchell—leap to their feet in resounding applause."[46]

By the time these words were written, Galbraith had already been sent home along with most of the rest of the 1,100-member team. The Survey's endorsement, drafted under Paul Nitze, in effect became the Emancipation Proclamation of the U.S. Air Force as an independent service.*

Back in New York with his family for Christmas, Galbraith enjoyed not only the holidays at home after months of grim war work, but the professional pleasure of seeing two important articles by him appear in print. In *Fortune*, "Germany Was Badly Run" set out an important part of the conclusions he and his Survey team had reached; that Germany had initially undermobilized and that war production had continued at a high and increasing pace until nearly the end of the war.[47] By carefully avoiding any mention of Army Air Force claims that "strategic bombing" had been vital in Hitler's defeat, the article focused its readers on the Nazis' problems in internal management and resource allocation and left serious doubts as to airpower's role in Germany's defeat.

In *Life*, Galbraith recapitulated, with less technical detail, essentially the same message. "The Interrogation of Albert Speer" set forth again the USSBS's fundamental conclusions about the Nazi-run German economy, and here too he avoided direct confrontation with the AAF and its claim of "victory" in practice and doctrine.[48] Still, a careful reader of either article would have understood Germany's failures in the economic conduct of the war.[49]

In "Japan's Road Back," which appeared in *Fortune* in March 1946, Galbraith again discussed wartime economic mobilization, but this time he specifically stressed the ineffectuality of strategic bombing.[50] He gave full credit to the Navy's interdiction of Japanese shipping and noted the survival rates of Japanese industrial plants and factories, railroads, and electrical generating

---

*Nitze's underlying views were well formed. As his biographers remark,

> Nitze was one of the first Americans to see the rubble of Hiroshima and Nagasaki. Curiously, however, he was not overwhelmed by the devastation. His task, he later recalled, was to "measure precisely" the impact of the bomb—"to put calipers on it, instead of describing it in emotive terms." While others saw the bomb as the ultimate proof of the futility of war, Nitze saw it as a weapon that could and probably would be used again. The damage in Hiroshima, he reckoned, was simply the equivalent of an incendiary bombing raid by 210 B-29s (Isaacson and Thomas, *Wise Men*, 485).

equipment—in stark contrast to the horrific civilian losses and barren devastation that U.S. bombing had wrought on Japan's cities.

GALBRAITH TOOK WITH HIM from the Bombing Survey many important lessons. Once again, as at OPA, events had driven home the sharp differences between economic theory (and policy) and actual economic performance. Roosevelt's often haphazard efforts at mobilization were in sharp contrast to the systematic preparations undertaken in Germany and Japan, and showed the differences between democratic power and authoritarian dictatorships. Yet the dictatorships, despite extensive and detailed planning, repeatedly misjudged crucial priorities and plans and often failed to implement them.

Galbraith also took from the Survey a new understanding of the limits of mathematically modeled behavior, a novelty in World War II. During the war years, a coterie of talented young American economists had gathered around a brilliant refugee figure, the Dutch economist Tjalling Koopmans, who had been trained in physics and mathematics and during the war worked in Washington at an obscure agency called the Combined Shipping Adjustment Board. In Holland, Koopmans, working under Jan Tinbergen, had pioneered the development of "linear programming," work that would later win him a Nobel Prize in Economics.[51] The young economists, using Koopmans's sophisticated mathematical modeling, had operationalized his work to solve shipping-allocation problems that had until then bedeviled the effort to supply American troops overseas. After the war, Koopmans and his team proudly pointed to this work as evidence of how rigorous new modeling tools could advance the understanding and planning of a host of peacetime problems.

During the war, the Army Air Force had drawn on several variants of Koopmans's early linear-programming models for shipping not only to analyze and optimize aircraft and weapons production and related resource allocations but to select and rank enemy targets.[52] This work was directed by a group of "Whiz Kids," ten preternaturally bright and intense young men, among whom perhaps the best known in later years was Robert McNamara, who went on to be the president of the Ford Motor Company, secretary of defense, and head of the World Bank.*[53] The relative precision that "linear programming" gave to decisions on allocating resources, when for any number of reasons options are constrained, was greatly admired, and a new generation of economists adapted it, helping to spread the "mathematicizing" of postwar economic theory.[54]

Galbraith, however, saw it differently. The seeming exactness of linear pro-

---

*McNamara's first job was to set up the system that, amazingly, told the AAF how many planes it had and mandated a daily inventory of the number, type, disposition, and condition of all aircraft, down to individual serial numbers. Transferred to England in 1943, McNamara persuaded the Eighth Air Force to concentrate on using the B-17 rather than the newer and more powerful B-24. Later, using carefully drawn statistics, he was able to convince Air Force commanders that the new B-29s were the "optimal instrument" for the firebombing of Japan, six times more effective than B-17s and B-24s. Nowhere, it seems, was the morality of firebombing cities raised as an issue. McNamara's ultimate disillusionment over the war in Vietnam led him to rethink this earlier work. "Had we lost World War II," he pensively told the filmmaker Errol Morris in 2002, "LeMay and I probably would have been tried as war criminals."

gramming might easily deceive its practitioners, he came to realize, especially in fluid or ambiguous contexts. At OPA, the problem had been the inevitable, very large one of contested power—between the government's attempts to restrain inflation on the one hand, and, on the other, the producers' inevitable resistance to these efforts and their desire to maximize their own interests. Workers, too, could be a problem for inflation fighters, when they saw others make what they viewed as "unfair" profits, or when their work was adversely rewarded if calculated in terms of income or consumer goods: unanticipated strikes or slowdowns or even routine "shirking" could disrupt the best-designed production flow charts. Consumers, too, were hard to account for—when, for example, they turned to black-market sources of supply to avoid rationing. The struggle to control inflation was a charged political problem as well as an economic one, and linear programming or mathematically elegant economic models could not anticipate the outcome of political battles. In such situations, they had the advantage of clarity but not of reality, and fell short of useful or stable applicability.

Linear programming could in theory work to better effect in the context of the military's logistical activity. Order and discipline could be imposed; goals were quantifiable in measurable terms of numbers of men, volumes and forms of equipment. But here, too, the apparent exactitude of priorities—in Koopmans's work, the optimal schedule for loading ships or calculating which harbors could handle what levels of traffic at given times was misleading: solutions were offered to problems that affected many trees in a much larger forest. Disagreement over strategies, coordination of conflicting goals, breakdown in achieving certain goals that then harmed others—all these affected economic performance, whether of specific allocation or of overall output.

Albert Speer's descriptions of the petty bickering and frequent incompetence of top Nazi officials impressed on Galbraith that the qualities and capacities of leaders also greatly affected a society's economic achievement. Linear programming and mathematically abstracted modeling of resource allocations nowhere captured these issues—or even asked questions about them.

"Economics" in short could not be considered in isolation from the human world of politics, institutions, and power. The behavior of individuals and groups repeatedly violated orthodox economists' prized axiom of "rational maximizing" of self-interest. On the one hand, the future had inherent uncertainties that no individual or group of individuals could successfully anticipate. On the other, constant negotiation and bargaining in decision making ensured that goals and preferences were subject to frequent and dramatic reevaluation and change, with less-than-optimal outcomes for all parties. Galbraith had learned these lessons before—the fight over the Agricultural Adjustment Administration's domestic allotments to black sharecroppers being the first dramatic example. But his war experiences broadened his understanding of their applicability.

The war also reinforced his Keynesian worldview. Private economic forces—businesses, corporations, labor, consumers—left to their own devices did not smoothly create even in peacetime the vaunted "economic equilibrium" that Marshall and his followers had claimed. Democratic societies needed government—even if flawed in the many ways that Galbraith had seen close up—to ensure the greatest possible benefit for the greatest number. Democratic governments at peace could not and should not exercise authority with the scale and scope they were allowed in wartime, but they could, Galbraith now firmly believed (and argued repeatedly at *Fortune*), influence economic growth, fluctuation, and distribution in ways that had seemed unimaginable even a decade earlier.

His service with the Strategic Bombing Survey left Galbraith with another, more troubling, question: What if a peacetime democratic government came under the influence of the armed forces and found its priorities shaped by the immense new "military-industrial complex" that had grown up during the war? Roosevelt had looked toward the years after the war with great optimism: it would be a time when the United States would prosper in new ways, he believed, and the government could assure Americans of a future that offered full employment, housing, medical care, and education; internationally, it could be a time of global peace, when American prosperity had the chance to be extended gradually around the globe. But a new and untried president now occupied the White House. And Galbraith had meanwhile seen close up the competitive rivalries among the armed services, and their ability to skew economic and national priorities. He had also seen how ostensibly "neutral" scientific research was reshaped to serve institutional and doctrinal goals. Appalled by the level of misrepresentation and concealment he had witnessed, he wondered what this might mean in peacetime—and for Roosevelt's vision of a postwar world.

Galbraith had no doubt about the American military's newfound power, and whatever he thought of "strategic bombing," he heartily endorsed its stunning achievements in defeating Germany and Japan. In May 1945, just three days after the German surrender, he had written his wife from Bad Nauheim:

> What a terrific thing the U.S. Army is. It is everywhere and everywhere it is a picture of enormous concentrated power. Great convoys—trucks, tank carriers, tanks, obtruding jeeps and guns—thunder along the *autobahnen*, mile after mile of them . . . Those that decided to play power politics are now having an impressive demonstration of what it takes to play that game . . .
>
> You can't see those men and machines roll without a tremendous sense of awe about the United States. I never realized before just what the United States is.[55]

10

A New War Beginning

1946 is our year of decision. This year we lay the foundations for our economic structure which will have to serve for generations.
—President Truman, addressing the nation, January 1946

[Soviet leaders today are] only the last of a long succession of cruel and wasteful rulers who have relentlessly forced their country on to ever new heights of military power in order to guarantee external security for their internally weak regimes.
—George Kennan, "The Long Telegram," February 1946

People in this country are no longer afraid of such words as "planning." . . . [P]eople have accepted the fact that the government has got to plan as well as the individuals in the country.
—Secretary of Commerce Averell Harriman,
October 1946

WHEN WORLD WAR II finally ended, on Sunday morning, September 2, 1945, with Japanese officials surrendering to Allied leaders on the deck of the U.S.S. *Missouri* as it lay at anchor in Tokyo Bay, much of Europe, Japan, China, and the Soviet Union was in unimaginable ruin, and more than 50 million human beings were dead. "PEACE," newspapers around the world headlined it, but the end of the war led to only a brief lull before a new and much longer struggle began. When the ceremonies aboard the *Missouri* concluded, more than 400 giant B-29s and 1,200 smaller carrier-based aircraft streaked by overhead—the symbol of the United States' awesome new military power, and symbol of what lay ahead. Over the next fifty years, a new kind of war consumed trillions of dollars and placed at risk billions of lives beneath a great nuclear shadow.

The United States changed greatly during the Cold War—in some ways more than it had during the New Deal or World War II. After shrinking precipitously, the government grew again, and with military programs consuming half of all federal spending for decades, America's economic structure, income distribution, and economic interests were remade. Modern economics as both a profession and a body of thought changed dramatically as well.

One evening in the autumn of 1971 over an Oxford high-table dinner, Thomas Balogh set himself the task of encapsulating that change for his fellow dons. The convivial Hungarian-born Lord Balogh, by then in his mid-sixties, was a prominent figure in economics who'd also been an adviser to Labour governments, and thus was someone who could claim familiarity with theory and policy. With a wry sense of symmetries, he remarked that to understand what had happened to his profession since the war, one needed to compare its history to the Bible, with Adam Smith cast as Abraham and Alfred Marshall as Moses. Malthus, he slyly suggested, might be likened to Jeremiah. John Maynard Keynes was like Christ, he said, who had come both to fulfill and transform the older teachings. And although Keynesianism had triumphed in economic theory and policy, much as early Christianity had triumphed in the Roman Empire after Constantine—whose role, he suggested, had been half-consciously played by FDR—it became immersed in the same sharp doctrinal conflicts that had riven the early church. These conflicts within the state's newly approved economic theology produced doctrines and beliefs that, while claiming Keynesian paternity, would have been unrecognizable at times to the faith's original teacher. Moreover, Balogh noted, the same period had produced a "real-world church" of policy and practice whose behavior, like that of the early Roman church and its papacy, bore only a distant resemblance to The Master's intended message.*

It is true, whether one accepts Balogh's mordant metaphor or not, that Keynesian economics did "triumph" after World War II and in a fashion that, while rooted in the older Marshallian tradition, did dramatically transform the profession, just as it transformed the function of government. It is also true that once *The General Theory of Employment, Interest, and Money* was established among scholars and policy-makers, its complexity and unresolved ambiguities spawned diverse, contentious interpretations whose adherents frequently found themselves at odds. The disputes were far-ranging and often vehement by academic standards: one group of followers, for example, came to call its opponents "bastard Keynesians."[1] The lines marking the divisions among the early "church fathers" of Keynesianism can't be perfectly drawn, but one must see where they are in order to understand the debates over the economy ever since, and Galbraith's distinctive place in them.

To begin with, outside the "church," a conservative pre-Keynesian econom-

---

*Balogh described this dinner to me in a tutorial meeting when I studied with him at Oxford. His comparison of Keynes to Christ was prefigured by Seymour Harris: in 1947, Harris wrote, "Keynes indeed had the Revelation. His disciples are now divided into groups taking sustenance from the Keynesian larder" (Seymour Harris, *The New Economics: Keynes' Influence on Theory and Public Policy* [New York: Knopf, 1947], 5).

ics endured. From Joseph Schumpeter, Friedrich von Hayek, and Frank Knight through Milton Friedman and George Stigler and eventually to figures such as Robert Lucas, James Buchanan, and Gary Becker, a vocal minority continued professing its faith in "neoclassical" economic thought in one form or another and continued believing that Keynes was a heretic and false messiah. Most remarkably, these "neoclassical" economists and their offspring, after being reduced to what seemed a broken remnant by the mid-1950s, would return with startling power in the 1970s and 1980s to launch a ferocious assault that, in conjunction with a resurgent conservatism in politics, for a time threatened the almost complete destruction of Keynes's legacy.

Though sharp differences also divided these "old believers," they were united in opposition to the Keynesian idea of liberal government's macromanagement of the economy.[2] Markets, whatever their minor imperfections, were best left untouched by public hands, they believed, and government was best when it spent and regulated least. (Outside university walls, of course, this was the enduring faith—if not always the practice—of both traditional Republicans and a majority of Southern Democrats.)

Conservative "neoclassicists" weren't the only pre-Keynesians who survived. There was also a somewhat more amorphous school of liberal economics that had evolved from the turn-of-the-century American branch of the German Social-History tradition and that had thrived during the New Deal.[3] Greatly reduced in numbers after Alvin Hansen led many of them away to Keynesianism, these progressive pre-Keynesians, while often supportive of the goals of Keynesian macromanagement, focused on institutional and structural issues of the market—monopoly and imperfect competition, the maldistribution of income and wealth—and largely eschewed mathematically sophisticated modeling. Its postwar proponents, Leon Keyserling and Clarence Ayers being two good examples, favored a continuing expansion of government regulation of business, an increase in spending on social programs, strong labor unions, and progressive taxation of income and wealth, all policies based on arguments and traditions that were well established long before *The General Theory* was published.

Whatever the differences among these various non-Keynesians, even larger fissures and disagreements divided the newly dominant Keynesians who never shared a homogeneously liberal worldview, as their critics often presumed.

The fledgling "business Keynesians," for example, who like Henry Luce had undergone a wartime conversion and now supported the Committee for Economic Development, represented a break with traditional Republican and business opposition to liberal government's expansion. They had been convinced, in part by the record level of profits that businesses had enjoyed during the war, that restoring a pre–New Deal laissez-faire posed undue risks. But the CED Keynesians weren't supporters of Keynes's social and political liberalism. Rather, they saw in *The General Theory* an argument for the potential use of government in managing capitalism's business cycles and in sustaining high business output alongside high (not necessarily full) employment. Although they were always opposed in the business community by traditionally ultraconservative groups such as the National Association of Manufacturers, a number of these CED Keynesians proved quietly but powerfully influential in the Republican administrations of Eisenhower, Nixon, and Ford.[4]

The liberal Keynesians—led most prominently by Alvin Hansen—considered themselves truer followers of Keynes's theory. They believed that full (or near-full) employment should be a basic goal of national policy, and assumed that it was government's responsibility, beyond macromanaging the economy's overall output, to address institutional and public-goods questions about education, housing, highways, and health care. But early division among the Keynesians wasn't just between Hansen's "liberals" and the CED's "conservatives." Soon after the war, a third group, led initially by the Harvard wunderkind Paul Samuelson, also appeared. More than the other two schools, whose concerns with economic theory were directly rooted in issues of real-world policy, this third group was composed of academics rather than Washington economists. As a consequence it lacked influence over public policy until the 1960s, when it suddenly seemed to redefine the entire liberal-conservative divide.

From the start, this third group had a complex, two-part goal. The first, exemplified in Samuelson's doctoral thesis, published as *Foundations of Economic Analysis* in 1947, was to bring postwar economics to an entirely new level of mathematical sophistication by incorporating econometrics, linear programming, computers, and game theory, and thereby to associate economics more closely with twentieth-century physics and other natural sciences. The second was to hybridize Keynesian macroeconomics with the older Marshallian microeconomic legacy into what Samuelson christened the "Neo-Classical Synthesis." Over the next twenty years, Samuelson, James Tobin, Robert Solow, Robert Dorfman, Franco Modigliani, Lawrence Klein, and Kenneth Arrow became this new group's most recognizable and enduring authorities, and made it into the reigning academic orthodoxy. If we extend Lord Balogh's metaphor, as the Neoclassical Synthesis coalesced into the dominant Roman Church, so Cambridge, Massachusetts, became the profession's new Rome, leaving Cambridge, England, behind as Jerusalem. Keynes's old venerated home was no longer the seat of power (much as Washington superseded London in global significance).

The arrival of advanced mathematics wasn't, however, the sole doing of the Neoclassical Synthesis. It came from several sources at once, not least two often overlooked institutions: the Cowles Commission and the RAND Corporation, although neither had a Keynesian agenda at its core. Cowles was the brainchild of Alfred Cowles, a Yale-educated investor and heir to the *Chicago Tribune* fortune. Having lost a great deal of money in 1929, he was much interested, in order to estimate stock-market performance, in the nascent field of econometrics.[5] In discussion with the Yale economist Irving Fisher (who'd also lost a fortune in the Great Crash), Cowles agreed to bankroll the Econometric Society, the journal *Econometrica*, and a new working group of economists and mathematicians interested in the often highly abstract problems of economic estimation.

Based from 1932 to 1952 at the University of Chicago, the Cowles Commission played a kind of Constantinople to Roman Cambridge. It largely stood apart from the Keynesian revolution, focusing more on developing estimation techniques than on solving the riddle of macroeconomic failure. Led by Tjalling Koopmans, Cowles pioneered rigorous modeling of causality in economics, adding the idea of "endogenous" and "exogenous" variables, as well as of "policy invariant parameters" and "structural parameters," to the economists' vernacular. Modigliani, Klein, and Arrow—all Cowles alumni—soon after helped import much of this new "Cowles style" into the Neoclassical Synthesis.[6]

The other great fount of postwar mathematicizing for economists was the RAND Corporation in Southern California. Set up by Robert Lovett and the Air Force (RAND is an acronym formed from *R*esearch *AN*d *D*evelopment) to expand on the success of the "Whiz Kids" and their wartime work in operational research, the richly funded think tank built on these strengths to develop systems analysis and contract-procurement evaluation for the armed forces. Soon after the Princeton mathematician John von Neumann and the economist Oskar Morgenstern published their revolutionary *Theory of Games and Economic Behavior* in 1944, RAND (along with Princeton) also became host to game theory's development; von Neumann, Morgenstern, John Nash (made famous to noneconomists in Sylvia Nasar's biography and the film *A Beautiful Mind*), and many others (including a young Daniel Ellsberg) participated.[7] RAND also encouraged the work at Cowles by providing (with the Navy) over half its income, and Cowlesmen were frequent visitors to Santa Monica, the seaside Los Angeles suburb where RAND operated in unmarked buildings close to the ocean.

Amidst this myriad of postwar research agendas, American economics as a profession now exploded. On the eve of World War II, the American Economic Association had counted barely 3,000 members, only 500 more than it had in 1912. Membership quickly doubled after the war; during the next thirty years, as the U.S. population itself doubled, the number of AEA members grew nearly sixfold, while the ranks of government economists increased even faster.[8] All of them were freshly equipped with new concepts, models, analytic techniques, and technology (most important, the computer) that left them full of optimism about what they could do to guide and shape the economy. By the late 1950s thousands of these economists began to foresee themselves leading America into an unprecedented, unending new Golden Age of prosperity.

It was amidst these profound changes in the American economy and in economics that Ken Galbraith rose to fame, even though he never joined the Neoclassical Synthesis, the CED "business" Keynesians—or even the "liberal" Hansen camp with which he has often been identified. Where exactly do his distinctive views fit in, then? The best clues to this puzzle lie in the Truman years, 1945 to 1952, for it was then that Galbraith established his core positions and passed from being known as a young (and for many, minor) agricultural economist and wartime price czar to being an admired pioneer in the Keynesian revolution.

First, on questions of domestic economic policy and of overall macroman-agement, he planted himself firmly in the Keynesian camp. He thereby served notice that he was no longer attached to his first book with Henry Dennison, with its vague aspirations for some sort of "national planning" system. Second, he made clear that he disagreed with the "business Keynesians" of the Com-mittee for Economic Development—another break with his past, since during the war in his *Fortune* articles he had openly praised the CED's "valuable con-tributions." Third, he began to outline his reservations about the unhesitating confidence of his fellow "liberal" Keynesians in full employment as a goal, reservations that owed much to his experience at the Office of Price Adminis-tration but that also can be traced back to his critique of Hansen's prewar proposals for managing wartime inflation.[9] In his view, the institutional requirements of firms and industries, and the ingrained habits and preconcep-tions of economic actors generally, imparted to the system what economists to-day call "sticky prices" and "sticky wages," with firms often electing to compete through advertising, branding, niche marketing, and the like rather than price. In these sorts of "imperfect markets," he believed, attempts to stimulate a slack economy through conventional Keynesian means risked a politically (if not economically) dangerous inflation well before full employment was reached.[10] In such a world, Galbraith suggested, it behooved Keynesians to re-examine the merits of using various means of wage and price controls in coor-dination with fiscal—and, to a more limited degree, monetary—policy. In the late 1940s, he had not yet outlined how such a control system might work, yet he repeatedly warned that fiscal policy alone could not be counted on to man-age imperfect markets smoothly, especially when actors were acting with im-perfect information.

These positions reveal only part of what became Galbraith's distinctive stance. He also foresaw (and more important, opposed) the dangerous connec-tion between the fortunes of the Keynesians' overall agenda and the process of Cold War rearmament, and he maintained a "Rooseveltian" position vis-à-vis the Soviet Union and in regard to the political-economic reconstruction of Europe and Japan; he emphasized that widely shared economic prosperity was more important as a counter to Stalinism than ideological and military strug-gle. His skepticism about military power and spending became a fixture of his work and his idea of economic analysis.

One memorable moment seems to have catapulted this "new" Galbraith to the early attention of his colleagues. In late January 1946, Galbraith, just thirty-seven and still an editor at *Fortune*, stepped off the train in Cleveland and caught a cab to the downtown hotel where the annual American Eco-nomic Association convention was getting under way—and where a furious row over the future of postwar economic theory was about to break out. The convention's most talked-about panel was assigned to discuss "New Frontiers in Economic Thought," and he was one of the speakers.

When the session began the next morning in the hotel's main auditorium, it was to a packed house that spilled out into the hallways.[11] The University of

Chicago's Frank Knight spoke first. Knight—by then in his sixties, with thinning hair, neatly trimmed mustache, and clear-rimmed glasses—was a formidable figure, having established his reputation in 1921 with his brilliant *Risk, Uncertainty, and Profit*, followed by a distinguished teaching career as well as editorship of the prestigious *Journal of Political Economy*.* To no one's surprise, Knight launched into a passionate defense of the old order's superior methodology and of the uncompromising claim that neoclassical economists, unlike the vulgar Keynesians, had to membership in the natural sciences.

All proper theory, he told his listeners, was based to begin with in axioms and "eternal and immutable laws." Then, in a vivid premonition of the later "Rational Expectations" and "New Classical" schools that emerged from Chicago in the 1970s, Knight said flatly and summarily that economics required assumptions of "rational and errorless choice, presupposing perfect foresight" and of "foreknowledge free from uncertainty," based on the "assumption of 'atomic' units negligible in size and hence continuous variability of all magnitudes." With these and a few other assumptions based on an idealized model of perfect competition, the essence of economic theory was complete. "There is no possibility," he imperiously concluded, "that new laws will be discovered comparable in generality and importance with the basic principles long recognized." Whatever the conditions of the real world, economic theory must presume the irrelevance of business cycles and the insignificance of monopoly ("one of the older branches of price analysis," he sniffed disdainfully) and imperfect competition. If Keynes had any useful insights, about which Knight was skeptical, they concerned only pedestrian policy issues, not elevated matters of economic theory.

Knight's attack on the Keynesian upstarts was then taken up by his partner on the panel, the no less theoretically certain (but less analytically gifted) Ralph Blodgett from the University of Illinois. Blodgett aggressively attacked what he saw as the *real* intentions of the Keynesians, theoretical disputes aside. The "leading economic issue of the day," he said, "has to do with the kind of economic system we will have in the postwar period," and he was certain that the Keynesians and their allies wanted nothing less than "the creation of a planned and controlled economy" (though "to be sure," he hastily added, "not many people are advocating a controlled economy as such"). With the Keynesians acting as cat's paws for such darker tendencies, "we are asked to approve such attractive and innocent-sounding things as full employment . . . a system of social security . . . higher minimum wages . . . and a high wage policy generally." This economists must not do.

Blodgett was hoping to rally his fellow economists against the new Visigothic hordes. "The advocates of such policies," he stoutly concluded, "contend

---

*Knight's general conservatism stands oddly against his own masterpiece. *Risk, Uncertainty, and Profit* in fact damaged neoclassical assumptions: by distinguishing the notion of roughly calculable "risk" from the incalculable idea of "uncertainty," Knight thought of entrepreneurs' profits as windfall rewards that violated the very equilibrium axioms of Marshallian economics. Since the late 1970s, a new generation of economists has grown interested in information problems, transaction costs, and contracts, reflecting Knight's pioneering work.

that they are necessary to the continued existence . . . of the free-enterprise system. I claim that they are more likely to result in the destruction of this system and to ensure the future existence of a controlled and planned economy."[12]

Amid concern about Stalin's intentions abroad, and with anti-Communist fervor at home building to a sustained crescendo (the House Un-American Activities Committee by then was in full swing), Blodgett's allegations that Keynesians were out to destroy capitalism were chillingly reckless and quite paranoid. Yet he was a luminous reminder of how many orthodox economists, far from achieving the scientific neutrality they so highly prized, were driven by partisan political allegiances.

Galbraith, along with Edward Chamberlin of Harvard and Clarence Ayres from the University of Texas, were the chosen responders to Knight and Blodgett. Both Chamberlin and Ayres were prominent economists at the time, but neither man could be fairly called "Keynesian": as codeveloper of "imperfect competition" theory in the early 1930s, Chamberlin imperviously still held to his pre-Keynesian views, while Ayres was one of Institutionalism's most prominent figures.

Galbraith was, in fact, the only real Keynesian on the podium. Yet his answer to the conservatives shows how distinctive his Keynesianism already was—in his explicit concern for social justice, and his belief that both economic theorists and policy-makers were obliged to search for it. These were in fact Keynes's own driving passions; Galbraith therefore saw no reason to answer Knight's claim that economics can work only when built on the positivist methods that men like Knight presumed were responsible for the success of the natural sciences.[13] Nor was the issue about choosing between "freedom" and authoritarian "planning," as Blodgett claimed. Rather, the difficult, practical question was how to balance the needs for freedom and security in a complex industrial society. Rigorous, logical thinking about the consequences of given policy choices should not be held prisoner to axiomatic principles that Knight and others claimed as the sole ground for economic theory.

Pointing to the New Deal's social security, minimum-wage laws, demand stimulation through fiscal policy, and legal protections for unions, Galbraith asked pointedly:

> Did the introduction [of these programs] in the Thirties change, in any very fundamental way, the structure of American capitalism? I think not. Entrepreneurs retained their control over investment and production decisions, and it is hard to see how their incentive to lower costs and extend their markets was impaired . . .
>
> The notion that free capitalist institutions and security are totally incompatible is, in my judgment, one of the most unfortunate cliches of our time. The problem . . . is not to issue a blanket indictment of all measures that enhance security. Rather it is to support those steps toward greater security of

income and employment that are consistent with free decisions by entrepreneurs and to indict those that are not . . .

I am not so blindly optimistic as to suppose that there is an easy formula. But I doubt that at the outset we should conclude that the task is impossible—at least so long as there is evidence from our recent history that the paths to freedom and security are at least partly convergent.[14]

After listening to the sustained applause Galbraith received, Frank Knight left the conference convinced that Keynesians were leading professional economists toward the worst sorts of apostasy.[15]

THERE WAS AN IRONY to Galbraith's apparent victory over Knight that became evident two weeks later, when the Senate passed the Employment Act of 1946: Keynes's followers were winning the battle for academic hearts and minds, but in the world of national politics and public policy, they were still being successfully resisted by alarmed congressional conservatives and influential sectors of the business community. And that resistance posed a dilemma that was to haunt "liberal" Keynesians for decades. Many small businessmen were still darkly convinced that Keynesianism was nothing more than a stalking horse for what they feared would be a second round of New Deal "collectivism" under Truman—or, worse, an encroaching American Stalinism. In the very first months after Japan's surrender, a great battle over postwar power and policy control had erupted in Washington, and the immediate issue was the Employment Act. The larger question was whether Keynesianism would in fact become the official economic doctrine of the U.S. government and, if so, in what form and with what powers and scope.

A year before, in early 1945, with Roosevelt still alive and enjoying his fourth-term victory, the Senate's liberals had introduced a Full Employment bill, which in its original form seemed the very embodiment of liberal Keynesian goals. It boldly declared that "all Americans able to work and seeking work have the right to useful, remunerative, regular and full-time employment," and that henceforth it would be the policy of the United States "to assure the existence at all times of sufficient employment opportunities to enable all Americans . . . freely to exercise this right." It mandated preparation of national economic forecasts, supervised by the Council of Economic Advisors, a specially charged new group in the White House. Using CEA forecasts and advice, the President was meant to recommend to an equally new Joint Economic Committee of Congress a "National Production and Employment Budget." (In today's terms, this was to be based on what economists would call a "full-employment GNP forecast.") This "NPE Budget" would then be used to set federal revenue and spending priorities and levels (including deficits, if necessary) to assure sustained optimal, full-employment output.

From the start, the Full Employment bill met redoubtable opposition. Apart from the Republican minority and not a few Southern Democrats, chief among the bill's opponents was the National Association of Manufacturers, which for years had represented the interests of the country's biggest corporations; even at the height of the New Deal's popularity, it had been an unyielding opponent of Roosevelt and Keynes alike.[16] The NAM attacked the Full Employment bill with every means at its disposal, warning that a virtual proto-Stalinism was stalking congressional corridors.[17] The table of contents of one of its briefing papers succinctly imparted the gusto with which NAM attacked the very idea of full employment itself.

> Section 1: The Full Employment Bill (S. 380) Means Government Controls.
>
> Section 2: The Full Employment Bill (S. 380) Destroys Private Enterprise.
>
> Section 3: The Full Employment Bill (S. 380) Will Increase the Powers of the Executive.
>
> Section 4: "Full" Employment Guaranteed—Criticisms—Terms.
>
> Section 5: The Full Employment Bill (S. 380) Legalizes a Compensatory Fiscal Policy—Federal Spending and Pump Priming.
>
> Section 6: The Full Employment Bill (S. 380) Leads to Socialism.
>
> Section 7: The Full Employment Bill (S. 380) Is Unworkable, Impractical, and Promises Too Much.
>
> Section 8: The Full Employment Bill (S. 380)—Items for Ridicule.[18]

What the NAM pamphlet lacked in rhetorical elegance, one Keynesian wryly observed at the time, was compensated for by its exploration of modernist poetics, "best appreciated if the list is incanted to the beat of drums." Yet these rhetorical excesses were far from ineffective among the conservative coalition of Republicans and Southern Democrats that dominated the Congress.

Throughout the debate over the bill during 1945, proponents of full employment were bedeviled not just by heated opposition but by unfortunate luck in their political timing. As the bill moved through early committee hearings, public attention was elsewhere—caught up first by Roosevelt's death in April, then Germany's surrender in May, by Hiroshima in August, and then victory over Japan in September. In consequence, two thirds of Americans told pollsters in 1945 that they favored a government guarantee of employment, but an equal number then said they'd never heard of the Full Employment bill; among those who had, only 8 percent could accurately describe its contents.[19] The business press provided much closer coverage of the bill, naturally—but only *Fortune* offered it support.[20] Yet competing events weren't the only reason for public inattention: although unemployment was starting to rise as a result of troop demobilization and cutbacks in defense contracts, it was still below 2 percent when the war ended.

Harry Truman had begun his presidency that April by declaring his unwavering loyalty to the Roosevelt agenda, and he restated it in a twenty-one-point message to Congress just days after Japan's surrender that one of Truman's biographers admiringly describes as "an all-out, comprehensive statement of progressive philosophy and a sweeping liberal program of action." In it, Truman called for "increased unemployment insurance, an immediate increase in the minimum wage, a permanent Fair Employment Practices Committee, tax reform, crop insurance for farmers, a full year's extension of the War Powers and Stabilization Act, meaning government would keep control over business, and federal aid to housing to make possible a million new homes per year."[21]

But this detailed postwar agenda, while undeniably liberal and Rooseveltian, wasn't Keynesian. And when it came to the Full Employment bill itself, Truman understood neither its principles nor its mechanics, and his message remarkably never mentioned it.

Another reason for the President's silence seems clear in retrospect: the challenges of ending the war and negotiating postwar international issues were consuming all his energies. Just as congressional cloak-room jockeying over the bill moved into high gear that summer, Truman was in Potsdam, negotiating with Stalin, weighing whether to use the atomic bomb on Japan, and trying to gauge where postwar global relations would head. Then, in early fall, he faced mounting domestic problems that taxed his new administration almost to the limit. Reluctant to retain price controls after the war, he decided to let them expire ahead of wartime wage controls, which led to a burst of inflation that brought down the fury of organized labor upon him, much to the dismay of the public and of OPA veterans like Galbraith.

By January 1946, just as the AEA was convening in Cleveland, that fury burst forth, first with a massive steel strike, swiftly followed by major strikes in the coal and automobile industries, then by a crippling nationwide rail shutdown. Truman in exasperation ordered the Army to take over the railroads (and came within moments of having soldiers take over the steel industry as well) before the strikes were settled. But all this carried a high price tag: popular support for the new President plummeted.[22]

Labor's reaction did nothing but confirm the worst fears of the NAM and most of the Republicans and Southern Democrats in Congress: for them, legislating full employment would only give more negotiating power to the hated unions. Republican congressional leaders sensed that they stood a real chance of capturing control of Congress in the coming November elections, which put them in no mood to bargain, especially given that the successor to the once mighty Roosevelt seemed to be growing politically weaker by the day.

When the bill in its final version passed the Senate in early February 1946—in the middle of the steel strike—it was a pale shadow of the original. The proposed new congressional Joint Economic Committee survived, but only as an advisory committee without bill-writing powers. The President's Council of Economic Advisors also remained, but like the JEC was now meant to be entirely advisory. Gone were the mandated goal of full employment and the presidential power to focus federal budgets and fiscal policy on achieving it; in their place, as one Keynesian caustically noted, was the pleasant but powerless suggestion that

> other things being equal; the federal government really ought to assist the industrious poor to find jobs, if other national objectives did not interfere. "Full" employment . . . vanished entirely . . . [A]lso sunk without trace was the notion of right to employment.
>
> A President was asked only to prepare one more report. Congress was directed to do no more than study it. Neither was compelled to do more than implement a policy so vague that it could be construed to mean almost anything at all.[23]

Here, then, was the hobbled beginning of Washington's postwar commitment to the new Keynesian era—hardly what its supporters (including Galbraith) had thought possible just months earlier. In academic economics, Keynes may have seemed everywhere triumphant. In the world of politics, policy, and power, however, nothing for the Keynesians was assured.

THAT SAME FEBRUARY—just a fortnight after his debate with Frank Knight at the AEA and ten days after passage of the watered-down Employment Act— Ken Galbraith arrived in Washington to start a new job. This began his second (and final) absence from *Fortune*—and, more important, his last direct service in American government for many years.

Galbraith had been back with his family in New York City for what seemed to them like only a few weeks since the Bombing Survey took him away the previous spring. Kitty had missed him—and knew their sons Alan and Douglas had missed him even more—while he was off in Germany and Japan. But having him home that Christmas had been a real joy for all of them, a joy they'd extended over the next several days as he and the boys commandeered the dining room in order to lay out the new toy train set Santa had brought.*

Kitty had thus been surprised at his willingness to return to Washington, especially since his final days at OPA had been so painful for both of them. She was sure, too, that Luce and Del Paine couldn't be too pleased that her husband was taking yet another leave so soon after returning from his Survey duties. Still, she knew that the Washington job was important, and perhaps her husband really could make a difference. So she gave her agreement—but then said she thought it might be best if she, Emily Wilson, and the boys stayed in New York, at least for a while; after all, decent housing was not easy to find in Washington, and she wasn't interested in making yet another move with two

---

*Kitty remembers that after Christmas dinner, she lay down, leaving Ken with the boys. He told them they, too, needed to take a nap before setting up the train set. To Alan he said, "Now, do you understand what you need to do?" Alan replied, "Yes, I need to take a nap." Turning to Douglas, he asked, "And do *you* know what we need to do?" To which the child replied, "Yes, move the dining room table."

small children, only to circuit back to New York expecting to find an apartment as nice as the one they now had.

True, unlike millions of other husbands and fathers, Galbraith had been abroad for only a few months at the very end of the war. But by now, five million soldiers, sailors, and airmen had been demobilized, and hundreds of thousands more were being released each month. Kitty and the boys were upset to lose husband and father to Washington—and to what were sure to be battles at least as intense as those he'd faced there before.

In his memoirs, Galbraith devotes a chapter to his new work as director of the State Department's newly formed Office of Economic Security Policy. The chapter, entitled "Cold Breath," explains that the office was charged with producing research and policy recommendations on the delicate subject of economic recovery for America's shattered enemies—especially Germany, but also Japan, Korea, and Austria. It also neatly lays out the opportunities the job offered him.[24] Here one could actually help to determine the reconstruction of these societies and do so with an extraordinarily free hand, thanks to the Allies' unconditional victory.

Although the OESP was new, American planning for postwar reconstruction had begun long before, in a mood of almost Wilsonian optimism: as one 1942 study put it, postwar Continental Europe would be a *"tabula rasa* on which can be written the terms of a democratic new order."[25] But *tabula rasa*, of course, the combatant nations were not, though, they were now certainly susceptible to unprecedented Allied influence.

In Galbraith's memoirs, the deeper currents in Washington affecting this evangelical mission—the shifting politics, the contending factions, the defining issues—were presented with such arch disdain for his State Department opponents, whom he called "the Secular Priesthood," that a reader might well be perplexed. The immense questions of how U.S. policy would relate to the Soviet Union and to Europe, of what Americans' diplomatic, military, and economic posture ought to be, are scarcely addressed except as a backdrop to Galbraith's frustrations with Foggy Bottom's bureaucrats. Oddly, for someone so precise, he was even vague about the dates he actually served.

In fact his tenure at the State Department lasted little more than seven months, from early February to mid-September 1946, when he abruptly resigned to return to New York and *Fortune*.[26] For someone of his energies, connections, and ambitions, the opaqueness of the memoir and the brevity of service are striking. "Perhaps I should have stayed and fought on," he has admitted, and then blames the State Department's clubby, Ivy League, and white-shoe WASP aristocracy for his departure.[27]

True, American foreign policy had for decades been the preserve of a small group of "well connected, upper-income Americans selected for their task by family membership and attendance at Groton, Exeter, Andover or St. Paul's and Princeton, Harvard, or Yale." The State Department was the place where such men felt they belonged, where "a true-blue gentleman" could work: "No

Groton man could serve in the General Accounting Office, the Bureau of Labor Statistics or the Department of Agriculture," Galbraith wrote.*

World War II had briefly forced these "secular priests" to share part of their hold over foreign policy with the labyrinthine bureaucracies assigned to manage various aspects of the war. But with the war over, Galbraith thought they were committed to reasserting their hegemony. FDR was dead, and Truman, a neophyte in foreign affairs, was "less sensitive than Roosevelt to their class aspirations and was more impressed by their superb assurance."[28]

Galbraith's focus on his bitter clash with the secular priests of the State Department is, finally, too simple an explanation for such an important moment in his and the nation's life.

Long before 1946, the debates over the shape of the postwar world had been rife with divisions and conflicts that extended well beyond the faults or ambitions (or even existence) of any secular priesthood at the State Department. Common to all these debates were the bitterly remembered legacies of World War I: the impact of reparation claims on Weimar Germany, the impotent League of Nations, Chamberlain's fatal equivocation at Munich. American leaders envisaged a healthier, more robust engagement in the world, especially those who, like Galbraith, had read Keynes's devastating *Economic Consequences of the Peace*. But what kind of engagement? In Roosevelt's wartime cabinet, opinion had divided over issues ranging from the future of Europe to decolonization to new international political and economic institutions to Soviet-American relations. Yet FDR felt strongly that the United States and its wartime allies must not fall into destructive diplomatic and military competition after the war.[29]

A central element in Roosevelt's vision of postwar cooperation rather than conflict—expressed most clearly at the Yalta Conference in February 1945—was the treatment of the Axis countries, Germany in particular. One group in his administration, led by Treasury Secretary Henry Morgenthau, wanted the nearly complete postwar destruction of German industry and the "pastoralization" of its population. Without significant industry, Morgenthau reasoned, the Germans could never again take up arms. But the "Morgenthau Plan" faced implacable cabinet opposition, not to mention that of Prime Minister Churchill. ("I had barely got underway," Morgenthau wrote in his diary about his presentation of his position at the Quebec Conference in September 1944, "before low mutters and baleful looks" came from the prime minister. "After I finished my piece he turned loose on me the full flood of his rhetoric, sarcasm and violence . . . I have never had such a verbal lashing in my life."[30]) The War

---

*They practiced a blue-blooded conservatism, certainly by New Deal standards. Franklin Roosevelt, Groton '00, Harvard '04, knew them well—and considered them "a bunch of phony Englishmen" (a charge echoed, amazingly enough, by the king of England himself, who complained to Roosevelt that he wished the United States were represented in London by Americans, not imitation Englishmen). Roosevelt once roared with laughter at I. F. Stone's *Nation* witticism that most State Department men were "trying hard to look like one of their own ancestral portraits."

After Pearl Harbor, FDR is said to have remarked to a friend that "his State Department was neutral in this war and that he hoped it would at least remain that way" (Weil, *Pretty Good Club*, 47, 84).

and Navy departments had by then also begun sounding alarms about what they perceived as Soviet intentions, and when their suspicions about Stalin's postwar goals grew darker, the "Morgenthau Plan" lost favor and after FDR's death it was basically buried with him. By the time of the Potsdam Conference, only France (always in favor of a weakened Germany) supported anything like it.

To those concerned more about Soviet expansion than about German reconstruction, a supine and pastoralized Germany would raise the costs (and risks) of Europe's postwar independence. It was bad enough in their minds that under the occupation agreements, the Soviet Union would control the eastern zone of Germany and the divided German territories east of the Oder-Neisse Line with Poland.

Roosevelt had worked mightily to focus these competing forces within his wartime administration and within the alliance on the vision of a *peaceful* postwar competition with the Soviet Union. At Yalta, though exhausted and ailing from the cardiovascular problems that led to his death two months later, he had finally gotten Stalin's and Churchill's agreement to create the United Nations, which he thought was an essential first step to avoid East-West confrontation.

But after his death, there had been a fundamental realignment of administration officials and attitudes. Part of this was due to inevitable personnel changes that any new presidency brings, but the transition hadn't gone well, and many of the New Deal's most prominent veterans privately agreed with former Secretary of the Interior Harold Ickes's acidic public evaluation of Truman's appointees as "a nondescript band of political Lilliputians."[31] At the State Department, turnover was especially high. Four different secretaries—Cordell Hull, Edward Stettinius, James Byrnes, and George Marshall—headed the department between December 1944 and January 1947. The resulting staff turmoil among subordinates meant the Truman State Department had little clear direction, and meant that the "secular priests" could hardly monopolize foreign policy.

During the war, State had grown enormously, from a $16 million budget in 1939 to nearly $120 million by 1946. But it had new competition in setting national foreign policies. The vastly larger War and Navy departments had acquired their own immensely influential voices in foreign affairs (which grew even stronger when the new Defense Department was created in 1947)—and the military, not State, was in official charge of the occupations of both Germany and Japan. The Pentagon, moreover, wasn't State's only competitor: further diminishing Foggy Bottom's hegemony over foreign policy, the orphaned Office of Strategic Services was about to be reborn as the Central Intelligence Agency, and a new National Security Council would be created in the White House to oversee these governmental bureaucracies for the President. (The U.S. Air Force, the Defense Department, the CIA, and the National Security Council were all the result of the massive National Security Act of 1947, introduced in Congress in February and—remarkably—signed into law just five months later.)

Amid these powerfully contending institutional forces in Washington, with their own internal and intramural debates about what American postwar strategy and priorities should be, Galbraith took up his new work.[32] At the outset, he seemed ideal for his job. (Assistant Secretary of State Will Clayton, who'd known him since the two had worked together to finance rationing plans after Pearl Harbor, certainly thought so. He wired Harry Luce on Christmas Day, 1945, asking Luce to "do your best" to arrange Galbraith's departure for "the very important job for him. We need him badly."[*][33]) After all, he had experience in economic macromanagement and policy, he was familiar with the German and Japanese economies, and he knew how to navigate Washington's treacherous corridors of power.

Yet soon Galbraith felt cut off from any meaningful decision making.

> [T]he consequence of my less than affectionate relationship with the renascent diplomats was less that I was unpopular than that I had very little to do. My staff handled all routine matters; all questions of policy, signaled by the so-called action copies of the telegrams, went to the priestly members, who often failed to advise me of their operations. I was left with what remained, which was largely nothing at all. My idleness was accentuated by an exceptionally spacious office, a very big desk, some expensive leather chairs and an uncomfortable leather sofa.[34]

However, this alleged idleness conflicts with Department records that show Galbraith actually maintained quite a hectic schedule, including several trips to Europe.[35] Also, Clayton in fact had gathered impressive talent to work together on questions of economic security and reconstruction. "Clayton's economists," as they were known, included brilliant young wartime veterans such as Yale's Walt Whitman Rostow (who in the 1960s returned to the State Department's Policy Planning staff under Presidents Kennedy and Johnson); the economic historian Charles Kindleberger; William Salant, an early and influential Keynesian; and Raymond Vernon. This was hardly a group inclined to merely passing time, let alone to being bureaucratically rolled over. And they weren't reticent about pressing their views, as a *Fortune* article in July 1946 made clear. "The political officers of the department are engaged in running warfare with the economic staff headed by Assistant Secretary Will Clayton. The Foreign Service men in the European and Near Eastern and African offices are generally committed to the idea of two blocs in the world . . . Mr. Clayton's men are more interested in exploring the possibilities of collaboration."[36]

Neither Clayton nor "Clayton's economists," including Galbraith, doubted for a moment that much was at stake. The terms established for German re-

---

*Clayton, a New England WASP who'd migrated to Texas, was the world's biggest cotton broker, and early in the New Deal had been a member of the virulently anti-Roosevelt Liberty League. He was brought to the State Department by Secretary Stettinius, in late 1944.

covery—and who set them—would help to decide how potential future conflict between Washington and Moscow might evolve. Just as important was the future of Keynesian-style policies at home, which now hinged in no small way on U.S. policy abroad: Delphic powers weren't needed to see that if a Cold War did unfold, it would lead to a very powerful American government, but one quite unlike any that New Deal liberals or Keynesians had envisioned. If Roosevelt's vision of a complicated but basically peaceful post-war competition with the Soviet Union did not materialize, the American economy would end up being driven not by the policies of either Keynes's "liberal" or "business" apostles, but by what its critics later called "military Keynesianism." The government would be fueled by arms budgets, not by full-employment priorities.

A year earlier, in the spring of 1945, President Truman had inherited a foreign policy that relied heavily on FDR's personal ability to convince Stalin and Churchill of the advantages of postwar cooperation among the Allies. Stalin's suspicions of Western, particularly British, intentions were well known. At the same time, Churchill's suspicions of the Russian leader (and Communism generally) ran deeper than FDR's, entwined as they were with his determination to preserve the British Empire as well as his belief in the ongoing durability of European "great power" politics.[37] This meant that Roosevelt's diplomatic juggling act was always a matter of infinite delicacy, a quality his successor lacked.

On May 23, less than two weeks after moving into the Oval Office, Harry Truman met with his first high-ranking Soviet official, Foreign Minister Vyacheslav Molotov, at the White House. Their chief topic was Poland, and whether the occupying Russians would permit free elections there. The conversation did not go well, and Truman ended up delivering a tongue lashing to Molotov that turned the Russian's face "ashy," as one participant recalled. Even Averell Harriman, who as ambassador to the Soviet Union had three days earlier briefed the new President on his own dark views about Stalin's "barbarian invasion of Europe," thought Truman had made "a mistake" in his handling of Molotov and the issues.[38]

Off to a bad start, just four months later, in August, Truman and Stalin collided at the Allied summit at Potsdam. Truman was nervous (he wrote his wife, "I sure dread this trip, worse than anything I've had to face"), and at the start of nearly two weeks of meetings outside Berlin, he felt he was making little headway with Stalin. In a letter to his mother written during the conference, the banty Missourian called the Russians the most pig-headed people he had ever encountered, and to his diary he confided that Stalin's regime was "a police government pure and simple. Still, Truman discovered he could do business with the Soviet dictator. He told a confidant that "Uncle Joe" reminded him of hard-boiled Tom Pendergast, the Kansas City Democratic machine boss who'd been Truman's first political patron. (A dozen years later he admitted he'd been naive at Potsdam, yet even so, he ruefully added, "I liked the little son-of-a-bitch.") As the August conference concluded he wrote his wife, "We have accomplished a very great deal . . . [Stalin] seems to like it when I hit him with a hammer."[39]

After Potsdam, Soviet-American relations became aggravated. At the end of the year, Truman confided to Secretary of State James Byrnes, a former senator from South Carolina and Supreme Court justice, that "unless Russia is faced with an iron fist and strong language another war is in the making. Only one language do they understand, 'How many divisions have you?' "*[40] Thus when 1946 began, Rooseveltian hopes of preserving some level of Soviet-American cooperation were growing dim. And the "iron fist and strong language" approach began to crystallize into new American policy terms that February. Two weeks after Galbraith arrived at State, George Kennan's famous "Long Telegram" arrived, in which the U.S. chargé d'affaires in Moscow and one of the principal Russian experts in the Foreign Service set out the reasons for what he described as a necessary new American "policy of containment."

Any hopes for peaceful competition with the U.S.S.R. were chimerical, Kennan declared starkly, because the Soviets were "committed fanatically" to the belief that there could be no long-term peaceful coexistence with the United States. Moscow was intent on assuring that "the internal harmony of our society [is] disrupted, our traditional way of life destroyed, the international authority of our state broken." Because Kennan's views largely reflected his own, Averell Harriman sent a copy of the lengthy telegram to Navy Secretary James Forrestal, like Harriman a former Wall Street investment banker, who was "the firmest of the firm" when it came to dealing with the Soviets.[41] He was so impressed by Kennan's reasoning that he had the still-classified telegram mimeographed and distributed to virtually all senior officials in Washington who had anything to do with military and foreign affairs.[42]

Two weeks later Winston Churchill arrived in Washington on his way to deliver a speech at tiny Westminster College in Fulton, Missouri.[43] Having been voted out of office in the midst of the Potsdam Conference the previous summer, Churchill was in the United States to speak as a private citizen, but he was treated as a visiting head of state. Truman, to underscore his own respect (and hoping to improve his dismal polling numbers by basking in Churchill's popularity), escorted the former prime minster to his home state in the Presidential railroad car and introduced him, glowingly, at the college. With Truman on the stage behind him, Churchill—resplendent in his Oxford cap and gown—delivered his famous "Iron Curtain" address. Russian leaders didn't want war, he told his audience, but they would incontestably take risks in their quest for "the fruits of war" and "the indefinite expansion of their power and doctrine." As a consequence, Moscow was lowering an "iron curtain" across

---

*Byrnes had also been one of Truman's competitors to replace Vice President Wallace at the 1944 Democratic convention. Shrewdly judging it better to keep a potential 1948 challenger close to him, Truman offered Byrnes the State Department job on the train back to Washington after FDR's Hyde Park funeral. Byrnes wanted the job so badly, he "almost jumped down my throat taking me up on it," Truman recalled. Both politicians understood that under presidential succession rules then, with no vice president, Byrnes would become President if Truman died or was incapacitated. (FDR, by contrast, had refused Byrnes his earlier requests for the State Department job. "He's nothing but a cocky bantam rooster. He has no international experience, and I would be remiss if I made him Secretary of State.") (On Truman's offer to Byrnes, Wittner, *Cold War America*, 5; on FDR's view of Byrnes, Weil, *Pretty Good Club*, 228.)

Europe, dividing the Continent in half and setting the stage for greater conflict as Stalin set out to probe the West's willingness and resolve to resist.

The "Iron Curtain" speech has legendary status today, but what is all but forgotten is that Churchill's warning was received with great hostility at the time. Editorialists from *The Wall Street Journal* on the right to *The Nation* on the left rushed to attack it, while Walter Lippmann, dean of American newspaper columnists, called it an "almost catastrophic blunder." (In London, *The Times* and the British government were similarly excoriating.) In Moscow, Stalin claimed that it amounted to a "call to war" against the Soviet Union. Truman was so stunned by the ferocious response that although he'd known what Churchill planned to say beforehand, he falsely claimed he hadn't. (He even wrote Stalin a letter offering to send the U.S.S. *Missouri* to bring him to the United States so that he, too, could speak directly to the American people. Stalin declined.[44])

To be sure, there were officials at both the State and War departments who believed that a "cold war" with the U.S.S.R.—some even darkly thought a "hot" war—was inevitable. But many others just as fully believed, as had Roosevelt, that there was time and room enough to find an alternative path. Secretary Byrnes was one, as was his top personal aide, the veteran New Deal lawyer, Benjamin Cohen.*[45] Below them, Assistant Secretary Clayton and most of "Clayton's economists" were also reluctant to assume the inevitability of Churchill's "Iron Curtain" and all it implied. At the Pentagon, although Forrestal was even more alarmist than Churchill, neither General Marshall nor General Eisenhower, representative of most of the Army's senior command, was eager for direct confrontation.[46] None of these men was by any stretch of the imagination "pro-Communist," as figures like Senator McCarthy in some cases later charged. But they all recognized the immense costs and peril in opting for military and diplomatic confrontation with the Soviet Union.

Byrnes himself had spent the war years in the White House as head of the team that coordinated U.S. military production at the highest level—and he and Roosevelt had talked frequently and in great detail about postwar plans.† He'd also accompanied Roosevelt to Yalta, and at Potsdam, when the inexperienced Truman stalled out in his negotiations with Stalin, he had smoothly

---

*Pressing by then, however, against both Byrnes and Cohen was Undersecretary of State Dean Acheson. After his appointment to the State Department by Byrnes in mid-1945, the dapper, mercurial lawyer had at first shown signs of Rooseveltian willingness to cooperate with the Soviet Union. In the fall of 1945, he'd even forced through the transfer of the OSS's Research and Analysis department to State, knowing that it included figures like the German academic Marxist Franz Neumann and his close friend Herbert Marcuse and that it was opposed to a hard anti-Soviet line. By mid-1946, however, Acheson was constantly counseling Byrnes to be tougher with the Soviets—a line Byrnes, bobbing and weaving throughout the year, resisted.

†Byrnes's official title as director of the Office of War Mobilization erroneously suggests the idea that he headed a bureaucratic behemoth. OWM was in fact a small, elite group, its dozen staff members based in the East Wing of the White House. Byrnes reported directly to FDR, OWM being a profoundly political job, concerned not only with assuring the supplies the Allied armed forces needed, but with settling the delicate balance of patronage and rewards among defense suppliers, their congressional patrons, the armed services, and the Allies. Byrnes was so effective that informally he was known as "Assistant President," which earned him the intense dislike of Vice President Wallace.

pulled Foreign Minister Molotov aside and hammered out a reparations agreement largely on American terms in exchange for surrender of German territory to Poland. In December 1945, at the Moscow Council of Foreign Ministers, he'd come close to restoring wartime Allied amity by successfully winning agreement on a thicket of issues ranging from Balkan treaty terms in the West to the structure for a Japanese occupation council and Korean unification in the Far East.[47] Thus, with Byrnes at State and with military commanders like Marshall and Eisenhower at the Pentagon, there was reason to believe that the U.S. and the U.S.S.R. could still find common ground for a workable competition.

The diplomatic and military risks of confrontation with Moscow, however, were not the only considerations being weighed in Washington; opportunity was another. The Soviets had suffered horrendous losses in the war: twenty million were dead and most of its industrial base west of the Urals had been completely devastated. The United States by contrast was unscathed at home, and its immense new productive capacities faced uncertain postwar demand. In the business community, Donald Nelson, the former Sears CEO who'd directed the War Production Board, along with the Chamber of Commerce director, Eric Johnston, met with Soviet officials repeatedly in 1945 in Washington and Moscow and talked in great detail about how major American corporations anticipated extensive trade with, and investment in, the Soviet Union as in the 1930s.

At State, Clayton was working just as hard as Nelson and Johnston for a Soviet-American trade future unlimited by competing ideologies. "Nations which act as enemies in the market place cannot long be friends at the council table," he argued.[48] And, as his deputy Willard Thorp wrote, most of the people "on the economic side who were busy trying to develop economic policies and so forth were not inclined to be strongly anti-Russian."[49] Like Clayton and Byrnes, they "opposed legislation that would restrict trade with Russia, pumped for substantial loans to *all* war-torn nations to enable them to restore their trading ability, and sought to prevent the establishment of 'closed blocs'—East or West—that would choke the flow of trade."[50]

IN GERMANY, the American military governor, General Lucius Clay, was equally worried about the direction of American foreign policy. Clay had almost daily contact with his Russian counterparts, and he knew that Germany was ground zero for the future of European affairs and for Soviet-American relations. Clay was a brilliant, West Point–trained forty-eight-year-old Georgia engineer who hardly inclined to naïveté or weakness about Communism, and to him, Germany was a miniature version of the larger looming storm. Relations with the Russians in their sector of occupied Germany were sometimes difficult, but, as he constantly reminded Washington, relations with the French in theirs were even worse. Europe's traditional rules of "great power" competition, with France wanting the weakest possible Germany, were as dispositive as any Washington-Moscow tension.

The immediate tasks for General Clay involved simply feeding the German people, who were surviving on rations of as little as 1,000 calories a day, getting the economy moving, and eventually overseeing the creation of a new and democratic government in the defeated nation. He also knew that he was hardly alone in his views about how to accomplish these tasks, or their end goal. During the war, General Marshall had made Clay his deputy chief of staff in charge of materiel. He'd brilliantly organized the vast production and transportation system that supplied the Army, and had swiftly risen to four-star rank. After D-Day, Marshall sent him to the White House to work as Byrnes's deputy, overseeing all of American war-related production. There Clay and Byrnes became friends; both men moreover shared the Presidents' postwar vision. Assigned to govern the American occupation zone in Germany at the war's end, Clay was consequently "one of the staunchest supporters of FDR's policy of accommodation with the Soviet Union. He worked diligently to make quadripartite government in Germany a success, and he blamed the French, not the Russians, for its initial failure. . . . [He] believed that a lasting accord could be reached with the Soviet Union."[51]

At the beginning of 1946, Clay's hopes for Allied unity were thus still high, and like Secretary Byrnes he was actively seeking to advance four-power cooperation. He'd been stunned by Kennan's "Long Telegram" (in fact, he'd gotten "pretty violent" about it, an aide recalled) and had reacted no less angrily to Churchill's "Iron Curtain" speech. "We have never and still do not believe for a minute in imminent Soviet aggression," he cabled Washington shortly after the Fulton speech. The Soviets "have been meticulous in their observance" of their promises and "cannot be accused of violation of the Potsdam agreements."[52] Realizing the effect Kennan's and Churchill's views were having, Clay repeatedly tried to steer Washington away from greater confrontation, but by late spring he sensed that he was swimming against the tide.

> By the summer of 1946, Clay had become dispirited. His problems with the French showed no signs of letting up; he was having great difficulty convincing Washington to provide the necessary food to prevent starvation in Germany; quadripartite government had gone off the rails; and to make matters worse, U.S. military headquarters in Europe was seeking once again to subordinate military government to tactical Army control.[53]

When Clay threatened to resign, both Byrnes and Secretary of War Robert Patterson brought the Army into line and reaffirmed Clay's authority.

Then in August, a new challenge emerged. Midlevel conservative bureaucrats at both the State and War departments once again tried to interfere with Clay's command. When Byrnes arrived in Paris for a meeting of Allied foreign ministers in mid-August, an angry Clay flew from Germany to brief him on what the subordinates were trying to do.

> In Byrnes's hotel suite that evening, he catalogued for the Secretary the array of problems suddenly confronting his military government: the War Depart-

ment wanted the quadripartite de-Nazification policy rescinded; the State Department was sending a group of experts to consult with Clay's staff about Occupation matters; and, worst of all, despite the inroads on German public opinion that Molotov had achieved [by suddenly calling for German re-unification, free elections, quick economic recovery, and political rehabilita-tion], no one in Washington wanted to approve the policy summary Clay had submitted in July [which sought the same goals along more pro-Western lines].

Byrnes heard Clay out and then responded as Clay had hoped. On every point mentioned by Clay, the Secretary of State was in full agreement.[54]

Realizing that the Secretary of State's agreement could be decisive in turning back "the confrontationists," Clay wanted to make sure Byrnes put those com-mitments on the record to prevent underlings from later reversing them. Would he, Clay asked, come to Germany in September and say publicly what he'd just said privately? Byrnes's answer was unhesitating: yes, absolutely, he would come.

Suddenly "Clay felt he was back on solid ground," his biographer writes. He then made a second request: Would Byrnes make sure one State Department official in particular wrote the speech for him? The secretary paused. Whom, Byrnes asked, did the general have in mind? The general knew exactly: a young man named John Kenneth Galbraith.

Clay had met him two months earlier, when Galbraith was in Germany on one of his trips for the Office of Economic Security Policy. He was there to ex-amine how to restore German coal production, and had asked to meet General Clay as a courtesy. But the two men had taken to each other almost instantly, and in several long subsequent conversations had ranged across the whole breadth of American foreign policy.[*55]

Byrnes already had noticed Galbraith at staff meetings in Washington and was also impressed by the young economist's grasp of the issues.[†] Although he had his own speechwriter, he agreed with Clay that Galbraith would be ideal for this particular job. He cabled to Washington ordering Galbraith to begin work on the address; the moment had come to lay out the goals of American policy in Germany and to confront the mutual suspicions in Washington and Moscow that were leading to the slow descent of Churchill's "Iron Curtain."

Shortly before eight o'clock on September 6, 1946, in Stuttgart's ornately Baroque opera house, Secretary of State Byrnes solemnly rose before an audi-ence of Allied Occupation officials and chosen Germans. Byrnes's aides had been priming the press for days to anticipate a major new declaration on U.S.

---

*General John Hilldring, whom Acheson recruited to State as Assistant Secretary for Occupation Affairs, as-signed Galbraith to a four-man special team that he sent to Germany in August to review and recommend what short- and long-term U.S. policy should be toward Germany. Galbraith and the Harvard economist Edward Ma-son (who had been in the OSS) cowrote the team's report, and met with Clay just before Clay flew to Paris to meet with Byrnes.

†Galbraith used Byrnes, as well as Leon Henderson and Will Clayton, as personal references during an FBI in-vestigation in 1950 (FBI Memo, July 15, 1950 Galbraith FBI files, in author's possession).

foreign policy. The audience thus also included Senators Arthur Vandenberg and Tom Connolly as well as dozens of reporters from the United States; technicians would broadcast the speech live to radio audiences across Europe and North America.

It would not be "in the interest of the German people or in the interest of world peace that Germany should become a pawn or a partner in a military struggle between the East and the West," Byrnes began. To prevent that required swift establishment of an elected provisional government, the drafting of a new constitution, and Germany's eventual admission to the United Nations. (These were all points Clay had sought over midlevel State Department objections.) Certain limits on industrial production would, however, have to remain in place, as would a limit on exports and on any German armed force. On each of these points, Galbraith—who had flown to Stuttgart with Byrnes and was standing offstage as the secretary spoke—had meticulously prepared the presentation of the issues.[56] The stance was even-handed, took allies and critics into consideration, and clearly signaled that the United States accepted its new global responsibilities, and would fulfill them on a basis that did not presume inevitable conflict with the Russians.

To reassure the Soviet Union and Poland, Byrnes reaffirmed that Germany's loss of territory east of the Oder-Neisse Line was permanent, and then, to reassure Germany, rejected any French claims to the Ruhr and the Rhineland. Above all, he stressed America's commitment to a democratic and prosperous Europe, undivided and open to all, a continent where trade and ideas could flow freely.

Byrnes's speech won standing ovations from the audience that night, and the next day was greeted enthusiastically throughout Germany. There was widespread approval in the United States as well—ringing endorsements appeared in many newspapers, including *The New York Times* and *The Washington Post*, which applauded its "middle way" position between confrontation and withdrawal: here, as the *Times* put it, were the seminal outlines of a viable U.S. foreign policy. (Four months later, signaling its own approval of "his great Stuttgart speech," *Time* named Byrnes its "Man of the Year."[57])

But barely a week later, the newly declared American foreign policy was blindsided by a domestic political row. On September 12, Secretary of Commerce Henry Wallace delivered a speech at Madison Square Garden in which he declared that the United States "has no more business in the political affairs of Eastern Europe than Russia has in the political affairs of Latin America" and that advocacy of "getting tough with Russia" was threatening the chance for peace in the postwar world.[58] " 'Get Tough' never brought anything real and lasting—whether for schoolyard bullies or businessmen or world power," Wallace insisted, to thunderous applause. "The tougher we get, the tougher the Russians will get." Wallace displayed here fewer illusions about Soviet conduct than he did later, declaring that Soviet "land reform, industrial expropriation, and suppression of basic liberties offends the great majority" of Americans. But he also went after the British: departing from his prepared text, he told his twenty thousand listeners that "the danger of [a new world] war is much less from Communism than it is from imperialism" and that Soviet cooperation would come "once Russia understands that our primary objective is neither saving the British Empire nor purchasing oil in the Middle East with the lives of American soldiers." The crowd—a gathering of labor, left liberals, and radicals—roared its approval.[59]

Coming as it did just days after Byrnes's landmark address, Wallace's speech suddenly cast in stark relief the unresolved differences within the administration—and apparent irresolution in the Oval Office. The issue was no longer just about *what* U.S. foreign policy should be, but *who* would determine it. Truman found himself besieged. Byrnes was livid: the commerce secretary was meddling in foreign affairs and, worse, had gone far beyond Byrnes's newly stated policies by attacking both the Soviet Union and Great Britain. Truman was no less upset, although, as with Churchill's Westminster College speech, he had seen Wallace's text in advance and had approved it. He now compounded the mess by insisting to reporters that he had only "glanced" at the speech and had trusted Wallace "to play square with me." (*Time* the following week called this "a clumsy lie"—and Truman knew it.)

The chaotic situation became worse when a long letter Wallace had written Truman two months earlier was leaked to the press. In it, Wallace went even further than at Madison Square Garden, claiming that certain unnamed U.S. military commanders were advocating a "preventive war" against the Soviet Union before it had time to develop its own atomic weapon. (He may have been alluding to General Curtis LeMay.)

Wallace and Truman had been edging for months toward open conflict, and both men's eyes were fixed on the 1948 presidential race. With the Madison Square Garden speech, Wallace had made it impossible to paper over their differences. Determined to reassert his presidential authority, and faced with a threatened resignation from Byrnes, Truman fired Wallace on September 20.

But the country was now shaken: Did Wallace's firing mean that Byrnes's policy was also out the window? Was the Kennan-Churchill "Get Tough" position now American policy? What of Roosevelt's goal—which most Americans still supported—of postwar cooperation to prevent the possibility of a new, possibly atomic, war? Veteran New Dealers were particularly aghast: Wallace had been the last Roosevelt holdover in Truman's cabinet. With this final tenuous connection between the two leaders now broken, what was left of FDR's vision for postwar America?[60]

Truman's approval ratings plunged to 40 percent, less than half what they'd been a year earlier, and *Time* spoke for millions when it declared, "If the world depended on the Truman Administration to keep it out of trouble, then the world had something to worry about."[61] Still, a few hoped something could be salvaged from the chaos. Byrnes, for one, briefly thought that Wallace's departure would strengthen his own voice in foreign policy. But an insecure Truman was by now privately as concerned about Byrnes as about Wallace, and began to plan the replacement of his Secretary of State.

A week later, a select list of senior administration officials found a top-secret report, "American Relations with the Soviet Union," on their desks. Drawn up several months earlier by two Truman aides, Clark Clifford and George Elsey, the report painted the darkest possible picture of Soviet intentions and the immediate need for a strong U.S. military response to them. "The language of military power is the only language which the disciples of power [in Moscow] understand," it declared. "Therefore, in order to maintain our strength at a level which will be effective in restraining the Soviet Union, the United States must be prepared to wage atomic and biological warfare."[62] Historians later concluded that the "Clifford-Elsey Memorandum" often grossly misinterpreted, even falsified, the record of Soviet behavior. Truman himself, after reading it, became so alarmed that he called Clifford at home on a Sunday and demanded it be locked away in a safe; it was only after firing Wallace that he reversed himself, ordering Clifford to send the paper to the administration's senior diplomatic, political, and military officials. Clifford nonetheless blandly cited in his cover note the "remarkable agreement" he'd found among his colleagues in preparing the paper. In power-sensitive Washington, that bold claim, coming directly from the White House, with Truman's obvious imprimatur, was itself a political masterstroke. Clifford and his readers knew that no such "remarkable agreement" had existed before the Wallace fiasco. But after that September, as one historian later observed, America's foreign policy "discussions would continue (as they have ever since) over issues of specific policy implementation. What ceased, however, was the debate over the basic ideological outlook. It was settled. The alternatives suggested by [Roosevelt at Yalta of peaceful competition] were to be ignored for a generation."[63]

AT HIS STATE DEPARTMENT OFFICE, Galbraith reluctantly grasped where Truman's foreign policy was headed. What had looked like a triumph at Stuttgart was going to dissolve. Immediately after Stuttgart, he had flown back to Washington, where he'd spent the next few days finishing the report on U.S. policy in Germany that General Hilldring had ordered him tp prepare. In the report's covering memo to Hilldring, Galbraith showed no illusions about Washington's rightward drift in policy that summer—and took exception to it: "Germany, however it may be regretted, is becoming the theater of an ideological struggle." To stop that, he advised two things: a rapid advance in German living standards, and a heightened respect by Occupation authorities for the rights and liberty of individual Germans. The size of Occupation forces also needed to be sharply reduced and German trade with any willing partners drastically increased. Galbraith finished his memorandum late in the afternoon on September 12, six days after Byrnes delivered his Stuttgart speech. That night, in a twist of fate, Henry Wallace delivered his explosive Madison Square Garden address.

In the 1930s, Galbraith had met several times with Wallace at the Agriculture Department, had drafted some well-liked policy memoranda for the Secretary, and had admired his courage and willingness to oppose conservatism generally. But with FDR gone, Wallace had been moving toward a politics Galbraith could not accept. His doubts had crystallized even before Stuttgart. "I recall attending a conference at Yale sometime shortly after the war, where Wallace spoke," he says. "He was advocating an advanced form of world government, in which the capital of this new system would alternate between Washington and Moscow. That's an exaggeration, but captures the effect Henry's speech had on me. I decided this was not for me."[64]

There seemed precious little left to do at the State Department, and little reason to wait until he was pushed out. The time had come to resign. By early October, he was back at *Fortune*'s Rockefeller Center offices in New York.

Byrnes's power steadily eroded over that fall, and in Germany Clay discovered that his opponents in the State and War departments weren't slowing down. He chose to fight a rearguard action, continuing to insist that the Russians could be worked with and that relations with them in Germany were improving.[65] Byrnes also fought to hang on, hoping, as one historian put it, that "the wartime amity between Washington and Moscow might still be restored and the momentum of the Cold War reversed."[66] But when Republicans swept the elections on November 5, recapturing both the House and Senate for the first time in two decades, he, too, realized that for those who valued Roosevelt's ideal of peaceful postwar competition with the Soviets, there was little left to do.

Shortly after Christmas Byrnes submitted his resignation, with a terse note chastising Truman and reminding him that "nations, like individuals, must respect one another's differences" and that "development of a sympathetic understanding between the United States and the Soviet Union" was "the paramount act of statesmanship." There was, Byrnes wrote, still time to "achieve a just peace by cooperative effort if we persist with firmness."[67] But Byrnes was wrong; for the United States, that time was now gone.

Back in New York and out of the government, Galbraith kept up his support for the goals that he had helped Byrnes articulate in Stuttgart, and that he and his fellow "Clayton's economists" had worked so hard for. In a widely read study that he wrote right after leaving the State Department, "Recovery in Europe," he made clear why he had resigned.[68] Unmentioned in his memoirs and "only dimly recalled" by him today, "Recovery in Europe" analyzed and made recommendations for European recovery that clearly sought to avoid increased tension with the Soviet Union if at all possible. Galbraith was keenly aware of—and opposed to—the steps the Soviet Union was then taking to expand its hegemony in Central and Eastern Europe, but he also recognized that the West was militarily in no position, let alone inclined, to "roll back" Communism there. The issue for him was, as Roosevelt had always argued, the rapid recovery of Europe's economies, most especially Germany's, and a restoration of prewar trans-European trade and investment—"in particular, in breaking down the barriers between eastern and western Europe and between Germany and Europe as a whole." To achieve that aim, the United States needed to move past the four-power occupation of Germany and instead pursue German unification, along with its demilitarization and neutralization. "A communist-controlled Germany would hardly fit this pattern," he noted, "nor would a Germany dominated by . . . France or the United States or the United Kingdom."

In short, Galbraith, like others loyal to Roosevelt's own views, still hoped to substitute economic recovery for armed competition or conflict, and to negotiate wherever possible with the Soviet Union in a way that both recognized its security interests and military power and yet firmly pressed for expanding and protecting democracies wherever possible. For such a plan to work, a vast expansion of American aid was crucial. Acknowledging U.S. assistance that had already been sent as "a start," he called for more of it, and for it to go to more of Europe. "No part of Europe, East or West, should be excluded a priori" from such assistance, he declared. A recovered and revitalized Germany could be "a bridge between eastern and western Europe—a community that buys, sells, and transports between the two." Galbraith then laid out a detailed ten-point plan: it is striking to note how closely the Marshall Plan, unveiled at Harvard's 1947 commencement eight months later, followed its points. Galbraith played no part in drafting the Marshall Plan, but people who did (such as Will Clayton) had read his report and were clearly influenced by it.[69]

In January 1947, in an article for *Fortune* bluntly titled "Is There a German Policy?," Galbraith tartly asserted that "the State Department, which in principle, makes German policy, and the Army, which in practice both executes policy and makes a good deal, have done little to explain their objectives."[70] He reiterated many of the points he'd made in "Recovery in Europe" and in Byrnes's speech, calling for German neutrality and reunification; for diminished emphasis on German reparations; for expanded Western aid, loans, and credits; and for German political and economic recovery as a cornerstone for a "new" Europe. "To split Germany," he warned, "would be to destroy one of the main bridges between eastern and western Europe and to confirm in economics American acceptance of two Europes."

But the policies he advocated were not to be. The President announced the Truman Doctrine that spring, formally committing the country to defeating Communism in Greece and Turkey. West Germany recovered economically, over the next years, but the nation remained divided for four more decades. And the United States proceeded on a course unlike any it had known before.

Recalling his 1946 foray into the world of diplomacy years later, Galbraith wrote grimly:

> I was not attracted by the thought of conflict, military or even political, with the Soviets. I believed that the divisive issues—reparations, Berlin, how Germany would be governed—could be negotiated. Patient effort was needed, effort that recognized that many Soviet attitudes were a cover for insecurity occasioned by the terrors of the recent past . . .

My more depressing memory of Berlin in 1946 was of the conversations that turned on the menace of the Soviet Union . . . [Many officers, diplomats and businessmen there] agreed that, although free enterprise was in all respects superior to Communism, only constant vigilance would save it from superior Communist wile . . . [T]o enter an opposing argument in evening conversation was often to be in the minority . . . A persistent expression of a minority view caused you to lose your effectiveness. Your dissent being predictable, it was not thought to add usefully to the discussion or deliberation. There was a patient pause while you spoke; then everyone got down to the real business.[71]

In Washington, many of FDR's progressive supporters were dismayed by Truman. Like many two decades later, when Lyndon Johnson became President after John F. Kennedy's assassination, they found the new, unelected President wanting in comparison to his predecessor. Truman's different style was part of it, but his choice of policy and policy-makers mattered more. (Among Truman's 125 senior appointees during his first two years, 49 were bankers, financiers, and industrialists, including his Secretaries of Commerce, War, and Defense, and his Undersecretary of State; 31 were generals or admirals; and 17 were corporate lawyers. As the journalist Howard K. Smith concluded, "[T]he effective locus of government seemed to shift from Washington to some place between Wall Street and West Point.")[72] And to the devoted New Dealers, there was also Truman's adoption of loyalty oaths and his support for purges of Communists in the government, unions, schools, and universities, a policy that left a bitter taste in many mouths. When archconservatives such as Congressman Martin Dies and his House Special Committee on Un-American Activities had attacked New Dealers for their "left" views, Roosevelt had risen to their defense. Now, under Truman, hundreds of federal employees were dismissed and nearly six thousand resigned "voluntarily" because of their alleged Communist affiliations.[73]

Galbraith viewed all this with quiet disdain. He himself, though he didn't know it at the time, had gotten his State Department job only over the objections of the department's internal security apparatus, which had formally disapproved of his appointment, warning that he would "draw sharp criticism to the Department . . . [and] jeopardize certain programs and appropriations."[74] Their opposition, though, wasn't because of "dubious" loyalties or "pro-Communist" leanings (although such charges were made) but because Galbraith had been too prominent at the OPA and had too visible an association with liberal groups and causes. It was an early measure of how "national security" was becoming mixed up with the punishment of dissent or, in Galbraith's case, of loyal support for an earlier administration's stated policies.[75]

Galbraith was about to watch former associates be dragged through unpleasant investigations. Paul Baran, his invaluable aide on the Bombing Survey, spent several years as a mendicant scholar, unable to find permanent employment despite his brilliance.* Charles Kindleberger couldn't get a government consulting job again until the 1960s.[76] And John Carter Vincent, the Far East specialist with whom Galbraith also worked at the State Department, was soon to find his career in ruins when he was vilified for being the diplomat who "lost China" during the toxic debate on that subject a few years later.[77]

Yet Galbraith remained unflinchingly committed to his Rooseveltian views. In January 1949, two months after Truman's upset defeat of Thomas Dewey, he returned to the topic of European economic recovery in a new study for the National Planning Association. In "Beyond the Marshall Plan," Galbraith made clear for the first time in his professional writings some of the central political assumptions underlying his economics.[78]

With the Cold War well under way, he was very concerned lest Washington's prejudices about the terms of European recovery undermine the effort. He warned of the dangers of advocating a doctrinaire American-style capitalism and showing an equally doctrinaire hostility toward Europe's social democrats and moderate socialists, as if they were no more than Bolsheviks in sheep's clothing.

> [I do not] suggest that the U.S. should associate itself with and support the moderate Socialists of Western Europe. This is not intended. What is insisted is that these parties are important for free and stable governments in Europe. Moreover, there is a half-century of experience to show that countries professing democratic socialism and those professing liberal capitalism can live amiably together. It is not even clear that after the concessions which a professedly capitalist country makes to social welfare and after the concessions which a professedly Socialist government makes to what is expedient, there is a highly consequential difference between the two.[79]

Galbraith thought the process of European economic integration should be accelerated and enlarged. He chided the soft conventional wisdom that nothing more than a customs union was the goal, and declared himself in favor of a centralized European government responsible for currency, customs, and taxes.

Measured against the European Union's advances in the years thereafter, his comments might seem unremarkable, but at the time, advocates of positions such as his, like the French diplomat Jean Monnet (whom Galbraith had met and admired), seemed wildly utopian to those who dominated U.S. policy. Yet as Galbraith presciently observed, "In this instance Utopia seems to accord also with the practical necessities of the case."[80]

He was also concerned lest American policy-makers believe that the Marshall Plan was sufficient for a *just* economic recovery. Although measurable ag-

---

*Baran was for many years coeditor of the independent Marxist journal *Monthly Review*, where he shared editorial duties with Paul Sweezy.

gregate economic progress had already been made by 1949 in many countries receiving U.S. aid, "differences in wealth and well-being are great; the costs of government bear heavily on the poorest of the people; ancient aspirations of workers to protect their welfare and of peasants to own the land they farm remain frustrated."

Galbraith was not alone in his views on these issues. More than two dozen NPA board members formally endorsed Galbraith's report; his views were shared by influential policy figures—including, for example, Lauchlin Currie, Leon Henderson, Isador Lubin, and John D. Black—and by robustly Republican figures such as Milton Eisenhower and Allen Dulles.

In 1949, however, as in 1946, Galbraith's warnings were not heeded. Although Marshall Plan aid to Europe eventually averaged $3 billion a year, it never reached either the levels he recommended nor did it take on the broad, tolerant outlines he advocated. Meanwhile, money at home for the U.S. military had begun to flow like water, most especially for the Air Force. Along with it flowed aid for European national armed forces as well as for covert CIA funding of Europe's conservative political parties.[81]

In 1949, U.S. military spending rose by nearly 40 percent over the previous year, to five times what it had been in 1940. In 1950, it surged upward again even before the Korean War broke out. Peace returned to the Korean peninsula in 1953, but American troops never left, and military spending (now fifteen times higher than in 1940) did not decline much; it certainly never dropped to the prewar levels. Over the next two decades, until the end of the Vietnam War era, U.S. expenditures on weapons and warriors accounted for well over *half* of the entire federal budget, and for several years approached two thirds of all Washington's spending. In lockstep, the federal budget's share of the total economy grew dramatically and reached more than twice the size of Franklin Roosevelt's largest New Deal peacetime budget. Put another way, between the end of World War II and the year Dwight Eisenhower left office fifteen years later, the United States spent more annually on its Army, Navy, and Air Force (*not* counting the Korean War years, *and* adjusted for inflation) than it had in World War II itself.[82] That transformation inevitably profoundly reshaped the entire country.

In 1998, the Brookings Institution published the most comprehensive independent estimate to date on the total cost of modern U.S. military spending. According to its figures (acknowledged to be understated for various methodological reasons), the United States had spent more than $18 trillion, nearly a third of that on nuclear weapons. It was far and away the largest single expenditure of the federal government for the previous sixty years; by comparison, the nation had spent $8 trillion on Social Security and $4.7 trillion servicing the national debt. (The figures are in constant 1996 dollars.) Money spent on nuclear weapons alone, the study noted, far exceeded the combined total spent on education; law enforcement; agriculture; natural resources and the environment; general science, space, and technology; job training, employment, and social services; community and regional development; and energy production and regulation since World War II.[83]

Harry Truman was right when, that fateful January of 1946, just four months after the end of the war, he told Americans that this "is our year of decision."

11

Back to Harvard: New Economics and New Voices

IN THE FALL of 1948, Ken Galbraith returned to Harvard—fourteen years after he first walked across the Yard and nine years after he reluctantly departed for Princeton. After his frustrating 1946 foray into the State Department, he had spent two years back at *Fortune*, writing and working as the magazine's senior economics editor, but the idea that Cambridge was his real home had never left him. He knew that someday he'd return to academic life.

A good measure of Harvard's attraction to him is seen in an episode in the spring of 1946, when David and Nelson Rockefeller tried to recruit him from his job at State to become chief economist for the Rockefeller family (and suggested a handsome reward if he would). When Galbraith politely declined, he cited his hopes of soon returning to university life and hinted that a job offer from Harvard, although "a long shot," might soon be in hand.[1]

By 1948, though, when he did finally return, academic economics was strikingly different from what he'd left behind. To begin with, there were many more students: thanks in no small part to the GI Bill, postwar enrollment in economics, as in higher education generally, had mushroomed.[2] Harvard's undergraduate enrollment had plummeted from 3,300 before the war to just 670 in 1945, then had shot up again to 5,300 by 1947, 4,000 of them veterans drawn from more heterogeneous backgrounds than Harvard's prewar classes and opening up the college in dramatic new ways.[3] With this enrollment boom came a demand for more courses and more faculty.[4] During the war 650 of Harvard's 2,000 faculty (including 80 percent of its physicists) had left for military or government service; although most eventually returned, hundreds more were needed. In economics, the new recruits had almost all gotten their first taste of Keynesianism as graduate students or young instructors before the war, and although older professors continued to resist the new paradigm, *The General Theory* was becoming the basic postwar agenda for research and teaching in economics.

But *The General Theory* wasn't the only factor shaping postwar economics.

Science at Harvard had matured during the war and lost much of its abstract innocence. Led by President Conant, who had become chairman of the National Defense Research Committee, the university had signed almost nine hundred military research contracts worth more than $33 million. Its scientists were leaders in the development of sonar, radar, cryptography, chemical and biological weapons, napalm, computers—and the atomic bomb.

This wartime work had had its effects. The physicist Kenneth Bainbridge, who'd accompanied Harvard's 85-ton cyclotron to Los Alamos after the government expropriated it for a rent of $1 per year, had watched, along with Conant and other Harvard scientists, as the first atomic bomb exploded at Alamogordo in the summer of 1945. (J. Robert Oppenheimer, Harvard '26, directed the scientific work of the Manhattan Project.) "I had expected only a lightning flash on the horizon," Conant wrote, but "it was more like . . . a giant star shell directly over head." Bainbridge caught the darker moral implications immediately. Twenty minutes earlier, he had been the one who threw the switches that began the countdown, setting the explosion in motion. Turning to Oppenheimer, he said simply, "We are all sons of bitches."

After Hiroshima and Nagasaki, the prestige of science—especially physics—was enormous, and it came to exercise a powerful indirect pull on economics. Linear programming and computers, game theory, advanced statistics and econometrics, and national income accounting burst now like Conant's giant star shell over the profession, just as *The General Theory* had a decade earlier.

"Burst" is perhaps an exaggeration. The postwar "mathematicization" of economics didn't come about because of a single author or single defining work, and its diffusion was subtle, elongated, and varied. But even a casual look at the leading journals of the day shows where the profession was heading. Most economists still relied on written English and logical reasoning conducted in English—not mathematical formulae—to make their arguments. In 1951, for example, just 2 percent of the pages in the *American Economic Review* contained a mathematical expression without an empirical use, compared to nearly *half* the pages thirty years later,[5] even though both the Cowles Commission and *Econometrica* had been pioneering for twenty years on behalf of sophisticated mathematics as a new economic "grammar."[6] But soon economists began to use that new grammar even as they acknowledged their uncertainty about it.

In an article for the *American Economic Review* in 1953, the young Robert Dorfman laid out the elements of linear programming and min-max theory, a topic that nowadays is taught in first-semester introductory textbooks. But in 1953, Dorfman apologized for the seemingly "difficult algebraic apparatus" these new techniques required, which he ruefully admitted "has impeded [most economists'] general acceptance and appreciation" of it. A year later, when he introduced another new technique known as input/output analysis, he switched strategies, promoting it with a salesman's enthusiasm: "There can hardly be an economist who has not watched with amazement that nova of economics, input-output," he began. But once I/O was properly understood and adopted, he promised it would revolutionize economics, ending forever what Dorfman called the profession's sad history of "individual research, piddling grants, and hand-me-down data."[7]

That same year, Galbraith's Harvard colleague Seymour Harris, himself a devout but nonmathematical Keynesian, set off a mini-firestorm over the insurgent mathematical supremacy. As editor of *The Review of Economics and Statistics*, he published a critical article by David Novick that chided economists for their hasty embrace of physics and advanced mathematics, for accepting mathematical formalism as superior to traditional logic exercised in English, and for neglecting the function of economists as observers of empirical realities in favor of deductive blackboard theorizing. Harris's eye for academic controversy was impeccable, because the brief article provoked a torrent of angry replies over the next year. Paul Samuelson, Lawrence Klein, Robert Dorfman, Jan Tinbergen, Robert Solow, Tjalling Koopmans, James Duesenberry, D. G. Champernowne, and George Stigler—a veritable who's who of modern American economics, including six future Nobel laureates and several of the central figures in the Neoclassical Synthesis—weighed in.

Samuelson archly noted that his fellow critics "had taken time out from their researches at the frontiers of economic science" to correct Novick's baleful arguments for nonmathematical economics in order that "error may beget truth." Klein claimed the article had depicted the mathematical economist as a "charlatan and dilettante," although it hadn't, then sweepingly countered that the work of nonmathematical economists "tends to be fat, sloppy, and vague," in sharp contrast to the "clarity of thought [which] characterizes mathematical economics." These were the milder responses.[8]

What these articles and dozens like them in the 1950s make clear is that "economic theorizing" in the sense in which economists use the term today— work laden with mathematical symbols and with arguments often dependent more on the logic of the formulae than on the observed empirical properties of the economy itself—was considered odd and rather recondite, and was still the exception to the rule.[9] Yet this new advanced "mathematical style," and the way it married Keynesian macroeconomics to the microeconomics of Marshall's marginalism, was responsible, in the "war of apostolic succession" then going on among Keynesians, for making the Neoclassical Synthesis the reigning faith of American economists for the next several decades. And Harvard, as it had been at many earlier moments in American economics, was at the heart of this enormous revolution. Paul Samuelson's *Foundations of Economic Analysis* was the new group's Magna Carta, and its leading figures included many Harvard graduates.

Yet the explosion of interest in mathematical economics ironically had the effect of diluting Harvard's lofty preeminence in the field for the next twenty years. No university ever enjoys a monopoly on the best theorists, and often an individual working alone produces a seminal or decisive work, or, as in much science, small groups of thinkers working together or adjacently will generate real change.[10] Also, mathematical economics had never been Harvard's strong suit, and now Yale, Chicago, and particularly MIT challenged—and began to share—Harvard's predominance. MIT's department was transformed in the 1950s principally by Harvard alumni, among them Paul Samuelson, Robert Solow, and Evsey Domar, and its reputation spread quickly after Samuelson's *Economics: An Introductory Analysis* became the leading introductory textbook after it appeared in 1948. But for a while in the early 1950s at least, Harvard economists held a visible edge over their crosstown rival.[11]

In September 1948, though, Ken Galbraith hadn't come back to Harvard to teach the new mathematical techniques—or even Keynesian theory. Instead, he was there to do agricultural economics, or so his colleagues thought.

Just as he had in the Depression, John D. Black meant after the war to maintain Harvard's vital role in shaping America's agricultural policies. Half a dozen undergraduate courses were now taught in agricultural economics, the most popular of which enrolled as many as ninety students. And it was Harvard's largest doctoral field in economics, too, making the university responsible for a quarter of the nation's Ph.D. degrees in the subject. (Between 1948 and 1953, Harvard awarded forty-three Ph.D.s in agricultural economics, compared to just twelve in economic theory and four each in econometrics and statistics.) Until Galbraith arrived, the indefatigable Black was almost single-handedly responsible for teaching all those students himself, aided only by a couple of untenured junior faculty.[12]

Although he'd recently turned sixty-five, the tireless Black was hardly ready for retirement. But he'd been thinking of the future and had decided that Galbraith would make his ideal successor. He realized that his protégé now cared and knew about a great deal more than farm credit, commodity marketing, and policies in the Department of Agriculture and American Farm Bureau, but also saw his multiple interests as a strength, and no doubt felt that Galbraith could be won back at least partially to the field in which he had built his own distinguished career.

Black had carefully kept his colleagues aware of Galbraith's wartime work by arranging for him to lecture at various department seminars, including the fabled "Fiscal Policy" seminar run by Alvin Hansen. Then, in 1946, he started vigorously promoting Galbraith for a newly created professorship, jointly sponsored by the Economics Department and the fledgling Littauer School of Public Administration.*[13]

There were several older, more prominent candidates for the post, however, and Galbraith finished third in the voting behind Jan Tinbergen and Theodore

---

*In December 1944, Galbraith sent his mentor a detailed memorandum entitled "Economics for the Public Administrator." In it he outlined a model course—tracing the elements of economic theory and public finance, administrative law, bureaucratic theory, accounting, and so on—for would-be senior public officials. Black undoubtedly circulated the memo among colleagues during his recruitment campaign (see Galbraith, "Economics for the Public Administrator," December 3, 1944, box 54, Black Papers, Wisconsin Historical Society, Madison).

Schultz. Black was frustrated and concerned when Ken was passed over. Throughout his career Black exemplified what the philosopher John Dewey called "the engaged scholar," someone who understood that the university's commitment to influencing public life was a civic and moral as well as an intellectual obligation. And especially because the new professorship was a joint appointment with the fledgling public administration school, he had no doubt which of the candidates was best suited for it.

He decided to raise his concerns directly with the university provost, Paul Buck, whose approval would be required in any final appointment decision. "The great weakness in our present situation," he wrote in a lengthy private letter, "is in persons qualified to train advanced graduate students in policy-making, who have the aptitude for it as well as the background." Yet with just a few such men, he went on, the Economics Department and Littauer working together had "a real opportunity to achieve greatness and become important influences in our national lives."[14] Galbraith, more than Tinbergen or Schultz, was such a man.

Then to everyone's surprise, Schultz turned down Harvard's offer, and the empty chair came up again in 1947—and once again Black pushed for Galbraith. This time the chief competitors were two younger scholars, Paul Samuelson and Arthur Smithies. By then an untenured associate professor at MIT, Samuelson's immense talents for the new mathematical economics were well established, and Smithies, an Australia-born former Rhodes scholar and Harvard Ph.D., had done work on Keynesian approaches to budgetary policy that was widely admired. (The breezy, athletic, hard-drinking Smithies also happened to be Errol Flynn's cousin, giving him a modest celebrity of a different sort.[15])

But to Black their candidacies raised a new issue: both men were part of what he called a "monetary-fiscal policy axis," and appointment of either, he cautioned Provost Buck, "would further unbalance the work in economics at Harvard." By "monetary-fiscal axis" Black meant Keynesians and their allies. "Of course none in this axis considers that he is narrow," he went on. "In their discussions, to be sure, they draw on all phases of the economy. But they organize it all in terms of a single framework of reference. They pour it all, as it were, through one narrow funnel, and do some sieving in the process."

Black had a second complaint: many of the more elegant mathematical "technicians," as he called them, were attached to what seemed to him often obscure theorizing. "If any economist of today is turning out articles or books presenting analysis of refinement, he is doing it because he lacks real power of analysis of the larger issues . . . or as a by-product of such analysis, or as a relaxation from the steady grind of his regular job." He thought Smithies and Samuelson fit in this category, and the postwar period was "no occasion for the refinements of theory and their applications; but rather for over-simplification and over-emphasis on a few vital elements."

Black also used his letter to the provost (which bypassed his own colleagues) to counter criticisms or doubts about Galbraith that he'd heard around the Economics Department and assumed Buck had heard, too. To those who sniffed that Galbraith wasn't skilled in the new mathematical economics, Black replied simply, "The simple truth is that a man of his breadth of comprehension is likely to find himself mainly absorbed in dealing with broad fundamental economic relationships," not just the new techniques. Another criticism was apparently that Galbraith was a poor speaker. "It is true that [Galbraith] often speaks haltingly when extemporizing," Black wrote, since he "needs time to find the exact word he wants." But he thought Galbraith was an excellent writer and teacher, with both an "uncanny sense for the vital points in a classroom discussion" and strong rapport with his students. (Subsequent student evaluations support Black: Galbraith consistently won excellent ratings throughout his years at Harvard.[16]) Lastly Black acknowledged a certain roughness in what he referred to as Galbraith's "public relations," but, he argued, "given time enough to plan for it in advance," Galbraith was "able to differ with his colleagues and associates in a pleasant and gracious manner; but not in haste and under pressure. No doubt a factor in his relations with others has been his urge to get on with the job and not waste too much time talking about it." Yet despite Black's intense campaigning, Galbraith in 1947 was passed over a second time, in favor of Arthur Smithies. (Samuelson shortly got tenure at MIT, having been passed over for this and then another chair at Harvard.*)

Black, a man who seldom took no for an answer, was not about to be deterred. "It was the summer of 1948," Galbraith wrote later, "when Black phoned me and asked me to come back to take over a new operation studying agricultural marketing. A big federal grant had just been made to Harvard for such a study on the assumption that maybe the farm program could be made cheaper—price controls diminished, that sort of thing—if there were a better, more efficient marketing system." There was a problem, however: "I would be a lecturer, a second-class citizen," a fact Black smoothed over by arranging for him to be paid out of the grant at the professor level.[17]

---

*Why Samuelson was passed over for that second chair is not clear, and whether anti-Semitism was involved is an open question. Seymour Harris was the department's only Jewish member at the time, and waited eighteen years to get tenure. Mason and Dunlop both deny the charge; Galbraith is less sure.

One person who certainly thought so was Joseph Schumpeter, himself an old-fashioned anti-Semite, raised in an era when ascription of ethnic group traits (both "good" and "bad") was commonplace. In 1932, for example, he expressed concern to Ragnar Frisch that "a clannishness of Jews and socialists" would block appointment of Erich Schneider as an Econometric Society fellow, then vehemently protested when Frisch criticized his prejudice. His private diary contains various outbreaks of real virulence against "niggers, Jews and subnormals," and he wrote of Keynes, "Just as the nigger dance is the dance of today, so is Keynesian economics the economics of today."

But Paul Samuelson was a favorite student, and when the department denied him tenure, it provoked Schumpeter's fury: "I could have understood if they didn't want to hire him because he is a Jew. But that wasn't it—he was just too brilliant for them!" Samuelson, very fond of Schumpeter, downplays allegations of his anti-Semitism (see Melvin Reder, "The Anti-Semitism of Some Eminent Economists," *History of Political Economy*, Winter 2000, 841–44; interviews with author on Mason's, Dunlop's, and Galbraith's views).

Hanging up the phone, Galbraith, who was vacationing with his family at the little Vermont farm he'd bought the year before as a getaway from New York,* pondered his options. He decided to take a long walk along the lane that ran past the farmhouse.[18] The afternoon had about it the sylvan quiet and warmth of a fine, windless New England summer day, and the woods were silent. This was in many ways the world he'd grown up in, and he felt at home in it—and at peace. *Fortune* and New York (like Washington) represented a different world, which also entranced him; it was full of activity and challenge and competition. He enjoyed many of his journalistic colleagues and was proud of his work at *Fortune*, yet its world was somehow incomplete.

The next day, he called Black and said he'd take the job. Several days later, he went to New York to tell both Del Paine and Harry Luce of his decision. He then spent the next few weeks wrapping up deskwork at the magazine and saying good-bye to New York friends, while Kitty arranged to sublet their apartment. Six weeks later, in mid-August, with his wife, their two young sons Alan and Douglas, and family housekeeper Emily Wilson, Galbraith decamped for Cambridge. Abandoning secure and very well paid employment at Time, Inc., was a career risk, but for him it was a matter of persuading Harvard to see things clearly.

GALBRAITH WAS OFFICIALLY part of the Harvard seminar on "Agricultural Forestry and Land-Use Policy," and he plunged into his new research and into his teaching assignments, meant to relieve some of Black's overload. Black simultaneously poised himself for the renewed battle to win a professorship for his protégé. The opportunity was not long in coming. Howard Bowen, dean of the College of Commerce and Business Administration at the University of Illinois, made Galbraith an offer that was worth pursuing: the chairmanship of the economics department. This was just what Black was waiting for: competing job offers, in time-honored academic tradition, were a means of leveraging one's colleagues— just as Black expected, the Economics Department tenure committee now decided there might be a professorship available after all.[19] This time, after only cursory discussion, the vote to approve Galbraith was unanimous.†

There matters should have rested. But congressional investigations of subversion were filling the front pages, and in certain quarters Galbraith was considered a man of dangerously controversial views. For the first time in modern memory, members of Harvard's governing Board of Overseers moved to block a recommended appointment. Black and Galbraith were stunned, to put it mildly, and so were the other professors in the Economics Department, not to

---

*In 1947, vacationing at the borrowed home of friends in southeastern Vermont, where the countryside was dotted with abandoned and little-used farms, the Galbraiths, on a whim, inquired about property for sale and were shown a 235-acre farm. The barn was long gone, but the house, built in the early 1800s, with irregular later additions, was charming—with wide pine floors, a massive fireplace, and five bedrooms. Outside, a broad meadow, surrounded by forest, slanted down to a large, beaver-filled pond. Ken and Kitty were enthralled. The owner was pleased to sell for $6,750.

†Ultimately, one dissenting vote was cast. The conservative Austrian-born economist Gottfried Haberler was absent the day of the vote; upon his return, he dutifully insisted on recording his lone vote in opposition.

mention the university's dean, provost, and president, who'd by then approved the appointment.

It was easy enough to uncover why the Overseers had taken this unprecedented action: the Boston lawyer Charles Cabot was leading the opposition, the very same Charles Cabot whose draft report Galbraith had cut up and rewritten three years earlier at the Bombing Survey. Galbraith recalled later, with some grace, that Cabot

> was not a mean man nor one to carry a grudge. But he had seen me behaving in an admittedly uncouth way and, as he saw it, on the wrong side. No brash civilian should have placed himself in opposition to the experienced wisdom of the Air Force or shown such a lack of respect for the acknowledged heroes of the Republic. This Charles Cabot knew, and therewith he knew his duty as a Cabot.[20]

Joining Cabot to oppose Galbraith's appointment were Sinclair Weeks, who'd briefly been a Republican senator from Massachusetts and was to be Eisenhower's Secretary of Commerce; Clarence Randall, the president of Inland Steel (and one of James Conant's oldest and closest friends); and Thomas Lamont, a senior partner in J. P. Morgan and the son of the recent donor of Harvard's Lamont Library. None of the three men had been involved with the Bombing Survey, but for all of them the names "Roosevelt" and "Keynes" crossed their lips with distaste—and Galbraith, in their minds, was publicly and dangerously coupled with both.[21]

In another organization and under other circumstances, four men out of thirty might have been politely ignored or outvoted. But this was Harvard, and these were Cabots and Lamonts and captains of finance and industry. Cabot's opposition was straightforward and specific as to Galbraith's role on the Bombing Survey. Weeks, Randall, and Lamont, who may have been uncertain as to what precisely a "Keynesian" was, nonetheless knew the term wasn't approbative among their class. For example, three years later, when Weeks declared that Eisenhower's election as President meant that "a climate favorable to business has most definitely been substituted for the socialism of recent years," his view was considered unexceptional.[22]

Randall, as chairman of the Overseers' Visiting Committee to the Economics Department, darkly reported the presence of "one or more Socialists, some zealous followers of British economist John Maynard Keynes, and some who advocate the extension of economic controls by Government." In the atmosphere of the time, Keynes's name, as Conant put it, was "like the proverbial red rag. In the eyes of many economically illiterate but deeply patriotic (and well-to-do) citizens, to accuse a professor of being a Keynesian was almost equivalent to branding him a subversive agent."[23]

As Cabot and his allies dug in, insisting on the Overseers' right to deny Galbraith a professorship, many feared Harvard was about to replay the two-year-long 1930s battle over Ray Walsh and Alan Sweezy. Anxious not to subject himself or Harvard for a second time in ten years to a public display of acrimonious divisions over economics, Conant persuaded all parties to keep the fight out of the press.*

Quietly, Galbraith's supporters among the Overseers—led by its chairman, U.S. District Court judge Charles Wyzanski—marshalled impressive support to block Cabot and his allies. From the State Department, Paul Nitze, his fellow director from the Bombing Survey, offered strong backing. Stuart Symington, then Secretary of the Air Force, assured the Overseers formally that the Air Force bore Galbraith no grudge. But the single most influential voice seems to have been that of General Orvil Anderson. In 1945, as commander of the Eighth Air Force, Anderson had clashed angrily and repeatedly with Galbraith over the Bombing Survey's draft conclusions, and Cabot had cited this as evidence both of Galbraith's "disrespect" for the military and of the clear prejudices that had shaped his conclusions. But Anderson completely undercut these charges: he considered Galbraith "sincere in every way" and "fearlessly honest," and while they'd most certainly disagreed, he'd never doubted that Galbraith's "motivations were rooted in logic and analysis."[24]

Throughout the fall of 1948 and into 1949, as this hidden Harvard war dragged on, Galbraith himself proved an able defender of his record in close-quarter combat. For example, reviewing the Bombing Survey reports he wrote or oversaw, he skillfully cast Cabot's views against his own. In a private memo addressed to his supporters (but certain to reach wavering Overseers), Galbraith wrote, "Mr. Cabot's purpose, I believed at the time, to be that of a mediator and one who sought to avoid offending the Air Force. My own concern was in having the history [of the bombing of Germany] told accurately. This controversy, subject to minor concessions of language, was decided in my favor." As to certain "rumors" that he'd let his politics and personal views shape the Survey's conclusions (Cabot had accused him of "intellectual dishonesty"—a charge that, if not refuted, was certain to be fatal to his appointment), he outlined in some detail the reasons why his politics had nothing to do with his conclusions, and why he thought that compromising in favor of Air Force sensitivities would have jeopardized the integrity of the report itself:

> While I set the greatest store by open-mindedness—the habit of mind that learns and unlearns—in scientific and scholarly pursuits, I do believe there are times when a man must be uncompromising. Facts cannot be compromised; neither can great issues of public welfare. I have no doubt that from my administration of price control considerable evidence of an uncompromising temperament could be adduced. In that context one could not compromise with a few; general compromise would have been fatal.
>
> The United States will suffer severely if it ever finds itself, in a period of danger, with public servants who believe otherwise and so pattern their behavior. The problem in the Bombing Survey was similar. The easy way would

---

*In Conant's autobiography, he maintained this silence and did not mention the episode.

have been to accept compromise where the record was troublesome or embarrassing. The result would have been a worthless report. It is to be recalled that along with the truth, the security of the country was at stake.[25]

Among the undecided Overseers, who of course listened carefully whenever a Cabot spoke, Galbraith's forthright defense was influential. Cabot and his allies were unrepentant, however, and Cabot refused to withdraw his accusations; it was months before his charges finally fell to the ground.

When they did, however, it meant only that one hurdle had been passed: there still remained Weeks, Randall, Lamont, and several other Overseers who were exercised over Galbraith's New Deal record and Keynesian commitments. In June 1949, the three nearly persuaded the Overseers to vote down Galbraith's appointment—this after the Harvard Corporation, the ultimate authority, had joined the department, dean, and provost in approving it, *and* after Conant had privately warned Randall that if the conservatives won, he would take it as a vote of no confidence in his leadership. Judge Wyzanski used his authority as the Overseers' chairman to delay a vote until the fall, but Conant by now was both shaken and appalled. By September 1949, when a new academic year began, many of those involved had come to realize that this fight was no longer about Galbraith's future alone.

To President Conant, the issue was now the fundamental one of academic freedom. A rock-ribbed Yankee Republican, he was disgusted by the attempted pillorying of Galbraith for his beliefs. "Much of what was being said about left-wing professors was nonsense," he noted later.[26] After the June meeting, he had realized no end was in sight, and so he "finally laid down the law, and fought for Galbraith on principle."[27] High principle, however, wasn't the only factor at play by then. The economist Edward Mason—a tough former OSS figure and supporter of Galbraith and now head of the new Littauer School—threw down a gauntlet. In a memo to Buck and the Corporation, he warned that if the Overseers didn't act soon, "a lot of dirty linen would be washed in public, and I feel certain it would not be Galbraith's linen."[28] In mid-November, Conant insisted that the question of Galbraith's appointment be called to a vote. This time he gave the Overseers a simple choice: they could either approve the decision—and, with it, the right of an academic department, the faculty, and him as President to appoint professors—or accept his resignation. With that, formal opposition to Professor Galbraith collapsed. Just before Thanksgiving, 1949—almost a year to the day after the Economics Department had first voted his appointment—Galbraith received a telephone call from Provost Buck telling him that his new professorship was won.[29]

Years later, in his memoirs, in much-refined understatement, Galbraith observed that to have been "so in limbo was not pleasant; in truth, it was very disagreeable." But, he wryly continued, it also taught a lifelong lesson:

> Often in academic and public life one wonders whether one must speak out on some issue where the emotions or pecuniary interests of the reputable are

in opposition to the public good . . . Always, when faced with such a decision,
I have thought of Sinclair Weeks, Clarence Randall, and Thomas Lamont . . .
[and then] do whatever possible to justify their forebodings.[30]

GETTING TENURE AT Harvard in November 1949 was a watershed in Galbraith's life. He was now forty-one, with a wife and two young sons, and until then, his career had been a blur of change and relocation: over the previous twenty years he'd packed up and moved from Ontario to Berkeley, to Washington, to Cambridge, to England, and then back to Cambridge; then it had been on to Princeton, Chicago, Washington, New York, Germany, Japan, New York, Washington, New York, and finally Cambridge again, always in rented apartments or houses. Tenure at Harvard transformed all that. In place of more than a dozen jobs, now he was to hold just one (save for his two years as ambassador to India): professor of economics, Harvard University. A year later, with his career now certain, Galbraith impulsively bought his family their first home, the redbrick three-story neo-Georgian house on Francis Avenue where he and Kitty have lived ever since. They had looked at it among several, but thought its large size was a problem and the first asking price too high. But when Kitty went into the hospital to give birth to their third child, Ken—who was as tired as she of the cramped second-floor apartment they'd occupied for three years—went ahead on his own, bargained down the price, and closed on the deal. Still in the hospital, Kitty was taken aback, needless to say, and worried about making the move with a newborn.

Once on Francis Avenue, she realized, first, that the house was just fine, and, second, that the ample bookshelves in the living room seemed rather bare for a Harvard professor's home. With the help of a friend, she filled them with sets of volumes of Dickens, Thackeray, Ruskin, and so on. One of the sets served a purpose other than decorative: her husband discovered Anthony Trollope. "Everything about the Victorian writer pleased him: Trollope's unabashed fondness for money; his satisfaction with politics; his mockery of the clergy; his disdain for the self-righteous; and, of course, his skillful pen. Ken has claimed an influence ever since."[31]

Built at the very end of the nineteenth century, the house, Galbraith proudly likes to note, cost just $26,500 in January 1951, roughly two years' salary. The ground floor consisted of a large oak-paneled living room with a fireplace; a study, which was soon piled with books and filled with photos of friends and celebrities; a large oval dining room with a fireplace; and a spacious high-ceilinged kitchen. At one end of the large central hall a wide staircase ascended to a landing amply lit by a ten-foot-high stained-glass window. On the second floor were three bedrooms and two baths, one still outfitted with a large claw-foot tub big enough to hold Galbraith's six-foot-eight-inch frame, and a small wing for servants. On the third floor were two more bedrooms and a large sunny playroom (that later, after the boys were gone, became Galbraith's place for quiet writing).

Tenure also brought with it important changes in Galbraith's work. First was the matter of sheer volume: he had written just one, coauthored book before 1949, and his published professional papers numbered less than two dozen, his magazine and newspaper pieces about three dozen. After 1949, it was as if a trickle became a torrent—more than forty books and more than a thousand papers and articles were to follow. And in them all one would find increasingly refined, even new, views and voice. Galbraith's work until then, despite several rather important insights, hadn't really stood out from that of many other young economists of his generation caught up in the Keynesian Revolution. His papers on agricultural economics for the most part followed, rather than led, in a field transformed by the parity-and-price-support revolution in which his mentor, John D. Black, had been so important. Likewise his writings on price control, industrial structure, and public-works spending were all within the broad mainstream of New Deal–inspired policies and beliefs. Although that New Deal influence alarmed conservative Harvard Overseers and orthodox economists such as Frank Knight, Galbraith's views were far from being highly unusual or progressive. His most Keynesian and most "Galbraithian" contributions lay ahead.

So, too, the Galbraithian style—the tone of ironic disdain, the arch syntax and meter, the skeptical eye for excessive self-regard among the rich and powerful, the driving concern about injustice—was still to come.

The temptation is to attribute the transformations in Galbraith's output, argument, and voice to the freedom and security of permanent academic employment. But there are complicating factors in this simple explanation, because the victory of tenure was followed almost immediately by tragedy.

In late March 1950, barely four months after his father received notice of his tenure, Douglas, the Galbraiths' six-year-old second son, suddenly fell ill. On an evening when Kitty was in New York, where her mother had just been hospitalized with a brain tumor, Emily Wilson had decided to take Douglas and his older brother, Alan, out to a movie in Harvard Square. Leaving the theater, the little boy told her that his legs hurt and he didn't want to walk home.

With Ken off early the next morning to join his wife for her mother's surgery and Douglas saying he felt no better, Emily decided to call in the family doctor. The doctor could find nothing wrong initially, but that evening, when Douglas seemed worse, she decided to contact a pediatric specialist. At nine the following day, after getting Alan off to school, Emily, on the doctor's instruction, took Douglas over to Children's Hospital in Boston for a battery of tests.[32]

Returning home later that same morning, Galbraith was surprised to find the house empty, then grew concerned when he read the note Emily had left. Why was Dougie so suddenly and so mysteriously ill? When he reached the hospital, the doctor asked to speak with Galbraith alone. Years later, Emily could still remember vividly the ashen look on Galbraith's face when he rejoined her in the waiting room.

Douglas, he said, likely had rheumatoid arthritis. Treatments needed to be started at once, though the doctors frankly were not certain of their diagnosis.

And so for the next three weeks, the child remained in the hospital undergoing tests, while Kitty shuttled back and forth to New York. Then, at the end of April, came worse news. Ken returned from the hospital late one afternoon to tell Kitty that the diagnosis of arthritis was wrong: Douglas had leukemia. For both parents, the pain must have at times been almost unbearable. Galbraith's parents were both dead, and now there was this sudden, incongruent prospect of the death of a son. For Kitty, both her child and her mother were dying at once.

Over the next two months, husband and wife both displayed great dignity and compassion. Friends recall Galbraith carrying Douglas downstairs each morning, his small body held by a wooden frame meant to minimize the pain, the father joking affectionately with his child, always tender, always loving. Every student in Galbraith's classes that term volunteered to give blood for Douglas, and so did many others.

It soon became clear that the efforts were to no avail, and the inevitable drew near. In early May, Kitty's mother died at her home in New York. Kitty was in anguish about leaving Douglas for her mother's funeral and did so only when her husband insisted she must go. While she was away, Douglas's condition worsened, and barely a week after Kitty returned to Cambridge, shortly after his seventh birthday, he passed away. For his birthday, Galbraith had bought his son the bicycle he'd asked for, knowing as he did so it would never be ridden.

Soon before, Kitty had discovered that she was pregnant, and Peter, their third son, was born that New Year's Eve. (James, the youngest of their three surviving boys, followed a year afterward.) Both for her and her husband, Alan and his two new brothers provided profound solace.

In his memoirs, Galbraith barely mentions the loss of his beloved second son. Two brief sentences in nearly six hundred pages tell us that "in the spring of 1950, our younger son Douglas, just seven and intelligent, determined and variously accomplished beyond his years, developed leukemia. His steady decline, accepted with unfrightened calm, is something on which after thirty years I do not care to dwell."[33] He has never added another word, but following his son's death the way he wrote changed forever.

AMERICAN CAPITALISM, FIRST published in early 1952, marks a turning point in Galbraith's career. Although it was less successful in sales and less daring in argument than some of his later books, it became a best-seller and is still in print a half century and 400,000 copies later.[34] Its success liberated Galbraith from what might have become an exclusively academic life. Like a slingshot, *American Capitalism* propelled him beyond the gravitational pull of university life and professional economics.

Never lacking in ambition, Galbraith was nevertheless unprepared for the public reaction to the book. He had written nothing like it before, and his work had never evoked such a reaction, even the articles he'd written for *Life*, which after all had reached millions of readers.[35] (In fact, he had been disappointed by the indifference that greeted his second book, *A Theory of Price Control*, published earlier the same year.) But if he hoped *American Capitalism* would be a popular and influential book, there was no evidence of this ambition in the way he negotiated its sale. Without a literary agent, he had simply approached an editor at Boston's old-line publishing house Houghton Mifflin, and, with no more than an oral presentation, got a quite standard contract, with a standard $1,000 advance. Galbraith told his editor that the book, with the working title *The Vested Ideas of Economics*, would "frame the pragmatic justification for a private economy. It does away with most of the cant about its relationship to freedom or its tendency to equate reward to marginal product. It substitutes, as the basic justification, the social efficiency of decentralized decision, especially in organization of production, and in providing a framework for innovation."[36]

He made the publishing arrangement in the spring of 1950, as his son lay dying, and one can still today feel in the book (which is dedicated "To Douglas") a ferocious, sublimated energy behind the wit and argument. The work represents a thoroughgoing break with what Galbraith had written before, not just in the scope and directness of its argument, but in its new authorial voice. It is a full-scale and quite original synthesis of a somewhat technical economic subject that also addresses broader political questions, and it is unified by a wide focus and by the freshness of its sometimes excoriating wit.

Galbraith's neighbor and friend Arthur Schlesinger, Jr., recognized the work's potential immediately. Schlesinger himself was no stranger to success or influence. A Pulitzer Prize–winning author by age thirty and (like his father) an eminent American historian, as he read Galbraith's manuscript in 1951, he foresaw the reception it would enjoy. It had "great force and clarity," he told Galbraith, and was "brilliantly illuminating. It ought to have great impact on American economic and political thinking."[37]

Schlesinger's estimate was handsomely correct. On publication, *American Capitalism* swiftly earned influential reviews in all the major newspapers and magazines.[38] *The New York Times* sweepingly declared that "London, Cambridge, and Oxford together would, indeed, be hard put to point to any recent attempt at a general reformulation of basic economic doctrine carried out with such verve and skill." Even *Business Week* hailed it as "a brilliant and provocative book, witty, irreverent, and utterly merciless."[39]

The few critical reviews were at least colorful in their dislikes. The troglodyticly conservative *Chicago Tribune* headlined its review "Fair Deal Trash in a Respectable Package." Its reviewer even suggested that Galbraith had cynically written the book only to seek favor (and a possible job) with the Truman administration, though why the book was seen as an endorsement of the Missouri Democrat was frankly not clear. The recently founded socialist journal *Dissent*, by contrast, scored *American Capitalism* for being too conservative, disliking its "economics of self-congratulation," and lumping Galbraith among those it dubbed "perennial faddists" and "hard-boiled eggheads of what might be called the devitalized center."*[40]

The book wasn't just a popular success: most economists greeted it with warm, respectful attention.[41] The *American Economic Review* thought it deserved the "careful attention of his professional colleagues," and *The Review of Economics and Statistics* declared that Galbraith "has produced a theory of capitalism which cannot be disregarded by anyone, though it will disturb many . . . [T]he new territory he has sighted needs to be explored, mapped, and occupied . . . Properly exploited, the bridgehead gained may serve as a starting point for a true twentieth century" economics. Britain's *Economic Journal*, often suspicious of upstart Americans, gave it high praise, pronouncing *American Capitalism* "shrewd, witty and forceful." Watchful of the virulent politics of Senator McCarthy, however, it noted that it would be "interesting to watch the fate of the ideology which [Galbraith] proposes with the audience to which it is addressed." Even conservative journals, while predictably objecting to its central arguments, glumly conceded that, as one observed, *American Capitalism* was exercising a dangerous influence on the nation's economists that "matches, or exceeds . . . any other book in our field since J. M. Keynes's *General Theory*."[42] This was far from hostile exaggeration: the American Economic Association designated *American Capitalism* as the subject for the opening panel of its 1953 national convention.

Time hasn't diminished *American Capitalism*'s power. It still possesses striking freshness today not only because the writing is witty and persuasive, but because its subject—the rationale for a capitalist market economy, and its economic and political meaning—remains so germane.

Conservative economists and political theorists alike have long equated markets with human freedom. In their view, private ownership and private control of property undergird the rights of individuals and their power to make independent choices; without such ownership freedom is impossible and the people are subject to the abuses of powerful governments, special interests, and their leaders. For several centuries Western (or at least Anglo-Saxon) liberalism shared in this view, and indeed did much to advance it against an older form of conservatism that favored the ancient power of kings and emperors to protect not only property but the inherited order accompanying it.

But as capitalism emerged along with new political freedoms in England, then in the United States, a new, modern liberalism developed, too. After the Civil War, American liberals went further, reconceptualizing government as an instrument of that popular will which could and should limit the new power of giant corporations and trusts, economic structures that had appeared during industrialization and that were taking on the often brutal and arbitrary power associated with political despots. Competing against socialists as well as laissez-faire conservatives, these modern liberals attacked the monopolistic

---

*The swiping reference was to *The Vital Center*, the recent book in which Schlesinger urged liberals and progressives to distance themselves from socialists and Communists, and thereby help to strengthen the tradition of a "vital center" in American politics.

power of the trusts and their baleful effects on economic competition and on democracy. But unlike the socialists and Communists, they sought to save and reform capitalism and private ownership of the means of production, rather than to overthrow it.

Like-minded economists embraced Alfred Marshall and his "marginalist" economics, which in its claim to "scientific" principles produced a new rationale for capitalism as a specific type of market relations. In Marshall's framework, rewards to individuals were distributed according to their contribution to marginal productivity, a process that optimized the efficient allocation and use of all resources. Monopoly was undesirable because it impeded optimal allocation, but by the 1920s economists presumed it was containable, and to a great degree was a secondary matter in the world of competitive equilibrium. After all, the fruits of industrialism seemed to be spreading quickly to all—the automobile, radio, and refrigerator were good examples.

The collapse and suffering of the Depression resurrected the passions of the trust busters as well as a generation of "national planners." Although these passions were largely suppressed during World War II, they reemerged (in a somewhat weaker form) among many postwar Democrats because economic concentration was growing rather than decreasing. By 1950, fewer than 150 companies, for example, controlled more than half of U.S. manufacturing assets, and in the economy overall, fewer than 400 firms out of several million controlled nearly 60 percent of corporate assets and employed more than a third of all American workers.[43]

Galbraith's startling originality in *American Capitalism* began with his attack on the conventional wisdom of all three groups: the conservatives with their property-equals-freedom argument, the claim of marginalists that competition equaled efficiency, and the liberals' belief that economic concentration inevitably undermined democratic politics. No less striking or controversial was his alternative analysis of modern capitalism's macrodynamics.

For any group to oppose the now century-old tendency toward business concentration and large-scale business was as hopeless as opposing gravity, entropy, or Darwinian selection, Galbraith argued. Concentration and bigness were inevitable, indeed "natural," in advanced capitalism. Thus the liberal belief in antitrust or 1930s-style "national planning" was a "less reliable faith than fetishism," while the marginalists' faith in a world of myriad "price-taking" firms, each too small to set a market's final price, was archaic, badly at odds with observable realities, and in need of major revision. (He thought the conservatives' dark belief that any "welfare state" inevitably would lead to modern-day "serfdom," in Friedrich von Hayek's inimitable term, was an anachronism hardly worthy of comment—a judgment he had to revisit in the Reagan era.)

The reason why both standard liberal and marginalist doctrines were now out of date was twofold: whatever its other faults, bigness presented clear advantage for achieving technological innovation; and the system of large institutions had its own tendency to checkmate its members, in forms and manners that were observable, although they had been largely ignored.

Galbraith admitted that business concentration led to all sorts of non-price competition that violated orthodox canons. But, he insisted, economists, as well as politicians and the public, needed to see that "efficiency" could be conceived in more than one sense, and that the societally acceptable tradeoff for reduced "allocational" efficiency based on price was increased "innovative" efficiency by the large corporation. Both Joseph Schumpeter and John Maurice Clark had already argued that bigness encouraged technological innovation, and that the loss of simple price competition was not an unalloyed market failure. But in *American Capitalism*, Galbraith refined their claims and made them central.[44]

The world no longer was in a depression, and, more important, the United States did not live in a nineteenth-century realm of absolute economic scarcity. With increasing output and rising living standards, an economic policy was needed that did not merely allocate resources and goods efficiently and determine competitive prices, but allowed for competition that fostered constant innovation through heavy expenditures on research and development, and that gave corporations the financial and managerial capacity to bring innovations to market. This capacity for innovative efficiency and the promotion of aggregate growth justified, Galbraith claimed, the large corporation, concentration, and the relative surrender of classic price competition.

These factors were vital to Galbraith's argument, but it was his "theory of countervailing power" that was *American Capitalism*'s real contribution, since he believed it would free liberals and economists to pursue new and better agendas. He told readers how important "countervailing power" was in the boldest of terms:

> The contention I am here making is a formidable one. It comes to this: Competition which, at least since the time of Adam Smith, has been viewed as the autonomous regulator of economic activity and as the only available regulatory mechanism apart from the state, has, in fact, been superseded. Not entirely, to be sure. I should like to be explicit on this point. Competition still plays a role . . .
>
> However, this is not the only or even the typical restraint on the exercise of economic power. In the typical modern market of few sellers, the active restraint is provided not by competitors but from the other side of the market by strong buyers. Given the convention against price competition, it is the role of the competitor that becomes passive in the market.[45]

Galbraith offered recognizable everyday examples. The labor unions' checkmating of oligopolistic industries was one; giant retail chains' countering the market power of large, concentrated producers was another; one large manufacturing industry, such as automobiles, bargaining with others, such as steel, was a third. Of course, not all markets or industries had these balancing forces. The home-building industry did not, for example, due to the quaintly old-fashioned fragmentation caused by tens of thousands of small builders; no one builder or group of builders was able to dominate even regional, let alone national, markets. Countervailing power would keep expanding in advanced American capitalism, because it was as much a "self-generating force" as the tendency to concentration itself. This means that, as a common rule, we can rely on countervailing power to appear as a curb on economic power."[46]

The overall implications of Galbraith's claims produced predictable reactions in the predictable places. Orthodox economists thought Galbraith meant to invalidate "competition" itself, at least as derived from Marshall's marginalist approach. Here Galbraith made no apology: Marshall's core insight may not have been wrong *in his time*, he allowed, but by now its utility was outweighed by its inaccuracies. To liberals, Galbraith seemed bent on killing off an older (and to him badly outdated) faith in anticorporate and anticoncentration doctrines that were meant to defend their own ideals of diffused power and citizen democracy. Here too he made no apology.

It went largely unremarked at the time, but later critics observed that the book almost inadvertently also threatened a third group. Where in this world of "countervailing power" was the dynamic government leadership, and its macromanagerial quest for continuous, stable growth, that Keynes advocated? If the new competition of "countervailing power" among market actors yielded acceptable—though theoretically unorthodox—results, why would a Keynesian-style government ever need to intervene?

Little wonder that *American Capitalism* quickly excited rebuttals from self-styled "pro-market" economists as well as from anxious liberals and Keynesians who thought the book seemed to celebrate capitalism as an astutely self-regulating system. As one otherwise sympathetic observer later judged it, *American Capitalism* was the only one of Galbraith's major books that had "about it an aura of complacency."[47] Yet "complacency" isn't the right word to describe the book, properly understood. *American Capitalism* is best read as a complex evaluation of the United States' dynamic political economy, showing Galbraith's strong sense of human beings' bounded rationality, and the profound interconnectedness of economics, politics, interests, and history at all levels. For Galbraith, strict "rules," even about the "natural inevitability" of concentration, aren't formal properties of the price system or of "nature." Economists aren't studying the "physics of social relations," but are grappling with trends and vectors whose force and direction can and do change over time, and which must therefore always be understood as contingent.

Galbraith's "economic" argument was thus integrated with an analysis of the political environment in which markets operated, because he believed, as the political theorist Charles Lindblom later put it, that "in all the political systems of the world, much of politics is economics, and most of economics is also politics."[48] And since he intended to draw a nonprofessional audience into the debate about choice among public policies and political values, the book's message was far from complacent. *American Capitalism* was an angry, caustic indictment of the intellectual and operational condition of American politics, especially liberal politics, at the end of the Truman era. (One can find in it parallels to Keynes's denunciation of the wartime English Liberalism of Lloyd George in *The Economic Consequences of the Peace*.) At the same time, Galbraith's style of argument and mode of analysis—his persuasion by means of English prose rather than of mathematics, his unwillingness to separate economic and political analysis, and his open advocacy for choice of certain values over others—make clear what he thought was the best way to analyze "economic" reality. He has sustained that claim throughout his career.

BY EARLY 1952, when *American Capitalism* reached bookstores, FDR had been dead for seven years, and his successor, the bespectacled former haberdasher from Missouri, had all too often disappointed Roosevelt's faithful followers. Galbraith had not actively worked in the 1948 Truman campaign, in contrast to both his earlier efforts in the reelection campaigns of FDR and his visible roles in subsequent campaigns. That inactivity was significant, and only partly explained by his move from New York to Harvard two months before the 1948 election. Now, four years later, with American troops fighting in Korea and with Truman about to announce his decision not to seek reelection, Galbraith was not hiding his frustration with the Democratic Party's behavior in recent years, especially its liberal wing.

> As this is written, American liberals have made scarcely a new proposal for reform in twenty years. It is not evident that they have had any important new ideas. Reputations for liberalism or radicalism continue to depend almost exclusively on a desire to finish the unfinished social legislation of the New Deal . . . On domestic matters, liberal organizations have not for years had anything that might be called a program. Rather they have had a file. Little is ever added. Platform-making consists, in effect, in emptying out the drawers.[49]

His accusations quickly became specific. Liberals' support for antitrust enforcement had failed not because the Truman administration hadn't supported such efforts, as many of them thought, but because, as Galbraith colorfully put it, "to suppose that there are grounds for antitrust prosecution wherever three, four or a half dozen firms dominate a market is to suppose that the very fabric of American capitalism is illegal."[50] That other old liberal nostrum, national planning, was equally bereft of hope, again not because of the administration's failings but because liberals (unlike the Communists, who had a wrong but specific alternative model in mind) had no idea what they really wanted.

> The truth is that much of the American liberal's modern advocacy of state intervention and planning has been general and verbal. [During the New Deal] it was a massive deployment of words which concealed, more or less successfully, the fact that he was a man who didn't quite know where he wanted to go . . .
>
> In fact, the pursuit of [national planning] has not been carried very far. It has been carried much less far than conservatives, in their worst dreams, have

been inclined to imagine. The most plausible alternative to competition is full public ownership of those industries where competition is ineffective. Few American liberals have even contemplated this possibility and some would indeed be worried were they forced to do so. Few of the halfway houses of control have even been investigated and it is a fair guess that they wouldn't be approved if they were. A minimum requirement of planning, for an economy where competition is no longer assumed to regulate prices, would be systematic price regulation by the state. Few contemporary liberals would find this palatable.[51]

The New Deal preoccupation with economic concentration per se was now pointless, Galbraith concluded, because the tendency toward immense corporate scale not only was inevitable but could be positive.

Why did Galbraith, whom so many think of as the quintessential liberal (and whom detractors such as Milton Friedman denounced as an out-and-out socialist) pen such words?

The political answer lies in the transformation of American liberalism in the immediate postwar years. Many historians and political scientists have dated the waning of New Deal liberalism's progressivism as early as 1938, when Republicans made inroads into the Democrats' enormous congressional majorities after the "little Depression" of 1937–38; others have pointed to Roosevelt's wartime compromises with big business; still others pinned it to the defeat of Henry Wallace's renomination for vice president in August 1944; many liberal Keynesian economists thought it was the immediate postwar months, when the Full Employment bill of 1945 became the much-diluted Employment Act of 1946. Whatever the starting point, Galbraith was surely right in judging that the robust progressive elements of New Deal liberalism were politically exhausted, and that younger Democrats (including himself) were in search of new directions, new policies, new agendas, and new leaders.

For these younger figures, the Truman administration was but a hollow shell of what had once been a vibrant Rooseveltian politics. At a Jefferson-Jackson Day dinner in early 1952, when Truman announced that he wouldn't seek re-election, Arthur Schlesinger, Jr., surprised himself by shouting "No, no," along with the audience—and then silently asked himself, "Why the hell I was shouting 'No,' since this is what I had been hoping would happen for months."[52] Illinois Governor Adlai Stevenson initially resisted even entering the presidential race, wondering, he wrote in his diary, whether it wasn't time for Republicans to run the country because Democrats had governed too long.[53]

But to Galbraith doubts about liberalism's future didn't mean that the New Deal's fundamental accomplishments could or should be rolled back. Contrary to some critics' ideas that *American Capitalism* somehow embraced a deterministic model of "natural" economic "laws" and thereby undermined support for government activism in the economy, Galbraith wrote:

At this point it becomes possible to answer . . . one of the questions with which this essay was launched. That is the meaning of the great expansion of state activity in recent decades, the expansion which conservatives have found so alarming and which many liberals have supported without knowing quite why. We can now see that a large part of the state's new activity—the farm legislation, labor legislation, minimum-wage legislation—is associated with the development of countervailing power.[54]

In other words, the conscious policy choices made by political leaders, acting with regard to the values of the constituencies that had brought them to power, were "neither adventitious nor abnormal" but an essential result of the matrix that shaped all economic institutions and actors.

Galbraith made it clear that voters, an informed public acting through their leaders, would determine—far more than neoclassical rules about marginal utility or competitive equilibrium could—whether "countervailing power" succeeded as a means of delimiting the abuses of economic concentration:

> Increasingly, in our time, we may expect domestic political differences to turn on the question of supporting or not supporting efforts to develop countervailing power. Liberalism will be identified with the buttressing of weak bargaining positions in the economy; conservatism—and this may well be its proper function—will be identified with positions of original power.[55]

Was Galbraith articulating for economists what became known among political scientists of the 1950s as "interest group pluralism"? In that influential model, the polity is described as consisting of competing interest groups struggling through the government to gain greater shares of power, privilege, control, and wealth.[56] That might have been an attractive theory for political scientists, but among economists it was no more than what Galbraith called "putting the skunk in the air conditioner."[57] If "countervailing power" emerged from government actions, it amounted to an exogenous interference in the market's power, not a "natural" working of the market, as some readers of *American Capitalism* thought Galbraith was claiming. This was no refutation or adaptation of Marshall's insights into market competition, only endorsement of government interference with it.

Galbraith, however, was not proceeding from Marshall's axioms of market rationality and optimal outcomes through competition in a world that incorporated government as an "exogenous" afterthought, as something "outside" economics. He was drawing on observations about contemporary reality that crossed from economics into politics, sociology, and history. And they were hardly his alone.

American government at midcentury was much larger and far more involved in the economy than in Marshall's time, and that involvement enjoyed a broad popular support. At the same time, the landscape of American business had steadily evolved from being a flat prairie dotted with millions of farms and small businesses to one punctuated with mountain ranges with peaks named General Motors and U.S. Steel and Alcoa towering over the prairie. As Galbraith bluntly put it,

> The large corporation is here to stay. Those who want to break it up or confine its operations within national boundaries are at war with history and circumstance. People want large tasks performed—oil recovered from the North Sea, automobiles made by the million to use it. Large tasks require large organizations. That's the way it is.[58]

American capitalism was thriving in this world of big government and giant firms. So what, then, if in both respects this new world diverged from marginalism's blackboard models? Galbraith's pragmatic question was straightforward: If our modern economic realities diverge from orthodox economic models, what are we to do? His refusal to respect academic boundary lines and to treat politics and economics as separate domains led to his answer: the benefit of "countervailing power" as an "economic theory" was not just that it better accorded with observable reality, but that it helped us reflect more deeply on the purpose of economic enterprise itself as a human activity within a democratic society.

Here Galbraith began to drive home a point of view he was to elaborate in *The Affluent Society* six years later: the focus of Marshall and the marginalists on optimizing output had been compelling when material goods and services were scarce relative to human needs. By the mid-twentieth century, with industry the source of an unending cornucopia of material goods and services, the issue for a much wealthier United States was whether more consumption of more goods—and a future of endless consumption of endlessly more goods—was in fact the height of human achievement. Galbraith, like Keynes before him, postulated an alternative goal for democratic capitalism that emerged from the very conditions that gave rise to "countervailing power."[59]

In the conventional theory of neoclassical economists, "the sufficient and only test of social change is whether, assuming organization and technology to be given, it reduces prices to the consumer." This, Galbraith admitted, was "not a test which countervailing power can always satisfy. The development of such power by workers or farmers may result primarily in a redistribution of returns. It may, by raising marginal costs, raise prices to the consumer."

Drawing on his experience in agriculture and wartime price controls, he suggested there was a different metric than simple "allocational efficiency" by which to judge an affluent democracy's economic performance:

> American society has not recently been threatened in peacetime (or even in wartime) by a shortage of food. There have been times when the tensions of the farming community were a threat to orderly democratic process. The evo-

lution of countervailing power in the labor market has similarly been a major solvent of tensions in the last half-century. Most would now agree, I think, that this has been worth a considerable price.[60]

This new metric he called "the minimization of social tension." He believed readers would see this as a demonstrable benefit in their new world governed by "countervailing power," especially when heightened social conflict was the alternative.

> On the whole, the appearance of countervailing power as a political issue cannot be considered especially unhealthy although it will almost certainly be so regarded. At first glance there is something odious about the notion that the poor and the excluded improve their lot in a democracy only by winning power. But so far there has been much less reason to regret that than to approve the results . . . Those who lost power cannot be presumed to have enjoyed their loss . . . Some, however, may have lived to see that, set against their loss of authority, is their greater prospect for an agreeable old age.[61]

Galbraith knew that conservatives nonetheless feared that the further expansion of "countervailing power" would bring only erosion of competition and loss of individual freedom. For them, he had a ready reminder:

> There remains, of course, the chance that power, developed and even encouraged to neutralize other power, will start on a career of its own . . . This danger may exist. No one can tell.
>
> It is only in light of history that our fears of the countervailing power of weaker groups dissolves, that their effort to establish their power in the market emerges as the stuff of which economic progress consists. It is by our experience, not our fears, that we should be guided.[62]

Some critics chose to view *American Capitalism* as, at most, a brief and unconnected episode in Galbraith's thought. As one put it, the concept of "countervailing power" was envisioned as a "way to explain why [capitalism] works; the task of [Galbraith's] subsequent books was to explain why it fails." In this critic's view, Galbraith "subsequently abandoned the theory. It does not appear again in his works."[63] But Galbraith denied ever having "abandoned" this core argument. In 1980, for example, he insisted that "as to countervailing power itself, I stand firm. . . . The concept of countervailing power does not deny the role of competition as a solvent for economic power. It does argue against efforts to dissolve positions of economic power as the principal remedy."*[64]

---

*He did, however, make an important qualification. "But in 1952, carried away by the idea, I made it far more inevitable and rather more equalizing than, in practice, it ever is. Countervailing power often does not emerge. Numerous groups—the ghetto young, the rural poor, textile workers, women clerical workers, many consumers—remain weak or helpless" (*A Life*, 284).

Yet *American Capitalism* concerns more than just "countervailing power." Galbraith also dwelled at length on the deleterious effects of certain ideas and ideology pervasive at the time, ideas held by influential business conservatives and their supporters in the Republican Party, the press, and certain academic circles. He pointed out their at times comic, at times poignant defense of a beleaguered yet heroic "free market," and their notion that they were noble warriors in an unending tournament of competition called "the market," facing "socialism" at every turn. The records of the Chamber of Commerce, the National Association of Manufacturers, and the Republican Party gave him ample evidence of conservatives' paranoia that despite unprecedented postwar prosperity and profits, business was facing "a last-ditch stand against disaster."[65]

The National Association of Manufacturers, he reminded readers, had long railed against Truman's moderate economic policies because it imagined they "would first hobble and then ultimately destroy the American business system." "Industry's ideas and ideals," NAM's president warned, faced an "unremitting battle against totalitarianism," totalitarianism *not* in the shape of Communism abroad but in the form of the Democratic Party at home. And the Chamber of Commerce, in a little book entitled *Socialism in America*, had likewise openly attacked Truman and the Democrats for taking a "backroad to socialism," or worse, citing as bipartisan proof the bitter rantings of the once loyally Democratic James Byrnes, who now claimed that Truman was leading America "over a bridge of socialism into a police state."[66]

Thanks to such Manichean convictions—part of a larger conservative view that held that government, universities, schools, unions, churches, peace and civil rights groups, and Hollywood were full of Communists and their equally dangerous sympathizers—a riotous march was now in full swing that made reasonable economic analysis and informed policy prescription all the more difficult, Galbraith said.[67] Ideological politics was hampering the ability to think about economics and to agree collectively and democratically on acceptable practices and purposes. Since using large frameworks to help shape our ability to reason is inevitable, the issue was not how to escape their influence but how to affect their content, and how to develop new frameworks that took better account of current circumstances and preferences, and of ideals and values transcending the present.

Galbraith was as impatient with his fellow liberals' antipathy to large corporations and industrial concentration as he was with business conservatives, because he thought both groups were indifferent to how the world actually worked. He was equally impatient with neoclassical economists, who insisted that price competition was the defining basis of modern markets and that efficiency considered only as "allocational efficiency" was the system's greatest contribution. They were hemmed in by out-of-date beliefs, the more so because they insisted that neoclassical economics was a "science" free of ideological blinders. To the contrary, neoclassical economics was laden with ideological assumptions and internal contradictions.

To begin with, its followers, whether they assumed the mathematically rigorous partial-equilibrium model of Marshall or the more complex general-equilibrium model of Marshall's French contemporary Leon Walras (increasingly favored in the 1950s), found it almost impossible to explain how simple price competition could survive in a world dominated by giant firms and highly concentrated industries.[68] To Galbraith, the observable reasons for the corporate concentration were inherent in the modern market: as young firms survive and grow, they gain technological expertise, economies of scale, a network of established selling and support structures, a set of banking, customer, and supplier relationships, and a certain "brand" recognition that later entrants find it hard to match. But their power creates a new kind of equilibrium—not the neoclassical paradigm with many small firms, each unable to influence price, but "far more typically [of] a few large firms together with a fringe of small ones. This equilibrium is apparently associated with a certain equality of strength among the major survivors coupled with a measure of equality of size that makes it difficult for any one large firm to buy another out."[69]

THE EXTRAORDINARY SUCCESS of *American Capitalism* provoked its critics to a hostility that a less influential book would have escaped, and this hostility found its clearest expression at the American Economic Association's annual convention in Washington, D.C., shortly after Christmas, 1953.[70] By pre-agreement, Galbraith was to start the session with an opening statement, to be followed by five critics, each assigned to focus on a different aspect of his argument. One young economist was overheard calling to his friend, just before the packed session in the Hotel Statler's main ballroom started, "Hey! Aren't you coming to see 'em clobber Galbraith?"[71]

The task of clobbering Galbraith fell principally to George Stigler.*[72] At six feet six inches, Stigler, like Galbraith, was an imposing figure, but apart from their height the two men had little in common. A committed economic and political conservative, the University of Chicago–trained economist had no doubts that Galbraith deserved a drubbing, and he intended to give it.

Stigler went right on the attack. Galbraith was guilty, he punned, of "playing with blocs," his theories not even worthy of the term since they amounted to prejudices rather than "scientifically defended" propositions. If subjected to scientific scrutiny, they fell apart:

> Two parts of the dogma of countervailing power might possibly be tested. The first part is that one concentration of economic power begets another and offsetting—or at least adjacent—concentration of economic power . . . The

---

*The other four panelists were Virginia's David McCord Wright, MIT's M. A. Adelman, John Perry Miller of Yale, and Frank Kottke from the Federal Trade Commission. Wright couldn't attend, but his paper, read to the audience, was even more vehement than Stigler's, calling *American Capitalism* the work of an "enemy of capitalist democracy."

Stigler was teaching at Columbia, but he soon returned to Hyde Park, where he became a pillar of the Chicago School. Stigler's dislikes weren't confined to Galbraithian economists; he was remarkably truculent with his colleagues. A younger colleague observed, "At Chicago the positivism was laid on thick, and conversations with the late George Stigler in particular were likely to be terminated by a positivist edict and a sneer."

second part of the dogma is that when bilateral oligopoly exists, socially desirable, or at least tolerable, results are obtained.

Stigler addressed two highly visible sectors in which Galbraith saw countervailing power at work: labor unions and retailing. The rise of labor unions—a historic trend that was then peaking, with 35 percent of the labor force unionized—Stigler dismissed as a function not of markets but of government. Their "strength, and often existence, was due to the New Deal," he said. "But what this shows is that governments often nurture some form of guild-cartel organization and that in the thirties the federal government nurtured a great deal of it." The matter of the unions' countervailing power was "a political rather than an economic" argument.[73]

In a strictly formal sense, Stigler was right. But he begged the question. His "refutation" acknowledged the unions' apparent countervailing power yet placed its origins "outside" the market system. But as countless economists knew, if uncomfortably—and as some, such as John R. Commons, had carefully examined—the market's borders were artifices concealing deep political presuppositions. And there was abundant evidence of governments' equally central role in helping to create modern capitalism.[74] If workers' unions (or farmers' price supports) were "artificial" and "exogenous" creations of governments, what then were corporations? What indeed were property laws, or contracts, or patents, or the banking system—or the courts and police (and the armed forces) that stood behind them? To dismiss one set of economic arrangements as artifices of government's "intervention" in "pure" markets, yet ignore government's centrality in defining, defending, and advancing the existence of markets themselves, or in giving shape and legally enforceable character to key business and financial institutions and arrangements, was a telling oversight for someone like Stigler, who claimed to be making "scientific" assumptions that somehow were socially neutral.[75]

Stigler's astigmatism was doubly embarrassing because another important Chicago School economist, Ronald Coase, had already undercut his argument. In 1937, the British-born Coase had written a path-breaking paper on the nature of the firm in which he asked a seemingly innocent question: "Why do business firms exist at all?"[76] Coase had spun out (not mathematically but with purely deductive reasoning) a compelling answer: firms exist because the purchase or hiring of "factors" in a market economy—labor, capital, natural resources, and so on—require contracts between parties; when the market costs of these contracts (and related knowledge) reach a certain level, coordination by means of a set of hierarchic institutions (firms) arises. With firms come the need for government to promulgate and enforce contract relations, which (though Coase didn't develop this) also gives parties to the contracts a definite interest in government's decisions, in its decision-making processes, and in competing for good treatment by government. Embedded in his idea—though he took his answer in a different direction—is the unmistakable need for modern government and law, at a minimum in setting out the terms and conditions by which firms could operate. (From Coase's work flowed various conservative specialties in economics: the economics of property rights, law and economics, and the debate over the idea of "transaction costs.")

However conservative in its conclusions this work remained (especially at Chicago), Coase's structural integration of government into the very heart of orthodox economic models served Galbraith's arguments better than it served Stigler's. A democratic government, charged with its obligations vis-à-vis the structural nature of actual markets, of necessity is obliged to act in consonance with the expressed values of its citizenry. Simply enforcing privately negotiated contracts when one of the parties is overtly more powerful than another is not acceptable—whether the issue is working conditions, race or gender discrimination, the distributed costs of pollution, or the provision of public goods such as education, parks, health care, or any other modern service in which democratic governments are engaged.[77]

Stigler then discussed instances where countervailing power seemed less dependent on the state. Galbraith thought that the cross-market power of large retailing chains showed a clear "countervailing power" to that of large manufacturers. Stigler agreed about the explosive growth of large chain stores, but did not think this had occurred in order to provide "countervailing power" to the concentration among producers of the goods sold by the chains. After all, grocery chains, for example, bought goods from many nonconcentrated suppliers, while many concentrated suppliers evaded concentrated-buyer markets. But Stigler's evidence was peculiar, because it came from a 1935 Federal Trade Commission study, an old survey tracking economic behavior at the height of the Depression (curiously, he ignored a 1948 FTC study that undercut his argument). Undaunted by the weakness of his evidence, Stigler went on to claim that "countervailing power" was no more than what economists call "bilateral oligopoly," which would have few of the advantages Galbraith asserted and was inferior to classical models of competition.

Stigler seemed to believe that bilateral oligopolies offered benefits only to the oligopolists themselves, not to the larger society. But economists had long since shown that oligopolies can exhibit maddeningly complex behavior that isn't predictably like that of a classic monopolist, and that often both serves a countervailing power function and distributes its benefits to many more than the immediate interest-holders in the oligopolies themselves.[78]

Galbraith had anticipated Stigler's critique, in any case. His point, he rejoined, was not to claim that competition had been destroyed by countervailing power but that the latter must be understood in conjunction with, and acting upon, competition. The countervailing power of concentrated retailers vis-à-vis concentrated manufacturers kept the latter from capturing super-normal profits, but competition among retailers (or the threat of it) also helped to transfer any potential above-average profits to the consumer.*[79]

---

*Recent studies of Wal-Mart, the world's largest retailer, show that it has consistently behaved as a "countervailing power," not as Stigler predicts (*The Economist*, "How Big Can It Grow?" April 17–23, 2004, 67ff).

Stigler left the meeting feeling he'd won the debate, just as he felt his mentor Frank Knight had beaten Galbraith in 1946. But the influence of Galbraith's "countervailing power" concept went on expanding. One economist observed in the early 1960s, "The use of the term 'countervailing power' has become so common in business and sociological writing about contemporary America that it is hard to find current popular discussions in print that do not make at least some use of the idea."[80]

NONETHELESS, THE ISSUES Galbraith raised about industrial structure and competition ironically did seem to recede, at least among mainstream economists, as the 1950s wore on. This was principally because a new group of theorists advancing Keynesian theories about national macropolicy took center stage. The proponents of the Neoclassical Synthesis by the late 1950s had largely shifted the profession from concern about the microeconomic issues of consumers, firms, and organizations to macroeconomic questions about aggregate employment, national income, and, especially, to the very Keynesian question of how government could manage the economy's sustained and stable growth.

With the rapid advance of their theories and of large-scale, computer-based economic models, the possibility of successful macromanagement seemed for a while within reach. By the 1960s, many economists were even prematurely proclaiming the arrival of the Golden Age of Keynesianism and, with it, the permanent successful public management of national economic growth. Their judgment was, needless to say, premature in the extreme. When confidence in mainstream Keynesianism fell dramatically in the 1970s, interest in microeconomic issues concerning consumers, firms, and industries renewed. As in the 1930s, this shift coincided with a downward shift in America's real-world economic performance, although the pressing issue was not depression but "stagflation," a haunting cycle of low growth, inflation, and high unemployment that the Keynesian theories had foreseen.

Among conservative economists who derided the Keynesians, the economy's disarray and stagnation was justification for new theory building, with their most famous accomplishment for a time "Rational Expectations" economics, a brand of theoretical fundamentalism that swept out from the University of Chicago and a few other equally conservative departments. Rational Expectationists applied a strict interpretation of the enduring orthodox view that human beings act as "rational maximizers" of their self-interest, which, when coupled with the theory of "efficient market clearing," allowed them to argue against Keynesian ideas that government policy could successfully fine-tune economic performance.

But then in the 1980s, a new kind of heterodox style arose, as young economists sought new ways of looking at theoretical issues, and in the process stumbled back onto issues that had preoccupied their intellectual fathers and grandfathers, including issues about power, knowledge, and structural concentration. This time, though, they were armed with all the mathematical rigor and sophistication that the Neoclassical Synthesis generation had deployed.

They used game theory, for example, to suggest that claims like Galbraith's about "countervailing power" might not be so implausible after all, by concentrating on situations of "uncertainty" and "interaction," in which traditional economics' rules for "rational actors" were not clear. A new understanding of "information" and its costs in economic transactions also seemed to support *American Capitalism*'s insistence that orthodox notions of "competition" were flawed. Coupled with these theoretical shifts was a new research focus on the actual behavior of firms and industries, rather than subordinating them to aggregate indices. Empirical studies of American manufacturing, for example, found that when industries were subdivided by both product and by degrees of industry concentration, one *could* see the significant and measurable effect of concentrated buyers on sellers' profit margins, particularly in consumer goods industries. As the Harvard economist F. M. Scherer concluded, "It seems clear that countervailing power can and does lead to lower transfer prices, at least in that middle ground of oligopolistic market structure where sellers are few enough to recognize their interdependence, but too weak to maintain a disciplined front against the whipsaw tactics of a strong, shrewd buyer."[81]

Though this new theoretical and empirical work seemed to vindicate Galbraith's claim in 1952 to have defined a new, more complex understanding of "competition," it did not close the gap between him and his orthodox contemporaries or their successors, or so at least the latter would claim. Many economists still sniff that perhaps Galbraith "got it right" but only by intuition rather than by the hard, rigorous work that requires mathematically shaped models or the examination of data using testing criteria such as the Herfindahl-Hirschman index or OLS regressions. To them, Galbraith is still a professional "outsider." But this dismissal, as we shall soon see, is complicated by the discovery that the mathematical modeling of economic reality is more elusive and less stable than was once imagined.

12

Stevenson and the Liberals

We cannot blink the fact that the party of Roosevelt is also the party of Bilbo and Rankin. But the fact remains that we have no practical alternative.*
—Chester Bowles, at the founding of
Americans for Democratic Action

BY THE SUMMER of 1952, Ken Galbraith found himself feeling oddly divided.

On the one hand, the extraordinary critical and popular success of *American Capitalism* had given him immense new recognition. And his family, after the painful loss of Douglas two years earlier, was healing and growing. Eleven-year-old Alan, who had been deeply affected by his brother's death, was once again thriving, along with his little brothers, Peter and James. (Galbraith was a doting father, but like most men of his generation, he left the child-rearing details to the women in the household. With three sons to care for, Kitty and Emily Wilson had their hands full. As his wife recalled years later, not without some annoyance, "John Kenneth Galbraith is the father of four sons—and never changed a diaper in his life."[1])

With the boys and a regular stream of lunch and dinner guests, the Galbraiths' home at 30 Francis Avenue by now was becoming a lively place. They had always enjoyed entertaining in Washington and New York, and Cambridge was no different. Arthur and Marian Cannon Schlesinger lived on Irving Street, just across the back wall of the Galbraiths' property.† Schlesinger, both because he was a prominent young professor himself, and because his father and father-in-law, Walter Cannon, were among Harvard's most renowned pro-

---

*Theodore Bilbo was a vitriolically racist Democratic senator from Mississippi (1935–47); John Rankin was the Democratic congressman, also from Mississippi, who was chairman of the House Un-American Activities Committee.

†Schlesinger's son Stephen recalls, "My father rarely played catch with me as a boy. But I could occasionally get him into a game when he was standing near the wall, talking to Ken."

fessors, knew interesting people throughout the university and enjoyed introducing Ken and Kitty to many of his and his wife's friends. The Galbraiths
also enjoyed the friendship of Professor Black, although there was always
that slight distance of the mentor relationship. Seymour Harris, Ed Mason, and
John Dunlop—all roughly Galbraith's age, and like him rising stars in economics—were also close. (And Galbraith quickly formed a warm friendship
with McGeorge Bundy, the brilliant young dean of the faculty, though he was
cool to Nathan Marsh Pusey, who became Harvard's president in 1953.)

The Harvard historian Bernard DeVoto and his wife, Avis, took a liking to
the Galbraiths and made them regular guests at "the hour," their famous Sunday afternoon "drinks party" at their rambling, book-filled home on Berkeley
Street. Benny DeVoto was not only a great (and controversial) historian of the
American West, but a novelist, essayist, pamphleteer, and perennial scourge of
intolerance, whether on the part of J. Edgar Hoover or American Stalinists.
Calling himself "a literary department store," he had been the editor of *The
Saturday Review* and was still a columnist for *Harper's*, producing the magazine's influential "Easy Chair" column each month for twenty years until his
death in 1955. DeVoto was a cheerful collector of people of all kinds, and his
Sunday party, which always reflected his eclecticism, made a lasting impression on the Galbraiths.

The same generous style of entertaining soon became a Galbraith trademark. Invitations to parties at Francis Avenue, unlike so many in Cambridge,
were welcomed because they promised a congenial hodgepodge of interesting
and engaged figures in the social sciences, humanities, sciences, and professional schools, as well as out-of-town friends from the Galbraiths' network of
New Deal veterans, liberal politicians, and journalists. Talk at these parties
was more likely to be about the latest novels or the politics of China or
the newest acquisitions at the Fogg Museum or the Boston Museum of Fine
Arts than the latest journal article or academic paper. Another key to the success of those parties (as well as to the success of much else about the Galbraiths' family and social life generally for nearly forty years) was the ebullient
personality of their housekeeper, Emily Wilson, beloved by the family and
guests alike.*

Work life at Harvard, too, was a source of pleasure and renewal. Galbraith's
teaching went well, and he was also directing the Harvard Economic Studies,
the Economics Department's prestigious book series, as well as sitting on the
editorial board of *The Review of Economics and Statistics*. Along with making
regular appearances in the professional journals, he was consistently sought
out to write articles for magazines and newspapers.

But on the other hand, while his personal life and career seemed rich,

---

*Galbraith and Emily early on formed a close bond, built in part on their shared humor. He was nearly two feet
taller than she, and it became an often-repeated family joke for him to stand next to her, then call out several
times to Kitty or the boys, "Where's Emily?" before peering down in mock surprise to "find" her scowling up at
him in equally mock annoyance. To Kitty's frequent embarrassment, they would challenge each other to see who
could recite more bawdy limericks.

America's political life gave him equally rich cause for frustration. Part of the frustration came from what he had discussed in his book, liberalism's postwar decay in economics and economic policy, but there was a second source as well. Galbraith, like many other New Deal liberals, was stunned by the vitriol that American conservatives were spewing into public debate.

Stalin's aggressive, even imperial policies in Central and Eastern Europe had mobilized most Americans into supporting a foreign policy that favored the "containment" of Soviet influence, but now there was a divisive toxin of anti-Communism at home. This was hardly new: after the Bolshevik Revolution in 1917 had prompted the United States (along with Britain and France) to dispatch troops to Russia in 1919, hoping to destabilize Lenin's new government and to support the "Whites" fighting the "Reds" in all the territories of the old Russian empire, fear of Bolshevism at home led to a nationwide Red Scare, with sweeping arrests of thousands of presumed radicals, including anarchists and socialists who in fact loathed Soviet Communism. Civil liberties were badly trampled, several thousand aliens were deported, and a young J. Edgar Hoover's career was launched. And during the Depression and the war, endless accusations of "Communist influence" were hurled at FDR and the New Deal, and not just from the far right. But after Roosevelt died, the domestic accusations—and the fervor of the accusers—took on renewed life when an ambitious new generation of men such as Joseph McCarthy and Richard Nixon found in them a path to political power.

Galbraith himself had twice personally felt the sting of this revitalized vituperation, but he was nonetheless eager to get back into the national political fray. When his friends George Ball and Arthur Schlesinger, Jr., urged him in July 1952 to join the presidential campaign of Adlai Stevenson as a speechwriter and adviser, he leaped at the invitation. Having sat out the 1948 campaign as well as any government service under Truman, he took this as an opportunity to reverse course and get involved, and—never an unappealing prospect—to do so at the highest levels. (The Republican standard-bearer in 1952 would be General Dwight D. Eisenhower, the immensely popular war hero, even though he faced opposition within the party from the isolationist wing, and notably from Senator Robert Taft, who disliked Eisenhower's alleged liberalism.) Eisenhower had refused until 1952 to identify himself with either party. Indeed, Truman approached him in 1947 with an extraordinary offer: to run as the Democratic nominee in 1948 with Truman as his vice president. As late as the fall of 1951, Truman was once again courting Ike, and liberals were actively advancing a "Draft Ike" movement. Senator Paul Douglas of Illinois even proposed that Eisenhower be jointly nominated by both the Republicans and Democrats.

When Galbraith signed on to the Democratic campaign, he had never met Governor Stevenson, although both of them had been recruited to the Bombing Survey by their mutual friend George Ball in 1945. Soon enough, they came to admire and like one another, and for the next eight years Galbraith hitched himself politically to Stevenson. "The grace with which he pictured himself as a harried, wavering intellectual lost in the harsh, demanding world of politics was one of his most engaging qualities," Galbraith remembered. Tall, with a bald head, prominent nose, and inquisitive, gentle eyes, this odd Princeton-educated Prince of Denmark "was committed to picturing not his strength in contending with harsh circumstance but his frailty, not his certainty but his doubts . . . It was an impulse in a politician for which no one was in the slightest prepared."[2]

Yet Stevenson was anything but frail. He was a wealthy corporate lawyer (George Ball had been a partner), had served as an aide to Secretary of the Navy Frank Knox during the war, then won the governorship of Illinois—a state not known for rewarding frailty in its politicians—and had in July won the Democratic nomination for president. "I came to believe that he loved every parade, every rally, every cheer, every band, every other moment of the great show," Galbraith wrote. "He was regarded as a liberal and perhaps is rightly so described. But he was also a committed elitist. He ran for President not to rescue the downtrodden but to assume the responsibilities properly belonging to the privileged."[3]

When Galbraith showed up in Illinois to work for Stevenson, for a moment the relationship seemed poised to end before it began. He hadn't counted on the fact that his own now-burgeoning national reputation would precede him and was thus taken aback when—on the very day he arrived in Springfield, where Governor Stevenson had his campaign headquarters, and within moments of checking into his hotel—he got a call from Schlesinger insisting that he stay in his room until further notice and talk to no one. "The reason was that at a press conference a day before, Stevenson had been asked if his campaign wasn't being taken over by radicals," Galbraith recollects, "specifically by dangerous figures from the Americans for Democratic Action." And Stevenson, who was admired for his speaking abilities, wasn't happy at having the press and public aware that others, especially a certain famous Harvard professor, were being recruited to write his speeches.[4]

The momentary "radicals-in-the-campaign" crisis passed and Schlesinger released Galbraith from his solitary confinement. But what about Stevenson's reluctance to acknowledge his Brains Trust? That, it turned out, proved to be one of the candidate's contradictions. When Galbraith left his hotel a free man and walked over to join the team he'd be working with, he realized that Stevenson's chief political aides, Wilson Wyatt and Carl McGowan, had been quietly assembling a quite lustrous cadre, whatever their boss's quaint misgivings about speechwriters. Known within the campaign as "The Elks" because the rented third-floor offices they occupied, three blocks from campaign headquarters and the Governor's Mansion, was otherwise the local Elks Club, the core group included, besides Galbraith and Schlesinger, John Fischer, editor of *Harper's*; W. Willard Wirtz, a law professor at Northwestern University (later President Kennedy's Secretary of Labor); David Bell, a senior Truman assistant (later Kennedy's budget director and then executive vice president of the Ford Foundation); Robert Tufts, a gifted young Oberlin political scientist; the Washington journalist Sidney Hyman; and John Bartlow Martin, a *Saturday Evening Post* reporter.[5] (Soon after arriving, Galbraith recruited his old friend Eric Hodgins from *Fortune* to join the team. Hodgins took particular pleasure in working for the Democrats as a "Luce man." Luce had already sent *Time's* publisher, C. D. Jackson, to work in Dwight Eisenhower's campaign as a senior strategist, just as he'd dispatched *Fortune* editor Russell Davenport to be Wendell Willkie's campaign manager in 1940. Leaving for Springfield, Hodgins sent Jackson a succinct little note: "Piss on you, C.D., I'm going to work for the right man."[6])

Galbraith quickly bonded with this hardworking and high-spirited group of young political warriors, who saw their job not only as electing a president, but in a deeper sense as renewing the vision and vitality of the Democratic Party. None of them doubted that it would be a hard-fought battle.

To begin with, everyone knew that General Eisenhower was extraordinarily popular. Stevenson himself had feared only Ike among his potential Republican opponents. Still, after the party conventions in August, an Eisenhower victory over Stevenson was far from certain: the hero of D-Day was leading Illinois's governor by only 6 percentage points (47 to 41 percent) in the polls.[7] Stevenson and his advisers knew that Truman had defeated Dewey in 1948 after much worse midsummer poll numbers, and they convinced themselves that there was a real possibility that the Democrats could capture the White House for a sixth consecutive term.

Galbraith shared their conviction, and so that summer in Springfield—and then in Cambridge after Harvard classes resumed in early September—he poured himself energetically into his ghostwriting duties, producing a steady stream of major and minor speeches on economic and agricultural policy, as well as helping edit and redraft the work of the other Elks.

The Elks' passion for Stevenson as the redeemer of the Democratic Party's liberalism was touched with a certain inescapable irony. Although for a generation of conservatives the bald-headed Stevenson came to epitomize all the foibles and dangers of "egghead intellectuals" in politics—a caricature that was endlessly invoked by McCarthy and Nixon—in 1952 he was, in fact, far from the darling of American liberalism. In truth, the governor was surprisingly conservative on issues ranging from Keynesian economics to civil rights, union power, and federal aid to education—litmus issues to younger Democrats such as Galbraith. To complicate matters, he had been resistant to running for the presidency at all.

The fact that he was the Democrats' nominee seems remarkable today, given the way the nominating process has changed. As a sitting President, Truman was the party's natural candidate, but when in early 1952 he decided privately not to run, he began a behind-the-scenes effort to have Stevenson win the nomination. Never personally enamored of the reserved and cautious governor, he nonetheless had calculated that Stevenson represented the party's best chance for holding onto the White House. But Stevenson—by turns coy, stubborn, and enigmatic—resisted the President's encouragement, to Truman's immense annoyance. In mid-March, with the primaries already under way Stevenson insisted he still hadn't made up his mind.

Truman wasn't alone in wanting the governor nominated. Hoping they could finally persuade him to enter the race, George Ball and James Loeb, the executive director of Americans for Democratic Action, arranged late that winter to dine with Stevenson during one of his brief stopovers in Washington.[8] Both men knew time was running out. Other candidates—including the quasi-populist Senator Estes Kefauver of Tennessee (whom Truman despised), Georgia's Senator Richard Russell, and the liberal millionaire New Yorker Averell Harriman, scion of the Union Pacific fortune—were already in the race or hovering at its edges, and Truman was under pressure to announce his own decision not to run. Harriman was rapidly gaining favor among northern liberals: FDR's ambassador to Russia in 1944–45, he'd succeeded Henry Wallace as secretary of commerce in late 1946, and Truman had trusted him enough to use him as an emissary to General Douglas MacArthur in hopes of avoiding what became a controversial collision over Korean War strategy; Truman had even encouraged him in the presidential race in order to fend off Kefauver. But Harriman had never run for public office and spoke woodenly on the stump because almost no one thought he could win in November.

The dinner did not go well. Stevenson was in a querulous mood and told Ball and Loeb he was both reluctant to run and resentful of Truman's pressure. What's more, he admitted, he didn't really believe in the "Fair Deal" goals of Truman's administration, and cited the issues, point by point, to highlight his disagreement. He opposed federal funding of public housing, he said, and opposed repeal of the anti-union Taft-Hartley Act (though he thought amending it might be acceptable). With the Korean War fueling inflation, he said he'd be tough about stabilizing the economy and would risk strikes if the unions opposed him in order to make wage gains. Schools were for states and localities to worry about, and federal aid to education should be considered only as a last resort. He told his dinner partners, who by now were picking distractedly at their food, that he opposed Truman's health reform proposals as "socialized medicine." As for a rapid expansion of civil rights for black Americans, the issue that had split the 1948 Democratic convention, that too was a matter for states to resolve, and Washington shouldn't be putting "the South completely over a barrel."

Despite being governor of a major farm state, Stevenson admitted to nearly complete ignorance of agricultural issues, but said he thought he opposed most of the New Deal's price stabilization plans. He also described himself as "orthodox" on economic policy and, while never mentioning Keynes, said he opposed deficits on principle. Only on foreign policy—meaning the tough bipartisan anti-Communist doctrine of the era—was he in accord with Truman.

Ball and Loeb were stunned, to say the least, and Ball drank too much scotch "to compensate for my chagrin"—and paid for it with a terrible hangover. He told other Democrats the next day merely that "the discussions did not go well." Loeb, much more alarmed, told several people he thought

Stevenson would make a bad candidate and poor president, and for a time even thought about having Americans for Democratic Action work to block Stevenson's nomination.[9]

Not long after this, Stevenson came to Massachusetts and sat down with Arthur Schlesinger, Jr., and a few others in Cambridge to talk about the race and to get better acquainted. Schlesinger encouraged Stevenson to enter the race, but after two hours of intense conversation he came away thinking that if the governor indeed ran, he would be

> the most conservative Democratic presidential candidate since [the Wall Street lawyer] John W. Davis [in 1924]. He thought Stevenson intended to aim his campaign at Southern Democrats and high-minded Republicans . . . groups for whom Schlesinger had little use and who were not numerous enough to elect a President. Stevenson seemed far more anxious to see Richard Russell than Averell Harriman. He once indicated that he was considering appointing John J. McCloy Secretary of State if he won.[10]

Ultimately, the shrewdly reluctant Stevenson rode out the entire primary season without entering the race, leaving Kefauver as the leader in primary votes but without a clear majority. When the Democrats gathered in Chicago for their convention in July, facing what many feared would be certain defeat in November if they chose Kefauver (whose womanizing and heavy drinking were sure to become front-page news), a "Draft Stevenson" movement emerged on the first day and quickly determined the nomination. The choice of Adlai Stevenson as the Democratic Party's standard-bearer provoked a crisis among many of the liberal party faithful, who longed for the dynamism and vision of Roosevelt yet feared what a Republican White House would do to FDR's legacy. Swallowing their concerns, they signed on with Stevenson, trying to convince themselves, as one of them put it, that "the logic of the situation would force Stevenson leftward as the campaign progressed."[11]

Once in the race, Stevenson did, in fact, move somewhat leftward. At the same time, his top aides and advisers had to come to terms with the exigencies of presidential politics: 1952 wasn't a good year for liberals. The United States had been at war in Korea since June 1950, and with no end in sight, part of Ike's appeal to voters was his presumed ability to find a solution. Meanwhile, the conservative anti-Communist campaign at home was crescendoing, with the red-baiting Senator Richard Nixon about to become Eisenhower's vice-presidential running mate. The New Deal coalition was effectively dead, its Southern wing having bolted the party in 1948 over civil rights, and organized labor loyal but angry at the party's increasingly rightward turn, symbolized by the Democrats' unwillingness to seek repeal of the hated Taft-Hartley Act.

A certain amount of a writer's and intellectual's freedom must sometimes be traded for access to power, and the price of power is sometimes an accession to certain established political truths, as Galbraith understood—the lesson wasn't new for him. The question now was whether to wring one's hands and lament one's fate, or dig out with the tools at hand. Galbraith the academic and author might be Keynesian in macroeconomics and redistributive in social policy, but Galbraith the speechwriter meant to persuade voters that a President Stevenson would not radically depart from the orthodoxies of the day.[12]

A good example of the pragmatic trade-off Galbraith was willing to make can be found in "The Control of Inflation," a speech he wrote that Stevenson delivered to party faithful in a sweltering Baltimore armory in late September. In it, he focused on a diagnosis of inflation and on how he as president would address it.[13] The speech reflected Stevenson's concern, after a swing through western states in which he had sounded traditional liberal themes, to express some conservative ideas when discussing the economy. "We haven't said a damn thing about the cost of government, efficiency, economy, anti-socialism, anti-concentration of power in Washington," he told his staff on September 13. "The impression is that we are moving more and more to the left. I don't want to be euchred out of that position. We mustn't let them [Republicans] preempt the position of fiscal responsibility."[14]

Knowing that Stevenson often overlooked details—and no doubt hoping to head off last-minute changes—Galbraith told the candidate that his proposed analysis of inflation for the speech had "no one remedy," and ranked each of the proposals he was going to make in terms of ascending "appropriateness and urgency." Attuned to Stevenson's innate caution and ignorance in economic policies, he stressed, "I am not identified with any extreme position in the controversy that rages over these issues."

The text of the speech, particularly its metaphors, was thus oddly, even painfully, "un-Galbraithian." Stevenson first blustered that "those who let their politics impeach their honesty tell you that inflation is the product of governmental waste and mismanagement . . . [A]s an explanation of the causes of inflation, it is pure poppycock." What then is the explanation? In a burst of un-Galbraithian simile, Stevenson insisted that inflation was

> like a husband coming into the kitchen, seeing one potato peeling that is too thick, and exploding that now he knows why you can't make ends meet. I'm for the Government's peeling its potatoes with a sharp knife and a miserly eye. And I've done some sharp and miserly peeling in Illinois myself. But I'm not going to fool myself or you that meeting a nation's inflation problem is that simple.

This patently inelegant analogy was then extended:

> The causes of inflation can, I think, be made plain. Let's stay in the kitchen a minute longer. It is as though we were making bread, and while we answered the phone, an evil neighbor dumped a whole cup of yeast into the bowl. That's the inflation story. In fact that *is* inflation.
>
> We have inflation today—not disastrous, but serious—because the gods of

war, working through their agents in the Kremlin, have dumped a barrel of yeast into the bread of our economy.

This may sound tinplate and false to the ear, but the policy recommendations Stevenson offered were even more un-Galbraithian. If elected president, his first step toward taming inflation would be to

> cut the Government's non-essential expenditures to the bare bones of safety. It is the biggest spending agency in the country and every dollar it spends adds to the inflationary pressure. It must spend every penny as though it were a five-dollar bill; and it must not spend a single penny for anything that is not needed right now.

And the second step? Washington would pledge to live by a balanced budget. The government, Stevenson insisted, must "keep itself just as close as possible to a pay-as-we-go standard. When we pay for these guns by borrowing money we contribute to inflation. When we collect taxes to pay for them we help stop inflation." Even this retreat from elementary Keynesian principles wasn't the end: Stevenson then assured voters, "I don't like taxes. I shall do everything I can to reduce them . . . And I'll bank on the American people, even in an election year, to understand straight talk and the need for a balanced budget."

Stevenson went on to warn that excessive private borrowing is as dangerous as government borrowing, and promised that as a third measure, he'd "work out with Congress a set of restraints upon excessive private credit which will keep the money market on an even, noninflationary, keel." This hint of possible government credit controls was a tepid Democratic measure: damaging to consumers, retailers, and real estate, such controls would surely give comfort to Wall Street and wealthy bondholders, hardly the heart of the New Deal constituency.

Then Stevenson proposed to retain the wage and price controls that President Truman had imposed as part of the Korean War effort, since however unpalatable and riven with loopholes they were, they were needed to keep the country from being "pulled or pushed any further into the twisting cyclone of inflation." But there would be no chance that such controls might linger in postwar seasons (a policy measure Galbraith had supported in his *A Theory of Price Control*). Reassuring his listeners of his "deep belief in a free economy," Stevenson insisted that he

> looked forward anxiously to the time when these casts on our economy— these price, rent and wage controls—can come off. I cannot tell you when that will be, for I can only guess as to the Kremlin's future course of conduct or misconduct. I can only say to you that I believe, with the modern doctors, that a healthy, but temporarily fractured economy, like a healthy patient, should get out of bed and get active again as quickly as possible.

With its medical metaphors, cooking conceits, twisting cyclones, and Kremlin as sorcerer's apprentice, the Galbraith speech for Governor Stevenson lacked the cool elegance and urbane humor that was becoming a Galbraithian trademark. Yet it was a political hit, and Stevenson later made a point of including it in a bound volume of his major addresses. (The well-received speech had little effect, however, because on the same evening, September 23, Richard Nixon was delivering his famous "Checkers" speech.) The question is whether it showed pragmatic adaptation to electoral requirements on Galbraith's part or bespoke something else running deeper in the currents of national politics.

BY 1952, THE DIVISIONS within American liberalism were nowhere more visible than in the Americans for Democratic Action, the nation's most influential liberal organization.[15] Founded in early January 1947, the ADA was an outgrowth of the Union for Democratic Action, a group formed in 1941, mainly by dissidents who broke with Norman Thomas's Socialist Party over its isolationism. The theologian Reinhold Niebuhr was the moving force behind it, and The Nation's editor, Freda Kirchwey, was chairman. Of the half-dozen major non-Communist progressive-left groups in the United States during the war, the UDA was the only one that formally barred Communists as members. Sensing a new urgency in 1946, and aware of the formation that year of the Progressive Citizens of America—Wallace's Progressive Party—UDA directors authorized the 1947 meeting that gave birth to the broader ADA.

At its inaugural meeting in Washington, at the elegant Willard Hotel, Eleanor Roosevelt and her son Franklin, Jr., led a roster of New Deal veterans that resembled, as one participant put it, "a government-in-exile." Along with Galbraith, Leon Henderson (who became the ADA's first chairman), Chester Bowles, Paul Porter, David Ginsburg, Richard Gilbert, Carl Auerbach, and Ed Pritchard—all of whom had served in the Office of Price Administration—were there; Elmer Davis, Isador Lubin, Gardner Jackson, and Ben Cohen also came (or joined soon after). From labor came the United Automobile Workers' Walter Reuther, David Dubinsky from the ILGWU, James Carey of the International Union of Electrical Workers, and Hugo Ernst. Urban reformers—Richardson Dilworth of Philadelphia, Hubert Humphrey of Minneapolis, and George Edwards of Detroit—joined the journalists Joseph and Stewart Alsop, Marquis Childs, James Weschler, Barry Bingham, and Kenneth Crawford, the two Arthur Schlesingers, father and son, and Reinhold Niebuhr. Though the ADA's primary goals concerned civil rights and civil liberties—as its energetic efforts on behalf of a civil rights plank at the 1948 Democratic convention had shown—the group wanted to affect the whole spectrum of liberalism's social and economic policies. For many of its members, one of the ADA's most important missions was to halt and reverse the influence of domestic Communists and fellow traveling radicals on postwar American liberalism.[16]

At the end of their inaugural meeting, the ADA's founders released a brief six-point statement of principles whose final point was: "We reject any association with Communists or sympathizers with communism in the United States as completely as we reject any association with fascists or their sympathizers. Both are hostile to the principles of freedom and democracy on which this Republic has grown great."[17] They made it clear that they were distinguishing the ADA from the Progressive Citizens of America and its leading figure, Henry Wallace. Like the ADA, the PCA boasted several New Deal–era luminaries, and was heavily influenced by organized labor, in its case the CIO, and by fellow travelers who rushed to make Wallace the PCA's leading light.*

The ADA and the Democrats were not spared the poisonous anti-Communism of the right, however. Leading the predictable attacks in the Congress were opportunistic GOP newcomers like Senators Joseph McCarthy and Richard Nixon, but GOP party elders never hesitated in their own denunciations. The veteran senator Robert Taft claimed that the Democrats were "so divided between Communism and Americanism" that "it made the United States the laughingstock of the world." The Republican party chairman railed that the Democrats were nothing but Southern racists, big-city bosses, and radicals bent on "Sovietizing" the country. Even Senator Arthur Vandenberg, once a pillar of bipartisanship in foreign affairs, wondered aloud whether working with the liberals "means more Chinas and more Hisses and more messes with Russian bombs hanging over us." By 1952, the immense hysteria that had grown out of what were a very few authentic cases involving Americans spying for the Soviet Union was reaching its apogee. Eisenhower uncomfortably accepted Nixon as his running mate in deference to it, and then, contemptibly, refused to defend General George Marshall from McCarthy's vicious attacks during the campaign. The impeccably honorable and loyal Marshall—Eisenhower's commander in World War II, and Secretary of State under Truman—was now tarred as being part of a Communist "conspiracy so immense, an infamy so black, as to dwarf any in the history of man."[18]

Galbraith found virtually every aspect of these right-wing assaults repugnant, but he also quietly blamed his fellow liberals in part for the success of the onslaught. Back in 1947, despite his deep misgivings about Truman's "get tough with the Soviets" policies, he had found it easy to join the ADA as his new political home, for he distrusted the woolly-minded Wallace and felt no inclination to defend the Soviet Union as a victim of U.S. aggression. Yet he worried that by steering too far toward the center, liberalism would lose its purpose and its political edge. As a consequence, while others in the ADA (including his good friend Arthur Schlesinger, Jr.) had worked to purge American liberalism of Communist influence—passionately working to defeat the PCA and Wallace's 1948 presidential campaign, backing prosecution and imprisonment of U.S. Communists under the controversial Smith Act—Galbraith lim-

---

*Some liberals initially saw the two new groups as divisive, Hans Morgenthau, Elliot Roosevelt, Marshall Field, and Max Lerner among the most prominent. Even Chester Bowles, who gave a stem-winding speech at the ADA's founding meeting, put off joining formally for nearly a year, while his wife joined the PCA. It wasn't until after the two groups clashed climactically in 1948 with the PCA openly supporting Wallace and the ADA (after initial reluctance) rallying around Truman, that the PCA waned (Hamby, *Beyond The New Deal*, 157–68).

ited his work for the ADA to advice on economic policy that echoed the spirit of the New Deal, and an expansive and generous vision of modern liberalism's goals.

For example, the ADA's first economic position paper, which in 1948 he cowrote, called for an increased minimum wage, tax reductions for low- and middle-income families, an expanded federal housing program, the extension of wartime farm price supports, and a price adjustment board that would try to find ways to lower prices 10 percent on a "voluntary" basis. And the paper steadfastly ignored any of the ADA's by then increasingly rote denunciations of Communism at home or abroad, and offered no endorsement for the vastly increased military spending that some ADA people thought was necessary for the United States to exercise global leadership.[19]

Similarly, after the Marshall Plan became fully operational, Galbraith, unlike several of his ADA colleagues, openly criticized those who wanted U.S. aid used to defeat not just Communism but Europe's social democrats and non-Communist Socialists. As he wrote in a policy paper in 1949, although the United States wasn't required to "associate itself with and support the moderate Socialists of Western Europe," it would be jeopardizing European democracy not to recognize that

> partliamentary government in most Western European countries is strong only where there is a strong Socialist or Social Democratic party . . . There is no certainty we can live amiably or even peacefully where, as a result of the decay of moderate socialism, people have manned the extreme bastions of political disunion.

The great questions of Europe's and the United States' future could not be reduced to a simple bipolar ideological calculus, because underlying issues of social and economic justice were never neatly divided:

> Reform in Europe means a surrender by the haves to the have-nots and it is partly for this reason that European political life tends to extreme and uncompromising positions. We will be risking serious disappointment in Europe unless we realize the extent of the social tensions which will persist in the absence of extensive reforms, and also the tensions which are certain to accompany the process of reform.[20]

International peace required continent-wide integration as well as domestic economic reforms achieved in an atmosphere of political tolerance. This meant more than customs unions or even currency integration, both fashionable topics; Europe needed to move with American support to full economic, social, and political integration.

This was Galbraith's answer to virulent anti-Communism at home and abroad—and it would remain so throughout his career. By temperament he avoided overtly ideological extremes, though he never feared to dissent from convention; his training as an economist focused him on improving economic conditions as an alternative to (and resolution of) inherited ideological combat; and his liberal disposition, based on his comfortable but modest rural upbringing, assured that he would favor the widest and most equitable distribution of better economic conditions.

By the time of the Stevenson campaign, these views were slowly regaining acceptance among fellow liberals, particularly regarding the domestic front. The reasons weren't hard to grasp: having worked in 1948 to defeat Wallace and the PCA, many of the ADA's staunchest anti-Communists were by 1952 themselves being attacked as "soft on Communism." The allegations were ironic, to say the least, but the natural outgrowth of the conservative rancor that Galbraith from the beginning had shrewdly judged couldn't be "controlled" or even "contained" (as many of his friends believed) by acceding to it—an accession for which he'd rightly foreseen that American liberalism would pay a deep price in influence, independence, and morale.

The implausible Republican charges that the "ultraleft ADA" controlled Stevenson's campaign, splashed repeatedly across front pages, were for Galbraith especially ironic. That Stevenson's campaign manager, Wilson Wyatt, had been the ADA's founding executive secretary (he left after two years) was enough for the Republicans to charge him with promoting "Socialist schemes in America." Senators Nixon, Dirksen, Mundt, and Case ludicrously alleged that Arthur Schlesinger, Jr., and "certain other Stevenson speechwriters" had associated with Communists and Communist organizations. McCarthy himself jumped in, ten days before the election, to claim that Schlesinger, Wyatt, James Weschler, and Archibald MacLeish, as well as Stevenson himself, were all tainted by "documented" red associations. Galbraith later told MacLeish that his greatest regret was not making it onto McCarthy's list.[21]

That November, Eisenhower won in a landslide, and the Republicans gained control of the Congress. Stevenson carried only nine states. Conceding defeat, he recalled President Lincoln's comment about losing an election: Lincoln said he felt "like the little boy who had stubbed his toe—he was too old to cry but it hurt too much to laugh." Afterward, to calm a distraught staff among whom many were in tears, he invited several of them to join him for champagne at the Governor's Mansion, declaring he had no taste for wakes, "especially when I'm the corpse." One woman offered comfort, telling Stevenson he'd "educated the country," to which he replied, "Yes, but a lot of people flunked the exam."

Many of those closest to Stevenson took the Democratic loss much less elegantly. George Ball wrote later that he "spent the next day numb and dreading the evening," and had to struggle to find the focus needed to return to his law practice. His friends Senator J. William Fulbright and the Washington lawyer Joseph Rauh went through the same experience.[22] They weren't alone in their reaction. The next morning, Galbraith awoke in Cambridge deeply depressed, "with the feeling that some cord—something vitally connecting my past with the present—had snapped."[23] Over the next several weeks his depression deepened.

Stevenson's defeat was no doubt a part of it, but in the past four years, Galbraith had been living through a roller-coaster experience of triumph and tragedy. There had been the yearlong pitched battle over his tenure, the nightmare as their beloved son slowly died of leukemia, the unexpected and disorienting success of *American Capitalism*. And now he had poured heart and mind for months into a failed presidential campaign.

As his depression worsened over the winter of 1952–53, Galbraith found that the lone predinner scotch he'd long enjoyed was becoming two or three scotches, and that at parties he was drinking more than he ever remembered. Unable to sleep, he'd gotten a doctor's prescription for Seconal, but then, because the recommended dosage didn't seemed to work, he kept increasing the number of pills he was taking—a dangerous move. Teaching that spring became a terrible burden, and the sense of permanent darkness felt at times almost overwhelming. Kitty was increasingly alarmed. Finally he sought the help of a psychiatrist neighbor, who quickly diagnosed his mood swings between depression and euphoria as latent manic depression, and started him on a regime of weekly therapy. The visits were kept "a beautifully guarded secret," he wrote later, in true 1950s style.

Gradually, the clouds of depression lifted. By the summer of 1953, the combination of weekly therapy and medication had dealt with most of the symptoms of Galbraith's struggles. And like so many of his generation, especially those familiar with the dawn-to-dusk demands of farm life, Galbraith used work itself as a balm. Politically, the work still involved Stevenson, on the assumption that he would run again in 1956.

Stevenson himself embarked on a six-month, thirty-nation, round-the-world tour that lasted from early March through August 1953. Writing a series of articles for *Look* magazine as he traveled, he used the trip to burnish his image as a statesman, to meet with government leaders and public notables wherever he went, to hold press conferences, and to opine on the United States' new global role and the world's reaction to it. The extended trip was an immense success, and 250 reporters and photographers greeted him when he landed in New York. Democratic leaders, including those who'd been lukewarm or hostile to him in 1952, were treating him as the leading candidate for president. Even Truman implored him to take command of the party.[24]

Galbraith and Arthur Schlesinger meanwhile thought they had a good idea: that is, they wanted to develop new ideas for the party and for Stevenson. Uncertain how the intellectually mercurial Stevenson would react to their advice, they turned to Thomas K. Finletter, an experienced lawyer and diplomat, to press their case. Highly regarded by Stevenson, who was his friend, Finletter was a generation older than Galbraith and Schlesinger—a rather slight, balding figure with penetrating eyes that signaled his penetrating intelligence—and had worked with Stevenson at the United Nations Conference on International Organization in San Francisco that set up the U.N. A senior partner at the Wall Street law firm Coudert Brothers, he had just stepped down as Truman's Secretary of the Air Force. A tough-minded "guns-and-butter" figure in the party, he was passionately anti-Communist internationally and supportive of an ever-expanding military budget, yet, in Schlesinger's words, "on domestic issues was a true radical. All-out. He was never perturbed by the things that perturbed Stevenson—civil rights, economic policy, and so forth. He was older than all of us. He was identified with air power and hard-nosed things like that. This gave weight to his views that Ken Galbraith and I did not have with Stevenson."[25]

Finletter listened carefully to their ideas and offered to arrange a meeting with Stevenson in August. In preparation for the meeting, Galbraith wrote Stevenson a letter about a talk he'd had recently with Averell Harriman on the "problem that has long been troubling me" (it was central to *American Capitalism*) and that was troubling Harriman as well. He asked Stevenson:

> How can we do the most to keep the Democratic Party intellectually alert and positive during these years in the wilderness? We have all told ourselves that mere opposition is not enough. Yet it would be hard at the moment to say what the Democratic Party is for. On domestic matters we are for good and against evil and for tidying up the unfinished business of the New Deal. We want an expanding economy but there are few who could be pressed into any great detail as to what this means or takes. We are solidly opposed to Hooverism and depression, but there wouldn't be much agreement and fewer new ideas as to what prevention or cure might require. In fact, we are still trading on the imagination and intellectual vigor of the Roosevelt era and that capital is running thin.

Alluding to the frustrations of his own speech-writing experience, he reminded Stevenson, "You will remember yourself the number of times during the last campaign when you found yourself rejecting (or on occasion reciting) ancient and flea-bitten clichés in the absence of anything involving thought." This was, he noted, "a disease of opposition parties, for initiative and imagination ordinarily lie with responsibility for action."

Fresh ideas were especially needed now to attract young people with little memory of the New Deal, and also to win support from the growing number of independent voters no longer wedded to the Roosevelt program. The answer, Galbraith thought, lay in "some organization in or adjacent to the Democratic Party" where leaders, policy-makers, and intellectuals could discuss and formulate policies. "As the party of the well-to-do, the Republicans do not hesitate to make use of their dough. As the party of the egg-heads we should similarly and proudly make use of our brains and experience." Papers would be written, then "sifted, discussed and worked over," with the winnowing process more important than the final product, and the ideas ultimately would be made available to members of Congress and to candidates.[26]

Like Finletter, Stevenson was immediately drawn to this proposal, and told Galbraith that it was "a perfect statement of our problem." But he was apprehensive about placing the operation within the party itself, given its fractiousness and disorganization. He didn't want it seen as a "Stevenson brain trust," but if some other venue could be found, he was ready to support it immediately.[27] Finletter's solution, after a weekend's discussion with Stevenson, Chester Bowles, and George Kennan at Bowles's home in Connecticut, was to offer to convene the group himself. He told Stevenson that Galbraith should be asked to draft two papers, one on the budget and taxes, the other on agricultural policies—and, given Stevenson's travel schedule, the first meeting should be held in New York just two weeks hence.

Galbraith hesitated only momentarily. The first meeting of what became known as "the Finletter Group" convened three weeks later. Galbraith led off its first discussion on U.S. agricultural policy; those listening included Finletter, Roy Blough (who had been on Truman's Council of Economic Advisors), Averell Harriman, Schlesinger, Richard Bissell (a Yale-trained economist then working at the Ford Foundation as its liaison to the CIA), the Democratic National Committee vice chairman Clayton Fritchey, Paul Appleby (who had been Henry Wallace's chief aide in the Department of Agriculture), and Richard Musgrave, an economist then at the University of Michigan. Stevenson missed the first meeting, but read the paper and the discussion notes with care, and wrote to thank Galbraith a few days later for his "splendid memoranda." (Typically, given his ambivalence, he privately told Finletter that while he thought the paper "quite fine," he wished more of "the other sides" of the argument had been included.[28])

The Finletter Group quickly grew, and it met every month or two for the next three years. (Bissell dropped out when he went to work full-time for the CIA.) The membership expanded to include, among others, Ben Cohen, Paul Nitze, Bernard DeVoto, Leon Keyserling, Arthur Maass, Alvin Hansen, Willard Wirtz, Isador Lubin, Henry Steele Commager, Chester Bowles, Roswell Gilpatric, Sam Rosenman, George Ball, Gale Johnson, and Seymour Harris, as well as invited guests such as Paul Samuelson, Walter Heller, Carl Kaysen, and Richard Rovere. The membership was heavy on economists (Galbraith privately considered himself the group's "academic dean") and Harvard professors. But the attendees also had a keen eye for applied politics: most of them went on to work on Stevenson's 1956 campaign (and eventually many of them were prominent on the New Frontier). The discussions were remarkably eclectic, geared toward developing "new ideas" on topics ranging from tax policy to wiretapping, and national security, from income distribution to disarmament to the U.S. position in Southeast Asia to the future of Social Security. The conversations were usually conducted over dinner at Finletter's elegant apartment or at one of his New York clubs, though on occasion the group gathered in Cambridge or Washington, D.C. (When the group met with Stevenson at Galbraith's home in March 1954, a young *Harvard Crimson* reporter named David Halberstam covered the gathering.)

As Stevenson's biographer observed,

> When the Democrats returned to power in 1960, these position papers, with their roots in the Finletter Group, became the basis of the New Frontier and the Great Society. Indeed, much of the legislation that became the law of the land under Presidents Kennedy and Johnson, particularly social legislation, can be traced back to those discussions in Tom Finletter's apartment. It was not that all the ideas . . . were original. Many had been in the air a long time. But these men got them on paper in agreed language, and Stevenson gave them public currency.[29]

Galbraith's work in the Finletter group was only one of his myriad extracurricular activities. The success of *American Capitalism* meant that editors at *The Atlantic*, *Harper's*, *The New Republic*, *The Reporter*, and *The Saturday Review* as well as at newspapers across the country called him constantly to solicit book reviews, opinion pieces, and articles. Galbraith responded generously, with a steady stream of pieces (more than two dozen in 1953 alone).

In the spring of 1954, John Fischer, the editor of *Harper's* (and a fellow Elks alumnus), called with an especially intriguing proposal: Would Galbraith write a piece that *Harper's* could publish that coming October, to commemorate the twenty-fifth anniversary of the stock market crash of 1929? Galbraith had never written on the subject but was intrigued by Fischer's idea, not least because a few weeks earlier, Arthur Schlesinger, then in the midst of writing his multivolume history of the New Deal, had happened to complain to him that no one had yet written a concise economic history of the Great Depression. Yes, Galbraith said, he would write the article.

By then, he had contracted with Houghton Mifflin to write a second book, tentatively entitled *Why People Are Poor*.[30] But he was having trouble getting started, and the more straightforward idea of narrating the history of the Great Crash captured his imagination. After doing several weeks of preliminary research for the *Harper's* piece, he decided there was much more than an article to write—in fact, there was a book here. So when Harvard classes ended in the spring of 1953, he decamped with his family for their farm in Newfane, Vermont. From there, after breakfast each morning, he drove to Hanover, New Hampshire, forty minutes north along the Connecticut River, where he ensconced himself in the Baker Library at Dartmouth College. Working steadily through the summer he not only completed the article for *Harper's* but finished both the research and the writing of a book on the 1929 crash.

Not surprisingly, Kitty Galbraith wasn't pleased that her husband was gone all day that summer—especially given his fearsome work schedule during the academic year—but with Emily Wilson she tended to the boys, playing with them in the fields outside their farmhouse, swimming in the pond, and going for walks down country trails. Her preoccupied husband would usually get back from Hanover by suppertime and relax for a couple of hours. Once the boys were in bed, however, he would often turn to further reading and research.

The Great Crash, 1929 is one of Galbraith's most entertaining and elegantly written books. It was an instant success—and has remained a steady source of royalties; still in print today, it has sold close to 800,000 copies.[31] Barely two hundred pages, *The Great Crash* sets out in vivid detail not the dry economic statistics but the colorful figures, the arcane (and often fraudulent) market manipulations, and ultimately the psychological mania that drove America's Jazz Age stock market to unprecedented highs—and then in a matter of months to a 90 percent fall.

Ever more confident as a writer after the success of *American Capitalism*, Galbraith put the knife edge of his caustic wit on full display, deftly piercing the pretensions, deceptions, and self-deceptions of the market manipulators, the wealthy, and their public defenders during the market's 1920s manic rise. Describing a moment shortly after the crash, when a prominent conservative senator spoke out in Congress to defend the "innocent community" of Wall Street from attacks by his populist colleagues, Galbraith dryly observed that "some hardened Wall Streeters may have been surprised when they realized that the 'innocent community' meant them." He observed tartly that the Federal Reserve, which failed to act once the scope of the looming collapse became apparent, was "helpless only because it wanted to be." He drew special delight not only in recounting the fall of Richard Whitney, the head of the New York Stock Exchange and a prominent and devoted Harvard alumnus, who ended up going to prison for fraud and embezzlement, but also in skewering what turned out to be the dead-wrong predictions of the Harvard Economic Society, that 1920s predecessor of modern-day for-profit forecasting firms founded by some of his department's esteemed figures:

> The threat to men of great dignity, privilege and pretense is not from the radicals they revile; it is from accepting their own myth. Exposure to reality remains the nemesis of the great—a little understood thing. All who articulate the convenient belief should never worry about their critics, only revelation of the truth.

Beyond the humor, however, was Galbraith's underlying reminder that the real world of economics can often be understood without advanced training, as well as his carefully argued case for the importance of activist government in regulating financial markets, and the superiority of Keynesian demand management as a means of growth compared to expansions driven by market booms and investor speculation. His arguments, his confident new style, his mordant humor, and his cool-eyed deflation of Wall Street's worst pretensions combined to make *The Great Crash* an instant best-seller—especially among the millions who still vividly remembered the crash and the decade-long depression that followed. Critics praised the book as well. *The New York Times* gave it a warm welcome; the *New York Herald Tribune* lauded Galbraith for telling his story "with all the verve, pace, and suspense of a detective story. For anyone who has ever dabbled, plunged, or professionally invested in the market . . . or for anyone who is interested in understanding the recent past . . . or for anyone who simply enjoys fascinating reading, this book will be of great interest." *The New Republic, The Nation,* and *The New Yorker* all recommended it to their readers, and *The Atlantic Monthly* called *The Great Crash*

> a trenchant and timely re-examination of the most spectacular boom-and-bust period in American history. Economic writings are seldom notable for their entertainment value, but this book is: Mr. Galbraith's prose has a grace and wit, and he distills a good deal of sardonic fun from the whopping errors of the nation's oracles and the wondrous antics of the financial community.

When the British edition appeared that fall, *The Times Literary Supplement* gave it a fat thirteen-hundred-word send-off, and the *New Statesman* in an equally lengthy review praised it as an "enthralling history."*[32]

Economists themselves welcomed the book generously—though occasionally with a cautionary note. *The American Economic Review* deemed it "thoroughly good," and "so well written and its lessons so clearly developed" that the reviewer faulted it only for not giving enough attention to details of business-cycle theories (which he then hastily admitted would have reduced the book's popularity and turned it into an economics history for professionals). *The Economic Journal* likewise called it "fascinating and topical," well worth reading as a clear-eyed reminder about the instability of stock markets and their susceptibility to economically "irrational" behavior, even though the reviewer chided Galbraith for not providing a more theoretically sophisticated structure for his arguments, especially those that linked the era's ultimately inadequate consumption, hindered by too slow an expansion of consumer credit, to the vast explosion in mass production as a partial underlying cause for the crash.[33]

GIVEN BOTH ITS enduring subject and Galbraith's superbly accessible and entertaining style, *The Great Crash*'s success was probably predictable. Yet, in another of those serendipitous coincidences that propelled Galbraith's career more than once, the book's initial sales were boosted by his appearance in a congressional hearing room six weeks before the book was published. He'd been invited to testify before the Senate Banking Committee by its chairman, J. William Fulbright; Fulbright was among many that spring who were concerned that the stock market was once again showing signs of an upward rush that seemed unsupported by real economic activity. In the previous six months

---

*Of all the reviews, Kitty Galbraith still loves to cite the judgment of Mark Van Doren: "History that reads like a poem."

the average stock price had risen by more than 50 percent, and although that was less than the run-up to the 1929 crash, Fulbright wanted to hear from economists, bankers, and Wall Street people about what they thought might be going on, and what might be done to prevent stock market mayhem.

When he showed up at the witness table wearing a conservative gray three-piece suit, red tie, and dark-rimmed glasses, Galbraith gave every appearance of being the cautious academic expert. But in his testimony, he warned openly that if another "boom" mentality developed (he carefully avoided saying it had already), the government should be prepared to step in before investors' myopia carried the market to dangerous and unstable speculative levels. He called on the Federal Reserve to be ready to impose a sharp hike in margin requirements (to 100 percent, if the boom didn't start to abate soon), and to give federal authorities discretionary power both to vary the length of time investors had to hold stocks in order to qualify for preferential capital-gains treatment as well as standby authority to levy a special surtax on capital gains. Knowing that his proposals wouldn't be well received on Wall Street or by Republican senators, he admitted that "these all look to be pretty horrible suggestions," but warned that unchecked speculation would lead to even worse results.

As he spoke, and unknown to him, the markets suddenly began to fall, shedding more than $7 billion in value (a significant sum in the mid-1950s) over the next several hours. The next morning *The New York Times* put Galbraith's picture on the front page, accompanied by a lengthy article summarizing his testimony; many readers inferred that his appearance had been the proximate cause of the markets' sharp slide.[34]

Conservatives, needless to say, were appalled. A flood of mail, "by far the heaviest of my lifetime," Galbraith recalls, "descended on Cambridge. It was denunciatory, defamatory, physically menacing or pious, the latter being from correspondents who said they were praying for my death or dismemberment." To get away from it all, Galbraith took his family on a weekend trip to Vermont, where in a turn of bad luck he promptly broke his leg skiing. "This being reported, I then learned that I had done something for religion: the pious read the news and wrote to tell me their prayers had been answered."[35]

Angry letter writers weren't the only ones furious with Galbraith's testimony; Senator Homer E. Capehart, an Indiana Republican who had taken great offense at it, decided to see what more could be learned about this dangerous Harvard professor. Capehart was a former manufacturer who'd become wealthy by inventing the modern jukebox, then selling his patents to the Wurlitzer Company. A reactionary even by the standards of the McCarthy era (three months earlier he had voted against McCarthy's censure by the Senate) he was also one of the Senate's dimmer members. (Lyndon Johnson once colorfully remarked of his colleague's intellect that "when Homer Capehart gets a bowel pain, he thinks it's an idea.")

In the voluminous internal security files amassed by the Congress, Capehart's aides soon located "Beyond the Marshall Plan," Galbraith's 1949 study for the National Planning Association, which had nothing to do with the stock market but included two paragraphs that, to Capehart at least, revealed the professor's true allegiances. Ten days after his appearance before the Banking Committee, Ken opened *The New York Times* to find himself on the front page once again. This time the headline was more menacing: "Capehart Charges Red Bias To Market Inquiry Witness."[36] Galbraith, the senator alleged, was a Communist sympathizer whose secret intention behind his recent testimony was to destroy stock market values and thereby "discredit American industry and the American economy."

The charges were ludicrous on their face. The paragraphs Capehart cited were lifted out of context, which had been Galbraith's argument for more vigorous American support of European economic reforms in order to damp down support for Communism, especially in France and Italy. But the preposterous charges bestirred several of Galbraith's old opponents, including Sinclair Weeks and David McCord Wright. Weeks, one of the men who had tried to block Galbraith's tenure in 1949 and was now Eisenhower's Secretary of Commerce, quickly requested an FBI investigation.* J. Edgar Hoover sent off an urgent handwritten note (a copy of which Galbraith later acquired using the Freedom of Information Act, and still treasures). "What do our files show on Galbraith?" the top G-man wanted to know. In due course, the disappointing report came back to Hoover, who forwarded it on to Weeks: "Investigation favorable except conceited, egotistical and snobbish."

Meanwhile, David Wright—who had debated Galbraith at the 1953 AEA meeting and still considered Keynesianism a stepping stone to Communism— wrote to Capehart from England, where he was on sabbatical. "I would be willing to fly home and testify if it is not too expensive and you feel that it would do any good," he declared. But, he cautioned Capehart, "Galbraith may try a general smear of my character and politics."[37]

By the time Wright's letter reached Capehart, Galbraith had long since sent telegrams to the major papers, wire services, and networks, following what was by then a standing rule of his (first learned at the Office of Price Administration): "Always counterattack strongly; that may discourage your enemy and it will surely please you and your natural allies." In his telegrams, he pointed out Capehart's highly selective editorial work, and noted that his original report had been endorsed by, among others, Milton Eisenhower and Allen Dulles, head of the CIA and brother of the Secretary of State. Then, cagily, he noted that his report had moreover been given as a lecture at Notre Dame: Was the senator from Indiana, he asked, impugning the patriotism of the state's best-known university or suggesting that Indiana Catholics were somehow also "soft on communism"?

---

*Galbraith testified late in the morning of March 9; at 4:30 p.m. Weeks's office called the FBI, looking for his security files—and demanding an immediate response (Sizoo to Clyde Tolson, FBI Deputy Director, March 9, 1955, Galbraith FBI File).

The telegrams did exactly what Galbraith hoped they would: Capehart was immediately put on the defensive, and while he sputtered on for a few more weeks, searching for more evidence of Galbraith's "pinkness," by then no one was listening.[38]

Millions more, however, were now listening to Galbraith.

13

The Affluent Society: *Parting Company with the Mainstream*

IN THE SPRING of 1955, Ken Galbraith began detailing the outline of a new book, one that he'd agreed to write for Houghton Mifflin three years earlier, just after *American Capitalism* appeared and shortly before he left to work on the Stevenson campaign. He was growing excited as the ideas took shape, and even allowed himself the thought that the book might equal *American Capitalism* in influence and popularity. In fact, he turned out to be wrong: *The Affluent Society* became his most famous and widely quoted work.[1] Yet that spring, his outline made no mention of affluence, because the book he planned to write, as he'd explained in his application to the Carnegie Corporation for research funds, was tentatively entitled *Why People Are Poor*.[2]

Poverty was much on Galbraith's mind, even though the United States was in the midst of an extraordinary economic boom. He was still teaching courses in agricultural economics, and John D. Black, now nearing the end of his own career, still hoped that Galbraith would take over as the department's leader in that field.[*] By now, however, he was also teaching courses on business organization theory, on the theory of consumption, distribution, and price, and on public regulatory policy, all subjects far afield from farm economics. More important to his new book, he was now also teaching "Problems of Economic and Political Development," Harvard's first course on "development economics," a burgeoning new topic. (He'd begun offering it in 1952; reflecting his distinctive view of how economics should be taught, it was the only department offering that used the word "political" in its title.) The question "Why are people poor?" was the heart of the class.[3]

Galbraith hardly qualified as an expert in development economics; his up-

---

[*]Between 1949 and 1960, "The Economics of Agriculture" (Ec 271) and "Agriculture, Forestry, and Land Policy" (Ec 279) were regularly offered. In the first four years Galbraith shared the teaching with Black; from 1953 to 1960, he taught them alone. Then, after six decades, instruction in American agricultural economics effectively ended at Harvard.

bringing, training, and research had not been in the immense regions of the globe soon to be known as the Third World. But in those early days, few other economists were any more experienced. A handful, such as Arthur Lewis (born in the West Indies), Raul Prebisch (from Brazil), and Alexander Gershenkron (a Russian émigré), could claim firsthand knowledge of the extreme poverty that beset the world's great majority; but most were, like Galbraith, Westerners whose efforts were driven by a combination of human compassion and intellectual challenge.

But for development economics Galbraith had two distinct assets: an intimate, personal knowledge of agricultural life, the Third World's primary occupation and chief source of national and export incomes; and detailed familiarity with the economic structures and reconstruction policies of war-devastated Europe. Both these realms of experience influenced and were influenced by his New Deal and Keynesian outlook. It's thus not surprising that along with most economists working on this subject, Galbraith began by assuming that if poor countries were to escape misery, let alone grow rich, governments—Western as well as Third World ones—would have to take the lead.

Direct comprehension of the economic, social, and political institutions that framed the many divergent "markets" making up Third World economies was essential, and the mathematically abstract models so popular among the younger generation seemed almost irrelevant. Markets in the Third World were nowhere near competitive equilibrium in the modern theoretical sense, since most were composed of subsistence agriculture on the one hand and a colonial legacy of extractive industries and export agricultural production on the other. The few imports and protected industries were dominated by a handful of often immensely wealthy families, who tended to control local politics or shared political power with the local military establishments. These economies in no way resembled the blackboard world of neoclassical economics, in which labor and capital move smoothly among profitable alternatives; and they had never made the fundamental investments in human capital (education, housing, and health care) or infrastructure (roads, dams, electricity, and communication) that by now were considered givens in the modern West.

Galbraith's first work on development issues had come in 1951, when the University of Puerto Rico asked Harvard's Economics Department to recommend someone to help evaluate the island's economic performance and prospects.

Puerto Rico had come under American control during the United States' late entry into the race for colonial empire in 1898, when victory in the Spanish-American War made Puerto Rico and the Philippines U.S. possessions. For fifty years the island had languished in the backwaters of American attention, briefly escaping "benign neglect" only in the late 1930s, when Roosevelt made his controversial aide Rexford Tugwell the island's governor in order to get Tugwell out of Washington. Tugwell had used agriculture as a progressive policy laboratory, first as Henry Wallace's undersecretary, then as head of the Farm Security Administration, but his views had fallen afoul of conservative congressional opponents.[4] But in his Puerto Rican exile, the tireless Tugwell had pressed for New Deal–style economic, political, and social reforms, though he never obtained the money or support to make many of them effective. Washington's neglect carried a price: in November 1950, Puerto Rican nationalists attempted to assassinate President Truman in broad daylight outside the White House.

The following year, at the invitation of Puerto Rico's reform-minded governor, Luis Muñoz Marin, Galbraith and a small team of researchers paid repeated visits to the island. With the Korean War on, Muñoz Marin and Galbraith understood there was little likelihood of major new funding from Washington, so the question became how to raise basic living standards quickly in some other way.

The answer was substantially to remake Puerto Rico's import and retail system. The island was classically underdeveloped: its economy was heavily dependent on sugar production, and it relied on the United States for food, medicine, and basic consumer goods, which arrived via an import system controlled by a cozy handful of wealthy San Juan–based businessmen who, in time-honored tradition, exacted substantial profit by marking up their basic costs without fear of challenge or competition. Further markups were added by the small retail merchants, well tutored in the "company store" legacy from the old sugar plantations. Nowhere could be seen anything so debilitating as price competition. By U.S. mainland standards, Galbraith observed, "the ultimate prices were frightful."

Marketing Efficiency in Puerto Rico, by Galbraith and Richard Holton—"by a substantial margin the least known of my books on economics," Galbraith has noted—sparked the formation of a government commission, on which he served, charged with implementing the practical reforms outlined in it.[5] San Juan's port facilities were expanded to increase competition among the importers, and new grocery chains and consumer cooperatives were encouraged to provide competition with the small retailers. Within a decade, the average difference between mainland and island retail prices had narrowed by more than half.

IN THE FALL of 1955 Galbraith took a bigger step in development economics. Having started on his first yearlong sabbatical that June, and equipped with both a Guggenheim fellowship and research funds from the Carnegie Corporation, he sailed with their three sons and Emily Wilson by freighter for Europe, intending to settle in Switzerland to write *Why People Are Poor*. Joined soon afterward by Kitty, who came by plane, the family spent the first several weeks vacationing on Lake Lucerne and then Lake Maggiore. Eventually they settled into a pleasant little apartment in Geneva, where he immersed himself in the United Nations' extensive library, a collection begun by the League of Nations in the 1920s, which contained a wealth of historical and comparative economic data available nowhere else. As he pored over the material, as well as the thick briefcase full of notes he'd brought from Cambridge, he tried to draft the first chapters of his new book.

But the writing didn't go well. "There were occasional flashes of hope" after several rough sketches, he later wrote. "But I was at a loss" for a central theme to unify the book.

> I did not have a convincing explanation as to why in either individual cases or in large rural and urban communities poverty persisted under conditions of general and improving well-being. Lacking such an explanation, my preliminary chapters were so devoid that I couldn't bear to read them myself. It was certain no one else would.
>
> The reason I came only later to understand. In the established or neoclassical tradition of economics to which I was still subject, poverty or something very like it remained for most people the normal condition. Labor, as also capital and other resources, were committed to production up to the point where any further contribution—input it has always been called in economics—served no longer to cover its cost. In nineteenth-century economics labor was assumed to be intrinsically, indeed biologically, abundant, and this abundance in competition for jobs kept wages at the minimum that would sustain life. Higher wages would enhance reproduction and therewith the abundance of toilers that would bring real wages back down.
>
> Nothing quite so Malthusian was believed by the 1950s. But deprivation was still the norm . . . In setting out to explain poverty, I was explaining what economics had always explained. My enterprise lacked novelty.[6]

With the book stalled and his anxieties mounting, happenstance provided an opening in the clouds of his frustration. The English economist Richard Kahn arrived in Geneva in late October, and invited the Galbraiths for dinner. The legendary Kahn, just three years older than Galbraith, had been Keynes's closest collaborator in *The General Theory* and had been no less important to Joan Robinson in her seminal work on imperfect competition. A friend since the Galbraiths' year in England in 1937–38, Kahn (by then a professor of economics at Oxford) brought along a tall, slender, finely featured Indian, Prasanta Chandra Mahalanobis, and his wife, Rani, when they all met for dinner.

Mahalanobis, then in his early sixties, had been a prizewinning physics student at Cambridge during World War I. An intimate friend of the great Bengali poet and painter Rabindranath Tagore (his wife had been Tagore's personal secretary), he returned to India in the 1920s to teach physics at the University of Calcutta but gradually shifted his interests first to meteorology, then statistics, then economics, and finally, in newly independent India, economic planning. Head of the Indian Statistical Institute and a member of the state Planning Commission, he had become over the years as close a friend to Prime Minister Nehru as he had once been to Tagore. Like Nehru and other Indian leaders of the time, Mahalanobis had been deeply influenced by the Fabian so-

Archibald and Kate Galbraith with their children in 1915: (left to right) Alice, Archibald, John Kenneth, William, Catherine, and Kate.

Ontario farm boys, 1918: Galbraith's brother Bill (standing), an unidentified cousin, and Galbraith (with glasses).

STOCK and MEAT JUDGING TEAM
ST. LOUIS - TORONTO - CHICAGO

R.H. GRAHAM

H.J. WATT

H.W. GOBLE

PROF. G.E. RAITHBY B.S.A. STOCK JUDGING

COACHES

PROF. R.G. KNOX B.S.A. STOCK JUDGING

E.C. STILLWELL B.S.A. MEAT JUDGING

H.P. AITCHISON

G.M. ENGEL

J.K. GALBRAITH

D.H. ROBERTSON

H.C. HARTLEY

E.A. INNES

A highlight of Galbraith's undergraduate years as an animal husbandry major was his appointment to the College Stock and Meat Judging Team, with a tour of campuses in the Midwest and a visit to the Chicago stockyards.

Galbraith's graduation picture, from his last year at Ontario Agricultural College, 1931.

Ken and Kitty Galbraith sailing for England the day after their wedding in September 1937. Their Model A roadster went with them, and was used for many trips during their year in Europe.

Galbraith was appointed wartime "price tsar" at the Office of Price Administration at the age of thirty-two.

The OPA staff at a congressional hearing: Leon Henderson (in a white suit) is testifying; behind him Galbraith and John Hamm listen; David Ginsburg, to Henderson's right, and Paul Porter (with glasses, in a white jacket) are also in attendance. The photograph was given to Galbraith by Henderson, who inscribed it: "This looks like an authentic picture of the price gang. Ken is dour. John is sniffing a phony. Dave just ate another canary. Paul is thinking of the widow and the salesman. And the boss has his mouth open."

A letter written by Richard Nixon for Galbraith when he was in charge of rubber rationing. Note carefully the lower right-hand corner with the "RMN" indicating his authorship.

ABOVE: *Galbraith in 1945, as a brevet colonel. He became a director of the Strategic Bombing Survey, which assessed the effect of American bombing of Germany and Japan during the war.* BELOW: *Galbraith and George Ball, then also a director of the Strategic Bombing Survey, in Germany in 1945; together they interviewed Albert Speer.*

President Truman gesturing at Galbraith; behind them are various administration figures, including, on the left, Seymour Harris.

Galbraith with Eleanor Roosevelt and two diplomats at the United Nations.

RIGHT: *The Galbraiths' first son, Douglas, died of leukemia when he was seven, in June 1950.*

ABOVE: *Kitty Galbraith in 1949.*

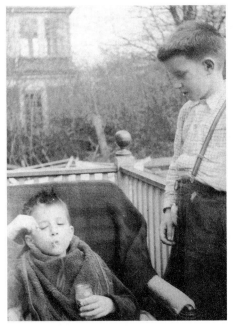

RIGHT: *Alan and Douglas, a few weeks before Douglas's death.*

Emily Wilson, the Galbraiths' housekeeper, maintained her spirit of independence and adventure through thirty-five years with the family. Here she is rowing on the Charwell, at Oxford.

The Galbraiths bought this farmhouse in Newfane, Vermont, in 1947, and have spent their summer holidays there ever since.

Galbraith with John F. Kennedy at the Democratic Convention in 1960.

Ambassador Galbraith arriving to present his credentials to the president of India.

Galbraith, hospitalized in Honolulu with a severe intestinal ailment, with the visiting Senator Robert F. Kennedy, 1962.

Galbraith with Prime Minister Nehru when he arrived in Washington in November 1961; at the right are Secretary of State Dean Rusk, Vice President Lyndon Johnson, and President Kennedy.

Galbraith and Prime Minister Nehru in Nehru's office.

The ambassador refreshing his skills as an agricultural economist.

The ambassador with a member of the new generation in India.

The ambassador in Leh, near the Chinese border, during the Sino-Indian War in October 1962.

Galbraith escorting Jacqueline Kennedy at a state dinner in New Delhi in 1962. They were good friends, and she gave him the photo in gratitude for his friendly solicitude at an awkward moment when she feared that her skirt was slipping.

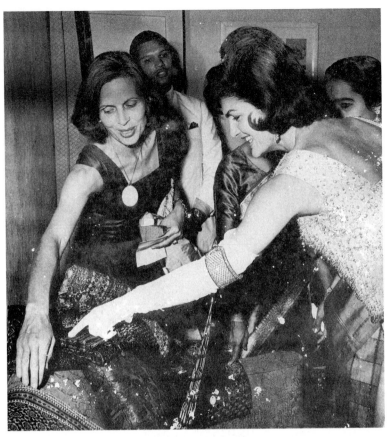

ABOVE: *Kitty Galbraith with Jacqueline Kennedy, shopping in India. The President later complained to Galbraith that his wife had spent too much money.*
BELOW: *An ambassador at rest.*

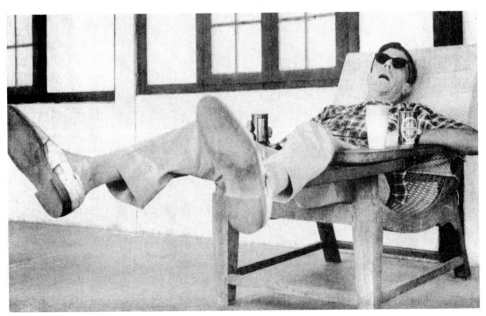

cialism of Sidney and Beatrice Webb, R. H. Tawney, G.D.H. Cole, and Harold Laski—a distinctively English sort of socialism that had long sought non-Marxist, democratic, and egalitarian solutions to the brutal legacy of the Victorian era's laissez-faire capitalism.

Galbraith was charmed. The Mahalanobises, he fondly remembered, represented "a world in which decency, compassion, and wide-ranging intelligence were combined with the belief that the nature of the economic order is, above all, a matter of moral commitment . . . I continue to believe that men and women of such decency deserved to be right."*[7]

Over dinner they talked about India's Second Five-Year Plan, and also about Mahalanobis's efforts to bring scholars from both the West and the socialist countries to advise on Indian social and economic development. Toward the end of the evening, Mahalanobis casually mentioned that the Eisenhower administration had sent Milton Friedman as an adviser but that he'd stayed only a few days. Galbraith "responded thoughtfully to the news, noting that to ask Friedman to advise on economic planning was like asking the Holy Father to counsel on the operations of a birth control clinic." Mahalanobis, amused, promptly invited him to come to India instead, and Galbraith accepted.

THUS, IN JANUARY 1956, Ken and Kitty Galbraith departed for India, with a brief stopover in Beirut for some lectures at the American University there (and, at Kitty's insistence, several hurried visits to the surrounding Greco-Roman and Crusader-era sites). They arrived in Calcutta by early February.

Calcutta represented the knotty challenge of development in its most acute form. "Few can forget their first sight of India," Galbraith wrote years later, "and certainly not if they come in through Calcutta."

> We passed in the late evening shadows from Dum Dum Airport to Barrackpore Trunk Road. Our way was through two peering, silent processions, white-clad with dark bare shoulders and dark bare legs, which moved endlessly, where one wondered, on each side of the road. Beyond the pedestrian chain, deeper in the shadows, were the hovels of those lucky enough to have a roof, here mostly refugees from East Bengal.
>
> Visible too were the charpoys or rope cots of those who lived and slept without shelter of any kind. Cattle, also silent, turned to view us as we passed. Heaps of refuse were everywhere. Soon it all became almost commonplace. A few days later driving into the center of Calcutta, my wife and I saw a baby, emaciated, half-prostrate, venting a long white stool beside the road. The infant was obviously very sick, but not until later did we react to what we had seen . . . Thus do one's eyes glaze on exposure to India.[8]

---

*Galbraith had been scheduled to visit India several months before he met Mahalanobis. In January 1955, Austin Robinson had invited him to lecture in India on problems of competition and economic structure. Galbraith had agreed, but during the brouhaha with Senator Capehart in late March, he had broken his leg skiing. Unwilling to put off his scheduled European sabbatical, he told Robinson that India on top of everything else would be too much.

But India's vivid miseries, rather than inuring or paralyzing Galbraith, fueled his desire to help. And at the large old vine- and palm-covered compound that housed the Indian Statistical Institute, he found an impressive group of fellow visitors filled with the same desire. MIT's Norbert Wiener, the brilliant father of cybernetics, was there helping design India's first attempt at computer-based planning. The Polish economist Oskar Lange, who after studying at Harvard, Berkeley, LSE, and Chicago had returned to Poland as a proponent of an anti-Stalinist "market socialism," was also in residence. From Stanford, Paul Baran likewise had journeyed to Calcutta, along with another Bombing Survey veteran, Nicholas Kaldor, from Cambridge University.

Although the group's collective talents made for memorable conversations, at times the political discussions made Galbraith uncomfortable. Over dinner and late-afternoon drinks, Lange, Baran, and Kaldor spared little in their criticisms of U.S. foreign policy under John Foster Dulles, including its hostility to India's policy of nonalignment; Galbraith, despite his own hardly favorable views of Dulles, found himself following Churchill's dictum about not criticizing one's government when out of the country, while never ceasing to do so at home.

Galbraith threw himself into researching and writing analyses of India's Second Five-Year Plan. By his own admission, with one exception "none was memorable and some were misguided."* That exception was a paper on India's public corporations. Unlike his fellow visitors and in contrast with India's own then highly regarded economic policy (influenced by the programs of the postwar British Labour government), Galbraith could find only weak merit in classic public ownership of major production capacities per se. In his view,

> The ultimate ownership of the very large industrial corporation, public or private, matters little. What is important is the autonomy that the management is accorded for operations and the rigor of the tests of performance to which management is made subject. Operating decisions or those on personnel . . . must never be second-guessed by civil servants or politicians . . . [Likewise] the management of the public enterprise must also be subject firmly to the test of earnings. This is because there is no other test—none that so comprehensively measures effectiveness in getting the most return for the least cost. Leadership should be undisturbed so long as it succeeds. When earnings fall, it should be changed and the new one left on its own to do better.
>
>   In India these rules were not followed . . . [T]he corporations sought decisions from the relevant civil servant or minister on a wide range of matters. They were not subject to the harsh test of earnings; it was not clear how performance was measured. I called this relaxed system "post office socialism."[9]

*In another paper he wrote at the same time he urged India to allocate space more efficiently on its railways by boosting passenger fares. Indian passenger trains, then as now, were vastly overcrowded, and freight trains carrying vital supplies were often delayed by the frequency of the passenger trains. The ensuing controversy killed the proposal (see *The Statesman*, April 28, 1956, 3).

In light of Galbraith's later sharp indictments of the managerial "techno-structure" of America's largest corporations, these conclusions are momentarily ironic. But his critique expresses his underlying pragmatism, and the belief that economic analysis and "rules" derived from theory must always take account of context. Indian development was decades behind America's, and the discipline of an independent management focused on earnings was a precondition for India's closing the gap. When India reached American levels of abundance, it, too, no doubt would have to wrestle with the same problems.[10]

Ken's skepticism about public ownership of large enterprises in India was ironic in another way. His paper and its conclusions were endorsed in Parliament by the opposition Popular Socialist Party and became the topic for several weeks of fierce public debate. The row over "post office socialism" brought Galbraith a measure of congenial celebrity: when Prime Minister Nehru met him, he "for a time regarded me with suspicion," Galbraith remembered, apparently convinced that "I was engaged in some peculiarly intricate proselytizing for American capitalism."[11]

By the late spring, the oppressive heat of the monsoon season was nearing, and both parents missed their sons, who had remained behind in Switzerland in Emily Wilson's capable hands. But they had also fallen in love with India, and with Indian art. Galbraith found himself entranced by Moghul-era miniatures, which he began collecting. They visited New Delhi, Bombay, Benares, Darjeeling, and Kashmir, which made a particularly indelible impression, as Galbraith later recorded. They arrived at the height of spring,

> when the sod rooftops and the Moslem cemeteries are thick with daffodils, the terraced paddies a fresh vivid green from the rice coming through the water, with the Himalayas as always reaching to their unbelievable white-clad heights in the near distance. The Alps, the Rockies, and all the other mountains are related to the earth, the Himalayas to the heavens.

Returning to Calcutta via New Delhi, they stopped to lunch with the U.S. ambassador, John Sherman Cooper, and his wife. Leaving the embassy that afternoon, Galbraith confided to Kitty, "When the Democrats get back in, I think I will get myself made ambassador to India."[12] Back in Switzerland by early May, the closed gates of Ken's imagination opened, and his book began to take on form.

With the children soon to be out of school, urban Geneva seemed the wrong place to spend the summer. Over the Christmas holiday, Ken and Kitty had spent a weekend in the little mountain village of Gstaad and enjoyed it greatly. So they returned to Gstaad and rented a pair of cozy flats, with space enough to house the family and provide room for Ken to write. Ideas now seemed to rush forth so rapidly that "often I thought [the book] was writing itself." But the book was no longer about why people were poor, or about poverty generally. India's crushing poverty and suffering had led him to reconsider the extraordinary abundance of the United States, an abundance that had seemed impossible to imagine just twenty years earlier.

> Much was now clear in my mind. The rich society was the new and interest-ing case; poverty was the still common but aberrant situation. However, since poverty had until now been the norm, it was affluence that had never been fully understood or examined.
>
> [Yet] the United States, the preeminent example of well-being, continued to make the increased output of privately produced goods the *summum bonum* of all social achievement. All progress was measured by the percent-age rate of increase in output.[13]

His new insight struck with the force of a thunderclap, Galbraith later re-called, even though he'd partially anticipated it in *American Capitalism*. Most orthodox economists were still focused on the efficient allocation of resources, and the relation of that efficiency to economic growth. This was the heart of the Marshallian legacy, after all, the inheritance from Adam Smith. In the 1930s, the conservative English economist Lionel Robbins had gone so far as to condense and generalize this into an axiom: "Economics," he declared, was above all else "the study of the allocation of scarce resources among unlimited and competing uses."[14] But what if Robbins was wrong? What if the assump-tions of two centuries of "modern" economics—assumptions apparently vali-dated by the grinding poverty that was the observable condition of most of civilization—needed to be changed, as poverty in the advanced industrial countries fell away?

That, Galbraith decided, would be the theme of his book. The writing now came swiftly and easily, and he never slackened his pace, getting up early every morning to write. By the time the family returned to Cambridge later that summer, in his briefcase was a completed first draft.

BACK IN THE United States, a new presidential campaign had started, and early in July Adlai Stevenson, seeking the nomination a second time, had written to Galbraith in Gstaad, asking for help in drafting his speech to the Democratic convention. Galbraith had written Stevenson to pledge his support before de-parting for Europe the previous summer; by the time Stevenson wrote, Ken had already drafted several well-received speeches for him during the prima-ries. "I marvel at the amount you accomplish in a year of 'leisure.' I wonder if the time has not come for me to unveil your conclusions in an acceptance speech in the event that I am nominated. In short, if you know what to do with the human race, I should be glad to make the announcement, at least to the Democrats."[15]

Now Galbraith obliged with a draft that was far more eloquent than the Baltimore speech he'd written in 1952. In the intervening four years he'd seen a lot of Stevenson and fellow Democrats both in the ADA and in the Finletter Group, and had worked especially hard to make sure that the group's recommendations were read and weighed by Stevenson himself. Stevenson clearly valued Galbraith's contributions and had sent him a steady stream of notes, letters, and newspaper clippings. And when he came to Harvard to deliver the Godkin Lectures in 1954, he had made a point of having Galbraith convene the Finletters at 30 Francis Avenue for an intensive discussion of his future options. Stevenson was impressed by the draft he reviewed and wrote back to Galbraith that he intended to use large parts of it.[16]

But then, in the final days before the Democratic convention, Stevenson decided to write his own acceptance speech, a decision that proved a disaster. Listening in the convention hall, Arthur Schlesinger called the address "a diffuse mass of words. After a few moments, the sense of excitement was trickling away." Ralph Martin, also in the hall, thought "the speech simply did not work." Senator Fulbright called it the worst he'd ever heard. Philip Graham, the publisher of *The Washington Post*, said he "thought the Democrats had a real chance to win until Adlai began to speak." In perhaps the cruelest cut, one reporter wrote that it was "no better than one of Eisenhower's speeches."[17] Once again, having started with high hopes, the Democrats watched forlornly as their dreams of recapturing control of the White House slipped away.

That fall, Galbraith played an important but somewhat more limited role in the campaign than he had in 1952. He served with Schlesinger and the writer John Hersey as one of the campaign's three principal speechwriters; but this time, although he still greatly admired Stevenson's many strengths, he also had a clearer sense of his weaknesses.[18] He recognized that Stevenson, for all his obvious intelligence, was not really interested in the hard details of policy. He used his influence on him more indirectly, therefore, in ways designed to compensate for the weaknesses he'd seen in the 1952 campaign. As Stevenson's biographer put it, "the research and writing operations of 1956 was less happy-go-lucky, less brilliant, but far more solid than the Elks Club of 1952. Grounded in the Finletter Group's work, which had drawn on some of the best Democratic minds in the country, the research material had been built up mountainously," and became a crucial in-house library for the campaign.[19]

Better research didn't compensate for other weaknesses, however. Galbraith's discontent over the attack strategy recommended by Stevenson's top advisers—a discontent he shared with Schlesinger and Hersey—broke into the open midway through the campaign. In *The New York Times*, James Reston reported the split under the headline "Struggle for Stevenson": the three speechwriters were deeply "unhappy about the tone of his public speeches to date and want him to revert to the noble themes of his 1952 campaign." Their fear, Reston said, was that Stevenson was losing independent voters with personal attacks on Eisenhower, charges of "legal corruption" in the administration, and "arguing that 'almost one-fifth' of the American people are living in poverty."[20] Stevenson tried to broker a compromise between the writers and the operatives, without much luck—though for a few weeks he did adopt a higher-minded tone.

Meanwhile the Republicans, and Vice President Nixon in particular, kept up their low-road attacks on Stevenson and the Democrats, just as they had in 1952, when Nixon lambasted Stevenson for "holding a Ph.D. degree from Acheson's school of the three Cs—Cowardly Communist Containment," and Eisenhower himself, standing beside Joe McCarthy, flatly accused the Truman administration of "treason."[21] Soon enough, the Stevenson campaign returned to the behavior the writers wanted to avoid.

That fall, Galbraith nonetheless loyally took time out from his Harvard work to travel with Stevenson and write speeches for him, darting back to Cambridge to meet with classes or work on revising his manuscript. After one especially successful speech in Los Angeles, in which the candidate's Galbraith-written attacks on Nixon repeatedly brought a roaring crowd to its feet, Stevenson told him he had wanted him for that speech because "about Nixon, Ken, you have no tendency to be fair."[22]

When Stevenson lost that November by an even bigger margin than he had in 1952—Eisenhower won 58 percent of the vote, and all but seven states— he was devastated, telling an old friend, "Oh, it hurts so badly." He announced he would never again run for office, and started talking about death and the arrangements he wanted made for his funeral. But few of his advisers, including Galbraith, had thought he would win, so although many were dismayed by the scale of Eisenhower's triumph, they were not as brokenhearted. The Democrats at least increased their majorities in Congress, and several new faces were emerging as possible candidates for 1960. To one, a freshman senator from Massachusetts who'd almost become Stevenson's running mate, Stevenson wrote, "I can think of no one to whom we should all be more grateful than you." John F. Kennedy replied graciously a few days later, praising Stevenson for the courage he'd shown in both campaigns.[23] Galbraith, too, had been impressed by Kennedy, who had sought out his advice before the convention on agricultural policy: here might be a Democrat who could win next time, he thought. But first there was his book to finish. This time there were no bouts with the depression that had plagued him in 1952, and the writing was going swiftly and well. By the time spring classes ended in May 1957, the manuscript was for all intents and purposes done, and he sensed that he had just completed what was going to be a major and influential piece of work.

IN THE OPENING pages of *The Affluent Society*, Galbraith acknowledged that he was hardly the first modern writer to imagine an end to human poverty or dwell on its implications. Beginning with Rousseau and continuing through the nineteenth century, thinkers as diverse as Henri de Saint-Simon, Charles Fourier, and Robert Owen in Europe, and Edward Bellamy, Henry George, and Orestes Brownson in the United States had conceived of such a world as more than simply imaginary. But the world they described was "utopian," literally "no place" in the actually existing world. It would come about, or so these writers believed, through the political and moral reorganization of human life, a project whose realization lay in the future, one toward which human beings could aspire but which could be reached only after centuries, not years.

As the industrial world's Dickensian factories and sweatshops churned out their cornucopia of goods, Marx of course took a darker measure of the new capitalism. But he, too, saw an end to human poverty, which he believed could be achieved through the rising of the new proletariat and its conscious seizure of the means of production. Marx was not alone in his analysis, as distinct from his prescription. By 1890 Alfred Marshall himself had openly worried in his *Principles of Economics* about the durability of capitalism, given its harsh inequalities, and declared that "the study of the causes of poverty" meant solving "the degradation of a large part of mankind," which should be for economists "their chief and their highest interest."[24] Even so cautious a figure as Harvard's Frank Taussig, after surveying turn-of-the-century poverty in America, declared flatly that "the institution of private property stands not only on the defensive but in a position that cannot long be defended."[25]

Keynes, too, left ample evidence that he envisaged a not-so-distant future in which the economic imperatives to work, to save, or otherwise to conform to what he called the "hag-ridden" theories of neoclassical economics could be put away.* In 1945, a year before his death, he had written that "we are entering into the age of abundance" when that transformation would begin to take place.[26]

Now, Galbraith pronounced a new judgment: goals that had hitherto seemed utopian in human history, in terms of total material output and its distribution, had largely been achieved. The triumph had come about not through proletarian revolution or even with a major lessening of inequality, but rather through a vast expansion of production. This was the very subject to which economists had devoted their theories, so one might conclude they had been right. What, then, justified Galbraith's attack on the economics of the past?

His answer was that economics in the United States had become a victim of its own success:

> The meaning of this is that elimination of insecurity in economic life can be a finished business. Nothing is more completely accepted in the conventional wisdom than the cliché that economic life is endlessly and inherently uncertain. In fact, the major uncertainties of pristine economic life (subject to a major qualification concerning the control of depressions) have already been eliminated. The ones that remain are of much reduced urgency . . .
>
> The ancient preoccupations of economic life—with equality, security, and productivity—have now narrowed down to a preoccupation with productivity and production. Production has become the solvent of the tensions once as-

---

*In his "Economic Possibilities for Our Grandchildren," published in *The Saturday Evening Post*, Keynes initiated a debate that foreshadowed the response to *The Affluent Society* a quarter century later.

sociated with inequality, and it has become the indispensable remedy for the discomforts, anxieties, and privations associated with economic insecurity. Here we have the explanation, or more precisely the beginning of the explanation, of a modern paradox: Why is it that as production has increased in modern times concern for production seems also to have increased?[27]

To Galbraith, the answer to this paradox, which he dubbed "the paramount position of production," was twofold. One he famously called "the conventional wisdom." The other expressed the nature of consumption, which, he argued, had changed: the world was driven not by consumers any longer but by producers.

Galbraith defined the "conventional wisdom" of any society—ancient or modern, capitalist, agrarian, hunter-gatherer, or socialist—as those general statements governing conduct that most of its members accept as true. The reason societies accept such "truths" is basically a functional one: agreement is needed to minimize social friction and to provide a narrative that allows members to make sense of their world. In modern societies, the conventional wisdom was observable: it could be seen and analyzed through surveys and interviews, in which one could discover what beliefs large groups held in common. (A society could have more than one "conventional wisdom": Galbraith was quick to distinguish the political differences between the "conventional wisdom" held by conservatives and liberals, for example.)

In its ritual presentation, "conventional wisdom" served abiding social purposes: psychologically it persuaded people that other, more famous and powerful figures shared their views, so they did not feel alone, and it served to evangelize the unpersuaded, adding to the dynamic strength of the group. In democracies especially, the high public official was expected, even required, to expound the conventional wisdom, and, as Galbraith noted, "his is, in many respects, the purest case."

> Before assuming office he ordinarily commands little attention. But on taking up his position he is immediately expected to be gifted with deep insights. He does not, except in the rarest instances, write his own speeches or articles; and these are planned, drafted, and scrupulously examined to ensure their acceptability. The application of any other test, e.g., their effectiveness as a simple description of the economic or political reality, would be regarded as eccentric in the extreme.[28]

But the job of articulating the conventional wisdom is not performed exclusively by elected officials in the modern capitalist society. It is shared by journalists, commentators, scholars, policy analysts, and, not least, business and financial leaders. Where once feathered and bejeweled sachems and shaman-priests were looked to for guidance in the cycles of planting and harvest, the explanation of lunar eclipses, and the supervision of the rituals of daily life, so today one turns to "the market" and its leaders to have them explain national affairs and recommend policies. In such a world, Galbraith quipped, the words of the Federal Reserve chairman exercised the function once filled by the Delphic oracle.[29]

Modern societies are especially vulnerable to attacks on the conventional wisdom, however. National communities comprising large populations dispersed geographically, divided by interests and needs, will find that time and changing circumstance, as well as changing conceptions of identity and relative group power, exact a heavy toll on any communitarian wisdom. (One has only to look at the shifts in attitudes toward women, blacks, and gays for such evidence; attitudes and relations toward each of these have shifted dramatically and measurably within only a few decades.) Galbraith was particularly interested to show how, since capitalism first emerged as a world force, "the conventional wisdom" of economics had been subject to such change.

> For decades prior to 1776 men had been catching the vision of the liberal state. Traders and merchants in England and in the adjacent Low Countries, and in the American colonies, had already learned that they were served best by a minimum of government restriction rather than, as in the conventional wisdom, by a maximum of government guidance and protection. It had become plain in turn that liberal trade and commerce, not the accumulation of bullion, as the conventional wisdom held, was the modern source of national power . . . These views were finally crystallized by Adam Smith . . . *The Wealth of Nations*, however, continued to be viewed with discontent and alarm by the men of the older wisdom.

And as the older mercantile view gave way and the robust energies of the factory system advanced, a new conventional wisdom emerged.

> Through the nineteenth century, liberalism in its classical meaning having become the conventional wisdom, there were solemn warnings of the irreparable damage that would be done by Factory Acts, trade unions, social insurance, and other social legislation. Liberalism was a fabric which could not be raveled without being rent. Yet the desire for protection and security and some measure of equality in bargaining power would not down. In the end it became a fact with which the conventional wisdom could not deal. The Webbs, Lloyd George, LaFollette, Roosevelt, Beveridge, and others crystallized the acceptance of the new fact.[30]

Yet the older order in any century gives way only with bitter resistance. "Ideas are inherently conservative. They yield not to the attack of other ideas but to the massive onslaught of circumstances with which they cannot contend," Galbraith wrote. As a result, "like the Old Guard, the conventional wisdom dies but does not surrender."[31]

In the 1930s, the conventional wisdom focused on the "natural" abilities of the market to rectify the errors of the Depression and on the devastating dangers of unbalanced public budgets in times of economic collapse. Then Keynes showed the way out in *The General Theory*, and it was to acceptance of Keynesian principles (albeit halting) that much of the West's postwar prosperity could be attributed. But events were once again overtaking theoretical convention, Galbraith darkly warned. Keynes "was also on his way to constructing a new body of conventional wisdom," he cautioned, "the obsolescence of some parts of which, in its turn, is now well advanced."[32] Public debate and scholarship on economics had focused on inequality, insecurity, and inadequate productivity, but in large measure, these concerns had been resolved, Galbraith wrote. Now, a new analysis and a new public agenda were needed.

There were three reasons, he thought, why economic inequality no longer pressed on Americans as it once had. First, inequality was indubitably *not* showing "the expected tendency to get worse." Income distribution comparisons between the pre- and postwar periods showed that inequality was *declining*. And between 1941 and 1950, federal data showed, the real after-tax income of the poorer half in the United States had grown by more than a third, while that of the richest 5 percent had somewhat eroded. Even more important, the poorest fifth of Americans had seen a percentage gain in their incomes five times greater than that of the richest fifth.[33]

Second, Galbraith thought the very rich were becoming less and less important in American life.

> As recently as a half century ago, the power of the great business firm was paramount in the United States, and so accordingly was the power of the individual who headed it. Men like Morgan, the Rockefeller executives, Hill, Harrington and Hearst had great power in the meaningful sense of the term, which is that they were able to direct the actions and command the obedience of countless other individuals.

Now, however, government's newfound power over economic life circumscribed that of the baronial corporate dynast. Anonymous and replaceable managers, not individual titans, ruled corporate America, and did so with a keener sense of the limits on their freedom of action. The truly wealthy were still with us, of course, but, Galbraith observed, they were wisely eschewing the vulgar display of the Gilded Age—the Newport "cottages," the liner-sized yachts, the mahogany-paneled private railway cars.

> The depression and especially the New Deal gave the American rich a serious fright. One consequence was to usher in a period of marked discretion in personal expenditure . . . Once a sufficiently impressive display of diamonds could create attention even for the most obese and repellent body, for they signified membership in a highly privileged caste. Now the same diamonds are afforded by a television star or a talented harlot. Modern mass communications, especially the movies and television, insure that the populace at large

will see the most lavish caparisoning on the bodies not of the daughters of the rich but on the daughters of coal miners and commercial travelers, who struck it rich by their own talents or some facsimile thereof.*[34]

Perhaps most important, the sheer increase in the volume of production itself, and its gradual dissemination into more and more hands, had transformed the whole scene. In earlier times, the benefits from any production gains accrued mainly to the wealthy; among the majority poor there had been no incentive (as distinct from coercion) to risk the known world of small-scale subsistence production for the larger one of capitalist abundance. But in modern societies, increased production offered an alternative to the radical version of redistribution of wealth precisely because it was mass production aimed at the mass market of worker-consumers. Not surprisingly, among the economically blessed, who were most attuned to radical redistribution's disadvantages this fact lent the doctrine of production "something approaching the standing of divine revelation." But this conclusion was not reached only among the well-off. Thanks to its tendency to spread its benefits wide, production had a dramatic effect on even the most vocal opponents of inequality. "As a result," Galbraith noted, "the goal of an expanding economy has also become deeply imbedded in the conventional wisdom of the American left."[35] (Interestingly, this observation about production and the American left caught the eyes of the CIA, which asked Galbraith's publisher for permission to reprint the chapter.)

Linked to inequality was the matter of insecurity. The age-old sources of economic insecurity—crop failures, invasions, natural disasters, epidemics—had been all but eliminated, only to be overtaken by new ones: constant price instability because of competition, with its adverse effects on profits and wages, which led businesses to oscillate between boom and bust, and the unequal, often exploitative differences between the powers of capitalist and of laborer. With the New Deal, the American government had sought to mitigate such insecurity systemically by creating old-age, disability, and unemployment benefits; by strengthening the hand of labor and trade unions; by creating public-sector jobs, and, for a time (through the National Recovery Administration), by discouraging price competition; and eventually by engaging in the Keynesian task of managing the overall level of consumption and investment in order to limit the length and severity of business downturns. But these defining new features of modern government, Galbraith emphasized, had only come after business's own attempts to gain security in the face of constant competition. Adam Smith himself, even while arguing the merits of competition, had caustically observed that businessmen "seldom meet together, even for merriment or diversion, but the conversation ends in a conspiracy against the public, or in some contrivance to raise prices"—an observation by his fellow Scotsman that

*In light of the second Gilded Age in the last years of the twentieth century, Galbraith said at the start of the new century that he regretted the seeming finality of this judgment.

Galbraith believed subsequent years had well borne out.[36] "From the very beginning of modern capitalist society," he wrote, "businessmen have addressed
themselves to the elimination" of price competition.

> Monopoly or the full control of supply, and hence of price, by a single firm
> was the ultimate security. But there were many very habitable halfway
> houses. Price and production agreements or cartels, price-fixing by law, re-
> strictions on entry of new firms, protection by tariffs or quotas, and many
> other devices have all had the effect of mitigating the insecurity inherent in
> the competitive economy. Most important, where the number of firms is
> small, a characteristic feature of modern industry, interdependence is recog-
> nized and respected, and firms stoutly avoid price behavior which would en-
> hance uncertainty for all.[37]

But, as he had in *American Capitalism*, Galbraith drew an unexpected conclusion. Government action had to a great degree removed the most pressing
economic insecurities for most citizens (although, he noted, health care had
yet to be dealt with); similarly the modern corporation, with its tendency toward concentration and control of markets, had removed the most debilitating
aspects of price competition (though not among small business and farmers).
Far from representing a "failure" of modern capitalism (and a violation of marginalist models), all this had been generally to the good.

> The desire for economic security was long considered the great enemy of in-
> creased production. This attitude was first grounded in the belief that the in-
> security of competition was essential for efficiency . . .
>   Not only is there no inconsistency between the mitigation of insecurity
> and the increase of production, but the two are indissolubly linked. A high
> level of economic security is essential for maximum production. And a high
> level of production is indispensable for economic security. So compulsive, in-
> deed, is the pressure to maintain output as a requisite of economic security
> that the economy is impelled to a level of performance which, as things now
> stand, it can sustain only with difficulty and at some cost and danger.[38]

So the key issue was Americans' (and economists') unreflective faith in an endless expansion of economic output as the measure of a healthy and successful
society. Galbraith's critical examination of this issue proceeded along a line
that can best be summarized as follows:

1. The central focus of orthodox economics had been (and still was) on
   "output" efficiency, measured by the rational allocation of resources via
   the private market.
2. Keynes, to our great advantage, shifted that focus to a second idea, that
   of a guided "growth" efficiency: the maximization of output through government's efforts at macromanagement of private markets. The resulting

full employment helped solve the twin issues of inequality and insecurity, which private markets and "output" efficiency had not.

3. The conventional wisdoms endorsing "this paramount position of production" in both models, however, were taking no account of the resultant postwar prosperity, and remained focused on maximization through private production for private consumption. The result was what Galbraith called "social imbalance," in which the market for privately sold goods and services was being saturated, while the demand for public goods—clean air, more parks and schools, better health care, less crime, less crowded transportation systems—remained unfulfilled.

4. The abundance of private goods and services was all the more anomalous because to a great degree, thanks to large corporations' advertising and marketing efforts, private "wants"—consumer demand expressed through Samuelson's "revealed preference"—which privately sold goods are meant to satisfy, are as much a corporate product as the goods sold to satisfy them. Far from being autonomously formed "rational maximizers," as in Marshall's world, consumers were being, perversely, transformed into the ultimate end goods of the corporation itself, through a process Galbraith calls "the Dependence Effect."

5. Finally, the "paramount position of production" made persistent inflation the inevitable rule. Operating near full capacity, a production-driven economy allowed its powerful actors to pass on wage and price increases to consumers, and resisted conventional fiscal and monetary policies that sought to brake inflation. Monetary policy made "only secondary contact with the problem of inflation," because although it could reduce aggregate demand through restrictive and inequitable means, it never challenged the substructure of corporately generated demand itself. Fiscal policy was at the same time ineffective because postwar Washington had shown no willingness to use tax increases to curb demand. "It was favored in principle," Galbraith jibed, "but not in practice."

For Americans to escape these traps would not be easy, because it wasn't simply a matter of attacking the vested interests of the rich and powerful, as earlier generations had. For better or worse, the country was captive to the "greatest of vested interests, those of the mind," Galbraith wrote. This hardly implied that there could be no escape; history didn't stop unfolding. The issue was how to take at least some preliminary steps—down payments on the larger purchase of greater human freedom.

One such step was to right the "social imbalance" of public scarcity amid private plenty by better financing of more public services, from education and health care to playgrounds and scientific research. But Galbraith recognized that, in the midst of the Cold War, with military spending greater than all state and local public expenditure combined, any increase in the federal income tax would merely be siphoned off into more military spending, and, given the tax code's many loopholes created by lobbyists for the rich, the next tax burden would fall heavily on the rest of Americans.[39] There was still a compelling case for greater public spending, but from what revenue source? Galbraith's answer was an increase in state and local sales taxes.[40] The merits of such taxes were ease of enforcement and direct funding where needs were the greatest; also, although state and local taxes were less progressive than the income tax, higher levels of consumption by the well-to-do would yield more revenue. As he anticipated, liberal critics accused him of callousness toward the poor, who would also have to pay any tax on purchased goods at retail; Galbraith's response was that the net transfer of benefits from newly financed public services would offset their tax burden.[41]

Galbraith also insisted that to claim that reduced private consumption meant reduced production and higher unemployment was to misunderstand his argument. The provision of decent housing, for example, entailed good city planning, prompt trash collection, well-maintained and well-lit streets, well-paid police and firefighters, nearby open space, good schools. Some of these public benefits would develop with increased public employment but also with the growing private-sector supply of needed services or production of socially consumed goods, and the employment that came with it. The mix and nature of consumption, rather than its level, was the issue. (In this, he anticipated the environmental debates of the 1970s and 1980s, when the "conventional wisdom" of conservatives and some economists claimed that new antipollution standards were nothing but a "tax," or "drag," on production; in fact, they often turned out to be a spur that generated new industries and job-creating technological innovations.)

Still, Galbraith understood that many people feared any change in the private production system because they feared the risks of their own unemployment. He underscored that America's new affluence hadn't itself abolished the business cycle, and that the imperative now was to decouple private production from insecurity. For laid-off workers, he ingeniously proposed a flexible new system of unemployment benefits, in which benefits would increase when overall unemployment was high but shrink when the aggregate level fell. Such a system, he argued, would give substantial support to individuals and to the recovery process during recessions, while removing any incentive for malingering when the economy was strong and jobs available.[42]

YET ONE READS these and other suggestions at the end of *The Affluent Society* with a certain disquiet. They seem only a starting point in solving the problems Galbraith was addressing himself to. Having identified a central cause of the endless generation of "superfluous" private demand in the way corporations created "want" for their products, he was silent on how to limit this behavior. In a competitive economy, why would General Motors stop promoting bigger tail fins if Ford did not? (Galbraith's recognition of this weakness led him to deal with it at length in both *The New Industrial State* and *Economics and the Public Purpose*.)

Galbraith could also be faulted on two further counts. The first was his assessment of the remaining poverty in the United States: in advancing his thesis about America's extraordinary new abundance, he remarked almost in passing that by now "poverty was more nearly an afterthought."[43] A few years later, when the Kennedy-Johnson era "rediscovered" poverty's extent and newly collected federal data concluded that a quarter of Americans were poor, Galbraith admitted that his remark had been cavalier and removed the offending sentence in later editions of *The Affluent Society*.

Yet his original chapter on "The New Position of Poverty" did not dismiss poverty's importance; it was an attempt better to define its nature and extent, compared to the widespread poverty of earlier times.*[44] He focused on two categories: "case poverty," as he called it, which included individuals who were poor because of poor education or health or substance abuse; and "insular poverty," where entire population groups were poor, irrespective of individual circumstances, in regions such as Appalachia or large areas of the Deep South. Neither kind of poverty was acceptable, and he advocated extensive public services and investment in education, housing, and job training to correct both.

The second issue on which Galbraith was criticized was his advocacy of the potentially transformative possibilities in what he called "the New Class." He was trying to define or create a plausible group of citizens who could help society make the transition away from the endless pursuit of private consumption. Marx in the nineteenth century had his key catalyst class, the proletariat (and his own different goals); for Thorstein Veblen in the 1920s such a transformative group were the engineers. Neoclassical economists had no such class, since their theory of economic man atomized social relations into a hurly-burly competition of individuals maximizing their own self-interest. Galbraith's thesis was that a new generation of Americans no longer worked simply to provide themselves and their families with necessities but because they drew intrinsic pleasure and reward from their work. With this shift, a New Class was appearing, a cadre of educated white-collar professionals and technicians that would be the vanguard in the search for satisfying work and for escape from repetitive, manual toil. Their values would spread more widely as opportunities for education reached the population as a whole. This development promised, or so Galbraith thought, a real opportunity for generating a better society and economy.

In making his point about the growing importance of rewarding work, as distinct from necessary labor, he also criticized the traditional neoclassical doctrines about the insatiability of demand. If material wants were everywhere and always insatiable, as so many conventional economists believed, why then

---

*Though the Great Depression was, of course, much on his mind, he also knew that even in the "prosperous" 1920s 60 percent of families had earned less than $2,000 per year, and that although the income of manufacturing workers had risen 8 percent (in line with the cost of living), for most farmers—because commodity prices fell throughout the decade—conditions had been far worse. By 1929, in fact, the top tenth of families were receiving 40 percent of all income—a level of inequality America wouldn't see again until the late 1990s. By comparison, when *The Affluent Society* appeared income equality was greater than it ever had been, or has been since.

had work hours declined steadily since the late nineteenth century, from seventy hours per week to barely forty? To be sure, one reason was increased productivity, the ability to create the same or more with less labor, but that couldn't be the whole story: if wants for goods were truly infinite, then people would have maintained the same work hours so as to buy even more.

History in the decades after he wrote *The Affluent Society* dealt blows to Galbraith's optimism about this New Class. Americans in general actually did increase their work hours over the last quarter of the twentieth century; U.S. workers, in fact, now work the longest hours in the industrial world (more even than the Japanese, who long held the record), and nowhere is this increase in hours more noticeable than among the New Class.[45] The rapid rise in the number of women in the paid workforce has meant that the number of total family work hours has grown even faster. And the private consumption habits of many of these New Class people do not encourage one to believe they are the vanguard Galbraith was hoping for. The 1980s "yuppies" and their 1990s successors—the SUV-driving, McMansion-dwelling suburbanites and habitants of chicly restored urban lofts, whose chief passions are for expensive restaurants, exotic vacations, and investment in the latest technological trend, and whose politics exhibit a quasi-libertarian contempt for government—show how wrong he may have been.

FOR ALL ITS LIMITATIONS, *The Affluent Society* hugely influenced the country's debates over its economic, political, and social future. It reached the best-seller list within weeks of its publication in the late spring of 1958 and stayed there for the rest of the year. Sales at home and abroad (it was swiftly translated into more than two dozen languages) soon passed the million mark, and it has never been out of print; a new revised and updated edition was issued in 1998, the book's fortieth anniversary.[46] The very phrase "affluent society" appears in most library reference books on the American language ("conventional wisdom" is almost as commonly recognized), and the book has shown up on virtually every list of the most influential works of the twentieth century.[47]

A torrent of reviews greeted *The Affluent Society*, usually with extraordinary enthusiasm, and even those that disagreed with one or another of Galbraith's arguments readily acknowledged their force and influence.[48] *The New York Times*'s page-one review, written by Edwin Dale, called it "a compelling challenge to conventional thought," its ideas "so daring and so convincingly argued that it deserves front rank in any debate in economics." Dale stated his "unequivocal belief that it is a very good thing indeed that this book was written." On the same day, Robert Heilbroner wrote in the *New York Herald Tribune* that *The Affluent Society* was "as disturbing as it is brilliant" and "impossible to dismiss," and praised Galbraith for raising issues of such "magnitude and importance." *The Washington Post*'s publisher, Philip Graham, wrote that paper's front-page review himself, a rare honor, and reported that it was a "brilliant . . . important, almost haunting volume. Few will read it and remain unshaken."[49]

In *The New Republic* the economist Robert Lekachman called it "this impressive book . . . written with all the charm, wit, and bite which makes Mr. Galbraith a rarity in his generation." Lekachman was "convinced that Galbraith has done an enormous service to the cause of intelligent economic and social debate" and perhaps "as substantial a service to the prestige of economics itself." To *The New Yorker*'s reviewer, *The Affluent Society* was deeply "provocative," and it advised readers that "anyone who thinks of economics as the Dismal Science should read Professor Galbraith." *The Atlantic Monthly* apologized for "the impossibility of doing justice to its intricate argument," while in *Commentary*, Irving Kristol effusively judged it a work of seminal importance, ranking it with Keynes's *General Theory of Employment, Interest, and Money* and two or three other modern milestones. These works "did not invincibly demonstrate a set of conclusions; their special quality was their ability to persuade people who had never even read them. They were, above all, plausible and reasonable and they allowed us to make sense of our social experience . . . *The Affluent Society* is such a book." *The Nation*'s reviewer quarreled with the book's seeming neglect of poverty but nonetheless considered *The Affluent Society* "exciting" and "valuable," concluding that "a more refreshing examination of the stereotypes of both liberal and conservative economic thought has not appeared in many a year." *The Yale Review* said it was "of the most vital significance for economic theory."[50]

Several months later, when *The Affluent Society* appeared in Britain, *The Times Literary Supplement* declared the work "of foremost importance" and the gifted creation of "a truly sensitive and civilized man," while John Strachey wrote in *Encounter* that "twenty years after its publication, *The Affluent Society* will be exercising an influence comparable, though of a very different kind, to that exercised by *The General Theory* today."[51]

There were, however, predictable critics. *Time*'s anonymous reviewer chided *The Affluent Society* for being "a vague essay with the air of worried dinner-table conversation"—a criticism so out of step with the general reaction that Galbraith quoted it in a preface to the book's second edition, along with his friend the novelist John Steinbeck's counsel to him that "unless a reviewer has the courage to give you unqualified praise, I say ignore the bastard."[52] The far-right weekly *Human Events* called it "a sniper attack" on liberty and progress, and rather perplexingly, an argument for instituting "a modern brand of Prussian feudalism"! From the left, *Dissent* rebuked him for not realizing that the inevitable conclusions of his argument could be solved only by socialism (though it appreciatively added that Galbraith's proposed solutions were the outlines for "a workable plan for a socialist society"). And George Stigler indignantly professed that he "considered it shocking that more Americans have read *The Affluent Society* than *The Wealth of Nations*." (This was a slap for which Galbraith had a ready answer: "I may conceivably be missing the deeper cause of Professor Stigler's sorrow," he deadpanned, "which may be not that so many read Galbraith and so few read Smith but that hardly anyone reads Stigler at all.")[53]

Other critics were grudgingly more generous: in the conservative *National Review*, Colin Clark, assessing "The Horrible Proposals of Mr. Galbraith," admitted that *The Affluent Society* was "a real contribution to economic theory" and agreed that "the facts about social imbalance so graphically here described, are, in many regions, correct."[54] Even the *Chicago Tribune* acknowledged, in a front-page review, that Galbraith had "never been in better form" and could "hit a vested interest at any range and shoot folly as it flies, in business thinking, in Washington circles, even in the professorate."[55]

The *Tribune*'s passing mention of "the professorate" was apt. With the immense success of *The Affluent Society*, Galbraith was no longer an ordinary professor, and to many economists he was no longer a fully acceptable member of their fraternity. To some, it seemed the time had come to spell out their differences with Galbraith and his dangerous dissent.

In an oft-quoted passage of *The Affluent Society*, Galbraith vividly summarized the "social imbalance" of private consumption amid public want, which was such an immense travesty of the nation's true capacities:

> The family which takes its mauve and cerise, air-conditioned, power-steered, and power-braked car out for a tour passes through cities that are badly paved, made hideous by litter, blighted buildings, billboards, and posts for wires that should long since have been put underground.
>
> They pass on into a countryside that has been rendered largely invisible by commercial art . . . They picnic on exquisitely packaged food from a portable icebox by a polluted stream and go on to spend the night at a park which is a menace to public health and morals. Just before dozing off on an air-mattress, beneath a nylon tent, amid the stench of decaying refuse, they may reflect vaguely on the curious unevenness of their blessings.
>
> Is this, indeed, the American genius?[56]

Galbraith later acknowledged that he'd worked hard on that passage but had always been troubled by it. "I thought it too patently contrived, too ripe, but in the end I let it stay."[57] For his academic critics, however, it symbolized what was wrong with the entire book—and with "Galbraithian economics." It showed a revolt against the style of reasoning they associated with their profession, and the "scientific" method they thought they utilized, their dispassion, rigor, careful presentation of evidence, adherence to core axioms inherited from marginalism, and a confirmation of arguments made in English by means of mathematical forms. By the 1980s, this economics style came under withering assault from a new generation of economists who accused it of being an impoverished modernist conceit.[58] But in the 1950s, the style in which Galbraith conducted his economic arguments seemed wrong or at best out of date.

To the reviewer in the *American Economic Review*, *The Affluent Society* might thus be "knowledgeable," but much of that part which purports to be factual and much that is interpretive seems grossly casual; and much of that part that takes the form of deduction seems somewhat loose and questionable . . . most awkwardly, haphazardly, and unreliably [done] as compared with the way modern statisticians do these tasks[, the work of] a political economist written in the tradition of Veblen.[59]

Somewhat less grudgingly, Kenneth Boulding in the *Review of Economics and Statistics* allowed that this "moving and important work, addressed to the conscience and good sense of our times," was still only a "penetrating tract," lightyears away from "serious" economic research.[60]

The most conservative economists were the most deeply offended. Friedrich von Hayek declared that once one exposed how Galbraith's colorful writing and sloppy reasoning concealed the economic illogic of the "dependence effect," with its claim that producers increasingly determined the wants of consumers, "the whole argument of the book collapses." Readers would then be free to see *The Affluent Society* for what it really was: the "latest of the old socialist argument."[61] (Hayek's revelation was lost on Irving Kristol, who wistfully lamented that while Galbraith might "be denounced in some quarters as a 'socialist,' he clearly hasn't the faintest interest in that doctrine."[62])

The University of Chicago's Harry Johnson was only slightly more accommodating.[63] Although he acknowledged that Galbraith was correct about an affluent society's having fewer urgent wants, he thought that from a neoclassical point of view this was nothing more than a marginalist tautology—"less urgent wants are those one satisfies only with greater income"—which Galbraith had then turned into a value judgment (forbidden to "scientific" economists) about an affluent society's inability to focus on maximizing private production.

Reasoning more strictly, he said, marginalist rules could be used to show that the preferences of the rich were of greater value than those of the poor— a theoretical position that Johnson acknowledged wasn't "the popular view." Galbraith's fatal fluency had led him into the gross theoretical error of believing that "the marginal utility of present aggregate output, ex advertising and salesmanship, is zero," which not only demonstrated his ignorance of Marshall's and Frank Knight's decisive work on consumer theory but, worse, amounted to "sheer semantic chicanery: one might with equal logic argue that the marginal utility of income is negative to a man who supports an administration which spends some of his tax payments on purposes of which he disapproves or to one who reduces his life expectation by heavy smoking."[64]

Galbraith was not ignorant of Marshall's and Knight's conclusions, but he disagreed with them and with the whole transposition of their work onto the conditions of postwar America. He was offering a new theoretical framework for understanding the contemporary world of affluence, and his "style" was an integral feature of his originality.

Some economists understood this right away, and admired Galbraith for what he was doing, even when they quibbled with this or that conclusion.

Paul Homan, for example, started his review of *The Affluent Society* by remarking:

> In the present century, the only English-speaking economists to achieve much of either fame or notoriety have been Veblen and Keynes. This did not happen because they were foremost in their scientific contributions to knowledge. It happened for two reasons: first, because they brought fresh thinking peculiarly applicable to the social and economic problems of their times, and, second, because they possessed a peculiar combination of shock-producing originality of mind and rhetorical persuasiveness.[65]

But to conservatives, Galbraith's style in economics was a first-order reason for refutation, a shibboleth that somehow "proved" that he wasn't a serious economist. In truth, they disliked his economic and political implications and assumptions as much as, if not more than, his style, just as they intensely detested Keynes. With *The Affluent Society*, dislike of its author's style took on new force and extended to a wider segment of professional economists. As the mathematically intense "model-building" style increasingly came to define how economists were supposed to express themselves in books and articles, Galbraith seemed to stand farther away from the new mainstream.[66]

This dispute turns out to be far from simple or clear-cut. The MIT economist Lester Thurow, for one, has written that many colleagues fault Galbraith stylistically on nothing more than what might seem to the laity a minor and formalistic point: "At least forty percent of economists' sometimes negative reaction to Ken can be traced to his not footnoting."

> Academics are egoists; when they write an article on a subject and you write an article on the same subject and don't footnote them, that makes them madder than anything. But being mature academics, they can't admit to getting mad about footnotes. So they have to be mad about something else— maybe about the way he exaggerates, stakes out a position which is probably a little stronger than reality would warrant.[67]

Thurow has a point. Shortly after *The Affluent Society* appeared, Galbraith found himself in just such a dispute with Alvin Hansen, who complained that it was he—Hansen—who had first coined the term "social balance," and developed it at some length before Galbraith made it a central concept in his own book. Hansen's complaint reached the ears of Paul Samuelson, who in turn made a passing reference to this claim of Hansen's in his presidential address to the American Economic Association.[68] The news added new fuel to the fire of Galbraith's critics, since it suggested a serious academic discourtesy, if not plagiarism.

But Hansen had been confused about the timing of his and Galbraith's books. He somehow thought *The Affluent Society* had been published in 1959, not the spring of 1958. Its first draft had been substantially complete, including the concept of "social balance," by the late summer of 1956, when Galbraith returned from Switzerland—a year before Hansen introduced his own use of the term "social balance." Hansen and Galbraith settled the matter congenially, but the story endured as folklore among many economists.[69]

Another part of the criticism concerns "style" in a way that a literature professor would understand better than a social scientist does. "Galbraithian style" often meant his authorial voice, including his long, often elliptical, sentences and paragraphs, and his deployment of wry, often mordant, humor. He consciously intended a specific effect, and his humor owed a great deal to a British tradition that while trading openly on an awareness of social class, spoke in the cultivated, educated, and socially confident voice of writers such as Lytton Strachey, Max Beerbohm, and Oscar Wilde. Despite its British antecedents, it also shared nineteenth-century democratic American roots with Mark Twain and Finley Peter Dunne. The subjects of his satire were inevitably the powerful and well-off, the promulgators and beneficiaries of the "conventional wisdom" in all its forms. Here he was closer to writers such as George Bernard Shaw than to Strachey, Beerbohm, and Wilde, and he shared Shaw's belief that the future is rich with democratic and egalitarian possibilities.

In *The Affluent Society*, we are reminded that "precisely because he lives a careful life, the executive is moved to identify himself with the dashing entrepreneur of economic literature," or that "as the rich have become more numerous, they have inevitably become a debased currency," or that "men of high position are allowed, by a special act of grace, to accommodate their reasoning to the answer they need. Logic is only required in those of lesser rank." A democratic and egalitarian sensibility is embedded in each of these aphoristic remarks. Other people may exercise power or influence over our lives or may harvest undue rewards from our common effort, but thanks to Galbraith's humorous deflation, we are invited to step through their veil of conceits and conventions. More important, Galbraith reminds us that we ourselves hold the power to create a more fully realized and generous democratic future. After all, "It is the good fortune of a rich country that, like a rich man, it has the luxury of choice. But it cannot avoid choosing."[70]

To Galbraith, choosing involves more than economists alone can help us with, especially when they insist that their work is "value-neutral" and "scientific." To realize fully the purpose of economic activity in a democratic society requires its citizenry to share a public commitment, "to consider its goals, to reflect on its pursuit of happiness and harmony and its success in expelling pain, tension, sorrow and the ubiquitous curse of ignorance." The country having reached an historically unprecedented level of material affluence, "the basic demand on America will be on its resources of ability, intelligence and education," not merely its capacity for material production. Thus, even Galbraith's choice of authorial voice is related to the way he conceives the project of economics itself and its connection to larger democratic purposes.

For one thing, he considered the boundaries separating economics from other fields—history, political science, sociology, and social and political philosophy—porous. The fact that these fields are divided in universities by department and training expresses only a very recent disciplinary and customary practice. A century earlier none of those specialties (save history, to a degree) existed at all: what academic economists there were taught their subject as a subdiscipline of moral philosophy or political economy.[71]

For another, rather than affirming the elegant descent of economic knowledge discovered by the most enlightened (theorists) to the less so (specialists in policy), and thence to political and financial or business elites, and eventually to an often ignorant "general public," Galbraith's style affirmed not only the right but the duty of a democratic public to participate fully in determining its economic priorities and rules. Throughout *The Affluent Society* and his works thereafter, an appeal to the public's "common sense," in the richest sense of that term, is mixed with abstract theory and applied policies; values are reaffirmed that endorse the citizen's skepticism about powerful, self-serving, pompous, and sometimes misguided elites; and goals are proposed that entail a substantial reordering of the economic system itself in the name of democracy and of greater economic and political equality.[72]

Galbraith knew that in *The Affluent Society* he was breaking not only with older pre-Keynesian economic doctrines but also in many ways from the postwar Neoclassical Synthesis. "Nothing in economics so quickly marks an individual as incompetently trained as a disposition to remark on the legitimacy of the desire for more food and the frivolity of the desire for a more elaborate automobile," he wrote.[73] But Galbraith also never doubted that he was firmly grounded in Keynes's own thought in several important ways. First, he willingly embraced the idea that the economist was directly obliged to speak to, and persuade, the nonprofessional public, just as Keynes had done. But in the decades since *The Economic Consequences of the Peace*, no economist but Galbraith came even close to producing such a volume for the public. Second, like Keynes, Galbraith sought to define economics not as a scientific field of "positive" assumptions that could be distinguished from the messier "normative" issues of policy but as an instrumental practice that was designed to achieve central moral and political ends and that was at its best when economists educated and persuaded the public. This had been true of Keynes's masterpiece *The General Theory*, despite its admitted complexity, and of many other short, accessible works, such as *How to Pay for the War* and *The Economic Consequences of Mr. Churchill*, the pamphlet he wrote in the 1920s castigating Churchill and the British Treasury for Britain's return to a prewar gold standard, because of its cruel effects in depressing workers' incomes.[74] And it was supremely true in Keynes's "Economic Possibilities for Our Grandchildren," with its prediction that in only a few generations a new and unimaginable level of material abundance would "lead us out of the tunnel of economic necessity into the daylight," and release us from the antiquated strictures of "maximizing" behavior in order to pursue other goals. In that new world, the economy's appearance of behaving according to natural law would break down in ways that showed how much unlike physics economics was. "If economists could manage to get themselves thought of as humble, competent people, on a level with dentists, that would be splendid!"[75]

GALBRAITH'S GROWING SEPARATION from mainstream economics concerned his fundamental and distinctive assumptions about the nature of economics and its theoretical underpinnings, as well as his ideas about democratic government, indeed about the ultimate purposes of democratic and economic activity in human society. In Marshall's theoretical legacy, as in Adam Smith's, the function of government was, broadly speaking, minimal and secondary to "market" forces. Government had to define the outer bounds of property relations through law, enforce those rules through the police and the courts, and provide for a national defense (and a stable national currency), but markets were central. Yet this adjunct relation of government to markets was never either empirically true or easily accepted.[76] Marx made the most concerted and visible assault on it, but he was only one of many thinkers who found the antecedents to marginalism unsatisfactory. In the United States, proponents of the sociohistorical and institutionalist legacy of Richard Ely, Thorstein Veblen, Wesley Mitchell, and John R. Commons were at least as skeptical of this simple division between government and markets.[77]

Marshall himself was consistently more supportive of a government active in the economy than his theory's more ardent apostles suggest.[78] Toward the end of his career he even openly asked whether the more richly complex model of biology, suffused with ideas of interdependence and feedback loops, wasn't a better starting point for economic theory than the mechanics of physics. He understood the effect of institutions, culture, and habit—as well as inertia, ignorance, and limited foresight—on economic behavior, and he carefully circumscribed many of his claims about "economic rationality" as being part of a long, complex social and cultural evolution. Marshall thought of optimization and equilibrium analysis as useful, but very rough, tools of often only transitory value.[79]

Marshall's followers were strongly encouraged to think in similar ways—that is, to recognize that the heuristic and proximate values of "pure theory" were incomplete when applied to "the art and ethics" of public policy—by Neville Keynes, John Maynard's father. Neville Keynes was a close and beloved protégé of Marshall's, and his *Scope and Method of Political Economy*, which appeared just a year after Marshall's *Principles*, was for many years considered an important guide to understanding and applying Marshall's theories.[80]

Similarly, Arthur Pigou, who followed Marshall as Regius Professor of Political Economy at Cambridge (and whose loyal dictum to students was "It's all in Marshall"), pioneered in developing "welfare economics," a branch of the neoclassical tradition that gave theoretical justification to even larger government interventions in markets. After World War I, Pigou underscored the many ways in which Marshallian markets "fail," identifying virtually all the modern notions of "externalities" that bedevil the updated model: congestion, pollution, resource exhaustion, imperfect information, and inventions. In each of these cases, Pigou concluded, expanded government interventions were essential to any solution.

But it remained for Keynes, in *The General Theory*, to advance the understanding of government's appropriate function in ways that solved more fundamental problems than Pigou's. The compelling challenge in the 1930s was to resolve not simply sectoral or industry-specific issues, but the generalized problem of marketwide failure, to restore aggregate demand in an environment that was showing less than Marshallian perfection, and then for Keynes to prepare for a world of abundance. It was this Keynesian springboard that gave vitality to Galbraith's critique of modern capitalism and anchored his ideas about democratic governments.

But of course Keynes and Keynesianism weren't synonymous. Developments after Keynes's death in 1946 showed that the doctrine of a large, macroregulating government was subject to widely differing interpretations, and was also intertwined with new political and economic issues extending far beyond Keynes's original thinking.[81]

At the policy level, the immense costs of the Cold War—both the military uses to which so much government spending was put and the political alliances and worldviews it sustained—took center stage. Federal spending had certainly risen under Roosevelt in the 1930s, when unemployment peaked at 25 percent of the workforce and never fell to less than 14 percent before the war. Yet the "vast" spending of the New Deal grew only from 7 percent of GDP in 1932 to just under 10 percent in 1940. Given that a quarter of that 10 percent in 1940 was for military rearmament, the popular idea that there was an "explosion" in federal spending under the New Deal is mistaken. And because expenditures by state and local government *fell* during the 1930s, total fiscal spending by American government over FDR's first two terms in fact barely rose at all.[82] This changed during World War II, when government came to account for nearly half the U.S. economy, but right after the war military spending briefly dropped. Then the federal government mushroomed again. By the time Eisenhower became President in 1953, Washington's 21 percent share of GDP was eight times higher than the 2.5 percent it had been when Herbert Hoover entered the Oval Office, and during Eisenhower's two terms never dipped below twice its average during the Great Depression.[83] Yet as the veteran *Wall Street Journal* economics editor Alfred Malabre observed, "If an economist from Mars were to descend tomorrow and peruse the economic data of the early post–World War II era, he or she (or it) would surely conclude that Keynesian economists . . . had little sway in those early postwar years."[84]

In fact, the 1950s did not reveal a consciously "Keynesian" policy approach to government spending in ways Keynes himself would have endorsed. Despite the government's immense enlargement under Truman and Eisenhower, the federal government ran surpluses much more frequently than deficits, even when unemployment was high by the standards of the time.[85] Compared to the avowedly conservative Reagan-Bush years to come—when "Keynesianism" was supposedly anathema and yet government's massive deficits nearly tripled the national debt as a percentage of GDP—one can wonder indeed what *was* Keynesian during the early Cold War.

For Galbraith, the unconscious presumptions underpinning this vast expansion of government under Eisenhower posed a dilemma. Traditional economics posited a limited government because in its theory of the market no one accumulated significant power over others thanks to endless competition. Then, with the evolution of the giant modern corporation and industries dominated by a few firms, the empirical evidence that economic power was stabilized in the hands of a few belied the model, and so government was called upon as a countervailing power—the idea behind the Progressive Era, the New Deal, and modern liberalism's economic credo. But Galbraith argued that contrary to the legacy of Woodrow Wilson, Theodore Roosevelt, Justice Brandeis, and other Progressives, one could no longer imagine dealing with bigness by breaking it up. Market failures narrowly conceived would not be eliminated by government, therefore, but be managed by it. Still, Galbraith stressed the "deep and enduring contradiction in modern industrial society. The public and the corporate purposes diverge." And the associated contradiction was that postwar governments were not autonomous from the private plans of major firms but, on the contrary, the two were deeply entwined.

One reason why so many corporate leaders after World War II accepted the expansion of government, however haltingly and grudgingly, was that they recognized the direct benefits of a business cycle moderated by "business Keynesianism." Memories of the Great Depression had won them over to the usefulness of the state as macromanager. They also understood that the government's concentration of expenditures on military affairs symbiotically linked it with big corporations. The armed forces' 70 percent share of federal direct spending on goods and services was far larger than their share of the total budget; it amounted to $501 billion between 1946 and 1960.[86] Rich defense contracts flowed out to Lockheed, Grumman, Hughes, Litton Industries, TRW, and big "nondefense" corporations like General Motors, IBM, and General Electric, and as research subsidies to universities and government-funded think tanks. Infrastructure investments were justified in military-needs terms. All this went beyond simple Keynesian macromanagement principles and showed a focused integration of the goals of the state and the giant corporations.

In 1947, Secretary of Defense James Forrestal declared, "Calvin Coolidge was ridiculed for saying . . . 'the chief business of the United States is business' but that is a fact." Time proved Forrestal right. Corporate profits soared after World War II, from $12 billion in 1945 to more than $50 billion by the end of the 1950s. And those profits went into fewer and fewer hands as the hundred biggest American companies reaped nearly 60 percent of all business profits. (The top thousand got 85 percent.) Profits for the biggest defense contractors were unusually high: for example, measured by corporate net worth in 1954, net profits at General Dynamics were 139 percent; at Boeing, 93 percent; at Douglas and North American, 80 percent. (That the government paid to build many of their plants, a practice begun in World War II and never abandoned, helped to create these astonishing margins.) "We are living under a curious kind of military Keynesianism," the historian Richard Hofstadter wrote, "in which Mars has rushed in to fill the gap left by the market economy."[87]

None of this had been anticipated by either the liberal or conservative tradition before World War II; the United States had never before maintained a large peacetime armed force or defined itself as a global superpower. But the new redefinition of government in heavily militarized terms carried great costs. Cold War conservatives were more than willing to use the cudgel of "Communist infiltration" and "Communist sympathizer" to delegitimize liberal candidates and programs, and to deem anything less than full support for the agenda of a heavily militarized government a "betrayal" of America.

There was a second challenge. Government, in the conservative view, was more than competent to maintain the defense of the United States and to blunt "Soviet tyranny" abroad, but at the same time it was thought incompetent or worse when it "interfered" in the workings of the "free market." Thus a limited sort of macromanagement was now acceptable, so long as private business was left "free" to operate within its self-defined boundaries. When liberals argued in favor of expanding government programs not devoted to defense, it was claimed that they were threatening a "burdensome" tax level that would impede optimal overall growth, and distort the legitimate allocation of goods and incomes as established by the efficient interplay of private supply and demand.

To Galbraith, this layered, interconnected relation between government and giant American corporations—and the conservative ideology that defended it—was *the* dilemma of modern liberalism and of Keynesianism. In a Cold War state, the government carried out its "Keynesian" macromanagerial mandate under circumstances heavily determined by military and strategic goals; meanwhile, the domestic economy was left to advertisers and marketers into an endless celebration of private consumption. This consumption increasingly met not needs so much as wants carefully manipulated by private-goods producers. Pressing public needs were not filled.

The Galbraithian way out of the dilemma was to fight to restore certain central liberal ideas about the public agenda, and to press the macromanagement of the economy and its underlying theory back into the service of a more expansive and hopeful Keynesian worldview. Democratic government relies on choices about values, which can't be made by markets alone. Freedom is essential, but so also are equality, security, social stability, reduced social tensions, and a quality of life that sustains creativity and that focuses the imagination on more than getting and spending. Freedom for Galbraith had both a "negative" dimension (the opportunity for independent action and autonomy) and a "positive" one (provision of basic resources and a social structure that protects negative freedom while promoting individual and collective ends).[88] The achievement of democracy and market capitalism was that both created the preconditions for the exercise of freedom, but at the same time market capitalism generated its own powerful limitations on freedom, promoting as it did the coarse ideological claim that ever-increasing consumption *is* freedom. To Galbraith this was "a false ideal." He argued, or hoped, that given affluence, more and more people would come to realize that "leisure, free time and intellectual achievement are the real thing."[89]

Corporations limit the effectiveness of government in ensuring the "positive" aspects of freedom, given their symbiotic relation with government's bureaucracies and interests and their often overt lobbying against the public interest. So, said Galbraith, "the role of government, when one contemplates reform, is a dual one. The government is a major part of the problem; it is also central to the remedy."[90] To promote both "positive" and "negative" freedom, governments should not install permanent programs, but have permanent goals aimed at enlarging freedom, as well as the equality and security necessary to it. Because different times require different programs, and the line between public and private realms can shift, "the test of public action is a practical one," Galbraith wrote. He argued pragmatically—in the sense John Dewey or Richard Rorty means the term—that "if needful good can be achieved only by government, or if it can be better achieved by government, the responsibility should be theirs."[91]

What, then, is the definition of "needful good"? True to Galbraith's underlying pragmatism, the answer is not abstract but lies in careful, reflective choices made in specific historical contexts. His answers can be inferred from the proposals he supported over the decades: major reductions in military spending; greater international cooperation for economic development and political freedom; welfare reform aimed at poverty reduction, including a guaranteed annual income; increases in the minimum wage; democratic trade unions; environmentalism; racial equality, including affirmative action; feminism and gender equality; major federal aid to education; urban reform; campaign finance reform; aid to and support of the arts; farm price supports; limits on financial speculation; progressivity in taxation, including sharp limits on windfall profits and executive compensation; increased public regulation of certain concentrated industries such as transportation, finance, utilities, weapons, and pharmaceuticals; and publicly financed health care.

Much more than correctly designed policies, he stresses, are needed to achieve such goals, however. Economists as public-policy professionals can't hope to see their technically proficient solutions simply implemented, and they do a disservice to themselves and the public by pretending to be simply "neutral" advisers. Governance is not a neutral activity, and successful democracies require advocates of authentic reform policies such as these to foresee and develop public understanding and support for their plans.

A key measure of success is the extent to which citizens participate in governance through voting, especially citizens who are disadvantaged by existing arrangements of power and wealth. Galbraith here warned against an overreliance on formal means to that end—changes in registration requirements, ab-

sentee balloting, and so on—which are only of modest value; real "reform begins . . . with belief, not with laws and the government."[92] For people to enjoy
real freedom they must individually and collectively participate in achieving
and maintaining it. "Emancipation of belief" is a necessary but not sufficient
step toward greater freedom. Galbraith recognized that democratic government is itself imperfect, particularly in an age of affluence, when it all too often becomes "a democracy of the contented and the comfortable" while "the
uncomfortable and the distressed do not have candidates who represent their
needs and do not vote."[93]

THIS PICTURE OF the modern possibilities for freedom and democracy is open
to many criticisms. From century-old works such as Max Weber's masterly
analysis of modern bureaucracy and Robert Michel's theory of "the iron law of
oligarchies" comes a pessimism about individuals' enjoying substantial freedom
or about democracies' working for the interests of more than a powerful few. In
the last quarter century, under the influence of the Reagan-Thatcher "revolutions," a market-affirming view posits the markets as the defenders of freedom
and government as its opponent. But in the 1950s, Galbraith was not contending with these views. He was, though, setting himself against mainstream
Keynesian economists, for whom government was of vital importance to the
economy, an opinion they anchored not in a political-philosophical framework
but in a mathematical one.

Many of the Keynesian mainstream pioneers broadly shared Galbraith's liberal beliefs. Samuelson, Solow, Modigliani, Klein, and Arrow (all eventual Nobel laureates) were also secular Jews who brought to economics not only
mathematical brilliance but a heritage of Jewish social justice teachings. Another decade passed before doubts were voiced among their own followers
about the telling differences between Keynes's theory and methodological approach and those of this group of apostles—and this occurred only after their
applied Keynesian prescriptions seemed to run aground.

In 1968, the economist Axel Leijonhufvud set out to distinguish between
"the economics of Keynes and Keynesian economics."[94] Keynes, he said, far
from advancing within Marshall's tradition assuming market-clearing behavior
by rational, self-maximizing individuals, had constructed a working model of
an economy fraught with all sorts of irrational behaviors that markets failed to
clear, for very human reasons. Exchange, in this formal interpretation, took
place in a world of uncertainty and disequilibrium prices, with the result that
individuals and firms faced many quantity restraints. Rather than prices adjusting quickly (whether for goods or labor), quantities often did so, with
prices lagging or remaining inflexible. Expectations were frequently inelastic or
very nearly so. This created, under certain circumstances, Keynes's famous
"liquidity trap": when a rising money supply led not to lower interest rates that
stimulated investment but to idle funds balances and inadequate investment
(and high unemployment)—and also created the larger problem of "intertem-
poral disequilibrium" because assets were mispriced. But if assets were so

often mispriced, as Keynes believed, then one could not validly construct conventional aggregate production function, covering both investment and consumption goods, as his mathematical followers had done. To do so ipso facto ruled out the very source of Keynes's insight that there was quite frequently—not just in times such as the Depression—an imbalance between output and capital-goods prices.

Leijonhufvud's critique of the postwar Keynesians raises important questions. How had this happened? Was it simply a result of mathematicizing? Or was it about something more specific in the selected mathematicized models?

The rise of the "model-building revolution" (to use Niehans's term) in academic Keynesianism perhaps owes most to three men: John Hicks, Paul Samuelson, and Kenneth Arrow. (There are other figures certainly, such as John von Neumann, Lawrence Klein, Ragnar Frisch, Jan Tinbergen, Tjalling Koopmans, Roy Harrod, James Tobin, Robert Solow, and Frank Ramsey.) Hicks, an English economist twenty years younger than Keynes, is best known to millions of economics students as the man who domesticated Keynes (though that term is never used). A prolific thinker who made several important contributions to modern economic techniques, Hicks in 1937, just months after The General Theory's first publication, formulated the "IS-LM diagram," which effectively reduced the core of Keynes's theory to two simultaneous equations. Represented graphically as cross-cutting lines, the equations linked changes in the real goods and money markets and produced an equilibrium point at their intersection between national income and the interest rate.

By the 1970s Hicks came to consider his IS-LM interpretation an error, recognizing (like Leijonhufvud) that he had misrepresented Keynes's preoccupation with uncertainty as a given condition of economic life.[95] But he had helped to launch generations of economists on an adventure that assumed the ability to subordinate Keynes's economics to the rigors of equilibrium modeling.[96] By itself, Hicks's formalization of Keynes wasn't enough to generate the new technical focus; yet one wonders whether, without it, postwar theoretical economics could have been so optimistic about the future.

After the war, Hicks's formulation of Keynes flowed neatly into the interest in a better mathematical formalization of the theory itself, and in a mathematically operationalized set of planning guidelines that policy advisers could use to influence government's effect on the economy itself (in turn inspired by Koopmans's development of linear programming). The instinct for formalization was embodied in Paul Samuelson's Foundations of Economic Analysis, with its extraordinary mastery of calculus and differential and difference equations that would not become standard for another decade or more.

Among his several contributions, Samuelson's early work dealt a heavy blow to the usual theory about how consumers form preferences for one set of goods over another. The nineteenth-century legacy of John Stuart Mill had been that the answer was "utility": consumers somehow rank-ordered their wants through an underlying (albeit imperfectly understood) psychological and moral system that eventually might be measured in units called "utils" like units of height, weight, or distance. When this proved illusory, a second formulation arose: if preferences couldn't be measured in absolute quantities such as "utils," they could at least be ranked so that the differences or intervals between them could be measured.

By the early twentieth century, the American economist Irving Fisher and his Italian contemporary Vilfredo Pareto recognized that both these notions of utility measurement were unnecessary. In their place, economics needed only "ordinal utility," a simple ranking of preferences, irrespective of their distances or intervals. From this knowledge alone, coupled with producer costs on the supply side, one could derive a theory of price.

But serious theoretical conundrums were associated with utility even in this form, and Samuelson set out to place the whole theory of consumer demand on the basis of simple observation of consumers' behavior. Saumuelson's contribution, called "revealed preference" theory, introduced a set of axioms (which he and others later refined) that established how, as revealed in their behavior alone, consumers "solved" the preference problem; economists could rely ex post facto on what consumers chose rather than having to postulate an ex ante schedule of utility. The theory argues that in effect consumers get what they want; if they wanted something else, they would (within income constraints) get it, and the fact that they don't "reveals" their preference. And that is all an economist needs to know.[97]

The effect of "revealed preference" was—gradually, not immediately—to remove the haunting problems about how consumer preferences were formed from the list of issues that model builders thought they had had to worry about. Why consumers chose to buy what they did, or what influenced them (advertising, ignorance, taste, status) became questions outside the domain of proper study, of concern to sociologists and business marketers, perhaps, but not to serious economists.[98]

Samuelson's pioneering efforts to "mathematicize" economics fit not just the profession's tendencies of the time, but those of the larger culture. College enrollment had skyrocketed after World War II and, with it, the demand for new professors, research, and methods that would secure for the academy the power, size, and influence that had been held forth as the promise of a rationally ordered world at least since the Enlightenment. Nowhere was the newfound prosperity and influence of the university more visible than in the sciences, and nowhere in the sciences more visible than in physics.

Albert Einstein had been an obscure young patent clerk in Switzerland when he wrote the papers that defined the new vision of physics; by the 1920s he was a world-famous celebrity, as well known as adventurers such as Charles Lindbergh, war heroes such as Black Jack Pershing, and actors such as Douglas Fairbanks. With the invention of the atomic bomb, physics gained an even greater, though darker, power over the modern world; it became quickly associated with an expansive vision of the atom's peacetime potential in energy, medicine, transportation, and other promising fields.

The amazing advances of physics coincided with those of technology. The automobile, radio, television, telephone, and airplane, new wonder drugs, even consumer products such as plastic wrap and frozen foods and nylon hose bespoke the agility of the scientific imagination and the endless bounty it devised. How could economists resist trying to be more like physicists? Many of them believed that to be more like physicists they must refine Marshall's foundations and substitute for them an abstractly deduced model of economic equilibrium at least as comprehensive as the gift Einstein had given physics.[99]

Technically, it was a matter of substituting a defensible, rigorously exact proof of general equilibrium for Marshall's partial equilibrium. Marshall had focused on the behavior of markets for single or paired commodities in isolation, ignoring the effects of changes in a commodity's price on other related market prices, though he intuitively recognized that such effects were there. Leon Walras and Pareto soon afterward sketched a more complete, general-equilibrium model that did better justice to this larger issue. Walras's solution—in effect an empirical-theoretical one—posited the process of *tâtonnement* (literally "tapping"), whereby buyers and sellers experimented continuously in response to prices called out by a hypothetical auctioneer, with an initial price for some arbitrary first commodity established as the *numéraire* for the others.

But Walras's solution was still troublingly incomplete by midcentury. Was such a system internally consistent, absent the arbitrary *numéraire*? Was the solution unique—that is, were there in fact a multiplicity of general equilibria rather than just one producible from a common starting point? And was such a system stable, so that it would return to equilibrium after a disturbance, such as a major new invention or supply shock?

To Keynes and his policy-oriented followers, such questions were of limited interest. After all, their foremost preoccupation was with problems of short-term aggregate behavior, the role of uncertainty, and the function of governments in managing the business cycle with the aim of steering economies toward stable long-term growth. But among the model builders, the matter of partial versus general equilibrium, and finding a serious mathematical proof for the latter, remained a seductive and haunting problem. Only by "unifying" Keynes's macroeconomic description with the microeconomic equilibrium theory did they think economics would achieve elegant, abstract cohesion.

Enter Kenneth Arrow. Arrow was the son of immigrants, born in New York City into a comfortable, book-filled home. But the Depression had ruined his father's business ventures, and so Arrow, a gifted child drawn to mathematics and logic, attended the City College of New York mainly because it was free. His family's circumstances focused him on the practical value of statistics, and led to summer employment as an actuarial clerk at an insurance company, where he learned about the problems of moral hazard and adverse selection. As a student at Columbia he earned first a master's in mathematics, then a Ph.D. under Harold Hotelling, a celebrated mathematical economist, in the new field of logic and social choice.

In 1954, Arrow (with Gérard Debreu) wrote a revolutionary paper that for the first time offered a rigorous mathematical "existence proof" for Walras's general equilibrium. The proof itself required a series of stylized, unrealistic presumptions (such as commodities in excess supply having a price of zero) and the use of sophisticated topological concepts unfamiliar to most economists. But the reasoning was elegant beyond a doubt. It was the overriding architectural *summum*, in effect, needed to make economics as comprehensively scientific as physics or the other natural sciences.*

The Arrow-Debreu existence proof summarized what the Neoclassical Synthesis was doing not only to Keynes but to professional economics generally. By the 1990s, even a historian of economic theory as sympathetic to the model builders as Jurg Niehans observed that

> from the point of view of analytical rigor, [Arrow and Debreu] were indeed revolutionary. In this respect they established entirely new standards, which could be met only by economists with much better mathematical ability and training than before. Up to that time the active use of a little calculus made one a mathematical economist. After that time mathematical economics became the preserve of those with the competence of a professional mathematician. In many respects, this was clearly a big step forward.

But this progress was not unalloyed:

> It came at a price, though. People with the mind and training of a mathematician are somewhat less likely to have a broad interest in social problems, and understanding of historical processes, and innovative economic ideas. As a consequence, the increase in mathematical competence was not associated with a marked acceleration in the progress of economic insight. The new mills could grind the corn more and more finely, but they did not process more grist.[100]

This wasn't apparent to most economists in the 1950s. The works of Hicks, Samuelson, and Arrow were fresh, rigorous, and seemed rich with promise. In the 1960s, their confidence burst forth in a new wave with the election of John F. Kennedy as President, but even in the 1950s economic theorists were increasingly confident they could deliver unimaginable prosperity.

Still, there were voices of dissent. On the libertarian right, Hayek continued to rail against any government infringement on the workings of the sacred market, while at the University of Chicago, an increasingly conservative economics department divided its time between embracing model building per se and abhorring the Keynesian component of the Neoclassical Synthesis.[101] It was left to Galbraith, first in *The Affluent Society* in 1958 and then in *The New In-*

---

*Whether or not Arrow and Debreu laid to rest all questions about the mathematical expression of Walrasian equilibrium came to seem less certain with time, especially after Amartya Sen's mathematically elegant work in the 1970s led many to conclude that economics' theoretical axioms were too impoverished to solve general questions of social welfare.

dustrial State a decade later, to articulate a full-blooded liberal dissent. In doing so he rejected the new acceptance of revealed preference and general equilibrium, as Keynes almost certainly would have done, had he lived.* He also insisted on the importance for economists of understanding history, power, and normative choice.

It wasn't until the 1970s that a counterrevolt coalesced against elements of the style of economics that attracted so many of Galbraith's critics. In late 1975, as the United States was stumbling economically after three decades of unprecedented expansion, Robert Gordon, a distinguished Keynesian of superior mathematical abilities, became president of the American Economic Association. In his inaugural address, he bluntly said that after three decades of the profession's hallowed model of perfect competition in its traditional and Neoclassical Synthesis forms, he considered it "the outstanding example of the failure of economic theory to adapt its analytical tools to the changing institutional environment." He called for a significant shift of the economics research agenda and the theorems governing it. The new agenda, he declared, should begin with the following assumptions:

> At the most basic level, a society is composed of individual human beings. The larger number of them sell the factor services they control to producing units ("firms" for short); and those who sell labor services must physically participate in the production process. A flow of newly produced goods and ser-

---

*Keynes once observed:

Mathematical [economics] has not, as a science or study, fulfilled its early promise. In the seventies and eighties of the last century, it was reasonable, I think, to suppose that it held great prospects. When the young [Francis] Edgeworth [a British pioneer in mathematical economics] chose it, he may have looked to find secrets as wonderful as those which the physicists have found since those days. But . . . this has not happened, but quite the opposite. The atomic hypothesis which has worked so splendidly in physics breaks down in [economics]. We are faced at every turn with the problems of organic unity, of discreteness, of discontinuity—the whole is not equal to the sum of the parts, comparisons of quantity fail us, small changes produce large effects, the assumptions of a uniform and homogeneous continuum are not satisfied . . . Edgeworth knew that he was skating on thin ice; and as life went on his love of skating and his distrust of the ice increased, by a malicious fate, *pari passu.*

And in 1937, reviewing a pioneering econometric analysis by Jan Tinbergen, he told his Cambridge colleague Richard Kahn, "I think [Tinbergen's econometrics] all hocus . . . But every one else is greatly impressed, it seems, by such a mess of unintelligible figurings. There is not the slightest explanation or justification of the underlying logic."

At the height of his powers and prestige, he wrote his friend Roy Harrod that "economics is a science of thinking in terms of models joined to the art of choosing models which are relevant to the contemporary world." The essence of building models was not to "fill in real values for the variable functions," as Keynes felt Tinbergen had done. Good economists were so few, he said, "because the gift for using 'vigilant observation' to choose good models, although it does not require a highly specialized intellectual technique, appears to be a rare one." The model builder who spends too much time refining the mathematics of his model will always fail "unless he is constantly correcting his judgement by intimate and messy acquaintance with the facts to which the model has to be applied."

I want to emphasise strongly the point about economics being a moral science. I mentioned before that it deals with introspection and values. I might have added that it deals with motives, expectations, psychological uncertainties. One has to be constantly on guard against treating the material as constant and homogeneous. It is as though the fall of the apple to the ground depended on the apple's motives, on whether it is worthwhile falling to the ground, and whether the ground wanted the apple to fall, and on mistaken calculations on the part of the apple as to how far it was from the centre of the earth.[102]

vices results. The distribution of these goods and services among potential
claimants depends on much more than the operation of "impersonal market
forces." It reflects a complex of institutional arrangements, which include,
among other things, the distribution of power among different groups to influence particular commodity and factor markets, both directly and through
government, how the ownership of wealth is distributed and for whose benefit it is used, the tax structure and network of government regulations that
emerge from the political process, and the total and distribution of net claims
by the rest of the world against domestic output.[103]

Here, finally, thirty years after the death of Keynes and the rise of the new
"model-building" Neoclassical Synthesis, it was being acknowledged that
something was seriously amiss in the way modern economics was done—and
that what was needed conceptually included the very elements Galbraith had
argued for. Institutional arrangements mattered, power mattered, the ownership of wealth mattered, the tax and regulatory structures mattered, how the
political process operated, under whose influence and for whose benefit—all
of this *mattered*. And modern postwar, Neoclassical Synthesis economics, with
the most sophisticated mathematical apparatus yet deployed, had somehow
not come to terms with these elemental facts.

14

Kennedy, Sputnik, and "Liberal Growthmanship"

My campaign for the presidency is founded on the single assumption that the American people are uneasy at the present drift in our national course, that they are disturbed by the relative decline in our vitality and prestige . . . If I am right . . . then those who have held back the growth of the U.S. during the last years will be rejected.

—Senator John F. Kennedy, campaigning in 1960

In 1956, after his nomination, Adlai Stevenson declared the vice-presidential selection open to a free vote of the convention. Kennedy was narrowly defeated by Estes Kefauver, and his position on agricultural policy . . . was believed, and especially by Kennedy himself, to have made the difference. In consequence, he came to regard my advice on agricultural and, by inference, on various other practical issues as impeccable.

—John Kenneth Galbraith

THE AFFLUENT SOCIETY made John Kenneth Galbraith America's most famous economist. The book spent nearly a year on *The New York Times* best-seller list—unheard-of for a book about economics—and as the title itself swiftly gained a permanent place in the English language, Galbraith was deluged with an almost unimaginable stream of requests for speeches, articles, interviews, and TV appearances.

The flow became so immense that to cope with the workload, he hired an attractive and very efficient young Smith College graduate who'd just spent several years in New York as the personal assistant to the president of a publishing house. Andrea Williams soon moved up to a more elevated role as the major domo of Galbraith's public life, editing his books and managing his affairs for the next forty years.

She quickly noticed how conscientious Galbraith himself was, replying to almost every inquiry, from the famous and unknown alike. She opened the mail, culled out the occasional crackpot, and presented her neatly organized pile to him when he came in, usually in the late morning or early afternoon. Galbraith by then reserved mornings for writing, whether his latest book or one of the countless articles, reviews, or speeches he was always crafting. He then took the next hour or two to read his mail and scrawl replies in longhand, leaving the finished pile for Mrs. Williams to type and return for his signature the next day.

The schedule was broken by trips, meetings, and teaching responsibilities (he taught three courses per semester in those days), but he would always turn back to his accumulated pile and plow through it. To editors, political figures, scholars, business executives, and friends the reply might be longer—usually three to five paragraphs—but everyone got an answer.

To a woman in California who wrote seeking comment on his use of the word "oligopsony" (economists' term for a market with few buyers) because she thought it her own neologism, he gently replied, "The word 'oligopsony' is indeed widely used in economics. It is interesting that you should have come on it independently. Yours faithfully." To a Maryland man who sent numerous pages from *The Affluent Society* with neat underlining and covered with marginalia, accompanied by a single-spaced memo of questions, Galbraith responded, "I very much appreciated receiving your letter. I gather you are doing something like the old-fashioned exegesis of the Bible. I am afraid I do not have anything to reply that would suffice. However, I do very much appreciate your nice comments and wish you luck in working your way through the rest of the volume. Yours faithfully." When a Boy Scout troop wrote collectively from Missouri and asked for his autograph, saying, "We are writing for our collection because we understand you are famous. If so, please reply," Galbraith did so the next day, inscribing a copy of his book as a gift.

After a sympathetic admirer informed him that DuPont's shareholder newsletter had taken him to task—"Professor Galbraith's 'The Abundant Society' [*sic*] takes the extraordinary view that 'needs' should be determined by government officials who are immune to advertising and selling. Papa knows best!"—Galbraith thanked the man, then, clearly enjoying himself, fired off a mock serious letter of complaint to the president of DuPont.

> You will recall that when I published my *American Capitalism* some years ago I had a prompt complaint from DuPont taking strenuous exception to some point I made about nylon. The same proposition subsequently served you well in an antitrust suit. If history repeats itself, you are again in trouble . . . This will be most embarrassing to you in the next lawsuit if, as before, the volume in question turns out to be useful.

A week later, a chastened P. S. du Pont III replied on the company's behalf, expressing "our distress that your new book was not given its correct title . . . and that the comment[s] upon its purport are in any way open to question . . . and apologize for the concern it gives you." (He assured Galbraith that this was only "the second such error known to have appeared in a DuPont publication.")

The letters Galbraith received and answered to the mighty and humble fill box after box at the Kennedy Library. The letter A alone in the General Correspondence file for the 1950s takes up five large boxes, filled with neatly stacked folders of letters and Galbraith's reply. And all these letters are testimony to the complexity of Galbraith's personality. Few authors are such diligent correspondents with such a range of correspondents, the effort itself bespeaking an old-fashioned, formal sense of courtesy and mutuality. They also show a side of the man incongruent with the arrogance of which he has often been accused. Arrogant and impatient he could be, especially in debate with accomplished or powerful opponents with whom he disagreed. And from *American Capitalism* on, in his writing he cultivated a voice that was withering in its *hauteur,* even when he wickedly undercut it himself. (An embroidered pillow sits prominently in his home, with the following advice: "Modesty is a Vastly Overrated Virtue," which he calls "Galbraith's First Law.")

Yet there is no doubt that Galbraith did have a certain reputation by then among those disinclined to like or agree with him. Harvard's dean, McGeorge Bundy, a strong-willed and forceful personality himself who got along quite well with him, wrote in a private note to Harvard's president, Nathan Marsh Pusey, one of those who got along least well with the university's best-known economist:

> I myself think that Ken Galbraith has one of the most imaginative and powerful minds in the Faculty of Arts and Sciences. I also think he shares this view. He is not a man distinguished by modesty, and in his map of the world its center is quite near himself. I wish these defects did not exist, because I am more and more persuaded that generosity is a cardinal virtue in university life. But intellectual distinction, energy, industry, and creative imagination are rare, and he has them all.[1]

Galbraith understood his reputation, and as his "first law" suggests, he accepted it and liked to play with it. Yet he also gave serious thought to the isolation brought by fame. In "The Perils of the Big Build-Up," written for *The New York Times Magazine* in 1954, as his own fame took off, he reflected on how societies elevate men to high esteem. He avoided any reference to himself, but the first-person experience can be inferred from his third-person examples. Often, he said, the process of isolation begins without its subject's seeking it.

> Perhaps he has earned a measure of public esteem for doing a difficult job or possibly he has made a more than ordinary showing of competence, diligence, good judgment or good nature. Sometimes—a common case of late—he has

just come to public office after a respectable, although unpublicized, private career.

For reasons that are no more explicable than why lightning strikes a particular tree, the man becomes the object of the build-up. The press and radio, and particularly the columnists, commentators and newsmagazines suddenly and unaccountably are stunned by his virtues. Qualities undiscovered one day are commonplace the next. New ones are invented and marveled at. Presently an ordinary, or perhaps somewhat better than ordinary, citizen, has become a superman and a cosmic philosopher.

What is the effect on the man himself?

With the build-up, even the man's personal life undergoes a remarkable transformation. His hobbies, for example, are no longer hobbies but the unique refreshment of an intense and active mind. His habits in tobacco, alcohol and attire become the marks of a striking personality—if he doesn't drink or smoke that is almost equally satisfactory. His wife is now a gracious, untiring and selfless partner, indispensable to his career. No hint of stress, strain or strangeness mars the perfection of their relationship.

The man so built up is not the only subject of Galbraith's interest:

We can only guess why we find it necessary to select men for this temporary deification. Perhaps we need heroes merely for the sake of having heroes. More likely, it is because we are afflicted these days with so many problems that seem or are insoluble . . . Since we couldn't possibly handle these questions ourselves, we find it comforting to suppose that there are paragons of wisdom who can.

If this fame making has serious costs for its object as well as the society that celebrates him, what is to be done? In truth,

there is no obvious antidote . . . Possibly we might solve the problem by agreeing, once a year, that one citizen of the republic would be selected for exclusive adulation by all media of mass communication. Then at the end of twelve months his shortcomings would be exposed, he would be retired in disgrace and given a generous pension.

For a moment, a more sobering idea—a reminder of what is at stake in a modern society that indiscriminately worships fame—causes Galbraith to summon up a core value camouflaged by his whimsy:

The only apparent alternative is to recognize that, in a democracy, leaders are only the first among equals. Nothing is gained by building extravagant images of their wisdom when they are bound to share our bafflement. On the contrary, to do so is to improve little on that other modern habit of casually asserting the disposition of leaders to utter venality and treason.[2]

The serious conclusion to this article offers another clue to the complexity of Galbraith's personality and of the period. The idea of 1950s America as an "affluent society" later became distorted and misleading, a simplistic fantasy about carefree suburban barbecue parties and America's first love affair with shopping malls, hula hoops, and Davy Crockett, a television world peopled by Ozzie and Harriet, Lucille Ball, and the Mouseketeers. America, of course, was never quite so innocent. The Korean War threatened a new global conflict between the United States, China, and Russia. And when Soviet forces invaded Hungary in 1956, while simultaneously British and French troops joined Israel's in an attempt to seize back control of the Suez Canal, nationalized by Egypt's powerful new leader, Colonel Gamal Abdel Nasser, and when, in October 1957 (just before *The Affluent Society* went to press), the Soviet Union launched *Sputnik* without warning, no one in America felt complacent. That the U.S.S.R. had been the first to develop the technology for the first space satellite at first stunned, then humiliated and horrified most Americans. How could this have happened? What did it mean? *Time* was blunt: "The U.S. takes deep pride in its technical skills and technological prowess, in its ability to get things done—first. Now, despite all the rational explanations, there was a sudden, sharp national disappointment that Americans had been outshone by the Russian moon."

"National disappointment" barely captured the mood. Senate Majority Leader Lyndon Johnson foresaw devastating consequences. "The Roman Empire controlled the world because it could build roads," he said on the Senate floor. "Later—when men moved to the sea—the British Empire was dominant because it had ships. Now the Communists have established a foothold in outer space."[3]

The Eisenhower administration tried to contain the damage by mocking the Soviet achievement. One White House official called *Sputnik* "a silly bauble," while another told reporters that the United States wasn't interested in "an outer-space basketball game." But the press had a field day when it discovered that Defense Secretary Charles Wilson, former chairman of General Motors, had known for at least two years that the Soviet Union had a major space program under way and had dismissed the idea of its winning a "space race": "I wouldn't care if they did." Awakening to the blunder, the White House rushed to promise Americans that a "crash program" would put the first American satellite in space within months. But Wilson's complacency left many infuriated: what did he have in mind for his satellite, Senator Johnson asked—chrome trim and windshield wipers?[4]

Not everyone saw the Russian achievement and the fumbling U.S. response as a disaster. Galbraith quickly grasped what *Sputnik* meant, and how it perfectly expressed *The Affluent Society*'s arguments about America's "social imbalance" and its neglect of the public sector despite its private affluence and excess. In a later edition, he commented, "No action was ever so admirably timed. Had I been younger or less formed in my political views, I would have been carried away by my gratitude and found a final resting place beneath the Kremlin Wall. I knew my book was home."[5]

GALBRAITH WASN'T THE only one to see opportunity in this new national crisis. The junior senator from Massachusetts quickly grasped the implications of *Sputnik*. John F. Kennedy had been in public office for more than a decade by 1957, having been first elected to Congress in 1946, then to the Senate six years later. Although popular with his constituents, he did not have a distinguished record as a legislator, and outside Washington and Massachusetts he was not well known. To most Washington insiders, he seemed little more than a charming backbencher.

> Elegant and casual, he sat in the back row [of the Senate] his knees against the desk, rapping his teeth with a pencil and reading *The Economist* and the *Guardian*. He was treated with affection by most senators, but he was ultimately elusive, finding his way in other worlds outside the chamber. Mythically wealthy, handsome, bright, and well connected, he seemed to regard the Senate grandees as impressive but tedious. In turn, he was regarded by them as something of a playboy, a dilettante.[6]

Kennedy's heroism as a PT boat commander in World War II had brought him fame, but dozens of other war heroes were more celebrated. Likewise, his first book, *While England Slept*, on Britain's lack of preparedness before the war, had won plaudits when it was published but was forgotten as Russia succeeded Germany as the country's national preoccupation. And even though his second book, the 1957 Pulitzer Prize–winning *Profiles in Courage*, set him apart, he had been far from courageous in facing the dangers of the demagogic Senator McCarthy. Influenced by widespread Catholic support in Massachusetts for McCarthy as well as by his father (and his younger brother Robert, who worked on the staff of McCarthy's committee), he was the only Democrat not to vote to censure him, when McCarthy's egregious behavior was finally a matter for discipline by the Senate in 1954.*

But Kennedy never lacked ambition and was born to a family that epitomized it. His wildly controversial father, Joseph Kennedy, had risen from humble roots—through a Harvard scholarship and a successful marriage—to enormous wealth, built on canny Wall Street stock choices, rum running during Prohibition, and shrewd investments in Hollywood. A major contributor to Democratic politics, Joseph Kennedy had been the first head of the Securities and Exchange Commission in the mid-1930s and then ambassador to Great Britain. But he'd destroyed his political career through his open support for

---

*The censure resolution was introduced by a Republican, Ralph Flanders of Vermont, and eventually passed the Senate 67–22. Kennedy was absent for the vote, which he explained as being due to his chronic back problems, caused by injuries sustained during the war.

U.S. isolationism and then, after the war began in 1939, by his vocal calls for British and American accommodation to Hitler. With his own chances for public office gone, he had turned his enormous energies and ambitions to the career of his oldest son, Joseph Jr., but the son's tragic death during the war ended those hopes and left the mantle to fall to Jack, the second son.

Though initially an awkward campaigner, Jack Kennedy had evolved in office. By 1956, Kennedy had thrust himself into the national spotlight by campaigning to become Stevenson's running mate. Although he lost narrowly to Estes Kefauver at the Democratic convention that summer, his activities—his address nominating Stevenson and the graceful concession speech he made to the delegates when his own nomination failed—stuck in people's minds.

After Stevenson's and Kefauver's lopsided loss that November, a Kennedy supporter casually remarked that at least the defeat had a silver lining: if nothing else, it meant that Kennedy could easily win the vice-presidential nomination in 1960. "I'm not running for Vice President any more," Jack crisply replied. "I'm now running for President."[7]

It was no off-the-cuff response. Three weeks after Stevenson's humiliating defeat, Joseph Kennedy had gathered the family at the Kennedy compound in Hyannis Port. He reviewed in detail how and why Stevenson had lost, and how in 1960 Jack could become the next president of the United States. His son listened intently, then countered with all the reasons why he wouldn't be elected (including the family's Catholicism), but the father forcefully answered each objection in turn. "Well, Dad," Jack concluded, "I guess there's just one question left. When do we start?"[8]

When to start was a minor question compared to how. What should the issues and agenda be that would make Kennedy stand out in a field that was sure to include veteran campaigners such as Stevenson, Hubert Humphrey, Stuart Symington, and Lyndon Johnson, all of them with formidable constituencies and issues of their own? And how would he then beat the Republican nominee, who was almost certain to be Vice President Richard Nixon, a fierce campaigner?

Suddenly came *Sputnik.* The opening that *Sputnik* gave to Kennedy and to all Democratic politicians and policy-makers was immense. In terms of economic policy, Herbert Stein's classification is helpful here in understanding why. Stein, an early and prominent "business Keynesian" economist who served as the Committee for Economic Development's research director (and as staff director of the Joint Economic Committee while Republicans controlled Congress), distinguished four important camps among 1950s Washington policy-makers and their economist allies.[9] "Conventional conservatives" was the first: men such as George Humphrey and Robert Anderson, Ike's treasury secretaries; the leaders of the National Association of Manufacturers; Arthur Burns, the chairman of the Council of Economic Advisors; most Republican and Southern Democratic congressmen. Second were "conservative macroeconomists" (Stein's preferred term, for political reasons, over "business Keynesians") such as Stein himself; Marion Folsom, CED's former director who became Undersecretary at the Treasury and then Health, Education, and Welfare Secretary; the CEA's Neal Jacoby and Gabriel Hauge; and Eisenhower himself, who had been a CED board member in the late 1940s.

Poised against them among the Democrats was the third group: "strict and exclusive Keynesians," which included younger congressmen of marginal influence and a bevy of economists working in the government or in think tanks. Here Stein was also thinking of Galbraith, Paul Samuelson, Seymour Harris, Alvin Hansen, and others marked as part of the Democrats' government-in-exile—idea makers for 1960 and beyond. The fourth group was the "reformers and planners" including those concerned most with antitrust, urban renewal, housing, welfare, and education, among whom Truman's former CEA chief, Leon Keyserling, stood out for his enthusiastic, panoptical focus on macroeconomic growth from a pre-Keynesian worldview. (Gardiner Means also fit here in many ways, but he was less visible than he had been in the New Deal.)

Among the GOP, the debate between the "old conservatives" and "business Keynesians" was always over budget balancing when recessions arrived, and on the "ideological" merits of lower taxes versus "tactical" tax cutting meant to stimulate a weak economy. On military spending, the Republicans were united, at least publicly, while none were especially keen on "soft" social spending; their preference always ran toward "hard" infrastructure projects like the National Defense Highway program, which built America's interstate freeway system.

Among congressional Democrats, especially with Lyndon Johnson in charge of the Senate and his fellow Texan Sam Rayburn running the House, support for social spending (unconnected to Keynesian assumptions but tempered by a keen eye for electoral impact) dominated. The party's Keynesians were left to shape their growth arguments by showing either how growth made the spending possible or how the programs contributed to growth. And, as among Republicans, defense spending was sacrosanct, its value or damage to the domestic economy left unexamined.

Although Democrats had regained control of the Congress in 1956 after losing it four years earlier, and although there was a rough bipartisan consensus on the increased size and purpose of military spending, when it came to domestic policy, traditional conservatives grudgingly shared power with the cautious business Keynesians in the administration. Because deficits were considered a prelude to the horrors of inflation, they were anathema to the traditionalists, while business Keynesians at least supported the preferred policy tools of those "automatic stabilizers"—unemployment insurance and tax brackets. The cobbled-together compromise policy goal became known as "growth without inflation." "Price stability," cautioned Raymond Saulnier, Eisenhower's second chairman of the Council of Economic Advisors, was a prerequisite for "sustainable economic growth," and the President himself made clear how he felt: the "deficit-producing, inflation-inviting, irresponsible-spending proposals of self-described liberal Democrats left him cold."[10]

Yet despite Eisenhower's seemingly clear position, sound politics occasionally trumped bad economics. Midway through Eisenhower's first term a break-through had occurred that to most Keynesians seemed monumental. When the economy slumped after the Korean War, Eisenhower actually agreed not to raise taxes—and therefore accepted a budget deficit. (In LBJ's administration, economists looked back to 1954 when, as they rosily put it, "the bipartisan character of expansionary fiscal policies was established for the first time, as the Republican Administration . . . adopted measures that had previously been linked to the New Deal and Keynesian economics.") Galbraith had praised the White House and CEA for "its considerable grace and ease in getting away from the clichés of a balanced budget and the unspeakable evils of deficit financing."[11]

Still, although Ike may have been the first Keynesian Republican Presi-dent—and although he never tried to repeal New Deal innovations such as so-cial security, banking and securities regulation, and large ongoing public-works campaigns—when it came to new civilian spending priorities, Republicans and Democrats were as divided as they had been in the 1930s. But now, generals, admirals, and defense contractors were the principal beneficiaries of Washing-ton's immense new largesse, combatting Moscow and Peking and their Third World allies being the rationale for bigger government.

And anti-Communism continued to be the Republicans' domestic political weapon of choice. They'd hobbled Democrats for more than a decade with the "soft on Communism" charge and showed no signs of abandoning it even after McCarthy's political demise in 1954. The Democrats, in fact, were far from "soft" on Communism at home or abroad, but convincing Americans that they were better at growing the economy *and* ensuring Cold War national security was not easy. That's why the news of *Sputnik* was a gift from the sky: now Democrats could plausibly argue that Eisenhower's administration had failed to establish the right priorities for research, education, and technology.

The Russian satellite was launched when the American economy was flag-ging badly. The recession that began in 1957 and carried over into 1958, the second in just three years, was the worst since the Depression. As unemploy-ment reached 7.6 percent after steadily creeping upward for years, critics claimed it was a clear sign that the Republicans were mismanaging the econ-omy. GNP growth, too, had been showing alarming signs, they pointed out: ac-tual GNP growth had matched its full employment potential as Keynesians would measure it for only a few months in late 1955, and by the time *Sputnik* orbited, it was running nearly 10 percent below its estimated optimum.[12]

The critics understood that Eisenhower's economists and policy advisers had accepted less-than-optimum growth in favor of price stability: inflation, after all, was their *bête noire*, and they weren't about to be misled by some the-oretically "missing" economic growth as measured by an abstract full-employment index. But *Sputnik* changed all that. What America's growth rate should be was no longer an important but esoteric issue for policy-makers and economists: it seemed to be about national survival.

New studies showed that the Soviet Union's economy was growing twice as fast as America's, perhaps even faster. Until *Sputnik,* most Americans displayed a curious ambivalence to their Cold War enemies. Moscow represented a clear and present ideological and military threat, but economically it was supposed to be a backward and primitive society. Its vaunted armed forces owed their might, it was believed, to the sheer size of the U.S.S.R., a grossly imbalanced economic system, and of course Communist duplicity. But now, Soviet technological prowess and economic might could no longer be laughed away as distant seconds to native American ingenuity and muscle. With *Sputnik's beep-beep-beep* echoing from the skies overhead, American views of the Soviet Union changed overnight.

When Congress's Joint Economic Committee convened hearings to evaluate U.S. and Soviet growth rates, journalists mobbed the hearing room. Lost in the ensuing press storm were the witnesses' cautious reminders that, as one put it, "firm conclusions about [growth] rates comparisons are fraught with many perils," or that, as several explained, the Soviet Union still lagged far behind the United States in total output. What splashed across front pages and television screens was the warning that if the Soviet Union and the United States sustained their current respective growth rates, "in time . . . the absolute gap would begin to narrow sharply."[13]

ADVOCACY FOR UNPRECEDENTED American economic growth and a convincing political strategy for achieving it, Senator Kennedy realized, could get him elected. But some Republican presidential contenders were just as quick to grasp *Sputnik's* implications. Nelson Rockefeller, preparing to run for the New York governorship as a springboard to the White House, had established through one of his family's foundations a special studies project on "national priorities," directed by thirty prominent and powerful citizens, its researchers led by a young Harvard professor named Henry Kissinger. And when the Russians launched the much larger *Sputnik II* into orbit a month after the first (this time with a dog aboard), the Rockefeller Commission on National Priorities wasted no time. In the spring of 1958 it told Americans they faced a stark choice: either quickly and permanently to agree to aim for an annual GNP growth rate of 5 percent as the U.S. target, or to risk losing not only prosperity but freedom. Rockefeller himself took to the airwaves to promote these conclusions. After his passionate warning on the *Today* show that "nothing less than the future of America and the freedom of the world" were at stake, nearly 200,000 people flooded NBC with requests for the report. That November, he beat New York's incumbent governor, Averell Harriman, in a landslide.[14]

To many Americans the Rockefeller report must have seemed at least reasonably plausible. During World War II, after all, the U.S. economy had burst upward at 20 percent annually, and wasn't the country again at war, even if it was a cold one? But to economists and policy-makers, the Rockefeller target came as a shock. Over the previous four years the U.S. economy had grown at little more than 2 percent; the average growth pace rose a little above 3 percent when measured since 1945, but 5 percent seemed to be reaching for the stars. And to help achieve it, the Commission was calling audaciously for a 50 percent increase in public spending over the next decade.[15]

The effect of the Rockefeller study was immeasurably multiplied by the almost simultaneous appearance of a Ford Foundation document called the "Gaither Report."[16] This top-secret work came from a blue-ribbon commission headed by Rowan Gaither, the chairman of RAND, and was mostly written by a RAND staff member, the mathematical economist Albert Wohlstetter, who had been working for some years on the "systems analysis" approach pioneered by the "Whiz Kids" of World War II, but now applied to Cold War policies.

The Gaither Report instantly became a second NSC-68 (the first was a top-secret presidential order, drafted by Paul Nitze in 1950, that called for swiftly tripling the military budget while maintaining a rapidly growing, high-employment domestic economy), and its analysis was enlarged and focused by Nitze's assistance. *Sputnik,* it said, had been carried aloft by a modified Soviet intercontinental ballistic missile. According to the Pentagon and CIA, the Soviet Union would have at least a dozen such nuclear-tipped ICBMs pointed at the U.S. within a year, capable of destroying three quarters of the Strategic Air Command's B-52s on the ground; deployment of American ICBMs was still two to three years away. Worse, this "missile gap" was magnified by a "bomber gap," since the Soviet air force was believed to be able to sneak over the Arctic Circle and cripple 90 percent of the U.S.'s bomber fleet.

The U.S. military budget, which had already tripled from 1950 to 1955 when the Korean War ended, needed to grow again, just as NSC-68 had prescribed, this time not just to buy more weapons (especially new ICBMs for the Air Force) but also to build a $30 billion civil-defense shelter system. No delay was possible; 1959 was pinpointed as the "year of maximum danger" from Soviet missile deployment.

Some senior officials were so shaken by the report's conclusions that they seriously advocated an immediate preemptive nuclear attack on the Soviet Union.[17] However, Eisenhower was appalled, knowing full well the politics and interests behind these claims, and ordered the report kept secret. Not surprisingly, it was leaked to the press days later, and the Gaither Report became front-page news.

Virtually every factual assumption the report alleged was false. The only "bomber gap" was entirely in America's favor: it had 1,600 B-52s and B-47s pointed at the Soviet Union, which had 500 bombers of inferior quality. The United States also already had the (albeit cumbersome) Atlas missile ready, with the much better Titan and the Navy's Polaris nearly ready; in virtually every respect, American technology was greatly superior. There was, in short, no "missile gap."

But the leak of the report did its job, and near panic ensued. The press helpfully mapped out cities "most at risk of nuclear attack," and private contractors rushed to fulfill demand for home fallout shelters. Eisenhower, furious over the report's dishonesty and facing the 1958 elections, did his best to calm public fears. Nixon and other GOP leaders followed suit, especially when con-

gressional Democrats tried to make the leaked report into a partisan indictment of the administration. Privately, the President was so irate at the manipulations of the Pentagon and its supporters that he decided that after
the elections, whatever their outcome, he would open serious arms talks with
the Soviet Union.

Senator Kennedy meanwhile concentrated his own career ambitions on the
"missile gap" and "bomber gap" alleged by Gaither. Drawing on research done
by Wohlstetter, he launched his reelection campaign in August 1958 with a
speech charging that Eisenhower's administration had squandered precious
time needed to prepare for these new Soviet threats—"the years the locusts
have eaten."[18] Other Democratic candidates joined Kennedy in denouncing
the GOP's reckless abandonment of national security, an issue Republicans
had been using since the 1940s to bludgeon them.

The Rockefeller Commission report represented a different challenge to
the GOP—and Nixon, most vulnerable to it, knew what it was: an internecine
challenge by Nelson Rockefeller to Nixon's presumed presidential nomination
in 1960. Alert to the raw politics behind the lofty call for 5 percent growth as
an absolute good, Nixon got Eisenhower to let him chair a cabinet-level task
force; acknowledging the importance of growth, the Cabinet Committee on
Price Stability for Economic Growth nonetheless fell back on familiar plati-
tudes about the dangers of inflation and "government interference" in the
economy. "Our Republican program seeks a strong rate of economic growth by
fostering private initiative," the group piously and vaguely declared, but "not by
resorting to vast public spending and loose money policies." It carefully
avoided naming any "target" growth rate as ideal or necessary.[19]

Nixon's caution was shared by the Committee for Economic Development,
but visible fissures were by now developing within the administration.* When
the CIA director, Allen Dulles, told Congress that the Soviet economy had
"been growing at a rate at least twice as rapidly as that of the United States
since 1950" and that "the gap between our two economies by 1970 will be
dangerously narrowed," his testimony was front-page news.[20] With this supposed economy gap now a matter of national security, the fissures between the
administration's economists and its military and intelligence spokesmen
widened into a chasm—and the press and Democratic politicians rushed to fill
the gap. Henry Luce, James Reston, and Walter Lippmann began to opine
darkly on the threat that Soviet growth rates posed, and editorial writers everywhere picked up their lead.

But American advocates for increased, military-led economic growth had no

---

*Nixon in 1960 was still ambivalent on the topic: "I would say that my goal and the only proper goal, for those
who do not buy the theory of government manipulated growth, the only proper goal is a maximum growth rate.
It might, in some instances be 3 percent, in some instances, 4 percent, in some instances 5 percent." Theodore
White notes that Nixon was forced by Rockefeller to accept "maximum growth" as a GOP goal just before the
party's 1960 convention, in the so-called Compact of Fifth Avenue. Neither Nixon nor Rockefeller, though, re-
ally trusted the other on this or anything else, and with reason. By then Nixon had planted John Ehrlichman as
Rockefeller's campaign chauffeur, the better to gather intelligence on his rival's strategies (see Theodore White,
The Making of the President, 1960 [New York: Atheneum, 1961], 434–36).

greater friend, it seemed, than Nikita Khrushchev. *Sputnik* emboldened the Soviet leader to brag about Communism's latent economic superiority, and its implications for the Cold War. In this he and Allen Dulles were as one. Like Dulles, Khrushchev singled out the year 1970 for his audience—as a moment not when the gap between the two nations would be "dangerously narrowed," as Dulles had it, but when the Soviet Union would "catch up and outstrip the United States" in industrial production. Growth would be "the battering ram with which we shall smash the capitalist system, enhance the ideas of Marxism-Leninism, strengthen the Socialist camp and contribute to the victory of the cause of peace throughout the world."[21] If the Soviet leader saw Russia's economic growth as a battering ram with which to defeat America, Jack Kennedy now saw acceleration of American growth as the battering ram with which he would win the presidential race in 1960.

In November 1958, Kennedy passed his first major hurdle, using his growth-equals-security platform to win reelection to the Senate by nearly 900,000 votes—the largest majority for any officeholder in Massachusetts history, and the biggest margin in any Senate race that year.[22] Across the country the roof fell in on the GOP: it lost twelve seats in the Senate, forty-eight in the House, and thirteen in gubernatorial races. Conservative Republicans had campaigned aggressively, but on the wrong issues: fearful that rapid growth would spark inflation or require stimulative deficits, they had backed anti-union right-to-work referenda in more than a dozen states as a cornerstone of their strategy. But this backfired disastrously, and led to defeat of nearly all the referenda and the candidates who backed them.

When Congress reconvened in January 1959, the slightly amazed Democrats found themselves with 64 seats in the Senate to the Republicans' 34 and dominating the House 283–153, their best showing in thirty years. It was, Richard Nixon admitted to reporters, "the worst defeat in history" for a party that controlled the White House. For liberals the victory was especially heartening. Swept into office was a coterie of solidly New Deal freshmen, including Senators Engle, Muskie, Young, Williams, Hart, Proxmire, McGhee, Moss, Cannon, Gruening, and Euguene McCarthy. Reading *The New York Times* the morning after the election, Galbraith was elated. Arthur Schlesinger was no less thrilled. Two years earlier, before *Sputnik,* he'd written Stevenson a lengthy memo entitled "The Central Idea for 1956." "Briefly stated, it is this: *We have a new age, a new prosperity, increasing leisure. Before us is a vision of a New America. What is the substance of this vision, and what are we doing, what can we do on a large scale, and practically, to realize it? We must act before it is too late, and before the Eisenhower administration sells our birthright down the river.*" Stevenson and the Democrats must align themselves "not with the New Deal, or the Fair Deal, but with the New America. Americans," Schlesinger continued, were "confident and optimistic as never before—but without national leaders who would point the nation to greatness." Stevenson had embraced the idea, had made it his campaign theme, and had failed. In 1958, Schlesinger thought the theme more relevant than ever.[23]

Translating his stunning Senate triumph into a presidential nomination and then into victory over a Republican opponent was now Kennedy's and his father's consuming concern. When it came to the voters, managing "the Catholic question" and shoring up his strength in the industrial states while holding onto the Democratic base in the South were tactically central tasks, but foremost was the issue of convincing elites that his presidency would "get the country moving again." As the liberal Democratic senator from Illinois, Paul Douglas, foretold in a prescient article for *The New Republic*, a new kind of "growthmanship" would be "at the heart of politics in 1960."*[24]

Kennedy read the Rockefeller commission report with great care, for he knew it was not just the work of a potential Republican challenger but a set of ideas vital to his campaign. In 1960, as one biography notes, "when some foreign policy question came up, Kennedy yelled to [press secretary Pierre] Salinger, 'Hey, Pierre, get the Rockefeller Brothers Study. It's all in there.' "[25] Also, the report represented the collective opinion of many powerful men, men whose support Kennedy wanted. (Once elected president, Kennedy recruited nearly a third of the Rockefeller commission's members into his administration, including Dean Rusk, Douglas Dillon, John J. McCloy, McGeorge Bundy, Chester Bowles, Walt and Eugene Rostow, Paul Nitze, Roswell Gilpatric, and General Edward Lansdale.[26]) Coopting his political rivals and courting their support base among America's elites was, however, only one part of Kennedy's electoral strategy. He needed his own ideas—economic ideas that would set him apart not only from his Republican but his Democratic competitors. And that meant Ken Galbraith was among the first he called.†

KENNEDY AND GALBRAITH had known each other since Kennedy's undergraduate days at Harvard in the 1930s, when Jack and Joe Kennedy spent three years in Winthrop House, where Galbraith was a tutor. And Galbraith's participation in Americans for Democratic Action and on Stevenson's presidential campaign staff in 1952 brought them into increasing, though irregular, contact. In 1956, Kennedy had sought out Galbraith's advice on agricultural policy, frankly admitting his urban innocence: "Where I grew up, we were taken out on a bus to see a cow." Impressed by the shrewd balance of economic theory and practical political insight in Galbraith's ideas, the young senator developed the habit of asking for Galbraith's thoughts on an ever-expanding range of economic matters.[27]

After the launch of *Sputnik* in the fall of 1957, Kennedy arranged more and more meetings with Galbraith in Boston and Cambridge. What did Galbraith think about America's real growth potential? What were the dangers of infla-

---

*Once a professor of economics at the University of Chicago (before the department became uniformly conservative) and one of Paul Samuelson's most beloved teachers, Douglas had done pioneering work in the 1920s and 1930s on growth economics. Today, his name is still associated with the Cobb-Douglas production function, an early modern attempt to express the components of growth and their interactions.

†Others on whom Kennedy initially relied came from either Harvard (Seymour Harris) or MIT (Paul Samuelson and Walt Rostow, with Rostow's advice focused on foreign, not domestic, policy).

tion under full employment? What about foreign trade, and the emerging balance of payments problem, which was starting to drain the huge U.S. gold reserves? Was monetary policy too restrictive, and what could a Democrat do about it without unduly upsetting Wall Street? Galbraith became part of JFK's inner circle, just outside the veteran "Irish Mafia" that formed its political core. When Kennedy came to Boston, he frequently asked Galbraith to meet with him, often for warmly remembered evenings at Boston's famed Locke-Ober's restaurant, "where never varying, he always ordered lobster stew." Those dinner conversations ranged from economic theory to policy and practical politics, and Kennedy's respect for Galbraith's judgment increased. After JFK's landslide Senate reelection in November 1958, Kennedy asked him to give him briefings before major appearances and to serve as his emissary to other Democratic Party leaders.[28]

Galbraith was spending more and more time with Kennedy, but his time was in shorter supply. For one thing, his Harvard duties were increasing in the ever-growing Economics Department, which now counted fifty-five faculty on its staff. (Most were junior men, and so Galbraith also spent a good deal of time in 1957 and 1958 lobbying his colleagues to hire Paul Samuelson back from MIT and James Tobin from Yale. The offers were made but declined; then the disappointed department scored a compensating coup by attracting Simon Kuznets from the University of Pennsylvania in 1959.)[29] For another thing, even before the huge success of *The Affluent Society*, Galbraith's calendar was filled with hectic travel, speaking engagements, and writing deadlines. In May 1958, for example (while awaiting the imminent appearance of *The Affluent Society*), Galbraith sailed to Europe for a tour of Poland and Yugoslavia, in the former as a guest of his friend Oskar Lange. Lange had returned from the University of Chicago to Warsaw shortly after the war, hoping to advance his theory of "market socialism" as an alternative to the Stalinist planning model that was largely, though not entirely, adopted by Poland. In 1956, a reform Communist regime had taken power in Poland under Wladyzla Gomulka, who navigated a limited East Bloc independence, thereby avoiding the fate of the more impetuous regime in Hungary, which lost its own reform attempts to Soviet tanks in the fall of that year. Lange and his ideas enjoyed under Gomulka a modest rehabilitation, and Galbraith's visit—Lange thought—might somehow help the process along.

This was Galbraith's first serious exposure to socialist planning and enterprise. Poland and Yugoslavia were, however, modest exceptions to the Stalinist model, having kept agriculture and a good deal of small business outside state ownership. (Stalin had foreseen problems with Warsaw years earlier, complaining that fitting the Poles to Communism would be like "putting a saddle on a cow." And Yugoslavia under Marshal Tito went much further toward "market socialism," as a consequence gradually becoming the most prosperous of Europe's Communist states.) On his return, Galbraith wrote *A Journey to Poland and Yugoslavia*, a modest essay-travelogue-analysis about the experience for the Harvard University Press.[30] The book eventually sold more than 10,000 copies—a delight to its publisher and a sign that in the aftermath of *Sputnik*, American curiosity about Communism and anti-Communist inquisitors was outdistancing fear. Galbraith sent a copy of *A Journey* to Kennedy when it came off the press, and JFK's charming "Dear Ken" note in reply was another sign of their growing friendship:

> It was a happy surprise on my return to Washington to find yet another Galbraith travelogue. Without doubt you have established yourself as the Phineas Fogg of the academic world, and I rather suspect that in the year of 1958 you ran a very good second to John Foster Dulles in international mileage. However, your impressions are indisputably more helpful . . . I understand you also were engaged in some egghead diplomacy on Rhodes this fall. Can we expect a homeric epic on your Aegean travels as well?[31]

Galbraith clearly enjoyed Kennedy, but more important, by now he had the germ of a big new book in mind, and Dean Bundy had given him leave for the spring terms of 1959 and 1960 to develop it. ("If you have another book in you as good as *The Affluent Society*," he told Galbraith, "I will certainly help you get it out.") Also, Bundy shuffled Gottfried Haberler out of the Paul M. Warburg chair in economics and awarded it to Galbraith. "Only an unconvincing sense of decency," Galbraith wrote some years later, "kept me from reflecting that I was replacing the man who had so righteously opposed my original appointment."[32]

Starting the first of his two leaves, Galbraith spent the spring term of 1959 working on his new book, taking occasional breaks to pepper Kennedy with advice on fiscal and monetary policy and on handling the press. In May, he stopped work on the book to pay a second, short visit to India (and Ceylon, added at the request of the island's prime minister). In both countries, his advice was sought out—in India, on public ownership and operations of the steel industry, in Ceylon, on development planning more generally. In New Delhi, he met once again with Prime Minister Nehru, on rather warmer terms than in 1957. Nehru had just finished reading *The Affluent Society*, and viewed Galbraith with new respect and affection, since he was appalled by the book's description of America's materialism and managed consumption. In Ceylon, Galbraith found his meetings with Prime Minister Bandaranaike pleasant, the country entrancingly charming—and his advice ignored.

From India, Galbraith flew on to Moscow, with a touristic stopover to photograph Samarkand, the great western terminus of the old Silk Road in Marco Polo's day. (At this point in his life he was pursuing photography as a serious hobby, and he even proposed a portfolio of his photos to Houghton Mifflin, but the publisher declined.) In Moscow, he was joined by his friend the Yale economist Lloyd Reynolds and, for part of his time there, Averell Harriman. They visited giant Soviet factories, universities, and planning bureaus in Moscow, Leningrad, and Tbilisi. Galbraith was unfailingly unimpressed—he found himself frequently defending the many virtues of capitalism—but the visit awakened in him a conviction that the industrial systems of the U.S. and the U.S.S.R. were gradually converging, as America's giant corporations grew ever more omnipresent and as the Soviet bureaucrats opened themselves—however slowly—to less rigid forms of control.

This idea of "convergence" won many apostles (not all of them liberal) during the next few years as more and more Americans came to believe that the financial, political, and cultural costs of the Cold War arms race had grown too high. In the mid-1960s, Galbraith and his friend the Nobel Prize–winning Harvard physicist and Eisenhower science adviser George Kistiakowsky convened a monthly working group of Cambridge scholars for discussions of the war, foreign policy, the arms race, and arms control. Henry Kissinger (then still a Democratic Party adviser) fully participated. After more than a decade as an advocate of the costly flexible-response defense policy that Kennedy adopted, Kissinger was ready to rethink the arms race and the possibilities of East-West convergence. Galbraith came to believe that the group was influential in eventually leading Kissinger and Nixon to seek "détente" with the Soviet Union and "normalization" of relations with China.[33]

Galbraith sent along his notes of his India-Russia trip, duly polished, to Kennedy in late 1959. Once again, a charming reply was forthcoming. Kennedy apologized for not having yet read the diary, given the press of Senate duties. "There were times when I would have liked to take it into [committee meetings] . . . to give the hours greater buoyancy," but he didn't, pretending to fear that if Republicans saw it, "you might be laid open to withering attacks . . . I shall take it along with me on my first journey after we fold our tents on Capitol Hill. I only hope that on arriving in Columbus, Ohio, I will be treated better than you apparently were in Alma Alta."* Kennedy told Galbraith they should meet soon to "take some soundings on the future."[34]

The tone of Kennedy's letters bespeaks his playfulness with friends and the relationship that he and Galbraith had built by then. Galbraith's letters were, by comparison, a mix of the light and the sober, reflecting in part the two men's age difference, but also the deference would-be political advisers judiciously maintain toward would-be presidents.

Yet even as the two men grew closer and their mutual admiration grew, Galbraith hesitated to declare himself a full-fledged Kennedy supporter. The possibility that Stevenson might run a third time still loomed, and even though it was unlikely, political protocol required that there be no public affirmation of support for another candidate.

---

*In Alma Alta, Galbraith had been attacked by a large dog, which "barely missed my private parts" and took a sizable chunk of flesh from his thigh. There was concern that the dog might be rabid, but Galbraith's inflexible Intourist schedule dictated proceeding on to Moscow. The local doctor promised to wire him there, saying either "the dog is sick" or "the dog is well." But the Intourist guide predicted a problem: "That telegram to an American will occupy our secret service for at least six months so you will never receive it." He was right, but fortunately the dog wasn't sick.

His long relationship with Stevenson wasn't the only constraint. As director of domestic policy for the Democratic National Committee's Advisory Council, he was obliged to maintain a modicum of intraparty nonpartisanship.

Nonpartisanship is an overstatement. The Democratic Advisory Council, formed by the DNC chairman Paul Butler after Stevenson's second defeat to offset the power of Southerners like Johnson and Rayburn in the national party, was the baronial club of the party's most powerful New Deal veterans—liberal leaders including Governor Harriman, Senator Herbert Lehman, Thomas Finletter, William Benton, and Dean Acheson. (Galbraith oversaw its domestic policy concerns, and Acheson directed its foreign policy work.)* Years later, Galbraith gently but slyly likened it to an Episcopal church vestry, a group "born comfortably to the faith, its accepted custodians." This faith

> was that the government, by innovative action on behalf of the old, unfortunate or poor, could ensure their employment, health and happiness at no great cost to the rich. Most or all of the needed revenue would come . . . from the better management of the economy. This the liberal experience had shown to be possible. If there were doubts, one could put them aside; in politics, as in the vestry, one does not raise difficult questions regarding divinity, the Trinity or even the personal dedication of fellow members to the Ten Commandments.[35]

Galbraith now found himself pressed into the middle of the Democrats' debate over economic growth and how to achieve it.

Among the group's members, there was no more tireless—and single-minded—advocate of growth as an unqualified economic and political virtue than the contentious, hard-driving Leon Keyserling. A Harvard-trained lawyer from South Carolina with an unfinished economics Ph.D. from Columbia and extensive legislative and economic-policy experience acquired as Senator Robert Wagner's aide in the New Deal, Keyserling had been chairman of the Council of Economic Advisors under Truman. His reputation for brashness and political savvy had been established on his first arrival in Washington in the spring of 1933. Rexford Tugwell, his mentor at Columbia, had sent him to Jerome Frank for a job at the Agricultural Adjustment Administration. Frank asked him what he knew about agriculture. "Ed Smith," Keyserling replied, naming the infamous "Cotton Ed" Smith, chairman of the Senate Agriculture Committee and, like Keyserling, a South Carolinian. Frank hired him on the spot.[36]

In 1949, the CEA's annual *Economic Report of the President*, written by Keyserling, had been (as one historian describes it) "growthmanship's declaration of principles," calling for "an increasingly focused, self-conscious, single-

---

*Herbert Lehman, heir to the Lehman Brothers fortune, was five-term governor of New York and, by 1949, a senator. William Benton, a legendary advertising executive, was owner of the *Encyclopædia Britannica*; as the senator from Connecticut he was an early opponent of Joseph McCarthy. Truman and Eleanor Roosevelt were members of the DAC but rarely attended meetings. Hubert Humphrey and John F. Kennedy were also members, and attended in part to court support for their 1960 presidential ambitions.

minded emphasis on growth as the overriding (but not sole) national economic goal." Daring in conception and presentation, it "came close to raising growth from an overriding economic goal . . . to a new organizing principle" for the United States.[37] But then, with the Korean War and Eisenhower's election, Keyserling's missionary faith in untrammeled growth had been sidelined by the Republicans' emphasis on price stability first. Politically benched for much of the 1950s, Keyserling took *Sputnik* as a coach's call summoning him back into the game. In a 1954 ADA handbook, Keyserling had deplored the "depression psychosis" he thought still influenced too many voters; even some liberals had "so little confidence as to think the American economy is going to be capsized again by every little puff of wind." "Good liberals" needed to embrace constant, rapid growth—America, he said, could raise living standards by a third by 1960 if they did.[38]

Keyserling was an advocate not just of growthmanship but also of guns-and-butter growthmanship. In 1950 he had helped Paul Nitze draft NSC-68, the now-famous but then top-secret Presidential security memorandum that systematically rationalized America's vast Cold War military budgets. In his zeal for "military Keynesianism," Keyserling showed no visible concern about inflation, or about the wastefulness of military spending, or about the consequences of militarizing American politics. He warned only that the country would need a thorough reeducation to overcome the mistaken public belief that "increased defense expenditures must mean equivalently lowered standards of living, higher taxes and a proliferation of controls."[39]

George Kennan, whose "Long Telegram" in 1946 had done so much to challenge the Rooseveltian postwar policies that Galbraith, Lucius Clay, and others were fighting to preserve, disagreed with this logic. The creation of the North Atlantic Treaty Organization, the acknowledgment of West and East Germany as separate states, the development of the hydrogen bomb, and growing domestic anti-Communism were already more than he had intended; NSC-68, with its goal of confronting "Communist threats" wherever and whenever they seemed to appear, went, in Kennan's view, too far. He loathed the secret finding because it determined the country's foreign and military posture, as the historian John Lewis Gaddis put it, summarizing Kennan's objections not "in terms of an independently established concept of irreducible interests" but instead on "its perception of the Soviet threat . . . The consequences of this approach were more than procedural: they transferred to the Russians control over what United States interests were at any given point."[40]

James Conant was as distressed as Kennan and feared that the document's assumptions might lead to World War III: America's goal should "instead be, he thought, to live on tolerable terms with the Soviet Union and its satellites." But after crisply arguing with Nitze, Conant backed off, as he did after having opposed development of "The Super," the world's first H-bomb. (As he later wrote a friend about "The Super," he hadn't resigned as a Pentagon science adviser despite his objections "because I didn't want to do anything that seemed to indicate we were not good soldiers."[41])

On the other hand, Robert Lovett, Deputy Secretary of Defense in 1950, was thrilled with NSC-68. The government's preeminent civilian advocate of air power saw immediately the growth implications for his beloved Air Force and its Strategic Air Command. "There was practically nothing the country could not do if it wanted to do it," he said, endorsing Keyserling's "guns-and-butter growthmanship" argument. Lovett thought it would be simple to accomplish the economist's call for "reeducation" of the American public: he counseled stating the document's conclusions "simply, clearly, and in . . . 'Hemingway sentences'. . . . If we can sell every useless article known to man in large quantities, we should be able to sell our very fine story in larger quantities." The State Department rallied to Lovett's support, outlining a two-step "public education" project, the first to build "awareness" of the issues, then "as soon as the atmosphere is right," a "psychological 'scare campaign'" to overwhelm opponents.[42]

Galbraith knew nothing about NSC-68 in the 1950s—it remained top-secret for years—but he vigorously and usually successfully resisted when Keyserling tried to incorporate the ideas behind it in ADA's policy statements.[43]

After *Sputnik*'s launch in 1957, he had a harder time of it at the Democratic Advisory Council. Keyserling had embraced the Rockefeller Commission's 5 percent growth target as his own goal (which in some genealogical sense it was), and now vigorously urged his fellow Democrats to make it the party's new official doctrine. So they sparred whenever DAC meetings turned to the issue of growth policy. (Keyserling "gave me frequent headaches," wrote Galbraith.[44]) Their clashes might have remained behind the scenes, but in late 1958, in response to the success of *The Affluent Society*, Keyserling made them public. In a series of heated articles for *The New Republic*, he attacked Galbraith, his runaway best-seller, and Arthur Schlesinger.[45]

Keyserling had five separate arguments. First, the United States wasn't an "affluent society" at all: Galbraith had vastly underestimated the extent of enduring poverty in the U.S. as well as low-wage near poverty. Second, he had ignored the world outside the United States and the even vaster scale of global poverty (as well as the American responsibility for alleviating it). Third, by assaulting the often fatuous, advertising-driven creation of consumer demand, Galbraith was ignoring the authentic function that private-sector growth and production could still perform in reducing poverty, satisfying real and reasonable consumer needs, and raising incomes. Fourth, he had bowed to conservative fears that full employment would produce intolerable inflation, and thus had allowed himself to accept moderately high unemployment as the necessary cost of "social balance." Last, in his haste to correct a perceived "imbalance" between private-sector "affluence" and public-sector "impoverishment," Galbraith—though he was right to advocate increased public-sector spending and investment—had violated core Democratic principles by favoring more sales taxes on food and other necessities as well as on luxuries, rather than an increase in the progressive income tax, to finance them.

Keyserling wrote at several points that Galbraith and Schlesinger were "my good friends," and this was true: the three men maintained their albeit always rocky friendship. But no reader could miss the sharpness of the criticism. Galbraith might well have ignored or dismissed such charges from a more conservative opponent; but coming from Keyserling, they necessitated prompt and thorough reply.

In his answer, published two weeks later, Galbraith explained that his differences with Keyserling were "less over the content of the liberal platform than over what comes first." The United States had indeed become affluent. Poverty remained, but it was the lowest in U.S. history, and in many cases was due to structural problems that private-sector growth alone couldn't solve. Too many of the poor were ill-educated, lived in chronically depressed regions or inner cities, were elderly (and hence out of the workforce), or suffered from personal afflictions; these people required public-sector programs and investment before the benefits of growth could reach them.

Nor was he oblivious to poverty elsewhere in the world; but *The Affluent Society* had been about the United States, and the subject of global poverty was outside its scope. Moreover, he did not agree that a faster-growing American economy would generate greater resources that the United States could then use to relieve such poverty. Postwar growth hadn't yet produced such a windfall: it was privately produced and dedicated to private consumption; only by finding the political will to divert resources to the public sector as part of a growth strategy could the United States make a difference to global poverty.

Galbraith, too, valued full employment as an ideal, but doubted whether economists and policy-makers could achieve it without generating inflation. The economy was too large and complex, and the skills of American leaders (and their advisers) too limited. He reminded Keyserling that, in *The Affluent Society*, he advocated an expanded, more generous system of unemployment insurance as well as targeted public programs to address "structural" poverty. Beyond that, the country needed "public intervention in wage and price setting" to limit the danger of inflation in large industries where business concentration and union power prevailed.

Who won this debate, and what influence did it have on Kennedy the candidate? At one level, Keyserling seems to have prevailed. At its 1960 convention in Los Angeles, the Democratic Party was to enshrine the goal of 5 percent annual growth as part of its platform. And soon, the problem of poverty exploded as a national issue. But it was Galbraith, not Keyserling, whom Jack Kennedy made his adviser.

Galbraith had personal reasons to believe Kennedy wouldn't adopt Keyserling's full-bore "guns-and-butter" strategy. JFK had early on expressed grave misgivings, even after *Sputnik*, about the arms race and U.S. support for colonialism and reactionary Third World governments. He wrote to Galbraith in February 1958,

> I quite agree with you that the emphasis of the Democratic Party, both in . . . the Advisory Council and in Congressional speeches, has tended to magnify

the military challenge to the point where equally legitimate economic and political programs have been obscured . . . With these narrow horizons, which take little account of economic aid or the United Nations, the political lessons you draw seem none too harsh. For my part, I intend to give special attention this year to developing some new policy toward the underdeveloped areas, a field in which I know you also have special interest and far greater competence.[46]

Kennedy attached a copy of the article he'd written for *The Progressive* on the need for a massive new aid program for India, a subject of real interest to him. He gave a number of important Senate speeches on the subject and cosponsored just such an aid bill with Kentucky's John Sherman Cooper, who'd been Eisenhower's ambassador to India. (Kennedy's passion for India was a factor in Galbraith's desire for the ambassadorship there. Of all the overseas government posts, this was first on Kennedy's list.[47])

Also, Galbraith was not alone in doubting Keyserling's unbending commitment to growth, which seemed like " 'more spending, more spending, more spending' by everybody," as James Tobin later recalled. "The group around Kennedy felt that a kind of unmitigated Keyserling or old-style Democratic liberalism in regard to economics and fiscal policy wasn't going to pay off politically both during the campaign and afterwards."[48]

Yet Kennedy's liberalism influenced Galbraith's willingness to shift his allegiance from Stevenson, who at the time was working as a lawyer for Reynolds Aluminum and the investment bank Henry Schroeder. Stevenson was angered by Kennedy's Senate floor attacks on French colonialism in Algeria, and was content to advance his clients' interests in Ghana, the Belgian Congo, and South Africa during a long tour of Africa—much to Galbraith's consternation.[49]

From mid-1958 on, however, as Kennedy used claims of a spurious "missile gap" in his Senate campaign to hammer the GOP, Galbraith grew concerned. Would campaign rhetoric become a trap for Kennedy's policies once he was elected?

SEVERAL HOURS AFTER JFK formally announced his presidential candidacy in January 1960, he had Galbraith and Schlesinger join him for a long evening at Locke-Ober's, which the three men devoted to campaign strategizing.[50] But a few days later Galbraith flew to Switzerland, where he spent his spring semester on leave, working on his latest book, and he thus missed the primary season. After returning to Harvard, he wrote Kennedy on June 1 "to let you know that I'm back in town again, though I can't say you are seriously in need of anything[51] (JFK was the clear front-runner by then). Kennedy in fact wanted to see Galbraith immediately, and so Galbraith and the Schlesingers drove to Hyannis Port for an afternoon—and another long strategy meeting. It was a hot, overcast day, and they went out for a cruise on the *Marlin*, the Kennedys' power launch, for more talk about staffing issues and next steps. Galbraith pressed Kennedy on civil rights, urging him to promise, if elected, to block the reappointment of Mississippi's Senator John Eastland, a pillar of segregation and racism, as chairman of the Judiciary Committee. Kennedy demurred. Galbraith and Schlesinger then urged him to avoid too much public association with Old Stevensonians like themselves. Kennedy demurred once again, and just as predicted, Senator Goldwater attacked the two by name at the GOP convention a few weeks later.

A few days later, borrowing a leaf from Schlesinger's instrumental "New America" memo to Stevenson in 1956, Galbraith sent Kennedy his own detailed strategy memo.[52] Unlike 1952 and 1956, he said the two parties' candidates would start their campaigns on a par with one another—which meant that Nixon would go on the attack early. Galbraith warned JFK against repeating Stevenson's frantic campaigning in response: focus on key cities and states, stick with key themes. Nixon would try to campaign on prosperity and peace, on the 1950s economic experience and the Democratic reputation as the party of war. The Vice President would also soft-pedal his old strategies of tarring his opponents as "pink," because by now the gambit was too badly tarnished. Still, Nixon was "a highly contrived and calculating figure," whereas Kennedy had succeeded in the primaries by "giving every indication of speaking from natural conviction," and giving "no impression that he was impersonating either his own or any other public image."

JFK would need to hammer away at three basic themes—that his presidency promised a new beginning at home and abroad; that Americans should not settle for "tension, conflict and economic distress at home" or for "life under the nuclear terror, to the indefinite prolongation of the arms race or to war"; and that the Democratic Party could not be, as the GOP had been, "the party of special interests."

In concrete terms, Kennedy should convey seven dramatically unified messages:

1. *Reducing international tensions*, with the goal of a less dangerous world.
2. *Tackling the arms race and disarmament*, along the lines of a Senate speech JFK had given in June.
3. *Forging a new development compact with the Third World*.
4. *Producing "Growth with balance"*: there should be criticism of slow growth, the Fed's tight money policy, unnecessary unemployment, the lack of important public services, and JFK should "reject the notion that the American economy is dependent on war production." (He noted that Seymour Harris was doing "important work on alternatives to defense spending.")
5. *Building Americans* and 6. *Rebuilding America* were interrelated: investment on schooling and health, medical research, housing and urban development, public transit, and the environment. (An attack on billboards "and other forms of aesthetic corruption" would also be well received.)

There was "an infinity of things to be done," and the rationale was "not a question of liberalism but of social strategy." Public spending across the board was not the goal: targeted, well-researched programs were.

7. *Advocating "Civil rights and full citizenship"*: "The important thing is not the gadgets or legislation but to make it clear that the full powers of the Presidency will be put behind the solution . . . Accomplishment is now the test."

Although Galbraith makes no claim that the memo influenced the fall campaign as powerfully as Schlesinger's had Stevenson's in 1956, Kennedy was clearly impressed by Ken's campaign skills. By the time of the Democratic National Convention in Los Angeles in July, JFK made sure that Bobby Kennedy assigned Galbraith to be one of their floor managers, in charge of more than a dozen western and northwestern state delegations—a visible sign of the Kennedys' trust in him.[53] His influence was important in Kennedy's nomination but even more so in winning liberal delegates to accept Senator Lyndon Johnson as his running mate. Talk of "betrayal" was rife among many until Galbraith, at Bobby Kennedy's behest, reminded them, "this is the kind of expedient Franklin Roosevelt would never have used"—pause, as heads nodded righteously—"except in the case of John Nance Garner."[54] With that, threats of revolt died out, and heads cooled quickly. The Democratic ticket for 1960 was now complete.

During the campaign, he wrote several crucial speeches for Kennedy—the "basic economic speech," given in myriad versions to different audiences, plus one on the federal budget and one on farm policy. (When Galbraith's economic speech was chosen over a less radical alternative at a campaign staff meeting, Joseph Kennedy was in attendance—and strongly supported Galbraith's version. An astonished JFK pulled Galbraith aside. "I would like to know," he said, a smile on his face, "what hold you have on my old man."[55]) Theodore Sorensen, Kennedy's principal speechwriter, also used Galbraith as a steady source of colorful quotations and short talking papers and press statements. Meanwhile, repeating the pattern he had established in 1952 and 1956, Galbraith taught at Harvard and rushed off to campaign when he could. (His activities between the convention and the election fill seven thick folders at the Kennedy Library.)[56] Given his surrogate duties, Galbraith didn't see much of Kennedy during all this, but just before the first televised debate between the two candidates, a Kennedy aide called saying that the candidate wanted him to "come over" for a predebate discussion in Chicago, apparently not realizing that Galbraith was at the moment in San Diego, about to speak on his behalf. Two weeks later, on the eve of the third debate, he got the same call, asking him to come immediately to the Carlyle Hotel in Manhattan. This time, he was only a few blocks away, so Kennedy, Sorensen, Schlesinger, and he had a protracted lunch, debating statements and answers to be used that evening.

But throughout the campaign, the candidate and his erstwhile teacher kept in touch by phone and letter—JFK peppering Galbraith with requests for short speeches he could give at whistle stops, advice on economic policy, ideas on strategy. Galbraith was not averse to offering advice, and he focused on what he thought were Kennedy's weaknesses. One was his speeches: right after the convention JFK received a two-page single-spaced letter on his acceptance speech. Galbraith praised Kennedy for its content—"The New Frontier theme struck almost exactly the note that I had hoped for in my memorandum. So did the low key reference to defense and Mr. K[hrushchev]"—but he thought it was "essentially unfinished . . . badly in need of editing and polish . . . superfluous words could have been drained out . . . the transitions could have been far smoother . . . images . . . sharper and more vivid." Like an old debate coach with a promising student, Galbraith went down his list. He reassured his pupil that although he'd been brilliant in front of the convention's caucuses, the acceptance speech was "a reasonable imitation of a bird with a broken wing. You do get off the ground but it's wearing . . . to keep wondering if you are going to stay up." It's a testimony to the depth of their friendship that Kennedy welcomed this review (Sorensen may have been less pleased).[57]

DURING THE FALL CAMPAIGN, Galbraith concentrated his advice on economic content rather than rhetorical style. One particular issue stands out because it became an emblem of the Kennedy administration's greatest policy challenge in economic, political, military, and diplomatic affairs—gold.

For thousands of years gold had been the inviolable backing of sound currencies, and nations that violated "the golden rule" by flooding markets with paper money unbacked by gold (or some combination of gold, silver, and copper) had paid for their abandon with inflation—and often collapse. Conservative economic policy thus always and everywhere opposed such fecklessness, and favored gold-backed "sound money." But as a capitalist economy appeared in the nineteenth century, the scarcity of gold held back its economic growth and sparked ferocious debates over paper money, credit, debtors, and democracy. Keynes had long been critical of the gold standard, and in 1944 he and Harry Dexter White used the Bretton Woods agreement to steer international trade and finance off it and onto a *de facto* "dollar standard," which substituted confidence in American economic, political, and military might for the metal.

By 1960, the early signs of a crisis could be seen—the U.S. economy wasn't growing as fast as many others, its trade surplus was shrinking, and inflation was a problem. Under Bretton Woods, foreign governments held massive amounts of dollars as reserves for their own currencies, while smaller private markets for gold (traded largely on industrial demand for the metal rather than on its use as a proxy for currency, which Bretton Woods effectively prohibited) had begun to drive its price up. This was an indirect signal of lack of confidence in Eisenhower's economic management and in his foreign and military policies, since by then the vast network of overseas U.S. bases and military commitments was draining the American trade surplus. Governments took notice.

The subject was esoteric for most voters but alarmed economists, bankers, and businessmen. The risk was not just economic but political: U.S. gold reserves were shrinking, as Fort Knox sent hundreds of millions in gold to foreign governments in exchange for dollars they no longer wanted to hold. But if Kennedy embraced conservative economic policies, it might well constrict growth at home and power abroad, and effectively destroy the vaunted promises he was making for the New Frontier.

Like Keynes, Galbraith disdained the "gold standard" economy, and like him thought it was conservatism's cat's paw. Economies grew with innovation, risk-taking, credit, and strong public and private leadership; to turn back to gold was to turn away from the modern age and the very idea of Keynesian management. Galbraith's advice to Kennedy was straightforward, and reiterated what he'd been saying to the senator for years: don't get caught in "golden handcuffs"; make the problem foremost a political one; connect it to GOP mismanagement of the economy; commit yourself and the country to grow the economy out of the problem with dynamic leadership. "Be concerned but not alarmed," he counseled JFK, adding that Karl Brandt, a conservative member of Eisenhower's CEA, had just contacted him, pleading with Galbraith to persuade Kennedy to help halt "the panic" in London gold markets by promising "sound policies" if elected. To this, Galbraith coolly noted, "I did not respond"—and told JFK he should do likewise.[58]

Kennedy largely followed Galbraith's advice on the topic of gold. Once in office, however, his administration's policies took a different course. According to Schlesinger, Kennedy "used to tell his advisers that the two things that scared him most were nuclear war and the balance of payments"; his Treasury Secretary thought that JFK's preoccupation became "almost phobia."[59]

To voters, growth, not gold, was the important issue. A recession was under way, and Kennedy embraced his party's commitment not just to ending the downturn but to accelerating growth. But he shared his advisers' doubts about Keyserling and his recommendations. His first question, for example, on meeting the economist Walter Heller during the campaign was, "Do you really think we can make good on that 5 percent growth promise in the Democratic platform?" Heller gave a nuanced and cautious answer, proudly reporting to Galbraith after the meeting that he had emphasized the trade-off between high-employment growth and inflation, described the potential effect of various growth levels on foreign trade, dollar balances, and gold reserves, and carefully distinguished in Galbraithian fashion between issues of "quality" and those of "quantity" in national output and consumption.[60]

On election night in November, Galbraith stayed up late with other supporters at Kennedy's Boston campaign headquarters, monitoring returns from around the country. It wasn't until well past midnight that victory was finally declared, but the wait seemed more than worth it.[61] After the frustrations and setbacks of the fifteen years since Roosevelt's death, and the emotional turmoil and pain of Stevenson's defeats in 1952 and 1956, here finally was cause for celebration.

As he went to bed shortly before dawn that Wednesday morning, Galbraith reflected on what the future was likely to hold. Jack Kennedy was a friend whom he liked and greatly admired, and over whom he felt he could exercise a degree of influence, especially when it came to shaping an authentic Keynesian effort to manage the economy and a liberal program that would advance beyond the conventional wisdom of the times. Yet he felt deep apprehension as well. Kennedy had promised not just "to get this country moving again," but to close the missile gap with the Soviet Union and to support Cuban "fighters for freedom" as well. Galbraith had felt acutely uncomfortable when Kennedy made his statement about Cuba in late October: Florida and New Jersey, two states with big Cuban émigré populations, were important for Kennedy's electoral strategy. Was this merely a hastily made stump promise in the final days of a close campaign, and would it be blunted or even forgotten? He sensed danger: not just for Kennedy and his new administration, but for the larger project in its best form, which, he hoped, might finally move onto history's center stage. The gold problem, he was sure, could be managed; a war could derail everything.

15

On the New Frontier

Dear Mr. President,

In an early two-volume work I intend to deal with the relation of a President to economists. I will naturally urge that he listen to them attentively, and indeed with a certain respect and awe. But I will also urge that the political winds in the willows are a safer guide to final action than the most enlightened conclusions of my craft. This is because the President (after all he got elected) must have a sense of what the people want. This is the best guide to action. Economists only know what they should want or, sometimes, what they used to want.

—Galbraith to President Kennedy,
August 1962

JANUARY 20, 1961: On the Friday morning of John F. Kennedy's inaugural, the weather in Washington seemed anything but welcoming to the new President. A bitter cold front had enveloped the city, and on Thursday snow began to fall. By evening, ice had encrusted the inaugural stand on the east steps of the Capitol. Soldiers were dispatched just before midnight; when chipping and digging failed, they were ordered to use flamethrowers to melt the ice. The searing flames did their job but in the night's howling wind left unseen damage. At noon on Friday, as Richard Cardinal Cushing concluded his lengthy invocation,* a thin trail of smoke began to rise from the base of the podium. Secret Service agents rushed beneath the platform, and the chief agent contemplated clearing the stands. Quickly determining that some electrical cir-

---

*The length of Cushing's invocation, noted by the press, amused Kennedy, because he knew New York's Francis Cardinal Spellman, the country's senior Catholic prelate, had wanted the pastoral moment for himself. But the arch-conservative Spellman was no friend of Kennedy or liberalism, and the invitation had gone to the Boston cardinal Cushing.

cuits had been damaged by the flamethrowers' intense heat, agents contained the problem, and the inauguration proceeded.

Shortly before one o'clock, Chief Justice Earl Warren finished administering the oath, and President Kennedy turned to the audience. Hatless and coatless, his breath frosting in the air, the young President solemnly began, "Let the word go forth from this time and place, to friend and foe alike, that the torch has been passed to a new generation of Americans . . . tempered by war, disciplined by a hard and bitter peace, proud of our ancient heritage." In the next few moments, the course of American history changed, and listeners across the country knew it at once. The elegance and panache of the speech and the speaker seemed to electrify Americans as no one had since Roosevelt. "Let every nation know, whether it wishes us well or ill, that we shall pay any price, bear any burden, meet any hardship, support any friend, oppose any foe to assure the survival and success of liberty," he declared to ringing applause. When he finished with his concluding injunction—"My fellow Americans, ask not what your country can do for you; ask what you can do for your country"— the ovation was tumultuous.

Wily old Sam Rayburn was as shrewd a judge of politics and character as any man in Washington. "That speech he made out there," the House Speaker said shortly afterward, "was better than Lincoln." (This was a sharp revision of his earlier views. In 1956, he'd called Kennedy "a little piss ant.") Having been elected by only a hair's breadth, the country's new leader found his popularity soaring after his inaugural.[1]

Seated near the podium with John and Elaine Steinbeck, Ken and Kitty Galbraith joined in the applause after Kennedy's speech, then—in a limousine provided by a network television crew that was making a documentary of the inaugural as seen in part through Galbraith's eyes—made their way up Pennsylvania Avenue.* The crowds were so thick that it took the limousine more than an hour to get to their VIP seats in front of the White House, and so they missed the start of the parade. In any event, none of the floats, drum majorettes, or marching units of National Guardsmen and police "could take my mind off the bitter cold," Galbraith remembered. The frozen Galbraiths discreetly abandoned the public festivities in favor of drinks at the home of George Ball, with whom they were staying.

Suitably warmed after an hour or so, they bundled up and made their way through a procession of private parties until around eleven in the evening, when they set off for the Inaugural Ball at the Armory. Traffic was as snarled as ever, though, and they abandoned their car to walk the last blocks in the cold.

---

*Galbraith by then was a figure of fresh renown in Washington, having been attacked by name by both Goldwater and Nixon during the campaign. He also was of some concern to figures like Robert Lovett, who had been alarmed by Galbraith's Bombing Survey conclusions and even more alarmed by *The Affluent Society*. Kennedy badly wanted Lovett in his administration, and offered him his choice of State, Defense, or Treasury. Lovett declined them all and "punctiliously informed Kennedy that he had voted for Nixon, apparently out of fear of J. K. Galbraith" (Schlesinger, *Thousand Days*, 125).

Once inside, the cameras of the TV documentary crew still in tow guaranteed them instant attention. Dancing and talking until 4 a.m., they had a "splendid time of it," with McGeorge Bundy urging Galbraith to take the Indian ambassadorship, which Galbraith had asked for but about which he now had second thoughts. Kennedy needed him, Bundy said, and there was much to be done.[2]

Galbraith knew that Harvard's rules would allow him only two years in New Delhi. He briefly toyed with giving up Harvard permanently and even discussed it with President Pusey. (Pusey, not a Galbraith admirer, raised no objection, asking only that he decide quickly so as not to disrupt spring course schedules.*) But Bundy and the economist Alexander Gerschenkron talked him out if it.

AS BUNDY SAID, there was indeed a great deal to be done. Kennedy's inaugural address was preoccupied with the Cold War, national defense, and the threat of international Communism—and didn't even refer to, let alone outline, a domestic agenda.[3] Yet he had promised throughout his campaign to "get the country moving again." How would this be done? Kennedy placed increased spending on military and space efforts at the top of the list of priorities. Such spending was eventually to account for 75 percent of all expenditure increases during his presidency, and funds for the space program rose from barely $1 billion in 1960 to $6.8 billion in 1964, while military spending in dollar terms rose even faster, from $46 billion to $54 billion.[4]

The boost in military and space spending was all the more remarkable because when Kennedy took office the Department of Defense was already operating 3,500 bases at home and abroad, and U.S. facilities covered 35 million acres (greater in area than Massachusetts, Connecticut, New Hampshire, Vermont, Rhode Island, Delaware, New Jersey, and Maryland combined). From its "missile gap" deficit at the time of *Sputnik's* launch, the country's nuclear arsenal had moreover grown to include 100 ICBMs and IRBMs, 80 submarine-based Polaris missiles, 1,700 intercontinental bombers, 300 carrier-borne aircraft, and almost 1,000 land-based supersonic fighters. In addition, the Army had thousands of its own tactical nuclear weapons, and was storing in one base alone enough nerve gas to kill the world's population several times over.[5]

Yet in Kennedy's less than three years in office, the number of battle-ready nuclear weapons grew by 100 percent and Polaris-armed submarines by 450 percent; U.S. tactical nuclear forces in Europe jumped 60 percent; and overall combat readiness in the Army rose by 45 percent.[6] It was, as his aide Theodore

---

*Pusey's regard for Galbraith was never warm and had cooled perceptibly in 1959, when Schlesinger and Galbraith launched a public broadside against Harvard over its choice of honorary degree recipients, which had been given to Republicans in public service five times more often than to Democrats since 1945. The GOP's list included Eisenhower, Dulles, Lovett, John McCloy, Henry Cabot Lodge, Jr.—and, not unnoticed by Galbraith, Sinclair Weeks. Pusey hated the ruckus the broadside created in the press and among the alumni. Ironically, its alternative recommendation of candidates bespoke the consciousness of the times. All were white males; Harvard had never in 320 years given an honorary degree to a black, Hispanic, or woman save one, the deaf and blind Helen Keller in 1955.

Sorensen later proudly wrote, "the largest and swiftest build-up in this country's peacetime history," even though much of it was the result of Eisenhower-era weapons systems finally coming on line.[7] Simultaneously Kennedy increased spending on many domestic programs: in his first six months alone, Congress approved new temporary unemployment benefits, an area redevelopment program, liberalization of Social Security benefits, aid for dependent children with unemployed fathers, and an omnibus housing bill—all while the country was recovering from another recession. Schlesinger grandly called it "a record of action on the domestic front unmatched in any single sitting since 1935."

But the dollars for these programs were a fraction of those spent on space and defense. Under Kennedy—as under Eisenhower—defense spending regularly outpaced all spending by state and local governments and was more than twice the magnitude of all federal domestic social expenditures. Meanwhile, Congress rejected many major New Frontier initiatives such as Medicare, aid to education, and a new Department of Urban Affairs. Despite Kennedy's efforts, the 1961 minimum-wage bill merely enabled workers to catch up with inflation and productivity gains since the last increase five years earlier; it extended coverage to 3 million new workers, but conservatives blocked further extension to the 16 million who were truly impoverished. For the elderly, the average monthly Social Security check was $75, while a day-care bill for 4 million children allocated $5 million—$1.25 per child. Under the Area Redevelopment Act eventually $1 billion was spent over four years on poverty-stricken Appalachia, but 80 percent of that went to road construction. The Pentagon, by contrast, was spending $1 billion a week.[8]

Kennedy, acutely aware of the country's needs, was especially touched by the plight of the young. According to Schlesinger, the President

> knew (and would rattle off the statistics) that each year 4 million boys and girls were born in the United States; that one of three who completed fifth grade would drop out before graduation from high school; that nearly 3 million in their teens would come every year into the labor market; that workers under the age of twenty-five, though less than one fifth of the labor force, were one-third of the unemployed; . . . that arrests of the young had increased 86 percent in a decade."[9]

He also grasped the scope of American poverty. Schlesinger credited his having read both *The Affluent Society* and Michael Harrington's *The Other America*, along with Galbraith's "unremitting guerrilla warfare in support of the public sector," with eventually convincing him that a major antipoverty program should be launched in 1964.

But at the start of his administration, poverty wasn't at the forefront of his agenda; getting the country moving again was, and "fiscal policy was the major [economic] weapon of the Kennedy administration," as Seymour Harris, who served as the Treasury Department's senior economist, observed. "The rise of spending was crucial, though the increase was only partly connected to economic objectives; the major part of the rise stemmed from increased needs to assure maximum security."[10]

Two weeks into office, Kennedy sent a special message to Congress about economic recovery and growth, outlining his ambitions. Soon after, on hundreds of desks and walls in the Commerce Department, a new sign appeared: "What have you done for Growth today?"[11] He also announced the formation of a new Cabinet Committee on Growth, which included the chairman of the Council of Economic Advisors, the head of the Budget Bureau, and the Secretaries of the Treasury, Commerce, and Labor. (The committee's title tellingly contrasted with Eisenhower's Cabinet Committee on Price Stability for Economic Growth.)[12]

Walter Heller, the new chairman of the Council of Economic Advisors, began calling the Kennedy policy "the New Economics." Growth, in his words, would henceforth be "both an end in itself and an instrumentality, both the pot of gold and the rainbow." As Heller's CEA colleague James Tobin put it, the Kennedy administration "regarded growth in national production and income not only as an end in itself but as the fount of economic and fiscal resources for meeting national ends" at home and abroad.[13]

As the agenda took shape, confidence abounded that the President and his economic advisers could realize their ambitious goals, and they seemed to reflect a fresh mood sweeping the country at large. To the journalist Theodore White, Kennedy and his men were part of "a new generation of Americans who saw the world differently from their fathers. [They were] brought up to believe, either at home or abroad, that whatever Americans wished to make happen, would happen."[14] And the heady confidence of Kennedy's economists soon seemed justified. By March the U.S. GNP began an expansion that eventually lasted 106 months, an achievement without precedent in the nation's history. Between 1961 and 1966 alone, one economic policy historian has noted,

> real GNP increased at a rate above 5 percent per year. Employment grew by 2.5 percent per year, and in January 1966 the unemployment rate sank to 3.9 percent. The percentage of Americans mired in poverty, according to official estimates, dropped from 22.4 percent in 1960 to 14.7 percent in 1966. As these advances unfolded, the rate of inflation remained below 2 percent per year through 1965. By all the usual measures, the economic policies of the early 1960s were an unambiguous success.[15]

Little wonder that New Frontier economists came to believe that their "New Economics" was ushering in a "Golden Age of Keynes"—and weren't alone in their praise. *Time* in 1965 put Keynes on its cover. "Today, some 20 years after his death," it declared, "his theories are a prime influence on the world's free economies, especially on America's." In Washington, "the men who formulate the nation's economic polices have used Keynesian principles not only to avoid the violent cycles of prewar days but to produce a phenomenal economic growth and to achieve remarkably stable prices." Even the monetarist Milton Friedman ruefully admitted, "We are all Keynesians now."[16]

Just how successful, in fact, was the New Economics, and what relation did Galbraith have to it?

Although Heller's term suggests a coherent whole, the New Economics was in practice a loosely coherent mosaic of policies. To begin with, its advocates were advancing activist management theories that had not been significantly tested. American economic policies in the 1950s had been nominally "Keynesian" by virtue of the government's sheer size, and by its efforts to "manage" the business cycle by following at best a cautiously conservative interpretation of Keynesian principles. Now, as Heller explained, there was meant to be a dramatic policy reorientation: "Gone is the countercyclical syndrome of the 1950s. Policy now centers on gap closing and growth, on realizing and enlarging the nation's non-inflationary potential."[17]

But Heller couldn't have foreseen that he and the administration's other mainstream Keynesians, centered in the CEA, were to spend a great deal of time struggling with non-Keynesians in the Treasury, Federal Reserve, and Congress. Kennedy himself wasn't fully won over to Keynesianism for quite a while. *Prospects and Policies for the 1961 American Economy*, a special report written for him by Paul Samuelson and others in December 1960, set forth these theories, but Kennedy hesitated to follow its recommendations.

Most important from Galbraith's perspective, the "New Economics" maintained a discreet silence on the armed forces' immense significance in the federal budget. Not giving more than passing mention to the Pentagon, instead the CEA's annual *Economic Reports* focused either on broad macroeconomic growth, or on specific domestic issues, or on gold and the balance of payments. (Samuelson's December 1960 report had observed that defense dollars were in a category all their own, and should be determined "on their own merits. They are not to be the football of economics stabilization."[18])

In their awkward silence, the New Economists reflected long-standing professional habit: America's Cold War consensus included most economists, after all. But consensus wasn't the only reason that U.S. military spending escaped rigorous scrutiny among those who valued their commitment to searching reason. The dark consequences of McCarthyism had reached deep into American academic life and exacted a certain discreet silence. The pioneering economic forecaster Lawrence Klein had faced repeated problems finding and keeping a teaching job because he'd briefly joined the Communist Party in college; Franco Modigliani, Don Patinkin, and Leo Hurwicz had all left teaching positions thanks to political harassment; Tjalling Koopmans, after brilliant wartime service, had been constantly scrutinized and criticized.

For others, the merits of self-censorship had become obvious. Kenneth Arrow, who'd been a Norman Thomas–style democratic socialist in college, in the 1950s "largely abstained from contemporary political involvements."[19] Herbert Simon found harassment the norm even then, and for years later, Samuelson recalled being acutely aware that "if you were a teacher at many a school around the country and the Board of Regents of your university was on your neck for using subversive textbooks, it was no laughing matter." After a young William F. Buckley savaged him in *God and Man at Yale*, he carefully reworked his popular *Economics* college text more than once:

> My last wish was to have an intransigent formulation that would be read by no one . . . As a result I followed an Aesopian policy of paying careful attention to every criticism of every line and word of my text . . . In a sense this careful wording achieved its purpose: at least some of my critics were reduced to complaining that I played peek-a-boo with the reader and didn't come out and declare my true meaning . . . I reread today, say the fifth edition of the book, with a certain irritation for the care with which many matters are formulated.[20]

Samuelson's textbook contained no more than a few words on American defense spending, and none on its size in relation to the federal budget or its effect on the economy. In this it was not alone: all the major economics textbooks did the same.[21]

Apart from the price they paid in analytic clarity and intellectual integrity, economists' decision to downplay or even ignore the size and effect of America's military budget came to have fateful consequences for Keynesian policy in the United States. And this was not a problem to which Galbraith had ever been blind or about which he now kept silent. Once Kennedy took office, he raised these concerns to a new level almost immediately. Military power, military spending, and a reliance on military intervention carried a terrible cost, he repeatedly warned the President.

And military spending was not the only issue that separated Galbraith from the "New Economics." Most "New Economists" by 1960 thought they had in hand the tools that would let them steer the economy. Their confidence was built on three cornerstones: an underlying mathematical model of stable growth, a trade-off theory of inflation and unemployment, and their practical index for measuring optimal performance.[22] With these three, as Tobin wistfully put it later, "We thought we could not only make the bicycle go faster but keep it at high speed and determine the path it would follow."[23]

The fundamental growth concepts of the "New Economics" owed much to the work of the Oxford economist Roy Harrod, Keynes's disciple and first biographer, and to the Harvard-trained Evsey Domar, a Russian émigré. The two men by the 1950s had ingeniously connected, through Keynes's "multiplier effect," the growth rates of the labor force and of investment in physical plant and equipment to measurably predictable changes in aggregate demand.[24] Using a combination of national income accounting definitions, statistical regressions, and algebraic and calculus-based manipulation, the "Harrod-Domar model" seemed to promise a way to calculate, predict, and, most important, manage overall economic growth. But the Harrod-Domar model had problems: among other things, it accounted poorly for technology's contribution to the productivity of labor and equipment—not a small weakness in modeling a modern economy. However, growth theory was something of a growth industry itself and attracted talented adherents.[25] Some thinkers, such as Robert Solow of MIT (who later served with Heller on Kennedy's Council of Economic Advisors), made brilliant contributions to unraveling the technology mystery, thereby mitigating the original model's productivity problem.[26] Others, such as James Tobin, improved on the original Harrod-Domar model by making labor and capital substitutable in the basic equations, thereby obviating what was called the "knife-edge" problem.[27]

Difficulties with the model persisted, especially the fact that it couldn't be made to match empirical data. Rigorous studies by the Joint Economic Committee of Congress and the Committee for Economic Development showed that increases in labor and capital together accounted, as Walter Heller himself admitted, for less than *half* of economic growth. That left Heller explaining that education accounted for almost all the rest—an analytically indefensible proposition. Still, the "New Economists" confidently assumed the fundamental correctness of their model, and believed they were free to focus on their second cornerstone, the trade-offs between inflation and unemployment that sustaining "managed" full-employment growth would bring.

Empirical work by the New Zealand economist A. W. Phillips, recalculated for the American experience by Samuelson and Solow, was decisive.[28] Using data on British economic performance dating back to the 1860s, Phillips had observed an inverse, stable relationship between rates of change in money wages and those in unemployment: rising inflation lowered unemployment and vice versa, with surprising predictability. This "Phillips Curve" was, as Solow put it, "really pretty astonishing."

> Here was evidence for a strong, and apparently reliable, relation . . . [that] did not appear to be a short-run transient affair as the [pre-Keynesian] macroeconomics of the 19th and early 20th centuries would have suggested . . . It seemed to say quite clearly that the rate of wage inflation—and, probably, therefore the rate of price inflation—was a smooth function of the tightness of the aggregate economy.

Samuelson asked Solow whether he thought the Phillips Curve meant "the economy can move back and forth along a curve like that," and Solow answered, " 'Yeah, I'm inclined to believe it,' and Paul said, 'Me too.' "[29]

Since the "New Economists" wanted both rapid *and* stable managed growth, their implicit policy challenge was to find an economic and political bargain that optimized growth somewhere between a strict "full-employment" goal and a modest rate of inflation. In theoretical terms, this was far more complicated than simply demanding that the American economy grow 5 percent per year, as Rockefeller and Keyserling had; in practical terms, Heller and the CEA set their Phillips Curve "bargain" at 4 percent unemployment and roughly 2 percent inflation.

The third cornerstone for these mathematical Keynesians—the "full-employment budget" concept—was a calculation of a hypothetical GNP level that assumed "full" (in reality, near-full) employment, then a comparison of this to actual economic performance. Keynes had introduced the idea in _How to Pay for the War_, and his back-of-the-envelope sketch had been greatly refined since then. The gap between the two—expressed in dollars of potential GNP "lost" by slow growth—was assumed to be the "room" that a country still had to grow before accepting fundamental restraints. Filling this gap, or "room," became the first order of business for Kennedy's "New Economists."

Kennedy's economic advisers were, however, cautious in spelling out their policy applications, at least at first. Sidestepping the 1960 Democratic platform plan calling for 5 percent GNP growth, Kennedy had been deliberately vague during his campaign about any hard targets—not just for tactical political reasons. Galbraith's and Heller's skepticism about 5 percent growth had impressed him, and when the President introduced his newly chosen CEA chairman to the press, he carefully told reporters only that he and Heller wanted a "faster" rate of growth, never saying what either of them thought "faster" might actually mean.[30]

Heller understood that winning JFK to the ideas of the "New Economics" was one of his primary tasks. By all accounts President Kennedy was a conscientious student of economics who occasionally even caught his own senior advisers in misstatements of arcane theory.* And most of the economists who knew and worked with JFK believed that he evolved both intellectually and politically while in the White House. Heller called him "my best student."[31] Kennedy's early behavior in office failed to match his often Keynesian-sounding rhetoric, yet seventeen months later, he seemed a full-fledged and fervent convert.

So why then was Galbraith the Kennedy administration's most prominent in-house critic of major elements of the "New Economics"? A partial answer can be found in the draft inaugural address Kennedy had asked Schlesinger and him to prepare. In it—roughly following the seven points Galbraith had given the candidate earlier—they laid out a domestic agenda of civil rights and economic opportunity, with expanded public investment in education, health, scientific research, and poverty reduction; internationally, they had Kennedy call for increased cooperation with allies, withdrawal of support for anti-Communist dictators, a major new partnership with Latin America, and heavily increased development aid for the Third World. Communism was to be confronted, but wherever possible peacefully—and containing the dangers of

---

*According to Heller, "We were often amazed at [Kennedy's] capacity for understanding a particular set of relationships in economics . . . [He] was capable of digesting rather lengthy and penetrating memos, and it was Ken Galbraith who tipped me off on that early in the game." Galbraith, of course, had tutored Kennedy in his own view of Keynesian essentials for years. In 1958, for example, he had written JFK, in the tone of a supportive thesis adviser, about the Senator's performance on _Meet the Press_. (He had spent the evening before it briefing Kennedy on policy and on its political framing.) On the program Kennedy had vigorously attacked restrictive Federal Reserve policies, pressed the alternative of wage-price guidelines to constrain inflation, and—best of all, from Galbraith's point of view—made the case for deficit spending when unemployment was high.

war was paramount.[32] But Kennedy and Sorensen had used almost none of this, eschewing mention of the domestic agenda and opting for the eloquent rhetorical challenge, simultaneously martial and peace-seeking, to restore America's greatness in the world.

Galbraith thought the final version brilliant, and brilliantly delivered. Yet its unspoken omissions underscored Kennedy's public caution, and he resolved to intensify his own education of the President. The most important of Galbraith's surviving contributions to the inaugural address was the line "Let us never negotiate out of fear, but let us never fear to negotiate."[33] His motives for writing such lines—and longer passages on the possibilities for mutual disarmament—reflected his well-formed worldview and his concern about the price the United States was paying for the Cold War.

Just before Kennedy's inauguration President Eisenhower had used his farewell address to the Congress to speak with remarkable candor of his concerns about the Cold War's enormous costs, warning Americans about the growing dangers of what he called the nation's "military-industrial complex."[34] Here, he said, were the Cold War's real and chief beneficiaries—and somehow they must be contained. To Galbraith this was no small irony: during Eisenhower's eight years in office, the United States had spent more on its armed forces than it had under Roosevelt to win World War II. Still, Eisenhower's speech had seemed wonderfully timed, and Galbraith had hoped the incoming Democratic administration would use it as a bipartisan foil to set new priorities. Kennedy, he felt, had to confront and contain the *de facto* "military Keynesianism" of his predecessors. If he managed to do so, he would make his administration as vitally important as the New Deal.

Getting economic policy "right" in a technical sense was only one contingent part of the challenge; finding the men who understood the problem was the real crux. Immediately after the November elections, Kennedy had assigned Galbraith, Arthur Schlesinger, and his own brother-in-law Sargent Shriver the job of recommending and vetting candidates for the incoming administration's top economic posts—the Treasury, the Budget Bureau, the Council of Economic Advisors, and so on.

For the chairmanship of the Council of Economic Advisors, Kennedy's first choice was probably Paul Samuelson, but Samuelson had always declined to live in Washington, and told the President that he would still decline.[35] Kennedy then thought of appointing Galbraith, and a few days after the election, had Schlesinger inquire whether he was interested. Yet no doubt also anxious about the reactions he'd have to face if he were to appoint his highly visible and controversial friend to the post, Kennedy "seemed far from distressed," according to Schlesinger, when told that Galbraith's answer was no.

Despite the job's obvious temptations, Galbraith declined because he still vividly remembered the trials and frustrations of both his OPA and State Department service in the 1940s. "I was little enchanted," he later recalled, "by the thought of doing with slight authority what I'd done twenty years earlier.

And equally I didn't wish to come every day to the same discussion of the same questions around the same oak table, mostly with the same people, not all of whom I wished to see."[36] For the CEA job he suggested Heller.

Galbraith's first choice wasn't the ambassadorship in New Delhi, though; his real hope was that Kennedy would arrange his appointment to the President-elect's now vacant Senate seat. Trial balloons suggesting the idea had appeared in the Boston papers and then in *The New York Times* right after the election (Galbraith has always insisted he wasn't the source for them).[37] But reaction to them made him quickly realize that JFK had another candidate in mind: his younger brother Robert. Then, under intense pressure from their father, he appointed Bobby as Attorney General, which left the still younger brother Edward as the designee. But Ted's youth (at twenty-eight) stood in the way of his appointment (the Constitution set thirty as the minimum age for a U.S. senator), and so Ben Smith, an old family friend, was tapped as the seat's place holder until the President's youngest brother became old enough to run in 1962.[38]

In New Delhi, Galbraith would of course be far away from Washington, but the President himself made quite clear that the distance was to be geographic only; he instructed his ambassador-designate to maintain frequent and broad-ranging contact on whatever economic, political, and diplomatic issues he might select. And whenever Galbraith so chose, the President added, the State Department's official channels to the White House should be ignored. This gave Galbraith a unique position. Encouraged by Secretary of State Dean Rusk, Kennedy formally ordered all U.S. ambassadors to channel their reports through State. According to Schlesinger, "Only Kenneth Galbraith ignored this injunction (and Kennedy was delighted that he did)." JFK wanted to hear from him directly and regularly, and to see him frequently in Washington. Until Galbraith left for India, he said, he wanted Galbraith nearby.[39]

BY CHRISTMAS 1960, Kennedy had already decided that it was politically advisable to reach out to moderate Republicans on economic policy. He teased his ambassador-designate that he was glad Galbraith was going to India, because "otherwise you and Heller would have me expounding a far too radical position. My policy is to be moderate and do much."[40] And contrary to Galbraith's advice, he chose the Wall Street investment banker C. Douglas Dillon as his Treasury Secretary and the New York Federal Reserve vice president Robert Roosa as Dillon's deputy. (Galbraith had favored a respected senior Democratic senator such as Paul Douglas of Illinois, himself a distinguished liberal economist, or Albert Gore, Sr., of Tennessee, or the Democratic congressmen Richard Bolling and Henry Reuss. Dillon had been Dulles's Undersecretary of State and a major Nixon donor.[41])

The consequences of choosing Dillon showed themselves immediately after the inauguration. When Kennedy, at his first cabinet meeting, asked everyone to explain briefly the most important issue each was facing, Dillon replied—in sweeping affirmation of the Wall Street worldview—that America's balance-of-payments deficit was "the nexus of all economic problems, at home and abroad."[42] He, along with Roosa and the Federal Reserve Board chairman, William McChesney Martin, lost no time in warning of the grave and extensive "dangers" posed by America's international economic situation.[43] Just as unsurprisingly, these men cast the problem in technical terms, requiring technically administered solutions that ignored or narrowly defined the overt political goals or the political implications for the administration's domestic aims and its supporters. In "Operation Twist," the two agencies cooperated to lower long-term interest rates while keeping short-term rates high, and to enact a string of related policies meant to deal with "the nexus of all problems" (the manipulation of the London Gold Pool and the Interest Equalization Tax, among others).

Right away Galbraith warned Kennedy that "Operation Twist" wouldn't work. "I know all about the gold outflow and I'm not ignoring it," he said, but Operation Twist was "mystic claptrap" and a "half-assed effort." His recommendation was to induce European central banks to lower their rates while the United States got its economy moving. This, he said, "will be called impossible or unwise" by those who profited from the high rates. "Meanwhile, the economy suffers and so do the people and so, potentially does this Administration." In office only a month, however, Kennedy wasn't willing to stymie his new Treasury Secretary, and Operation Twist continued. Soon enough Galbraith was proved right.[44] But the policies were swallowed without much resistance at the CEA, despite Keynes's well-known contempt for the gold standard and for letting international economic relations determine domestic economic policy. Heller and the others understood they were making a devil's bargain.[45] As Heller later put it, "One couldn't do as much as one might like to have done to stimulate the economy . . . because short-term interest rates had to be held up to keep money from flowing overseas. To stimulate the economy, you just had to do it by fiscal policy, and tax cuts were the only promising path in Congress."[46]

Even Paul Samuelson argued that the country's gold outflow "without question" had to "affect our choice among activist policies to restore production and employment." He urged the CEA to identify employment-generating policies with the least effect on the balance of payments—a quest, as one economist later put it, that was like "looking for needles in the proverbial haystack."[47] But Galbraith kept pressing Kennedy to resist these directions.

As an alternative, he gave Kennedy a list of wide-ranging recommendations for measures meant to solve what he considered a relatively small problem. Foreign aid, for example, could be tied to the recipients' purchase of U.S. goods and services; Americans could be gently encouraged to buy American (though the government should avoid "jingoistic appeals"); a wealth surtax could be placed on rich American expatriates; an increased duty should be imposed on tourist purchases brought home.

In January, Kennedy put Galbraith in charge of drafting the economics section of the State of the Union message, as well as a separate special message to Congress on the balance of payments. After sharp debates with Dillon, Heller, and others, Galbraith thought he had prevailed on the gold issue and several others. And of the speech as the President delivered it, he wrote,

> From any point of view, I don't think it could be better. The economic sec-
> tions are excellent and do not spare the Eisenhower Administration in their
> review of unemployment, declining product, business failures, farm income
> and continuing price advance. The affirmative part portends good legislation,
> even if some is yet to be devised or thought out . . . My views on foreign aid
> and development, perhaps not unnaturally, are strongly articulated.[48]

But, Galbraith noted in his diary, apart from the President, the new administration might "be too professional—too aware of criticism, too sensitive to
what cannot be done. There are no political buccaneers with a fine enthusiasm
for action—in the manner of Harold Ickes or Hugh Johnson. The [State of the
Union]—or a late draft—has a passage calling for some spirit of adventure in
the public servant. It could be addressed to the Cabinet."[49]

Galbraith himself never flinched from advising on controversial issues, and
he repeated the worries he put in his diary directly to Kennedy. He was himself, perhaps, the kind of "political buccaneer" he recommended President
Kennedy favor. The President should rigorously evaluate the economic cost of
troop deployments abroad, he said, and be prepared to cut back bases and
troops; he should just as rigorously review American military and economic
support for certain foreign governments such as those of South Korea and
Taiwan.[50]

Galbraith also thought the President should consider establishing capital
controls of some sort on any large movements of private U.S. funds abroad.
(He returned to this issue repeatedly; it was the subject of his last letter to
Kennedy, written a week before the President's assassination.[51]) He also urged
him to use American power to advance fundamental economic reform in the
Third World, not just in the interests of justice, but to strengthen the U.S.
economy. In 1962, he was to write, "In Latin America, it is land reform, above
all, that the people want. Those who own the land have already been paid for
it a thousand times. In the absence of reform our aid does not help the people
or even much postpone revolution. Rather it buys the way temporarily around
the crisis in the process of which dollars are funneled into Rio and squirreled
out to Paris."[52]

Until he left for India in early April, Galbraith was given Secretary of State
Cordell Hull's spacious old office in the Executive Office Building next to the
White House, whence he could be easily called to the Oval Office or to the
upstairs family quarters, as he repeatedly was. And Kennedy made sure that
Galbraith attended virtually all of the crucial first meetings at which the administration's economic policies were formulated. JFK's instructions were
clear: Galbraith's job was to "tell me not what I should do but what I should
tell others to do—and be specific."[53] For three months Galbraith thus met

frequently with the President one-on-one as well as with Heller, Treasury Secretary Dillon, and Federal Reserve Chairman Martin and their deputies to discuss and debate issues from tax cutting and domestic spending priorities to
foreign aid and balance-of-payments problems, and he was called upon repeatedly to draft speeches and papers.[54]

These economic policy duties were only one part of his exhausting schedule; by late February, more and more of Galbraith's time was being taken up in
State Department and CIA meetings, plowing through the thick briefing books
meant to prepare him for his Senate confirmation hearings in March. It was
frustrating work—his dislike of the State Department hadn't lessened over the
years and was exacerbated by his newfound dislike of Dean Rusk, who seemed
only a modest improvement over John Foster Dulles. The bad feelings between
him and Rusk probably started in early January, after Galbraith sent Rusk a polite note suggesting that Rusk might want to inform the current Indian ambassador, Ellsworth Bunker, of his impending India posting. Rusk sent back a
stiffly worded note on protocol, advising Galbraith to talk less about this possibility. But personal feelings aside, they disagreed on fundamental policy on India and Pakistan, on the U.S.S.R. and China, and on Vietnam.[55] At one point
Galbraith even drafted a letter offering to remove his name from consideration
for the post in New Delhi, but was talked out of it by McGeorge Bundy.

President Kennedy, like Roosevelt, wasn't keen on the State Department,
and he had appointed Rusk, whom he didn't know, because he came highly
recommended by Robert Lovett, who'd overseen Rusk's presidency of the
Rockefeller Foundation as a board member. Lovett assured Kennedy that Rusk
would not make policy on his own and would faithfully follow the President's
lead. But in the President's private letters to his new ambassador in India, he
repeatedly made his distress over Foggy Bottom clear, and he was delighted
when Galbraith observed to him that it was a good thing they were writing to
each other directly, because trying to communicate through the State Department was "like trying to fornicate through a mattress."

At the Senate hearings, Galbraith almost lost the posting when a conservative Republican senator interrogated him about China. "The shit hit the fan,"
he wrote later, when he mildly suggested that the United States might well
consider diplomatically recognizing China, once its government accepted the
right of Taiwan to exist independently. In the 1960s, for many on the right
wing this was an admission of virtual treason, and it earned Galbraith front-
page coverage the next morning. With some difficulty senior Democratic senators on the committee, unwilling to embarrass President Kennedy by rejecting
his nominee, were able to salvage the appointment.[56]

AMBASSADOR GALBRAITH AND his wife stepped off a plane at New Delhi's Palam
Airport on the evening of April 8, 1961. That same day, in a secret jungle camp
in sweltering eastern Guatemala, 1,400 heavily armed Cuban exiles in camou-
flage fatigues gathered for what their CIA trainers said was an important announcement. In forty-eight hours, the advisers told them, they would begin

moving to ships waiting on Nicaragua's Caribbean coast, the first step in what would be "a great, heroic struggle." This was the moment the exiles had waited, prayed, and trained for: "Operation Zapata," their invasion of Cuba, was about to begin. For the first time, some of the men were now also told they would land at a remote spot on Cuba's southern coast known as the Bay of Pigs.

A few of them, hearing of the location, were alarmed. The Bay of Pigs, they knew, was backed by a great, marshy swamp, terrible fighting terrain in the best of circumstances. They swallowed their doubts, though, when the Americans told them that top specialists in the CIA and Pentagon had chosen the spot and planned every detail of the invasion. Moreover, U.S. bombers and fighter jets would be overhead as they landed, with President Kennedy's personal blessings, and 10,000 to 15,000 crack U.S. troops would follow in a second wave, if needed.

Yet the Americans confidently said they were counting on the Cubans alone to do the job. "You will be strong, you will be getting so many people to your side that you won't have to wait for us," CIA agent Frank Bender told them. "You will go straight ahead. You will put your hands out, turn left, and go straight into Havana." The Nicaraguan dictator Luis Somoza was equally confident. When the Cubans shipped out several days later, he came to the docks. "Bring me a couple hairs from Castro's beard," he said.[57]

They didn't, of course.

Under withering fire, most of the invasion force nine days later never got past the beaches at the Bay of Pigs, and Fidel Castro's well-disciplined troops quickly rounded up the few who made it into the swamps. Cubans never rose up to greet the exiles as the CIA had promised, and the American planes meant to support the invasion never took off—on Kennedy's direct order. On the ground, the invasion of Cuba was a fiasco; it was no less so in Washington.

From New Delhi, Galbraith watched in horror as the disaster unfolded: here was exactly the sort of foreign misadventure that could derail Kennedy's presidency. President Truman had been led into a deeper and costlier war in Korea in 1950 by advisers who persuaded him to let General Douglas MacArthur advance U.N. troops to the Yalu River. It was a "mopping up" operation in a war then nearly over, he was told, but instead it brought a million Chinese soldiers streaming across the China-Korea border, prolonged the war for three more years, and ultimately cost Truman any chance of reelection. In 1960, President Eisenhower had similarly listened to advisers, chief among them the CIA chief, Allen Dulles, who'd convinced him to permit a U-2 spy plane to fly over Russia just weeks before a major U.S.-Soviet summit meeting in Paris, at which Eisenhower had hoped to cap his presidency by convincing Nikita Khrushchev to embrace a major reduction in the arms race between the U.S. and the U.S.S.R.

The scale of the Bay of Pigs disaster shocked Galbraith, but he had known about the proposed Cuban invasion before he left Washington. His old friend Chester Bowles, now Undersecretary of State but not a key decision maker in the Cuban plan, had told him about it. Deeply alarmed, Galbraith had immediately written to the President on April 3, warning him of the risks and recalling what had happened to both Truman and Eisenhower—though without mentioning Cuba by name in order not to compromise Bowles.[58] Senator J. William Fulbright had also given Kennedy arguments against invasion. In a March 23 memo, he wrote bluntly, "To give this activity even covert support is of a piece with the hypocrisy and cynicism for which the United States is constantly denouncing the Soviet Union in the United Nations and elsewhere. This point will not be lost on the rest of the world—nor on our own consciences." But the die was cast, and JFK didn't reply to Galbraith.

On April 4, however, when Kennedy met with Rusk, Robert McNamara, and the Joint Chiefs of Staff to finalize plans for the operation, the warnings must have been on his mind, because he unexpectedly invited Senator Fulbright to join the top-secret meeting. The senator delivered a blistering critique of the invasion plans, as Kennedy knew he would. According to Schlesinger, "Speaking in an emphatic and incredulous way, Fulbright denounced the whole idea. The operation, he said, was wildly out of proportion to the threat. It would compromise our moral position in the world and make it impossible for us to protest treaty violations by the Communists. He gave a brave, old-fashioned American speech, honorable, sensible and strong; and he left everyone in the room, except me and perhaps the President, wholly unmoved."

The President then asked whether, rather than invasion, infiltration of smaller groups of guerrillas might be a better alternative, clearly testing the waters. But the others reaffirmed their support for invasion. Despite his advisers' agreement, Kennedy said he wanted to give matters further thought before giving his final authorization. After Kennedy adjourned the meeting, he called Arthur Schlesinger aside to ask his off-the-record opinion; Schlesinger told him that he, too, was now opposed to invasion, especially after hearing Fulbright. The President nodded once or twice but said little.

Early the next morning, Schlesinger hastily prepared a memo arguing for continued support of anti-Castro operations but against invasion, and carried it by hand into the Oval Office. A tired-looking Kennedy pored over the document intently, then looked up and said, "You know, I've reserved the right to stop this thing up to 24 hours before the landing. In the meantime, I'm trying to make some sense out of it. We'll just have to see." But Schlesinger thought the young President was by then a prisoner of events and of the advice he was getting.

> The advocates of the adventure had a rhetorical advantage. They could strike virile poses and talk of tangible things—fire power, air strikes, landing craft and so on. To oppose the plan, one had to invoke intangibles—the moral position of the United States, the reputation of the President, the response of the United Nations, 'world public opinion' and other such odious concepts . . . I could not help feeling that the desire to prove to the CIA and the Joint

Chiefs that they were not soft-handed idealists but were really tough guys, too [influenced Kennedy's key advisers].[59]

Three weeks later, with the disaster evident to all, Galbraith in New Delhi was furious with himself for not having pressed harder—and pledged that in India at least he would curtail or end CIA covert operations. He could not wholly succeed, but they were cut back during his time in New Delhi.[60]

It took Galbraith only days to realize that although nonaligned India posed a real challenge to American foreign policy, Southeast Asia was a matter of urgent danger. He had never been to Southeast Asia and until then, like most Americans, had paid little attention to it. But India was at that point chairing the International Control Commission, a three-nation body (Canada and Poland were the other two members) that supervised the shaky armistice in Laos, which had been torn by a long-running civil war. Galbraith was supposed to keep a close watch over the ICC—and thus Laos—for the State Department. Indeed, JFK had specifically ordered Galbraith to leave early for India in anticipation of this Laotian crisis.[61]

Laos at that point barely qualified as a nation—it was more like a collection of loose tribal alliances held together by a king whose sovereignty was sketchy at best. Most Americans knew little about it or about the fighting that had been going on there for years, nor did they know much more about the two larger nations adjoining its eastern border, North and South Vietnam, still embroiled in a related conflict.

Laos, the two Vietnams, and Cambodia had once made up French Indochina, a nineteenth-century colonial construct of rubber, rice, and hardwood plantations that had collapsed in 1954 with the defeat of the French army at Dien Bien Phu at the hands of Communist nationalist insurgent forces. Few Americans knew that the U.S. government had been involved in Indochina since 1946, when President Truman agreed to let France use surplus U.S. guns, planes, and ships to restore its control there after Japan surrendered. Equally few realized that in the year leading up to France's 1954 surrender, Eisenhower had provided nearly $1 billion to Paris to prevent French defeat— or that the Joint Chiefs had seriously proposed using nuclear weapons to stop the Vietnamese rebels (Eisenhower had vetoed the proposal, fearing a second war with China just months after the Korean armistice).[62]

Having visited Indochina as a congressman in 1951 when the area was filled with an immense deployment of French troops, Kennedy had been an early critic of French policy there. After the Geneva peace accords of 1954, Washington took over Western "responsibility" for Indochina when France withdrew, but it quickly found it was having no luck in bringing peace to the region. Believing that the North Vietnamese leader, Ho Chi Minh, was a puppet of the Soviet Union—as they mistakenly imagined Mao Tse-tung was in China—the Americans began to violate the peace agreement by installing and paying for a separate anti-Communist regime based in Saigon, by blocking reunification of the two Vietnams, and by arming both South Vietnam and Laos.

Despite this, Ho Chi Minh's forces kept advancing, and now they were Kennedy's problem.

Poring through diplomatic and intelligence reports on Laos, Galbraith in New Delhi swiftly grasped that the risks of misadventure there went far beyond what had just happened in Cuba. Three weeks after the failed Cuban invasion, he sent JFK a private back-channel letter in which he realistically admitted that Laos was in danger of "falling to Communism" just as Cuba had "fallen" to Castro two years earlier. This time JFK should not so quickly let advisers persuade him that America could easily use force to change the situation.

Laos, Galbraith observed acutely, was "a jungle regime" where "the writ of government runs only as far as the airport," and it was "going to be a hideous problem for us in the months ahead."

> The rulers do not control or particularly influence their own people; and they neither have nor warrant their people's support. As a military ally the entire Laos nation is clearly inferior to a battalion of conscientious objectors from World War I. We get nothing from their support and I must say I wonder what the Communists get.

What then did Galbraith recommend that the President do?

> One answer, no doubt, is that the Communists will do a better job of organizing existing leaders out. Nevertheless I am convinced that in these primitive countries we cannot always back winners and we cannot be sure that the winners we back will stay on our side. For the same reason we should never assume that anyone is lost to the Communists.
>
> We must above all face the probability of gains and losses and certainly no single loss will be decisive. Most of all we must not allow ourselves or the country to imagine that gains or losses in these incoherent lands are the same as gains or losses in the organized world, that of France or Italy—or India.[63]

Galbraith's letter reached the President at a crucial moment. His Pentagon and national security aides had been meeting almost daily to decide whether, despite the disaster at the Bay of Pigs, to airlift 11,000 heavily armed American troops into Laos to supplement the 25,000-man Laotian Army (the entire budget of which was being paid for by Washington—making Laos the biggest per-capita recipient of U.S. aid in the world). Favoring intervention were Defense Secretary McNamara, Secretary of State Rusk, National Security Advisor Bundy, their principal deputies, and the Joint Chiefs of Staff. McNamara confidently calculated he could have an initial vanguard for the 11,000 troops moving into Laos less than a week after the order was given. The Chiefs, however, saw the 11,000 troops only as the first wave of a 60,000-man force, and urged Kennedy to use nuclear weapons if Laotian guerrillas, whose numbers were far smaller, proved resistant to this massive incursion. (Air Force Chief of

Staff Curtis LeMay had even larger goals: the President, he told the group, should be prepared to use Laos as the start of an all-out war with China.)[64]

Only Kennedy himself opposed sending U.S. troops to Laos. He'd been chastened by what had just happened in Cuba, and though he wouldn't say so, was very angry about the advice he'd gotten. His real feelings were probably expressed by his brother, during one National Security Council meeting after the Bay of Pigs, when the young Attorney General had shouted, "Goddamn all of you! You're supposed to be so bright, and you helped get the President elected, and now you've got us into this situation, and the Russians will think we're a paper tiger!"[65] Right after the Bay of Pigs, when Richard Nixon had urged on him a full-fledged U.S. invasion of Cuba—and intervention in Laos—Kennedy had replied, "I just don't think we ought to get involved in Laos, particularly where we might find ourselves fighting millions of Chinese troops in the jungle."[66]

Just before Galbraith's letter reached him, Kennedy held up his advisers' invasion plans because the warring Laotian factions and their backers had agreed to a cease-fire negotiated under intense pressure from the International Control Commission, chaired by India. (India was joined in its efforts by Great Britain and by Averell Harriman, who as Kennedy's ambassador-at-large in Geneva, representing the United States at the ICC, also sought to avoid intervention.) Indeed, Galbraith's letter also reported on his discussions with Prime Minister Nehru and the Indian government to help negotiate the cease-fire.[67]

WALTER HELLER AND his colleagues on the Council of Economic Advisors were, not by accident, unaware of the debate over an invasion of Laos as they pored over budget figures for fiscal 1962 and tried to estimate economic growth. Their ignorance of crucial foreign-policy debates was fundamental to the structure of the administration: the Council of Economic Advisors worked in isolation from the National Security Council, and it does not seem to have occurred to anyone that this was a problem.*

Fifteen years earlier Leon Keyserling had considered it the CEA's duty to be involved in the shaping and defining of America's military expenditures and of integrating them into planning for domestic economic growth. But under Eisenhower, the CEA chairman, Arthur Burns, had constructed an impermeable wall between White House economists and the armed forces. The Pentagon's ever-growing budget was not subject to CEA discussion or critique.

Kennedy's economists prided themselves on being "political," but they weren't so in a geopolitical sense, nor were they experienced veterans of Washington infighting, as Galbraith was. (James Tobin had been quite frank when JFK first interviewed him: "I'm afraid I'm only an ivory-tower economist."

---

*Of course, Heller spoke informally with NSC aides such as the Harvard economist Carl Kaysen. But CEA records and Heller's files at the Kennedy Library show little sign of detailed knowledge of the planning process prior to U.S. foreign-policy actions being taken. Theodore Sorensen, in an interview with the author, confirmed that the two groups had no regular direct interaction, and Heller acknowledged the same in a memo to LBJ's aide Jack Valenti in 1965.

Kennedy disarmingly replied, "That is the best kind. I'm only an ivory-tower President.") What they meant by "political" was that they gradually learned how to lobby in the administration for their policies and viewpoints, and how to help lobby both Congress and the press when the President chose to proceed on an issue within their area of expertise and responsibility. (Heller frequently did so, as one economist noted, by "seeking public support for deficit spending by invoking not John Maynard Keynes but Henry Ford II and [IBM chairman] Thomas Watson, Jr.") But in the larger context of Cold War politics, the "New Economists" were supremely *un*political. Cut off from foreign policy and military strategy debates, they lacked what really counts in Washington: the political ability to influence those commitments *before* they began shaping (however ominously) the very economy the economists proudly planned to manage for optimum growth. Heller acknowledged later, "When [JFK] was involved in [foreign crises such as] the Bay of Pigs, I might not see him for three weeks."[68]

Ironically, Galbraith, in distant New Delhi, was in the opposite position. He had held more senior government posts than they (Heller and Tobin—like Gardner Ackley, who succeeded Heller under Lyndon Johnson—had worked as junior economists in the Office of Price Administration), and he had intimate and regular epistolary contact with the President as well as with White House and State Department aides such as Schlesinger, Harriman, Ball, and Bowles. He saw the future of Keynesian policies on the New Frontier with a quite different eye than Heller.[69]

In July 1961, Galbraith wrote to Kennedy of his latest concern in Southeast Asia:

> South Viet Nam is exceedingly bad. I hope, incidentally, that your information from there is good [as] I have an uneasy feeling that what comes in regular channels is very bad. Unless I am mistaken [South Vietnamese President Ngo Dinh] Diem has alienated his people to a far greater extent than we allow ourselves to know.
>
> This is our old mistake. We take the ruler's word and that of our own people who have become committed to him. The opponents are thieves and bandits; the problem is to get the police. I am sure the problem in Viet Nam is partly the means to preserve law and order. But I fear that we have one more government which, on present form, no one will support.[70]

Once again, Galbraith had shrewdly grasped the pressures Kennedy was under and the risks he faced. The unstable Laotian armistice of May had kept Kennedy from ordering a massive U.S. incursion into Indochina for the moment, but the State and Defense departments and the Joint Chiefs of Staff were still convinced that American diplomacy would have to give way to American military force in Southeast Asia.

Only the month before, Kennedy had returned from his first summit meeting with Nikita Khrushchev, in Vienna, and Galbraith became even more convinced that the immense costs of the Cold War posed even graver dangers than he had hitherto thought. Within the White House, one group of advisers was debating foreign-policy actions without considering their domestic economic effects; a few doors away, talented economists were constructing economic growth plans that took no account of what Galbraith called the "culture of foreign misadventure"—either the enormous size of the military budget and its particular stimulative effects, or the domestic economic risks posed by a costly commitment of U.S. resources abroad. To Galbraith, this was the worst kind of folly.

Khrushchev, confident that the inexperienced JFK could be bullied, had savagely berated him, demanding that all Allied troops be withdrawn from Berlin and darkly threatening "firm measures" if they weren't. Kennedy had been shaken, and to show his resolve, he put the armed forces on alert, mobilized the reserves, and announced that the government would spend an unbudgeted extra $3.2 billion on military outlays, including 200,000 new troops. This came as a complete shock to Heller and the CEA, but it was mild compared to his dismay when Kennedy then laid plans for a $3 billion tax increase to pay for the spending. With the nation just pulling out of recession, Heller feared the tax would jeopardize any chance for quick recovery. He and Samuelson eventually persuaded Kennedy not to seek the increase but accepted that, as a trade-off, they would aim to have the budget in balance in 1962.[71]

In a nationwide television address Kennedy warned that he would not permit the Communists "to drive us out of Berlin, either gradually or by force." To underscore his determination, he called for a massive construction program of fallout shelters, and told the country that "if war breaks out, it will have been started in Moscow and not Berlin." Overnight, to millions of ordinary citizens, the United States seemed closer to nuclear war than at any time since 1945. When the Soviet Union began to construct the Berlin Wall in mid-August, Kennedy called General Lucius Clay out of retirement, and Clay prepared for a second Berlin Airlift. The East Germans briefly held a U.S. diplomat, so Clay sent American tanks to Checkpoint Charlie—and the Russians responded in kind. For a few hours, war seemed imminent, until the diplomat was released.* By late summer the crisis in Germany eased—others would develop soon enough—but the unexpected $3.2 billion in new military spending stayed, twice as much as all the new stimulative measures the administration undertook that year for unemployment, housing, and public-sector construction.

Vice President Johnson was sent on a tour of Asia meant to reassure American allies of U.S. commitments to them. Stopping in Saigon, he passionately reaffirmed America's commitment to Vietnam's "freedom," and incautiously pronounced President Diem "the Winston Churchill of south Asia." From Vietnam, Johnson came to India, where Galbraith raised with him his concerns

---

*Clay in the crisis proved as shrewd a judge of the Soviets as he had been in 1946. "These were Russian tanks, not East German tanks," he later remembered. "It was obvious that the Russians did not trust the East Germans in this situation. As soon as they did that, I was no longer concerned. The Russians had come out of hiding, and I was sure they were not going to do anything" (Smith, *Lucius D. Clay*, 660).

about Laos, but LBJ proved more interested in speech making and hand shaking with the locals than in discussing Laos with Galbraith. Galbraith arranged a visit with Nehru, where LBJ and the prime minister "spoke rather formally on education which they favored, peace which they wanted and the Third Five-Year Plan which they praised. The rest of us listened with respect and drank tea." Johnson did let out a memorable Texas "yee-hah" at the Taj Mahal; the trip's diplomatic achievements were less remembered.[72]

Galbraith drew no comfort from Johnson's militant hyperbole, and was further shaken that fall when he found out that the Pentagon and the President's civilian advisers were now pressing Kennedy to send 40,000 U.S. troops to Vietnam. Kennedy was resisting, eager to find a way to negotiate his way out of what he called this "dangerous mess." But in Washington, none of his top advisers were offering him the policy options he wanted.[73]

Galbraith, however—hopeful that he could win Kennedy to a more robust domestic expansion program than the CEA advocated and simultaneously persuade him to reduce the risk of further costly and dangerous commitments abroad—was already laying out for the President his own sophisticated synthesis of foreign, domestic, and economic policies.[74]

To begin with, Galbraith placed greater emphasis on solving structural deficiencies in the American economy than on simply increasing aggregate growth per se.[75] He was following the arguments he had developed in *The Affluent Society*, especially those concerning the "social imbalance" between "private affluence" and "public poverty." He colorfully (and, to economists, heretically) reminded Kennedy that the idea of aggregate economic growth

> is extremely important to economists and about two thousand other people in all the land. This enlightened minority knows that growth is really important. The rest can't remember whether the growth rate is three per cent, six per cent or ten per cent. And instinct tells them that the expanding element in Gross National Product doesn't include the really vital things like food, clothing or fornication which are already excessively available. Nor does it include medical care, schools, or unemployment compensation which they do want but which they know requires some legislation by what Billy Graham once called the Christ-bitten Congress.

Complimenting Kennedy on a recent speech on economic policy, Galbraith added,

> I couldn't help noticing that immediately after you got through with the charts you got down to child, medical and unemployment care. This is the old political instinct at work. With the principal exception of housing, growth adds the least essential (and most superfluous) privately-produced goods since we naturally provide ourselves with the most important things first. Needless to say, the addition of more and better depilatories has nothing to do with national health and vigor.[76]

Galbraith also stressed the need to do something about poverty, a problem whose solution required significant, targeted government aid and investment, since it had so far shown itself immune to reduction by aggregate growth, especially in inner cities and regions like Appalachia. In an early memo to the President, he had urged him to propose a "Special Assistance Act of 1961, a bill that would include supplementary aid for families of the unemployed; emergency grants and loans targeted to areas with chronic unemployment; a system of grants or low-interest loans for unemployed families to fix up their homes; and a youth conservation corps for unemployed teenagers."[77] The bill was never introduced, but Kennedy did add $215 million for supplementary family aid, $40 million for area redevelopment, and $10 million for low-income and rural housing to his first budget.

Second, Galbraith declared himself suspicious of tax cuts as a stratagem for stimulating economic growth, though he knew Heller was eager to try them. "Once we start talking about tax cuts we will take the pressure off the rest of your program . . . We now say that housing, school building and urban renewal are needed both for themselves and for their effect on employment. Given the tax cut conservatives will not be slow to say that this will do the job." Nominal tax rates might appear burdensome—and certainly conservatives always bewailed them as oppressive, especially the 91 percent top marginal rate on incomes, unrevised since World War II. Yet, he pointed out, the top nominal rates were fictitious: the system was so riddled with loopholes that no one paid anything like those rates. Better that a Democratic administration increase federal domestic spending—deficit spending, if need be—targeted where it was needed most and investing in schools, hospitals, and roads, where the federal government spent too little, especially in comparison to its spending on defense.[78]

Third, Galbraith argued that monetary policy should be used to lower both long- and short-term interest rates, in order to reduce consumer credit and mortgage costs. This was in opposition to the CEA's and Treasury's view that short-term rates needed to stay high to encourage foreign depositors.

Fourth, concerning America's international balance of payments, and the related question of increased U.S. gold outflows, Galbraith argued for a strategy of what amounted to "benign neglect." Giving them a high priority would constrain the President's abilities to act purposefully in the domestic economy, he argued.[79]

Galbraith had been alarmed when he heard Kennedy suddenly assert, just before the election, that a Democratic White House would vigorously defend the dollar against foreign demands for payment in gold from Fort Knox. Though hardly a compelling issue to most voters, the nation's balance-of-payment deficits and the resulting drain on U.S. gold supplies were of great concern to economists, bankers, and Treasury and trade officials. To Galbraith, they risked braking any robustly Keynesian domestic program, just as the Pentagon's immense budget did. He warned Kennedy against being caught in a trap. "We should be concerned but not alarmed," and should concentrate instead on growing the domestic economy.[80] In the $500-billion-plus American economy, after all, the balance-of-payments deficit amounted to barely $3 billion—a fraction of 1 percent of total GNP. Conservatives would try to use the issue to attack Democratic expansion plans, of course, but any instinct to cut back should be resisted. He reminded Kennedy that Franklin Roosevelt had been similarly persuaded to believe there was a "gold crisis" when he was fresh in office in 1933, and had vainly wasted precious time and political resources on it—and he had faced a much greater problem than Kennedy in 1960. Better politically and economically to blame the gold problem on Republican policy under Eisenhower and carry out a Keynesian program at home.

Two weeks after the election, he warned Kennedy again not to emphasize the issue—and especially not to let opponents or well-meaning but cautious advisers use it to trim back domestic expansion plans. The better alternative was to focus on cutting overseas troop commitments and increasing exports to reduce the payments deficit. At home, he advised, Kennedy should close tax loopholes, install a wage-price policy, encourage productivity advances, and use federal farm payments to strengthen U.S. agricultural sales overseas. At the same time he should advocate support for a European Common Market and a similar structure in Latin America. Most important, he should recommend closer multilateral central-bank cooperation (as Keynes had envisioned at Bretton Woods in 1944) to combat pressure for higher interest rates as the means to control inflation as well as trading imbalances.[81]

Kennedy responded enthusiastically, asking Galbraith for details on wage-price guidelines and advice on setting up a task force to reform U.S. tax policies, including who should serve on it. Significantly, however, he didn't respond to Galbraith's concerns about the gold issue.

Finally, Galbraith emphasized that no attempt to improve the domestic economy could succeed unless there were more stable relations with the Soviet Union. "New Economists" too often acted as if they thought of growth as growth and government stimulus as government stimulus; in their forecasting models, building a missile silo was the same as building a school in dollar and GDP terms, opening a naval base the same as opening a new park. And their theoretical neglect of foreign policy spilled over in practical terms. In the nearly 400 memoranda it sent to JFK, the CEA never highlighted nor evaluated differences in the composition or end purposes of federal spending, or the economic trade-offs and aggregate implications of military spending. These were theoretical and practical limits that Galbraith was unwilling to accept. But he knew that his influence on Kennedy had its limits, that Kennedy heard competing advice and was subjected to the pressures of prevailing opinion.

In June 1961, on his first return trip from India, Galbraith discussed all these points and issues with Kennedy—occasionally in some unusual locations. Once, Galbraith found himself briefing Kennedy in the White House family quarters as the President took a bath, now and then interrupting their conversation to adjust the hot-water tap with his foot. On another occasion, this time in the President's bedroom, he and the President, along with Dillon, Heller, and a few others, skillfully pressured Fed Chairman Martin into foregoing an interest-rate hike.[82]

AS THE ADMINISTRATION lurched from one dramatic foreign crisis to another its first year—from the Bay of Pigs to Laos, from the Congo to the Vienna Summit, and Berlin—Galbraith realized more and more how closely the domestic economic agenda was linked to the country's foreign policies. This meant that at every turn he needed to encourage the President to resist advisers who favored costly military engagements and foreign economic policies that subordinated Keynesian interests at home.

Galbraith returned again to Washington in early November 1961, in order to accompany Prime Minister Jawaharlal Nehru of India on an official state visit. After barely six months in New Delhi, he had already forged a close friendship with Nehru, both men being "much too intelligent and sophisticated to let diplomatic differences undermine their mutual personal admiration," as Nehru's biographer later wrote.[83] But Galbraith's closeness to the Indian leader and his easy, independent access to President Kennedy were a constant source of worry—and no small consternation—for State Department bureaucrats. For example, as part of Nehru's visit Galbraith decided the two leaders might enjoy a relaxed private conversation somewhere outside Washington before taking up their official meetings. He arranged for Hammersmith Farm, the Newport, Rhode Island, estate of Jacqueline Kennedy's mother and stepfather, to be the locale—and then didn't bother to include anyone from the State Department on the guest list. A flurry of anxious, envious interoffice memos discussed "what Galbraith was really up to."

There were reasons for State's bureaucrats to worry. On November 6, over a lengthy, intimate luncheon at the estate, Kennedy and Galbraith pressed Nehru and his foreign minister, J. M. Desai, to take active leadership to neutralize the situation in Vietnam. This was a foray that Galbraith knew Secretary of State Rusk would not approve. Using the talking points Galbraith had given Kennedy, the President urged Nehru and Desai to talk directly with Ho Chi Minh, to support a U.N. observer corps in Vietnam, to strengthen the International Control Commission, even—this was a proposal from Chester Bowles— to help create a "belt of neutrality" girdling Southeast Asia.[84] Nehru listened carefully but "was not responsive," Galbraith wrote later, "partly because our ideas on how to bring the Viet Cong insurrection to an end were far from precise."[85] Nehru was clear on one thing, though: "We should not send in soldiers."[86] Galbraith went to bed that evening determined to keep doing what he could to dampen the smoldering embers he feared might burst forth into a consuming war in Southeast Asia.

In Washington the next day, there were several hours of formal talks with Nehru and Kennedy in the Oval Office joined this time by Rusk, Assistant Secretary of State Phillips Talbot, and the National Security Council deputy chief, Walt W. Rostow. The talks didn't go well, for Nehru showed no sign of being willing to back U.S. policy, and immediately afterward Kennedy talked privately with Galbraith about what to do next. Galbraith quickly headed for Rostow's office.

Rostow and Galbraith had known each other since 1946, when they worked together as two of "Clayton's men" at the State Department. They had agreed then that a prolonged military struggle with the Soviet Union was inadvisable, but in the intervening years Rostow's attitude toward the Communist world had hardened dramatically. A brisk, owlish, Yale-trained economic historian, Rostow had joined the economics department at MIT in 1950. During the 1950s—although they saw each other socially, shared a common interest in Indian economic development, and served as Kennedy advisers—the two men had gone in very different directions. In Rostow's case, his policy shift fit well with work being done by other MIT economists. MIT's president, James Killian, was eager to build his economics department around Samuelson into a world-class faculty, on the level of its science and engineering departments. As part of his strategy, he had created the Center for International Studies, an interdisciplinary research program led by economists but including other social scientists. To fund it, he relied not only on conventional sources such as the Ford Foundation but also (a decision he later came to regret) on secret and quite lucrative research and consulting contracts with the newly formed Central Intelligence Agency.[87]

At CENIS, Rostow began work under a CIA grant on his famous theory about the stages of economic growth. Through his research, he was introduced to the problems of Southeast Asia, and soon was advising Nelson Rockefeller and the Eisenhower administration on covert action as well as economic development policies. Gradually he synthesized a near-seamless Cold War vision of Third World economic and political development coupled with a tough-as-nails anti-Communism predicated on using counterinsurgency forces as freely as aid dollars. In 1961, as deputy director of Kennedy's National Security Council, Rostow saw his job as applying the lessons he'd learned, and South Vietnam was the perfect laboratory.[88]

Rostow's closest ally at the White House was the retired general Maxwell Taylor. Taylor, a former Army chief of staff, was President Kennedy's personal military adviser, a handsome, self-confident former paratrooper who'd chafed during the Eisenhower years over the vast amounts of money that had flowed to the Air Force and Navy and the neglect (in his view) of the country's ground forces. The Defense Department's emphasis on "more bang for the buck"— and thus the intensive funding of the Strategic Air Command and the Air Force's and Navy's long-range missile programs—had left the Army resentful of what it felt amounted to garrison duty in Europe, Japan, and South Korea. Taylor believed that replacing the Eisenhower era's so-called New Look doctrine of massive nuclear retaliation with a multilevel strategy of "flexible response" would allow the United States to fight two large and one small war simultaneously, with heavy emphasis on the Army rather than on missiles and bombers.[89]

Rostow shared Taylor's belief in "flexible response" as America's new war-fighting doctrine, and both in turn were enamored of the Army's top specialist in "unconventional warfare," General Edward Lansdale. Lansdale's success in the 1950s in helping suppress the Communist-inspired Huk rebellion in the Philippines had convinced Rostow and Taylor that South Vietnam was the next place to utilize Lansdale's counterinsurgency skills in the global war against Communism.[90] Lansdale's analysis of "the Vietnam question" was completed shortly before Kennedy took office, and the Army passed it on to Rostow. After reading it—and already convinced that Vietnam and Laos were "the most dangerous challenge" the West had faced since World War II—Rostow arranged an Oval Office meeting a week after the President took office. There, he, Rusk, and Lansdale laid out the "crisis."

Kennedy expressed interest in the possible use of U.S. Special Forces to train the Vietnamese in counterinsurgency techniques and perhaps in sending Lansdale as ambassador to Saigon; but he perspicaciously scoffed at the idea that paying for a bigger army for President Diem would make much difference, and he ignored the arguments favoring the introduction of U.S. combat troops. After their meeting, Rostow and Lansdale found themselves temporarily isolated. The Joint Chiefs weren't keen to send Green Berets to Asia, State vetoed Lansdale as ambassador, fearing he was "a lone wolf operator," and President Diem ignored Lansdale's ideas for reforming the South Vietnamese army.

But the crisis in Laos in April and May, and then the Berlin crisis over the summer reignited Rostow's effort to focus the White House on Vietnam. When Kennedy in May rejected his advisers' call for 60,000 U.S. troops (and possible use of atomic weapons) in Laos, he had given way slightly on Vietnam, ostensibly to help control cross-border incursions by Communist troops. He approved American bankrolling of an additional division for the South Vietnamese army, and agreed to send a few hundred U.S. soldiers to Saigon for training purposes, but the Pentagon's proposal to insert a U.S. division in Vietnam, along with naval and air units, went nowhere.

By September, Diem was asking for money for 100,000 new troops, the new U.S. ambassador in Saigon, Frederick Nolting (fresh from NATO), was supporting the request, and McNamara increasingly now saw Vietnam as "a laboratory for the development and procedures for the conduct of sub-limited war," a cornerstone of Taylor's flexible response doctrine. (Air Force General Curtis LeMay was equally enthusiastic, hoping to test out his newly created "Jungle Jim" system of heavily armed tactical air support for counterinsurgency.) With McGeorge Bundy warning him against any "appeasement" of the Soviet Union over Berlin, Kennedy finally approved Rostow's oft-repeated request to send Maxwell Taylor, Lansdale, and him to Saigon to "review U.S. options." But the President was apprehensive, knowing what they'd likely propose on return: Rostow by then wanted JFK to create a new Truman Doctrine for Southeast Asia.[91]

Galbraith meanwhile was lobbying the President as hard as Rostow to go in the opposite direction. He'd written Kennedy six pointed memos since April on policy in Southeast Asia, and on both his return trips to Washington, he had met with the President to discuss these concerns. He'd also talked at length with Chester Bowles and George Ball, and he'd talked with Harriman in Geneva; all were as worried as he about the direction the President's closest advisers wanted to go in Saigon.[92]

Galbraith had noted in June that "the fundamental division in American policy is coming to be over foreign policy," with those opposed to armed intervention "under suspicion of being appeasers." In August, he'd had a long conversation with Bowles in New Delhi, during which "I was admirably instructed on what I already knew, didn't believe or couldn't remember," as he told the President. "He thinks he has aroused bureaucratic enmities by firing too many people; I said it was my impression he had aroused yours by not firing enough . . . Chet promised to do his best but says he is boxed in. In government people get boxed only when they won't kick their way out." He added, "If the State Department drives you crazy you might calm yourself by contemplating its effect on me. The other night I awoke with a blissful feeling and discovered I had been dreaming that the whole Goddamn place had burned down. I dozed off again hoping for a headline saying no survivors."[93]

By early October, Galbraith was more worried about Vietnam than Berlin, having read a State Department cable indicating that Diem now wanted a U.S.-Vietnamese defense treaty, a virtual guarantee of U.S. intervention. After his friend Jerome Wiesner, JFK's science adviser, arrived in New Delhi and described the advice the President was getting, Galbraith cabled the President again about the impending Taylor mission.

> Dear Mr. President:
> I keep seeing stories that we are to have a serious review of foreign policy. Men of wisdom will applaud this. When things are not good, it is usually imagined that a review, or possibly a reorganization, will make them better. No one ever asks whether the best is being made of a lousy situation . . . However, a good review will create a lot of needed employment for the State Department.

But obviously bureaucratic reviews seldom got to the heart of real problems:

> Foreign policy, like domestic policy, is a reflection of the fundamental instincts of those who make it. All of us have been reared with the same instincts, more or less—that we should combine courage with compassion, suspect pompous or heroic stances, respect our capacity to negotiate, refuse to be pushed and seek solutions in social stability rather than military prowess.

He then connected the risks foreign intervention posed for Kennedy, American liberalism, and a successful liberal Keynesianism—the threads that bound together his own views.

I do worry a good deal about the domestic political position in which our foreign policy will be placing us. Ahead of us, in fact, are the same difficulties that beset the Truman Era. The right, in the United States, will always criticize reasonableness as softness. To be sensible is to appease. And to knock the Soviets or the Chicoms [Chinese Communists] into the gutter is not the least bit warlike. It is the only thing they understand and respect. Democrats are warlike because they are weak-kneed.

The Truman Administration never developed a way of dealing with this dialectic. Sometimes it brought Republicans, including Dulles, into the Administration with the hope that this would blunt the attack. Sometimes it tried to show that it could talk as pugnaciously as the Republicans. Neither worked.

The answer, I am sure, is to pin the label of warrior firmly on these goons. This is not an emotional reaction but a sound political tactic to which they are vulnerable. When they speak of total victory they invite total annihilation. They aren't brave but suicidal. There is a curious superficial pugnacity about the American people which, I am persuaded, does not go very deep. They applaud the noisy man but they reconsider if they think him dangerous. We must, I feel, make it clear that these men are dangerous. They survive because we have let them have the best of both worlds: they could appeal to the pugnacity as a defender of the peace.

Then, in a paragraph that can only chill the heart of any American who lived through the years that lay ahead, he told the young President,

Although at times I have been rather troubled by Berlin, I have always had the feeling that it would be worked out. I have continued to worry far, far more about South Viet Nam. This is more complex, far less controllable, far more varied in the factors involved, far more susceptible to misunderstanding. And to make matters worse, I have no real confidence in the sophistication and political judgment of our people there. Harriman, incidentally, shares my view.[94]

This was advice that Kennedy was getting from almost no one else in his administration. (The three exceptions—whose directness hardly matched Galbraith's—were Chester Bowles, George Ball, and as the cable notes, Averell Harriman. All of them were longtime friends of Galbraith's.)

Galbraith's October cable reached Kennedy's desk just as the President formally authorized Taylor to go to Vietnam. Two days later, JFK unexpectedly sent Taylor amended instructions: he and his team were no longer to "evaluate what could be accomplished by the introduction of SEATO or United States forces into South Vietnam" (as the President's original instructions, written by Taylor for JFK, had said), but simply to survey "courses of action which our Government might take to avoid a further deterioration in South Vietnam." Making himself perfectly clear, the President added, "You should bear in mind that the initial responsibility for the effective maintenance of South Vietnam rests with the people and government of that country. Our efforts must be evaluated and your recommendations formulated, with that in mind." Political, economic, and social factors were "equally significant" to military ones. Kennedy was boxed in by his advisers, but he was kicking back.[95]

As luck would have it, when Galbraith arrived in Washington on November 1 to prepare for the Nehru visit Rostow had just returned from Vietnam, an intensive review of the "Taylor report" was getting under way before it went to Kennedy.[96] Galbraith knew he needed to talk to Rostow as soon as possible— and says the first White House meeting with Nehru six days later provided the perfect opening. Galbraith went to Rostow's office that afternoon, and after initially chatting about Nehru's visit, turned the conversation to Taylor's mission. What had Rostow learned in Vietnam? What sorts of recommendations would he and Taylor make to the President? After seeing the situation at first hand, were they now urging caution or greater commitment?

Rostow said he was reluctant to talk about the group's findings because Kennedy himself hadn't yet seen the report, and because it was so heavily classified, Galbraith wryly recalled, as "to limit access to God and the President of the United States; specifically excluded were the other members of the Trinity." But Rostow gestured to a pile of memos on his desk where the Taylor report sat in plain view. Galbraith asked to see it; Rostow demurred. Then the phone rang. When Rostow momentarily turned to it, Galbraith instantly decided what to do. "My authorized access as an ambassador being equal to that of the authors of the report, I simply picked up the copy and walked out."[97] For whatever reasons,* Rostow did not stop him—and Galbraith left the White House with the Taylor report tucked under his arm. Rushing to his room at the Hay-Adams Hotel, he began to read—and was soon appalled. After glancing through just the first few pages, he began furiously scribbling notes on a legal pad. Here, he realized, were outlines for what could become America's next great war.

Taylor and Rostow were calling for the initial dispatch of 8,000 to 10,000 American troops in the guise of "flood relief workers." Covert operations, cooperation between the CIA and Vietnamese intelligence, and U.S. training of South Vietnamese soldiers were all to be "radically increased." Toxic herbicides—including a compound called Agent Orange, which Galbraith had never heard of and which Dean Rusk was shortly to describe to Kennedy as a benign "weed killer"—were to be used for the first time to defoliate vast swaths of jungle.†[98] U.S. helicopters and light aircraft squadrons, manned by uni-

---

*With the press office nearby, one deterrent to stopping Galbraith is obvious. Rostow could not have welcomed the headline "Ambassador Arrested at White House; Top-Secret Document Theft Charged."

†Rusk told the President reassuringly that defoliants didn't violate international bans on chemical weapons, and remarked that the British had used them against Malaysian insurgents in the 1950s. Yet Rusk knew how explosive the plan was: His deputy, U. Alexis Johnson, had warned him that "the key is not making this an operation in itself . . . We must also stay away from the term 'chemical warfare' and any connection with the [Army's] Chemical Corps, and rather talk about 'weed killers'. Defense and the Chemical Corps entirely agree on this." Rusk removed these comments before sending the memo to the President.

formed American personnel, were to be sent out in support of what would henceforth be South Vietnamese operations jointly planned with the Americans. U.S. air and naval forces were to prepare for direct but unspecified "harassment" of North Vietnam itself.

Whatever the cautionary proscriptions and initial limits and caveats the report contained, here was the rationale for an open-ended American commitment to military engagement in Southeast Asia. But Galbraith had already let the President know his own views on this folly, and even before going to Newport with Prime Minister Nehru, Kennedy had read his memo, which, presciently, functioned as a point-by-point reply to the Taylor report.

On November 1, Galbraith had met with George Ball. By then Ball had read the first draft of the Taylor report, and he may well have outlined it to Galbraith at lunch. Later that afternoon, President Kennedy met with Galbraith and former President Truman. During that meeting, Bowles came in with two other State Department officials who were both hardliners on Vietnam, U. Alexis Johnson and Walter McConaughy, to discuss Laos, where ongoing negotiations to neutralize the country were at their end point.

Harriman, as the U.S. negotiator, wanted a peace accord, which would cut off State's and Defense's continuing eagerness for troops, but the Soviet Union was insisting that International Control Commission reports of future accord violations should be unanimous, which meant that its satellite Poland would have veto power over them. Rusk favored rejecting the accord if necessary, and he needed Kennedy's instructions. Picking up the phone, the President called and awakened Harriman in Geneva at midnight. Assured by Harriman that India and Canada could always publish any minority view on the ICC, Kennedy told the delegation from State that he was going to support Harriman, but he did this with "such tact," Galbraith recalled, "that I doubt they knew."

Having rescued the Laos accord from collapse, Kennedy called Galbraith aside when the group adjourned. The Taylor mission was due to see him in just forty-eight hours; Kennedy asked Galbraith how quickly he could produce a memo of his opinions on Vietnam. This became the memo Galbraith provided two days later, which mentions "the Taylor Commission [*sic*] and some of the accompanying press accounts," but doesn't indicate Galbraith had yet seen the actual report.

"The situation in South Vietnam is perilously close to the point of no return," Galbraith wrote. "Serious thought is being given to a military operation in South Vietnam which would entail all the risks of the operation in Korea ten years ago, without the justification of a surprise attack across the boundary, without the support of the United Nations, and without a population determined to fight for independence." To prevent such a disaster, Galbraith thought the President should initiate a program that would end the fighting, yield a neutral and democratic Vietnam, and put a U.N. presence in place to supervise the peace.

To that end, he told Kennedy he should promptly replace Ambassador Nolting with Ambassador Harriman or George McGhee in Saigon, persuade the U.N. to dispatch observers there immediately, put the few U.S. military advisers already in Vietnam since the Eisenhower days under U.N. command, and open talks with the Soviet Union to help stop the fighting. Thereafter, Galbraith urged negotiations on renewed trade between Hanoi and Saigon, reciprocal diplomatic relations, and major U.S. economic assistance to U.N.-supervised reconstruction. These actions would avoid "the high risk and limited promise of armed intervention," but would also help greatly to contain Soviet and Chinese influence in Southeast Asia.[99]

KENNEDY READ GALBRAITH'S memo immediately—and was apparently impressed, for he supported a number of the points during his subsequent talks with Nehru. But at an interdepartmental meeting on November 4, called to discuss the Taylor report the day after it was given to the President, Secretary of Defense McNamara lobbied hard for readying not just 8,000 to 10,000 men for Vietnam duty but six to eight Army *divisions*—roughly 220,000 troops, he estimated. In support of McNamara, Assistant Secretary of Defense William Bundy (an older brother of National Security Adviser McGeorge Bundy) invoked what came to be called "the domino theory," declaring that if Vietnam "fell to the Communists" it would lead to the fall of all of Southeast Asia, "right down to Indonesia." "The strategic implications worldwide," he gravely asserted, "would be extremely serious."[100]

But the group knew that convincing Kennedy of their views would not be easy. As Taylor cautioned them, the President was still "instinctively against introduction of U.S. forces."[101] And when they discovered that Galbraith not only knew the details of the Taylor report but was pressing the President to resist its recommendations, they were livid. It was a breach of the secrecy in which they'd tried to wrap the report, yet Galbraith's relations with Kennedy meant that nothing would happen to him. They were in a bind.

But Kennedy was in a much more terrible bind. On the one hand, his own instincts, not to mention his fresh memories of the Bay of Pigs and the Pentagon's eagerness to invade Laos, told him to hesitate; on the other, he was once again under near-uniform pressure from his national security advisers, who were arguing that anything less than a major engagement in Vietnam would risk disastrous consequences.* First the one, then the other delayed on November 7 and 8 the formal White House meeting meant to review the Taylor report and decide on a course of action. The President meanwhile started leaking word to the press that he opposed sending troops to Asia: articles by Arthur Krock, James Reston, and others suddenly carried news "from senior White

---

*After reading the Taylor report Kennedy compared, to Schlesinger, the troop commitments that Taylor and the others wanted with an alcoholic's need for drink. "'They say it's necessary in order to restore confidence and maintain morale. But it will be just like Berlin. The troops will march in; the bands will play; the crowds will cheer; and in four days everyone will have forgotten. Then we will be told we have to send in more troops. It's like taking a drink. The effect wears off, and you have to take another.' The war in Vietnam, he added, could be won only so long as it was their war. If it were ever converted into a white man's war, we would lose as the French had lost a decade earlier" (*Thousand Days*, 505).

House officials" expressing these views. As one *Times* front-page headline put it, "Kennedy Remains Opposed to Sending Forces after Hearing Report."[102] His advisers meanwhile drafted and redrafted the top-secret National Security Action Memorandum in which he would set forth his directive for action on Vietnam, trying to gauge just how much they could get the President to agree to, and thrashing out remaining disagreements among themselves.

They also lobbied the President relentlessly to take up arms. On November 8, McNamara sent his own top-secret memo to Kennedy, upping the ante from Taylor's proposal for 8,000 to 10,000 men to 205,000 (a slight revision down from his earlier estimates). In the memo, McNamara carefully deleted a paragraph in his draft version that had told Kennedy he needn't commit all six divisions immediately; now he said that two divisions should be sent almost at once. Even so, he added, with these 70,000 men, there was still only a fifty-fifty chance of success. In short, if the United States wasn't willing to make a massive troop commitment, it should expect to lose Southeast Asia to Communism. (Kennedy read the same message in a separate joint memo from McNamara, Rusk, and the Chiefs the next day. Taylor, it turns out, was coordinating these various drafts behind the scene.)

Also on November 8, after a small dinner party that President and Mrs. Kennedy gave in the White House family quarters to honor Galbraith and the British ambassador, David Ormsby-Gore, JFK and Galbraith talked about Vietnam and India. Kennedy had gotten the proposal for 205,000 troops that afternoon. Galbraith offered to stop over in Saigon on his way back to India, and Kennedy accepted at once. They had talked almost incessantly about Vietnam for more than a week—on October 31, November 1, 5, 6, 7, and at 2 a.m. that very morning, when Kennedy had telephoned—and they would talk again the next day.

At noon on Saturday, November 11—eight days after JFK was formally given the Taylor report—the President and his National Security Council finally sat down together in the Oval Office.[103] That morning Rostow had given JFK a memo on what the President's advisers would recommend; he pleaded for the largest possible U.S. intervention not only in South Vietnam but in North Vietnam as well. After reading the memo, an alarmed Kennedy sat down and hastily scribbled out a list of questions in anticipation of the noon meeting:

1. Will this program be effective without including the introduction of a U.S. troop task force?
2. What reasons shall we give Diem for not acceding to his request for U.S. troops?
3. Under what circumstances would we reconsider our decision on troops?[104]

This was not a President ready to take up American arms in Southeast Asia, and the others knew it. So when Rusk presented their consensus view—in essence embodying the core recommendations of the Taylor report—he hedged in such a way as to make the President feel he was being given a string of distinct options and exit points along the policy path.

Over the next two hours, Kennedy remained aloof, as members of the group commented, one by one, on Rusk's presentation. But their plan broke apart when Robert Kennedy kept insisting, "We are not sending combat troops. Not committing ourselves to combat troops," and the President himself then refused to accept Rusk's advice that he formally declare "saving Vietnam" as a stated national policy goal. "Troops," JFK coldly told his advisers, "are a last resort." And if they were ever to be sent, he added, he wanted them to be a multilateral force, not U.S. troops alone.

After more discussion, during which his aides kept pressing on him the need at least to follow Taylor's advice, if not McNamara's, the President changed course: he now abruptly said he would endorse the various short-term military recommendations Taylor had made—sending a few thousand U.S. soldiers (as advisers but not combatants), more economic aid, and stepped-up cooperation between American and Vietnamese armed forces and their intelligence services. But beyond that, he said firmly, he would not go.*[105] McNamara's proposed commitment of more than 200,000 troops was not up for discussion.† Then he adjourned the meeting.

This wasn't what Taylor, McNamara, or the others wanted. So, rather than taking the President's careful proscriptions as clear limits, they took them as openings. For an eager McNamara, Kennedy's sharply hedged agreement was all he needed to hear. The next day, Sunday—without waiting for the President to approve the formal National Security Action Memorandum—McNamara drafted orders for the Pentagon. First, the Chiefs were to proceed immediately on the limited new deployments of noncombat troops to Vietnam that Taylor had recommended; more important, they were to review and update contingency plans to move more troops to the western Pacific in preparation for a larger engagement.[106] At State, Rusk's aides drafted a telegram to the American embassy in Saigon, carefully dancing around the distinctions the President had settled on the day before.[107]

On Monday morning, Rusk met separately with the French and British ambassadors to brief them on the decisions President Kennedy had taken on Saturday. He soothingly (and falsely) reassured Herve Alphand—whose government was firmly opposed to introduction of any kind of U.S. forces in Vietnam, combatant or not—that while there was no plan to send troops now,

---

*Kennedy's words were: "I am ready to approve 3. Will not accept 1. Will go for 3." Point 1 in the Rusk memo was about U.S. willingness to commit U.S. and SEATO combat troops in Vietnam; point 3 was a ten-point list of assistance, from provision of military equipment and more economic aid to the administrative training of Vietnamese bureaucrats.

†After Kennedy refused to commit the U.S. to "saving" South Vietnam, but approved limited deployment of non-combat troops and a warning to Diem about the necessity of government-wide reform, he seemed almost as an afterthought to give an OK to Pentagon contingency plans for what became known as the "McNamara option." McNamara assured the President he would do the planning only, but take no action. But as the group adjourned, U. Alexis Johnson, with a keener eye to what had just been achieved, noted for the record that "the line has clearly been drawn in Vietnam."

the possibility would not be discarded. To Sir David Ormsby-Gore, Rusk was more candid: he detailed the plans to send the 8,000 to 11,000 noncombatant troops Taylor had recommended and roles they were to play, acknowledging that their presence in Vietnam would clearly violate the Geneva Accords. Then, contrary to what Kennedy had ordered Saturday, Rusk said that while the United States had "no immediate plans" to send combat troops to Vietnam, it might well decide to do so "depending on the situation some weeks hence."

On Monday afternoon, as McNamara's orders made their way through the Pentagon bureaucracy, Galbraith was flying westward, headed back to India via Hawaii, Bangkok, and Vietnam. That morning he'd called Kennedy to say good-bye, but instead of pleasantries, the President had reiterated his direct instructions given earlier: Galbraith was to reach Saigon as quickly as possible and report back personally to Kennedy alone, using the CIA as back channel, on what he learned there, including his own recommendations for what should be done next. The President didn't tell him the details of the National Security Council meeting, only that he should report back immediately.[108]

A WEEK AFTER leaving Washington, Galbraith was back in New Delhi, having spent several days talking with U.S. and Vietnamese officials in Saigon, as well as with American military officials in Hawaii and Bangkok. It had been an edifying experience. Ambassador Nolting and senior U.S. military officials were optimistic, junior officers guardedly less so. One briefing Galbraith described as "geared to the mentality of an idiot, or more likely, a backwoods congressman." There were few signs of combat in Saigon itself, although someone had thrown a bomb at Nolting a few weeks earlier. Driven out of town under heavily armed escort along a new multilane highway paid for by U.S. AID, Galbraith dryly observed that it was hard to tell "friendly jungle" from "Vietcong jungle."[109]

Through the CIA he'd sent a short report from Bangkok telling the President there was "scarcely the slightest possible chance that the administrative and political reforms now being pressed upon Diem will result in real change." With his characteristic gift for analogy, he added, "While situation is indubitably bad military aspects seem to me out of perspective. A comparatively well-equipped army with . . . a quarter million men is facing a maximum of 15–18,000 lightly armed men. If this were equality, the United States would hardly be safe against the Sioux." ("Incidentally," he added, "who is the man in your administration who decides what countries are strategic? I would like to have his name and address and ask him what is so important about this real estate in the Space Age.") Back in New Delhi, in a second top-secret cable Galbraith outlined what more he'd found—none of which can have given the President much comfort.[110]

The cable dealt with twenty-four separate issues, from the popularity of the Viet Cong among Vietnamese peasants to the fighting capacities of the South

Vietnamese army, from the political problems of Diem's regime to the ineffectiveness of existing American policies. The Diem regime, Galbraith warned, suffered the multiple liabilities of being corrupt, incompetent, and unpopular—and it was playing on America's anti-Communist fears to perpetuate itself in office. U.S. diplomatic and military officers in Saigon were pressing Diem to reform his government, but they weren't pressing hard enough.

Galbraith did not advocate "abandoning" Vietnam, however. He urged Kennedy to probe the Russians for signs of a negotiated solution. Meanwhile, he said, the time had come to allow a change of regimes in Saigon (just as in 1960 Eisenhower had helped force out President Syngman Rhee in South Korea), in hopes that a successor to Diem might create a more democratic and less corrupt government—"nothing succeeds like successors," he quipped— while the U.S. pressed forward on every available diplomatic front.

Kennedy gave a copy of Galbraith's cable to Rostow, who was predictably incensed. He had "no objection" to Galbraith's idea about replacing Diem, and he suggested quiet contingency planning "if Diem does not perform." But Rostow then recited his figures on enemy infiltration, and sneered that "to heighten his political argument Ken has grossly underestimated the military significance of the infiltration process; he has ignored Diem's record down to 1959; and he has ignored the brutal basic arithmetic of guerrilla war"—none of which was true. Rostow also falsified his own extensive ambitions for U.S. combat troops, and concluded by darkly warning that the Communists had to be stopped at all costs. "The New Frontier will be measured in history in part on how that challenge was met. No amount of political jiu-jitsu is going to get us off that hook."

For good measure, he fired off an equally ferocious letter to Galbraith in New Delhi, telling him, "We should not kid ourselves that we are up against a serious and major offensive mounted from Hanoi; and it will take hard and purposeful labor on many fronts, both inside and outside South Vietnam, to save that area without a war."[111]

Galbraith soon came to regret his advice about regime change in Saigon— against which he had in fact counseled before the Taylor report appeared. Several weeks earlier, at a dinner party with Harriman and Schlesinger in Washington, Harriman had shrewdly complained that "the trouble with the State Department is that it always underestimates the dynamics of revolutions." Someone wondered whether removing Diem might be the answer for South Vietnam, to which Galbraith had replied, "Our trouble is that we make revolutions so badly."[112]

But in the weeks since that dinner party, much had changed between the United States and Vietnam. By the time Galbraith's cable reached Kennedy, Pentagon officials were already executing McNamara's orders, and embassy staff in Saigon were reporting to Rusk on President Diem's hostile reactions to Kennedy's limited new instructions. Still, JFK had been pushing back on his advisers. On the day Galbraith reached Hawaii, Kennedy had caught wind of what amounted to insubordination, and realized that his insistence on taking no action on longer-term measures to involve the U.S. in Vietnam had fallen on deaf ears.

The record of the four days after the November 11 NSC meeting makes this crystal clear: in memos and conversations among Rusk, McNamara, Rostow, and their deputies, the discussion was all about "losing a strategic moment for the introduction of U.S. troops," and why it was "unwise and contrary to the lessons of history" even to think about negotiations with the North Vietnamese Communists until President Kennedy had shown the world that "the U.S. is serious about saving South Vietnam."[113] Several administration officers were also very worried about Galbraith's conversations with the President, and about what his report after visiting Saigon could do to their plans. For example, just as Galbraith left Washington on Monday, November 13, U. Alexis Johnson told Rusk that Taylor had succeeded in arranging for a second NSC meeting in order to pressure the President to reverse his decision prohibiting U.S. combat troops, but that they would "have to move quickly" because "Galbraith has been working hard on this."[114] Johnson told Rusk he was "worried" because Galbraith had gotten hold of a copy of Rusk's latest instructions to Ambassador Nolting, which supposedly summarized what the President had decided on November 11, but which they both knew were in fact a very aggressive interpretation of Kennedy's decision: Rusk had told Nolting to inform Diem that the President was promising no troops, but simultaneously to leave Diem believing that the matter was still open. This was entirely contrary to the tenor of Kennedy's actual decision.[115]

Kennedy seems to have caught wind that same day of what his aides were up to, and was so alarmed that on Tuesday, November 14, he sent a brisk, clear order to Rusk and McNamara:

> I think we should get our ducks in a row . . . I believe we should make more precise our requests for action. In the papers which I have seen [Defense and State orders supposedly based on the NSC decisions he approved on November 11] our requests have been of a general nature.

He made it very clear once again that negotiations, not expanded fighting, were his first priority. And he also told them he wanted a proposal that Averell Harriman had given him to be taken up immediately.

For Rusk and McNamara, who had just read it, this was *not* good news. Galbraith, they knew, had stayed with the Harrimans in Washington, and had no doubt apprised Harriman of the contents of the Taylor report and the President's fears. Harriman was as opposed to sending troops as Galbraith and Kennedy—and in some ways knew even better than the President just how determined Washington bureaucrats worked to get what they wanted from elected leaders.

On Sunday, November 12, the day after the first NSC meeting, Harriman's memo had asked Kennedy for immediate permission to contact the Russians in Geneva. The goal was to start talks that would lead to a cease-fire in Vietnam, open trade between North and South Vietnam, and create a revamped, strengthened ICC to monitor the accords.[116] Kennedy had reacted enthusiastically, and on Tuesday bluntly told Rusk and McNamara he was thinking seriously of sending Harriman to Geneva by the end of the week to start talking with the Russians.[117] For a moment, President Kennedy seemed to have the upper hand.

But the next morning, just before the second NSC meeting that Taylor had arranged, McGeorge Bundy weighed in.[118] In a memo to the President, he apologized for having left so much about Southeast Asia up to Rostow until now while concentrating on Europe and the Soviet Union. But, he reminded JFK, "the other day at the swimming pool you asked me what I thought and here it is." He told the President he was absolutely convinced it was right to send fully equipped combat troops to Vietnam, starting with one full division, or about 20,000 to 25,000 men, immediately, and that the promise of these troops (and of more to come) should be used as a bargaining chip with Diem to force reform of his regime, as well as a signal to the Soviet Union and China of the United States' determination to counter the Communists. A division wasn't much, Bundy admitted, but worth sending to see if it would shift the tide of battle. Besides, he soothed the President, "the odds are almost even that the commitment will not have to be carried out."

Bundy's intervention seems to have tipped some invisible balance in Kennedy; with the secretaries of state and defense, the Joint Chiefs of Staff, and now his NSC adviser all in agreement, when the NSC met a few hours later, Harriman wasn't present, and Kennedy didn't mention the idea of sending him back to Geneva. In effect, the advisers had won this round. Yet the President was still upset, and got into a stiff-backed exchange with Rusk in front of the group. The tension in the room is quite apparent from the meeting's notes:

> Mr. Rusk explained the Draft of Memorandum on South Viet Nam. He added the hope that, in spite of the magnitude of the proposal, any U.S. actions would not be hampered by lack of funds nor failure to pursue the program vigorously.
>
> The President expressed the fear of becoming involved simultaneously on two fronts on opposite sides of the world. He questioned the wisdom of involvement in Viet Nam since the basis thereof is not completely clear. By comparison he noted that Korea was a case of clear aggression which was opposed by the United States and other members of the U.N. The conflict in Viet Nam is more obscure and less flagrant.
>
> The President then expressed his strong feeling that in such a situation the United States needs even more the support of allies in such an endeavor as Viet Nam in order to avoid sharp domestic partisan criticism as well as strong objections from other nations of the world. The President said that he could even make a rather strong case against intervening in an area 10,000

miles away against 16,000 guerrillas with a native army of 200,000, where millions have been spent for years with no success.

The President repeated his apprehension concerning support, adding that none could be expected from the French, and Mr. Rusk interrupted to say that the British were tending more and more to take the French point of view. The President compared the obscurity of the issues in Viet Nam to the clarity of the positions in Berlin, the contrast of which could even make leading Democrats wary of proposed activities in the Far East.[119]

Kennedy by now fully understood his dilemma and immediately afterward talked with Harriman by phone. Right after that call, he ordered Bundy to see Rusk that afternoon. His instructions were blunt: Bundy was to tell Rusk that "the Pres. is still thinking hard and has spoken to Harriman and Taylor." Specifically, Bundy was to inform Rusk that the President needed people around him who were "wholly responsive to his policies." Therefore, he wanted Harriman to be made Assistant Secretary of State for Far Eastern Affairs and George McGhee (also opposed to intervention) to replace Ambassador Nolting in Saigon; Galbraith was to be ordered to put all possible pressure on India as chair of the International Control Commission to help find alternatives to U.S. military intervention.

But Rusk fought back at his meeting with Bundy, point by point: Harriman was needed in Geneva to complete work on the Laos peace accords; Nolting should stay in Saigon because "he has Diem's confidence"; and before Galbraith pressed the Indians on the ICC, the United States first needed to decide that "we mean to hold in Southeast Asia." He was implying that Kennedy, at the NSC meeting on November 11, had failed to make such a decision—and that Galbraith would undermine reaching it.

As Bundy drafted his report to Kennedy on his meeting with Rusk, he understood that his own relationship with the President was suddenly in jeopardy. Realizing the scale of the policy schism between JFK and his most senior advisers, Bundy grasped that if he stood with Rusk and McNamara now, he would forfeit Kennedy's confidence, which is death for any presidential adviser. He thus added to his report something that might placate the President: a list of proposed personnel changes, a musical-chairs shuffle of Rusk's subordinates, adding that Rusk "won't do this unless you tell him to." Bundy's recommendations served their goal. Reading them a few hours later, Kennedy nodded his head repeatedly as he scrawled notes in the margins.[120]

Two weeks later—a week after Galbraith's cables reached the White House—Kennedy reshuffled the top posts at the State Department, making Harriman Assistant Secretary for Far Eastern Affairs and promoting George Ball to Undersecretary; but Bowles was pulled out of State and Nolting was left in Saigon to placate a bruised Rusk. Whether or not these changes would make the difference Kennedy sought remained to be seen, but Harriman and Ball (like the sacrificed Bowles) were far more sympathetic to Kennedy's (and Galbraith's) views. In his diary, after learning of the shuffle, Galbraith recorded his own shrewd assessment of what JFK had—and hadn't—achieved: "It is all excellent and not a moment too soon; but then Kennedy left in place at his right hand McNamara, Bundy, Rusk, and Taylor."[121]

SEVERAL WEEKS AFTER the shake-up, *The New York Times* reported from Saigon on the arrival of the first of McNamara's troop deployments, carefully described in official press releases as U.S. Army "flood relief specialists." The next day, just as the aircraft carrier U.S.S. *Core* arrived bearing new helicopters, light aircraft, and their U.S. pilots and mechanics, the *Times* noted that the International Control Commission was considering ceasing operation in Vietnam as a result of the "increase in United States assistance to South Vietnam." The article mentioned that 1,500 U.S. military personnel were now in the country, and then added, "Many more are expected."[122]

16

India

India is not the sort of post to which rich, socially minded, and prestige-oriented men and women aspire. Ken's predecessors, John Sherman Cooper, Chester Bowles, and Ellsworth Bunker, had all been intelligent, literate, thoughtful men, drawn to India's ageless beauty and culture and bent on addressing her vast problems. Ken felt fully equal to his succession. And the whole idea of having the letters A, E, and P after his name delighted his soul. Ambassador Extraordinary and Plenipotentiary bespoke a grandeur perfectly cut to suit his larger-than-life frame.

—Peggy Lamson, *Speaking of Galbraith*

INDIA HAD WON her freedom from British rule only thirteen years before Kennedy became President, and antique habits of state and diplomacy still lingered. Shortly after arriving in New Delhi in April 1961, Galbraith went to present his credentials at the President's Palace, riding in a handsome motorcade, flanked by motorcycles and patrol cars. He cut a formidable figure, outfitted in an elegantly tailored suit, gray silk tie, and black silk top hat, which brought his overall height to well over seven feet.

At the palace he was met by a detachment of Bengal Lancers mounted on perfectly matched bay horses and was escorted in by an honor guard of Sikh officers, "perhaps the best turned-out soldiers in the world," as he described them. The ceremony that followed—the speeches, the military band and the anthems, the presentation of papers, the champagne toasts—was "exceedingly well done; the Indians approach ceremony as though they meant it, rather than, as in the United States, in a kind of abashed reluctance . . . When we emerged to come home, my automobile flag was unfurled for the first time."[1]

The Galbraiths' arrival by plane several days earlier had been no less elegant—though the welcoming committee proved a bit slapdash, since the plane arrived an hour ahead of schedule. Weighted down with garlands of flowers, and met by a sizable crowd, Galbraith found it "not, I am happy to say, without fanfare. I should have preferred arriving, as did the Viceroys, from the sea at the Gateway of India in Bombay and a triumphal train passage to New Delhi, but one must make do with the twentieth century. And it wasn't too bad. Certainly better than the average landing at Logan [airport in Boston]."[2]

These comments come from the book that Galbraith wrote about his work as U.S. ambassador to India. *Ambassador's Journal* is his longest book, and it shows him in his early fifties at the height of his years as a public figure and writer. For anyone who aspired to be what he later called "a useful economist," blackboard mathematical models might illuminate glimpses into the lived world of economic relations, but one needed to engage more intimately and directly with the world.

Galbraith proved supremely self-confident—and, by most accounts, remarkably successful—in discharging his ambassadorial duties. "Some may have felt that he was less bent on representing the views of the United States than the views of John Kenneth Galbraith," one observer put it, "but even so, they looked upon him as a very effective and influential force. He was extremely popular with the Indians, who cherished him for his intellect, his candor, and his ever present tendency to debunk received truths."[3] He was no less popular with the U.S. press: major profiles of his ambassadorship in *Life*, *Look*, *Time*, and half a dozen other leading publications portrayed him as successful, popular, and charmingly iconoclastic.

Impatient with the administrative routines and responsibilities of his post, he quickly delegated supervision of what was then America's largest Third World embassy, with more than a thousand staff, and focused himself on major policy issues. "The necessary tasks, I soon discovered, could be accomplished in around two hours of official work a day. Any more time involved ill-concealed idleness. However, in the press, among Indians and in Washington, I acquired, with very little fraud, a reputation for exceptional diplomatic diligence."[4] He made it a point to travel frequently and to meet as many people as possible—local maharajahs, villagers, politicians, and bureaucrats. Thanks to his two previous visits, he already knew many of India's leading figures from Prime Minister Nehru on down, and was comfortably familiar with the domestic and foreign-policy issues that preoccupied them.

Under Eisenhower, the United States had not enjoyed the best of relations with India: John Foster Dulles had been hostile to Nehru's stance of nonalignment between the United States and the Soviet Union, and U.S. support for Pakistan, along with India's acceptance of Russian aid and the Fabian worldview of many Indian leaders, had chilled the relationship. But President Kennedy was personally eager to see that change. In the Senate, to hone his reputation in foreign policy, he had become a vocal champion of closer and more extensive ties with India, and in 1958, with Republican Senator John Sherman Cooper (Eisenhower's former ambassador to India), he had co-authored a major bill to help fund Indian economic development. In various

Senate speeches he rightly observed that India was crucial to the future of Asia and the "free world," a competitor to China whose friendship the United States could not afford to lose. He even described a "development gap" as dangerous as the "missile gap" he claimed existed with the Soviet Union, and he called on the United States to help make India *the* non-Communist model of industrial development, efficient agriculture, advanced education, and ever-rising living standards.[5] Galbraith supported these views, though with less emphasis on anti-Communist competition, and within weeks of arriving in New Delhi he could tell Nehru with great pleasure that President Kennedy would shortly announce a record billion-dollar development assistance package for India.

But in sharp contrast to the warm relations he was developing with Nehru and other Indians, Galbraith quickly got himself involved in a major dust-up with Dean Rusk and State Department officials in Foggy Bottom. When Pakistan's president, Ayub Khan, paid a state visit to Washington in July 1961, the joint U.S.-Pakistani communiqué talked about "mutual friendship" and the promise of "extensive aid," which convinced Indians that a new round of U.S. military aid for Pakistan was forthcoming. Galbraith called a press conference to allay Indian fears, earning himself front-page coverage—then, to his dismay, learned from classified cables that indeed the United States was about to deliver F-104 fighters to Karachi. He was not pleased. He caustically noted in his diary that the planes, after being off-loaded from a U.S. aircraft carrier, were supposed

> to be trundled through the streets at night in secret when no fewer than 10,000 people will see them. I warned Washington to make the matter public—and then be braced. These planes will contribute nothing to our security in the area. They will be another complication in India-Pakistan relations and another source of suspicion so far as we are concerned.

When the planes did indeed arrive in Pakistan, Galbraith was colorfully livid about them in a private letter to Kennedy. The F-104s, he wrote, "were unloaded in all the secrecy that would attend mass sodomy on the BMT at rush hour . . . When the thing promised to get out of hand here the Department cabled me sympathy. Eventually I wrung authority to release the number [of planes delivered] out of [Assistant Secretary Phillips] Talbot more or less by physical violence." (Galbraith was no fonder of Talbot than he was of Dean: working with him was "like playing badminton with a marshmallow. You could never tell if he was going to stick to the racket or go with the net.") The ensuing uproar largely erased the goodwill in India generated by the billion-dollar aid announcement and simultaneously enraged the Pakistanis, whose government had been told the aircraft shipment would be secret.

Of greater concern to Galbraith was a subject on which he was required to keep silent for many decades. In September 1961, anticipating that China would soon be testing a nuclear weapon, State Department planners recommended, in a top-secret memo to Rusk, that the United States "beat the Chinese Communists to the punch" by persuading India to test its own atomic bomb first—if need be, by overtly supplying American technology and materiel. This would, they said, "be seen as a great victory for free Asia." As the memorandum acknowledged, however, the plan was vehemently opposed by Ambassador Galbraith, who reckoned there was hardly a chance that Nehru would agree to it and the very suggestion would greatly damage U.S.-Indian relations. The planners noted that Galbraith, in a spirit of unexpected compromise, suggested that Jerome Wiesner, the President's science adviser, stop in New Delhi after his planned upcoming visit to Pakistan, where he could meet the Indian science adviser and perhaps obliquely raise the question of nuclear weapons in Asia.

This is in fact what happened. Wiesner arrived in New Delhi early that October, whereupon Galbraith immediately recruited his old friend into opposition to the plan. In *Ambassador's Journal*, Galbraith—sworn to secrecy—mentions only that he gave Wiesner "an earful on needed reforms in our diplomatic representation," while noting obliquely that the future M.I.T. president recounted his own frustrations about his day-to-day battles in Washington on behalf of a ban on nuclear testing, and describes Wiesner's meeting with Nehru as one in which he "gave a very effective and thoughtful exposition of the disarmament problem." Finally free to discuss this forty years later, Galbraith says that Wiesner, just as appalled as he was by State's proposal, delivered their views to President Kennedy, who agreed with them about its manifest dangers; the plan to help India go nuclear was never revived (although declassified records show that Pentagon and State Department planners continued for some years to draw up plans for a preemptive nuclear attack against Chinese weapons facilities).[6]

Galbraith's skepticism of official U.S. foreign policy and its planners wasn't helped by the near invasion of Laos, undertaken soon after the disaster at the Bay of Pigs. This dubious activism contrasted with what he felt was American passivity about India. In a back-channel letter to Kennedy, he noted, "I think I dislike most the uncontrollable instinct for piously reasoned inaction. When the Department does respond to telegrams it is invariably to recommend evasion of issues that cannot be evaded. The result is that we get the worst of all available worlds."[7] He voiced his concern about keeping peace in Laos and preserving the kingdom's neutrality, and he warned that to convince India, as head of the International Control Commission, to risk its prestige in support of U.S. aims in Laos was "an uphill battle. The Department expects me to explain our devotion to neutrality in Laos one day and our supersonic toys for the Pakistanis the next. This is called policy."

YET LIFE IN INDIA had more to it than disputes with the State Department or long-distance advice on the direction of the New Frontier. The parties, the travels, the encounters with statesmen and villagers that Galbraith so enjoyed are all richly described in *Ambassador's Journal*; his confident, poised voice can be heard on every page, even when confessing his own foibles or weaknesses with his characteristic self-assurance and self-deprecatory charm. Kitty and their sons are more present than in his other writings, and we see for the first time the facets of a man in a family.

His oldest son, Alan, by then a junior at Harvard, remained behind in Cambridge. But for ten-year-old Peter and nine-year-old Jamie, India was an exotic and majestic adventure. To amuse them, their father amiably suggested that a pet or two might be welcome, and overeager Indian staffers outdid themselves in response: a pair of peacocks was installed in the backyard, but had to be removed after they started bashing their heads against the garden walls and required medical attention. A leopard cub was the next visitor, against Kitty's better judgment, but it too was soon gone. Nehru heard of it and, fearing for the boys' safety, personally threatened to have it "sequestered" if not removed. His decision distressed the boys, but the Galbraiths' housekeeper, Emily Wilson, who had accompanied them to India, was relieved even though she had installed a litter box, not wanting to "have leopard shit all over my house."

As a fourth-grader at the international school Jamie also composed an essay on his parents in which he wrote, "My father is Ambassador to India, or the chief United States official here. He does many different types of work. He writes reports for the United States Government on Indian conditions. He has conferences with the Indian Government to improve diplomatic relations. And Dad makes speeches to make a little better the understanding between the U.S. and India and he represents the President on official occasions. Mother doesn't do much except arrange entertainment and administer the household." Kitty used this adventure in premature chauvinism to lead off an essay she wrote for *The Atlantic Monthly* entitled "Mother Doesn't Do Much," in which she delightfully described "all the things Mother *did* do while not doing much."[8]

Even while doing the official work his son's essay described, and conscientiously keeping up his voluminous journal, Galbraith also wrote three other books: *The Scotch*, a beautifully crafted recollection of growing up in rural Ontario; *The McLandress Dimension*, his first satirical novel under the pseudonym Mark Epernay; and, with the Indian art critic Mohinder Singh Randhawa, a serious study of Moghul painting of the sixteenth to eighteenth centuries.

Literary skill and enthusiasm alone hardly explain the man we find in these diverse pages. Thirty years earlier, Galbraith had been a lanky Canadian farm boy studying agricultural economics and destined, one might imagine, for a serviceable career as a teacher (like his father or older sister) or farmer or perhaps adviser to a provincial farm bureaucracy. But here he is, a sophisticated, socially well-connected figure whose long list of friends and acquaintances glitters with names representative of American, European, and South Asian industry and wealth, society and the arts. Scattered decoratively through the pages of *Ambassador's Journal* are descriptions of encounters and friendships with dozens of fascinating people—Acheson, Rockefeller, Harriman, Nehru, de Gaulle, Fulbright, Graham, Menon, Desai, Murrow, Reischauer, Reuther, Schlesinger, Shriver, Vidal, Steinbeck, the Duke and Duchess of

Windsor*—and above all, President and Mrs. Kennedy. The Kennedys themselves legendarily embodied this same sophistication, and the fact that Galbraith was at ease in their world helps to explain the depth and intimacy of their friendship. But Galbraith hadn't acquired his extraordinary rolodex of connections through the Kennedys; he had made them on his own. How?

Harvard is one answer—and not to be underestimated. Kennedy's was a consummately Harvard administration, with many of its senior officials drawn from Crimson alumni and faculty, including McGeorge Bundy, Arthur Schlesinger, Douglas Dillon, Robert McNamara, James Tobin, and Seymour Harris; Kennedy in fact ended up imposing an informal "Harvard quota" on new appointees. (Galbraith was probably the only graduate of the Ontario Agricultural College to serve JFK—or, for that matter, any White House.)

The crucibles of New Deal politics, wartime Washington, and postwar liberal politics were no less important. He'd first met Chester Bowles, a Yale man and former Connecticut governor, during the Second World War; the two had worked closely in Americans for Democratic Action, on Adlai Stevenson's campaigns, and on the Democratic Advisory Council.[9] On Stevenson's campaigns he'd also come to know Philip Stern, a Harvard-trained lawyer and journalist who was heir to the Sears & Roebuck fortune and was now a deputy assistant secretary in the State Department. Averell Harriman, scion of one of America's great railroad fortunes, was another acquaintance from wartime days. George Ball's friendship dated from the Bombing Survey and the Lend-Lease Administration.

The fact that these powerful men were rich was not lost on Galbraith. Wealth had never been his own driving ambition, and in his books he was often at pains to remark on the social distance between him and his upper-class friends and acquaintances. When Nikita Khrushchev came to the United States in 1959, a group of businessmen and financiers awaited him at Harriman's elegant New York townhouse, among them David Rockefeller, John J. McCloy, David Sarnoff, and W. Alton Jones; Galbraith was present, in his words, as "representative of the proletariat." Over champagne and caviar, the men discussed politics, business, and disarmament. Khrushchev felt he was in the presence of America's real "ruling class" and said so. As Galbraith recalls, "Somebody demurred, but in perfunctory fashion."[10]

But Galbraith's network wasn't limited to the rich. He and John Steinbeck had met by accident in the mid-1950s in the Virgin Islands, where the two men and their wives happened to be vacationing at the same resort. Philip and Katherine Graham had become friends at about the same time, following Graham's enthusiastic review of *American Capitalism* in *The Washington Post*. And Galbraith knew Edward R. Murrow, the country's best-known broadcast journalist and the new head of Kennedy's U.S. Information Agency, because Kitty

---

*The Duke of Windsor's advice on India Galbraith found worth recording: " 'I hear you are going to In-jea,' he said. 'A most interesting country. I had a very good time there in my early youth. You must do the pig-sticking in Rajasthan . . . And you will find the people most agreeable in their own way. They have been most uncommonly decent to my niece.' " This advice was proffered at a dinner party where the two men were seated with Henry Luce, Perle Mesta, Mrs. William Randolph Hearst, Jr., and John D. Rockefeller III.

Galbraith and Janet Murrow had been school classmates and close childhood friends.* The two men had reconnected in wartime London, where Murrow was making his celebrated broadcasts for CBS Radio and Galbraith was working on the Bombing Survey, and then later in New York. An evening at the Murrows' apartment in 1948, when the two couples peered at a flickering little television screen to watch the Democratic Convention nominate Harry Truman, was the first time Galbraith had watched television. Murrow assured him it would someday be very important; Galbraith wasn't so sure.[11]

Galbraith's books would have guaranteed him a certain authorial fame, but it would not have been so broad or lasting had he not also enjoyed this network of acquaintances and friendships, which his journalism amplified—the work at *Fortune*, well-received articles for *Life*, plus book reviews and pieces for *The New York Times*, successes that led to articles in *Harper's*, *The Atlantic Monthly*, and dozens of other publications.

In his glittering network of acquaintances, in this voluminous written work, and in his insider-outsider relation to government service, Galbraith resembled no other economist so much as John Maynard Keynes, strikingly different as their social backgrounds were. Galbraith acknowledged the parallels but denied any conscious emulation. "My admiration for Keynes, as I've often told, is immense, as is my intellectual debt," he remarked.

> What I drew from him was his commitment to intellectual rigor, his skepticism about the market's self-correcting capacities, and his belief that economists should concern themselves with more than the refinement of mathematical models. On reflection, perhaps my admiration for him did encourage me to spread his and my own ideas through public service and journalism, but it was not conscious at the time.[12]

As Galbraith's appearances in newspapers and magazines became more frequent, complaints grew, just as they had with Keynes. Some academic colleagues predictably grumbled about his suspect "popularizing" and growing "arrogance," a charge that Keynes, too, often faced. Galbraith was hardly oblivious to these views, but far from disowning the accusations of vanity, he turned them into opportunities for genial self-deprecation. He delighted, for example, in retelling the story of his White House breakfast with President Kennedy shortly before departing for India. While reviewing policy matters, Kennedy paused to ask "how I had liked an article about me in the morning's *New York Times*. It described my election memos as 'sharp, funny and mean.' I said I objected to the *Times* describing me as arrogant. He said, 'I don't see why. Everybody else does.' "[13]

The anecdote itself is telling, and beautifully layered, as Galbraith in-

---

*Kitty affectionately recalls working with Janet in student government and on the class yearbook, and notes that she was asked to pour the tea—a distinct social honor in those days—at Janet's engagement party.

tended. It cautioned his critics that he knew better than they about the quality the Indians call *darshan*—"the beneficial glow of being in the presence of the great," he explained. *Darshan* is "sought in all societies," he mildly observed, "but only the Indians are candid enough to endow it with a name."[14]

The fullness of Galbraith's time in India, and the richness with which he told of the experience and revealed for the first time his own life and personality, was always measured by the important issues of the day. He meant Galbraith the man and Galbraith the actor on a public stage to be understood as inseparable, and he wanted to suggest a metric by which we may judge our own engagement and commitments.

In India, the ever-present subtext was Vietnam, which came through in the dozens of letters and cables Galbraith exchanged with the President, and also in his recurrent attempts to involve India in a negotiated Vietnamese settlement. But war in Southeast Asia was not the only war he faced while in New Delhi. Two Indian conflicts—one quite serious—broke out during his years there, and though neither proved as bloody or as dangerous as other conflicts of the time, each in its way was extremely significant.

Shortly before Christmas 1961 Galbraith suddenly found himself in the midst of the first of these two wars—though the term "war" itself seems misapplied. On December 20, 1961, the Indian Army invaded Goa, the tiny Portuguese colony on the west coast of India that was a remnant of Lisbon's now long-eclipsed empire, known mainly in guide books as the resting place for the founder of the Society of Jesus, St. Francis Xavier, and for its idyllic beaches, cobblestone streets, and charming Ibero-colonial architecture. Ever since 1947, New Delhi had demanded that Portugal abandon this minor indignity, and Lisbon had ignored the request; the U.S. tacitly backed Portugal, in return for its allowing NATO airbases in the Azores.

When Galbraith returned from Washington and Nehru's state visit there, and from his embroilments in trying to stop implementation of General Taylor's report on Vietnam, war in Asia was on his mind, and he was dismayed to learn that the Indians were considering it over "the Portuguese pimple," as he called it. But it quickly became clear that an invasion was exactly what New Delhi was planning, and for many reasons—national pride, a perceived need to flex India's muscles, and domestic politics.[15]

Two weeks of escalating Indian rhetoric followed, with belligerent Portuguese replies and feckless State Department inaction that largely enraged Galbraith. His own proposal—to put the matter before the U.N. and to seek a negotiated settlement leading to Goa's eventual return to India—was ignored in Washington. Publicly the State Department condemned India's aggression, and Secretary Rusk, meeting with Portugal's foreign minister, failed to persuade Antonio Salazar that perhaps finally the time had come to step back, even slightly, from his antiquated colonial habits.

The outcome seemed preordained, although Galbraith did his best to prevent it. In the middle of the month,

The American Ambassador, Professor Galbraith, who for days had been trying to head Nehru off from an invasion, made his point with such effect that the Prime Minister was deterred. When Galbraith left, Nehru told [Defense Minister] Krishna Menon that the order for the troops to advance into Goa . . . should be suspended . . . Menon replied that it was too late; the troops, he said, had already begun their advance—although in fact they had not.

On December 20, as two Indian Army columns marched into Goa, Galbraith's three military attachés put up a big map in the chancery and covered it with great sweeping arrows showing troop movements. This all seemed faintly ridiculous to Galbraith, rather like a map "plotting the movement of the governor through the Iowa State Fair." The attachés solemnly predicted that though the operation would probably be bloody, it would be over in about ten days. Galbraith shook his head. "The operation will be over by tonight," he insisted. In fact, the fighting was over, save for a random skirmish or two, by noon—and the casualties were one man shot and one man drowned accidentally. "It was the last such briefing I ever got," Galbraith observed. "My officers thereafter never thought to challenge my military acumen."[16]

The State Department continued to chastise India for the invasion, and the Indian press—rather too gleefully, Galbraith thought—responded by quoting back the pious justifications that State had given for the Bay of Pigs invasion of Cuba six months earlier.

The stress leading up to this incident—the frustrations with the State Department and with Indian officials, as well as the terrible pressures of his November trip back to Washington, the fight over the Taylor report, the disturbing stopover in Saigon, and his subsequent warnings to Kennedy about the risks in Vietnam—began to show their effects. Galbraith found himself fighting off severe migraine headaches and feeling at times deeply depressed. This was a familiar pattern: there had been episodes of overwork and depression during his wartime days at OPA and after the death of his son Douglas and Adlai Stevenson's defeat in 1952.

Shortly after Christmas, Galbraith decided it was time he took a break. Leaving his wife and sons behind, he flew to Switzerland for a few days of vacation, then returned to Boston and Washington. In Gstaad, with lots of old friends around, he felt better, then experienced a new wave of depression. In Boston, the pleasure of friends lifted his spirits, and he had a chance to spend some time alone with Alan. Yet he still felt "in mental and physical disrepair" and talked seriously with at least one or two close friends about resigning his ambassadorship.

In Washington, the symptoms were bad enough that the White House arranged for the President's personal physician, Dr. Janet Travell, to examine him; after a series of tests at Bethesda Naval Medical Center, he was diagnosed with a badly infected sinus, a bad liver, and signs of amoebic dysentery. He ended up staying in the hospital for more than a week.[17]

But even bed rest proved less restful than might have been hoped, for while in the hospital, he got himself in the middle of a nasty little front-page row. The Cosmos Club, Washington's most elite private club, had refused to admit as a member the black journalist Carl Rowan, whom Kennedy had appointed deputy assistant secretary of state for public affairs; by coincidence the President, too, had recently been proposed for membership in the Cosmos, his sponsors being none other than Galbraith (who had joined it during World War II) and James Conant. Galbraith's solution to the potential embarrassment to Kennedy—who couldn't now accept membership himself but didn't want a needless sideshow fuss with the club—was to resign and thereby invalidate his sponsorship of Kennedy. He was immediately joined in his resignation by Ed Murrow, Arthur Schlesinger, Jr., and Harlan Cleveland. In power-sensitive Washington, a point had been made, and soon after the club began admitting African Americans as members.

Back out of the hospital a few days later, he then tangled with Rusk's deputy, Phillips Talbot, over U.S. policy in Kashmir. The outcome eventually was passably to Galbraith's liking, but the struggle with Talbot and "the vast Estates-General" of policy bureaucrats only confirmed his prejudices about Rusk and the State Department. All in all—despite several opportunities to see Kennedy alone and catch up with friends—it was not the restful trip it might have been.

Two months later, though, Galbraith celebrated the social triumph of his ambassadorship (and the quintessence of *darshan*): a state visit to India by the first lady, Jacqueline Kennedy. Given its own lengthy chapter in his journal, entitled "Great Fun," the ten-day visit in March 1962 shows a side of Galbraith invisible in his work until then. Every detail of the planning that went into the visit—her arrival, her choice of clothes, the immense state dinners, the visits to India's famed tourist sites (from Fatehpur-Sikri and the Taj Mahal to Agra and Benares), as well as the vast carpet of onlookers and admirers who turned out wherever she went—is retold.

The night before her arrival, we see the Galbraiths presiding over a full dress rehearsal of the dinner they were to host in her honor, with forty-five embassy staffers playing the role of invited guests and the tables perfectly decorated and arranged, with exactly the same food and wine, so that each item could be tested for taste, temperature, and appearance and each of the small string orchestra's pieces timed.

Jacqueline Kennedy was unquestionably not only beautiful and intelligent but entrancing, and Galbraith's descriptions hover on the edge of rhapsodic. A dinner party organized by Prime Minister Nehru, its guests drawn from what Galbraith called "the gayer members of the community," finds J.B.K. (as he referred to her throughout) "in a long dress of pale turquoise which responded brilliantly to the lights," the dinner party itself a near fairy tale "that would last in anyone's memory."

> You must imagine chairs stretching across the lawn and lit by the half moon
> and the reflection of the stage lights. These flashed on a stunning array of

saris—every woman present had chosen from many and spent hours on the choice. In front of the chairs was a little canopied area for the supreme guests, the canopy being made of flower petals. Finally before all was the stage, dancers, musicians in vivid or sometimes wild costume, the women being especially sinuous as they turned and twirled.[18]

Mrs. Kennedy's travels across India are lovingly described, the sumptuousness of their accommodations and travel befitting the era of the Raj, and everywhere J.B.K. the center of attention and admiration. In Jaipur, for example, the famed City Palace was opened for her by the maharajah who owned it for a special midnight tour. There, she, the ambassador, and a small party

> spent a couple of hours roaming its exquisite environs—the various courts and audience chambers, the gardens where the fountains had been turned on, the armory and the museum with its wonderful miniature paintings. The lights gleamed on the red walls, the swords and also on the saris of the party. And rugs and tapestries which are a bit vivid in the daytime seem fine and subdued at night. It was all most romantic.[19]

If at times this languid idyll sounded more like the work of a budding nineteenth-century British novelist on her first grand tour of the Jewel in the Crown, Galbraith repeatedly rescued it from romantic banality with deftly self-deflating humor. The chapter begins not as Mrs. Kennedy's plane touched down, for example, but an hour earlier when nine-year-old Jamie Galbraith accidentally locked the keys to the ambassador's limousine inside it. Forced to abandon "the Queen Elizabeth"—as Galbraith named the immense Cadillac—the family rushed to the airport unceremoniously in a Ford sedan.*

Meeting with a group of Peace Corps volunteers, Galbraith slyly noted that, when asked their impressions of India and of the value of their own preparatory training, the young men earnestly recommended

> (a) a better preliminary language instruction and (b) a better balance between the sexes. Most of them do not find the Punjabi girls, beautiful though they are, a sufficiently available substitute. The point is a good one and I will take it up with [Sargent] Shriver [Peace Corps director and Kennedy's brother-in-law]. Youngsters this age cannot be expected to take kindly to monastic chastity, however good the purpose.[20]

Even Mrs. Kennedy herself came in for an occasional sly, albeit gentle, jibe:

> The President had told me that the care and management of Mrs. Kennedy involved a great deal of attention, and he is quite right. One of the minor foot-

---

*As Jamie tells it, Emily Wilson ingeniously succeeded in picking the lock, and "the Queen Elizabeth" was delivered to Palam Airport in time for the First Lady's arrival.

notes of the trip was some shopping in Benares. On my advice, J.B.K. bought a couple of handbags and, while she was looking at the textiles, she whispered as to whether she should buy some silk brocade and a couple of jeweled brocade bags. In the rush, neither of us inquired the price. I assumed they were 200 or 300 rupees. In fact, they were Rs. 3,000. The papers made something of the fact that she had spent some $600 in less than five minutes. Actually, it couldn't have been more than ten seconds. She was annoyed at my carelessness.[21]

SIGNIFICANTLY, "GREAT FUN" ended not with Mrs. Kennedy's departure but a month later in early April, with Galbraith back in Washington on official business, where he made a telling juxtaposition. Jackie invited him to join the Kennedy family for a weekend at Glen Ora, the family's rented estate in the Virginia countryside; he wrote of "the well-televised and widely reported kiss" she gave him at National Airport, and then of the evening spent watching an hour-long NBC special about her Indian visit, which duly impressed her husband. Then, disrupting the mood of intimacy and innocent charm, he related his discussion with the President about Vietnam, his subsequent talk with Mc-Namara, and the memo he left behind.

In the memo, Galbraith recapped point by point his opinion of the risks and faulty assumptions behind the policies Kennedy's advisers were advocating. He openly and directly urged the President to have Averell Harriman seek Soviet help in arranging a major pullback by North Vietnam "in return for phased American withdrawal, liberalization in the trade relations between the two parts of the country and general and non-specific agreement to talk about re-unification after some period of tranquillity." And he counseled JFK "to resist all steps which commit American troops to combat roles" and to back away immediately from newly implemented State and Defense department policies that called for forcing South Vietnamese peasants into "strategic hamlets" and for using defoliants such as Agent Orange.[22]

What he didn't write about in his book—and the details emerged only when the relevant documents were declassified in the 1990s—was that Kennedy followed his advice almost to the letter.

Harriman, six months into his new role as Assistant Secretary of State for Far Eastern Affairs, was called into the Oval Office on April 5, the day after Kennedy got Galbraith's memo. There the President read him what it said, and told Harriman he wanted the Russians contacted about the deal Galbraith was proposing. Harriman was also told to instruct Galbraith to ask the Indian government to open simultaneous conversations with the North Vietnamese on the same terms.[23] That same afternoon Kennedy also sent a copy of Galbraith's memo to Secretary McNamara, who instructed his aides to prepare a detailed response that explained why JFK should give his support to the strategic-hamlet program and the use of chemical defoliants. Kennedy's advisers continued to put up quite powerful resistance to his clear intentions.

Kennedy expected this by now; what caught him off guard was Harriman's response. During the debate over the Taylor report in the fall, Harriman had pressed the President to send him back to Geneva to open discussions with the Russians. Now, as Assistant Secretary of State, Harriman stoutly defended the department line, and told JFK that "while he agreed with some of the conclusions" in Galbraith's memo, he was opposed both to using the Geneva talks to open conversations with the Russians and to any "neutral solution in Viet-Nam."* When Kennedy nonetheless insisted that he wanted Galbraith instructed to get the Indians to open up channels to Hanoi, Harriman said he would—and then he never did, despite the President's direct orders.[24] Galbraith never received the President's instructions, and no such orders can be found in State Department files. Later in April, after learning that Harriman had rejected the idea of talking to the Russians, Galbraith sent a blistering telegram in dissent—which was, predictably, ignored.[25]

From the Pentagon came even stronger resistance. McNamara soon forwarded to Kennedy a bitter rejection of Galbraith's proposals written by General Lemnitzer, chairman of the Joint Chiefs of Staff. Lemnitzer concluded that although the U.S. should never reject the idea of talking with the North Vietnamese, the problems in Vietnam were entirely the result of Communist aggression, and he approvingly quoted Dean Rusk's claim that "there can be peace overnight in Vietnam if those responsible for the aggression wish peace. The situation is just as simple as that." Meanwhile, Lemnitzer continued, American policy was "to support the government of President Diem . . . to whatever extent that may be necessary to eliminate the Viet Cong threats"— exactly the policy Kennedy refused to support. This confidently blunt conclusion left Kennedy no room for doubt about where his senior military advisers stood: "The Department of Defense cannot concur in the policy advanced by Ambassador Galbraith, but believes strongly that present policy toward South Vietnam should be pursued vigorously to a successful conclusion." McNamara indicated on his file copy that Lemnitzer's memo to Kennedy was not to be sent or shown to Galbraith. The Joint Chiefs "were already concerned that negative evaluations of the war's progress might undermine the president's resolve. Ken Galbraith was particularly lethal because he presented his views with the wit Kennedy relished."[26]

---

*Harriman's views throughout the Cold War mixed tough anti-Communism with a more flexible liberalism, and shifted frequently depending on his judgment of the situation and his own position—and vulnerability—in the U.S. political and foreign-policy establishment, as well as on his peculiar blend of aloofness and insecurity. Two journalist-historians have noted,

> Mac Bundy began calling Harriman "the Crocodile." ("He lies there on the riverbank, his eyes half closed, looking sleepy. Then, *whap*, he bites.") The nickname caught on: Bobby Kennedy gave Harriman a gold crocodile, and Harriman's staff gave him a silver one, "from your victims" . . . Aides described his negotiating style as "water torture" . . . When the North Vietnamese, the most devious of the lot, spoke, Harriman would ostentatiously read *The New York Times*. When a North Vietnamese representative began calling the U.S. a warmonger, Harriman "accidentally" hit the "talk" button on his microphone and said to an aide, "Did that little bastard say we started World War II?" (Isaacson and Thomas, *Wise Men*, 618).

Galbraith understood Harriman's curious personality: "All his life Averell needed reenforcement of his self-esteem," he said (Abramson, *Spanning the Century*, 16).

Kennedy, however, kept bringing up Galbraith's memo.[27] On May 1 once again State, Defense, and CIA officials vehemently attacked it, Harriman taking the lead.[28] In New Delhi on May 5, without receiving official instructions from Washington, Galbraith raised the issue of negotiations with the Indian representative to the International Control Commission. He sent back word that indeed the Indians thought there was reason to explore bilateral talks; the White House quickly responded that the President was definitely interested and that Galbraith should see what the next steps might be.[29]

Then, in the complex chessboard that was Southeast Asian politics, the situation in Laos suddenly blocked movement on Vietnam. For months the Laotian king and his right-wing government had been frustrating all attempts to form a neutralist coalition government that would include the Communist Pathet Lao. Kennedy, like Galbraith, believed that such a coalition represented the little kingdom's only hope, and he told the king that the United States would not defend his government if he kept refusing to join a coalition. On May 6, after negotiating fruitlessly for five months, the Pathet Lao overran a government outpost, which prompted fears in Washington that full-scale war might resume. Fearing a loss of any bargaining power if the government collapsed, and with the Joint Chiefs calling once again for a massive American intervention, Kennedy ordered 4,000 U.S. troops to Thailand and preparations for intervention into Laos. This eventually persuaded the Laotian government to agree to the long-sought coalition in July, but it carried with it another price: it quickly convinced the wary North Vietnamese that they should not negotiate with the Americans.*[30]

Just as this latest Laotian peace accord was being signed in Geneva on July 23, two remarkable meetings took place that showed that Kennedy had not given up on Galbraith's recommendations. In Honolulu, McNamara stunned General Paul Harkins, the U.S. commander in Vietnam, by telling him to draw up a plan "for training and equipping the South Vietnamese armed forces and phase out [of] major U.S. combat, advisory, and logistics support." According to Deputy Secretary of Defense Roswell Gilpatric, the President had "made clear to McNamara and me that he wanted to not only hold the level of U.S. military presence in Vietnam down, but . . . to reverse the flow . . ."[31]

A day earlier, in Geneva, just as amazingly, the skeptical Averell Harriman had met with North Vietnamese negotiators for the first time. He and the North Vietnamese foreign minister quickly reached what seemed a tacit agreement to keep their forces out of Laos but then fell into a tit-for-tat exchange

---

*Until then, they had apparently thought a similar neutral model might be adopted for South Vietnam. North Vietnamese officials contacted neutralist supporters in Saigon and Paris about negotiating a tripartite coalition government in South Vietnam, but the State Department rebuffed any action until the Laos accords took effect in October and Hanoi's troop infiltration ceased. Ho Chih Min came to fear the imminent invasion of North Vietnam by U.S. forces and went to Beijing to seek military assistance. Chairman Mao—with China weakened by his disastrous Great Leap Forward policies, and with his own fears of an imminent war with Taiwan and of conflict along the Sino-Indian frontier—decided he needed a strong ally on his southern flank. He agreed secretly to provide Ho with enough weapons and ammunition to arm 230 infantry battalions.

about Vietnam, each blaming the other for violating the 1954 Geneva Accords. Harriman abruptly broke off the discussion, telling his surprised listeners that Rusk was waiting for him. He reported to Washington that, for the time being at least, there was in his opinion no further need to pursue talks. Better, he said, to wait and see who honored or violated the just-signed accords on Laos, rather than undertake a new diplomatic offensive immediately.[32]

AFTER ALL GALBRAITH'S often fruitless work on behalf of a negotiated peace in Vietnam and a U.S. exit, he found the summer of 1962 a "mostly dull" interlude on the diplomatic front. The dominant issue he worked on concerned India's negotiations with the Soviet Union to acquire MIG fighters, intended to offset the F-104s Washington had insisted on sending to Pakistan the year before. But congressional voices were threatening massive cuts in the U.S. aid program to India if the MIGs were acquired. To Galbraith, this was largely routine Cold War jockeying by all parties. In a halfhearted attempt at fence mending, he spent an hour or two with Rusk in Bombay, and sardonically reported to Kennedy that while he still didn't find Rusk "the easy, confident, forthcoming, eclectic and commanding figure with which in my imagination I associate the diplomacy of the New Frontier, we get along much better than hitherto . . . But as you are aware I grow mellower by the month."[33]

This was so much nonsense, as Galbraith was carrying on his own second war on the home front, and the conflict was anything but mellow. What concerned him most that summer was not diplomatic but economic issues—specifically the advocacy of Heller, Tobin, Samuelson, and other "New Economists" for a major tax cut. For the President's economists, the cuts not only were good policy but also represented their best chance to demonstrate what their particular style of activist Keynesianism could do to create sustainable full-employment growth—a style that up to that point was untested. Kennedy had resisted them, with almost as much vigor as he'd shown toward the State and Defense departments on the subject of troops in Vietnam, having bluntly told Heller in December 1960, "I understand the case for a tax cut but it doesn't fit very well with my call for sacrifice." Samuelson had been instructed to omit any mention of a tax cut when he laid out his pre-inaugural economic report to the President-elect because "it would be embarrassing and it would not take place."[34]

Throughout 1961 and early 1962, Heller had nonetheless kept raising the issue, only to be rebuffed.[35] By March, however, the economy's recovery had slowed, so he now argued that "a quick, sure way of adding to purchasing power . . . would be a temporary reduction of personal income taxes." Kennedy demurred once again, but then in April he collided with the U.S. Steel chairman, Roger Blough, over proposed steel price increases. He forced Blough to back down, but in the process he soured his fragile relations with the business community. ("My father always told me that all businessmen were sons of bitches, but I never believed it until now," he famously remarked. But after besting Blough, Kennedy said to Schlesinger, in a more jocular mood, "I told him that his men could keep their horses for the spring plowing"—an echo of Grant's words to Lee at Appomattox.)

When the stock market dipped suddenly shortly thereafter, Heller quickly urged at minimum a $5 billion tax cut to prime the economy and bolster business confidence; this was a much larger figure than he had proposed in 1961. This time, more sure-footed in political and economic argumentation, Heller shrewdly invoked Kennedy's problems with the business community as justification for a tax cut.[36] Conservative outrage had boiled over about the President's dressing down of the steel companies, and in early June, a reluctant but realistic Kennedy was persuaded that he needed to mend fences; he announced that the following January he would propose a tax cut as part of his legislative agenda for 1963. A week later, Galbraith, who was back in Washington and participating in meetings with the White House's economic advisers at Kennedy's request, weighed in heavily against this idea.

Galbraith had come back to the U.S. in mid-May because he was ill again—"bad stomach and no sleep"—and doctors had advised another round of tests to follow up on those he'd undergone in January. He'd then spent a week resting on his farm in Vermont, interrupted by an urgent call from Kennedy over the sudden sharp drop in stocks on May 28. He dissuaded the President from going on television to calm jittery nerves but agreed to come to Washington post haste. He cautioned Kennedy against thinking the drop signaled a general slump—"As you said rightly the other day, sometimes they [falling stock prices] do, sometimes they don't"—but added that it would likely have a negative effect on automobiles, housing, real estate and large-ticket consumer goods. "Accordingly all forms of budget liberalization and any steps to keep money rates easy and encourage investments are of increased urgency. As usual, I would be against a tax cut."[37] This was exactly contrary to what Heller was recommending.

On June 5, when Galbraith met with Heller, Tobin, Samuelson, Solow, and others to discuss a tax cut, he and David Bell, the head of the Bureau of the Budget, were the only skeptics in the room. The next day, in a private discussion with Kennedy just before the President met with the same group, Galbraith leaned hard against the proposal.[38] At the end of their talk, Kennedy asked him to help draft a major speech on economics that he was scheduled to give in New Haven that Sunday.

Galbraith's lobbying had effects. On June 11 Kennedy delivered his now famous Yale commencement address, in which he laid out the argument for Keynesianism more fully than any president had before him: it was the turning point in Kennedy's conversion to Keynesianism, and Heller called it "a truly remarkable document—undoubtedly, the first complete speech on economic policy—and modern economic policy at that—that a President had ever made."

Significantly, the speech made no mention of tax cuts, even though Kennedy had just announced his tentative plans for a 1963 tax cut. Instead it concentrated on demolishing what the President told his Yale audience were popular "myths" that stood in the way of sustained economic growth—myths such as the necessity of balanced budgets, the evils of "big government," and the dangers of public debt. He left open the choice of preferred fiscal stimulus: tax cuts or increased spending. This silence was no accident: both Heller at the Council of Economic Advisors and Galbraith (working with Schlesinger) had prepared separate drafts of the speech, and Kennedy on the flight up to New Haven had worked on Sorensen's composite version in great detail, writing between a quarter and a third of the final text himself. The emphases and omissions were his.[39]

Heller knew he had not won the day for his cuts, and thought he knew why. "Among [New Frontier] economists," he ruefully admitted, "there's no question that Galbraith was closer to the President"—and Galbraith was still pressing Kennedy to combine increased spending with tax reform in lieu of an across-the-board tax cut. Heller needed a new line of attack, and needed to wait until Galbraith was out of Washington.

A month later, with Galbraith safely back in India, the CEA met with the President on July 13, this time with Paul Samuelson and Robert Solow. The latter two invoked their abilities as economic forecasters to shape the meeting's outcome: they had already warned Kennedy on June 6 that "only an early tax cut appears to be capable of giving the economy the stimulus it needs"; now they ominously described current economic conditions as "even more unfavorable than we had expected." Heller's tax cut was essential "to avert the developing recession," and in their view the need to cut immediately was so great that the President should "divorce all cuts from *any* [tax] reform."[40]

Even so, Kennedy remained extremely reluctant to cut taxes. Galbraith had weighed in once again on July 10 with a lengthy warning that cuts would neither win him friends in the business community nor deliver political benefits to voters before the November midterm elections. In a briefing memo of July 11 to prepare Kennedy for the July 13 meeting with the CEA, Sorensen echoed Galbraith, arguing that the President should favor a tax cut only if a downturn actually started; if the cuts were sure to go to consumption rather than savings; if the resulting deficit was smaller than Eisenhower's $12 billion 1959 deficit; and if Congress and the business community went along. He reluctantly agreed that some sort of cut was likely going to be needed, but the conditions he proposed were close to a tax-cut veto.

After his meeting on the morning of July 13, Kennedy lunched with a group of businessmen who favored a tax cut but disagreed about its timing. That afternoon, he talked separately with Treasury Secretary Dillon and Congressman Wilbur Mills, the powerful chairman of the House Ways and Means Committee. Both said they wanted no immediate actions on Heller's proposal—Dillon because he feared it would interfere with Treasury's pending tax reform proposals, Mills because Congress was unlikely to support it and he himself opposed immediate action.

As it turned out, Samuelson's and Solow's prediction of recession was wrong: the economy ended up growing a booming 5.8 percent in 1962 (and then 4 percent in 1963) without any tax cut, and the stock market saw the start of a long bull market. But the "scientific" forecast had its effect, and Kennedy in August went on national television to propose a tax cut more dramatically. Yet even then the President kept hedging, since he once again put the idea off for a year and combined it with a comprehensive program of tax reform. This wasn't the Heller scenario at all, which called for immediate tax cuts to fend off a putative recession.

In New Delhi, Galbraith was pleased, and in late August congratulated Kennedy on his televised address. He was now "the most Keynesian head of state in history," he wrote, and should hang a portrait of the master "in your bathroom or some other suitably secluded place." Anyway, Kennedy was right that tax reform and more spending were the issues. "The only people who do really feel strongly about Federal taxes are the Republican rich who are in the high surtax rates and those who would be were it not for the loopholes. The first will fight for reductions. The second will fight for their loopholes."[41]

According to Theodore Sorensen, the President throughout the summer and fall of 1962 "remained unenthusiastic, if not skeptical, about tax reduction," and viewed a tax cut "not as a bold Keynesian program of economic stimulation, but rather as a sweetener, a secondary device designed to ease the passage of the tax reforms, which remained uppermost" in his mind.[42] And Kennedy himself made a point of telling Heller, "You know I like spending money. What I want from you are good programs by which money can be spent effectively." As JFK put it to Heller a year later, "First we'll get your tax cut, then we'll get my expenditure programs."[43] Kennedy's attitude did not show a "lingering fiscal conservatism," as some have argued, for he *had* indeed become a Keynesian. But he had *not* become a New Economics Keynesian.

IN THE MIDST of the debate over tax policy, suddenly a much larger threat loomed: On October 16 John F. Kennedy found himself facing the prospect of nuclear war with the Soviet Union. The Cuban Missile Crisis posed the greatest danger to peace since World War II—and promised far greater destruction.[44] And on that same day the chance of a second war also loomed, as thousands of troops massed along the border in the Himalayas between China and India. There was a risk of immense human slaughter: prolonged conflict between the world's two largest countries could easily take the lives of millions.

On the morning of October 16, McGeorge Bundy opened his daily briefing book. In it he found two urgent memoranda: the first, from the State Department, warned that "fighting on the Sino-Indian border has become much more serious."[45] The United States was supplying modest amounts of nonlethal military aid to New Delhi for the time being—transport aircraft, radios, and spare parts. But the situation was dangerous, and Bundy was told that State and Defense were studying what additional aid might be necessary, should India request it. Bundy glanced through it quickly.

The second, more alarming memo came from the CIA. After analyzing reconnaissance photos taken by U-2 overflights of Cuba two days earlier, the agency said that it appeared certain the Russians were building missile sites in Cuba. The night before, Ray Cline of the CIA had called Bundy and told him to expect the memo. Bundy had decided not to inform the President at the time, wanting more information and fearing that a nighttime meeting in the Oval Office might tip off the press. As he now read the CIA memo, his mind raced over the elements of Operation Mongoose, the Kennedy administration's top-secret effort to destroy Castro's regime.

Over the past year, General Edward Lansdale had been working tirelessly to foment an uprising on the island. Agents had been infiltrated, small attacks had been launched against military and civilian targets, and attempts by the Mafia and others to kill Castro had been made—with little, as Bundy knew, to show for the efforts. Seven weeks earlier Bundy therefore had gotten Kennedy's approval for NSAM 181, a Presidential directive that ordered Lansdale to step up his efforts, and to develop "with all possible speed" plans to foment an internal revolt against the Castro government as well as a possible U.S. invasion, tentatively proposed for October. After that directive was issued, photos from another U-2 flight had identified a site being prepared for Russian surface-to-air missiles—defensive weapons—which became added reason for spurring the effort.

The Castro government had quickly gotten wind of Lansdale's new orders, though, for the Miami exile community had been extensively penetrated by Cuban agents. Castro in September had even publicly warned that the United States was planning an invasion, a charge that the President had heatedly denied as "a frantic effort to bolster his regime." Yet Bundy and the President well knew that Castro was right. Lansdale was in fact preparing options for such an invasion, with a tentative launch that October.

At 8:45 a.m., Bundy carried his briefing book into the Oval Office and told President Kennedy for the first time that the CIA had "hard photographic evidence" that the Soviets now had IRBMs in Cuba. A stunned Kennedy then ordered Bundy to convene a meeting of the National Security Council's executive committee (called Ex Comm) for 11:45 that morning. (At almost the same moment, Galbraith in New Delhi happened to send a cable to Kennedy. Worried about the growing signs of war between China and India, he began, "I remember well when I was running price control the only news ever passed up to me was of major disasters. The intelligence reaching your office must be much the same.")

Kennedy then called his brother Robert. The attorney general expressed surprise at Bundy's memo, although he, like Bundy, was a member of the task force overseeing Operation Mongoose. The President also consulted John McCloy, a Republican Wall Street lawyer, in New York, and one of the administration's unofficial "Wise Men." McCloy recommended the United States take immediate and forceful action, if necessary including air strikes and an invasion. Shortly before the Ex Comm meeting started, Kennedy met with another "Wise Man," Charles Bohlen, the former U.S. ambassador to the Soviet

Union, who was about to leave for Paris as Kennedy's ambassador there. "There seemed to be no question in [JFK's] mind, and certainly none in mine," Bohlen wrote later, "that the United States would have to get these bases eliminated . . . the only question was how."

At the Ex Comm meeting (which Bohlen joined at JFK's request), a senior CIA photoanalyst showed the damning evidence. Further U-2 flights were ordered for that afternoon, and participants began reviewing U.S. options—from surgical air strikes on the Soviet bases to full-scale invasion to a blockade. Ambassador Kohler in Moscow was ordered by cable to meet Premier Khrushchev immediately. (The Soviet leader, who didn't know of the U-2 evidence, falsely insisted that all Soviet activity in Cuba was purely defensive.)

Over the next two days, Kennedy and his advisers met repeatedly to review new intelligence reports and to consult with more outside "Wise Men," including Dean Acheson (who counseled a surgical strike) and Robert Lovett (who favored a blockade). By now U-2 flights had identified SS-5s, a Soviet missile with a 2,200-mile range, much greater than the SS-4s already confirmed.

Meanwhile, Galbraith in New Delhi was monitoring the worsening Indian situation, knowing nothing of the missile crisis in Cuba. In a cable on October 18, he alerted Washington that signs of war were growing. With winter coming in the Himalayas, action would be delayed, giving time for talks, but Nehru, in a private meeting, had been very firm that "the Chinese must be driven out whether it takes a year, five years or ten." The prime minister wanted this made very clear to Kennedy.[46]

By Friday afternoon, Kennedy and the Ex Comm were leaning toward Lovett's idea of a blockade against Cuba. Simultaneously, Galbraith, skeptical that fighting would break out immediately in the Himalayas and eager to talk with the President, had boarded a plane in New Delhi bound for London, where he planned to deliver a long-scheduled lecture at the Guildhall, and then go on to Washington.

As he flew west, it was afternoon in Washington and an urgent Ex Comm meeting was under way.[47] Maxwell Taylor, whom Kennedy had recently appointed chairman of the Joint Chiefs, was outlining the Pentagon's recommendations: to bomb the missile sites immediately and impose a naval blockade that would prevent any more missiles from arriving, and to prepare for a full U.S. invasion to follow. Taylor admitted he wasn't sanguine about the effects of the bombing, however—and expressed concern about the reactions of both the Soviet Union and U.S. allies.

The President worried aloud that an air strike would be an invitation for the Russians to invade Berlin and that such an invasion would force him to reply with nuclear weapons. It was, he told the group, "a hell of an alternative. But if we do nothing, we will have problems in Berlin anyway. So, we have to do something." (Air Force Chief of Staff LeMay helpfully compared any attempt at negotiations before bombing to "appeasement at Munich," and said that an immediate, overwhelming military strike was the only alternative.) After much deliberation, Sorensen was told to abandon the "air strike" speech he'd been writing and prepare a "blockade" speech—which he finished in draft for Kennedy at 3 a.m. That same night, a coordinated schedule of military and diplomatic moves was prepared for White House approval.

On Saturday, the speech and the operational plan for a blockade were amended and approved. After the meeting adjourned at 5:10 p.m., the President told Sorensen to redraft his new speech, then told his aide privately that he'd wait to make a final decision on Sunday morning, after talking with Air Force officials about air-strike options. McNamara, either told or sensing that the President's mind wasn't made up, ordered four tactical fighter-bomber squadrons put on alert. As deployment orders went out through the Pentagon that night, rumors swept across the capital that war might be imminent. Press calls flooded in, but the White House, citing national security, urged reporters and editors to publish nothing for forty-eight hours, by which time the Navy would be in place and Kennedy could address the nation.

Among the orders that went out that night was a "top-secret/eyes-only" message from Kennedy to Galbraith, and Galbraith was awakened in the middle of the night in London to receive it. It wasn't about Cuba, though. He was being ordered back to New Delhi by the quickest possible means: preparing for battle in Cuba, Kennedy had just learned that war had broken out between China and India.

Aboard an eastbound jet by noon, Galbraith read the cable traffic and messages delivered by courier from the London embassy. Chinese troops had swept across India's Himalayan border in two areas a thousand miles apart: in Ladakh, to the west, and at several points in the Northeast Frontier area that stretched from Bhutan to the Burmese border. Indian troops were falling back, their forward units captured or destroyed, across most of the battle lines. By 6 a.m. Monday, Galbraith was back in New Delhi and was being briefed by his aides on the military and political situation.

The suddenness and strength of China's attack had come after months of confrontations and skirmishes, part of escalating tensions between the two powers since 1959. The root of the problem lay in the so-called MacMahon Line, drawn by a British surveying team in 1914 to define disputed borderlines in several remote areas between then-British India and Chinese-dominated Tibet. No treaty ever made the line official, however, and by the time Nehru came to power in an independent India and Mao Tse-tung in the People's Republic of China, neither leader was keen to follow the dictates of imperial British surveyors.

After China occupied Tibet militarily in 1950, India took the position that indeed the MacMahon Line was its border, a view China vehemently rejected but did nothing practical to overturn. Within a few years, to Beijing's great annoyance, the CIA was funding the Dalai Lama and running an active insurgency movement in Tibet; after China brutally put down a Tibetan revolt in 1959, the Dalai Lama and thousands of his followers fled to the safety of India, and relations between Beijing and New Delhi deteriorated.[48] By 1961, India was operating what it called a "forward policy," the echo of an old British imperial strategy, placing troops at the very edges of disputed areas along its 2,000-mile-long Himalayan frontier to block incursions or attempted land grabs. Skirmishes occurred with growing regularity.[49]

Nevertheless, no one in New Delhi expected the Chinese invasion when it came, and the government's political and military leaders were in disarray and near panic by the time Galbraith got back from London. At least, Galbraith consoled himself, Defense Minister Krishna Menon—a brilliant and mercurial left-wing politician who was no favorite of either Galbraith's or Washington's—was being bypassed, since Nehru had effectively taken direct command of the army.

The army's problems weren't confined to the Himalayan battlefront. B. M. Kaul, chief of the general staff (and a cousin of Nehru), was, as one observer politely put it, "in an agitated state of mind." Fearing the outbreak of general war, he began excitedly calling for a temporary military dictatorship in India, for South Korea and Taiwan (with U.S. assistance) to invade China, and for the United States not only to provide air cover for Indian cities but to "launch massive air attacks on China from bases in India."[50]

Galbraith over the next few days incongruously divided his time between the India-China war and the Indians' reaction to the Cuban Missile Crisis— with the Indians on the one hand initially hostile to a U.S. blockade in the Caribbean and on the other inclined to seek U.S. military assistance in their own war, as it rapidly became clear that Russia wouldn't help and India's non-aligned "friends" were silent. A letter from Kennedy to Nehru, carelessly drafted by an aide to explain the U.S. position, was intercepted and redrafted by Galbraith, fearful that its elementary illiteracy would only exacerbate Nehru's feelings. Within a few days, with the two armies fielding nearly 60,000 troops, the Indians had taken 4,000 casualties (Chinese losses weren't known), were still falling back, and now were well behind the MacMahon Line. Chinese troops were undeniably in Indian territory and moving forward.[51]

In Washington on Thursday the head of the Strategic Air Command, acting without the President's knowledge or authority, ordered SAC on DEF CON 2, the highest state of war readiness the United States ever reached during the Cold War. At the White House, intense discussions were going on about invading Cuba and "eliminating" Castro, using Operation Mongoose teams. Because there was virtually no time for Washington to think about China and India, Galbraith was in an extraordinary situation for a twentieth-century diplomat. He "had a considerable war on my hands without a single telegram, letter, telephone call or other communication of guidance."[52] With a remarkably free hand to shape U.S. policy and only the sketchiest of instructions, he took the opportunity to do just that. He assured India of U.S. support for its claim of the MacMahon Line as its boundary; he got his attachés to work on contingency planning for the delivery of U.S. military aid; and he laid out how the State Department needed to deal with Pakistan (which was making pro-China noises, so that three divisions that India needed against China were tied down on the Pakistan border), the Soviet Union (which India didn't want to offend), and Krishna Menon (who kept insisting that Pakistan, not China, was India's greatest enemy). In an almost nonstop barrage of visits, he saw General Kaul, Krishna Menon, Foreign Minister Desai, and other Indian leaders to assure them of U.S. support and to hear their inside assessments. He also met with Nehru, whose physical condition caused him alarm: under the stress, his friend "was frail, brittle, and seemed small and old. He was obviously desperately tired."

Kennedy and Khrushchev had been exchanging tense letters, and the situation seemed to get closer and closer to war. Kennedy authorized U.S. planes in Europe to load nuclear weapons, targeted on Russia. The CIA reported that the first Cuban missiles were operational. On October 25, Galbraith updated Rusk, McNamara, and Bundy on the Indian war in a "top-secret/eyes-only" cable. The next morning Kennedy approved arms shipments as required and met that afternoon with the Indian ambassador; Rusk cabled Galbraith with details and further instructions.[53]

Using their CIA back channel, Galbraith sent two messages to Kennedy on how the war might be used to force out Defense Minister Menon. Kennedy replied the next day with an "eyes-only" cable, agreeing; he told Galbraith that he was "leaving next steps up to you." Rusk, who had flown to Karachi to assure General Khan that U.S. military aid to India would not represent a policy tilt against Pakistan, cabled back his considered opinion that "Sino-India border dispute is second only in importance to Cuba in present global confrontation between the Free World and Sino-Soviet bloc." The next day Kennedy sent a long personal letter to Khan, assuring him of abiding U.S. support.[54]

Then suddenly from Washington, late on October 28, came good news at last: Khrushchev had backed down, and the Soviet Union would remove its missiles from Cuba. At 5 p.m. that afternoon Russian technicians began dismantling the first bases; by November 1 all of them were gone.

The next day, however, the Sino-Indian war entered a new and dangerous phase. With the Chinese continuing their advance, India formally requested U.S. military assistance; airlifted U.S. weapons began arriving within a week, followed by several shiploads of weapons bearing a million rounds for machine guns, 40,000 mines, and 100,000 mortar rounds, as well as hundreds of two-way radios and other equipment. (More than $60 million in arms and supplies—enough to equip ten Indian mountain divisions—were eventually sent by the United States, with more from Britain, and smaller amounts from France, Canada, and other countries.)[55] Over the next ten days, the situation grew ever more complex. As Western condemnation of China's action increased, the Chinese advance came to a halt, but this news was offset by furious new rumblings about Kashmir from the Pakistanis, who feared that India might turn its new stockpile of Western arms on them. Back in Washington, Rusk wired the U.S. ambassador in Pakistan: "It is clear that Paks have whipped themselves into near hysterical state and that next few weeks will be very difficult for all of us."[56]

The State Department was now back in touch with Galbraith, who chafed at much of its advice; he was more inclined to act on what he knew to be true in front of him. Not incidentally, he was enjoying the immense influence he was now exercising over the Indian government. When a CBS News crew showed up in New Delhi, Galbraith hesitated to grant them an interview, because, he said, he was "not fond of the role of a professor masterminding a war." Yet that was in fact what he'd become, and later he admitted that he quite enjoyed it but at the time "did not want to seem so."[57] Besides, with China hesitating, he sensed that the fighting might quickly wind down; India's position wouldn't be helped if it was seen as overly influenced by the American ambassador.

Amid the conflict, though, there were a few pleasures in which he let himself take delight: Krishna Menon was finally dismissed from the government, while from California came news that Richard Nixon had lost the election for the governorship and appeared to be leaving politics for good, telling the press bitterly, "Now you won't have Richard Nixon to kick around any more." A third pleasure was moving into the new ambassador's residence, designed by Edward Durrell Stone. Until then, he and the family had been living in two modest-sized nineteenth-century bungalows, awaiting completion of their new quarters. To Galbraith, the new home "lacked warmth but not beauty," despite a constantly running fountain that gave the impression "of a toilet out of control." Once the India-China war was behind him, though, he occasionally amused himself by climbing the latticed stone screens that divided some of the rooms, with Peter and Jamie—to Kitty's dismay—climbing behind him.

On November 13, Galbraith sent a long letter to Kennedy outlining the new political and military situation. He was remarkably prescient on a number of points. Though confident that the war would not become a general conflict, he warned the President that the fighting might not yet be over.[58] Indeed, the Chinese suddenly resumed their advance in a series of lightning strikes and overran Indian positions in both the western and the eastern combat theaters. As one after another Indian position fell under the onslaught, it set off alarms in Washington and near hysteria in New Delhi. By then China had offered to open "unconditional negotiations" to end the fighting. The Indians, who took the term "unconditional" to mean that the talks would open up boundary claims in a way inimical to their own position on the MacMahon Line, rejected the offer.

Rusk, in another "eyes-only" cable, told Galbraith ominously,

> I am convinced that we are on the front end of large and unpredictable events affecting many parts of the world and that earlier frames of reference will require radical review by many governments including our own . . . If the situation in the subcontinent should take a rapid and adverse turn, India must surely recognize that geography restricts our ability to act promptly in the area.

He raised the possibility that Pakistan might break with the West and conspire with Beijing against India.[59] Nehru dispatched two personal letters to Kennedy, in which he described the situation as "really desperate," and called on the U.S. to send a dozen squadrons of all-weather U.S. fighter jets to protect India's cities, and for B-47 bomber squadrons to strike at Chinese bases.[60] That same day, Kennedy and the NSC heard an intelligence report from John McCone on Chinese troop strength and movements; Rusk worried that American aid wasn't moving fast enough, and that India might lose Assam. The situation deteriorated so quickly that by November 20, Galbraith wrote, "it was the day of ultimate panic in Delhi, the first time I have ever witnessed the disintegration of public morale . . . The wildest rumors flew around town, the most widely believed that a detachment of 500 [rebellious Indian] paratroopers was about to descend on New Delhi" to depose Nehru and install Krishna Menon as prime minister.[61]

The United States began to prepare for a major new confrontation with the Communists, not quite certain whether or not this was somehow linked to what had happened in Cuba. A few weeks earlier, in talking about the missiles there, Kennedy had spoken of them as a "Sino-Soviet" threat, though there was no evidence, then or now, that Beijing had anything to do with the arms in Cuba. After the CIA told Kennedy and the Ex Comm at a meeting on November 19 that China could easily support a force of 300,000 troops against India, the United States and Britain drew up plans to ship at least $60 million each in weaponry to India, and Rusk advised Galbraith that State thought it very possible that "Peiping is now engaged in an all-out assault on India." A diplomatic mission headed by Averell Harriman, a special military team headed by General John Kelly, and a congressional delegation headed by Senate Majority Leader Mike Mansfield had all by then either reached New Delhi or were on their way.

Then, on November 22, with the Americans and British weighing the logistics of a massive arms airlift to reinforce the Indians, just as suddenly as the Chinese attacks had begun Beijing announced that it was ordering a unilateral cease-fire and would withdraw behind the MacMahon Line by December 1.

To Galbraith—who, as one historian put it, had found himself during the past six weeks in the occasionally awkward position of being both American ambassador and "in effect a privy councillor to the Indian government, a role [he] played with zest and tact"—the cease-fire and withdrawal came as a relief.[62] The stress had been killing, and, he later candidly admitted, he'd been taking "large amounts" of barbiturates and sedatives in order to sleep.[63] It was Thanksgiving Day in the United States, and he hadn't even noticed. With peace arriving "like a thief in the night," Galbraith's wife and children were left to dine on turkey and stuffing while he spent the day with the British ambassador, the visiting senators, Prime Minister Nehru, the new army commander-in-chief, the American press corps, and then the delegation headed by Harriman.

Galbraith continued to be a shrewd adviser to the Indian government, as he had been throughout the conflict, counseling Nehru to buy time, to hold all Indian forces in place, to damp down nationalistic talk in the Parliament, to wait and see what the Chinese in fact did.[64] When they withdrew as promised on December 1, there was rejoicing throughout India, and a immense outpouring of affection for the United States and its ambassador. According to one poll, just 7 percent of Indians replied "very good" when asked their opinion of America before the crisis; by December, the number had skyrocketed to nearly 65 percent.[65]

But Galbraith was also a remarkably adroit protector of U.S. interests, carefully advancing them without stepping too hard on Indian toes and creating what at the time seemed the beginning of a new era in U.S.-Indian relations. Even Rusk grudgingly expressed thanks, albeit briefly: "Deeply appreciate your handling present crisis," he wrote in a cable.[66]

It was an achievement President Kennedy thoroughly admired, however. He invited Galbraith in December to come back to Washington as much to celebrate as to debrief him personally. He and Mrs. Kennedy gave a small informal dinner party for Galbraith with the Shrivers upstairs at the White House, followed by an evening at the theater (much noticed in the papers). Kennedy then had Galbraith give a briefing to the Joint Chiefs of Staff ("in brilliant beribboned uniform") and attend a lengthier meeting with the Ex Comm (at which he attacked the Joint Chiefs for their proposed air-defense plan for India). "The President, after listening to me, stamped on the Joint Chiefs with both feet. One enjoys arguing a good case—and also winning." Galbraith claimed to feel reassured when he heard that Rusk "continues to regard me as a major inconvenience in an otherwise placid organization."[67]

Three days later Galbraith flew to Nassau, where the President and British Prime Minister Harold Macmillan were reviewing a variety of Anglo-American commitments. The major issue was nuclear weaponry—the Skybolt missile and the provision of Polaris submarines to Britain (decisions that provoked de Gaulle's eventual withdrawal from NATO). JFK asked Galbraith to lead off the session that the two leaders devoted to "the Sino-Indian dispute" and its aftermath. Before it began, he and Kennedy went for a swim, then lunched with Macmillan. The British delegation, including the prime minister, failed to impress him.

Characteristically, during the session itself Galbraith not only took the lead but shifted the discussion to the future settlement they should effect between India and Pakistan on Kashmir, which he considered a much greater danger to peace than supposed Chinese ambitions to expand southward. He offered a critique of recommendations of both Kennedy's and Macmillan's aides that would heavily expand India's military budget and almost certainly increase tensions among China, Pakistan, and India.[68] "By later afternoon," unfortunately,

> all imagination had been removed from the exercise. A great opportunity to bring India into much closer working association with the western community (and to save a great deal on independent Indian defense expenditures),

an opportunity sensed only by the President, [Undersecretary of State Phillips] Talbot and myself, had been largely dulled over. I felt discouraged. By twilight, a dismal paper had been agreed to by the group—one that largely missed the point.[69]

All things considered, it seemed to Galbraith to be a good time to move on.

In late November, Kennedy had asked Galbraith whether he would object if he wrote to Harvard President Pusey to see if he'd agree (against Harvard's rules permitting faculty only a two-year leave) to Galbraith's staying on as Indian ambassador. Galbraith had politely declined the offer. Now, in Nassau, "I arranged with the President to return home about June." Kennedy was not surprised, and took his friend's decision to go back to academic life graciously, though this didn't prevent him from asking Galbraith in January 1963 whether he'd like to be U.S. ambassador to the Soviet Union. That too would have posed a risk to his Harvard tenure and given him no relief from Rusk; Galbraith declined, though not easily.*

Galbraith returned to New Delhi for a family Christmas and spent the early months of 1963 doing mostly routine duties, awaiting announcement of his replacement (it turned out to be Chester Bowles). Predictably futile talks between India and Pakistan about Kashmir made no headway, and the fruitless banality of British and American discussions of this failure provoked Galbraith's contempt. He and his wife made a brief and interesting side trip that spring for the wedding of the American socialite Hope Cooke to the prince of Sikkim; there were lectures in Japan, visits from both Chicago economist Milton Friedman and Dean Rusk (the former proved less irksome), and an exquisite trip for the whole family to Simla, in the Himalayan foothills, via private railway car.

It was time to go home.

THE SITUATION IN VIETNAM was growing worse. Publicly President Kennedy downplayed his doubts, though with remarkable ambiguity. For example, he told a White House news conference in December 1962 that "we don't see the end of the tunnel but I must say I don't think it is darker there than it was a year ago, and in some ways lighter." Privately, his assessment was filled with both tension and foreboding. Although the official assessments he was given emphasized all the "progress" being made in containing and pushing back the Viet Cong, the Pentagon wanted more money for the next year's fighting—a quarter billion dollars, in fact, twice its previous estimates. Moreover, the generals wanted to push the fighting northward. ("We should do something to make the North Vietnamese bleed," one Joint Chiefs report put it.[70])

After Senate Majority Leader Mike Mansfield returned from a tour of South Vietnam—shortly after Kennedy's December news conference—he said

---

*Alan Galbraith, then a Harvard senior, remembers the serious consideration his father gave to taking this post.

publicly that President Diem was no closer to peace than he had been in 1955 and that American aid might be required for years; he urged the withdrawal of U.S. troops. At first furious with him, Kennedy a few days later confessed, "I got angry with Mike for disagreeing with our policy . . . and I got angry with myself because I found myself agreeing with him." He called Mansfield to the White House and told him he was determined to have all U.S. troops out of Vietnam in two years, shortly after what he expected to be his reelection in November 1964.[71]

In May 1963, clearly on the White House's directions, Secretary McNamara met again with U.S. military commanders in Asia, as part of their ongoing review of the situation in Vietnam. This time he told them not only that their request for the doubling of funds would not be met, but more important that he wanted new, much firmer plans for U.S. withdrawal than they'd given him the previous spring. He said these plans had to include the first thousand troops out by the end of 1963, and all the rest out by early 1965. The United States, it seemed, was not going to go to war in Southeast Asia after all.

A month later, in a public indication of the direction he now wanted his administration to move, Kennedy on June 10 delivered a commencement speech at American University, in which he announced that the United States, Britain, and the Soviet Union would soon negotiate an atmospheric nuclear test-ban treaty, and declared that he saw it as the first building block in what he believed could be a new era in East-West relations. Using language that Americans hadn't heard from any President in memory, he declared,

> I have chosen this time and this place to discuss a topic on which ignorance too often abounds and the truth is too rarely perceived—yet it is the most important topic on earth: world peace.
>
> What kind of peace do I mean? What kind of peace do we seek? Not a Pax Americana enforced on the world by American weapons of war. Not the peace of the grave or the security of the slave. I am talking about genuine peace, the kind of peace that makes life on earth worth living, the kind that enables men and nations to grow and to hope and to build a better life for their children—not merely peace for Americans but peace for all men and women—not merely peace in our time but peace for all time.
>
> I speak of peace because of the new face of war. Total war makes no sense in an age when great powers can maintain large and relatively invulnerable nuclear forces and refuse to surrender without resort to those forces. It makes no sense in an age when a single nuclear weapon contains almost ten times the explosive force delivered by all the allied air forces in the Second World War. It makes no sense in an age when the deadly poisons produced by a nuclear exchange would be carried by wind and water and soil and seed to the far corners of the globe and to generations yet unborn.
>
> Today the expenditure of billions of dollars every year on weapons acquired for the purpose of making sure we never need to use them is essential

to keeping the peace. But surely the acquisition of such idle stockpiles—which can only destroy and never create—is not the only, much less the most efficient, means of assuring peace.

I speak of peace, therefore, as the necessary rational end of rational men. I realize that the pursuit of peace is not as dramatic as the pursuit of war—and frequently the words of the pursuer fall on deaf ears. But we have no more urgent task.

The President had been mulling over this remarkable text for several months. According to Arthur Schlesinger,

> Kennedy began to feel in the spring of 1963 that there was a possibility for some kind of new movement in our relations with the Soviet Union, and he began to look for an opportunity to make a "peace speech." That was the way it was described, and this was a project which was kept extremely confidential in the White House . . . The draft was not shown to the State Department or to the Defense Department until the Saturday before it was given.[72]

That is, halfway through his presidency, Kennedy decided that he must redefine the nation's Cold War posture and, with Russia, begin moving toward new and less dangerous relations. Yet even then General LeMay was still seeking White House authorization of a U.S. "first strike" capacity—which showed, Kennedy thought, that the military planners were "living in total dreamland." And knowing how controversial the speech would be to many in his administration, the President kept its preparation top secret.

In late May, as Ted Sorensen prepared a near-final draft, the President and Mrs. Kennedy gave another private dinner at the White House with Galbraith, who was back in Washington on his last official duty, a state visit of the President of India.[74] Kennedy talked at length to Galbraith about the speech and what it might mean, and he pointedly asked once again whether Galbraith would accept the ambassadorship to Russia. Galbraith was thrilled that Kennedy seemed willing finally to step away from advisers whose thinking, he believed, was at the core of America's worst problems. For a moment, he even wondered whether he'd made the wrong decision in declining the ambassadorial post.

But he also knew how passionately committed many of Kennedy's aides were to the habits and suspicions of the Cold War era, and he vividly recalled how President Roosevelt's hopes and ambitions for U.S.-Soviet relations had come undone in 1946 after his death. Still, that night, over dinner and then over cigars and brandy, the conversation kept reminding Galbraith that Kennedy was alive, vigorous, and only halfway through his first term, with a good likelihood that he'd be elected to a second in 1964. With six years ahead, Galbraith felt full of hope that this would become the presidency he had so long waited for.[75]

17

Tragedy, Triumph, Tragedy

Of all the changes in American life wrought by the cold war, the most important by far, in my opinion, has been the massive diversion of energy and resources from the creative pursuits of civilized society to the conduct of a costly and interminable struggle for world power. We have been compelled to reverse the traditional order of our national priorities, relegating individual and community life to places on the scale below the enormously expensive military and space activities that constitute our program of national security . . .

To a very considerable extent the American people are not now exercising effective control over the armed forces; nor indeed is the Congress . . .
— J. William Fulbright, chairman,
Senate Foreign Relations Committee,
April 1964

NOVEMBER 22, 1963: Out of the terrible first days that followed her husband's assassination at Dealey Plaza, Jacqueline Kennedy carried treasured memories of the kindnesses that many people extended to her. One in particular she always cherished.

With the death of the President in Dallas, the White House was suddenly no longer her home—and the matter of where she and her two children might go was for a moment uncertain in those first stricken, desolate hours. The delicate question was answered when Averell Harriman telephoned, shortly after she returned to Washington, and offered his Georgetown home for as long as she and the children might need it.[1] Some weeks later Bobby Kennedy told her that it was Ken Galbraith who'd thought to contact Harriman, asking him in turn to call Mrs. Kennedy. "That," she said softly of Galbraith, "is the kind of man he is."[2]

It was a gesture the Kennedys never forgot. When Jackie died of cancer in

May 1994, the night before her public funeral in New York a private service for the family was held in her Fifth Avenue apartment. Only a tiny handful from outside the immediate Kennedy family were invited: Ken and Kitty Galbraith were among them.[3]

WHEN THE FIRST news of the President's assassination came in that Friday in November 1963, Galbraith was in New York at the offices of *Newsweek*, about to sit down for lunch with Arthur Schlesinger, Katharine Graham, *Newsweek's* new owner (and *The Washington Post's* publisher), and the magazine's senior editors. The purpose of the lunch was to discuss ideas for an editorial redesign. Mrs. Graham had just recently taken over the management of the family publishing company, following the suicide of her husband, Philip, and she was looking to Galbraith, with his political savvy and experience at *Fortune*, and to Schlesinger for advice.

A staffer rushed in with news from Dallas that President Kennedy had been shot and was being taken to a hospital. A stunned silence fell in the room, and a sickening feeling came over Galbraith. "It all sounded much too real to be a mistake, and I confess that I gave up hope. Imagining what it means to be shot in the head, mentally destroyed, I wished momentarily that the news might have been that he was dead."[4] When the President's death was confirmed, Galbraith, Schlesinger, and Mrs. Graham rushed to La Guardia airport, where they boarded her private plane to fly immediately to Washington.

They reached the White House by midafternoon, and what Mrs. Graham noticed first was both the grim sorrow and the atmosphere of controlled chaos, as aides tried to function without a President, Vice President, or Cabinet (most of whose key members were over the Pacific on their way to a conference in Japan). Many White House staffers were red-eyed from crying and fighting to control their emotions. After a short while, Mrs. Graham felt awkward being there with no official role, and out of place as a newspaper publisher. She also lost track of Galbraith and Schlesinger, who had gone to be with Ted Sorensen, who had taken temporary unofficial charge of the White House staff while everyone waited for Lyndon Johnson to arrive from Dallas.[5] She decided it was best for her to leave.

The rest of the day "was full of activity," Galbraith later said, "but I now can barely recall what it was we were doing."[6] Early that evening, he and others were driven to nearby Andrews Air Force Base to meet *Air Force One*, returning from Dallas with President and Mrs. Johnson, Mrs. Kennedy, and the body of the late President.

By the time the plane arrived, the considerable crowd had swelled, with several dozen congressmen and senators along with a swarm of reporters and TV cameras. Bobby Kennedy escorted his sister-in-law and her children off the plane first, followed by President Johnson and the rest of his party. Galbraith thought it incongruous and undignified to see JFK's coffin removed using "a lift arrangement of the kind used to put food aboard." Mrs. Kennedy insisted on going to Bethesda Naval Hospital with the coffin instead of returning to the

White House, as the staff had arranged, and LBJ and his family went home to the vice president's residence. That left Galbraith and the others he'd come out with to go back to the White House on their own.

About nine, he and Schlesinger finally had a bite to eat in the White House mess, and Galbraith then went to Averell Harriman's home in Georgetown, where he could "rarely remember a deadlier or drearier" group of friends. Then sometime after midnight, he proceeded to Mrs. Graham's house, since she'd generously told him that, under the circumstances, he was welcome to stay as long as he wanted. Settling into an unfamiliar bed in an unfamiliar room, a terrible pain now suddenly washed over him, and he found that he needed several sleeping pills before he could even close his eyes, and even then slept fitfully.[7]

The next morning, Galbraith stayed at Mrs. Graham's house to work on a memorial piece for *The Washington Post* (the article, "A Communication," appeared in the *Post* the next day). After turning it in, he went to the White House to visit the Kennedy bier with Kitty, who had arrived from Boston. From there the two walked to the nearby Occidental restaurant, where they lunched in a deeply somber mood with Walter Heller, Paul Samuelson, Schlesinger, and a few other friends. He returned to the White House to see Ted Sorensen, who was still "badly broken up," and to help work on funeral arrangements.

About three that afternoon Galbraith was walking between the White House and the old Executive Office Building when he suddenly ran into President Johnson, who had just held his first Cabinet meeting.[8] Johnson, grabbing his arm, pulled Galbraith into his EOB office, evicting a Texas judge anxious to see him. A few minutes earlier, Galbraith had passed the Oval Office. Glancing in, he had realized that everything there was still Kennedy's—the war memorabilia, the model sailboat, the pictures of Jackie and the children. As he sat down with Johnson now, he imagined that they were somehow in a dream and that President Kennedy would be returning momentarily.

He and President Johnson plunged into an intense conversation, as LBJ sipped an orange soda. The Texan observed that both of them were "Roosevelt liberals," that he wanted to continue the Kennedy policies, and, most important, that he wanted Galbraith's support and advice, especially about what he should be doing first.

Characteristically, Galbraith did not hesitate, though the question was unexpected and his answer unplanned. "Well, I think there are two things," he replied, "one domestic, one foreign." Civil rights was the domestic issue, and they both knew LBJ would do well on it. "As for the foreign problem, I said that he had to worry about the military and about Indochina," Galbraith recalled. "But on that second observation I got no response at all from Johnson. His response to the first was very immediate and warm, but on the second, nothing."[9]

What Galbraith didn't know as they spoke was that in the Cabinet meeting Johnson had just come from, Vietnam had been high on the agenda, and that LBJ already was thinking ahead to his meeting the next day with Henry Cabot

Lodge, Jr., the ambassador to South Vietnam, and was uncertain about what to say to him. Two weeks earlier President Diem had been overthrown and then assassinated by dissident South Vietnamese generals supported by the United States; McNamara and Rusk, in memos LBJ had read moments before he ran into Galbraith, had underscored that the generals were anxiously watching the new President for signs of his intentions in Southeast Asia. What were they?

LBJ had never been part of Kennedy's inner circle on foreign policy, and was uncomfortable with the patrician Lodge, who had been Nixon's running mate against Kennedy and Johnson in 1960. And so the next afternoon LBJ began the meeting with Lodge sounding almost like Galbraith, emphasizing that he'd never been happy with U.S. operations in Vietnam, especially the overthrow and murder of Diem; but then, anxious to show Kennedy's people that he was in full command, he shifted abruptly, instructing Lodge to tell waiting reporters that he'd made "his first decision of substance—that American aid to the Saigon regime would continue at present levels."[10] Johnson apparently thought he was doing no more than giving a response designed to show continuity in U.S. policies to its allies, not initiating any new "Johnson Doctrine" for Southeast Asia.

Afterward, his aide Bill Moyers came in, and LBJ privately shared over scotches what he thought he'd communicated. "I told [Lodge]," the new President said, "to go back and tell those generals in Saigon that Lyndon Johnson intends to stand by our word, but by God, I want something for my money. I want 'em to get off their butts and get out in those jungles and whip hell out of some Communists. And then I want them to leave me alone, because I got some bigger things to do right here at home."[11] It was pure Johnson—and the worst miscalculation of his presidency.

But the comment throws a light on LBJ's silence about Vietnam when he encountered Galbraith—and on why he asked for his help. He knew that Galbraith had long advised against further commitments in Southeast Asia, but that Kennedy's senior advisers had disagreed. Those advisers were Johnson's now, and their best course for the moment was not to change course. The domestic front was a different matter, where LBJ was much surer of himself—and where he and Galbraith had much in common, having known each other since the New Deal.* And so he asked for specific help at the end of their meeting: would Galbraith work with Sorensen on the speech Johnson would give to Congress in four days, his first as President?[12] In that speech—which

*The two men had first met in 1941 when Galbraith was at the Office of Price Administration and Johnson was an awkward, raw-boned young congressman from Texas. They had been introduced by Clifford and Virginia Durr, neighbors and good friends of the Galbraiths. The Durrs were that extraordinary rarity at the time: Southern white integrationists who supported expanded civil rights and opposed lynch laws and poll taxes. Durr became a prominent New Deal lawyer. When he and his Wellesley-educated wife returned to Alabama after the war they became a constant irritant and goad to the white establishment there, and were early supporters of the Montgomery bus boycott (Durr was Rosa Parks's lawyer) as well as of a young black minister named Martin Luther King, Jr. Johnson later told Galbraith that one of his proudest moments in the Senate came in the early 1950s, when he warned Senator Joseph McCarthy to "lay off" the Durrs or face Johnson's considerable wrath. McCarthy was eager to tar the Durrs with accusations of "red influence," but he complied.

opened with Sorensen's memorable words, "All I have I would have gladly given not to be standing here today"—he chose to talk of those "bigger things to do right here at home," of unifying America, of racial healing, and of building on the New Frontier's incandescent promise. Significantly, he never mentioned Vietnam. As the speech concluded, and members of Congress rose in thunderous bipartisan applause, from the gallery Galbraith briefly imagined that, just perhaps, Johnson might not drag the country further into the war.

GALBRAITH'S UNQUESTIONABLE LOYALTY TO and affection for President Kennedy and his family did not prevent him from seeing a potential for greatness in Johnson. Unlike many in the Kennedy administration who viewed the former Vice President with disdain, Galbraith felt that, despite his many flaws, he might well have the talent to achieve what Kennedy had only been able to set out as goals.

Johnson, of course, agreed. "Hell," he confidently told aides after just six months in the Oval Office, "we've barely begun to solve our problems. And we can do it all."[13] Reviewing Johnson's achievements during his first year in office one can certainly understand the confidence. By the summer of 1964 he had pressed through Congress the landmark Civil Rights Act, the billion-dollar beginnings of the War on Poverty, and then the legendary tax cut that Walter Heller had campaigned for since 1962.

Anxiously aware at first that he'd reached the White House because of a horrible tragedy, Johnson fretted constantly about his public and political support, especially among Kennedy loyalists. Several hours after his chance encounter with Galbraith the day after Kennedy's assassination, for example, he had met with Walter Heller and enthusiastically talked about launching a great assault on poverty. Heller was very impressed. Johnson ended the meeting by urging Heller with great earnestness to "tell your friends—Arthur Schlesinger, Galbraith, and the other liberals" that he wasn't "a conservative who is likely to go back to the Eisenhower ways or give in to the economy bloc in the Congress . . . I am a Roosevelt New Dealer. As a matter of fact, John F. Kennedy was a little too conservative to suit my taste."[14]

By July 1964, when the Republicans nominated Senator Barry Goldwater of Arizona as their candidate, the savvy LBJ realized that his own election that coming November was no longer a question of whether but by how much. Goldwater's record—with his calls for breaking diplomatic relations with the Soviet Union, for abolishing the graduated income tax, for making Social Security voluntary, for withdrawing from the United Nations, and for using tactical nuclear weapons in Vietnam—bespoke a politics that most Americans disliked. (When he insisted he wouldn't mind "lobbing one into the men's room of the Kremlin," a pundit quipped that Goldwater—who proudly maintained his officer status in the Air Force Reserve while serving in the Senate—"looked at the world through rose-colored bombsights."[15])

Goldwater's supporters didn't help whatever slender chances he might have had. They loved his contempt for moderate Republicans, indeed, for moderates of any kind. At the Republican National Convention in San Francisco, they roared their approval for his claim that "extremism in the defense of liberty is no vice." And when the moderate New York governor, Nelson Rockefeller, tried to address the convention, they booed and hissed with frightening vehemence. The millions who saw this on national television were stunned. The journalist Richard Rovere described the Goldwaterites at the convention as "hard as nails. The spirit of compromise and accommodation was wholly alien to them . . . They wished to punish as well as prevail."[16] Drew Pearson, the nation's most widely read political columnist, was even harsher: the next day he wrote, "The smell of fascism has been in the air of this convention."[17]

The performances of Goldwater and his supporters at the convention sealed his fate. Days after his nomination, polls showed him trailing Johnson by 33 percentage points, a gap that never really closed. By November, despite the defection of Mississippi, Georgia, Louisiana, and South Carolina from the Democratic column, Johnson went on to win 61 percent of the vote nationwide. Riding his coattails, the Senate and House, long Democratic, became overwhelmingly so, the Senate by 68 to 32, the House by a stunning 295 to 140.[18]

It was a historic nadir for the GOP, and some pundits began to write of America's "one-and-a-half-party system," predicting it would take a generation for the Republicans to recover, if they ever did. In the eight presidential elections since 1932, the GOP had won just twice and had controlled the Congress for only four years. But Galbraith was increasingly concerned about his own party. He was a delegate to the Democratic National Convention in Atlantic City that August, and understood that the floor fights and demonstrations that erupted over which delegates from Mississippi would be seated were laying bare unbridgeable rifts in the old New Deal coalition. He also understood that the tumultuous twenty-minute-long ovation the delegates gave Robert Kennedy, and the film about his late brother that he introduced, only excited the worst in LBJ's suspicious nature.

Johnson's subsequent victory margin and the size of the Democrats' new congressional majorities were mixed blessings, Galbraith decided: Johnson had a better chance to reshape the nation's political agenda than anyone since Roosevelt in 1936, yet just as FDR had overreached when he tried to pack the Republican-dominated Supreme Court in 1937, LBJ now might also dangerously overreach.[19] But few shared Galbraith's concerns.

What worried him most was what Johnson had done just three weeks before the convention. On August 4, the President had ordered reprisals taken against alleged attacks made on two U.S. destroyers, the *Maddox* and *C. Turner Joy*, on patrol off North Vietnam. The *Maddox* had indeed been under some sort of attack on August 2, but the circumstances and actual nature of any further engagement were clouded in ambiguity and uncertainty. Johnson had nonetheless ordered preparations for a U.S. air assault on North Vietnam the next day, and simultaneously ordered the State Department to draft a resolution for congressional approval that authorized him to "take all necessary measures" to repel attacks against U.S. forces and to "prevent further aggression" in the area. That document (which in fact had been in the works for several months) was to become famous as the Gulf of Tonkin Resolution. With its near-unanimous passage three days later on August 7, Congress seemed to give unalloyed consent to the administration's actions in Vietnam—and some would argue gave the de facto mandate, if not the de jure approval required by the Constitution, for the United States to declare war on another sovereign nation.

The participants in this flurry of activity in Washington, as well as historians, have debated heatedly ever since whether a second attack actually occurred; whether U.S. actions in the days prior had provoked it; whether the White House knowingly lied in presenting its case to Congress; and what the legal implications of the resolution really were. (LBJ himself days later said he always doubted there had been an attack. "Hell," he told George Ball, "those dumb, stupid sailors were just shooting at flying fish."[20] But he had knowingly taken advantage of the moment. McGeorge Bundy later wrote, "Lyndon Johnson didn't want to fight a war without congressional authorization," and "attacks on ships on the high seas were a perfect reason for getting a resolution through Congress." Almost immediately Johnson "committed himself to having a resolution and a speech and had the airtime . . . and the last thing he wanted to do was reexamine that."[21]) It is clear that whatever the final answers to those questions are, the immense war machine the United States had built since World War II was finally going to find its use.

THE UNITED STATES had never entered a war so well prepared. Until 1941, geographic isolation, not a large peacetime army, had been its best defense. But by the mid-1950s American troops and ships were stationed from Berlin to Bangkok, and defense treaties linked the United States with nations around the globe. By the time Johnson took office there were more than 1,500 American military installations outside the United States, far more than the British had at the height of their imperial power.

Under President Eisenhower, nuclear weapons and the ability to deliver them had formed the heart of America's global "deterrence" strategy. The "New Look" posture, as the Pentagon's aggressive new military stance was called, was undeniably expensive—and explained why so much of the federal budget went to the armed forces. But expensive as it was, "New Look" was cheaper than other options. Eisenhower understood this—and had consciously elected to underfund the vast manpower and weapons requests of the Army and Navy in favor of the Air Force's more "economical" nuclear weapons.

His choice carried hidden costs, however: in material terms, for one, it represented certain trade-offs in terms of domestic development. Eisenhower had grown up poor, and understood why "New Look" wasn't truly "cheap." As he put it during his first term, in almost Old Testament terms, "Every gun that is made, every warship launched, every rocket fired signifies, in the final sense, a theft from those who are hungry and are not fed, by those who are fed and are not cold." He then went on in specifics:

The cost of one modern heavy bomber is this: a modern brick school in
more than 30 cities.

It is two electric power plants, each serving a town of 60,000 population.

It is two fine, fully equipped hospitals.

It is some 50 miles of concrete highway.

We pay for a single fighter plane with half a million bushels of wheat.

We pay for a single destroyer with new homes that could have housed
more than 8,000 people.[22]

A second cost was less tangible, but no less important to the former general, who had grown up a small-town Republican, inherently suspicious of bigness in government, for whatever ends. As the historian John Lewis Gaddis has written, Eisenhower feared that the military's "unrestrained spending could alter the very nature of American society, either through the debilitating effects of inflation or through regimentation in the form of economic controls."[23] But having abandoned his party's traditional isolationism, the President could not resolve how to balance overwhelming, globe-girdling military power and real domestic security. (Leon Keyserling's advice to Truman had been to deny any such paradox: military Keynesianism would yield bombers *and* schools, fighters *and* food, destroyers *and* homes. Eisenhower never believed it.)

There was a third strategic cost to "New Look," with implications for American values that were no less profound. Ike's reliance on a policy that threatened massive nuclear retaliation had produced a military force structure that was top-heavy in its nuclear capacity aimed at Russia or China but feeble in its ability to deter lower-level challengers by nonnuclear means. Still, the U.S. hardly lacked conventional forces: the Army alone by the mid-1950s was twelve times larger than it had been before World War II. But with hundreds of thousands of American ground forces assigned to Western Europe, Japan, and South Korea, the economic logic behind "New Look" had also dictated an "extramilitary" strategy toward other areas of the world: the extensive use of covert political and paramilitary operations. In Iran, Guatemala, Tibet, and the Congo, when the United States perceived serious threats to its now far-flung national interests, subversion, rather than invasion, became the modus operandi meant to compensate for the thinness of rapidly deployable conventional forces. Whatever the moral price was for a democracy, the budgeting effect of this strategy had led the Yale economist James Tobin (soon to be on Kennedy's CEA) to his observation that "New Look" was a policy "made as much in the Treasury as in State."[24]

By the late 1950s, though, Ike's "New Look" posture had begun to seem alarmingly outdated to a growing cadre of geo-strategic thinkers. They saw a clear need for a major realignment of military forces, and of diplomatic and military thinking, to meet the problems posed by the steady liquidation and dissolution of Europe's old colonial empires in the Third World. America, they argued, needed a new strategy, one that continued to build and refine the country's keystone nuclear arsenal but that also included new capacities for the Army, Navy, and Marine Corps, allowing for new and more flexible responses.

In his 1957 *Nuclear Weapons and Foreign Policy*, Henry Kissinger, then a young instructor in Harvard's Government Department, had recommended releasing the Pentagon from the fiscal limits of "New Look" military policy in order to fight more limited nuclear wars. Kissinger also argued for a more robust economy that could sustain a more robust, varied military and diplomatic system. Amazingly, the book unexpectedly took off, selling 70,000 copies, spent fourteen weeks as a best-seller, and became a Book-of-the-Month Club selection. Kissinger by the mid-1960s abandoned his thesis, convinced that "limited, nuclear" wars were—as critics had warned—impossible to contain; but in the 1950s, by breaking with "New Look" (and moral) taboos, he was thrust from the still-tiny new world of "Cold War intellectuals" to the status of nuclear celebrity.

The book also brought Kissinger the patronage of Nelson Rockefeller, who appointed him director of the Rockefeller studies that called for 5 percent growth. His view, as it turned out, happened to coincide as well with those of the Army's frustrated chief of staff, Maxwell Taylor, who was then outlining what he called the "strategy of flexible response" as the needed alternative to the "New Look" doctrine. Together the decorated ex-paratrooper and young academic went on to have a dramatic effect on the Democratic Party—and on Kennedy's, Johnson's, and the country's future.

Taken up by Democrats eager to steal a march on the Republicans' domination of the defense issue, Taylor's vision was enshrined in the 1960 Democratic platform. Appointed first as Kennedy's personal military adviser, then as chairman of the Joint Chiefs of Staff, General Taylor passionately encouraged the New Frontiersmen to couple their commitment to economic growth to his equally growth-oriented vision of American military policy. After Kennedy's death, LBJ then named Taylor ambassador to South Vietnam; in doing so he also approved the strategic outlines for a major nonnuclear American land war in Southeast Asia, which Eisenhower had long resisted and which his asymmetrical "New Look" force structure was incapable of carrying out.[25] Once embraced, Taylor's "flexible response" strategy meant more than just developing new military options. In the minds of the Kennedy policy-makers, most of whom Johnson inherited, it began dictating military and diplomatic action.

Shortly after taking office in 1961, Kennedy had been given a detailed memo by Walt Rostow outlining what needed to be done in Southeast Asia:

> We must somehow bring to bear our unexploited counter-guerilla assets on the Viet-Nam problem; armed helicopters; other Research and Development possibilities; our Special Forces units. *It is somehow wrong to be developing these capabilities but not applying them in a crucially active theater.* In Knut Rockne's old phrase, we are not saving them for the Junior Prom.[26] [emphasis added]

At the Pentagon, Robert McNamara, no less enthusiastic, implemented the White House's newly authorized lifting of the fiscal constraints inherited from Eisenhower, even as he sought to "rationalize" military spending economically by imposing rigorous cost-benefit analysis, pioneered at RAND in the 1950s.[27] As the Defense Department's 1962 *Annual Report* proudly put it, the Pentagon was now applying the new military doctrine "in accordance with the President's directive that military requirements should be considered without regard to arbitrary budget ceilings."[28]

All this came to a head under President Johnson, and it led Galbraith from being a senior administration insider to being a passionate government outsider and critic in just two years. From the very first he had voiced his alarm at the interweaving of fundamental economic growth policy with a costly, aggressively expansive new military doctrine, and by the summer of 1963, he had thought his views were finally making headway with President Kennedy.

As we have seen, in the spring of 1962 Kennedy had ordered aides to work several of Galbraith's ideas—for containing the Indochinese conflict and avoiding further U.S. troop commitments—into proposals for Harriman to discuss with the Russians at Geneva. And in the spring of 1963, Secretary McNamara had ordered General Harkins and other senior military commanders in the Pacific to lay out a detailed plan for withdrawal of all American forces from Southeast Asia. As now-declassified U.S. records show, six months before his death Kennedy was in fact prepared to begin a first withdrawal of a thousand American troops by the end of 1963, and planned to have the rest withdrawn shortly after his anticipated reelection in November 1964, and he made the withdrawal a formal objective of his administration with National Security Action Memorandum 263 a month before his death. Henceforth, all Pentagon planning was to "be directed towards preparing [South Vietnamese] forces for the withdrawal of all U.S. special assistance units and personnel by the end of calendar year 1965."[29]

But all that had changed after Dealey Plaza. Four days after President Kennedy's assassination, on November 26, at the urging of his advisers, President Johnson approved a top-secret NSC action memorandum, NSAM 273, that reaffirmed Kennedy's order to remove the thousand troops but then declared that the "central object of the United States in Vietnam [is] to assist the people and Government of that country to win their contest against the externally directed and supported Communist conspiracy." This was the carte blanche that Kennedy had refused to give in November 1961, and it eventually spawned its fateful consequences.

Whether Johnson understood that he was reversing Kennedy's policies has never been clear—and remains controversial. Some historians have concluded that Kennedy's troop withdrawal was merely a tactical move intended to pressure Diem to reform his government. After Diem's assassination, they argue, Kennedy would necessarily have reexamined the situation and been prepared to reverse course. And Kennedy's aides were certainly encouraging a reversal: McGeorge Bundy had drafted NSAM 273 for Kennedy's consideration just before Dallas. But there is no evidence or reason to believe that Kennedy would have approved it; he had repeatedly overridden his advisers before. The historian Robert Dallek, for example, has concluded that it was the aides who "encouraged Johnson to believe that he was essentially following JFK's lead. JFK's three principal foreign-policy advisers echoed each other's advice on Vietnam as if it were the received wisdom."[30]

Although Galbraith took pains to persuade President Johnson against the path he chose, beginning with their first meeting twenty-four hours after the assassination, it was two years before he broke publicly with Johnson. Surprisingly, given LBJ's normally ruthless insistence on total loyalty from aides and advisers, throughout 1964 and into 1965 Galbraith remained close to him, campaigning in more than twenty states for the President's election, writing speeches, and working actively in designing the new War on Poverty.

Despite their steadily increasing differences over the Vietnam War, the relationship between the two men had its share of colorfully memorable moments. One occurred in mid-1965:

> We were up in Vermont one summer day, the telephone rang, and LBJ summoned me, asked me to come down to Washington. He had a couple of speeches, he said, and "everybody down here is tired, come on down, write me a couple of speeches." So he sent a plane up to Keene, New Hampshire, and I went down and spent the day in the West Wing, just outside his office.
>
> One was just a diplomatic speech of no consequence. I dashed that off and then went to work on a major speech on economics for an AFL-CIO group. And I worked on it through the day, put in everything I believed that I thought he could be persuaded to accept, and a good deal of rhetoric, and at the end of the day I had finished the speech.
>
> And he came in, put his foot up on the chair, threw away the speech that was of no consequence, and settled in for the main speech. I could see he liked it. He nodded his head and smiled. Finally, he put the speech down and he said, "Ah, Ken," he said, "just what I want to say. I'm not going to change a word. It's just a wonderful speech."
>
> Then his expression changed and he said, "But nobody else will think so. Did it ever occur to you that making a speech on economics is just like pissing down your leg? It seems hot to you, but not to anybody else."[31]

Yet Galbraith and Johnson could not avoid the tension and danger that was Vietnam.

> In meetings with LBJ and also with McNamara and Bundy, I came back often, even tediously, to the subject. Johnson was not a great listener, although at times I thought him sympathetic. Repeatedly, as to others, he said that he was really being a force for restraint. "Ken, have you any idea what Curtis LeMay would be doing if I weren't here to stop him?"[32]

Galbraith remembered the gruesome human devastation left behind by the B-29s' indiscriminate firebombing, under LeMay's command, of civilians and soldiers in Japan. And he had heard talk of LeMay's repeated attempts as Air Force chief of staff to persuade President Kennedy to consider nuclear war with China as part of any plan for American intervention in Southeast Asia. Johnson's pleas held Galbraith in check before the November 1964 election, as they did others for much longer. Given the alternatives, there were compelling reasons for silence, even during the Gulf of Tonkin fiasco.

> But eventually and sadly I came to the conclusion that Johnson was on a hopelessly different course . . . The early months of 1965 were, for me, an especially sad time. After campaigning joyously for LBJ and against Barry Goldwater as a warmonger, I had to watch the long-resisted introduction of combat troops and the first bombings of North Vietnam. I felt very angry . . . Gradually and reluctantly, I realized that the only honest course was open opposition, unpromising as that seemed to be.[33]

The most noticed of Galbraith's early public protests against the war in Vietnam appeared in *The Atlantic Monthly* in February 1965. Titled "Foreign Policy: A Stuck Whistle," it was a sweeping critique not simply of the administration's Vietnam policy, but of what he deemed the conservatism underlying all U.S. foreign policy. Galbraith was careful to compliment President Johnson on his domestic programs and to stress the support he himself had given to LBJ's election campaign, but he made his own dissent from U.S. policy overseas indelibly clear:

> People are tired of the litany of our foreign policy—with its endless calls for vigilance, the pious assertions of our own virtue, the repeated promises of prompt improvement in our affairs in Saigon and Paris. The never-ending reports of fruitful diplomatic missions and useful diplomatic talks when it is evident that nothing was accomplished, and the continuing assurances that we are tough-minded and hard-headed and will never allow our better instincts to prevail.[34]

Vietnam wasn't the issue as such: it was only one part of America's overall foreign policy rigidities that included everything from an unwillingness to enter serious arms-reduction negotiations with the Soviet Union to refusal to give diplomatic recognition to China and to support for tin-pot dictators and juntas across the Third World. And these rigidities were condoned and even encouraged by Democrats and Republicans alike.

There were echoes here of Galbraith's deep-seated resentment of the State Department's "secular priesthood," a sentiment reinforced at the Democratic Advisory Council in the 1950s by his constant clashes with Dean Acheson. Acheson, the son of an Episcopal bishop and a consummate Ivy Leaguer, embodied everything about the Democrats' foreign policy that Galbraith disliked.

Equally important was his dislike of the "new" State Department, still bureaucratic, self-protectively cautious, and dissembling on important issues. Dean Rusk was a Georgian who hardly met the "secular priesthood" profile, but he displayed what Galbraith considered the department's worst characteristics. By 1965 he was convinced that the soft-spoken, bald-headed Rusk and some of his deputies were impediments to a sensible foreign policy.

> His excessive respect for military men and military power made him dangerously sanguine about military accomplishment. And he had a strongly dichotomous view of the world. On the one hand, the free nations; on the other, the comprehensively united Communists . . . When, with the passage of time, the rifts began to appear between the Chinese and the Soviet Union, Rusk was unperturbed. He merely adjusted the facts to his faith. Were the Communist states divided, he insisted, it was only over how best to destroy the free world.[35]

The appearance of the *Atlantic* article was impeccably timed. In mid-January, Peter Grose, the *New York Times* correspondent in Saigon, privately warned White House aides that "the next six months may mark the end of the road" for the American intervention and urged them to tell President Johnson to explore "every opportunity to withdraw with honor." The very next day, the Saigon government of General Khanh, which had overthrown the Diem regime fourteen months earlier, was itself overthrown by a new group of dissident Vietnamese generals. (This pattern was to be repeated several more times.) Two weeks later, LBJ ordered commencement of "Rolling Thunder," the first systematic bombing campaign against North Vietnam, and in March, student protests against the war began in earnest. The nation's first "teach-in" convened at the University of Michigan and was replicated at more than one hundred campuses over the next few months. Galbraith was among the very earliest teach-in participants, and got more attention than most.[36] In April the first student-led antiwar march took place in Washington.

Press coverage of that first march suggests just how isolated opponents of the war were in early 1965. As one critic later wrote, *The New York Times*'s coverage of the April march on Washington "deprecated, marginalized, trivialized, and polarized" not only the march but the movement itself.[37] Polls showed that LBJ's Vietnam policies were supported by two thirds of the country, and when the President in May sought his first really big boost in Vietnam-related spending, Congress amply reflected, even magnified, this public support: the vote in the House for the spending bill was 408 to 7, that in the Senate, 88 to 3.[38] That winter and spring, Galbraith was knowingly and deliberately distancing himself from the prevailing wisdom of the times.

As the war escalated that year, he unhesitatingly escalated his own dissent even as LBJ tried to draw him closer. On July 16, after attending the Washington funeral of Adlai Stevenson, Galbraith was asked back to the White House by McGeorge Bundy, so that Johnson could probe to see whether Galbraith might be willing to succeed Stevenson as Ambassador to the United Nations. Galbraith quickly turned the conversation to other candidates, Arthur Goldberg in particular. Goldberg accepted.

A week later, Galbraith returned to the issue of Vietnam. On July 22, he wrote President Johnson a blisteringly frank memo that began, "I assume the following to be true, much official crap to the contrary."

(1) Vietnam is of no great intrinsic importance. Had it gone Communist after World War II we would be just as strong as now and would never waste a thought on it.

(2) No question of high principle is involved. It is their rascals or ours. Both sides would lose in free elections!

(3) The basic issue is that we must show that we can't be thrown out—that we don't give up under fire. This would also be bad here at home.

(4) It is right to consider the politics of the problem. A great many people who make policy do not have to take the political heat. Rusk ran the Korean War and his career was made by it. [Rusk was in charge of the Korean desk at State during the war]. Stevenson ran for office during the war and was destroyed . . .

(5) Political questions are partly what we make them.[39]

He then laid out, step by step, his alternative, urging the President to order U.S. officials "to stop saying the future of mankind, the United States and human liberty is being decided in Vietnam. It isn't; this merely builds up a difficult problem out of all proportion." They should also be told to "stop saying we are going to reconquer the whole country. We are not going to pacify Chicago or Harlem [the locus of recent race riots]." Johnson should focus on pulling troops back to a small number of enclaves, including Saigon, that could be held militarily, suspend the bombing of the north and south, and keep emphasizing American willingness to negotiate a peace. Negotiations might not start quickly, he noted, but they would come. This policy would avoid outright "defeat" and neutralize the Republicans while letting Johnson make progress with the Russians on arms control and other more important issues.

> In the past there were two difficulties with this program. It would have undermined the South Vietnamese government and required the commitment of our troops. Now there isn't any South Vietnamese government worth worrying about and our forces are committed.
>
> The great problem is our own eager beavers who do not consider the mood of our own people come the next election, and whose political teat is not in the wringer.

Johnson didn't explode at or ignore this memo, as one might have expected. A day after receiving it, on July 25, he instead made it central to a hastily convened late-afternoon meeting at Camp David, an intimate discussion that proved pivotal to the escalation of the war. He invited just three people to Camp David: Robert McNamara, Clark Clifford, and Arthur Goldberg, who had just resigned from the Supreme Court to become ambassador to the United Nations; *not* included were Rusk, Bundy, Rostow, or any generals.

After five months of intensive bombing of North Vietnam and the shift of U.S. ground troops to active combat status, but with no real progress toward peace, President Johnson was being counseled to make further massive increases in U.S. military commitments, increases that he realized would effectively "Americanize" the war. He was dubious at best, but Rusk, McNamara, Bundy, Rostow, and the Joint Chiefs were pressing for 100,000 to 150,000 more troops. The week had been taken up in almost back-to-back meetings on the next steps in Vietnam, and a crucial National Security Council meeting was set for July 26, at which LBJ's aides expected him to decide whether to take this new step from which there could now be no turning back.

Notwithstanding Rolling Thunder and the nearly 80,000 U.S. troops already in Vietnam or on the way there, Johnson still did not consider that he'd made irrevocable commitments, and he kept hesitating, demanding that he be given options other than escalation. In a sign of the pressure he was under, a few months before the Camp David meeting he'd exploded at Army Chief of Staff Harold Johnson:

> Bomb, bomb, bomb. That's all you know. Well, I want to know why there's nothing else. You generals have all been educated at taxpayers' expense, and you're not giving me any ideas and any solutions for this damn little piss-ant country. I don't need ten generals to come in here ten times and tell me to bomb. I want some solutions. I want some answers.

Poking his finger into the officer's chest, he growled, "Get things bubbling, General." Shortly after, he complained in agony to his press aide, Bill Moyers, "Light at the end of the tunnel? Hell, we don't even have a tunnel; we don't even know where the tunnel is."[40]

Notes taken at Camp David show that early in the meeting, Johnson suddenly pulled Galbraith's memo from a file folder and began reading it aloud, point by point. None of the other men had apparently seen it beforehand. What, LBJ somberly asked when he finished, did the others think of this advice? Was this the way to go?

For a long moment, there was silence.

The elegant and normally understated Clifford spoke first. He was one of the capital's fabled "Wise Men," a former key aide to Truman and by then a wealthy Washington lawyer, one of those whose real influence rarely involved a courtroom appearance or even a legal brief. The work that men like Clifford did—and for which they were highly paid—was done with well-placed phone calls, or *sotto voce* conversations at intimate dinners and cocktail parties, or over drinks in private clubs where the important agreements reached rarely required a written record afterward. Although he was to succeed McNamara as secretary of defense two years later, at that point he had no official position in the government despite Johnson's repeated pleas that he join the administration. Clifford wasn't a "dove"; to the contrary, he'd done key work in formulating Truman's hard-line approach to Stalin in the 1940s. But neither was he a "hawk."

Clifford was shaken when he considered the consequences of further escalation. Galbraith's memo was identical to his own dark assessment of where the war was heading and what its consequences would be at home, and he urged the President not to send the fresh U.S. troops that had been requested. Instead, as the meeting's cryptically worded notes show, he passionately concurred with Galbraith:

> Don't believe we can win in SVN. If we send in 100,000 more, the NVN will meet us. If the NVN run out of men, the Chinese will send in volunteers. Russia and China don't intend for us to win this war. If we don't win, it is a catastrophe. If we lose 50,000+ it will ruin us. Five years, billions of dollars, 50,000 men, it is not for us. At end of monsoon, quietly probe and search out with other countries—by moderating our position—to allow us to get out. Can't see anything but catastrophe for my country.

When Clifford finished, again there was silence.

It was McNamara's turn. Speaking without notes or briefing book, he vehemently countered Clifford's and Galbraith's arguments. Unleashing a torrent of data, he said his own conclusion was that a U.S. victory was possible—and quite soon—if only Johnson would give him and the Joint Chiefs what they were asking for. The Defense Secretary's legendary self-confidence, here as elsewhere, belied the fact that by then he already had ample warnings about the trustworthiness of his data.

Ambassador Goldberg followed McNamara. Uncertain which way Johnson was leaning and without directly challenging the Defense Secretary's military assessment, he pleaded with LBJ to let him try to open negotiations with the North Vietnamese through the United Nations.

After nearly two hours of often heated discussion and no clear conclusion, Johnson stopped the meeting, walked outside, and for the next two hours first drove and then walked around the grounds of the Camp David compound, lost in apparent pain and uncertainty about the decision he was about to take. Late that evening, he returned to the White House without saying what he would do, although Clifford sensed that his and Galbraith's arguments had lost.

When the NSC meeting convened the next day, at the White House, his intuition was proved right: Johnson opted to support McNamara and the Joint Chiefs, not Clifford and Galbraith. But the President then emphatically told everyone present that the full scale of what he was doing was to be kept secret until they could better gauge the results, and that he would go no further in making any commitments until the end of the year. (Interestingly, he refused the Pentagon request that he begin calling up the reserves, as Galbraith had advised. This seems to have been an attempt not just to limit public reaction but to keep a manpower brake on the generals.) He expected that by year's end—as McNamara and the Joint Chiefs assured him—he would have clear evidence of major progress and that the war would soon be over. (Rostow didn't think it would take so long. "The Vietcong are going to collapse within weeks," he confidently declared in July. "Not months but weeks."[41]) The war in Vietnam—and with it both the nation's politics and economy—now entered a new and fateful phase.

GALBRAITH'S CONCERNS ABOUT Johnson's policies in 1965 weren't confined to America's great war machine in Vietnam. He was also alarmed about the effects of the $12 billion "Keynesian" tax cut that had passed the House shortly before Kennedy's death, and then in the spring of 1964, with LBJ's strong support, finally became law.[42] To Galbraith, the tax cut was only slightly better than Eisenhower's "military Keynesianism"; at worst it threatened what he believed should be the Democrats' Keynesian goals, especially since any attempt to reform the tax code had been abandoned. All the dangers he'd foreseen were showing signs of coming true.[43]

First, Congress and special interests had made sure that the tax reductions were heavily weighted to America's most affluent citizens. Among the wealthy and corporate classes, the law was hailed as an unparalleled achievement. (One sign of their enduring affirmation is that Ronald Reagan invoked it in 1981 when he, likewise, proposed massive tax cuts that even more noticeably favored the powerful and well-to-do.) While *Fortune*'s readers had reason to be pleased—the stock market boomed, and a new group of market investors called mutual funds soared with it—Galbraith saw a transparent lack of equity, and a profound political miscalculation, because the millions who benefited least were primarily Democratic voters, after all.

Signs abounded that many of those voters were not convinced that the tax cuts directly benefited them. ("Tax shifting" was a large reason why most families felt less benefit than Heller had promised. Washington's receipts from the progressive income tax fell modestly from 19 percent of GDP in 1960 to 18 percent in 1965, but *total tax revenues* at all levels of government *rose* slightly: regressive taxes—Social Security payments and state and local levies—jumped from 11.4 percent to 12.7 percent, more than offsetting the cut in federal income taxes, and fell hardest on middle- and low-income families.) Unemployment had fallen, but most Americans had not experienced noticeable wage and salary gains, whatever the aggregate indicators showed, and the poverty rate had barely moved.[44] Claims for the tax cut's macroeconomic effects notwithstanding, it did not seem to show a measurable microeconomic consequence and did not put as much income back into people's pockets as promised. From 1961 through 1965, nominal wages and salaries rose 18 percent, while corporate profits soared 76 percent.[45] The result was that in 1965 President Johnson faced big new wage demands from the unions (along with hefty price-hike demands from business) well before war pressures kicked in.

The steelworkers were the most demanding, but construction, airline, auto, lumber, and chemical workers were also restive.

LBJ had inherited from Kennedy a "voluntary" wage-and-price guideline policy set up by Heller's CEA to damp down wage increases, but it relied on presidential pressure rather than legal enforcement mechanisms of the sort Galbraith had administered in World War II. With a goal of holding increases in both wages and prices to 3.2 percent, and with Kennedy's occasionally high-profile actions (most memorably, his confrontation with Roger Blough of U.S. Steel), the guidelines had been fairly successful. Johnson and his CEA naively assumed that, with the increased growth promised by the 1964 tax cut and with the money it put into consumers' pockets and then into spending, the guidelines would hold. They didn't. Consumer purchasing soared in late 1964 and 1965, but the sheer volume was a surprise and was heavily concentrated on big-ticket items such as cars bought by affluent customers. Consumer debt soared, too. Business and banks were well pleased, but the torrid pace was outstripping the CEA's predictions and would, if not contained, create inflationary pressures whatever the result of blue-collar-wage talks.

At the same time, despite all the attention given to LBJ's new War on Poverty, Galbraith realized that congressional funding for it so far was still very modest relative to the problems it aimed to solve. By one estimate, the billion-dollar Economic Opportunity Act of 1964 represented less than one tenth of the dollars administration economists wanted spent to cut poverty in that year alone; LBJ boosted the number only to $1.5 billion in 1965.[46] To be sure, he was advocating other programs of which Galbraith approved—from Model Cities and minimum-wage increases to clean-air and clean-water bills and new federal funding for education—but with war pressures building, the estimated new revenues that Heller and others believed would flow from the additional growth of GNP would not persuade conservative Southern committee chairmen or Republicans in Congress to fund these programs, especially given the race of the citizens most likely to benefit from them.

Privately Johnson seems to have shared Galbraith's views. By the fall of 1965, according to Johnson's biographer Robert Dallek, LBJ, looking at Congress, "had little expectation that a strong economy would mean much in the way of additional Great Society reforms. His goal was to maintain the economy at a level that would fund the war in Vietnam and domestic programs in place. If he could get any other major reforms passed, all the better. But this was a third priority."[47] Sargent Shriver, LBJ's chief of staff in the War on Poverty as director of the Office of Economic Opportunity, tried to maintain a game face, telling Congress as late as 1966 that poverty could still be eliminated within a decade. But by 1967, he backtracked dramatically, admitting that "the war on poverty will not be won in a generation."[48]

Galbraith was dismayed that fellow Keynesians such as Heller, whom he otherwise liked, were opting for the tax cut rather than holding out, as he would have preferred, for passage of substantial expenditure programs that would be as stimulative as the cuts. By mid-1965, as a major war in Southeast

Asia came closer, the surrender of progressively oriented revenue-raising authority meant the loss of the government's chief tool to counter economic overheating. His years at the OPA had taught Galbraith an indelible lesson about the economic and political benefits earned when governments controlled war-induced inflation pressures through means the public saw as fair. It was bad enough that the United States was now escalating its military intervention in Vietnam; worse would come when the financial costs escalated, and the administration was unable to limit war-induced inflation. It was no surprise to Galbraith that it took almost three years before Johnson and the Congress passed new tax increases with any bite to them—long after inflation had taken hold. The only macromanagement alternative until 1968 was a blunt one: it would be up to the Federal Reserve to raise interest rates, the very action likeliest, in Galbraith's view, to derail the economy further and delegitimize both the Democrats and Keynesian theory itself.[49] Predictably, late in 1965, the Fed began to raise rates.

Oft-repeated stories surrounding the 1964 tax cut make it harder to understand the debates and circumstances that enveloped it, the motives behind it, and its consequences. To proponents such as Heller, and its defenders since, the bill proved that Keynesian analysis and policy were right: by prolonging the expansion that began in early 1961 and pressing the economy close to its full-employment capacities, it demonstrated the correct principles behind Heller's claims about economists' abilities to fine-tune the U.S. economy. When this accomplishment fell prey to overstimulation because of increased spending for Vietnam, it was the fault of others who made demands of the economy that could only spark inflation. And the villain in all this was LBJ.[50] Had President Johnson not hidden his intentions to expand the Vietnam War from his economic advisers, many if not all the subsequent problems could have been avoided. The CEA's economists, as Hobart Rowen put it, were "sold down the river by Johnson and McNamara, who were masters of deceit."[51]

This comforting story, like similar ones shared over dinners and cocktails at faculty clubs and academic conferences for years, has a flaw: Johnson's economists themselves repeatedly denied being misled. Gardner Ackley, who succeeded Walter Heller as CEA chairman in December 1964, just before the first big Vietnam buildup began, later insisted he would "try very hard to disillusion anybody who believes that [story]." Apart from a brief period in the summer of 1965, Ackley claimed that the CEA "knew what [Vietnam buildup] numbers were being talked about, and we also knew very well that, whatever those numbers were, they weren't nearly big enough in terms of what was going to happen to defense expenditures . . . There was certainly no question about absence of sufficient information to reach a policy judgment."[52]

Press coverage of the war also makes it hard to defend the idea that Johnson was hiding his plans. *Fortune*, for example, published a lengthy article entitled "Guns, Butter, and Then Some" in late 1965 to explain the economic effect of the war escalation. It traced where the defense contracts would go, where shortages would likely appear, what the pressures on the economy would be, what the likely options were. None of the CEA members raised an alarm. "There's more room to go," one commented to *Fortune*.[53] In November twenty American economists predicted that the economy would grow strongly the next year. "With a few dissenters," one participant noted, "there was no great concern that the economy was overheated and would require restrictive monetary policy."

Yet two weeks later, without warning the White House ahead of time, the Federal Reserve raised interest rates. Suddenly the CEA began to worry about overheating, and Ackley told LBJ that a tax increase—a flat surtax on income—would be necessary. LBJ refused even to discuss the idea.[54]

As the war grew ever more expensive in 1966 and 1967, the ability of the "fine-tuners" to recommend coherent economic options failed them. It was not easy to explain the economy's actual performance: after beginning to overheat, it slowed, then started to overheat again. None of this made sense in the models, nor to the modelers.* Adopting a pose of Delphic ambiguity, the CEA admitted that "policy will have to be made carefully to avoid the dangers on both sides—a new inflationary surge or an excessive slowdown"—hardly advice the President could use. When Johnson asked Heller, by then back in academe, what he should do, Heller replied that he hoped "you will get Divine guidance on the question of a 1967 tax increase, since economic guidance gives you no very firm answer at the moment."[55]

Still, in a deeper sense, Ackley and Heller *had* been kept more in the dark than they cared to admit. Following the pattern set under Eisenhower and Kennedy, no CEA member attended an NSC meeting under Johnson, nor did the NSC ever ask the CEA for advice.†

Arthur Okun, who took over from Ackley as CEA chairman in February 1968, poignantly recalled only one exception to this "remarkable degree of compartmentalization" (his words) between the two groups. In early March 1968, with both the war and the economy spinning out of control and the Tet Offensive under way, the President told Okun he wanted the CEA to analyze immediately for him the economic effects of any further commitment of

---

*Later critics asked whether the economic models used by the CEA were correct from a technical point of view. The economist Martin Prachowny argues that in trying to gauge the effects of the proposed tax cut, the CEA used a fairly simple "multiplier" or "multiplier-accelerator" model rather than a better-suited IS-LM model, which would take better account of the effect of a tax cut on interest rates and monetary policy.

A critique of this sort is telling, but it doesn't address the larger political-economic points that Galbraith raised about the overall size and effect of the military budget, the related Cold War mind-set, the demands that playing global hegemon placed on U.S. gold reserves and the balance-of-payments, and the consequent failure to see beyond those dangerous limits to politically acceptable alternatives that would alter the fundamental economic assumptions built into the models and policy debates.

†On the day Congress passed the Gulf of Tonkin resolution, Heller asked the White House aide Jack Valenti to persuade LBJ to make the CEA chairman an adjunct member of the National Security Council. He claimed that Eisenhower had routinely brought in the CEA "whenever there were economic overtones to national security matters," and that he himself had been brought in during both the Berlin Crisis and Cuban Missile Crisis by Kennedy. But none of the standard histories or CEA internal records support such claims. LBJ ignored Heller's request (see Heller to Valenti, August 7, 1964, Heller Papers, JFK Library).

troops. Okun thought that Johnson was grasping for some reason, any reason, to say no to his generals. The CEA produced the necessary calculations, but by the time their report was ready the advice was beside the point: it reached the Oval Office just days before LBJ suddenly announced his plans to retire.

Galbraith's objections to the tax cut were well known by 1968, but only one part of his larger objection to what he considered the CEA's fixation during the New Frontier and Great Society eras on boosting rapid "economic growth" per se. In 1962 he had warned Kennedy,

> The glories of the Kennedy Era will be written not in the rate of economic growth [n]or even in the level of unemployment. Nor, I venture, is this where its political rewards lie. Its glory and reward will be from the way it tackles the infinity of problems that beset a growing population and an increasingly complex society in an increasingly competitive world. To do this well costs the money that the tax reducers would deny.[56]

Three years later his views hadn't changed. As he had constantly said for over a decade, to focus on greater private-sector growth when the real needs were for spending on nonmilitary public-sector goods and services was to risk trivializing and marginalizing the legacy of their time in office.

Heller and the others thought Galbraith was wrong. The tax cut stimulated GNP growth further, and the eventual government revenue gains would more than replace any revenues initially lost, they insisted. Indeed, the social programs that Galbraith most wanted and that Heller, too, wanted could be funded from the growth. But Galbraith never believed that politicians would use the revenues in the ways he and Heller preferred, unless the White House led the way and mobilized constituencies of the kind Roosevelt had created in the New Deal. With more than 70 percent of the federal budget in the mid-1960s devoted inter alia to military programs, the space program, and interest payments on the national debt, his question was simple: given the dominant political coalitions, ideology, and interests in Washington, what would assure that increased tax revenues would be redirected to domestic civilian priorities? For too long, the CEA's "New Economists" paid only passive attention to defense costs and avoided a critical examination of the constant foreign-policy and military pressures that laid claim to so much of the budget. What would shift public support to the social balance the country needed? To this Heller had no immediate answer, but he thought Galbraith dogmatic and overly idealistic.

Yet few besides Galbraith recognized the problems until too late. In February 1964, for example, just days after Senate passage of Heller's landmark tax cut, Gaylord Nelson, a young reform-minded senator from Wisconsin, rose to ask why, after months of careful, meticulous debate over this $12 billion tax-cut bill, the Senate was now passing a $17 billion defense spending bill without debate.

> Why are we expected to pass this bill in two or three hours—before commit-
> tee hearings on the bill have even been printed; before any senator not on the
> Armed Services Committee has had an opportunity to study the testimony;
> within twenty-four hours after we had an opportunity at all to know what the
> Committee recommended . . .
>
> I am questioning what is apparently an established tradition, perhaps a na-
> tional attitude, which holds that a bill to spend billions of dollars for the ma-
> chinery of war must be rushed through . . . in a matter of hours.[57]

No senator bothered to answer Nelson, and the bill cleared the Senate the
same afternoon on a 97-to-2 vote. It was the first of many such votes over the
next years.

In the forty years since its passage, the 1964 tax cut has spawned, in policy
circles at least, much debate over its impact and legacy. For example, in the
1980s Ronald Reagan—to the horror of many Keynesians and liberals—repeatedly cited it to validate his far larger "supply-side" tax cuts, even though he
denounced Keynesian-style macromanagement in the same breath. Looking
back from 2000, the economist Martin Prachowny tried to assess just how effective the Kennedy-Johnson cuts actually were, without taking sides in this
fierce ideological debate. Prachowny's critique was important for economists,
because he used modern techniques to revisit the growth models of New Economics and their estimates of the tax cut's effect, ante and post facto. Surprisingly, he found the CEA's model, and the form and values of the multiplier
principle it applied, hard to identify. And he showed that the Council had serious doubts about their predictions, which they never shared with noneconо-
mists in the government or with the public.*[58]

After the tax cut passed in 1964, Arthur Okun, the economist most responsible for designing the models the CEA relied on, examined the results.
He calculated that by mid-1965, GNP was $24 billion larger than it would
have been without the tax cut—a huge success. Yet Okun was troubled by his
conclusions, and worried privately whether he'd accounted for the effect of
monetary policy at the time, and whether he'd ignored the inflationary pressures that such a large GNP increase might lead to. Slowly it dawned on
him that his pre–tax cut model and post–tax cut evaluation were very problematical.[59]

---

*James Duesenberry at the CEA, for example, candidly told Seymour Harris at Treasury in 1963 that their pro-
posed tax cut models made "a return to full employment by 1966 possible but the odds are against it." If each
dollar's worth of tax reduction led to two dollars' worth of GNP growth (what economists call a multiplier of
two), "expansion would peter out," while a multiplier of three would give results that were "highly implausible."
To sell the cuts, the Council anxiously ended up using, depending on the audience, multipliers from less than
one up to five, which led to GNP growth estimates that made Heller, in his own words, privately "rather skeptical of these numbers." Yet he felt that the CEA's job was to test its theories in order to prove the worth of the
New Economics. "The idea was to get all these people [in the administration] to understand that we knew what
we were talking about, that Kennedy would make a better policy if he listened to us, that they ought to be clued
in on what we were trying to do in spite of the fact that this was an arcane subject to a bunch of lawyers. In that
sense, the first job was to become an accepted part of the inner circle."

Yet when Prachowny used newer modeling techniques to re-estimate the tax cut's effects, he concluded that in fact it was "a stunning success and that alternative routes to full employment [such as Galbraith's public spending strategy] were less likely to achieve the same goals." This would seem a ringing endorsement of the New Economists—if growth was the only goal, and if it was measured in otherwise antiseptic circumstances. But the circumstances weren't antiseptic, and the chief source of infection was presumed to be Johnson's escalation of the Vietnam war spending. Having assumed an invariant 1.5 percent inflation rate following the tax cut, Okun's model surprised him when inflation burst upward soon after.[60]

But Vietnam was merely the conventional and encompassing explanation. At a deeper level, other important forces were at work. For one, the composition of the workforce was changing as more women entered job markets along with the huge numbers of the baby boom generation, representing a stimulative factor on the demand side (and a productivity drag on the supply side). As Robert Solow admitted many years later,

> The basic fact is that we overestimated the growth of productivity in the 1960s . . . We tended to be simple labor-and-capital people. As I have confessed, we may have paid less attention than we should have to the changing age-sex composition of the labor force and its effect on both the productivity trend and the definition of full employment . . . We expected more from the pick-up in investment than we got . . . Where did real life go wrong?[61]

Consumer markets and the supply of easy consumer credit were also changing. For example, between 1964 and 1967 the number of banks in the credit card business grew from 60 to 800, and 32 million new cards were issued in 1967 alone. By 1970, outstanding consumer credit was more than $100 billion, double what it had been when Kennedy took office.[62] Thus, the freer attitudes of a new generation of Americans, *The Affluent Society* generation, toward consumption and debt seem to have played as much a part in stoking inflation as the cost of the Vietnam War, and far more than the much maligned but far smaller spending LBJ assigned to his War on Poverty or the difficulties faced with wage-price guidelines.

Yet neither Okun's econometric models nor Prachowny's reinvestigation of them took account of these demographic, credit, and psychological shifts. A new generation had never known the Depression's poverty nor World War II's fears; what it knew were the suburbs, the golden, advertising-drenched world portrayed on television, and the eagerness with which retailers and banks promised to make that world their own. With political leaders pledging first a New Frontier and then a Great Society, citizens at the lower edges of the promised worlds moreover believed they too had every right to be part of them and to see the end to barriers that stood in the way.

Prachowny ironically concluded that in the end, Galbraith's strategy for spending would have been the wiser one. As Galbraith repeatedly told JFK, Prachowny likewise acknowledged, "The tax rate is the clumsiest and least reliable instrument that can be used" to stimulate growth. "It would be more sensible to depend on variations in direct government demand for goods and services than to manipulate private disposable income to achieve the same result."*[63]

IN EARLY JANUARY 1966, Galbraith was nonetheless still trying to exercise some direct influence on the administration's Vietnam policies, even though by now he was among its most prominent opponents. Taking a break from the intensive final work on his next book, he sat down in his third-floor study late on a snowy afternoon that month to write a detailed nine-point memorandum for LBJ.[64] It was, he wrote the President, an attempt to see the war not "in light of my own preferences . . . but as it concerns the Presidency and the whole country."

The central reality was that "we have no major national interest in Vietnam . . . It is a practical problem and not the focus of a holy crusade against Communism. It calls for consideration in the light of practical politics and not by anti-Communist zealots." Galbraith reiterated the risk of war with China, and warned Johnson that while he had majority support in the country, "you owe a lot to the feeling that you are the great restraining force in the situation." The obvious danger was that "this miserable conflict is monopolizing headlines that properly belong to your domestic achievements and energies that should properly go to our domestic problems."

In his memo Galbraith did not mention a remarkable dinner he'd had with McNamara just three days earlier in Washington, although it was an important catalyst for his writing to the President. The Secretary of Defense had said things that had left him deeply shaken: the war, according to McNamara, was now spinning out of control and would lead to a major American defeat. At the dinner, which Arthur Schlesinger had organized at McNamara's request and which Richard Goodwin and Carl Kaysen also attended, the Defense Secretary became very emotional, describing the constantly escalating troop demands from General Westmoreland and the failure of U.S. bombing to halt the constant resupply of enemy troops. To Galbraith this latest admission of the bombing's negligible results came as no surprise. What surprised him was McNamara's admission that the only viable alternative now left for the United States seemed to be withdrawal with honor.

McNamara also said that the President was torn about what to do and was depressed; he had even talked of resigning. Two weeks earlier, McNamara had persuaded Johnson to announce a halt in the bombing at Christmas and had drafted cables that sent American diplomats racing around the globe in hopes

---

*After rediscovering in 2000 a truth clear to Galbraith four decades earlier, Prachowny went on to lament "the extravagant claims and promises that economists make when they become policy advisors"; but lacking Galbraith's larger theory of political economy which links economic change to constant political struggle and popular education, his solution was to wonder openly whether the CEA itself should be abolished. "The prestige of the Council of Economic Advisors has fallen considerably since its heyday of the 1960s and the giants of the economics profession are no longer beguiled by the prospect of serving as members" (Prachowny, *Kennedy-Johnson Tax Cut*, 174–81).

of using the halt to open negotiations that might settle the war. But if no breakthroughs came quickly, the distraught McNamara warned his dinner companions, Johnson would escalate the war yet again.[65]

Recognizing that by now Johnson would not pull back the troops he'd committed even if diplomatic talks with North Vietnam could commence, Galbraith urged him, as he had six months earlier, to adopt an "enclave" policy, focusing the troops on holding the major Vietnamese cities and a portion of the countryside, while pressing ahead for negotiations and the beginnings of a staged withdrawal. "Our military will not like this," he acknowledged. "Nor would Republicans and some of the columnists. This . . . will work strongly to your advantage. Without pulling out or losing ground, you are . . . the man who stands against impatience and a big war." He acknowledged that negotiations would not come easily, but "as Churchill used to say, most wars in history have been avoided simply by postponing them."[66]

It was in some sense too late, of course. When the Christmas bombing pause didn't induce the North Vietnamese to come to the negotiating table, Johnson raised U.S. troop levels and intensified the bombings, just as McNamara had warned. In April Galbraith again urged Johnson to step back from the abyss. A Buddhist uprising in Vietnam gave the President a chance to halt the fighting and open negotiations, Galbraith argued—"an opportunity only the God-fearing deserve and only the extremely lucky get."

Johnson never replied.

In late May, Galbraith tried a third and final time, offering to draft a speech that would set the stage for an early withdrawal. This time he received an answer—written by Walt Rostow for Johnson's signature. "I have never doubted your talent for political craftsmanship," the letter began, "and I am sure you could devise a script that would appear to justify our taking an unjustifiable course in South Vietnam." The President then noted that Galbraith had just delivered a commencement address that was critical of the war. "Did I misread your admonition to quit talking about Viet Nam and discuss the gains of the Great Society?" he asked. "Then why don't *we*?"

Galbraith took this stinging rebuke personally, and responded tartly, reminding the President that among his own advisers, "the people who want to invest more and more in this war have nothing to lose. They will end up working for a foundation."[67] His unmistakable reference was to McGeorge Bundy who, having long encouraged the escalation of the Vietnam War, had come to realize its folly and departed the White House for the presidency of the Ford Foundation.

Clearly there was nothing left for Galbraith to say directly to President Johnson, and so he now concentrated on public protest.* Accepting more and

---

*Galbraith nonetheless maintained a limited contact with the White House, through LBJ aides Joseph Califano and Jack Valenti. In April 1967, he used it to help rescue the imprisoned Greek political leader Andreas Papandreou. Papandreou was a Harvard-trained economist who'd taught for many years at the University of Minnesota and at Berkeley before returning to Athens at the behest of his father, who was Greece's prime minister. When the government was overthrown in spring 1967 by a junta of reactionary army officers, they imprisoned Papandreou and hundreds of others.

more speaking engagements across the country (with a special affection, he says, for invitations in Texas), he also gave more and more interviews and poured out more and more articles against the war, using his prominence to legitimize and expand dissent.[68] Surveying these efforts, the veteran *New York Times* political columnist James Reston judged him "the most articulate spokesman of the scattered Vietnam peace forces in America . . . who is just old enough and big enough . . . to turn the peace movement into a political movement if that is what he decides to do." *Newsweek* concluded that although Galbraith had worn out his welcome at the White House, he was "one of the few men with both the intellectual and political cachet to command the attention and respect of a wide spectrum" of the country.

The White House realized the danger Galbraith posed, and worried that Reston was right about his ability "to turn the peace movement into a political movement." Hoping to isolate him, the political scientist John Roche, a former Americans for Democratic Action president who had joined Johnson's staff as a prowar intellectual-in-residence assigned to containing the increasingly rebellious academic community, scoffed to reporters, "Ken's trouble is that he feels an elite from academe should be the saviors of the country."[69]

By the spring of 1967, Galbraith had developed a full-fledged proposal for a negotiated settlement that built on the outlines he'd described to Johnson. As a paperback book entitled *How to Get Out of Vietnam*, it sold out its 250,000-copy first printing, and the proposal was taken seriously enough (everywhere but the White House) for *The New York Times* to ask him for a condensed version as an article in its Sunday magazine.[70] This not unexpectedly enraged President Johnson, and aides demanded that the *Times* allow the State Department's William Bundy to reply in the same issue with Johnson's reasons for opposing the plan.[71]

By then Galbraith, just as Reston had prophesied, was planning to challenge Johnson's reelection in 1968, convinced that there was no other way to stop the war. Elected president of the 50,000-member ADA in March, he persuaded the group to stand openly against the war. (As a result, the president of the AFL-CIO, George Meany, a strong supporter of Johnson and the Vietnam War, pulled union financial support from the ADA in retribution.) At the same time, Galbraith joined Schlesinger, Richard Goodwin, Theodore Sorensen,

---

Fearing his execution, his American-born wife, Margaret, personally appealed to Galbraith to intervene, thinking that as a former ambassador as well as an economist, he could best persuade President Johnson to do something, as the colonels were anxious to cultivate U.S. support. Dozens of other economists, including Kenneth Arrow, Robert Dorfman, Stanley Sheinbaum, and Leonid Hurwicz, rallied to Papandreou's support.

Galbraith phoned Califano, knowing it was useless to phone Rusk at the State Department; it had quickly recognized the new military government, and had expressed only muted concern about the overthrow of a democratic NATO ally. It was mid-evening, and Califano agreed to pass Galbraith's plea on to Johnson that night.

Before dawn the next morning a call from Undersecretary of State Nicholas Katzenbach awakened Galbraith. He said he had a message from the President. Galbraith stiffened, fearful of rebuff. Then, with an audible chuckle, Katzenbach quoted LBJ verbatim: "Call up Ken Galbraith and tell him that I've told those Greek bastards to lay off that son-of-a-bitch—whoever he is." Papandreou was released shortly thereafter and was allowed to leave Greece. Others wired or called the White House, but Papandreou and his wife always credited Galbraith with saving his life (see Galbraith, *A Life*, 459–60; Margaret Papandreou, interview with author).

Joseph Rauh, and several others in a new antiwar organization, Negotiations Now, intended not only to raise the pressure on Johnson but ideally to serve as a launching platform for an opponent willing to run against LBJ in 1968 if one could be found.

For a brief moment Galbraith was entertained by the improbable idea of running for President himself. In Berkeley for a speech and discussions with the liberal California Democratic Council, he was asked to meet with a delegation of liberal antiwar activists led by Allard Lowenstein. Lowenstein, a former head of the National Student Association and a controversial figure in the student antiwar movement, seemed to bridge the gap between rebellious students and older figures such as Senator Kennedy and Galbraith. He too had been canvassing among the handful of politicians who might be persuaded to run against Johnson, but with no success. Would Galbraith himself, he asked, consider the race? The economist quickly pointed out that since he was a Canadian by birth, he was constitutionally ineligible to run.[72]

Galbraith also endorsed "Vietnam Summer," a massive student-led attempt through door-to-door canvassing and face-to-face meetings to reach the millions of Americans who hated the war but at the same time distrusted the students and academics who opposed it. It met with limited success, and so after school resumed that September, Galbraith and Rauh decided that it was time for them to canvass Capitol Hill.

Inside the administration, the war by then had taken its toll. President Johnson was in constant anguish over it and talking with his wife and closest advisers about retiring. At the same time, McNamara, finally convinced that the war could not be won, told the President he favored an enclave-and-negotiation strategy not dissimilar to the one Galbraith had proposed. To many (including Johnson) McNamara seemed near emotional collapse, and his revised views and overwrought emotions only heightened what amounted to a near schizophrenia in Johnson. Resentful of his Defense Secretary's shift in position (and alarmed by his increasingly erratic behavior), in November LBJ suddenly and without warning dismissed him from the Cabinet and made him head of the World Bank. Then, reversing course, he appointed Clark Clifford as McNamara's successor and began laying plans to get the United States out of Southeast Asia, going so far as to have General Westmoreland testify to Congress about the new "withdrawal" strategy.[73] For a moment, the moves left LBJ's antiwar critics stunned and confused. What should they do?

Finding a well-known Democrat who was willing openly to challenge a sitting President from his own party was nearly impossible, Galbraith and Rauh discovered. Senator Robert Kennedy declined, and so did George McGovern, who insisted that Kennedy was the only realistic choice. What Kennedy did do, however, was suggest someone else: Minnesota Senator Eugene McCarthy. And so Galbraith made his way to McCarthy's office. The two men had known each other since McCarthy's election to the House in the 1950s (introduced by Congressman Henry Reuss of Wisconsin, an old OPA colleague).

In his office that day, McCarthy listened, I thought sympathetically, to my plea and told me he was coming to Boston in a few days. We would discuss it further then. I went on to speak at a significant meeting against the war at the University of Chicago—significant, for it had been organized by a group of local trade unions . . . Returning to Cambridge, I introduced McCarthy at a gathering of young Democrats . . . Afterward outside he was cheered by an impressive gathering of Harvard students whose attendance and enthusiasm were partly my inspiration . . . We then adjourned to our house to consider the prospect . . . The discussion was not prolonged. Gene had already decided to run.[74]

18

The New Industrial State

It is the genius of the industrial system that it makes the goals that reflect its needs—efficient production of goods, steady expansion of their output, a steady expansion in their consumption, a powerful preference for goods over leisure, an unqualified commitment to technological change, autonomy for the technostructure, an adequate supply of trained and educated manpower—coordinate with social virtue and human enlightenment.

—John Kenneth Galbraith,
The New Industrial State

Believe it or not, the most popular book in the country at this moment is The New Industrial State. *The success of its predecessor,* The Affluent Society, *prepared book people for its success, but who would expect a highly intelligent book on economics to sweep the country?*

—*Book Buyers Guide,*
Summer 1967

AS THE VIETNAM WAR escalated, Galbraith found himself in a dilemma: he was tempted to increase his public opposition to the war, but at the same time he sought the nurturing privacy of writing. In the end, he did both.

The 1960s were a prolific decade for Galbraith as a writer. During little more than two years in India, he had somehow found enough time amidst his ambassadorial duties to produce a set of essays, *Economic Development*; *The McLandress Dimension*, his first novel; as well *The Scotch*, a gently evocative memoir of growing up in Canada that he considers his finest piece of writing. All the while he kept recording the voluminous diary notes that became *Ambassador's Journal*, which was published in 1969. Back in Cambridge by the fall of 1963, he increased the decade's already exceptional output to a torrential pace over the next few years. On top of his teaching duties and producing magazine and newspaper articles, lecturing nationwide against the war, and involvement in the 1964 and 1968 presidential campaigns, he wrote a second novel, *The Triumph*, a blistering satire of the State Department that became a *New York Times* best-seller; a coauthored book on Indian Moghul painting (a passion he'd discovered in New Delhi); and two tracts on the war and the U.S. military establishment (*How to Get Out of Vietnam* and *How to Control the Military*).[1]

Yet even then he was not done.

Galbraith's return to academic life after two and a half years* didn't mean that he was ready to stop serving and advising presidents; in the summer of 1963, he had, among other things, at Kennedy's request taken over the negotiations on (and settled) a thorny civil air treaty between the United States and Canada, and he had kept up a steady stream of memos and meetings with JFK on economic policies and Southeast Asia.[2]

Just before classes started in the fall of 1963, Galbraith retrieved a set of rough manuscript chapters from his safe-deposit box at Cambridge Trust—the partly finished draft of a book begun in 1959. Enjoyable as the distractions of India and the perquisites of his time there had been—not to mention the new pleasures of writing a novel, a memoir of childhood, an art-history work, and a literary-political diary—the carefully wrapped onionskin pages he'd left tucked away in that bank vault represented something even more important to him—the beginnings of a book on economics and politics that, he believed, would overshadow the influence and reputation of *The Affluent Society*.

Getting back to normal campus life wasn't easy, however, and attending to those pages wasn't easy either. A *Newsweek* reporter showed up to appraise his first day back in the classroom (positively, it turned out: "Galbraith met his first class—Ec 169, Theory and Problems of Economic Development—and blasted off with an hour lecture, which both the professor and his 200 students clearly enjoyed"). Committed to teaching three courses and a seminar, Galbraith told the reporter he planned nonetheless to "devote three hours each day to writing" his new book.[3]

By mid-1965, Galbraith had abandoned much of the early draft. The writing, editing, and rewriting dragged on, but in the summer of 1967 the reward came. From the moment *The New Industrial State* appeared in bookstores, it seemed to fulfill its author's hopes and expectations. The book glided onto *The New York Times* best-seller list and remained there for a year, including two months at the top (and joined for a time by his novel *The Triumph*).[4] Foreign editions quickly appeared in nearly two dozen countries, and reviewers for major newspapers and magazines rushed to offer their opinions.[5]

It is hard to say whether *The New Industrial State* had the same effect in the 1960s as *The Affluent Society* had had in the 1950s, and to assess its lasting influence. To begin with, it is more difficult in its argument, incorporating

---

*Galbraith's official absence from Harvard included a six-month extension based on an exception allowed for "wartime" service—a condition that Galbraith invoked in light of the Sino-Indian war in the fall of 1962.

a greater number of separate strands—a complexity Galbraith justified by calling it an entire "house" of ideas about the American economy and economics, compared to which the *The Affluent Society* was but a "window."[6] The book also demands more of readers not trained in economics. And it struck centrally at the business and public-sector organization of modern America, in contrast to the less antagonistic views of large corporations expressed in *American Capitalism* fifteen years earlier. Also, it appeared at a time when preoccupations with Vietnam, with poverty, with race relations, and with turbulent social and cultural changes offered daunting competition for attention.

It is abundantly clear, however, that *The New Industrial State* provoked hostility among many of Galbraith's fellow Keynesians. The animosity of most conservative economists to him had been a given since *American Capitalism*, but now new voices joined these detractors, including several of the most prominent figures of the Neoclassical Synthesis. The surprising vehemence of some of their arguments bespoke resentments that had been smoldering for some time.

The most vocal of these new critics was Robert Solow of MIT. Solow could hardly be mistaken for an economic or political conservative. He'd been on the staff of Kennedy's Council of Economic Advisors, and with Paul Samuelson had done much of the path-breaking work that defined the Neoclassical Synthesis. Sixteen years Galbraith's junior, the wiry, intense, Brooklyn-born Solow was forty-three when *The New Industrial State* appeared, and already had a reputation as a pugnacious debater. For several months before *The New Industrial State*'s appearance, he and Samuelson had been embroiled with Joan Robinson, Piero Sraffa, and Nicholas Kaldor of Cambridge University in the legendary "Cambridge v. Cambridge" debates, or "Cambridge capital controversies."[7]

The "Cambridge v. Cambridge" debates—carried out over several years in letters, journal articles, books, and public fora—may seem recondite to noneconomists, involving as they did extremely sophisticated logical and mathematical claims about, among other things, capital's "switching" and "reswitching" characteristics under different economic conditions. Yet although the topic was abstruse, none of the parties doubted that something fundamental was at stake.[8] Samuelson and Solow were, in essence, being called upon to defend the Neoclassical Synthesis (and, by implication, the Kennedy-Johnson era's "New Economics") at the most fundamental theoretical level. Just as gifted technically as the two Americans, Robinson, Sraffa, and Kaldor were vocal proponents of a more radical and to them more authentic reading of Keynes and his legacy, one that was free of what they saw as the confining (and dishonest) strictures that the Americans' incorporation of Marshallian microprinciples and mathematical model building had placed on Keynesian policy and theory.

The English trio had about them a pride of place in the Keynesian tradition that led them to look upon the Americans as upstarts. Robinson and Sraffa had been members of "the Circus" in the 1930s, the intimate little group around

Keynes at Cambridge who'd helped him refine *The General Theory*, and they felt they best understood what Keynes had intended.[9] Robinson especially was Solow's equal as a debater. The daughter of a British brigadier general famed for denouncing Prime Minister Lloyd George during World War I, she had her father's courage, a rapier wit, and a finely developed hauteur, well exhibited when she indelicately took to referring to her American opponents as "bastard Keynesians." At one point, when she, Samuelson, and Solow appeared together to debate their differences, the arguments got so heated that Samuelson (who disliked personal confrontations) walked off the stage while Solow spoke.[10]

The Cambridge controversies weren't the only problem on Solow's mind. More visibly, the 1964 Kennedy-Johnson tax cut, which Solow had helped Heller design as the totem of New Economics, was facing dismemberment as inflation began surging through the American economy. Worse, the process of amending or replacing the 1964 act was humiliating the "fine-tuners." The economists who had succeeded Heller and Solow in the White House had realized that a more anti-inflationary fiscal policy was needed, but work on the necessary new legislation was proceeding by fits and starts, resisted in turns by LBJ, then by the chairman of the House Ways and Means Committee, Wilbur Mills, then by key interest groups, and even by the press.[11] The New Economists' inability to persuade political leaders to shape tax policy quickly to fit the rapidly changing economic environment—a *sine qua non* for "fine-tuning" to work in practice—was just as difficult as Galbraith had warned it would be when Heller first proposed the cut in 1962.[12] And a key theoretical assumption undergirding the policy confidence of "fine-tuners" was also being undermined.

In the spring of 1967, Paul Samuelson proudly reminded an economics symposium that the Phillips Curve was "one of the most important concepts of our time." But as he spoke, a promising young Yale-trained economist named Edmund Phelps was completing a landmark paper challenging its vaunted explanation of the trade-off between employment and inflation.[13] In effect, Phelps argued, there was an irreducible "natural rate" of unemployment that couldn't easily be lowered, even by accepting a higher rate of inflation. If Phelps's conclusions held up, the rosy prospect that policy-makers could engineer a stable, ever-growing full-employment economy—a prospect fed by Solow's and Samuelson's pioneering work on the Phillips Curve—would be severely constrained, to say the least.

Milton Friedman shortly thereafter piled on in his inaugural address as president of the American Economic Association.[14] He insisted that Samuelson and Solow had been fundamentally wrong not to recognize this "natural rate of unemployment,"* which Keynesian policies couldn't reduce without sparking intolerable inflation. Friedman had been arguing elements of this point for years to no great effect—partly because the "natural rate" idea was

---

*The academic term is "NAIRU," for "nonaccelerating inflation rate of unemployment."

hardly new, having been popular in the early nineteenth century before being abandoned by the new faith in Marshall's "smoothly clearing market" world. But now the alignment of the stars was changing.

As mainstream Keynesians found themselves in a cross-fire from Keynes's progressive English disciples on one side and a conservative monetarist such as Friedman on the other, and with the achievement of the 1964 tax cut turning to dust before their eyes, the gnawing idea that there might be errors in their theoretical work and its policy applications haunted many of them.[15] Set against this background, the tone of Solow's review of Galbraith's new book in 1967 is easier to understand, as is Galbraith's response to it. Until then he had mostly met his critics with cool indifference and even a certain lèse-majesté. But after seeing an advance copy of Solow's review for The Public Interest, he insisted to the magazine's editors, Daniel Bell and Irving Kristol, that he be given the unprecedented right to reply in the same issue. They tried to demur, claiming the issue was typeset and almost on the presses, but Galbraith prevailed by offering to pay personally to avoid any delay at the printers.[16] It was evident that for both economists, otherwise allied in so many ways, much was at stake.

Solow started by deconstructing The New Industrial State into a half dozen separate theses, then criticizing them one by one. Although Galbraith's reply contested Solow's characterization of several of these points, Solow's divisions are useful, and are followed here with only slight modifications.

Thesis 1: The giant corporation, for Galbraith, is the "characteristic organization" of modern capitalism. Tiny in number among the millions of U.S. corporations overall, a thousand or so giants dominate the economic landscape, not only because of their advantages of size (due largely to what economists call "returns to scale") but because the complexity and cost of advanced technological investment requires extensive bureaucratic organization. Economists in Galbraith's view had inadequately investigated the consequences, especially when the behemoth's behavior undermined their idealized model of competition.[17]

Thesis 2: Shareholders, the nominal owners of the corporations, have little power over corporate decision-making compared to the top managers and senior specialists in operations, marketing, and research and development, whom Galbraith calls collectively "the technostructure." Members of the technostructure are, in his opinion, a central feature of the giant corporation because they have the power to shape its culture, goals, and behavior.

Thesis 3: The members of the technostructure for the most part don't own significant blocks of stock themselves and, disliking uncertainty in the company's prospects, seek to reduce risk by giving up classic "profit-maximizing" principles so beloved by economists in favor of growth with predictable profits. They do this by various means that introduce a new level of corporate-led "planning" into the market as a whole—Galbraith explicitly identifies it collectively as "the planning system"—which overtly tries to manipulate demand as well as supply. They also pay millions to politicians and lobbyists to manipulate public regulation and laws that influence their industry and market performance. Despite, or perhaps because of, these payments, they have largely come to accept government's primacy in macromanagement of the economy's business cycle.

On the production side, the technostructure's successful planning and risk reduction lead to corporations' vertical integration, heavy reliance on internal financing (rather than bank borrowing or issuance of bonds), and co-optation of labor unions (which no longer represent a "countervailing power," as Galbraith described them in *American Capitalism*).[18]

On the demand side, the technostructure's ends are achieved by a steady barrage of advertising and marketing that generally induces consumers to buy what the corporation wants to sell at the price it prefers. This "revised sequence" of demand formation, as Galbraith calls it, in which the corporation shapes demand rather than demand emerging uni-directionally from the "sovereign" consumer, stands in stark contrast not only to classical Marshallian economics but to mainstream Keynesianism's absorption of its older microeconomic rules.[19]

Thesis 4: In lieu of classical "profit maximizing," the giant corporation pursues its end of survival and independence by concentrating on steady but maximal sales growth, consistently predictable earnings, technological virtuosity, and insulation from what it considers adverse interference (though not assistance) from government. Once these conditions favored by the technostructure's leaders seem secure, the large corporation will acknowledge other objectives if they improve the "corporate image"—sponsorship of the arts and charities, for example.

Thesis 5: Advertising, plus a national ideology that praises the constant growth of privately consumable goods and services, may serve the giant corporation and its technostructure, but it misdirects the collective energies and attention of citizens away from the truth that the United States for the most part is already awash in affluence. The poverty visible in our midst is no longer a function of an inadequate aggregate supply but of a maldistribution of income and wealth that misshapes demand for private and public spending. This remaining poverty notwithstanding, the goal of the giant corporations' "planning system" is to satisfy the technostructure's desire to manage fully all aspects of its market environment, to reassure citizens they are getting what they "want," and to convince government bureaucrats and leaders (and the press) that in accepting the "planning system" even while preaching the virtues of "free markets," they are serving the larger national purpose and ideal.

Thesis 6: The key resource of the modern economy is no longer its huge industrial capacity for producing goods but the capacity to mobilize organized intelligence. (Here Galbraith was anticipating what others were later to christen the new "information economy.") Central to this new economy is the modern "educational and scientific estate": the scholars, teachers, and researchers who work in universities and nonprofit research centers whose innovations in science, technology, and social organization are woven into the work of big corpo-

rations, which provide research funds, endowed chairs, and lucrative consul-
tancies in exchange for these valuable new technologies and techniques.

This educational and scientific estate no longer sees itself as standing apart
from the corporations, pursuing its own agenda of pure "scientific" ends and
general public knowledge. Its members may not be as centrally or overtly motivated by personal financial rewards as the technostructure's elites, but they
are not suspicious or hostile to them either. And their work in generating policy proposals and various tools for social innovation is generally welcomed by
the technostructure—as long as it does not directly challenge the fundamental
power and order of the corporate "planning system." The two groups are now
symbiotically linked. They share social status, educational and class backgrounds, frequent social contact, and love of technological virtuosity.

This new sense of common interest and identity notwithstanding, Galbraith
argued at surprising length that the educational and scientific estate (unlike
the technostructure) still values the prestige and rewards that derive from
sources other than corporate power or wealth. Because it also maintains and
champions certain values not identical to those of the technostructure, he
posited the possibility that leaders and ideas might emerge from it to encourage the country to abandon its monotheistic worship of an ever-growing GNP
as the ultimate test of a good society.

Having given this synopsis of *The New Industrial State's* principal theses,
Solow set about his criticism of them. First, however, he observed that "jeal-
ousy" had often been "a real factor" in many economists' dislike of Galbraith
and his ideas.

> Galbraith, after all, is something special. His books are not only widely read,
> but actually enjoyed. He is a public figure of some significance; he shares
> with [Federal Reserve Chairman] William McChesney Martin the power to
> shake stock prices . . . He is known and attended to all over the world . . . It
> is no wonder that the pedestrian economist feels for him an uneasy mixture
> of envy and disdain.[20]

Galbraith is a "big-thinker," Solow went on, the normal economist a "little-
thinker," and the two were like the couple whose husband makes all the "big"
decisions, such as "what to do about Jerusalem, whether to admit China to the
U.N., how to solve crime in the streets," while the wife makes the "little" ones
about where to live, what job to take, and how to raise the children. Galbraith,
Solow tartly concluded, was guilty of declaiming on "Whither We Are Trend-
ing" and in *The New Industrial State* had produced what he called "a book for
the dinner table and not the desk," because, as "real economists" knew, in each
of his major claims Galbraith was simply wrong.

Galbraith's first thesis, that the giant corporation was the "characteristic"
modern organization, was, Solow believed, incorrect: "only about 55 percent of
the Gross National Product" was even in the nonfinancial corporate sector,
"and not nearly all of that is generated by the giant corporation." While power-

ful in manufacturing and utilities, the behemoths were much less important in trade and services, the fastest-growing parts of the American economy. As these nonmanufacturing sectors became more important, "the role of the large corporation may be limited," he predicted.[21]

Solow's conclusion has not aged well. Business data forty years later show that manufacturing remains as highly concentrated as it was then: just half of 1 percent of all manufacturing firms employ more than half of all manufacturing's workers, and the largest four hundred firms employ more men and women than the bottom 97 percent. Solow's prediction of a "limited" role for gigantism in trade and services has proved hollow. Computer software giants such as Microsoft, fast-food chains such as McDonald's, and megaretailers such as Wal-Mart and Home Depot, as well as dozens of other once smaller firms outside the old world of manufacturing have become dominant presences in their own fields—even more dominant than manufacturing firms were in theirs when *The New Industrial State* was written. For example, in retailing, one half of 1 percent of companies employs more than 60 percent of all retail workers.* In burgeoning new sectors such as information technology and health care, the concentration is even higher—more than 70 percent.[22]

In the era of the global economy, the supercorporation has similarly come to dominate international trade and business. Much of this new worldwide business concentration has been fueled by the spectacular explosion of mergers and acquisitions. In 2000 alone there were mergers worth nearly $2 trillion— all part of the gigantism one finds in virtually every sector of the economy. Significantly, while mergers have been touted by their proponents for enhancing the merged companies' potential for profits (which Solow would take as proof of the power of orthodox market imperatives) studies of postmerger company performance consistently show poor bottom-line performance, with the real gains accruing to the executives, financial advisors, and holders of large blocks of the acquired company's stock at the time of sale—a pattern that Galbraith's theories explain.

When it came to Galbraith's claim that the independent technostructure sets corporate goals different from those of the profit-maximizing firms of standard economic theory, Solow's argument was that "market forces" largely constrained many, if not most, of these enterprises from behaving in a new and different way. He granted Galbraith's point about the separation of ownership from management but faulted him for not providing "convincing evidence."

Here one has to say in retrospect that Solow had the advantage, even though neither economist anticipated America's "financialization"—the vast growth of the financial sector—or the country's political appetite for business deregulation and lower taxes. To give one example, investment funds of all sorts—from the more than ten thousand mutual funds (in which nearly half of

---

*Wal-Mart, a tiny regional retailer in 1967, is far larger than any manufacturer. Today, it is the *world's* largest corporation, visited by 100 million customers each week, and with 1.5 million employees. Its $256 billion in sales equals 2.4 percent of U.S. GDP.

all Americans now invest) to often esoteric hedge funds made famous by figures such as George Soros—have come to define a new competitive marketplace that is in some ways more traditional than the one described in *The New Industrial State*. The power of these funds and of the financial sector as a whole is hailed as a triumph of "markets," though in truth it has also resulted from changes in the legal and regulatory environment. And it has placed the managers of America's largest companies under pressures that were much less common from 1945 to 1965, the period discussed by Galbraith and Solow.[23]

Neither man foresaw the sweep of "globalization" that by the 1980s was fostering important new overseas sources for workers, finance, sales, competitors, and products, and that has reshaped the relevant meaning of "national" and "international" markets ever since. And no one in the 1960s could have anticipated the enormous range of effects "globalization" and "financialization" combined would have on U.S. corporate culture and performance.

Yet glimmers of Galbraith's insights still shine through today. For example, the consistently greater benefits mergers bestow on the technostructure's senior managers and outside financial advisers than on the corporation's shareholders support Galbraith's claim about the ability of managers to optimize their advantage compared to that of the company's legal owners to do so.[24] So, too, the use of stock options and other incentives in management pay schemes, intended by their proponents to align the divergent interests of managers and owners more closely, has led to managerial practices that have boosted short-term performance at the cost of the long-term health of the stock and the company, a recipe for managerial misbehavior and predatory financial market practices. These options, a major element in technostructure compensation, have let managers do spectacularly well even while their companies failed. That senior corporate executives have raised their total compensation in ways indicating that they have insulated themselves from competitive market forces is a development that better accords with Galbraith's views than Solow's.[25] When *The New Industrial State* appeared, CEOs at major U.S. corporations, relying heavily on straight salary and bonuses, were annually earning roughly 20 times the average U.S. worker; by the mid-1990s, after performance-tied compensation became common, that factor had jumped from 20 to more than 400.[26]

Solow also chastised Galbraith for claiming that big-business "hostility" toward government was in decline, that it was a remnant of small-business attitudes largely absent from megacorporations' attitudes under the technostructure leadership. The large corporations, he argued, were at least as hostile to public macromanagement as other segments of the business community. Yet it can be said that Solow failed to distinguish between business rhetoric and practice. If in fact the big companies were "hostile" to government, how then could one explain, as one political economist pointed out, the 12,000 business lawyers, the 9,000 business lobbyists, the 42,000 trade associations, the 8,000 public relations consultants, and 3,500 business affairs consultants who were making a very good living in Washington, not to mention the tens of thousands more in similar positions at the state and local levels? Surely their efforts—and the hundreds of millions spent annually by corporate PACs and business donors—couldn't all be simply for the textbook end of "profit maximization." Whether the giant corporations were hostile to government macromanagement or symbiotic with it was a question that needed more complex analysis than Solow offered.[27]

Solow devoted his closest attention, and greatest ire, to Galbraith's third thesis, that the modern giant corporation, under the "planning" strategies of its technocratic leadership, is to a large degree risk-averse and that as a result—the fourth thesis—large firms no longer primarily seek to maximize profits. These theses are also the most difficult to evaluate, then and today, because economists in truth have no satisfactory and comprehensive theory of profits or of risk and innovation. But Solow was peremptory in his overall judgment: they were "so much an exaggeration that it smacks of the put-on."[28]

On the supply side, Solow argued, companies were still beholden to external capital markets—for financing, for example—and thus subject to "market discipline": bankers and bond markets would enforce corporate profit maximizing, whatever the "technostructure" might want. Yet Solow knew that his refutation lacked the rigorous theoretical consistency he faulted Galbraith for failing to provide: banks and bond markets might well not finance a corporation whose profits fell below prevailing rates or that had a substandard credit rating (not the same thing as a substandard profit margin). But if Galbraith was right that the prevailing profit rate of large companies was below a Marshallian optimum (which derives from constant head-to-head competition between firms that cannot influence prevailing prices by themselves), it was still the case that banks and bond markets would have to provide financing, since that was the market reality they faced. (As a theoretical matter, the best examples of just such a situation are found in the Japanese economy, as Martin Bronfenbrenner and others have pointed out.[29])

In discussing what Galbraith called the "revised sequence" of consumption, Solow fell back on a peculiar combination of anecdotal refutation and allusion to a long-held (but weakly investigated) microeconomic belief among economists that "advertising serves only to cancel other advertising, and is therefore merely wasteful."[30] While this fit standard blackboard assumptions, including Paul Samuelson's theory of "revealed preference," whether it accords with reality is another matter. To begin with, the very idea that for decades corporations have consciously, systematically, engaged in "wasteful" behavior seems unlikely in a world of "rational" economic behavior. As the economist Robin Marris put it, if economists were so "sure that most advertising results in a stand-off, the profession has clearly been guilty of a grave dereliction of duty to the public. They should have been shouting loudly and with one voice, 'Here is an activity that has no significant economic effect, good or bad; it is a total waste; it should be prohibited like arson.' "[31] In reply to Marris, Solow quickly backpedaled, claiming he meant to say only that advertising had no real effect on the choice between spending and saving—a very different (yet still contestable) argument. Of course, economists have long stressed that spending on advertising is a small part of overall gross domestic product—2.5 to 3 percent is usually cited—and, while perhaps wasteful, is not significant. But that doesn't resolve the argument, since in the $10 trillion American economy today that small percentage works out to roughly $250 billion to $300 billion—more than the country spends on public primary education annually.[32]

In any case, GDP probably shouldn't be the relevant denominator: government, after all (which advertises little) accounts for one third of GDP and much of the private-sector activity below the retail level requires little or no advertising for sales. As a percentage of consumer sales (a more relevant denominator), advertising spending is much larger, a "surcharge" on consumption effectively amounting to several thousand dollars per household per year, someone like Galbraith might insist. Last, that $250 billion to $300 billion figure is too low, based as it is on advertising expenditures reported by major corporations and advertising agencies. There is a vast netherworld of local consumer advertising that is never reported in these surveys, and the more inclusive term "marketing and promotion expenditures" would be a better measure than traditional "advertising."

The truth that products advertise themselves in their packaging, as any trip down a supermarket aisle reminds us, is a good example here. Sports stadiums named for corporations, schoolbooks subsidized by companies that insert their brand names into school texts, "buzz marketing"—hiring young promoters to pitch products to target audiences without revealing their employment relation—and of course "product placement" in television shows and films have all become weapons in the arsenal of modern marketing.* And consumers themselves have joined this promotion-saturated world. When *The New Industrial State* appeared, few Americans wore name-"branded" clothing. Nowadays, a walk down any American street brings you face to face with an endless stream of fellow citizens willingly dressed as marquees for L. L. Bean, the Gap, FUBU, Ralph Lauren, Land's End, Nike, and other such companies. All those individuals are working at no cost for the nation's biggest corporations, and at some cost to themselves to boot, since branded merchandise carries a price premium. The street sales-promotion efforts are neither charged to producers' advertising or promotion budgets nor captured in GDP data.

Economists who have tried to study the effects of advertising in some detail acknowledge the difficulties of fitting their models and mathematical techniques to the world as it is. As Richard Schmalensee wrote, "We still know relatively little about how advertising affects consumer behavior."[33] Econometric modeling is especially unreliable at assessing advertising effects not just be-

---

*In an article wonderfully entitled "How to Brand Sand," for example, three management consultants laid out step-by-step advice on how to escape the "prison of price competition" (Sam Hill et al., "How to Brand Sand," *Strategy and Business*, Spring 1998, 22–34).

cause of conceptually and empirically inadequate data, but also because of simultaneous equation difficulties and survey methods that are inadequate to measure even such elementary relations as advertising-to-sales ratios.

Even so, plenty of evidence suggests that advertising violates standard assumptions of "rational" behavior. Economists would at least like to believe that ads serve some sort of "informational" function, but this claim often seems implausible: the soft-drink companies—Coca-Cola, Pepsi Cola—are among the most aggressive advertisers and marketers in the world, but they employ such informationally contentless slogans as "It's the Real Thing" and "Join the Pepsi Generation." Yet for some reason (strangely elusive to economists), their advertising seems effective—Americans today now drink more soft drinks than water—though what information "The Real Thing" imparts defies comprehension. That said, Schmalensee acknowledges that researchers have found clear empirical evidence that, roughly speaking, the higher the advertising-to-sales ratio, the higher the profits.[34]

On *The New Industrial State*'s fundamental argument that profit maximization is only one goal among many for large firms, Solow hedged his own views even as he criticized Galbraith's, in unspoken recognition of modern theory's problems and uncertainty on the issue. On the central question of whether modern corporations seek to maximize sales provided they meet a certain required return on capital, Solow admitted, "These are intrinsically difficult theories to test against observation" and acknowledged that, as Galbraith claimed, big firms probably weren't as rigorous and single-minded about profit maximizing as economic theory assumed. Then, reversing himself, he insisted he was certain they did follow a "rough" approximation of that theory. But "rough" is not an adjective to use when making a reasoned claim of the sort that Solow said he valued and that must be subjected to the testing he claimed Galbraith had avoided.

Unfortunately, neither Solow nor Galbraith delved in their debate into the works of William Baumol and Robin Marris, who were already detailing the complex motivations of modern managerial capitalism and, like Galbraith (who acknowledged their influence), showing the need to revise "profit maximizing" theories in ways that would better explain the role of growth in managers' decision making as more than an instrument of profit.[35] Also unfortunately skipped over were Herbert Simon's theories of "satisficing" and "bounded rationality" (for which he later won the Nobel Prize) and the work Cyert and March did in extending Simon's theories to the firm; at the highest theoretical level these offered plausible rationales for just such "mixed" behavior.[36]

The final two theses of *The New Industrial State*—on pervasive affluence and the moral responsibility of educators and scientists in the emerging "information economy"—drew almost no comment from Solow. Perhaps this was because he thought it showed Galbraith the "big-thinker" at his worst—not really worthy of comment. Yet he couldn't resist a jibe: Galbraith could afford to write as he did about a postaffluent world because he did so from the luxury of a chalet in Gstaad, "where he occasionally entertains the muse," he wrote.

In sum, Galbraith was less an economist than "fundamentally a moralist," who wanted people to believe his subjective moral values were "objective, and opposition to them merely ideological." Galbraith might try to show us that "the economy does not efficiently serve consumer preferences," but "as theory, this simply does not stand up, a few grains of truth and the occasional well-placed needle notwithstanding."[37]

The Galbraith-Solow exchange may seem an artifact of its time and the issues preoccupying it almost antiquarian. The resurgence since then of microeconomics, the rise of monetarism and of the New Classical and supply-side schools, the political ascendancy of an American conservatism that assumes the normative and objective superiority of "market-based" decisions for almost all issues—these all have contributed to a changed intellectual climate in economics and politics.

But to view the Galbraith-Solow debate as of solely historical interest is to misunderstand its significance. For one, it was a battle for the controlling metaphors of economics and for a dominant rhetorical form that defines what is and isn't properly acceptable as "economics." Solow asked his readers to see economics first and foremost as a "scientific" project, consisting of hypotheses that can be formulated as mathematical statements to be tested by mathematical techniques, and since Galbraith was unable to provide such tests, he was to be disregarded. "Counting noses or assets and recounting anecdotes are not to the point," Solow insisted. "What is to the point is a 'model'—a simplified description—of the economy that will yield valid predictions about behavior."[38] This powerful indictment of Galbraith's ideas has been echoed repeatedly. But it conceals a complex host of arguments that aren't so easily or quickly decided in Solow's favor. (This is quite apart from the fact that Solow more than once in his review made the very errors he accused Galbraith of: economists, he claimed, had "long known" their models to be only "approximations" of the observable world, but he did not specify to what degree or by what metric they established this truth.)

In the decade just before The New Industrial State, some highly regarded economists, several just mentioned, had independently developed analyses that gave greater weight to Galbraith's argument than Solow was allowing, analyses that eroded the power of the very standard he set as the criterion of "successful" economics: the ability accurately to predict future behavior. For example, Richard Lipsey's work on "second-best" optima, or Herbert Simon's theory of "bounded rationality" and "satisficing" as an alternative to "maximizing" behavior, and Harvey Leibenstein's identification of "X-efficiency" goals for the firm (which by coincidence was published almost simultaneously with The New Industrial State) all pointed in separate, fascinating ways toward Galbraith's ideas and away from Solow's notion that even if firms weren't always classic profit maximizers, they did "approximate" such behavior.

At the very least, these theorists underscored just how difficult it is to determine blackboard-elegant "optimal" behavior paths in real-world practice. Simon's theories underscored the practical impossibilities associated with actually calculating optimizing behavior in a useful way, and helped to inspire a new generation to study the economics of information and transaction costs. Likewise, Harvey Leibenstein's "X-efficiency"—with its emphasis on recognizing the effect of habits, customs, moral imperatives, discretion, standard procedures, emulation, and incomplete contracts in undercutting textbook models of straightforward profit-maximizing behavior—underscores the major points about big corporations that Galbraith hammered home in *The New Industrial State* and that Solow argued were "refuted" by "economic theory."[39]

IN HIS REPLY to Solow, Galbraith addressed the issue of their quite different methods and theoretical frameworks head-on. He responded point by point to what he called "Professor Solow's error and his use of *obiter dicta*" and to what he considered gross misreadings of his own argument and misrepresentation of his theoretical approach.*

The "point of it all," he said, was this question: What lay ahead for "economics in general and . . . the highly prestigious work with which Professor Solow is associated in particular"? Solow and his allies believed that "the best society is the one that best serves the economic needs of the individual," but in a particular way that served a particular analytic "frame" as well. In Solow's world,

> wants are original with the individual; the more of these that are supplied the greater the general good. Generally speaking the wants to be supplied are efficiently translated by the market to firms maximizing profits therein. If firms maximize profits they respond to the market and ultimately to the sovereign choices of the consumer.
>
> Such is the frame and given its acceptance a myriad of scholarly activities can go on within. Any number of blocks can be designed and fitted together in the knowledge that they are appropriate to—that they fit somewhere in— the larger structure. There can be differences of opinion as to what best serves the purposes of the larger structure. Mathematical theorists and model builders can squabble with those who insist on empirical measurement. But this is a quarrel between friends.[40]

This was not, however, Galbraith's analytic frame. From quite different assumptions (which, he reminded readers, he—more than Solow—shared with Keynes) flowed a quite different analysis:

> Should it happen that the individual ceases to be sovereign—should he become, however subtly, the instrument or vessel of those who supply him, the

---

*Galbraith's reply earned him praise from a surprising quarter: Milton Friedman, who on December 12, 1967, wrote him to say that "on substance, I probably come closer to agreeing with Bob . . . than with you. But on form and professional manners, I am wholly in your camp and delighted that you spanked Solow so gently yet effectively. Keep it up."

frame no longer serves. Even to accommodate the possibility that humans are better served by collective rather than by individual consumption requires the framework to be badly warped. Should the society no longer accord priority to economic goals—should it accord priority to aesthetic accomplishment or mere idleness—it would not serve. And no one quite knows the effect of such change.

One can only be certain that, for a long time, economics, like the lesser social sciences, will be struggling with new scaffolding. And the work of economists will be far less precise, far less elegant, seemingly far less scientific than those who are fitting pieces into a structure the nature of which is known and approved and accepted. And if social priority lies elsewhere, it will be less prestigious.[41]

The effect of this loss of prestige, Galbraith slyly cautioned, would be felt in the daily life of academic scholars. The best students liked working with "men of precise and well articulated mind like Professor Solow," but they also needed to feel some sense of "social purpose." (Some, he allowed, were drawn to modern economics solely by the lure of being "technical initiates," an attraction to the recondite and esoteric not unlike those of "a fraternity, lodge, or chess club.") In the past, the claim of economics to enhance individual well-being had offered just the valid "social purpose" the young sought, but today, "to assist the individual in his subordination to General Motors will not be so regarded."

The motivation of talented students aside, there was a larger and more serious issue to weigh. "The sanctity of economic purpose," Galbraith observed, "will also be questioned if well-being as conventionally measured continues to improve and leaves unsolved the problems associated with collective need—those of the cities and their ghettoes and the by-passed rural areas—or if this progress involves an unacceptable commitment to the technology of war." To readers in 1967, after three summers of urban race riots and a darkening prospect in Vietnam, his warning was sharply aimed.

If Solow found little of value and much nonsense in The New Industrial State, others did not, even when the book discomfited them. Fortune better than most showed its readers just what Galbraith had done in The New Industrial State that made Solow so uncomfortable. Its reviewer disagreed with several of Galbraith's arguments but admitted that no major work of economics had been so forcefully put forth since Keynes:

What is truly significant about this book is that, for the first time, it ingeniously combines the tradition of moral-social criticism with a professional and plausible economic analysis. In doing this, The New Industrial State goes beyond liberal reformism, beyond Marxist or even neo-Marxist socialism, and—the boldest leap of all—beyond [conventional] economics itself. For Professor Galbraith raises the question of whether the American people actually want the particular kind of material progress their system delivers. His answer, which is negative, will be good tiding to the entire spectrum of dissenters . . . who despise "the power structure" and embryonic central planners. Professor Galbraith patiently explains to them all that they are right in attacking the system, though not always for the right reasons. It is predictable that his book will become one of their sacred texts.[42]

But *Fortune* underestimated the book's enduring appeal—and not just to "dissenters" who despised "the power structure." By 1980, a survey article in the *Journal of Economic Literature* identified more than 150 different works that used the historical and institutional approach that Galbraith advocated to analyze the behavior of corporations, and although they did not all reach Galbraith's conclusions, they departed from the "profit-maximizing" model of conventional theorists.[43] By then, more and more economists found themselves echoing Galbraith's complaint about the sacrifice of "relevance for rigor." In a telling example, Robert Gordon, in his presidential address to the American Economic Association in 1976, affirmed Galbraith's critique of conventional economic thought. "We economists," he declared, "pay too little attention to the changing institutional environment that conditions economic behavior. We do not often enough reexamine our basic postulates in light of changes in this environment, and, perhaps more important, we shy away from the big questions about how and why the institutional structure is changing—and where it is taking us."[44]

By the mid-1980s, even Solow appeared to be experiencing doubts. At the 1984 AEA convention, in a paper with the deceptively simple title "Economic History and Economics,"[45] he revisited the distinction he'd drawn between "big-thinkers" like Galbraith and "little-thinkers" like himself and most economists. He'd come to believe, he said, that "the attempt to construct economics as an axiomatically-based hard science is doomed to failure" because "all narrowly economic activity is embedded in a web of social institutions, customs, beliefs, and attitudes. Concrete outcomes are indubitably affected by these background factors, some of which change slowly and gradually, others erratically." From this, he had decided that

> the true functions of analytical economics are best described informally: to organize our necessarily incomplete perceptions about the economy, to see connections that the untutored eye would miss, to tell plausible—sometimes even convincing—causal stories with the help of a few central principles, and to make rough quantitative judgements about the consequences of economic policy and other exogenous events. The function of the economist in this approach is still to make models and test them as best one can, but the models are more likely to be partial in scope and limited in applicability. One will have to recognize that the validity of an economic model may depend on the social context. What is here today may be gone tomorrow, or, if not tomorrow, then in ten or twenty years' time.

This was a powerful admission, to say the least, from one of the nation's foremost mathematical economists and model builders.

It was not the judgment of a lone apostate. Three years later, when the American Economic Association gathered in 1987 in Chicago (home to the Vatican of conservative economics) to celebrate its centenary at the height of the Reagan era, of all the works written by economists over the preceding century only one was given a panel of its own.[46] It wasn't Alfred Marshall's *Principles* or Keynes's *General Theory* or Samuelson's *Economics*, or Milton Friedman's *Monetary History of the United States*. It was *The New Industrial State*. Galbraith said he was pleased.

19

Collisions

In those months [in the mid-1960s] . . . I was deeply engaged on The New Industrial State. *When my work on the book was over for the day, I took up my obligatory concern about Vietnam. One has a tendency to imagine oneself alone in such a worry. It is never so.*
—John Kenneth Galbraith, *A Life in Our Times*

If there are differences of opinion, there should be men to represent them.
—John Kenneth Galbraith,
February 1968

IT IS IMPOSSIBLE to pinpoint what pushed modern America's unresolved tensions—economic, racial, political, generational, military, regional, diplomatic, ethnic, and sexual—into brutal public confrontation. By 1968, though, an avalanche of confrontations had started rolling. The political litany of that year—the vicious fighting of the Tet Offensive in Vietnam, North Korea's seizure of the U.S.S. *Pueblo*, the Kerner Commission's stark conclusion after four summers of bloody urban race riots that the United States was a racist society, the sudden decision by President Johnson not to seek reelection, the assassination of Martin Luther King, Jr., the tumultuous student demonstrations at dozens of universities, the murder of Robert Kennedy, the violence at the Democratic National Convention in Chicago, capped finally with the election of Richard Nixon with just 43 percent of the vote and majorities in only fourteen states—has been told often and well.[1] Less well remembered are the economic events that occurred in 1968, although they are as important to the history of that time, and even more so to what followed.

In March 1968, the United States faced an extraordinary gold crisis, a speculative run on the government's supply of the metal that, *Time* warned its readers, represented "the largest gold rush in history, . . . a frenetic speculative stampede that . . . threatened the Western world."[2] Although many in the press agreed with *Time*, the general public, caught up in the bad news from Vietnam and the early presidential primaries, never grasped the scope of the danger.

But in Washington, policy-makers were shaken as they watched the failure of a decade's worth of efforts to control the danger created by an underlying balance-of-payments deficit. Pressure was so intense that at one point Treasury Secretary Henry Fowler, an otherwise methodical and reserved man, found himself yelling orders to his aides to airlift half a billion dollars in gold bars from Fort Knox to New York on a "crash basis" without even insuring the shipment. And Treasury officials weren't the only frightened ones. The crucial London gold market set a single-day record when 200 tons of the metal changed hands, and fistfights broke out on the Paris Bourse when ten times the usual number of buyers jammed into the gold pit.[3] "Everybody was just petrified," Treasury Undersecretary Joseph Barr later recalled. "It was a hair-raising period . . . We literally had to watch the gold markets day by day and hour by hour."

National Security Advisor Walt Rostow bluntly warned President Johnson that a single American misstep "could set in motion a financial and trade crisis which would . . . endanger the prosperity and security of the Western world."[4] His words seemed neither strained nor hyperbolic to those around him, but by then Washington's collective political nerves were already fraying under the weight of news from Vietnam. Just as the gold crisis broke in March, the Tet Offensive that the North Vietnamese had launched a month earlier reached the height of its savagery (including a then-unnoticed U.S. counterassault on a tiny hamlet named My Lai). Analysts later concluded that the Tet Offensive was a military defeat for Hanoi's forces, but at the time their entry into Saigon, their attack on key government and allied buildings (including the U.S. embassy and officers' quarters), and their simultaneous and sustained assaults across South Vietnam stunned Americans watching all this on the evening news.

President Johnson's administration had been pledging for years that progress was being made and that an American victory would soon be at hand. In November 1967 General William Westmoreland had testified to Congress that he'd "never been more encouraged" by the situation in Vietnam and that the United States would certainly "win" the war.[5] But now, as bad news kept pouring in, a notoriously impatient people were reaching their own conclusions.

Most Americans hadn't supported the protests of dissident college students and liberal intellectuals during 1965, 1966, or even 1967. By 1968, however, anger and distrust had spread from the academy into factories, offices, and homes. As Clark Clifford, who succeeded Robert McNamara as Defense Secretary, wrote later, "The most serious American casualty at Tet was the loss of the public's confidence in its leaders."[6] What real "progress," after all, had the United States to show for its efforts, with a half million troops stationed in Vietnam, and U.S. casualties after five years of combat approaching 200,000, including nearly 30,000 dead? By the end of March 1968, the Tet Offensive had driven the American public to a new judgment of the war and of its leaders; a Gallup poll reported that only one in four Americans now supported LBJ's policies on Vietnam, and nearly two out of three opposed them.[7]

As if simultaneous economic and war reversals weren't enough, on March 12, the upstart antiwar senator from Minnesota, Eugene McCarthy—a man who by his behavior seemed to prefer poets to politicians, and who had considered the Catholic priesthood before choosing a career in public life—did something amazing: "Clean Gene" McCarthy came close to matching a sitting President of the United States in the New Hampshire primary (42 percent, as against 49 percent for Johnson), having trailed Johnson in national polls two months earlier by a seemingly hopeless 18 percent to 71 percent. Four days later, his near victory prompted the better-known Senator Robert Kennedy of New York to enter the race. Little wonder that Clark Clifford remembered that March in near-apocalyptic terms.

> The pressure grew so intense that at times I felt the government itself might come apart at its seams. Leadership was fraying at its very center—something very rare in a country with so stable a governmental structure. In later years, almost every one of the men who lived through the crisis claimed that he had reacted calmly to events. In fact, everyone, military and civilian, was profoundly affected . . . There was, for a brief time, something approaching paralysis, and a sense of everything spiraling out of control of the nation's leaders.[8]

Weighed down by these political, economic, and military setbacks, President Johnson was at the far edge of exhaustion and, some feared, near collapse. His old friend Senator Richard Russell of Georgia later said that when the two met to talk privately as they had for years, LBJ sometimes sobbed uncontrollably, making their meetings unbearably painful for both men.[9]

Ultimately, March came to an end without North Vietnam's triumph in Saigon and without the meltdown of the Western financial and trade system that Rostow and others had feared. But nothing was getting better in Southeast Asia, and the country was experiencing the worst pressure on the dollar since World War II, narrowly averting a formal devaluation (something the once-indomitable British pound was unable to escape). Wall Street and global financial markets were so frightened that stocks took their worst plunge since the Depression, beginning a fifteen-year-long slump.

Something else, however, did end that March—the political career of Lyndon Baines Johnson. At 9 p.m. on the evening of March 31, the President went on network television to announce that he would not meet the demands of his generals for 200,000 more troops in Vietnam. For forty minutes he detailed the challenges in Southeast Asia, no longer suggesting that an easy or immediate victory lay ahead. Peace—not victory—was, he insisted, now his paramount goal. As he neared his conclusion Johnson paused, and took off the glasses he'd been using to read his text. Facing the cameras directly, his face drawn and tired, he quietly but firmly declared that, because campaigning for reelection would interfere in his quest for peace, "I shall not seek, and I will not accept, the nomination of my party for another term as your president."[10]

It seemed like the most breathtaking reversal in modern U.S. politics. Just four years earlier, this consummate career politician had been elected to the presidency of the United States by the greatest majority in American history and then gone on to achieve some of the nation's greatest legislative triumphs. Now he would not even seek a second term.

That same evening, Ken Galbraith was speaking to college students in northern California in opposition to the war and in support of the presidential candidacy of Gene McCarthy. As he began, someone passed him a note about Johnson's stunning announcement. His audience broke into cheers and applause when he shared the news, but the speech itself then turned into "a minefield," as he swerved back and forth through the text, incorporating on the fly the political implications of LBJ's move.[11]

It was ticklish for several reasons. Principal among them was Galbraith's recognition that Johnson even now wasn't calling for an immediate armistice, let alone withdrawal from Vietnam. (He had actually said he was sending 13,000 more troops there.) And so the war would go on.* That in turn meant that the race for the Democratic nomination, and the race to become the next president, were still up for grabs. And he was torn between two candidates.

Galbraith could rightly claim to have had an important hand in creating the opposition that precipitated Johnson's decision to retire. He'd been a public leader of the antiwar movement for three years; his little book *How to Get Out of Vietnam* had detailed a negotiating strategy for a U.S. exit from Vietnam which he hoped Johnson might be pressured into accepting. *Time* had singled out Galbraith's importance to the antiwar movement by putting him on its cover and devoting a remarkably supportive article to his accomplishments as "the most quotable—and possibly influential—critic of U.S. society." What most distinguished him, according to *Time*, was that he "offers more convincingly than almost anyone else the respectable alternative that Lyndon Johnson has repeatedly demanded of his attackers."[12] He was, the magazine assured its readers, "no Mary McCarthy, who fatuously insists that it is the intellectual's duty merely to oppose the war, without deigning to suggest how it ought to be ended. Nor does he resemble those clergymen whose justifiable indignation at the war's barbarities is diluted by the fact that it is usually directed solely at the U.S. . . ."

Four months earlier, in "The Importance of Being Galbraith," the journalist David Halberstam—in one of the canniest assessments ever written of Galbraith as public actor—had already used the phrase "respectable alternative" to describe this quality, but added a subtle observation. The Harvard economist, he said, had emerged "as a critic who manages to keep as many lines open as

---

*Seventy thousand combatants—35 percent of all U.S. casualties—were killed or wounded in 1968, making it the worst year of the entire war.

possible" yet who "denies vehemently any Establishment association," a balance made possible by a little-observed fact:

> The Establishment's position on Vietnam has never been entirely clear, and there is some evidence that the Establishment has never really approved of Southeast Asia, preferring Europe as a more civilized and predictable continent. Thus, there is a subtle Establishment opposition to the war, based not on the qualms about napalm but on the idea that the war is costing too much for too little.

He then drew a telling distinction: "Fulbright made the mistake of attacking this country's arrogance of power in its commitment there. If he had said, instead, 'We can use this arrogance and power much better somewhere else,' he might have been successful." Galbraith, Halberstam went on, "will not make this mistake. His opposition to the war is tough, consistent, and pragmatic. He has become, in American life, a very respectable figure and a successful one. Hence the question on many people's lips: Will success spoil John Kenneth Galbraith? The likely answer: No, it will only make him more so."[13]

LYNDON JOHNSON'S SUDDEN withdrawal from the presidential race that March, however, posed an unenviable challenge to Galbraith's successes as an antiwar critic, which he had to face the night after McCarthy's near victory in New Hampshire. He'd created an exhausting schedule for himself by crisscrossing the state for weeks beforehand stumping at campuses, churches, union halls, and house parties on behalf of McCarthy and then rushing back to Harvard to teach. On primary night he happily celebrated with McCarthy and other advisers, then raced down to Cambridge the next day; his 200 students stood in thunderous applause when he entered the lecture hall. At home that Wednesday night and relaxing for the first time in weeks, he and Arthur Schlesinger were going over the primary results, plotting out what McCarthy should do next, when the phone rang.

It was Ethel Kennedy, Bobby's wife; she was calling to tell them that her husband was now seriously close to entering the race. Would Ken and Arthur, she delicately asked, phone him directly and encourage him to do so?[14]

This wasn't quite the literal truth: Robert Kennedy had already decided to run. Earlier that same day he had met with McCarthy in his brother's Senate offices, hoping to persuade him to drop out, but McCarthy had coolly refused, and the meeting had broken up after just twenty minutes. With a hastily planned announcement of his own candidacy only three days away, Kennedy knew it was urgent to ensure that prominent Kennedy veterans like Galbraith and Schlesinger were pulled back into the Kennedy circle.

That night, Galbraith and Schlesinger talked excitedly about what Kennedy's entry into the race would mean. It seemed evident to both that he would be the stronger candidate. Schlesinger felt it was imperative they back the strongest candidate, but the idea of switching support now seemed nearly impossible to Galbraith. He'd campaigned for Bobby Kennedy's Senate election in 1964, and there was no question of his loyalties to the Kennedy family. But Senator Kennedy's intensity—what Galbraith saw as his lack of ambiguity, indecision, or middle ground—made him uncomfortable. John Kennedy had been the master of an elegant balance between commitment and detachment, which Galbraith admired and indeed strived for himself. But in Bobby's mind, as Galbraith put it, "You were either for the cause or against it, with the Kennedys or a leper."[15]

Yet saying no to Kennedy wasn't easy. Galbraith had already broken with scores of friends and fellow Democrats over the war. And the choice was a matter not simply of personal relations but of fundamental political values and possibilities. He had long ago come to believe that a liberal Democratic president and Congress were the most natural, certainly the most preferable, of political arrangements, and the 1960s had begun with great hopes. John F. Kennedy's election in 1960 had marked the end of a long string of disappointments, and despite the tragedy of his assassination, for a time LBJ's domestic agenda promised to fulfill what Kennedy had been able only to promise—and even to reconnect the Democratic Party and the country with the New Deal legacy. Then the Vietnam War, it seemed, had first enveloped and then suffocated liberal programs, hopes, and legacies.

But Vietnam wasn't simply a cruel accident. It had developed out of an encompassing worldview and policy decisions and judgments about the future dating back to World War II, when Henry Luce had hubristically first outlined "the American Century." Now in 1968, that dream was coming to a tragic end, and the intertwined costs of Vietnam and America's dwindling gold supply were its emblems.

The entanglement of the U.S. gold crisis with Vietnam, and of the country's chronic balance-of-payments problems with what many came to see as the general failure of the New Economics, was not yet fully played out, however. Indeed, the year 1969 saw a respite from the pressures on the balance of payments and on the U.S. economy generally. But in 1971, when President Nixon announced to general amazement that *he* was now a Keynesian, and then completely severed the connection between gold and the dollar, history really did change radically. Why were these international finance and trade structures so closely connected with American diplomatic, economic, and military policies? And what was it about this connection that made the Nixon revolution virtually inevitable?

IN 1945, WHEN World War II ended, the United States enjoyed a unique circumstance among the combatants. Relatively unscathed, its economy immensely robust and doubled in size, it was enormously wealthy, and it owned, among other things, almost 90 percent of the world's roughly $40 billion supply of monetary gold. Washington policy-makers reviewed the disasters that had befallen the world after World War I and assured one another that this time the United States would not retreat into isolation but instead would be an engine for economic recovery, not simply for charitable reasons but because it was in the national interest. Through the Marshall Plan, bilateral aid programs, the newborn World Bank, the International Monetary Fund, and the General Agreement on Tariffs and Trade (GATT), the United States proceeded to help war-torn Western Europe, Japan, and other regions of the globe to achieve rapid economic recovery. Although government-to-government foreign and military aid were the more-debated issues, trade was the essential cornerstone of American policy. With just 5 percent of the world's population, the United States accounted for more than half the world's trade, an unhealthy asymmetry that underscored the dimensions of the devastation for the other combatants. Expanded global trade, in which the U.S. took a smaller share, would be better for America's long-term economic health.

Essential to rapidly expanding trade was the financial system that was designed at the Allied conference at Bretton Woods, New Hampshire, in 1944. John Maynard Keynes had led the British delegation and was the conference's most celebrated participant, but it was Harry Dexter White, a less well-known U.S. Treasury official, who defined the agreement's final architecture. Yet American economic power, not the intellectual force of White's arguments, was what carried the day.

The systemic choices made in 1944 in favor of Harry White's "American Plan" at Bretton Woods (over Keynes's doubts and objections, as well as his closely argued alternatives for an international system less dependent on a single nation) became, over time, the heart of the dilemma the United States faced in 1968. Shortly after the Bretton Woods conference adjourned, Keynes wrote, with more than a hint of exasperation, to Richard Kahn,

> The Americans have no idea how to make these two institutions [the IMF and World Bank] into operating international concerns, and in almost every direction their ideas are bad. Yet they plainly intend to force their conception through regardless of the rest of us. [They] think they have the right to call the tune on practically every point. If they knew the music, that would not matter so much, but unfortunately they don't.[16]

In March 1946, Keynes returned to the United States for the inaugural meeting of the International Monetary Fund and World Bank in Savannah, Georgia; he'd been appointed the British governor of both. He was filled with foreboding. Churchill had delivered his Iron Curtain speech, which Keynes thought appalling, shortly before the meeting convened. Then Treasury Secretary Fred Vinson opened with what Keynes felt was "a long and turgid speech full of emotional and fundamentally insincere expressions of hope" for the postwar world. The American delegation showed just how insincere Vinson had been, as it overturned every one of Keynes's proposals to make the two new financial institutions generous and humane sources of credit for a global recovery and development. Instead, he concluded, the Americans wanted a tough financial policeman, under *their* control. "I went to Savannah to meet the world," Keynes remarked privately, "and all I met was a tyrant." The triumphant Americans celebrated on the final evening, with an oblivious Harry White leading "a 'Bacchic rout of satyrs and Sileniuses' from Latin America into the dining room with 'vine leaves'—or perhaps cocktail sticks—in his hair and loudly bellowing 'Onward Christian Soldiers.' "

The Savannah conference broke Keynes physically. He awoke the next morning short of breath and collapsed soon after. Laid out on a table, he seemed to be hovering near death. Miraculously he recovered after two hours, and several days later sailed back to England. He spent much of the voyage struggling to write a paper "condemning American policy with great ferocity and passionately recommending H.M. Government to refuse to ratify the Fund and Bank agreement." The unfinished paper was never delivered; Keynes died three weeks later, on Easter Sunday.

With Keynes gone, a new international financial reserve system evolved that made the U.S. dollar interchangeable with gold in settling nations' trade accounts and with the dollar, as a proxy for gold, backing the value of other national currencies. The much greater availability of the dollar compared to gold at first assured steady and rapid growth for major industrial countries in a generally inflation-free environment. The superiority of this new Bretton Woods gold-and-dollar system over its predecessors lay not least in its greater flexibility. When rapidly recovering and expanding international trade called for a rapidly expanding global money supply, it was easier to print dollars than mine gold.

But therein lay a temptation. The United States' own economic behavior internationally was shaped by two important factors: its costly global deployment of troops and network of alliances around the world, and its commitment—high- and low-minded at once—to dismantling the residual European empires (and their imperial trade preferences) which impeded the global aspirations of American businesses.

Cold War deployments—major U.S. bases in Europe, Japan, and Korea, smaller bases in more than sixty other countries, and global fleet and air deployments—guaranteed that billions of dollars a year moved overseas. At first Washington focused on creating and developing this system of bases and assuring the treaty relations underlying them (NATO, SEATO, CENTO, ANZUS); the steady U.S. capital outflow associated with it was mostly overlooked. Meanwhile, foreign demand for U.S. goods and equipment brought more money into U.S. accounts than was going outward. By the early 1960s, however, things had grown economically much more complex. U.S. military commitments had matured, and hundreds of thousands of troops, their families, and a dense network of supporting civilians were stationed semipermanently overseas. At the same time U.S. business interests abroad had grown in scale and complexity.

Historically, American trade patterns had stressed the exchange (primarily with Europe) of agricultural commodities for merchandise and equipment—with a steady flow of capital and technology moving westward across the Atlantic (primarily from Britain) to supplement domestic investment. Then, when America's Industrial Revolution thrust it ahead of Britain, U.S. investment in the distribution of American goods in Europe, even in Europe-based manufacturing, modestly but steadily grew, with U.S. capital flowing eastward across the Atlantic.

When Galbraith was born, in 1908, the biggest American corporations had pushed their overseas sales, manufacturing operations, and investment to what then seemed almost unimaginable levels. For example, by 1914 two U.S. corporations, Singer Sewing Machines and International Harvester, were the largest companies in imperial Russia, with Russian manufacturing plants, thousands of employees, and a sales and distribution network stretching from the Urals to Siberia. In Britain, a spate of books appeared anguishing over "the American challenge"—the first of many such cycles of anxiety that swept across Europe in the twentieth century. But the drive of these giant U.S. corporations to create overseas operations and find overseas markets to sustain their growth and profitability really took off only after World War II. The Harvard business historian Alfred Chandler notes that after 1950 American firms vastly enlarged their European-based manufacturing operations not only to support European sales but, in many instances, also to supply U.S. markets. Here, in short, was the birth of the modern era of multinational corporations.

Chandler's figures for U.S. manufacturing operations in Great Britain and Germany, two of America's most important foreign markets, are illustrative. Over the fifty years between 1900 and 1950, U.S. companies created roughly two hundred such overseas operations in the two countries; in just twenty years after 1950, the number in Britain and West Germany quadrupled to 800. In dollar terms, the post–World War II jump was even more noticeable—and seemed to be rising almost asymptotically as Europe's economies recovered: U.S. investment in West Germany, for example, jumped 165 percent between 1960 and 1965 alone, with similar sharp rises in France, Italy, and the Low Countries. No less important, nearly two-thirds of these post-1950 expansions were done not through start-ups but purchase of existing foreign firms.[17] That sort of international corporate growth had tremendous implications for U.S. capital flows, as well as for development of global capital markets, when billions of private American dollars went abroad in direct investment opportunities, alongside the public dollars supporting U.S. overseas military operations.

By the 1960s, the effect of the public and private forces on America's international trade accounts was concerning Treasury officials, Wall Street bankers, and some economists. The so-called current account (which basically measures the sale and purchase of goods and services between the United States and other countries) wasn't a problem: the U.S. had run sizable surpluses in it throughout the century. The concern was about the new deficits in the capital account (which measures private investment flows, dollars spent by U.S. tourists abroad, and government flows, especially for the armed forces). The combined deficits were overwhelming the surpluses in the current account, thereby creating chronic and growing deficits in the overall U.S. balance of payments.

In a standard economics textbook, the simplest solution to this imbalance is straightforward: devaluation of the currency. A reduction of the dollar's value relative to other currencies through conscious government policies would make the foreign imports more expensive and U.S. exports cheaper, thereby increasing the American current accounts surplus, at the same time making overseas assets more expensive (discouraging U.S. corporate investment abroad) and U.S. assets cheaper (encouraging domestic and foreign investment here). But as so often happens, standard textbooks and their theories were hard to apply to the actual economic and political world.

The United States, first of all, had no intention of even considering devaluation. To begin with, it was bound *not* to do so by the Bretton Woods agreements of 1944, and anyway, the success of any devaluation depended crucially on trading partners' not following suit, for if all partners devalued equally, the original imbalances would simply be reinstated with only the price level changed. Most European currencies hadn't even become fully convertible until the late 1950s, and the thought of provoking tit-for-tat revaluations was anathema to the United States and its allies. (When, shortly after the war, the United States had forced Britain to reinstate convertibility as a precondition for obtaining a massive U.S. reconstruction loan, the immediate flight of billions of pounds into dollars had been disastrous for Britain and the pound: no one had forgotten.)

The "American Plan" of Harry Dexter White further complicated matters. By permanently tying the dollar to gold and allowing the simultaneous use of both to settle trade accounts, dollars had been piling up overseas as America's trade partners recovered economically. The dollars were part of the official reserves backing local national currencies, and in private hands they were unconverted surpluses in foreign corporate (and wealthy individuals') accounts.

If the U.S. devalued to solve its own balance-of-payments problems, under White's Bretton Woods arrangements it would noticeably (and painfully) reduce the wealth of allied foreign governments. With the reserve backing for their own currencies reduced, their central banks might well be forced into contracting the monetary supply in order to avoid inflation. But in cutting the money supply, the banks would risk precipitating recessions which, in domino-like order, might trip off a worldwide recession.

At the same time, reducing the value of dollar-holdings of wealthy foreigners (and wealthy Americans living abroad) might encourage these individuals to prefer gold or currencies such as the Swiss franc or West German mark. Although this involved a small number of people, their wealth and influence over corporate and financial market attitudes and decisions could not be taken lightly. As one historian put it, devaluation was "to private commercial bankers, government finance ministers, and public central bankers what 'Edsel' is to the Ford Motor Company. Devaluation is not only to be eschewed but not even mentioned; it is the synonym for monetary failure. A currency devalued is a currency debauched."[18]

Thus by 1968 the United States was falling victim to the danger in its hegemonic leadership of the West—not just because of the war in Vietnam, but also because it was caught between its political role as a global superpower and the limits of the international financial system it had helped to create. As the author and enforcer of a new would-be Pax Americana, America was now damned if it acted—and damned if it didn't.

President Kennedy's "New Economists" had put off this moment of reckoning by opting for technical fixes that did not address the fundamental ideological and structural tensions. Often sweetly elegant on their surface, the programs were not reasoned and well-coordinated strategies but, in the end, as one economic historian put it, "pure ad-hocery."[19]

For example, under Douglas Dillon the Treasury and Federal Reserve first launched Operation Twist, that sophisticated attempt to raise short-term U.S. interest rates while lowering long-term rates in order to attract foreign depositors, and then won passage of an "interest equalization" tax, meant to erase the difference between domestic and foreign credit costs. But the Pentagon (well before the expenses of the Vietnam war kicked in) increased its already massive NATO expenditures, and U.S. trade officials were spurring more global trade through the Kennedy Round of tariff cuts—without attending to the consequent outflows of U.S. capital.

Galbraith had never doubted the risks to the United States inherent in the capital account deficits and the gold problem. His first memo to President-elect Kennedy in November 1960, as well as the last one, which reached Kennedy's desk the day before he left for Dallas, were on this subject.[20] But Galbraith also felt it was dangerous to give too much visible attention to the matter. He feared that too much apparent White House focus on gold and the balance of payments would spark fears on Wall Street and in overseas markets that would only worsen the problem.

Galbraith was clear about his preferred solutions, although the details changed as the situation changed, and as one after another of the administration's technical fixes were tried but failed to produce the hoped-for results. Initially, he pressed JFK for an aggressive expansion of U.S. trade—for example, an export drive, pressure on allies for freer American access to the Common Market, and construction of a Western Hemisphere trading area. Despite the sound of this, he wasn't merely a conventional free-trader. Simultaneously he was urging Kennedy to campaign for a domestic wage and price policy; targeted agricultural subsidies to make U.S. food exports more competitive; closure of a long list of corporate tax loopholes; coordinated central-bank policies by the U.S., Europe, and Japan on interest rates and monetary policies; and, most important, major cutbacks in overseas military spending and troop deployment. None of this, he warned Kennedy privately, would happen in the right way if he appointed as Treasury Secretary "a banker-statesman," as "the Establishment is so energetically urging."[21] After Kennedy appointed Dillon to the Treasury post, the disappointed Galbraith nonetheless kept up his campaign.[22]

Just as he'd warned, the execution and coordination of foreign economic policy during 1961 failed to achieve the promised results. In spring 1962, he sent JFK a memo bluntly entitled "The Gold Flow Again." The issue wasn't "technical" problems needing "technical fixes," he told the President, but something fundamental that Kennedy—and, more important, the voters—could understand: "strong vested interests, pecuniary and ideological" lay at the center of the matter, and

> every conceivable action will thus be in conflict with one of those vested interests—with the liberal view of trade and aid, the Rockefeller Brothers *cum* Establishment view of troop deployment, and anticommunist strategy, the businessman's preferences on taxation and investment, the rich man's preferences for the Costa Brava and the serviceman's preferences on connubiality and love.[23]

This colorfully summed up Galbraith's view of real-world economics and of blackboard theory in relation to it. Politics was inescapably interwoven with economic policy and economic realities. The political power of wealth needed to be part of the President's and the public's calculations. Defining economic problems in terms of mathematically robust models that disregarded political power and then proposing "technical" solutions that satisfied the models would, in the end, risk the presidency, the health of American democracy, and the well-being of the American people.

People who told the President that trade liberalization was the solution would disagree with his prognosis, Galbraith admitted, but "for them trade liberalization is not a policy but an altar." Those who wanted devaluation of the dollar were no less misguided (even though for some economists it was "as alcohol to the Iroquois"). When it came to satisfying foreign bankers' demands for U.S. gold, the President should consider them as "egotistical reactionaries" governed by "their always myopic and often medieval instincts." Galbraith proposed instead a nine-point program to integrate short-term policy measures into a consciously progressive political-economic analysis. It was far from orthodox or even mainstream Keynesian models.

Galbraith's recommendations included controlling leakages in the foreign-aid program and encouraging Americans to buy U.S. products (while avoiding jingoism). Then, in direct challenge to the "vested interests," he urged Kennedy to seek some form of capital controls on U.S. investment abroad, and to close the loopholes on expatriation of wealth and on Americans living abroad so as to escape U.S. taxes. And he pressed Kennedy again to reduce the country's overseas troop deployments and its heavy subsidies of authoritarian regimes. U.S. policy should focus on accelerating the kind of economic and political reform that was "far more urgent and also much cheaper than [foreign] aid":

In South America it is land reform, above all, that people want. Those who own the land have already been paid for it a thousand times. In the absence of reform our aid does not help the people or much postpone revolution. Rather it buys the way temporarily around the crisis in the process of which dollars are funneled into Rio and squirreled out to Paris.

What some might call naive idealism was, he thought, on the contrary a matter of hard-nosed understanding of the costs of "ideological idealism" on the part of conservatives.

I am aware of the difficulties here and the ease with which one can counsel perfection. But I also gravely suspect the legitimist tendencies of the State Department. In any case we must someday ring the bell on the big, unpremeditated loans to Latin American governments which do no good and buy only a few weeks' time for governments that are as likely to be replaced by . . . worse.[24]

The White House did implement several of these recommendations, though there was little progress on the harder points.[25] Dillon's deputy, Robert Roosa, meanwhile suavely promised the American Bankers Association in 1962 that the United States was "moving forward toward a restoration of equilibrium and surplus in the American balance of payments." It was a promise one economic historian, Ray Canterbery, later likened to "viewing the U.S. finger in the dike as proof of the viability of the system."[26]

Kennedy by 1963 shared this dim assessment. He sent a special message to Congress on the balance of payments, which noted signs of progress while warning of the need to make further "inroads into the hard core of our continuing payment deficits."[27] Uncertain how to proceed—or even how seriously to take the problem—and dissatisfied with the advice he was getting, he then turned to Galbraith.

August 1963 was an especially bitter month for President Kennedy. At the end of July, he had scored a singular diplomatic triumph—the Senate had passed and he had signed the nuclear test-ban treaty he had called for a year earlier at American University. But August had opened with personal tragedy: his prematurely born son, Patrick, died after less than two days of life. Politically, his cautious approach to civil rights was challenged by Martin Luther King's "I Have a Dream" speech to a massive Washington audience at midmonth, while in Vietnam the promises of "progress" his advisers had made to him that spring were turning hollow, as Buddhist uprisings against the Catholic president, Diem, wracked the country. (To Americans' horror, Buddhist monks were setting themselves afire in Saigon—and Diem's sister-in-law was gaily telling the press she applauded every time they did so.) By Labor Day Kennedy seemed ready to abandon Diem and, if need be, Vietnam.[28]

Galbraith was the President's weekend guest at Hyannis Port in the middle of August, and Kennedy took Galbraith and Walter Heller sailing for an afternoon on Nantucket Sound. The three talked at length about taxes, the war on poverty that Kennedy said he wanted to launch in 1964 (after passage of what he pointedly called "Heller's tax cut"), and gold and the balance of payments. Galbraith limited his criticisms of the tax bill, registered his strong support for a major antipoverty program, and concentrated on the gold and balance-of-payments question. When the sloop docked, Kennedy, clearly intrigued by several of Galbraith's suggestions, asked him, to Heller's ill-concealed concern, to write up the points he'd raised.[29]

On August 28, Galbraith sent his views to the White House in two detailed memoranda.[30] Although he expected JFK to circulate them for comment, he typically minced no words. In Galbraith's view, the President had to recognize the lack of policy coordination among various government departments and their conflicting interests, which, he said, had to end: "Someone's ox must be gored."

Having reviewed the President's classified files on the balance-of-payments and gold, Galbraith emphasized that little progress was being made using the "technical fixes" favored by White House advisers, thanks to the factional problem, and he said he knew that hostility would greet his proposals:

> The person who comments responsibly on the balance of payments problem is like the herald who brings bad news: He is a figure for popular execution, and in this case each department will have its own gibbet. There are, indeed, grave difficulties with everything here urged. I hope these will not be considered decisive for they must now be measured against the alternative courses of action, which are few and worse, and the consequences of inaction, which would be worse yet.

What Kennedy needed, he counseled, were bold strokes on five related fronts. The most important was to establish the White House's willingness to use long-term capital controls over U.S. private investment abroad, if needed, and in the short term to impose a mandatory freeze. Next was to order a delay in the Kennedy Round of tariff-reduction negotiations; Galbraith even thought a modest tariff increase aimed at European nations that were maintaining or raising their own tariffs on U.S. goods might be in order. Third, he should order a significant redeployment of American troops back to the United States and substitute greater airlift capacity for their basing overseas. Fourth, a surtax should be placed on tourist travel abroad; and fifth, a much closer connection should be drawn between America's foreign aid and the recipient's expenditure of that aid in the United States.

By early September, clearly influenced by Galbraith's advice, President Kennedy sent a draft memorandum to Dillon, McNamara, Rusk, Heller, and Galbraith that read almost as if Galbraith had written it himself. He ordered Dillon to increase efforts to "dissuade American investors from committing funds abroad, including both large scale direct investments and large scale purchases of foreign securities," and to arrange immediate meetings with

European finance ministers and central bankers "to slow U.S. direct invest-ment in Europe." McNamara meanwhile was told to produce "further savings of overseas expenditures," while the State Department was told to review the Kennedy Round of tariff cuts and prepare options for "emergency use of tem-porary countervailing duties," and the Agency for International Development was instructed to recommend forthwith how to implement "Ambassador Gal-braith's proposal for super-tying of aid." Kennedy added that he wanted all the departments to report back to him "at the earliest possible date" and be pre-pared to meet with him thereafter.[31]

The President's memorandum set off a veritable panic among his senior cabinet officers and aides, who lobbied fiercely to make sure the final version of his instructions was toned down. Rusk in particular opposed any reduction of U.S. forces abroad, while other (unidentified) aides reworked or deleted the President's insistence on specific actions.[32] Even so, Kennedy pointedly kept turning to Galbraith for further advice. On November 15, Galbraith sent a let-ter to JFK encouraging his willingness to act boldly on the economic front that began: "Dear Mr. President, As the years pass, you must be growing accus-tomed to my communiqués which, largely in the interests of science, draw at-tention to my foresight and prescience in economic matters."[33] He noted that there had been a momentary respite in the balance-of-payments problem, thanks to Kennedy's demands for an interest equalization tax, which, while not a favorite with Galbraith, at least showed "that the control of long-term capital movements is basic to the strategy for the control of the balance of payments and . . . that [contrary to Dillon's advice] the problem will yield more readily than we suppose to energetic action." In this, Galbraith colorfully added, pres-idential firmness "represents a considerable moral gain over the ass-kissing of the French central bankers and the Swiss private bankers that is otherwise required."

The success of Kennedy's action on the tax, along with Galbraith's persis-tent encouragement and tutoring, moved the President to reconsider once again his reluctant deference to Treasury's views. According to Theodore Sorensen, JFK by then "had some evidence to back his suspicions that the gloomy rumors which triggered the gold withdrawal of 1960 had been deliber-ately spread by American bankers to embarrass him politically . . . He did not want to be vulnerable to the same tactic in 1964."[34] Shortly after receiving Galbraith's letter, he told Sorensen he wanted an all-day planning session scheduled with his economic advisers at Camp David to consider more strin-gent capital controls. Sometime early in December, he instructed, made the most sense—right after he got back from Texas.[35]

After Kennedy's assassination, President Johnson was not well served by the financial advisers he inherited. Secretary Dillon, for example, on December 2 wrote LBJ a detailed memo recapping Kennedy administration policy on the balance of payments. While broadly accurate in describing the major early ef-forts in 1961 and their disappointing results, and Kennedy's renewed push in

July 1963, it omitted entirely the firm new directions Kennedy had ordered in September, largely following Galbraith's recommendations. Instead, Dillon pressed the official Treasury view that progress was being made with cautious technical measures and that by 1965, the U.S. balance-of-payments deficit would be cut by 70 percent or more.

After Dillon's prediction proved wrong, and the situation grew worse, President Johnson gradually acted over the next three years on the points Galbraith had proposed to Kennedy. He slapped new and tighter restrictions on U.S. investments abroad; restricted overseas loans by U.S. banks; ordered cuts in military and economic assistance to American allies (Vietnam, however, which by then was taking in half of all AID funding, was exempted from the order); and called on Americans to cut back their overseas travel and spending.[36] But with Vietnam, new weapons production, and the space program (carried out largely by the same defense contractors) draining the federal budget, and with the biggest and politically most powerful American corporations drawing more and more of their sales and profits from their foreign investments, Johnson's efforts were too little and too late.

By 1968, sales by overseas affiliates of U.S.-based manufacturing companies alone were, by one estimate, equal to nearly a third of all U.S. manufacturing exports.[37] At the same time, those same corporations were learning quickly how to finance their operations overseas as well as how to protect foreign profits from the Internal Revenue Service. "Eurodollars"—the billions of U.S. dollars that had migrated abroad in the previous decades and that had stayed abroad when the stability of the dollar meant that holding them was as safe as holding gold—were by the late 1960s being offered as offshore loans on better terms than those offered by U.S. banks, which were subject to Federal Reserve and government restrictions of various kinds. The resulting "Eurodollar market," at first a trickle and then a flood, reshaped U.S. banking markets and the world of international banking and corporate finance.* It was harder and harder for the U.S. government to control that behavior, or determine ultimately the fate of its own currency.

During LBJ's term, the Eurodollar market mushroomed from $9 billion in 1964 to more than $40 billion, forcing the administration to step away from at least some of its hegemonic burden as "reserve banker to the world." A new set of "special drawing rights" (SDRs) were created that pooled and expanded funds placed by nations with the IMF, which member countries could then draw on in times of financial crisis. Typically, Johnson took credit for this innovation, which in theory at least moved toward relieving some of the pressures on the United States, but SDR funds weren't large compared to U.S. reserves, let alone subsequent global demand, and ended up as minor assistance rather

---

*The Eurodollar market was initially an unintended byproduct of Cold War tensions. When the Soviet Union sold natural resources in the West it was paid in dollars. Fearful that the United States might freeze or seize those funds at some point, Moscow set up a London-based trading bank, and it seems to have initiated the Eurodollar lending system.

than major relief. Meanwhile the gargantuan outflow of dollars that had inevitably resulted from Harry White's American Plan kept accelerating. By the late 1970s, the Eurodollar market would soar to $475 billion; by comparison, U.S. government financial reserves remained constant over the same period at $16 billion, a figure far short of any American ability to back the dollar with gold from Fort Knox.[38]

Keynes had foreseen these consequences of the American Plan. He had urged instead the adoption of what he called his "bancor" system, in which member nations would pool funds deposited with a multilateral agency—contributing in dollar terms five times what White proposed—which they could use as needed in times of financial crisis or for more growth and development. His generously internationalist "bancor" model didn't go over with the American delegation at Bretton Woods, however, thickly populated as it was with conservative bankers and politicians. It meant having to cooperate and compromise with international partners in too many ways, and didn't explicitly advance the self-interested American goal of breaking open older established trading networks on behalf of U.S. business interests. Worse, it placed clear responsibility on wealthy creditor nations to aid the debtors. Keynes's "bancor" system looked like the "special drawing rights" regime that the United States finally and reluctantly adopted two decades later, but by then the global problems were too advanced to cure.

What President Johnson did was but a pale shadow of Lord Keynes's original plan. Worse, he left office vainly claiming that he'd solved the country's international financial problems:

> Monetary strength now is spread more widely over the world than in the early postwar years, when the dollar dominated affairs. That is healthy. But the world does not work well if there is uncertainty about the stability of the dollar. Although many tasks remain ahead in the field of international monetary reform, one of my comforts as I left the White House was that the dollar was once again strong.[39]

The world soon discovered that he'd no more "solved" America's fundamental international economic problems than he'd brought "an honorable peace" to Vietnam. To the contrary, much more pain and humiliation in both realms lay ahead.

FIVE YEARS AFTER Kennedy's assassination, the balance-of-payments and gold problems were no longer manageable in the ways Galbraith had advised in September 1963, for the crisis was now at an almost unimaginable level of tension. Under Kennedy, net U.S. gold outflows had averaged $750 million annually, but by March 1968, those numbers looked like pocket change. Over the three days that followed the New Hampshire primary, speculators and panicky foreign dollar holders stripped the U.S. government of more than $1 billion of its fast-shrinking gold reserves. Under pressure from Washington, governments closed gold and currency markets around the world, hoping to stem the gold panic and the losses.[40]

Yet the dangers of America's steadily eroding economic situation were playing a distant second to its political crises.

Johnson was out of the race; Sirhan Sirhan and James Earl Ray, both once unknown loners, were now known around the world; the French government of Charles de Gaulle had almost fallen after students and workers rose up in a series of demonstrations unrivaled since the Paris Commune a century earlier; and the Soviet Union had invaded Czechoslovakia. Gene McCarthy was competing with Hubert Humphrey, Richard Nixon, Nelson Rockefeller, Ronald Reagan, and George Wallace to become the Oval Office's next occupant.

In the GOP primaries, Nixon had done well, winning some states such as Wisconsin with 80 percent of the vote. But at the Republican National Convention in Miami in August, the party's fault lines were fully on display, with the waning Northeast-business-moderate tradition behind Rockefeller arrayed against the hard-right Goldwater conservatives of the South and Southwest, whose mantle had been bestowed on Reagan. Nixon ultimately won the nomination, but by a razor-thin margin—ten votes out of more than 1,300 cast.

Meanwhile, the segregationist former governor of Alabama, George Wallace, faced no primary or competitor for his third-party creation, the American Independent Party. But he still needed to qualify for the ballot in the fifty states, and to broaden his appeal to white voters outside the South he chose as his running mate the retired Air Force chief of staff, Curtis LeMay. Their ticket—which should have run under the slogan "no to Negroes, yes to Nukes," one pundit suggested—couldn't possibly win, but it promised to create mayhem for the two leading parties' candidates.

Meanwhile at the Democratic National Convention the climactic event of a chaotic year's chaotic presidential race took place. Gathered at the Chicago Amphitheater on the city's South Side in August, the Democrats had to choose between Eugene McCarthy and LBJ's vice president, Hubert Humphrey.

Hubert Humphrey had entered politics in the 1940s as a liberal reformer, first as mayor of Minneapolis and then as a U.S. senator from Minnesota, and like Galbraith was a cofounder of Americans for Democratic Action. But in accepting the vice-presidential slot in 1964, he had wedded himself to Lyndon Johnson and to the Vietnam War. Humphrey had long harbored doubts about the war, but at the convention he could not escape Johnson's powerful hand. Governor John Connally, head of the Texas delegation, was LBJ's point man, assigned to ensure that neither Humphrey nor the delegates broke with a White House–approved platform plank that supported the President's conduct of the war.

Galbraith went to Chicago as Eugene McCarthy's floor leader and foreign-policy spokesman.[41] But he knew that McCarthy had almost dropped out of the race. In June, hoping to dissuade him, Galbraith had gone to Washington to talk with him at his home right after attending Robert Kennedy's funeral at St. Patrick's Cathedral in New York:

Gene was deeply depressed; the death of Robert Kennedy showed the hope-lessness of the game. What had been real would now be pretense; what had been pleasure was now pain. Supported by Abigail, his politically acute and rather less romantic wife, I pleaded that he carry on. The banality of my argu-ment still rings faintly in my ears. Gene remained sad and unmoved but pro-posed another talk in Cambridge a few days later. This we had with Coretta King and a number of McCarthy's local supporters present. His mood was better . . . [but] I don't believe that Eugene McCarthy's heart was ever again wholly in the battle.[42]

Wherever his heart had gone, McCarthy stayed in the race, and arrived in Chicago still battling for the nomination. But the battle in Chicago turned out to be far broader, and fought not just on the convention floor.

Outside the convention hall, the National Mobilization Committee to End the War in Vietnam—called MOBE, a loose assemblage at best of the com-plex, often mutually hostile components of the antiwar movement—had gath-ered their own protesting forces. A risk of violent clashes in Mayor Richard Daley's city was there from the start, and police and demonstrators had started skirmishing even before the convention got under way. Organized in theory by the veteran pacifist David Dellinger and the SDS leaders Tom Hayden and Rennie Davis, MOBE competed for supporters and media attention with the Yippies, an anarchistic, almost dadaist, group best known for its two most telegenic figures, Abbie Hoffman and Jerry Rubin. In Lincoln Park on Sunday a noisy crowd of exuberant young people ignored an 11 p.m. curfew in favor of listening to rock music, paying boisterous tributes to Pigasus for President, and much "om"-ing while seated in the lotus position, which, the poet Allen Gins-berg assured the crowd, would immobilize the police. Chicago cops in riot gear then waded into the crowd, clubs swinging.* Then in Grant Park on Tuesday night, several hundred demonstrators surrounded a huge equestrian statue and draped it in Viet Cong flags and protest banners. Police pulled down one young man who climbed atop the statue, breaking his arm in the process, while once again Ginsberg chanted "om" nearby. Emotions on both sides flared, as stones and curses flew on one side, and batons on the other.[43]

At several points Galbraith tried personally to hold the potential for vio-lence in check, which produced at least one light moment. One night he crossed Michigan Avenue from the Hilton Hotel where most of the McCarthy delegates were staying, and then from an improvised platform addressed the young demonstrators in the park facing the hotel. He spoke of the struggle for peace, of the need for patience, of the necessity of avoiding violence even in response to violence. He assured them that the young National Guardsmen,

---

*Ginsberg didn't confine himself to the Chicago parks. He tried at one point to enter the convention hall with credentials as a reporter for a countercultural journal named *Eye*. Galbraith happened to be behind the bearded poet when a guard took one look at Ginsberg and refused to let him in. A police captain was called over. "What's the matter, Jack?" he asked the guard. "He wants to come in." "Has he got credentials?" "Hell," the guard snapped, "he ain't even got shoes."

heavily armed and in full battle uniform behind him, were not the enemy. Like the demonstrators, he said, they, too, were against the Vietnam War and, in proof of their feelings, had joined the Guard to avoid service in Southeast Asia. The demonstrators loved this, and briefly cheered the soldiers. When Galbraith turned to make his way back to the hotel, however, a large, muscular sergeant rushed toward him, and he stiffened, expecting the worst. The sergeant instead grabbed his hand and pumped it furiously in appreciation. "Thank you, sir," he said. "That was the first nice thing anyone has said about us all week."

Inside the convention hall, little was going well—and all of it was on national television. Under strict security conditions devised by Mayor Daley, the hall had been packed so tightly that movement of any kind across the convention floor involved shoving, bumping, and occasional angry pummeling. Though he denied it, President Johnson had maintained control of the platform committee, insisting on a "peace plank" that satisfied no one. Angry accusations by dissident delegates that the dais refused to recognize them added to the bitterness. Galbraith, who had testified for a strong Vietnam plank at the platform hearings, watched as LBJ's supporters rammed through what the President wanted.

Convention week itself started with a ham-fisted challenge to Galbraith's seating as a delegate, even though the Massachusetts delegation eventually voted for McCarthy 70–2. (When it came time to vote on seating one of two contending delegations from Alabama, Galbraith turned the tables. He forced the former Massachusetts governor Endicott "Chubb" Peabody, a leading Humphrey supporter, to back the more integrated group, reminding Peabody in front of the TV cameras of his mother's fabled support for civil rights.)

Governor Harold Hughes of Iowa placed Senator McCarthy's name before the delegates, and Galbraith and the civil rights leader Julian Bond offered formal seconds. As Galbraith stepped down from the dais, he saw in horror that television sets in the waiting rooms behind the platform were broadcasting in gruesome detail the bloody riots that were simultaneously breaking out downtown. (The mayor and police blamed them on the antiwar demonstrators, but official investigations ultimately placed responsibility on the city's shoulders.[44]) It was mayhem, as people rushed to escape the stones and bottles of protesters or the batons and tear gas loosed by the police. Demonstrators, onlookers, reporters, even convention delegates were attacked, and nearly two hundred police were reported injured. Humphrey and McCarthy were slightly tear-gassed, and well after authorities seemed to have unquestioned control of the streets, police charged the Hilton Hotel and invaded Galbraith's room as well as McCarthy's and several others'—allegedly in search of protesters.

In the midst of this unimaginable chaos, the voting began in the convention hall. Throughout the evening, television cameras constantly cut back and forth between the voting in the hall and the rioting in the streets, creating a surrealistic montage of democratic engagement. Just before midnight Humphrey won the nomination by a final ratio of nearly three to one, although

McCarthy succeeded in carrying California, Massachusetts, Oregon, New Hampshire, and Iowa, and only narrowly lost New York. In protest against Humphrey's silence about the events outside, McCarthy refused to enter the hall to offer his endorsement of the winning candidate.

Democrats left Chicago bitterly divided, enormously angry, and aware that Humphrey's convention victory had taken place amidst a scene that would almost surely guarantee his ultimate defeat. The next day, as McCarthy's plane took off, the pilot announced over the intercom, "We are leaving Prague."[45]

Facing the prospect of Richard Nixon as President of the United States, Galbraith and, with his encouragement, ADA within a matter of weeks announced their support of Humphrey, as did other peace and civil-rights groups and, finally, McCarthy himself. After a face-to-face appeal from Humphrey, Galbraith actively campaigned and raised funds for him.[*]

Toward the end of the campaign, Nixon, fearing a resurgence of support for Humphrey, began claiming that he had a plan to bring peace to Vietnam. Americans would soon discover that it was a lie. What they couldn't know at the time was that Nixon, through intermediaries, was secretly trying to persuade South Vietnam's then president, General Nguyen Van Thieu, to resist any attempt President Johnson might make to arrange a cease-fire or to bring South Vietnam to the negotiating table with North Vietnam. It was a grotesque, and likely illegal, interference in U.S. national security affairs, and cloaked in hypocrisy when Nixon piously told reporters, "We do not want to play politics with peace." President Johnson, who thanks to FBI wiretaps and leaks in both the United States and Saigon basically knew what Nixon was doing, failed to make an issue of this during the campaign (probably because his evidence wasn't ironclad, and the fact that it relied heavily on wiretaps was in itself questionable and might redound to Nixon's benefit).

Two days before the election, as the polls tightened with a last-minute surge for Humphrey, Nixon, fearful that President Johnson might still make a peace announcement at any moment, personally phoned the White House. In fact, no such announcement was in the offing, but to a skeptical LBJ he passionately insisted that whatever Johnson knew about secret contacts between Thieu and certain Nixon supporters had not been ordered by him and he was not privy to them. His claims didn't persuade the savvy President, but dissuaded him at least from going public with what he knew so close to the election itself. "When he finally hung up, Mr. Nixon and his friends collapsed with laughter. It was partly in sheer relief that their victory had not been taken from them at the eleventh hour."[46]

On November 5, 1968, Richard Nixon won 43.3 percent of more than 73

---

[*]For a campaign that included so much bitterness, there was at least a moment of levity at the end. When, a few days before the election, Galbraith spoke from a podium in New York in support of Humphrey, he "looked down to see a totally naked man and a handsome young woman clad only in old sneakers handing me up the head of a pig. This was an accepted mark of disfavor in those days; the decision to support Humphrey had not met with universal approval." Police quickly bundled the pair away, but the scene was captured by a news photographer, and Galbraith displays the photo prominently in his study, to the enduring embarrassment of his wife.

million votes cast; Humphrey finished behind him by fewer than 500,000 votes; and George Wallace placed a distant third.

Years afterward, *The New York Times* columnist and former Nixon aide William Safire wrote, "When people later wondered why Nixon thought so highly of President Thieu, they did not recall that Nixon probably would not be President were it not for Thieu. Nixon remembered."

And so out of the chaotic events of 1968, Richard Nixon emerged as President, and both the war and the economy that had been Lyndon Johnson's now became his.

NIXON'S INAUGURATION BROUGHT no relief from the protesters who'd done so much to drive out Lyndon Johnson, however. In 1968, Columbia University had been the site of the year's most famous protests; Harvard's turn came in 1969. The disruptive, wounding student strike that Harvard went through in the spring of 1969 fractured campus opinion along dozens of incongruent lines.[47] Partly a protest against the Vietnam War, partly about civil rights and Harvard's treatment of African Americans and other minorities, partly about the university's governance, partly an explosion of the inchoate anger of a new generation against the power and institutions of the time, the 1969 strike left emotions polarized across the campus. Among many faculty members, sympathy for those who sought tenure while espousing Marxist, Marxian, quasi-Marxian, or just radically dissenting views was in short supply.

In 1969 the nation's largest Students for a Democratic Society chapter was Harvard's, with more than 200 members, and it was headily self-confident. In 1966, its members had surrounded Robert McNamara on the street outside Quincy House during his visit to the campus. They hoped to prompt a debate over the war, but the affair had ended up with the Defense Secretary climbing onto the hood of a car, where he (rather imprudently) sneered that he was "tougher" than they were and that America would prevail in Vietnam. This predictably further aroused the crowd, and McNamara, however tough, decided that retreat was the superior strategy in the moment. Guided by a young graduate student named Barney Frank, he retreated into Quincy House and then fled through the legendary maze of Harvard's underground steam tunnels.

A year later, in 1967, angry students locked a Dow Chemical Company recruiter in the Chemistry Department. (Dow was widely reviled for producing the napalm then being used in Vietnam.) They effectively held him prisoner for several hours before ejecting him from the campus. The episode angered and embarrassed the Harvard administration, conservative alumni, and supporters of the war. In the aftermath, the administrators' tempers cooled enough that, instead of expelling the malefactors, they placed 74 of them on probation and sent formal letters of admonishment to another 170. The faculty had supported this decision by a wide margin, but President Pusey and his deans misread the support as carte blanche for a tougher handling of student protesters in the future. Pusey began to refer in print to radical students as "the Walter Mittys of the left" who "wanted to play at revolution," not perhaps the best tone to adopt to calm a volatile campus. Harvard then awarded an honorary doctorate in 1968 to the Shah of Iran, just weeks after Columbia University had endured its legendarily acrimonious student takeover.

In the summer, Pusey was caught off guard when the left-leaning Social Relations Department suddenly announced that it would offer a radical critique of American society as a course that coming fall; at first he thought it was a hoax and then was horrified when 750 undergraduates registered for the course. Without success, he spent weeks trying to scuttle it.

By February 1969, with Nixon in the White House, the faculty was increasingly restive. They had just voted against discontinuing the Reserve Officers' Training Corps (ROTC) as Pusey had wanted, but then denied course credit to students who enrolled in it—a decision that satisfied no one and aggravated all. This ROTC decision seems to have been the immediate catalyst, and the Nixon presidency the deeper cause, for the massive student strike that gripped Harvard two months later. That April, hundreds of student protesters, after weeks of peaceful protests, seized University Hall, where the offices of the college's deans were located, and declared the university "shut down." Pusey responded, after a brief (and by most accounts desultory) attempt at negotiations, by calling in more than 400 heavily armed, club-wielding state and local police to evict and arrest the students. Much of the resulting melée was caught by radio and television reporters, and news of the strike was broadcast across the nation. The rage and conflict that had shaken hundreds of colleges and universities had reached the country's oldest and most prestigious center of higher learning—and it sent a tremor that seemed to shake America. *Time* later tried to capture the reaction millions had had on learning that the police had swept through Harvard Yard, their batons flying, while legions of students—including some of the brightest in the country—fought back, and onlookers stared on in horror. "The great temple of learning on the Charles," the newsweekly observed, "will never be the same."

To no one's surprise, Harvard's best-known economist was at the forefront of the strike of 1969, including almost every one of the debates that preceded the strike, and the heated faculty exchanges during and after it. He had written about many of the issues in an article for the *Harvard Alumni Bulletin* in December 1968, where he argued for a greater faculty involvement in the university's governance, especially in appointment of the Harvard president and its deans (he did not recommend greater student involvement). The article kicked off a tempest, enraged Pusey, became the subject of a front-page *Wall Street Journal* article, and elicited a howl of alumni protests.[48] As one of the leaders of the faculty's "liberal" faction, he did not condone the students' seizure of university buildings in April but strongly opposed the administration's decision to call in police to evict the students, and subsequent plans to discipline them harshly.

Harvard being Harvard, most of the faculty opposition to this "liberal" faction was itself a moderate liberal group of professors who viewed the strike as a fundamental threat to Harvard as an institution and to measured discourse and academic freedom. Many who spoke most passionately for this position were European émigrés, whose first-hand experiences with right-wing, Nazi, or Communist regimes made them appreciate American freedom and academic rights the more. Even when they sympathized with some of the student positions (and they often did), the seizure of buildings, the heated rhetoric, and the constant possibilities for violence appalled them. They viewed democracy and the university as more fragile than figures like Galbraith did.

Henry Rosovsky was in this group. A Jew whose family fled the Nazis during the 1930s, he'd gotten his doctorate in economics at Harvard in the late 1950s, and was recruited back to Harvard in 1967, in part, he now says half jokingly, because he'd been teaching at Berkeley for many years and "some of my colleagues thought that, as a Berkeley veteran, I would have some insight into student protesters that would help Harvard avoid the same sorts of clashes." Rosovsky liked Galbraith, but the strike and its aftermath put strains on their relationship. "I simply couldn't understand Ken's position. I thought he was entirely too cavalier at points, and too harsh toward President Pusey. Overall, the administration frankly hadn't behaved terribly badly, in my opinion."[49]

The economic historian Alexander Gerschenkron, a close friend of Galbraith's for decades, reacted more vehemently than Rosovsky to Galbraith's sympathy for the students. Their friendship was already badly strained by Galbraith's antiwar activism, for Gerschenkron thought it highly improper for a scholar to publicize his political opinions. Born into a White Russian family that had fled the Bolsheviks for Austria, Gerschenkron was a highly regarded historian of economic development and a revered teacher, who treasured the university's freedom and who loathed the student rebels and, even more, the colleagues who sympathized with them. As his biographer (and grandson) observed, he "hated many things about the late 1960s, but more troubling to him than the excesses of drugs, sex, foul language, or anything else the students were experimenting with was the way many of his Harvard colleagues were swept up in a culture of youthful permissiveness. [He] was sure that the university was going over to the barbarians."[50]

In tumultuous faculty meetings convened during and after the 1969 strike, Gerschenkron became an outspoken defender of the university administration and its willingness to have student protesters arrested and expelled. When at one impassioned meeting Dean Franklin Ford likened the students to "storm troopers," his language provoked an outcry from some professors. But Gerschenkron rose in defense of Ford and declared,

> This business must not be allowed to go on, because if it is allowed to go on, then anyone in this room . . . can be dragged out, carried like a sack of potatoes out of your lecture room and dropped over the stairs of Emerson Hall or Sever [Hall] . . . unless he submits meekly to preposterous demands, and is willing to allow himself to be raped, symbolically . . .

He turned toward his estranged friend Galbraith, sitting nearby, and pointedly continued.

> Let us take once, once a candid look at ourselves, at this faculty and see why the faculty is not really apt to protect academic freedom and must leave it at critical times to the administration . . . There are middle-aged popularity kids who have done considerable damage to this university . . . I know quite well that there are many things wrong in the United States, many things in America that are horribly wrong, but I also know that there are many things that are wonderfully right with the United States . . . and among those things are the great universities of this country . . . And to try to destroy, to disrupt, to destroy, to attack this university, this is criminal. [Those who attack it] attack something that is really the finest flower of American culture.[51]

The two men's twenty-year-long friendship became one of the many casualties of the 1969 Harvard strike, and although a dismayed Galbraith tried several times to restore it, Gerschenkron would not consider it.

> He regarded my views on Vietnam as wrong and beyond the pale, not subject to discussion. There was absolutely no chance of talking about it with him. Similarly, my tolerance of the student revolt. Alex Gerschenkron could not separate difference of belief from friendship. If you were different in belief, you could not be on good terms. He lowered the curtain.[52]

The 1969 strike was the most violent protest at Harvard, but not the last. A year later, the U.S. invasion of Cambodia ordered by President Nixon led to a rally of more than 30,000 in the football stadium. Smaller groups also organized demonstrations against South African apartheid, pressing Harvard either to divest its huge portfolio of stock in companies that did business in South Africa or to vote its shares publicly against apartheid policies. Dean Ford, after suffering a heart attack, resigned in 1970; the first woman and the first African American were appointed to the Board of Overseers; parietal rules were virtually abandoned*; and the university agreed to support the construction of low-income housing in Cambridge.

Yet Chairman of the Overseers Douglas Dillon and some of his colleagues were nonetheless alarmed. Student admission applications and alumni donations were falling for the first time since the Great Depression. In June 1971, President Pusey announced that he, too, was retiring.

The selection of Derek Bok, dean of the Law School, to succeed him was praised when it was announced soon after. Galbraith was delighted; he and Kitty counted the Boks as good friends. Everyone knew that the immensely talented Bok, like several other deans, had privately disagreed with Pusey's deci-

---

*The College's parietal rules were those "by which," Galbraith once said, "Harvard distinguished the circumstances in which its students might fornicate, and those in which they might not."

sion to send in the police during the strike. A labor law expert, he believed Pusey hadn't exhausted the opportunities to negotiate a peaceful settlement. And he was a striking choice for Harvard in other ways. Scion of the Curtis publishing fortune, he drove a Volkswagen Beetle and had not attended Harvard as an undergraduate. More troubling to conservative alumni was that his father-in-law was the social-democratic Swedish economist Gunnar Myrdal, who with his wife, Alva, not only supported what many American conservatives reviled as "Swedish socialism" but were prominent European opponents of the Vietnam War.

Bok himself was considered tough-minded yet balanced in his views, and committed to reasoned debate about the purpose and future of both the university and society. He was also passionate about opening the ranks of Harvard students and faculty to those who "historically had perhaps not been as welcomed at the College" (as one historian genteelly put it), and about encouraging Harvard to engage the world around it. One professor later quipped about the Bok-era faculty's response that it behaved like the Strategic Air Command: a third were airborne at any moment.[53]

Harvard's recommitment to reasoned engagement wasn't taken up by American society as a whole, however. The 1960s had released the tectonic plates on which its connecting elements fragilely rested and allowed them to collide once again. Darker emotions—of betrayal, of resentment, and of revenge— now bubbled up, as power, wealth, and privilege realigned. An anger and a sourness surfaced over the dislocation of "traditional" values and mores, and it foretold a backlash not only against the rebellious 1960s but against the traditions and values that had emerged in the 1930s to reform American society. Those values had their own roots deep in the nation's past, but would soon be treated as alien and corrupting. As the 1960s ended, with them went the heady optimism so many had felt as the decade began—and a new American politics and economics began to take shape, even though only a few were bold enough to imagine where they might lead.

20

Galbraith and Nixon: Two Keynesian Presidents

The first months of 1971 were the lowest point of my first term as President. The problems we confronted were so overwhelming and so apparently impervious to anything we could do to change them that it seemed possible that I might not even be nominated for reelection in 1972.

—Richard Nixon

I remember the year 1971 with great fondness.

—John Kenneth Galbraith

TWO DAYS AFTER CHRISTMAS, 1971, as he listened to the warm applause from more than 1,500 fellow economists when he stood to speak, John Kenneth Galbraith could be pardoned for a sense of quiet, but almost complete, satisfaction. He and his colleagues were in New Orleans for the eighty-fourth annual meeting of the American Economic Association, and the gathering that first night already promised to be the rewarding high point of what for Galbraith had been a very good year.

He had spent the winter term at Trinity College, Cambridge, as a fellow of the college, at the invitation of its master, R. A. "Rab" Butler, a former chancellor of the exchequer. The conditions for writing at Trinity proved "rather too perfect"—and he used the time to make substantial progress on the first draft of *Economics and the Public Purpose*, the book that, after *The Affluent Society* and *The New Industrial State*, completed what he now considers the "informal trilogy" of his major works.[1] Given comfortable rooms at Nevile's Court with an elegant view looking out onto the library designed by Christopher Wren, Galbraith settled into the long-established pleasures of a Cantabrigian bachelor-scholar's existence, writing uninterrupted in the mornings, then emerging for lunch, calls, letters, long walks across the Backs, late-afternoon tea and sherry with friends, followed by the college's elegant dinner.

The only weekday interruptions in this pleasant routine were a series of un-demanding lectures, occasional informal talks for students and the public, and a steady stream of press interviews. On weekends, he went to London, where Kitty had taken an apartment for them, because she refused to re-immerse herself in the misogyny of British academic life in Cambridge.*

By mid-spring, the Galbraiths were back in Boston, and then went on to summer at their farm in Vermont, where Galbraith made even more progress on his book. In September, he resumed teaching at Harvard, and continued to work on the book each morning. Christmas that year was especially pleasant, though more hectic than usual. On December 21, Kitty flew to New York to appear on the television show *To Tell the Truth*, where contestants tried to guess which of several women was the real Mrs. John Kenneth Galbraith. The next day she and her husband enjoyed late-afternoon cocktails with old friends, followed by a round of caroling. On December 23 they gave a small lunch at Boston's Ritz-Carlton for the editor of *The Boston Globe*, Thomas Winship, with Jerome Wiesner and his wife and the columnist Mary McGrory; they left for their farm in Newfane that evening. The Galbraiths' two younger sons were now students at Harvard—Peter a junior majoring in government; Jamie a sophomore majoring in social studies—and both were at home in Vermont for the holidays. (Alan, the oldest son, was a junior partner at the law firm of Williams, Connolly, and Califano in Washington; he and his wife, Sarah, were expecting their first child and had decided to stay and celebrate Christmas there.)

On a snowy Christmas Eve, with their two younger sons and a guest, a pretty Radcliffe undergraduate from Pakistan named "Pinky" Bhutto, they trimmed a freshly cut tree and feasted on Emily Wilson's oyster stew. The next morning, they all opened Christmas presents in front of a crackling fire, took a long walk, and came back to dine on a twenty-five-pound turkey and trimmings. That evening, they made a point of going to bed early, for early the next morning, Galbraith and Kitty were to rendezvous with their friends James and Emily Tobin, who'd been staying with friends nearby, and drive back to Boston, where the four of them would board a flight to New Orleans.

Galbraith had attended his first AEA meeting in 1933 in Philadelphia as a Berkeley graduate student hoping to find work; now he was about to succeed Tobin as president of the organization. From the warmth and duration of the applause that greeted him that first night, one could tell that he was hardly the "outsider" that some of his critics were so fond of claiming. Of course, he had his share of detractors even here, and academics being academics, predictably some of the notable ones were expected to skip his inauguration ("unexpect-edly called away," "feeling ill," "scheduling conflict"). As it turned out, though, absentees were few. By and large, even economists who disagreed sharply with

---

*Galbraith muted his wife's objection slightly by stretching Trinity's rules: by the 1970s "women of distinction" were welcome at High Table, though scholars' wives weren't. Galbraith thus invited the college chaplain's wife as his guest, and the chaplain invited Kitty.

him showed up—his old nemeses from Chicago, Milton Friedman and George Stigler, for example, and Robert Solow (who was overheard remarking that Galbraith's election owed more to his prominence as an antiwar Democrat than as an economic theorist).[2]

A privilege accorded the AEA's incoming president is that of organizing the convention's program, setting the topics and speakers. Galbraith had taken the privilege quite seriously, and produced a program that sent shockwaves through the profession's conservative members. *Business Week* reported that for many the New Orleans meeting was no less than a subversive attempt "to change economics from within by using the establishment's convention to focus on non-establishment subjects."[3]

The magazine wasn't wrong, yet the topics Galbraith put on the agenda conveyed quite brilliantly the tectonic shifts then going on within the profession, shifts that at the time seemed as large as those that had occurred in the late 1940s, when most American economists converted to Keynesianism.[4]

But from the point of view of charter apostles like Galbraith, too much of Keynes's originality had been tamed since then, even neutered, by the reintroduction of pre-Keynesian microeconomics. Starting in the Eisenhower years, AEA conventions had increased their emphasis on complex methodological and mathematical-technique questions, and moved away from public policy and empirical research. Much of this emphasis on method and mathematics served the hopes of "mainstream" Keynesians that they would be able to "fine-tune" the American economy. But from the mid-1960s onward, as the U.S. economy grew ever more resistant to "tuning" of any kind, and as monetarists such as Friedman relentlessly attacked the intellectual underpinnings of Keynesianism, the "mainstream" increasingly fell into disarray.

In a telling sign of that disarray, at the 1970 AEA convention in Detroit, some economists had freely admitted to reporters that the profession was in crisis—even worse, many said, in simultaneous crises that were afflicting theory, useful policy advice, and even academic organization. In its coverage of that meeting, *The New York Times* concluded that such talk underscored how clear it was that "the golden age of economics had peaked in 1965," and no economists knew when a new one might appear.[5]

This disarray clearly influenced Galbraith when he designed the New Orleans agenda. In a sense, this meeting was his answer to the questions raised the year before about how and when the profession's decline would stop. He knew that his answer would provoke controversy, but to no one's surprise, he was determined to give it anyway. To escape their crisis, Galbraith had long believed, economists needed to turn away from pursuing the latest in technique and come back to substantive debate over public policies and the implicit relation of economics to essential democratic values. Decline would end, he planned to tell his colleagues, only when they showed the world that "our age of scholasticism is ending."[6]

Galbraith knew that many of his own generation would resist his message, but he also knew that a new audience would welcome it. Sprinkled among the suits and sport coats in the hallways and meeting rooms were denim shirts and even a Nehru jacket or two, and a sudden variety of hair lengths and styles— the outward signs of a big change going on among young people. In 1968, some younger economists had even insisted on forming their own caucus within the AEA, The Union for Radical Political Economics, whose ungainly initials, URPE, were pronounced with equal infelicity, "ehr-pee." By 1971, the group had nearly 1,500 dues payers (and substantially more nonmember sup- porters). URPE's interests covered a range of liberal and progressive concerns, from income inequality and race to feminism, arms control, the environment, and Third World development. Some were trying to "update" certain Marxian ideas, but many more were using Keynesian and institutionalist theories, as well as their own syncretic creations, to criticize—and remake, or so they hoped—their intellectual inheritance.[7]

Galbraith was sympathetic to much of what this new generation believed in, and he knew a number of URPE's founders who came from Harvard. Yet, at sixty-three, he was not one of them. Many in URPE in turn admired Galbraith and the way he'd used his own variant of the Keynesian tradition to criticize the assumptions of the postwar "mainstream," but they wanted to go further in reforming both theory and practice.[8]

Galbraith's distance from the young radicals and from his own contempo- raries gave him a good position from which to design the convention's program, which caught the tensions and divisions among economists almost perfectly. To show what he thought the "end of scholasticism" should look like, and to highlight problems that a quarter century of attention to economic growth had not solved, he focused on economic inequality, making it the explicit subject of seven different panels and a prominent factor in three others.

This might have been seen as a personal mea culpa, since many people thought the subject had been minor in Galbraith's writing. But in truth that charge better applied to the economics profession as a whole. Between the end of World War II and 1964, when LBJ's War on Poverty began, of the nearly 800 articles in the *American Economic Review* only three dealt with poverty or inequality in the United States. In 1959, the Joint Economic Committee of Congress asked Robert Lampman, a University of Wisconsin economist (he became the CEA's specialist on poverty from 1961 to 1964), to assemble a complete bibliography of postwar books and articles by economists on modern poverty; his typed list required only two pages.[9] In December 1964, six months after Lyndon Johnson's War on Poverty bill was signed into law, in belated em- barrassment Theodore Schultz, the University of Chicago economist and fu- ture Nobel Laureate, chided his colleagues, "Poverty has no room in the house modern economists have built."[10] Growth, not distribution, had been the siren song, and it had taken years with television cameras and newspaper reporters following civil rights workers into the Mississippi Delta and into inner cities in the North for the full dimensions of America's poverty of race and region to be "rediscovered." Even then, it was not economists but those such as the writer and activist Michael Harrington who showed the persistent scale and scope of poverty, by his estimates a condition that affected a quarter or more of Americans.[11]

Starting in the mid-1960s, economists finally "rediscovered" poverty themselves, with an outpouring of research papers and conferences (accelerated by a large outpouring of federal and foundation research funds). By 1970, a researcher was able to fill a 442-page bibliography with more than 8,300 entries on poverty (although this included work by sociologists, political scientists and urban planners as well as economists).[12]

Given the profession's slow awakening to poverty, what stands out is that from 1958 onward, Galbraith highlighted the subject, which is why it is no surprise that President Johnson appointed him in early 1964 to the White House task force charged with formulating policy and direction for the Office of Economic Opportunity, the cornerstone agency of the War on Poverty.* His ideas about intensive early education for poor children were taken up by Wilbur Cohen, John Gardner, and Francis Keppel as partial inspiration for the Head Start program, while his proposal for a nationwide teachers' corps was put forward as part of the antipoverty program by Senators Kennedy and Nelson.[13] Unlike many fellow liberals, however, Galbraith always maintained a sharp distinction between the specific problem of poverty and the much larger issue of economic inequality, and, further, the influence of power and ideology on both.†

By 1971, both conservatives and liberals were willing to debate the means to "abolish poverty"; for example, Milton Friedman's proposal for a "negative income tax" was widely discussed in the Nixon administration as well as among liberals such as Galbraith. But inequality—and what relation it might have to poverty and to many other economic, political, and cultural problems—was not. He was now determined to move his colleagues and the public to take up that much thornier issue.

At the New Orleans meeting, two panels focused on poverty and inequality among African Americans; two others explored the condition of women, and that of workers and trade unions—two groups suffering not so much from poverty as from inequality. Others looked at overall income differences in the United States and at the specific effects of taxation on inequality in ways that

---

*Even after the two men parted company over Vietnam, when Sergeant Shriver's duties at the OEO grew heavy enough that he could no longer also run the Peace Corps, LBJ asked Galbraith to take over the latter (Galbraith, *A Life*, 454–55).

†The government's economists quickly turned to the Defense Department as their model for planning and analysis, this being a politically safe alternative to the messy rough-and-tumble of political organizing and social mobilization of the poor and middle classes that Galbraith thought essential for the War on Poverty's success. The Office of Economic Opportunity's planners early on imported wholesale the systems analysis and operations research methods that McNamara had brought to the Pentagon in 1961 and that in turn dated back through the RAND Corporation's work in the 1950s to the Army Air Force's strategic bombing plans in World War II.

Using these models gave the OEO planners a measure of analytic clarity, but it concealed from them "life on the ground" for the American poor and the effects of the roiling debates that the War on Poverty, like the Vietnam War, provoked in the American public and among politicians. Historians have since argued that this beguiling analytic clarity, and the bureaucratic rationality it helped to impose on government programs, indirectly contributed to the effective stabilization of poverty rates for the next three decades.

challenged traditional views that the tax system was benignly "progressive." The panels' titles themselves underscored Galbraith's expectations: "The Economics of Full Racial Equality," "What Economic Equality for Women Requires," and "Inequality: the Present Tendency and the Remedy" left little doubt about what he thought economists ought to be saying and doing beyond analyzing these problems.

Galbraith also had panels representing empirical and theoretical challenges to marginalism and the reigning models of Keynesianism: "The Future of Consumer Sovereignty," "Some Contradictions of Capitalism," "The Corporation, Technology and the State," "Have Fiscal and/or Monetary Policy Failed?" and "On the Status and Relevance of Economic Theory." To some, these panels might represent "a good deal of criticism of the system, more of the profession, and some self-flagellation," he dryly noted. But they also reflected "an exceedingly determined search [that] is now underway not only for solutions but for a better theoretical framework in which to place them."[14]

Despite his own strong views, expressed in the convention's panel topics, Galbraith made sure that many voices were heard, more than most AEA presidents normally invited. He made a point of singling out friends, of course: Paul Samuelson (who the year before had become America's first Nobel Laureate in economics), Simon Kuznets (Galbraith's Harvard friend and colleague, who won the 1971 Nobel Prize), and Gunnar Myrdal (who was to receive it in 1974) and his wife, Alva (who would become a Nobel Peace Prize recipient in 1982), were all honored with celebratory lunches.

But Galbraith just as readily made sure those with whom he disagreed were well represented. He asked Milton Friedman—who routinely pronounced Galbraith a "socialist" or worse (a claim always softened for Galbraith by the fact that Friedman also deemed Social Security and the income tax "socialist")—to deliver the lead paper for the keynote panel on fiscal and monetary policy. Alongside Friedman, Galbraith put Arthur Okun, a staunch defender of the New Economics from which Galbraith so often vehemently dissented. And he invited Gottfried Haberler—the only Harvard economist who had opposed giving tenure to Galbraith twenty years earlier—to speak on the Nixon administration's wage-price guidelines. (The Austrian's legendary conservatism hadn't faded in his retirement; he denounced labor unions as the primary cause of inflation, and urged a flood of cheap imports to undercut wages as well as the repeal of minimum wage laws and other "privileges," as he called them, that workers enjoyed.)

For the prestigious Richard Ely lecture, named after the AEA's founder,* Galbraith arranged for his old friend Joan Robinson to discuss "The Second Crisis of Economic Theory."[15] It proved a shrewd and powerful choice, for she drew "an overflow audience with an enthusiasm rarely seen at academic gath-

---

*Ely, a vehement opponent of marginalism and laissez-faire, founded the American Economic Association in 1885 as an explicitly progressive group to combat Social Darwinism, conservatism, and "capitalist apologetics." "The avenues of wealth and preferment are continually blocked by the greed and combinations of men and by

erings."[16] As James Tobin, himself a pioneer of the Neoclassical Synthesis that Robinson so disliked, later acknowledged, she finally found in America "the prime-time audience appropriate to her towering stature in the profession."[17] Trim and diminutive at sixty-eight, with short-cropped white hair, a fair complexion devoid of makeup, and a clear preference for the sensible over the fashionable, Robinson might have been mistaken for a matronly English-woman of the upper middle class, but when she spoke, the listeners knew they were in the presence of a world-class intellect.*

The first sentence of her lecture left no doubt as to her assessment of the current state of the profession: "When I see this throng of superfluous econo-mists—I am using that word, of course, in the Shakespearian sense—I am re-minded how much the profession has grown since the thirties and how many more there are now to suffer from the second crisis than there were to be dis-credited in the first." This "second crisis" of the 1970s, like that of the 1930s, she believed came from conventional economic theory's inadequacies when faced with the real world, and from its willful concealment of its own failure.

The "first crisis" had arisen when orthodox Marshallian theory had no expla-nation for, or solution to, the Great Depression, or for the massive unemploy-ment and underutilization of productive capacities. Now economics faced a second crisis because, in its "bastardized" synthesis of Keynes and Marshall, it still "had nothing to say on the questions that, to everyone except economists, appear to be most in need of an answer," namely what full employment is sup-posed to be for, and how income and wealth are to be distributed.

As she detailed her accusations over the next half hour, vigorous applause kept forcing her to pause. Galbraith, listening from his seat on the platform just behind her, led the sustained standing ovation at the end. Her challenge to mainstream Keynesians and their conservative colleagues obviously delighted him. In barely thirty minutes, she had elegantly crystallized the rationale be-hind the focus of his weeklong program provocatively emphasizing real-world inequality, the tenuous social rationale for unlimited production itself, and conventional theory's failure to analyze, let alone solve, such issues. It wasn't surprising that she was a hit with the members of URPE; what pleased Gal-braith, he later recalled, was the number of older economists who said how much they agreed with her, too. Even Tobin admitted, "The targets of her in-dictment loved every word."[18]

A further reason for Galbraith's pleasure was that she was reminding the

---

monopolists," he wrote. "We hold that there are certain spheres of activity which do not belong to the individual, certain functions which the great cooperative society, called the state—must perform to keep the avenues open" (quoted in Eric Goldman, *Rendezvous with Destiny* [New York: Vintage Books, 1977], 88).

*A hint of the edgy coolness that many mainstream Keynesians felt toward her had been given a few hours ear-lier. The economist Paul Davidson joined her for an early dinner, and "while we were eating, in walked about a dozen people—Samuelson and his wife, Arrow and his wife, the whole establishment, and they take a huge table, and we're the only two tables [occupied] in the whole dining room . . . Well, they walk right past us, and not one of them said, "Hello, Joan" . . . Not a word was spoken . . . We must have overlapped for forty minutes" (Davidson quoted in Turner, *Joan Robinson*, 183).

gathering that women needed to be taken seriously as economists. Academic economics had always been steadfastly unwelcoming to women and to minorities: Harvard's Economics Department, the oldest in the United States, had never in its hundred years found a single woman (or, for that matter, a male African or Hispanic or Asian American) who qualified for tenure, and the same was true at virtually every other major university; barely 2 percent of tenured university economists in the early 1970s were women. And because no woman had ever delivered a major address at an AEA convention, in this as in many other respects, the 1971 AEA convention was a major breakthrough. Robinson's address created just the climate Galbraith wanted, and he quickly made the most of it. At the normally pro forma business meeting the next evening, he proposed a series of resolutions on the status of women that set forth a detailed program for ending sex discrimination in the profession.

Passing these resolutions turned out to be harder than he anticipated, for they faced significant opposition. Part of the opposition was a matter of ingrained habit and privilege, and an inherent discomfort with change. A number of conservative economists had even responded to the "women's movement" with scholarly articles defending the economic logic behind gender discrimination. Others were simply uncomfortable with Galbraith, whatever the issue; Herbert Stein told a reporter that Galbraith "ran [the meeting] like a jerk."* Arthur Okun groused that "it was amateur night and Galbraith was completely unprofessional in running things."[19] It wasn't until midnight that the resolutions finally passed, and this only after some deft maneuvering on Galbraith's part. But the next day's *New York Times* headlined the midnight decision to its readers.[20] A new era, it seemed, was dawning in American economics.

TWO NIGHTS LATER, as Galbraith and his wife flew home to Cambridge, he settled into his airline seat with the same satisfaction he'd felt at the start of the week. If the success of this convention was an indication, 1972—even perhaps the decade—was going to be very good indeed. Sipping a scotch, he turned to a stack of newspapers he'd purchased at an airport kiosk just before boarding, and his mood darkened considerably. The massive U.S. bombing of Hanoi and the mining of Haiphong harbor, which President Nixon had ordered at Christmastime, was still ongoing.

Nixon's presidency was now almost three years old. Yet despite repeated promises by both him and Henry Kissinger, peace in Southeast Asia seemed no closer than it had been under Lyndon Johnson. To the contrary, as the

---

*Bernard Collier, interviewing economists about Galbraith for a *New York Times Magazine* article in 1973, found that all but one at least admitted that Galbraith was an excellent writer, even when they disagreed with him. "The single exception" was Stein, "who was very ill-natured about discussing Mr. Galbraith instead of Mr. Stein. His comments concerning Mr. Galbraith's economics and praise were sincerely nasty, and shortly he turned my attention to a dull article in *The Ladies Home Journal* full of praise for President Nixon. 'See,' he said disagreeably as he pointed to his name on the credit line. 'I'm a writer too' . . . As a final criticism, Mr. Stein said, 'Galbraith's economic stuff is a lot of crap.' "

papers made clear, this latest escalation—with more than 3,000 sorties and 40,000 tons of bombs dropped—was tearing apart not only Vietnam but the United States, and it almost guaranteed further prolongation of the war.

To Galbraith, it seemed part of an unchanging pattern: Nixon had ordered the secret bombing of Cambodia in 1969, his first year in office; in 1970, he had ordered the invasion of that tiny country, which had drawn Cambodia directly into the war and set off massive new student protests around the world, including at more than four hundred American universities; and in the spring of 1971, Nixon had escalated again, ordering a major incursion into Laos that turned into a rout, despite his claims to the contrary. Now B-52s were pounding North Vietnam. (Kissinger called the tactic "jugular diplomacy," and Nixon left no doubt about what he was seeking: he told the chairman of the Joint Chiefs of Staff, "This is your chance to use military power effectively to win this war, and if you don't, I'll consider you responsible."[21])

Yet, as Galbraith well knew, something was now different about the war: U.S. troops were being withdrawn. From a high of 530,000 troops in 1968 under Lyndon Johnson, Nixon had reduced the total by two thirds, to 184,000, and had pledged more cuts ahead. With withdrawals, U.S. casualties had fallen and so had intensive news coverage—especially television coverage. Nixon liked to call his combination of escalated air power plus troop reductions "Vietnamization," and he had convinced himself that he could successfully extract the United States from ground combat, continue the fighting in South Vietnam, *and* win the support of American voters.[22]

But "Vietnamization" wasn't going according to plan. Use of U.S. airpower in Cambodia and Laos, whose purpose was to maneuver the Viet Cong and North Vietnamese into a settlement that Nixon and Kissinger thought acceptable, had instead widened the war. It had also widened opposition to it in the United States. In June 1971, 61 percent of Americans said they wanted all U.S. troops out of Vietnam before the next presidential election.[23] Nixon's "Silent Majority," it seemed, had had enough of his Vietnam policies.

Congress could sense the discontent. In the Senate, Robert Dole was still denouncing the President's opponents as "a Who's Who of has-beens, would-be's, professional second-guessers and apologists for the policies which led us into this tragic conflict in the first place,"[24] but Dole's vitriol, like that of Vice President Spiro Agnew and Nixon's speechwriters William Safire and Patrick Buchanan, was losing its appeal. When Senator Edward Kennedy in mid-1971 introduced an amendment that severely curtailed the President's ability to send more draftees to Vietnam, it passed the Senate 78–4.[25] By the end of the year, a Gallup poll of voter preferences in the upcoming election showed Kennedy, who wasn't even a declared candidate, running almost neck-and-neck against Nixon.[26]

The President's problems weren't just centered on Vietnam, however. The American economy's ever-escalating problems were haunting him as well. Nixon had never been especially interested in economic policy as such; political strategies and the grand design of U.S. foreign policy were what he liked best. (Paul McCracken, CEA chairman, thought Nixon had "an almost psychological block about economics," and approached everything about the subject "like a little boy doing required lessons."[27]) Yet this consummate politician knew that he had won the White House because the New Deal coalition assembled by FDR was falling apart, and he was doing everything in his power to hasten its demise. Having understood and appreciated the immense grassroots energies behind Goldwater's failed 1964 campaign, he grasped that civil rights, Vietnam, and the youth counterculture were hitting discordant notes among millions of Americans, especially millions of white Southerners who had never before considered voting Republican. Cultivating defection of these "genetic Democrats" in the South and their migratory descendents in the southwestern Sun Belt was the cornerstone of Nixon's vision of a "great party realignment" following his election in 1968.[28] With such a shift, he told his aide H. R. Haldeman, the right conservative could create a new, perhaps even permanent, Republican majority. He would "need to build our own new coalition based on Silent Majority, blue-collar Catholic, Poles, Italians, Irish. No promise with Jews and Negroes." A new kind of appeal had to come from a conservative who was "not hard right-wing, Bircher, or anti-Communist."[29]

With someone like Haldeman, the President could talk with this sort of back-room frankness, but more often he used a higher-minded tone to describe his political program. For example, he wooed Daniel Patrick Moynihan away from the Democrats, and in turn this savvy Irish Catholic former Harvard professor flattered his boss to a fare-thee-well, in particular encouraging Nixon to compare himself to Benjamin Disraeli.[30] Always insecure around Ivy Leaguers—even non-WASPS like Moynihan, who'd fought his way up from the hardscrabble world of Hell's Kitchen in New York—Nixon adored this comparison. The great Victorian conservative Prime Minister and the twentieth-century American President both, as Nixon expanded on the idea, had begun life as outsiders; through sheer effort, will, and ambition, each had overcome major midcareer defeats to reach the apex of politics as head of the most powerful government of his time. Moreover, as Nixon noted to Moynihan, Disraeli achieved his resurrection by breaking through old party alignments and divisions. In the great struggle to expand the voting base of British democracy, his sponsorship of the 1867 Reform Bill had enfranchised many more common people than a competing Liberal initiative would have. This Disraeli model held a profound lesson, Nixon thought. "Tory men and Liberal policies," he loftily confided to Moynihan, "are what have changed the world."[31]

Nixon's dream of becoming an American Disraeli turned out to have revolutionary consequences for American politics, the American economy, and the American economics profession. The most memorable example of this self-proclaimed American Disraeli's ideal of "Tory men and Liberal policies" was his recognition of the nation then known as "Red China," a paradox he himself underscored to Mao Tse-tung when they finally met in Beijing. "In America, at least at this time," he boasted to the Chinese leader, "those on the right can do what those on the left can only talk about."[32] Yet by then Nixon had already demonstrated his capacity for conflating the conventional notions of "left" and "right" on the domestic front.

Eager to publicize his "Tory-man, Liberal-policy" persona, Nixon (without consulting his advisers) in January 1971 remarked to the television reporter Howard K. Smith, "I am now a Keynesian in economics."[33] This was, to put it mildly, a surprise to everyone, including Smith, who hadn't asked about Keynes.

The incongruous conversion signaled trouble. Nixon himself was uncertain why he'd said what he did. Herbert Stein claimed he meant he had converted to Stein's "business Keynesian" view, which allowed for a "high-employment federal budget" and permitted a stimulative deficit when unemployment rose above target levels (although under the influence of Milton Friedman's "natural rate" theory, the target levels were kept deliberately vague, but still well above levels activist Keynesians considered "full" employment).[34] It is more likely that the politically feral Nixon understood that he would need to have some big and dramatic things happen in 1971 if he was to be reelected in 1972 and build his dreamed-of "new Republican majority." Yet there is no question that in 1971 he was about to break in unprecedented fashion with traditional conservative policies.

When Nixon took office in 1969, he had followed what his CEA chairman Paul McCracken dubbed "gradualism," accepting his advisers' counsel to initiate largely undramatic economic maneuvers that were supposed to slow down the overheated economy, but not so swiftly that it provoked a recession.* At first, "gradualism" seemed to work: after eight years of expansion, the economy slowed in 1969. But then in 1970, beset by strikes at General Motors and other big corporations, unemployment and inflation suddenly and unexpectedly rose side by side, something economics textbooks said was almost impossible. In November 1970, Republicans did badly in the midterm congressional elections and Nixon now feared the worst about 1972 unless the economy im-

---

*The economy they inherited from LBJ gave some reason for caution. It was showing two surprising—and, as it turned out, misleading—signs of recovering health: in 1968, there were surpluses in both the federal budget and the balance of payments. But the budget surplus was largely an accounting chimera. Thanks to a change in the budgeting process, the Johnson administration that year had presented a new "unified" federal budget that incorporated the Social Security and highway trust funds, which along with a few others had until then been held "off-budget," in separate government accounts, since they were funded by designated taxes (the payroll tax and the gasoline tax) and were for designated purposes. Both funds were running surpluses, and the political gains from mixing those surpluses with the "operating budget"'s burgeoning deficits, and thereby producing an apparent overall governmental surplus was too tempting for the White House to resist. By 1969, however—even with the trust funds now included—Washington once again ran a deficit, and it would continue to do so for the next thirty years.

The balance-of-payments surplus in 1968 likewise was a temporary artifact of circumstance. After the near collapse of the French government that spring in *"les évènements de Mai"* (during which President de Gaulle briefly fled riot-torn Paris for the safety of a French military base in West Germany), and then the Soviet invasion of Czechoslovakia in August, billions of francs, pounds, and marks held by European capital, as well as American capital in Europe, rushed to the United States as a safe haven. When Nixon's early economic policies showed little sign of proving effective against U.S. inflation, and with the war in Vietnam dragging on, White House policy drove those funds back out, and the downward pressure on the dollar and upward pressure on gold resumed.

proved. "A Republican administration with any kind of economic slowdown," he growled to Haldeman right after the 1970 elections, "is a disaster. Without economic drag, [we] would have carried both House and Senate." Soon, Haldeman noted in his diary, the frustrated President started "seriously considering complete change of advisers . . . Doesn't want to take any chance on screwing up 1972."[35]

Nixon's search for new economic advisers, for men tough enough to make the business cycle work for his reelection, dictated his conversion to his own peculiar brand of "Keynesianism." And the best evidence for this is the man he made Treasury Secretary and put in charge of economic policy three weeks after announcing his embrace of Keynes: the former Texas governor John Connally.

Overnight the lanky Texan became the most visible sign of Richard Nixon's new world. Yet Connally hardly represented a fresh set of "liberal," let alone "Keynesian," views that America's Disraeli was incorporating into a grand new "Tory-liberal" synthesis. He was pro-business, pro–Vietnam War, and above all else a consummate pragmatist of power and interest-group politics, Texas-style. "I can play it round or I can play it flat," he was fond of saying, "just tell me how to play it."[36]

Most of the White House press corps remembered Connally only as the man who'd been sitting in front of JFK when the presidential motorcade entered Dealey Plaza in November 1963, and who had taken a near-fatal bullet meant for Kennedy. In 1968, he had resurfaced briefly as Lyndon Johnson's personal floor boss and strategist at the tumultuous Democratic convention in Chicago. How had that same John Connally suddenly become Nixon's new Treasury Secretary?

Out of office, increasingly conservative, and still immensely ambitious, Connally had impressed Nixon at a White House conference in late 1969, where this millionaire son of poor sharecroppers took control of figures and issues as easily as he did the others in the room. Nixon had been smitten. According to the always envious Henry Kissinger, "Connally's swaggering self-assurance was Nixon's Walter Mitty image of himself. He was the one person whom Nixon never denigrated behind his back."[37]

Kissinger may well have been right, but Mittyish idol or not, there was a simpler explanation for Nixon's admiration. Connally was Nixon's fourth try in two years to find a man who could drive White House economic policy the way Kissinger and Nixon drove foreign policy. And from the moment of his arrival at Treasury in February 1971, Connally did just that: ignoring the bickering among Nixon's other economic advisers, he plowed ahead with a Texas-sized confidence that he could do what they hadn't. After just four months on the job, through a combination of competence, ruthlessness, and unctuous flattery, he won Nixon's complete confidence. What neither man fully understood, however, was that in forcing the economy into the service of a President's electoral needs they were setting in motion forces that would revolutionize American and global economic behavior and policy. For it would ultimately be these two politicians—both conservative, neither trained in economics, each elusively pragmatic as only the very ambitious can be—who, after Nixon's announced conversion to Keynesianism, would instead effectively end the Keynesian policy era in America.

IRONICALLY, THE END of Keynesianism and of Richard Nixon's presidency began in almost simultaneous and unconnected events. On Sunday, June 19, 1971, *The New York Times* began publishing excerpts from the Pentagon Papers, a dense, 7,000-page, top-secret Defense Department history of the Vietnam War, which had been shown secretly to the *Times* by an ex-Pentagon official, Daniel Ellsberg. Even though Nixon rightly surmised that the Pentagon Papers' contents would do greater harm to the reputation of his Democratic predecessors then to himself, he was livid about the leak itself and, egged on by Henry Kissinger, viewed it as part of a larger pattern of government leaks that had to be plugged. An example needed to be made of Ellsberg.

First Nixon tried to have the courts force the *Times* to cease publication. When that failed, he ordered the creation of a top-secret group of break-in and dirty-tricks operators to find incriminating information on his enemies; it became infamous as "the Plumbers." By then, he had already used the FBI to wiretap senior aides whom he suspected of leaking to the press. That had been minimally legal, whereas, as everyone involved understood, nothing about the Plumbers was: G. Gordon Liddy might be a former FBI agent and Howard Hunt an ex-CIA man, but the barest figleaf of legally permissible covert activity ceased when this merry band of right-wing "black ops" veterans began their new career by breaking into the office of Daniel Ellsberg's Los Angeles psychiatrist, hoping to find information with which to smear Ellsberg. The L.A. break-in was bungled, which should have been a warning to Nixon, but wasn't.

Four weeks after the Pentagon Papers appeared and "the Plumbers" were organized occurred what Nixon counted as the crowning achievement of his foreign policy. In mid-July, after months of covert discussions and a top-secret trip by Kissinger to Beijing, the President dramatically announced that the United States and China would inaugurate a new era and that early in 1972 he would go to meet Mao Tse-tung in Beijing. This stunning reversal of decades of enmity and intransigence on both sides—enmity to which Congressman, Senator, and Vice President Nixon had contributed—promised to remake the landscape of American and global politics.

Yet Nixon's problems continued as the summer wore on and, since he had believed that his China breakthrough would be universally hailed, he was stunned to find the public and Congress truculent and critical instead. At a special White House briefing on China for congressional leaders, the legislators listened politely, then insisted on talking about inflation and unemployment.[38] Beyond the Potomac, Americans were dismayed by the war, but they were even more frustrated by the economy. It was their number one issue—and three out of four thought the administration was mishandling it.[39]

In short, nothing was going as planned by the summer of 1971, and Nixon's chances for reelection, let alone for creating the "new Republican majority," were hanging in the balance.

For months, the clamor for the White House to "do something" about the domestic economy had been building, in particular pressure to impose the sort of wage and price controls Nixon publicly denounced; internationally, the situation was just as tense. West Germany had devalued the mark that spring, and by late July the British were secretly warning Washington that a second devaluation of the pound might be imminent. At a meeting with the Business Council the ever-pragmatic John Connally had been stunned by the intensity of criticism from David Rockefeller and other business leaders for Nixon's failure to control spiraling wage increases. Even George Schultz at the OMB—who as a former University of Chicago professor was far more hostile than Connally to any idea of government intervention—came back from the same meeting abashed by what he'd heard. A few days later, he told his aides to "get stuff together on what controls would look like."[40]

At the same time, pressure was rising to "do something" to fix the United States' chronic balance-of-payments problem, with its attendant drain on U.S. gold supplies and confidence in the dollar. It could no longer be dealt with by the "technical" measures that had preoccupied the "New Economists" a decade earlier.

On the afternoon of Tuesday, July 28, Nixon sat down for nearly four hours of Oval Office meetings to map a way out. At 3 p.m. he met with Treasury Secretary Connally, OMB Director Schultz, and his White House aides John Ehrlichman and Charles Colson; the subject was the economy. As recently released (but never before published) White House tapes show, an anguished Nixon was frustrated and angry about the unrelenting protests against his presidency, and spent much of the time mulling aloud about his great list of real and imagined "enemies."[41] He and his aides rambled angrily across a range of topics, from the state of the bond market to organized labor's lukewarm support to the vexing hostility of "the Negroes and the Jews." He derided America's top union leaders as a mediocre clan of "uneducated Irish Catholics . . . who can't put three words together in grammatical sequence"; he pronounced the nation's university presidents "a bunch of shits" and contemptuously dismissed the country's corporate CEOs as "sad damn sacks . . . taking a beating from their kids and not standing up." None of them understood that America, as a result of the tumult and chaos of the 1960s, was now "facing the greatest moral crisis in its history" or seemed to realize that destiny had left to him alone the responsibility of reversing the vast consequences of that crisis.

Among this grab bag of enemies, a few stood out, as Nixon made clear. To Connally he urged, "The next time out, whenever you have the opportunity—I know you often use your principle 'It's nice to have an enemy'—well, one of the best ones I can think of is John Kenneth Galbraith." Apparently alluding to Galbraith's congressional testimony on July 20, which had harshly criticized the administration's mishandling of the economy,[42] the President snarled that "this son-of-a-bitch has unmasked what these bastards, all these bright New Dealers, want. They want another OPA, they want to control the economy, they want to control wages and prices." He told Connally, "You get out there and make an issue of it—and destroy him on it."

Secretary Connally, unctuous in Nixon's presence and sensing his anger, reassured the President of his sagacity. "I couldn't agree more with you and I will *really* take him on," he drawled laconically. "He testified in Washington and made snide remarks, smart-acre remarks, and I was prepared to take him on when I testified in the House but they didn't ask the question." This wasn't enough for Nixon, however, who warmed to the topic of the hated Galbraith. "There ought to be a concerted effort by the whole administration to *blast* him—not just to blast him, to say he's the economic spokesman for the left wing of the Democratic Party, er, the ultra-liberal wing, or the liberal wing, here he's their chief economic guru." On the tapes one can hear Nixon pounding the desk. "I sure think we ought to take him on, don't you? Make the Democratic candidates and spokesmen repudiate him. They ought to be asked questions, force the Democratic candidates to say, 'Do you support John Kenneth Galbraith on wage and price controls?' Let 'em say, make 'em say."

Connally by this point can be heard in the background, chanting like an evangelical congregation in thrall to their preacher, "Yes, sir. Yah, sir. Yes, sir. Yessss, sir." Nixon continued railing against the OPA (where he'd worked before joining the Navy) and "controlled economies, socialism," and saying he wanted to "scare the hell out of the unsophisticated person who, at first blush," might support Galbraith's views on the need for different kinds of economic measures. "It's political as much as anything else—how, whether we play that game."

George Schultz, spinning out the President's plan to denigrate Galbraith, shifted the conversation to the question of how to maneuver usually Democratic union leaders into supporting the Republicans, how to use blue-collar support of Nixon to force their leaders into line. Schultz's idea was to "really embarrass [AFL-CIO president George] Meany with Galbraith." That, he said, should be the White House's new goal. Nixon listened for a while and then broke in, this time to rail again about his "enemies." The problem, he said, was that the Negroes, the Jews, the ungrateful university presidents, the weak-willed CEOs, and America's liberal religious leaders refused to follow the supportive example of his friend, the Reverend Billy Graham, an observation that produced yet another chorus of "Yes, sir"s from Connally.

The group then turned to strategies for popularizing the administration's economic policies, but soon enough they drifted back to cursing Nixon's enemies. Schultz urged that Galbraith be made into the principal target on economic matters, which seemed to delight Nixon; he suggested that they should make Galbraith into "a terrible goblin." "The way you do it is to talk up 50,000 OPA cops, telling everybody, messin' in your business and so forth . . . everything is fixed, you can't change jobs, rationing . . . ruination . . . socialist, throw in the word 'socialist' . . . this is a socialist scheme, a scheme to socialize America. Now the intellectuals won't like it one bit but *stick* it to 'em, that makes votes."

At 4:30, Schultz, Ehrlichman, and Colson left, and Nixon and Connally—now joined by H. R. Haldeman—spent a half hour on the troubles of Vice President Spiro Agnew, who was facing criminal indictment for corruption charges that predated his vice presidency. The three men weighed the possibility that Agnew would be forced to resign by the end of the year. (Running through the conversation was the clear but unspoken implication that Nixon's choice to replace Agnew would be Connally.) Shortly after 5 p.m., Connally left, and Nixon and Haldeman continued to assess the Agnew-Connally situation, before moving on to the President's upcoming schedule, and then to China.

But Galbraith was still on Nixon's mind, because he suddenly told his top aide angrily, "It's really ironical to have these symps, these crawling bastards like Galbraith and Kennedy" complaining about his dramatic new opening to China. Haldeman urged his boss to look on the bright side: "You've put a bullet-proof shield around yourself," he said, referring to political benefits that had been won by this audacious shift in the administration's foreign policy, which for the foreseeable future would trump the losing card of Vietnam.

Just before 6 p.m., Colson returned with National Security Advisor Henry Kissinger in tow, and the four men spent another hour evaluating the political and diplomatic impact of the China opening. Kissinger dwelt at length on how he planned to use it in the Paris peace talks with the North Vietnamese—he and Nixon agreed that it would make their negotiators more pliant—and on how it was simultaneously undercutting the ability of the Soviets abroad and the Democrats at home to criticize the White House. Exquisitely attuned to Nixon's insecurities, Kissinger compared the China move to what he called Kennedy's inept handling of the Cuban Missile Crisis; he lauded Nixon for his boldness and genius, in contrast to what he described as Kennedy's incompetence in causing, then mishandling, the earlier confrontation.

Kissinger confidently told Nixon that he had recently talked privately with Galbraith, who had admitted that the Democrats were going to be hamstrung on foreign policy in the upcoming presidential election, and that they would be able to campaign against Nixon only on the domestic economy's poor performance—exactly what Nixon was hoping. The President was delighted to hear that his "enemy" Galbraith was acknowledging Nixon's strategic brilliance.*
The men discussed plans for a Soviet-American summit and Kissinger's upcoming return trip to Beijing, where he would plan for Nixon's state visit there in 1972, before adjourning for dinner.

Yet as the President's meetings came to a close that summer's day, it was

---

*Galbraith had been assessing the damage the China opening was doing to the Democrats. Kissinger's telling Nixon he'd learned this from Galbraith in *private* conversation bespeaks both men's love of conspiracy and secret dealings. Galbraith remembers seeing Kissinger shortly after testifying before Congress, but does not recall the substance of their conversation. He and Kissinger had gotten along reasonably well in eartlier years, when, along with George Kistiakowsky and some Harvard and MIT defense intellectuals, they had many off-the-record discussions about the dangers of nuclear war and the need to forge a new sort of relations with the Soviet Union.

clear to Nixon and his top aides alike that while the remarkable China opening he and Kissinger had made was indeed a political master stroke, Galbraith was also right: the performance of the U.S. economy was going to be the prime battleground for the 1972 elections, and Nixon had no master stroke like the Chinese opening on this front. Finding one became his overriding preoccupation.

He first told aides how he "loved the long ball over three yards and a cloud of dust"; then, changing his metaphor, he told them the time had come for "total war on all economic fronts."[43] What he didn't tell them was that for the past six months, for all his railing about the ruination and socialism that would arise from wage and price controls, he and Connally had been secretly evaluating that very option but had deliberately stalled on taking action, waiting for exactly the right moment to maximize the benefits for Nixon's reelection.[44]

That moment came at the beginning of August, just five days after his lengthy strategy meeting. On August 2, Connally gave the President a long briefing about a detailed package of supposedly anathema proposals. "I am not sure this program will work," he told Nixon. "But I *am* sure that anything less will not work."[45] Connally's genius in that meeting was to overcome Nixon's uncertainty about and aversion to measures that were sure to hurt him with many voters in his Republican base. Listening with an attentiveness he almost never showed for such matters, the beleaguered President signed off on everything Connally proposed, with only a handful of minor caveats. That night, Bob Haldeman confided to his diary that the President had made "a huge economic breakthrough."

Nixon and Connally badly needed a precipitating threat from abroad that would justify to Congress and the public the actions they were about to take, and late the following week, London provided it. In a phone call to Treasury Undersecretary Paul Volcker, British officials warned him that on that coming Friday (August 13), to defend the pound they would present $3 billion worth of British government–held dollars and U.S. Treasury securities, and they expected Washington to provide gold in return. Both sides anticipated panic in the financial markets when this happened, as it would be instantly apparent that the United States' closest ally was in effect voting against the legacy (and price) of Washington's global leadership since World War II. The humiliation the British had suffered in 1946—when in a matter of days American financial markets had stripped away the billion-dollar postwar recovery loan from Washington that Keynes had negotiated—was now about to be felt in Washington itself.

That same Friday afternoon, a Marine helicopter lifted off from the White House lawn and scuddered north toward Camp David. The presidential speechwriter William Safire was on board but didn't exactly know why. Finding to his surprise that Herbert Stein was with him, Safire asked what this urgent clandestine meeting was about.

"This could be the most important weekend since March 4, 1933," Stein replied gravely, referring to the day when Franklin Roosevelt, three days after taking office, shut down the country's banks in order to stem the panicked withdrawals that were threatening to destroy the nation's financial system. Stein said something else about "domestic controls" and "closing the gold window," but with the roar of the helicopter's motors, Safire (who'd never studied economics) wasn't sure what he was talking about.

At Camp David, along with the President, Haldeman, and Ehrlichman, Safire found the men who made up Nixon's economic team: Treasury Secretary Connally, Fed Chairman Arthur Burns, CEA Chairman Paul McCracken, OMB Director Schultz, and Stein. (Connally's deputy, Paul Volcker, was also there, as was trade adviser Peter Peterson, but, significantly, neither Henry Kissinger nor Secretary of State William Rogers.)

Connally started the discussion by summarizing the positions he and Nixon had already decided on. The often-quarrelsome economics team showed less disagreement than one might have expected. Burns was recalcitrant about the idea of suspending the convertability of dollars and gold, but he was enthusiastic about domestic wage and price controls, having been a lonely advocate of them for some time.[46] The fact that the meeting amounted to a forced plebiscite rather than an authentic debate meant that discussion moved swiftly—and with surprisingly modest dissent. After only a few hours, the group adjourned, its work turned over to aides like Safire who were to draft a presidential address announcing the historic turn the country was about to take.

Years later, Stein reminisced about what he called "the unreality" of that fateful meeting:

> The whole atmosphere, and particularly the isolation from the outside, served to separate the group from the realities of economic and political life. They acquired the attitudes of a group of scriptwriters preparing a TV special . . . for Sunday night. The announcement—the performance—was everything. It had to be as dramatic and smooth as possible . . . But it was not regarded as a step in a continuing process of government. After the special, regular programming would be resumed.
>
> This suspension of realism enabled the participants to overlook a number of questions that would have been considered at length if the decision had been made in a less exotic environment.[47]

Nixon most of all seemed to embrace the peculiarly hermetic "suspension of realism."

Haldeman found the President the next night alone in his cabin "in one of his sort of mystic moods." With the lights off and a fire blazing despite the August heat, Nixon gestured to Haldeman to join him. "We're at a time where we're ending a period where we were saying the government should do everything," he said, pensively staring into the fire. "Now all of this will fail unless people respond. We've got to change the spirit . . . You must have a goal greater than the self, either a nation or a person, or you can't be great."[48] The next day the Camp David meeting adjourned. As the helicopters lifted off, the fact that it had happened at all, as well as the decisions taken, was still momentarily wrapped in the utmost secrecy.

Ever fearful of leaks from even his closest advisers, Nixon (with Connally's encouragement) had already notified the networks that he'd want prime time for a major address that Sunday night. Within hours of returning to the White House, the President stared into a teleprompter and began speaking.

The time had come for "a new economic policy for the United States," he told the nation. "We are going to take action, not timidly, not half-heartedly, and not in piecemeal fashion."

America would now be governed by his "New Economic Policy," under which he would impose across-the-board federal controls on wages, prices, and rents. The controls—administered by a pay board, a price board, and later a cost-of-living council—would be implemented in two phases, beginning with a ninety-day "freeze" period, followed by a longer phase (it ended up limping along until the spring of 1974). These controls, he said, would give the country the breathing room it needed to slash inflation, help reduce unemployment, and begin reestablishing stable growth. Secondly, Nixon announced a tax-reduction package that focused on greater depreciation allowances and a hefty investment tax credit, a tax shelter for exporters, and a repeal of LBJ's auto excise tax. To offset these revenue losses, he ordered $5 billion in spending cuts from domestic programs.

Internationally, he went on, the United States would cease converting dollars for gold (in economics jargon, he was "closing the gold window") and would impose a 10 percent surtax on all imports. Suspending convertability would stop the hemorrhaging of U.S. gold supplies caused by unnamed "international money speculators" who'd been "waging all-out war on the American dollar," he assured Americans. (In fact, it was America's major trading partners who, after watching U.S. inflation eat into the value of their dollar holdings, were insisting on holding gold.) The surtax would meanwhile significantly reduce "excessive" imports caused by the "unfair exchange rates" of certain American allies (Japan, unmentioned, was number one on this list). According to Nixon, having used American generosity after World War II to rebuild their own economies, these allies were behaving "unfairly" toward a beneficent U.S. But the value of the dollar would now find a "fairer" level. New U.S. exports and new U.S. jobs would follow from America's realigned balance of trade.[49]

To judge from opinion polls over the next few days, most Americans were delighted that Nixon had finally done something about the economy: 68 percent said they approved of Nixon's New Economic Policy; only 11 percent were opposed.[50] A few editorials embarrassed Nixon by pointing out that "new economic policy" had been Lenin's name for his reform policies in the early days of the Soviet Union, but overall the press was favorable, and Wall Street voted its approval with the biggest one-day increase it had ever had, followed by a record-setting week.[51]

Democratic Party leaders floundered at first, fearing that Nixon had deftly "stolen" the economic issue from them just as his opening to China had stolen foreign policy. But within days they focused on what they sensed voters would see as NEP's fundamental unfairness: the wage and price controls included no controls on profits or dividends for the wealthy, while the tax package included too much for business and too little for the average consumer. The AFL-CIO was even harsher, convinced that the inflation-fighting burden would fall disproportionately on workers' wages rather than prices. George Meany openly threatened to boycott mandatory wage controls, and let it be known that union leaders were willing to go to jail, if necessary.

Galbraith's home phone started ringing even before Nixon finished that Sunday night, and he was still answering reporters' questions at midnight. In *The New York Times*'s lead story the next morning, readers found him declaring that the NEP was "one step forward and two steps backward." Wage and price controls could be supported, he said, but the business-tilted tax reductions and the dismantling of Bretton Woods could not; he feared most the job losses that would result.[52] (Paul Samuelson, in the same article, said "he approved of everything" in the President's package except the federal spending cuts, while Arthur Okun praised the NEP as "a leap forward into realism.") For *The Washington Post*'s readers, Galbraith gave a more colorful response. Asked how he felt when he first heard about Nixon's new policies, he replied, "Like the streetwalker who had just learned that the profession was not only legal, but the highest form of municipal service." He took pleasure in reminding reporters that just three weeks earlier, Paul McCracken had publicly assailed him after his testimony favoring such controls, and had said vehemently that "the difference between Professor Galbraith and the Nixon Administration on the matter is clear."[53]

Still, several fellow Democrats—especially his friends in organized labor—were more than a little surprised by his apparent approval of Nixon's economic package, even though he repeatedly staked out his differences with the White House. In an interview that *Business Week* misleadingly entitled "Galbraith Gives Nixon an A-minus," for example, he made a point of underscoring the broader view of wage-and-price controls that he'd maintained for thirty years. He defended them as a legitimate part of an anti-inflation policy mix that also included sharply progressive taxation on earned and unearned income, surtaxes targeted to troublesome sectors, wage and price increases closely tied to productivity gains, and better unemployment compensation to soften the effect of rising joblessness when inflation slowed.[54]

To economists who snickered or pulled back in horror at the thought of such controls because of their effects on market efficiency, Galbraith replied that the issue for him was not about restoring optimal efficiency to an otherwise smoothly operating, equilibrium-based economy, but about leeching inflation out of an economic system that wasn't equilibrium-based, that concentrated significant economic power in a few hands, and in which producers, retailers, and creditors endlessly sought to stimulate consumers to make additional purchases in order to maintain their own profits.

With such an economic system, government had limited choices for controlling inflation. The orthodox alternative was usually to cut off inflation through the monetary system, by having the Federal Reserve raise interest rates. But this carried the heaviest costs for those least able to survive them, by causing a Darwinian purge of small businesses, high unemployment for workers, and mortgage and consumer credit contractions that might bring those at the bottom to their knees. As a Democratic (and democratic) economic policy adviser, Galbraith found that deplorable. What's more, as he pointed out, that sort of monetary medicine could be expected to work fastest, with the least harm, in the smoothly functioning system that traditional equilibrium-based theorists liked to imagine. But Galbraith held no such view of the American economy's actual structure, and disdained "the meat-ax of monetarism," since some business sectors and income groups were better placed than others to capture its non-equilibrium-based advantages, which in turn would eventually work themselves into the system once again as inflationary pressures.

The additional merit of wage and price controls, he noted, was that they forced out into the open the otherwise hidden trade-offs built into the economic structure. In a sense, they revealed the "political" dimensions present in an economy such as the United States', in which more than just idealized and abstracted "market forces" operated. Required to justify wage or price hikes, large corporations and unions would face public evaluation of their claims.

In short, Galbraith's overall interest in wage and price controls was fundamentally different from "Nixonian Keynesianism." It was not a reelection strategy, but a macromanagement strategy meant to deal with a glaring weakness in conventional full-employment Keynesian strategies. He was willing to support Nixon's shift to wage and price controls not as an end in itself, but as a step toward public support for a more liberal strategy. His deepest fear was that if inflation went on unchecked, it would gradually erode not only living standards, but public support for Keynesianism and for liberal, activist government. The Vietnam War had already done immense damage to public confidence in government; losing control of the fight against inflation would carry even weightier consequences.

As Phase I took effect that fall, both Nixon and Galbraith were thus pleased to see prices and wages quickly begin to level off. In mid-November Phase II took over, and both large companies and unions were required to seek government approval before enacting any significant wage or price increase. As more and more details of Phase II were released, however, Galbraith swiftly moved back onto the attack, repeatedly faulting Nixon's new system for its many weaknesses, from its announced temporary status to its lack of social equity to the specific decisions the control boards actually took. The whole effort amounted, he thought, to "one of the most cynically successful political actions" in modern American history.[55]

By the year's end, the news was dominated by the U.S. bombing campaign in North Vietnam. It was too early to tell how well the system would do its job, but, sensing that wage and price controls might just work at least for his purposes, Nixon began shaking off the worst of his fears and became increasingly optimistic that he would win reelection. Back from New Orleans and his installation as the AEA's new president, Galbraith was no less convinced that Nixon could be defeated, and was determined to do all he could to bring this about.

21

The Price of Hypocrisy

AS 1972 BEGAN, both Nixon and Galbraith fully understood the political and economic importance of the presidential election that lay ahead. For Nixon, the task was to convince Americans that the White House was making significant strides on both the Vietnam War and the economy, and that the worst was now behind. So in early January, within days of ordering a halt to his brutal two-week bombing campaign against North Vietnam, the President assured CBS reporter Dan Rather during an exclusive hour-long interview that the U.S. military role in the Vietnam War was finally all but over. It would not be an issue in the upcoming elections that November, he said, "because we will have brought the American involvement to an end." When Rather asked him to be more specific, the President declined to elaborate, but three weeks later he in effect answered Rather by announcing that in secret Paris peace negotiations, Henry Kissinger had outlined the U.S.'s terms for its full withdrawal. Now, Nixon insisted, it was up to the North Vietnamese to decide the next step, but as far as he was concerned, peace could very well be at hand. It was another political masterstroke that once again disarmed his critics, and it was capped triumphantly two weeks later when he and Kissinger landed in Beijing to begin talks with Mao Tse-tung and Chou En-lai on "normalizing" U.S.-Chinese relations.

The next step to reelection now rested on success in managing the economy. Nixon believed his policies were making headway, economically as well as politically. Under Phase II, inflation was still decreasing, and the administration scored valuable points among independent voters (and even Democrats) when the Price Council took a firm stand against price increases by some of America's biggest companies. (Unemployment, by contrast, remained persistently high, drawing the ire of organized labor, which kept threatening to boycott the wage controls.) At the Federal Reserve, the politically savvy Arthur Burns meanwhile began sharply boosting the money supply in a bid to push the economy upward in anticipation of November's election.* And Nixon, not trusting the effects of his New Economic Policy alone, ordered his Cabinet to accelerate spending to help feed the expansion the Fed was stirring. (Melvin Laird at the Defense Department loyally followed Nixon's orders by purchasing a two-year supply of toilet paper for the armed forces.)[1] America's would-be Disraeli was even trying (unsuccessfully) to convince his Council of Economic Advisors that this priming of the economic pump was not politics but simply part of his new Keynesian commitment to high employment growth, and would lead to the long-term economic growth and stability that had eluded Kennedy and his "fine-tuners" a decade earlier.

Galbraith meanwhile started 1972 by announcing his support for Senator George McGovern of South Dakota as Nixon's Democratic opponent. McGovern, tall and lean, with a broad round face, brown hair, and a distinctively protruding chin, spoke softly with the steady cadences and flat intonations of a Midwesterner. Fifteen years younger than Galbraith, he grew up in South Dakota, the son of a small-town Methodist minister. During World War II, McGovern served with distinction as a B-24 pilot in Europe, then came back to get a doctorate in American history and teach at his alma mater, tiny Dakota Wesleyan. South Dakota had been a firmly Republican state for years, but in the 1950s, along with a handful of other young veterans, McGovern set out to change that. Crisscrossing the state in his car, sleeping on couches in the homes of supporters, giving hundreds of speeches at fried-chicken-and-potato-salad dinners, he rebuilt the state Democratic party and won South Dakota's single congressional seat in 1956.

He and Galbraith had been acquainted since early in the Kennedy administration, when McGovern was director of the Food for Peace program, which distributed hundreds of millions of dollars' worth of surplus U.S. food supplies across the Third World. After his election to the Senate and Galbraith's return from India, their shared rural background, rise from modest beginnings, committed liberal politics, and early opposition to the Vietnam War helped them form an extremely close bond.

Consequently, from almost the moment Nixon won in 1968, Galbraith had been clear that he would support a McGovern presidential bid if and when he declared his candidacy. In fact, he did his own share in encouraging McGovern's entry in the 1972 race. Each summer since returning from India, Galbraith had gathered a circle of influential friends at his Vermont farm to discuss the future of the Democratic Party and of liberalism generally; Arthur Schlesinger, Richard Goodwin, Gloria Steinem, and McGovern were regulars. As Galbraith recalls it, "From the beginning [the group] assumed that McGovern would (or should) be the next presidential candidate," a choice made all the easier when Hubert Humphrey, Edmund Muskie, and George Wallace emerged as McGovern's chief opponents.[2]

---

*Burns later indignantly denied any political motives behind his actions, but his expansionist policies in 1972 closely reflected the advice he had given Nixon in 1960, when Burns was an economic adviser to Eisenhower, who had refused to press Burns's position on the Fed, to Nixon's near-hysterical distress. Nixon convinced himself that had the Fed been expansionary in 1960 as Burns recommended, he would have defeated Kennedy.

Displaying the same energy and passion he'd shown for presidential campaigns since Stevenson's in 1952, Galbraith threw himself into McGovern's in 1972. He began just as he had for FDR, Stevenson, Kennedy, Johnson, and McCarthy—by writing speeches; but McGovern was also clear about his respect for Galbraith's advice, and the sheer pleasure he took in his company. "I discussed everything with him in '72, from the war in Vietnam to farm price supports to feeding the hungry to cutting military expenditures—in fact, to converting military expenditures to civilian alternatives, beating swords into plowshares." And he got "more laughs and more good ideas and more stimulus out of Ken than anyone else I can think of."[3] Galbraith returned the compliment, calling McGovern "a man of kindness, fine intelligence, humor and stubborn honesty of liberal purpose." (After JFK's death he considered McGovern one of his two closest friends in politics; the other was Edward Kennedy).[4]

It was a feverishly busy year for Galbraith. He put the finishing touches on *Economics and the Public Purpose* and composed nearly two dozen articles and reviews. He testified on behalf of Daniel Ellsberg at the Pentagon Papers trial in Los Angeles, where he argued that prosecution of Ellsberg was illicit, since revealing secrets as Ellsberg had was a routine function of government, not a threat to the republic, and he testified to the instances when he had leaked secret government information while serving in the OPA and the Bombing Survey, and during his ambassadorship to India. He went to Paris at the invitation of Valéry Giscard d'Estaing to deliver the keynote address of a three-day-long French government conference on the future of industrial society, and with James Tobin and Kenneth Arrow, spent two weeks traveling and lecturing in China as guests of the Chinese government—they were among the first Americans allowed in after Nixon's visit four months earlier.[5]

He even briefly allowed his name to be floated as a possible Massachusetts candidate for the Senate, withdrawing only when fellow liberals pressured him not to run against the Republican incumbent, Edward Brooke, a Nixon regular who also happened to be the only African American in the Senate.[6] (Eugene McCarthy, running a quixotic and short-lived presidential campaign of his own that year, got Galbraith in momentary hot water with the McGovern people by announcing that if elected, he'd name Galbraith Secretary of the Treasury. Galbraith hastily assured McGovern that McCarthy had never consulted him on the presumptive appointment.)

Most important, he spent a great deal of time speaking on McGovern's behalf all over the country, serving on various policy committees, fund-raising, and giving dozens of interviews. He even showed up as the featured guest at a McGovern fund-raiser in Paris.[7] On the Democratic Party platform committee he led an insurgent campaign to stiffen top-bracket income and inheritance taxes, withdrawing only when McGovern said it would make him too vulnerable to Republican attack. At the Democratic National Convention in Miami that August, he helped draft McGovern's acceptance speech, served as a

Massachusetts delegate and caucus leader for his candidate—and proved to be a lightning rod for McGovern's critics within the party. AFL-CIO President Meany in particular so disliked McGovern that he withheld the group's endorsement, a first in its history, and at the convention singled out Galbraith for a blistering attack—many disliked Galbraith's Vietnam views as much as his support for wage and price controls. Galbraith and Walter Heller were part of an elite in the party, Meany fulminated, a pair of "economic jitterbugs"* who, along with gay rights and abortion rights activists, were destroying the party.[8]

Inadvertently, Galbraith had a hand in the disastrous choice of Senator Thomas Eagleton of Missouri as McGovern's running mate. McGovern's first choice was Kevin White, mayor of Boston, but White had headed the Muskie ticket in the state's primary and Galbraith, fearing a political gaffe of the first order, called McGovern to urge him to make a different choice. McGovern agreed, and said he'd move on to his second choice, Senator Gaylord Nelson of Wisconsin. When Nelson declined the offer, Eagleton was called.

Galbraith also worked as a paid political commentator for NBC, appearing each morning during the Democratic and Republican conventions with his conservative friend the *National Review* editor William F. Buckley. The two provided a predictably acerbic yet witty commentary on the candidates, the parties, and the goings-on at the conventions. The distinction between their respective styles was captured by one reviewer who observed, "Galbraith may be arrogant, but he doesn't look arrogant, whereas Buckley manages to look positively haughty. On the *Today* program, [Galbraith] at least seemed a benign, langorous rustic. In contrast, Buckley somehow always contrived to tilt his head in such a way that he appeared to be looking down at whomever he was addressing." They were a smash hit, and Galbraith later recalled that he loved the job most because Buckley was "the ideal opponent—pleasant, quick in response, and invariably wrong."

As late as April polls showed Nixon and McGovern tied at 41 percent, with the former Alabama governor George Wallace trailing at 18; but after Wallace was severely wounded by a would-be assassin in May and withdrew, Nixon courted his voters by attacking affirmative action and "quotas"—and never surrendered the lead thereafter. To woo moderate swing voters, Nixon tried simultaneously to demonstrate his "statemanship," to focus on the benefits of détente with the Soviet Union, and to contrast this with McGovern's "radicalism." Even though polls soon gave him a commanding lead, the ever-insecure Nixon left nothing to chance, probing the darker side of politics at every opportunity to ensure his victory. For example, hours after learning that Governor Wallace had been shot, he ordered aides to circulate the patently false story that Arthur Bremer, the gunman, was a McGovern supporter. His infamous "enemies list" grew constantly, and he ordered the IRS to review McGovern's tax returns as well as those of his top aides. Gal-

---

*Meany never made clear what he meant by this.

braith is proud that he appeared on not just one, but two, of Nixon's "enemies lists," "an achievement which accorded me significant standing—and envy among my friends."

Then in June, almost a year to the day after *The New York Times* began publishing the Pentagon Papers, the Plumbers were discovered while breaking into the Democrats' Washington headquarters at the Watergate complex. Although *Washington Post* reporters quickly established a White House connection to the Plumbers, at the time most American journalists treated it just as Nixon's aide, Ronald Ziegler, described it: "a third-rate burglary" with no relation to his campaign. Convinced he could ride out the scandal, the President privately justified the act to Haldeman by vilifying McGovern as "a damn socialist with a blind spot for communists," and let John Connally reassure him that the Democrats were "going through the throes of a suicide, which was fine" for Nixon and the country.[9] Two weeks before the election, worried because McGovern's numbers were starting to creep up, Nixon had Kissinger announce that "peace is at hand," although both men knew it wasn't.

In November Nixon swept to victory with 61 percent of the vote, winning 49 states. Galbraith (like millions of other liberals) was very disappointed, but dismay over the outcome of presidential campaigns was by now familiar, and he took a bit of solace in the fact that Massachusetts was the one state that supported McGovern. For Nixon, however, his 1972 landslide seemed to vindicate his entire career, the perfect answer to the critics who considered him out of touch with the American people. (Henry Kissinger, sensing Nixon's mood, had a handwritten note left on Nixon's pillow that night in which he told the President what a "privilege" it was to work for him, and how brilliant Nixon had been to "take a divided nation, mired in war, losing its confidence, wracked by intellectuals without convictions, and give it a new purpose and overcome its hesitations."[10])

Yet true to Nixon's haunted nature, rather than proving a source of joy, victory quickly produced one of his darker moods. The next day he demanded resignation letters from his Cabinet and staff, and told Kissinger that henceforth the conservative columnists Rowland Evans and Robert Novak were the only journalists he might talk to without Nixon's prior approval. The rest of the press corps, the President said, were to be treated as enemies. (Unconvinced that Kissinger would obey, he began talking to Haldeman soon afterward about dumping Kissinger as soon as Vietnam was "resolved.") But as November wore on with the United States and North Vietnam unable to reach terms, Nixon and Kissinger decided that it would take another massive bombing of the North Vietnamese to "resolve" Vietnam—to produce their preferred settlement terms. Kissinger told Nixon that the regime in Hanoi was "just a bunch of shits. Tawdry, filthy shits. They make the Russians look good, compared to the way the Russians make the Chinese look good when it comes to negotiating in a responsible and decent way."[11] He ordered the bombing of Hanoi and Haiphong at Christmas; this time it was far more ferocious than the year before, with 20,000 tons of bombs dropped, the most concentrated bombing campaign of the entire war.

FOUR DAYS AFTER Christmas, Ken Galbraith went to the podium before an expectant audience of 2,000 fellow economists, just as he had a year earlier in New Orleans. This time, though, he was in the ballroom of the York Hotel, in Toronto, his term as president of the American Economic Association about to end, his post to be taken over by his Harvard colleague and friend Kenneth Arrow. Normally, the president's departing address is noncontroversial, but the bombings were going on as he spoke and were much on his mind, as was George McGovern's defeat, not to mention a dismaying tenure decision his Harvard colleagues had just made. So he decided that in his final address, "Power and the Useful Economist," he would say as clearly and directly as he ever had what so troubled him about his beloved profession and its relationship to the world.

The haunting problem at the core of modern economics was, he said, "the willful denial of the presence of power and political interests" in both its blackboard theories and its attempted real-world applications. In both the neoclassical and neo-Keynesian traditions,

> by insisting that the individual firm or industries—no matter how large—are at the mercy of the market, and that the state and the interests of the most powerful and wealthy are at the mercy of the sovereign citizenry, conventional economists have presumed away the most compelling questions of our time—whether about growth, inequality, global development, the environment, resource use, or consumer protection.[12]

The Nixon-McGovern race had been a struggle about power, he said, and about the ability of the corporate "planning system" and its allies to bend the government to its purposes. Yet conventional economics insisted on remaining "neutral" on the central issues represented in the contest. He was not seeking a "partisan" economics, he insisted, though he knew many would find the comment sardonic. Quite the contrary: he was seeking "a more honest understanding" of intellectual "neutrality," one that taught that power and politics did matter and that a democratic government needed "emancipation" from powerful economic interests in order to be truly democratic. To do less was in truth "not neutral," and inescapably made economics "the influential and invaluable ally of those whose exercise of power depends on an acquiescent public."[13]

Remarkably, the applause was sustained when he finished, and most of the audience rose to its feet. A sizable crowd came up to him after the session adjourned, eager to talk. He wasn't able to stay as long as he would have liked, however, because he was due shortly at the business meeting, where more controversy awaited. The Wellesley economist Carolyn Shaw Bell was scheduled to report formally on the preliminary findings of the committee on the status of women in economics (appointed in New Orleans the year before). Galbraith had seen the results, data from the first-ever survey of women in the profession, and like Bell and her committee colleagues, he was appalled. Barely 2 percent of tenured economists were women.

The meeting was tense, the room packed. Announcing that they had received a Ford Foundation grant to disseminate the results of the study and to monitor progress on future hiring and promotion of women economists, Bell crisply noted that she and others who supported equality for women were prepared to use "other means to redress" the situation if progress wasn't made soon.

Galbraith fully supported Bell, and endorsed the idea of having an AEA standing committee on the status of women in economics that would press for rapid, radical change. At the Toronto meeting, there already had been quite a discussion of a related proposal that he and Lester Thurow of MIT had made and of draft legislation drawn up to implement it: under the Galbraith-Thurow plan, large corporations would be obliged to ensure that women and minorities were promoted or hired so that they held jobs at all salary levels in the company in rough proportion to their overall employment levels.[14]

The other topic discussed in Toronto that night was the fate of two young Harvard faculty members, Samuel Bowles and Arthur MacEwan. Both men had just learned that Harvard intended to let them go, and their case was about to become a new national cause célèbre.[15] The facts were straightforward enough—and, to those old enough to remember, eerily reminiscent of the Walsh-Sweezy imbroglio twenty-five years earlier. Both Bowles and MacEwan had Harvard doctorates in economics, both were well-regarded teachers, and both had been founding leaders of the Union for Radical Political Economics in 1968. As Bowles told the *Crimson*, the 15–5 departmental vote against his tenure "hardly came as a surprise," since the decision showed that the department's senior professors were determined "to defend the structure of power and privilege, both within the Economics Department and in the larger capitalist society." He and MacEwan had made it no secret that they intended to "serve those who suffer under the capitalist system, not those who run it." Bowles noted that their dismissal followed the department's release of two other young radicals, Herbert Gintis and Thomas Weisskopf, and the department's repeated refusals to award tenure to at least one radical theorist despite numerous requests made unanimously by the graduate students.[16] The facts of the case, and the underlying issue of academic freedom, concerned the AEA enough that in Toronto that night, after some heated debate, executive committee members voted overwhelmingly for a stiff resolution condemning "political bias" in hiring and promotion decisions, and "discrimination against radical economists or any others." Harvard narrowly escaped being mentioned by name—but no one doubted the resolution's principal target.

The fate of the four young leftists was also an urgent matter to Galbraith and to Wassily Leontief, Kenneth Arrow, and other senior men in the department. None of them particularly agreed with their junior colleagues' Marxist-oriented ideas, but they thought the young men were technically competent, Bowles and Gintis especially, with critical minds whose views were worth including in a department that after all had nearly two dozen tenured members.

Galbraith especially had good reasons for his concerns. The animus of conservative Harvard alumni toward both him and the other Keynesians had never really abated after his own tenure fight in 1948–49. An impromptu group calling itself the Veritas Foundation had formed in the Eisenhower years around Teddy Roosevelt's grandson Archibald, a prominent CIA officer at the time. (His brother Kermit, also in the CIA, had directed the agency's overthrow of Iran's democratically elected government in 1953 and the installation of Reza Pahlavi as the Shah of Iran.) Veritas and Archie Roosevelt dedicated themselves for the next twenty years to exposing the darker machinations of Cambridge Keynesians. "No matter what phase of left-wing infiltration we study," one of their studies reported, "be it in government, in information media, in foundations, in labor unions, whether we deal with Keynesian socialism, neo-Marxist socialism, or with Bolshevik communism, the tracks lead inevitably to Harvard." Galbraith, they said, was "the new crown prince of Keynesianism" who "had planted a swarm of their followers in government, and advanced his Keynesian views solely as a stalking horse for British Fabian Socialism, which was itself in turn nothing more than a stalking horse for Soviet Communism." Galbraith, the leaders of Veritas assured their fellow Harvard alumni, was a long time "extremist . . . and favorite of the Kremlin."

From the mid-1950s onward for two decades, Archie Roosevelt had also maintained an extensive personal correspondence with FBI director J. Edgar Hoover on the myriad dangers Galbraith posed, all of which Hoover added to Galbraith's already-thick FBI file and thanked Roosevelt for in appreciative personal notes. Always amused more than alarmed by the vitriol he provoked, Galbraith kept a copy of the Roosevelt group's lunatic exposés in his office library for many years, and reread them whenever he needed encouragement to intensify his efforts on behalf of American liberalism.[17]

By the time of the Bowles-Gintis debate, Galbraith also had learned something he hadn't known during the Walsh-Sweezy affair about Harvard's preference for orthodoxy in its economists. In the mid-1960s, his friend Paul Buck, the university's long-serving provost, had edited a remarkably forthright history of the social sciences at Harvard that revealed the embarrassing circumstances under which the Economics Department had been created in the 1870s.[18] It showed that President Eliot, the great modernizer of the university, had set up America's pioneer department of political economy by dismissing Francis Bowen, the university's lone teacher of economics, and replacing him with Charles Dunbar, an ambitious young Harvard graduate who had no formal training in economics but, as editorial writer for *The Daily Advertiser*, one of Boston's leading newspapers, was a vociferous supporter of both free trade and a gold-backed currency. Several wealthy Boston merchants who would benefit directly from lower U.S. trade barriers, and who were appalled at any weakening of the dollar, "made it clear," as Buck's study put it, "that Harvard should teach political economy and teach it correctly."

Bowen, who had taught Harvard's lone political economy course since the 1850s, had apparently incurred their wrath because he'd publicly supported the then-conventional wisdom among most Yankee Republicans, which favored tariffs (the GOP didn't really embrace free trade as a doctrine until after World War II). The tariffs, Bowen argued with some correctness, were needed to protect America's emerging industry from European competition. It was bad enough to these merchants that Bowen was advocating what amounted to long-term national gain at the cost of their short-term advantage; worse, he supported the apostate idea that the nation's massive Civil War debt shouldn't all be repaid to the private creditors who held it (Bowen thought the debt ought to be repaid, but below par). For America's farmers, workers and small businessmen—on whom the burden of repayment fell most sharply—debt repayment was serving to exacerbate the sharp recession that had taken hold after the Civil War. Bowen's quite popular view was also part of a larger "radical Republican" hostility toward financiers, which drew both on earlier Jeffersonian and Jacksonian Democratic ideals and on ancient roots of democratic opposition to the public costs of war financing. But to the Boston merchants—among whom many had bought government bonds as a lucrative wartime speculative investment in what they anticipated correctly would be a sharp postwar deflation—the idea of payment below par was not just anathema, but a sign of larger revolutionary danger that needed no encouragement from Harvard.

Seeking to rescue their alma mater from such self-evident heresies, these men, who included a number of influential Overseers and major donors, had thus pressed young Dunbar on President Eliot. Moreover, they offered to guarantee Dunbar's salary and to pay for an annual public lecture series on the merits of "sound money." Eliot, newly installed in office, succumbed to their blandishments and poorly concealed threats, despite a certain disquiet. He hired Dunbar (but sent him to Germany to study economics before allowing him to teach) and reassigned the indignant Bowen to a less dangerous position teaching Christian ethics.

When the Bowles-Gintis case reawakened controversy at Harvard over the "proper" teaching of economics, the hundred-year-old Bowen-Dunbar case was all but forgotten. But Galbraith was determined not to allow the frustrations he'd endured in the 1930s and 1940s to be replayed. Moreover, he had a fondness for several of these young scholars, especially Bowles, who was the son of Chester Bowles, whom he'd known for thirty years. Throughout the late 1960s, Galbraith and Bowles had kept up a lively correspondence on topics that ranged from the administrative details of U.S. aid to India to progress of the antiwar movement to the challenges facing liberalism from Nixon and the new Sun Belt conservatives. Both men were also proud fathers, and their letters made repeated references to Sam's progress from his Harvard doctorate in

1965 to assistant professor and then associate professor in 1971. Galbraith reported much as a guardian uncle would on Sam's latest papers and classes; a proud Bowles confessed that his son's work was too abstruse and its mathematics too dense for him to understand.[19]

Like many others of his generation, Sam Bowles was deeply affected by the civil-rights movement and by the war in Vietnam (from which his father, like Galbraith, had been one of the earliest dissidents). But of course the 1960s had done more than inspire youthful idealism. By the time the formal tenure vote for Bowles and MacEwan came up in December 1972, the white-hot emotions fanned by the strike of 1969 were finally cooling, but they had left scars, nowhere more clearly than in the Economics Department, now chaired by James Duesenberry. Duesenberry was a talented, tough-minded macroeconomist known for the sophisticated computer-based forecasting models he'd developed with Otto Eckstein and Lawrence Klein, and he had no use for radical economics. As he bluntly told graduate students after Bowles left, he "could not think of any Marxist who would have been given tenure and that the department didn't consider 'Radical Economics' to be a legitimate field of study."[20]

So perhaps it was no surprise that Bowles and McEwan were let go. Then, two months later, the department, in what appeared a reversal of policy, announced it would offer Herb Gintis a four-year nontenured post; but a month after that, seemingly out of the blue, the University of Massachusetts announced it was hiring both Bowles and Gintis with tenure. Galbraith had been covertly encouraging the University of Massachusetts to do just this, once it was clear to him that Harvard would never change its mind.[21] Simultaneously he stirred up a second hornet's nest by leaking word to the *Crimson* that Otto Eckstein, his full-time colleague drawing full-time pay, was allegedly devoting most of his time to running Data Resources, Inc., a company that he and a group of venture capitalists had set up to sell computer-based economic forecasting to business clients.* (Two other professors, Dale Jorgensen and Martin Feldstein, were also shareholders, and the firm employed other department members and graduate students on a part-time basis.)

Galbraith insisted that he objected to Eckstein's dual role as professor and businessman on principle. (Some years before, he had in fact proposed that the department itself incorporate its own for-profit economic research unit, so he understood the value of these enterprises. But his idea called for such a unit to generate additional income that could be used for offices, computers, and research assistance.)[22] And it was not the matter of full-time academic pay for part-time academic work that bothered him, he said, but rather that Eckstein sat on the department committee that oversaw appointments. (He had been among the stronger opponents of tenure for Bowles and MacEwan and

---

*Paul Samuelson mistakenly believed that the break between Galbraith and Gerschenkron dated to this episode. "Alex said to me that 'tattletaling was the unpardonable sin both at the shipyard and when I was a worker in the Social Democratic party in Vienna,'" and was furious with Galbraith "for the unforgivable sin of tattling on a coworker." But as Gerschenkron's biographer points out, this simply is incorrect (Dawidoff, *Flyswatter*, 306).

was contemptuous of "radical economics" generally.) To Galbraith, there was at the least the serious appearance of a conflict of interest. "Business ties necessarily impair the faculty's ability to impartially judge economists, especially radical economists," he told Duesenberry.

His complaint touched off a reappraisal of the department's unwritten rules on outside work. Not illogically, many of Eckstein's defenders saw Galbraith's protest as retribution for the Bowles affair and, more important, petty.[23] Derek Bok, still settling in as Harvard's president, was among those most distressed. "One might think that Ken would have felt vulnerable to the charge he raised against Otto," Bok notes, "given the amount of time he spent away from the university," although, he freely admits, there was a key difference: long before the DRI issue came up, Galbraith had asked to have his own salary frozen. "I think he felt he was doing quite well with his royalties and speaking fees," Bok says, "and wanted to give something back to Harvard as his intellectual home. It remains, in my experience, the only example of a Harvard professor surrendering a substantial portion of his salary."[24] Eckstein eventually switched to part-time status, and was cleared of any implications of wrongdoing by a department committee headed by Duesenberry, who said, "Galbraith is annoyed because his boy did not get promoted."[25] In 1979 Eckstein sold his share of DRI to McGraw-Hill for more than $20 million.

Galbraith's continuing dissatisfaction with what he considered his colleagues' unwillingness to accept a wider range of economic views led him, along with Arrow, Leontief, Albert Hirschman, and Stephen Marglin to float the idea of Harvard's creating a separate Department of Social Economy, where issues of income and class "would be taken more seriously," as he put it. Planning papers were written, a few meetings were held, an approach was made to Dean Rosovsky and to Bok, but nothing came of it. There was too little support and too extensive an opposition for the idea to make headway.[26]

In June 1973, Galbraith wrote Bok about what he had concluded after all these struggles:

> The harmony which one now foresees in the discipline is based on a general commitment to neoclassical economics or its applied refinements. Accomplishment in model-building and refinement is, I think nearly all would agree, an increasingly stern requirement. We would not again hire a labor economist who, like Professor Dunlop or Professor Schlicter, made his career out of a practical association with the unions and the problems of labor mediation. Professor Leontief, were he now showing the experimental tendencies that marked his early career, would be in trouble. Even his work, when firmly established, was not strongly supported. We would not have an economist who was too much preoccupied with the practical details of tax reform—unless he protected his flank by suitable theoretical or econometric exercise. My own past tendencies would certainly not be acceptable for promotion . . . What is not in doubt is that we are now very strong in the journals but much less

strong in the obscenely practical matters on which many people, including many students, expect economists to be useful.[27]

Galbraith sent copies of his letter to all the members of the Economics Department, although he knew by then that little would happen. Kenneth Arrow, however, was allowed to set up a small committee to review the curriculum. The "Arrow Report" modestly urged some new courses to explore "the relationship between society [and economics], as well as the hiring of people qualified to teach this field from coherent alternative perspectives." But this recommendation was ignored, and Duesenberry bluntly told Arrow there was "zero chance" of hiring the proposed faculty. Likewise the department's Visiting Committee called on the department to provide radical alternatives to the dominant curriculum, but was ignored. "It was all very civil," reported the *Crimson*, describing the meeting that tabled the Arrow Report, but "few had really expected any other outcome."[28]

It was no surprise, then, that in the fall of 1973 Galbraith was in a restless mood. He turned sixty-five in October, and sixty-seven was the age when Harvard customarily expected its professors to retire. His old friend Kuznets had announced his retirement, and Seymour Harris had just died. Arrow, who was fifty, was increasingly restive, too, and talked openly of leaving for Stanford. Leontief, who won the Nobel Prize that fall, the third Harvard economist in a row to do so, had been thinking about retiring, and ultimately left Harvard for New York University, where he continued his teaching and research into the 1990s. It seemed to be time for a change. In the new Harvard Economics Department, there seemed less and less room left for men like Galbraith, and there were no successors in sight.

Henry Rosovsky years later characterized the shift that took place: "Harvard's strength had always been in a certain academic eclecticism and an attention to applied problems," he said. "In fact, it wasn't until [Robert] Dorfman was recruited from Berkeley [in the 1950s] that Harvard really acquired a first-rate mathematical economist, and frankly it wasn't until the mid or late 1970s that I'd say we reached a competitive parity as a department with MIT. With all the retirements in the mid-1970s the department finally had room to make the shift complete."[29]

And the shift toward ever-greater emphasis on mathematically oriented model building was paralleled after Galbraith and the others left by a falling confidence in Keynesianism and the idea of activist government-led macroeconomic intervention. Martin Feldstein (who, in the 1980s, would become chairman of Ronald Reagan's CEA) soon became chairman of the department. Several years later, Robert Barro, a brilliant, young, and ultraorthodox pioneer in Rational Expectations and New Classical theory, was recruited from Chicago, along with some promising MIT graduates, all outstanding in their mathematical abilities but untested in the policy realm. But the recruitment of these gifted new colleagues (some, like Barro, were at least as conservative as

Feldstein, and others, such as Gregory Mankiw, were moderates who grew more conservative) was not balanced by the addition of strongly liberal, let alone "radical," faculty once Galbraith's generation was gone.

So perhaps after all it was time to retire. But what to do next?

THE FALL OF 1973 was a hectic time to plan a retirement, especially since public affairs were in such disarray. Less than a year after Nixon's overwhelming reelection, his administration was crumbling under the pressures of Watergate. Within three weeks in October, Vice President Spiro Agnew had to resign, Nixon's attempt to fire Special Prosecutor Archibald Cox prompted the famous Saturday Night Massacre, and war broke out in the Middle East. With that war came an Arab oil embargo and then a fourfold oil-price increase that effectively recast the world's economies and financial system. The hunger for Galbraith's comments from reporters and editors seemed insatiable. And at the same time he was marking the publication of *Economics and the Public Purpose*, the third book in what he now considers the central trilogy of his major works, which required the usual book-promotion efforts.[30]

This new book was Galbraith's most radical work, as befitted the times. Far more prescriptive than *The Affluent Society* and *The New Industrial State*, *Economics and the Public Purpose* was his boldest and farthest reaching attempt to set forth an alternative set of principles for organizing the modern American economy. Conceived in the wake of Richard Nixon's election in 1968, and finished after Nixon's 1972 reelection, it conveyed his sense of immense frustration with contemporary economics, and with contemporary politics and society. He wanted to break through the "conventional wisdom" on dozens of fronts.

What is surprising is the enthusiasm with which critics greeted the book. *Time* called it "one of the most important books of the year" and pronounced Galbraith "that rarest of social critics—a reformer whose new ideas are cheerfully anticipated even by people whose wordly holdings may be swept away if his programs are put into practice." *The New York Times*'s lengthy front-page review boldly promised that the book would "help create the kind of new political climate needed to break the hold of the great corporations on our national life."[31] According to *The Washington Post*'s reviewer, it demonstrated that "Galbraith and Paul Samuelson are the great teachers of economics in our time,"[32] and *Newsweek* judged it a "witty, trenchant, myth-destroying" proof that "Galbraith knows that economic systems are supposed to reflect reality; he also knows that ours does not."

> His books have been searching efforts to separate economic fact from theory. In his new book he has found what he has been looking for . . . Since he believes the Republican Party is "the instrument of the planning system," Galbraith's hopes repose in the McGovern wing of the Democratic Party. Will Galbraith's idea, which may be "radical" but certainly sounds sensible, work? Maybe time will tell [but it] sounds like an idea whose time has come.[33]

Even *BusinessWeek*, in a review written by the Republican economist Murray Weidenbaum, called it "a provocative book raising important issues of public policy," and clear demonstration that "Professor Galbraith succeeds admirably in the basic task of the teacher . . . to goad his student/readers into rethinking accepted notions and concepts and thus perhaps coming up with better answers to the serious problems which continue to beset us."[34] Six months after it appeared, *Economics and the Public Purpose* was nominated for the 1974 National Book Award in contemporary affairs.

In contrast, economics journals for the most part opted to ignore it. The *Journal of Economic Literature*'s reviewer, Barbara Bergmann, was, however, critical of the silence. "Though there is much to set the teeth of most economists on edge, one would have to be living in a Tibetan monastery, with one's only information about the American economy supplied by a subscription to the *Journal of Economic Theory*, to be able to doubt that major features of the Galbraithian picture of the economy accord with elements to be observed in the actual economy," she said.[35] Some prominent economists did offer their opinions: Herbert Stein found time to write a caustic review for *The Wall Street Journal*. But the fullest, most thoughtful consideration, by James Tobin, wasn't read by most economists because it was published in the *Yale Law Review*.[36]

That so many critics welcomed Galbraith's latest book from so many points of view suggests the roiling mood and divisions of the country in 1973, the more so because for the first time Galbraith was, shockingly, proposing "socialism" as a means to solve America's economic problems. He did this conscious of the predictable conservative and liberal reactions. Schlesinger had warned Galbraith not to use the term,[37] but Galbraith was adamant. "I'm tolerably experienced in the polemical aspect of economic discussion," he remarked to an interviewer. "If one doesn't use sharp categories, one is said to have left things unclear. And if one does use sharp categories, one is said to be simplistic."[38]

Yet as was quickly obvious to any reader of his book, "socialism" for Galbraith wasn't Soviet-style socialism or Chinese or Cuban; it wasn't even revolutionary. In Western Europe and Japan, he pointed out, governments had adopted one or another of his proposals without great disaster either for democracy or markets. But for the United States, which had always been at the conservative end of modern democratic capitalism's spectrum, he chose the provocative word deliberately. As far as he was concerned, the 1970s called for not one but *five* different kinds of socialism, each focused on different problems.

"Public Service Socialism" was a call for direct public authority over health care, public transportation, and housing; this would follow the patterns used in Britain, Germany, and Scandinavia, and would break through the tangle of partly public, partly private elements in an American system that functioned poorly in all three areas.

"Defense Socialism" grew from Galbraith's long-standing hostility to the "military-industrial complex": it was time, he said, to make defense contractors publicly owned enterprises, to destroy the destructive symbiosis between the

Pentagon and the contractors that led to wasteful weapons systems, bloated bureaucracies, and overseas adventurism.[39]

"Technostructure Socialism" reflected his conviction that stockholders of the largest corporations no longer exercised meaningful control over management and the technostructure. Better now to have the Treasury buy them out with government bonds, and place the largest several hundred corporate giants under public ownership, as Western Europe had already done in many industries ranging from steel to automobiles. Rich stockholders would be fully compensated but over time their fortunes would lessen, which would decrease wealth and income inequality. Management's salaries and benefits would be reduced but otherwise would be only modestly affected by the change.

"The Socialism of Ends" concerned the matter of direct public "planning" and the "coordination" of the nation's overall economic output based in democratic common values and public goals, beyond simply increasing aggregate production. The lack of such coordination—and instead the economy's merely responding to private plans reflecting the goals and interests of the great corporations—had led to what he saw as repeated shocking failures in the mix and quantity of private goods and services, and in the public sector.

By way of example, he noted that talk of the "energy crisis" focused on "shortages," which were in no small part the direct result of the private planning system's long-standing promotion of energy-inefficient vehicles and appliances, and by its manipulation of state support for the vastly expanded highway system while starving railroads and metropolitan bus systems. Private ends had captured public institutions and worsened the problems that the private-consumption fixation created. Unless the United States accepted that it already had a nationwide "planning system" in place, based in the giant corporations, it could not begin to move toward public coordination of resources and planning for public purposes.

Finally, there was "Socialism in Support of the Market," in which Galbraith called for increased public support for small business and for most American workers, which functioned outside the planning system of the giant corporations.[40] Here Galbraith showed how he understood his several "socialisms" as a mechanism of democratic influence over certain economic sectors that he was convinced had escaped the control of authentic market mechanisms. Both the market mechanisms and the public good had suffered. His call was for "actions by the state to provide the small firm with research and technical support, capital and qualified talent [to] reflect not preferential but compensatory treatment . . . [and] to reduce the inherently unequal development as between the two systems." He also favored affirmative "government intervention to stabilize prices and profits in the market sector," as an additional means to reduce sectoral inequality between large and small firms.[41]

But these several "socialisms," even in Galbraith's idiosyncratic use of the term, weren't his only agenda. *Economics and the Public Purpose* advanced a score of other nonsocialist proposals for a new American economy. For example, he called for an expanded and increased minimum wage; a return to a more progressive taxation system; a guaranteed annual income for the poor; sharply increased revenue-sharing with states and cities; abandonment of "full" employment, narrowly defined, as a federal policy goal; heavily increased funding for the arts; radically diminished power for monetary policy and the Federal Reserve; greater government support for unionization; international commodity price stabilization; the advancement, under certain specified conditions, of a "fair trade" policy, rather than doctrinal support for unqualified "free trade"; and an effective (rather than Nixonian) wage-and-price-control system.

Even so sweeping an agenda did not complete Galbraith's answers to the question, "What is to be done?" There were dozens more suggestions in *Economics and the Public Purpose*, covering issues from agricultural technology development to options for structuring the workweek. In effect, the last third of the book (the first two thirds gave the analysis underpinning his program) was a kind of left-liberal Baedeker's guide for remaking the nation, a reform agenda that rivaled in scope the New Deal itself—and even went beyond it.

He singled out two subjects for chapter-length attention, topics that were for many readers no less frightening or controversial than "socialism": feminism and environmentalism.

Modern capitalism, he bluntly declared, had transformed women into a "crypto-servant class," and he made his objections to their condition clear in epigraphs drawn from Betty Friedan and Lenin.[42] Within the modern-day culture of affluence, he said, women had become managers of consumption, but managers who served the ends of the producing goals of the corporate system, not their own. To remedy this, and to create authentic modern liberation for women, required new antidiscrimination laws in employment, public mandates and financial support for professional child care to working mothers, greater work-time flexibility, and affirmative action for women in higher education and the job market, especially equal access to its better-paid realms.[43] From such equality, he said, many of the changes he wanted would flow:

> It follows that, if women are no longer available for the administration of consumption and the administrative task must thus be minimized, there will be a substantial shift in the economy from goods to services . . . There are few matters on which the mind can dwell more appreciatively than on the changes that would occur if women were emancipated from their present service to the consumer society and the planning system.[44]

Concerning the environment Galbraith was no less progressive, expressing concerns he'd first addressed in 1958 in *The Affluent Society*, before environmentalism became a pressing national issue. There he warned of the "burgeoning" global population and the need for "space to live with peace and grace," as well as the rapid "depletion of the materials which nature has stocked in the earth's crust and which we have drawn upon more heavily in this century than in all previous time together."[45] This was in accordance with the book's overarching theme of bloated consumption. In 1960, in *The Liberal Hour*, he attacked the way America's "automobile culture" assaulted the environment with what he called "the ghastly surgery of the superhighway."[46] In 1967 in *The New Industrial State*, he discussed the private planning system's inability to incorporate the public goods expressed in environmental values within its goals. And in 1970, assessing President Nixon's environmental policies in an essay for *Life*, he argued for new environmental taxes, direct and indirect regulation of polluters and land and natural resource use, and a sharp reduction in production of polluting and energy-intensive goods, notably the automobile.[47] Now he integrated those concerns into his larger analysis and his prescriptions for change.

Damage to the environment, he argued, was a byproduct of systematically related problems: the constant, unreflective quest for technological innovation; an advertising culture supported by big corporations that met accusations of pollution with deceitful paeans to corporate "green" sensitivities; the dominant, unequal power of the forces of private consumption when compared to the forces that advanced the fulfillment of public needs; and the worship of aggregate growth at the heart of modern economic organization and economic theory. Only through an enlightened citizenry who forced its political leaders to pass laws establishing a new system of incentives and regulation could environmental damage be limited; left to themselves, markets would not find the necessary solutions.[48]

Galbraith characteristically introduced a strong cautionary note: environmentalists (like other reformers, left or right) would fail if they argued their case too absolutely. The public needed to be educated in environmental values, of course, but it helped to recognize the trade-offs. Some externalities could be regulated back into the operating costs of the polluting firms, and here markets and regulators could work hand in hand. But burdensome regulation that took no account of the potential worsening of income distribution (due, say, to plant closures and lay-offs, or to the increased costs of "green" goods) needed to be addressed head-on: reduction of economic inequality, not its increase, Galbraith insisted, had to be a central metric of any environmentalist and otherwise reforming agenda.[49]

The success of *Economics and the Public Purpose*, in both critical and sales terms, buoyed Galbraith.[50] It remained on the best-seller list for nearly five months, and was translated into seven languages. Although he later admitted to the datedness of some of his proposals by saying "time has proved kinder to certain of my writing than to others," most writers with a best-seller earning lavish reviews might have paused to savor their success—but that had never been a Galbraith habit. In fact, by the summer of 1973, he had already started negotiating the terms of his next project, the one that would let him crystallize his plans for retirement from Harvard.

The catalyst for the project came from an unexpected quarter: a telephone call from London that summer. A young man named Adrian Malone was on the line. Galbraith didn't recognize the name, but Malone quickly explained that he was a senior BBC producer whose credits included *Civilization*, with Sir Kenneth Clark, and *The Ascent of Man*, with Jacob Bronowski. Malone said he wanted next to do a series on economics, and was looking for a host who "had a sense of wholeness and who could cut across intellectual boundaries," someone who also understood that "television is a blunt instrument" and who could both write and narrate effectively within its stringent form. Would Galbraith be interested in being that person?

Normally shockproof, Galbraith was caught off guard, and for a moment his mind raced. How long would doing such a series take? Two or three years, Malone replied. Would it all be shot in Cambridge or London? Malone explained that it would be shot at dozens of locations around the world, so Galbraith would have to spend a good deal of time away from home, sometimes even for months at a time. After more discussion, Galbraith promised to think seriously about the offer and told Malone to ring back the following week.

Galbraith was most certainly interested by Malone's offer, but he also knew that Harvard would never approve his taking a leave to complete the series. Yet if he suddenly resigned at the end of the upcoming 1973–74 academic year—two years before his retirement was expected—some might wonder whether pique was involved, given his abundant and public frustrations with the Economics Department. The solution he reached, after much thought, proved elegant in terms of both Harvard's rules and public appearances. Officially, he would remain at Harvard for the next two years, and retire, as custom mandated, in June 1975. But in reality he would teach only in the fall of 1973, and devote the remaining eighteen months to this television series.[51]

Malone decided he could work with that schedule so long as Galbraith agreed to spend several periods in London on preproduction, which he did. Over the fall of 1973, Galbraith and Malone hammered out contractual details and began to rough out the thirteen-part series. In late January 1974, Galbraith flew to London to meet with Malone; his director, Richard Gilling; and two associate directors, David Kennard and Mick Jackson. Together, they settled on the program's structure, the predominant theme of each episode, and the series title: *The Age of Uncertainty*.

Working by turn in Cambridge, Gstaad, and Vermont that winter and spring, by mid-1974 Galbraith had created a detailed essay for each episode. (These essays, polished and reworked, became the text for the show's companion volume, also entitled *The Age of Uncertainty*; one essay, on the history of money, much expanded, became a book of its own, *Money: Whence It Came, Where It Went*.)[52]

With the essays done, a shooting script needed to be written. Here the work became more collaborative: Galbraith produced a first draft, which the television people pared and shaped to fit the medium. The job here was to create the lines for Galbraith's stand-ups and voice-overs and the dialogue for actors playing the parts of Marx, Keynes, et al. "There wasn't a sentence that didn't have three or four ideas in it," Malone recalled. "Sometimes they got so dense that the viewer would miss the point." The producer and his team spent a good amount of time trimming down drafts that Galbraith already thought lean.

Preparing Galbraith to narrate on-camera eventually required just as much attention from the director and crew. Never a patient man, Galbraith had to learn to put up with the stop-start-wait rhythm as the crews set up, waited for just the right light, paused if a cloud passed overhead, and shot and reshot scenes until Gilling and Malone thought they had it just right.

There were other irksome requirements that were new to Galbraith, minor but essential to the production. His hair, for example, was very fine and had a tendency to slip down over his forehead; when shooting began in the spring of 1975 it had to be secured repeatedly with hair spray. The need for consistent hair length throughout the series also meant that at the start of production, a BBC hairstylist spent what seemed hours to Galbraith seeking tonsorial perfection. Finally achieved, this masterpiece was then photographed from all angles, the photos serving as a template over the eighteen months it took to complete shooting, with Galbraith firmly enjoined to allow no one else to trim his hair during that time.

Clothing was also an issue: obviously, he couldn't show up in a scene one day wearing a red tie, and return to shooting it the next wearing a blue one. With parsimonious efficiency, Galbraith solved this problem by ordering his London tailor to make two identical grey-flannel suits, and buying several identical blue shirts and dark blue ties. Thus equipped, he spent a year and a half narrating scenes from Vermont to Singapore, "dressed as consistently as a clergyman."[53]

The greatest single annoyance over the period turned out to be Malone's "no skiing" rule. It wasn't actually Malone's but Lloyds of London's, which was insuring the production and which prudently felt that the accidental disabling of the program's star was not in its best interests. Thus, for two winters in a row, Kitty would go off to Gstaad's slopes each afternoon without him.

While Galbraith became involved in planning and preparation for the BBC series, his formal career as a Harvard professor moved inexorably toward its end, four decades after he first strode through the Yard. Having arrived anonymously, he was leaving a legend. Henry Rosovsky still tells what he insists is a true story that illustrates why Galbraith by then was considered, in Rosovsky's words, "the most famous professor at Harvard." Waiting once in Hoboken, New Jersey, for his car to be serviced, Rosovsky says, "In this squalid garage, in a squalid part of town, the grease-covered mechanic asked about my place of employment. 'I teach at Harvard' was my reply. 'Ah,' said the mechanic, in a muffled voice from underneath the car, 'do you happen to know Professor Galbraith?' "[54]

Of course Galbraith's impact had been at least as great in Cambridge itself. For someone who had spent as much time away from Harvard as he had—he freely spoke in a farewell address to students of "the forty-one years that I have been at Harvard, or, as some of my colleagues would prefer, the forty-one years

I have been frequently not at Harvard"—he was leaving behind a university with a high level of affection and respect for him.

Among students, Galbraith had become an Olympian figure, yet warmly regarded. In June 1975, the senior class voted him their Class Day speaker—the person they most wanted to hear at graduation, not the speaker chosen by the administration, because, as the class marshal put it, "He is respected because of his scholastic endeavor, but more than that, though he is not often available to students, when he is, he is totally devoted to them."[55] It was a commencement honor that hadn't been bestowed on a faculty member in years. In 1976, the Harvard *Lampoon* officially pronounced him still "the funniest professor at Harvard," and presented him with an enormous old purple and gold Cadillac convertible with just the sort of enormous tail fins that had been the object of his famous philippic against excessive consumption in *The Affluent Society.**

Another measure of his popularity among students can still be found in old copies of *The Harvard Crimson's* famed *Confidential Guide's* to Harvard courses.[56] In 1953, when he still shared responsibility for teaching Ec 1, the big introductory survey course, the *Confi Guide* advised, "The best lectures were by Galbraith and Baldwin who drew accolades for strikingly well organized, natural and rapid fire delivery." Two years later Galbraith's and John Dunlop's lectures "gave us a chance to hear some of the department's best people." By 1958, the course's reputation overall was suffering, and "students found the lectures worthless . . . Only Galbraith and Samuelson received any praise."

Galbraith also won praise in courses that he designed himself. About Ec 169, his class on Third World development, the *Confi Guide* declared, "A course with JKG is always enjoyable and informative and this is probably his best . . . [His] emphasis on the social and political problems facing the underdeveloped nations infuriated the orthodox Ec majors, but the uninitiated found themselves delighted with the broad perspectives gained."

By the late 1960s, the divisions bedeviling the campus showed themselves in the reviews of Galbraith's biggest course, Soc Sci 134, "The Modern Industrial Society." In its first review one *Confi Guide* writer acidly complained that the course was "more or less a summary of JKG's most recent book, *The New Industrial State* . . . The long ambassador, as he was known affectionately in India, has failed in all his past courses to demonstrate either economic vigor or an interest in undergraduates. And this new course will probably be no different. It will draw freshmen, awed by the name and reputation, and seniors by JKG's extemporaneous witticisms." But a year later a new reviewer reversed course: "Galbraith is a man who knows an awful lot and whose mouth relates with a great deal of clarity. He would, if our country decided such matters on these merits, make an excellent president."

Yet it was also true that, however warmly regarded he might be by some students, he was leaving behind few signs in his own department of influence

---

*Galbraith donated the Cadillac to WGBH, the local PBS station, for a fund-raiser at which it was auctioned off for a record $19,000.

comparable to that he had had outside academic economics. He had never been chairman of the department, for nearly two decades had not worked collaboratively with department colleagues, since the 1950s hadn't nurtured and cultivated doctoral students as teachers like Samuelson, Solow, Friedman, and others did as a matter of course. Meanwhile his output for academic journals virtually disappeared with the start of the Kennedy administration. Still Galbraith was well liked by most of his colleagues, and although they did not consider his work part of the profession's mainstream (a judgment Galbraith readily accepted), it was reasonably well respected. "Ken was gone so often," Rosovsky has recalled, "and appeared in the press so often with the sorts of celebrated people most of us economists never imagined we'd meet, that we thought of him as from another world. And yet any time he was asked to do something for the department or to help a colleague, he always responded generously."[57]

That said, Rosovsky quickly admits that there were "one or two exceptions" in the department in this attitude toward Galbraith. He declined to name them, but they undoubtedly included Gerschenkron after 1969, and likely Duesenberry and Eckstein after 1973.

Gerschenkron's stance was a special case, and his colleagues were often embarrassed and troubled by his attitude toward Galbraith. For example, the econometrician Zvi Griliches, who had voted against keeping Sam Bowles but considered it "a close decision," sent Galbraith a handwritten note in late 1973, apologizing for Gerschenkron's behavior toward Galbraith during a particularly unpleasant meeting that followed Bowles's tenure denial. "Alex's behavior" at that meeting was "entirely uncalled for," he wrote, and assured him that the rest of the committee thought Galbraith had been "very fair" and collegial throughout. He was sorry about the "obvious distress" Gerschenkron had caused, valued Galbraith's presence in the department greatly, and felt his work had "expanded my view of the world even when I disagreed with it." He ended by assuring Galbraith that "you are appreciated by many people here, more than you might think."[58]

Yet at Galbraith's retirement dinner,* there was a palpable sense that the Economics Department was changing fundamentally once again as it had in the mid-1930s when he first arrived. The retiring older generation included some of the leading lights of their generation, liberal economists who had proudly worked for Roosevelt and Kennedy, and who had supported and vastly refined the ways in which modern government helps to macromanage the national economy. Griliches's impulse to add a final reassurance by writing to Galbraith implicitly acknowledged the difficulties.

If Galbraith was dismayed, he did not let it show. Instead he reflected on what he would like to leave behind. In 1967, he had given Harvard a very gen-

---

*Gerschenkron forced the department to break the amiable tradition of holding a collegial dinner in the spring to honor all the men who were retiring or leaving. To everyone's embarrassment and distress, Gerschenkron insisted that separate dinners be held because he would not attend any event honoring Galbraith.

erous gift that for many years he insisted be kept anonymous: he assigned title to all royalties from the second edition of *The Affluent Society*, specifying that the funds be used for Harvard and Radcliffe students "facing an unexpected crisis in their lives," a polite circumlocution that meant Harvard was to use the money primarily to help with unexpected student pregnancies. Then when a fire damaged several colleagues' offices, he offered the royalties from *Economic Development* to help finance repairs. Subsequently, he gave the university's Fogg Art Museum his valuable collection of seventeenth- and eighteenth-century Moghul miniatures.

To mark his retirement, Galbraith settled on something more distinctive: he decided to establish an annual $10,000 prize for the best teacher in the Economics Department, to be awarded by a vote of the department's graduate students. Yet in his last talk as a Harvard professor, he firmly if gently told his listeners that it was not teaching alone that counted. In his Class Day speech he declared,

> Harvard has always had two kinds of professors, the inside people and the outside people. The insiders make their lives within the university community; the outsiders are only associated with it. The outside men—most of us, alas, have been men—are the best known; the insiders the most useful. They serve on the committees, help in the administration, know the students, attend at the Houses, see the university as the embodiment of their own lives.

But unfortunately, too many of "these truly unselfish scholars retreated from involvement with public issues and opted instead for the hassle-free comforts of academic routines."[59]

No one was left with any doubt about the choice Galbraith had made, or why.

22

The Great Unraveling

Many reformers—Galbraith is not alone in this—have as their basic objection to a free market that it frustrates them in achieving their reforms, because it enables people to have what they want, not what the reformers want. Hence every reformer has a strong tendency to be adverse to a free market.
—Milton Friedman

The modern conservative is engaged in one of man's oldest exercises in moral philosophy; that is, the search for a superior moral justification for selfishness.
—John Kenneth Galbraith

SHORTLY BEFORE LABOR DAY IN 1974, Galbraith's assistant, Andrea Williams, phoned him at his farm in Vermont to say that a special-delivery envelope had just arrived from the White House. It contained a letter from President Ford that he might want to answer promptly. Would Galbraith, the new President wanted to know, come to the White House to meet with him and his advisers? The subject was the American economy, and Ford would very much appreciate hearing Professor Galbraith's thoughts and advice.

Galbraith paused for a moment before dictating his reply to Mrs. Williams. Less than two weeks had passed since Richard Nixon's resignation, and now his successor was seeking Galbraith's advice! It was a fair measure of just how uncertain the country's new leaders were, he thought, that a Republican White House was asking for his views. After all, *The New York Times* had reported on his strenuous objections to Ford's proposed economic policies.[1] And yet he'd been expecting this letter ever since the unelected former Michigan congressman took office.

President Ford's invitation arrived, as luck would have it, almost exactly three years after Richard Nixon had launched his New Economic Policy, promising that with it he would banish the nightmare of "self-doubt" and "self-disparagement" that seemed to haunt America's economic future. Now, out of the wreckage of Watergate, Gerald Ford was being called to address the failures of Nixon's policies and the economy's continued great unraveling while his shattered predecessor brooded in San Clemente.

It was Watergate that destroyed Nixon's presidency, of course, but the failures of his economic policies were never far away and were always intricately related to his political maneuverings. Ironically, some of his supporters would soon highlight the linkage in an effort to rewrite history in his favor. Raymond Price, a former speechwriter, claimed that by "crippling" his presidency, Nixon's "enemies" had helped to "destroy" the American economy.[2] This wild, exaggerated claim was one more reminder of the anger felt on all sides of America's political divide. Yet Price was pointing to something profoundly important but barely understood by most Americans: the deep connections between Nixon's economic policies and his political strategies, and their consequences. His legacy wasn't just the shame of Watergate; another Nixon legacy was the fact that most Americans, as polls indicated, were no longer confident about the nation's future or trusted their elected government to lead them.

As the journalist and political historian Michael Barone has noted, "By early 1974, about 75% of Americans were saying that the country was headed in the wrong direction," a pessimism that was "wildly out of line" with even the worst of the Depression years, "when a confidence in the fairness of the system" still existed. Moreover those doubts couldn't be blamed on Watergate alone, because Americans' confidence levels didn't improve thereafter.

> The problem for the voters was not just discontent with their leaders—though that was part of it. The problem was that their way of life seemed threatened, the promise of continuing economic growth on which people had based their lives had been broken, the underpinnings of economic security which they had taken for granted had been undermined and it was becoming painfully apparent that the stratagems which had been relied on to provide economic security—rapidly rising wage contracts, Social Security and other cost-of-living adjustments, government aid and intervention programs—were only making the problem worse. The solutions and the theories which had produced economic growth and personal security no longer seemed to work. Neither the Republicans who had presided when they failed nor the Democrats who reaped the immediate political benefits of their failure seemed to have the solutions and theories to replace them.[3]

Yet leaders are expected to lead in such circumstances, and so to begin restoring that fundamental confidence, one of President Ford's first acts was to announce plans for an unprecedented "domestic economic summit," which, given the parlous condition of the economy, he insisted on convening in late September, just six weeks after taking office. At it, he promised Americans, he would gather leading economists, businessmen, union officials, and elected representatives; he was sure that together they could hammer out a plan to solve the problems Nixon and the NEP had left behind. He also announced plans for a series of "miniconferences" beforehand, each designed to air the very best ideas for curing the nation's economic woes. At the first of these smaller meetings he said he would set "the nation's top economists" to work "drawing up . . . a battle plan" against inflation. Hastily engraved White House invitations were express mailed to Galbraith, Paul Samuelson, Walter Heller, Milton Friedman, Paul McCracken, and fifteen others.

But the economists' meeting—like the other miniconferences and the summit, with its 800 participants—turned out to be a grim failure that cost Ford dearly because it produced no answers or solutions (unless buttons proclaiming "Whip Inflation Now" counted as such). His approval ratings plunged from 71 percent in August to 50 percent in October and never recovered thereafter. Yet the failure couldn't fairly be blamed on the President (though it was) because haunting all the gatherings was a fundamental question: *What* exactly was the problem? Ford and his advisers believed that inflation was "domestic public enemy number one," as he put it, which threatened to "destroy our country's homes, our liberty, our property, and finally our national pride as surely as any well-armed wartime enemy." With the Consumer Price Index rising that summer at an annual rate approaching 15 percent, its fastest pace since World War I, most Americans (almost nine out of ten, according to polls) agreed with Ford.[4]

To the surprise of many, Galbraith at the economists' miniconference agreed with Ford, too, which put him in the odd position of also agreeing with Milton Friedman, which the press noted gleefully the next day. But Galbraith's reasons sprang from a different analysis and entailed different prescriptions than Friedman's or the President's.[5] He focused at their White House meeting on two aspects of the political context in which the economy was then functioning—the public's conviction that inflation was the critical problem, and the inherently distinct groups and interests the two political parties served. The foremost challenge, he told the President and his fellow economists, was to control inflation as an economic problem—but to do so in a way that restored public confidence in government's capacity for leadership. This meant a dual struggle that called for a non-doctrinaire yet liberal-aimed Keynesian strategy of a specific kind, since standard conservative policies for dealing with inflation—tight money, budget balancing, high unemployment—had already failed.

Inflation, as he saw it, was being driven in complex ways by five major factors: the money supply was growing too rapidly; the federal budget wasn't taxing enough purchasing power away from consumers; a wage-price "arms race" was under way between big business and big unions; dangerous structural problems afflicted the food and energy sectors; and, most important politically as well as economically, the public's fear of more inflation was feeding inflation itself. Yet getting control of this sort of inflation wasn't a "matter of faith nor of ideology"; it "requires the same action of conservative governments and liberal." In truth, no single "economic policy" would suffice, because tactical flexibility was paramount.

Galbraith, to make that point, even allied himself with Friedman and President Ford in agreeing that the Federal Reserve had to tighten the money supply, although he said it must be very short-term, since its effects were "the most depressive, discriminatory, and dangerous of remedies." He also called for redesigned wage and price controls, arguing that Nixon's use of them showed not that they always "failed" but that they hadn't worked when "irresponsibly administered by men who opposed the policy, set up no organization for administration or enforcement, went, lunar-fashion, from one phase to another and fatuously promised that all controls would soon be ended." Taxes also needed to be raised, specifically through a graduated surtax on upper incomes, an increase in top corporate rates to capture windfall gains, and an environmental excise tax introduced to discourage energy consumption. Once prices stabilized, lower-income groups should then be targeted for major tax relief. Most important, what Ford, Friedman, and other conservatives were eager to do—force an immediate budget balancing by cutting spending, and accept higher unemployment as the inevitable price for their monetary policies—was completely wrong.

Galbraith knew that his ideas would get little support from his mathematically adept liberal colleagues at the miniconference. And indeed, Paul Samuelson spoke for them when he replied that Galbraith and Friedman were wrong to focus so heavily on inflation. "The number one thing wrong," he insisted—intent on resolving what he considered the theoretical crisis alongside the actual one—was the mistaken belief that "our number one problem is inflation."[6] He meant to underscore the extraordinary situation they saw all around them that September, the unthinkable conjunction (in economic-textbook terms, at least) of rising unemployment and skyrocketing inflation. With the jobless count more than 6 percent (and headed past 9 percent) even though inflation was nearly 15 percent, Samuelson wasn't alone in his stunned amazement at this repeal of the Phillips Curve. Even Fed Chairman Arthur Burns admitted that whatever this new condition was, it was virtually inconceivable to his once-confident profession. "I have been a student of the business cycle for a long time," he grimly declared, "and I know of no precedent for [this mix of inflation and unemployment] in history."[7]

Among economists at least, there was a name for what was happening, "stagflation"—even if none of them could quite explain it or knew how to make it go away.* Like scientists tracing some mysterious new plague, they thought they'd seen the first signs of this new illness in Nixon's first term, but because

---

*For the public, the name "stagflation" was new: *The New York Times*, for example, mentioned it only half a dozen times that year. And on Wall Street, just naming the problem was worthless. Traders there were in a near panic: the stock market had fallen almost 50 percent from its level a year earlier, and hit a new low as Ford and the economists talked. It was the biggest, fastest collapse since the 1930s, the start of a slump that would last nearly ten years.

their theories made no provision for its possibility, they had assumed it was some sort of temporary and transient anomaly.[8] Even as the problem worsened, most of them went on treating it as a mystery, while the few who ventured answers usually cited "anomalous" causes and circumstances rather than any "natural" workings of the economy.

One anomaly had come directly out of Nixon's New Economic Policy. By redrawing the international economic order created at Bretton Woods, NEP in 1971 had destroyed the old system of fixed exchange rates among the major nations and replaced it with "floating" rates, which most economists had applauded at the time. But the change hadn't produced the new order that theorists such as Samuelson (who supported the float) had anticipated. Instead a new world of quasi-mercantilism emerged, in which countries scrambled to protect their economies even as they professed higher loyalties to "free trade" and "flexible" exchange rates. The United States was as guilty as its allies in letting this happen, and John Connally jokingly expressed the Nixon administration's cynicism about the results, after the devaluation of the dollar and Nixon's 10 percent import surtax: "We had a problem, and we're sharing it with the world—just like we shared our prosperity. That's what friends are for."[9]

NEP's dynamiting of the old international order in 1971 was only the start; natural disasters over the next two years were compounded by more economic mismanagement. In 1972, extraordinary grain crop and fisheries failures, influenced by the then little understood El Niño current, occurred all over the world. The Soviet Union, hit especially hard, was forced to make massive, initially secret purchases (with Nixon's approval) in U.S. wheat and corn markets, which when combined with shortages elsewhere drove up food prices everywhere. Ongoing shortages and mishandling of farm surpluses by Agriculture Secretary Earl Butz a year later compounded the problem: in one month alone in 1973, the price of wheat skyrocketed 22 percent, corn 30 percent, and soybeans 45 percent. Nixon, panicked, ordered a new price freeze only to abandon it in embarrassment a month later when it visibly worsened the situation.[10]

Administration officials such as Treasury Secretary George Schultz repeatedly argued that in almost all of this, the White House was the victim of uncontrollable circumstances. But Galbraith just as consistently replied that nearly all these calamities owed just as much to the administration's missteps.[11] "Crops have been bad this year," he told a reporter, "but no one should blame anything on God as long as we have Nixon in the White House."[12]

Then in October 1973, as congressional Watergate investigators closed in on the besieged White House, a series of new crises struck. The coincidence of domestic political chaos and international danger could hardly have been worse. On October 6, Egyptian troops without warning swept across the Suez Canal toward Israel, while Syrian troops threatened the Golan Heights. As war raged in the Middle East, Spiro Agnew resigned as Vice President, having pleaded no contest to tax charges connected with bribes he'd taken. On October 20, Nixon tried to fire the Watergate Special Prosecutor, Archibald Cox, after Cox demanded access to the White House's secret tape recordings. Both

Attorney General Elliot Richardson and Deputy Attorney General William Ruckelshaus resigned rather than carry out Nixon's order to fire Cox; ultimately Solicitor General Robert Bork did his bidding. This "Saturday Night Massacre" produced a new firestorm of protests, and turned Watergate into a full-fledged constitutional crisis.

But by then, news had broken that sealed the President's fate: on October 17, America's oil-producing allies in the Middle East had announced they were embargoing all oil shipments to the United States in retaliation for its support of Israel. For Nixon's presidency—and for any hopes of a recovering U.S. economy—the end had now come. The following week, the House of Representatives agreed to convene formal hearings on Nixon's impeachment. Nixon now had just ten months left in his presidency. For the economy, however, the agony would go on much longer, as oil prices spiked from $3 a barrel to $12 by the time the embargo was lifted in March 1974.

For orthodox economists, everything about this litany of "anomalies"—from wage-price controls, through the food-price crisis, to the oil embargo and the subsequent price explosion—helped to "explain" stagflation. This was no neo-classical blackboard economy, with thousands of small producers and millions of consumers, each acting competitively out of rational self-interest to produce the equilibrium and optimal allocation of resources that Marshall and his followers took as the signal genius and beauty of capitalism.

Conventional Keynesians were even more perplexed. They had always doubted the self-correcting capacities of Marshallian markets, but all the sophisticated techniques they'd devised depended nonetheless on a certain predictability in the economy's response. Nothing about *this* economy seemed predictable, though. The Brookings Institution's Joseph Pechman, one of Walter Heller's "best and brightest" in the 1960s, spoke for many when he forlornly admitted that "the high rate of price increases during the recent periods of sluggish demand is a mystery that most economists have not solved."[13]

To Galbraith, however, the situation was hardly surprising or confusing, and perhaps he could be pardoned for feeling vindicated. In his diagnosis of stagflation and the remedies he proposed there was no break between Galbraith the economist and Galbraith the citizen and political activist. To him, the "anomalies" of stagflation could be understood by a "useful economist"—one who integrated politics, power, ideology, and historical circumstance to explain the actually lived economic world. Policies, he agreed with conservatives, had a lot to do with the problem, but this was a commonplace observation, since the modern economy was inconceivable except in the context of public policies and programs (despite most economists' presumption of the beneficent and omniscient operation of markets, with governments and public policies an unwelcome intrusion).

Failures by the conservative Nixon made up only one facet of the dilemma. Equally problematic was that no comprehensive progressive alternative had been proposed. Galbraith's mainstream Keynesian allies had largely failed in their attempts to fine-tune the economy in the 1960s for very specific reasons, he thought. First, they had analytically neglected until too late the economic effects of the vast American military complex, with its interdependent industrial and political base, and had underestimated the fragility of the Cold War trade and monetary system that accompanied it. Second, by insisting that economic policy was the province of technical specialists, they had helped veil the truth that most economic debates are ultimately political ones, and had helped vitiate both democracy and the ideal of an informed and engaged electorate. Third, by advocating tax cuts under Kennedy that took too long to reverse when spending on the Vietnam War soared and inflation appeared under Johnson, they had encouraged the public to distrust their right as professionals to manage the economy. Worst, their analyses lacked comprehension of the politics and ideology that undergirded the choices the government was making, both in its arms race with the Soviet Union and in its handling of the post–Bretton Woods economic system. And finally they either were unwilling to offer their own normative judgments about possible alternatives, or cloaked them in technical jargon.

Ironically, Galbraith noted, economists had contributed the tools of game theory and cost-benefit analysis to nuclear-war planning and military procurement, which increased the technical efficiency of the nation's gargantuan war machine, without ever truly asking for what end this efficiency was intended and at what cost. Whatever their personal preferences, conventional Keynesians, in pursuit of full-employment growth, had been fighting all these years for a bigger federal budget without clearly differentiating—for themselves or the public—the value of spending money on schools and hospitals from spending on tanks and guns, or raising the Galbraithian question of when exactly our affluence would release us from the treadmill pursuit of growth itself. In a perverse twist on their theory of "revealed preference," when it came to the Cold War, they had effectively left the selection of such ends to "the political process," treating the government's "taste" for arms and confrontation as an exogenous given, unexamined and outside their scope. On domestic economic matters, narrowly conceived, when they actually addressed "normative" issues such as targeted federal aid to reduce poverty, they had too often insisted on technical quantitative measures of "efficiency" and little more, replicating the then-fashionable (but later discredited) "Program Planning and Budgeting" models that Robert McNamara had introduced at the Pentagon. Galbraith was convinced that their narrow criteria had reshaped, and helped to destroy, a more encompassing theory of political economy that would take account of all the inherently complicated social, cultural, and political factors that shape American lives.[14]

Galbraith was thus unwilling to categorize the consequences of Nixon's wage and price controls as "anomalous." Unlike his Keynesian colleagues, he had repeatedly advocated the use of controls to limit inflation, "the clear and present economic danger that is potentially more destructive [than depression] of our values and amenities of democratic life."[15]

The Keynesian preoccupation with full employment suffered two failings that were now putting the whole Keynesian vision at risk, he thought. The first, which he had outlined in *The Affluent Society*, involved theoretical presumptions that Keynes himself had not made but that had become standard in postwar "Keynesian" theory. The Neoclassical Synthesis, affirming endless aggregate growth as the central measure of success, failed to break with the axiomatic celebration of the markets' "self-justifying commodity production," which had been the hallmark of pre-Keynesian microeconomics. This left its advocates pursuing the policy goal of planned "full-employment equilibrium" but without sufficient regard for what Galbraith believed were the structural problems the modern economy and its politics presented.

As Galbraith saw it—he outlined this analysis in *American Capitalism*, added to it in *The Affluent Society*, and in *The New Industrial State* incorporated it systematically into his theory of the "planning system"—the ability of the corporate planning system to manage aggregate demand through advertising's artificial creation of wants allowed it to pass on cost increases quite easily. This meant that the system resisted both conventional market-based pressures and Keynesian policies to reduce prices, and put tremendous pressure on the residual "market system" and its millions of smaller firms (responsible for half of U.S. employment), where prices and wages reflected consumer demand more closely and increases could not so easily be passed on.

In various, often dauntingly complex ways, this dualist structure in the American economy was at the heart of the "anomaly" of stagflation, he felt. In its crudest schematic form, prices rose in the planning system while unemployment rose in the market system. This meant that Nixon's conservative version of wage and price controls, cynically misconstructed from the start, had been doomed to fail because it made no effective distinction between the "planning" and "market" systems and, worse, lacked authentic support from Nixon's own advisers.*[16] The ninety-day Phase I "freeze" had "worked" simply because wage and price increases were temporarily made illegal, but Phase II had barely worked at all, just as Galbraith had warned. As soon as Nixon was reelected in 1972, it was effectively abandoned, which naturally prompted new wage and price increases.

Yet the truth—bitter for Galbraith and for millions of other liberal Americans—was that the cynically conceived New Economic Policy had been a great success as a *political* maneuver, for it had contributed to Nixon's overwhelming 1972 reelection. This in turn challenged the liberal conception of democratic politics and power at the heart of Galbraith's economics.

Galbraith had always focused on democracy—the intelligence and informed engagement of a country's citizens—as the engine meant to drive not just the part of human life designated as "political" but much about the "economic" sector as well. His oft-repeated insistence that "economics does not

---

*Nixon's Phase II controls did require the nation's 1,500 largest firms to get specific permission to raise prices, and the pay board focused on large union contracts. But enforcement was so weak that the companies found myriad ways to evade public control. As the chairman of the Price Commission sheepishly admitted, "My knowledge of economics and past price controls was abysmal."

usefully exist apart from politics" expressed his abiding commitment to a concept of democracy that owes much to pragmatists such as the philosopher John Dewey and to Galbraith's vivid sense of the tangible successes that liberal Democrats had achieved after Roosevelt won office in 1932. But with Nixon's reelection in 1972, there had been signs of a fundamental political realignment, of a permanent unraveling of the electoral coalition on which Roosevelt's accomplishment, however unsteadily, had once rested.

The white South held the key to this new world. Fervently Democratic as a result of the Civil War, white Southerners had become and remained part of the New Deal coalition thanks not only to their antipathy toward Republicans but also to an endless stream of subsidies—public works and farm supports in the 1930s, military base and plant sitings during and after the war—and to Roosevelt's calculated inaction on racial discrimination. But by 1972 most white Southerners could no longer abide the national Democratic Party and certainly not George McGovern. Everything about Yankee liberals like this presidential candidate seemed alien, especially the "traitorous" positions they took on civil rights, the Vietnam War, and the noisy, rebellious counterculture of the 1960s. In 1960, despite widespread misgivings, the South had overcome its historic anti-Catholicism to help elect John F. Kennedy as President; in 1972, just one in eight white Southerners voted for McGovern.[17] Despite Watergate and Nixon's humiliating departure, it was evident that liberal politics were still unable to claim influence or leadership—and economic policy and theory kept moving rightward, too.

The hard question was how to rebuild the Democratic Party—and Nixon's ignominy created what seemed a golden opportunity. In November 1974, the GOP was humiliated for a second time in three months, losing forty-six seats in the House and four in the Senate, almost all of them outside the party's new Confederate heartland.

But the new generation of Democratic leaders, the affluent and educated sons and daughters of Galbraith's generation, brought with them a new politics; they were bonded much more by their loathing of Nixon and the hated Vietnam War than they were committed either to the old New Deal coalition or to voters of the Democratic blue-collar base who had supported the war. Their instincts were anti-authoritarian and, while culturally egalitarian, disconnected from the bread-and-butter lunchpail issues and traditional values still so central to millions of Americans. Environmentalism, feminism, and limits on the growth and abuse of executive power were their mantras. The party's elders railed against them, convinced that whatever road the Democrats should take—with or without the South—theirs was not it. In the context of this divided, drifting Democratic Party, a resurgent New Right (which hated Nixon almost as much as it hated liberal Democrats) moved to fill the void in politics.

FOR GALBRAITH, THE two most visible apostles of the new post-Watergate era were Gerald Ford's Treasury Secretary William Simon and CEA Chairman Alan Greenspan. Simon, a millionaire Wall Street bond trader, was tall, angular, and intensely combative—an economic conservative of near-religious zeal. The difference between the GOP and its Democratic opponents was nothing less than "the difference between freedom and socialism," according to Simon, and liberalism was a mere "hash of statism, collectivism, egalitarianism, and the anticapitalism" that rendered "even the most innately brilliant of men stupid."[18] When Ford's economists urged a modest budget deficit in order not to worsen the economy's contraction, Simon would have none of such leftward apostasy. The required policy was old and simple, he thundered: "Balance the budget, period!"[19]

Simon's worldview, as Galbraith often pointed out, was in many ways reminiscent of an earlier Republican era, of Calvin Coolidge and Herbert Hoover, and especially Hoover's Treasury Secretary, Andrew Mellon, the millionaire banker-industrialist who after Wall Street's collapse in 1929 urged further firings and forced bankruptcies as a cure for the Depression. Simon's views were in fact so antediluvian that more sophisticated GOP economists like Herbert Stein caustically referred to them as the party's "old-time religion."[20]

Alan Greenspan, though more subtle than Simon, was the other new-policy apostle. President Ford's rumpled, stoop-shouldered chief economist shared Simon's overall view that now was not the time for a loose or accommodative fiscal policy along Keynesian lines. The origins of Greenspan's views on this were different than Simon's: he was a former jazz musician who'd come to economics circuitously, via the exotic libertarianism of the novelist-philosopher Ayn Rand, the author of *Atlas Shrugged* and *The Fountainhead*. Like Simon, however, he eventually built his career in business, and their corporate experience had brought them to roughly the same judgments. (Greenspan had one advantage over the needlessly antagonistic Simon: his capacity for tactically inspired ambiguity. As one frustrated Washington journalist put it, "he had a rare talent for exuding gobbledygook."[21])

Galbraith watched Simon and Greenspan carefully at Ford's economic summit in September 1974, and he wasn't surprised when their influence on the hapless President meant that Ford's first budget assumed that, as the price for defeating inflation, the nation would have to endure a recession twice as deep as any since World War II, with unemployment averaging at least 7 percent for the rest of the 1970s and no hope of growth above 1 percent. Even under these draconian conditions, the budget made no promise that inflation would come down any time soon to the 2 to 3 percent postwar levels once considered dangerously high.

This stunning economic projection came with an equally stunning rejection of the idea that government policy could do much more than administer the castor oil. Yet in defending the new White House policy line, for once Greenspan unwisely eschewed gobbledygook. The function of economic advisers was, he told the press, "not to think up a report to restore confidence—our job is to tell it as it is."[22] As Galbraith correctly predicted in *The New York Times*, reality would resist this harshly narrow conception of government's macromanagement function: Greenspan's "tell it as it is" policy vanished after

President Ford, in faithful obedience to it, refused to bail out a nearly bank-rupt New York City, producing the famous *New York Daily News* headline, "Ford to City: Drop Dead." When the city came near to defaulting soon after, spreading panic in the very bond markets where Simon had made his fortune, a wiser politics reasserted itself. (By the time Washington eventually stepped in, however, the bailout cost the market billions of dollars more than it would have had the White House acted sooner and more wisely.)

Yet to Galbraith's dismay, the drifting and divided congressional Democrats offered no alternatives. As the *Washington Post* reporter Hobart Rowen noted, "For all the noise Democratic politicians made about the inadequacy of Ford's economic programs, they pretty much bought his line. There was little to dis-tinguish [their] unemployment and budget deficit targets from Ford's. Both parties more or less accepted Greenspan's analysis that excessive stimulation would merely regenerate inflation."[23] The failure by Democrats to challenge an unpopular president underscored again the isolation of the traditional liberals, and its consequence: a broken party that could produce only verbal dissent and programmatic cooperation.

There was one notable exception, but it was to prove star-crossed: Shortly before Nixon resigned, Augustus Hawkins, a veteran African American con-gressman from Los Angeles, had introduced in the House what became known as the Humphrey-Hawkins Bill, touting it as "finally doing what the Full Em-ployment Act [*sic*] of 1945" had always intended: mandate full employment as a national policy, with the federal government legally obliged to achieve it. But in the nearly four years it took for the bill to become law—midway through the Carter administration, in 1978—its odyssey expressed much of liberalism's chaotic disorganization.

In virtually every respect, from Galbraith's point of view, Humphrey-Hawkins represented the worst of liberal remedies. It was built on the simpli-fied premise that stagflation was the result of underconsumption caused by maldistribution of income, and argued wrongly that by encouraging economic growth through government spending with little regard for inflation and by mandating employment as a legally enforceable right, the United States could restore itself to vigorous economic health. (Leon Keyserling was among the bill's most vocal proponents, because, as Galbraith quipped, it was "all Keyser-ling and no Keynes.")

After Jimmy Carter came to the White House in 1977, passage of the bill unfortunately became a test of strength that pitted a cautious Democratic president preaching "hard choices" and "national austerity" (in echo of Gerald Ford) against congressional liberal lions such as Humphrey and Kennedy, as well as the Congressional Black Caucus and the major trade unions. Passage of Humphrey-Hawkins from its draft to final form replayed in slow motion the evisceration of the Full Employment Bill that occurred under Truman: the fi-nal version contained no enforcement powers and offered little more than symbolic commitment to full employment.

To Galbraith, Humphrey-Hawkins was a mistake from the start, not only

A collage made by Mrs. Kennedy after her trip to India, showing Galbraith atop an elephant.

The Galbraith family in the early 1960s, at home in Cambridge: (left to right) Kitty, James, John Kenneth, Alan, and Peter.

President Johnson and Galbraith, walking past the Rose Garden in January 1966. Unlike many New Frontiersmen, Galbraith worked energetically for Johnson until he broke with him over the Vietnam War.

Galbraith and Johnson discussing economic policy in May 1966.

Galbraith greeting President and Mrs. Johnson in May 1966. On the right, FBI Director J. Edgar Hoover watches carefully; the Bureau maintained extensive, often wildly inaccurate, files on Galbraith for more than forty years.

After supporting Senator Eugene McCarthy in the 1968 Democratic primaries, Galbraith reluctantly but energetically campaigned for Hubert Humphrey against Richard Nixon that autumn. A group of protesters organized by Abbie Hoffman sent this "streaker," carrying the head of a pig on a tray, to protest Galbraith's speech at a Humphrey fund-raiser.

Galbraith showing an aspect of his Scotch-Canadian heritage at one of the annual Jimmy Fund skating events at Harvard, which raise money for pediatric cancer care and research.

Gloria Steinem and Galbraith, at the Galbraiths' home in Vermont in 1970.

Galbraith with his friend and sparring partner William F. Buckley, Jr., before a television appearance.

Galbraith walking Senator George McGovern to his car as he leaves the Galbraiths' home at 30 Francis Avenue in 1972. The South Dakota senator was a presidential candidate that year, and Galbraith president of the American Economic Association.

Galbraith on a parked motorcycle in Paris. He was there to work on The Age of Uncertainty.

Professor Galbraith in Paris, 1977.

Galbraith with President Jimmy Carter during the Camp David meetings in 1978.

*Galbraith with his old friend, neighbor, and colleague Arthur M. Schlesinger, Jr.,
at Galbraith's home in Cambridge.*

Galbraith with Alan Greenspan and Senator Daniel Patrick Moynihan, his old Harvard neighbor, before testifying on Reagan's budget before the Senate Finance Committee in 1983.

To Prof. and mrs galbraith, what a wonderful return to cambridge! affectionately, Benazir

The Galbraiths and Senator Edward Kennedy with Prime Minister Benazir Bhutto of Pakistan, when she visited Cambridge in 1989. The Galbraiths had enjoyed "Pinky" Bhutto as an undergraduate at Harvard years earlier; she inscribed the picture: "To Prof. and Mrs. Galbraith, what a wonderful return to Cambridge! affectionately, Benazir."

Galbraith with Mikhail and Raisa Gorbachev, on their visit to Cambridge in 1992. Senator Kennedy is at the back, on the left.

Ken and Kitty Galbraith with Barbra Streisand, after she spoke at the Kennedy School in 1995.

The Galbraiths with President Bill Clinton, when Ken received the Presidential Medal of Honor.

With the Canadian novelist Robertson Davies, at Galbraith's eighty-fifth birthday party, held at the Boston Public Library in 1993.

With Julia Child at the birthday party. The Galbraiths and the Childs were longtime neighbors and friends.

With the publisher of The Washington Post, *Katharine Graham, a friend for nearly fifty years, at Galbraith's ninetieth birthday party.*

With former Labor Secretary Robert Reich at the birthday party. The diminutive Reich likes to say that he was as tall as Galbraith until he began studying economics.

The Galbraiths, their sons and daughters-in-law, and their grandchildren, at his ninetieth birthday party.

Photograph by John Goodman

Kitty and Ken Galbraith in Vermont.

bad policy but bad politics. Ham-fisted full-employment policies risked corrosive inflation, which in turn would erode support for authentic Keynesianism and for Democratic liberals. It would be better, Galbraith thought, to bring inflation quickly under control while paying out generous unemployment benefits. But this view left him in an awkward situation: to the consternation of friends, he and Milton Friedman once again were on one side of the argument, while allies like Senators Humphrey and Kennedy were on the other.

LIBERAL POLITICS AND Keynesian public policy weren't the only casualties of the great unraveling that Nixonian Keynesianism had unleashed. In academic circles, Keynesianism as theory was undergoing the most sustained and powerful assault since *The General Theory*'s appearance forty years earlier. New and gifted critics known as "rational expectationists" were declaring the final demise of Keynesianism as policy *and* as theory, which even Schumpeter, Hayek, and Friedman had never imagined possible. At the University of Chicago, one of Friedman's brightest students, Robert Lucas, betrayed no hint of doubt or qualification as he announced what he and fellower "rat-exers" believed they had finally demonstrated: "Keynesian orthodoxy is in deep trouble, the deepest kind of trouble in which an applied body of theory can find itself," he declared. "It appears to give seriously wrong answers to the most basic questions of macroeconomic policy."[24]

Lucas shed no tears about this pronouncement. He and his allies were aggressive new fundamentalists who saw their most pressing duty as sweeping the Augean stable of economics clean of the Keynesian waste that had accumulated over forty years. In fact, they looked at the problems of American economics rather as the newly insurgent religious fundamentalists led by Jerry Falwell and his Moral Majority viewed the state of American morals. To "rat-exers," Keynesianism had corrupted economics by ignoring the "eternal truths" embodied in microeconomic axioms of an earlier era and in the process had dragged the United States into a quagmire of sloth, inefficiency, and bloated government. So passionate were they in their new convictions that, amazingly, even Milton Friedman and monetarism were suspect sinners. Galbraith, needless to say, was beyond the pale.

For young economists like Lucas, the old "truths" were easily summarized. Human beings are always and everywhere rational maximizers of their individual self-interest; markets, left to themselves, optimize economic outcomes; and government acts (with only a handful of exceptions) to distort markets and, therefore, the economy's efficient operation. Keynesian attempts at macromanagement were the worst kind of market interference (short of socialism) because they deceitfully promised that under the tutelage of intelligent economists, public policy could somehow override or repeal these "eternal" rules. Keynesians were, in effect, liberal necromancers who had gulled the public into thinking they could control the motion of the sun and stars.

In their hostility to Keynes, Lucas and his fellow rat-exers were hardly breaking new ground. What set them apart from, say, a *Wall Street Journal* editorialist like Robert Bartley or a conservative economist-turned-politician like Phil Gramm of Texas were their theoretically sophisticated refinements, the most important of which involved the idea of "rational expectations" itself. If one presumes that individuals are rational self-maximizers, it follows that they will fully incorporate all available information in evaluating their economic environment. As a simple deduction from the premise of rational self-maximizing, this claim seems almost trivial, but it contained a dangerous trapdoor for mainstream Neoclassical Synthesizers, who prided themselves on welding Keynes's macroeconomic focus to pre-Keynesian microeconomic assumptions.

For years the mainstream Keynesians believed that with their large-scale computer-based models of the U.S. economy, they could eventually forecast economic performance accurately, which in turn would let them modulate government macromanagement to optimize total output. As the sophistication of their computers and their mathematics advanced in the late 1950s and 1960s, they believed they were nearing their goal. But by the mid-1970s, stagflation, oil shocks, monetary instability, and the newly complicated international environment played havoc with their models. To some Keynesian modelers, the solution was to change a few equations and assumptions; to rational expectationists, however, the havoc was a function of a fundamental flaw in Keynesianism itself.

All the old models required estimates of what the economic actors expected as well as of their current behavior. The Keynesians used what they called "adaptive expectations," meaning that individuals and firms formed their expectations about future inflation by looking at past inflation rates—in other words, adapting what they learned from history to form judgments about the future. But if individuals and firms maximize rationally, then people don't use merely "adaptive expectations." Instead, they fully incorporate not just historical patterns but all the currently available information, which makes their behavior more nimble than "adaptive" models would predict. In the case of inflation, if people come to expect that it will soon fall, they will rationally alter their own behavior accordingly, even before inflation actually begins to fall.

The argument had devastating implications for activist government policy of the kind that liberal Keynesians supported. The policies couldn't possibly exert the powerful long-run effects they claimed for them because people, using "rational expectations," would perceive the government's intention and the likely reactions of others and then act in ways that inevitably blunted the policies' effectiveness. This "Policy-Ineffectiveness Proposition" meant that the true goal of government should be not *better* economic policy but *less* policy, leaving markets free to work their magic unburdened by regulatory interference.

As a rigorous, mathematically accomplished defense of pre-Keynesian orthodoxy, Rational Expectations was a stunning success, and it did the Keynesians what seemed terrible, some thought fatal, damage. One rat-exer gloated,

> It means that hundreds of laws and thousands of dissertations, books, and articles . . . have been pointless. It means that all macroeconomic models that

business and government rely on for their economic planning are useless except in the narrowest of circumstances. And that's the *good* news for the Keynesians!

Confident that the battle had been decided, he continued:

> Rational expectations, in sum, avoids the errors of Keynesian economics by applying a few well-established classical principles. It corrects the Keynesian assumption of irrational ["adaptive"] expectations with the established assumption that agents optimize or, in other words, form the best expectations possible with the information available to them. It avoids Keynesian inconsistencies by building all its theoretical structures on the same foundation, on coherent assumptions about optimizing agents. Finally, it avoids arbitrary Keynesian goals that are only proxies for individual welfare, such as economic growth, by seeking to improve individual welfare in more direct ways.[25]

The sheer theoretical beauty and rigorous internal consistency of Rational Expectations—its "blackboard seductiveness," as one economist put it—gave birth to a "New Classical Economics," a buoyant school of thinkers (including Lucas, Robert Barro, and Thomas Sargent) who saw themselves as the rightfully dominant replacement for the failed Keynesians.[26] Yet the fact that even classical, pre-Keynesian economics was intimately concerned with issues of wage and price rigidities, non-market-clearing prices, irrational expectations, and the strong real effects of money in the short run seemed to elude the New Classical fundamentalists, who went beyond the core Rat-Ex insights to develop an elaborate system that emphasized the constant "market clearing" of all economic actors and a consequent constant equilibrium of markets. But in doing so, they were sure they were purging economics of the false idols that devilish Keynesians had introduced—claims about economic behavior grounded in ideas like liquidity preference and the Phillips Curve, which Keynesians could observe in real life but couldn't derive analytically from purified microeconomics' foundational assumptions.[27]

"The goal of the New Classical revolution," wrote Gregory Mankiw, "was to rebuild macroeconomics beginning with microeconomic primitives of preferences and technology."[28] The Keynesian world acknowledged the messiness of human history, the reality of ignorance and miscalculation, and the inescapable uncertainty of life, whereas the New Classical fundamentalists' pristine creation was a macroeconomic universe that ran solely according to microeconomic principles. It was like a version of eighteenth-century deism's extraordinary philosophical creation "the universe that runs like a clock," from which God's presence was purged save only as the infinite watchmaker who set the process in motion.

The rigorous, conservative, self-confident puritanism of 1970s anti-Keynesians seemed almost unstoppable, especially as it advanced into the heart of Cambridge itself, which for forty years had been the Keynesian Rome.

Led by Stanley Fischer and Rudiger Dornbusch, whom MIT had imported from the University of Chicago, Cambridge economics underwent an internal housecleaning. "They were bringing the latest thinking in," a star Fischer pupil later wrote. "They had absorbed a lot of the Chicago approach" from Friedman and Lucas. Working alongside Harvard's Martin Feldstein at the prestigious National Bureau of Economic Research, which Feldstein brought from New York to Cambridge, the transplanted Chicagoans inaugurated a new era in Harvard-MIT economics. Their students included Olivier Blanchard, who eventually became chairman of the MIT department, and Maurice Obstfeld and Ben Bernanke, the department chairmen at Berkeley and Princeton, respectively; other prominent young stars included the Stanford "New Growth" theorist Paul Roemer; the Berkeley husband-and-wife team David and Christina Roemer; Columbia's Frederic Mishkin; Jean Tirole, an industrial organization expert; and Gregory Mankiw and Paul Krugman.

Although most of this new generation never embraced Rational Expectations as such, they acknowledged the powerful influence of Lucas and Chicago (via Cambridge).* By 1980, Lucas claimed, in fact, that "one cannot find good, under-forty economists who identify themselves or their work as 'Keynesian.' "[29] His claim wasn't pure hubris; as Princeton's Alan Blinder, a gifted doubter of the Rat-Ex faith, later remembered about those times, "New Classical economics enjoyed spectacular success in the intellectual world of the late 1970s and early 1980s. It was the main reason why 'Keynesian' became a pejorative term. In the academic world of those years, it took either valor or indiscretion, perhaps both, to admit being a Keynesian. Few did."[30]

One important exception was, of course, Ken Galbraith. And his position was simple: he paid no attention to Rational Expectations. For one thing, its proponents were unknown outside academic circles. (*The New York Times* didn't mention the theory or Robert Lucas until late 1979, for example, and then only briefly.)[31] For another, Galbraith was far more worried about the greater danger posed by the new popularity of another Chicagoan, Milton Friedman, and his distinctive theory of monetarism.

Monetarism and Friedman were all too familiar to Galbraith by then. It was the rare 1970s newspaper or magazine article on problems of the U.S. economy that did not feature him and Friedman together: in 1975, *Time* described

---

*Fischer later left MIT in the 1990s to become chief economist of the IMF, where his enforcement of the era's pre-Keynesian economic orthodoxy, especially during the Asian financial crisis, prompted furious criticism, particularly from the World Bank's chief economist, Nobel laureate Joseph Stiglitz.

The Fund's multi-billion-dollar rescue operation, which was intended to solve the Asian crisis but instead helped to provoke even more severe unemployment and recession, had been favored by President Clinton's Treasury Secretary, Robert Rubin. When Rubin left office in 2000, he became chairman of Citigroup, the nation's largest and newest financial conglomerate, which had come into existence almost overnight after New Deal prohibitions on such conglomerates were overturned with Rubin's backing. As it happened, Citigroup had been heavily exposed during the Asian financial crisis, when the Treasury, under Rubin (and his deputy Lawrence Summers, a former Fischer student), as well as the IMF under Fischer, showed themselves in Stiglitz's view to be far friendlier to Western banks and investors than to the Asian poor and their governments. Fischer soon thereafter became Citigroup's vice chairman. Stiglitz asked, "Was Fischer being richly rewarded for having faithfully executed what he was told to do?" (Stiglitz, *Globalization and Its Discontents,* 208).

them, alongside Keynes and Adam Smith, as the modern world's most important economists. But that sort of attention, let alone accolade, for Friedman represented a seismic shift, while from the appearance of *The Affluent Society* in 1958 until well into Nixon's second term fifteen years later, it had been Galbraith who was far better known.[32] But Galbraith and Friedman had known each other personally since the early 1950s, when Galbraith took an early and quite tough stand against monetarism, with the result that the two occasionally crossed swords.* Galbraith knew that Friedman was a first-rate economist, well regarded for his work developing the "permanent income" hypothesis, his studies of risk aversion, and his restatement of the quantity theory of money. He also knew that Friedman's prestige had been enhanced by his landmark history of U.S. monetary policy, which appeared while Galbraith was in India, and that he'd used his presidential address at the AEA in 1967 to attack the Phillips Curve and the Keynesian New Economists, an attack he then brought into general public discussion through a monthly column he wrote for *Newsweek* during the Nixon years. Yet even then, Friedman's views remained largely without real influence on public policy, Galbraith knew. With Nixon's fall, however, that changed rapidly. Indeed, what dismayed Galbraith and most other Keynesians during the Ford-Carter years was how swiftly Friedman and monetarism gained new supporters in Washington.

The diminutive, bespectacled Friedman had first set out his basic doctrine in 1948, building on the Depression-era work of his Chicago predecessor Henry Simons and Columbia's James Angell. (The roots of the theory were traceable to eighteenth-century European work on what economists refer to as "the quantity theory" of money.[33]) But during the heyday of postwar Keynesianism, the tiny band of monetarists who coalesced around the combative Friedman were marginalized, since their theory rejected virtually all of Keynes's claims that fiscal policy could be used to macromanage an economy, with monetary policy consigned to a much reduced function (if any at all). This was sheer heresy to Friedman: to him, "money mattered," and the optimal freedom for markets, with a stable management of the money supply, was the supreme responsibility for an otherwise small and limited government.† Among main-

---

*Friedman's early career benefited from powerful patrons: both Frank Knight and Friedrich von Hayek actively promoted him. Hayek brought Friedman into the Mont Pélérin Society, his legendary annual summer gathering in Switzerland of conservative economists, political scientists, and businessmen. Friedman in turn claimed a hand in arranging the publication of Hayek's *The Road to Serfdom*.

Unknown to Galbraith, his nemesis Clarence Randall, the head of Inland Steel, also was an early admirer of Friedman's. After failing to block Galbraith's tenure at Harvard in 1948–49, Randall pressed President Conant repeatedly to hire a "sensible-minded" economist such as Friedman to "balance" the presence of Galbraith (Herbert Stein and Arthur Burns were Randall's two other recommendations). Conant weighed the request but finally refused to follow the advice (Kellers, *Making Harvard Modern*, 84).

†As Galbraith frequently pointed out, Friedman's passion for smaller government never included military spending, whose gargantuan scale and effects he disregarded. In his most widely read work, *Free to Choose*, Friedman for example singled out Social Security, the Federal Reserve, and the Departments of Agriculture; Education; Energy; Health, Education and Welfare; Housing and Urban Development; Justice; Labor; and the Treasury for rebuke, but did not mention the much larger Department of Defense (save for a passing swipe at the public works projects of the Army Corps of Engineers).

stream Republicans his theory had almost no supporters, and his brief prominence in 1964 as Barry Goldwater's economic adviser didn't help his reputation; even Nixon kept him at arm's length. He occasionally read some of the endless stream of memos Friedman sent to the White House, but the only assignment he ever gave him was on a committee investigating an all-volunteer armed forces. (Characteristic of the wariness Nixon's economists felt toward Friedman, CEA Chairman Paul McCracken smiled broadly when asked by a business reporter whether his economic policies were "Friedmanite," and coyly replied, "Friedmanesque.")*[34]

Yet in the early 1970s conservative bastions such as the *Wall Street Journal* editorial page began to pay serious attention to the monetarist cause.[35] Then as U.S. and global economic performance worsened, and doubts about Keynesian policies spread, Friedman's rock-solid confidence in his theory and his unflagging attacks on the Keynesians stood out like beacons to those who by conviction believed that government policies were at the root of the economy's problems. Cutting through the uncertainty and confusion, Friedman boldly insisted that monetarism had not only the explanation but the cure for stagflation, based on one unshakable truth: all Keynesians—mainstreamers as well as dissidents like Galbraith—were completely and utterly wrong, and for easy-to-use reasons.

First, Friedman argued, the mainstream had always been wrong to think that the Phillips Curve bargain—the famous discovery of a trade-off between unemployment and inflation—worked as they believed. There was no such elegant and simple trade-off, he insisted, because instead modern economies had a "natural rate of unemployment" which resisted when fine-tuners tried to alter it in pursuit of their full-employment ideal. Inflation would merely accelerate when this "natural rate" was reached and unemployment would decline no further.[36]

When pressed, Friedman acknowledged his theory could not determine a priori a preordained percentage number for jobless workers, because the "natural rate" was determined by a multiplicity of factors including existing union contracts, job search and mobility costs, technological changes, and so forth.†
Yet he insisted that the Keynesians' quest for "full employment" was not merely a chimera, but a major cause of the nation's economic problems. This mesmerized conservative politicians and policy-makers.

Having gone that far, Friedman had no intention of stopping: the "natural rate" hypothesis, he said, could be linked back to his overall monetarist agenda

---

*Nixon's intuition about keeping his distance from the volatile economist wasn't entirely misplaced. Friedman later denounced him as "the most socialist president" in American history (although he also considered him the brightest public official he'd ever met). Friedman especially detested Nixon's wage and price controls. When George Schultz brought Friedman to the White House to talk with the President shortly after the controls were put in place, an uneasy Nixon awkwardly tried to lighten the moment by telling Friedman "not to blame Schultz" for the controls—to which Friedman bluntly replied, "Oh no, Mr. President, I don't blame George. I blame you." The two men never spoke again.

†The a priori indeterminacy of the natural rate would by the late 1990s become a haunting weakness for the theory when growth soared and unemployment plummeted, yet inflation remained inconsequential. Was it 6 percent? If not, was it 4 percent? And just how and why did it change over time without affecting inflation?

to show that the Keynesians were wrong in an even larger way. They had been seduced into believing that fiscal policy could substantially alter aggregate demand, but, according to Friedman, that prescription in times of recession—stimulative government spending financed by sale of government bonds—"crowded out" private borrowing and investment from the existing money supply, which in turn reduced the stimulative effect of the government's deficit and, worse, distorted the sacred free functioning of the market.[37]

Just as bad, the Keynesians' faith in fiscal policy to macromanage the business cycle meant using an instrument full of flaws. Without mentioning its origin, Friedman adopted Galbraith's strategic and tactical indictment of Heller's 1964 tax cut and raised it to axiomatic status in the monetarist canon: passage of tax bills was a politicized and time-consuming process of drafts, hearings, debates, and compromises only weakly tied to the needs of the business cycle at a given moment. Special interests could easily distort the bill's final effects, and by the time the law was passed, business conditions might well have changed—yet repeal or revision of the legislation would require another long political cycle.

Monetary, not fiscal, policy was thus the means by which a modern economy could be managed, he insisted. The money supply's effect on aggregate demand was much larger, and in theory at least it could be more rapidly expanded or contracted by the Federal Reserve System, which operated outside the legislative process. But to work as Friedman wanted it to, monetary policy needed to follow certain very strict rules. In its earliest form, Friedman's theory had included an "activist" role for the Fed not dissimilar to the fiscal "fine-tuning" prescriptions of mainstream Keynesians.[38] But by the 1970s, Friedman abandoned Federal Reserve "activism" for a new doctrine of Fed "stability" and "predictable consistency."[39]

What that meant was a slow growth of the nation's money supply, governed largely by the underlying growth of population and productivity. The Federal Reserve was no longer supposed to try to raise or lower interest rates to "manage" the business cycle, but rather to concentrate on the size of the money supply itself, and to guide it by this "slow growth" rule.* Most important, government was to abandon entirely what Friedman considered "the useless and misguided acrobatics" of fiscal fine-tuning.

Under these new rules, and with the Federal Reserve also required fully to publicize its monetary growth targets, monetarists argued that business and consumers would no longer face the uncertainties of fluctuating government policies and would adjust their own behavior accordingly. Inflation would fall, business cycles would resume their "rational" rhythms, and the old pre-Keynesian ideal of "natural" equilibrium would be restored, deviations from it being limited to the effects of exogenous "shocks" to the system.

---

*Defining "the money supply" (M) turned out to be trickier than first imagined, and different definitions were classified as $M1$, $M2$, $M3$, $M4$, and so forth. The inability of the monetarists to agree among themselves on which M to use turned out to be a "technical" problem of enormous consequence and embarrassment for them.

In the environment of the post-Nixon years, monetarism's audacious simplicity, backed with sophisticated economic arguments set in the context of neoclassical economic theory, began to exercise an almost hypnotic effect on conservative (and many moderate) policy-makers, politicians, and journalists. Here was not only an antidote to the Keynesians and the apparent failures of their policy prescriptions, but the kind of firm, simple policy rules that everyone could understand.

But monetarism wasn't simply a case of the "right" scientific theory suddenly carried to the fore by inexorable logic at the "right" time to rescue the economy and economic theory from further Keynesian depredations. Much of its attraction along the Potomac clearly rested on its vindication of the Republican Party's new political and economic conservatives. More, it internalized a brand of libertarian conservatism that Eisenhower-era Republicans had rejected but that now was about to become the milk-and-honey dream of "the new GOP" emerging under Ronald Reagan. This libertarian monetarism promised to be an immense cudgel in the hands of those who'd long chafed under what they viewed as a heretical "liberal hegemony" in politics and economics, Democratic and Republican alike.

Friedman had no hesitation about spelling out his ideals for modern society, starting with small government, low taxes, and reduction to the greatest degree possible of government involvement in the economy. But that wasn't all. He was, as one sympathetic reviewer summarized it, also in favor of

> the abolition of industrial regulation, security and exchange controls, farm price supports, minimum wages, public schools, national parks, compulsory military service, corporate income taxes, progression of income taxes, fractional reserve banking, fixed exchange rates, import duties, the Federal Reserve System, price and rent controls, interest regulation, licensing of physicians, and Social Security in its present form.[40]

More than a value-neutral theory in academic economics, this brand of monetarism was a conscious weapon in the larger debate on political ideas that could define American society. As Alfred Malabre, the veteran economics editor of *The Wall Street Journal*, later acknowledged, Friedman and his colleagues were not the "scientific" ideal of economists as cool, value-neutral theorists, but

> super salespeople, merchandising, after much frustration, an economic medicine that promised far more than it could possibly deliver . . . Though Friedman would later deny it, his argument . . . came close to guaranteeing recession-free growth—if only Washington would follow his recommendations . . . With the benefit of hindsight more than two troubled decades later, these claims seem wildly utopian. In [the 1970s], however, they sounded to many of us remarkably credible and highly desirable.[41]

Vanguards of a counterrevolution against not only the Keynesian Revolution but also the growth of government and its expansion, Milton Friedman and his monetarist apostles and conservative political allies now encountered—much to the consternation of Ken Galbraith—an ever-weakening opposition wherever they pressed forward.[42]

In the academy, mainstream Keynesians went on the defensive, insisting that they'd been misunderstood all along, that they'd always grasped the importance of monetary policy, and that elements of monetarism could be usefully accepted without embracing Friedman's ultraconservative version of its implications.

For example, shortly after Gerald Ford took over the presidency, Yale's James Tobin, who had advised the McGovern campaign two years earlier, adamantly denied any symmetrical polarity between Keynesian "fiscalists" on the one hand and Friedmanite "monetarists" on the other. "There are no such [extreme] fiscalists," he argued, since they would have to claim that only fiscal policy mattered and that money was irrelevant, and none did. "The only extremists are the monetarists," he went on—an irony, he added, since "there is no inherent logic that places monetarists to the right of the New Economists. They have different models of economic mechanism, but they need not have different political values. A conservative can be a Keynesian and a liberal a monetarist."[43]

Tobin blamed the press, with its love of "drama, conflict, and novelty," for promoting monetarism and Friedman with such alarming fervor. Fortunately, he added, such irrationalism would never prevail against transparent, reasonable New Economics. Tobin was confident that Friedman's day had come—and gone. "Now that the monetarist tide is waning," he reassured colleagues, "I must conclude that little lasting harm has been done, unless the time of economists on both sides is heavily valued." Battle-scarred (and chastened) it might be, Tobin concluded, but "the New Economics lives after all."[44]

In the history of economists' predictive errors, Tobin's doesn't equal Irving Fisher's claim that "stock prices have reached what looks like a permanently high plateau" just weeks before the Great Crash of 1929, but it comes close. The reality was that monetarism was now about to enter its own (albeit briefer) golden age of intellectual respectability, and in the 1980s would be put into practice in both the U.S. and Great Britain. And contrary to Tobin, it was mainstream Keynesianism that was about to go into exile—alive perhaps, as Tobin averred, but ignominiously consigned to a Siberian wilderness.

That a brilliant economist and liberal Keynesian such as Tobin, who'd learned real-world policy and politics first-hand, could so misjudge the world around him underscores the difference between economics' view of itself as a branch of the natural sciences and Galbraith's conviction that it could not escape in analysis or operation from the political world surrounding it. Intellectually Tobin was of course right on one point in a strict and formal "scientific" sense: nothing about monetarism, once shorn of Friedman's libertarianism, prevented liberals from being monetarists. Yet the unexplained empirical fact was that virtually every major monetarist was a passionate political conserva-tive, and *that* had tremendous implications.

Since monetarists were convinced they were at war with Keynesians over theory and with liberals and "big government" over policy and politics, they conducted themselves accordingly, wanting not just a "scientific" victory about superior explanatory hypotheses, but a near-religious "redemption" of a society that had fallen prey to what Friedman called liberalism's "tyranny of control."*[45]

Galbraith had long before identified not only what he felt were monetarism's fundamental intellectual errors but the dangers they posed to Keynesianism and political liberalism with his sharp rebuttal to monetarism in 1957.[46] He had been debating Friedman ever since. Neither of them ever retreated. Friedman routinely made a point of deriding Galbraith in his *Newsweek* column, and fought hard against Galbraith's election to the AEA's presidency in 1971. When he discovered in 1976 that Galbraith's BBC series *The Age of Uncertainty* was about to air, he even flew to London to deliver a vehement broadside to a think tank so conservative that it denounced Margaret Thatcher as too liberal. There—to wild applause from his audience—he "exposed" what he called "the factual inadequacy of the Galbraithian view and the dogmatic confidence with which he asserts it."[47] (Despite these public clashes, the two men nonetheless maintained cordial personal relations, making a point each summer of getting together in Vermont, where both owned summer homes.)

Galbraith's objections to the monetarists were fundamental: he thought their single-minded emphasis on the money supply in order to manage the economy was haunted by conceptual confusions, dauntingly hard to imple-ment technically, and profoundly inequitable in its consequences. In 1973 he warned (with prescient clarity, as monetarist policy experiments by the Federal Reserve and the Bank of England in the early 1980s demonstrated) that mon-etarism was,

> as a technical matter, highly uncertain in its effects. No one knows what the response to a greater or less availability of funds for borrowing will be or when that response will occur, for the reason that the factors that govern such response are never the same from one time to the next. This uncertainty is concealed, in turn, by intense and solemn discussion employing arcane terminology—rediscount rate, prime rate, open market purchases, spreads, twists—under conditions of priestly seclusion. The public wrongly assumes that this discussion proceeds from knowledge. In fact where there is knowl-edge and certainty . . . there is little to discuss.[48]

The price that citizens would have to pay for the monetarist experiment was, to Galbraith, evident:

*In waging their war, they recognized no borders. Friedman and several other Chicago economists rushed to Chile to advise General Augusto Pinochet after Pinochet—with the encouragement and assistance of the Nixon administration—overthrew the democratically elected socialist Salvador Allende. Democracy was, in Friedman's view, not a requirement for the freedom to choose.

Such policy works by reducing or increasing, directly or indirectly, the amount of money available for lending. Those who least need to borrow and those who are most favored as borrowers are in the planning system. Those who most rely on borrowed funds, or are least favored by the banks are in the market system. The planning system is the most highly developed part of the economy, the market system the least developed. Monetary policy thus favors the strongest and the most developed part of the economy, and discriminates against the weakest.[49]

But Galbraith was sailing against the wind. The United States in the 1970s was fundamentally realigning itself, not only in electoral politics and the economy, but in its worldviews. As it approached its bicentennial in the summer of 1976, the most obvious signs of that shift were visible in the presidential campaigns. By then "neither political party," one historian sharply concluded, "wanted much to do with its own recent partisan traditions."[50]

INSIDE THE DEMOCRATIC PARTY, faith in Keynesian policies and in the durability of the New Deal's legacy—the hard-won liberal coalition of labor, northern big cities, and ethnic voters, uneasily wedded to a conservative white South—was everywhere in tatters. When the 1976 convention opened in New York's Madison Square Garden that July, Galbraith, attending as a Massachusetts delegate, caustically reminded a *New York Times* reporter how different this gathering was from the ones in 1968 and 1972. The party's post-McGovern leaders, he said, had "an uneasy desire to compensate for their compromises, and their constant references to 'courage' attempt to persuade the speaker that he isn't doing what he is doing." The convention's eventual nominee, Georgia governor Jimmy Carter, came in for Galbraith's especially harsh judgment: when it came to defining his policies, "what Carter substitutes for specificity is piety."[51] That November his discontent with Carter was replicated throughout the North and West as record numbers of liberal Democrats stayed away from the polls.[52]

For the dwindling number of moderates in the GOP, the discontent was equal, for signs of deep and adverse changes abounded in their own party. Although President Ford finally won the nomination, he didn't do so unopposed. The centrist traditions of corporate-oriented, eastern Republicans and their small-town Midwestern allies—of Willkie, Dewey, Eisenhower, and Rockefeller—were everywhere being overturned by the angry, conservative Sun Belt followers of Barry Goldwater, led in 1976 by the former actor (and former liberal) Ronald Reagan, who proved a dangerously effective challenger to Ford.*

Outside the parties, even more dramatic change was evident. The loose bi-

---

*Desperate to hold on to the GOP's "new conservatives" in 1976, Ford dumped Vice President Nelson Rockefeller in favor of Senator Robert Dole. Even so, Ford barely held off Reagan at the party convention, by 1,187 votes to the Californian's 1,070. In the two decades after 1976, GOP primary voters' self-identification as "moderate" plummeted from half of the party to barely a third, while identification of Republican voters with the religious right soared, amounting in some Southern states to two-thirds or more of the party's 1996 primary voters (exit poll data 1976–96, Roper Center, University of Connecticut).

partisan coalition of big business, big labor, and big government—the great practical postwar coalition of "countervailing powers" that Galbraith identified in *American Capitalism*—was falling apart. At the AFL-CIO, George Meany felt they'd been abandoned by their big business "partners" in the midst of stagflation, and betrayed by the Democrats' failures to defend workers facing unemployment and eroding incomes. As well he knew, his bargaining position was the weakest it had been in forty years: union membership now amounted to barely 25 percent of the labor force. With unemployment undercutting union ranks and inflation eating away at the standard of living, he was desperate for action and furious that congressional Democrats could produce no viable programs. (Hoping to break the impasse, Meany supported Carter strongly in 1976 but soon regretted it, calling the Georgian by the end of his term "the most conservative president I've seen in my lifetime." A sardonic Arthur Schlesinger, with a longer view of history, observed that in the two-century history of the Democratic Party, at least Grover Cleveland had been more conservative.[53])

Big business felt equally betrayed and abandoned. In what the political historian David Calleo labeled the "New Economic Disorder" of the late 1970s—a world of stagflation, tough new global competition, harsh interest rates, and aggressive new corporate "raiders"—executives found labor's wage demands unconscionable, coming as they did on top of the monumental new energy costs resulting from OPEC's fourfold price increases. Overall, business profits were lower than in the 1960s (profit margins in 1975, an especially tough year, were the worst in seventeen years). Worse, behind these lower aggregate profits, an unprecedented new sectoral pattern of profit distribution among firms had emerged.

Small- and medium-sized companies were predictably faring worst: affordable credit was hard to find and these firms had little ability to pass through price increases without damaging sales. But also at the upper reaches of the nation's largest corporations—the world of Galbraith's "technostructure" and "planning system"—unforeseen changes had altered the landscape. Awash in record sales and pretax profits, Exxon suddenly displaced General Motors as the largest U.S. corporation; Texaco was now the third largest, Shell was glowingly described as "a money machine" by *Forbes*,[54] and Mobil was so awash in cash that it was snapping up distantly related companies such as the retailer Montgomery Ward.

But as these energy giants thrived, many big and powerful non-oil firms were struggling for their very existence. CEOs in the immense durable-goods manufacturing, motor vehicle, and retail trade sectors also watched in horror as their profits, adjusted for inflation, fell by more than half. Even in the machinery, primary and fabricated metals, food, and wholesale trade industries profits were barely keeping up with inflation.

In the petroleum industry, meanwhile, profits soared tenfold in the 1970s. In 1970, petroleum industry profits amounted to a modest tenth of all profits in U.S. manufacturing; but thanks to OPEC's price hikes in 1973 and then again in 1979, oil and gas profits were half of all manufacturing profits by the time Ronald Reagan was elected President. As he entered office, the oil business was the most profitable industry in the country, its total profits five times larger than those of its nearest competitor.[55] In the boardrooms of Big Oil, the 1970s were a spectacular decade—all the caviling about nationalized oil fields overseas, energy regulation, and windfall profits taxes notwithstanding.* In marked contrast, the pervasive sense of crisis that gripped the rest of America's business leaders was captured in a mid-decade *Time* cover story apocalyptically headlined, "CAN CAPITALISM SURVIVE?"†[56]

This amazing reversal of fortune among the Fortune 500 fueled a change no less important in the relations big business had with Washington. As one political journalist wrote,

> Throughout the 1970s, the chief executive officers of major corporations began to play a much more personal and direct role in the political arena than ever before. They became profoundly disillusioned with the post–World War II consensus. Federal regulatory agencies, they believed, hampered productivity; government expenditures, under the rubric of Keynesian economics, produced inflation; and taxes inhibited investment.[57]

This new level of personal engagement was anything but spontaneous. A year before the first OPEC price increases, Treasury Secretary John Connally and Fed Chairman Arthur Burns had secretly persuaded a small group of the nation's most powerful CEOs to form the Business Roundtable, designed both to support Nixon's policies and to consolidate the CEOs' abilities to shape public policy.[58] Its membership restricted to the two hundred biggest companies in the country, the Business Roundtable, along with the Trilateral Commission and the World Economic Forum, was much more sophisticated than the antediluvian National Association of Manufacturers, and more adroit at exercising influence in Washington than the more moderate Committee for Economic Development. "You see a changed type of person who's the chief executive officer of a major corporation than when I came here in 1958," one Washington policy-maker told *The New York Times* early in the Carter era. "They were extremely competent executives then but wore blinders, and couldn't see . . . that what is happening in the public arena can have more impact on your company than anything else you do. But you don't have to tell them that now—they have learned the lesson well."[59]

In the roiling economic cauldron that was the 1970s, the Business Round-

---

*The cartelization of oil has kept on producing an unprecedented wealth transfer. *The Economist* in 2003 estimated that "OPEC has managed to transfer a staggering $7 trillion in wealth from American consumers to producers over the past three decades by keeping the oil price above its true market-clearing level," adding that "that estimate does not include all manner of subsidies doled out to the fossil-fuel industry, ranging from cheap access to oil on government land to the ongoing American military presence in the Middle East" ("The end of the Oil Age," *The Economist*, October 25, 2003, 11).

†*Time*, for all the attention-grabbing fear in that headline, assured readers that it ultimately foresaw no end to capitalism, though it highlighted calls by Galbraith as well as Henry Ford II for a new era of public economic planning and leadership to compensate for the market's large and systemic failures.

table's new leaders weren't interested in maintaining a trilateral concordat or countervailing-power arrangements. Labor costs were too high, were still rising, and needed to be brought down. New opportunities for investment and expanded sales to restore profits were needed, plus a government both willing to wring inflation out of the system and provide those new opportunities. This wasn't just a matter of "getting government off our backs," but something more subtle and complicated, and the Business Roundtable understood that it required both less and more "government" at once.

Domestically, there were three goals, all about "less" government: lower taxes on business and upper incomes; a cap on wage inflation; and deregulation of industries such as transportation, finance, energy, and telecommunications. Internationally, there were also three goals—but they required "more" government. Washington was expected to intervene on behalf of American big business, first, for expanded (but politically supervised) markets for sales and production, while subtly maintaining a mercantilist advantage at home; second, for reduced tumult (and a favorably weighted dollar) in foreign exchange markets by means of "orderly marketing arrangements"; and third, for cooperation in forging a post–Bretton Woods world that would lift global (and more important, American) business and finance to unprecedented new heights.

The question for business was how to persuade the White House and Congress to seek those goals. The first giant step toward an answer came in 1976, when the Supreme Court ingeniously ruled in *Buckley v. Valeo* that corporate spending to influence elections and legislation was a form of "free speech" and thus fully protected by the First Amendment. With that, deep business coffers opened, beginning a race in political contributions that remade the American political landscape. Spending by corporate and business association political action committees (PACs) in federal elections soared from $8 million in 1972 to $85 million ten years later. (Apart from sizable contributions made by individual member corporations, the Business Roundtable itself became one of Washington's most powerful lobbying groups.)[60] A new rule (as yet unbroken) emerged in U.S. presidential races: whichever candidate raised the most money before the first primary became his party's nominee for the White House.[61]

Money also started pouring into the American Enterprise Institute, the Heritage Foundation, and other new conservative think tanks, which took as their job the creation of a more business-friendly climate in the nation. These new think tanks never aspired to the "objective" and "nonpartisan" research style of older public-policy centers such as the Brookings Institution; instead they embraced the rules of what Irving Kristol, a former liberal turned neoconservative, called "the adversary culture."

As founding coeditor of *The Public Interest* in 1965, Kristol had published both liberal and conservative articles, but a decade later his newfound conservatism became lapidary; he denounced universities and foundations as "left-wing asylums" guilty of fostering among the young and naive "a climate of opinion wherein an anti-business bent becomes a perfectly natural inclination." The only solution to this "utopian romanticism," he advised, was for conservatives boldly to create their own intellectual "counter-establishment," with its own think tanks, conferences, journals, and magazines, all to "take back" the public agenda.

In the economic policy debates, Galbraith, a popular whipping-boy for these energetic new conservatives, loomed large. The way the Heritage Foundation compared Galbraith's and Friedman's abilities was typical. Galbraith, Heritage explained, was guilty of having an "imagination that is thoroughly selective: he can conjure up examples of marketplace failure, but he fails to notice the palpable evidence that government controls have not produced any ameliorating influence." In contrast, Friedman was a model of dispassionate lucidity:

> In *Free to Choose*, Milton and Rose Friedman produce the hard facts that [Galbraith] so conveniently elides. The history of government forays into the marketplace has been a history of unmitigated failure . . . In a telling appendix, the Friedmans reproduce the Socialist Party platform of 1928 and note that virtually every suggested reform has been adopted in the U.S. since that time.[62]

To summarize the history of business-government relations as nothing more than an "unmitigated failure" was certainly bold revisionism, but the accolade for the Friedmans' idea that modern American public policy has been an ongoing enactment of the Socialist Party's agenda better showed how intellectually outlandish both Heritage and the Friedmans could be. Yet the new think tanks displayed no embarrassment in making such claims; they believed their larger goal—of harnessing Washington to their aims—was within reach. As William Baroody, head of the American Enterprise Institute, proudly announced in 1978, "The prevailing theology of liberalism, providing a common intellectual core of beliefs that many leaders in Washington could rally behind, has broken up." A jubilant Irving Kristol was more succinct: "the liberal center has begun to crumble."[63]

For conservatives in the late 1970s, being able to pose the modern economic debate as a clash between two titans, Friedman and Galbraith, one rising, one falling—rather than as the David and Goliath struggle in which Friedman had long seen himself—was a godsend for their campaign against "the prevailing theology of liberalism." Galbraith, after all, wasn't merely the country's best-known Keynesian economist, but a former anti–Vietnam War activist, a supporter of the rebellious 1960s young, a Harvard and East Coast elitist, and (like that other hated ex–Harvard professor, Henry Kissinger) traitorously in favor of détente with the Soviet Union: Who could be easier to despise? Meanwhile the press embraced the same personification of Keynesianism versus monetarism because it made for a lively one-on-one conflict that was far easier to describe than the technical intricacies of monetary or fiscal policy. (When Friedman won the Nobel Prize in 1976, the story became even easier to tell and added luster to monetarism's new intellectual legitimacy.)

THE PERSONALIZATION OF the clash between Galbraith and Friedman ended up nastily intruding directly into Galbraith's life when he and his producers were finally ready for his BBC documentary series, *The Age of Uncertainty*, to be broadcast in the United States in 1977. By then, it had taken more than $2 million and three and a half years of work; Galbraith and the crews had gone to nineteen countries, with stops in (among other places) Death Valley, the Pentagon offices of the Joint Chiefs of Staff, the Jardin des Tuileries in Paris, the Scottish Highlands, Karl Marx's boyhood home in Trier, Germany, the archives of the Spanish empire in Seville, and a 13,000-acre Arizona "graveyard" for military aircraft; they even took a Mississippi cruise on the paddle-wheeler *Delta Queen*. There had been months of shooting at the Ealing Studios in London, where elaborate sets were constructed to portray one or another abstract idea pictorially: a carnival shooting gallery, where financial innovators who had come to a bad end could be picked off like tin ducks; a roller-coaster ride, meant to symbolize the boom and bust of business cycles; and a large relief map of Europe, on which life-sized cut-out figures of generals, kings, the tsar, and the kaiser were moved like chess pieces to illustrate the changes wrought by World War I.

To cap the series, Adrian Malone built the final episode around a wide-ranging conversation among Galbraith, Henry Kissinger, the former British prime minister Edward Heath, the *Washington Post* publisher Katharine Graham, the *Boston Globe* editor Thomas Winship, Arthur Schlesinger, the then-director of the London School of Economics Ralf Dahrendorf, the Soviet government adviser Georgi Arbatov, the English labor union leader Jack Jones, and the former prime minister of Thailand Kukrit Pramoj. As Kitty described it, "Twelve programs were the views of Galbraith. Program thirteen would be the views of others on issues of current concern."[64] Shot with the guests seated in white Adirondack chairs on the lawn outside Galbraith's Vermont farmhouse in the summer of 1976, the episode posed nightmarish logistics, with heavily armed Secret Service agents and local police patrolling the woods to protect Kissinger, and guests crammed into the two small inns in Newfane that could accommodate them, ten miles away down a long, bumpy dirt road.

The admirably challenging topics that Galbraith and Malone chose included the future of the modern corporation, the relations of rich and poor nations, the trade-offs between inflation and unemployment, and the risks of nuclear war. The weather held, though there were other inevitable mishaps: a car ran into a ditch, one jet-lagged guest fell asleep during filming, and the sound track wasn't quite synchronized with the film. There were also moments of humor: according to Galbraith, when aides to Kissinger went looking for him to warn that a new crisis was brewing in Lebanon, a local sheriff overheard them and offered to help. He said he knew quite a few people across the river in Lebanon, New Hampshire, and thought that if the Secret Service called them, the local police there were quite capable of handling whatever the crisis might be.[65]

The series was broadcast in England in the late fall of 1976 to a mixture of warm and cool reviews. "British critics on the whole disapproved," Galbraith recalled. "They thought it overillustrated; more should have been heard, less seen." And there were sharp dissenters from the content, too, including the English historian J. H. Plumb.[66] Eventually *The Age of Uncertainty* appeared in dozens of other countries thanks to French, German, and Japanese translations, and to accompany the series Galbraith wrote a companion volume of the same name, which quickly became an international best-seller in its own right, as well as a Book-of-the-Month-Club selection in the United States; sales in Japan alone topped half a million.[67]

Before it could be aired in the United States, *The Age of Uncertainty* started drawing aggressive, bitter denunciation from American conservatives, who'd been alerted by news of Milton Friedman's dramatic flight across the Atlantic to denounce the show's patent heresies and inaccuracies. A decade earlier, the overt bias behind Friedman's charges might have been laughed off, but in the political climate of the late 1970s, such objections were taken seriously by PBS, which had cofinanced the series and was financially dependent on an increasingly hostile and budget-minded Congress.

Late in 1976, managers at KCET, the Los Angeles PBS affiliate in charge of U.S. distribution, decided that after each hour-long segment of the series a conservative critic must be allowed to "respond," which the BBC had felt no need to arrange. They did so moreover without telling the show's host or producer, who first learned about it at a private screening in New York just prior to the series' scheduled U.S. debut. Needless to say, both Galbraith and Malone were deeply offended, and they both protested vehemently.[68] But when faced with the implicit possibility of cancellation, they grudgingly acceded. KCET's managers then papered over their unilateral action by releasing a statement saying that Professor Galbraith "was for anything that would stir things up and encourage people to think about the issues" and announced that his conservative "respondents" would include William F. Buckley, the philosopher Sidney Hook, Herbert Stein, and, for the final episode, Ronald Reagan.[69]

It isn't clear whether Milton Friedman was more put off by Galbraith's ideas generally, or by the fact he and monetarism were never even mentioned in the series, or that he was not one of the respondents selected by KCET. What is clear is that, playing off the by then well established "Galbraith vs. Friedman" trope, he skillfully parlayed Galbraith's series into one of his own. Sponsored by a tiny PBS affiliate in Erie, Pennsylvania, whose manager hated *The Age of Uncertainty* and refused to broadcast it, and funded by a handful of rich ultraconservative foundations,* Friedman created *Free to Choose* as his answer to *The Age of Uncertainty*. The series, with Friedman as its narrator, began airing on PBS in 1980, just as Ronald Reagan started campaigning for the presidency.[70] Curiously, this time PBS required no "balancing" response by liberal critics of Friedman, while Reagan from the campaign trail gave the new series a ringing endorsement, calling it "superb," required viewing "for everyone— from the President to the private citizen—who is concerned with the future of America."[71]

The fact that PBS deliberately altered Galbraith's series during the Carter presidency and not, as one might have thought, in the Nixon or Reagan era, when public funding for PBS, NPR, and the National Endowment for the Arts all came under ferocious Republican attack, is a small but telling indication of how the conservative tide rose and even accelerated during that Democratic period.[72] Jimmy Carter in his quest to reconstitute the Democrats as a "centrist" party that could hold on to its Southern white base—just at the moment when the Republican Party, in pursuit of that base, was veering very far to the right itself—never seemed to understand the larger currents sweeping around him. With his love of "technical" solutions to problems that were also political and ideological, Carter could not keep the party's—and the nation's—problems from steadily worsening.

His "technician" approach found ready acceptance in Washington, however. Thanks to the immense expansion of public policy research inside and outside government, thousands of people, a great many of them economists, pored over endless reams of data, applying computer models and cost-benefit analyses to everything from farm output to weapons procurement to school-lunch programs. (The Office of Management and the Budget counted thirty-six separate federal agencies devoted to research, planning, and evaluation—and admitted it was a partial list.[73]) In its sophistication, the work was the embodiment of everything the 1950s model-building revolution launched by the mainstream Keynesians had dreamed of.

But there was a catch. The rise of all this technically sophisticated research produced something none of the 1960s "best and brightest" could ever have imagined: "the widely held opinion that social research is essentially negative, destructive, and not particularly helpful to society."[74] Here was a level of dismay among domestic policy's practitioners—whether in transportation, housing, poverty reduction, education, or financial and fiscal issues—that had been seen hitherto only among the diplomatic and military planners distressed about the Vietnam War. Worse, the most talented of them, such as the Brookings Institution economist Henry Aaron, were saying something even more disturbing: that the research process as it was being conducted seemed "to

---

*Including the Olin Foundation, headed by William Simon. *Free to Choose* was one part of a new conservative education agenda, spearheaded by Olin, that included funding dozens of new "market-friendly" professorships, research centers, and entire new "law and economics" departments; sponsoring an endless stream of books, magazines, pamphlets, and conferences; even creating a *Sesame Street*–like TV puppet show that extolled the virtues of capitalism to preschoolers.

corrode any simple faiths around which political coalitions are ordinarily built."[75] Public faith in government's ability to do its work competently had been falling like a stone since the mid-1960s, when nearly three out of four Americans still trusted Washington to "do the right thing" all or almost all the time; by the late 1970s, that percentage had fallen to 40 and was still falling.[76]

To Galbraith's vocal dismay, the response to this huge crisis of confidence in democratic government from the Carter Democrats was more "technical" schemes and favored acronyms—the SPR ("strategic petroleum reserve"); an unimaginably complex energy price and tax policy, TIPS ("tax-based incomes policy"), to slow wage increases; and OMAs ("orderly marketing agreements") to manage foreign trade. Under Carter, hopes that Democrats might recover a vibrant liberalism never stood a chance. The "ultimate policy President," as his chief speechwriter later described him, held

> explicit, thorough positions on every issue under the sun, but he has no large view of the relations between them, no line indicating which of these goals (reducing unemployment? human rights?) will take precedence over which (inflation control? SALT treaty?) when the goals conflict. Spelling out these choices makes the difference between a position and a philosophy, but it is an act foreign to Carter's mind.[77]

Carter's economic policies dismayed Galbraith almost from the start.* To Alan Greenspan, Carter had "moved in the right direction" because he'd followed his innate conservative instincts.[78] Liberals disagreed, and they watched as their new President failed to develop a coherent, let alone liberal, agenda or leadership style. By 1978, the tension between liberal economists such as Galbraith and once-liberal, now more cautious colleagues such as CEA Chairman Charles Schultze, Joseph Pechman of the Brookings Institution, and Walter Heller became itself a minor cause célèbre in Washington, with *BusinessWeek* jeering that Galbraith and other "ultra-liberals" were stubbornly refusing to recognize, as Schultze, Pechman, and Heller had, that "the doleful economic climate of the '70s has spurred a movement to the right among practitioners of the dismal science itself." Fortunately, it said, Galbraith exemplified only the tiny remaining handful of "outspoken left-of-center economists" whose devotion to "controls and central planning" made it impossible for them to see the "evident signs" of the revolt against liberalism all around them, including in the Democratic Party.[79]

In 1978 *The New York Times* offered a more nuanced interpretation: the country was in the midst of "a revolt against taxes by the middle and upper income groups," but this was far from being the "revealed preference" of a majority of voters; quite the contrary, the *Times* noted, it was to no small degree the

---

*Galbraith's feelings toward Carter likely weren't helped after he wrote the candidate offering to assist in the campaign—and got a mimeographed note of thanks in return.

result of the conscious work done by "critics of government intervention in the economy [who] now dominate the intellectual debate," and it added that the dominance of those critics owed much to the systematic subvention of their views by big business. The *Times* highlighted the millions of dollars that the corporations that had financed the Business Roundtable—such as General Electric, Goodyear, Mobil, and Phillips—were now pouring into remaking American politics. "Whatever the reasons, there is little doubt that the current upsurge in conservative thinking owes much to the newly aggressive attitude by American business. A higher level of corporate support has been instrumental in the transformation of [conservative think tanks] into an influential center of policy analysis."[80]

For President Carter and his "new" economic and political "centrism," disaster arrived in late 1978, when OPEC struck for a second time in the decade, raising oil prices 15 percent overnight. From $1.50 a barrel in 1971, the benchmark cost of crude oil had now risen to over $20; it would peak at $34 a barrel by 1980. Carter had made a national energy policy a centerpiece of his administration, but these increases only underscored his weaknesses, and his public support plummeted to barely 25 percent over the next several months, lows that hadn't been seen since the darkest days of the Truman administration. Desperate to regain momentum, the President decided to convene a weeklong, closed-door retreat at Camp David, to which he invited 130 guests drawn from a who's who of business, politics, religion, journalism, and academia—all meant to advise him on the nation's future. Dressed in a cardigan sweater and jeans, with a legal pad in hand for taking notes, day after day the President of the United States sat on the floor of his cabin as small groups of his guests were escorted in to opine on the state of the nation and the world.

This was the first opportunity Galbraith had had for a face-to-face discussion of policy with Carter,* and it didn't go particularly well. The President assiduously took notes as others in his little group spoke. When it came Galbraith's turn, he suggested that, among other things, a gasoline rationing system might be in order. The note-taking stopped, and he sensed that he "was being viewed as rather eccentric."[81]

The Camp David retreat did have one memorable consequence. It inspired Carter, hoping to rally a desperate and demoralized country, to deliver his infamous "malaise" speech, in which (unlike Ford and Nixon before him) he sternly refused to promise that America's nightmare would soon be over. He met, of course, with the same success as his predecessors. A year later, as his one-term presidency slouched to a close, unemployment was at nearly 8 percent, inflation was soaring (in March 1980 the Consumer Price Index touched 16 percent), prime interest rates topped 18 percent and liberal Democrats were more on the defensive than they had been at the start of Nixon's presidency. As the economy seemed to spiral out of control, public anger and fears

---

*Only six economists were among the 130 guests that week. The other five were Walter Heller, Arthur Okun, forecaster Lawrence Klein, business economist Marina Whitman, and labor economist Eli Ginsberg.

were further exacerbated by the humiliating seizure of the American embassy in Teheran in November 1979, followed by a failed rescue attempt. Yet there was still no retreat or reevaluation of the Democrats' new "technical" approach to governance. Vice President Walter Mondale bluntly put to his party the direction he and the President saw ahead: The time had come, he said, to give up nostalgia for the Rooseveltian past and "adjust liberal values of social justice and compassion to a new age of limited resources."[82]

Among Washington policy-makers, chastened mainstream Keynesians had already made that adjustment by abandoning hopes of "fine-tuning" a buoyant, ever-growing economy; instead they warned Americans to face up to "the big trade-off" that needed to be made between "equality and efficiency" (as the title of Arthur Okun's influential book put it).[83] Most then came down hard on the side of "efficiency," which required greater freedom for market forces. "Economic deregulation" became the latest Washington enthusiasm, beginning with the airline industry, then swiftly moving into banking, the stock market, communications, railroads, and trucking. In the test case of the airlines, not only conservatives but even Ralph Nader and Senator Kennedy (the latter persuaded by his aide Stephen Breyer) supported this new policy.

For ordinary Americans, inflation and unemployment were the great preoccupations. More ominously—yet almost unmentioned at the time—income and wealth inequality were accelerating, beginning an uninterrupted, twenty-five-year trend that turned the United States into the most inegalitarian of the world's advanced economies. The country's once-unrivaled manufacturing sector—the engine that had made its economy the world's largest and that had been the backbone of postwar blue-collar economic security—reeled from foreign competition, while the service sector, where by now most Americans worked, was intensifying a brutal bifurcation between well-paid jobs for the best-educated and low-wage work with few, if any, benefits for the rest. Hardest hit were big cities in the East and Midwest, where decently paid blue-collar jobs evaporated as older plants shut down or moved away. Crime and drug addiction soared as stable communities disintegrated (this was amply documented by the sociologist William Julius Wilson).[84]

Galbraith hadn't been alone in warning that Nixon's abandonment of Bretton Woods and fixed exchange rates—which most economists had thought would bring greater rationality and efficiency to global markets—would lead to just such consequences; Richard Cooper of Yale, one of the country's best international economists, had been sounding the same warning for years, but the two had been rare in their dissent.[85] The U.S. government's dollar policies, in particular, forever caught up in conflicting demands as a domestic currency, international reserve currency, and a political/policy tool for exerting Washington's leadership, oscillated between expansion and contraction. Those U.S. policies kept other currencies on their own roller-coaster ride that created a global instability, which along with inflation, drove soaring gold prices (they peaked at more than $800 per ounce as the decade ended, up from little more than $30 ten years earlier), and left U.S. trade balances steadily decaying.

Yet out of all this instability a deceptively autonomous revolution was gathering speed: the revolution of global finance. Galbraith had pointed to major elements of it in both *The Age of Uncertainty* and *Money: Whence It Came, Where It Went*. Although much of *Money* was taken up with a lengthy history of money and associated manias dating back to the ancient kingdom of Lydia, Galbraith kept returning to two central tenets that, he argued, applied across time and cultures: that money and finance inevitably suffer from cycles of speculative expansion followed by collapse; and that it is a fallacy to imagine that the possession and/or management of great sums of money implies a supernormal intelligence. Money, he wryly warned, "is a singular thing. It ranks with love as man's greatest source of joy. And it ranks with death as his greatest source of anxiety. Over all history it has oppressed nearly all people in one of two ways: either it has been abundant and very unreliable, or reliable and very scarce."[86]

It was the first of the two tenets that was about to shake the world, even as he was writing the book. The new financial economy of Wall Street (mutual funds, credit cards, mergers and acquisition) was starting to explode with unprecedented force in size and power relative to the everyday world of the goods economy, where tangible things (cars, tools, toothpicks, clothes, and computers) were made. And it was exploding into a vast global market that seemed outside the reach of any central bank's control.

A number of markers blazed the way to this revolution: the invention of money market funds, followed by the deregulation of brokerage fees, and then the application of computer technology to facilitate a global trading market. But the defining moment had come midway through the 1970s, when the nation's biggest banks found themselves awash in more cash than even the Exxons and Texacos had. This immense new liquidity—a result of "petrodollar" deposits from the record earnings of the oil companies and the OPEC states, the immense trade-generated Eurodollar pools, and the accomodative policies of the world's major central banks—created a gigantic crisis. The deposits by themselves were no blessings—in the upside-down world of banking, deposits are liabilities, not assets—and finding familiar, blue-chip customers to lend to was harder and harder (loans, after all, are bankers' assets).

As the banks looked farther afield, beyond the AAA-rated companies they had preferred to lend to in duller times, they found that Third World governments and risky American companies already laden with debt were the only customers willing to borrow. Citicorp CEO Walter Wriston and other banking executives praised themselves for their "ingenuity" in opening these new markets, and they forecast a brave new world of sophisticated risk management and a global customer base. Wriston famously argued that because sovereign nations did not go bankrupt, lending to them represented no real risk. But, Galbraith warned, the false linkage by the public, journalists, and politicians of "unusual intelligence with the leadership of the great financial institutions" almost inevitably preceded disastrous financial reverses.[87] Starting with the collapse of the Mexican peso in 1982, it took less than half a decade before an avalanche of default by the banks' new overseas clients led the world into a vast global debt crisis and, for a time, the haunting specter once again of worldwide economic collapse.[88]

Foreign governments were far from being the only source of the banks' soon-to-be spectacular woes. In 1974, New York's Franklin National Bank had been declared insolvent as a consequence of mismanaged bets placed in the new foreign currency markets that followed Bretton Woods's demise. It was the biggest bank failure since the Depression, yet it went largely unnoticed because on the same day Gerald Ford granted Richard Nixon—to much greater uproar—"a full, free, and absolute pardon." In retrospect Franklin National turned out to be the banking industry's miner's canary, the harbinger of the death of thousands more American financial institutions over the next fifteen years and of major banking crises in three quarters of the world's nations.

Meanwhile, smaller banks and, more ominously, savings and loans found themselves caught in their own dead-ends with no apparent escape route. Carrying long-term loans, especially mortgages, made when interest rates were low, they were trapped into paying depositors new high interest rates, in part to stem flight of the cash to the new money market funds. (These funds had held less than $2 billion in 1974, but soared to $75 billion by 1980—and then to $500 billion by 1990, and to $1.2 trillion by 2000).[89] As these seismic structural shifts occurred in the financial system, much else shuddered and shifted as well.

Since currencies were now traded as commodities, speculators in London, New York, Chicago, and elsewhere—as they'd long done with pork bellies and corn—began to borrow on the margins in order to place huge bets on movements of the dollar, mark, yen, and pound (and eventually the baht, rial, and peso). As the computer and telecommunications revolutions unfolded, twenty-five-year-old currency traders—the first of a new generation the novelist Tom Wolfe would satirize as "Masters of the Universe"—focused on turning a quick day's profit for their employers by moving billions around the planet in ways that thirty years earlier no treasury or central bank could have imagined. America's foreign-exchange markets alone exploded to trading nearly $25 billion a day by 1980. (That was just the start: by 1990 the U.S. foreign-exchange markets were trading more than $150 billion a day, and they passed $350 billion by 2000.[90])

In this new world of volatile global finance, Washington found its power waning and its economic leadership faring no better than the banks'. Once-businesslike trade negotiations with long-term allies now echoed with accusations of "trickery" and "deceit," as nations jockeyed to protect their domestic industries and interests while simultaneously (and desperately) expanding their exports to compensate for the new high costs of energy and sagging domestic demand.

The Europeans and Japanese were especially angry that, in the wake of the 1973 oil price hikes, Nixon and Kissinger, rather than seeking to break the OPEC cartel, successfully persuaded OPEC to make customers pay for all oil purchases in dollars. Kissinger called the first OPEC price hikes "one of the pivotal events in the history of this century," but the fact that he and Nixon never seriously considered forcing a price rollback was the true pivot. The reason was that they both—geopolitical strategists, not economists—feared Middle Eastern instability for Israel and for America's feudal allies in Saudi Arabia and Iran. Eager to build up the Shah of Iran's power as a regional enforcer of the Soviet-American détente, in 1972 they had offered him virtual carte blanche to purchase an unlimited flow of American arms (to the consternation of the Saudis). But as the Iranian budget became bloated with arms purchases (and was simultaneously bled by corruption), the vexing question of how the Shah would pay was unanswered—until the war with Israel in 1973.

By then Libya had extorted an unprecedented new pricing arrangement from Occidental Petroleum's Armand Hammer—and to the surprise of the Arab world Muammar Qaddafi had faced no American reprisals. Hammer was intimately connected to Nixon, a connection he cemented through illegal payoffs and contributions.* The shah and the Saudi king, who were bitter that the dollar's 1971 devaluation had curtailed the purchasing power of their royalty payments from American oil companies, decided that the upstart Qaddafi's audacity could be safely emulated, and war with Israel provided their excuse to claim support from the Middle East's masses.

Even though a cutoff of U.S. arms sales was one logical weapon the United States could have used to lower oil prices when the war ended, Nixon and Kissinger instead let Iran and Saudi Arabia use their gargantuan price increase to buy even more arms, in effect "recycling" an oil surtax to finance the American arms industry and the U.S. balance of payments. More than $50 billion in weapons were sent to the Middle East in the next ten years, and much more have been sent since. (As part of this arms trade, a series of multi-million-dollar CIA arms shipments were made to Iraqi Kurds, who used them to harass the shah's nemesis, Saddam Hussein. When the shah reached a new accommodation with Hussein in 1975, Kissinger cut off the Kurdish shipments, which allowed Hussein to slaughter thousands of Kurds and force the evacuation of hundreds of thousands more into Turkey and Iran.)

The echoes of Nixon's and Kissinger's response to OPEC were not limited to the Middle East, however. Their policy of mandatory dollar-denomination had many striking effects.†[91] First, it insulated U.S. oil imports from the steady decline of U.S. purchasing power abroad, as the dollar's value depreciated worldwide. Second, it made importing oil more challenging for the Europeans and Japanese, because they had to acquire an ever-growing stream of dollars to

---

*The bribes were discovered by Watergate investigations and eventually led to Hammer's being convicted and sentenced to prison. (Neither Ford nor Reagan would grant him a presidential pardon, but the first President Bush did.)

†The United States' power to insist that not just oil but other commodity prices as well as financial assets and trade transactions of all kinds be denominated in dollars has steadily increased. The IMF reported that by 1999 sixty-five of the world's seventy major traded commodities, 40 percent of international private assets, 60 percent of official currency reserves, and 45 percent of international commodity invoicing were counted in dollars.

finance their oil purchases.[92] Third, in the so-called NOPECs of the Third World—developing countries that lacked indigenous oil supplies—it brutally whipsawed their economies. When the West's demand for their agricultural products and natural resources fell as Western economies went through recession, it drove down their currencies, which raised the cost of imported oil, and simultaneously raised the cost of repaying the loans they'd taken out from Western banks.

No wonder that economists came to call this "the Great World Inflation." (Combined average inflation rates of the major industrial countries reached an unprecedented 13 percent a year by the mid-1970s, compared to barely 2 percent in the late 1960s.[93]) Yet when it gave way to the "Great World Recession" in 1975–77, after oil prices cut further into domestic purchasing power throughout the West and central banks tightened credit, Washington blamed its allies rather than its own policies for the problem. Allies, it complained, were engaging in restrictive trade practices to limit U.S. export sales and in "dirty floating," not letting their own currencies adjust realistically against the dollar, thereby thwarting the achievement of "natural" trade levels. Washington also claimed that the allies, preoccupied as they were by their own struggles against domestic inflation, had overdone their efforts to damp down national demand levels, and that this was exacerbating the global recession.

The solution, from Washington's point of view, was what it always had been since World War II: growth, with the United States as the locomotive driving new international expansion, as it had in the postwar years.[94] Nothing but more growth, it was argued, would break through the "beggar-thy-neighbor" behavior of nations shaken by the recent shocks and uncertainties of the 1970s.

But Galbraith continued to warn that this by itself was a recipe for more crises. In article after article he argued that a big growth push would create further rounds of inflation unless fundamental economic structural changes were made, because it simply was not the case that "markets always know best." Yet as the 1970s wore on, getting to such a politics seemed harder and harder. Nations, companies, workers, and consumers had all become accustomed to inflation in a way that promoted a continuous circle of anticipatory price and wage increases meant to deflect its damage onto others.

In such a world, stimulative government policies directed toward a simple expansion of output would be ineffective—and even countereffective. In Galbraith's view a carefully conceived combination of policies was needed—wage and price controls on the biggest companies and unions, restrained monetary growth, plus tax increases on the well-to-do that would yield revenues to be spent on public goods and services.[95] Given the decade's dramatic increase in mergers and acquisitions, Galbraith even gave up his traditional hostility toward antitrust efforts, arguing that at least for the time being a restraint on the consolidation of the country's biggest businesses would loosen price rigidity and the tendency toward price-led inflation, most especially in the energy sector.

Here, however, the "free market" gospel and the new global private financial system intervened. Dollars in circulation overseas—the so-called Eurodollar market, born initially of the chronic trade deficits the United States had run in the 1960s—had become gargantuan with the ever-larger U.S. trade deficits. From an estimated $11 billion Eurodollar pool in 1965, dollars outside the U.S. had by 1970 reached $60 billion, were by 1975 pushing past $200 billion, and would by the end of the decade soar past the $500 billion mark.[96] These were dollars outside the direct oversight and limits of the Federal Reserve, yet they strongly affected both the U.S. and world economies. Conservative economists, especially monetarists like Milton Friedman, had for years called for just such a world of international monetary freedom, believing that private financial markets would find ways not only to lend funds but also to regulate national currencies' relative valuations much more efficiently than the old Bretton Woods system or the central banks.

The reality was quite different. Awash in lendable funds from 1975 on, the big banks in London and New York had kept pouring out loans to Poland, Mexico, Argentina, the Soviet Union, and dozens of other countries, a practice that came to be called "petrodollar recycling." But as commodity prices fell and financial controls weakened, Galbraith had no difficulty assessing the system's obvious flaw:

> This recycling, as it was imaginatively called, was considered innovative and imaginative at the time as well as an operation at the highest level of financial respectability. Its legacy, so sadly apparent since, was either default or an oppressive burden of debt for the countries so favored, a burden gravely threatening their living standards and the stability of their governments. Some, perhaps much, of the borrowed money was further recycled, without local benefit, to Switzerland or back to New York.[97]

But the bankers, focused on booking the fees they earned for originating the loans, and thinking themselves clever for denominating their loans in dollars and making the interest rates variable rather than fixed, foresaw only an endless stream of profitable new business ahead.

At home, they also undermined financial restraint by hawking easy credit just as relentlessly. When the public discovered the elixir of credit cards, the giant Visa and MasterCard bank networks raced to convince as many Americans as they could that the seemingly limitless opportunities for spending with plastic, not "real," money were the nation's latest God-given right. Prudential, rapid repayment was no longer the banks' goal, since profits now came from the interest and fees charged on unpaid balances.

In a carnival-like orgy of direct marketing, banks sent out hundreds of millions of cards to hastily assembled mailing lists (which often included the newborn, the incarcerated, the dead, even family pets). The number of credit-card holders soared from barely a few million in 1968 to more than 60 million ten years later, and the value of an average card purchase had more than tripled.

The change that credit cards brought to Americans' consumption patterns and attitude toward debt was enormous: from 1970 to 1980, purchases on credit cards went from barely $7 billion to $60 billion, leading one delighted credit-card executive to boast that "the traditional values espoused in *Poor Richard's Almanack* have been turned upside down." Americans, he said, were learning new rules that bankers should encourage:

1. It doesn't pay to save for a rainy day.
2. Buy now, not later; prices will invariably go up and the purchasing power of your dollar will inevitably go down.
3. Stretch your financial obligations over as long a period as possible.
4. Borrowing improves your credit rating.
5. Pay your bills as late as you can (without jeopardizing your credit rating).[98]

As Americans plunged on in this new consumption campaign, something darker lurked behind their anxious spending. The pollster Daniel Yankelovich found that the country had all but abandoned "an older post–World War II attitude of expanded horizons, a growing psychology of entitlement, unfettered optimism, and unqualified confidence in technology and economic growth" and replaced it with "lowering expectations, apprehensions about the future, mistrust in institutions, and a growing psychology of limits."[99]

Those doubts and limits took on dramatic and humiliating expression during the Iran hostage crisis in 1979–81, when for 444 days beginning in November 1979, Iranian students held more than four dozen U.S. citizens prisoner in Teheran in reprisal for the U.S. government's support of the deposed shah. America, it seemed, now needed dramatic change, and it would not be to Galbraith's liking.

AFTER HIS OFFICIAL RETIREMENT from Harvard in 1975, Galbraith continued to stay as involved in public life as ever through lectures, travels, congressional testimony, his articles and interviews for newspapers and magazines, and of course his books. Having taught himself script-writing for *The Age of Uncertainty*, he wrote the series' companion volume and *Money*. And even before the series went on the air, he was back at work each morning in the third-floor study of his home on Francis Avenue, where he spent 1977 to 1979 producing four more books, and more than six dozen magazine and newspaper pieces.

Although he seemed more prolific than ever, critics began to notice a difference: none of the new books rivaled the power or scope of *American Capitalism* or *The Affluent Society* or *The New Industrial State*. One, *Almost Everyone's Guide to Economics*, was a slender, breezy introduction to economics that consisted of interviews with his friend Nicole Salinger, the then wife of President Kennedy's former press secretary, Pierre Salinger. Not inaccurately, *BusinessWeek* dismissed it as a book "only for those with a compulsion to read absolutely everything that John Kenneth Galbraith writes. Even they could beg off because Galbraith didn't actually write this sub-primer."[100] Another, *Annals of an Abiding Liberal*, was a collection of previously published lectures, articles, and reviews written on a hodgepodge of topics, from economics to train travel in India to his own uproarious views on his forty-year-long FBI file.

The Nature of Mass Poverty, however, was a serious book, on a subject worthy of Galbraith's close attention, the title being the one he had planned to use for the book that became *The Affluent Society*.[101] Although it was a slender reworking of lectures he gave in 1978 at both Radcliffe and the University of Geneva, it won accolades from normally critical magazines such as *The Economist*, which complimented him for bringing to it his "great intellectual energy and one of the sharpest pens economics has known."[102] In it he took on several presumptions in development economics—the importance of outside investment in infrastructure, the cultivation of foreign aid and private foreign investors, and faith in application of the latest Western technology—and suggested that they did not necessarily make for the optimal path to development and the reduction of poverty. He had come to many of these conclusions twenty years before, but they seemed important to expand in a new context. Again he emphasized the significance of elementary education (especially for women), democratic and relatively corruption-free political regimes, the application of "appropriate technologies" that were inexpensive and easy to operate, and greater reliance on internal capital and skills. Economic development theory was about to undergo a major reorientation toward "market-based solutions" and the application of "structural adjustment programs"; it would take another fifteen years and the repeated failure of these policies before aid agencies, the IMF, and the World Bank rediscovered the essential wisdom Galbraith brought to the problem of global development.

Galbraith himself realized that none of these works with the exception of *The Nature of Mass Poverty* had a compelling thesis to rival those of his important earlier books. In effect, the new books were Galbraithian Baedekers, offering *tours d'horizon* of modern economic and political history leavened by dashes of economic theory that made them engaging, entertaining, and informative to the general reader, but they lacked distinctive new intellectual contributions. More than a few critics began wondering aloud whether Galbraith's powers as a writer and critic were finally waning.

Late in 1979, a single moment seemed to encapsulate the inevitable transition going on at several levels at the very end of the decade. In Boston the John F. Kennedy Presidential Library opened to enormous fanfare. President Carter flew up to keynote its dedication, seven thousand guests were served box lunches in the library's parking lot, and throughout the city, weekend parties celebrated the Kennedy legacy. But, *The Washington Post* noted, the party at the Galbraiths' was "the ultimate Camelot reunion."[103]

The term seems exactly right, for Galbraith symbolized the party's past and not its future to the "new Democrats" around Jimmy Carter. The Democratic Party, the nation, the world were coming to accept the idea that a new market-driven philosophy was replacing the older liberal balance between markets and governments. Yet that change—if it was happening—was not coming easily. Galbraith meanwhile did not think that his brand of liberalism needed to be abandoned, as so many people implied that it must. For him, the new ways of thinking in the Democratic party weren't new at all, and they certainly weren't persuasive. The GOP was undergoing its own shift rightward under Ronald Reagan—and America didn't need two conservative parties. Milton Friedman and Galbraith stood on opposite sides of an enormous ideological and political divide, and nothing in the values that Friedman professed inspired him. The Chicagoan's brand of ideological conservatism that Reagan embodied politically reminded Galbraith of a remark Keynes had once made about Hayek and *The Road to Serfdom*: the book was, Keynes dryly observed, "an extraordinary example of how, starting with a mistake, a remorseless logician can end up in Bedlam."[104]

When a year later Jimmy Carter lost the presidency to Ronald Reagan, and an even more conservative time in American politics and economics got under way, Galbraith celebrated the dawn of the Reagan era by publishing his memoirs, *A Life in Our Times*. At more than 560 pages, it was the longest work he'd ever written. Suffused with his trademark wit, keen character sketches, and intimate descriptions of encounters over the years with the century's leading political, literary, and academic figures, it rose swiftly on the best-seller list and won raves from most critics.

Yet the very fact that it was a memoir rather than a work of economics meant something, for Galbraith made no attempt to propound new economic ideas or even comment on Reagan's election. In fact, the final chapter gave the reader an unmistakable (and for his admirers, rather melancholic) impression that its author believed his ability to contribute more new ideas was at an end.

> Readers and more especially authors should be warned as to books written after sixty; the creative impulse survives more powerfully, I'm persuaded, than the critical judgment of what is written. If you continue to write, you have especially to be on guard against the tendency to plagiarize yourself. Words come to mind that are resonant in their meaning or expository power. The idea so framed is a thing of clarity and brilliance. Presently you discover, although sometimes you do not, that one reason it is so wonderful is because you have said it before.[105]

Galbraith used the next few pages to discuss the writing of *Economics and the Public Purpose* and creation of *The Age of Uncertainty*, but the brief review he gave both—and his almost complete silence on the array of troubles that had beset liberal politics, Keynesian economics, and the economy itself in the previous decade—suggested disengagement and even a hint of a disillusionment that he'd never before shown.

At the end of the book, he recalled the influential financier Bernard Baruch, who in old age declined into a political version of the Norma Desmond character in *Sunset Boulevard*, the forgotten silent-screen actress who still imagines herself an important star insisting, "I am big. It's the pictures that got small." By World War II, for young men like Galbraith then, Baruch was "to all of us ancient but still determined to obtrude, be at the center. We thought him something of a bore."

Galbraith was now almost seventy-three. He noted that he had opposed Jimmy Carter's nomination in 1976 and had done so again in 1980, the second time by supporting Senator Kennedy. The price of his opposition to Carter was that he ended up watching the Democratic National Convention proceedings from the stands rather than from the convention floor where he'd been for so many years. He closed the book with these bittersweet words: "I have noticed that those who write their memoirs have difficulty in knowing when, on public matters, they should stop. The obvious stopping point is when the view is from the stands."[106]

23

The Economics of Joy

For more than 35 years, economic theory—the skein of Cambridge (U.K. and U.S.A.) economics woven by Alfred Marshall, John Maynard Keynes, and Paul Samuelson—has been a powerful force directing economic policy. Today, there is general agreement that government economic management and policy is in disarray.

Many economists argue that prescriptions derived from previous historical situations no longer apply, but there is little consensus as to new prescriptions. Indeed there is emerging a prior question about the fundamental postulates of this neoclassical economics—about the model of a competitive equilibrium, and about the guiding assumptions as to how individuals, firms, and governments behave.
    —Daniel Bell, *The Crisis of Economic Theory*, 1981

Do we really need a Council of Economic Advisors?
    —President Ronald Reagan, 1981

BY THE 1980s, few economists could ignore how noisily quarrelsome their profession had become. In the 1950s, Paul Samuelson had famously been able to insist that a broad postwar consensus had emerged, a sort of Keynesian version of medieval Europe's Catholic unity. But now—though the Church of Keynes remained—a much more raucous world of competing evangelists prevailed.

Samuelson himself acknowledged that much had changed in the preface to his legendary textbook's twelfth edition. *Economics* had introduced millions to the field since it first appeared in 1948, but now Samuelson had to explain how drastically the profession had shifted. Recognizing that his colleagues sounded more like a cacophony than a choir, he promised his young readers that he had undertaken his textbook's "most sweeping revision" ever. One key change, he assured them, was that he had now "integrated different schools of thought—Keynesian, classical, monetarist, supply-side, rational-expectations, and modern mainstream" theories as well as "post-Keynesian eclecticism, . . . Chicago libertarianism, . . . Marxism and radical economics" into the work. He also paid more attention to Galbraith's ideas about the affluent society and technostructure, and gave him a notable compliment. Galbraith's critics, he said, "miss the point . . . In the history of ideas, the thinker who creates a new synthesis and speaks in telling fashion to a new age is the one who plays the pivotal role in history." *Economics*, he promised, now represented "an *authoritative* statement of the accumulated knowledge of generations of economists."[1]

His use of the verb "integrate," however, was a literary sleight-of-hand. In truth, it meant only that he'd incorporated summaries of these otherwise often totally incompatible theories into his massive text. Real "integration"—in the sense of a stable intellectual synthesis—was beyond even Samuelson's unquestionable genius.

In fact, Samuelson's list was incomplete: one could easily expand it with "traditional" and "revisionist" Keynesians of various schools, neo-Keynesians, post-Keynesians, environmental economists (some favoring "limits-to-growth," some not, some bitterly antimarginalist, some convinced all environmental problems were simply "externalities" questions, capable of solution by the marginalist model), feminist economists (of varying views), liberal Institutionalists (and, to confuse matters, the more conservative New Institutionalists), old Austrians and neo-Austrians, New Classicals, "new-micro"-economists (and for good measure a dissenting group of "new-new-micro"-economists), advocates for "industrial policy" and proponents of Real Business Cycle theory, and even, at the dimmer margins, a handful of resurgent gold-standard cranks, an ineradicable nuisance.

Hoping to cast the best possible light on their disarray and disagreements, the young Harvard economist Gregory Mankiw, a rising star in the profession, diplomatically suggested that perhaps the nation's economists were merely undergoing "a period of confusion, division, and excitement," implying that from all this a grand new synthesis might arise.[2] Older and wiser about his colleagues, Princeton's Alan Blinder was more forthright—and offered no such hope of reunification. "Contemporary macroeconomics," he complained, "is fractious, argumentative, and frustrating. The schisms among Keynesians, monetarists, rational expectationists, and supply siders . . . are real. And they are giving economics a bad name."[3] But the great MIT veteran Robert Solow offered perhaps the most telling admission, even though it amounted to faulting the patient rather than the doctors: "The economy," Solow remarked, "simply isn't very predictable."[4]

Galbraith might have been forgiven a hint of *Schadenfreude* at all this turmoil, but instead he felt foreboding. "It was not difficult by 1980 to see that American politics and the economy were as turbulent as economic theory," he says. "After Senator McGovern's defeat, we liberal Democrats had lost standing in the party and the country as a whole. A new generation without experience of the Depression or New Deal emerged. Business lost all confidence in government's ability to manage the business cycle. And the oil shocks and stagflation played havoc with the public's confidence."[5]

To Galbraith, economics' intellectual disorder wasn't to be explained by the "unpredictability" of the economy, since he didn't consider it an independent variable; instead he understood its erratic performance by focusing on the one hand on theory, and on the other by relating the connection between the structure of the economy and politics and ideology in the real world. On the theoretical level, Galbraith thought the failure to comprehend the economy's erratic behavior was due to the intellectual "bargains" that mainstream Keynesians had made. He once again faulted the Neoclassical Synthesis for wedding Keynesian macroeconomics to neoclassical microeconomics, rather than developing a clearer role for the influence of power, ideology, and group interests—and a model of policy-making that emphasized the complex social and political foundations of choice. In the 1960s, this had left New Economists unprepared for the consequences of the Vietnam War; in the 1970s, it had left them unprepared for stagflation and paved the way for their conservative opponents.

> The separation of microeconomics from the purview of Keynesian economics and policy thus preserved a microeconomic model that could not be accorded an inflationary role. This separation was important; it was at the very heart of the great compromise of Keynes with the classical tradition, the compromise that preserved the market nexus. To admit of the inflationary role of the wage-price spiral was to destroy that compromise. Worse still, it was to invite policies—wage and price restraints—that surrendered the market, in greater or lesser measure, to the authority of the state.[6]

So when the New Economics' policies "failed" in the 1960s, and Nixon's wage-price policies failed in the 1970s, there was only the hammer of monetary policy left. Because wage-price controls (however designed) had never been part of mainstream Keynesian theory, their misuse in Nixon's New Economic Policy helped delegitimize any role for them.[*]

The global economy by the 1980s was consequently going through a new stage of highly uneven integration, Galbraith believed, which owed as much to politically negotiated relations as to Marshallian "market forces." Economies that once had been only distantly connected (the American and Japanese for example) were now closely linked, and so-called Asian Tigers such as Taiwan and South Korea—which thirty years earlier had been in a sense precapitalist, based on agricultural subsistence, with only limited urbanization, industrialization, and modern financial structures—were now increasingly competitive as their products often quite disruptively flooded the West. The development

---

[*]Galbraith was not alone in advocating serious use of wage and price controls to stem inflation. Barry Bosworth and Bruce McLaury of Brookings, James Tobin at Yale, Francis Bator at Harvard, and Wall Street economist Henry Kaufman all supported such controls, though several still saw the need as ad hoc rather than permanent.

process in these Asian countries bore little resemblance to textbook theory, with oligopolistic firms dominating the lucrative export markets and governments constantly intervening in violation of marginalist tenets. (Japan's *keiretsu* and South Korea's *chaebols* were the clearest examples in Asia, and Raul Prebisch's import-substitution programs the signature form in Latin America.) OPEC's cartelization of oil was a further violation, both in the enormous surtax it levied on economic growth and in the "petrodollar recycling" problem it created for global financial markets.

In the United States, Galbraith traced out the political elements of economic policy, from Nixon's "Keynesianism," and the "WIN" buttons of Gerald Ford, to the stop-start inconsistency of policies under Jimmy Carter. "None of these efforts" to address poor economic performance, he argued, "was serious or legitimate. They were temporary steps, wise or not so wise, meant to serve until the Keynesian macroeconomic policy came somehow to perform its established function in combining reasonably full employment with stable prices." But restoring Keynesian order hadn't been possible because the social trust underpinning the postwar economic bargain among business, labor, and government had vanished. Once it was gone, neoclassical logic, which has actors acting out of self-interest and in which accounting for behavior based on mutual trust is dodgy at best, had rushed into the breach.* "Since neither unions nor business firms . . . were inclined to accept government interference with wages and prices, the traditional defenders of the integrity of the microeconomic market had decisively powerful allies."[7]

Yet explaining the ways in which the United States and global economies were changing in terms of abstract neoclassical behavior seemed preposterous to Galbraith. A real explanation required understanding the larger political-economic context of Cold War competition, the new multinational dimensions of corporate power, and America's behavior as what political scientists call a "hegemonic force" that generated, consciously or inadvertently, certain path dependencies—for example, by persuading OPEC to denominate all oil sales in dollars, or by ignoring the statist, oligopolistic development practices of favored exporters such as South Korea or Taiwan or Mexico, which hardly produced textbook market behavior or relations.

Domestically, one had to see that a system of huge organizations—big corporations, unions, government—had partially supplanted and contained the power of traditional markets. This was the precondition for understanding the wage-price spirals and resulting stagflation. "From the interaction of these entities had come a new and powerful inflationary force: the upward pressure of wage settlements on prices, the upward pull of prices and living costs on wages."[8] It was in this context, a struggle as much political as economic, that

---

*Game theory does a better job of accounting for mutual trust leading to otherwise seemingly sub-optimizing behavior. Elements of the new "information theory" approaches also offer abstract explanations, but, like game theory, say little about how actual real-world power, persuasion, and ideology affect mutual accommodations. It is Galbraith's central claim that historically informed "political economy" still does the best job of coherent explanation.

the dismal performance of the U.S. economy was occurring. For Galbraith, improvement could come only when citizens chose to support new democratic governments, here and abroad, that were committed to an equitable and efficient new global economic balance.

In one sense, Galbraith, in what to many seemed pure idealism, was actually being a modern pragmatist: the "truth" of an economic theory ultimately lay in its "success" or failure when applied as policy. But a well-designed policy's success was contingent on its supporters' abilities to persuade and/or coerce its recognition and acceptance by other economic actors. Public policy, at the simplest level, required, first, government action and then a certain set of anticipated reactions by investors, producers, workers, and consumers to create a "virtuous" growth cycle. But abstractly "correct" Keynesian actions by government might produce the "wrong" outcomes if the others reacted in unanticipated ways. For example, given a tax break, investors might hesitate to invest if they anticipated that taxes would soon rise again. Or consumers with a heavy debt load might use their tax breaks to cut their debt rather than make new purchases. Either of these responses would stymie the expansionary effect of the tax break. Beliefs and expectations, in other words, were central to the success of public policy and thus to the validity of Keynesian theory. And beliefs are held, influenced, and communicated by groups. Each time government set a new policy, the policy was filtered through preexisting beliefs and expectations of those groups. If it was at odds with the interests or beliefs of significant, powerful groups, the likelihood of failure increased.

Something like this, in Galbraith's view, had happened during the 1970s, when distrust and hostility toward activist government had grown precipitously for various reasons, including political ones ("Vietnam," "civil rights," "Watergate"). At the same time, new economic factors such as the oil price hikes, the explosive growth of consumer credit and corporate debt, the multinationalization of large corporations, and development of the Eurodollar market were shifting the terms of reference (beliefs) and horizons (expectations) of investors, producers, workers, and government. Under the circumstances (many of them clearly international in scope and nature), government policies were met with suspicion, hostility, and even resistance. With millions of angry voters cynical about government, and encouraged in that anger and cynicism by a rising New Right, policies were doomed to be only weakly effective, especially if they addressed international problems with national, rather than cooperatively international, solutions.

Conservative economists and political scientists such as Gordon Tullock, James Buchanan, and Anthony Downs had reached much the same analytic conclusion about the increasing ineffectiveness of government policies. But they had done so through neoclassical assumptions of radical individualism, and their remedy went in the opposite direction. Galbraith's remedy involved the restoration of liberalism and Keynesian government; theirs was to scorn liberalism and reduce government's role for achieving liberal ends in the economy to a minimum. The resurgence of this conservatism and its consequences became the subject of most of Galbraith's work in the 1980s. He offered less analysis of the economy's structure (his focus in *The Affluent Society* and *The New Industrial State*) and almost no prescriptive alternatives (as in *Economics and the Public Purpose*). The reason why was simple enough: the urgent political task, he thought, was to oppose this new conservative movement. If liberals lost the political battle, and public consensus shifted even further right, Keynesianism's policy and theory risked permanent irrelevance. It was no surprise that all the fractious debates among academic economists thus annoyed Galbraith as never before, and produced some of his sharpest jibes.

> One of the astonishing and little-examined aberrations of academic, professional, and business life is the prestige that is accorded without thought to the specialist . . . [Yet] there can be no doubt that, in economics, specialization is the parent not only of boredom but also of irrelevance and error. Certainly, this is so in all practical matters. Widespread influences, many of them from far outside the "field" as it is commonly defined for classroom convenience, bear on every important economic decision . . . [But] the specialist, by his or her training, righteously excludes what it is convenient not to know. The specialized economist is thus spared the relatively modest expenditure of energy and intelligence that would bring most of economics and much of the relevant politics, social relations, and psychology within his grasp.[9]

To Galbraith, the only virtue of intensive economic specialization was that few people besides economists cared about it.

That didn't mean Americans weren't concerned about economic issues. To the contrary, the economy was issue number one in almost every poll taken during the 1980s. But just as Galbraith warned, the arguments over economics that dominated Washington, think tanks, and the press were shaped by a politicized, ideological, and highly partisan agenda, and fueled by the ambitions and interests of those who led the conservative revolution not just in Washington, but across America on a dozen fronts at once.*

Like many before it, that revolution (or counterrevolution, depending on one's point of view) was actually at most a loose alliance of often contentious, incongruent groups and individuals. Some of them, like Galbraith's friend William F. Buckley, were charter members from the mid-1950s; millions more joined as recent converts, caught up in the evangelism of Goldwaterites or in the backlash against civil rights and Vietnam activism. But they came together in support of an alliance that had acquired a name that helped conceal its disparate and discordant strands: "The Reagan Revolution," in recognition of the President who better than anyone else had come to articulate the values that shaped it.[10]

---

*Simultaneously, a similar revolution was occurring in Britain, marked by Margaret Thatcher's ascendancy. How widely the conservative revolt spread around the planet is a question worth complex debate.

By any conventional standard, the amiable ex-actor (and former New Deal Democrat), just three years younger than Galbraith, hardly seemed to qualify as a revolutionary.* But as one Republican chronicler of the decade put it,

> By 1980 the country was ready for a more radical turn of economic policy to the right than had been seen since 1896—possibly ever. There was a greater feeling than at any time in forty years that prevailing policy had failed—and that was conventional liberal policy. And the country elected a President who was devoted to such a radical turn. He was no "modern" Republican or "moderate" conservative—terms which in his world had come to mean liberal in disguise.[11]

One of Reagan's own Council of Economic Advisors economists was even blunter: "Views that were once regarded as those of right-wing extremists became the views that would elect a president."[12]

One historian has summarized the stunning goal Reagan set out to achieve—and in some ways accomplished:

> In winning the presidency, this erstwhile movie actor performed one of the most striking political feats of the modern era: he stole the growth issue that had for a generation been a Democratic staple, repackaged it, and made it his own. What Richard Nixon sought to do by stealth and indirection, Reagan did with flare and fanfare. In the 1980s, Reagan used the growth issue to alter fundamentally, in ways both good and bad, intended and unintended, the political economy of modern America . . . in an effort to drive a stake through the heart of modern liberalism.[13]

Unlike Nixon (or Ford), Reagan entered the White House with no Washington experience, a fact that he wore as a badge of honor. Jimmy Carter had done this, too, but as an engineer-president who tried to micromanage too many elements of his own policies and got lost in their intricacies. Reagan had no intention of repeating this mistake. What he brought to Washington were powerfully simple convictions, central to which was the belief, as he often put it, that Washington itself "is the problem, not the solution." Government at all levels, this new President insisted, had grown too large, too rich, too regulatory, and too intrusive—and he intended to use his presidency to reverse that cancerous trend. He told voters that they had a choice "between two different visions of the future, two fundamentally different ways of governing—their government of pessimism, fear, and limits, or ours of hope, confidence, and

---

*Reagan's victory margin in 1980 spoke more to the willpower of the revolutionaries than initial popular support for the revolution he was leading. He won narrowly in 1980, with 50.7 percent of the popular vote, the worst showing by any Republican elected president in the twentieth century save Nixon in the three-way 1968 campaign. Reagan fared much better in 1984, garnering 58.8 percent, but even that solid performance ranked him behind FDR, LBJ, Nixon in 1972, and even Warren Harding and Herbert Hoover.

growth." Twenty years earlier, the gifted sociologist Daniel Bell, pondering the large trends of the twentieth century, had concluded that America was entering a new age defined by "the end of ideology." If so, it was somehow a thesis that had escaped the notice of Reagan and his allies.

IT'S SAFE TO SAY that virtually everything about "Reaganomics" and the Reagan Revolution appalled Ken Galbraith. He had known Reagan personally, though not well, from their days in Americans for Democratic Action in the late 1940s, when he had found the actor pleasant but little more. He had lost touch with Reagan in the 1950s and was mildly surprised to find him at the 1964 Republican convention, fervently endorsing Barry Goldwater's nomination.[14] He was more surprised in 1966, when Reagan defeated California's popular two-term liberal governor, Edmund "Pat" Brown. But like many others at the time, he assumed Reagan's political career would end there, scuttled by the "extremism" of his views.[15]

Two days after Reagan's inauguration in January 1981, Galbraith laid out in detail his concerns not only about Reagan's announced plans but also the broader rightward political and ideological shift under way. In "The Conservative Onslaught," a long essay for *The New York Review of Books* (to which he frequently contributed), he derided the coming consequences of the "Reagan Revolution," and correctly named Arthur Laffer's supply-side ideas, Milton Friedman's monetarism, and William Simon's hyperconservative commitment to tax cutting for the wealthy and corporations, and their shared contempt for the public sector, as the basic concepts that would guide it.[16] He was willing to allow that much was imperfect about modern government and its macromanagement efforts by now, in particular its attempts to end stagflation in the 1970s. But he was excoriating toward those who thought that the country's redemption merely required a higher devotion to "the genius of markets" to remedy the situation. The new administration, he warned, in "its design for economic management incorporates all of the old elements of failure in a somewhat exaggerated form."[17]

Not surprisingly, Reagan and his supporters disagreed. Liberalism and Big Government were "the old elements of failure" which Reaganomics was going to purge, starting with the government's hand in the economy, and especially the "socialistic" federal tax code that collected nearly 20 percent of GDP each year. Barely a month into office, the President introduced the Economic Recovery Tax Act, a sweeping proposal meant to slash tax brackets by 30 percent over three years, with its benefits strongly and unapologetically weighted toward the upper-income brackets and corporations. Republican advocacy of tax cuts favoring the well-to-do was of course an idée fixe of all modern GOP fiscal policy-makers.*[18] What distinguished Reagan's 1981 tax bill and his first

---

*In the 1920s, a decade after the federal income tax became constitutional but was still levied only on the top 2 percent of households, Andrew Mellon, Calvin Coolidge's multimillionaire Treasury Secretary, became the GOP's first supply-sider. Ignoring the rising overall tax burden imposed by states and localities on the bottom 98 percent, he successfully cut the federal income, estate, and capital-market taxes. Unlike Arthur Laffer's

budget were startling new features that neither Eisenhower, Nixon, nor Ford had attempted: the tax cuts were of unprecedented size; the spending cuts in nearly 300 domestic programs were equally huge; these domestic cuts were more than offset by massive new military spending; he proclaimed an intention to balance the budget by 1984, his first three goals notwithstanding; and he made novel arguments in defense of his plans.

During the primaries, Reagan had not hidden the scope of this agenda. Alarmed by his radicalism, more traditional Republicans launched blistering attacks. George Bush's charge of "voodoo economics" was the most famous, while Senator Howard Baker suggested that Reaganomics was "a riverboat gamble." But once Reagan was in the White House, Republicans closed ranks; Bush was now Vice President and Baker, Senate Majority Leader (and by 1985 White House chief of staff). Even so, one veteran GOP economist admitted that the new President's plans represented "the rejection of traditional Republican policies." Indeed, it was "more than that—by denying that the objectives being pursued had any costs," Reagonomics risked becoming a dangerously delusional "economics of joy."[19]

Reaganomics indeed indisputably, passionately, and eagerly broke with traditional Republican policies. Reagan represented a new Republican Party, one that now closely resembled Richard Nixon's dream of a "new Republican majority"; it was solidly based in the South and Southwest and wanted nothing to do with the compromises of "Tory men and liberal policies." Sun Belt Republicans from booming cities and suburbs were calling the political tune. In place of old-guard "Yankee Republicans," it was "Cowboy and Confederate Republicans" who controlled the party, and Ronald Reagan was their Jefferson Davis.[20]

That Reagan's "economics of joy" was consciously and strategically political didn't mean that it lacked intellectual underpinnings. As Galbraith emphasized when Reagan took office, it leaned heavily on the ideas of Galbraith's nemesis Milton Friedman and on his reputation as a prophet among these rebellious new conservatives (burnished by Friedman's support for their hero Barry Goldwater). The old country-club shibboleths of Yankee Republicans—the moral and civic virtue of lower taxes for the well-to-do, balanced budgets, and as little government regulation and social spending as possible—took on a new intellectual respectability, thanks to their association with monetarism's alleged theoretical superiority to "failed" Keynesianism. Even though those who held to these older GOP premises soon shouldered aside Friedman's core monetarist goals—predictable and stable money supply growth—Friedman proudly claimed the Reagan program as his own.

The intellectual patrimony of Reaganomics also drew heavily on a newer conservative "theory" called "supply-side economics" that had been advanced by a brash young Stanford-trained business economist named Arthur Laffer.

1980s plan, Mellon's didn't spark deficits because the government's budget was already heavily in surplus, and with Coolidge limiting spending, the cuts increased the surplus; instead its stimulative effect was to spark the stock market's wild run-up, which ended in collapse in 1929 and launched the Great Depression (see Hession and Sardy, *Ascent to Affluence*, 680–83).

After a stint working under Donald Rumsfeld in the Nixon administration, Laffer had gone on to teaching at the University of Chicago's business school. As the oft-told tale had it, Laffer first sketched out his famous "Laffer Curve" on a cocktail napkin at a Washington restaurant. One of his two dinner companions was Richard Cheney, who'd worked with Laffer under Rumsfeld during the Nixon years and who apparently needed the napkin diagram to follow Laffer's arguments; the other was a zealous young *Wall Street Journal* editorial writer named Jude Wanniski.[21] Drawing a little curve that resembled a round hill, Laffer explained to Cheney and Wanniski that it represented tax rates and their relation to overall tax revenues. On the rising left side of the curve, where tax rates were low or moderate, a tax increase might increase revenues; but past the midway turn and on the falling right side of the curve, as rates went higher further increases in taxes would only lower revenues.

By itself, the insight underlying the Laffer Curve was nothing new to economists, as Galbraith and others frequently pointed out: it was the application of the old microeconomic "law of diminishing returns" to the macroeconomics of public finance. It said simply that if tax rates became confiscatory, people would reduce their efforts to earn additional income. Laffer's innovation, as he passed the napkin to Cheney and Wanniski, was to convince them—and over the next few years, an army of conservative journalists, think-tank analysts, and politicians—that America was already so burdened by confiscatory taxes that it had passed the summit of the curve.

(Another account of the origins of modern supply-side theory features the brilliant Robert Mundell as the person responsible for its theoretical development and for inspiring Laffer's interests in the subject. Wanniski was always well aware of Mundell's importance. But Mundell's eccentricities—his long hair, use of alcohol and other stimulants, and bouts with emotional instability—made him a poor poster child for supply-side theory among conservatives, though he won the Nobel Prize in 1999.[22])

Politically, supply-side theory intoxicated the right, because it promised that most perfect of dreams: profound change without pain. The Laffer Curve implied not only that lower taxes were virtuous in and of themselves (the established Republican faith), but that they would promptly increase the total amount of goods and services supplied to the economy (hence the "supply-side" appellation) and thereby drive growth. Even more important, it would satisfy a second great pillar of Reaganomics: the increased government revenues from this new growth would finance the immense military expenditures Reagan wanted to undertake.

In short, according to supply-siders, this new generation of Republican conservatives could have it all. They could cut taxes on the well-to-do and corporations *and* increase U.S. military and covert operations to confront the "Evil Empire" of Soviet Communism, not to mention the rampant and expanding Communist influence stretching from El Salvador and Nicaragua to Angola and Mozambique to Afghanistan. All the while Republicans could take political credit for growing the economy faster.[23]

The Laffer Curve never won widespread support among economists (although it did seduce a vociferous minority) for the embarrassingly simple reason that a vast amount of empirical evidence contradicted its central claim that Americans were overtaxed. Europeans paid substantially higher taxes than Americans, yet during the three decades after World War II, Europe's economies showed steadily better growth rates.[24] In the United States, most higher-tax states such as Massachusetts and California showed better growth rates than lower-tax states.[25] The clear implication was that major tax-cutting would not produce a burst in economic supply and hence the public revenues that Laffer predicted—meaning that big deficits would be the inevitable consequence. But thanks to the near-evangelical zeal of Wanniski, who sold Laffer and supply-side to his editorial-page boss Robert Bartley at *The Wall Street Journal*, and thereby to a receptive business community; to the neoconservative intellectual Irving Kristol, who touted it to intellectuals in *The Public Interest*; and to Jack Kemp, the ebullient former Buffalo Bills quarterback turned conservative Republican congressman, who preached it to party colleagues, supply-side economics was almost overnight transformed into GOP doctrine.*[26]

As the supply-siders' star rose, they brought a second gift to the conservative policy table to match their promise of painless growth: a "solution" to the employment-inflation dilemma. Most economists had backed away from the mainstream Keynesians' Phillips Curve "trade-off" model in favor of Friedman's "natural rate" theory of unemployment; yet they were still convinced that bringing down persistently high inflation would entail a sharp, painful, and prolonged increase in unemployment before the economy settled into equilibrium. Supply-siders now ingeniously argued that the increases in productive output, savings, and income that would follow from their proposed tax cuts would almost instantaneously bring demand-supply relations into equilibrium, and therefore require no such massive layoffs. Asked whether he really thought such increases would come so quickly, Laffer blithely replied, "How long does it take you to reach over and pick up a fifty-dollar bill in a crowd?"[27]

Here, truly, was the heart of Reagan's "economics of joy." If Laffer was right, it meant no one would have to suffer while the inflation inherited from the 1970s was wrung out of the economy. The GOP's old "castor oil" approach that accepted slow growth and sustained unemployment (which Gerald Ford had endorsed under the tutelage of Alan Greenspan and William Simon, and which contributed heavily to Ford's defeat in 1976) would henceforth be a thing of the past, as alien to modern Republican economic policy as surgery without anesthetics.

By January 1981, all that remained was to put supply-side theory into practice—and under Reagan that was assured. Laffer and Kemp had been key eco-

*Conservative Democrats were also deeply enamored. Senator Lloyd Bentsen of Texas (who later became President Clinton's first Treasury Secretary) called it "the start of a new era in economic thinking," and the Democratic-controlled Joint Economic Committee issued a number of studies that generally endorsed it.

nomic advisers during the campaign, and persuading Reagan was like "pushing on an open door," his aide Ed Meese later said. "Reagan was a supply-sider long before the term was invented."[28]

Galbraith steadfastly warned that the truth was that most of the Reagan people were motivated by an unprecedented greed matched only by their indifference to the poor. To him, the clearest evidence was the 1981 Economic Recovery Tax Act's unapologetic favoritism toward the well-to-do set alongside the stiff $45 billion in cuts Reagan demanded at the same time in Medicaid, low-income housing, and school lunch programs (the last best remembered for the President's defense of ketchup as a school-meal vegetable for children).

Four months after Reagan took office, congressional Democrats were wringing their hands over how to react to his tax- and budget-cut proposals, but Galbraith wasn't. In *The New York Times Magazine* that spring he labelled the new Reagan era as what he saw it to be: the modern resurrection of the nineteenth century's Gilded Age. "The Uses and Excuses for Affluence" opened with the description of a lavish ball organized in 1897 in New York City. At a cost of $400,000 (roughly $4 million in 1980s terms), Mrs. Bradley Martin had had the Waldorf Hotel ballroom transformed into a replica of Versailles and invited several hundred guests to attend in period costume. In the midst of a severe economic recession, her ostentatious display itself was mind-boggling, but was outdone by the hostess's apparently sincere explanation for it: Somehow she had learned that the poor of New York were facing great distress that winter and her thought was that a grand party's exuberant display of enjoyment of life might somehow, if properly reported, lessen the burdens of those who heard about it—and might also helpfully give direct employment to the legion of cooks, florists, waiters, carriage drivers, and dishwashers retained for the occasion.

Supply-side economics was born that night, Galbraith deadpanned, and he compared Mrs. Bradley's ball to Reagan's economic agenda and worldview. This was Galbraith at his witty and polemical best, drawing out historical precedents, deftly deflating the pretensions of the well-to-do and the vacuousness of their defenders. For Galbraith, the Reverend Jerry Falwell, in claiming that wealth was God's way of "blessing those who put Him first," was no different from that great Gilded Age Social Darwinist William Graham Sumner (himself a clergyman), with his claim that millionaires were "a product of natural selection." The indifference of the Social Darwinists toward the poor may have been muted for ninety years, he added, but it had found new expression in the 1980s. Nowhere was this better captured than in Reagan's Budget Director's curt defense of massive cuts in social spending: "I don't think people are *entitled* to any services."

Galbraith accurately predicted that a vast stream of deficits would flow from the supply-siders' nostrums, that the economic well-being of the majority would show no gains, and that simultaneous adherence to monetarist doctrine would indeed push inflation out of the system, but only by provoking a severe recession. It was only by masking these likely consequences—and relying on Mrs. Martin's vindication of the indulgences of a few as a benefit for all—that Reaganomics could hope to succeed. Wryly he called on the President to speak "candidly," urging him to tell Americans straightforwardly "that wealth is enjoyed, that more is always wanted . . . so it has always been, so it is now. The present income tax reduces this pleasure . . . and that is why it isn't liked by most of those who have to pay the most."[29]

Galbraith's energy for campaigning against Reagan seemed boundless right from the start. He published thirty-eight articles in Reagan's first year alone, hammering away at the administration's economic, foreign, and military policies. In the first four weeks after the inaugural, his byline appeared in *The New York Times*, *The Washington Post*, *The Times* of London, *The New York Review of Books*, *The Des Moines Register*, and the Los Angeles *Herald Examiner*, and he delivered five speeches in three countries. Over the next seven years, Galbraith never broke stride.

Reagan supporters quickly returned fire. One of the President's most vehement defenders was Robert Nisbet, a onetime left-liberal sociologist turned neoconservative, who lambasted Galbraith in *Commentary* that fall in a mood of high dudgeon: "More than anyone else I can think of John Kenneth Galbraith is the nearly perfect exemplar of American liberalism. No one comes close to Galbraith in the exquisite fit of his mind and its limitations to the essential theme and the varied idols of the liberal cause in our times."[30] To begin with, Galbraith "was not and never will be noted as an economist," and was clearly inferior to "the Mises, the Hayeks, the Friedmans, Haberlers, and Fellners of this world" because his truth was contained in "a triangle formed by the names of Marx, Veblen, and Keynes." It wasn't enough that Galbraith was intellectually inferior and a partial Marxist; he was, Nisbet added, a terrible writer, too. "The patterning of words means more to him than the fusion of words to thoughts . . . which is the true test of style." Galbraith's writing was merely "*Weltschmerz*, with *fin-de-siècle* pretensions, but not enduring, memorable, or evocative literature." With his mind "befuddled or else muddied by liberal dogma," Galbraith's sole economic goal was "the eradication of as much of the private free enterprise system as possible."

The fact was, Nisbet decided, Galbraith suffered from the clinical psychopathology of "cognitive dissonance . . . a phenomenon characteristic for example of pre-millenarian religious groups," the woolly, wild-eyed sort that predict the imminent end of the world, then, when faced with its continued existence, simply advance the date rather than question their faith. The consequence of his preaching was that "through tracts like Galbraith's *The Affluent Society* the expectations [of Americans] multiplied and grew grander, ever harder to gratify," resulting in "social and moral chaos, reflected in the exponentially rising number of security guards, security dogs, alarm systems, and, of course, handguns."

Nisbet's charges were heady even by the harsh new rhetorical standards of the 1980s. None of Galbraith's earlier critics—Solow, Friedman, the Harvard Overseers who tried to deny his tenure, Stigler, or even Hayek—had ever leveled such a sweeping indictment, or its claim of mental illness. "Accused of many things in my life," Galbraith recalled with a smile, "I do not ever remember thinking myself responsible for social and moral chaos or an increase in handgun sales."[31] The attacks by Nisbet—soon followed by George Gilder, Arthur Laffer, Milton Friedman, William F. Buckley, *The Wall Street Journal*, *Forbes*, and even at one point by Vice President Bush during a face-to-face debate in Geneva—fazed him not at all.

In fact, they seemed to energize him to concentrate on bigger political game—and in that hunt, he showed all the experience he'd acquired playing Washington power politics since the 1930s. In one particularly deft *Washington Post* op-ed, Galbraith described a recent lunch he'd had at the American Enterprise Institute, where he was to debate George Gilder, "the new high priest of high (and romantic) capitalism." His lunch was with three "old friends" of his generation: Arthur Burns, former head of the Federal Reserve; Gottfried Haberler; and William Fellner, a former CEA member under Nixon, "and before that, the best-loved professor of economics at Yale." He related the conversation with these three old lions of conservative economics to make it clear that not one of them had ever supported Reaganomic-style monetarist or supply-side policies, and had long condemned the sorts of deficits they knew Reagan's tax cuts would produce. Galbraith's question was "why these and other good conservatives are so quiet," when faced with a "conservative" President willing to "play so fast and loose with the conservative economic and fiscal faith." After all, it should not be left to liberals alone to oppose policies "that in much milder form conservatives in past times found unwise, even alarming."[32]

Defections from the Reagan revolution gave him further opportunities to weigh in against the administration. When Reagan's Budget Director David Stockman abandoned the revolution soon after engineering the enormous 1981 tax cut, horrified by the huge deficits it inevitably produced, Galbraith once again underscored the dangers of radical zeal on the left or right. The youthful Stockman, by his own admission a steadfast devotee of a shifting ideological rainbow, had always been an ideologue. Starting in the 1960s as an antiwar protester, he'd moved gradually by the mid-1970s to a hard-edged conservatism, committed to wielding, he said, "a sword forged in the free market smithy of F. A. Hayek."* Elected to Congress from a conservative district in Michigan when Reagan became President, Stockman threw himself into Reagan's service as a "new conservative warrior." Yet Stockman by 1982 expressed shock at the red ink resulting from Reagan's tax cuts and, even more, at "the pigs feeding at the trough," as he characterized the special interests who had helped behind the scenes to shape Reagan's tax policies. The 1981 tax cut had reduced federal revenues by an estimated $2 trillion over the 1980s, and com-

---

*The process began while he was a Harvard Divinity School student. He was hired to babysit the children of Daniel Patrick Moynihan, and soon became a young protégé of Nixon's favorite Democrat.

bined with Reagan's $2 trillion military budget, generated deficits so immense that they lifted the total federal debt from $700 billion to $3.5 trillion.[33]

For Galbraith, Stockman's and Reagan's devotion to ultraconservative principles was a public reminder that "if you hear someone in public life say that he is going to stand firmly on principle, you should take cover and warn others to do the same. There is going to be suffering." He continued more somberly: "Rigorous ideological commitment is of a greatly negative value for governing a country, especially for making economic policy, and is a positive threat to social tranquility and economic well-being." Here Galbraith succinctly offered the essence of his own approach to economic theory and policy generally:

> Economic and social institutions are in a constant process of change; ideological commitment, by its nature and strongly avowed virtue, is static. Accordingly, guidance therefrom is likely to be obsolete, obsolescent, or irrelevant. Never is it so comprehensive in guidance as to take account of the greatly diverse circumstances of real life. The United States has survived, at least until now, by the willingness of governments, large and small, to make practical concessions to change and to diversity. A reluctant pragmatism has been our salvation.[34]

President Reagan's contrasting philosophy, he jibed, should be easy enough for most Americans to understand: "In recent years, the rich have not been working because they have had too little money, and the poor have not been working because they have had too much."[35] So to remedy this perceived injustice, the White House gave enormous benefits to the well-to-do while innocently insisting that its goal was economic growth for everyone. This, he slyly counseled, was a mistake on the President's part. Americans, he said, needed to see that there was nothing intrinsically wrong with a President or party benefiting its chief (and most powerful) benefactors. Reagan was unfairly being forced to treat his rewards to the rich as "a dirty secret." Better to have everyone agree that the effects of monetarism, supply-side tax cuts, and the run-up in military spending was "services to the affluent by the Reagan Administration." To claim otherwise was "to reject our proud claim to clear thought and plain speech."[36]

IF JUDGED BY the sheer volume of his writing, the number of his speeches, the extent of his travels, and the breadth of his active support for progressive groups and causes, the 1980s were as productive as any decade in Galbraith's life. He wrote seven more books, including *Economics in Perspective*, a critical study of modern economic theory, policy, and practice, which sold more than half a million copies worldwide; *The Anatomy of Power*, on power in politics and economics; *Capitalism, Communism and Co-existence*, a dialogue on Soviet-American relations with the Soviet reform economist Stanislav Menshikov; and *The Voice of the Poor* and *A View From the Stands*. (Collectively, these books sold more than 1.3 million copies in the 1980s, hardly a bad showing for an author whose ideas were allegedly passé in the conservative decade.)

The press still called him with astonishing regularity for interviews, comments, and opinion pieces. Over the decade, he appeared no less than 663 times in *The New York Times* alone,[37] and his assistant, Mrs. Williams, found that a regular feature of her work involved coordinating times for interviews, often late at night or early in the morning when foreign reporters on deadline or live radio shows called for comments; Galbraith rarely turned them down, whatever the hour.[38]

Book reviews were another regular venue, as they had been for years, and in his retirement he wrote not just on works in economics but with equal panache on biographies, novels, the arts, India, and modern U.S. and European history; on Californiana, Scotch whiskey, the environment, and the CIA. The reviews were turned out at the rate of one every six to eight weeks for newspapers and magazines all over the world. (On occasion, even conservative journals such as *Forbes* and the *National Review* invited articles.) His review subjects included books on James Thurber, H. L. Mencken, John O'Hara, Robert Kennedy, Rudyard Kipling, Walter Annenberg, John Hay Whitney, and Clare Boothe Luce; the modern history of Pakistan and British portraiture in colonial India; the collected works of Keynes; and half a dozen books by economists on American economic conditions.

A constant stream of speaking invitations, as many as two hundred per year, also continued to pour in. Some involved sizable fees from corporations, conventions, or trade associations; others—from governments and think tanks in Europe, Asia, Latin America (and occasionally the Soviet Union and Eastern Europe)— generally offered very modest speaking fees but first-class airfare and accommodations, and the opportunity to meet with national leaders. Colleges, universities, and dozens of liberal cause–related groups also courted him relentlessly. In 1982—a fairly representative year of his "retirement"—he flew to Vienna for a speech at the Austrian Finance Ministry, "Economic Policy and the Social Left"; to London to give a lecture entitled "Economics and the Arts" at the Arts Council of Great Britain; to Canada to speak on the global arms race at McGill University and the U.N. Association of Canada, on ideology and economics to the Royal Society of Canada, and on the future of Social Security at Laval; and to Chicago to address the American Bar Association's convention that year on the topic "Capitalism in the Age of Organization." (The last was a reworking of a speech he'd given to the Direct Mail/Marketing Association's convention in Los Angeles four days earlier.)

Never reluctant to recycle his own work, he gave that same basic talk twice again that year: as his annual lecture to Harvard undergraduates taking Ec 10, the college's very popular introductory economics course, and more lucratively at a business conference in Tokyo. For especially handsome fees he also shared his views on the economy's troubled performance with both the Midwestern Frozen Foods Association and the Academy of Dental Science, and even debated his old friend William F. Buckley in that cultural Valhalla, Las Vegas. For Washington, he worked in an address to a packed National Press Club on journalists' failures in covering Reaganomics, then at the Smithsonian he recalled his days as price tsar in World War II. His New York audiences included participants in a U.N. conference on arms control and the state's AFL-CIO central labor council.

Colleges and universities at which he spoke in 1982 included Brown, Stanford, Berkeley, Arkansas, New York University, Indiana, Goucher College, Reed College, the College of New Rochelle, and tiny Greenfield Community College in western Massachusetts. He also gave a talk at FDR's summer home in Campobello for Roosevelt's birthday centenary. Closer to home he spoke at Harvard's medical and law schools, to undergraduate classes in economics and government, and gave the Phi Beta Kappa oration at commencement in June. In all, that year he gave nearly sixty speeches in fourteen states and six countries.[39] The topics were at least as varied as his book reviews: one was on conservation and the restoration of the Charles River; another was a remembrance of his long friendship with Archibald MacLeish; a third was a memorial service address for George Kistiakowsky, the Nobel laureate Harvard chemist with whom Galbraith had worked closely for many years on Vietnam, arms control, and reducing the defense budget.

For all their variety, most of his speeches that year, and throughout the decade, returned to certain central themes. First was the hypocrisy of Reaganomics, especially the tax and budget cuts, the inevitable deficits, and the inequities and outright harm they were imposing on millions of people at home and abroad. Second was the danger of a new generation of conservative politics and economics—a larger phenomenon than Reagan's administration—and the shibboleths of an affluent, anxious American elite that strived incessantly to portray its values and interests as universal ones.

Above all, Galbraith spoke out against Reagan's encouragement of the Cold War's newly reignited arms race and the vehement anti-Communism that was used to justify it. Even as he slashed social programs, Reagan had launched a buildup of U.S. armed forces that eventually pushed total federal spending to 25 percent of GDP, a record exceeded only once in U.S. history, by the gargantuan costs of World War II. Along with the outdated World War II battleships Reagan recommissioned and the new billion-dollar bombers he built, there was his Star Wars agenda, a program that exemplified the cost overruns and underperformance of the era's new weapons.* Defense Secretary Casper Weinberger, who had won the nickname "Cap the Knife" as a budget-cutting aide to Governor Reagan in California, was rechristened "Cap the Shovel" at the Pentagon as the largesse poured forth.

But Secretary Weinberger was only one part of the problem. In a constitutional system supposedly built on checks and balances, the fact is that no one ever really fought to control those military budgets, famous for their gold-plated toilet seats and $500 hammers. Stockman freely acknowledged that

---

*The overruns and underperformance of defense expenditures became so routine that they were said by defense policy types to be governed by "Augustine's Law." Norman Augustine, a highly regarded defense engineer, insisted after he conducted an in-depth study of 1980s procurement contracts that there was never more than a 10 percent chance that a defense program would meet its budget, a 15 percent chance it would meet its schedule, and a 70 percent chance it would meet its performance goals.

when he was head of the Office of Management and the Budget (whose duty it was to review every item in the President's budget),

> the only cabinet officer [he] did not challenge was, of course, the secretary of defense. In the frantic preparation of the Reagan budget message, delivered in broad outline to Congress on February 18 [1981], the OMB review officers did not give even their usual scrutiny to the new budget projections from Defense. Reagan had promised to increase military spending by 7 percent a year, adjusted for inflation, and this pledge translated into the biggest peacetime arms build-up in the history of the republic—$1.6 trillion over the next five years, which would more than double the Pentagon's annual budget while domestic spending was shrinking. Stockman acknowledged that OMB had taken only a cursory glance at the new defense budget, but he was confident that later on, when things settled down a bit, he could go back and analyze it more carefully.[40]

Stockman was pushed out of Washington before he had a chance for that second look.

Martin Feldstein, who was Reagan's CEA chairman from 1982 through 1984, was no less candid, once he was back at Harvard, about the defense budgeting process on his watch. "Economic analysis and economists had little influence on the overall level of defense spending," he wrote. "The overall level of defense spending was not the result of adding up a series of individual decisions. The administration's target level for total defense spending was decided by the President and the Defense Secretary Casper Weinberger and then negotiated with the Congress." In office, Feldstein maintained the studied silence that the CEA kept throughout the Cold War years—though he knew what Reagan's military budgets were doing to the deficit and the U.S. economy. The silence, he said, was based on his ignorance: "When I was CEA chairman, I recognized that I didn't have the expertise to judge the proper amount of defense spending. My view, which I repeatedly stated publicly, was that the nation could certainly afford the current and projected levels of defense spending if we were willing to pay for them by raising taxes or cutting other spending." (In his otherwise comprehensive and brilliant *American Economic Policy in the 1980s*, published in 1994, Feldstein made no mention of the defense budget or its economic, social, or political impact. The words "military spending" or "defense spending" don't appear in the index.)[41]

Even the most conservative of Reagan's economics advisers were at times appalled. William Niskanen, Feldstein's libertarian successor at the CEA, echoed Stockman and Feldstein after leaving office, rather scornfully describing the Reagan defense budgets as "little more than a stapled packet of the budget requests from the services."[42] Eventually even a few senior Republican officials in the Pentagon, such as Assistant Secretary of Defense Lawrence Korb, left government and made well-informed public criticisms of the enor-

mous waste involved, as did lower-level defense industry engineers and officials. But by then Reagan and Weinberger had spent the $2 trillion.

Galbraith had no reluctance about speaking out. In June 1985, he found
himself on the speaker's platform at a conference in Geneva attended by both
Vice President Bush and the ultrahawkish Assistant Secretary of Defense,
Richard Perle. As both men squirmed, he gave a lengthy, carefully argued, and
impassioned address on arms control in which he excoriated the Reagan administration not only for the immense size and wastefulness of the U.S. military budget, but the primitive anti-Communism directed against the Russians
(though not the Chinese), the destabilizing role of Star Wars, the development
costs of arms sales to the Third World, and Vice President Bush's view that
nuclear war was winnable. Both Bush and Perle were visibly furious by the
time he finished, and grew more so when the audience gave him a standing
ovation.[43]

A quarter century earlier, Galbraith had been instrumental in the creation
of an arms-control group, the Washington-based Council for a Livable World,
originally conceived by Leo Szilard and other nuclear scientists alarmed by all
the failures to control or reverse the Cold War arms race. In the early 1970s,
along with George Kennan and Pepsi-Cola's chairman, Donald Kendall, he'd
helped to found the American Committee on East-West Accord, a smaller
group that did much of its work behind the scenes. ACEW's membership included Averell Harriman, George Kistiakowsky, J. William Fulbright, Jerome
Wiesner, Harrison Salisbury, George Ball, and the Reverend Theodore Hes-
bergh; it counted at one time seven former American ambassadors to the Soviet Union as endorsers of its program. In 1988, Galbraith and a few others
founded Economists Allied for Arms Reduction and persuaded a veritable pantheon of postwar economic giants that included Paul Samuelson, Robert
Solow, James Tobin, Kenneth Arrow, Franco Modigliani, Wassily Leontief, and
Lawrence Klein to sign on as directors. After the profession's silence on the
arms race and the military budget for so many years, the group aimed to do
what Galbraith had long argued for: provide detailed economic analysis that
demonstrated the merit of sharp cuts in military spending worldwide, and of
redirection of monies saved to domestic public needs across the globe.

> In the past, economists have tended to regard war as an external disruption of
> the normal peaceful course of events. Yet war and large military budgets have
> reduced human welfare and harmed the environment far more than inflation,
> business cycles, and many other factors that economists regard as the busi-
> ness of their profession. ECAAR encourages economists to apply the tools of
> economic analysis to questions of war, security, and peace.[44]

Beyond the sheer size and wastefulness of the Pentagon's budget, what
most concerned ECAAR was the enormous expansion of arm sales to the
Third World, with the United States proudly in the lead. President Reagan had

eviscerated the Carter administration's halting attempts to set sharp limits on such sales; between 1981 and 1989 total arms sales to underdeveloped countries rose to nearly $350 billion, and Reagan turned a blind eye when at least $50 billion more in covert arms sales flowed alongside. In those eight years, less developed countries in Africa, Asia, the Middle East, and Latin America bought, on official account, 37,000 surface-to-air missiles, 20,000 artillery pieces, 11,000 tanks, 3,200 supersonic aircraft, and 540 ships and submarines. Off the books, the CIA shipped weapons to dozens of allies from Angola to Afghanistan—by one estimate, 65,000 tons annually to Afghan rebels alone, even after it became clear that deadly shoulder-fired Stinger missiles were being resold to Islamic radicals in the Middle East.[45]

Galbraith's disgust for Reagan's military policies was matched by his scorn for the bipartisan embrace of Friedman-inspired monetary policies. But for this, he knew, Reagan was not entirely to blame.

In 1979 when the American economy was reeling from the second great OPEC price hike, it had been Paul Volcker, chairman of the Federal Reserve, who imposed the policies Friedman had long sought. This supremely self-confident career civil servant towered over colleagues at six feet, seven inches (an inch shorter than Galbraith) and was famous for the immense cigars he loved to puff on, especially in meetings he found tiresome (at least until federal health regulations banished the practice even at the Fed). As a senior deputy to Treasury Secretary John Connally, Volcker had helped to devise the 1971 Camp David accords that repealed Bretton Woods' legacy of fixed exchange rates. Now at the Federal Reserve, Volcker announced that the Fed would henceforth manage the dollar on the basis of money supply volumes, as Friedman had long advocated, not of interest rate targets. And he imposed a stringent new tightening of that money supply designed to choke off inflation—another Friedmanesque policy prescription.[46] Like the "castor oil" policies Alan Greenspan and William Simon prescribed for Gerald Ford, Volcker's medicine helped to destroy Jimmy Carter's chances for reelection.

More important, the consequences of this monetarist policy was a devastating recession, as Galbraith accurately warned in 1981, when he offered up the outlines of a liberal alternative.[47] Not surprisingly, Volcker and Ronald Reagan ignored his recommendations. Once Reagan took office, Volcker, determined to make his policies work, had tightened again, forcing benchmark interest rates to an unimaginable, record-shattering 20 percent—and then kept them at or above an equally unprecedented 12 percent average for much of Reagan's first term. With the economy strangled, inflation was indeed choked out of the system, falling between 1980 and 1982 by over 12 percentage points to under 4 percent—but at an immense cost. Volcker's policies, just as Galbraith predicted, produced a brutal recession—the worst, in fact, since the 1930s, with real GDP falling more than 3 percent, industry operating at 60 percent of capacity, and unemployment skyrocketing to nearly 11 percent.[48]

As the scope of the debacle became clear, the new Friedmanite rules proved too extreme for the Fed (though not to Friedman or to acolytes such as Treasury Undersecretary Beryl Sprinkel, who continued to deplore any loosening of the tight-money regime). In late 1982, Volcker abandoned his monetarist experiment and returned to more conventional money-supply theory and to expansionary interest-rate cuts. The U.S. economy then roared to life, and this broke the seductive thrall that Friedman's theory had held over many economists—if not over the true believers on the political right and in the administration, who held up the recovery as proof that their theories worked. (Margaret Thatcher insisted that England continue on its own Friedman-inspired monetarist experiment for another three years, thereby prolonging Britain's economic stagnation. The Bank of England finally followed the Fed's example, after which the British economy also, predictably, took off.[49])

The ultimate irony for Friedman, however, came after Alan Greenspan succeeded Volcker as the Fed's chairman in 1987. Greenspan's past as a devotee of Ayn Rand, and his toughness as Gerald Ford's CEA chairman, had earned him a glowing reputation among conservatives. But he soon became anathema to doctrinaire monetarists such as Friedman, for he refused to follow their prescription of "fixed rules" focused on the money supply (rather than interest rates) and provide a steady, slow growth of that supply. Instead he turned out to be a devoted empiricist who pored over the most arcane details of America's economic performance and then set much more flexible policies; he was also politically adept enough to pour money into the system when the stock market suddenly plunged in October 1987. Despite the monetarists' fury, he politely ignored Friedman's most fundamental theoretical claims. "Monetary aggregates," Greenspan explained, simply "do not appear to be giving reliable indications of economic developments and price pressures."[50] Some years later Alan Blinder, having served as Greenspan's vice chairman, put the matter even more succinctly: "Alan Greenspan has demonstrated that what we once called fine-tuning is indeed possible"—which, Blinder noted, ran against all the conventional wisdom of economics after the fall of Keynesianism. "What Greenspan has accomplished probably eclipses Walter Heller's fondest dreams."[51]

Using unorthodox means for orthodox ends, Greenspan produced results on inflation and in the stock and bond markets that made him a figure approaching cult veneration status in Washington and on Wall Street, and gradually won even Galbraith's qualified admiration.[52] He reached much the same conclusion as Blinder, who several years earlier, had cleverly dubbed Greenspan a "monetary Keynesian." In an era of partisan gridlock over taxes, budgets, and deficits, Greenspan shrewdly used the Fed rather than fiscal policy to steady, and continually expand, the economy. "Keynes himself," Galbraith later averred, "under the circumstances would have found much to admire in Alan Greenspan's policies."[53] To Galbraith's great amusement, Greenspan's successes reduced Milton Friedman to a dyspeptic claim of "bafflement." "What I'm puzzled about is whether, and if so how, they [at the Fed] suddenly learned how to regulate the economy," he was to grouse. "Does Alan Greenspan have an insight into movements in the economy and the shocks that other people don't have?"[54]

THROUGHOUT THE 1980s, the increasingly scandal-ridden behavior of America's private sector gave Galbraith a rich field of opportunities for attack. Long before Enron, Tyco, Worldcom, Global Crossing, and their accountants caught the public eye by producing the largest bankruptcies in American history as well as the richest CEOs, Galbraith was reviewing the tarnished careers of Ivan Boesky, Donald Trump, Michael Milken, Boone Pickens and other transiently stellar figures who had become the 1980s' most famous "paper entrepreneurs." "Pay, corporate perquisites, . . . congenial corporate-paid recreation . . . and a relaxing delegation of thought" were even then hardly new phenomena at the higher reaches of big corporations; he now alluded to a central thesis of *The New Industrial State*:

> Some twenty years ago I developed the case—I called it "the approved contradiction"—that traditional economic theory contains an inescapable anomaly with respect to maximizing profits in the case of the great corporation. According to traditional theory such maximizing of profit is the central and inescapable motivation in all economic life, and, in the case of the large corporate enterprise, not for management but for stockholders . . . The management, in other words, has a powerful commitment to maximizing profits but where its own interest is concerned a surprising and improbable detachment from this commitment. My point, I venture to think, has gained a substantial measure of popular acceptance.[55]

At the end of the Reagan presidency, he rather gleefully revisited the famous excesses of a $2 million seventieth-birthday party that was organized in Morocco for the publisher Malcolm Forbes, and the $1 million party on Long Island for the financier Saul Steinberg's fiftieth. Reprising the tale of Mrs. Bradley Martin's party in 1897, he sardonically comforted himself with his prescience and congratulated Forbes and Steinberg—and, most important, Ronald Reagan for giving such generous tax concessions to such men. "Not only have Mr. and Mrs. Steinberg and Mr. Forbes been stirred from the alleged lethargy of the affluent, but with better treatment of capital gains the experience shows that we will almost certainly have yet more costly such events.[56]

Galbraith also drew attention to the vast explosion of corporate debt that came as a result of the "leveraged buyout" mania from which Steinberg grew rich (before going bankrupt), and which Forbes celebrated in his magazine. The idea was simple enough: an LBO raider borrowed heavily from banks and other financial sources to buy a target company, and then placed the debt on the company's books, paying off the purchase by selling off units of the business, by massive layoffs, and frequently by transferring business activity overseas to low-wage countries. When nearly a third of the 1980s LBOs ended up in default,[57] the enthusiasm for the most highly leveraged acquisition styles faded. But the fever behind the merger-and-acquisition model never really went away, despite the eventual evidence that it was the LBO artists—the investment bankers advising on the deals, and the managers and shareholders of acquired companies who took payment in cash—who were the prime beneficiaries. (By the end of the century, total merger-and-acquisition values passed $2 trillion, before the stock market's collapse abruptly reined in activity.)

Galbraith warned early on that CEOs at the acquiring companies and their highly rewarded investment advisers often did not know what they were doing.

> Even very simple circumstances tax the mental resources and the perception of many of those involved. A great deal of money changes hands, and we have an aberrant but inescapable tendency to associate the presence of the handling of money—of large financial transactions—with acute intelligence. One has only to know some of those so concerned or even to wait and watch their ultimate fate to see how odd this is. In the highest of high finance, as we have recently seen once more, the paths of presumed financial intelligence lead regularly, if not to the grave, at least to the minimum security slammers.[58]

AS THE 1980s PROCEEDED, honors and awards poured in on Galbraith. In 1982 he was elected to the fifty-member American Academy of Arts and Letters, to the chair once occupied by his old friend the poet (and one-time *Fortune* editor) Archibald MacLeish. Galbraith was the first economist ever so honored; in 1984, the Academy elected him president.[59]

Then shortly after Christmas 1987, when the American Economic Association convened in Chicago to celebrate its centenary, Galbraith's *The New Industrial State* was chosen from among the thousands of books published by American economists during that century for a featured panel discussion. Galbraith admitted to being greatly pleased by this, but insisted that two other related events gave him even greater pleasure. The first was that a panel was devoted to the political economy of the arms race, a topic the profession had barely touched until Galbraith had opened the issue for debate in 1971. The second was that Alice Rivlin, an economist at the Brookings Institution, had just completed her term as the AEA's president, the first woman ever chosen for the post.[60]

In June 1988, Harvard added to Galbraith's long list of academic honorifics by awarding him an honorary doctorate. In awarding doctorates to Arthur Schlesinger in 1987 and now to him,* Harvard perhaps finally was "trying to rectify all those decades of error," Galbraith sardonically allowed. Three months later, the Galbraiths flew to the Soviet Union, where he was given an honorary degree by Moscow State University. Kitty Galbraith quipped, "Not even John Reed had gone from crimson to red as quickly as Kenneth."

To celebrate his eightieth birthday that October, not one but four glittering

---

*"Those decades of error" were a sly reference to the 1959 study he and Schlesinger did that showed that three quarters of Harvard's honorary doctorates in public service went to conservatives.

parties were organized, the largest and most elegant held at the Century Association in New York City. Ken and Kitty welcomed the nearly one hundred guests, he in a well-tailored blue suit, she in a white Indian silk dress; the guest list bespoke the range of accomplished men and women who had become old friends. Next to Galbraith at the head table were Jacqueline Kennedy Onassis on his right, and the actress Angie Dickinson on his left. (Galbraith had first met Dickinson by chance as he departed from Washington for Saigon in November 1961, following the struggle over the Taylor Mission report. Always attracted to beautiful women, he switched his Washington-to–Los Angeles flight so they could travel together. "By halfway to Los Angeles," he later wrote, "I was deeply in love . . . [and] was heart-broken when Los Angeles came up under the wing." Their flirtatious transcontinental friendship endured thereafter.) Lauren Bacall and Marietta Tree added more glamour. From the Kennedy era there were George Ball, McGeorge Bundy, Richard Goodwin, Orville Freeman, Ted Sorensen, Stephen Smith, and Arthur Schlesinger. Katharine Graham had flown up for the party from Washington, and *The Boston Globe*'s Thomas Winship and his wife likewise from Boston. James Hoge, then editor of the *New York Daily News*, and his wife, Sharon King (they were married in the Galbraiths' living room), chatted with Harold Evans, former editor of the *Sunday Times* of London, and his wife, Tina Brown, the editor of *Vanity Fair*. Robert Silvers of *The New York Review of Books* and Clay Felker of *New York* magazine joked that the evening's list resembled a press conference more than a party, as they swapped stories and gossip with David Halberstam, Louis Auchincloss, Tom Wicker, Gail Sheehy, Harrison Salisbury, and Doris Kearns Goodwin.

George Kennan and Roy Jenkins, Britain's former chancellor of the exchequer, talked with William Luers, a former ambassador who was head of the Metropolitan Museum, about the state of American diplomacy, while Wassily Leontief and Lloyd Reynolds chatted with Galbraith's youngest son, James, about the state of the economy. Galbraith's old OPA friends David Ginsburg and Congressman Henry Reuss, and the former ADA chairman Joseph Rauh and his wife assessed life in Washington under Reagan.

In his toast Rauh told the story of his grandson's reaction to a party that had been held for his own seventieth birthday. Rauh had asked the boy which of the speakers he had liked best. "Oh, I liked Mr. Galbraith the best," the youngster replied firmly, "because all the other people talked about you, and I already know all about you. But Mr. Galbraith talked about himself, and I didn't know about him, so I thought he was the best."[61]

As a further honor, Houghton Mifflin in 1988 published a Galbraith Festschrift, *Unconventional Wisdom: Essays on Economics in Honor of John Kenneth Galbraith*, in which nearly two dozen economists—including Paul Samuelson, Wassily Leontief, Jan Tinbergen, Albert Hirschman, Shigeto Tsuru, Kenneth Boulding, Lester Thurow, Mancur Olson, Lloyd Reynolds, Walter Adams, Barbara Bergmann, Samuel Bowles, Herbert Gintis, Henry

Rosovsky, and his son James—paid tribute to his contributions.[62] (Two more *Festschriften* have since appeared.)

Yet the outpouring of affection and admiration for him notwithstanding, the reality was that Galbraith's influence in American public life, like that of his generation of Keynesians generally, was waning. The Keynesian tradition of activist fine-tuning of the economy that figures like Heller, Samuelson, and Solow had once embodied was being taught less and less. Pre-Keynesian microeconomics, couched in ever more sophisticated mathematical abstractions, enjoyed a prestige it hadn't had since the 1920s. Even younger economists who were drawn to the Keynesian legacy cautiously described themselves as "neo-Keynesians" or "post-Keynesians," to avoid direct association with the alleged errors and tainted assumptions of an earlier generation.

The neo-Keynesians in particular set themselves the Herculean task of wedding elements of the old Keynesianism (for example, the idea of "sticky wages" and price rigidity) to the rigors of the rational expectationists' faith in "market clearing." They introduced ideas such as the "efficiency wage" to explain why empirical evidence showed that wages frequently exceeded what strictly interpreted competitive markets would sustain, and singled out contracts and imperfect information to explain deviations from the rat-exers' blackboard model in financial and real-goods markets.[63]

But the neo-Keynesians also eschewed much of the activist and liberal government leadership that was central to the Keynesian legacy, or when they acknowledged it, they did so timorously. Deregulation and increased competition were for them the preferred solution for economic failures, inequalities, and misallocations. "Markets"—curiously abstracted from any social, political, or historical particularities of late-twentieth-century American capitalism—were once again to be the guide, not public policy. When *The Washington Post* asked a young Harvard economist what the general public should know above all else about economics, the unhesitating reply came back, "Markets are beautiful!"[64]

But Galbraith's own aging and these changes within economics only partly explain why his prominence in America public life was waning. Shortly before his eightieth birthday, a book entitled *The Last Intellectuals*, in which he figured prominently, offered a further explanation. Its author, the intellectual historian Russell Jacoby, claimed that the robust American tradition of "the public intellectual"—an archetype embodied in the careers of men such as Lewis Mumford, John Dewey, Archibald MacLeish, Edmund Wilson, and Galbraith and, before them, Ralph Waldo Emerson, Henry David Thoreau, and Walt Whitman—was passing from the scene. Jacoby distinguished between the larger universe of "intellectuals" who "cherish thinking and ideas" and the smaller world of public intellectuals, men and women "who contribute to public discussions . . . the writers and thinkers who address a general and educated public."

Vibrant democratic cultures, Jacoby argued, need public intellectuals at least as much as they need intellectuals. But in their place, he said, a new generation of campus-bound academics had emerged. Their writings were not directed to the general public, because their goal was to persuade only their university-based peers. "The professors share an idiom and a discipline. Gathering in annual conferences to compare notes, they constitute their own universe . . . As intellectuals became academics, they had no need to write in a public prose; they did not, and finally they could not."[65]

To Jacoby, Galbraith was the rare academic exception: a superb, even defining, example of the public intellectual. Basing his assessment on sociological studies of elite-group influence, he noted that by the early 1970s, Galbraith had established himself as one of the nation's ten leading intellectuals—a status no other economist enjoyed. But by the late 1980s, no new generation of comparable intellectuals had come forward to replace this elder generation. Galbraith was especially important because he stood distinctively apart from so many younger social scientists who adopted "economistic worldviews" in their work. Citing as an example the profound effect econometrics and neoclassical modeling were having on his own field, American history, Jacoby highlighted Robert Fogel's and Stanley Engerman's *Time on the Cross*, a then much-discussed econometric analysis of American slavery. Using the new methods, the two authors had startlingly claimed that slavery was a much more benign system, with less coercion and brutality employed by slave owners, than previously thought. Fogel and Engerman had concluded, after studying one large Louisiana plantation's records, that the slaves as a group had only received "an average of 0.7 whippings per hand per year." This was their evidence of slave owners' caring attitude toward their slaves. For the two historians, Jacoby wrote, "This was almost scientific proof that slaves were not driven to work by punishments, since the whippings were too infrequent to be effective." Dissatisfied by their methods, Herbert Gutman, a noneconometric historian, had not only pointed out Fogel's and Engerman's calculation errors, but translated what the figures actually meant: the "0.7 whippings" figure meant that on that plantation, three slaves were whipped each week. What, asked Gutman, would other slaves have thought of their master's benignity watching those whippings three times a week, year after year? And what should one do with the analogous fact that "on average 127 blacks were lynched every year between 1889 and 1899. How does one assess that average? . . . Is it useful to learn that 99.9997 percent of blacks were not lynched annually?"[66]

Jacoby considered *Time on the Cross* an egregious example of the dangers in the so-called dispassionate rigor of academic specialization, but his argument about public intellectuals and their decline rested on more than the institutionalization of thought. He noted that conservatives, too, found little of useful public value in academic intellectuals, but for a different reason: in their view, most universities had become malignant hotbeds for every manner of left-wing and protest movement, and were busily undermining higher education and society itself. "This is the conservative nightmare: while radicals and liberals have been chased from public and visible posts, they actually staff the education system, corroding the Republic from within."[67] He went to great lengths to make sure his views were not mistaken for theirs.

Galbraith himself offered a view of academic life in many ways identical to Jacoby's at almost the same time. In *Economics in Perspective*, which also appeared in 1987, he looked back over the history of economics since Adam Smith, and its evolution into a tightly walled and highly mathematicized discipline. By now, he said, all too much of what academic economists did constituted "esoteric" knowledge, "of high prestige but low practical effect." By contrast, he once again affirmed the value of what Thorsten Veblen called "exoteric" knowledge, knowledge "of low prestige but high practical effect." Agricultural economics, for example, was "rather sordidly exoteric," yet was the fount of enormous and proven practical achievements worldwide. But *The New York Times*, in its review of the book, written by Leonard Silk, well caught the atmosphere of the 1980s— and the predicament it posed for Galbraith. Silk dismissed Galbraith's proposal for a useful "political economy" as "not being exactly a fresh thought for the day" and scored him for failing to see that "the market" was an efficient allocator of resources and creator of growth, "an appreciation" that "liberal economists have come to share with conservative economists," he noted pointedly.[68] Galbraith, in short, was both too old and too outside the new era's consensus to be relevant.

GALBRAITH HAD LAST attended a Democratic National Convention in 1980, when he supported Ted Kennedy's challenge to Jimmy Carter. He was dismayed when Walter Mondale and Geraldine Ferraro lost in 1984, having hoped that the dismal economic picture in the first Reagan term might push a Democrat into office. But four years later when Michael Dukakis lost with just 45 percent of the vote, he felt little surprise. As he wrote in the *Times*, much of the greed and careless indifference toward vulnerable fellow citizens that characterized the 1980s was, in a way, the fault of a liberal misjudgment.

> The unarticulated assumption of American liberals, as of social democrats in other countries, [once was] that the newly affluent—blue-collar workers with middle-class incomes, the new, vastly enhanced professional class, the modern, relatively well-paid white-collar bureaucracy, those protected from the trials of unemployment, old age and illness—would, in gratitude, have political attitudes different from those of the older rich. And so, presumably, would their offspring.

But explaining Reagan's successes entailed a darker, more dismaying conclusion.

> The liberals were wrong. In light of history it is far more probable that those who led in the designs for modern security and affluence were contriving their own political decline . . . I do not predict that with increasing affluence, conservative administrations will always be in power . . . There are other things that decide elections, including voter turnout, the differing interests and votes of women, the pervading suspicion of overseas adventure and the yet more compelling fear of nuclear war. I *do* suggest that one effect of affluence is a continuing conservative trend in politics, and that those who dismiss

the pro-affluent movements of these past years as a temporary departure from a socially concerned norm are quite wrong.[69]

Something fundamental seemed to be ending, in short, something about the liberal spirit of democracy and compassion. Three weeks after Galbraith's glittering birthday party, George H. W. Bush, Reagan's Vice President, not Michael Dukakis, was elected president.

Affluence, which Galbraith once thought the American people could learn to understand, tame, and even transcend in order to release themselves from the endless treadmill of material consumption—seemed to be more powerful and seductive than ever. And government of the kind Galbraith most admired—democratic, activist, inventive, practical, egalitarian, Rooseveltian—now seemed an achievement of the past, buried under the onslaught of popular mistrust and resentment that had cascaded out of the Vietnam era and then been carefully nurtured and exploited by the new Republican leaders for their own ends. Markets, markets, markets were now the omniscient, the omnipotent, the omnipresent metrics by which all was to be measured. Those who could not meet the market's exacting standards were either reeducated or abandoned by it.

All this reminded Galbraith of his childhood in Canada, after World War I, when his father would talk about America—to the south, across Lake Erie—with Harding and Coolidge and Hoover and a booming economy that nonetheless left so many behind, and about what it had been like for earlier generations of Galbraiths in Scotland, when the landowners had taken their land to raise sheep, and English Victorians had come north to build woolen mills.

In those days, Social Darwinism was the approved orthodoxy of the upper and upper-middle classes, comforting its adherents with "the exceptionally convenient thesis that poverty is the socially therapeutic agent that eliminates the unfit." A century later, Galbraith could see the outlines of a neo-Darwinian ethic in America's domestic and foreign policies, most easily visible "in the feeling that gifts to the undeserving poor, even to insolvent relatives, are somehow bad for their character. Social Darwinism has also a comfortable association with one branch of fundamentalist theology, which holds that property expresses God's approval of the worthy. The relevant texts can be had from the religious broadcasters and the spokesmen for the Moral Majority."[70]

Perhaps now indeed finally it was time to retire to the stands.

24

Joy Fades

*Today, it is as if the world were born anew . . . By reducing taxes and regula-
tory bureaucracy, we have unleashed the creative genius of ordinary Americans and ushered in an unparalleled period of peacetime prosperity. The
world is safer, and more prosperous, than it was eight years ago. And the
America of today is, once again, brimming with self-confidence and a model
for other countries to emulate.*

—Ronald Reagan, 1989

*Tax reduction oriented to the affluent, unduly enhanced defense expenditure
and a large deficit in the federal budget were the prime manifestations of error. Related was a large and persistent deficit in the American balance-of-
payments account, causing the United States to shift from being the world's
largest creditor to being, by a wide margin, its largest debtor. There was erosion of the nation's competitive position, social tension in the big cities, financial speculation and manipulation extending on to widespread and unsubtle
larceny and, in the end, the painful recession cum depression of the early
1990s . . . [Yet this] is a view that seriously understates what the Reagan administration, given its purpose and that of its supporters, accomplished.*

—John Kenneth Galbraith, 1994

TO RONALD REAGAN'S SUPPORTERS, his successes were gigantic: he had, through
vision and determination, recast the direction of American and world history.
Thanks to him, the American economy was soaring, and around the world millions now longed for lives like those lived in America. President Bush, his successor, having denounced Reagan's "voodoo economics" in 1980, was bravely
campaigning for reelection on his promise to continue the Reagan Revolution
in 1992 against an upstart young Arkansas governor.

The passionate faith of Reagan's supporters masked what Galbraith and others believed was evidence of harder truths. At the most fundamental level, the simple fact was that the U.S. economy's growth had *not* taken off under Reagan. Instead growth had been slower in the 1980s than in the 1950s, 1960s, or even the troubled 1970s, and the United States' economic performance had lagged behind that of major U.S. competitors, including Japan, France, West Germany, Canada, and Sweden, in terms of real growth per capita. (Only Britain, where a similar conservative experiment was tried by Mrs. Thatcher, had done worse.[1]) These were countries that had all developed quite different forms of capitalist democracy, maintaining larger public sectors than the United States, with more welfare support in all forms for their citizens, and more regulated private markets—precisely the "diseases" that Reagan and his fellow conservatives denounced as "drags" on economic growth.

But weak overall economic performance was only one of the problems Reagan had left. No less damning was the shape of the country's income and wealth distribution. From Franklin Roosevelt's presidency through Lyndon Johnson's (three decades when, as Galbraith always pointed out, the size of government steadily grew and tax rates were far more progressive), the gap between America's rich and poor had first narrowed dramatically and then stabilized, with the country's middle class growing larger and more prosperous, and the number of America's poor diminishing. But starting slowly under Richard Nixon and then sharply accelerating throughout the Reagan years, American income and wealth distribution went in exactly the opposite direction. By the early 1990s the United States was the most inegalitarian of all the advanced industrialized countries.[2] (Galbraith sardonically allowed that post-Communist Russia was more unequal.[3]) Moreover, America's middle classes were working harder—in terms of both total hours worked and the number of workers per household—just to maintain their median incomes.[4]

The standard conservative defense of Reaganomics was to point to all the increases in individual opportunity. At the top of the income and wealth pyramid, there was certainly no question about new opportunities, but Reagan's and Bush's tax and regulatory cuts had not produced for the rest of society what most Americans would normally call greater opportunity (let alone greater security) amidst all the abounding signs of change. For example, nearly 50 million jobs had disappeared. Those lost jobs had been replaced by many more jobs: there had been a net increase in jobs in the 1980s, but the net job growth, like GDP growth, was slower in the 1980s than in any other decade since World War II, and the new jobs routinely paid less, provided fewer benefits, and offered less job security than those they replaced.[5] The profound disruptions Americans endured in the 1980s hadn't been equaled since the 1930s. By the end of the Reagan-Bush era, 75 percent of Americans were reporting that they or someone close to them had been laid off since Reagan first took office, and 30 percent were saying they had taken on extra work just to maintain—not improve—their incomes.

As for becoming winners in this "new world of opportunity," just one in five said they were better off, half the country reported no measurable gains, and 30 percent said they were falling backward. Half of all Americans additionally said they weren't earning what they had expected to at this point in their careers, and only 11 percent thought it very likely that young Americans would be better off than their parents. Much more optimistic answers had once been given to similar questions. Also, more than half of Americans said there was now an "angrier mood" at work, half of all workers worried about losing their jobs in the next twelve months, and three in four feared they lacked sufficient savings to retire.[6]

Those who benefited most were the best educated, and college degrees became a crucial predictor of lifetime financial success as well-paid blue-collar jobs disappeared by the millions. Americans always say they value "better education," especially as a means by which the less fortunate may eventually catch up in the new "opportunity economy." But from the 1970s to the early 1990s, the college graduation rate for young adults from the richest quarter of the population rose from 40 percent to almost 80 percent, while for young adults from the poorest quarter it remained frozen at 8 percent.[7] Inequality of basic opportunity had become even greater than inequality of economic outcomes.

None of this should have come as a surprise, Galbraith reminded his readers. The claim that "the 1980s saw an exercise in innocent economic error" was "badly misguided. These years saw, in fact, a largely deliberate and, in its own terms, successful economic policy." The Reagan administration served "a well-defined community consisting of the comfortably rewarded in life extending on to the admittedly rich." For this small community there had always been "two well-recognized threats to its continued comfort, one domestic and real, one foreign and verging on religious belief"—and Ronald Reagan had attacked both with great energy and purpose.[8] The first was the federal government and its taxation of the nation's upper classes and corporations. The second was "the Evil Empire" of Soviet Communism and whomever the White House considered the Evil Empire's allies, such as the Sandinistas in Nicaragua. But Galbraith was convinced that in trying to deal with both threats—simultaneously to overthrow progressive taxation and Communism—Reagan had created long-lasting and damaging contradictions.

Reagan never tired of denouncing government as "the problem, not the solution," but federal spending actually grew more under him than under any other president since World War II, in his second term reaching a record peacetime level of 25 percent of GDP. But as far as Galbraith was concerned, there was little to commend in government's growth during the 1980s, because so much was allocated to increased military spending and interest payments on Reagan's massive annual deficits. Setting aside Social Security and Medicare payments, financed directly and exclusively by Social Security taxes on wages, military spending and interest payments still took up nearly half of total federal funding.* Social and infrastructure spending (apart from the particular and, for economists, complicated case of rising Social Security and Medicare payments) had meanwhile remained stagnant. Put more strikingly, under Reagan, the federal government spent more of the nation's GDP on the Pentagon alone than Roosevelt had on all New Deal social and economic recovery programs during the Great Depression.

What also didn't keep pace with Washington's spending was Washington's income. Under Reagan, federal revenues consistently fell well behind expenditures. Instead of the predicted investment, savings, and growth, the result of Reaganomics was an unbroken string of enormous deficits, and ever-growing massive interest payments that consumed an ever larger share of the budget.† By one estimate, federal debt accumulated in the 1980s exceeded all the public debt the United States accumulated in the two centuries since George Washington's presidency—and yet all that stimulus never sparked a proportionately massive growth explosion.

Instead, the deficits led to a more intricate and complicated dance of economic consequences and political and policy responses than had been anticipated.

Giving a name (or names) to that dance was not easy, since many overdiscussed terms were attached to several different domestic and international changes occurring at the same time. The term "globalization," to pick one famously overused example, was coined to encompass a network of interconnected shifts in which economic, political, and cultural values and institutions associated with the West seemed, for better or worse, to be penetrating the South and East. The idea of the "Information Age" as replacing the "Industrial Age" was likewise intended to describe the importance of the computer, telecommunications, and the Internet both to production and consumption, and to culture and identity. The "New Economy," related to the "Information Age," encompassed larger shifts in the organization of work, income, production, and competition toward a more purely "market" economy.

Galbraith, after sixty years of studying and debating modern politics and economics, was not impressed by the claims of the absolute novelty of these phenomena.[9] Profound changes had indeed occurred, but new "conventional wisdoms" were obscuring as much as they explained. He believed that well-established analytic concepts of modern political economy could be used to

---

*The federal government officially calculates "defense spending" as the Department of Defense's part of the total federal budget, including Social Security and Medicare, but this itself involves what Galbraith has called "the politics of counting." A broader-based accounting of "defense spending" would include the portion of the Energy Department's budget allocated for nuclear weapons research; the Veterans' Department budget for retired military personnel and their health care; foreign military training and weapons sales; and the pro-rated portion of the interest payments attributable to prior-year military budgets. This nearly doubles the official "defense spending" total.

†The deficits ended only in 1998, when the Clinton administration produced the first surplus since 1969, but they resumed at record levels under President George W. Bush after just three years. In percent-of-GDP terms, annual interest payments on the accumulated federal debt since Reagan have been nearly three times what they were from Eisenhower through Carter. The United States spends more each year to service federal debt than it does on K–12 public education.

understand the new shifts in income and wealth, relative institutional power, benefits for some interest groups versus others, and so forth. But a politically committed response, attuned to preserving democratic power and broad-gauged equality, was required.

To begin with, the political setting and effect of the budget deficits needed to be analyzed. Galbraith and others argued that they had set in motion a ferocious political debate between Republicans and Democrats. The political scientist Aaron Wildavsky exaggerated only slightly, Galbraith thought, when he said that Reagan's budgets were to the 1980s "what civil rights, communism, the depression, industrialization, and slavery were at other times." Likewise, his former Harvard colleague and neighbor Senator Moynihan wasn't far off the mark when he insisted that they had wrongly become "the first fact of national government."[10]

By the time President Bush faced Governor Clinton in the election of 1992, this "era of the budget" had scrambled the core ideological tenets of the two political parties once again, on the one hand playing havoc with the GOP's traditional abhorrence of deficit spending, and on the other doing away with Democrats' support for activist-Keynesian-style, deficit-fueled growth. Conservative politicians and journalists tried to blame the Democrats for the deficits because they had resisted Reagan's proposed cuts in social spending—though many economists forcefully explained that this notion completely failed the evidence test. (Spending levels authorized by Congress were routinely quite close to Reagan's and Bush's original proposals; the deficits had already been built into the presidential budgets.[11]) The internally divided Democrats, meanwhile, found themselves in the strange position of sounding more like Calvin Coolidge than Franklin Roosevelt, Galbraith causticly noted, making moralistic calls for balanced budgets.

The dangerous posturing around the endless budget battles was clearly illustrated in the notorious Gramm-Rudman "balanced budget" act of 1985, the work of two conservative Republican senators, Phil Gramm of Texas and Warren Rudman of New Hampshire. Gramm-Rudman tried to make deficits illegal and budget balancing automatic by setting annual targets for smaller and smaller deficits each year until a budget balance was achieved. If Congress and the President failed to agree on a budget that met those targets, the new law mandated computer-driven formulas that would cut all federal programs in equal proportion until the goal was reached. One Washington policy-maker later reflected,

> Almost no member of Congress had anything good to say about Gramm-Rudman; Rudman himself called it "a bad idea whose time has come." The Secretaries of Defense and State fought it on national security grounds. Most economists opposed it. Lawyers declared it of dubious constitutionality. Few Americans in or out of Congress thought it wise . . . Yet the bill sailed through both houses of Congress with huge majorities . . . Somehow an unholy alliance of Republicans and conservative Democrats took utter nonsense and

treated it like gospel; if you opposed Gramm-Rudman, you were in favor of big deficits. In this circus atmosphere, you had to be brave to be responsible. Few were.[12]

To make things more complicated, the White House and Congress agreed to a string of tax *increases*, in a gingerly (and ultimately unsuccessful) attempt to halt the budgetary bleeding. In Washington policy parlance, the big 1981 Reagan tax cut known as ERTA was followed by smaller but cumulatively significant tax increases: TEFRA in 1982, a gasoline tax hike, Social Security financing reforms in 1983, DEFRA in 1984, TRA in 1986, and the Omnibus Reconciliation Act in 1987. Although the deficit was still over $150 billion a year when Reagan left office, those intervening increases staved off outright fiscal disaster.*

More than a political price was paid for these compromises, though, as Galbraith frequently commented. For one, the compromises preserved substantial advantages for wealthy individuals and corporations, and the immense benefits they'd received in the 1981 "supply-side" bill were never fully rolled back. By the end of the Reagan years, the top marginal income tax rate paid by the wealthiest American families was roughly a third of what it had been under Eisenhower.[13]

Further down the income scale, no one did nearly as well. The decade's largest revenue-raising bill by far was the 1983 Social Security Reform Act, but since it increased the tax only on wages, its burden fell hardest on the country's middle and working classes.† The 1983 bill accomplished something else: it ended Social Security as a "pay-as-you-go" plan. Congress for the first time deliberately raised Social Security rates high enough not just to cover payouts to current retirees but to generate an annual surplus, which in turn was used to cover the huge operating deficit Reagan had created in the rest of the government budget. Soon, those Social Security surpluses were financing an increasing share of Washington's annual deficits, as hundreds of billions of dollars flowed from Social Security's bank accounts to the U.S. Treasury to buy bonds that covered the shortfall.

Forcing Social Security to cover deficits in the rest of the federal budget had two large, very dangerous consequences. First, by concealing the actual scale of the deficits it confused most Americans about their effect on the burgeoning total federal debt. Traditionally, the most important measure of federal debt had always been the "debt held by the public," which doesn't count the

---

*Without them, some economists have since estimated that the deficit would have swelled to half of the federal budget, a political as well as economic disaster of unimaginable magnitude; with them, at least the Reagan deficits were held to something closer to a fifth of the budget.

†Not well understood by most Americans is the fact that Social Security is also a "capped" tax, meaning that no additional tax is paid once preset wage limits are reached, with the percentage growing smaller as top wages grow larger. This means that the top 10 percent of wage-earners routinely pay less than the bottom 90 percent of earners as a percentage of their wages. The Social Security tax increase was engineered by a presidential commission chaired by Alan Greenspan.

small portion of the federal debt held by the government itself. The distinction had been academic, since until Reagan the public traditionally held the lion's share (80 percent or more, on average) of total federal debt. But after the Greenspan Commission reforms, the total federal debt skyrocketed from a publicly held debt of barely $700 billion (and government-held debt of $200 billion) to reach a combined public-private $6 trillion by 2003, with Social Security holding over half that enormous total.

Whether it is a problem to have a government agency own such a huge government debt is an issue that passionately divides economists along partisan as well as technical lines. But in the ideologically poisoned atmosphere after the Greenspan reforms, one surpassing irony is that although those surpluses "rescued" Social Security from insolvency, with Greenspan promising a "financially healthy" program for the next seventy-five years, conservatives ever since have questioned Social Security's long-term solvency and called for its abolition (an idea first proposed by Barry Goldwater in 1964, at the urging of Milton Friedman). That is, they have fostered and then exploited the public's confusion and fear over the Social Security surpluses, their uses, and the eventual deficits the system may face. The same conservatives—with generous financial support from the Wall Street firms that would benefit enormously from the change— offer up "privatization" of Social Security as the way to escape the system's alleged "low returns" and the "high risk" of its ultimate "bankruptcy," despite a well-documented myriad of risk and return problems tied to putting pension funds into stock markets.

The second corrosive effect of forcing Social Security to cover the deficits was that it increased distrust of the accuracy of federal budgets and the transparency of the process that created them. As the highly regarded MIT economist James Poterba observed, "Phantom attempts to achieve deficit targets by camouflaging spending as loan guarantees, by instituting tax policies that yield short-term revenue gains but long-term losses, and by invoking accounting tricks to balance one budget at the expense of the next only make budget balance more difficult."[14]

The effect of the Reagan deficits "spilled over" in many crucial ways, transforming both the U.S. and global economies. The heart of the change was in what some economists called the "financialization" of modern economies, a typically infelicitous term that nonetheless underscores the importance of trading in financial assets, compared to the fundamental production of goods and services. Signs of this shift were visible at the start of the Reagan era, but then accelerated so dramatically that the concept of "financialization" itself became a new "conventional wisdom." Consider, for example, the size of the stock market in relation to the overall economy: The total dollar value of U.S. stocks in the quarter century after World War II was usually about half the size of GDP; over the 1980s, that value trebled to 150 percent (at the height of the 1999 stock market peak it reached nearly $20 trillion, or 200 percent of GDP). The total debt of America's households and corporations meanwhile grew likewise: having risen in line with GDP growth in the pre-Reagan years it took off on its own path, rising from 160 percent of GDP in 1981 to 225 percent by 1989 (and nearly 300 percent today).

Internationally, the "financialization" process was even more dramatic: soon after Nixon's dismantling of Bretton Woods, currency trading rose to what then seemed the enormous sum of $18 billion traded per day in 1978. By the time Reagan left office, $600 billion was traded daily (by the end of the century the figure was $1.5 trillion). Global derivatives contracts, an esoteric "hedging" device initially sold by banks to multinational corporations anxious to manage their post–Bretton Woods currency-exchange risk, evolved into a full-fledged speculative market, soaring from near zero in the Ford-Carter years to $20 trillion by 1990 and to $120 trillion by 1999. (This $120 trillion is roughly three times the sum of all nations' GDPs combined.) In such an environment, not surprisingly, the profits of U.S. financial corporations likewise rose much faster than those of nonfinancial corporations. In the old Bretton Woods days, total industry profits for financial corporations averaged about 15 percent of those for all nonfinancial corporations; that figure has grown steadily to nearly 50 percent in the post-Reagan years.[15]

The very non-Galbraithian assumption is that such changes represent the "natural" and efficient workings of "markets" released from government constraints. This badly misrepresents what actually occurred when Reagan and Bush were in office. To Galbraith, consciously designed public policies—and their indirect consequences, often poorly understood or willfully ignored by their designers—were as important as "markets" in making this new world.[16] For example, it was policy that helped to sustain high real (that is, inflation-adjusted) interest rates throughout the 1980s. After Paul Volcker and the Federal Reserve used their short-lived monetarist experiment to choke off inflation, interest rates did not return to the historic long-term levels that economists assumed they would; instead record-high real interest rates averaged over 5 percent, more than twice the long-term U.S. average.[17]

Those high interest rates should have choked off growth by discouraging borrowing for new investment and consumption, caused a second recession, and forced the White House to choose between tax cuts for the wealthy, and economic growth. But they didn't—and the question was why? The most important answer, Galbraith believed, lay in the new global financial markets. With major industrialized and oil-producing countries awash in cash, global markets had funneled into the United States hundreds of billions of dollars from wealthy foreigners and their governments, drawn to the high interest rates and vaunted security of U.S. capital markets.[18]

One could say that these high rates acted as an economically "rational" market magnet drawing funds to America (thereby saving Reagan from making the hard choices his otherwise "irrational" deficits required), but in fact politics were always the markets' partner. By the 1980s Japan was running a huge trade surplus with the United States, and American officials made it clear that an implicit price for allowing the surpluses to continue was that Japanese profits be reinvested in U.S. Treasury bonds; Japan thus became America's largest foreign creditor. Similarly Washington made sure that Saudi Arabia and Kuwait understood that the United States would act against the gigantic dollar surpluses they were building up unless they, too, made major commitments to buy both American bonds and military hardware.

Despite the scope and scale of these manipulations and interventions, little understanding of what was happening overall—or how its disparate parts were connected—seeped into public consciousness in America. Much more discussed, because they fit the country's long-standing conventional wisdoms about technology, were all the new computer and telecommunications systems that linked New York trading screens to Paris, São Paolo, and Singapore, permitting a simultaneous explosion of foreign-exchange trading, arbitrage, and hedging.[*19] This rush of foreign investors to U.S. bonds was manna to America's bankers, especially since their once-profitable opportunities to lend to the Third World were now mired in rancorous debates over renegotiation and repayment.

Because the banks, in their reckless rush to lend out petrodollars in the 1970s, had protected their own interests first by requiring that Third World loans be calculated in dollars, and then by attaching floating interest rates that soared when the Federal Reserve forced U.S. rates to record highs, it had become completely impossible for debtor nations to meet the banks' repayment schedules. Mexico's disastrous financial implosion in 1982 was the precipitating moment in global debt crisis that now unfolded. A near fiasco followed when countries from Argentina and Brazil to Hungary and Poland suspended their own repayments of more than a quarter trillion dollars in loans. The banks' devastated balance sheets played an important part in encouraging both government regulators and the banks to maintain higher interest rates as a means to restore their capital base while searching for ways to work off the nonperforming loans.[†]

But something quite predictable then happened: the value of the dollar soared against other currencies, initially by nearly 30 percent, and by as much as 50 percent by 1985. With such extraordinary dollar appreciation, the sales of suddenly cheap foreign cars, steel, and electronics soared while U.S. exports sagged, widening the trade deficit. Thus the huge budget deficits drove up an equally huge trade deficits, which produced unprecedented domestic havoc in key sectors of the U.S. economy. Conservative economists then shifted, just as

---

[*]The explosion in cross-border financial markets was also helped by new economic theories about risk and risk management. Work done by Modigliani, Black, and Merton is often cited; they led to the hiring of mathematicians and economists to write computer programs for risk management for banks and trading houses. The meltdown in 1998 of Long-Term Capital Management, where Merton was a senior partner, was a paradigmatic cautionary tale.

[†]Nevertheless, the big banks remained saddled with half a trillion dollars or more (estimates varied) in uncollectible Third World loans throughout the 1980s.

they did on the significance of budget deficits, to claiming that trade deficits didn't really matter.[20]

The United States had been a "creditor" nation for more than a century, running a surplus in its current-account trade with the rest of the world. That had ended under Richard Nixon in 1971. When Reagan took office, the trade deficit was already $27 billion; two years later, however, it had soared to $60 billion; it then reached a breathtaking $123 billion two years after that. Although by 1990 it shrank slightly, it ended up totaling over $900 billion during Reagan's eight years in office (and it has taken off to even higher levels ever since).[21]

The consequences were not abstract. A harsh domestic recession at the start of the 1980s, followed by surging imports, hit America's manufacturers very hard. In the "Rust Belt," the heartland of American manufacturing north of the old Mason-Dixon Line and stretching roughly from Pennsylvania west to the Mississippi River, thousands of what would have been competitive plants were shuttered, leaving millions of highly skilled and highly paid workers searching for jobs at the local McDonald's or Kmarts at wages that were often less than half of what they had previously earned, and without the health and pension benefits they had once enjoyed. By the end of Reagan's second term, as much as 40 percent of U.S. manufacturing jobs in the Rust Belt had simply disappeared.[22]

At the same time, thanks to the dollar's appreciation caused by the deficits and the high interest rates, combined with a fall in demand for U.S. food exports in the developing world, whose purchasing power had collapsed, America's farmers began their own prolonged collapse. Galbraith watched in horror as the Farm Belt fell into the worst economic crisis since the Great Depression. Domestic agricultural prices slumped and food exports fell nearly 50 percent during Reagan's first term, forcing hundreds of thousands of farmers into outright bankruptcy, prodding hundreds of thousands more to abandon farming as a way of life, and precipitating a nationwide collapse of rural land values. By Reagan's second term, America's 2 million remaining farmers were earning nearly half their net income—more than $20 billion a year—in federal aid. The damage was so extensive that farmers' income did not return to its level under Jimmy Carter until the mid-1990s.[23]

In a speech to the National Governors' Conference in the summer of 1987, Galbraith went beyond explaining the roots of the farm crisis in Reaganomics to offer a series of concrete proposals to solve the crisis. Leaders in the United States and abroad, he said, needed to recognize that the global agricultural system had changed because of myriad new farm technologies. Management of surpluses, not the fear of scarcity, was now the problem agricultural policies must solve, and modern price-support systems in the U.S., Japan and Europe weren't capable of doing so. Galbraith warned of a taxpayer revolt against the increasing farm subsidies that would worsen the situation. Before that happened, the major farm-export countries—the United States, Canada, Brazil, Argentina, and Australia, in particular—should negotiate a global network of production agreements and phase out their domestic price-support systems.* Consumers would likely see some increase in food costs, but he argued that the net increase would likely be minor and in any case more than bearable vis-à-vis the total cost of direct and indirect government subsidies.²⁴

THE RUST BELT and Farm Belt weren't the only victims of Reaganomics. Another "pro-market" experiment, the early-stage deregulation of the American financial sector itself, resulted in the great savings and loan crisis. A year after Reagan took office, Washington abruptly lifted limits put in place during Roosevelt's administration to prevent a repeat of the 1929 financial market's collapse, including limits on banks' and savings and loan companies' interest rates, geographic expansion, and the types of loans and customers. For nearly four decades, those limits had promoted a remarkable stability in the U.S. financial system; in 1981, in what amounted to the policy equivalent of a "perfect storm," that stability evaporated.†

The banks and S&Ls tested their new freedom by raising the interest rates they paid on deposits in order to lure back the billions that had been siphoned off by money-market funds, that Nixon-era invention which, free of federal regulations and insurance, had exploded in popularity and cash deposits. But this meant the banks needed to make high-return loans in order to pay depositors the same rates as their new competitors, and that in turn meant—as it had with Third World lending—going after riskier loan customers, with what turned out to be the same disastrous results.

At first, new policy changes seemed to come to the rescue, by creating just such opportunities in commercial real estate. The 1981 tax cut was loaded with dozens of lobby-driven "sweeteners"—special tax breaks for particular economic interest groups. Commercial real estate had won some of the sweetest—and now one could suddenly "write down" the economic life of a skyscraper or shopping mall not in forty years but in as little as fifteen years.‡ This extraordinary rapid depreciation (which bore slender relation to the buildings' actual physical or economic "life") shielded enormous amounts of investor income from taxation and set off a gold rush of lending for new commercial con-

---

*Congressional Republicans, ignoring Galbraith's advice, passed the Freedom to Farm Act in 1996. This "free market" bill was supposed to end all government aid to U.S. farmers over ten years, but it made no attempt to coordinate global production. The predictable result came swiftly: farm commodity prices collapsed a year later, Congress backtracked and in political panic voted temporary "emergency" farm assistance that ended up totaling $23 billion. By 2002, that "emergency assistance" totaled nearly $100 billion—and American farmers were still dependent on Washington for half their net income.

†The push to "deregulate" banks and S&Ls began under President Carter, with passage of the 1980 Depository Institutions Deregulation and Monetary Control Act. The process accelerated dramatically with passage of the sweeping Garn–St. Germain Act in 1982, and then through deregulatory decisions energetically pushed by the White House and by Alan Greenspan, who was a paid consultant to Lincoln Savings, one of the most notorious of the failed S&Ls. The result—new laws that weakened capital requirements, encouraged accounting fraud, and even deliberately blocked federal auditing oversight—combined with repeated denial and concealment of the looming disaster by the White House and its regulators, made the eventual S&L bailout under President George H. W. Bush ten times larger.

‡The 1981 tax cuts also permitted accelerated depreciation, which made the write-offs even larger at first. Worse, they even allowed this sort of high-speed write-off on existing real estate, not just new construction.

struction. By one estimate, more square feet of new commercial building space were built in the 1980s than during the entire previous history of the country.

Then, as with all such gold rushes, after excessive speculation came collapse, when real estate prices across the country gave way (especially in feverish markets in California, Texas, and Florida), leaving thousands of shopping malls and office buildings empty and the thousands of S&Ls that had financed them bankrupt.[25] In trying to explain what ended up as a $300-billion clean-up of the industry by taxpayers, politicians and journalists made much of the outright fraud and chicanery perpetrated by some of the industry's most colorful figures, such as Lincoln Savings Bank's Charles Keating. Since then, however, most economists and policy analysts have come to agree that the crisis was more fundamentally a systemic one bred by public policy, richly encouraged by lobbyists, and compounded by government regulators' unwillingness to change course once the problems became evident, in hopes that a "market-led" recovery would solve the disaster.[26]

When rescue finally arrived in the form of President George H. W. Bush's Resolution Trust Corporation, a public agency charged with closing thousands of S&Ls, selling off their assets, and then using taxpayers' money to make good on millions of federally insured deposits, a chorus of complaints arose from conservative economists that most of the blame for the disaster should be laid on the "moral hazards" created by government's insuring the deposits in the first place. Absent such insurance, they argued, depositors would have been more cautious and would have constrained the institutions' reckless behavior.

But this theoretically plausible explanation (at least in standard neoclassical terms) overlooked several realities. Wall Street firms had acted on their own virtuous "market instincts" to create a market for "loan securitization" that allowed ailing bankers and S&Ls to bundle the loans they made, repackage them, and sell them off as tradable securities (akin to stocks or bonds) to pension funds, insurance companies and others. The buyers considered the securities risk-free, because federal deposit insurance backed the underlying deposits. This allowed the S&Ls to turn over their reckless lending activity even faster. It also overlooked the creation of a "bundled deposits" market by many of the same Wall Street firms, which brokered billions of dollars to the S&Ls most desperate for cash, thus helping to hold up interest rates. And it overlooked the fact that although deposits were insured up to only $100,000, once an S&L failed, the Reagan administration simply ignored that legal limit and repaid the much larger depositors, who in most cases had known full well the risk they were running.

And, of course, most fundamentally, the conservative critics of the "moral hazard" problem overlooked the political suicide that any White House—liberal or conservative—would commit if it were to announce to millions of American voters that their vanished savings accounts and certificates of deposit were no longer insured because it was inconsistent with neoclassical economic theory to insure them. About all this, Galbraith observed,

Few exercises in our time are so ingenious and, when examined, so engaging as our language to grace an inconvenient economic tendency or necessity. In past times, loans that were not repaid went sour or were in default. Now they are rolled over. Or rescheduled. Or they become problem loans. Or, best of all, they become nonperforming assets. (I heard the other day of a banker whose son had had a bad accident with the family car. The lad told his father that the car wasn't totaled, only rendered permanently nonperforming.)[27]

Galbraith, writing these words in 1985, before the full scale of the S&Ls' "nonperforming asset" problem was known, warned that what Reagan's economic policies were creating was a novel form of "socialism" for the nation's largest enterprises. He noted the past decade's history of federal rescue of Chrysler, Lockheed, Conrail, Amtrak, the Continental Illinois bank; also of the then early-stage bailout of a few high-profile S&Ls, and of Mexico and Argentina (and thereby of Citicorp and Chase Manhattan). While smaller firms and weaker industries were now supposed to be left to the harsh winds of the market, he observed, the principle of "too big to fail" was the Republican watchword, despite remonstrations to the contrary.

Time proved Galbraith right. Unwilling to learn the lessons offered by their disastrous lending to the Third World, or in their real estate lending, banks compounded their errors with massive forays in energy lending, based on the erroneous idea that oil and gas prices would take off once the Reagan administration had abolished Ford- and Carter-era controls. When in the 1981 tax bill energy suppliers were given generous new tax breaks, especially to encourage new production, Reagan promised simultaneously to release the companies from the inordinately complicated (and flawed) bureaucratic contraption of earlier "energy policy," with its various grades of "new," "old," and "old old" oil, its lackluster "alternative energy" programs, and its contradictory price limits and production incentives. But the oil and gas price explosion failed to materialize, and hundreds of energy producers went under, including a youthful George W. Bush, who started his business career with a string of unsuccessful oil exploration ventures. (Unlike most of his small Texas competitors, however, the future president was repeatedly and generously rescued by business and political supporters of his father.) So did their lenders—first Penn Central, one of the nation's twenty largest banks, and then Continental Illinois, the nation's sixth-largest. The fact that the crisis for the banks never reached the scale of the S&L crisis owes much to the stubborn resistance of a few regulators who failed to toe Reagan's line, notably William Seidman, chairman of the FDIC, who later was put in charge of the Resolution Trust Corporation.[28] This "Mr. Clean" ended up being loathed by the White House for his stubborn independence, which Treasury Secretary Donald Regan sneeringly called Seidman's "fuck-you money."[29] Yet even with figures like Seidman charting their own course, after each collapse more shock waves washed through the financial system. In the United States, the net effect of all this risk taking and consequent volatility was that the number of banks fell precipitously, banking assets were concentrated in fewer and larger banks, and no gain in economic efficiency or profitability was recorded.[30]

THE CHARACTERISTIC of Reaganomics least celebrated (or mentioned) by its supporters was the central, indisputable activism of the federal government in all of this, as Galbraith over and over loved to point out, with malicious glee at times. The Reagan era, far from being a time when government power over the economy was rolled back, was one in which government's hand was ever-present, precipitating the decade's dramatic shifts and then working to rescue its political leaders and their business supporters when the shifts went awry.

The federal government's well-known and costly bailout of the savings and loans was only one of countless examples of aggressively active manipulation of "the market" by a nominally conservative White House that publicly was pledged to freeing markets from state manipulation.[31] The global debt crisis, for example, was the subject of repeated and costly rescue efforts and rule changes by the White House throughout the 1980s, beginning with the bailout of Mexico after its abrupt "standstill" on the $80 billion it owed foreign lenders in 1982 and Argentina's $44 billion "standstill" (half of which was due to capital flight) soon after. Needless to say, these rescues in turn helped America's biggest banks, which were the countries' biggest lenders.

Solving Third World default in fact became the subject of ongoing White House salvage efforts in the Reagan-Bush years, most prominently first the Baker Plan (named after its author, James Baker, Reagan's second Treasury Secretary) and, when that failed, the Brady Plan (named after Nicholas Brady, Baker's successor). Baker offered his plan in 1985 after his predecessor, Donald Regan, the former head of Merrill Lynch, had spent nearly three years unsuccessfully and desultorily trying to solve the debt problem country by country. Baker, a tough, wealthy Houston lawyer schooled in John Connally's tradition of conservative pragmatism, had begun the 1980s as the head of George Bush's primary campaign against Reagan; he had negotiated Bush's withdrawal when Reagan's victory became likely so successfully that Reagan took both men into his administration (Baker was Reagan's first White House Chief of Staff). After Baker and Don Regan swapped jobs, Baker proposed that Western banks renew lending to Third World countries in exchange for the commitment to tough new economic reforms, and their working-down of massive existing debt through a "menu" of options, including debt-for-equity swaps and increased matching lending by the IMF and World Bank.

The better decision would have been outright debt forgiveness, as far as Galbraith was concerned. But that was too much for either the ideological Reagan or even the more pragmatic Baker to swallow.[32] And the Baker Plan eventually worked in one brutal sense: pressured by the IMF and World Bank, Third World countries *did* increase their repayments to Western lenders. But they did so by imposing singularly harsh new "structural adjustments" on their citizens: cutting spending on health and education to balance budgets, opening their economies to Western imports that ravaged small domestic producers, adopting monetary policies that crushed inflation but also growth, and pressing for export-led growth rather than increased domestic consumption. The strategy of "structural adjustment" became known among economists and development specialists as "the Washington Consensus," not just because the World Bank and IMF were headquartered in Washington but because the White House and Treasury Department had been central in leveraging the two big multilaterals into their new position. Despite its promises, however, the Washington Consensus didn't lead to more Western bank lending, and it was soon pronounced an outright failure by both the World Bank and the IMF (although not before it had wreaked further havoc on some of the poorest economies and most vulnerable human beings in the world; development economists speak of the 1980s as "the Lost Decade" in global economic development).[33]

By the time Reagan's second term came to an end in early 1989, many observers already thought the Baker Plan was a disaster. Money was flowing to and from the Third World, but it was devastating global economic development: by some estimates more money was being sent from the poor countries to Western banks than was being spent on the combined health and education budgets of the entire Third World. Faced with the untenable domestic politics bred by such policies, Brazil suddenly announced it would stop servicing most of its $108 billion debt. Argentina and other nations threatened to follow suit, and riots over onerous debt-servicing conditions broke out all over, promising a whole new round of financial and political crises.

Bush's newly installed Treasury Secretary, Nicholas Brady, pressed by his deputy, David Mulford (whose sophistication for the *realpolitik* element in international economics owed much to his prior service as economic adviser to Saudi Arabia), in 1989 finally opted for outright debt relief rather than renegotiation as a means to kick-start the Third World's stalled economies. This represented a dramatic break in the policy line, so much so that the administration's conservative ideologists forced Brady to talk about the banks' offering "voluntary relief," and to make sure that his plan provided $30 billion in support from the IMF, World Bank, and Japan as the sweetener for them to do so.

Galbraith had consistently derided the Baker Plan and was no less caustic when the Brady Plan took its place, comparing them to the failed Dawes and Young Plans in the 1920s, two onetime famous U.S. efforts meant to finance continued reparations payments by the defeated Germans.[34] At one point, he became so annoyed with Baker that he described his economic policies as nothing better than "a marvelous exercise in fantasy and obfuscation."[35] And in 1984, in a major address to the U.N. General Assembly, he urged Third World countries, as an alternative to embracing "the Washington Consensus," to focus on the interim goals of boosting agricultural production to feed domestic populations, increasing education and opportunities for women, and avoiding government policies that deliberately held down farm prices in order to encourage rapid urban and industrial development.[36] A year later, when the Argentine government invited him, along with Franco Modigliani and Paul

Volcker, to offer on-site recommendations for cutting inflation and restoring the nation's battered economic health, he vociferously argued again for resistance to "Washington Consensus" policies.[37]

By 1986, his disgust with the consequences of "the Washington Consensus" in all its forms provoked a dramatic personal gesture that ended up playing a small but important part in forcing the White House to move beyond the Brady Plan. Invited to give a series of lectures in Brazil, he arrived to find the country in near chaos, with thousands of protesters battling soldiers and riot police in Brasilia, and the finance minister on the verge of resigning over his IMF-dictated austerity program. Galbraith first privately advised President José Sarnay—and then, with Sarnay's encouragement, publicly said at a press conference—that Brazil should stand up to the pressures from the North, estimating that by then Brazilians had much more leverage than they thought, and less to fear from defying the New York bankers who wanted a new round of debt repayments and the domestic budget cuts to make them. His encouragement stiffened the resolve of the Brazilians in their dealings with Washington, and it earned him headlines across Latin America—and, after it was reported in the States, the fury of Baker and the White House's economic apostles.[38]

But it wasn't just the Third World that was paying the international price for global "financial capitalism." Japan was by then the world's second largest economy and a ferociously successful exporter, whose products were scything through their competition in the U.S. automobile, machine tool, steel, semiconductor, and consumer electronics industries. Once, "made in Japan" had been an American sneer for poor-quality products; but by the mid-1980s, "made in Japan" had become a gold standard. With the value of the dollar and U.S. real interest rates at record highs, the United States sucked in Japanese products, leaving a huge trade deficit on the U.S. side of the ledger and thousands of U.S. companies and millions of U.S. workers unable to compete. Analyzing the nature and meaning of "the Japanese Miracle" for Americans became an academic and policy boom industry, as scholars and policy-makers ferociously debated its significance and the question of whether the United States should (or could) emulate—or defeat—it.[39] (No simple consensus emerged.) But in any case the pain that Japan's exports were inflicting was a volatile political and economic issue. In Detroit, irate and frightened auto workers were vandalizing Japanese-made cars, and state and local governments, pressed by angry voters, were refusing to buy Japanese goods as part of a new "Buy American" grassroots revolt. Reading the polls, the Reagan administration weighed the political risks and then intervened repeatedly in U.S.-Japanese trade relations. As early as 1982, it began pressuring the Japanese to accept "voluntary restraint agreements" first on automobile, then on steel, and then 100 percent tariffs on semiconductor exports; simultaneously it pressured them to import American products, as Japan was alleged to be blocking "free trade" in U.S. goods.[40]

Intervening in trade was only the start; soon the administration was engaged in manipulating international financial markets against Japan. Japan, awash in an enormous savings pool earned in part from its massive trade surpluses, was, as already noted, pouring hundreds of billions of dollars back into U.S. bond markets, and eventually became the largest single foreign financier of the federal deficits. With the dollar drastically overvalued, the dollar-yen exchange rate soared above 250, which in turn primed the flood of Japanese goods into the U.S. and helped to cripple America's ability to export to Japan. To remedy this untenable situation, James Baker convened a meeting of G-5 finance ministers at the Plaza Hotel in New York City in September 1985. There, behind closed doors, he pushed through a package of government interventions designed to drive down the overvalued dollar and forced Tokyo to accept a massive upward revaluation of the yen, which halved the value of the yen against the dollar in less than a year. This was clearly an attempt to fix by government intervention (in a way that Baker's fellow Texan John Connally would have recognized and supported in an instant) the failures of the same government's misguided domestic policies, while publicly maintaining its fealty to the genius of the markets.

But soon the Plaza Agreement backfired. Japan, finding U.S. bonds (and real estate, Tokyo's other popular American investment) too expensive for the revalued yen, poured money instead back into its home market, into Japanese real estate and the Tokyo stock market. The speculative bubbles set off in both sent the Nikkei Index to nearly 40,000 and made downtown Tokyo real estate the most expensive in the world. (It was so expensive that, for a brief time, a single block in downtown Tokyo's fashionable Ginza District was briefly worth more than all the commercial real estate in Canada.) When the twin bubbles inevitably burst in the early 1990s, as Galbraith had vocally warned they would, the Japanese stock market, real estate sector, and banking industry were left in a slump so deep that, unimaginable to conventional Western economists, it persists well into the twenty-first century.[41]

Japan wasn't the only country that went through this boom and bust thanks to the Republicans' devotion to market rhetoric and mercantilist policies. Japanese investors also poured billions into Southeast Asia and mainland China, where Tokyo's capital, technology, and management expertise fueled the growth of the already prospering "Asian Tigers"—Hong Kong, Taiwan, South Korea, and Singapore—and of Indonesia, Thailand, Malaysia, and the Philippines. This was hailed as brilliant, a spur to an "Asian Miracle" (in nations that effectively ignored the free-market policies pressed on the rest of the world by the "Washington Consensus"). By the mid-1990s, the "Asian Miracle" was overtaken by the Asian Financial Crisis—which set off a chain reaction in Latin America and Russia, and further retarded Japan's own recovery.

By the time the Japanese bubble burst during the first President Bush's term, however, several years before the major Asian Financial Crisis, the destruction of national financial systems had become an almost pedestrian commonplace. Globally, the IMF reported the astounding fact that 144 of its 181 member countries had gone through a major financial crisis (in many Third World countries, more than once) between 1980 and 1992.[42] In a separate study of fifty major currency crises over the same period, the IMF documented the damage, estimating that the affected countries GDPs had fallen by an average of 15 percent.[43]

In the fall of 1987, America's stock markets plunged into a bubble-bursting financial crisis of their own—a sharp reminder that the world's largest and most powerful economy wasn't any more immune than Japan or the Third World to the viruses of the 1980s. On October 19, 1987, Wall Street went into sudden free fall, with the Dow Jones average plunging a stomach-wrenching 22 percent—its greatest one-day collapse ever, and nearly double the worst day faced in 1929, when the panic in the markets had helped usher in the Great Depression.[44] Soon London, Paris, Frankfurt, Hong Kong, and Tokyo began tumbling as well.

Fearing a disastrous collapse of the securities industry and a global crisis of confidence, Alan Greenspan ordered the Federal Reserve to pump billions of dollars into the financial system and promise still more if needed. Even so, it was touch-and-go: the next Monday, October 26, the market cascaded downward again by 8 percent, the second worst day on Wall Street since the Great Depression. The Fed's swift action—based, as luck would have it, on a contingency plan completed only weeks earlier that anticipated just such a crisis—slowly halted the slide, but it took another two years for the markets to recover the levels they had achieved before the drop began.[45]

Galbraith's office and home phones were ringing almost continuously by late afternoon on Black Monday, as reporters rushed to transcribe his opinions about what had happened and would happen—and they did not stop ringing for weeks. Asked disingenuously by a young London *Times* reporter whether he'd been getting many other calls, an amused Galbraith replied, "Have I been rung up? Good God! On one day last week I was called twice by *The New York Times*, once by the *Boston Globe*, once by the *Boston Herald*, once by the *Washington Post*, once by the *Philadelphia Inquirer*, once by the *Miami Herald*, once by the *Denver Post*, once by the *Los Angeles Times*, twice by *The Wall Street Journal*, twice by the French newspapers, once by a journal in Norway of all places, twice by newspapers in Japan whose names I could not understand." (He wasn't exaggerating: in the first week, he appeared in seven different *New York Times* articles, repeatedly in the *Washington Post, The Times* of London, the *Financial Times*, and in more than three dozen other newspapers and magazines.)[46]

Reporters were especially keen to reach him because the previous January he had warned openly that the stock market was overvalued and headed for a crash. When "The 1929 Parallel" appeared in *The Atlantic*, conservatives had howled in derision, and the unfortunate *U.S. News & World Report* just days before the crash had called him a "merchant of gloom," no better than the little boy who cried "wolf."[47] But Galbraith hadn't argued that the 1929 crash and the Great Depression were about to repeat themselves; he had simply said that structural dangers were visible in the stock markets for those who wished to see them. To him they guaranteed with almost perfect certainty that there was about to be a precipitous drop, from which various consequences might flow.

The first danger, the ancient one, stemmed from what he called "the dynamics of speculation," which exuberant markets exhibit once investors become accustomed to share-price increases and to "the thought that they can take an upward ride with the prices and get out before the eventual fall." The stock market had been rising steadily after bottoming in the 1982 recession—indeed, several times faster than the overall economy, let alone corporate sales or corporate profits.

The second danger was newer: recent years had seen an explosion in new financial instruments—securitized loans, hedging and derivatives, and junk bonds. What they had in common was that they helped drastically to increase corporate debt as well as the leveraging of that debt, especially given the many mergers and acquisitions then taking place. Comparing these instruments to the closed-end trusts and pyramiding operations of 1920s firms such as Goldman Sachs and corporate buccaneers like Samuel Insull and the Van Sweringen brothers, Galbraith focused on a more elemental truth: that "the mergers, acquisitions, takeovers, leveraged buy-outs, their presumed contribution to economic success and market values, and the burden of debt they incur are the current form" of society's durably repetitive capacity for self-delusion about money. "Nothing," he remarked, "so gives the illusion of intelligence as personal association with large sums of money."

He also observed that Reagan's tax and interest-rate policies, like Andrew Mellon's in the Roaring Twenties, had greatly "lessened the tax bite on the most bitten," but unlike Mellon's had shown none of the promised increases in real capital formation or consumer demand. Instead, much of the money that was returned to the rich in the 1980s simply flowed into the stock market rather than into building the underlying goods economy on which it rested. Although he didn't cite figures for his claim, the empirical record of Reagan-era business investment in plant and equipment certainly supports his view: after rising slightly as the 1982 recession ended, it fell sharply and then stayed well below the average until the mid-1990s.[48]

Galbraith missed highlighting the participation of pension and mutual funds in this debacle, celebrated as "the democratization of the stock market." The percentage of American households that owned stock rose from less than 25 percent of families to more than 40, thanks to mutual funds. In fact, much of this participation was involuntary, occurring when companies abandoned their old "defined benefit" pension funds (in which the company effectively guaranteed a return to the retiree) and substituted "defined contribution" plans (in which return was dependent on financial market performance, with companies assuming responsibility only for their contributions, not the returns).

When the crash he'd foreseen arrived in October, just after his seventy-ninth birthday, Galbraith carefully told the *Financial Times* that although it was "fully comparable to the crash of 1929 and in some respects worse," he did not believe it would "lead to another depression" because "it was substantially a financial crash, not a reflection of the real economy." He nonetheless quickly upbraided the "sophisticated stupidity" of financial markets, gave a quick lashing to Arthur Laffer and Milton Friedman, and declared his (vain as it turned out) hopes that this would mark "the last chapter of Reaganomics."[49] (Characteristic of Galbraith, as the bad news was breaking he was found by the *Financial Times* not at home but at a conference in Turin, Italy; on his way there, a more enterprising London *Times* competitor in London had scooped the *Financial Times* with a Galbraith interview conducted at the Ritz.)

Over the next two years, the markets gradually recovered, but financial regulators barely had time to catch their collective breaths before a new crisis set in. Michael Milken had already won notoriety as the United States' "junk-bond king" when he directed the Beverly Hills offices of the New York brokerage firm Drexel Burnham Lambert. A model to Galbraith of the buccaneer financier of the time, Milken had revolutionized the market for low-grade, high-risk corporate bonds to draw in investors impressed by their high returns; he then used the proceeds to underwrite hundreds of hostile corporate takeovers in which the new owners saddled their targets with responsibility for paying off the junk bonds used to acquire them. Milken made a fortune almost overnight (he was paid $300 million in 1986 and $550 million in 1987), and he also made some of his allies and clients, such as his fellow buccaneer Ivan Boesky, very rich indeed; the employees of the take-over targets seldom fared well.* In 1989, a ninety-eight-count criminal racketeering and fraud indictment and a massive civil case were filed against him by the SEC. Little more than a year later, Drexel Burham was bankrupt and the junk bond market had gone into free fall, dragging down many of the companies that raiders had "ingeniously" acquired using the bonds. Milken plea-bargained his way out of more than a century of jail time in exchange for paying a $600 million fine and agreeing to spend ten years in jail (he spent only two), and accepting banishment from the securities industry for life.

Then, to close out the decade, the Bush administration, having kept the full scope of the S&L crisis out of view during the 1988 election, announced that it was closing down more than seven hundred ailing thrifts, called for setting up the Resolution Trust Corporation to dispose of their assets, and acknowledged that the cost of the industry clean-up would likely be at least $75 billion. (This fell far short of the final estimate of $250 billion to $500 billion, but was a substantial step forward from the $15 billion Reagan had said was the full extent of the problem.)

When the scope of the financial overreach became evident, confidence in Wall Street plummeted, real estate prices dropped, and the leveraged-buyout mania was deemed just that. Under hapless "Poppy" Bush, the nation slid into

---

*The Milken protégé Gary Winnick, a telecom billionaire, built Beverly Hills–based Global Crossing into an industry giant in less than a decade, then walked away from it with several hundred million dollars before its spectacular bankruptcy in 2001.

a recession that destroyed his chance of reelection in 1992, even though his approval ratings had been stratospheric after the Gulf War, in 1991. Out of all this soon came what Galbraith considered a new bipartisan inanity—the Beltway decision in the 1990s once again to try to balance the budget as a matter of neoclassical economic rules, rather than through Keynesian tactics.

A final striking feature of the decade's global "financialization" had been its effect on the structure, culture, and outlook of American corporations. New technologies and new managerial styles were often given prominent credit at the time, but many of the changes had a simpler explanation: they were directly initiated or indirectly accelerated by Reagan and Bush administration policies. This had major consequences for American economic performance—and for Galbraith's theories of the large firm.

In 1967, in *The New Industrial State*, he had divided America's business landscape between, on the one hand, an elite minority of a few thousand immense, stable, and powerful corporations that were able to exercise self-protective influence over their environment and, on the other hand, millions of smaller enterprises left to compete largely according to traditional market rules of neoclassical competition. The corporate elite, he'd argued, was one in which a "technocracy" steadily innovated through superior R&D and sales efforts, worked to influence demand through advertising and branding, paid their managers well, retained earnings to finance expansion rather than turning to credit markets, and were for the most part free of outside control, not least that of their shareholders. To Galbraith, the emergence of this technocratically managed world showed just how far capitalism had evolved since the era of the robber barons, stock market touts, and cutthroat competition.[50]

Whatever the validity of these earlier arguments, the portrait of a clubby, orderly world of "technocratic managerial" capitalism seemed out of date. The corporate landscape was now a different system. Many described it as a bold, adventurous new evolutionary stage on the way to a "new corporation" and a "new economy" that were part and parcel of the Reagan Revolution.

This new world was described with different features, depending on the author. For one, "new" referred to the market environment in which the corporations operated, the competition-inducing pressures created by expanding international trade and investment, the "new" financial markets for credit, and the actively managed stock portfolios of giant pension and mutual funds. For another, the giant corporations had restored entrepreneurial zeal and excitement among managers, with consultants such as the ubiquitous Tom Peters and McKinsey & Company preaching a gospel of "leadership for excellence" based on continuous innovation and attention to quality-based production. In thousands of business books and articles, young MBAs were prepared for heroic new roles, for which they were drilled like Marine recruits. "Intrapreneurship," "zero defect" manufacturing, "just-in-time delivery," "getting close to the customer," "total quality management," and "reengineering" became the watchwords of the new era. Peters's book *In Search of Excellence* sold nearly 5 million copies and spent two years on the *The New York Times* best-seller list.[51] Dozens of similar tomes, the religious tracts of a materialist era, broke the million-copy sales level.

These consultants and coaches wanted their warrior-hero managers to face up to what they considered the "realities" of the new global marketplace. Nothing could ever again inspire comfort or complacency, they warned: there would always be a dangerous competitor, a constantly volatile market, a hard-to-motivate labor force, an unexpected breakdown in the economic environment, an adverse Wall Street analyst's report, a threatening corporate raider. To succeed in this world, managers had to treat their companies not as an earlier generation had, as a careful assemblage of core competencies in equipment, labor, managerial skills, and products, but as a "bundle of financial assets," each asset measured for its potential profitability and financial-market appreciation. Rather than focusing on nurturing a company's established markets, and expanding them by innovating technologically and reinvesting retained earnings (as Galbraith had described the earlier "technostructure" as doing), managers were expected constantly to acquire new divisions, new companies, new product lines, new markets, and to shed old ones, whatever the (often destructive) consequences for employees and community stakeholders. Managerial success was judged on the company's short-term income and balance-sheet performance, the quarterly numbers on which portfolio managers made their decisions to buy, hold, or sell the company's stock. (By itself, this sort of system wasn't entirely new: it had been pioneered by conglomerates such as Textron in the 1960s. But the performance of the original conglomerates failed to meet their promise and the model fell out of managerial and investor fashion.)

This "new corporate" vision of the adaptive, flexible corporation and its bold new managerial leadership swept through the nation's business press, business schools, and corporate suites. The "new corporate" manager was moreover soon being touted as a model of leadership for the nation—if only more of the country were run like a business. Such managers were also offered up as proof that a textbook-classic dynamic competition had been fully restored to the United States after the grim stagflation and decay of earlier decades.

Its supporters thought the "new corporate" world of the 1980s should rightfully reward managers whose passionate commitment was to the bottom line and to the growth of "shareholder value." These new allegiances, it was said, constituted one more way in which the "new economy" had overturned the clubby "technocratic managerial" corporatism that Galbraith had once described. There was no more room for clubbiness when facing powerful, institutionally based stockholders, who had more aggressive attitudes toward management's performance, were more demanding about short-term gains, and weren't reluctant to dump stocks that didn't "perform" to their standards.

At first, the evidence for this "new world" seemed compelling. In *The New Industrial State*, Galbraith had made much of the point that managers exercised enormous control over their companies because ownership of shares was diffuse, and only in few companies were shares so concentrated (for example, among a founder's heirs) that management could be effectively challenged from outside. Critics like Solow notwithstanding, empirical evidence suggests that Galbraith was correct in many of his observations about 1960s corporate ownership structures. Corporate stock was owned by wealthy families and individuals, with the top 10 percent of households holding almost 90 percent of stocks. But that world had disappeared, and the structure of stock ownership had dramatically changed. Pension funds, mutual funds, and other institutional investors controlled nearly 60 percent of U.S. stocks, which was effecting two revolutions simultaneously. First, they were spreading stock ownership among millions of Americans who'd never owned stocks before—"taking Wall Street to Main Street," as business writers enthused. Here Reaganomics' supporters (especially Jack Kemp, Arthur Laffer, Robert Bartley, and other supply-siders) proudly declared that a new "people's capitalism" was being created within the markets themselves, and would now forever unite the interests of capital with the majority. Second, the big new institutional players, pooling the holdings of millions of small shareholders, seemed to be strong new neoclassical regulators of corporate managers' performance, with the funds keenly focused on companies' quarterly performance.

The fund managers, under competitive pressures to perform for millions of middle-class clients, were not reluctant to dump the stock of companies that didn't meet their expectations—or even to challenge management more directly. In the 1960s, most wealthy investors had patiently focused on solid, steady dividends and long-term capital appreciation, as Galbraith explained, and they rarely showed any intoxication with quarter-by-quarter results. In the Kennedy-Johnson era, "turnover" on the New York Stock Exchange—the volume of shares bought and sold in relation to the total shares outstanding—averaged 20 percent per year. By the height of the Reagan era, fund managers' addiction to quarterly numbers had driven turnover rates to more than 70 percent, and the average stock was held by fund managers for a year or less.[52]

As if all this weren't enough to stimulate a neoclassical-style "competitive focus" among corporate managers, adding to the pressure on executives was a new breed of takeover and buyout specialist, many of them financed by Michael Milken's reinvention of "junk" bonds. Corporate takeovers became not only commonplace but often hostile affairs that struck hard at companies whose managers weren't "making their numbers," that is, managing their corporations for the short-term profitability that fund managers watched, whatever their long-term prospects or performance strategies.

To escape the clubby old habits and to align the interests of shareholders and managers, there was also a huge increase for top managers in the use of stock options and performance bonuses tied to company performance. This was supposed to end forever the conflicts of interest long ago identified by Berle and Means, its proponents argued. Stock options weren't new, however: they had been used modestly in the 1960s, then had fallen out of favor as stock markets stagnated. When markets took off in the 1980s, neoclassical financial economists celebrated the reemergence of options as the perfect remedy for the "misalignment of interests" which, they admitted, led to managerial behavior that failed to maximize "shareholder value." That was all ancient history, they now believed.

The stock-options movement had a more complicated effect on corporate America than "new economy" proponents anticipated. Among America's top 100 CEOs, for example, *Forbes* found that income from options and performance bonuses rose from 22 percent of total compensation in 1980 to more than half of compensation in 1988, and the total dollars paid rose even faster. In the Nixon era, as previously noted, the total pay of top CEOs was roughly 40 times the earnings of an average American worker; by the end of the Reagan administration it had soared to 220 times. Meanwhile, the average worker saw no increase at all, in inflation-adjusted terms.*

All this emphasis on short-term, bottom-line performance thrilled conventional economists, the business press, and Reagan administration officials, who saw the "natural" outburst of entrepreneurial zeal as just what they had promised would follow from tax reduction and deregulation. Galbraith, by contrast, warned Americans about the instabilities and economic dangers inherent in what he called "this self-deluding model" of how a viable capitalism should really work over the long term—and in the process found himself ever more isolated. Then, gradually, evidence began to accumulate showing that the "new corporation" wasn't performing as well as expected.

To begin with, there was the matter of corporate debt: between 1984 and 1989, nonfinancial corporations took on $1 trillion in new debt to finance or defend against corporate takeovers. Overall, during the 1980s corporate debt more than doubled as a percentage of net corporate assets and interest payments. But this freshly accumulated debt didn't raise productivity growth, investment in research and development, or even corporate profits, all of which were below the levels of earlier decades. What it *did* do was force corporate managers to disgorge enormous amounts of cash in the form of interest payments, and to repurchase company stock as a defense against raiders rather than retain that cash for future investment. In fact, interest payments were consuming a record-high 30 percent of total corporate cash flow by 1990, while stock repurchases consumed another 20 percent. This was "impatient capitalism" in an extreme form, but it appeared to be the inescapable new norm.[53]

Impatience also forced managers to pursue "efficiency" with a newfound ruthlessness toward employees that, while thrilling to Wall Street, created enormous pain and dislocation for the large majority of American workers. An astounding two thirds of them said they had made cutbacks in their spending

---

*Because the IRS did not require corporations to book options as costs against corporate earnings, the companies reported much fatter profits than they should have. *Fortune* reported on August 12, 2002, that—even after the stock market collapse that reduced both stock and options values—the Standard & Poor's 500 companies had overstated earnings by 25 percent by not including real options costs. In the high-tech world the figure was astronomically higher: Dell's earnings (absent options costs) were overstated by 60 percent; Intel's, 90 percent; Cisco's, 170 percent.

because of uncertainty about their economic future; 42 percent of Americans (most of them salaried) reported having to work added hours to make do, while another 25 percent (mostly wage workers) said they'd taken reduced hours or pay cuts in order to keep their jobs. Uncertainty bled into the workers' core self-confidence about their ability to hold on to a job, and begins to suggest why wages for the bottom 80 percent of Americans had been stagnant for nearly twenty years. By 1992, nearly three quarters of Americans were convinced that ongoing layoffs and job losses were now a permanent fact of life, 44 percent of workers told the *Times* they'd be willing to take a smaller salary to keep their current job, 71 percent were willing to reduce their vacation days, 53 percent would willingly take reduced benefits, and half admitted they were much less likely to disagree with their bosses. Americans also offered pollsters a striking self-appraisal of where they stood in the class pyramid that made up the American dream. For a nation that had thrived for decades on an image of itself as a triumph of the middle-class, only slightly more than a third of Americans thought they belonged to the middle class; 55 percent now said they were "working class."[54]

25

Century's End

When statistics do not make sense I find it generally wiser to prefer sense to statistics.

—John Maynard Keynes

In making economics a nonpolitical subject, neoclassical theory destroys the relation of economics to the real world. In that world, power is decisive in what happens. And the problems of that world are increasing both in number and in the depth of their social affliction. In consequence, neoclassical and neo-Keynesian economics relegates its players to the social sidelines. They either call no plays or use the wrong ones. To change the metaphor, they manipulate levers to which no machinery is attached.

—John Kenneth Galbraith

FOR KEN GALBRAITH, born in the first decade of the twentieth century, its final ten years were among his least favorite, in part because of his own aging, which he found annoying. In an article written for *The Boston Globe* on his eighty-fifth birthday, "The Still Syndrome,"[1] he spoke openly about how he dealt with growing old. "The end is here, but not yet in sight," and younger people needed to learn how to "refrain from the uncontrollable tendency to re-mind us of how certain, assured and even obvious" is the slow decline of aging. He dubbed this tendency "The Still Syndrome," epitomized in the inevitable questions: "So are you *still* exercising? So are you *still* driving? So are you *still* writing?" He claimed to be waiting for someone to ask, "So are you *still* alive?" (He got almost as many congratulatory letters on that one *Globe* article as on any book he'd written—almost all from men and women over seventy.)

Yet despite his complaints, it was hard to find evidence that Galbraith let age get in the way of the life he wanted to lead. Most days until quite late in the century, he went out for a stately mile-long walk through the neighborhood, frequently with Kitty or a friend in tow, often ambling across familiar paths on the Harvard campus for lunch at the Faculty Club with old friends and acquaintances at the Long Table.[2] Three times a week he also went across the Charles River to swim at the university's Olympic-sized Blodgett Pool, a twenty-five-minute exercise routine—no more, no less—that he had maintained for years. (Age here served him well: once he found the pool unexpectedly closed but was determined to swim anyway. When a surprised young attendant found him stroking laps and demanded that he leave, Galbraith paused long enough to announce loftily, "My name, sir, is Blodgett," before continuing down the lane. The attendant, after one look at the craggy features and flashing eyes and hearing the tone of authority, quickly disappeared.[3])

One activity that Galbraith finally did give up—but only at the insistence of his doctors—was skiing during his annual winter vacation in Switzerland. (He proudly liked to note that Kitty, five years younger, kept skiing through most of the 1990s despite a broken hip and metal pins meant to hold the bones in place. "She takes it a bit easier," he allowed.) Actually, Galbraith had never been a particularly good skier, a fact of merry amusement among his friends. After watching him make his way down the slopes at Gstaad some years earlier, his friend William Buckley dryly inquired how long he'd been at the sport. "About thirty-five years," Ken replied. "Ah," Buckley shot back, "about as long as you've been doing economics."

One might have thought that the Galbraith home on Francis Avenue would be quieter than in the years when he was still teaching at Harvard, his three sons and their friends raced up and down the stairs, and visitors from all over the world passed regularly through the front door. By now many of his generation were dead or in nursing homes, and his sons were grown and married, with wives and children of their own, and well established in their careers.

Alan, the oldest, was now in his fifties, tall, balding, slightly round-shouldered, and perhaps the softest-spoken of the Galbraith sons. After graduating from Harvard in 1963 and from the University of Michigan Law School, and after a stint clerking in Sacramento for the California Supreme Court justice Stanley Mosk, he and his wife, Sarah (a Radcliffe graduate who was also a lawyer), moved to Washington, where he was now a senior partner specializing in patent, malpractice, and contract disputes at Williams & Connolly, one of the capital's best-connected firms; he and Sarah had a son and two daughters, all of whom during the 1990s attended Harvard. The middle son, Peter, sharp-eyed and quick-tongued, with a coiled energy that one friend said "makes him look like he's always ready to pounce," was almost ten years younger than Alan; he got his B.A. in government at Harvard shortly before his father's retirement, then spent several years living in Vermont, teaching at Windham College and getting himself elected as the state's Democratic Party chairman before going on to Oxford. But like Alan (and their parents before them), he, too, eventually went to Washington, where he spent nearly fifteen years as a senior staffer on the Senate Foreign Relations Committee, and during the mid-1980s did key, and courageous, work in exposing Saddam Hussein's genocidal campaigns against the Iraqi Kurds. In the Clinton administration, he served for five years as the U.S. ambassador to Croatia, during the worst of the Balkan wars, where he worked to blunt the Serb military attacks, deliver humanitarian aid, and negotiate crucial peace agreements leading up to, and including, the Dayton Accords. Peter has one grown son, and two smaller children with his second wife, a Norwegian anthropologist.

James, the Galbraiths' youngest son, chose perhaps the most daunting career of the three. Tall and big-boned, with the Galbraith gene for reddish hair, he majored in social studies at Harvard, then went to study at Cambridge as a Marshall Scholar. He got his doctorate at Yale under Sidney Winter, then spent several years working in Washington, too, eventually becoming staff director of the Congressional Joint Economic Committee. Following a stint at the Brookings Institution in 1985, he decamped for the University of Texas, where he is now the Lloyd M. Bentsen Jr. professor of government/business relations at the L.B.J. School of Public Affairs, in Austin. There, with his Chinese-born wife, Ying Tang, he has raised four children. Far better trained in mathematical economics than his father, he maintained his own Galbraithian skepticism about its uses; he coauthored a progressive Keynesian textbook with Robert Heilbroner. For several years he also advised China's State Planning Commission.

Although none of the sons lived nearby, the closeness of the Galbraith family, as well as their love of friends and visitors, meant that 30 Francis Avenue was never really quiet. Usually one or two Harvard students lived upstairs, in exchange for modest household chores and errand running. The Galbraith sons and their families, frequently with friends in tow, regularly showed up for holidays and summer visits, and the grandchildren who attended Harvard treated the rambling redbrick house as a second home. Little had changed from the 1950s or 1960s: there were still "the visitors"—the endless stream of old and new friends, scholars, politicians, reporters, writers and artists—who dropped in for lunch or dinner or drinks and, if from out of town, occasionally stayed overnight. Visitors were usually put up in the oval blue bedroom on the second floor, with its fireplace, big windows looking onto the backyard, stacks of books, comfortably worn chairs—and the guest book that Kitty always asked them to sign.

The Galbraiths' housekeeper, Sheela Karintikal, like her predecessor, Emily Wilson, was used to the routine. Told unexpectedly in midafternoon to plan on five, or seven, or nine, for dinner that night, she would grumble with good-natured weariness that "Sir and Madam don't change," then turn on the stove. Sheela had joined the Galbraith household in 1977, following Emily Wilson's retirement after thirty-five years with the family. (The Galbraiths purchased a nearby condominium for Emily, and passed her duties on to Sheela.) Indian-born, Sheela had heard of the famous ambassador, but was introduced to the Galbraiths only in the 1970s, through a mutual acquaintance. After several years she was joined by her son, daughter-in-law, and their two children. This extended second family took up a wing of the second floor, which had been vacant with the Galbraiths' three sons gone.

Little else about Ken Galbraith's well-established routines changed over the years, then. There was the trip to Gstaad each winter, usually for a month, starting in late January or early February. Summers brought another month or two at the family farm in Vermont, with its own steady stream of family and friends. As for diet, Galbraith ate sensibly but not cautiously ("I am genetically gifted with low cholesterol," he observed), and frequently took a glass of wine or two with dinner. With friends, he might also enjoy a good single-malt before dinner—or if dining out, a margarita. "I believe in the old Scottish adage 'Some men are born a couple of drinks below par,' " he liked to say, "and need a glass or two from time to time for their health."[4] He had given up smoking thirty years ago, after the first Surgeon General's report. Rare among men his age, he had no bladder or prostate problems. "All my unmentionable parts are in good condition," he volunteered with a grin, and he slept well each night, going to bed at around eleven, and waking at seven-thirty.

After breakfast and a look through *The New York Times* and *The Boston Globe*, the centerpiece of his daily life began, in a routine he'd maintained faithfully for half a century. About eight-thirty or nine, he ascended the stairs to his sunlit, book-lined writing room on the third floor. Working in longhand on a yellow legal pad—with a pause now and then to consult a book or article—he wrote steadily until just before lunchtime, which Sheela served with clocklike regularity at one. In the afternoon, he most often walked over to his two-room Economics Department office, and turned first to the accumulated correspondence, returned phone calls, and set his schedule. He would then pass his completed legal-pad pages to Andrea Williams, who in a concession to modern technology would enter what he'd written onto her computer, returning the printout to him the next morning for further editing and additions in his careful longhand, a process that was repeated again and again until he felt his wording was just right. Galbraith has always been grateful for Mrs. Williams's keen eye and sharp pencil. "Few writers in any language have been so favored. My spelling is often impressionistic; my punctuation is erratic; so more rarely is my syntax; my memory, though generally good, is subject to lapse, often under conditions of the greatest certainty; my sense of taste is fallible; and so too is my impression of what is or is not clear. All these faults are corrected to near perfection by Andrea Williams. Nothing, literally nothing that I have written for publication has escaped her scrutiny."[5] Galbraith frequently insisted that the air of freshness and spontaneity readers admire in his writing emerged only after the fifth draft has been reworked by her.

During the 1990s the morning routine yielded five new books, as well as several hundred articles, op-ed pieces, speeches, and interviews. In the spring of 1990, at age eighty-one, he wrote his third novel, *A Tenured Professor*, in which he took richly comic aim at the rational expectationists, their intellectual cousins the "random walk" theorists in finance, the merger-and-acquisition gunslingers who ruled Wall Street, and the Washington politicians, Republican and conservative Democrat alike, who promoted deregulation and laissez-faire as certain remedies for the economy's ills. The lead character is a Harvard economist named Montgomery Marvin who invents "the Index of Irrational Expectations" and accumulates an extraordinary fortune by shorting all the major economic bubbles of the 1980s—real estate, currency, banking, and energy. Marvin then turns his fortune to reformist ends by using it to finance political rectitude committees (PRCs) to blunt the power of PACs, and to buy up and then shut down a large part of the defense industry. These latter actions, however, cause him to run afoul of the SEC, which has seen no harm in his earlier rapacious speculations in capitalism's follies but won't countenance his progressive corrections of them, and eventually strips him of his empire.

If age was impairing Galbraith's writing abilities, more than a few critics seem not to have noticed. *Time* lauded *A Tenured Professor* as "the mandarin author's slyest satire yet," *The New York Review of Books* said it showed that Galbraith was "a latter-day Voltaire," and *The Atlantic Monthly*, *The Washington Post*, *The Boston Globe*, and a dozen others added equally fulsome praise. *The New York Times Book Review* cheered it as "great fun at the expense of the powerful and their all-too-numerous admirers. Conservative Congressmen are shown braying against the Marvins' plan to 'deface the pastoral fringe of the pristine California and Texas fields' with toilets for the field hands. Leading liberals, confronted with an effective version of their own beliefs, fall back into idle chin-stroking." In the daily *Times*, Herbert Mitgang found the book "ingenious and humorous even as it is chilling and cuts close to the bone about banking and the roller-coaster stock market." Of Galbraith's three novels, it was "by far his wittiest and wisest. Lurking in the background of his story is enough economics to satisfy Wall Street game players and enough of a cheerful fairy tale for grown-ups to please the most liberal dreamers."[6]

Before the year was over, Galbraith had a second book out, *A Short History of Financial Euphoria*, commissioned by the entrepreneur Christopher Whittle as part of a series called "The Larger Agenda," and distributed to 150,000 opinion makers before being released in bookstores. Galbraith himself thought the work "a bit light," but felt no compunctions accepting the $75,000 Whittle paid him. Despite its brevity, *A Short History* won its own string of positive reviews that summer, including two in one week from the *Times*, and its sales easily covered Whittle's advance (in Canada, which hadn't been flooded with free copies, the book became a best-seller).[7] After the markets' many troubles in the 1980s, readers found it sobering to consider his warning that the times augured another massive market run-up that would end in a spectacular bust.

GALBRAITH WAS NOT solely preoccupied with his books, however: the collapsing Soviet empire and Washington's uncertain, even hostile, response to this momentous development commanded attention. Having advocated expanded arms control and détente between the two superpowers since the Eisenhower years, not surprisingly he had been among the first to welcome Mikhail Gorbachev's unexpected attempts at reform of the sclerotic Soviet economy and its repressive social and political system. In 1985, at the height of the Reagan administration's arms buildup, Gerard Smith and Cyrus Vance, the chief U.S. negotiators of the SALT I and SALT II arms-limitation treaties, respectively, publicly called on the President to inaugurate a new round of negotiations with Gorbachev at a planned summit meeting in November. Galbraith, along with former CIA director William Colby and former Secretary of the Army Stanley Resor, were among the two dozen Americans who cosigned the Smith-Vance proposal. Two years later, in 1987, Galbraith went to Moscow for a three-day conference on peace and disarmament, where Gorbachev joined the Soviet physicist Andrei Sakharov in appealing for a new global commitment to nuclear arms reduction, not just for its own sake but as a linchpin of Soviet reform. The conference provoked great debate in the West, and exerted real pressure on Reagan to curtail his Star Wars plans.[8]

But most American conservatives then (and not a few liberals), caught up in Reagan's "Evil Empire" rhetoric, went on distrusting Gorbachev, however clear it was that he was trying to institute authentic reforms in the Soviet system. Galbraith decided to publish *Capitalism, Communism and Coexistence: From the Bitter Past Toward a Better Prospect*, an edited transcript of a lengthy and lively conversation he'd had at his Vermont farm with the Soviet economist Stanislav Menshikov, whom he had first met in 1964 and whom he admired for his intelligence and his refreshing independence of views during the stultifying Brezhnev years. Menshikov, twenty years younger than Galbraith, was more than just a "Soviet economist": his father had been Soviet ambassador to the U.S. in 1958–62, and the Menshikov family in Tsarist Russia included a long line of princes and nobles dating back to Peter the Great. Stanislav, a rising star in Soviet intellectual circles, had been deputy director of a prominent Moscow think tank, a senior United Nations staff member, and, most recently, editor of a Marxist academic journal in Prague.

In their 1988 book—which *Foreign Affairs* deemed "a good sophisticated primer" and Dimitri Simes in *The Washington Post* called "a testament to the new Soviet openness" (it was published simultaneously in Moscow)—the two economists shared in respectful praise of *perestroika* (reform) and *glasnost* (openness).[9] But whereas Menshikov viewed Gorbachev's sweeping reforms as means for renewing a socialism based on "true democratic centralism," Galbraith argued that they needed to go further toward authentic capitalism and social democracy, by allowing more room for markets, prices, and entrepreneurs, as well a freer press, freer culture, and a vibrant multiparty politics.

Menshikov, it turns out, wasn't the only Russian interested in Galbraith's ideas about transforming the Soviet Union. To Galbraith's surprise, Gorbachev himself unexpectedly added his own strong voice of support. In Washington for a summit meeting with President Reagan, he arranged a Soviet Embassy reception for a small, remarkably eclectic group of Americans that included Galbraith, Henry Kissinger, Paul Newman, Yoko Ono, the Reverend Billy Graham, George Kennan, Robert McNamara, and a few dozen others. During

Gorbachev's remarks to the group, he smiled at Galbraith and told the audience he'd long been a Galbraith admirer, having studied several of his books over the years, and would value especially his advice on Soviet reform.[10] (Galbraith has fondly recalled that Kissinger grimaced on hearing this.[11])

Galbraith was soon invited to Moscow, where he met with Soviet economists such as Leonid Abalkin and Oleg Bogomolov, who favored radical reforms but who like Galbraith opposed the overnight introduction of "shock therapy," as favored by a younger generation in both Moscow and Cambridge, notably Anatoly Chubais, who was to direct Russia's controversial privatization program, and Jeffrey Sachs, the young Harvard economist who was the leading American shock therapist.

But Gorbachev's hold over the Soviet Union was slipping by the time of Galbraith's visit, and Galbraith grew alarmed that a too-rapid collapse of the old order promised growing, perhaps catastrophic, danger for the new. Impoverishment, corruption, and political instability would undermine the chances for democracy. And were some misunderstanding to lead to a nuclear war, the "Evil Empire" would not be the only one to suffer. "Not even the most accomplished ideologue will be able to tell the difference between the ashes of communism and those of capitalism," Galbraith remarked.

He thus welcomed Gorbachev's decision the following year to permit the East German regime to open the Berlin Wall, releasing Eastern Europe nonviolently from a half century of Soviet domination. But he still feared what might happen if the Soviet government should itself collapse, particularly if the West refused to give major economic and technical support to it. But after Gorbachev resigned and was succeeded by Boris Yeltsin in late 1991, Galbraith's and Menshikov's ideas quickly fell out of favor, vigorously denounced by a self-confident new generation of Russian reformers. (Grigory Yavlinksy, for one, called Galbraith "a Marxist.") Yet, just as he had predicted, after Yegor Gaidar, Yeltsin's first prime minister, launched a massive opening of the economy, inflation soared by 2,500 percent in little more than a year, the life savings of most Russians disappeared, and the vouchers handed out to share the corporate wealth of the old economy among its citizens ended up in only a few hands. Few were prepared to listen to Galbraith's prescient warnings at the time; if not quite "Marxist," they were at least considered delusionally liberal. But Gaidar himself was forced from office, and Yeltsin's reformers went on to preside over a decade of severe hardship for most Russians and to produce a vast web of corruption that, far from nurturing democracy, created a new oligarchic class and an embittered public distrustful of the very idea of democracy. With the Bush and Clinton administrations unwilling to furnish economic aid and in the new "Wild West" atmosphere the reforms had created, crime at all levels of Russian society spread uncontrollably, GDP plunged by 40 percent (greater than the U.S.'s Great Depression collapse), the life expectancy of the average Russian male dropped from sixty-seven to fifty-eight, and a new economic "oligarchy," in many cases abetted by a burgeoning criminal "mafia," took control of the economy's commanding heights.[12]

After the Russian economy collapsed a second time in 1998, many of Galbraith's most respected colleagues became as openly critical of the Yeltsin transition as he had been at its start. Nobel laureates Kenneth Arrow, Lawrence Klein, James Tobin, and Joseph Stiglitz offered devastating reviews of the costs of the mishandled reforms and the reformers' misplaced hopes in neoclassical theory.[13] And when Gorbachev returned to the United States in 1992 for his first visit as a private citizen, he went first to Washington where he pleaded unsuccessfully for significant economic aid for Russia and its new government, and then to Boston, where, speaking at Harvard, he singled out Galbraith (once again in the audience), to praise him for his long-standing commitment to what Gorbachev said were the ideals guiding his own reforms: to avoid superpower confrontation and thereby to release the resources that the superpowers had once spent on the arms race to fight disease, hunger, poverty, and war throughout the world instead.[14]

Galbraith never lamented the passing of the old Soviet regime. Indeed he celebrated the collapse of Soviet Communism as the "greatest transformation on the world scene in the last half century." Even so, he was appalled by the human consequences for 350 million former Soviet citizens, and rejected the triumphalist belief of Western conservatives that with the Soviet Union's demise, the world had entered "the end of history," where markets and middle-class democracy would swiftly and easily span the globe. Instead, he reminded people that the United States and Britain suffered themselves from the liabilities of economic inequality, racial and social conflict, environmental neglect, and a messianic view of their position in the world not dissimilar to those that had marked the old Soviet Union.

Communism, he believed, had failed to accommodate its rigid doctrines to its subjects' widespread hunger for freedom and material comfort; under Reagan, Bush, and Thatcher, the "free market" rhetoric in the U.S. and Britain had failed to acknowledge the realities of a market system that was now permanently entwined with government, and had been used to break the modern social contract that balanced freedom with security and fairness. "The comfort and short-run convenience of [those] who are secure, contented and, in greater or lesser measure, affluent has been served," he grimly observed, while "action on the budget, taxes and needed civilian expenditure important for the longer-run has been forgone. Ideology is, by both nature and purpose, a substitute for thought, and thought, alas, is what is required if we are to accommodate to changing reality."[15]

By the spring of 1992, Galbraith had crystallized his indictment of American conservatism's ideological blinders in *The Culture of Contentment*. It was easy to detect in the book a harsh note of dismay at the results of twelve years of the most conservative national leadership since the 1920s. And for the first time Galbraith openly indicted his fellow citizens for betraying what he considered America's most cherished ideals and values: The United States had become "a culture of contentment, . . . wherein the majority of those who vote are socially and economically advantaged and will fight . . . to maintain that advantage." These privileged voters would naturally vote "against increased taxation that would reduce the federal deficit and respond to aching social problems. The result is government that is accommodated not to reality or common need but to the beliefs of the contented."[16] This majority of voters was *not* a majority of all Americans, of course. But in 1992 little more than half of the bottom three fifths of Americans bothered to turn out to vote, although those who did voted strongly Democratic. By comparison only 38 percent of the most affluent fifth gave their vote to the Democrats, but with an 82 percent turnout, these voters could effectively neutralize the Democratic margins below them.[17]

Having argued in *The New Industrial State* that members of the "technostructure" and the "educational and scientific estate"—society's best-educated white-collar workers—could be a vanguard to help free the country from economic error and misallocation, he now acknowledged that most would not do so, and that as a consequence, American democracy was facing a crisis.* All too often, managers, professionals, and small-business owners (as well as professors, researchers, and intellectuals), whom he had once expected to offer dissenting leadership and challenges to the "planning system" of the great corporations and their allies and servants in government, were silent. "The future for the contented majority is thought effectively within their personal command," he observed, and their commitment to the public as a whole has dimmed. "Their anger is evident—and, indeed, can be strongly evident—only when there is a threat or possible threat to present well-being and future prospect . . . This is especially so if such action suggests higher taxes."[18]

But the real danger to democracy was in the leaders who helped guide voters to these views, those passionately reactionary politicians with their soaring rhetoric about how "unleashing markets" would solve the nation's problems, and their summary dismissal of government as the "problem, not the solution."

To better-off and better-educated men and women—many of them too young to remember or know Roosevelt or Keynes except through books, if they knew of them at all—comfortable affluence was a given, a normal condition, far from the hard-won achievement that Galbraith's generation knew it was. Over thirty years, the antiauthoritarian rebelliousness of the Sixties generation had oddly blended with the antigovernment (though not anticorporate) ideology of the new conservatives to create a public rhetoric that cut across older divides. The new presumption was that any public needs that could not be met by private solutions could safely be ignored or even ridiculed. Asked whether they trusted their government to "do the right thing" all or most of the time, by the end of the Bush administration in 1992, three out of four Americans said they *didn't*.[19]

---

*As for Galbraith's original "technostructure vanguard" thesis and his revision of it, election data show that professionals and managers voted Republican consistently after World War II, most heavily in 1972, against McGovern; 1964 was the one year when, rejecting Goldwater, they voted Democratic. But as the two groups grew larger, and women and minorities entered their ranks, their support for the GOP steadily fell; since 1992 they have been voting Democratic (National Election Survey data 1952–2000; author's analysis).

The effect of this distrust on voting behavior was manifest. Not long after *The Culture of Contentment* appeared, the conservative American Enterprise Institute published a study entitled *Income Redistribution and American Politics*. It reported (with commendable frankness, under the circumstances) that since the 1970s, "American politics has become increasingly polarized around a . . . conflict [that] is basically over income distribution" and that "party identification has become more closely linked to income, with the Republicans becoming a party of the better off; the Democrats, the poor."[20] (This conclusion wasn't quite accurate, as the study's own data showed. Setting aside the fact that voting itself by then was increasingly an activity of the upper and upper-middle classes, AEI found that "the poor"—the bottom *60 percent* of American voters, a singularly capacious definition of "the poor"—remained mostly Democratic. Still, the AEI's data were clear that among the top 40 percent there *had* been a significant rightward shift.[21])

The shift was largely a by-product of the massive defection of middle- and upper-income white Southern and Sun Belt Democrats to the GOP, the very realignment that Richard Nixon had shrewdly sought to encourage as key to a "permanent Republican majority"; the AEI rightly concluded that it made the Congress "the most ideologically-divided" one in a century. The division was highly asymmetric: between a militantly conservative right, which dominated the Republican Party, and a divided and disorganized liberal-moderate Democratic opposition. About this new generation of GOP leaders and the new "contented" voting majority, Galbraith noted the surpassing irony that "the substantial role of government in subsidizing their well-being" had been conveniently forgotten.[22] Public investment from which they'd directly benefited—in education, health care, roads, science, and trade, not to mention in the high technologies originally financed by government—were now being celebrated as the singular achievement of "market-driven entrepreneurs."* Yet this was taken as no more than the contented majority's "just deserts." The common faith was that "what the individual member aspires to have and enjoy is the product of his or her personal virtue, intelligence and effort. Good fortune being earned or the reward of merit, there is no equitable justification for any action that impairs it—that subtracts from what is enjoyed or might be enjoyed."†[23] True, he added, among the affluent were numerous "scholars, journalists, professional dissidents, and other voices" who agitated against the new Gilded Age's feck-

---

*The federal government's role in financing the affluence of its conservative critics was not just in income and wealth transfers by class alone. Studies of the federal budget show that states that consistently voted Republican got billions more dollars from Washington than they paid into the federal coffers, while heavily Democratic states received less in benefits than they paid in total federal taxes. See Tax Foundation, "Federal Tax Burden and Expenditure by State," special report 105 (Washington, D.C.: Tax Foundation, August 2002).

†A decade after Galbraith wrote these words, Vice President Richard Cheney offered a memorable reminder of their relevance. In a cabinet meeting that discussed proposed massive tax cuts in the George W. Bush administration, Treasury Secretary Paul O'Neill protested that the cuts would be certain to fuel massive deficits. Cheney curtly dismissed this objection. "Reagan proved deficits don't matter. We won the midterms. This is our due." The cuts stayed, O'Neill was pushed out, and the deficits soared past half a trillion annually the following year.

less narcissism, and against the harm done to vulnerable citizens and to the common needs of society. Ironically, though, "by their dissent, they gave a gracing aspect of democracy to the ruling position of the fortunate."[24]

Galbraith was adamantly unwilling to serve as "a gracing aspect" for this new Gilded Age, and was unsparing in his indictment of its failures in *The Culture of Contentment*, one resting on a detailed cataloguing: despite Republicans' endless promises to the contrary, under them, economic growth had been the worst since the Great Depression; their tax cuts had principally benefited the well-to-do; those cuts, combined with an extraordinary surge in arms expenditures, had produced an unbroken string of budget deficits without precedent in the nation's history; America's trade balance, once long in surplus, had been running its own unprecedented and unbroken deficits; and the nation had gone from being the world's greatest creditor nation to the world's largest debtor. Meanwhile the gap between America's rich and poor, in terms of both income and wealth, had grown larger, while middle-class incomes had stagnated or eroded. Officially, Galbraith noted, the number of Americans living in poverty during the Reagan-Bush years rose by nearly 30 percent: by 1992, one out of five American children was born into poverty. About all of this Galbraith, notwithstanding the elegant detachment he still affected, was irate.

Intellectually most appalling to him were the forthright encomia to inequality that were being expressed, the conservatives' presumptuousness to outline philosophical (even theological) foundations for conservative policy. George Gilder's *Wealth and Poverty*, in Galbraith's view, served as the bible of the country's second Gilded Age, as surely as had William Graham Sumner's cruel Social Darwinism in the 1880s. Gilder was a hero to the Reagan White House: he had helped draft Reagan's acceptance speech at the 1980 Republican National Convention, vociferously promoted Laffer's supply-side tax cuts in *The Wall Street Journal*, championed Reaganomics at the Manhattan Institute, and proudly noted that he was the living author most frequently cited in Reagan's speeches.[25] Galbraith quoted verbatim Gilder's claims that "regressive taxes help the poor"; that, in order to succeed, "the poor need more of the spur of their poverty"; and that the "ineluctably elitist" nature of progress "makes the rich richer and increases their numbers, exalting a few extraordinary men who can produce wealth over the democratic masses who consume it."[26] Of Gilder's arguments and their applications, Galbraith caustically allowed that in quoting them, "none of this should be taken as criticism; Mr. Gilder's achievement, as he himself so generously conceded, [has been] to serve not rationality but faith. He saw a demand and filled it."*[27]

---

*In 2003, Gilder bought *The American Spectator*, a scathing right-wing monthly that in the 1990s thrived on anti-Clinton, take-no-prisoner diatribes, most famously the work of David Brock. The magazine had grown so extreme that its readers abandoned it in droves, leaving it in bankruptcy by the decade's end. As the *Spectator's* new owner, Gilder announced in his first issue that he intended to remake the magazine into "a vessel for the views of the investor class," then went on to denounce the second President Bush's $1.3 trillion tax cut as neither large enough nor skewed enough toward the rich. Tracing his own economic philosophy back to divine foundations, he declared that "supply-side economics has a moral source . . . a religious belief ultimately, hearkening [sic] back to our own creation as free creatures." Gilder opined that among temporal champions of such

Galbraith was also unambiguous in his dislike for the "neoliberals" who by then dominated the Democratic Party. "In 1988," he reminded readers,

> the Democratic candidate, Michael Dukakis, largely abandoning the issues that might be adverse to the culture of contentment, made as his principal claim his "competence." Not surprisingly, the traditional and seemingly more reliable exponent of comfort won. Many decades ago President Harry S. Truman observed in a memorable comment that when there was a choice between true conservatives and those in pragmatic approximation thereto, the voters would always opt for the real thing.[28]

Still, Democratic Party leaders' turning away from their traditional liberal values and traditional bases among the nonwealthy majority toward the new "contented majority" daunted Galbraith. In *The Culture of Contentment*'s final chapter, entitled simply "Requiem," he wondered openly what it would take for them to fight once again for greater economic equality and for the public goods he believed the nation required—stronger environmental limits, health care for 40 million uninsured Americans, better schools, better unemployment and welfare benefits, rehabilitation rather than incarceration for the addicted, and protection rather than privatization of Social Security. "In the past," he wrote, "writers, on taking pen, have assumed from the power of their talented prose must proceed remedial action. No one would be more delighted than I were there similar hope from the present offering. Alas, however, there is not."[29]

To him, "the contented majority" and the dominant political actors were basically deluded in their strident rhetorical rejection of government's vital relation to the American economy and their professed earnest determination to reduce its size. Their arguments seemed a travesty to him. In the 1980s, as Galbraith pointedly insisted, the size of government hadn't shrunk at all; to the contrary, it had grown to a peacetime record high in U.S. history. In any event, it was not size of government, but the reordering of its revenue and spending priorities that angered him. Along with the increased benefits to the few had come a brittle sense of privileged entitlement that allowed them to ignore impoverishment at home and abroad; to accommodate themselves to deficits; to celebrate the merger-and-acquisition mania; and to be silent about the resultant financial crises, including the unprecedented collapse of the savings and loan industry. Also, their support for the country's militant international unilateralism was a disgrace; Galbraith emphasized the internal decay of the Soviet Union's oligarchy as a cause of its collapse, rather than the Reagan arms buildup so celebrated by Republicans—which actually had so much to do with the decade's enormous fiscal deficits.

Predictably, conservative critics, bold and unrepentant, rushed to excoriate Galbraith and *The Culture of Contentment*. In the *National Review*, William F.

---

divine views, Rush Limbaugh was "the most important and effective Republican leader today and the most interesting"—a "genuine intellectual."

Buckley caviled that "nothing penetrates his comprehensive illusion" that America needed to "expand the public sector at a faster rate than we are do- ing." Buckley concluded, "It is fortunate for Professor Galbraith that he was born with singular gifts as a writer. It is a pity he hasn't used those skills in other ways."[30] *The Wall Street Journal*'s Robert Bartley accused Galbraith of wearing impenetrable armor when it came to the "facts" of President Reagan's great achievements. Chiding him as an unrepentant defender of "centrally planned economies," Bartley argued that though it might well be true that there was too much "contentment" in America, it was because too many gov- ernment programs protected undeserving welfare recipients, teachers, retirees, and the like. The idea that income and wealth had grown more unequal was "debatable," he thought, and even if true, was merely a just reward for efforts and risks taken by the talented. As for rising poverty, Bartley was frank: "The underclass presents a quandary Harvard dons have no ready formula to solve"; as for the middle classes, they enjoyed "too much political protection," which needed to be undone by cutting entitlement programs such as Social Security and education spending.[31]

BY CONTRAST, in *The New York Times* Robert Bellah said he "knew of no book . . . that treats more incisively or more convincingly the profoundly injurious consequences of these policies to our economy." *The Washington Post*'s chief book critic, Jonathan Yardley, praised it as "measured, ironic . . . yet angry" about the "complacency for which sooner or later we will pay a heavy price." Across the country, nearly two dozen major papers and magazines rushed to praise the book, and its sales quickly passed the 100,000 mark.[32]

Before 1992 was over, American politics took a dramatic turn for what to Galbraith seemed the better, a turn that suggested "the culture of content- ment" might not be permanent after all. That November, voters rejected the incumbent President George H. W. Bush and elected a Democrat to the White House, only the second time they had done so in almost thirty years. Twenty years earlier, Bill Clinton had toiled, like Galbraith, for George Mc- Govern's candidacy (as head of the campaign in Texas), and in the 1992 pri- maries, he campaigned on a platform that seemed at sharp odds with the conservative Republican agenda of the Reagan and Bush administrations, its essence provided by campaign manager James Carville's legendary phrase, "It's the economy, stupid." Governor Clinton himself promised to "put people first," and declared that in seeking universal health care, lifelong learning opportuni- ties, major investments in public works, welfare reform, economic expansion, and a tax system in which "the rich will pay their fair share," he was "fighting for the forgotten middle class."[33] Here, finally, was a Democrat Galbraith could embrace. Asked shortly after the election whether Clinton might be favorably compared to John F. Kennedy, Galbraith replied, "The greatest thing they share is that they represent a younger generation taking power, and I'm all for that, bringing a new group of eager people to Washington, people who regard gov- ernment as an opportunity and not a burden."[34]

But in truth, Democratic leaders—even young, charismatic figures like Governor Clinton—were, in practice if not promise, becoming more and more unrecognizable to liberal party lions like Galbraith. The change had begun decades before, in 1972, when the Texas lawyer and deal-maker Robert Strauss had taken over the financially bankrupt Democratic National Committee following George McGovern's lopsided defeat.

After his 1972 loss to Nixon, McGovern generously offered to give the Democratic National Committee his 600,000-name direct-mail donor list, which had raised $26 million for his campaign, to help pay off the party's debts and generate desperately needed new revenues. Strauss (who had already arranged Galbraith's removal from the Democratic Policy Council) accepted the huge list, and thanked McGovern profusely for his loyalty and support; then he put it in a closet and never sent out a mailing to the names to solicit a dime for the party.[35] For men like Strauss, the liberal New Deal–New Frontier–Great Society era was over, and the sooner the party was clear on that, the better. Strauss's stature as a conservative inside-the-Beltway player led the first President Bush to appoint him ambassador to the Soviet Union in 1991.[36] By then his attitudes toward Democratic liberals were defining a new party. The Reagan years had reenforced the native belief of party satraps like him that the Democrats needed to tack rightward in order to govern, a lesson underscored by the huge explosion in campaign costs—an unprecedented "dollars-for-votes arms race," as one observer called it—that was drawing the Democrats ever closer to the rich individual and corporate donors who had long been stalwarts of the GOP. (Between 1972 and 1992, PAC contributions had gone from $8 million to more than $190 million. During the 1980s, labor unions PAC contributions grew fourfold, while corporate and trade association PAC dollars grew elevenfold.[37])

Embodying this new view of the party, the Democratic Leadership Council, a Washington-based "ideas and action" group, as it styled itself, enjoyed substantial influence in the party. Created in 1984, funded by business and trade groups, and chaired by conservative Southern Democrats such as Sam Nunn of Georgia, Charles Robb of Virginia, and John Breaux of Louisiana, the DLC's goal was to "save" the Democratic Party from the "excessive liberalism" of its past and return it to what the "New Democrats" deemed America's "vital center," an appropriation of Arthur Schlesinger's term—ironic, given that forty years earlier he had coined the term when he, Galbraith, and other New Deal liberals had created the Americans for Democratic Action to rescue the party from excessive conservatism. No small part of the DLC's claim was that it could return large parts of the South to the Democratic fold.[38]

Bill Clinton had served as the DLC's chairman shortly before he began campaigning for the presidency, and once in office he appointed many DLC figures to key White House posts, much as Kennedy had appointed ADA supporters in 1961. Yet, as Galbraith and other liberal skeptics pointed out, Clinton's electoral victory hardly seemed to endorse the "right-turn" strategy the group advocated: he had won only 43 percent of the vote in a three-way race against President Bush and the Texas billionaire Ross Perot (the weakest victory margin since Woodrow Wilson's 41 percent in 1912). And far from regaining the South, he had carried only four minor states there, and had lost heavily in Florida and Texas, the South's richest prizes.

A month after his election Clinton reached out in what seemed an encouraging sign to party liberals: he convened an unprecedented "economic summit" in Little Rock, where for two days three hundred economists and economic policy-makers participated in a "national seminar" to debate the depressed state of the U.S. economy and the policy options for generating a recovery. Liberal participants were optimistic. As *The Boston Globe* columnist David Nyhan put it, "We all knew Clinton was smart, articulate, a maestro of the mike in talk-show settings. But even his enemies have to admit the man is brilliant. He knows all these intellectuals. He's actually read a lot of their books. He can handle the abstruse notions of economics. How about this shocker: He can talk in complete sentences! Wow." Galbraith was especially pleased to hear about the President-elect's exchange with the veteran economist Henry Aaron of the Brookings Institution. In the Carter administration, Aaron had been an influential advocate of fiscal caution; at Little Rock, he urged Clinton to resist the urge for spending and to concentrate on deficit reduction. But Clinton firmly replied, "All spending is not the same. There is plainly a difference between spending money and investing it. We have got to change the character of federal spending" toward investment in people.[39]

It also didn't hurt, especially in Cambridge and Boston, that Clinton had asked his friend and fellow Rhodes scholar the Harvard public policy expert Robert Reich to organize the Little Rock conference. When he then appointed Reich Secretary of Labor, it was taken as a further sign that his administration was more promising than Jimmy Carter's had ever seemed. Reich was also a friend of Galbraith's and called on him frequently for advice. When they shared a podium, the diminuitive Reich was fond of remarking, "When I first started studying economics, I was as tall as Professor Galbraith."

Once in office, however, Clinton stumbled repeatedly, as he was relentlessly attacked by the Republicans and abandoned by fellow Southern Democrats, first on his new policy about "gays in the military," then on a modestly stimulative economic package meant to help the country recover from the recession. As he backed away from his defeats in late 1993, his avowed "New Democrat" strategy seemed maladroit to Washington insiders, and a full-fledged retreat from core Democratic values to Galbraith.

Galbraith was hardly being naive about the constraints on the White House. In 1960 President Kennedy had come to office with one of the narrowest majorities in history, and constantly felt the pressure of conservatives in Congress restraining his initiatives. Yet to Galbraith, Ross Perot's performance in 1992, the best third-party showing since Teddy Roosevelt lost to Wilson in 1912, signaled just how deep the discontent was among the American people, and it represented an opportunity for the Democrats, if only they would take it. In 1980, Ronald Reagan, winning with another paper-thin majority, had promised in his own variant of anti-Washington populism to lift the burden of government and substitute the "freedoms" of the market. But benefits had flowed forth so inequitably during his term in office that voters in 1992 were as disillusioned with corporate America as they were with Washington bureaucrats. Most Americans clearly distrusted government, and even more stunning, nine out of ten said they now distrusted corporate America and believed that the wealthy and corporate elites had captured effective control of the government. As Galbraith saw it, the new conservative devotion to market "freedom" had not supplanted the distrust of government's burdens; most Americans now found *both* oppressive, alienating, and, worse, in collusion.[40]

Yet President Clinton was doing almost nothing politically to capitalize on this distrust of concentrated wealth and corporate power and to fend off the relentless antigovernment attacks of the GOP. Instead, after his initial humiliations, he opted for a more cautious strategy of governance than he'd promised in the campaign. Having to dig out from the sharp recession he'd inherited, and out from under the daunting legacy of massive Reagan-Bush deficits, Clinton was in fact opting more and more to abandon old Rooseveltian and Keynesian ideals. Cutting the deficits and limiting public spending were to be this President's new "middle way" to economic health.

Galbraith recognized that, as a political matter, the size of the deficits Clinton inherited had to be addressed. After all, he himself had more than once quipped that "politics consists in choosing between the disastrous and the unpalatable." He thus admired Clinton for engineering a difficult and complicated tax increase that at least raised effective rates on the top income brackets to 29 percent while it simultaneously expanded the Earned Income Tax Credit for the working poor.*[41] The new rates on top incomes were still far below the 38 percent they'd been in 1980 (let alone the 92 percent top statutory rate under Truman and Eisenhower, when, as Galbraith loved to remind audiences, American economic performance was far better). "Like the post-election Bill Clinton," he told an interviewer, "I would go further than increasing taxes on those with incomes above $200,000. I too would have no hesitation going down to $100,000. I am not going to weep for anyone who has an income of $100,000 or more."[42] Still, Clinton politically was forcing Republicans to confront their hypocrisy on the deficit and debt issues. After years of preaching fiscal probity, the GOP under Reagan had discovered the joys of deficits and were now so enamored of them that Clinton's tax bill passed the House by a three-vote margin, 218–215, with every Republican voting against it.[43]

But Galbraith was concerned about Clinton's hesitation to restructure federal spending priorities. He wanted to see a clear shift away from military programs such as Star Wars, America's vastly redundant military system of bases

---

*Clinton's 1993 tax increase had been preceded by President George H. W. Bush's larger increase in 1990, the one that broke his "Read my lips" pledge in the 1988 campaign and fueled conservative enmity toward him over his "betrayal."

all over the world, its exorbitant arms exports, and other repellent remnants of the Cold War. The shift should favor domestic programs, and furnish the foundations for a post–Cold War multilateralism in which (as Roosevelt had envisioned fifty years earlier) the United States might lead, but not alone.[44] Instead, he saw Clinton stealing a page from GOP Holy Writ and tilting rightward, seeking budget balance rather than the right mix of Keynesian stimulation that would have the broadest impact on the economy. Galbraith repeatedly pointed out that Washington's domestic discretionary spending—a key to Keynesian stimulus, because it encompasses everything from cancer research and veterans' benefits to housing, the environment, agriculture, and the justice system—had fallen by nearly a third between 1980 and 1992. But under Clinton it kept falling, until it reached a twenty-year low in 2000, and was slated to fall even further in the administration's long-term budget projections, despite massive anticipated surpluses.[45]

Clinton had committed himself to balancing the budget on the advice of his economic adviser and Secretary of the Treasury, Robert Rubin, a former Goldman Sachs chairman who believed that restoring the federal government to long-term budget balance was a key to national prosperity and growth. To Galbraith, this echoed too much of the standard Treasury advice that he'd fought against thirty years earlier, when another Wall Street banker, Douglas Dillon, held the office under President Kennedy. As Rubin pressed his case, what initially heartened Galbraith were signs of a clear alternative advanced by other members of the new White House team. Championed on the policy side by Labor Secretary Reich, and initially also by Laura Tyson and Alan Blinder on the Council of Economic Advisors and Gene Sperling on the National Economic Council, this second group took seriously Clinton's campaign promise of massive public investment in human capital and physical infrastructure—the "most dramatic economic growth program since the Second World War."[46] Galbraith saw this as an updated version of early New Deal supply-side stimulus programs, not a resurrection of Keynes—but it would be a start. Half a dozen Nobel laureates in economics endorsed it, and for a time it seemed to enjoy the upper hand in the debate: Clinton himself sarcastically complained to his staff that in following Rubin's advice, "We're the Eisenhower Republicans here . . . Isn't that great?"

As the battle between public investment and budget balancing was fought out, it often turned bitter. Galbraith noted that Paul Begala and James Carville, the campaign advisers who had helped to focus Clinton on the platform of "Putting People First," were especially appalled by both the policy and the political message it sent. Rubin argued that his plan would soothe Wall Street's bond markets, which looked at the deficits as an invitation to inflation (and thus lower bond values); but the markets' response was to keep interest rates high, which slowed economic recovery. In a White House staff meeting, Carville sarcastically remarked that if Rubin was right, he wanted to come back in his next life not as president or pope, but as the bond market because "then you can intimidate anyone." He also began referring to Rubin as "Nick," pretending to confuse him with President Bush's Treasury Secretary Nicholas Brady; Begala less obliquely called the Office of Management and Budget director Leon Panetta, a Rubin ally, "the poster child for economic constipation."[47]

But the deficit—and the reaction of the Federal Reserve and the bond market to it, maintaining high interest rates that slowed economic recovery—ultimately convinced Clinton to follow Rubin's advice. But he did it grudgingly: after listening to a presentation by his economic advisers, Clinton turned bright red with anger and shouted, "You mean to tell me that the success of the economic program and my reelection hinges on the Federal Reserve and a bunch of fucking bond traders?"[48] By persuading the President that that was indeed the case, Rubin and the hawks beat the campaign team and the policy officers such as Reich. By the end of 1993, to Galbraith's dismay, Clinton had largely abandoned the public investment programs he'd outlined as a candidate. Worse, the President seemed to embrace deficit reduction as a principle, not a tactic. "I have a jobs program," he proudly declared, "and my jobs program is deficit reduction."[49] This was not a program Galbraith could support.

The year 1993 was frustrating for its political setbacks, but it brought Galbraith a number of lighter personal pleasures. First, although he completely lacked musical talent he was invited to play a bass drum with the Boston Pops, along with Michael Dukakis on gong and Mayor Ray Flynn of Boston on cymbals, in a tribute to John Williams, the Pops conductor. He and Kitty flew to Washington to see their son Peter sworn in as ambassador to Croatia by Vice President Gore. A lovely show of Indian paintings, including the Moghul miniatures they had donated to Harvard, opened at Harvard's Sackler Museum, to rave reviews. And in October there was a gala eighty-fifth-birthday party organized for him by his publisher, Houghton Mifflin, and held in the frescoed great hall of the Boston Public Library on Copley Square. Four hundred guests dined by candlelight on smoked salmon, beef tenderloin, and pears poached in port. President Clinton sent personal regards, and Senator Kennedy delivered his own elegant toast. Among the guests were Harvard's president, Neil Rudenstine, and his predecessor, Derek Bok; Boston's mayor and the ex-mayor Kevin White, who chatted amiably with the former New York City mayor John Lindsay; Arthur Schlesinger and his wife; Gloria Steinem, Kitty Carlisle, and Pat and Bill Buckley, all from Manhattan; the actress Angie Dickinson, who flew in from Los Angeles; the editors of *The Atlantic* and *Foreign Affairs* as well as the former editor of *The Boston Globe*; Paul Samuelson and Wassily Leontief; the filmmakers Ismael Merchant and James Ivory; Richard and Doris Kearns Goodwin; and the Canadian novelist Robertson Davies. For Boston, the evening was a major gala and was so reported by the press. Galbraith wryly saw it merely as another reward for following his First Law—that modesty is vastly overrated.

But early in the new year, politics from both Clinton's and Galbraith's perspectives started to worsen. For the President, the problem lay in the arcane design of the health-care reforms proposed by the commission headed by his wife, Hillary Rodham Clinton. It was a singularly complex construction of private and public initiatives, and it never won support (or even understanding) from the public. The health-care industry lambasted it in their "Harry and Louise" ads and sent $25 million in campaign contributions to Clinton's opponents in Congress. Meanwhile, Congressman Newt Gingrich, who had predicted three years earlier that "the next great offensive of the Left" would be "socializing health care," was secretly planning to scuttle *any* health reforms as a prelude to winning control of Congress in November 1994.[50]

To Galbraith, the bill's defeat epitomized neoliberalism's failures, although publicly he still avoided attacking the young President. Asked in the summer of 1993 by a *Boston Globe* editor, H. D. S. Greenway, whether like many other liberals he was growing pessimistic about Clinton, Galbraith gave a deftly sympathetic reply: "I was in the [Kennedy] White House in the early weeks of the administration, and I remember this as a period of unalloyed confusion. Nothing in the early months of the Clinton administration has been comparable with the disaster at the Bay of Pigs, which people have conveniently forgotten."[51] (A week later, Galbraith's mail brought a personal note of thanks from the Oval Office; his remark had not gone unnoticed.) Yet in November 1994, Galbraith was dismayed, though unsurprised, by the scale of the Democrats' disastrous losses in the midterm election, as the hapless, drifting party lost control of Congress for the first time in forty years.[52]

For the GOP, there was no dismay, needless to say. Their congressional victory now showed that defeat of Mrs. Clinton's health-care package had been anything but a disaster. With his party suddenly in control of both House and Senate, Newt Gingrich, the newly elected Speaker of the House, assured supporters that their poll-crafted "Contract with America" represented a Second Coming for the GOP's Sun Belt right-wingers; they would have no need for compromise of any kind with the hated Democrats. "I think one of the great problems we have in the Republican Party is that we don't encourage you to be nasty," he told his colleagues. "We encourage you to be neat, obedient, loyal and faithful and all those Boy Scout words, which would be great around a campfire but are lousy in politics." There would be no more Boy Scout politics, Gingrich assured them, while he was their scoutmaster.[53]

Clinton now heeled rightward, following the "triangulation" strategy recommended by his political adviser Dick Morris. Desperate to get out ahead of Gingrich, the President called for a balanced budget, radical welfare reform, a middle-class tax cut, and reductions in Medicare and Medicaid. When he promised that "the era of big government is over," the DLC celebrated it as proof that Galbraith's sort of liberalism was finally dead in the Democratic Party. As the political journalist Joe Klein put it, the nation's political debate had finally and permanently "changed from left-right to moderate-right, with Clinton commanding the middle."[54]

Clinton's "New Democrat" embrace of balanced budgets, domestic spending cuts, massive welfare reform, and smaller government was unquestionably a brilliant short-term tactical move to rescue his presidency from the ideologically blinkered Gingrich, who started 1995 in a Jacobin mood. The Speaker sweepingly called for the elimination of 280 federal programs, deep cuts in Social Security, Medicare, and environmental spending, and the outright abolition of the Departments of Energy, Education, and Commerce, and the Council of Economic Advisors. But he and his revolutionary allies had misjudged the mood of the American people. A month after the November elections, the publishing house HarperCollins, owned by the conservative media mogul Rupert Murdoch, gave Gingrich a $4.5 million book advance; Murdoch's fortunes were directly tied to pending legislation that the incoming Congress would take up, yet after news of the deal broke, it took the Speaker many long weeks to realize that the huge preferred payment was a public-relations disaster.*

In April, after Timothy McVeigh bombed the Murrah Federal Office Building in Oklahoma City, killing 168 people, Clinton eloquently spoke of the dangers of antigovernment extremism of the kind Gingrich represented, and of the importance of public service. "There is nothing patriotic about hating your country," he declared, "or pretending that you can love your country but despise your government." In the wake of the terrible bombing, many in the country were willing to hear Clinton's message and gave up some of their hostility toward Washington, but the Speaker and his allies pressed on with their attacks.

That fall, they shut down the federal government itself as part of their refusal to compromise on Clinton's balanced budget plans. But the shutdown was a monumental miscalculation on Gingrich's part: polls showed that the public hated it and hated the partisan vitriol that lay behind it, and blamed the Republican Congress for it by nearly two to one. The backlash was also personal: the Speaker's disapproval ratings shot from 29 to 56 percent; *The Washington Post* called him "the most disliked member of Congress."[55]

Even before then, Galbraith had sensed that the tide of public opinion was turning against Gingrich and his incendiary allies, though not necessarily toward Clinton. He was sure that the Speaker and his colleagues had disastrously overplayed their hand by trying to reverse sixty years of liberal political achievements. In a *New York Times* op-ed, he mischievously even feigned remorse that apparently America's conservatives had fooled themselves into thinking they were slaying liberalism by attacking Social Security, unemployment insurance, Medicare and Medicaid, and the GI Bill. These weren't "liberal" successes at all, he solemnly averred, but rather simply the "necessary accommodation" of democratic government to the challenges of the times. "We have allowed conservatives and the public at large to credit us with social action that was not our initiative," he dead-panned. "We were merely accommodating to the great thrust of history. History compelled the changes for

---

*Gingrich's obtuseness was ironic because he had risen to power in part by driving the Democratic House Speaker James Wright from office because of a book deal: in 1984 Wright had let the Teamsters Union purchase a thousand copies of his compilation of speeches.

which we took, and were given, credit—and for which we are now being blamed. And history cannot be reversed."[56]

BY THE TIME Clinton bested Senator Robert Dole in his reelection campaign a year later, Galbraith had written two more books—*A Journey Through Economic Time* and *The Good Society: A Humane Agenda*—which showed the distance that stood between him and this new generation of Democrats. *A Journey Through Economic Time* was his latest *tour d'horizon*, an engaging essay surveying twentieth-century economic and political history in which he repeated a cautionary tale he'd long told, but now pressed forcefully. It was about the abiding significance of error in human history, especially in the realm of policy, from the Treaty of Versailles and Churchill's 1925 return of England to the gold standard to Ronald Reagan's "reckless appropriation of Keynesianism" in the 1980s. *The Good Society* was quite different, an attempt to sketch out the principles and visions that had guided him over the years and to establish their relevance for the future.

Given the harsh conservative climate in Washington, it pleased him that *The Washington Post's* Jonathan Yardley was among the most sympathetic of its reviewers. "At an hour of right-wing reaction it is useful to be reminded that alternatives still exist and can even be argued in a civil fashion, and Galbraith's stubborn insistence on his old convictions is a refreshing reminder that human resistance to opportunism has not entirely vanished." But Yardley, reflecting the disillusionment that had led so many to Clinton-style neoliberalism, assessed critically what he saw as the book's flaws. He quoted Galbraith's list of essential goals for a good society:

> Employment and an upward chance for all. Reliable economic growth to sustain such employment. Education and, to the greatest extent possible, the family support and discipline that serve future participation and reward. Freedom from social disorder at home and abroad. A safety net for those who cannot or do not make it. The opportunity to achieve in accordance with ability and ambition. A ban on forms of financial enrichment that are at cost to others. No frustration of plans for future support and well-being because of inflation. A cooperative and compassionate foreign dimension.

"Generalizations so broad as these are not much different from what one finds in a political platform or a 'Contract With America,'" Yardley wrote. "Even Patrick Buchanan would have trouble taking exception" to Galbraith's general points.

> His view that there is such a thing as unacceptable wealth surely is shared by the millions of Americans who are appalled at the bloated fortunes raked in by junkbond shysters and golden-parachuted CEOs. Similarly, his concern about the wild disparity that now exists between not merely the rich and the poor but the rich and everybody else is not the mad raving of a lone lunatic

howling in the forest; it is becoming a central, if as yet imperfectly articulated, element in the American political mix.

The Good Society, Yardley concluded forlornly, was "in the end, an offhand piece of work, and that is a pity."[57]

In *The New York Times*, Matthew Miller thought the book displayed "the best and the worst of modern liberalism," and like Yardley, he was impatient. One could no longer "pretend that the bromides of the left aren't ready for rethinking," he wrote, though which bromides Miller wanted rethought wasn't clear (he mentioned "complacency on the deficit" and "a reluctance to control costs on Medicare and Social Security," but little more). Oddly, he said nothing of the political struggle that had been under way between the left and the right for the last twenty years, and gave no explanation of how the deficits had emerged or of how to solve the Social Security problem.[58]

In both these books Galbraith steered clear of attacking Clinton administration policies head-on, although he was making little secret of his growing disenchantment, and he would not keep it bottled up forever. The moment came, appropriately enough, at a memorial ceremony on April 12, 1995, in Warm Springs, Georgia, to mark the fiftieth anniversary of FDR's death. There, with Clinton, Jimmy Carter, Andrew Young, Elliot Richardson, and Lane Kirkland among those on the podium, and several thousand people in the audience, Galbraith pointedly made clear that in his view President Clinton was no Franklin Delano Roosevelt. FDR may have welcomed the hatred of his enemies, Galbraith jibed, but not to the point of embracing them; did Clinton, he wondered aloud to the audience, really have the stomach for a good fight? Arthur Schlesinger, following Galbraith, was no warmer, suggesting that the accommodation Clinton kept offering to the GOP risked becoming appeasement.

When it came his turn to speak, a chagrined President Clinton gamely struggled through his own remarks, insisting that FDR would favor Clintonomics were he alive. But few that afternoon looked convinced—and Clinton knew it, and so did the press, which sensed a wounding fight in the making. Hoping to head off any such coverage, the President told reporters aboard *Air Force One* on the way back to Washington that his policies had been "misunderstood" by the two New Deal veterans. Still, the contretemps made the front page of *The Washington Post* the next day. Clinton hastily arranged a small private luncheon at the White House that included Galbraith and Schlesinger, after which a presidential spokesman firmly insisted that Galbraith and the President had had a "lively" conversation and that "cordiality had been fully restored."[59]

Galbraith had a decidedly mixed opinion of Clinton, but Clinton's victory over Senator Dole in November showed him that the President was clearly a new master of political campaigning—and now he was the first Democrat elected to two terms since the great New Dealer himself. His reelection, and the policies and politics he pursued as he presided over what turned out to be the longest uninterrupted expansion of the economy in U.S. history, posed an unavoidable challenge to Galbraith's critique of Clinton's neoliberalism.

Popular political histories, Galbraith sagely understood, would start discussion of Clinton's second term with the Monica Lewinsky scandal and the impeachment trial that grew out of it, but for most economists, the story would begin quite differently, because after a quarter century of slow growth, lagging productivity, and worsening income distribution, the country had awakened, and its economy was exhibiting dramatic strengths that some had thought might be lost forever. Of even more compelling significance for most citizens, the real incomes of the middle and working classes were now growing as well, albeit modestly, after a quarter century of stagnation. Even the number of poor Americans started to decline for the first time since Richard Nixon held office.[60] Despite the seemingly endless orgy of political vitriol, clashes, and scandals, a chorus was proclaiming that, after years of conflict, struggle, and repeated setbacks, the nation was finally "reinventing" itself; it was creating a dynamic "New Economy."

The economy was "new" because it was built not on the industrial prowess the United States had first shown in the nineteenth century but on a flexible postindustrial frame that relied on the computer, telecommunications, and other new technologies. It also relied on what observers perceived as a new attitude toward work itself, which reflected the higher education and entrepreneurial ambitions of millions of workers who seemed willing to embrace, rather than resist, the constant, rapidly changing demands of global competition. Nimble high-tech companies based in Silicon Valley, along Boston's Route 128, and in Austin, Seattle, North Carolina's Research Triangle, and even Manhattan, were to this "New Economy" what the factories of Pittsburgh, Detroit, Buffalo, and Chicago had been to the old.[61]

Proponents of America's "New Economy" claimed that workers now were no longer mere "workers" in any traditional sense. Significant accumulation of wealth, a privilege long reserved for a few, was said to be the majority's opportunity, there for the taking. In the 1990s, "Wall Street came to Main Street."[62] Investing in stocks and bonds, most especially in dazzling and very new high-tech companies, was deemed commonplace for soccer moms and shop clerks, firefighters and truck drivers. As the Dow Jones Index trebled, from less than 3,500 to 10,000, the proportion of American families owning stock soared, rising to almost one in two by the late 1990s (it had been just one in ten in the 1960s).*[63] Excited talk of the dazzling 20, 25, even 30 percent annual returns

---

*The dollar value of these holdings remained quite skewed throughout the 1990s. By the decade's end, while the average value of stocks held by the bottom 40 percent of those households owning stock was less than $2,000, and by the middle 20 percent, less than $10,000, the top 1 percent owned an average $2.5 million. Also, most Americans who chose stock market investing had done so involuntarily. Thanks to Reagan-era changes in pension system regulations, thousands of large corporations, eager to offload responsibility for paying workers' pensions, shifted in droves from "defined-benefit plans," in which retired workers are guaranteed certain payment levels, to "defined-contribution" plans such as 401(k)s, in which employers make pre-agreed contributions alongside workers themselves; the value of these plans is subject to financial market fluctuations and can well fluctuate during retirement, too, depending on the funds in which they were invested. (In the Nixon era, only one in

to be made in their new mutual funds and 401(k) pension accounts, rates once unimaginable to most Americans, had supplanted talk of the World Series, high-school proms, and the latest television series at family dinner tables.

Galbraith thought he saw something all too familiar: his fellow Democrats, especially those in the White House, were still fully coming to terms with the consequences of two decades of conservative policy and politics. He hammered especially hard on income and wealth inequality, which kept rising, and on the adverse domestic and international effects of economic deregulation, which exacerbated the trend. The matter of inequality was not only a moral failing but an economic one, he kept saying, because overconcentration of wealth in a few hands fed, and fed on, a psychology of speculative excess that encouraged a volatile boom-bust cycle, severe economic dislocation, political and social conflict, and greater inequality, which only perpetuated the process. He pointed once again to the vast increase in the pay of senior managers tied to stock options, which did almost nothing to improve their workers' pay or benefits. This was the perverse consequence of setting the once-cosseted technostructure free to "compete," while unfairly weighting the rewards of competition.* Rather than demonstrating the large corporation's "return to competition," as many economists believed, Galbraith argued that the past two decades had produced a hybrid corporate structure that was harsher than the one he had described in the 1960s. In this new hybrid form, the big corporation's top managers were skilled at preserving (and multiplying) oligopoly-like wages and benefits for themselves while subjecting everyone else, through layoffs, pay freezes and benefit cuts, to the harsh winds of the market.[64]

Thus the income of America's top corporate executives, by then anchored to stock performance, kept soaring under President Clinton. By the end of his presidency, the ratio of their earnings to that of the average production worker was more than 400 to 1.[65] And these corporate elites extended their power over and into the public sector. The ability to turn democratic governments into the allies and handmaidens of big companies, domestically and internationally, was to Galbraith patent evidence that the "New Democrats" had failed in declining to challenge the "conventional wisdom" that in the 1980s and 1990s there had been a simple, dramatic return to classic models of market-based competition. Despite the talk of Wall Street coming to Main Street, and despite the surge in the number of Americans investing in stock markets, the markets' gains flowed overwhelmingly into the hands of a few. For example, between 1989 and 1998, 35 percent of the markets' gains went to the top 1 per-

---

nine workers had pension plans in "defined-benefit" programs; by the end of the Clinton era, half of them were.) And because fewer than half of all workers participate in any kind of pension plan, most Americans will have to rely on Social Security, their savings, and any gains realized from sale of their homes for their retirement income.

*Sales, technical, and administrative supervisors were not remunerated as well as the most senior corporate officials, but compared to the rest of American workers they did very well in the 1980s and 1990s. The incomes of the top fifth of Americans, which effectively includes all such personnel of the technostructure, grew by 42 percent between 1979 and 1999, nearly five times more than did the incomes of the bottom 80 percent. In contrast, during the first three decades after World War II, the incomes of *all* income groups rose more or less in tandem, which is why President Kennedy could speak of a rising tide lifting all boats.

cent of households, 86 percent to the top 20 percent—and 4 percent to the bottom 60 percent. And thanks to dividends and gains from stock sales, almost all the broader growth in total household income accrued to the richest 5 percent of Americans.[66]

For most middle-class families, the 1990s were in fact a time not of surging stock market portfolios but of surging personal debt. Over the decade, they received less than 3 percent of the markets' gains, but took on nearly 40 percent of the increase in all households' debt. For all families, the new scale of their indebtedness was breathtaking: for the first time in U.S. history, total household debt in fact exceeded total disposable income. As millions of families struggled to keep up with mortgage and credit card payments, the number of bankruptcies soared, doubling from their already high 1980s levels, and even when the economy picked up in the second half of the 1990s, indebtedness kept rising.[67]

At the bottom end of the economy, the big news was also not about stock market gains but the landmark revisions in the nation's tattered and much-reviled welfare system, a fulfillment of Clinton's 1992 campaign promise to "end welfare as we know it." The bill he signed in 1996, after two vetoes of earlier versions, met his promise, but in harsher and riskier terms than his advisers had ever envisioned. Even so, Clinton's controversial decision soon seemed vindicated: within two years, welfare rolls had been cut by one third to one half, and employment rates among the poor were at record highs. (Poverty rates among African Americans fell nearly six percentage points between 1995 and 1999, among Hispanics by nearly eight points, and among minority children by nine.) Yet for all these much-ballyhooed consequences, the truth was that by the end of Clinton's presidency the percentage of Americans living in poverty was no lower than it had been in 1973 (when the real progress that had been made in reducing American poverty effectively ceased). Even more disturbing to Galbraith in human terms was the fact that the *number* of Americans officially living in poverty—33 million—was no lower than it had been the day John F. Kennedy died.*[68] In an America that proudly counted its millionaires in the millions, this was to Galbraith an almost unspeakable indictment of the nation for failing to create a truly humane society.

Clinton also used his second term to pursue a "New Democrat" course internationally, pressing hard to expand U.S. trade through new "free trade" agreements. In his first term, with the help of congressional Republicans, but the opposition of most Democrats, he'd pushed through the North American Free Trade Agreement, and in his second he led the campaign to create the World Trade Organization. Critics of both abounded, especially among liberal members of Congress and the trade unions, who watched the President reluc-

---

*The poverty rate (percentage of Americans living in poverty) was 22 percent in 1959, 11 percent in 1973, and 11 percent when Clinton left office. The Clinton administration's success was in cutting the rate after its 50 percent increase in the 1980s. The actual number of Americans living in poverty in 2000, 33 million, was 11 million more than it had been under Richard Nixon.

tantly add a largely toothless codicil to NAFTA that, he claimed, would protect labor and environmental rights. The trade agreements produced violent protests around the world, in the United States most famously in the "battle of Seattle" in 1999, but seemed to have little positive impact on the U.S. trade deficit. Instead, the deficit tripled in size to almost $400 billion over the decade. Despite NAFTA, bilateral trade deficits with both Mexico and Canada grew, but overall the increase was accounted for mainly by voluminous new trade with China, as Kmart, Toys 'Я Us, and Wal-Mart stocked their shelves with Chinese-made goods. Along with Japan, China accounted for more than half the U.S. trade deficit, yet neither country behaved in any way like the "free trade" regime the Clinton administration said it was seeking. China did, however, join Japan in the same sort of "political economy" bargain Treasury Secretary Baker had forced on Tokyo through the Plaza Agreement in the late 1980s. Under Clinton, the two Asian giants became the largest owners of U.S. government bonds in the world. With the stock market soaring and the dollar rising, Asian investors also returned billions to the United States. The issue, apart from the quite non–"free trade" character of all this trade, was about its sustainability.

The President, basking in the low-inflation, high-employment growth the United States was enjoying by 1997—nearly 4 percent per annum—exulted in the rewards of his new policy direction: "If we can keep interest rates down with the deficit-reduction package and a balanced budget, keep investing in education and technology and keep expanding trade, I'm not sure we'll be as victimized by the business cycle as we have been in the past. We may be able to have much more stable and much longer-term growth than we ever had before." Treasury Secretary Rubin was even more enthusiastic. "The most likely scenario far and away," he declared, "is a continuation of solid growth and low inflation as far into the future as you feel comfortable in making this kind of judgment." Federal Reserve Chairman Alan Greenspan openly blessed the combination of healthy growth plus high employment and low inflation (to the fury of his fellow Republicans), declaring it "as impressive as any [performance] I have witnessed in my near half-century of daily observation of the American economy."[69] Briefly, then, the dreams of Walter Heller and the New Economists seemed to be coming true; this would be the beginning not just of a New Economy but of a new era in Western civilization and global economics.

But the New Economy as "the bridge to the future," as President Clinton called it, had barely opened for traffic before deep cracks in this remarkable structure began to show. Shortly after Clinton's reelection, chairman Greenspan remarked almost in passing that the booming stock market was "perhaps" exhibiting signs of "irrational exuberance," but he then declined, as maestro of the nation's money supply, to do anything that might rein in any of the market's excesses. The historical long-term price/earnings ratio of stocks was 10 to 12, but by Clinton's second term stock prices were running at 30, 40, 50 times earnings. (Among the most highly prized dot-com and new technology stocks, many had p/e ratios over 100, even 200 and 300, and for some of the most sought after, there were *no* earnings to measure against the stock price, meaning in strict arithmetic terms that they had price/earnings ratios of infinity.) Everything about the New Economy's Wall Street performance, in other words, was signaling a major bubble in the making.

Despite the warning signs, the proud Fed chairman (like the grateful President) did not take away the party's punch bowl. No taxes or interest rates or margin requirements were raised; no other signals that a classically unstable boom was under way were sent. Yet neither the Fed nor the White House, as Galbraith observed, had been responsible for starting the bubble: the low-tax, high-leverage, quick-profit investment climate, built on the cold-eyed management credo of running companies as "asset bundles," had been born in the 1980s, and while the leveraged buyout artists and junk-bond salesmen had already fallen hard once, the thousands of lawyers, accountants, and investment bankers who had learned how to jury-rig their high-flying deals, with built-in fat fees and quick exits for the savvy, were still at work and eager to do new business in the 1990s. (The number who'd been sent to jail for financial chicanery during the collapses of the 1980s, which Galbraith believed might have been modestly prophylactic for a time, was insignificant.)

The New Economy had whole new industries in which these men could work their financial magic—foremost the explosive, deregulated world of telecommunications. In just nine years, from 1992 to 2001, that industry's share in the GDP doubled, and was responsible for providing two thirds of the decade's new jobs and a third of its new investment.[70] Where once stolid AT&T had ruled (and provided widows, the elderly, and the wary with modest yet clockwork-certain dividends and appreciation), now new companies— Worldcom, Covad, Northpoint, Lucent, Nortel, Cisco, Alcatel—that hadn't existed a decade earlier were suddenly Wall Street's latest darlings, their stocks doubling, tripling, quadrupling, quintupling so swiftly that few investors had time to grasp what "second-generation wireless" meant before the third generation loomed on the horizon, and "fiber optics" somehow promised near-zero communications costs around the planet. The "near-zero" claim, Galbraith noted, itself should have been a warning to intelligent market watchers, but wasn't, as a new generation of fast-moving companies, deploying battalions of high-priced lawyers, accountants, and investment advisers, leveraged purchase of competitors with all-stock deals and then raced to install the latest, often barely tested or debugged, technologies in the marketplace.

The market frenzy was, worse, abetted by government, as the Federal Communications Commission joined in by auctioning off the nation's airwaves, doing its part to "revolutionize" the world of telecoms. The commission faithfully followed the models that a new generation of pro-deregulation economists had tested and retested on their blackboards and computer programs, and that they and the backers of the Telecommunications Act of 1996 promised would optimize use of the market in ways that old-fashioned public regulation never had. When one especially big segment of the airwave frequencies—the so-called "C block"—was sold in 1996, the feverish bidding led to a record $10 billion paid for the spectrum sold, nearly three times what the FCC's economists had estimated. But to the government's chagrin, the purchasers' checks began to bounce, no small matter since the FCC had, amazingly, *lent* most of the $10 billion to the bidders. Within months, the bidders declared bankruptcy and more than $7 billion of the $10 billion that the cash-strapped federal government had advanced to them vanished. And yet the prevailing boom psychology meant that few investors—let alone the American public—understood or even noticed what had just happened. "This was to be a strong and especially damaging example of the error in substituting broad principle, verging as ever on theology, for relevant, if always painful, thought," Galbraith sharply observed. And, he added, it was, not without prior warning. The travails of airline deregulation under President Carter and the deregulation of banks, savings and loans, and energy under President Reagan had been there for all to see. Yet major new deregulation—of broadcasting, finance and insurance, and electricity—was just getting under way.[71]

Likewise little noticed by the public, a hail of campaign contributions and a herd of lobbyists descended on Washington when the Financial Accounting Standards Board, the nonprofit oversight group charged with setting accounting rules for America's corporations, proposed in 1995 a new set of standards that would tighten up what its experts felt were dangerously loose practices being used by some of America's fastest-growing new companies, especially the telecoms. ("Fictitious profits" was too strong a term for so prudent a body.) Securities and Exchange Commission Chairman Arthur Levitt favored the new rules, but Commerce Secretary Ron Brown and Treasury Secretary Lloyd Bentsen (Robert Rubin's predecessor) both denounced the reform proposals. When key Democrats in Congress such as Senator Joseph Lieberman weighed in against them, the FASB's effort quickly waned. The regulations, which would have prohibited companies from overreporting net income by, among other things, obliging them to accurately detail the costs of unexercised stock options held by senior executives, were turned back.[72]

Outside the United States there were also plenty of signs that all was not well. After participating in the Great Global Lending Explosion of the 1970s and then barely surviving the Great Global Debt Collapse in the 1980s, Third World countries and their New York and London bankers were once again facing monumental crises.[73] Mexico, whose 1982 debt crisis had triggered the 1980s collapse, reprised its role in 1994 by spawning a second round of crises when it defaulted once again. But the Clinton administration reacted as the Reagan administration had, bailing out the lenders with $40 billion in direct loans (and, extralegally, providing an even bigger amount through the so-called Emergency Stabilization Fund, which had never been intended for this purpose). In the aftermath, this White House, like its predecessor, prematurely took credit for "saving" both Mexico and the global financial system from even greater disaster.*

Just two years later, however, the greater disaster arrived. A new round of massive debt default occurred in the booming economies of Southeast Asia, and this "Asian crisis" quickly and wildly spread outward from Thailand, Malaysia, Indonesia, and the Philippines to envelop first South Korea, and then even Russia and Latin America (and for a moment the United States itself, through the directly related collapse of the big hedge fund Long-Term Capital Management). To Americans who'd grown accustomed to the notion that "markets know best" and that the coerced "opening" of dozens of Third World and former Soviet Bloc economies in the 1980s and early 1990s under the rubric of "structural adjustment" and "shock therapy" had all been for the good, something once again was terribly wrong.

For Galbraith, this was all part of the post–Bretton Woods system that Richard Nixon had created. Two decades later, there were the open markets, the instantly mobile global financial systems, and the voluminous international trade—all the ingredients that first-year economic students learned were seminal virtues. But once again the world was in grave trouble. This time Asia required a $95 billion rescue operation from the IMF; support for Russia and Latin America needed more than that. Savage debates ensued among economists and policy-makers over the cause of these latest crises and over the efficacy and appropriateness of the treatment that the IMF was prescribing, given how much suffering the treatment induced. (In Indonesia, for example, unemployment soared tenfold and poverty rates doubled in barely a year; in more affluent South Korea, unemployment quadrupled and poverty tripled, while some of the nation's biggest corporations went bankrupt.[74])

Unlike many on the left, Galbraith drew conclusions that rejected neither the process of globalization nor the leadership of the IMF and World Bank. The deepest lessons of the twentieth century were to him incontrovertible: more global integration of economies, cultures, and political systems offered many more and better potential benefits to mankind than the violent nationalisms that had helped cause two world wars and that, in toxic combination with ethnic, racial, and religious prejudice, had unleashed more than 220 smaller ones and taken the lives of more than 100 million human beings.[75] The question was how to increase international cooperation, how to coordinate liberal economic and social policies across borders, and how to use multilateral institutions on behalf of the poor. He was unsparing when it came to the so-called Washington Consensus—with its demands for free trade, cuts in government spending that harmed education, health, infrastructure, and antipoverty measures—that the World Bank and IMF had embraced and then

---

*Mexico barely grew for the rest of the decade, poverty massively increased, the middle class was decimated, millions fled to the U.S. in search of work, and the Mexican banking sector and large parts of the country's industrial base became American-owned, yet Washington took away a different lesson: as the Treasury Secretary proudly noted, the U.S. government made a profit on its Mexican loans (see Larry Summers, in Frankel and Orszag, *American Economic Policy in the 1990s*, 263).

imposed on the Third World majority. They had failed on their own terms, he pointed out repeatedly, producing a rolling string of financial crises across Asia, Latin America, and Africa; half the world's population was still needlessly living on less than two dollars a day per person, and in dozens of countries hundreds of millions of people were suffering more in the 1990s than they had in the 1970s. Most starkly, he often emphasized, more than a million children under the age of five were dying *every month* from preventable malnutrition or disease.

True, there had been major advances in reducing poverty globally, but Galbraith liked to point out that almost none of the countries that had done best had relied on the prescriptions advocated by the Washington Consensus. The biggest success story by far, measured in terms of the total number of people no longer living in abject poverty, was China, which moved far away from the Maoist model but came nowhere near resembling the economic models advocated by U.S. policy-makers and mainstream economists. And the stunning performance of the Asian Tigers owed more to principles of development Galbraith has supported since the late 1950s, such as strong central government direction of investment and education, than any of the neoclassical blackboard models.

AS THE CENTURY came to an end, global poverty, corporate crime, and income inequality seemed far from the minds of most Americans. Thanks to the unwavering focus of the American press, they were spending time on the matter of Monica Lewinsky, Kenneth Starr, and the impeachment trial of President Clinton. To Galbraith, Clinton's conduct seemed distasteful but hardly criminal, and the round-the-clock media attention was both "a great bore" and one more destructive distraction from the fundamental issues the country needed to face. "Economics, politics, social welfare all require a certain amount of knowledge and intelligence to be effective," he said. "But on sex every body has an equal start. Therefore this is the opportunity for people who don't know anything about anything else . . . to appear on television. That has been the basis of the whole Lewinsky affair."[76]

Never a television watcher save for a regular thirty minutes of evening news, Galbraith occupied himself in late 1998 and early 1999 by working on a little memoir—a sketchbook, really—about some of the people he had known, worked with, and in some cases befriended. "Before I even started writing it, I knew I had a winning title," he said, his eyes twinkling. " 'Name-Dropping.' " When the book appeared, *Name-Dropping: From FDR On* was precisely the success he'd anticipated, proving that although he had no taste for scandal, he had one for the press. In the *Times*, Godfrey Hodgson praised it warmly, calling it "as fresh and lively as the work of a thirty-year-old"—no mean achievement for someone who was now ninety.[77] In it, Galbraith offered more than a dozen vivid little cameo descriptions, from Franklin and Eleanor Roosevelt through Truman, Kennedy, and Johnson, with Nehru, Pierre Trudeau, Albert Speer, and a few other foreign figures added to round out the work. It was

Mrs. Roosevelt—and Mrs. Kennedy—for whom he claimed he said he felt the most affection, and in an important act of personal reexamination he urged readers to see the greatness of Lyndon Johnson, at least on the domestic front. (In November 1999 Galbraith flew to Austin, Texas, where he gave a speech at the LBJ Library in which he revised his judgment of Johnson, admitting, "This is something I've wanted to talk about for years": the late President's commitments to civil rights, social spending, and poverty reduction. "Those of us" who fought him on Vietnam "have done far too little to correct [this] history since," he said.[78])

Galbraith wasn't the only one doing some reexamination. In June 1999, the London School of Economics, which in the 1930s, when Galbraith first visited it, had been a bastion for conservative economics, decided to award him an honorary doctorate. Lord Roll, the investment banker and historian of economics, presenting his old friend to LSE's Court of Governors, likened Galbraith to Oliver Goldsmith as described by Dr. Johnson: "He did not touch anything that he did not adorn."

Galbraith thanked LSE for having given him the opportunity in 1937–38 to hear Friedrich von Hayek lecture and to participate in the discussions that followed. Class time, he recalled, "was given over, all but exclusively, to [students] telling him he was wrong. I found myself in support of this correction . . . Over the years I've often presented myself to ardent conservatives as a student of Hayek. It has added in an agreeable way to their normal confusion."[79] But he did not neglect to recapitulate "the unfinished business of the century": the growing inequality of income, the lack of broad opportunity for leisure, the excessive attention to material goods, the persistence of poverty, the continued presence of war and nuclear weapons. He was given a sustained standing ovation.

Conclusion

The Galbraith Legacy

For too long we seem to have surrendered personal excellence and community value in the mere accumulation of material things. Our gross national product now is over 800 billion dollars a year, but if we judge the United States of America by that, that gross national product counts air pollution, and cigarette advertising, and ambulances to clear our highways of carnage. It counts special locks for our doors and the jails for people who break them.

It counts the destruction of the redwoods and the loss of our natural wonder in chaotic sprawl. It counts napalm, and it counts nuclear warheads, and armored cars for the police to fight the riots in our cities. It counts Whitman's rifles and Speck's knives and the television programs which glorify violence in order to sell toys to our children.

Yet the gross national product does not allow for the health of our children, the quality of their education, or the joy of their play; it does not include the beauty of our poetry or the strength of our marriages, the intelligence of our public debate or the integrity of our public officials. It measures neither our wit nor our courage, neither our wisdom nor our learning, neither our compassion nor our devotion to our country. It measures everything, in short, except that which makes life worthwhile. And it can tell us everything about America except why we are proud that we are Americans.
—Robert F. Kennedy, 1968

Ken Galbraith . . . will be remembered, and read when most of us Nobel Laureates will be buried in footnotes down in dusty library stacks.
—Paul Samuelson

ON A QUIET TUESDAY in mid-August 2000, Ken Galbraith left his home in Cambridge for Boston's Logan Airport and Washington, D.C., reversing the direction of the ocean voyage he had taken in September 1934 to begin his life at

Harvard. Over sixty-five years, he'd made this trip hundreds of times, a regular commuter on the "Bos-Wash corridor." But the coastal steamers of the old Merchant & Miners Line no longer sailed the route, and Amtrak's service for years had borne only faint resemblance to the elegant overnight Pullman express he'd long preferred.

At Logan, navigating the plane's narrow center aisle with a cane (meant to help with the aftereffects of a fall—a broken hip and three broken ribs) was difficult. Settling his six-foot-seven-inch frame into his seat wasn't easy, either, the cramped quarters yet another reminder of why airline deregulation had been ill-advised in the first place, he quipped.[1] But the flight attendants were accommodating, Kitty was there to help, and quite a few of his fellow passengers recognized him, many smiling or simply staring in admiration, a few others reaching out their hands to welcome him aboard.

One passenger asked what was taking him to Washington, and he modestly allowed that he'd been asked to attend "a small ceremony."

The next afternoon, in the high-ceilinged East Room of the White House, Kitty, her three sons, their wives, and Mrs. Williams, were among the audience of several hundred who gathered for that "small ceremony." As President Clinton read out his name, Galbraith stood, steadied by a young Marine guard, then leaned forward as the President placed America's highest civilian award, the Medal of Freedom with its bright blue ribbon, around his neck.[*]

For Galbraith, the White House ceremony had the air of a homecoming of sorts, since among his fellow recipients were men and women he knew well: George McGovern, Daniel Patrick Moynihan, Jesse Jackson, Marion Wright Edelman, the Reverend George Higgins, and Millie Jeffries, all veterans of the defining liberal political and social struggles of the previous half century.

Galbraith's old friend Sargent Shriver—President Kennedy's brother-in-law, the Peace Corps' first director, George McGovern's running mate, and himself a Medal of Freedom recipient—caught the moment for many at the crowded reception, when he pulled a photocopy of Richard Nixon's resignation letter from his pocket. On that same day a quarter century earlier, Nixon delivered the letter to Secretary of State Henry Kissinger, formally ending his presidency. "Here it is," roared Shriver who wore a McGovern-Shriver button on his lapel. "Twenty-five years later! We've made a lot of progress since Richard Nixon . . . We didn't win, but, by God, what we stood for was really auspicious."[2]

Conservatives had their own reasons to find the ceremony auspicious. Singling out Galbraith and calling his award a "Presidential Medal of Ignorance," the *Forbes* columnist Virginia Postrel raged that "Galbraith had spent his career peddling nonsense" and that "his work, long scoffed at by serious economists of all political stripes, has been utterly discredited by the experience of the

---

[*]This was Galbraith's second Medal of Freedom, a distinction he shares only with Colin Powell. In 1946, President Truman wanted to present him with the same medal for his service to the Bombing Survey, but Galbraith, who had just resigned from the State Department and was not warmly inclined to Truman's foreign policy, declined to come down from New York to receive it. The White House ended up mailing it to him.

past several decades." To the libertarian Postrel, it was "as though Ronald Reagan had given a Medal of Freedom to his wife's astrologer."[3] After reading her column, a bemused Galbraith opined that his only concern was that, by likening astrologers to him, Postrel might have limited their usefulness to future Republican presidents.[4]

To the reporter covering the ceremony for *The Washington Post*, the awards ceremony had about it a sense of passing time. "John Kenneth Galbraith. Jesse Jackson. George McGovern. Daniel Patrick Moynihan. Marian Wright Edelman. Each is an icon, reflecting some aspect of our collective life as a nation—benchmarks of history whose names we instantly recognize."[5] The contributions of these men and women—Galbraith the oldest among them—were now part of American history, and it was hard to see Galbraith as relevant to the new century and to what pundits were calling the New Economy. That summer, after touching their all-time highs a few months earlier, U.S. stock markets were "drifting like yachts off the Hamptons," as one news report soothingly had it, waiting for the next breeze to take them higher still. Unemployment and inflation were at near-record lows, and the gross domestic product was growing at a stunning annual pace—nearly 6 percent. Did Galbraith and all his "Old Economy" ideas matter anymore? It was an attitude that perplexed and frustrated him.

Even during the following spring, the same attitude still prevailed when a conference with a hundred top economists and policy-makers convened at Harvard to assess the 1990s and the New Economy. Stock markets had been falling continously for months by then, but the panelists overlooked the fact and concentrated on the successes of the decade just ended. After twenty years of largely anemic economic progress, the 1990s represented good news the participants wanted to celebrate.

The conference's co-organizer, who had worked at the Council of Economic Advisors in both the Reagan and Clinton administrations, captured their mood.

> How will historians—or economic historians, at any rate—remember the 1990s? It is not too soon to predict.
>
> Unquestionably, history will remember this period as a time of economic achievement. Between 1993 and 2000 the United States exhibited the best economic performance of the past three decades. In 2000 the U.S. economic expansion surpassed in length the expansion of the 1960s, and thus became the longest on record. During Clinton's second term, real economic growth averaged 4.5 percent per year, and unemployment fell to 4 percent . . . Strong growth and low unemployment were particularly remarkable because they were accomplished by structural budget surpluses and low inflation . . . And for the first time in three decades, productivity growth rose substantially in late 1990s, despite the length of the expansion . . .
>
> To be sure, some observers found cause for concern . . . Overall, however, the U.S. economic performance during the 1990s was outstanding.[6]

In such a dazzling new world, where was the need for Galbraith's old cautions about "conventional wisdoms" or his critique of the fundamental distortions that, he claimed, the American economy congenitally produced in tandem with American politics and foreign policy? Among the participants were economists he'd worked with and knew well, men and women who'd served in every presidential administration since 1960—and yet the country's best-known economist, who lived only a short walk from where they were meeting, hadn't been invited. To most at the conference his sort of liberal Keynesianism seemed quaintly antiquarian remnant. In the fast-paced new world of global competition, sophisticated finance, constant technical innovation, and "limited" government at home (even as it spanned the world as its only military superpower), what possible lessons could Galbraith's ideas and experience offer?

Yet by the time that upbeat Harvard conference published its results a year later, in the spring of 2002, the glow of the New Economy was fading fast. In the twenty-four months since Galbraith received his Medal of Freedom, stock markets fell dramatically, and many of the New Economy's vaunted dot-com and telecom stocks lost 90 percent of their value and wiped out more than $8.5 trillion in financial wealth. Former corporate stars with names like Enron, Worldcom, Global Crossing, Adelphia, and Tyco now had a different reputation, "the world's only superpower" was under violent military and intellectual attack—and John Kenneth Galbraith, now ninety-three, was back in the news. More than six dozen newspapers, from *The New York Times* and *Boston Globe* to the Columbus *Dispatch* and San Antonio *Express-News* in the United States, from the *Financial Times* and *The Economist* in London to the *Straits Times* in Singapore and *Asahi Shimbun* in Tokyo, rushed interviews and profiles of him and op-eds by him into print. *The Wall Street Journal*, which had banished him from its editorial pages for years, now put him on its front page.[7] Galbraith had been cautioning for five years that the markets were overvalued and companies undermonitored, so he was more than happy to oblige, and in passing announced that he'd set to work on his forty-third book, *The Economics of Innocent Fraud*, in order to detail his conclusions.[8]

The Washington Post suddenly remembered why Galbraith was worth honoring:

> In the boom years, many chose to forget the simple genius of the American proposition. It is rooted in what economist John Kenneth Galbraith saw as a system of "countervailing power." We put limits on government because we don't want it to dominate our lives. But, in turn, we rely on government to check concentrations of private power. Americans have always been suspicious of excessive power residing anywhere—in government or in parts of the marketplace.[9]

Even Bill Clinton decided that Galbraith had important ideas worth sharing with a new generation. Shortly after leaving the White House, he wrote Galbraith a long personal letter in which he proposed that together they write a book about American government and enduring liberal values. (Galbraith gave the idea serious consideration for several months but then declined, citing age and health as his reasons.)[10]

By 2002 the disappearance of $8.5 trillion in falling markets wasn't the only economic agony. During Clinton's last two years in office, the government's budget had begun showing a surplus—the first since Lyndon Johnson held office, and projections showed nearly $5 trillion more to come in the decade ahead. That forecast had made it possible to imagine both retiring the enormous public debt accumulated largely under Clinton's Republican predecessors and, at last, undertaking important new public spending on long-deferred national domestic priorities. But now, under President George W. Bush, that $5 trillion vanished. In its place were vast deficits projected far into the future, created by government revenue losses due to Bush's tax cuts and by resurgent military spending meant to finance a new security doctrine that would forever guarantee America's unilateral military preeminence. Under George W. Bush, "Keynesianism, Republican-style," Galbraith remarked with more than a hint of anger in his voice, seemed to be back with a vengeance, and with such baleful consequences that "I never imagined I would look back on the Reagan era with nostalgic fondness."[11]

Unemployment, too, was on the rise, reaching by 2003 a more familiar and chronic 6 to 7 percent, and 2 million jobs, half of them in the nation's long-suffering manufacturing sector, disappeared in just twelve months. The incomes of most citizens were once again stagnating—even though, by official measure, Americans were working the longest hours, taking the shortest vacations, and receiving the poorest job-related benefits offered by any advanced economy in the world. Personal savings rates were also stalled at dismally low levels (a phenomenon first seen in the 1970s that continued in the 1980s despite the introduction of tax-favored saving devices such as IRAs and 401(k)s, and actually worsened in the 1990s), while personal bankruptcies hit an all-time high of 1.6 million households (principally married couples with children).[12] Economic growth, such as it was, was explained largely by unsustainable household consumption fueled by cheap home refinancing, an "opportunity" created by interest rates that the Federal Reserve cut to record lows in response to declining economic activity.

Although the trauma of September 11, 2001, plus the war in Afghanistan and the pending invasion of Iraq, overshadowed much of this forlorn economic news, the reports of myriad Enron-style accounting frauds revealed an unprecedented pattern of fraud among Wall Street mutual funds and brokerage houses. It was clear that a significant portion of the New Economy's "remarkable" performance had in reality been based on accounting chimeras, lax regulatory oversight, slippery rules, and analysts' willful connivance in hiding the real state of corporate balance sheets and income statements from the public. Economists, Wall Street, and the press—a once unified chorus singing the praises of the 1990s—now glumly tried to guess how long the "hangover" from the decade's "irrational exuberance" would last, and who would be hurt the most.

Despite these revelations, much about the new century's travails seemed easy to explain to many Americans (Democrats especially), who laid the blame at the doorstep of the White House and its Republican occupant, George W. Bush. His $477 billion tax cuts—the largest in America's history, bigger even than the fabled Reagan tax cuts that in 1981 inaugurated their own string of record-shattering budget deficits—were, in this view, the heart of the problem.[13] The cuts—over half of whose benefits went to the richest 1 percent of American households—had combined with the President's equally extraordinary buildup of military might (another echo of the Reagan years), part of a new national security doctrine of "permanent overwhelming military superiority," to create the mess. Had Al Gore, the candidate who won the popular vote in 2000, become President, the new century would have begun differently, the argument went. Be that as it may, virtually all economists agreed that the underlying "New Economy" boom of the Clinton years was due for major correction downward. Why was that? What had created the boom? How had its benefits been distributed? What problems had it helped to create? What arguments had been used to explain it, and how persuasive did they now seem? What alternative explanations were there? And what might lie ahead? And in *this* debate, what was still relevant and important in Galbraithian economics?[14]

There was no lack of critics rushing forward with explanations, including some of the best economists in the country—Paul Krugman, Robert Shiller, and Joseph Stiglitz among them. Stiglitz, a brilliant Nobel Prize winner who'd been chairman of Clinton's Council of Economic Advisors and then as chief economist of the World Bank, was among the most excoriating.[15] "Luck," he said, had been far more important in the "New Economy" boom than anyone imagined at the time, "luck" aided by the Clinton administration's single-minded focus on reducing the federal deficit, which in turn produced effects that few understood. The White House commitment to deficit reduction had encouraged Alan Greenspan and the Federal Reserve to lower interest rates, which in turn allowed the nation's biggest banks to recapitalize themselves after the debacles of the 1980s had pushed them near to collapse. Once recapitalized, they began lending again.

Thanks to a wave of economic deregulation, especially in the telecommunications and energy sector, and some important technological innovations, the banks had found no dearth of would-be borrowers. Stock markets began to soar as managers of giant funds, under intense competitive pressure to boost their returns for investors, started to value the prospective earnings of the deregulated companies at multiples far beyond the immediate ability of earnings to match them. Wall Street demanded that company executives produce ever-better and brighter earnings and growth stories to justify the multiples, which encouraged the use of dubious accounting techniques that would show the best possible earnings and underreport the increasingly enormous liabilities companies were taking on. As the popularity of massive stock options offered to senior management helped cut into whatever real net earnings the companies were actually making, accountants found reasons to bend their reports as consulting fees paid by the same companies they were auditing swelled their own earnings.

In the midst of this classic bubble-in-the-making, the Clinton administration had gone ahead with deregulation of banking, insurance, and investment banking by repealing the Glass-Steagall Act of 1933. Glass-Steagall had been passed to remedy the pernicious self-dealing and backroom trading of the 1920s that many believed had led to the bubble that ended in the Great Crash of 1929. In the New Economy, allowing commercial and investment banks to merge and permitting banks and insurance companies once again to sell stocks and mutual funds was supposedly "different," but of course it was not. The consequences spread beyond U.S. shores, as banks and investors, anticipating Glass-Steagall's repeal, had sought new profits overseas. Investment in emerging markets in the Clinton years jumped sixfold, and billions of dollars poured into economies that were rife with crony capitalism and bereft of strong regulators. After barely dodging a global economic collapse in 1994 when Mexico's financial system failed for a second time, the world experienced the panic that began two years later in Southeast Asia and spread across Asia, Latin America, and Russia. The poor in those societies, Stiglitz reminded his readers, paid a far higher price than Americans who saw their IRAs and 401(k)s melt down.

Stiglitz's critique, not surprisingly, drew fierce criticism from veterans of the Clinton administration, the World Bank, and the IMF. Yet left unanswered by Stiglitz's critics as well as by Stiglitz were some profound questions: How did we get to such a worldview? What might replace it? And in what context, and across what longer history, should we view the achievements and failures of the 1990s? To answer these questions we must reintroduce Galbraith's economic and political beliefs, for, not surprisingly, his answers hinge on the larger issue of what one expects from the future and how one judges the somewhat longer past. He always insisted that was the only proper context in which to do economics.

For more than half a century Galbraith argued that the truly important economic issues must be evaluated through the lens of economics, politics, sociology, law, ideology, and history simultaneously, that the work of economics is far messier than the blackboard mathematical models that claim hegemony, and that economic analysis and prescription must always keep front and center both the factors of power and the narratives that societies use to tell their economic stories. That understanding of what economics is can explain why Galbraith is proudly a liberal—in his politics, his economics, and at the core of his moral beliefs. The intellectual ground of his liberalism rests not in his reactions to immediate circumstances, but in beliefs that go back to his Canadian youth and the reform liberalism of the Progressive Era, when twentieth-century liberalism broke decisively with its nineteenth-century predecessor.

The earlier laissez-faire liberalism had conceived its central project to be the extension and defense in the economic realm of Lockean and Enlightenment ideas about individual political freedom. Adam Smith, Ricardo, Malthus, and Herbert Spencer all believed that by optimizing individual freedom, a laissez-faire economy solved not only economic problems but also social and political problems, which in turn optimized economic well-being for all and thereby set in motion an endless, virtuous circle of ever-growing freedom and well-being.

The tenets of this earlier liberalism were at the philosophical foundations of neoclassical economics and its various leaders, from Alfred Marshall right up to the present day—from Frank Knight, Lionel Robbins, and Friedrich von Hayek to Milton Friedman, George Stigler, Robert Lucas, and Arthur Laffer. The core assumptions have been compactly summarized:

> The market is a natural, non-coercive and self-regulating sphere of voluntary behavior that rewards people according to their contribution to the welfare of others. As a result it produces the maximum possible levels of freedom, equality, and welfare. People are self-contained, have mostly contractual links or responsibilities, and are largely uninfluenced by others. Each person seeks her or his own advantage and is equally able to enter markets and bargain. Pursuit of individual want satisfaction and self-interest leads to spontaneous order or natural harmony, social advantage, the common good, and benefit to others. Companies produce what the consumer—collectively—wants, in the quantities and qualities wanted, and at prices they will pay. In a market free of government intervention, no one person, group, seller, buyer, or manufacturer determines what is produced or what prices are paid. Large and small participants are equally subject to the market. As no one controls production, prices, or what is offered, no identifiable individual has power over any other identifiable individual, each of whom voluntarily participates or not at the prices and quantities offered, thereby protecting freedom. Competition regulates behavior, preventing self-interest from harming others. Competition thus becomes the key moral imperative—one lacking in government—and means to organize society. If free, markets take over and de-politicize many of the distributive and regulatory functions others assign to government. Non-interventionist public policy, limited government, and leaving people to their own devices follows.[16]

By the time Galbraith was born in 1908, however, "reform liberalism" was challenging these laissez-faire axioms. The "dark satanic mills" of early capitalism, the brutality of the new global colonial economy, and Social Darwinist claims that poverty was the natural condition of the weak and wealth the natural reward of the strong had shattered their confidence. The realities of capitalism had decoupled the promise of human freedom from the consequences of economic freedom—a break famously captured in Anatole France's bitter jibe that the rich and the poor were equally free to sleep under bridges and beg in the streets. Capitalist markets hadn't dissolved abusive power, in the view of reform liberals, because the private economic power of corporations and their owners now represented a danger as least as great as the odious hand of monarchy and mercantilism. They thus spearheaded the creation and defense of "the regulatory state" as a counterweight, referee, and overseer of private economic power in the name of democratic liberty and individual rights. Beginning in the United States at the state and municipal level, then moving on to the national capital, Progressive Era reformers worked to set in place new rules governing wages and working conditions, the regulation of "natural monopolies," the breakup of business "trusts," the removal of urban slums, urban zoning, the guarantee of unadulterated food and medicine.

To realize government's new functions, reformers—and in the United States they came from both the Republican and Democratic parties—created the income and wealth tax, a central monetary authority, and a network of laws, regulations and public commissions that would oversee trade, transport, power, and communications. To guarantee the democratic nature of this new governance, they opened the Senate to direct election, created the modern civil service, authorized direct referenda, and gave women the right to vote. The modern professional classes, meritocratic higher education, formal training for public service, and government and academic support for research and development in the natural and social sciences all became institutional cornerstones of a new society.

Born in the very heart of the Progressive Era, Galbraith as a child unquestionably imbibed its values directly. His father was a devoted supporter of Canada's preeminent Liberal Party prime minister and campaigned locally for the Liberal Party in Ontario. Besides being a successful middle-class farmer who utilized the best practices of modern scientific agriculture, Archie also set his son a model in his public service—as a schoolteacher, as the head of local phone and insurance cooperatives, and as a politician. His willingness in World War I to chair the local draft board so as to be able to exempt young men from the slaughter of the Somme and Flanders Field, his willingness to abandon the badly fractured Liberal Party and help found the United Farmers party and elect a reformist provincial government—all bespoke an independence and loyalty to principle that merged seamlessly with a passion for public life and politics.*

The second catalyst for Ken Galbraith, as for most of his generation, was unquestionably the Great Depression—a searing experience that he explored first as an agricultural economist, notably under the tutelage of his Harvard mentor, John D. Black. Black himself had trained at the University of Wisconsin, an intellectual cathedral for liberal reformers, which in the Progressive Era had pioneered the controversial idea that university-based social scientists could serve the public directly in designing reform programs for government. The University of Wisconsin's economists were a model for engaged policy in-

---

*Galbraith in later life professed to see parallels between himself and the Progressive Era economist Thorstein Veblen. Some of Galbraith's admirers have expanded on the comparison, but Veblen, as Galbraith readily admits, played no part in the early development of his intellectual vision, since he wasn't exposed to Veblen (or Marx or Marshall) until he reached Berkeley in the early 1930s.

tellectuals. Under the progressive Republican governor Robert La Follette, they helped the laws that created the country's first unemployment program and workers' compensation insurance and produced model regulatory bills for the railroads and utilities; after World War I they helped staff the federal government with its first professional economists, chiefly in the Department of Agriculture, where their ideas about farm reform quickly became the common wisdom.[17]

But it was Keynes's *The General Theory of Employment, Interest, and Money*, published in 1936, that made the most important mark in Galbraith's intellectual life. Pressure to expand government spending on public welfare had previously rested on moral arguments about social justice or concern for the poor; arrayed against it were equally powerful conservative arguments about the various "iron laws" of human nature that reformers couldn't overturn without disastrous results. After repeated cycles of victory and defeat, reformers by 1936 had learned enough about the weaknesses of these conservative arguments to generate their own "rational efficiency" arguments for expanded government. Spending on large-scale public works during economic recessions and restricting monopolies by then satisfied both sides. Nevertheless, the battle between the two camps raged as strongly as it ever had—and in the 1930s with a new urgency, thanks to the rise of Soviet Communism and German and Italian Fascism. Unions' rights, minimum-wage laws, maximum hour and overtime laws, unemployment insurance, Social Security, the income tax, health and safety regulation, consumer product protection all were still controversial elements of what reformers took to be minimal social justice and efficiency but that conservatives denounced as "big government" or "socialism."

Keynes's genius was to reformulate the old debate using the very "laws" Alfred Marshall and his contemporaries had used to defend a largely unrestricted capitalism. Keynes demonstrated that, far from always seeking out an "equilibrium" that optimally used all available resources, market economies could very easily operate for long periods at quite suboptimal levels that left unemployment and underproduction widespread. If this was true, then enormous government spending was required to correct the inefficiencies. Claims of morality, generosity, compassion, fairness, or equality were no longer needed to justify a strong public sector; the "conservative" laws of economics, once properly understood, would be sufficient.

For Galbraith, as for so many young economists of his generation, these conservatives' complaints were just that: complaints. Keynes's central insight about government's function in the macromanagement of the economy—deficit spending in times of recession and fiscal constraint in times of inflation—was quickly established as the cardinal rule by which Galbraith and his peers could organize their economic vision. In such a world, the passionately argued goals of earlier reformers—once cast as political and moral obligations about democracy and equality and rights, to be fulfilled by an engaged and informed citizenry—could now be achieved through the cool application of scientific reason and an updated set of economic "laws" applied by citizens' (self-) appointed proxies—dispassionate, "scientific" economists.

But with World War II, concerns about unemployment and stagnation were replaced first by fears of war-induced inflation under conditions of scarce labor, and then by apprehension that the postwar world might collapse again into depression or stagnation. Keynes adapted his own ideas to these challenges in two very practical ways. First, he laid out a means for Britain to finance its part in the war that was vastly more equitable than what had occurred during the First World War, and was less likely to lead to economic collapse when the war ended. Second, he designed postwar multilateral financial institutions—which, radically altered by the Americans, became the International Monetary Fund and the World Bank—that he hoped would create conditions for a lasting, democratic global financial system, end the inequitable tyranny of the gold standard, avoid repeating the old disasters such as Weimar Germany's hyperinflation, and allow for rapid, generous economic development in the postcolonial world.

Galbraith's wartime experience left indelible marks, too, and left him with similar hopes despite similar frustrations. At the Office of Price Administration, he saw first-hand the tangled behind-the-scenes negotiations of government and business, as businessmen—or congressmen willing to do their bidding—swarmed his office seeking exemptions from this or that price limit. When he and his boss, Leon Henderson, failed to go along with enough of those self-interested pleadings in the middle of the war and were fired, the dismissals underscored to him as nothing else could the permanent interconnectedness of government and the markets. His midwar move to *Fortune* deepened his awareness of their constant interplay, but this didn't leave him cynical. Keynesian policies, he argued over and over again, would still benefit business by reducing the risks of recession and inflation, and would not have a direct impact on normal managerial prerogatives. This was an important strategy, especially after the 1945 Full Employment bill was emasculated by its conservative opponents in both parties.

The Cold War brought entirely new challenges, when the explosion of military spending hugely increased the size of the federal government and produced extraordinary new alliances. Massive expenditures on weapons and troops, and new foreign and domestic bases to house them, created America's first gigantic peacetime military force, which became the locus of the large public spending that Keynes and his followers considered essential to stabilizing capitalism's inevitable fluctuations. The new "military Keynesianism" turned the remnants of Roosevelt's supposedly temporary war-making machine into Eisenhower's "military-industrial complex," and helped fuel (and was fueled by) the political paranoia of McCarthyism. It also drove a new American foreign policy of global containment and confrontation that eventually ran amok—with terrible consequences.

Yet it was in this unprecedented new Cold War America that Galbraith's most enduring ideas crystallized in their most powerful and challenging form. Its most easily recognized feature was the *way* he wrote about economics, and for *whom*. Just as Keynes had recognized that doing economics entailed far more than deriving the correct blackboard model, so Galbraith understood that reaching a large public was more important than debating the professional colleagues whose work was driven mostly by mathematics. From *American Capitalism* on, Galbraith's insistence was that however correct their mathematical models might be (in the simple scientific sense of providing accurate predictions), they were formal descriptions of human behavior that, in their abstractness and complexity, failed to meet their promise of scientific prediction and also excluded millions from participating in understanding and shaping their own destinies.

To many economists, this seemed a weak, even frivolous, argument. After all, the "old economics" was fraught with error and confusion, and the natural sciences has been contributing for centuries to human progress, even though most people couldn't tell the difference between a neutron and a neuron. But to Galbraith, the very fact that the natural sciences had led not only to vast opportunities for human progress but also to the power to end human life—perhaps all life—on the planet, showed that the tale was not the simple, oft-told one of Science's Contributions to Progress. If war was too important to be left to generals, then the sciences meant to serve generals were also too vital, in the nuclear age, to be left to scientists, or to scientifically inclined economists and the political elites of both parties who were, in Galbraith's view, manipulating the assent of American citizens as they risked the world's survival.

IF ONE LOOKS at the direction of Galbraith's life and the choices he made before he was fifty, one sees something fundamental about his character, sees where his separation from mainstream economics and mainstream liberalism would carry him. He had faced more than half a dozen major junctures in his early career: he had given up a safe position in agricultural economics to strike out on a new career as a Keynesian macroeconomist; he had chosen to stand by two young radical colleagues when maintaining discreet silence might have better served his own academic ambitions; while in the government, he'd refused to alter his tough-minded behavior toward powerful business and congressional interests; at *Fortune*, where he might have followed Harry Luce's advocacy of "American Century" internationalism, he had pressed for a fuller embrace of Keynes; at the Bombing Survey, he had insisted on challenging the claims made by powerful military and civilian individuals for the "success" of strategic bombing; at the State Department, he had fought against the alleged inevitability of a militarized global confrontation with the Soviet Union; and at Harvard he had refused to trim or apologize or recant in the face of those who wanted to deny him the right to teach there because of his "radicalism." In short, he had demonstrated a willingness to choose the harder path, to risk his career, in order to maintain the independence of his own critical judgment. But he had also refused to be marginalized.

Even after Harvard finally gave him tenure, he refused to settle for professional safety, because the imperative in the 1950s was clear-cut: the scale of the issues determined his choice, and the life of Keynes in some ways became his guide. On the one hand he emulated Keynes's use of the press and its popular audience, writing to expand rather than limit the circle of public debate over technical issues of macroeconomic domestic policy and over the United States'—and the world's—future. His trademark elegance and humor were not simply signs of a budding author's aesthetic preference for the well-turned phrase or an obscure professor's hunger for commercial popularity, but a means for conveying his arguments to the largest possible audience.

Yet to pose many of the central questions was still quite difficult, given the political climate. Even after the Korean War ended and McCarthy had been disgraced, the saber-rattling stridency of Republican anti-Communists was matched—missile for missile, megaton for megaton—by veteran Democrats. This only highlighted for Galbraith how bipartisan the Cold War mind-set had become in American elites. He could now see that the connection between military expansion and domestic economic growth was no longer a matter of unpleasant coincidence but, increasingly, a cornerstone of conscious policy and an assumed key to American prosperity. Guns now meant butter, and butter, guns. The shift—from what had once been a "defensive" rationale for stopping Soviet "expansionism" to a "growth" rationale that presumed such military spending would continue uninterrupted and could be harnessed to a permanent national economic strategy—appalled Galbraith.

American Capitalism, with its emphasis on "countervailing power" and the need for government to nurture it, was Galbraith's first major attempt to reconcile liberal aims with a market economy dominated by large corporations. His point to fellow liberals was that given the new circumstances, they could no longer keep hoping to use vigorous antitrust or some vague democratic "national planning" to return America to a Brandeisian or Wilsonian dream economy where millions of small consumers and producers maintained neoclassical competition. The large corporation, he argued, was *the* defining economic institution of modern capitalism, possessing a capacity for technical innovation and constant progress that justified a cautious acceptance of it.

Here the conservative Schumpeterian element in Galbraith's thought was at its strongest, as he argued that Marshall's model of "resource-allocative efficiency" had been replaced by the "innovation efficiency" of the giant corporation. In this new land of giants, the key was to see that cross-market competition—the "countervailing powers," of unions versus manufacturers, of consumers versus retailers, of retailers versus manufacturers—could, if properly nurtured by an activist and *liberal* Keynesian government, be a successful proxy for the virtues of Marshall's model.

Showing the ways that the American economy no longer conformed to either neoclassical or "mainstream" mathematical Keynesian models was thus at the fore in Galbraith's work. And it was no longer simply a matter of understanding how the large corporation made for a new type of economy, but of considering the meaning of American affluence and the Cold War world in which it had emerged.

Affluent America in the 1950s was still far from achieving Keynes's post-scarcity ideals. Corporate America with its marketing dominance and massive advertising had chained the country to an endless treadmill of consumption that flooded the market with private goods, while the conservative politics with which the corporation was intimately intertwined left government unable to fulfill the public's desire for "public goods" or to achieve a final, permanent elimination of residual poverty. Galbraith understood that any chance of creating a *liberal* Keynesian future required more than just tinkering at the margins by changing growth-rate assumptions and diverting some of the billions spent on arms to schools, roads, and hospitals. Something much larger was called for, something that challenged society's "conventional wisdom" across the board—from its habits of consumption to its domestic political alignments to its costly international behavior.

Setting out with *The Affluent Society* on what some of his critics thought was a Quixotic course, he often found himself recalling one of his favorite lines of Keynes: "Words ought to be a little wild, for they are the assaults of thoughts on the unthinking." But *The Affluent Society*'s humorous puncturing of social pretensions saved it from being a jeremiad—although that was what it really was. Americans had lost control of their freedom, Galbraith was saying, even as they'd reached an economic security unprecedented in human history. What kind of people considered a shopping mall "the public square" or thought that roaring down littered roads through a polluted countryside in gas-guzzling, chrome-covered, tail-finned behemoths was the achievement of the American Dream? Galbraith's critique was launched nearly a half century before the country discovered that two thirds of its citizens were overweight, or suburban "soccer moms" started piloting 6,000-pound SUVs (with worse gas mileage than the Model T) to the playground and supermarket, or bottled water and gourmet food became multi-billion-dollar industries, or men and women began serving voluntarily as corporate billboards, sporting designer labels on everything from their shoes to their sunglasses. That all lay in the future.

Galbraith thought he saw in John F. Kennedy a possibility for change. Here was a candidate clearly intelligent enough to grasp his arguments about the interconnectedness of anti-Communism and the underprovision of public goods and services, someone who might be still young enough and bold enough seriously to challenge the nation's conventional wisdom on any number of fronts. From 1956 until JFK's death, Galbraith worked to realize through Kennedy at least a partial break with the habits and convictions of the Cold War and with their domestic and international consequences.

By November 1963, however, Galbraith had realized just how deeply military power and a new hegemonic mind-set had come to govern the nation. He had passionately and persistently warned President Kennedy about the dangers of Vietnam in letter after letter and meeting after meeting. And as declassified records show, Kennedy paid far closer attention to Galbraith's advice than many of his aides assumed at the time. Simultaneously, Galbraith also noted that Walter Heller's advocacy of a tax cut as a Keynesian stimulus (rather than deficit-financed public spending as Galbraith wanted and Kennedy himself preferred) not only contributed to the rapid expansion of the economy that they all wanted, but then, as Galbraith warned, helped accelerate a ruinous inflation. That, in tandem with the war, eventually destroyed Johnson's presidency and the activist Keynesians' reputation in Washington and among voters for years to come.

The New Industrial State reflected his experiences in the Kennedy and Johnson administration—his sense of the sheer power of the giant corporations and also their intricate connections to the government, the media, and the universities. Two decades of the Cold War and nearly a decade of combat in Southeast Asia had taught him to revise his estimate of the significance of "countervailing powers" (especially those of unions versus management or of consumer versus producer). In this new world, where corporations often (though not always) managed consumer demand rather than simply responding to it, the technostructure's values—its appreciation of technical innovation, its lack of interest in pure, textbook-style profit "maximization," and its preference for stable, controlled rates of growth—gave capitalism a new "style," one different from its early "entrepreneurial" period.

As he was finishing *The New Industrial State,* Galbraith's political life was changing almost as much as his thinking. He was moving away from conventional establishment power centers. When he supported Eugene McCarthy and then George McGovern, his focus was not just on ending the Vietnam War but also on gradually finding some sort of larger resolution to the Cold War, confronting the power of the "administered society" and moving the world toward post-scarcity democracy, as he and Keynes had always been convinced was possible.

Richard Nixon's 1968 victory and landslide 1972 reelection—and his decision to become a "Keynesian" himself and then to dismantle Bretton Woods—to Galbraith meant much harsher circumstances. Nixon's foreign policy, with its conservative détente that made American relations with China part of a triangulation policy pressuring the Soviet Union, and its encouragement of "regional powers" closely allied with Washington, showed its baleful effects after Nixon permitted OPEC's massive oil price increase in the fall of 1973 to stand. The orderly remnants of Bretton Woods completely dissolved, and the White House's refusal to break the car-tel shifted the world into an unstable global economy characterized by endless lines at gas stations (which preoccupied the press and voters) and, far worse, beggar-thy-neighbor trade patterns, currency instability, massive reckless lending, and grotesquely uneven development in the Third World. Thus began a financial roller-coaster ride of inflation and recession, feckless monetary policies, financial market bubbles, commodity market collapses, and heedless lending practices followed by financial collapse—a manic ride that repeated itself over and over again for three decades.

In many ways, it was the Nixon era—and "Nixonian Keynesianism"—that undermined the relative stability in Galbraith's model of the American economic system as outlined in *The New Industrial State*. Unions could no longer exert the powers they'd once had as one third of the informal postwar triumvirate of government, big business, and labor—which in conjunction with Washington's "military Keynesian" spending had once guaranteed the country's economic stability before it tipped over in Vietnam. Corporate leaders, faced with destabilizing inflation, slow growth, uncertain currency values and risky global markets, and then the crushing cost of the energy "taxes" levied by the OPEC cartel, simply seceded from that triumvirate and began to look for their own political solution to the nation's economic problems.

This new world of "Nixonian Keynesianism" eventually almost finished off mainstream Keynesianism in the university. Neoclassical economics had survived the Great Crash and the Keynesian Revolution by wedding itself to a style of analysis that Keynes had never advocated; this Neoclassical Synthesis had well expressed the mathematically modeled methodology that accorded no value to Galbraith's "old-fashioned" political economy. But in the 1970s it was itself overturned by more conservative economic theories that kept the new mathematical style but returned to pre-Keynesian assumptions. Many academic Keynesians sought to fend off attack through compromise—only to find that the attackers had no interest in compromise, so sure were they that they were finally expunging Keynes's "failed" notions from the future of the profession.

Galbraith, by contrast, engaged in repeated counterattacks, focusing on Friedman and monetarism because they carried the greatest political clout, but by then he had become isolated from the academic "mainstream." The irony, in retrospect, is that the rebellious economic conservatives ended up facing their own firing squads, as Reagan's government abandoned first supply-side economics, then monetarism, and then Rational Expectations, leaving them only as theory surviving in the classrooms where their most devout apostles taught. White House and congressional Republicans retained their own version of supposedly "Keynesian" deficits, with massive tax cuts for big business and the wealthy and an equally massive rearmament campaign. In the Alice-in-Wonderland world of modern GOP economics, they also simply denied the deficits and their effects.

Here was "Keynesianism" stood on its head—"turbocharged Keynesianism," *The Economist* once called it, though no reputable Keynesian ever endorsed such practices. Under it, the new global economy of finance swiftly outgrew the world of trade and real goods that finance was historically meant to support. And the tsunami of cash, options, futures contracts, and securitization created in the 1980s, coupled with a systematic deregulation of energy, real estate, banking, savings and loans, and telecommunications led to a speculative fever that created its own (wildly uneven) "growth." The only sense in which the growth pattern was systematic was that it made for a radical income and wealth redistribution, as the fortunes of the rich increased, the poor stagnated, and the middle class suffered through the longest drought of real income gains since the Great Depression. Internationally, this new generation of Republicans—far removed from their ancestors' habits of caution and prudence—tried to conceal their domestic recklessness by encouraging trade deficits almost as large as their budget deficits, then using the earnings of rich trading partners such as Japan and the revenues from hefty increases in Social Security taxes (which taxed all *but* the rich) to buy hundreds of billions of dollars' worth of Treasury bonds, which allowed the budgetary deficits to continue.

Galbraith felt no reason, academic or political, to restrain his criticism of all this, and he never hesitated to excoriate the Republicans' "politics of joy" for the damage it caused and the hypocrisy with which they defended themselves. From the very first months of the Reagan administration, he showed remarkable acuity in anticipating the strategies the White House would follow, the defenses the GOP would raise, and the social, political, and economic effects the strategies would have, whether on aggregate growth, income distribution, job creation, deficits, or financial crises. His criticism flashed with new anger whose edge was only barely softened by the arched eyebrow and sardonic voice that had so long been his stylistic signature.

Yet the situation at the turn of the century suggests a paradoxical incompleteness in Galbraith's career, in political liberalism, and in liberal Keynesianism. Despite decades of ferocious conservative criticism, a great deal of the world that Galbraith and his fellow reform liberals created between 1900 and 1980 endured into the new century: the minimum wage, workers' rights, vastly expanded and publicly financed health care, prohibitions on discrimination based on race and gender, an influential environmental movement (and environmental laws), a major reduction in poverty, a large middle class, expanded educational opportunities, Social Security. Government as a percentage of GDP is larger today than it was when Galbraith last served in it, and has shown no sign of growing smaller. The issue is not its size but the purpose to which its spending is put and the sectors from which its revenues are collected.

Thanks, however, to the political power of liberalism's opponents (especially since the shift of the white South to the GOP) and the conservatives' narrative about government's excessive size and inefficiencies, reform liberalism's most cherished programs are incomplete, and cautious "New Democrats" have resurrected the nineteenth-century liberal idea that markets offer the true path to prosperity and security. Galbraith has consistently chided this "New Democratic" attitude. After all, the economy, which produces more than $12 trillion in goods and services each year, has not enabled 44 million Americans to get health insurance, or 33 million Americans to rise out of poverty, even as it generated fortunes for the thousand richest Americans that, when combined, exceed the GDP of dozens of poor countries. What once seemed to be reform liberalism's victories now seem uncertain: the country's middle class is working harder, with less security, and greater insecurity about its future than ever before, conservative philippics against liberalism have convinced them that "government" in the reform liberal sense of the word is to blame. Although the Cold War has been over for a long time, New Democrats have yet to find their voice. To the contrary, and to Galbraith's great dismay, many "New Democratic" politicians sound like their predecessors at the height of the Cold War, anxious not to be seen as "weak" on defense or accused of practicing "redistributionist" politics at a time of crisis.

Galbraith's hope has always been that real liberal political leaders would have the courage to express an alternative vision and that liberal economics might play its part in guiding them to it. For much of his career after World War II, however, his peers were at odds with him, thinking that economics should aim at a different goal, in which neutral, objective, factual science could somehow overcome the deep divisions of human interests and classes. But time has taken its toll on those dreams of economics as a "pure science," just as "science" itself is now understood as being deeply entwined in humanity's social, political, and power relations.

In the early 1990s, in what turned out to be an indictment of those dreams, the American Economic Association appointed a commission of twelve economists, representing a range of often-conflicting economic "schools," to undertake a multiyear study of their profession.[18] Surveying more than 3,000 senior American economists, it found that nearly two thirds believed that they had for too long mistakenly "overemphasized mathematical and statistical tools at the expense of substance," and that the time had come to overhaul and revise economics' core suppositions. The study found "an absence of an empirical and applied base in the entire economics curriculum," which left the students to learn mathematically derived theories characterized by an "absence of facts, institutional information, data, real-world issues, applications, and policy problems." (The students themselves, when asked what they believed would assure them a successful career, cited "excellence in mathematics" and "being good at problem-solving" as the key factors, whereas "having a thorough knowledge of the economy" was "unimportant."[19]) The worried commissioners noted that companies such as GE, IBM, and Kodak were disbanding their economics departments, and the private-sector use of economists was declining everywhere but on Wall Street; too many prospective employers found that economists weren't being trained for "anything but other graduate programs." Even on Wall Street few people believed that academic training prepared young economists for the real world. Morgan Stanley's chief economist said that his firm, like many others, insisted "on at least a three-to-four-year cleansing experience to neutralize the brainwashing that takes place in these graduate programs."[20] They offered this chilling conclusion: "The commission's fear is that graduate programs may be turning out a generation with too many idiot savants skilled in technique but innocent of real world economic issues."*

Many other voices by then could be heard questioning the overemphasis on

---

*Galbraith was not surprised by the findings, and admitted to personal pleasure on hearing that Milton Friedman rather forlornly acknowledged not only the failings of monetarism (in policy "it has not been a success" and

mathematical technique. Lawrence Summers, once at the Treasury Department and soon to become president of Harvard, wrote that "econometric results are rarely an important input to theory creation" and that "attempts to make empirical work take on too many of the trappings of science render it uninformative."[21] His harsh conclusion was echoed by the Nobel laureate Ronald Coase, who chided econometricians for "data mining" habits that "resembled the Spanish Inquisition," quipping that they were all too often merely proof that "if you torture the data long enough, Nature will confess."[22] These warnings seemed all the more troubling after a comprehensive study of articles published in the *American Economic Review* showed that most of them didn't even use statistical inference methods correctly. Little wonder that by 1996, 95 percent of economists declared themselves often skeptical of the mathematically derived empirical findings published in the profession's leading journals.[23]

Fortune had a long assessment of what, in mainstream economics, remained valuable after the conservative assaults on the once-vaunted Keynesian consensus. It concluded:

> The pitched battles of [the 1970s and 1980s] are over, but nobody really won. Academic economists have indeed attained a state of relative peace and consensus, but they have done so by diminishing their expectations. They use similar analytic tools and come up with similar answers to narrow questions. But when it comes to explaining the behavior of the world economy, economists can't agree—in fact, most of them no longer seem to believe there is a single correct explanation . . . Analytical techniques are becoming ever more sophisticated, but it is looking ever less likely that they'll someday add up to a coherent, reliable science of economics.[24]

Even *The Economist*, which had championed neoclassical economics and Reagan-Thatcher politics, in a special series on where the profession stands sounded no less dismayed by the state of conventional economics:

> For roughly twenty-five years after 1950, despite all the clichés about economists never agreeing, it was fair to talk of a broad economic consensus on the big economic questions. Almost all economists were believers in what they called the "neoclassical synthesis." In the mid-1970s, thanks to a mixture of theoretical argument and unhelpful economic events, this consensus broke down. Economists have been trying to repair it ever since, but with little success.[25]

"I'm not sure I would as of today push it as hard as I once did") but also that in modern conservatism's quest for smaller government, after three decades of ideological ascendancy, "it is hard to say that there has been any improvement." And Galbraith lauded Robert Solow for admitting that mathematical economics, after a half century of frustration in search of scientific certitude, might be more accurately seen as an example of "the overeducated in pursuit of the unknowable."[26]

Today, there are promising signs that at least some economists are finally once again taking up the "institutional" and "structural" questions at the core of Galbraith's work. Their answers well help the profession move past the old assumptions, as they discuss the very issues—and experiment with the very methods—that Galbraith has long claimed were most important.

These innovations cover a lot of territory: the "new growth theories" developed by Paul Roemer and his colleagues, suggesting new ways that economies might escape the constraints of scarcity; the "asymmetric information" ideas of George Akerlof and Joseph Stiglitz, which demonstrate the structural imperfections in markets that undermined the chance for achieving neoclassical equilibrium; the "new trade theory" work of Paul Krugman, which overturns some of the central tenets of Ricardo's legacy; Brian Arthur's ideas about "path dependency," which show that institutions use their power to "lock in" patterns of often-"inefficient" technologies; the "new institutionalism" of Oliver Williamson, which reinterprets corporate structure and behavior in new ways that recognize the power of "corporate cultures"; the "new institutional history" pioneered by figures such as Douglass North, which refutes the idea that general equilibrium models and neoclassical axioms can explain how real world economies have evolved; and the new "political economy" theories in macroeconomics as well as in political science and economic sociology.[27]

Perhaps the most telling sign that economics is being forced to rethink its mainstream models and axioms has been the extraordinary advance in "behavioral economics," led by such noneconomists as the Princeton psychologist Daniel Kahneman, whose work shows the myriad ways in which people reject what economists long considered "rational" choice. He has prompted renewed interest in Herbert Simon's earlier theories of "bounded rationality" and forced economists to reexamine the effects of habits, customs, common beliefs, ideology, class, status, status goods, even the so-called winner-take-all system of economic rewards practiced by modern-day CEOs, professional sports figures, and entertainers. The fact that Kahneman, a psychologist, was awarded the Nobel Prize in economics in 2002 speaks volumes.

Still, none of these recent advances has yielded an overarching new theory on the theoretical order of neoclassical equilibrium analysis or mainstream Keynesianism. That in itself may be a blessing, because it leaves economics in the twenty-first century obliged to work much as Galbraith worked for seventy years in the twentieth. If in fact "understanding economics" requires not only specific tools to explain individual prices (which economists are generally still good at doing) but willingness to approach the questions of why societies allocate rewards in ways that frustrate and elude standard models, why some societies develop thriving economies quickly while others lagged far behind (and in some cases go on lagging further and further), or why all too often the public goods and services that citizens want and need are not supplied, then in truth economics does indeed concern the fundamental issue of how societies and civilizations work. It is here that Galbraith challenges not only his colleagues but all of us. For in societies that claim to treasure democracy as their ideal (so new in human history), defining of "democracy"—and with it, "freedom" and "equality" and "justice"—supersedes in importance issues of price and efficiency.

Of all the economists who have taken up that challenge, the Indian-born, Cambridge-educated Nobel laureate Amartya Sen is perhaps the best known and most highly honored. Sen—who for many years taught economics *and* philosophy at Harvard, then was Master of Trinity College, Cambridge, before returning to Harvard once again—believes that the issue of "social choice," a long-standing matter of great technical interest to economists, is of concern not just to economists but is an issue with which the public must engage. Sen's view is that the goal not just of economics but of society in general is the enlargement of what he calls "positive human freedom" and the capability to enjoy it.

"Capability," for Sen, has a specific meaning, one that lies somewhere between raw intrinsic human capacity and a cultivated ability that is provided by specific kinds of social interaction and institution. In a simple sense, anyone capable of speaking English may be able to say "The sky is blue," but a certain kind of social training is required before one can go on to distinguish aquamarine from turquoise. So, too, in creating just societies, human beings may have an intrinsic capacity and raw hunger for freedom, but without the right set of skills individually and collectively to negotiate its acquisition, maintenance, and expansion, they will never fully achieve it.

Sen's insistence on making larger moral and cultural concerns preconditions for answering "economic" questions has enormously influenced theorists, not least because his mathematical sophistication allows him to carry on the debate without rejecting the modern discipline's most prized methodological tools. Yet Sen has also repeatedly made clear that this technical discussion, of value to its participants, morally requires a parallel conversation carried out in language and using ideas broadly accessible to as many people as possible.

This second line of work for Sen has led him to the forefront of the great debates on economic development strategies, debates in which he has forcefully distinguished between what "markets" do, on the one hand, and what on the other hand governments, NGOs, culture, institutions, and customs do to generate "freedom." He has forcefully shown, for example, that widespread starvation has seldom if ever taken place because of a "market failure," that is, the failure to produce and have on hand enough food to feed the hungry. Rather the failure has been a political one, of not getting the food to those who most need it because of inadequate income on the part of the poor, greed among the owners of the food supplies, and/or corruption and incompetence of public officials. Large-scale famine, Sen points out, hasn't happened in democracies, only in authoritarian systems. For reasons such as these, he has chided colleagues who claim to see "markets" as either the precondition or the *summum bonum* of substantive freedom, and he constantly stresses the interconnectedness of that freedom with a generous concept of "development," with the larger goals toward which "development" presses, and with the people and means by which those ends are chosen.

For anyone familiar with John Kenneth Galbraith's work and life, the work of Amartya Sen today is a reminder that gifted economists willing to look beyond the dream of economics as a science can recover the fundamental questions that so many people have always hoped economics might answer. When Sen declares that "we need the power and protection of [many types of] institutions, provided by democratic practice, civil and human rights, a free and open media, facilities for basic education and health care, economic safety nets, and of course, provisions for women's freedom and rights—a neglected area which is only now beginning to receive the attention it deserves," we hear the echoes of Galbraith's fundamental claims.

With more than three billion people living on less than two dollars a day, with more than half the world's population having access to neither safe water nor a telephone, with more than 800 million people malnourished and at risk of starvation, Sen's practical work—his attempt to actualize the meaning of "capability"—has been done on a global scale, unlike so much of Galbraith's, which concentrated on the United States. (Sen was a prominent advocate of the Millennium Development Goals, which set the reduction of world poverty by half over the next fifteen years as its challenge. He also was an architect of the United Nations' *Human Development Report*, an annual country-by-country survey of global progress across a range of fronts, from literacy rates, disease control, and gender discrimination to the spread of democracy, the impact of arms spending, and the quality of the environment.) Yet Galbraith's analysis of the international consequences of American economic, political, diplomatic, military, and cultural power is ultimately international, too. His critique of "the affluent society" was meant to open the debate on how democratic societies should organize themselves to achieve goals beyond those offered by the private market. His indictment of the Vietnam War and of "military Keynesianism" was "international" in the fullest sense of the word, indicting the United States for heedlessness and incaution in world affairs. So, too, his excoriating criticisms of Ronald Reagan, George Bush, and the "New Democrats" of the second Gilded Age—with its radical redistribution of wealth, income, and opportunity, and the self-satisfied "culture of contentment" validating it—were never limited to their effect on the United States alone. Galbraith's constant insistence on the democratic quest to achieve that full range of what Sen calls "capabilities" for "positive human freedom" in the United States and across the globe has always informed his hopes for humankind.

Galbraith has also maintained an optimistic belief that human beings construct the world they live in and that human reason—cognizant of human limits, and attuned to the claims of power and privilege, yet committed to creating a world that seeks to expand freedom and security, justice and hope, equality and compassion—can continue to gain ground. He took from Keynes the structure of what he saw as a powerful means to that end, and he amended it when circumstances created new challenges. To him, understanding the material world was, as it was for Keynes, not the goal but the means by which to realize a dream. What lay beyond the mere production and possession of things was always more important.

There is a new breadth in economics today that casts fresh light on Galbraith's career and its significance. Yet, as Amartya Sen has noted, Galbraith's contribution still "doesn't get enough praise." In June 2000, Sen gave the commencement address at Harvard on the subject of globalization, and he used it to offer an eloquent articulation of the "capability" challenges the world needed to meet. In order to do this, he said, we must fully understand how to balance and direct competing power in societies, which have conflicting interests and unevenly distributed strengths, for power is at the center of achieving true freedom. The "great importance" of this topic had first dawned on him as a young college student in Calcutta almost half a century earlier, he added, sitting in a coffeehouse reading a little book entitled *American Capitalism* by an American economist named Galbraith—and it had never left him since.[28]

Some months later a reporter asked Sen whether he thought that Galbraith's work would enjoy lasting influence, and if so, why. Sen's reply was that Galbraith and his work would indeed endure, and for a simple reason that could best be seen in *The Affluent Society*. The book was an example of Galbraith's "great insight," he said, which "has become so much a part of our understanding of contemporary capitalism that we forget where it began. It's like reading *Hamlet* and deciding it's full of quotations. You realize where they came from."[29]

NOTES

INTRODUCTION: ON FIRST COMING TO CAMBRIDGE

1. Peggy Lamson, *Speaking of Galbraith* (New York: Ticknor & Fields, 1991), 35, and Galbraith, interview with author.
2. On his days at Willey's School, see John Kenneth Galbraith, *The Scotch* (Boston: Houghton Mifflin, 1964), 80–91.
3. Galbraith, interview with author.
4. J. R. Kearl et al., "A Confusion of Economists?" *American Economic Review*, May 1979, 30.
5. Galbraith, interview with author.
6. John Kenneth Galbraith, *A Life in Our Times: Memoirs* (Boston: Houghton Mifflin, 1981), 43.
7. Details of the strike are from front-page contemporary accounts in the *Boston Evening Transcript* in September 1934, and from *Time*, "Idle Answer," September 17, 13; "Second Week," September 24, 22; and "Claims and Credits," October 1, 11.
8. See national income in Department of Commerce, Bureau of the Census, *Historical Statistics of the United States, Colonial Times to 1970* (Washington, D.C.: Government Printing Office, 1975), v. 1, 235–36; the foreign trade figures are from Charles Kindleberger, *The World in Depression, 1929–1939* (Berkeley: University of California Press, 1973), 172.
9. Charles Hession and Hyman Sardy, *Ascent to Affluence* (Boston: Allyn & Bacon, 1969), 629–31.
10. Hoover quoted in Ibid., 630.
11. Joseph Schumpeter, *Business Cycles*, 20 (New York: McGraw Hill, 1939), v. 2, 911.
12. Mellon quoted in Herbert Hoover, *The Memoirs of Herbert Hoover: The Great Depression, 1929–1941* (New York: Macmillan, 1952), 5, 16, 30.
13. Eleanor Roosevelt quoted in Arthur Schlesinger, Jr., *The Coming of the New Deal* (Boston: Houghton Mifflin, 1959), 1–2.
14. FDR quoted in ibid., 2–3.
15. Galbraith, *A Life*, 34.

16. Ibid., 34.
17. Schlesinger, *The Coming of the New Deal*, 20–21.
18. "Federal Reserve for Exchange Curb as in Pending Bill," *The New York Times*, March 24, 1934, 1. The allegations, made by William Wirt, a prominent conservative Indiana educator, were based on conversations he supposedly had had with unnamed members of Roosevelt's "Brains Trust."
19. "Growth of Membership and Subscribers," *American Economic Review*, January 1949, 314.
20. Marshall personally was often more realistic about the limits of his model than his followers, and as a moderate Victorian-era reformer saw room for limited state action on behalf of the disadvantaged. See A. K. Dasgupta, *Epochs of Economic Theory* (Oxford: Blackwell, 1985), ch. 7 (on Marshall's policy views and his partial equilibrium analysis). Dorothy Ross, *The Origins of American Social Science* (New York: Cambridge University Press, 1991), ch. 6, gives a thoughtful overview of neoclassical economics' ascendancy—and its many challengers—among U.S. economists in the late nineteenth and early twentieth centuries.
21. Fisher, Lawrence, and the HES are all quoted in John Kenneth Galbraith, *The Great Crash*, 3rd ed. (Boston: Houghton Mifflin, 1988), 70–71.

CHAPTER 1: GROWING UP IN SPECIAL PLACES
1. Galbraith, *The Scotch*, 11.
2. Ibid., 5–6, 1–2.
3. On the *Globe*'s local influence, ibid., 79. For a sense of its views during Galbraith's youth, see its great Scots-Canadian editor James Macdonald's *The North American Idea* (Toronto: McClelland, 1917). Macdonald was a Social Gospel Presbyterian minister as well as a journalist who was revered among the Scots of Canada.
4. See Robert Craig Brown and Ramsay Cook, *Canada 1896–1921: A Nation Transformed* (Toronto: McClelland & Stewart, 1974), 186–87.
5. The classic work on the Progressive Era is Richard Hofstadter, *The Age of Reform* (New York: Knopf, 1955), which sees Progressivism as a liberal middle-class reform movement; James Weinstein, *The Corporate Ideal in the Liberal State, 1900–1918* (Boston: Beacon Press, 1968), and Martin Sklar, *The Corporate Reconstruction of American Capitalism* (New York: Cambridge University Press, 1988), are more radical analyses that echo John Chamberlain, *Farewell to Reform* (New York: Liveright, 1932), and Matthew Josephson, *The President Makers* (New York: Harcourt, Brace, 1940), in their critique of big business and its impact on politics and reform. Robert Wiebe, *The Search for Order* (New York: Hill & Wang, 1967), offers an insightful account of the struggles to organize a modern urban society out of agrarian roots; Morton Keller, *Regulating a New Economy* and *Regulating a New Society* (Cambridge, Mass.: Harvard University Press, 1990 and 1994), provide detail on the era's reforms, comparing them to similar reforms in England at the same time.
6. See Brown and Cook, *Canada 1896–1921*, ch. 1.
7. Ibid., 3–4.
8. Ibid., 101.
9. The study, written in 1904 by the assistant relief officer of Toronto, is cited in ibid., 100.
10. Formally, the UFO appeared in 1913, but this was a renaming of a group formed

in 1907 that resulted from the merger of the Grange and the Ontario Farmers' Association. See L. A. Wood, *The History of the Farmers' Movement in Canada* (Toronto: University of Toronto Press, 1924), 147–55.

11. On the railroad, see Galbraith, *The Scotch*, 8.

12. Galbraith's version, in *A Life*, is ambiguous. It traces the Canadian family branch to Archibald Galbraith, born in 1771, but doesn't say when he arrived in Canada. Lynda Galbraith, the wife of Galbraith's nephew, who has assembled more detailed family records, suggests that the arrival was in 1818 or 1819. Lynda Galbraith, interview with author.

13. D. W. Meinig, *The Shaping of America*, 3 v. (New Haven: Yale University Press, 1986–98) v. 1, 289 (on Scottish migration in the 1760s to 1770s).

14. Galbraith, *A Life*, 1.

15. Richard Altick, *The English Common Reader: A Social History of the Mass Reading Public, 1800–1900* (Chicago: University of Chicago Press, 1957), 69–72.

16. The letter, dated December 17, 1851, is from Galbraith family papers in the possession of Lynda Galbraith.

17. Immigration from Great Britain to Canada was actively encouraged by British policy after the War of 1812, particularly along the border, to block immigrants from the United States, who might one day support Canada's annexation to the U.S. See Meinig, *Shaping of America*, v. 2 (1993), 50–51.

18. See C. O. Ermatinger, *The Talbot Regime* (St. Thomas, Ont.: Municipal World, 1904).

19. Lamson, *Speaking of Galbraith*, 7.

20. Galbraith, *A Life*, 5.

21. Lamson, *Speaking of Galbraith*, 3.

22. Ibid., 4.

23. Catherine Galbraith Denholm, interview with author.

24. On reading and the Dutton Library, Lamson, *Speaking of Galbraith*, 4, and Catherine and John Kenneth Galbraith, interviews with author. He takes great pride in the fact that the library was named after him in 2003.

25. Galbraith, *A Life*, 2. In Galbraith, *The Scotch*, he never mentions her.

26. Catherine Galbraith Denholm, interview with author.

27. "Funeral Was Largest Seen in Years," *The Dutton Advance*, October 25, 1923.

28. Galbraith quoted in Lamson, *Speaking of Galbraith*, 15.

29. The first quotation is from an unnamed eulogist at the funeral, reported in *The Dutton Advance*, January 22, 1938; the second from E. A. Smith, in the *Advance*'s report of Galbraith's accidental death, January 17, 1938.

30. Catherine Galbraith Denholm, interview with author.

31. Ibid.

32. Galbraith, *The Scotch*, 44–46.

33. *The Dutton Advance*, January 22, 1938.

34. On Laurier's loss, by 40,000 votes among 1.3 million cast, see Brown and Cook, *A Nation Transformed*, 183ff. Canada's parties drew on the model of Liberal/Conservative politics in Britain, the party division that shaped English politics in the nineteenth century. In England, the prewar years were similar when the Liberal Party reached new heights of power under Lloyd George, yet in fact was poised at the edge of imminent decline, about to disappear as a major force. See George Dangerfield, *The Strange Death of Liberal England* (New York: H. Smith & R. Haas, 1935), for the definitive account.

35. Joseph Schull, *Ontario Since 1867* (Toronto: McClelland & Stewart, 1978), 214.

36. John English, *The Decline of Politics: The Conservatives and the Party System, 1901–20* (Toronto: University of Toronto, 1993), 194.

37. See W. R. Young, "Conscription, Rural Depopulation and the Farmers of Ontario, 1917–1919," *Canadian Historical Review*, September 1972, 289–320.

38. Hendrie's charge and the allegations of links between the United Farmers, Bolshevism, and Sinn Fein are quoted in English, *Decline of Politics*, 218.

39. Drury quoted in Brown and Cook, *A Nation Transformed*, 319.

40. Good quoted in ibid., 316.

41. E. C. Drury, *Farmer Premier* (Toronto: McClelland & Stewart, 1966), 108.

42. On the government's record, see Schull, *Ontario Since 1867*, ch. 11. On the general context of Ontario politics, see Graham White, *The Government and Politics of Ontario*, 5th ed. (Toronto: University of Toronto Press, 1997), and Hugh Thorburn, *Party Politics in Canada* (Scarborough, Ont.: Prentice-Hall, 1991). On parallels between the UFO and western Canada's several United Farmer parties, see Robert Vipond, *Liberty and Community* (New York: State University of New York Press, 1991). Vipond is especially good on how interwar provincial governments operated as social-reform laboratories, comparable to La Follette's experiment in Wisconsin, the Farmer-Labor Party in Minnesota, and the Nonpartisan League in North Dakota.

43. Lamson describes the travails at Dutton High in *Speaking of Galbraith*, 10–16.

44. The description of life at OAC, unless noted, is from Galbraith, *A Life*, 6–17; Lamson, *Speaking of Galbraith*, 17–25; and Galbraith, interview with author.

45. See Lamson, *Speaking of Galbraith*, 23–25 (on Galbraith's remarks to *Time*, dismissing OAC). Ultimately, tempers cooled, and the degree was not rescinded although talk of naming a campus building after him died, and the university sealed its files on the matter. See Ontario Agricultural College, *Calendar, 1926–27* (Guelph, Ont.: OAC, 1926), 4–5 (Ph.D.'s listed among faculty), 20 (admission requirements).

    The University of Guelph, which OAC was eventually renamed, carries on OAC's traditions on a higher plane today. In 1999, it reported that its researchers had created three genetically modified piglets, trademarked "Enviropigs." The excrement of the animals was said to be significantly milder in aroma, according to the researchers, who were at the time waiting to see whether this trait could be passed on by natural breeding. See "Brave New Pigs," *Chicago Sun-Times*, June 28, 1999, E1.

46. Galbraith, *A Life*, 12.

47. Galbraith quoted in Lamson, *Speaking of Galbraith*, 18–19.

48. Galbraith quoted in ibid., 29 ("maximum offense"): in *A Life*, 11–12, he says "side of safety." In the citation accompanying the honorary degree he received in 1965 from the University of Guelph, bemused mention is made of *The OACIS* under his editorship. "Not only did it draw down upon itself the wrath of two College presidents, but it also earned for itself the attention of a reporter from the Toronto *Globe*, and we suspect, tart inquiries from the Department of Agriculture."

49. Galbraith, interview with author (on nicknames). Galbraith described the trip—which he made officially as a member of the college's Fourth Year Stock Judging Team—in *The OAC Review*, December 1930, 155. Michigan State's agricultural

facilities, he averred, "showed sound judgment from a College viewpoint. They are plain, utilitarian and complete." Purdue had "an air of more advanced maturity than Michigan," especially in the swine department, from which he came away "with a profound respect for the progress the United States is making in the direction of a stretchy, smooth . . . type of market hog." Illinois seemed especially vast and the best equipped, with its own grain elevator and a judging pavilion so enormous it "would nicely house . . . the Ontario Provincial Winter Fair with some space to spare."

50. Galbraith quoted in Lamson, *Speaking of Galbraith*, 21.

51. Galbraith, *A Life*, 15; a clue to Galbraith's earliest and unformed thoughts about economics appears in a little essay, "Depression and the Student in Agriculture," *OAC Review*, March 1932, 440–42. Eager to demonstrate his own seriousness and to encourage it in his fellow students, he tries to explain the farm crisis as one of overproduction, amidst a "competitive armaments" race of technological innovation. He urges students to study economics as a means of dealing with the situation, rather than remaining focused merely on how to increase production further.

52. Galbraith, *A Life*, 12.

53. Galbraith's graduate life at Berkeley, including his trip west, are from his essay "Berkeley in the Thirties," in Galbraith, *A Contemporary Guide to Economics, Peace and Laughter* (Boston: Houghton Mifflin, 1971), 344–60, and from Galbraith, interview with author.

54. Ibid., 346.

55. Ibid., 348.

56. The agriculture-related courses were mostly joint offerings of the Giannini Foundation and the Department of Economics; the others were in the department itself, save for political science. See Galbraith's application to the Royal Society of Canada, 1933, in Early Correspondence, box 1, Galbraith Papers, John F. Kennedy Library, Boston.

57. Galbraith, "Berkeley in the Thirties," 351–52. For a conservative's assessment of Berkeley in the 1930s, see Robert Nisbet, in *Teachers and Scholars* (New Brunswick, N.J.: Transaction Press, 1992), on his own student days there.

58. Galbraith, "Berkeley in the Thirties," 352.

59. The nature and extent of Silvermaster's spying is not clear, and he was never arrested or charged with espionage. The allegations against him—that he directed a Washington ring of Communist Party members and sympathizers working in the government—were made by Elizabeth Bentley, a Communist Party courier turned FBI informer. Her charges were repeated at numerous congressional hearings and in the press, but many proved inaccurate on further investigation. In the 1990s, partial declassification of the Venona Papers, a collection of government wiretaps and electronic intercepts from the earlier period, gave new weight to her charges—and, among a small coterie of academics still following the issue, an opportunity to fling back and forth their own accusations, eerily reminiscent of the earlier period.

60. Galbraith, *A Life*, 23.

61. Galbraith, *A Life*, 30. Veblen's influence on Galbraith's mature thought is more complex than this suggests. Galbraith's insistence on treating correct economic theorizing as a process that incorporates concepts drawn from sociological, historical, political, scientific, and cultural-anthropological sources—and that

downplays the role of mathematical modeling—is certainly Veblenian. The two men's use of biting satirical humor, their subversive distrust and denigration of received authority and "conventional wisdom," are also shared characteristics. But Galbraith's energetic engagement in economic and political reform, his trust in democratic ideals and belief that democratic governments can direct the energies of capitalist markets toward the creation of a more just society go beyond Veblen. In this, the influence of Galbraith's father, of Keynes and Roosevelt, and of the New Deal ethos are closer to Ely and Commons than to Veblen.

62. Galbraith, "Berkeley in the Thirties," 354–55.
63. Galbraith to Alice Galbraith, May 16, 1933, Early Correspondence, box 1, Galbraith Papers, JFK Library.
64. Catherine Galbraith Denholm, interview with author.
65. Hepburn's promise turned bitter for men like Archie Galbraith. Once in office, he veered sharply rightward and was turned out at the next election by an overwhelming margin. His term delegitimized the Liberal Party and led to Conservative Party dominance of Ontario for the next four decades. It was a traumatic enough memory that Galbraith made a point of lambasting Hepburn on the very first page of his memoirs, a point perhaps lost on his readers, since he did not explain Hepburn's role as a protégé of Archie, or the history of the UFO and Archie's involvement in it. On Hepburn's impact on Ontario and Canadian politics, see Schull, *Ontario Since 1867*, ch. 14, and Richard Alwey, "Mitchell F. Hepburn and the Liberal Party in Ontario," Ph.D. diss., University of Ontario, 1965.

CHAPTER 2: HARVARD IN THE 1930s

1. For a succinct departmental history see Edward Mason, "The Harvard Department of Economics from the Beginning to World War II," *Quarterly Journal of Economics*, August 1982, 383–433, and Robert Church, "The Economists Study Society," in Paul Buck, ed., *Social Sciences at Harvard, 1860–1920* (Cambridge, Mass.: Harvard University Press 1965), 18–90 (especially 29, on Harvard's first economics Ph.D., awarded to Charles Dunbar). Dunbar had been appointed Harvard's first full-time economics professor five years before his doctorate was earned. His thesis was only marginally about economics in the modern sense: he wrote it under Henry Adams, on Anglo-Saxon legal procedures.

2. Lowell's architectural contributions were significant: he oversaw construction of Widener Library, the Business and Medical schools, and the Law School's Langdell Hall, in addition to the residential houses along the Charles River. The *Harvard Alumni Bulletin* noted on his retirement, "Many people are of the opinion that the University will never again go through so great a physical expansion in so short a time." Lowell was intensely competitive about his reputation and legacy: he had an "antipathetic obsession" with his predecessor Eliot (warmly reciprocated), and he opposed the appointment of Conant as his successor, his enthusiasm for the chemist "measured by micrometer." Conant's assessment of Lowell's style quoted Lowell's own words about Harvard administration: "tyranny tempered by assassination." (He might have recalled Eliot's advice that the most important attribute of a successful college president was "the capacity to inflict pain.") See Morton and Phyllis Keller, *Making Harvard Modern* (New York: Oxford University Press, 2001), 13–17; James Hershberg, *James B. Conant: Harvard to Hiroshima and the Making of the Nuclear Age* (New York: Knopf,

1993), 56–59; and Henry Aaron Yeomans, *Abbott Lawrence Lowell, 1856–1943* (Cambridge, Mass.: Harvard University Press, 1948).

3. Hershberg, *James B. Conant*, 57; Kellers, *Making Harvard Modern*, 15, 18, 22.

4. Conant was focused on retiring the old guard. During his first month in office, he told a professor, "I am sure you know that I feel as strongly as anyone about the desire of filling this institution with brilliant and productive young men." And he was only mildly amused when the University of Chicago's president, Robert Maynard Hutchins, sent him a newspaper clipping on Harvard's Entomology Department. The headline was "Harvard Has Insects 60 Million Years Old," next to which Hutchins had scrawled, "We retire ours at 65." Kellers, *Making Harvard Modern*, 24, 27. For Conant's views on Harvard's Economics Department, see James Bryant Conant, *My Several Lives: Memoirs of a Social Inventor* (New York: Harper & Row, 1970), ch. 32.

5. Church, "Economists Study Society," 88.

6. For a short introduction to Taussig and his work, see Ben Seligman, *Main Currents in Modern Economics* (New York: Free Press, 1962), v. 3, 623–28, and Redvers Opie, "Frank Taussig," *Economic Journal*, June–September 1941, 347–68.

7. See Mason, "Harvard Department of Economics," 402 (on Carver and Lowell's comment about him); 400 (Eliot's advice); 406–7 (on Gay). Gay taught sociology as an economist because Harvard, curiously, didn't create a separate Sociology Department until 1933, long after most other large universities.

8. Richard Swedberg, *Joseph A. Schumpeter: His Life and Work* (Cambridge: Polity Press, 1991), 113–17.

9. The importance of the University of Wisconsin in the early history of American economics should not be overlooked. The economist Richard Ely—after founding the AEA in 1885 as an explicitly reformist group opposed to Social Darwinism, and in favor of labor unions, activist government, and indeed Christian socialism—was pushed out of Johns Hopkins University and ended up at Madison. There he drew influential followers, including John R. Commons, a powerful reform figure in his own right and a pillar of Institutionalist economics. Alvin Hansen and John D. Black studied under Commons, and at Harvard graduate students Lauchlin Currie and Harry Dexter White worked under Allyn Young, who had revised and edited Ely's textbook, which until the 1930s was, as noted earlier, *the* introductory American economics textbook, far outselling Marshall's *Principles* everywhere but in the Ivy League. See Robert Lampman, *Economists at Wisconsin, 1892–1992* (Madison: University of Wisconsin Press, 1993).

10. Harris's scholarly productivity owed much to his ability to direct graduate students as researchers for his books. At one celebrations dinner, the host is said to have remarked, to great laughter from the audience, "Seymour needs no introduction. All of you have either read or written his books." Despite his productivity, Harris was not well treated by the department: it took eighteen years for him to get tenure, and the stress produced a nervous breakdown when it was finally awarded. Kellers, *Making Harvard Modern*, 81 (on treatment).

11. Mason, "Harvard Department of Economics," 429.

12. On the *Crimson* poll, see John Bethell, "Frank Roosevelt at Harvard," *Harvard Magazine*, November–December, 1996, 48.

13. Mason, "Harvard Department of Economics," 401–2.

14. Galbraith, *A Life*, 45.

15. Ibid., 48.

16. Douglass Brown et al., *The Economics of the Recovery Program* (New York: McGraw-Hill, 1934).

17. "Harvard Experts Condemn the NRA," *The New York Times*, January 2, 1934, 16. Quotations from the book cited here all appear in *The Times*' article.

18. The letter was signed by John Cassels, Lauchlin Currie, John Crane, Robert Lamb, Alan Sweezy, and Raymond Walsh. See "Six Harvard Men Back Gold Policy," *The New York Times*, February 25, 1934, 2.

19. Viner, who later grew more conservative, was then working at the Treasury Department as a senior economist. He hired Currie and White as part of his "Freshman Brains Trust," in 1934, shortly before Galbraith arrived in Cambridge. Currie and White were good friends, and as early as 1932, in prefigurement of their coming influence on the New Deal, had written an important working paper on anti-inflationary policies that fully anticipated Keynes's *General Theory*. See David Laidler and Roger Sandilands, "An Early Harvard Memorandum on Anti-Depression Policies," *History of Political Economy*, Fall 2002, 515–32.

20. Galbraith, interview with author. By 1935–36, Galbraith says his networking had done the trick: forty students, many assured by other young instructors that agriculture was a "big thing" in the Roosevelt administration, enrolled. This proved to be too enthusiastic a success for the department, he adds, and Black was called in to serve as teacher with Galbraith as assistant.

But Harvard's course catalogs show Galbraith teaching only two graduate courses in 1934–35, both with Black—Econ 43, "Economics of Agriculture," and Econ 44, "Commodity Distribution and Prices"—and co-teaching only Econ 43 in 1935–36. In 1936–37, courses were renumbered, and he taught three courses: one on his own for undergraduates (Econ 71, "Economics of Agriculture"); and two for graduate students with Black, Econ 106, "Economics of Production," and Econ 107, "Commodity Prices and Distribution" (Harvard Course Catalogs, 1934–37, Harvard University Archives). Enrollment records for 1935–36 show his class had seven students, not forty (no figures for his 1934–35 or 1936–37 classes were found). But most graduate economics courses enrolled fewer than seven students; only three enrolled more than twenty and none more than thirty (*Report of 1936 Visiting Committee*, Board of Overseers, appendix II, 364–65, in Harvard University Archives). It would appear that the enrollment jump he describes thus actually was from a small graduate class in 1934–35 to his undergraduate class in his third year.

21. When Black arrived at Harvard in 1926, Harvard had three Ph.D. candidates in agricultural economics; by 1930, it had thirty-one, about half Cornell's number ("Candidates for Ph.D. Degree in Agricultural Economics," undated [1932?], box 52, Black Papers, Wisconsin Historical Society, Madison).

22. Galbraith, *A Life*, 55. For the "insulting economist" comment mentioned in the footnote, see Galbraith, introduction to *Economics for Agriculture: Selected Writings by John D. Black*, ed. James Calvin (Cambridge, Mass.: Harvard University Press, 1959).

23. J. K. Galbraith and J. D. Black, "The Quantitative Position of Marketing in the United States," *Quarterly Journal of Economics*, May 1935, 394–413. Black's interest in marketing grew out of a large project he was directing for the Social Science Research Council.

Galbraith's published pre-Harvard papers include "The Concept of Marginal

Land" (with G. M. Peterson), *Journal of Farm Economics*, April 1932; two monographs, *Honey Marketing in California* and *Economic Aspects of the Bee Industry*
(both with E. C. Voorhies and F. E. Todd), Giannini Foundation Research
Monographs (Davis: California Agricultural Experiment Station), July 1933
and September 1933, respectively; "Some Aspects of the Overseas Markets
for Canadian Honey," *Scientific Agriculture* (Ottawa, Ont.), December 1933;
"Branch Banking and Its Bearing on Agricultural Credit," *Journal of Farm
Economics*, April 1934; *California County Expenditures*, a new draft of several
chapters from his Ph.D. dissertation, Research Monograph of the Giannini
Foundation (see above), August 1934; and part II, sections III and VIII, of "A
Program for Permanently Tax-Delinquent and Tax-Reverted Land" (with K. H.
Parsons), Galbraith's study for the National Resources Board, Land Planning
Committee, in *Report on Land Planning* (Washington, D.C.: NRB, 1935).

24. Galbraith and Black, "The Quantitative Position of Marketing," 412–13.

CHAPTER 3: AMERICAN AGRICULTURE AND THE NEW DEAL

1. Schlesinger, *Coming of the New Deal*, 87.
2. See Theodore Saloutas, *The American Farmer and the New Deal* (Ames, Iowa:
   Iowa State University Press, 1982), 254. Ch. 18, "New Deal Farm Policy: An
   Appraisal," offers a well-balanced assessment.
3. The economics team was quietly assembled in the 1920s (ironically, but signifi-
   cantly) to deal with the chronic postwar depression in farm prices. On "best-
   established" economists, see Stephen Baskerville, "Cutting Loose from
   Prejudice: Economists and the Great Depression," in Stephen Baskerville and
   Ralph Willett, eds., *Nothing Else to Fear: New Perspectives on America in the
   Thirties* (Manchester, England: Manchester, 1985), 276. Arthur Schlesinger and
   William Leuchtenberg in their seminal works underscore agriculture's critical
   importance in FDR's thinking and in the evolution of New Deal attitudes.
4. On Brookings' attitude toward the New Deal, which at first was warm, then
   cooled quickly, see James Smith, *The Idea Brokers: Think Tanks and the Rise of
   the New Policy Elite* (New York: Free Press, 1991), ch. 4.
5. See Galbraith and Black, "The Production Credit System of 1933," *American
   Economic Review*, June 1936, 235–47; Galbraith, "The Federal Land Banks and
   Agricultural Stability," *Journal of Farm Economics*, February 1937, 48–58; Galbraith, Macy, and Malenbaum, "Farm Mortgage Loan Repayment," *Journal of
   Farm Economics*, August 1937, 764–82; Galbraith, "The Farmer's Banking System: Four Years of FCA Operations," *Harvard Business Review*, Spring 1937,
   313–20; and Galbraith and Black, "The Maintenance of Agricultural Production
   during the Depression," *Journal of Political Economy*, June 1938, 305–23.
6. Schlesinger, *Coming of the New Deal*, 42–44 (lynch mob, "Russia now"); 27
   (revolution in countryside).
7. See Murray Benedict, *Farm Policies of the United States, 1790–1950* (New York:
   Twentieth Century Fund, 1953), for overview. FDR's Republican cousin
   Theodore set many of the precedents for the New Deal's regulatory policies.
   Basing his decision on both claims to "scientific management" and the imperatives of conservation, TR oversaw creation of the Agricultural Extension Service
   and passage of the Newlands Reclamation Act, a significant revision to Lincoln's
   Homestead Act, and a host of other measures. Even price supports predated the
   New Deal: under Woodrow Wilson, Congress passed the Corn Production Act,

which guaranteed minimum prices and used the wartime Food Administration to oversee agricultural production, marketing, and distribution, and the 1919 Cotton Reduction Act foreshadowed the New Deal's AAA. Having served as the head of the Food Administration, Hoover was—as his own backing for the Federal Farm Board shows—far less anti-"interventionist" than Harding or Coolidge. See Keller, *Regulating a New Economy*, ch. 7, on policies in early twentieth century.

8. Galbraith, *A Life*, 60.

9. See Lionel Robbins, *An Essay on the Nature and Significance of Economic Science*, 2nd ed. (London: Macmillan, 1935).

10. Galbraith, "Farmer's Banking System," 313–20.

11. Galbraith et al., "Farm Mortgage Loan Repayment," 764–82.

12. Galbraith, "Farmer's Banking System," 321.

13. Galbraith and Black, "Maintenance of Agricultural Production," 322–23.

14. See Mancur Olson, *The Logic of Collective Action: Public Goods and the Theory of Groups* (Cambridge, Mass.: Harvard University Press, 1971).

15. See John Kenneth Galbraith, *The Anatomy of Power* (Boston: Houghton Mifflin, 1983). The book got, predictably, much better reviews from sociologists and political scientists than economists.

16. Galbraith, *A Life*, 35. Though Galbraith made getting an AAA job sound easy, in fact the agency was overwhelmed with applicants: in its first two weeks, it received 25,000 job applications, according to the AAA's first director. See George Peek and Samuel Crowther, *Why Quit Our Own* (New York: Van Nostrand, 1936), 104–5.

17. Galbraith and Parsons, "Program for Per Monthy Tax-Delinquent Land," *Report on Land Planning*.

18. Galbraith, *A Life*, 37.

19. Ibid., 36–37.

20. Schlesinger, *Coming of the New Deal*, 46. For the history of the American Farm Bureau's role in the 1930s cotton issue, see Christina McFayden Campbell, *The Farm Bureau and the New Deal: A Study of the Making of National Farm Policy, 1933–40* (Urbana: University of Illinois Press, 1962), ch. 3.

21. Schlesinger, *Coming of the New Deal*, 48.

22. On the divisions among AAA staffers, see Saloutas, *American Farmer and the New Deal*, ch. 4. Tolley himself said of the "Pragmatists" around Wallace, "I belonged to that group if I belonged to any" (quoted in Saloutas, *American Farmer*, 82).

23. Black personally was neither indifferent to nor unaware of conditions tenants and sharecroppers endured. In the late 1920s he had written a study of migrant farm labor conditions for the Rosenwald Fund (created by the Sears Roebuck magnate Julius Rosenwald). In 1934–35, the fund carried out a new study of tenants and sharecroppers, to which he contributed. The study got extensive press coverage for its documentation of the dire condition of Southern farm laborers and its call for a "complete reformation of the South's land tenure system." On the 1920s study, see Rosenwald Fund Papers, box 14, Black Papers, Wisconsin Historical Society, Madison; on the Rosenwald Fund's sharecropper study, see "South's Land Evils Assailed in Report," *The New York Times*, March 21, 1935, 25.

24. Wallace quoted in Hession and Sardy, *Ascent to Affluence*, 725.

25. See Katie Louchheim, ed., *The Making of the New Deal: The Insiders Speak*

(Cambridge, Mass.: Harvard University Press, 1983), 239. The young lawyer quoted is Alger Hiss.

26. On the 700,000 evicted, see Hession and Sardy, *Ascent to Affluence*, 726; see Schlesinger, *Coming of the New Deal*, ch. 7, esp. 77–83, and H. I. Richards, *Cotton and the AAA* (Washington, D.C.: Brookings Institution, 1936), ch. 9, on the 1934 tenant battle and its consequences for the AAA.

27. Michael Barone, *Our Country: The Shaping of America from Roosevelt to Reagan* (New York: Free Press, 1990), 121.

28. Tolley Papers, Columbia University Oral History Project Microforms (Lamont), microfiche W 286, vol. 2, 347–48, 349–50.

29. Schlesinger, *Coming of the New Deal*, 71.

CHAPTER 4: GETTING READY FOR KEYNES

1. Galbraith, *A Life*, 50.

2. See Hession and Sardy, *Ascent to Affluence*, 636; for more details, see R. L. Nelson, *Merger Movements in American Industry, 1859–1956* (Princeton: Princeton University Press, 1959), 61.

3. Robert Triffin, *Monopolistic Competition and General Equilibrium Theory* (Cambridge, Mass.: Harvard University Press, 1940), 17.

4. Galbraith, "Monopoly Power and Price Rigidities," *Quarterly Journal of Economics*, May 1936, 472.

5. Ibid., 474.

6. Berle and Means quoted in Jordan Schwarz, *Liberal: Adolf A. Berle and the Vision of an American Era* (New York: Free Press, 1987), 60.

7. See Adolf Berle, assisted by Gardiner C. Means, "Corporations and the Public Investor," *American Economic Review*, March 1930, 71.

8. Schwarz, *Liberal*, 67.

9. Preface to Berle and Means, *The Modern Corporation and Private Property*, quoted in ibid., 67.

10. Review quoted in ibid., 59–62.

11. See W. C. Crum, "On the Alleged Concentration of Economic Power," *American Economic Review*, March 1934, 69–87. It should be noted that Berle's views were influenced by one of Crum's former colleagues, William Z. Ripley, who chose to leave the Economics Department for the Harvard Business School. In 1927, Ripley's critical analysis of corporate finance, *Main Street and Wall Street* (Boston; Little, Brown, 1927), had stirred a debate after it was serialized in *The Atlantic Monthly*.

12. Galbraith, *Economics in Perspective* (Boston: Houghton Mifflin, 1987), 198–99.

13. See Henry Dennison, "The Need for Development of Political Science Engineering," *American Political Science Review*, April 1932, 241–55, for a sample of his thinking. For evaluation of his views, see Kim McQuaid, "Henry S. Dennison and the 'Science' of Industrial Reform, 1900–1950," *American Journal of Economics and Sociology*, January 1977, 79–98.

14. Galbraith, *A Life*, 64–65 (on Dennison and his group).

15. Ibid., 63.

16. See ibid., 64. The idea that Galbraith sought only "increased competition" seems peculiar in light of the two papers he'd just written in which he called for "smoothing" prices by accepting (indeed, broadening) oligopolistic behavior, and his rejection of antitrust.

17. Ibid., 65.

18. Ibid.

19. Ibid., 66.

20. Ibid.

21. Henry Dennison and John Kenneth Galbraith, *Modern Competition and Business Policy* (New York: Oxford University Press, 1938), 105–7. For an assessment of Dennison's influence on Galbraith, see Kyle Bruce, "Conflict and Conversion: Henry S. Dennison and the Shaping of John Kenneth Galbraith's Economic Thought," *Journal of Economic Issues,* Winter 2000, 949–67, and Bruce's chapter, "The Making of a Heterodox Economist: The Impact of Henry S. Dennison on the Economic Thought of John Kenneth Galbraith," in Michael Keaney, ed., *Economist with a Public Purpose: Essays in Honor of John Kenneth Galbraith* (New York: Routledge, 2001), 25–50.

22. See, for example, Kenneth D. Roose, "The Recession of 1937–38," *Journal of Political Economy,* June 1948, 239–48.

23. Horace White, review, *Modern Competition and Business Policy,* by Dennison and Galbraith, *American Economic Review,* December 1938, 755–56.

24. Samuelson quoted in Lamson, *Speaking of Galbraith,* 39.

25. Samuelson quoted in Galbraith, "How Keynes Came to America," in *Economics, Peace and Laughter,* 49. David Colander and Harry Landreth, *The Coming of Keynesianism to America* (Cheltenham, England: Edward Elgar, 1996), interview a dozen of Keynes's American pioneers (including Galbraith). David Laidler, *Fabricating the Keynesian Revolution* (New York: Cambridge University Press, 1999), carefully sifts through the interwar pre-Keynesian antecedents to *The General Theory.* Don Patinkin, "Keynes and Econometrics," *Econometrica,* November 1976, 1091–1123, is especially good on Keynes and the emergence of national income accounting, and on Keynes's prickly, skeptical views toward econometrics and mathematical modeling more generally. Donald Winch, *Economics and Policy in Historical Perspective* (New York: Walker, 1970), still gives one of the best overall introductions to *The General Theory*'s impact.

26. See Swedberg, *Joseph A. Schumpeter,* 118–19.

27. Bertrand Russell, *Autobiography,* 2 v. (Boston: Little, Brown, 1951), v. 1, 97.

28. Keynes quoted in Winch, *Economics and Policy,* 189.

29. Samuelson quoted in ibid., 187.

30. See John Hicks, "Mr. Keynes and the 'classics': a suggested reinterpretation," *Econometrica,* April 1937, 147–59, and W. A. Young, *Interpreting Mr. Keynes: The IS-LM Enigma* (Cambridge: Polity Press, 1987).

31. Lamson, *Speaking of Galbraith,* 43.

32. "Manhasset Bridal for Miss Atwater," *The New York Times,* September 18, 1937, 16.

33. Lamson, *Speaking of Galbraith,* 43.

CHAPTER 5: GOING TO THE TEMPLE

1. Galbraith, *A Life,* 73.

2. See Hession, *John Maynard Keynes,* 302–8. Robert Skidelsky, *John Maynard Keynes: Fighting for Freedom 1937–1946* (New York: Viking Press, 2000), ch. 1 goes into much greater detail on his health and treatments.

3. Galbraith, *A Life,* 70.

4. Ibid., 74.

5. Oddly, SSRC's records list Galbraith as a Ph.D. from the University of Chicago. For the quoted description of the purpose of his fellowship see the 1937–38 Social Science Research Council, *Annual Report*, 11.

6. Galbraith, *A Life*, 79.

7. See the letters between Galbraith and Harold Burbank, in Economics Department Files, Correspondence, 1937, Pusey Archives, Harvard University.

8. "It was pretty awful because, before we got to Cambridge, England, I had never heard of John Maynard Keynes, and *The General Theory* had just been published, and all I met were his [Ken's] economist friends. So you know I was quite quiet and so I decided one day after we were talking about *The General Theory*, given I was supposed to be fairly intelligent, to pick it up. I started with the introduction, but early on in the book he explains that he hasn't quite thought through all his ideas. So I thought, I'll wait until he writes his next book, and that's where my economics rested. There was a lecture 'Is There a Rate of Interest?' and I thought that if these people don't know there is a rate of interest, why do they talk about it? And forty years later that same lecture was on the bulletin board in Cambridge because in a lecture someone asked a lecturer 'Is there a rate of interest?' " (Catherine Galbraith interview in Stephen Dunn, "The Origins of the Galbraithian System," *Journal of Post-Keynesian Economics*, Spring 2002, 351).

9. Catherine Galbraith, interview with author.

10. Calculated from citations of Keynes in economics journals, 1934–40, in JSTOR, the Mellon Foundation–funded Web site of academic journals.

11. On Eccles, see Sidney Hyman, *Marriner S. Eccles: Private Entrepreneur and Public Servant* (Palo Alto, Calif.: Stanford University Press, 1976) and Marriner Eccles, *Beckoning Frontiers* (New York: Knopf, 1951); on Currie, see Roger Sandilands, *The Life and Political Economy of Lauchlin Currie* (Durham, N.C.: Duke University Press, 1990). Currie's work as a Keynesian fifth-columnist turned sour after the war, when various congressional committees subpoenaed him, charging without impressive foundation that his loyalties had been much further to the left. Currie departed for Venezuela, where he became a wealthy rancher, businessman, and economic adviser to the government. He died in 1984.

12. See Richard Gilbert et al., *An Economic Program for American Democracy* (New York: Vanguard, 1938). Shortly before Currie became his White House adviser, FDR created a temporary Monetary and Fiscal Advisory Board, describing its purview as "the whole range of a great many problems that relate to fiscal and monetary policies in respect to sound and orderly recovery, and conditions essential to avoiding the peaks and valleys of booms and depressions."

   The Board's creation predates by eight years the President's Council of Economic Advisors, which came into being only under Truman, as part of the Employment Act of 1946. It testifies to the speed with which, after "the Little Depression" of 1937–38, "Keynesian" thinking began to permeate White House economic policy (Franklin D. Roosevelt, *The Public Papers and Addresses of Franklin D. Roosevelt*, compiled by Samuel Rosenman, 13 vol. [New York: Random House, 1938–1950] v. 7, 602).

13. See James Roosevelt to FDR, February 2, 1939, and FDR's reply, February 12, 1939, in Elliott Roosevelt, *FDR: His Personal Letters* (New York: Duell, Sloane,

1950), v. 4, 857–58. The Gilbert book in fact wasn't a summary of pre-Keynesian thinking or the early New Deal record, but FDR's enthusiasm for it in late 1938 shows how far he had evolved in his views.

14. See Lauchlin Currie, "The Keynesian Revolution and Its Pioneers," and Alan Sweezy, "The Keynesians and Government Policy: 1933–1939," in *American Economic Review*, May 1972, 116–24 and 134–41.

15. Keynes, letter to Roosevelt, February 1, 1938, quoted in Hession, *John Maynard Keynes*, 305–6.

16. The economist Don Patinkin notes of Keynes, "For some periods of his life . . . it would be more appropriate to say that in addition to being a publicist he was also an economist." The historian of economics Wayne Parsons commented, "Certainly, it is the case that Keynes's views on economic policy actually predate the attempt to formulate a theoretical model which could win over academic economists. And, as far as Keynes was concerned, the activity of theoretical proof was closely related to that of convincing those who disagreed with him. . . . There is a sense in which it could be argued that all of Keynes's work was essentially journalistic; that is, concerned with current problems and events. This must include *The General Theory* itself." See Patinkin's quote and Parsons's comments in Wayne Parsons, *The Power of the Financial Press* (Aldershot, England: Elgar, 1989), 52–53.

17. In "How to Pay for the War" Keynes proposed to prevent wartime inflation by siphoning off excessive consumer demand through compulsory savings; to provide universal family allowances paid in cash; to link wage and pension increases to a price index keyed to rational consumer goods; to maintain low interest rates; and to have a general levy on capital at the end of the war to help pay off the national debt. Not all of this became British policy, although interest rates were kept low, pay was deferred through forced savings (though less than he proposed), and family credits were provided. Keynes thought his proposals were applicable beyond wartime, "a first installment of a comprehensive social policy to regulate the general level of spending so as to avoid the disastrous alternations of boom and slump which will otherwise continue to undermine the foundations of society" (Hession, *Keynes*, 314–16). Skidelsky, *Keynes, Fighting for Freedom*, chs. 3 and 4, offers greater detail and works to convince us of Keynes's "middle way" approach to war finance.

18. Galbraith, *A Life*, 79.

19. Robert Solow, interview with author.

20. Galbraith, "Fiscal Policy and the Employment-Investment Controversy," *Harvard Business Review*, Autumn 1939, 27.

21. Ibid., 29.

22. Hansen to Galbraith, October 17, 1939, General Correspondence, box 5, Galbraith Papers, JFK Library.

23. Galbraith, *A Life*, 80.

24. Ibid., 81. On the influence of Myrdal's *An American Dilemma*, see the special issue of *Daedalus* devoted to it and its legacy, Winter 1995.

25. On his European travels during his year in Cambridge, Galbraith, *A Life*, 79–89, and Catherine Galbraith, interview with author.

26. Ibid., 86.

27. The following summer, Galbraith published his research as "Hereditary Land in the Third Reich," *Quarterly Journal of Economics*, August 1939, 465–76.

28. See "William A. Galbraith and Murray McNeil Killed by Wabash Train at Crossing," *The Dutton Advance*, January 17, 1938. The article noted that Archie "was the father of Kenneth Galbraith, one of the most brilliant young men Canada has produced."

CHAPTER 6: MOVING ON—TOWARD WAR

1. Galbraith, *A Life*, 96.
2. For the events surrounding The Walsh/Sweezy affair, see *The Harvard Crimson*, 1937–38; Harvard University Corporation, Committee of Eight, "Report on the Terminating Appointments of Dr. J. R. Walsh and Dr. A. R. Sweezy," May 1938, UAI10.500, Harvard University Archives; Irwin Ross, "The Tempest at Harvard," *Harper's*, October 1940, 544–52. The 131 faculty who signed the open letter, and its organizers, were all junior men (Committee of Eight, "Report," 16, 62). Headlines the first week after the announced firings included: "Labor Unionist Leaders Stir Harvard Row" (*Chicago Tribune*); "Leaders in Teachers Union Face End of Harvard Career" (*Baltimore Sun*); "Harvard Teachers Union Leaders to Lose Jobs" (*St. Louis Post-Dispatch*); and "Harvard Agitators to Lose Jobs" (*Los Angeles Times*). *The New Republic's* headline was "Harvard Starves the Social Sciences"; and *The Nation's*: "Economic Heresy at Harvard" (see ibid., 64–69).
3. On Conant's "teaching ability" rationale, see *The Crimson*, April 12, 13, 15, 1937, 1; on libel action threatened, *The Crimson*, April 16, 1937, 1; on formation of the Committee of Eight (originally nine, but Elmer Kohler died before their report was complete), *The New York Times*, May 28, 1937, 19. Committee of Eight, "Report," 13–17, offers a useful chronology.
4. Galbraith, *A Life*, 96–97 (a summary of the case). In Mason, "Harvard Department of Economics," 425–29, Mason (already tenured) shared Galbraith's skepticism about the "neutrality" of Harvard's decision.
5. On the reactions to the Committee of Eight's first report, in May 1938, see Ross, "Tempest at Harvard," 545–47. By then, Walsh and Sweezy had formally submitted their resignations, Walsh in September 1937, Sweezy in January 1938, although technically Conant originally had offered them two-year terminating appointments.
6. Hershberg, *James B. Conant*, 108–10, 117. (Hershberg, otherwise excellent, misidentifies the member of the faculty who petitioned Conant, and the name of one of the Committee of Eight.)
7. See Galbraith to Black, April 12, 1938, and Black to Galbraith, June 18, 1938, in box 7, Black Papers, Wisconsin State Historical Society, Madison. Black wrote candidly that in a private meeting, Conant had told him "there can be very few promotions in the Department in the next year or two. . . . He is aware of the serious consequences of letting very able young men go while hanging on to a good many relatively ineffectual full professors in their declining years but sees no way to help the situation." Black urged Galbraith to consider a job at the Department of Agriculture as acting head of the Division of Farm Finance, which Black was confident he could arrange.
8. In Galbraith's letter to Stanley Howard, chairman of the Princeton Economics Department, April 13, 1939. It's clear he had been offered a job by Princeton; he wanted to make sure that it was a tenure-track offer, argued for a higher salary, noted that he had offers from the University of Pennsylvania and a second, un-

named, school, and said that Harvard might still vote to keep him. See Galbraith to Howard, April 13, 1939, in General Correspondence, box 5, Galbraith Papers, JFK Library.

9. Galbraith, *A Life*, 97.

10. Mason, "Harvard Department of Economics," 428. Several of the generally conservative economists went to great efforts to help those whom Conant let go. Harold Burbank, for example, actively sought good jobs for them. After Galbraith moved to Princeton, W. L. Crum was telling Yale of his merits, describing him as "a brilliant man" and "a very brilliant teacher, . . . [with] an unusual capacity for getting a grip on students and writes well," although, he added, it was "difficult to agree with him on some of his views but that may merely reflect the fact that my views come largely from what is now called the horse and buggy era." To Johns Hopkins, Crum wrote that "Galbraith came to us from California with very high recommendations and in all respects lived up to them. We were immensely pleased with his performance and . . . deeply regret our having failed, largely because of budgetary difficulties, to compete against the Princeton offer" (Crum to Westerfield, December 20, 1939; Crum to Johns Hopkins, no date [1940–41?], Department of Economics files, Harvard University Archives).

11. The other adviser was Beardsley Ruml, a brilliant businessman and economic theorist who helped to advance his own variant of "Keynesianism." See Robert Collins, *The Business Response to Keynes, 1929–1964* (New York: Columbia University Press, 1981), 84 (on Ruml and CED, where he became the group's "most fecund idea-man and intellectual catalyst").

12. Broadus Mitchell, *Depression Decade* (New York: Rinehart, 1947), 44.

13. Hession and Sardy, *Ascent to Affluence*, 741.

14. National Resources Planning Board, *The Economic Effects of the Federal Public Works Expenditures, 1933–1938* (Washington, D.C.: NRPB, June 1940). Roosevelt's order for the study, dated January 26, 1939, is quoted in the study's transmittal letter to the President.

15. Galbraith, *A Life*, 94.

16. See National Resources Planning Board, *The Structure of the American Economy*, parts I and II (Washington, D.C.: NRPB, 1939). Part I, written by Means, set out his arguments and analysis; Part II included the views of Hansen, John Maurice Clark, and Mordecai Ezekiel. The debates between Means and Hansen, and Means and Keynes—and their significance for the triumph of Keynesianism—are discussed in Theodore Rosenof, *Economics in the Long Run: New Deal Theorists and Their Legacies, 1933–1993* (Chapel Hill: University of North Carolina Press, 1997), ch. 6. See also Philip Warken, *A History of the NRPB, 1933–1943* (New York: Garland Press, 1979).

17. On Keynes and Means, see Rosenof, *Economics in the Long Run*, 69–74. Oddly, Skidelsky's magisterial biography of Keynes ignores the entire exchange; indeed, he fails to mention Means and Hansen, despite the latter's being America's first eminent Keynesian.

18. Rosenof insightfully though incompletely observes that Galbraith can be viewed as "the pivotal figure in both the Meansian institutionalist and Hansensian Keynesian Traditions . . . after World War II" because he was "something of an institutionalist in his stress on corporate structure and power; he also continued and amplified Hansen's emphasis on public versus private use of resources." Rosenof also notes that although Galbraith "continued" the two disparate

positions—reflecting Means in *The New Industrial State* and Hansen in *The Affluent Society*—he developed his own ideas in the context not of the Depression but of the abundant 1950s and 1960s. In suggesting that this focus on abundance is what made Galbraith so vulnerable to critics in the 1970s, when stagflation appeared, Rosenof fails to contextualize the larger collapse of mainstream Keynesianism, which makes the matter more complex (see Rosenof, *Economics in the Long Run*, 126–27).

19. In a retrospective evaluation, Galbraith's NRPB study is cited as one of two key federal studies that exemplified the "self-confident, crusading spirit" of the administration's young Keynesians (see Alan Sweezy, "The Keynesians and Government Policy, 1933–1939," *American Economic Review*, 1972, 122).

20. Galbraith, *A Life*, 97. Albert Einstein, who lived and worked in Princeton in those years, shared some of Galbraith's feelings about Princeton, calling it "a wonderful little spot, a quaint and ceremonious village of puny demigods on stilts" (quoted in Otto Nathan and Heinz Norden, eds., *Einstein on Peace* [New York: Simon & Schuster, 1960], 245).

21. Galbraith to Aaron Gordon, February 28, 1940, General Correspondence, box 5, Galbraith Papers, JFK Library.

22. Galbraith to Henry Wallace, "Memorandum to the Secretary of Agriculture," October 1939, General Correspondence, box 5, Galbraith Papers, JFK Library.

23. Poll cited in Michael Barone, *Our Country: The shaping of America from Roosevelt to Reagan*, 128.

24. Black to Galbraith, February 22, 1940, Early Government Service, box 10, Galbraith Papers, JFK Library.

25. Galbraith, *A Life*, 101.

26. Ibid., 99.

27. Ibid., 102.

28. Poll data cited in William Manchester, *The Glory and the Dream*, 2 v. (Boston: Little, Brown, 1974), v. 1, 276.

29. Galbraith, *A Life*, 109.

30. Ibid., 106.

31. David Brinkley, *Washington Goes to War* (New York: Knopf, 1988), 133.

32. Galbraith, *A Life*, 109.

33. See William O'Neill, *A Democracy at War: America's Fight at Home and Abroad in World War II* (New York: Free Press, 1993), ch. 5, on Washington's haphazard preparations for war. A year before he created NDAC, Roosevelt had authorized formation of the War Resources Board in May 1939, but the first New Deal attempt at war planning lasted only seven months. Key New Dealers including Currie opposed it because it was dominated by businessmen, and FDR's political advisers felt it hurt him among voters still clinging to neutrality (O'Neill, 75–79).

34. Galbraith, *A Life*, 110.

35. Galbraith to Princeton's Dean Root, February 14, 1941, Early Government Service, box 2, Galbraith Papers, JFK Library. Galbraith had told Root in 1940 that he'd left the American Farm Bureau for war work in Washington, and Root had replied that "your new plans have our full approval" (Galbraith to Root, August 5, 1940, and Root to Galbraith, August 15, 1940, Early Government Service, box 1, Galbraith Papers, JFK Library).

36. Galbraith to O'Neal, August 30, 1940. Early Government Service, box 1, Galbraith Papers, JFK Library.

37. *Public Papers of Franklin D. Roosevelt, 1940* (Washington, D.C.: GPO, 1941), 568–69.

38. "Germans Don't Wait," *The New Republic*, September 30, 1940, 446.

39. Alan Brinkley, "The Idea of the State," in Steve Frazer and Gary Gerstle, *The Rise and Fall of the New Deal Order* (Princeton, N.J.: Princeton University Press, 1989), 93.

40. "Mr. Mumford and the Liberals," *The New Republic*, April 29, 1940, 564.

41. FDR in Boston, quoted in Barone, *Our Country*, 141.

42. O'Neill, *Democracy at War*, 31.

43. See Arnold Offner, *The Origins of the Second World War* (New York: Praeger, 1975), ch. 7; O'Neill, *Democracy at War*, 18.

44. Transcript of Roosevelt's fireside chat, *The New York Times*, May 12, 1940, 12.

45. Galbraith to Twaddle, August 30, 1940, Early Government Service, box 1, Galbraith Papers, JFK Library.

46. Galbraith, *A Life*, 111.

47. Ibid., 111.

48. See Galbraith, "The Economic Effects of the Federal Public Works Expenditures, 1933–1938," especially ch. 2 and 48–51.

49. Galbraith to Davis, August 15, 1940, Early Government Service, box 1, and untitled speech (probably written for Davis), April 10, 1941, Early Government Service, box 2, Galbraith Papers, JFK Library.

50. Galbraith, *A Life*, 111.

51. Ibid., 111–12.

52. "Asserts Goodyear Aided in Violence," *The New York Times*, July 12, 1936, 8.

53. Galbraith, *A Life*, 113.

54. Ibid., 114.

55. Ibid.

56. Ibid., 114–15. For a third-party account, see Harold Stein, *Public Administration and Policy Development: A Case Book* (New York: Harcourt, Brace, 1952).

57. Eliot Janeway, *The Struggle for Survival* (New Haven: Yale University Press, 1951), 12–13. On the early efforts at economic mobilization, see Lester Chandler and Donald Wallace, eds., *Economic Mobilization and Stabilization* (New York: Holt, 1951), and David Novick et al., *Wartime Production Controls* (New York: Columbia University Press, 1949).

58. Ibid., 162.

59. Ibid., 244.

60. Galbraith, *A Life*, 122; Catherine Galbraith, interview with author.

CHAPTER 7: NOW COMES WAR

1. Joseph Goebbels, *The Goebbels Diaries, 1939–1941* (New York: Putnam, 1983), 336.

2. Barone, *Our Country*, 134–35.

3. On Huxley, see Ronald Clark, *The Huxleys* (New York: McGraw-Hill, 1968).

4. See Galbraith, "Memorandum to Mr. Huxley," December 15, 1939, in Early Government Service, box 2, Galbraith Papers, JFK Library. (There is no reply from Huxley in the papers.) One feature of Galbraith's surviving correspondence

from before Pearl Harbor is how little he mentions the war. His memoirs make no mention of this letter-memorandum.

5. Not surprisingly, O'Neal accepted Galbraith's resignation regretfully. See O'Neal to Galbraith, December 18, 1940, Early Government Service, box 3, Galbraith Papers, JFK Library.

6. For examples, see Black's note to Galbraith, February 5, 1941, Early Government Service, box 2, Galbraith Papers, JFK Library, about lecturing at joint meetings of Black's Agriculture Seminar and Hansen's Fiscal Policy Seminar. Galbraith also taught a Harvard summer-school session in June 1940; the subject is lost. Throughout, Galbraith oscillated between being an agricultural expert and a macroeconomist. See conference program, George Washington University, March 14, 1941 (Early Government Service, box 2, Galbraith Papers, JFK Library), at which Galbraith spoke on "Agriculture and the Defense Program." Other panelists on defense and various economic issues included Hansen, Gardiner Means, John Maurice Clark, and Richard Gilbert; Arthur Burns chaired.

7. Alvin Hansen, "Defense Financing and Inflation Potentialities," *Review of Economic Statistics*, February 1941, 1–7.

8. On price rises, see Richard Lingeman, *Don't You Know There's a War On?* (New York: Putnam, 1970), 269.

9. Galbraith, "Memorandum to Professor Alvin H. Hansen," February 13, 1941, Early Government Service, box 3, Galbraith Papers, JFK Library.

10. Galbraith, "The Selection and Timing of Inflation Controls," *Review of Economic Statistics*, May 1941, 82–85. The article is a revised version of the memo.

11. O'Neill, *Democracy at War*, 84.

12. Ibid., 84–85.

13. Ibid., 85.

14. Galbraith, *A Life*, 124–25.

15. Catherine Galbraith, interview with author. She had already boxed up their Princeton belongings the year before in preparation for Chicago; then she found a furnished apartment in Washington, waiting to see what came of the NDAC assignments. Hoping to escape the worst of Washington's heat, she'd worked out a move to summer quarters on Seminary Hill in Alexandria. At summer's end they moved once again, to a house on P. Street, in Georgetown, where they settled in for three years.

16. For overviews of OPA and related issues of management of the wartime economy, see Novick, *Wartime Production Controls* and Chandler and Wallace, *Economic Mobilization and Stabilization*. See also Harvey C. Mansfield et al., *A Short History of the OPA* (Washington, D.C.: Office of Temporary Controls, OPA, 1948), and Seymour Harris, *Price and Related Controls* (New York: McGraw-Hill, 1945). Donald Nelson, *Arsenal of Democracy* (New York: Harcourt, Brace, 1946) gives a personal account of the controversial executive director's work at OPM (ch. 9 deserves reading because Galbraith gave Nelson extensive comments on it before publication).

17. The concentration of the government's contracts in a handful of companies was investigated by a Senate committee chaired by Harry Truman in the middle of the war. Just fifty-six companies, it found, controlled 75 percent of the value of all federal war-related contracts, which perforce had a marked effect on the

overall shape of the economy. Given the size both of those contracts and of overall federal spending (half of GDP during the war), the growth of big business's share of the economy was dramatic. In 1940, 175,000 firms accounted for 70 percent of manufacturing outputs; by 1943, 100 firms controlled 70 percent. See John Morton Blum, *V Was for Victory* (New York: Harcourt Brace Jovanovich, 1976), 123.

18. Detroit's use of resources and Henderson's remark are from Doris Kearns Goodwin, *No Ordinary Time: Franklin and Eleanor Roosevelt* (New York: Simon & Schuster, 1994), 231–32.

19. Ibid., 225–31.

20. Taft quoted in Richard Polenberg, *War and Society* (Philadelphia: Lippincott, 1972), 185.

21. Galbraith, *A Life*, 142.

22. Ibid., 139.

23. Ibid., 134–35. Government price controls didn't start in November when OPA was finally established; Roosevelt had already given that (legally dubious) power to OPACS in his executive order establishing it in the spring. Price ceilings had thus been set before Pearl Harbor on machine tools and a few other war-related items, but the consumer markets (apart from sugar and textiles) were left untouched until war began in December. The prewar controls worked smoothly enough, but largely because there was excess capacity in each market or because oligopolies were in control. ("It is easiest to administer administered prices," Ken quipped in one of his memos to Henderson.) By November, Galbraith warned presciently that danger lay ahead, and he urged Henderson to prepare for civilian rationing as well as expanded price limits (Galbraith to Henderson, November 19, 1941, in Early Government Service, box 3, Galbraith Papers, JFK Library).

24. Galbraith to Henderson, August 17, 1942, Early Government Service, box 4, Galbraith Papers, JFK Library.

25. Eleanor Roosevelt, Winston Churchill, and FDR quoted in Goodwin, *No Ordinary Time*, 288–91. "Day" became "date" in FDR's final text.

26. Galbraith, *A Life*, 146.

27. Ibid., 147, and Galbraith, interview with author.

28. Galbraith, *Great Crash, 1929*, 139.

29. Marquis Childs, *I Write from Washington* (New York: Harper, 1942), 242.

30. Galbraith, *A Life*, 151–52. Galbraith's version in "A Letter to the Historian of the OPA from J. K. Galbraith, Sometime Assistant and Deputy Administrator for Prices of the OPA," unpublished memorandum, July 27, 1943, at 23–24, in the OPA Records, National Archives, tells a slightly different version of both the first commodity controls and the cottonseed clash.

31. Galbraith to Henderson, November 19, 1941, Early Government Service, box 4, Galbraith Papers, JFK Library.

32. Galbraith, "Letter to the Historian of the OPA," 25–29 ("went home," 28); see 152–55, for a slightly amended version, giving greater credit to the role of Harold Leventhal, an OPA lawyer. Galbraith, *A Life*.

33. The data on staffing are from Chester Bowles, *Promises to Keep* (New York: Harper & Row, 1971), 43. Bowles became director of OPA in the fall of 1943 and ran it until 1946. Budget data are from Mansfield, *Short History of the OPA*, 223.

34. For a revealing look at Nixon's time at OPA, and why for years he denied that he'd worked there, see Milton Viorst, "Nixon of the O.P.A.," *The New York Times Magazine*, October 3, 1971, 70 ff.

35. Goodwin, *No Ordinary Time*, 358.

36. O'Neill, *Democracy at War*, 92.

37. Galbraith, "Letter to the Historian of the OPA," 12–13. The *Fortune* poll of business attitudes is cited in O'Neill, *Democracy at War*, 101.

38. OPA, "Chronological Outline of Events and Situations in OPA History to July 1, 1943" (Washington, D.C.: OPA Historical Records Office, January 1944).

39. Personnel figure in unpublished memo from Galbraith to Prentiss Brown, "Informal Guide to the Price Operations of the Office of Price Administration," January 23, 1943, Early Government Service, box 2, Galbraith Papers, JFK Library.

40. Galbraith, *A Life*, 136.

41. Galbraith, "Personal Memorandum to Mr. Henderson," undated 1942, Early Government Service, box 2, Galbraith Papers, JFK Library.

42. Galbraith to Henderson, undated 1942, Early Government Service, box 2, Galbraith Papers, JFK Library.

43. OPA, "Chronological Outline," 21.

44. Galbraith, *A Life*, 167. The complexity of enforcing General Max is described in great detail in Galbraith to Brown, "Informal Guide."

45. Galbraith, "Letter to the Historian of the OPA," 52.

46. Henderson quoted in Goodwin, *No Ordinary Time*, 394.

47. Michael Straight, "Why Henderson Goes," *The New Republic*, December 28, 1942, 847.

48. I. F. Stone, *The War Years 1939–45* (Boston: Little, Brown, 1988), 144.

49. Galbraith, *A Life*, 180, and interview with author.

50. See ibid., 180–91 (on his final months at OPA).

51. "Galbraith, OPA's Price Chief, Quits in Middle of Maxon Feud," *The Washington Post*, June 1, 1943, 1. *The New York Times* ran the story on the front page of its business section as "Galbraith Quits As OPA Price Head," June 1, 1943, 21. (See *The New York Times Index 1943* for the various pre-firing stories cited.)

52. Lamson, *Speaking of Galbraith*, 71.

CHAPTER 8: LUCE, KEYNES, AND "THE AMERICAN CENTURY"

1. Robert Elson, *The World of Time, Inc.* (New York: Athaneum, 1973), xiv.

2. Ibid., 6.

3. Ibid.

4. Ibid.

5. Ibid., 9.

6. "The American Century," *Life*, February 17, 1941, 61–65.

7. Elson, *World of Time*, 18.

8. Quoted in Geoffrey Perrett, *Days of Sadness, Years of Triumph* (Baltimore: Penguin, 1973), 283.

9. Galbraith, *A Life*, 259.

10. Ibid., 258.

11. Dwight Macdonald, "Against the Grain," *Writing for Fortune* (New York: Time, Inc., 1980), 150.

12. Luce set up the Q unit after *Fortune*'s "Tenth Roundtable on Problems of Postwar Transition," the gathering of about thirty industrialists, union officials, and

government economists on September 5–7, 1941, at which Luce, Paine, and Galbraith first met. The group's reflections appear as a supplement in *Fortune*, November, 1941.

13. Robert Herzstein, *Henry R. Luce* (New York: Scribners, 2000), 269. The aide most worried about spies at Time, Inc., was Charles Stillman, who authored the crucial Q Department memo on Keynesianism.

14. See Elson, *World of Time*, 18–19. Though Luce eventually changed the name of this outfit to the more inoffensive "Postwar Department," he kept Raymond Buell as its director. Buell had been head of the Foreign Policy Association and had deeply impressed Luce with his book, *Isolated America*. In it, Buell declared, "If we want to, America can replace Britain as the world's dominant power. We should utilize our strength, not on behalf of imperialism or power politics, but in support of a new concept of world organization, which has become absolutely essential to the maintenance of democracy in the present age," sentiments Luce incorporated into "The American Century."

15. Stillman quoted in Elson, *World of Time*, 20–21.

16. Luce quoted in Herzstein, *Henry R. Luce*, 269–70. The larger contexts in which Luce's—and not just Luce's—ideas evolved are taken up in Charles Maier, "The Politics of Productivity," in Maier, ed., *The Cold War in Europe* (New York: Wiener, 1991), 169–201. Maier's argument is that for both domestic and international reasons, American elites gradually embraced a view of productivity and constant growth as an alternative to class-based politics and economic redistribution.

17. Galbraith, *A Life*, 256.

18. Ed Lockett to Ralph Paine, March 7, 1942, Galbraith File, Time, Inc., Archives, New York City.

19. Paine to Galbraith, April 16, 1942, Galbraith File, Time, Inc., Archives.

20. Galbraith to Paine, April 20, 1942, and Paine to Galbraith, May 7, 1942, Galbraith File, Time, Inc., Archives.

21. Paine to Galbraith, August 18, 1942, and Galbraith to Paine, August 21, 1942, Galbraith File, Time, Inc., Archives.

22. Galbraith to Paine, June 13, 1943, Galbraith File, Time, Inc., Archives.

23. Paine to Galbraith, telegram, June 21, 1943, Galbraith File, Time, Inc., Archives.

24. Galbraith to Stettinius, August 31, 1943, Early Government Service, box 5, Galbraith Papers, JFK Library.

25. Galbraith, *A Life*, 257.

26. Lamson, *Speaking of Galbraith*, 75.

27. [Galbraith], "Transition to Peace: Business in A.D. 194Q," *Fortune*, January 1944, 83ff.

28. See Paul Samuelson, "Full Employment After the War," in Seymour Harris, ed., *Postwar Economic Problems* (New York: McGraw-Hill, 1943), 53, and Samuelson, "Unemployment Ahead," *The New Republic*, September 10, 1945, 309–12.

29. Paine to W. D. Geer, office memorandum, December 22, 1943, Galbraith File, Time, Inc., Archives. Geer was *Fortune's* publisher.

30. "U.S.A. Goes Republican," *Life*, November 16, 1942, 33–40.

31. Barone, *Our Country*, 165–66.

32. Samuel Rosenman, *Working with Roosevelt* (New York: Harper Bros., 1952), 463–68.

33. Goodwin, *No Ordinary Time*, 526–27.

34. See Perrett, *Days of Sadness*, 291–94.

35. Yet labor did well during the war in dramatically expanding worker benefits such as health and pensions, which were not subject to the government-imposed wage limits. Prior to the war, fewer than 10 percent of workers had access to company-provided medical benefits. See Jacob Hacker, *The Divided Welfare State* (New York: Cambridge University Press, 2002) for a detailed history of this wartime policy and its postwar effects.

36. Alan Brinkley, "The Idea of the State," in *Rise and Fall of New Deal Order*, 103.

37. David Lilienthal, *The Journals of David Lilienthal*, 7 v. (New York: Harper & Row, 1964), v. 1, 43.

38. James Weschler, "The Last New Dealer," *Common Sense*, September 1943, 163–64.

39. On Galbraith's optimism, see his steady correspondence in 1944–46 with Chester Bowles, who replaced Prentiss Brown as head of the OPA in late 1943. In his letters he ranged from issues involving the economic theory behind price control to the political tactics for defending the OPA, down to such arcane details as the appropriate price ceiling for cattle and women's clothing. Bowles appreciated the letters and regularly sought out further advice. See, for example, Galbraith to Bowles, December 8 and 29, 1943, and June 4 and October 17, 1944, and Bowles to Galbraith, January 17, 1945, in General Correspondence, box 5, Galbraith Papers, JFK Library.

40. [Galbraith], "Public Regulation Is No Dilemma," *Fortune*, February 1944, 132–133.

41. [Galbraith], "Retreat from the Pentagon," *Fortune*, March 1944, 132–35.

42. [Galbraith], "Baron Keynes of Tilton," *Fortune*, May 1944, 147ff.

43. On *Time*, Friedman, and Nixon, see Herbert Stein, *Presidential Economics*, 113 and 135. Friedman insisted he was misquoted, according to Stein.

44. See "Lord Keynes' Bunk," January 1, 6, and "Bunkitas," August 17, 1943, 8, in *The Wall Street Journal* for representative samples of its opinion of Keynes.

45. Stein, *Presidential Economics*, 75; Walter Heller, "CED's Stabilizing Budget Policy After Ten Years," *American Economic Review*, September 1957, 634.

46. See Robert Collins, *The Business Response to Keynes, 1929–1964* (New York: Columbia University Press, 1964). NAM's views were summarized by its chief's declaration in 1943: "[T]he Hansen debt philosophy is a job-destroying concept . . . [T]hose who advocate socialistic proposals should do so openly." Another NAM official went further: "The Hansen theory should be hit and hit hard. Either industry will expose the Hansen theory, or extravagant government spending will be with us forever" (87–88).

47. Ibid., 88. For a larger view of the Chamber's attitudes toward Keynesianism, see chs. 4 and 5.

48. Benton to Galbraith, September 29, 1944, cited in ibid., 249, footnote 45; William Benton, "The Economics of a Free Society," *Fortune*, November 1944, 163ff.

49. *Fortune* Management Polls are from *Fortune*, November 1941, 12ff; October 1943, 12ff; and May 1944, 8ff. In the 1944 poll, 57 percent of top executives favored Thomas Dewey as President versus 8 percent who favored Roosevelt.

50. *Fortune* Management Poll, *Fortune*, August 1945, 20ff.

51. James A. Smith, *The Idea Brokers* (New York: Free Press, 1991), 108–9.

CHAPTER 9: SURVEYING THE CONSEQUENCES OF WAR

1. Goodwin, *No Ordinary Time*, 604–5.

2. On Roosevelt's death, see ibid., 601–4; the press reaction is in Manchester, *The Glory and the Dream*, v. 1, 426–32.

3. Galbraith was recruited by Paul Nitze, on the advice of George Ball, who had met Galbraith during the latter's brief sojourn at the Office of Lend-Lease Administration in the summer of 1943, when Ball was Lend-Lease's general counsel. He gave Nitze several possible names and added, "If you decide to tackle Ken Galbraith (who is now on the editorial staff of *Fortune*) you might mention my name as I know him quite well. Galbraith is an extremely energetic fellow of first rate intellectual capacity and a good deal of experience in running large research projects. He would, I think, do a very good job" (Ball to Nitze, February 3, 1945, quoted in MacIsaac, *Strategic Bombing in World War II* [New York: Garland, 1976], 96. Ball described his Bombing Survey days with Galbraith in his autobiography, *The Past Has Another Pattern* [New York: Norton, 1982], 42–68).

4. Galbraith, interview with author.

5. Goodwin, *No Ordinary Time*, 605 (on Churchill and Stalin).

6. Manchester, *Glory and the Dream*, v. 1, 433.

7. On bomb tonnage, see MacIsaac, *Strategic Bombing*, 107; the 1.4 million tons dropped on Germany was half the total dropped in Europe during the war.

8. Fred Ikle, *The Social Impact of Bomb Destruction* (Norman: University of Oklahoma Press, 1958), was the first major discussion of this issue. There is now a voluminous literature, with Ronald Schaeffer, *Wings of Judgment: American Bombing in World War II* (New York: Oxford University Press, 1985), among the most thoughtful studies. Wesley Craven and James Cate, eds., *The Army Air Force in World War II*, 7 v. (Washington, D.C.: Office of Air Force History, 1983) is the official version. Stephen Garrett, *Ethics and Airpower in World War II* (New York: St. Martin's Press, 1985), and Eric Markusen and David Kopf, *The Holocaust and Strategic Bombing: Genocide and Total War in the Twentieth Century* (Boulder, Colo.: Westview Press, 1995), are focused on the moral questions. The German writer W. G. Sebald has sparked intense debate with his reexamination of Allied bombing from the German perspective; see his *The Natural History of Destruction* (New York: Random House, 2003).

9. See Walter Isaacson and Evan Thomas, *The Wise Men* (New York: Simon & Schuster, 1986), 202–9. On Lovett and the origins of the USSBS, see MacIsaac, *Strategic Bombing*, chs. 3–4.

10. For a full account, see Robert Frank Futrell, *Ideas, Concepts, Doctrine: A History of Basic Thinking in the US Air Force, 1907–1964* (Maxwell Air Force Base, Ala.: Air University Press, 1974).

11. Many historians believe FDR "pulled the number out of the air." It appears, however, that General H. H. "Hap" Arnold, commander of the Army Air Corps, was the source (MacIsaac, *Strategic Bombing*, 11), though Isaacson and Thomas credit Lovett as the real mastermind. The figure of 1,700 planes in the 1940 Air Corps included *all* aircraft it controlled; General Marshall warned FDR that in fact he had only 160 combat-ready fighter planes, should war come. And these appalling deficiencies weren't the Air Corps's alone. Marshall exaggerated only slightly when he testified to Congress that the United States had 80,000 combat troops (O'Neill, *Democracy at War*, 18).

12. The Army Air Force's overall war operations plans were set out by its Air War Plans Division in a directive labeled AWPD-1, which remained the basic frame of AAF thinking throughout the war (Ray Cline, *Washington Command Post* [Washington, D.C.: Office of the Chief of Military History, 1951], especially 60–61).

13. On early Luftwaffe and RAF bombing experience, see Sir Charles Webster and Noble Frankland, *The Strategic Air Offensive Against Germany* (London: Her Majesty's Stationery Office, 1961), v. 1.

14. O'Neill, *Democracy at War*, 452, note 6.

15. Ibid., 306.

16. Ibid., 309.

17. On Arnold's willingness to accept horrific casualty levels in order to prove the value of strategic bombing, see Thomas Coffey, *Decision over Schweinfurt* (New York: David McKay, 1977), 265, and H. H. Arnold, *Global Mission* (New York: Harper Brothers, 1949), 294 and 495. The AAF's casualties were indeed horrific: 55,000 of America's total 291,000 battle deaths were in the Army Air Force; another 35,000 AAF personnel died from service-related accidents (O'Neill, *Democracy at War*, 309).

18. O'Neill, *Democracy at War*, 311–12.

19. See W. W. Rostow, *Pre-Invasion Bombing Strategy* (Austin: University of Texas Press, 1981).

20. On "small committee," see General Carl Spaatz's memo of April 5, 1944, quoted in MacIsaac, *Strategic Bombing*, 31; on discussions leading up to Spaatz's memo, dating back to early 1943, see ibid., ch. 2; on eventual size and organization of USSBS, see ibid., ch. 4.

21. Ibid., 44.

22. Ron Chernow, *The House of Morgan* (New York: Simon & Schuster, 1990), ch. 10 (on the firm's World War I role), ch. 27 (on Alexander).

23. For assessments of their importance, see Mark Blaug, *Great Economists Since Keynes* (London: Harvester, 1985).

24. One of the two safe crackers was Sergeant Paul Baran, a brilliant multilingual Russian refugee who had earned a doctorate from the Humboldt University in Berlin, studied economics as a postdoctoral student at Harvard, worked at the Brookings Institution, and for a time under Galbraith at the Office of Price Administration, before joining the Office of Strategic Services. Baran was a leading American Marxist, but thoroughly anti-Soviet, economist during the 1950s and 1960s.

    His Harvard connections were vital to his Berlin exploits in 1945. Through a German friend he had known in Cambridge, Baran was led to Albert Speer's chief economist and statistician, who gave him a 130-page report on the history of the Nazi economy up to the surrender; it was invaluable background for interviewing Speer. See James Beveridge, "History of the United States Strategic Bombing Survey," unpublished (on microfilm) (Washington, D.C.: Office of the Chief of Military History, July 1946), v. 2, frames 1037–42, and Paul Sweezy, ed., *Paul A. Baran: A Collective Portrait* (New York: Monthly Review Press, 1965), ch. 2.

25. USSBS, "The Effects of Strategic Bombing on the German War Economy," report (October 31, 1945), 278–79. Also useful is Burton Klein, *Germany's Economic Preparations for War* (Cambridge, Mass.: Harvard University Press, 1959),

which compares English, American, and German war production. Klein, Galbraith's deputy on the Bombing Survey, completed his Ph.D. thesis (which this book is, slightly revised) under Galbraith's supervision.

26. USSBS, "Effects of Strategic Bombing," 277. See also [Galbraith], "Germany Was Badly Run," *Fortune*, December 1945, 173ff. Galbraith's conclusions never became a subject for Luce's publications. During the war, Robert Lovett had convinced Luce, his fellow Yale Bonesman, of strategic bombing's effectiveness, and Luce's magazines and newsreels enthusiastically reflected Lovett's view (Isaacson and Thomas, *Wise Men*, 207).

27. USSBS, "Effects of Strategic Bombing," 283. The increase of German war production *after* Allied bombing began in earnest is impressive: of a total 30,000 Me-109s, the Luftwaffe's fabled fighter aircraft, built after 1939, half were built in 1944 and early 1945. Fourteen hundred Me-262s (the world's first jet fighter) were built in 1944 and 1945. Five thousand U-2 rockets were launched in the last months of the war; annual tank production rose from 3,000 to 17,000 between 1941 and 1944; munitions tonnage rose from 540,000 to 3,350,000 in the same period. In 1944 alone, Speer's war production machine produced enough for the Wehrmacht to equip or reequip 225 infantry and 45 armored divisions, more troops than it had in the field. See Dan Van Der Vat, *The Good Nazi: The Life and Lies of Albert Speer* (Boston: Houghton Mifflin, 1997), 177–79 and 197–98.

28. Galbraith and Ball described their encounter with Speer for *Life* magazine, in "The Interrogation of Albert Speer," December 17, 1945, 57–63; see also Galbraith, *A Life*, ch. 14. Galbraith's declassified notes of Speer's interrogation were published in "The Origin of the Document," *The Atlantic Monthly*, July 1979, 50–57. Speer provided his own version of his interrogation in Speer, *Inside the Third Reich* (New York: MacMillan, 1971), ch. 1.

29. D'Olier, Alexander, and a few others soon arrived for the interviews with Speer. The parties agreed to a slightly surreal schedule: Speer would attend the cabinet meetings of Dönitz's Potemkin government in the morning, then join the Americans at 2 p.m. for five hours of what Galbraith later called their "bombing university." (Speer arrogantly called it their "bombing high school.") One afternoon, Speer pulled out from under a table a dozen volumes of aerial photos mapping every hydroelectric facility in the western Soviet Union. "I give you this," he said, "because sooner or later, you are going to have to fight the Russians. It's too bad we Germans couldn't have made common cause with you. The Russians are the enemies of us both" (see Ball, *Past Has Another Pattern*, 54).

Paul Nitze makes no mention of Ball's or Galbraith's presence in his description of "my interrogation of Speer." He was convinced of air power's superiority and also does not mention Ball's and Galbraith's dissent, or their work on the final report. See Paul Nitze, *Hiroshima to Glasnost* (New York: Grove Weidenfeld, 1989), 32–34 and 16 (on Speer). An architect of Truman's Cold War policies and as author of NSC-68, Nitze was a Pentagon hawk during the Vietnam War and grew even more hard-line during the Reagan years. Galbraith maintained a pleasantly civil relation with him, but left no doubt about his views: Nitze became, he said, "a Teutonic martinet happiest in a military hierarchy" (Isaacson and Thomas, *Wise Men*, 484).

30. Ball, *Past Has Another Pattern*, 51–53.

31. Galbraith, *A Life*, 215.

32. MacIsaac, *Strategic Bombing*, 97–98.

33. Ibid., 99–102.

34. Ibid., 217–18. The Bombing Survey's complete papers, including working documents, take up nearly 1,000 linear feet in the National Archives; the index alone is over 300 pages long.

35. Galbraith, *A Life*, 226.

36. Ibid., 226–27.

37. Hanson Baldwin, "Civilians Gauge Air War," *The New York Times*, September 2, 1945, 18. On effect of this and Pearson article, see MacIsaac, *Strategic Bombing*, 139–41.

38. For Alexander's statement, Anderson's fears, and resulting newspaper headlines, see MacIsaac, *Strategic Bombing*, 141–43.

39. Ibid., 118 (on when cities were bombed); 107 (on comparative tonnage dropped [1.4 million tons hit Germany, 160,000 on Japan, excluding the two nuclear bombs], and the 22 percent that were directed at industrial targets). On the invention at Harvard of the magnesium-napalm bombs used, see John Bethell, "Harvard and the Art of War," *Harvard Magazine*, September–October 1995, 45.

40. MacIsaac, *Strategic Bombing*, 106.

41. USSBS, "The Effects of Strategic Bombing on Japan's War Economy" (Washington, D.C.: USSBS, December 1946), 2, 56.

42. USSBS, "Summary Report (Pacific War)" (Washington, D.C.: USSBS, Chairman's Office, July 1, 1946), 26.

43. See MacIsaac, *Strategic Bombing*, 204, note 12.

44. USSBS, "Air Campaigns of the Pacific War" (Washington, D.C.: USSBS Pacific, study no. 71a), 69.

45. USSBS, "Summary Report (Pacific War)" (Washington, D.C.: USSBS Pacific Report no. 1), 28.

46. MacIsaac, *Strategic Bombing*, 147.

47. [John Kenneth Galbraith], "Germany Was Badly Run," *Fortune*, December 1945, 173ff.

48. John Kenneth Galbraith and George Ball, "The Interrogation of Albert Speer," *Life*, November 22, 1945, 18–24.

49. A technical debate over Galbraith's conclusions developed later. See Emile Despres's critical review of the Galbraith report in *The Review of Economic Statistics*, November 1946, 253–56, and Galbraith's reply (with Paul Baran), *The Review of Economic Statistics*, May 1947, 132–34. Despres had been part of the Survey team.

50. [John Kenneth Galbraith], "Japan's Road Back," *Fortune*, March 1946, 132ff.

51. For an insightful summary of Koopmans's life and contributions to economics, see Jurg Niehans, *A History of Economic Theory* (Baltimore: Johns Hopkins University Press, 1990), 408–20. Koopmans became a powerful critic of much deterministic modeling—that is, the belief that given precise inputs, the programs could yield equally precise conclusions. At best, the answers were probabilistic, he argued. He was also a strong critic of the core neoclassical assumptions that markets optimize outcomes, and he frequently argued for the superiority of public allocation of resources.

52. On the use of mathematical modeling by the AAF in Europe, see Charles McArthur, "Operation Analysis in the U.S. Army Eighth Air Force in World War II," in *History of Mathematics* (New York: American Mathematical Society,

1990), v. 4. For its postwar effect—a vital yet curiously neglected part of the history of economics—and the ways in which Cold War military ambitions helped drive the new "mathematical" style, see Philip Mirowski, "Cyborg Agonistes: Economics Meets Operations Research in Mid-Century," *Social Studies of Science*, October 1999, 685–718, and Mirowski, "Cowles Changes Allegiance: From Empiricism to Cognition as Intuitive Statistics," *Journal of the History of Economic Thought*, Spring 2002, 165–93.

53. See John Byrne, *The Whiz Kids* (New York: Doubleday, 1993), 48–51.

54. The Whiz Kids' leader was Charles "Tex" Thornton, a brash college dropout from a dirt-poor Texas family who had learned statistics as a junior clerk in the Agricultural Adjustment Administration. Looking for wider horizons by mid-1940, he was introduced by a friend to Robert Lovett, who took an instinctive liking to him and hired him for the Army Air Force (the very same week that Lauchlin Currie hired Galbraith at the National Defense Advisory Commission).

After the war, Lovett, who had awarded the Ford Motor Company billions in wartime defense contracts, persuaded Henry Ford II to hire Colonel Thornton as head of corporate planning (along with Robert McNamara as his deputy). The Whiz Kids performed brilliantly at Ford, which was haunted by management failures that had taken place under Ford's father. But when the ever-brash Thornton protested noisily after being passed over for company president, Ford fired him. Once again Lovett intervened: Thornton went to Hughes Aircraft in 1948, as vice president in charge of helping rescue development of the F-92 Starfire, a jet fighter that Lovett, by now Secretary of Defense, wanted ready for potential war with the Soviet Union as soon as possible. Thornton, with the technical support of Chet Raymo and Dean Woolridge, did the job. Hughes's military business soared from $2 million to $200 million and from 1,000 employees to 17,000 over the next four years, and to a profit margin of better than 35 percent on its investment. But his brightest managers chafed constantly under Howard Hughes's erratic leadership.

Raymo and Woolridge left to found their own firm, the legendary TRW, which went on to supervise development of ICBMs and spy satellites for the Air Force. Thornton himself bought Litton, Inc., a small California electronics firm that produced key components for missile guidance systems. It was a masterstroke—Thornton understood not only how defense contracts would build his business, but how profitably. (Litton was even more profitable than Hughes, with a 40 percent profit margin in its early years.) He also foresaw that electronics would be the key, and that the fragmented new industry, much of it created by the proverbial engineers working in a garage, was ripe for consolidation. Over the next ten years, Litton Industries became one of America's most powerful defense contractors, built on wave after wave of conglomerate acquisitions that relied on Thornton's vision of what he called "synergy."

By 1960, when McNamara became President Kennedy's Secretary of Defense (hired on the advice of Lovett), he reintroduced to the armed services the same ferocious statistical and operational scrutiny that he and the Whiz Kids had developed at Ford. Litton, like TRW and Hughes, prospered in the McNamara era, and Thornton became an adviser both on the "pacification program" in Vietnam and financing the war there (he arduously opposed any tax increase to pay for it). On Thornton's career at Ford, see Byrne, *Whiz Kids*, 123–38; at Hughes, 231–44; at Litton, 379–90; as McNamara adviser, 450–54.

55. Galbraith to Catherine Galbraith, May 11, 1945 (letter in Mrs. Galbraith's possession).

CHAPTER 10: A NEW WAR BEGINNING

1. For the first use of the term "bastard Keynesians" in print, see Joan Robinson, review of *Money, Trade, and Economic Growth*, by Harry Johnson, *Economic Journal*, September 1962, 690–92.

2. "Old believers" weren't all "Marshallians"; the more accurate word is probably "marginalist," or perhaps Veblen's term, the "neoclassicals." (Keynes confused matters by calling them "classical," a term usually reserved for figures beginning with Adam Smith, and including Ricardo, Mill, and Malthus, but not Marshall.) For one insider's account of their lives in the Keynesian era, see George Stigler, *Memoirs of an Unregulated Economist* (New York: Basic Books, 1988). An accessible, nontechnical introduction to their diverse views can be found in Conrad Waligorski, *The Political Theory of Conservative Economists* (Lawrence: University Press of Kansas, 1990). Niehans, *A History of Economic Theory*, in discussing what he calls "the leitmotiv of marginalism" (159ff.), gives a short summary of the terminological question, and the confusions.

3. These progressive alternatives to Marshall's marginalism had been proposed in the late nineteenth century by figures such as Richard Ely (founder and first president of the American Economic Association), the labor economist John R. Commons, and (in his iconoclastic way) Thorstein Veblen; they are referred to with only passing accuracy as "social-historical economists," or Historicists. Despite the Marshallians' ascendancy, this group exerted immense influence on public policy and many universities in the Progressive Era. Ely's introductory textbook, as noted earlier, outsold Marshall's *Principles* until the late 1920s.

   By the New Deal, the Historicists had evolved into several different policy camps, notably the "national planners" (of whom Rexford Tugwell and Adolph Berle were representative) and the "trust busters" (Thurman Arnold). There were distinctive subcamps as well, for example, in agricultural economics, where the Agricultural Adjustment Administration and "domestic allotment" programs developed by John D. Black and others held sway. But by the end of World War II, however influential in the policy realm, the legacy of the Historicists (and their 1920s progeny, the Institutionalists) was in eclipse. For an introduction, see J. Ronnie Davis, *The New Economics and the Old Economists* (Ames: Iowa State University Press, 1971).

4. See Collins, *Business Response to Keynes*, ch. 6.

5. On Cowles and his family's publishing fortune, see James Alcott, *A History of Cowles Media Company* (New York: Creative Publishing, 1998). Cowles's ancestors had cofounded the *Chicago Tribune* with the Medill family, and Alfred Cowles was the paper's second largest shareholder. The family's media empire also included *Look*, the *Minneapolis Star-Tribune*, and *Harper's* magazine most prominently. On Cowles, econometrics, and the Commission, see C. F. Christ, "History of the Cowles Commission, 1932–52," in *Economic Theory and Measurement* (Chicago: Cowles Publishing, 1952), and Roy Epstein, *A History of Econometrics* (Amsterdam: North-Holland, 1987). The best interpretive works are Philip Mirowski, "Cowles Changes Allegiance," and Mirowski, "Cyborg Agonistes."

   Economists will benefit from James Heckman, "Casual Parameters and Policy Analysis in Economics: A Twentieth Century Retrospective," *Quarterly Journal of Economics*, February 2000, 45–97, for its rich handling of the Cowles legacy, the Commission's recognized failures, and the responses it provoked—including the rise of Rational Expectations. The frustrations and dead ends that econometricians have faced—and the inconclusive value of econometrics to economic theory and policy—are well told.

6. Overemphasis on estimation techniques hides the controversial politics that went with them. Koopmans and his mentor, Jan Tinbergen, were both inclined to democratic socialism, and were influenced by the Polish economist Oskar Lange, then teaching at the University of Chicago. Lange believed that planners could recreate the market's efficiency through a system he called "market socialism," and Koopmans was convinced he could use the new estimation techniques to realize Lange's theory; as a consequence, in the late 1940s, "Cowles was ground zero of Walrasian market socialism in America" (Mirowski, "Cowles Changes Allegiance," 166ff.).

    Life became hard for the postwar group at times in the McCarthy era. Klein had a difficult time getting work, and was pushed out of the University of Michigan after being subpoenaed by a state version of HUAC. Modigliani, Hurwicz, and Patinkin left the University of Illinois after local businessmen raised a ruckus. As Herbert Simon later recalled, "Communists and supposed Communists were being discovered under every rug . . . Any graduate of the University of Chicago, with its reputation for tolerance of campus radicals, was guaranteed a full field investigation before he could obtain a security clearance," an important factor for Cowles economists who wanted to work at or visit RAND (ibid., 168–70).

    The Cowles Commission, along with Koopmans, left the University of Chicago for Yale in 1955, in response to ongoing harassment by Milton Friedman, Frank Knight, and Arthur Burns, who loathed the techniques as well as the politics of the Cowlesmen.

7. Our understanding of RAND's influence on postwar economics is incomplete because much of its work remains classified. Von Neumann's interests were only partly in game theory; he was also involved in development of the atomic and hydrogen bombs, and originated the science of large compressions critical to the new bomb making.

    RAND came to have tremendous influence over the armed forces, especially after its director, the Berkeley economist Charles Hitch, went to work for Robert McNamara in John F. Kennedy's Pentagon. Hitch pioneered the application of an updated operation research program, which McNamara used for cost-cutting, weapons program consolidations, and—more darkly—his statistically derived belief that the United States was winning in Vietnam. See Mirowski, "Cyborg Agonistes," 691–701; Mirowski, *Machine Dreams* (New York: Cambridge University Press, 2002), gives a fuller exposition. The role of Harold Hotelling, godfather to the work of Friedman, Stigler, and the rough-and-ready pragmatism of the Chicago School, mediated through RAND's development of operations research, is provocatively interesting.

8. "Growth of Membership and Subscribers," *American Economic Review*, January 1949, 314 (on prewar figures); vanderbilt.edu/AEA/org.htm (postwar figures).

9. See Galbraith, "The Selection and Timing of Inflation Controls," *Review of Economic Statistics*, May 1941, 82–85.

10. See Galbraith, "Reflections on Price Control," *Quarterly Journal of Economics*, August 1946, 475–89; Galbraith, "The Disequilibrium System," *American Economic Review*, June 1947, 287–302; and his panel comments, on "Problems of Timing and Administering Fiscal Policy in Prosperity and Depression," *American Economic Review*, May 1948, 442–43.

11. See "New Frontiers in Economic Thought," *American Economic Review*, May 1946, 93–153 (complete panel discussion); 152–53 (Galbraith comments).

12. Ibid., 129.

13. For a classic defense of the conservative ideal, see Milton Friedman, *Essays in Positive Economics* (Chicago: University of Chicago Press, 1953); for a representative dissent, see Alexander Rosenberg, *Microeconomic Laws: A Philosophical Analysis* (Pittsburgh: University of Pittsburgh Press, 1976); for a comprehensive bibliography, see Deborah Redman, *Economic Methodology: A Bibliography with References to Works in the Philosophy of Science, 1860–1988* (New York: Greenwood Press, 1989).

14. Galbraith, "New Frontiers," 152–53.

15. On Knight's long-running opposition to Keynesianism, see the chapter on Knight, "Frank H. Knight: Philosopher of the Counterrevolution in Economics," in W. Breit and R. L. Ransom, *Academic Scribblers: American Economists in Collision* (Chicago: Dryden Press, 1982).

16. On the National Association of Manufacturers' animosity to the New Deal, see Richard Tedlow, "The National Association of Manufacturers and Public Relations During the New Deal," *Business History Review*, Spring 1976, 25–45; on NAM's problematic leadership place in American business, see Alfred Cleveland, "NAM: Spokesman for Industry?" *Harvard Business Review*, May 1948, 357ff.

17. For assessment of the quite different reactions of the NAM, the Chamber of Commerce, and the Committee for Economic Development, see Collins, *Business Response to Keynes*, chs. 4–5.

18. NAM cited in Robert Lekachman, *The Age of Keynes* (New York: Random House, 1966), 168. For a fuller account of the bill's passage, see Stephen Bailey, *Congress Makes a Law* (New York: Columbia University Press, 1950).

19. Poll cited in ibid., 169.

20. See Milton Gilbert, "Toward Full Employment," *Fortune*, October 1945, 151ff. However, *Fortune* ran an opposing article by Sumner Schlicter in the same issue. Gilbert was a friend of Galbraith's, the brother of Richard Gilbert of the OPA, and worked under Galbraith at the Bombing Survey; Schlicter was one of Harvard's more dedicated anti-Keynesians.

21. David McCullough, *Truman* (New York: Simon & Schuster, 1992), 468–69.

22. On Truman's initial New Deal agenda, and the subsequent labor strikes, see ibid., 468–510.

23. Lekachman, *Age of Keynes*, 171 (things being equal); 174 (also sunk).

24. Galbraith, *A Life*, ch. 16.

25. Council on Foreign Relations, "Studies of American Interests in the War and Peace" memorandum of discussion, Economic and Financial Series, no. E-A 36, October 27, 1942. The Council's powerful behind-the-scenes role in setting America's postwar agenda began in 1939, and closely paralleled in many respects the work and views of Luce's Q Department (though in much greater detail and with much more direct effect on Washington policy-makers).

Five months before Pearl Harbor the CFR's high-level committees of senior government officials, academics, and businessmen formally defined America's postwar "national interest" as part Keynes, part Ricardo: "(1) The full use of the world's economic resources—implying full employment and a reduction in business cycle fluctuation; and, (2) The most efficient use of the world's resources—implying an interchange of goods among all parts of the world according to comparative advantages of each part in producing certain goods" (see G. William Domhoff, *The Power Elite and the State* [New York: Aldine, 1990], 126). Domhoff, a political sociologist, also notes the CFR's centrality in the creation of the World Bank and the International Monetary Fund. Alvin Hansen was a key member of the CFR's Economic and Financial Group, and he met with Keynes in London in late September 1941 (officially as a State Department representative) specifically to discuss plans for postwar economic cooperation between the United States and Great Britain. He carried with him proposals prepared by the Economic and Financial Group for an International Economic Board and an International Development Corporation that went far beyond the free trade policies that the United States was then trying to force on Britain as part of a Lend-Lease quid pro quo. Coincidentally, Keynes had just set down for the first time his own views on these matters, and he enthusiastically welcomed Hansen's ideas, incorporating the "global full employment" position CFR had set out in his second draft. When Hansen returned to the United States, he met with Vice President Wallace, Secretary of State Hull, and Treasury Secretary Morgenthau to outline the CFR plan and Keynes's proposals; he then recapped all his meetings for the CFR. Hansen and the CFR formalized their proposals, and, working with Jacob Viner, sent them on December 5—two days before Pearl Harbor—to Lauchlin Currie at the White House. (Hansen also sent a summary letter directly to Roosevelt.) A week later, on Sunday morning, December 14, Morgenthau called Harry Dexter White and ordered him to begin work immediately on the American outlines for what became the IMF and World Bank. See Domhoff, *Power Elite*, ch. 5, especially 159–81, and Skidelsky, *Keynes: Fighting for Freedom*, ch. 6, especially 202–9, 218.

26. Galbraith was already writing his State Department boss Will Clayton about leaving in early July. See Galbraith to Clayton, July 12, 1946, Early Government Service, box 4, Galbraith Papers, JFK Library.

27. Galbraith, interview with author. Galbraith's claim of a "secular priesthood" in State wasn't entirely unfair: three quarters of new Foreign Service officers hired between 1914 and 1922 came from prep schools, especially St. Paul's and Groton. But the imposition of civil service requirements in 1924 changed the Department's hiring practices: by the end of World War II, three quarters of its officers were *not* the Ivy League types Galbraith so disliked, although among the top 120 officials, according to *Fortune*, "99% enjoyed private incomes" that supplemented their government salaries. One measure of their political conservatism was that before the war "New Dealers condemned Chamberlain for excessive appeasement, the Europeanists [in State] for too little," since the Europeanists viewed Hitler's anti-Communism as "a point in his favor" (Martin Weil, *A Pretty Good Club* [New York: Norton, 1978], chs. 1–3, esp. 46, 102); "The U.S. Foreign Service," *Fortune*, July 1946, 81ff.

28. Galbraith, *A Life*, 243, 245. Within the State Department, the road back to power came through Stettinius's naive and bumbling mismanagement in 1944 of

a major reorganization plan, which FDR had intended to contain the power of the conservatives once and for all; instead they increased their power. Then, after Yalta, through a series of ruses they grasped back the responsibility to lead in the definition of postwar policies. See Weil, *Pretty Good Club*, ch. 12 (on reorganization), 198–99 (on Yalta aftermath).

29. See Daniel Yergin, *Shattered Peace: The Origins of the Cold War and the National Security State* (Boston: Houghton Mifflin, 1978), chs. 1 and 2 on the tensions between FDR's tough yet fundamentally Wilsonian "Yalta axioms" and the confrontational and conservative "Riga axioms." See also Melvyn Leffler, *A Preponderance of Power* (Stanford, Calif.: Stanford University Press, 1992), ch. 2. John Lewis Gaddis, *Strategies of Containment* (New York: Oxford University Press, 1992), ch. 1, succinctly assesses FDR's quite sophisticated geopolitical strategy.

30. John Morton Blum, *From the Morgenthau Diaries*, 3 v. (Boston: Houghton Mifflin, 1967), v. 3, 369–70.

31. Ickes quoted in Manchester, *Glory and the Dream*, v. 1, 505.

32. See Leffler, *Preponderance of Power*, chs. 3–4, especially 105 (on the military's contempt for State), 50–53 (on U.S. calculations regarding Soviet intentions and toward European construction).

33. Clayton to Luce, [December 1946], Galbraith File, Time, Inc., Archives.

34. Galbraith, *A Life*, 246.

35. Walt Rostow and Charles Kindleberger recalled Galbraith as very energetic and engaged in his work. Rostow called him "very helpful, very active, a whirlwind at times" (Rostow and Kindleberger, interviews with author).

36. "The U.S. Foreign Service," *Fortune*, July 1946, 153. On the tensions between "Clayton's economists" and the political officers in State, also see Weil, *Pretty Good Club*, 203.

37. On Stalin's views, and Churchill's views of Stalin, see Adam Ulam, *Stalin: The Man and His Era* (New York: The Viking Press, 1973), 623–24, 640–52.

38. See Charles Bohlen, *Witness to History 1929–1969* (New York: Norton, 1973), 213.

39. McCullough, *Truman*, 451–52. For Truman's letter to his wife, see Robert Ferell, ed., *Dear Bess* (New York: Norton, 1983), 520–21.

40. McCullough, *Truman*, 480; on Truman's offer to Byrnes, see Wittner, *Cold War America* (New York: Praeger, 1974), 5; on FDR's view of Byrnes, see Weil, *Pretty Good Club*, 228.

41. For "firmest of firm," see Walter Isaacson and Evan Thomas, *The Wise Men*, 377–78. The two authors note that Forrestal, like Harriman, thought Roosevelt and American policy had been too accommodating to Stalin during the war, and they welcomed Kennan's telegram because they wanted very tough—but ultimately businesslike—relations with the Soviets after the war. By the fall of 1946, however, as the United States embarked on its military confrontation, both men were expressing private doubts. "Harriman," according to Forrestal's diary, "did not believe the Russians would provoke war in the near future, but there was a chance of finding an accommodation which would be the foundation for peace provided they realized we would not make an unending series of concessions." Regarding his own attitudes, Forrestal wrote Harriman that fall that "just as you and I felt there was too great a swing pro-Russia three years ago, I am a little fearful that it may swing too strongly the other way now."

42. McCullough, *Truman*, 490–91. Interestingly, it's not clear how closely Truman paid attention to Kennan's telegram initially.

43. According to Keynes, Churchill's real purpose in coming to America was to lobby for the $3.75 billion loan that a nearly bankrupt Britain was seeking from Washington. Its approval was bottled up in fractious congressional debates, and Keynes told former Treasury Secretary Morgenthau that Churchill "was trying to pressure his friend [the financier Bernard] Baruch not to testify against the British loan" (Keynes to Morgenthau, March 2, 1946, quoted in Weil, *Pretty Good Club*, 186).

44. McCullough, *Truman*, 488–90.

45. Galbraith and Acheson were reunited in the late 1950s as cochairmen of the Democratic Advisory Council, where they clashed repeatedly. On 1946, see Dean Acheson, *Present at the Creation* (New York: Norton, 1969); on the Democratic Advisory Council, see Galbraith, *A Life*, 359–60.

46. As Yergin, *Shattered Peace*, notes, "The Army was the one service that continued to base its postwar outlook on the Yalta axioms" of viable, though difficult, cooperation with the Soviet Union (211).

47. See Jean Edward Smith, *Lucius D. Clay: An American Life* (New York: Henry Holt, 1990), 411.

48. Clayton speaking to the Detroit Economic Club, quoted in Wittner, *Cold War America*, 7.

49. Thorp quoted in Weil, *Pretty Good Club*, 205.

50. Ibid., 204. For more on Clayton, see Frederick J. Dobney, ed., *Selected Papers of Will Clayton* (Baltimore: Johns Hopkins University Press, 1971).

51. Smith, *Lucius D. Clay*, 550. For a closer view of Clay's policies in Germany, see John Backer, *Winds of History: The German Years of Lucius Clay* (New York: Van Nostrand Reinhold, 1983). Clay's views after 1948, when the Russians restricted access to Berlin, hardened into a more conventional anti-Soviet position.

52. Clay's political adviser, Robert Murphy, quoted in Yergin, *Shattered Peace*, 191, 212–13.

53. Smith, *Lucius D. Clay*, 376.

54. Ibid., 384–85.

55. Galbraith, interview with author.

56. Galbraith's text closely followed many of the points Clay had outlined in a July 19 memo on Germany's future, as he acknowledged to Clay's biographer. Charles Kindleberger helped in the drafting, and Benjamin Cohen, the State Department's counsel, reviewed it, and made additional changes. "I then took it on to General Clay in Berlin. He read it while smoking the usual six cigarettes" (Galbraith quoted in Smith, *Lucius D. Clay*, 387; on Clay's July 19 memo, see 379–81).

57. "Man of the Year," *Time*, January 6, 1947, 23ff. See also Elson, *World of Time*, 166.

58. For Wallace's views of the speech and his firing, see John Culver and John Hyde, *American Dreamer: The Life and Times of Henry A. Wallace* (New York: Norton, 2000), ch. 22; for a view more favorable to Truman, see McCullough, *Truman*, 513–20; for policy context, see Alonzo Hamby, *Beyond the New Deal: Harry S. Truman and American Liberalism* (New York: Columbia University Press, 1973), ch. 5.

59. The speech was not an unalloyed success. Wallace sharply criticized recent Soviet actions in Eastern Europe, which earned him boos and hisses from many in the crowd.

60. On New Dealers' reactions, see Hamby, *Beyond the New Deal*, 130–33.

61. See "'This Great Endeavor,'" *Time*, September 30, 1946, 20.

62. See Leffler, *Preponderance of Power*, 133–34, and Clark Clifford, oral history interview, April 13, 1971, Truman Library. trumanlibrary.org/oralhist/cliford2.htm. The full text of the Clifford-Elsey memo wasn't made public until the late 1960s, when *New York Times* columnist Arthur Krock published it. It appears in Thomas H. Etzold and John Lewis Gaddis, eds., *Strategies of Containment: Documents on American Policy and Strategy, 1945–1950* (New York: Columbia University Press, 1978). The document's claims drew most heavily in fact on controversial assessments done by the Joint Intelligence Committee, a CIA precursor set up during the war by the Joint Chiefs of Staff. On the powerful but forgotten influence of the JIC, see Larry Valero, "An Impressive Record," *Studies in Intelligence*, Summer 2000, at cia.gov/csi/studies/summer00/art06.html.

63. Yergin, *Shattered Peace*, 255.

64. On Galbraith's attitudes toward Wallace's politics, Galbraith, interview with author.

65. See Galbraith to Black (on Hilldring's appointment of him), August 5, 1946, and Galbraith and Mason to Hilldring, "Some Recommendations on German Policy," September 12, 1946, Early Government Service, box 4, Galbraith Papers, JFK Library. In November, on the same day the GOP won control of Congress, Clay briskly told reporters that Byrnes's policies were still in place as far as he was concerned. Even after General Marshall replaced Byrnes in January, Clay remained indefatigable in his efforts to contain Washington's new direction. When Marshall called him to Moscow for a foreign ministers' meeting that spring, he encountered John Foster Dulles, the vehemently anti-Communist Republican lawyer whom Marshall had brought along, hoping to cultivate the GOP's new congressional majority.

    Clay and Marshall knew that military intelligence reports had secretly concluded the devastated Russians wouldn't be capable of launching a major war for more than a decade. Even George Elsey, coauthor of the Clifford-Elsey memo six months earlier, worried that "there has been no overt action in the immediate past by the U.S.S.R. which serves as an adequate pretext" for the just-proclaimed Truman Doctrine. Nevertheless, Dulles saw Soviet-American relations in millennial terms, as a clash between "godless Communism and the Christian West," as he brusquely informed Clay.

    But Stalin was conciliatory throughout the conference, and Clay correctly judged the degree of Soviet bargaining weakness: the Russians, he told Marshall, could be led to negotiate satisfactorily across a range of issues. Dulles would hear none of it. Clay "turned white with anger" and unleashed a tirade to Dulles's face, his eyes flashing like steel. "Blood was all over the floor," one aide remembered.

    Marshall, whose respect for Clay was enormous, was in a trap: he needed Republicans in Congress to approve his budget for the Truman Doctrine, and Dulles was their suspicious eyes and ears. Clay was unceremoniously sent back to Berlin. The Cold War was finally truly on. (Hoping to mollify Clay, Marshall helped to arrange a fourth star for the three-star general.) See Leffler, *Preponder-*

ance of Power, 151–57; Smith, *Lucius D. Clay*, 413–20. See also "Clay Sees Amity Gaining in Berlin," *The New York Times*, November 5, 1946, 2 (on his Election Day comments). Elsey quote is from Isaacson and Thomas, *Wise Men*, 397.

66. Smith, *Lucius D. Clay*, 411.

67. Byrnes quoted in ibid.

68. Galbraith, "Recovery in Europe" (Washington, D.C.: National Planning Association, 1946). See "Prolonged U.S. Aid Held Europe's Need," *The New York Times*, December 3, 1946, 2.

69. Even Kennan subscribed by then to a view very close to Galbraith's. In a confidential report to the Secretary of State shortly before the Marshall Plan was announced, Kennan stressed that American aid to Europe "should be directed not to combatting Communism as such but to the restoration of the economic health and vigor of European society." (Kennan quoted in McCullough, *Truman*, 562.)

70. [John Kenneth Galbraith], "Is There a German Policy?," *Fortune*, January 1947, 126–27.

71. Galbraith, *A Life*, 247, 254–55.

72. Smith quoted in Wittner, *Cold War America*, 22.

73. McCullough, *Truman*, 552.

74. Galbraith, *A Life*, 242.

75. Galbraith's eight-inch-thick security file, which he obtained in the late 1970s under the Freedom of Information Act, makes for chastening reading. First formally investigated by the FBI for his National Defense Advisory Commission and Office of Price Administration jobs before the war, he was reinvestigated by State Department security officials in 1946 and then several times more by the FBI in the 1950s, 1960s, and 1970s. The State Department's investigators talked to dozens of sources and examined reams of records, going all the way back to his childhood.

Congressman John Taber, a reactionary upstate New York Republican with whom Galbraith tangled while at OPA, was scathing: "GALBRAITH had made many mistakes while at the OPA; had been fired . . . from his job as Professor at Princeton University because he was a Communist; . . . was a member of many Communist front organizations and was mixed up with a man named SMITH who is a noted West Indian Communist." Another source called him "One of the long-hair boys" at OPA, and while "I don't think he was a Communist or Red . . . you will always hear the word 'Pink' or 'Commy' or something in that sense." Although the vast majority of sources from Harvard, the OPA, Bombing Survey, and *Fortune* attested to Galbraith's loyalty, energy, intelligence, and diligence, these few wild accusations led to the security department's opposition to his 1946 appointment. See Boston FBI to J. Edgar Hoover, July 5, 1950 (summarizing the 1946 findings), in the Galbraith FBI Files. (Galbraith was never given his actual State Department files.)

76. See Charles Kindleberger, *The Life of an Economist* (London: Blackwell, 1991), 45.

77. On Galbraith's relation to Vincent, see Galbraith, *A Life*, 246–47. On Vincent, see Leffler, *Preponderance of Power*, 127–30.

78. Galbraith, "Beyond the Marshall Plan" (Washington, D.C.: National Planning Association, 1949); for press coverage, see "ECA Year Is Hailed by Planning

Group," *The New York Times*, February 14, 1949, 2, and "Marshall Plan Won't Solve Social Unrest, Report Warns," *The Washington Post*, February 14, 1949, 9.

79. Galbraith, "Beyond the Marshall Plan," 13–14.

80. Ibid., 21.

81. See Peter Grose, *Operation Rollback* (Boston: Houghton Mifflin, 2000).

82. Calculations on defense spending are from OMB data in Stein, *Presidential Economics*, tables A-3 and A-7.

82. See Stephen Schwartz, *Atomic Audit: The Costs and Consequences of U.S. Nuclear Weapons Since 1940* (Washington, D.C.: Brookings Institution, 1998).

83. See Stephen Schwartz, *Atomic Audit: The Costs and Consequences of U.S. Nuclear Weapons Since 1940* (Washington, D.C.: Brookings Institution, 1998).

CHAPTER 11: BACK TO HARVARD: NEW ECONOMICS AND NEW VOICES

1. Galbraith, interview with author; Galbraith to David Rockefeller, April 6, 1946, and Rockefeller's reply, April 16, General Correspondence, box 5, Galbraith Papers, JFK Library. Neither letter describes the job offered; however an aide to Rockefeller says, "The approach to Professor Galbraith was part of the Rockefeller Brothers' effort to modernize and shape the Rockefeller Family office to answer their needs rather than those of their father in the period immediately after World War II. One part of the reorganization was the creation of an economic research unit capable of providing financial research on investment opportunities in the United States and abroad as well as basic research on the general economic situation in parts of the world in which individual brothers had an interest. Stacy May, Nelson's economics professor at Dartmouth in the 1920s and a vice president at the Rockefeller Foundation in the 1930s, was eventually chosen for the position" (Peter Johnson, Rockefeller Family Office, letter to author, August 5, 2003).

2. In 1940, total U.S. university enrollment stood at 1.5 million; by 1947, some 1.2 million ex-GIs alone were enrolled, the first wave of more than 7.8 million World War II veterans who took advantage of the GI Bill. See Department of Commerce, Bureau of the Census, *Historical Statistics of the United States*, 2 v. (Washington, D.C.: GPO, 1975), v. 2, 383.

3. See John Bethell, "Harvard at War," *Harvard Magazine*, September–October 1995, 32–48. For more detail, see Conant's memoirs, *My Several Lives*, and Hershberg, *James B. Conant*.

4. AEA membership soared after the war. From 1910 to 1940 it had stagnated between 2,000 and 3,100; in 1946, it reached 4,300; in 1948, over 5,700. See *American Economic Review*, "Annual Directory," January 1949, 315.

5. See Grubel and Boland, "On the Efficient Use of Mathematics in Economics," *Kyklos*, v. 39, 1986, 419–42. Their figures are 2.2 percent of *American Economic Review* pages in 1951 versus 44 percent of pages by 1978.

6. As early as 1912, the Yale economist Irving Fisher—one of the founders of the Econometric Society and *Econometrica* in the 1930s—had envisaged a society that would unify economic theory, mathematics, and statistics into an integrated methodology, but nothing came of his idea. In 1926–27 Fisher revived his plan, after getting responses to one of his own mathematically sophisticated papers from several journals: one economics journal accepted only the economics part; a statistical journal wanted the economics and higher math removed; and a mathematics journal declined to publish a work on economics and statistics. See

Niehans, *History of Economic Theory*, 410. For a short blow-by-blow history see C. F. Christ, "The Founding of the Econometric Society and *Econometrica*," *Econometrica*, January 1983, 3–6.

7. See Robert Dorfman, "Mathematical, or 'Linear' Programming: A Non-mathematical Exposition," *American Economic Review*, December 1953, 797–825, and Dorfman, "The Nature and Significance of Input-Output," *American Economic Review*, May 1954, 121–26.

8. See *Review of Economics and Statistics*, November 1954, for David Novick's article and eight initial responses, plus responses by Enke, Stigler, "Mathematics: Logic, Quantity, and Methods," and Wilson in the May and August 1955 issues, and by Schoeffler in the February 1956 issue. (Novick was a senior economist at RAND, and thus had early exposure to the new mathematical style.)

9. Even so, many economists still hesitated to adopt a fully mathematicized strategy, as Howard Bowen's extensive survey of 1950s graduate economics training made clear. Practical skills, including accounting, plus economic history and intensive empirical methods, were the widely favored norm in Ph.D. programs. Forty years later, when the American Economic Association again surveyed graduate programs, the situation was completely reversed: abstract theorizing was paramount, and economic history, empirical familiarity with the economy, and applied skills were virtually gone. By then, the consequences of the shift were apparent: nearly two thirds of graduate-level economics professors claimed that the profession was "overmathematicized" and "too unrelated to the real world" (see Howard Bowen, "Graduate Education in Economics," *American Economic Review*, September 1953, supplement, 1–223, and Anne Krueger, et al., "Report of the Committee on Graduate Education in Economics," *Journal of Economic Literature*, September 1991, 1035–53).

10. For a nontechnical discussion of this "cluster effect" on development of game theory, see Sylvia Nasar, *A Beautiful Mind* (New York: Simon & Schuster, 1998).

11. Samuelson first published *Economics: An Introductory Analysis* in 1948, but it took several years (and editions) for it to become the best-selling economics textbook, a position it held from the mid-1950s to the mid-1970s. It is still in wide use though not in first place. See E. Cary Brown and Robert Solow, eds., *Paul Samuelson and Modern Economic Theory* (New York: McGraw-Hill, 1983) for an introduction. For sales figures, see "Play It Again, Samuelson," *The Economist*, August 23, 1997, 58. Judging by the number of speakers and papers delivered at AEA annual conventions during this period, Harvard economists outpaced MIT by a ratio of six to one. See Daniel R. Fusfeld, "The Program of the AEA Meetings," *American Economic Review*, September 1956, 643.

12. Black taught five courses with the assistance of one part-time instructor, supervised his graduate students, and presided over an extensive federally financed study of U.S. agricultural policy. As he noted to Provost Buck, with some justifiable pride, 12 of 120 Ph.D.'s in economics (not just agricultural economics) conferred in the United States in 1946–47 were his students (Black to Buck, December 22, 1947, Black Papers, Wisconsin Historical Society.) *The Behavioral Sciences at Harvard*, prepared in 1954 for the Ford Foundation, gives the figures on Harvard economics Ph.D.'s in various fields (table 1, p. 66).

13. Unlike other Harvard graduate schools, the Littauer School, founded in 1937, was in modern parlance a "virtual" institution (and remained so until reconsti-

tuted as the John F. Kennedy School of Government in the late 1960s). It had no faculty of its own, relying instead on the Economics and Government departments, and no campus, and never enrolled more than 100 students. Created from a $2 million donation by the glove manufacturer and former GOP congressman Lucius Littauer, it was meant, in Littauer's words, to train cautious bureaucrats who would resist "the heavy hand of government descending on us" thanks to FDR and the New Deal (see Kellers, *Making Harvard Modern*, 130–33).

14. Black to Buck, December 22, 1947.

15. On Smithies and his work, see G. C. Harcourt, "Arthur Smithies," in John Eatwell, et al., eds., *The New Palgrave* (New York: Stockton, 1987), v. 4, 375–76.

16. See *The Harvard Crimson*'s annual *Confidential Guides*, in which Harvard students rate faculty for their teaching abilities. Galbraith's Ec 1 teaching in 1953 was rated "the best lectures of the year" with "strikingly well-organized material and rapid-fire delivery" (*Confidential Guide to Courses* [Cambridge, Mass.: Harvard Crimson, 1954], Harvard University Archives).

17. Lamson, *Speaking of Galbraith*, 92; Galbraith, *A Life*, 269. His memoirs omit mention of the efforts Black made in 1946 and 1947 to bring him back to Harvard, as well as the fact that he and Black were in close touch about this new research-based appointment from at least the spring of 1948 (see Black to Galbraith, May 13, 1948, Black Papers, Wisconsin State Historical Society).

18. Galbraith, interview with author.

19. Galbraith and Bowen had been Social Science Research Council fellows together in England the same year, Bowen in London, Galbraith in Cambridge. The offer from the University of Illinois, moreover, wasn't from a second-tier department; Bowen had hired already Don Patinkin, Franco Modigliani, and Leo Hurwicz from the Cowles Commission. The three left, however, in the early 1950s, after a nasty anti-Communist purge, as noted earlier. See Mirowski, "Cowles Changes Allegiances," 169; Galbraith, *A Life*, 273.

20. Galbraith, *A Life*, 274–75.

21. Lamont may well have had his own strong views on the Bombing Survey's conclusions. Early in the war, his powerful father had served on the Army Air Force's Committee of Operations Analysis, which established the targeting priorities used through much of the bombing of Germany. See MacIsaac, *Strategic Bombing*, 25–26.

22. Weeks quoted in Galbraith, *American Capitalism* (Boston: Houghton Mifflin, 1952), 4.

23. Conant, *My Several Lives*, 437 (Randall's report), 440 (Conant's reply).

24. "Report to Overseers, November 21, 1949," memorandum, in Papers of Walter Edmonds, box 3, Harvard University Archives.

25. "Memorandum from: J. K. Galbraith," undated in 1949, Harvard University, box 70, Galbraith Papers, JFK Library.

26. Conant, *My Several Lives*, 445.

27. On Conant's ultimatum, John Dunlop, interview with author.

28. Mason quoted in Hershberg, *James B. Conant*, 613; Hershberg gives a full account of the events in 1949 and their context in ch. 31.

29. John Dunlop, interview with author.

30. Galbraith, *A Life*, 275–76.

31.   Lamson, *Speaking of Galbraith*, 103.

32.   Emily Wilson was far more than a "housekeeper" to the family. At her memorial service in 1999, James Galbraith depicted her place in the family:

> Emily Wilson joined our family in 1940. There was an incident not long after, when she was arrested on the bus in Alexandria, Virginia, for refusing to give up her seat. There was a little bit of the essential Emily in that. She knew what was right and what was wrong, and she was steadfast in acting on her convictions.
>
> I once asked her why she left Washington to follow my parents to New York in 1943, and later to Cambridge. She said, "I fell in love." And so she did. And then came Alan, and Douglas, and when Dougie died, Peter was born and, as Emily told it to me later, she told my parents they had to have another one, and here I am.
>
> In my childhood she was everywhere. I spent my childhood in her kitchen, smelling the bread and the cakes and the spaghetti sauce and the casseroles, and drying the dishes and putting out the washing, and listening to the stories of her friends—Ana and Eunice and Ivin and George—and of my parents and how she used to go crying to my Mother after Dad had put all the dishes on the top shelf, complaining, "He's so tall he must be crazy." There is a "Happy Home Recipe" in her scrapbook, written out in her marvelous hand: 4 cups of love, 2 of loyalty, 3 of forgiveness and a barrel of laughter. That was her formula, all right, but how I wish I knew how to make her bread.
>
> She had no false modesty; as the sign in her bathroom said, "When you're as great as I am, it's hard to be humble." Her cooking was the best in the world, and she wanted to hear you say so. She had the habit of command . . .
>
> She was at home in the world. She was a great figure in Newfane, in Gstaad, and in that house on Ratendon Road in New Delhi where she trained the ferocious leopard cub whose name, as I remember, was Jumna, to a box. She had skied in the Alps and ridden a mountain pony to the high Himalayas in Kashmir, and she had pictures to prove it. But she was a working person mainly, and she worked incredibly hard. And her friends were working people too, and through her and them we learned something about that.
>
> She could be a fierce person too, with that implacable sense of what was right and wrong, especially in the raising of children . . .
>
> There were occasions when you got her going just a little bit, and she would start to say "I always knew I was going to kill one white man before I died . . ." And you would know then that it was probably smart to get out of the way and lie low for a little while.
>
> Well, we are grown up now, and each of the Galbraith children has three children of his own, and she knew and loved them all. We carry her values and her humor and her love forward to each of them.

James K. Galbraith, "Remarks at the Memorial Service for Emily Wilson," St. Paul's AME Church, Cambridge, August 10, 1999 (unpublished, courtesy of James Galbraith).

33.   Galbraith, *A Life*, 278.

34.   Houghton Mifflin had recorded sales of 236,000 copies by 1994, two thirds do-

mestic, but its records, as the house noted to this author, systematically under-report sales because British and foreign publishers provide sales figures only after their advances against earnings are earned out. The Houghton Mifflin totals also don't include book-club sales, or sales data for certain other publishers who relicensed rights.

In the case of *American Capitalism*, this relicensing was caught up in Cold War propagandizing, to Galbraith's benefit. At the urging of the U.S. Information Agency, in 1955 New American Library bought the British and Commonwealth rights from Hamish Hamilton, his London publisher, in order to produce a special 25,000-copy, 50-cent edition for India, designed, as the NAL's chairman wrote Galbraith in strictest confidence, "to counteract the flow of Russian literature in [Indian] academic circles." Ignoring the letter's awkward phrasing—the NAL chairman surely didn't mean Gogol or Dostoyevsky—Galbraith agreed. Two years later after immense success in India, the NAL expanded sales to include Burma, Indonesia, Japan, Pakistan, Ceylon, Egypt, Greece, Iran, Iraq, Jordan, Lebanon, Syria, and Turkey.

Reminded of this arrangement forty years later, Galbraith sardonically observed that he regretted not sharing royalties with John Foster Dulles, in hopes of even greater sales (Wiggins to Galbraith, October 17, 1955, and April 10, 1957, General Correspondence, box 63, Galbraith Papers, JFK Library; Galbraith, interview with author).

35. See Galbraith, "The Cure at Mondorf Spa," *Life*, December 17, 1945, 57–66, and Galbraith and Ball, "Interrogation of Albert Speer," *Life*.

36. "Chapter Outline," box 54, folder 1, Houghton Mifflin Papers, Houghton Library, Harvard University.

37. Schlesinger to Galbraith, April 19, 1951, in Galbraith's office files, Littauer, not catalogued.

38. See especially Stuart Chase, "Capitalism Without Tears," *The Reporter*, March 4, 1952, 33–35; Daniel Bell, "The Prospects of American Capitalism," *Commentary*, December 1952, 603ff. (The reviews are of Galbraith's *American Capitalism: The Concept of Countervailing Power* [New York: Houghton Mifflin, 1952].)

39. "Clobbering Theory," *BusinessWeek*, January 9, 1954, 93.

40. Michael Hoffman, "The Weights in the Balance," *The New York Times Book Review*, February 24, 1952; Stuart Chase, "Capitalism's New Mantra—Economic Optimism," *New York Post*, February 17, 1952; John Harriman, "About Big Business," *Boston Globe*, and Melchior Palyi's *Chicago Tribune* review are cited in Charles Hession, *Galbraith and His Critics* (New York: New American Library, 1972), ch. 3; Bernard Rosenberg, "The Economics of Self-Congratulation," *Dissent*, Winter 1954, 92.

41. Paul Homan, *American Economic Review*, December 1952, 925–28: Adolf Berle, "American Capitalism," *Review of Economics and Statistics*, February 1953, 81–84; Joan Robinson, *The Economic Journal*, December 1952, 925–28; C. L. Christenson, *Journal of Political Economy*, June 1952, 275.

42. Simon Whitney, "Errors in the Concept of Countervailing Power," *Journal of Business*, October 1953, 238–53.

43. See Otis Graham, *Toward a Planned Society* (New York: Oxford University Press, 1976), ch. 1 (on the New Deal history of the national planners); see Edward Mason, *Economic Concentration and the Monopoly Problem* (Cambridge, Mass.: Harvard University Press, 1957), 1 (on the volume of professional literature on

the subject as "a Niagara" during the 1930s and 1940s). The Federal Trade Commission's official warnings about the scale of post–World War II mergers are in Federal Trade Commission, *The Merger Movement: A Summary Report* (Washington, D.C.: GPO, 1948); Justice William O. Douglas's opinions in *Columbia Steel v. United States* in 1947 and *Standard Oil v. United States* in 1948 use similar data. On concentration by 1950, see M. A. Adelman, "The Measurement of Industrial Concentration," *Review of Economics and Statistics*, November 1951, 275–77.

44. John Maurice Clark had advanced the idea of "workable competition" as an alternative to classic competition in 1940, and included in it a suggestion about "innovative" efficiency almost in passing. Three years later, Joseph Schumpeter offered his own explanation for the role in technological change in increasingly concentrated (and non-classically competitive) markets. Galbraith briefly explains why his own concept differs from those of Schumpeter and Clark in *American Capitalism*, 58 (on Clark), 86 (on Schumpeter).

45. Ibid., 112.

46. Ibid., 113.

47. Myron Sharpe, *John Kenneth Galbraith and the Lower Economics* (White Plains, N.Y.: M. E. Sharpe, 1974), 8.

48. Charles Lindblom, *Politics and Markets: The World's Political-Economic Systems* (New York: Basic Books, 1977), 8.

49. Galbraith, *American Capitalism*, 11.

50. Ibid., 55.

51. Ibid., 55–56.

52. Schlesinger quoted in John Bartlow Martin, *Adlai Stevenson of Illinois* (New York: Doubleday, 1976), 547.

53. Stevenson quoted in David McCullough, *Truman*, 891.

54. Galbraith, *American Capitalism*, 151.

55. Ibid., 151.

56. David Truman, *The Governmental Process* (New York: Random House, 1951), represents the classic "interest group pluralism" defense, although V. O. Key, *Politics, Parties and Pressure Groups* (New York: Thomas Y. Crowell, 1944), comes closer to Galbraith's views.

57. Galbraith, interview with author.

58. Galbraith, *The Age of Uncertainty* (Boston: Houghton Mifflin, 1977), 277.

59. For Keynes's most accessible explanation of similar views, see his "Economic Possibilities for Our Grandchildren," in Donald Moggridge, ed., *The Collected Writings of John Maynard Keynes*, 30 v. (London: Macmillan, 1971), v. 9, 321–32. See Wayne Parsons, "Keynes and the Politics of Ideas," *History of Political Thought*, Summer 1983, 367–92, and Peter Hall, "Keynes in Political Science," *History of Political Economy*, Spring 1994, 137–53.

60. Galbraith, "Countervailing Power," *American Economic Review*, May 1954, 3.

61. Galbraith, *American Capitalism*, 152.

62. Ibid., 152–53.

63. Sharpe, *Galbraith and the Lower Economics*, 8.

64. Galbraith, *American Capitalism*, 3rd ed. (White Plains, N.Y.: M. E. Sharpe, 1980), v–vi.

65. Ibid., 2.

66. By 1950, the Chamber—for complicated internal as well as external reasons—

had retreated from the moderately progressive support it had given at the end of World War II to a Keynesian-style government. On the Chamber's shifting views on Keynesianism, see Collins, *Business Response to Keynes*, chs. 5 and 6. Byrnes quoted in Galbraith, *American Capitalism*, 3.

67. Galbraith knew firsthand. In late 1950, he suddenly learned that he was under investigation by the government's serpentine new security apparatus. The reason? Nearly a year earlier he'd submitted an expense reimbursement form after participating in a one-day Commerce Department meeting on farm subsidies and the economy. Unknown to him, the paperwork was processed as if he were an ongoing consultant to the Department. By then, any such government appointment required a screening check, and this one soon turned up the fact that in 1944 Galbraith had been a founding supporter of the National Citizens Political Action Committee, and, more darkly, that he "had participated in an effort to curtail drastically the amount of paper available to a free press." (NCPAC was a liberal group organized by the CIO's Sidney Hillman to support Roosevelt, and the ominous paper allegation traced back to OPA days, when wartime price controls were placed on newsprint.)

By 1950 the charges were enough to launch an F.F.I.—a "Full Field Investigation," in FBI parlance—that would go on for the next nine months, and end up three inches thick. The cost to taxpayers must have run into the tens of thousands of dollars, because reports poured in from FBI agents in Washington, New York, Boston, Chicago, Newark (meaning Princeton), Detroit, San Francisco (for Berkeley), Richmond (covering suburban Washington), Birmingham, Albany, and St. Louis, as well as consular officials in Toronto and London. Galbraith's books, reviews, and articles were read, though found "not to reflect any information that may be pertinent to this investigation" (save one: his suspiciously favorable review of Merle Miller's *The Sure Thing*, a novel dealing with the witch hunting of the period, was clipped and attached).

Galbraith's friends rallied to affirm his loyalty. FBI informants in the Communist Party swore no knowledge of him. Lou Maxon, who had forced his dismissal from the OPA, helpfully described him as "a 'fly-by-night' economist who seemed determined to inject a Socialist trend" into OPA policies, and the research director of the House Un-American Activities Committee, after combing his files, found a dangerous-sounding "connection with one of the Communist books, magazines, and other literature," although the only remotely qualifying candidate was *Fortune*. There were slapstick moments: the State Department's personnel office couldn't find his employment records, but its security office found its files, including Galbraith's alleged dismissal from Princeton for being a Communist, and word of the elusive "Doctor Ware."

Shortly before Christmas, Galbraith—who knew none of this at the time and wouldn't know the details for another quarter century—received a peremptory letter from the Commerce Department's Loyalty Board, demanding to know whether he'd ever been associated in any way with any "Totalitarian, fascist, communist or subversive" group or had ever advocated the overthrow of the government. It also demanded to know his relationship with three men, none an alleged Communist. One, Corliss Lamont, had been a neighbor in New York; another was the late head of the National Planning Association and a friend; the third he did not know. Rather indignantly, he wrote back, "Few people have made their social and political convictions more thoroughly a matter of record than have I. As a boy I learned to wear my politics, as my ancestors wore the tartan, on my shoulder for all to see. For the past fifteen years in books, reports, and monographs . . . I have stated my views. You will find that I have never doubted the rightness of a society in which one is free to do so." After receiving his reply, the government terminated the consulting appointment he'd never actually held and the investigation ground to a halt. (Commerce Department 1950, Galbraith FBI file, in author's possession; see also Galbraith, "My Forty Years With the F.B.I.," *Esquire*, October 1979, 122ff.)

68. For economists, the issue is that of "increasing returns to scale," which in Marshall's theory justifies large corporations by the advantages inherent in great size—technological gains, market power, and so on. But why don't such "increasing returns to scale" eventually undermine competitive equilibrium? How can smaller firms compete and survive? And why shouldn't they lead to a single gigantic corporation's monopolizing an entire industry, or even all business activity in the economy? Marshall's more empirical work (such as *Industry and Trade*) suggested a practical recognition of this problem, but his theoretical assumptions in *Principles of Economics*, and the tensions between his concepts of decreasing and increasing returns, were never resolved to his own (or later economists') real satisfaction. See George Stigler, "The Division of Labor Is Limited by the Extent of the Market," *Journal of Political Economy*, June 1951, 185–93. For a more recent discussion of the enduring "increasing returns" problem and work on it, see Stigler, "Increasing Returns to Scale," *The New Palgrave*, v. 2, 761–64.

69. Galbraith, *American Capitalism*, 36. Galbraith in ch. 4 chose not to press the theoretical implications of "increasing returns to scale," and in a period when mergers were overwhelmingly "friendly," did not anticipate the ruthless 1980s and 1990s world of "new technology" industries (computers, telecoms, and so on), and of hostile takeovers and unfriendly mergers. Whether events in recent decades refute Galbraith's thesis or represent a cyclical phase, similar to the railroad experience after the Civil War, or the automobile experience around World War I, remains to be seen. In the earlier instances, the new technologies also introduced many small firms that competed intensively on price, but the competition proved ruinous and led to rapid industry consolidation and domination by a few companies. On the related issue of the modern evolution of business and bankers' attitudes toward mergers, see Ron Chernow, *The House of Morgan*.

70. The statements of Galbraith and the respondents are in "Fundamental Characteristics of the American Economy," *American Economic Review*, May 1954, 1–34.

71. "Clobbering Theory," *BusinessWeek*, January 9, 1954, 93.

72. Donald McCloskey, *Knowledge and Persuasion in Economics* (New York: Cambridge University Press, 1994), 12. For a brief Stigler biography, see Mark Blaug, *Great Economists Since Keynes* (Brighton, England: Wheatsheaf, 1985), 239–41; for Stigler's rambling remembrances see his *Memoirs of an Unregulated Economist* (New York: Basic Books, 1988), in which he never mentions Galbraith.

73. Stigler, "Playing with Blocs," *American Economic Review*, May 1954, 11.

74. See Thomas McCraw, ed., *Creating Modern Capitalism* (Cambridge, Mass.: Harvard, 1995).

75. Two useful conceptual studies that examine the international context for govern-

ment's hand in markets are John Zysman, *Governments, Markets, and Growth* (Ithaca: Cornell University Press, 1983), especially "four views of the state and the economy" in ch. 6; and Zysman and Laura Tyson, *American Industry in International Competition: Government Policies and Corporate Strategies* (Ithaca: Cornell University Press, 1983). Since the 1980s, the growth of this "new political economy" analysis has been asymptotic, deeply influencing a younger generation trained by the Neo-Classical Synthesis generation. See Robert Gilpin, *Global Political Economy* (Princeton: Princeton University Press, 1991).

76. Ronald Coase, "The Nature of the Firm," *Economica*, November 1937, 386–405. Coase, like Stigler, wasn't on the Chicago faculty in 1953, but his theories have long since made him a pillar of "Chicago School" reasoning.

77. On the economics of property rights, see Harold Demetz, "Toward a Theory of Property Rights, *American Economic Review*, May 1967, 347–59; and Demetz and Armen Alchian, "Production, Information Costs, and Economic Organization," *American Economic Review*, December 1972, 777–95. For the economics of the law, the early classic is Richard Posner, *Economic Analysis of the Law* (New York: Little, Brown, 1973). Economic work on "transaction costs" has had much wider influence. See Jurg Niehans, "Transaction Costs," *The New Palgrave*, v. 4, 676–79, for an introduction.

78. As F. M. Scherer has put it, "Economists have struggled with the oligopoly problem for more than a century without achieving a unified behavioral theory" and must "strive to learn as much as we can through a constant interplay between theorizing and observing how real-world oligopolists behave" (F. M. Scherer, *Industry Structure, Strategy, and Public Policy* [New York: HarperCollins, 1996], 12).

79. Galbraith expanded this point in the 1956 revised edition of *American Capitalism*.

80. R. J. Monsen, *Modern American Capitalism, Ideologies and Ideas* (Boston: Houghton Mifflin, 1963), 29–30.

81. F. M. Scherer, *Industrial Pricing: Theory and Evidence* (Chicago: Rand McNally College Publishing, 1970), 122. See also F. M. Scherer and David Ross, *Industrial Market Structure and Economic Performance*, 3rd ed. (Boston: Houghton Mifflin, 1990). Steven Lustgarten, "The Impact of Buyer Concentration in Manufacturing Industries," *Review of Economics and Statistics*, August 1975, 125–32, and Ute Schumacher, "Buyer Structure and Seller Performance in Manufacturing Industries," *Review of Economics and Statistics*, May 1991, 277–84, provide additional data.

CHAPTER 12: STEVENSON AND THE LIBERALS

1. Catherine Galbraith, interview with author.

2. Galbraith, *A Life*, 372 (grace); 288 (committed to picturing).

3. Ibid., 289.

4. Ibid., 289–90, and Schlesinger, interview with author.

5. The roster of men who worked in Stevenson's campaign reads like a who's who of the era's liberal intellectuals and policy-makers: the historians Henry Steele Commager and Bernard DeVoto; the poet and journalist Archibald MacLeish; Norman Cousins, the editor of *Saturday Review*; the playwright and FDR aide Robert Sherwood; the New Deal veterans Rexford Tugwell, Ben Cohen, and Samuel Rosenman; Leon Keyserling, the head of Truman's Council of Economic Advisors; Seymour Harris; Thomas Eliot, chancellor of Washington University, a

former Congressman who played a key role in the creation of Social Security (and the grandson of Harvard's famous president Charles Eliot); Yale's Eugene Rostow; Walter Johnson and James Arnold of the University of Chicago; John Palfrey of the Columbia University School of Law; the economics journalist Stuart Chase; the *New York Post* editor James Weschler; and Herbert Agar, former editor of the *Louisville Courier-Journal*. See John Bartlow Martin, *Stevenson of Illinois*, 630–34.

6. Galbraith, *A Life*, 294.

7. Barone, *Our Country*, 256.

8. Martin, *Stevenson of Illinois*, 539–40; also Ball, *Past Has Another Pattern*, 116–17.

9. Charles Murphy, a senior White House aide, dropped by after dinner to join the conversation, and ended up no less exasperated. In fact, Ball had organized the dinner at the request of Murphy, who in turn was acting on Truman's instruction, as Stevenson knew. Ball, *Past Has Another Pattern*, 116.

10. Schlesinger quoted in Martin, *Stevenson of Illinois*, 638.

11. Ibid.

12. Galbraith, *A Life*, 294–98. Galbraith observed that Stevenson "had heard of Keynes but largely from people who supposed him subversive. Stevenson's own views on economic policy, to the extent that they existed, had been formed at Princeton thirty years before in an economic atmosphere dominated by a stalwart resistance to the twentieth century" (296–97).

13. Adlai Stevenson, *The Major Campaign Speeches of Adlai E. Stevenson* (New York: Random House, 1952), 165–72; Galbraith to Stevenson, September 17, 1952, General Correspondence, box 59, Galbraith Papers, JFK Library.

14. Martin, *Stevenson of Illinois*, 677.

15. See Stephen Gillon, *Politics and Vision: The ADA and American Liberalism* (New York: Oxford University Press, 1987), 10–16.

16. That shift, however, was fraught with struggles, doubts, and recriminations, especially over loyalty boards, the Smith Act, and the Hiss-Chambers issue. See ibid., 72–82.

17. See Clifton Brock, *Americans for Democratic Action* (New York: Public Affairs Press, 1962), 52. The ADA eventually became so influential that nearly four dozen of its top members went into senior positions in the Kennedy administration in 1961. Besides Galbraith himself, active or former ADA members in the Kennedy Administration included Theodore Sorensen, Arthur Schlesinger, Arthur Goldberg, Orville Freeman, Abraham Ribicoff, Chester Bowles, G. Mennen Williams, Averell Harriman, Eleanor Roosevelt, and Thomas Finletter (Brock, *Americans for Democratic Action*, 11–12).

18. McCullough, *Truman*, 521 (Taft and GOP chairman); Vandenberg and McCarthy quoted in Eric Goldman, *The Crucial Decade and After: America, 1945–1960* (New York: Vintage Books, 1960), 132, 213.

19. Gillon, *Politics and Vision*, 29. The plan was drafted with Chester Bowles, Alvin Hansen, Seymour Harris, Richard Gilbert, and Robert Nathan. Leon Keyserling, then chairman of Truman's Council of Economic Advisors, was among those who endorsed a military buildup as beneficial to the liberal agenda.

20. John Kenneth Galbraith, "Beyond the Marshall Plan," 11–12, 14.

21. Galbraith, interview with author.

22. Ball, *Past Has Another Pattern*, 130–32.

23. Galbraith, *A Life*, 304, and interview with author.
24. Martin, *Stevenson of Illinois*, 75–79.
25. Ibid., 82–83.
26. Galbraith to Stevenson, September 23, 1953, General Correspondence, box 59, Galbraith Papers, JFK Library.
27. Stevenson to Galbraith, October 16, 1953, General Correspondence, box 59, Galbraith Papers, JFK Library.
28. Martin, *Stevenson of Illinois*, 84–89.
29. Ibid., 89.
30. Galbraith proposed the book that became *The Affluent Society* six months after *American Capitalism* was released and just before he left for Illinois to work on the Stevenson campaign. See Galbraith to Houghton Mifflin, July 8, 1952, Galbraith File, box 54, Houghton Mifflin Papers, Houghton Library, Harvard University. It is interesting that for a time Galbraith considered titling it *Political Economy*.
31. According to Houghton Mifflin, 540,000 copies were sold by 1994. These sales figures, provided to the author by Houghton Mifflin, are very conservative because British and foreign publishers reported only sales *after* author advances were paid out of sales, and no book club sales are included; also in later years, Galbraith sublicensed additional editions to other houses whose sales weren't recorded to Houghton Mifflin.
32. Reviews cited are *The New York Times Book Review*, April 24, 1955, 3; *The New York Herald Tribune Book Review*, April 24, 1955, 4; *The Atlantic Monthly*, June 1955, 79; *The Times Literary Supplement*, October 28, 1955, 17; *New Statesman*, October 22, 1955, 516.
33. *American Economic Review*, September 1955, 687–88; *Economic Journal*, March 1956, 126–28.
34. "Stock Inquiry Told of Boom Psychology; Economist Recommends 100% Margin," *The New York Times*, March 9, 1955, 1. The headline on *The Harvard Crimson* front-page story, by a young Christopher Jencks, was even more explicit: "Market Declines After Galbraith Testifies."
35. Galbraith, *A Life*, 310.
36. "Capehart Charges Red Bias," *The New York Times*, March 21, 1955, 1.
37. Curiously, Capehart read Wright's letter into the *Congressional Record*. See U.S. Congress, Senate, Committee on Banking and Currency, "Stock Market Study," 84th Congress, 1st session, 1955, 298.
38. Galbraith, *A Life*, 309–12.

CHAPTER 13: *THE AFFLUENT SOCIETY*: PARTING COMPANY WITH THE MAINSTREAM

1. See Galbraith file, box 54, file 4, Houghton Mifflin Papers, Houghton Library, Harvard University.
2. The Carnegie Corporation gave Galbraith $8,000. Galbraith, interview with author. By 1955, though, Galbraith's plan for the book was shifting away from why people were poor, toward some broader concept. In a letter to Adlai Stevenson in May 1955, Galbraith wrote that the book's working title was *A New Treatise on Political Economy*. Galbraith to Stevenson, May 26, 1955, General Correspondence, box 59, Galbraith Papers, JFK Library.
3. In the fall of 1958, Galbraith finally shed agricultural economics. By then he was teaching "The Social Theory of Modern Enterprise" as a semester course

and wanted to add a new one, "Economic Theory and Institutional Change," to reconcile theories of the markets and the firm with the realities of the modern corporation. Galbraith to Seymour Harris, September 18, 1958, General Correspondence, box 70, Galbraith Papers, JFK Library. Galbraith taught "Consumption, Distribution, and Prices" (Ec 107 and 207) with Black from 1949 to 1953, and "Business Organization and Control" (Ec 161) on his own from 1949 until 1952. He also cotaught a seminar on public regulatory policy with other faculty until 1955. "Problems of Economic and Political Development" (Ec 287) was initially taught by Galbraith and Black; Galbraith continued with it until 1965, sometimes alone, sometimes with Edward Mason, and, for one year, with Simon Kuznets. See Harvard course catalogues, 1949–60, Archives, Pusey Library, Harvard University.

4. See Michael Namorato, *Rexford G. Tugwell* (New York: Praeger, 1988), ch. 6.

5. Galbraith, *A Life*, 316; the study is John Kenneth Galbraith and Richard H. Holton, *Marketing Efficiency in Puerto Rico* (Cambridge, Mass.: Harvard University Press, 1955). See, for a fuller sense of the work's scope, Project Files, boxes 66 and 67, Galbraith Papers, JFK Library. Galbraith remained involved until the late 1950s.

6. Galbraith, *A Life*, 307 (convincing explanation); 323 (came later to understand). Chapter 21 tells of his first India visit in detail.

7. Ibid., 323–24 (on the Kahn-Mahalanobis dinner, including quotes). Also, Galbraith to Robinson, January 26 and April 11, 1955, General Correspondence, box 53, Galbraith Papers, JFK Library.

8. Galbraith, *A Life*, 326.

9. Ibid., 332–33.

10. For his larger views on Indian planning, see John Kenneth Galbraith, "A Foreign Economist Looks at Second Plan," *Hindustan Standard*, April 15, 1956, and his later "Rival Economic Theories in India," *Foreign Affairs*, July 1958, 587–96.

11. Galbraith, *A Life*, 331.

12. Ibid., 334 (ambassador); 335 (sod rooftops).

13. Ibid.

14. See Lionel Robbins, *An Essay on the Nature and Significance of Economic Science*, 15. On the many problems with the formalist definitions, see Daniel Hausman, *The Inexact and Separate Science of Economics* (New York: Cambridge University Press, 1992).

15. Stevenson letter quoted in Lamson, *Speaking of Galbraith*, 132.

16. John Bartlow Martin, *Adlai Stevenson and the World* (Garden City, N.Y.: Doubleday, 1977), 110. The Godkin Lectures, published as *Call to Greatness* (New York: Harper Bros, 1954), became a best-seller.

17. Ibid., 351–52.

18. Allen Drury, "10 Ghost Writers Serve 4 Nominees," *The New York Times*, September 23, 1956, 10.

19. Martin, *Stevenson, and the World*, 234.

20. James Reston, "Struggle for Stevenson," *The New York Times*, September 17, 1956, 8.

21. See Martin, *Stevenson of Illinois*, 713.

22. Stevenson quoted in Lamson, *Speaking of Galbraith*, 133.

23. Martin, *Stevenson and the World*, 392–95.

24. Alfred Marshall, *Principles of Economics* (London: Macmillan, 1890), 2, 4.
25. Marshall and Taussig are cited in Galbraith, *The Affluent Society* (Boston: Houghton Mifflin, 1958), 39.
26. In "Economic Possibilities for Our Grandchildren," in Keynes, *Collected Writings*.
27. Galbraith, *Affluent Society*, 93 (finished business); 99 (ancient preoccupations).
28. Ibid., 21.
29. He mischievously singled out, as an example of hollow "conventional wisdom" bombast, an address by the chairman of Inland Steel, Clarence Randall, one of the overseers who opposed his tenure. Ibid., 21 n.
30. Galbraith, *Affluent Society*, 22–23.
31. Ibid., 26. Galbraith here is mildly rebuking Keynes for his famous aphorism that "we are all ruled by ideas and little else."
32. Ibid., 25. Galbraith was signaling his abiding concerns not only about a single-minded focus on output and on inflation's adverse effects on the economy, but about the political and popular consensus supporting the government as macro-manager. Many Keynesians, he felt, in wrongly imagining that Keynes's essential message was about ever-increasing output, and wrongly believing they could fine-tune the U.S. economy to run at full employment, risked introducing a steady inflationary tendency. This would destroy their claim to leadership. (This is in fact what happened in the 1970s.) Better, Galbraith suggested, to accept some modest level of unemployment and support fully those affected through generous government programs. On Keynesian attitudes toward output, see 153–56; on inflation, see 175–76.
33. Ibid., 74–75. For both views on the New Deal era's "great compression" of inequality and for a longer-run comparison of U.S. income data that shows large cyclical trends rather than a simple linear improvement, see Jeffrey Williamson, *American Inequality: A Macroeconomic History* (New York: Academic Press, 1980), and Kevin O'Rourke, *Globalization and History* (Cambridge, Mass.: MIT Press, 1999).
34. Galbraith, *Affluent Society*, 76 (power of great firm); 79 (serious fright).
35. Ibid., 81–83.
36. See Adam Smith, *Wealth of Nations* (London: Random House, 1991), book 1, ch. 10.
37. Galbraith, *Affluent Society*, 85–86.
38. Ibid., 94 (desire for society); 96 (no inconsistency).
39. For example, state and local government spending in 1958 was 8.6 percent of GDP, and defense, 10.6 percent. See Stein, *Presidential Economics*, 417–18.
40. Galbraith, *Affluent Society*, 245–49.
41. See Michael Reagan, "Private Wealth and Public Poverty," *The Nation*, June 14, 1958, 548.
42. Galbraith called this "Cyclically Graduated Compensation," or CGC. See Galbraith, *Affluent Society*, 231–33.
43. Ibid., 250.
44. See Lawrence Mishel et al., *The State of Working America, 2000–2001* (Ithaca: Cornell University Press, 2001) (on postwar inequality and poverty trends).
45. See Juliet Schor, *The Overworked American* (New York: Basic Books, 1991), although her methodology has been criticized. For an independent assessment of her and her critics, see Jerry Jacobs, "Measuring Time at Work," *Monthly Labor*

Review, December 1998, 42–53; Jacobs's findings generally support Schor. See also Tibor Scitovsky, *The Joyless Economy*, 2nd ed. (New York: Oxford University Press, 2000); Scitovsky's later work supports Galbraith's original views. See also Scitovsky, "Growth in an Affluent Society," *Lloyds Bank Review*, January 1987, 1–14, or Scitovsky, *Human Desire and Economic Satisfaction* (New York: New York University Press, 1986). Robert Frank, *Microeconomics and Behavior* (New York: McGraw-Hill, 2002), is a rich, up-to-date survey of the relevant issues, as well as the weaknesses of standard economics in explaining them.

46. U.S. and overseas sales data from Houghton Mifflin. It was made a Main Selection of the Book-of-the-Month Club, and there was a New American Library paperback edition.

47. See R. B. Downs, *Books That Changed America* (New York: Macmillan, 1970).

48. *Book Review Digest* in 1958 listed nearly two dozen reviews, and Galbraith's files contain dozens more from newspapers, journals, and magazines not covered by the *Digest*.

49. Edwin Dale, "Are We Living Too High on the Hog?" *The New York Times Book Review*, June 1, 1958, 1; Robert Heilbroner, "Economist's Provocative Challenge to Certain Cherished Beliefs," *The New York Herald Tribune Book Review*, June 1, 1958, 3; Philip Graham, "The Folly of America's Faith in Chain Belt Living," *Washington Post Book World*, June 1, 1958, 1.

50. Robert Lekachman, "Galbraith's New Economics," *The New Republic*, June 9, 1958, 18; *The New Yorker*, June 28, 1958, 93–94; Phoebe Adams, "The Atlantic Bookshelf," *The Atlantic Monthly*, July 1958, 85ff.; Irving Kristol, "Our Boondoggling Democracy," *Commentary*, August 1958, 176–77; Michael Reagan, "Private Wealth and Public Poverty," *The Nation*; Robert H. L. Wheeler, "American Advertising: The Perils of Abundance," *Yale Review*, "The Affluent Society," September 1958, 128ff.

51. *Times Literary Supplement*, November 21, 1958, 675; John Strachey, "Unconventional Wisdom," *Encounter*, October 1958, 80.

52. "The Affluent Society," *Time*, June 2, 1958, 78–80; Steinbeck quoted in *The Affluent Society*, 2nd rev. ed. (Boston: Houghton Mifflin, 1969), xxix.

53. George Reisman, "Galbraith's Modern Brand of Feudalism," *Human Events*, February 2, 1961, 77; Ben Seligman, "Where Do We Go from Here?" *Dissent*, Winter 1959, 84; George Stigler, "The Intellectual and the Marketplace," in A. Klassen, ed., *The Invisible Hand* (Chicago: Regnery Press, 1965), 34; Galbraith, "Economics Versus the Quality of Life," *Encounter*, January 1965, 34.

54. Colin Clark, "The Horrible Proposals of Mr. Galbraith," *National Review*, October 11, 1958, 237.

55. Gerald Carson, "A Man of Wit Challenges Current Economic Ideas," *The Chicago Sunday Tribune Book Review*, June 1, 1958, 1.

56. Galbraith, *Affluent Society*, 199–200.

57. Galbraith, *A Life*, 340.

58. The literature is vast: the best starting point remains Donald McCloskey, *The Rhetoric of Economics* (Madison: University of Wisconsin Press, 1985), especially ch. 1, "The Poverty of Economic Modernism." See also Phillip Mirowski, "The When, the How, and the Why of Mathematical Expression in the History of Economic Analysis," *Journal of Economic Perspectives*, Winter 1991, 151.

59. Rutledge Vining, "The Affluent Society: A Review Article," *American Economic Review*, March 1959, 112.

60. Kenneth Boulding, review, *Review of Economics and Statistics*, February 1959, 81.

61. Friedrich von Hayek, "The Non Sequitur of the Dependence Effect," *Southern Economic Journal*, April 1961, 346–48. Galbraith seems to have haunted Hayek. In 1960, the Mont Pélérin Society, which Hayek had first convened after World War II as an exclusive gathering of conservative economists, political scientists, and philosophers (leavened by a few politicians and wealthy businessmen-benefactors), met to review, lament over, and excoriate Galbraith and *The Affluent Society*. Hayek, Stigler, and David McCord Wright reprised their by-then familiar arguments. See Henry Hazlitt, "Galbraith Revisited," *Newsweek*, October 9, 1961, 89; the *Mont Pélérin Quarterly*, April–July 1961, was devoted to the subject.

62. Irving Kristol, "Our Boondoggling Democracy," 178. Kristol had not yet converted to neoconservatism.

63. H. G. Johnson, interview, *Current Economic Comment*, August 1960, 3–10.

64. Ibid., 7. A useful survey of *The Affluent Society*'s early critics can be found in Charles Hession, *John Kenneth Galbraith and His Critics* (New York: New American Library, 1972), chs. 4–5. J. R. Stansfield gives a strong defense in "The Affluent Society after Twenty-five Years," *Journal of Economic Issues*, September 1983, 589–608; a fuller defense is Stansfield, *John Kenneth Galbraith* (London: Macmillan, 1996), in which *The Affluent Society* is discussed in chapter 2. (Stansfield, however, is an Institutionalist, and pulls Galbraith further into his own camp than necessary.) The British sociologist-economist David Reisman's *Galbraith and Market Capitalism* (London: Macmillan, 1980) interweaves themes from Galbraith's major works into a comprehensive argument, and synthesizes earlier critics with his own critiques. Sharpe, *John Kenneth Galbraith and the Lower Economics*, ch. 3, casts a cool eye on Galbraith's arguments, but presents his criticisms only briefly. John Gambs, *John Kenneth Galbraith* (New York: St. Martin's Press, 1975), and Frederick Pratson, *Perspectives on Galbraith* (Boston: CBI, 1978), are less useful; so, too, C. Lynn Munro, *The Galbraithian Vision* (Washington, D.C.: University Press of America, 1977). Loren Okroi, *Galbraith, Harrington, Heilbroner* (Princeton: Princeton University Press, 1988), offers helpful comparisons between these three figures.

   Four *festschrift* volumes contain useful articles: *The Journal of Post-Keynesian Economics*, May 1984; Samuel Bowles et al., eds., *Unconventional Wisdom* (Boston: Houghton Mifflin, 1989); and Helen Sasson, ed., *Between Friends: Perspectives on Galbraith* (Boston: Houghton Mifflin, 1999); and Michael Keaney, ed., *Economist with a Public Purpose* (New York: Routledge, 2001).

   Economists may especially want to review Robert Solomon, "Galbraith on Market Structure and Stabilization Policy," *Review of Economics and Statistics*, May 1958, 164–67, and Allan Meltzer, "A Comment on Market Structure and Stabilization," *RES*, November 1958, 413–15, which reply critically to Galbraith's earlier *RES* article, May 1957, 124–33, in which Galbraith previews for professional colleagues his *Affluent Society* ideas on market structure, inflation, and the inadequacies of conventional fiscal and monetary policies. Edmund Phelps, ed., *Private Wants and Public Needs* (New York: Norton, 1965), gives a judicious review of the "social balance" and induced-consumption themes.

65. Paul Homan, "Galbraith's Affluent Society," *California Management Review*, Spring 1959, 97.

66. For standard examples of critics of Galbraith's style of argument, see Scott Gordon, "The Closing of the Galbraithian System," *Journal of Political Economy*, July–August 1968, 635–44, and Gerard Gafgen, "On the Methodology and Political Economy of Galbraithian Economics," discussion paper 49 (Konstanz, Germany: University of Konstanz, 1974).

67. Thurow quoted in Lamson, *Speaking of Galbraith*, 138–39.

68. Paul Samuelson, "Economists and the History of Ideas," *American Economic Review*, March 1962, 7.

69. Alvin Hansen to Galbraith, May 8, 1969; Galbraith to Hansen, May 27, 1969, in Galbraith's private papers. In 1958, Hansen had written that *The Affluent Society* was "brilliant and skillful writing . . . not seen since the great days of Keynes." Hansen to Galbraith, December 23, 1958, General Correspondence, box 33, Galbraith Papers, JFK Library.

70. These *Affluent Society* quotes are collected in Pratson, *Perspectives on Galbraith*, 250–53.

71. See Dorothy Ross, *The Origins of American Social Science* (New York: Cambridge University Press, 1991), and Mary Furner, *Advocacy and Objectivity* (Lexington: University of Kentucky Press, 1975), for an introduction to the evolution of academic social sciences.

72. An important milestone in understanding the public's "common sense" is Benjamin Page and Robert Shapiro, *The Rational Public* (Chicago: University of Chicago Press, 1992). In the 1920s, Walter Lippmann had argued that the public was fickle, incoherent, and unstable in its opinions, a view passed along for decades in the academic literature. Page and Shapiro reviewed fifty years of public opinion polls in the 1990s, and came to the opposite conclusion. The American public was, they said, in fact prudential, generous, and consistent on a host of issues across time, and while often not closely informed on details of public policy, guided by stable and coherent views (that were often at odds, it should be noted, with those of top policy-makers, academics, and opinion elites). Race was the one area where views changed markedly in the half century, toward greater tolerance. The chapter on economic policy and values is especially relevant.

73. Galbraith quoted in Pratson, *Perspectives on Galbraith*, 252.

74. "How to Pay for the War" and its policy effects are summarized in Skidelsky, *John Maynard Keynes: Fighting for Freedom*, chs. 2–3; in the earlier work Keynes wrote, "On the grounds of social justice no case can be made out for reducing the wages of the miners. They are the victims of the economic juggernaut. They represent in the flesh the 'fundamental adjustments' engineered by the Treasury and the Bank of England to satisfy the city fathers" (Keynes, "Economic Consequences of Mr. Churchill," quoted in Charles Hession, *John Maynard Keynes* [New York: Macmillan, 1984], 218).

75. See Keynes, "Economic Possibilities for our Grandchildren," 323.

76. See Douglass North, *Structure and Change in Economic History* (New York: Norton, 1981), David Landes, *The Wealth and Poverty of Nations* (New York: Norton, 1998), and Karl Polanyi, *The Great Transformation*, 2nd ed. (Boston: Beacon Press, 2001).

77. See Ross, *Origins of American Social Science*, and, for greater detail, Joseph Dorfman, *The Economic Mind in American Civilization* (New York: A. M. Kelly, 1966).

78. Marshall's *Industry and Trade*, published thirty years after *Principles of Eco-*

nomics, is an excellent source on his mature attitudes. As his biographer notes, Marshall, like Adam Smith, wasn't as conservative as many of his followers. Marshall's view was of "a complex, evolutionary process of combined economic, social and individual change in which each individual's abilities, character, preferences and knowledge developed along with social institutions, markets and the technologies of production and communication." See J. K. Whitaker, "Alfred Marshall," *The New Palgrave*, v. 3, 353.

79. Keynes's short biography of Marshall in *Essays in Biography* (London: Macmillan, 1933) is the best introduction to Marshall's character and complexities, especially when read in conjunction with Talcott Parsons, "Economics and Sociology: Marshall in Relation to His Time," *Quarterly Journal of Economics*, February 1932, 316–47. See J. Maloney, *Marshall, Orthodoxy, and the Professionalization of Economics* (Cambridge: Cambridge University Press, 1985) for a more recent evaluation.

80. John Neville Keynes, *The Scope and Method of Political Economy* (London: Macmillan, 1891). See also Phyllis Dean, "John Neville Keynes," *The New Palgrave*, v. 2, 42; and Arthur Pigou, *Wealth and Welfare* (London: Macmillan, 1912), effectively revised as *Economics and Welfare* in 1920—the book went through many editions. Whether Viner and Coase "solved" Pigou's problems is a matter of ongoing debate. (See Jurg Niehans, *A History of Economic Theory*), 318–23.

81. See Axel Leijonhufvud, *On Keynesian Economics and the Economics of Keynes* (New York: Oxford University Press, 1968), and Robert Clower, *Economic Doctrine and Method: Selected Papers of R. W. Clower* (Brookfield, Vt.: Elgar, 1995); on Leijonhufvud's influence in the 1970s, and on John Hicks's revisions of his own original IS-LM interpretation of Keynes in the 1930s and its effect on mainstream Keynesianism, see Roger Backhouse, *Interpreting Macroeconomics: Explorations in the History of Macroeconomic Thought* (New York: Routledge, 1995).

82. Although total *government spending* rose little as a percentage of GDP during the 1930s, total *federal debt* rose by more than 45 percent in dollar terms between 1933 and 1939—the result of serious shortfalls in federal income versus expenditures. In percentage terms, however, the striking rise of Depression-era federal debt occurred under Hoover, not Roosevelt, going from 16.7 percent in 1929 to 39.6 percent in 1933; from 1933 to 1939, the debt rose only to 46 percent. See Herbert Stein, *Presidential Economics*, 458 (table A-4).

83. Ibid., 456 (table A-3). Thanks to wartime imposition of payroll withholding taxes, the number of federal taxpayers rose from 7 million in 1941 to 42 million by 1944—and never fell thereafter. See O'Neill, *Democracy at War*, 94.

84. Alfred Malabre, Jr., *Lost Prophets* (Cambridge, Mass.: Harvard Business School Press, 1994), 45.

85. The federal budget was in surplus nine of the first fifteen years after World War II, and the federal debt, which stood at an immense 114 percent of GDP, was whittled to 47 percent by 1961. Unemployment, by contrast, chronically averaged 5 percent. See Stein, *Presidential Economics*, 456 (table A-4, on surplus and debt), and 454 (table A-2, on unemployment).

86. Wittner, *Cold War America*, 117.

87. Ibid., 115–18 (on Forrestal, profit data, and Hofstader).

88. See Conrad Waligorski, *Liberal Economics and Democracy* (Lawrence: University Press of Kansas, 1997), 82.

89. John Kenneth Galbraith, "Economic Freedom," speech given at Wellesley College, Wellesley, Mass., October 13, 1954, Speech File, box 104, Galbraith Papers, JFK Library.

90. Galbraith quoted in Waligorski, *Liberal Economics and Democracy*, 85. For a left-Marxist-neo-Hegelian critique of Galbraith on these issues, see Paul Diesing, *Science and Ideology in the Policy Sciences* (New York: Aldine, 1982), ch. 8. Diesing's work—a sometimes brilliant systematic attack on liberalism, social-science methods, and capitalist ideology—hits Galbraith especially hard on a daunting question for all liberal critiques of the modern era: if the ideology of markets so powerfully dominates government and citizens, how can "public reeducation" and a reassertion of democratic control and democratic values ever succeed? Diesing's own answer, emblematic of the modern academic left, totters into a discussion of how to reform academic social science in order to produce "better answers," better theories, and better models. His prescriptions do no more than formalize the analytic method that Galbraith practiced for a half century. See ch. 14, especially 391–98.

91. Galbraith quoted in Waligorski, *Liberal Economics and Democracy*, 86.

92. Ibid., 88.

93. Ibid., 89–91.

94. Axel Leijonhufvud, *On Keynesian Economics*. On the book's influence—it was cited by other economists in more than 500 articles in the subsequent thirty years—and its author's later shift in viewpoint, see Backhouse, *Reinterpreting Macroeconomics*, ch. 12.

95. John Hicks, *The Crisis in Keynesian Economics* (Oxford: Blackwell, 1974).

96. See John Hicks, "Mr. Keynes and the 'Classics': A Suggested Interpretation," *Econometrica*, April 1937, 147–59. For others who likewise tried to shape *The General Theory* back into a marginalist mold, see D. G. Champernowne, "Unemployment, Basic and Monetary: The Classical Analysis and the Keynesian," *Review of Economic Studies*, February 1936, 201–16; Roy Harrod, "Mr. Keynes and Traditional Theory," *Economica*, February 1937, 74–86; and James Meade, "A Simplified Model of Mr. Keynes's System," *Review of Economic Studies*, February 1937, 98–107. Backhouse, *Reinterpreting Macroeconomics*, ch. 9, provides useful insights.

97. Whether or not "revealed preference" purged economics of ordinal utility theory is still contested. Amartya Sen drew attention to the ways game theory—especially the Prisoner's Dilemma game—undercuts the core assumptions of revealed preference in *Collective Welfare and Social Choice* (San Francisco: Holden-Day, 1970). See also Sen's "Behaviors and the Concept of Preference," *Economica*, August 1973, 241–59, and "Personal Utilities and Public Judgement: Or What's Wrong with Welfare Economics?" *Economic Journal*, September 1979, 237–58. (Sen credits *The Affluent Society* as an important early influence on his thinking [interview with author].) The classic Chicago refinement is George Stigler and Gary Becker, "De Gustibus Non Est Disputandum," *American Economic Review*, March 1977, 76–90. See Hendrik Houthakker, "On Consumption," in Cary Brown and Robert Solow, eds., *Paul Samuelson and Modern Economics* (New York: McGraw-Hill, 1983), 57–68 (an overview, albeit one sympathetic to Samuelson). See also Robert Kuttner, *Everything for Sale* (New York: Knopf, 1996), 41–44, for an easily read critique of the effects of revealed preference on debates over markets' efficiency. See also Daniel Hausman,

The Inexact and Separate Science of Economics, chs. 1, 2, and 13, for more technical evaluations.

98. I have perhaps downplayed the work of the MIT economist Franco Modigliani, his Harvard contemporary James Duesenberry, and others in developing the life-cycle and permanent-income models of consumption and savings. By focusing on aggregate household income, and refining a formalized model of individual consumption in the terms of an idealized "rationalizing" behavior, they shifted the grounds on which model builders analyzed consumption issues. There is now concern about the predictive usefulness of such models. Angus Deaton, *Understanding Consumption* (New York: Oxford University Press, 1992), 214.

99. Whether what physicists do is what economists think they do is debated among philosophers of economics and science. See Donald McCloskey, *Knowledge and Persuasion in Economics* (New York: Cambridge University Press, 1994), chs. 9–11; Hausman, *Inexact and Separate Science*, ch. 15; and Alexander Rosenberg, *Microeconomic Laws: A Philosophical Analysis* (Pittsburgh: University of Pittsburgh Press, 1976).

100. Niehans, *History of Economic Theory*, 492.

101. A strong tradition at the University of Chicago, best exemplified by Friedman, favors simple modeling. See Milton Friedman, "The Methodology of Positive Economics," in Friedman, ed., *Essays in Positive Economics* (Chicago: University of Chicago Press, 1953). Friedman flatly asserted that the goals of a science such as "positive" (versus "normative") economics are exclusively predictive, a claim that had enormous influence in the 1950s. But his untrained venture into the philosophy of science has been savaged repeatedly over the years by other economists, and his own practices did not match his preaching. See Hausman, *Inexact and Separate Science*, 162–71.

102. Keynes on "mathematical economics" is quoted in Arthur Pigou, *Economics in Practice* (London: Macmillan, 1935), 262–63. Where the word "economics" appears in brackets, Keynes used the word "psychics," referring to Edgeworth's slender but important little book, *Mathematical Psychics*. The word "economics" is substituted here to avoid confusing readers. Keynes on Tinbergen, Kahn, and Harrod quoted in Robert Skidelsky, *John Maynard Keynes: The Economist as Savior, 1920–1937* (New York: Allen Lane/Penguin Press, 1992), 618–21.

103. Robert Aaron Gordon, "Rigor and Relevance in a Changing Institutional Setting," *American Economic Review*, March 1976, 10–11.

CHAPTER 14: KENNEDY, *SPUTNIK*, AND "LIBERAL GROWTHMANSHIP"

1. Bundy to Pusey, January 6, 1958, Overseers: General, box 131, Archives, Pusey Library, Harvard University. Bundy was not the first Harvard colleague to speak like this about Galbraith. John D. Black, as mentioned earlier, had noted a certain roughness in Galbraith as far back as 1947: "Given time enough to plan for it in advance," he wrote to Provost Paul Buck in support of Galbraith's candidacy for a professorship, Galbraith "is able to differ with his colleagues and associates in a pleasant and gracious manner; but not in haste and under pressure. No doubt a factor in his relations with others has been his urge to get on with the job and not waste too much time talking about it" (Black to Buck, December 22, 1947, Black Papers, Wisconsin Historical Society).

2. Galbraith, "Perils of the Big Build-Up," *The New York Times Magazine*, March 7, 1954, 12ff.

3. See Manchester, *Glory and the Dream*, v. 2, 965 (*Oregonian*, *Time*, and Johnson quotes.)

4. Ibid., 964.

5. Galbraith quoted in ibid., 965.

6. Harry McPherson, *A Political Education: A Washington Memoir* (Boston: Houghton Mifflin, 1988), 41. George Ball, who admired Kennedy and was his Undersecretary of State, was equally critical about JFK before he entered the White House: "Kennedy's political assets were far less impressive [than Eisenhower's]. In Congress his reputation had been more for absenteeism than serious achievement. He had never belonged to the inner circle of senators; nor was he confident of an always capricious public support. His major assets were his good looks and the glamour of a golden boy" (George Ball, "JFK's Big Moment," *New York Review of Books*, February 13, 1992, 16). For a closer look at Kennedy's economic views in the Senate, and the influence on him of Galbraith and other Cambridge economists, see Hugh Norton, *The Employment Act and the Council of Economic Advisors, 1946–1976* (Columbia: University of South Carolina Press, 1977), ch. 6.; also E. Ray Canterbery, *Economics on a New Frontier* (Belmont, Calif.: Wadsworth, 1968), especially chs. 3, 4, 6.

7. Manchester, *Glory and the Dream*, v. 2, 944.

8. Doris Kearns Goodwin, *The Fitzgeralds and the Kennedys* (New York: Simon & Schuster, 1987), 428–29.

9. See Iwan Worgan, *Eisenhower Versus "The Spenders": The Eisenhower Administration, the Democrats and the Budget, 1953–1960* (New York: St. Martin's Press, 1990), ch. 1 (for detailed examination). For a synoptic introduction, see Herbert Stein, *Presidential Economics*, 78–81.

10. Raymond Saulnier, *The Strategy of Economic Policy* (New York: Fordham University Press, 1962), 21; Eisenhower quoted in Collins, *MORE*, 45.

11. *Economic Report of the President* (Washington, D.C.: GPO, 1966), 173; Galbraith quoted in Herbert Stein, *Fiscal Revolution in America* (Chicago: University of Chicago Press, 1969), 283.

12. Hession and Sardy, *Ascent to Affluence*, 812–13.

13. Cited in Collins, *MORE*, 46.

14. Frank Gervasi, *The Real Rockefeller* (New York: Atheneum, 1964), 195–96.

15. Rockefeller Brothers Fund, *Prospect for America: The Rockefeller Panel Reports* (Garden City, N.Y.: Doubleday, 1961), v. xv, 251–53. In its call for public spending, the Commission echoed Galbraith's indictment of America's "social imbalance." Tracing the history of public infrastructure spending, the report showed that in the period 1915–40, per capita spending on schools, roads, waterworks, et cetera, grew 4.5 percent annually (adjusted for inflation). During the Depression spending fell and did not recover until 1936; but between 1936 and 1957, there had been no growth at all.

   The MIT economist Francis Bator reached the same conclusion via a different methodology: measuring nondefense public spending as a share of the nondefense-related portion of the GNP (the so-called civilian GNP). Bator found that in 1929 such spending was 7.5 percent; by 1939, 13.4 percent; and by 1957, 10.3 percent. Once again, it appeared that in America's new, "affluent society," there was money for guns but not butter. Bator cited in Hession, *Galbraith and His Critics*, 113.

16. This account of the "Gaither Report," its origins, the accuracy of assessment,

and its impact, is from Strobe Talbott, *The Master of the Game* (New York: Knopf, 1988), 66–74.

17. Stephen Ambrose, *Eisenhower, Volume Two: The President* (New York: Simon & Schuster, 1984), 434–35.

18. Kennedy quoted in Desmond Ball, *Politics and Force Levels* (Berkeley: University of California Press, 1988), 39–40. Kennedy used an early draft of Wohlstetter's impending *Foreign Affairs* article, "The Delicate Balance of Power," that summarized his arguments in the "Gaither Report."

19. Nixon report quoted in Seymour Harris, *Economics of the Kennedy Years* (New York: Harper & Row, 1964), 181.

20. Allen Dulles, in Joint Economic Committee, *Comparisons of the United States and Soviet Economics*, 86th Cong., 1st session, 1959, hearings, 6 and 11.

21. Khrushchev quoted in Collins, *MORE*, 46.

22. Manchester, *Glory and the Dream*, v. 2, 1034.

23. Ibid., 1034 and Barone, *Our Country*, 302–6 (on Republican losses); Martin, *Stevenson and the World*, 197–98, and Schlesinger, interview with author (on Schlesinger memo to Stevenson).

24. Paul Douglas and Howard Sherman, "Growth Without Inflation," *The New Republic*, September 26, 1960, 22.

25. Peter Collier and David Horowitz, *The Rockefellers* (New York: Holt, Rinehart, 1976), 329 n.

26. Gerard Colby, *Thy Will Be Done* (New York: HarperCollins, 1995), 338.

27. Galbraith, *A Life*, 53–54 (on Winthrop House); 356 (for Kennedy quote and early advising).

28. Ibid., 375–76, describes Galbraith's amusing work as JFK's emissary to Eleanor Roosevelt.

29. On his 1950s Harvard workload, see Galbraith to Mason, October 4, 1954, where he lists teaching six classes per year, co-supervising 10 to 15 doctoral theses, the direction of the book series Harvard Economic Studies, and working on graduate admission and fellowship applications, trusteeship duties at Radcliffe, and "some minor Harvard committees." On cutting his workload, Galbraith to Harris, September 18, 1958. On his lobbying for Samuelson and Tobin (to get them, Galbraith wanted to offer at least $20,000 a year—much more than he earned—but Dean Bundy was reluctant), see Galbraith to Department Chairman Ed Mason and to Bundy, November 4, 1957, and their replies, November 7, all in Harvard 1948–1965, box 70, Galbraith Papers, JFK Library. On the size of the department and recruiting Kuznets, see Kellers, *Making Harvard Modern*, 222–23.

30. See Galbraith, *A Life*, 349–53, and Galbraith, *A Journey to Poland and Yugoslavia* (Cambridge, Mass.: Harvard University Press, 1959).

31. Kennedy to Galbraith, January 21, 1959, in Galbraith, *Letters to Kennedy* (Cambridge, Mass.: Harvard University Press, 1998), 61. Sales figures provided to author by Harvard University Press.

32. Galbraith, *A Life*, 363 (on the big new book [it was *The New Industrial State*], leave, and Warburg chair).

33. Ibid., 364–71 (on his trip to India, Ceylon and Russia); on his photography, see Galbraith to Houghton Mifflin, December 16, 1958, Galbraith file, box 54, Houghton Mifflin Papers, Houghton Library, Harvard University; on the 1960s Cambridge policy group and Kissinger, see Walter Isaacson, *Kissinger* (New

York: Simon & Schuster, 1992), 104–5; on Kissinger's shift from "Flexible Response" to détente, see Gaddis, *Strategies of Containment*, ch. 9.

34. Kennedy to Galbraith, September 11, 1959, in Galbraith, *Letters to Kennedy*, 8; Galbraith, *A Life*, 366–67 (on the dog attack); the India-Russia diary, mimeograph, Publications: Book MSS, box 94, Galbraith Papers, JFK Library.

35. Galbraith, *A Life*, 358.

36. Collins, *MORE*, 38.

37. Ibid., 20–21.

38. Leon Keyserling, "Full Employment," in Quincy Howe and Arthur Schlesinger, Jr., eds., *Guide to Politics, 1954* (New York: Dial Press, 1954), 9–13.

39. Keyserling in Gaddis, *Strategies of Containment*, 94.

40. Ibid., 98. Ch. 4 discusses NSC-68 and its consequences, and Keyserling's work in creating its economic justification.

41. Hershberg, *James B. Conant*, 482–84.

42. Lovett and "scare" plan quoted in Gaddis, *Strategies of Containment*, 107–8.

43. Gillon, *Politics and Vision: ADA and American Liberalism*, 113 (on Keyserling's expansive claims for growth in ADA's 1956 platform).

44. The DAC's lengthiest policy statement on the failings of, and alternatives to, Eisenhower-era economics was reported on the front page of *The New York Times*, just three weeks after *Sputnik*'s rockets roared aloft. Galbraith, its author, gave visible ground to Keyserling on the importance of growth, then knotted up the claim with Galbraithian particulars on corporations' managed pricing, the Fed's tight-money policies, structural bottlenecks, and so forth—themes central to the soon-to-be published *Affluent Society*. See W. H. Lawrence, "Democrats Take a Strong Stand for Civil Rights," *The New York Times*, October 21, 1957, 1 (the full text of the DAC's economic statement is on 20).

  Three months later, Keyserling issued his own recommendations, free of Galbraith's moderating hand. He advocated "sharply higher wages, higher consumption, much larger government spending on both defense and civilian programs, and a tax cut to lower-income groups." The growth would, he said, balance the budget quickly and actually dampen, not sharpen, inflation. There was no need to choose between "missiles and tail fins," he told the *Times*; growth would pay for both. "Pay Rises Called a Recession Cure," *The New York Times*, January 15, 1958, 13; Galbraith, interview with author; also Galbraith, *Ambassador's Journal*, 68.

45. See Arthur Schlesinger, Jr., "The Death Wish of the Democrats," September 15, 1958, 7–8; Leon Keyserling, "Eggheads and Politics," October 27, 1958, 13–17; "Galbraith and Schlesinger Reply to Leon Keyserling," November 3, 1958, 14–15; and "Leon Keyserling on Economic Expansion," November 17, 1958, 16–17, all in *The New Republic*.

46. Kennedy to Galbraith, February 4, 1958, 1960 Presidential Campaign, box 74, Galbraith Papers, JFK Library.

47. On Kennedy and India, see Mark Haefele, "Walt Rostow, Modernization, and Vietnam: Stages of Theoretical Growth," Ph.D. diss., Harvard University, 2000, 254–55.

48. Tobin, in "CEA Oral History," 34, 49, JFK Library.

49. Martin, *Stevenson and the World*, 411–16 (on Stevenson's client and Africa tour); Galbraith's reaction, interview with author.

50. Galbraith, *A Life*, only briefly mentions the dinner, 378; Schlesinger, *Thousand*

Days, 27–28 (on Locke-Ober's meeting), 34–36 (on Schlesinger detailing the influential public petition that he and Galbraith, along with Henry Steele Commager, Allan Nevins, Arthur Goldberg, James MacGregor Burns, and a dozen other former Stevenson backers used to endorse Kennedy for the nomination). On Galbraith's sense of guilt about switching to JFK and Stevenson's reply, see Galbraith to Stevenson, August 12, and reply, August 18, 1960, General Correspondence, box 59, Galbraith Papers, JFK Library. Some Stevenson supporters, including Agnes Meyer (widow of Eugene Meyer), Alicia Patterson of *Newsday*, and Tom Finletter's wife, were more reproachful at the Democratic convention. See Galbraith, *A Life*, 380–81.

51. Galbraith to Kennedy, June 1, 1960, 1960 Presidential Campaign, box 74, Galbraith Papers, JFK Library. Schlesinger, *Thousand Days*, 36–38 (on Hyannis Port weekend).
52. [Galbraith], "Confidential Memorandum Campaign Strategy, 1960," 1960 Presidential Campaign, box 74, Galbraith Papers, JFK Library. Boxes 74 and 75 contain three other important strategy memos by him: "Financing the Democratic Program," "Re Presidential Assistants," and "The Issue of Experience in the 1960 Campaign," the last on Nixon.
53. Galbraith, *A Life*, 378.
54. Schlesinger, *Thousand Days*, 62.
55. Galbraith, *A Life*, 385.
56. See 1960 Presidential Campaign, boxes 74 and 75, Galbraith Papers, JFK Library.
57. Galbraith to Kennedy, July 16, 1960, 1960 Presidential Campaign, box 74, Galbraith Papers, JFK Library. For Kennedy's inaugural address and Johnson's speech to Congress and the nation five days after Kennedy's assassination, Sorensen effectively torpedoed Galbraith's drafts in favor of his own, which were stellar. See Michael Beschloss, *Taking Charge* (New York: Simon & Schuster, 1997), 38–41, on LBJ's and Sorensen's discussion of Galbraith's draft.
58. Galbraith to Kennedy, October 20, 1960, 1960 Presidential Campaign, box 74, Galbraith Papers, JFK Library.
59. On Kennedy and gold in brief, see Irving Bernstein, *Promises Kept*, 121–22; for a fuller account, Ray Canterbery, *Economics on a New Frontier*, chs. 7, 8, 13. Samuelson was an opponent of Galbraith on both the gold question and monetary policy. Samuelson's comments underscore his emphasis on pure theory over politics. Both issues were for him technical ones; for Galbraith, they were always simultaneously economic and political. Tobin complained of Galbraith's influence on JFK's interest-rate policies and wondered aloud whether Kennedy knew about Roosevelt's handling of the gold issue in 1933, which of course he did, from Galbraith's memo to Kennedy. See Samuelson in "CEA Oral History" JFK Library, 51–68 and 61–63.
60. Walter Heller, in Edwin Hargrove and Samuel Morley, eds., *The President and the Council of Economic Advisors: Interviews with CEA Chairmen* (Boulder, Colo.: Westview, 1984), 173–74. He summarized the discussion in a memo for Galbraith, Samuelson, and Seymour Harris, to emphasize their shared views.
61. Shortly after midnight, Nixon went before reporters and supporters to concede, if "the present trend continues." But he never admitted defeat formally. He lost with 49.55 percent of the vote to Kennedy's 49.71 percent, and remained convinced that Mayor Daley in Illinois and Lyndon Johnson in Texas

had stolen the election (Kennedy won Illinois by 4,500 votes and Texas by 28,000).

CHAPTER 15: ON THE NEW FRONTIER

1. Details of inauguration from Schlesinger, *Thousand Days*, 11–14, and Manchester, *Glory and the Dream*, v. 2, 1089–91.
2. Galbraith, *Ambassador's Journal: A Personal Account of the Kennedy Years* (Boston: Houghton Mifflin, 1969), 17–18.
3. According to Sorensen, Kennedy focused on foreign and military issues because domestic affairs were felt to be too divisive and partisan. See Theodore Sorensen, *Kennedy* (New York: Bantam Books, 1966), 272.
4. See Seymour Harris, *The Economics of the Kennedy Years* (New York: Harper & Row, 1964), 197 (75 percent data); "Military and Civilian Space Budgets," *Air Force Magazine*, August 2000, 37 (on space budgets); Gaddis, *Strategies of Containment*, 359 (on military dollars).
5. Wittner, *Cold War America*, 145–48.
6. Harris, *Economics of the Kennedy Years*, 236. Kennedy's acute awareness of the link between defense spending and domestic politics explains why he was in Dallas on November 22, 1963, to shore up support among conservative Democrats in advance of his 1964 race. In the speech planned for that afternoon he planned to remind his skeptical listeners,
   > In Fort Worth, I pledged in 1960 to build a national defense which was second to none—a position I said, which is not "first, but," not "first, if," not "first, when," but first—period. That pledge has been fulfilled. In the past 3 years we have increased our defense budget by over 20 percent; increased the program for acquistion of Polaris submarines from 24 to 41; increased our Minutemen missile purchase program by more than 75 percent; doubled the number of strategic bombers and missiles on alert; doubled the number of nuclear weapons available in the strategic alert forces; increased the tactical nuclear forces deployed in Western Europe by 60 percent; added 5 combat ready divisions and 5 tactical fighter wings to our Armed Forces; increased our strategic airlift capabilities by 75 percent; and increased our special counterinsurgency forces by 600 percent. We can truly say today, with pride in our voices and peace in our hearts, that the defensive forces of the United States are, without a doubt, the most powerful and resourceful forces anywhere in the world.

   Anchoring the South to the Democratic Party had for Roosevelt been a matter of supporting rich cotton subsidies and silence on race; arms spending was the Cold War's currency.
7. Sorensen, *Kennedy*, 608.
8. Schlesinger, *Thousand Days*, 878; on spending, Wittner, *Cold War America*, 204–5.
9. Schlesinger, *Thousand Days*, 607 (on JFK and children); 921–23 (on starting war on poverty).
10. Harris, *Economics of the Kennedy Years*, 14.
11. James Tobin, *The New Economics One Decade Older* (Princeton, N.J.: Princeton University Press, 1974), 13.
12. Collins, *MORE*, 52.
13. Heller and Tobin quoted in ibid., 54.

14. Theodore H. White, *In Search of History* (New York: Harper & Row, 1978), 493–94.

15. Collins, *MORE*, 53.

16. Friedman quoted in "We're All Keynesians Now," *Time* (cover story on Keynes), December 31, 1965, 64–67. Friedman later insisted he'd been misquoted. "What Friedman had actually said was this: 'We are all Keynesians now and nobody is any longer a Keynesian,' meaning that while everyone had absorbed some substantial part of what Keynes taught no one any longer believed it all" (Stein, *Presidential Economics*, 113).

17. Walter Heller, *New Dimensions of Political Economy* (Cambridge, Mass.: Harvard University Press, 1966), vii–viii.

18. Samuelson quoted in Irving Bernstein, *Promises Kept* (New York: Oxford University Press, 1991), 122.

19. Mirowski, "Cowles Changes Allegiance," 169–71.

20. Samuelson, "Liberalism at Bay," in Hiroaki Nagatani and Kate Crowley, eds., *The Collected Scientific Papers of Paul Samuelson* (Cambridge, Mass.: MIT Press, 1977), v. 4, 871–72. On Buckley's effect, see Samuelson interview in David Colander and Harry Landruth, *The Coming of the Keynesian Revolution* (Brookfield, Vt.: Edward Elgar, 1996), 171.

21. See Seymour Melman, *The Permanent War Economy* (New York: Simon & Schuster, 1974), 147–51; textbooks surveyed include those by Caves, Chalmers and Leonard, Dernburg and McDougall, Dorfman, Eckstein, Gordon, Hailstones and Brennan, Harris, Heilbroner, McConnell, Nichols and Reynolds, Peterson, Reynolds, Samuelson, and Schultze.

22. See Robert Solow and James Tobin, introduction to the 1961 reprint edition of *Economic Report to the President*, in James Tobin and Murray Weidenbaum, eds., *Two Revolutions in Economic Policy* (Cambridge, Mass.: MIT Press, 1988), 3–16. The 1961 and 1962 *Economic Reports* are the clearest manifestos of New Economics thinking of the time.

23. James Tobin, interview with author.

24. Harrod's growth model grew from his study of Keynes's "multiplier principle" and of the "accelerator" ideas of John Maurice Clark. Domar developed similar ideas while studying under Alvin Hansen during World War II. Harrod relabeled the "accelerator" the "capital/output ratio," set the marginal propensity to save equal to the average propensity, and thereby showed that steady-state or smooth growth caused total income to grow at a rate equal to the savings rate divided by the capital/output ratio. Distinguishing between what he called "natural" growth rates (roughly, at full employment) and "warranted" (roughly, steady-state equilibrium) growth rates, he was led to the so-called knife-edge problem, arguing that "warranted" growth was inherently unstable because departures from it were cumulative. This was a subject of intense debate, to which economists like Tobin thought they had found an answer; Harrod never really agreed. See H. Phelps-Brown, "Sir Roy Harrod: A Biographical Memoir," *Economic Journal*, March 1980, 1–33.

25. See, for example, Paul Samuelson and Robert Solow, "A Complete Capital Model Involving Heterogeneous Capital Goods," *Quarterly Journal of Economics*, November, 1956, 537–62.

26. Solow's contribution, the so-called "T" or "Solow constant" sign for technological change, was first advanced in his "Technical Change and the Aggregate Produc-

tion Function," *Review of Economics and Statistics*, August 1957, 312–20. See also Solow, "Technical Progress, Capital Formation, and Economic Growth," *American Economic Review*, May 1962, 76–86.

27. See James Tobin, "A Dynamic Aggregative Model," *Journal of Political Economy*, April 1955, 103–15. Tobin's solution to the knife-edge problem became the key to creating what some economists consider a full Neoclassical Synthesis model of growth, reliant less on Keynes than on pre-Keynesians such as Alfred Marshall and Knut Wicksell.

   Growth theory took another step with Edmund Phelps's articulation of "the golden rule," which concluded that the optimal rate of economic growth was equal to the rate of interest. See Phelps, "The Golden Rule of Accumulation: A Fable for Growth Men," *American Economic Review*, September 1961, 638–45. For several reasons, however, the "golden rule" turned out to be more seductive theoretically than practically applicable. Since the 1960s, growth theory has shown tenuous connection to practical applications. See Frank Hahn and R. C. O. Matthews, *Surveys of Economic Theory*, v. 2 (New York: St. Martin's Press, 1965) for an overview of the postwar growth theory debate.

28. See James Knowles, "The Potential Economic Growth in the United States," in *Study of Employment Growth and Price Levels* (JEC, 86th Cong., 2nd sess., 1960), and Edward Dennison, *The Sources of Economic Growth in the United States*, Supplementary Paper No. 13 (New York: Committee for Economic Development, 1962). For Heller's comments, see Canterbery, *Economics on a New Frontier*, 67–68; A. W. Phillips, "The Relation Between Unemployment and the Rate of Change of Money Wage Rates in the United Kingdom, 1861–1957," *Economica*, November 1958, 283–99; and Paul Samuelson and Robert Solow, "Analytical Aspects of Anti-Inflation Policy," *American Economic Review*, May 1960, 174–94.

29. Solow quoted in Daniel Bell, "Models and Reality in Economic Discourse," in Daniel Bell and Irving Kristol, eds., *The Crisis in Economic Theory* (New York: Basic Books, 1981), 66–67.

30. See Heller interview, in Hargrove and Morley, *The President and the CEA*, 173.

31. See Canterbery, *Economics on a New Frontier*, ch. 1, and Heller interview, in Hargrove and Morley, *The President and the CEA*, 174–75.

32. Inaugural Address, box 76, White House 1961, Galbraith Papers, JFK Library. Sorensen's "Inaugural Address" file at the library shows the speech's evolution to its final form.

33. Galbraith's surviving contributions also included Kennedy's call to aid underdeveloped countries "not to defeat communism, not to win votes, but because it is right," as well as the rhetorically powerful closing, "Let us begin" (Galbraith, *Ambassador's Journal*, 15).

34. Eisenhower had planned to decry "the military-industrial-congressional complex," but changed this because, "It was not fitting, [Ike] thought, for a president to criticize Congress. It may have also seemed to him particularly ungracious, since he was about to be succeeded by one of the loudest congressional drumbeaters for higher military spending" (Lars-Erik Nelson, "Military-Industrial Man," *New York Review of Books*, December 21, 2000, 6).

35. See Samuelson on the CEA offer from Kennedy, which he says Galbraith strongly urged him to accept, in *CEA Oral History*, 101–2; on JFK's willingness to appoint Galbraith, which Samuelson says Galbraith made clear to him he

wouldn't accept, see 82, 107. Samuelson suggests that Seymour Harris may have wanted the post, but was quite ill at the time, and Kennedy some weeks later made him Dillon's senior economic adviser at Treasury (109). Interestingly, Heller, who barely knew Kennedy (and had supported Humphrey in the primary), was taken aback to learn that Galbraith had ever been under consideration. "I didn't know that Ken . . . I would have not thought that the president would have wanted Ken in this job," he sputtered. "I'm a little surprised to hear that he could have had it if he wanted it" (107).

36. Galbraith, *A Life*, 389–90.

37. Galbraith, *Ambassador's Journal*, 1. See John Fenton, "Furcolo Believed Likely to Name Kennedy Choice to Senate Seat," *The New York Times*, November 11, 1960, 24.

38. See Adam Clymer, *Edward M. Kennedy: A Biography* (New York: William Morrow, 1999), 25–35 for details.

39. Galbraith, interview with author; Galbraith, *Ambassador's Journal*, 20–21; Schlesinger, *Thousand Days*, 394 (for "ignored the injunction"). Kennedy took pleasure in his correspondence with Galbraith. In late 1963 he suggested to the editors of *Life* that they ought to publish them. Approached by *Life* after Kennedy's assassination, Galbraith declined to proceed with this plan, but later included many of his letters in *Ambassador's Journal*. In 1998, Harvard published a near-complete version as *Letters to Kennedy*.

40. Galbraith, *Ambassador's Journal*, 26.

41. See Galbraith to Kennedy, November 17, 1960, in Galbraith, *Letters to Kennedy*, 33. In *Ambassador's Journal*, 1, Galbraith wrote that he favored McNamara for Treasury, after getting a strong recommendation from an old mutual friend, W. H. "Ping" Ferry. Katharine Graham vividly recalled a dinner at her home shortly after the election, at which her husband advanced the case for his friend Dillon and got Galbraith's impassioned adverse reaction. See Katharine Graham, *Personal History* (New York: Knopf, 1997), 271.

42. Canterbery, *Economics on a New Frontier*, 89. Galbraith didn't know at the time that Dillon's case for gold and its linkage to national security had already been made by Paul Nitze during the campaign. Asked to chair a task force on national security, Nitze reported to Kennedy that "all those whom we consulted in the New York business community had listed gold as the nation's top issue," and that Nitze's friends in State and Treasury thought the problem was worse than Eisenhower admitted. "The earliest appointment of a Secretary of the Treasury who enjoys the highest respect and confidence in the international financial world," he concluded, should be Kennedy's first priority. See Schlesinger, *Thousand Days*, 129.

43. The Sproul Report, organized by Roosa to counter Keynesian goals for the administration, is the fullest first statement of the Treasury-Fed view.

44. Short-term interest rates rose more than long-term rates fell. By 1964, the price paid for Operation Twist drawing in every $1 of short-term foreign capital was an estimated $12 loss in GNP. See Galbraith to Kennedy, February 16, 1961, box 76, White House 1961, Galbraith Papers, JFK Library; on Operation Twist's failure, see Canterbery, *Economics on a New Frontier*, 164.

45. At a meeting of Kennedy's top economic advisers on January 18, 1961, Tobin especially supported Dillon's views on reducing the reserve requirement. Galbraith opposed them, feeling "the discussion was dominated—too much, I thought—

by the problem of gold outflow" and believed mistakenly that by the end of the discussion that he'd gotten the issue shelved. See Galbraith, *Ambassador's Journal*, 14–15.

46. Heller interview, in Hargrove and Morley, *President and the Council of Economic Advisors*, 202.

47. Canterbery, *Economics on a New Frontier*, 100. For details of Samuelson's positions, see his *New Frontiers of the Kennedy Administration: The Texts of the Task Force Reports Prepared for the President* (Washington, D.C.: Public Affairs Press, 1963), 24ff.

48. Galbraith, *Ambassador's Journal*, 22. Galbraith did not highlight the military section of the speech, which called for a major weapons buildup, where the tone and content cut directly against all of his instincts and beliefs. See "State of the Union, January 30, 1961," in *Public Papers of the Presidents, John F. Kennedy, 1961* (Washington, D.C.: GPO, 1962), 19–28.

49. Galbraith, *Ambassador's Journal*, 23.

50. See Galbraith to Kennedy, February 2, 1961, White House 1961, box 75, Galbraith Papers, JFK Library.

51. Galbraith to Kennedy, November 15, 1963, in Galbraith, *Letters to Kennedy*, 58.

52. Galbraith to Kennedy, May 31, 1962, in ibid., 48–52.

53. Galbraith, *Ambassador's Journal*, 33.

54. Ibid., chs. 1–2.

55. Ibid., 11–12.

56. Ibid., 45–48.

57. Cited in Manchester, *Glory and the Dream*, v. 2, 1098. See also Haynes Johnson, *The Bay of Pigs* (New York: Dell, 1964), Peter Kornbluh, *Bay of Pigs Declassified* (New York: New Press, 1998), and Peter Kornbluh and James Blight, *Politics of Illusion* (Boulder, Colo.: Lynne Rienner, 1998).

58. Galbraith to Kennedy, April 3, 1961, in Galbraith, *Letters to Kennedy*, 64–65.

59. See Schlesinger, *Thousand Days*, 235–40; the full text of his April 5 memo, notes of the April 4 meeting, and Fulbright's arguments are in United States Department of State, *Foreign Relations of the United States, Cuba 1961–63* (Washington, D.C.: GPO, 1997), documents 79, 80, 81.

60. See Galbraith, *A Life*, 396–97. The view of his CIA station chief, Harry Rositzke, is different. Rositzke, in an interview with the author, confirmed that some but not all covert agency activities were curtailed. Rositzke noted that the CIA's support for the Dalai Lama and Tibetan refugees, who were living in India, continued. This program included the training of young Tibetan guerrilla fighters in secret bases in Colorado, then airlifting them back in to Tibet. The program was a disaster, and almost all the guerrillas were captured, tortured, and killed by the Chinese, who were infuriated by the United States' role. (The Chinese were no less furious about U-2 flights over their territory, but the spy planes took off from Pakistani bases.) At the end of Galbraith's ambassadorship, after the Sino-Indian War in 1962, New Delhi secretly allowed Washington to place a string of highly sensitive listening devices in the Himalayas, along the Chinese border. Because many of the CIA's other activities, involving domestic Indian politics, are still classified, Rositzke offered no further details.

61. Galbraith, *Ambassador's Journal*, 48.

62. Covert U.S. involvement in Indochina's future actually predated the 1946 aid commitment. At the Allied meeting in Potsdam in the summer of 1945, Truman

and Churchill secretly agreed that, once the Japanese surrendered, the initial postwar Allied occupation of Indochina would be divided between the British in the south and the Nationalist Chinese in the north, with the line of division at the 16th Parallel. Stalin seemed unperturbed when he learned of this arrangement made by his allies, but both the French and the Indochinese nationalists (including Ho Chi Minh) were outraged. See Leffler, *Preponderance of Power*, 92–94; McCullough, *Truman*, 452. On U.S. covert support in 1954, see Wittner, *Cold War America*, 161.

63. Galbraith to Kennedy, May 10, 1961, in Galbraith, *Letters to Kennedy*, 70–71.

64. See Kaiser, *American Tragedy: Kennedy, Johnson, and the Origins of the Vietnam War* (Cambridge, Mass.: Belknap/Harvard, 2000), 48 (on McNamara's estimate); 43 (on the Joint Chiefs' views); 52 (on LeMay). See Wittner, *Cold War America*, 230 (on U.S. aid to Laotian army).

65. Robert Kennedy quoted in A. J. Langguth, *Our Vietnam: The War, 1954–1975* (New York: Simon & Schuster, 2000), 127.

66. See Richard Nixon, "Cuba, Castro, and John F. Kennedy," *Reader's Digest*, November 1964, 281–300.

67. See Schlesinger, *Thousand Days*, 315.

68. Canterbery, *Economics on a New Frontier*, 127 (on Heller's lobbying technique); Heller interview, in Hargrove and Morley, *President and the Council of Economic Advisors*, 192.

69. See Hugh Norton, *The Employment Act and the Council of Economic Advisors* (Columbia: University of South Carolina Press, 1977), 177, 199.

70. Galbraith to Kennedy, July 11, 1961, in Galbraith, *Letters to Kennedy*, 76–77.

71. Heller interview, in Hargrove and Morley, *President and the Council of Economic Advisors*, 199–200; Canterbery, *Economics on a New Frontier*, 105, notes the CEA's exclusion from NSC discussions.

72. Galbraith, *Ambassador's Journal*, 121–24.

73. See Kaiser, *American Tragedy*, 100–5.

74. See Galbraith, *Letters to Kennedy*, ch. 2.

75. "While the Department of Labor, the Commerce Department, and Federal Reserve Chairman Martin were concerned with training workers in order to eliminate 'structural' unemployment, the CEA was more concerned with economic growth" (Canterbery, *Economics on a New Frontier*, 73); Canterbery's evidence for this view follows (73–77).

76. Galbraith to Kennedy, August 20, 1962, in Galbraith, *Letters to Kennedy*, 54–56.

77. Galbraith to Kennedy, March 25, 1961, in ibid., 39–42.

78. On Galbraith's repeated counsel that stimulative spending rather than tax cuts should be favored, see Galbraith, *Ambassador's Journal*, ch. 1.

79. See the speech he wrote for Kennedy, "Special Message to the Congress on Balance of Payments," January 29, 1961, and his State of the Union address, in *Public Papers of the Presidents, John F. Kennedy, 1961*, 10–28; Galbraith's drafts are in White House 1961, box 76, Galbraith Papers, JFK Library. Between 1945 and 1960, of the thousands of articles that appeared in the top two dozen economics journals, only twenty-seven used the word "defense" or "military" in their text, and only three of those meaningfully addressed the structural effects military spending had on the economy. JSTOR search by author. When Kennedy-Johnson CEA veterans wrote a *festschrift* for Heller in 1982, none mentioned this problematic linkage of defense spending to successful economic expansion

before Vietnam, and Heller again dismissed the very idea as "a canard that dies mighty hard" (Joseph Pechman and N. J. Simler, *Economics in the Public Service: Papers in Honor of Walter W. Heller* [New York: Norton, 1982]; Heller's comment, 242).

80. Galbraith to Kennedy, October 20, 1960, in Galbraith, *Letters to Kennedy,* 29–31.

81. Galbraith to Kennedy, November 17, 1960 in ibid., 32–34; Galbraith, *Ambassador's Journal,* 13–14. The definitive—though very British—treatment of Keynes at Bretton Woods is Robert Skidelsky, *John Maynard Keynes: Fighting for Freedom, 1937–1946,* chs. 10–13.

82. Galbraith, *Ambassador's Journal,* 136.

83. Stanley Wolpert, *Nehru: A Tryst with Destiny* (New York: Oxford University Press, 1996), 479.

84. Galbraith to Kennedy, "A Plan for South Vietnam," November 3, 1961, *Foreign Relations of the United States, Vietnam 1961* (Washington, D.C.: GPO, 1988), document 209 (hereafter, *FRUS Vietnam 1961*).

85. Galbraith gives slightly different versions of the sequence and dates of Nehru's visit to Hammersmith Farm and events in the following week in *Ambassador's Journal,* ch. 8, and *A Life,* 470–77. The "lack of precision" in what he and Kennedy said was partly due to the deep hostility among Kennedy's other foreign-policy advisers to opening negotiations with the North Vietnamese. The next day in Washington, Dean Rusk gave Desai a stern lecture on "Communist duplicity" after Desai mildly suggested that both the United States and Russia were at fault in the failures of the Geneva Peace Accords. See "Memorandum of a Conversation, Department of State," *FRUS Vietnam 1961,* document 229.

86. Galbraith, *Ambassador's Journal,* 246.

87. On CENIS, the CIA, and MIT, see Dorothy Nelkin, *The University and Military Research: Moral Politics at MIT* (Ithaca, N.Y.: Cornell University Press, 1972); Mark Haefele, "Walt Rostow, Modernization, and Vietnam: Stages of Theoretical Growth," Ph.D. diss., Harvard University, 2000; and James Killian, *The Education of a College President* (Cambridge, Mass.: MIT Press, 1985), 63–68. Noam Chomsky, *The Cold War and the University: Toward an Intellectual History of the Postwar Years* (New York: New Press, 1997), and Christopher Simpson, ed., *Universities and Empire: Money and Politics in the Social Sciences during the Cold War* (New York: Free Press, 1998) give a broader overview.

88. See George Rosen, *Western Economists and Eastern Societies: Agents of Change in South Asia, 1950–1970* (Baltimore: Johns Hopkins University Press, 1985).

89. See Wittner, *Cold War America,* 145.

90. See W. W. Rostow (with Richard Hatch), *An American Policy in Asia* (New York: John Wiley, 1955), for his early views on guerrilla warfare and Lansdale. See also Haefele, "Walt Rostow," ch. 4.

91. See Kaiser, *American Tragedy,* ch. 3, for this chronology, and his rebuttal to David Halberstam's long-accepted claim in *The Best and the Brightest* that it was Kennedy himself who by then wanted Vietnam used as a testing ground for U.S. military power to deter the Russians.

92. Galbraith, *Letters to Kennedy,* 65–88, and Galbraith, *Ambassador's Journal,* 131–37, 203–8.

93. Galbraith to Kennedy, August 15, 1961, in *Letters to Kennedy,* 79–82.

94. Galbraith to Kennedy, October 9, 1961, in *Letters to Kennedy,* 86–88.

95. The cable from Ambassador Nolting to the State Department, October 1, 1961, was shared with half a dozen key U.S. embassies, including that in New Delhi. See *FRUS Vietnam 1961*, document 142; on Wiesner's visit and Galbraith's subsequent cable to Kennedy, October 9, 1961, see *Ambassador's Journal*, 222–25. On October 5, Chester Bowles sent a dissenting memo on Vietnam to Rusk, outlining his strategic arguments for neutralizing Southeast Asia generally rather than fighting; he also sent a copy to Adlai Stevenson, the American U.N. ambassador, noting that Ball and Harriman agreed with him. Rusk ignored Bowles's memo, as he increasingly ignored Bowles, and there is no indication that Kennedy ever saw it. See *FRUS Vietnam 1961*, document 145. The October 11 draft instructions Taylor wrote for Kennedy to sign are document 157, and should be compared with Kennedy's significantly amended October 13 version of them in Maxwell Taylor, *Swords into Ploughshares* (New York: Norton, 1972), 225–26.

96. On Galbraith's November schedule, *Ambassador's Journal*, 241–71. Officially, the "Report of General Taylor's Mission to South Vietnam, 3 November 1961." The Taylor-Rostow party left Washington on October 15 and returned two weeks later; it was in Vietnam October 18 to 25. See Kaiser, *American Tragedy*, 102.

97. Galbraith, *A Life*, 470.

98. See Rusk to Kennedy, November 24, 1961, *FRUS Vietnam 1961*, document 275; Alexis Johnson to Rusk, November 22, is quoted in this document, at n. 1. On the Vietnam defoliant program, see Walter Boyne, "Ranch Hand," *Air Force Magazine*, August 2000, 84–89.

99. See Galbraith to Kennedy, "A Plan for South Vietnam," November 3, 1961, FRUS 1961, document 209. Note the memo's November 3 date, which contradicts Galbraith's first published account of these events, in *Ambassador's Journal* (1969), where he says he first read the Taylor report at the State Department on November 11 (254), and met with Rostow on November 4, not November 7 (242); he makes no mention of purloining the report, although he says obliquely, "I rather frightened Walt with the responsibility he was assuming" (243). His account of meeting Rostow on November 7 and walking out with the report is from *A Life*, written in 1981 (470). Galbraith, in interview with author, says that in 1969 he was reluctant to name Rostow as his unwilling source for the Taylor report. He may also not have wanted to reveal how he got hold of the document; when *Ambassador's Journal* appeared, Richard Nixon was President, and the possibility of prosecuting a prominent antiwar figure such as Galbraith might have been tempting. By 1981 Galbraith had perhaps confused the dates; in any case, he gave President Kennedy his memo on November 3, the same day Taylor formally presented his report. In separate interviews with the author in 2002, neither Galbraith nor Rostow could clarify their discrepant memories.

On Galbraith's November 1 meetings with Ball, and with Kennedy, Truman, and Bowles, see *Ambassador's Journal* (242–43). Mann, *Grand Delusion* (240–53), recounts the 1961 dissenting views of senators Fulbright and Mansfield (including the latter's memo to Kennedy on Taylor's report, delivered the same day as Galbraith's), and of George Ball's warnings to Kennedy about the report at almost the same time.

100. See Draft, McNamara to Kennedy, November 5, 1961, *FRUS Vietnam 1961*, document 214. The pressure to recommend more troops to Kennedy was so

great that George Ball went along—despite his later recollections to the contrary. See Howard Jones, *Death of a Generation* (New York: Oxford University Press, 2003), 120–21.

101. See "Memorandum for the Record," November 6, 1961, *FRUS Vietnam 1961*, document 211, and Kaiser, *American Tragedy*, 109–10. The hawkish November 8 draft basis of the November 11 decision memorandum presented to the President called for committing 205,000 troops, and declared that "the chances are against, probably sharply against, preventing the fall of South VietNam by any measures short of the introduction of U.S. forces on a substantial scale"—a sentence that was deleted from the final memorandum. See "Draft Memorandum for the President," November 8, 1961, *FRUS Vietnam 1961*, document 228. McNamara's memo to JFK the same day, with his and the Joint Chiefs' equally hawkish views, are in striking contrast to the final decision memo of November 11. See *The Pentagon Papers, Gravel ed.*, v. 2 (Boston: Beacon Press, 1971), 108–10.

102. E. W. Kenworthy, "President Is Cool on Asia Troop Aid," *The New York Times*, November 4, 1961, 1; see also Kaiser, *American Tragedy*, 108.

103. "Notes of a meeting, the White House," *FRUS Vietnam 1961*, document 236; the notes are General Lyman Lemnitzer's. Interestingly, *The Pentagon Papers* doesn't include this document and consequently shows some confusion about the meeting and what happened (116–17).

104. "List of Questions Prepared by President," *FRUS Vietnam 1961*, document 235.

105. See "Memorandum for the President," November 11, 1961, *United States–Vietnam Relations* (Washington, D.C.: GPO, 1985), book 11, 359–67.

106. See the two memos by McNamara to Lemnitzer, November 13, 1961, *FRUS Vietnam 1961*, documents 245, 246.

107. On State's instructions, see State to Embassy Vietnam, November 15, 1961, document 257, in ibid. But by then, Ambassador Nolting had already heard from the French and British ambassadors in Vietnam of Rusk's earlier conversations with their counterparts in Washington and was aware of the discrepancies in Rusk's descriptions of U.S. plans to commit troops. He complained about hearing of Washington's decisions after the French and British had, and warned that the South Vietnamese government had no doubt been similarly informed, thus diminishing his stature and influence, and muddying the United States' true intentions in the eyes of Diem. On Nolting's reaction, see Embassy to State, November 15, 1961, document 255.

108. See ibid., on Rusk's discussion with the French ambassador, document 241 (Memorandum of Conversation, November 13, 1961), and with the British ambassador, document 243 (Memorandum of Conversation, November 13, 1961). Galbraith, *Ambassador's Journal*, ch. 12; that Kennedy never told Galbraith about the November 11 NSC meeting is from an author interview with Galbraith.

109. Galbraith, *Ambassador's Journal*, 259–61.

110. Ibid., ch. 8. Galbraith's top-secret President's-eyes-only cable from Bangkok is dated November 20; from New Delhi, there was a back-channel cable on November 21 and a lengthier memo on November 28. See Galbraith, *Letters to Kennedy*, 89–97 (New Delhi documents), and *The Pentagon Papers*, v. 2, 121–22 (Bangkok cable).

111. Rostow to Kennedy and Galbraith, November 24, 1961, *FRUS Vietnam 1961*, document 274.

112. The dinner is described in Schlesinger, *Thousand Days*, 506.

113. *FRUS Vietnam 1961*, documents 251 (Rostow to JFK) and 252 (JFK to McNamara).

114. Ibid., document 242 (Johnson to Rusk).

115. Rusk sent the instructions on November 14. *The Pentagon Papers*, 117.

116. On the background for Harriman's memo and the progress he had made that October with the Russians over Laos, and the aftermath, see Rudy Abramson, *Spanning the Century: The Life of W. Averell Harriman, 1891–1986* (New York: William Morrow, 1992), 586–91.

117. *FRUS Vietnam 1961*, document 252 (Kennedy to Rusk and McNamara, November 13, 1961), and document 239 (Harriman to Kennedy, November 12, 1961). It is very possible that Sir David Ormsby Gore, the British Ambassador who was very close to Kennedy, leaked Rusk's briefing the day before about sending troops "depending on the situation some weeks hence."

118. Ibid., document 253 (Bundy to JFK).

119. Ibid., document 254, notes of NSC meeting. The draft NSAM of November 13 (ibid., document 247) includes a section that follows Galbraith's and Harriman's advice on opening discussions with the Russians in Geneva, and with the North Vietnamese through the Indians. In the final version (ibid., document 272), NSAM 111, issued on November 22, the section was deleted.

120. Bundy to Kennedy, November 15, 1961, *FRUS Vietnam 1961*, document 256; compare to 281, which lists the personnel changes Kennedy made on October 26.

121. Galbraith, *Ambassador's Journal*, 265–66. Three days after Kennedy shook up the State Department, he did the same at the CIA, replacing Allen Dulles with John McCone. The next morning the President then peremptorily informed McCone—along with Taylor, Rusk, McNamara, and Lemnitzer—that he'd put General Lansdale in charge of Operation Mongoose, the White House's top-secret effort to destroy Fidel Castro and his government. (Six months later, in May 1962, Castro responded to Operation Mongoose by agreeing to the first placement of Soviet missiles in Cuba. Deployment began in July, setting the stage for the Cuban Missile Crisis that October.)

122. See Jacques Nevard, "U.S. 'Copter Units Arrive in Saigon," *The New York Times*, December 12, 1961, 21, and Robert Trumbull, "U.S. Aid to Saigon Irks Truce Group," *The New York Times*, December 13, 1961, 12.

Chapter 16: India

1. Galbraith, *Ambassador's Journal*, 79.

2. Ibid., 61.

3. Lamson, *Speaking of Galbraith*, 158. The Indian press clipping file, assembled by the Embassy press office, takes up eight sizable boxes at the JFK Library.

4. Galbraith, *Ambassador's Journal*, 393.

5. See Mark Haefele, "Walt Rostow, Modernization and Vietnam," thesis, 252–60. Rostow advised Kennedy in the late 1950s, and drafted at least one of his most important Senate speeches on India.

6. See Lamson, *Speaking of Galbraith*, 160–61 (on Indian press coverage of Galbraith's press conference, and his opinion of Talbot); Galbraith, *Ambassador's Journal*, 174–75 (on his concern about the F-104s); Galbraith to Kennedy, August 15, 1961, in Galbraith, *Letters to Kennedy*, 80 (on physical violence). On State Department plan for Indian atomic bomb, see George McGhee to Secretary Rusk, "Anticipatory Action Pending Chinese Communist Demonstration of

a Nuclear Capability," September 13, 1961, Records of Policy Planning Staff, 1957–61, RG 59, National Archives, Washington, D.C.; Galbratih, *Ambassador's Journal*, 222 (on Wiesner talks) and 225–26 (on Wiesner and Nehru). William Burr and Jeffrey Richelson, "Whether to 'Strangle the Baby in the Cradle': The United States and the Chinese Nuclear Program, 1960–64," *International Security*, Winter 2000/01, 54–99, outlines U.S. policy and planning, including ongoing plans for preemptive strike.

7.	Galbraith, *Ambassador's Journal*, 187.

8.	See Lamson, *Speaking of Galbraith*, 165–67 (on boys' life in India, Kennedy's note, and May 1963 *Atlantic* article, which Galbraith prints in full as an appendix in *Ambassador's Journal*).

9.	Bowles, *Promises to Keep*, offers an informative view of their friendship.

10.	See Rudy Abramson, *Spanning the Century*, 575.

11.	Galbraith, interview with author.

12.	Ibid.

13.	Galbraith, *Ambassador's Journal*, 52; the article is "A Professor-Politician," *The New York Times*, March 29, 1961, 19.

14.	Galbraith, *Ambassador's Journal*, 318.

15.	India's complicated motivations are ably summarized in Neville Maxwell, *India's China War* (New York: Pantheon, 1970), 227–28; "Portuguese pimple" comment, Lamson, *Speaking of Galbraith*, 162.

16.	Quoted in Lamson, *Speaking of Galbraith*, 164.

17.	Galbraith, interview with author.

18.	Galbraith, *Ambassador's Journal*, 320.

19.	Ibid., 329.

20.	Ibid., 330.

21.	Ibid., 333.

22.	Galbraith to Kennedy, April 4, 1962, in ibid., 342–44.

23.	See *Foreign Relations of the United States, Vietnam 1962*, document 148 (*FRUS Vietnam 1962* hereafter). The day before, Chester Bowles had submitted a lengthier report on Vietnam and the Far East, expressing much the same position as Galbraith's. But Kennedy made no allusion to it when meeting with Harriman, and likely had not read it. The 54-page document is in Bowles, Secret, Schlesinger Papers, JFK Library (Washington, D.C.: GPO, 1990).

24.	Isaacson and Thomas, *Wise Men*, 618; Abramson, *Spanning the Century*, 16. There were ample precedents for "The Crocodile's" flip-flopping and apparent disobedience, though Kennedy probably didn't know them. For example, shortly after Truman took office, in 1945, Harriman as ambassador to Moscow—eager to overturn what he considered Roosevelt's "naive" hopes for postwar cooperation with the Soviet Union—delivered a hard-nosed warning to the new President about the duplicity of Soviet intentions, but then claimed to be shocked when Truman read Soviet Foreign Minister Molotov the riot act a few days later. During the Korean War, sent by Truman to deliver a tough message to General Douglas MacArthur, Harriman apparently fudged the message, causing Truman to send an even sterner one by cable, which incensed MacArthur and helped to provoke their famous subsequent clash. See Abramson, *Spanning the Century*, 394–96 (on Truman-Molotov), 451–54 (on Truman-MacArthur); and 581 on Galbraith's and Schlesinger's efforts to get Harriman into the New Frontier despite JFK's initial concerns that he was too old and too independent.

25. Galbraith, interview with author, and *FRUS Vietnam 1962*, document 148, f. 4. Galbraith's caustic reply is document 164. He was especially annoyed because he'd spent several days in Geneva with Harriman the previous July, and felt they were in agreement. Galbraith, *Ambassador's Journal*, 176–78; and interview with author.

26. *FRUS Vietnam 1962*, document 156 contains Galbraith's memo, Lemnitzer's reply, and McNamara's notes; A. J. Langguth, *Our Vietnam*, 172.

27. A useful condensed narration is in Kaiser, *American Tragedy*, 131–44.

28. "Both Harriman and I vigorously opposed the recommendation," the State Department's chief intelligence officer, Roger Hilsman, minuted, referring to Galbraith's proposal, "and the President accepted it." Kennedy's motivation for his apparent acquiescence became clear several days later, after he talked with CIA Director John McCone, and the White House national security aide Michael Forrestal: former President Eisenhower had just been briefed by McCone about Laos and Vietnam, and had reiterated (rather disingenuously) what he said had always been his own policy—that if the U.S. sent combat troops to Southeast Asia, it should be prepared to win at all costs, including using tactical nuclear weapons if necessary. Kennedy, horrified, feared his predecessor might say this publicly. See Kaiser, *American Tragedy*, 131–36; and *FRUS Vietnam 1962*, documents 176, 178 n., 356, and 359.

29. Kaiser, *American Tragedy*, 133.

30. See William Duiker, *Ho Chi Minh* (New York: Hyperion, 2000), 529–31 (on the North's interest in neutralization); and Qiang Zhai, *China and the Vietnam Wars* (Chapel Hill: University of North Carolina Press, 2000), 116 (on Mao's supplies to Hanoi).

31. Kaiser, *American Tragedy*, 139–40.

32. Ibid., 139–43.

33. Galbraith, *Ambassador's Journal*, 372; Galbraith to Kennedy, July 13 and August 6, 1962, in Galbraith, *Letters to Kennedy*, 106–10.

34. JFK's comment to Heller quoted in Schlesinger, *Thousand Days*, 577; on Sorensen's instruction to Samuelson, see Bernstein, *Promises Kept* (New York: Oxford University Press, 1991), 126–27.

35. In 1961, Heller had talked only of a small "temporary" cut, meant to kick-start the economy out of the recession inherited from Eisenhower. In 1966, when Heller gave the Godkin Lectures at Harvard (and basked in praise for the much bigger tax cut that finally passed after Johnson became President), he downplayed his frustrations over Kennedy's resistance to his tax-cutting policy. But in 1982, he admitted that 1961 was an un-Keynesian "supply-side" year, with only a "mild dose of demand stimulus in an early 1961 antirecession package." The supply-side measures he was alluding to were the investment tax credit (ITC), depreciation guideline liberalization, voluntary wage-price guidelines, job training programs, the Treasury's Operation Twist, and acceptance of the "Cambridge–New Haven Growth School."

  This makes curious reading. The ITC and depreciation liberalization weren't adopted until 1962, so had nothing to do with economic stimulation in 1961; new spending on job training was tiny (by comparison, unemployment payments were nearly half a billion dollars); the weak wage-price guidelines were dubiously effective; Operation Twist pushed up short-term rates far more than it lowered long-term ones and so was more costly to GDP growth than imagined;

and no one except the CEA had yet accepted the new growth model as a basis for policy.

Omitted, also, is the hefty $3.4 billion in new and unbudgeted military spending that Kennedy ordered in the midst of the Berlin Crisis in the summer of 1961. Heller mentioned defense spending only to denounce its significance: "The idea that [we] got the economy moving again through a defense buildup is a canard that dies mighty hard."

His argument was that official defense spending rose by only 10 percent (or $4 billion) between 1960 and 1965. But more accurately counting from Eisenhower's last budget (FY 1961) to Kennedy's last (FY 1964), military spending rose $6 billion in just three years. Adding space-program spending (much of which had military as well as civilian uses and largely went to the same defense contractors) raises the total to $10 billion, 2.5 times Heller's figure. By comparison, New Frontier combined spending on health, education, housing, employment, and transportation rose barely $1 billion.

Paul Samuelson, who'd strongly recommended more defense spending in his December 1960 report to the President, in 1962 was franker in acknowledging that the 1961 growth stimulus occurred as "a result of two or three new upward revisions of our defense budget, and not as a result of a cool decision on the part of the New Team to disregard ideology and prescribe for the nation what its sound economic health required." See Samuelson, "Economic Policy for 1962," *Review of Economics and Statistics*, February 1962, 4. For Heller's Godkin Lecture views see *New Dimensions in Political Economy* (Cambridge, Mass.: Harvard University Press, 1967); his 1980s comments are in his "Kennedy Economics Revisited," in Joseph Pechman and N. J. Simler, eds., *Economics in the Public Service* (New York: Norton, 1982), 240–42. Budget figures for 1960s are from Office of Management and Budget, *U.S. Budget 2004*, Historical Tables, table 4, at omb.gov.

36. Heller confidentially told the rest of the CEA that he thought "the President has been educated out of his previous thinking on fiscal policy." But he cautioned them that meant only that "he may be receptive to new philosophy" and that they "should start [drafting] a series [of memos for JFK], with proposals emerging." But the economists bogged down in uncertainty about how the economy was going to perform, and what size tax cut they should recommend. Was immediate tax cutting really necessary? Was a $4–5 billion cut—much smaller than the $12 billion eventually proposed—the right size? The economists just weren't sure. Heller worried aloud that Galbraith had just sent Kennedy another of his own memos—how were they to respond? Should the scheduled Social Security tax *increase* be deferred, as Galbraith advised? What about his support for the Treasury's tax-*reform* package? Arthur Okun, then a young staff member for the Council (he later became LBJ's third and final CEA chairman) expressed the group's doubts: "If we come out of this with . . . $2 billion [in cuts] and a deferment of [Social Security] taxes, we'd have a major victory, even bigger than our Berlin non-increase in taxes. Well, I can dream." This was exactly contrary to what Heller was recommending. Okun, "To the Records and Tobin," June 1, 1962, Budget and Tax Policy 1962, CEA Papers, JFK Library.

37. Galbraith to Kennedy, May 29, 1962, in Galbraith, *Letters to Kennedy*, 46–48.

38. Galbraith, *Ambassador's Journal*, 381–82.

39. Schlesinger says the decision to focus the speech on economic myths was

Kennedy's, inspired by a conversation he had had with André Malraux a month earlier in which the two discussed the persistence of myth in the modern world; Kennedy then tried out the theme at a White House conference on economic priorities, and afterward with Schlesinger outlined quite specifically what he wanted to say at Yale. Schlesinger wrote a first draft; Kennedy asked it be "sharpened"; he wrote a second with Galbraith's help, which became "too sharp"; and Sorensen produced a draft, drawing on advice from the CEA, "that wasn't right either," so McGeorge Bundy and Schlesinger wrote still another; Kennedy asked for more changes, and finally rewrote parts of it himself, adding several paragraphs on the plane to New Haven. See Schlesinger, *Thousand Days*, 592–93; Galbraith, *Ambassador's Journal*, 381–82.

40.   See Samuelson and Solow to Kennedy, "The Changed Mid-Year Outlook," June 6, 1962; and "That Second Look at Need for a Tax Cut," July 13, 1962, and Sorensen to Kennedy, "Tax Cut," July 12, 1962, both in Sorensen Papers, JFK Library; Galbraith to Kennedy, July 10, 1962, in Galbraith, *Letters to Kennedy*, 52–53.

41.   Galbraith to Kennedy, August 20, 1962, in Galbraith, *Letters to Kennedy*, 54–56.

42.   See Sorensen, *Kennedy*, 425–26; Robert Collins, *The Business Response to Keynes*, 180–95; Irving Bernstein, *Promises Kept*, 146–59.

Heller and the CEA spent the next five months working more as a lobbying firm than a policy research operation, and without help from Kennedy. In several key instances, the work was a matter of pushing on open doors: the Chamber of Commerce, for example, by summer favored an immediate $7.5 billion cut, emphasizing business tax cuts. Heller conveyed their text to Kennedy, observing that "good economics makes strange bedfellows," but failing to tell him of the Chamber's proposal for an offsetting $5 billion cut in federal domestic spending.

Heller also went to work on the Treasury Department, and in late August persuaded JFK to let him be the chair of an interagency working group on growth with the Treasury, Commerce, and Labor departments and the Budget Bureau. Its mandate was to study investment in education, civilian technology, and manpower training (exactly the sort of programs Galbraith and Kennedy wanted), but Heller skillfully made his tax cut its centerpiece by recruiting Harvey Brazer, the Treasury's head of tax analysis, as his ally. Brazer's report in late October concluded that a $10 billion 1963 tax cut—twice what Heller wanted, and three times what he'd asked Kennedy for in July—would promote significant growth without inflation. Treasury's tax reforms would now come in tandem with these tax cuts.

With Dillon persuaded to join this united front, Heller's attention turned to Congress, in particular to Wilbur Mills. By then Mills was "cautiously optimistic" that no recession was coming (as Samuelson and Solow had confidently predicted in July), and saw no need for quick cuts. But he was now inclined to favor permanent reductions so long as the White House pledged "a maximum effort to hold down non-defense expenditures." On tax reform, he was decidedly cooler, especially reforms that closed corporate loopholes.

Heller presented his working group's recommendations on December 2. Kennedy gave no clues as to his reaction, but on December 14, he spoke before a group of businessmen in New York, largely reprising his Yale speech, this time including a defense of tax cuts "not to incur a budget deficit, but to achieve the more prosperous, expanding economy which can bring a budget surplus." Signaling his willingness to make a deal with Congressman Mills, he also pledged not to increase fiscal year 1964 civilian spending. Galbraith was appalled, calling it "the most Republican speech since McKinley," while Sorensen said "it sounded like Hoover, but . . . was actually Heller."

Yet the President was thrilled to be scoring points among businessmen; he told Heller he'd given them "straight Keynes and Heller, and they loved it." Even the head of the National Association of Manufacturers declared himself "encouraged" by the President's approach. Heller sent the President a just-published CED study that called for a business-oriented two-step tax cut that also capped federal civilian spending. According to Heller, Kennedy "was much impressed by it."

But then the President started backsliding. He asked Heller once again to explain why cuts were preferable to Galbraith's recommendations for spending and Dillon's for tax reform. Heller replied swiftly. In a lengthy memo entitled "Recap of Issues on Tax Cuts (and the Galbraithian alternative)," he answered each of the President's concerns—or so he thought.

A week later it came time for JFK to make a final decision on the tax package he would present to Congress. On December 26, he convened his advisers at the Kennedy family compound in Palm Beach. Once again, the President backed Dillon and reform first, Heller and cuts second; Galbraithian spending was put on hold until the White House could see what deals it would have to strike with Congress. Heller was "stunned and disappointed, but he did the only thing he could short of resigning; he defended the program with all possible vigor." (See Hobart Rowen, *The Free Enterprisers* [New York: Putnam, 1964], 237, on Heller's reaction.)

43. Kennedy's "I like spending money" is quoted in Schlesinger, *Thousand Days*, 597; Kennedy's remark to Heller is quoted in Heller, "Kennedy Economics Revisited," in Pechman and Simler, *Economics in the Public Service*, 246.

44. The narrative and citations involving the Cuban Missile Crisis are drawn from Ernest May and Philip Zelikow, eds., *The Kennedy Tapes: Inside the White House During the Cuban Missile Crisis* (New York: Norton, 2002), and from Laurence Chang and Peter Kornbluh, *The Cuban Missile Crisis, 1962* (New York: New Press, 1998). The best analytic work remains Graham Allison, *Essence of Decision*, 2nd ed. (New York: Longmans, 1999).

45. Brubeck to Bundy, October 15, 1962, *Foreign Relations of the United States, 1961–63 South Asia* (Washington, D.C.: GPO, 1996), document 165 (*FRUS 1961–1963 South Asia* hereafter).

46. Galbraith to State, October 18, 1962, *FRUS 1961–1963 South Asia*, document 177.

47. The question of why the Soviets moved to install the missiles is still debated, and linked by some to Operation Mongoose, the covert program to undermine/ overthrow Castro, initiated by Kennedy after the Bay of Pigs. Declassified U.S. records now make it clear that nine months before the missile crisis, General Edward Lansdale, in charge of Mongoose, was scheduling an "uprising" in Cuba for October, and that just two months before the crisis he was pushing for a U.S. invasion—and assassination of the Cuban leadership—to follow the uprising. Meanwhile CIA Director John McCone interestingly had begun warning of possible placement of Soviet missiles in Cuba as early as April, and by August the President was taking him seriously enough to link U.S. Jupiter missiles in

Turkey to Soviet motivations for placing their own missiles in Cuba. See James Hershberg, "Before 'The Missiles of October': Did Kennedy Plan a Military Strike Against Cuba?" *Diplomatic History*, Spring 1990, 163–98.

48. See Kenneth Conboy and James Morrison, *The CIA's Secret War in Tibet* (Topeka: Kansas University Press, 2002), and John Kenneth Knaus, *Orphans of the Cold War: America and the Tibetan Struggle for Survival* (New York: Public Affairs, 2001).

49. Neville Maxwell, *India's China War*, is still the definitive work on the war, and the source of the summary here. As late as August 1962, Galbraith had reported to President Kennedy that Nehru "expects to have negotiations with the Chinese" starting in the early fall, and while he was dubious that these would resolve anything, Nehru "thinks they will calm the atmosphere." See August 10, 1962, memo from State Department Executive Secretary Brubeck to McGeorge Bundy, National Security Files, Countries Series, India, General, August 1–21, 1962, Confidential, JFK Library. Galbraith, in a letter to the President on Indian politics (frank enough to be omitted from *Ambassador's Journal*), downplayed the Chinese threat, focused on the impending Russian sale of MiG fighter jets to India, and strategized on how to use a slowdown in U.S. aid to gain a more influential hand in New Delhi. Galbraith to Kennedy, August 6, 1962, in Galbraith, *Letters to Kennedy*, 108–110.

50. See B.M. Kaul, *Untold Story* (New Delhi: Allied Publishers, 1967), 397, and S. S. Khera, *India's Defence Problem* (Bombay: Orient-Longman, 1968), 230–31.

51. Estimated troops and losses are from CIA/State estimates presented to President Kennedy by his NSC deputy Carl Kaysen, November 3, 1962, in *FRUS 1961–1963 South Asia*, document 190.

52. Galbraith, *Ambassador's Journal*, 435.

53. Galbraith to State, October 25 (update); Kaysen to Kennedy, October 26 (arms shipments); Rusk to Galbraith, October 27, 1962, *FRUS 1961–1963 South Asia*, documents 180, 181, 182.

54. Embassy in Pakistan (Rusk) to State, October 27 (on significance of the war); White House to Embassy in India, October 27; State to Embassy in Pakistan, October 28, all in ibid., documents 184, 185, 186. Document 185 summarizes but does not reproduce Galbraith's two back-channel messages to Kennedy.

55. Data on initial weaponry, Kaysen to Kennedy, November 3; on eventual arms shipped, Rusk to Galbraith, December 8; NSAM 209, December 10; and memorandum of Kennedy-Macmillan meeting, December 20, 1962, in ibid., documents 190, 221, 223, 230.

56. State to Embassy in Pakistan, November 18, *FRUS 1961–1963 South Asia*, document 201.

57. Galbraith, *Ambassador's Journal*, 451.

58. Galbraith to Kennedy, November 13, 1962, in ibid., 473–76.

59. Rusk to Galbraith, November 18, 1962, *FRUS 1961–1963 South Asia*, document 200.

60. Telegram from Embassy in India to the Department of State, November 19, 1962, *FRUS 1961–1963 South Asia*, document 203.

61. Galbraith, *Ambassador's Journal*, 487.

62. Maxwell, *India's China War*, 420n.

63. Galbraith, interview with author, and Galbraith, *Ambassador's Journal*, 503.

64. See Galbraith, *Ambassador's Journal*, chs. 20–21; Maxwell, *India's China War*, ch. 7, provides assessment of Galbraith's influence.

65. Galbraith, *Ambassador's Journal*, 512 (citing U.S. Information Service poll).

66. Rusk to Galbraith, November 18, 1962, *FRUS 1961–1963 South Asia*, document 200.

67. Galbraith, *Ambassador's Journal*, 519–21.

68. The Indian issues at the Nassau Conference are in ibid., 521–22, and discussed more thoroughly in *FRUS 1961–1963 South Asia*, documents 230 and 231.

69. Galbraith, *Ambassador's Journal*, 502.

70. General Harkins's "Comprehensive Plan for South Vietnam" suggested that military-assistance spending in FY 63 should be boosted from the previously budgeted $130 million to $234 million. The "Wheeler Report" is the source of the "make them bleed" statement. See Kaiser, *American Tragedy*, 188–89. See also 198–212 (for useful context, including the critical point that Diem that spring also wanted a reduction in U.S. forces because he resented U.S. "interference" and "spying" on "his war").

71. Mansfield's report, Kennedy's reaction to it, his discussion with Mansfield, and McNamara's orders on beginning a U.S. withdrawal are in A. J. Langguth, *Our Vietnam*, 208–9. JFK news conference, and other reactions to Mansfield, in Howard Jones, *Death of a Generation* (New York: Oxford University Press, 2003), ch. 10.

72. Arthur Schlesinger, Jr., *John Fitzgerald Kennedy . . . As We Remember Him* (New York: Atheneum, 1965), 192.

73. The phrase is McGeorge Bundy's, describing his and Kennedy's reaction to LeMay's proposal, cited in Kaiser, *American Tragedy*, 199.

74. Galbraith, *Ambassador's Journal*, 577.

75. Galbraith, interview with author.

CHAPTER 17: TRAGEDY, TRIUMPH, TRAGEDY

1. Galbraith, *Ambassador's Journal*, 595–96. Galbraith met privately with Mrs. Kennedy late Sunday afternoon, November 24, at her request to discuss funeral arrangements. On the floor below, LBJ was having the fateful meeting with Lodge described here.

2. See Lamson, *Speaking of Galbraith*, 183–84.

3. Galbraith, interview with author.

4. Galbraith, *Ambassador's Journal*, 588; ch. 27 describes in detail the days around the assassination.

5. See Katharine Graham, *Personal History* (New York: Knopf, 1997), 353; Galbraith reported to the White House aide Ralph Dungan, not to Sorensen. See Galbraith, *Ambassador's Journal*, 589, and interview with author. For Schlesinger's recollections, see *Thousand Days*, 935–36.

6. Galbraith, interview with author.

7. Ibid.

8. Johnson's White House calendar shows that he met with Galbraith at 3:05 p.m. for ten minutes, in the Executive Office Building's room 274. An aide's notation adds that the President drank "dietetic orange drink." See President's Daily Diary, November 23, 1963, LBJ Library, Austin, Tex.

9. Galbraith quoted in Merle Miller, *Lyndon: An Oral Biography* (New York: Putnam, 1980), 337.

10. Ibid., 331. For notes of LBJ's meeting with Lodge, see *Foreign Relations of the United States, Vietnam, August–December 1963* (Washington, D.C.: GPO, 1991), document 323.

11. Bill Moyers, "Flashback," *Newsweek*, February 10, 1975, 11; Langguth, *Our Vietnam,* 267–69.

12. Galbraith, *Ambassador's Journal*, 592. The speech delivered was Sorensen's, with small contributions from Galbraith.

13. Quoted in Richard Goodwin, *Remembering America* (Boston: Little, Brown, 1988), 270.

14. Notes on Meeting with LBJ, November 25, 1963, Heller Papers, JFK Library.

15. Barone, *Our Country*, 374–76.

16. Rovere quoted in Richard Hofstadter, *The Paranoid Style in American Politics* (New York: Knopf, 1965), 112.

17. Drew Pearson quoted in Bernstein, *Guns or Butter*, 130.

18. Electoral data in Barone, *Our Country*, 377–80.

19. Galbraith, interview with author.

20. Quoted in George Ball, *Past Has Another Pattern*, 379. Ball opposed the resolution, knowing that if in fact the two U.S. ships were attacked, the North Vietnamese were likely acting defensively in reaction to covert U.S. incursions under Op Plan 34A.

21. Quoted in Robert Dallek, *Flawed Giant* (New York: Oxford University Press, 1998), 155.

22. Dwight D. Eisenhower, speech to American Society of Newspaper Editors, April 16, 1953, *Public Papers of the Presidents, Eisenhower (1953)* (Washington, D.C.: GPO, 1960), 182.

23. Gaddis, *Strategies of Containment*, 134. Ch. 5 explores "New Look" and its myriad problems in detail. Eisenhower's most famous refinement of this view was his 1961 Farewell Address on "the military-industrial complex," in which he voiced his realization that the militarization of American society had produced powerful, interlocking economic and political interests that made the country's gargantuan military budget a troubling cornerstone of national existence.

24. James Tobin, "Defense, Dollars, and Doctrines," *The Yale Review*, March 1958, 324–25.

25. See Maxwell Taylor, *The Uncertain Trumpet* (New York: Harper, 1960), esp. 137–39. For background, see Douglas Kinnard, *The Certain Trumpet: Maxwell Taylor and the American Experience in Vietnam* (Washington, D.C.: Brassey's, 1991).

26. Rostow memo to President Kennedy, March 29, 1961, box 192, National Security Files, JFK Library. See also George Kahin, *Intervention: How America Became Involved in Vietnam* (New York: Knopf, 1986).

27. See John Byrne, *The Whiz Kids* (New York: Doubleday, 1993), ch. 26, on McNamara's applications of mathematical modeling, game theory, etc., to military resource planning. See also his deputy Alain Enthoven, "Economic Analysis in the Department of Defense," *American Economic Review*, May 1963, 413ff. Philip Mirowski, *Machine Dreams* (New York: Cambridge, 2002), chs. 4, 5, offers a brilliant ex post facto investigation of modern economics and the needs of the Cold War military.

28. U.S. Department of Defense, *Annual Report for Fiscal Year 1962* (Washington, D.C.: GPO, 1963), 3.

29. See "Proceedings of 8th SecDef Conference on Vietnam," May 6, 1963, Taylor Papers, box 1, National Defense University, Washington, D.C.

30. Dallek, *Flawed Giant*, 101. William Gibbons, *The U.S. Government and Vietnam* (Princeton, N.J.: Princeton University Press, 1986), William Rust, *Kennedy in Vietnam* (New York: Da Capo, 1986), and Stanley Karnow, *Vietnam: A History* (New York: Viking Press, 1983), all interpreted Johnson's policies as continuing Kennedy's, even though *The Pentagon Papers* (v. 5, 211–46) showed that LBJ's policies broke with Kennedy's withdrawal plans. John Newman, in *JFK and Vietnam* (New York: Warner, 1992), reopened the issue, arguing that Kennedy was serious about withdrawal, having solidified his spring 1963 position in October, after McNamara and Taylor returned from Saigon with a new report. Newman focused on NSAM 263. Robert McNamara's memoirs, *In Retrospect* (New York: Times Books, 1995), gave first-hand credence to this argument. The release of long-classified government documents added to those in *The Pentagon Papers*, in particular the *FRUS Vietnam* volumes for 1963, the relevant Joint Chiefs papers, and audio tapes of 1963 Oval Office meetings on Vietnam. On October 4, 1963, JCS Chairman Taylor codified the President's instructions, explicitly ordering that all military planning henceforth "be directed towards preparing [South Vietnamese] forces for the withdrawal of all U.S. special assistance units and personnel by the end of calendar year 1965" (Taylor to JCS, "Vietnam Action Plans," October 2, 1963, JCS CM935-63, box 1, Taylor Papers, National Defense University, Washington, D.C.). As Howard Jones, in *Death of a Generation*, concludes, "President Kennedy, as this document attests, had decided on a major disengagement that rested on a greatly restricted definition of 'victory'—so restricted, in fact, that it was tantamount to an admission of defeat" (384). James K. Galbraith's "Did John F. Kennedy Give the Order to Withdraw from Vietnam?" (unpublished paper, University of Texas, 2002) is an invaluable guide to the withdrawal controversy, published in revised form as "Exit Strategy," *Boston Review*, October–November 2003, at bostonreview.net.

31. Galbraith, interview with author; see also Galbraith, *A Life*, 449–50.

32. Galbraith, *A Life*, 479.

33. Ibid.

34. Galbraith, "Foreign Policy: A Stuck Whistle," *The Atlantic Monthly*, February 1965, 64–68.

35. Galbraith, *A Life*, 404.

36. See "U.S. Liberals Using 'Teach-In' against Mr. Johnson," *The Times* (London), April 14, 1965, for coverage of his participation at Harvard's first.

37. See Melvin Small, *Johnson, Nixon, and the Doves* (New Brunswick, N.J.: Rutgers University Press, 1988), ch. 2. Small notes the handful of demonstrations that preceded the University of Michigan teach-in, but emphasizes their modest size and infrequency, and the lack of public and press attention to them.

38. Ibid., 42–43. See also Melvin Small, *Covering Dissent* (New Brunswick, N.J.: Rutgers University Press, 1994), ch. 4.

39. See Galbraith, *A Life*, 455–57, and Johnson, *Vantage Point*, 543 (on U.N. ambassadorship and Goldberg). Galbraith's memo, notes on the subsequent Camp David meeting, and the record of the NSC meeting—actually, three consecutive meetings convened over that weekend—are in *Foreign Relations of the United States, Vietnam June–December 1965* (Washington, D.C.: GPO, 1991), document 79 (Galbraith memo); document 85 (Camp David notes); on aftermath of

meeting, Kaiser, *American Tragedy*, 479–83. See also Mann, *a Grand Delusion*, 454 (on Camp David).

40. Dallek, *Flawed Giant*, 254–55 (General Johnson and Moyers).

41. Rostow quoted in Lamson, *Speaking of Galbraith*, 188.

42. See Martin Prachowny, *The Kennedy-Johnson Tax Cut: A Revisionist History* (Northampton, Mass.: Edward Elgar, 2000).

43. Galbraith, interview with author.

44. See OMB and BEA data in Stein, *Presidential Economics*, 417, 419. For early recognition that poverty would not be easily reduced by the Heller tax cuts, see Henry Aaron, "The Foundations of the 'War on Poverty,' " *American Economic Review*, December 1967, 1229–40.

45. Wittner, *Cold War America*, 206.

46. Bernstein, *Guns or Butter*, 102.

47. Dallek, *Flawed Giant*, 308.

48. Wittner, *Cold War America*, 251.

49. Galbraith to Kennedy, July 10, 1962, in Galbraith, *Letters to Kennedy*, 52–54.

50. Bernstein, *Guns or Butter*, ch. 14, gives examples of this view.

51. Hobart Rowen, *Self-Inflicted Wounds* (New York: Times Books, 1994), 10.

52. Ackley, interviewed in Hargrove and Morley, *The President and the Council of Economic Advisors*, 247–48.

53. Gilbert Burke, "Guns, Butter and Then Some," *Fortune*, December 1965, 119ff. The business press was full of detailed looks at the economic impact of Vietnam from then on.

54. See Bernstein, *Guns or Butter*, 164–65. For Ackley's crucial December 26, 1965, memo to LBJ, see Prachowny, *Kennedy-Johnson Tax Cut*, 196–98.

55. The CEA and Heller quoted in Dallek, *Flawed Giant*, 310–11.

56. Galbraith to Kennedy, July 10, 1962, in Galbraith, *Letters to Kennedy*, 53.

57. Nelson quoted in Julius Duscha, *Arms, Money, and Politics* (New York: Ives Washburn, 1964), 2–3.

58. See Prachowny, *Kennedy-Johnson Tax Cut*, ch. 4.

59. Ibid., 77ff (Okun's doubts); 67 n. (Dusenberry to Harris); 58 (Heller's skepticism); 75 (Heller on CEA's job).

60. Ibid., ch. 5.

61. Solow, "Economic Growth in the 1960s," in Pechman and Simler, eds., *Economics in the Public Service*, 73–74.

62. See Joseph Nocera, *A Piece of the Action* (New York: Simon & Schuster, 1994), ch. 2.

63. Prachowny, *Kennedy-Johnson Tax Cut*, 174. With hindsight, Heller and his 1960s colleagues became much more temperate in their claims for what the Kennedy-Johnson tax cut achieved. See comments by Heller, Tobin, Solow, Samuelson, and Ackley in Pechman and Stimler, *Economics in the Public Service*, chs. 1–2, 6–7.

64. Galbraith, *A Life*, 482–83.

65. See Kai Bird, *The Color of Truth* (New York: Simon & Schuster, 1998), 345. Bird says the dinner was in Cambridge; Schlesinger and Galbraith, in interviews with author, confirmed that it was at Schlesinger's Georgetown home. On Johnson, McNamara, and the Christmas 1965 bombing halt, see Langguth, *Our Vietnam*, 406–14.

66. Galbraith, *A Life*, 482–83.

67. These Galbraith-Johnson letters are in Confidential, box 71, White House Files, April–May 1966, LBJ Library. Following Bundy's decision to resign, White House aide Jack Valenti remembered that "when Rostow's name began to float, Ken Galbraith called me for an 'urgent appointment,' to see me and talk about the vacancy. Galbraith came to my office and eloquently, possibly desperately, cited a catalogue of laments about Rostow in that spot. It was pretty clear that Ken and Walt Rostow were not what one could describe as *en rapport*. Ken left my office in an unhappy frame of mind" after realizing that Rostow's appointment as National Security Advisor could not be stopped. Jack Valenti, *A Very Human President* (New York: W. W. Norton, 1975), 251.

68. For a summation of these efforts, see Galbraith, "An Agenda for American Liberals," *Commentary*, July 1966 (originally a keynote address to ADA in April 1966). Anthony Lewis's interview with Galbraith, "The World Through Galbraith's Eyes," *The New York Times Magazine*, December 18, 1966, 13ff., is also informative.

69. Reston, *Newsweek*, and Roche cited in "The Galbraith Dimension," *Newsweek*, October 7, 1967, 24.

70. Sales figures for the book are cited in "John Kenneth Galbraith: The All-Purpose Critic," *Time*, February 16, 1968, 32.

71. "Galbraith Plan to End the War" and "Bundy Comments on Galbraith's Plan," *The New York Times Magazine*, November 12, 1967, 29ff.

72. Galbraith, interview with author.

73. Dallek, *Flawed Giant*, 494–98.

74. Galbraith, *A Life*, 488–90.

CHAPTER 18: *THE NEW INDUSTRIAL STATE*

1. *Economic Development* (Cambridge, Mass.: Harvard University Press, 1962); *The McLandress Dimension* (Boston; Houghton Mifflin, 1963), under the pseudonym Mark Epernay; *The Scotch* (Boston: Houghton Mifflin, 1964); *How to Get Out of Vietnam* (New York: New American Library, 1967); *The Triumph* (Houghton Mifflin, 1968); with Mohindur Singh Randhawa, *Indian Painting: The Scene, Themes and Legends* (Boston: Houghton Mifflin, 1968); *How to Control the Military* (New York: New American Library, 1969). *Economic Development* is especially noteworthy.

2. Galbraith, interview with author. See *Foreign Relations of the United States, Foreign Economic Policy, 1961–63* (Washington, D.C.: GPO, 1995), General Foreign Economic Policy, documents 24 to 39, and the relevant microfilm appendices. The issues were gold and the balance of payments, and reforms in the foreign aid system. (Hereafter *FRUS/FEP*.)

3. "Truants' Return," *Newsweek*, October 7, 1963, 76.

4. Lamson, *Speaking of Galbraith*, 200. *The New Industrial State* has sold 650,000 copies since it first appeared, and *The Triumph* has sold nearly 50,000 copies, according to Houghton Mifflin's records.

5. Hession, *Galbraith and His Critics*, ch. 7, provides a useful summary and citation of reviews.

6. In his foreword, Galbraith wrote that *The New Industrial State* "stands in relation to [*The Affluent Society*] as a house to a window. This is the structure; the earlier book allowed the first glimpse inside."

7. Marjorie Turner, *Joan Robinson and the Americans* (Armonk, N.Y.: M. E. Sharpe, 1989), chs. 8–10.

8. Ibid., 143 (on Solow's clear sense of its significance).

9. Robert Skidelsky, *John Maynard Keynes: The Economist as Savior 1920–1937* (New York: Viking, 1994), 447–52 (on Robinson, Kaldor, and "the Circus").

10. See G. C. Harcourt, *Theory of Capital* (Cambridge: Cambridge University Press, 1972), and Turner, *Joan Robinson and the Americans*, 120.

11. See Bernstein *Guns or Butter*, ch. 14.

12. Solow acknowledged Galbraith's key criticism twenty years later, even as he mischaracterized it. "The Council did not agree with Galbraith, who preferred no stimulus to a tax cut. His motto, never give away tax revenues because you may need them later, looked good in 1966–68 when President Johnson escalated Vietnam War spending without raising taxes" (see James Tobin and Murray Weidenbaum, eds., *Two Revolutions in Economic Policy*, 11).

13. Samuelson quoted in Bell and Kristol, eds., *The Crisis in Economics*, 66. Phelps's paper was published several months afterward as Edmund Phelps, "Phillips Curves, Expectations of Inflation and Optimal Unemployment over Time," *Economica*, August 1967, 254–81.

14. Milton Friedman, "The Role of Monetary Policy," *American Economic Review*, March 1968, 1–17. Though much of his criticism took direct aim at Samuelson's and Solow's work, Friedman avoided attacking them by name.

15. See Robert Solow, "A Hard Year for Economic Policy," *The Public Interest*, Fall 1966, 9–12.

16. Solow's review, "The New Industrial State or Son of Affluence," Galbraith's reply, "A Review of a Review," and Solow's "A Rejoinder" are in *The Public Interest*, Fall 1967, 100–19. See also Robin Marris, "Galbraith, Solow, and the Truth About Corporations," and Solow, "The Truth Further Redefined: A Comment on Marris," *The Public Interest*, Winter 1968, 37–52. On the delays at the printer, author interview with Galbraith. For a heated but less edifying exchange between Galbraith and a conservative critic, see Scott Gordon, "The Close of the Galbraithian System," *Journal of Political Economy*, July–August, 1968, 635–44; Galbraith, "Professor Gordon on 'The Close of the Galbraithian System,'" *Journal of Political Economy*, July–August 1969, 494–503; and Gordon, "'The Galbraithian System'—Rejoinder," *Journal of Political Economy*, November–December 1969, 953–56. Gordon, an admirer of the rigorously orthodox Frank Knight, launched a sweeping attack, claiming that Galbraith thought corporations now "had unlimited power" and "control completely all important elements of its environment"—which Galbraith did not think. Gordon unfortunately then undercut himself, acknowledging that "the modern large corporation *is* largely free of stockholder control; it *does* supply internally a large part of its capital requirements; it *is* run by its managers; and the managerial bureaucracy *is* a coherent social-psychological system with motives and preferences of its own" (639). Still, he can be credited with noting in passing at least one large force that later damaged Galbraith's arguments: the rise of pension and mutual funds as challengers to managerial independence.

17. The primacy of advanced technology as a determinant of the size of a corporation is dialectical: "In examining the intricate complex of economic change, technology, having an initiative of its own, is the logical point at which to break

in. But technology not only causes change, it is a response to change. Though it forces specialization, it is also the result of specialization. Though it requires extensive organization, it is also the result of organization" (Galbraith, *New Industrial State*, 20). Technology also isn't comprehensible simply as Schumpeter described it—a "perennial gale of creative destruction" driven by competition. Galbraith identified six different imperatives working interactively to determine specific technological developments.

18. On the predicament of the unions, see Galbraith, *New Industrial State*, chs. 23–24, where he argues that unions are no longer a countervailing power because corporations have learned how to pass on wage increases; blue-collar workers are less important to the overall production process and less numerous than (hard-to-unionize) white-collar workers; and general affluence and high employment have reduced the confrontational element. Yet, he adds, unions won't disappear or become irrelevant because they perform functions useful as much to the corporation as to the workers themselves in minimizing conflict and supporting the planning system's goals.

19. Galbraith cites Samuelson: " 'The consumer is, so to speak, the king . . . Each is a voter who gets things done that he wants done' " (*New Industrial State*, 194).

20. Solow, "New Industrial State," 101.

21. Ibid., 103. Solow's claim "only 55 percent of GNP" suggests his own rhetorical bias: 30 percent of GNP was in the public sector and hence reasonably to be excluded from his denominator. Likewise, to be more fair he should probably have used GDP rather than GNP, which by excluding the net foreign trade balance was also a better denominator (though the subsequent rise of multinational corporations lets that argument cut both ways). Finally, GDP and GNP both exclude a large volume of sales below the final sales level, in order to avoid double counting in the national income accounts. Reintroducing total transactions and large corporations' size in them would have been more revealing. All these adjustments would have favored Galbraith's point regarding concentration.

22. Calculated from "Number of 1999 Employees, Firms and Corresponding Establishments," "Statistics of U.S. Business," U.S. Census Bureau Web site, census.gov.

23. Solow makes a passing reference to the influence of mutual funds and large-scale institutional investors in his reply to Marris, "Galbraith, Solow, and the Truth About Corporations," 51.

24. See Neil Fligstein, *The Transformation of Corporate Control* (Cambridge, Mass.: Harvard University Press, 1990); Michael Useem, *Investor Capitalism: How Money Managers Are Changing the Face of Corporate America* (New York: Basic Books, 1996); and Margaret Blair, *Ownership and Control: Rethinking Corporate Governance for the Twenty-First Century* (Washington, D.C.: Brookings Institution Press, 1995).

25. See the foreword to the revised third edition of *The New Industrial State* (Boston: Houghton Mifflin, 1978).

26. See Graef Crystal, *In Search of Excess: The Overcompensation of American Executives* (New York: Norton, 1991), which pioneered this research. Pinketty and Saez, using newer data, estimate the ratio of top executive earnings to that of the average worker was 39:1 in 1970, 101:1 in 1980, 222:1 by 1990, and 1046:1 in 1999. Thomas Pinketty and Emanuel Saez, "Income Inequality in the United

States," working paper W8467 (Cambridge, Mass.: National Bureau of Economic Research, 2001).

27. See Robert Reich, "Regulation by Confrontation or Negotiation?" *Harvard Business Review*, May–June 1981, 84. Reich makes clear why the federal government's bailout of firms such as Lockheed or Chrysler, entire industries such as the savings and loans, or even nations such as Mexico is integral to the modern "planning system" and its integration of private and public goals. On Washington's nexus of money and politics, the literature is voluminous: public-interest groups from Public Citizen to the Center for Responsive Politics to Independent Action routinely report on the business-political axis, and book-length studies by Rick Smith, William Greider, Kevin Phillips, and Thomas Edsall provide extensive interpretive overviews.

28. Solow, "New Industrial State" (review), 104.

29. See Martin Bronfenbrenner, "Japan's Galbraithian Economy" (working paper wp-70-69-7, Carnegie Mellon University, School of Industrial Administration, no date).

30. Solow, "New Industrial State" (review), 105.

31. Marris, "Galbraith, Solow," 38–39; Solow, "Truth Further Defined," 48–49.

32. See Stuart Elliott, "Advertising," *The New York Times*, June 18, 2003, C8 (noting that with 6 percent of the world's population and 25 percent of total GDP, the United States accounts for half of global advertising spending).

33. Richard Schmalensee, "Advertising," *The New Palgrave*, v. 1, 34.

34. See Richard Schmalensee, *The Economics of Advertising* (Amsterdam: North-Holland, 1972).

35. William Baumol, *Business Behavior: Value and Growth*, 2nd ed. (New York: Macmillan, 1967), and Robin Marris, *The Economic Theory of Managerial Capitalism* (London: Macmillan, 1964).

36. See Herbert Simon, *Models of Man: Social and Rational* (New York: John Wiley, 1957), and R. Cyert and J. G. March, *A Behavioral Theory of the Firm* (Englewood Cliffs, N.J.: Prentice-Hall, 1963).

The theoretical and empirical literature has expanded enormously since the 1960s. Although much of this newer work has not supported the specifics of Galbraith's argument, it has shown him to be correct in insisting that the dominant economic tradition was inadequate to explain the behavior of the modern corporation, or its internal motivations, or the effects of its action on the economy and society. Most important, in Oliver Williamson's words, all the new research has shown that the corporation can no longer be treated as what economists call "a production function"; it rather has to be seen foremost as "a governance structure." The corporation, in its modern multidivisional form, or conglomerate or multinational forms, as much as, if not more than, abstract "markets" variously blends elements of technology, price-setting, and governance issues under the overall supervision of its managers; these are all central arguments in *The New Industrial State*.

Compare Oliver Williamson's and Adrian Wood's path-breaking works and the historical analysis of Alfred Chandler in the 1970s, and in the 1980s the cross-industry and cross-national comparative research of Michael Porter, as well as the shift in the 1980s and 1990s to what economists call "transactional," "signaling," and "informational" problems on the one hand, and the disputed matter of rationality in financial markets on the other, and their combined functions. See Oliver Williamson, *Corporate Control and Business Behavior* (Englewood Cliffs, N.J.: Prentice-Hall, 1970), Adrian Wood, *A Theory of Profits* (Cambridge: Cambridge University Press, 1975), and Alfred Chandler, *The Visible Hand* (Cambridge, Mass.: Harvard University Press, 1977). See also Williamson, *The Economic Institutions of Capitalism* (New York: Free Press, 1985), ch. 15.

37. Solow, "New Industrial State" (review), 108.

38. Ibid., 103.

39. Harvey Leibenstein, "Allocative Efficiency vs. 'X-efficiency,'" *American Economic Review*, June 1966, 392–415. See also the survey of more than fifty studies supporting the theory in Roger Frantz, *X-Efficiency: Theory, Evidence, and Applications* (New York: Kluwer-Nyhoff, 1987), as well as Edna Ullmann-Margalit, *The Emergence of Norms* (New York: Oxford University Press, 1977), and Leibenstein, *Inside the Firm: The Inefficiencies of Hierarchies* (Cambridge, Mass.: Harvard University Press, 1987).

40. Galbraith, "Review of a Review," 117.

41. Ibid.

42. Irving Kristol, "Professor Galbraith's 'New Industrial State,'" *Fortune*, July 1967, 90ff.

43. Robin Marris and Dennis Mueller, "The Corporation, Competition, and the Invisible Hand," *Journal of Economic Literature*, March 1980, 32–63.

44. Robert Gordon, "Rigor and Relevance in a Changing Institutional Setting," *American Economic Review*, March 1976, 1–14.

45. Robert Solow, "Economic History and Economics," *American Economic Review*, May 1985, 328–31.

46. The AEA's panel "'The New Industrial State' After Twenty Years," with Galbraith as speaker and Robert Solow, Barry Bluestone, and F. M. Scherer as discussants, appears in *American Economic Review*, May 1988, 373–82. Also relevant is Galbraith's introduction to *The New Industrial State*'s fourth edition (1995), in which he addressed himself to major trends that had affected the book's analysis: the rise of mergers and paper entrepreneurship; the uneven competence of management, particularly in older industries such as steel and autos; foreign competition; the instability provoked by Reagan-era fiscal and monetary policies; and the evidence of the declining salience of the educational and scientific estate.

CHAPTER 19: COLLISIONS

1. Jules Witcover, *The Year the Dream Died* (New York: Warner Books, 1997), is a good introduction to 1968; for election data, 437.

2. *Time*, March 22, 1968, quoted in Robert Collins, "The Economic Crisis of 1968 and the Waning of the American Century," *American Historical Review*, April 1996, 396.

3. Ibid.

4. Ibid.

5. Westmoreland testimony, in November 11, 1967 (transcript), Congressional Briefings on Vietnam, box 1, LBJ Library.

6. Clark Clifford, *Counsel to the President* (New York: Random House, 1971), 474.

7. Gallup data cited in Barone, *Our Country*, 432.

8. Clifford quoted in Mann, *Grand Delusion*, 475–76.
9. Dallek, *Flawed Giant*, 526–27.
10. Lyndon Johnson, *Vantage Point* (New York: Holt, Rinehart, 1971), 435.
11. Galbraith, interview with author.
12. "The Great Mogul," *Time*, February 16, 1968, 24–28.
13. David Halberstam, "The Importance of Being Galbraith," *Harper's*, November 1967, 54.
14. See Galbraith, *A Life*, 496–98. Schlesinger's version of her phone call is in *Robert Kennedy and His Times* (Boston: Houghton Mifflin, 1978), 847. Schlesinger recalls the call coming on the Sunday before the New Hampshire primary, not the Wednesday after it. Ethel Kennedy's March request was repeated by Richard Goodwin, who left the McCarthy campaign when Robert Kennedy announced his candidacy. Goodwin called Galbraith in the middle of the night from Los Angeles on June 5, just as Kennedy's primary victory there became certain. Galbraith said he was sympathetic but needed to talk with McCarthy to see what his plans were. Moments later, Sirhan Sirhan fired his fatal shots.
15. Galbraith, *A Life*, 495.
16. Keynes to Kahn, and events in Savannah, cited in Robert Skidelsky, *John Maynard Keynes: Fighting for Freedom*, 467–70.
17. See Alfred Chandler, Jr., *Scale and Scope: The Dynamics of Industrial Capitalism* (Cambridge, Mass.: Harvard University Press, 1990), 200 (on Russia); 158–60 (on postwar expansion in Europe).
18. Canterbery, *Economics on a New Frontier*, 81. See Thomas Schwartz, *Lyndon Johnson and Europe* (Cambridge, Mass.: Harvard University Press, 2003), ch. 5, for a sympathetic summary introduction to the Johnson White House's handling of "the gold crisis" in 1968 and its relations to the end of fixed exchange rates.
19. David Calleo, *The Imperious Economy* (Cambridge, Mass.: Harvard University Press, 1982), 20–21.
20. Galbraith to Kennedy, November 17, 1960, and November 15, 1963, in Galbraith, *Letters to Kennedy*, 32–34, 58. See also ch. 2, showing their ongoing discussions of gold and balance of payments.
21. Galbraith to Kennedy, November 17, 1960, in ibid., 32–34.
22. Galbraith, *Ambassador's Journal*, ch. 2. Kennedy's first major statement on the balance of payments was his special message to Congress on February 6, 1961. An important declassified record of the administration's debates is in *Foreign Relations of the United States, 1961–63, Foreign Economic Policy* (hereafter *FRUS 1961–63*, Foreign Economic Policy). Dillon would prove less conservative than Galbraith initially feared, and at several points the two found themselves allied. They both opposed Heller's tax cut proposals in 1961 and 1962, worked together on reform of foreign aid as late as fall 1963, and in general embraced the utility of deficit stimulation. They weren't identical in their views: Galbraith wanted public spending while Dillon sought tax reform over Heller's tax cuts, and Dillon was a cautious CED "business Keynesian" on deficits. See Canterbery, in *Economics on a New Frontier*, 85–89 (for explanation for Dillon's views).
23. Galbraith to Kennedy, May 31, 1962, in Galbraith, *Letters to Kennedy*, 48–50. Galbraith wasn't alone in his view; Carl Kaysen, the Harvard economist who was deputy to McGeorge Bundy, Undersecretary of State George Ball, and James Tobin agreed on the political dimensions of the gold question. According to

Schlesinger, "The issue, in their view, was whether the control of high financial policy should rest with central bankers and currency speculators or with responsible governments" (Schlesinger, *Thousand Days*, 653).

24. Galbraith to Kennedy, May 31, 1962, in Galbraith, *Letters to Kennedy*, 51–52.

25. See Canterbery, *Economics on a New Frontier*, 184–88.

26. Robert Roosa, *The Dollar and World Liquidity* (New York: Random House, 1968), ch. 4; Canterbery, *Economics on a New Frontier*, 184.

27. *Public Papers of the Presidents of the United States: John F. Kennedy, 1963* (Washington, D.C.: GPO, 1964), 574–84.

28. On the impact of August 1963 on Kennedy's determination to pull back from Diem and Vietnam, see Jones, *Death of a Generation*, chs. 13ff., and Kaiser, *American Tragedy*, chs. 8–9. The significance of the August 24 cable to Saigon signaling U.S. willingness to support Diem's overthrow, which was written by Kennedy's advisers in an end run around him, set in motion Diem's overthrow and murder three months later.

29. Galbraith, interview with author.

30. Galbraith to Kennedy, August 28, 1963, *FRUS/FEP*, section 3, documents 30 and 31. Neither of these memos appeared in *Ambassador's Journal* or *Letters to Kennedy*, because Galbraith thought they were "too technical" to be of general interest.

31. Kennedy's original September 12 memorandum, as well as the heavily modified final version actually sent out by the White House on September 19, are in National Security Files, Subject Series: Balance of Payments and Gold, Secret, JFK Library.

32. See *FRUS/FEP*, section 3: Galbraith's memos to Kennedy (documents 30, 31, 32); Kennedy's September 12 memo and aides' changes to it (document 33); Rusk to Kennedy, opposing troop cuts, September 18 (document 34); and State Department editorial notes, summarizing the much-edited presidential memo of September 12 as it finally was sent on September 19, on McNamara's recommended defense cuts, and Kennedy's agreement with Rusk to override 70 percent of the cuts, September 19 and 23 (documents 36 to 38).

33. Galbraith, *Letters to Kennedy*, 58.

34. Sorensen quoted in Canterbery, *Economics on a New Frontier*, 234.

35. Ibid., 235.

36. See Dillon to Johnson, December 2, 1963, Memos to Presidents, Dillon Papers, JFK Library. For LBJ's actions, felicitously self-described, see Lyndon Johnson, *Vantage Point*, 315–17; for Vietnam's share of AID funding, see Walter McDougall, *Promised Land, Crusader State* (Boston: Houghton Mifflin, 1997), 193.

37. Data are from Robert Lipsey, "Outward Direct Investment and the U.S. Economy," in Martin Feldstein et al., *The Effects of Taxation on Multinational Corporations* (Chicago: University of Chicago Press, 1995), 7–33.

38. Data on Eurodollar market are from Bank of International Settlements, *Annual Reports* (Basel, Switzerland: IBS), and Council of Economic Advisors, *Economic Report of the President* (Washington, D.C.: GPO), for relevant years.

39. Johnson, *Vantage Point*, 321.

40. Collins, "The Economic Crisis of 1968," 407–8.

41. On Galbraith at the Chicago convention, interview with author, and Galbraith, *A Life*, ch. 31.

42. Galbraith, *A Life*, 499.
43. For a definitive account of the 1968 Democratic convention see Daniel Walker, *Rights in Conflict, Convention Week in Chicago, August 25–29, 1968* (New York: E. P. Dutton, 1968).
44. Galbraith, *A Life*, 504–5.
45. See Bernstein, *Guns or Butter*, 514–15.
46. *The Sunday Times* (London) cited in Dallek, *Flawed Giant*, 590.
47. See Kellers, *Making Harvard Modern*, ch. 14 (the 1969 strike, events before and after, and Galbraith); see ch. 13 (underlying changes at Harvard that led up to the strike).
48. "Harvard Alums Fume as Galbraith Attacks School's Leadership," *The Wall Street Journal*, February 12, 1969, 1.
49. Henry Rosovsky, interview with author.
50. Nicholas Dawidoff, *The Fly Swatter: How My Grandfather Made His Way in the World* (New York: Pantheon, 2002), 302.
51. Ibid., 314–15.
52. Ibid., 308–9.
53. See Kellers, *Making Harvard Modern*, 318–58.

CHAPTER 20: GALBRAITH AND NIXON: TWO KEYNESIAN PRESIDENTS

1. Galbraith, *A Life*, 526.
2. See Lamson, *Speaking of Galbraith*, 209.
3. "Convention That Went Galbraithian," *BusinessWeek*, January 1, 1972, 16–17.
4. The full agenda of the 1971 AEA meeting is in *American Economic Review*, March 1972, 465–69.
5. See Marilyn Bender, "Worldly Prophets: Economists Mull Job Situation, Power and Relevance," and Sandra Salmans, "Boat Gets Rocked in Economics," *The New York Times*, December 27, 1970, section 3, 1, 2.
6. Rendig Fels, "Editor's Introduction," and Galbraith's foreword to the convention's papers in *American Economic Review*, May 1972, ix.
7. URPE's initial prospectus, drafted at Ann Arbor by a group primarily from Harvard and the University of Michigan, said it would seek "first, to promote a new interdisciplinary approach to political economy which also includes relevant themes from political science, sociology, and social psychology. Secondly, to develop new courses and research areas which reflect the urgencies of the day and a new value premise. Such areas include the economics of the ghetto, poverty, imperialism, interest groups, and the military-industrial complex. And thirdly, political economics should be sensitive to the needs of social movements of our day, and have more group research that links all issues to a broad framework of analysis." See "History and Nature of URPE," at urpe.org/history, and Martin Bronfenbrenner, "Radical Economics in America," *Journal of Economic Literature*, September 1970, 747–66.
8. Samuel Bowles and Richard Edwards, "Varieties of Dissent: Galbraith and Radical Political Economy," in Samuel Bowles, Richard C. Edwards, and William G. Shepherd, eds., *Unconventional Wisdom: Essays in Honor of John Kenneth Galbraith* (Boston: Houghton Mifflin: 1989), 39–52.
9. Galbraith, *The Affluent Society*, 2nd rev. ed. (Boston: Houghton Mifflin, 1969), xxiv–xxvii, and Galbraith, "Let Us Begin: An Invitation to Action on Poverty,"

Harper's, March 1964, where he remarks, "Because, a few years ago, I wrote a book which described our society as affluent I have ever since been accused of believing that there are no poor people left in the United States. This charge comes, to be sure, from those who have not read the book" (16). The count of three articles in the *American Economic Review* was by author, using JSTOR, querying for all articles with the word "poverty" or "inequality" in the title or abstract. Of the three, the most important was Simon Kuznets's 1954 AEA presidential address, "Economic Growth and Economic Inequality" (*American Economic Review*, March 1955, 1–28), in which he claimed that postwar growth was reducing inequality and poverty alike—heady news for a generation raised in the Depression, and correct for the previous ten years; it became less true as time went on. In 1955, almost the entire AEA program was devoted to "growth," and neither "poverty" nor "inequality" was mentioned (*American Economic Review*, March 1956). Lampman's bibliography is noted in Bernstein, *Guns or Butter*, 84.

10. Theodore Schultz, "Investing in Poor People: An Economist's View," *American Economic Review*, March 1965, 510–20. Schultz notes that while modern economists "have made room for economic stability and for growth . . . poverty for want of a theory is lost in economics." Robert Lampman's chapter on poverty in the 1964 *Economic Report of the President*, LBJ's first, inaugurated the CEA's focused, detailed, and coordinated attention to poverty and, to a lesser degree, inequality (see Bernstein, *Guns or Butter*, ch. 4); the Heller interview in Hargrove and Morley, *Presidents and CEA*, ch. 4, offers a firsthand account.

11. Michael Harrington, *The Other America* (New York: Macmillan, 1970), and Irving Howe's review of Harrington's book in *The New Yorker*, read by President Kennedy, dramatized the issue for JFK. See also Schultz, "Investing in Poor People," 511.

12. Bernstein, *Guns or Butter*, 84; see also Alice O'Connor, *Poverty Knowledge* (Princeton, N.J.: Princeton University Press, 2001), ch. 7.

13. See Galbraith, *A Life*, 450–52 (on his early involvement in War on Poverty); Johnson, *Vantage Point*, 72 (on LBJ's eagerness to involve Galbraith). Johnson's determination to have Galbraith help design the War on Poverty comes across succinctly in a phone conversation LBJ has with Kermit Gordon, the director of the Bureau of the Budget. Johnson had talked with Galbraith earlier in the day, and he tells Gordon three times in the space of a minute that he wants Galbraith flown down to Washington immediately, and put to work with Gordon and Walter Heller on the strategy, organization, and message for launching the War on Poverty (President and Director Gordon, January 29, 1964, 12:20 p.m., LBJ Library). On Galbraith's hand in the birth of Head Start, see Eric Goldman, *The Tragedy of Lyndon Johnson* (New York: Knopf, 1974), 299. He first suggested the teacher corps in Galbraith, "Let Us Begin," *Harper's*, January 1964, 16–24. On Kennedy's and Nelson's translation of the idea into legislation the next year, see Bernstein, *Guns or Butter*, 199.

14. Galbraith's introductory comments are in *American Economic Review*, May 1972.

15. Marjorie Turner, *Joan Robinson and the Americans* (Armonk, N.Y.: M. E. Sharpe, 1989), ch. 13. See also Ely's autobiography, *Ground Under Our Feet* (New York: Macmillan, 1938).

16. Fels, "Editor's Introduction," ix.

17. James Tobin, "Review of Joan Robinson's *Economic Heresies*," *The Public Interest*, Spring 1973, 102.

18. Ibid., see Joan Robinson, "The Second Crisis in Economic Theory," *American Economic Review*, May 1972, 1–10; Galbraith, interview with author.

19. Stein and Okun quoted in Bernard Collier, "A Most Galbraithian Economist," *The New York Times Magazine*, February 12, 1973, 12ff.

20. Eileen Shanahan, "Sex Bias Is Seen for Economists: Galbraith Will Work Against Discrimination in Field," *The New York Times*, December 30, 1971, 35. The proposals Galbraith introduced became the work of a year-long study by a group chaired by Wellesley College's Carolyn Shaw Bell, who presented its findings at the 1972 AEA convention.

21. Richard Nixon, *RN: The Memoirs of Richard Nixon* (New York: Grosset & Dunlap, 1978), 733–74.

22. On Nixon's and Kissinger's plans for Vietnam after American troops left, see Larry Berman, *No Peace, No Honor* (New York: Free Press, 2001).

23. Gallup poll, June 25–28, 1971, quoted in Barone, *Our Country*, 492.

24. Dole in 1971 *Congressional Quarterly Almanac* (Washington, D.C.: CQ News, 1972), 282–83.

25. See Mann, *Grand Delusion*, 681–82.

26. Polling data cited in Barone, *Our Country*, 485.

27. Paul McCracken quoted in James Reichley, *Conservatives in an Age of Change* (Washington, D.C.: Brookings Institution Press, 1981), 206.

28. See Earl Black and Merle Black, *The Rise of Southern Republicans* (Cambridge, Mass.: Harvard University Press, 2002) and their *Politics and Society in the South* (Cambridge, Mass.: Harvard University Press, 1987). See also Kevin Phillips, *The Emerging Republican Majority* (New York: Arlington House, 1969). Phillips, a Goldwater supporter who became a Nixon campaign adviser, generally gets credit for the detailed strategic analysis undergirding Nixon's grand ambitions; *Newsweek* called the book "the bible of the Nixon strategy."

29. Nixon quoted in H. R. Haldeman, *The Haldeman Diaries* (New York: G. P. Putnam, 1974), 117–18.

30. Stein, *Presidential Economics*, 139 ("It was Moynihan who spelled out for Nixon the concept of the conservative man with liberal policies and introduced him to the classical models of that man—Lord Melbourne and Benjamin Disraeli").

31. Nixon quoted in Daniel Patrick Moynihan, *The Politics of Guaranteed Income: The Nixon Administration and the Family Assistance Plan* (New York: Random House, 1973), 215.

32. Nixon, *RN*, 562.

33. "Nixon Reportedly Says He Is Now a Keynesian," *The New York Times*, Jan. 7, 1971, 19. Taken aback, Smith told the *Times* it was like "a Christian saying Mohammed was right."

34. Stein, *Presidential Economics*, 170–75.

35. Cited in Allen Matusow, *Nixon's Economy* (Lawrence: University of Kansas Press, 1998), 83.

36. Connally quoted in Stein, *Presidential Economics*, 162.

37. Henry Kissinger, *White House Years* (Boston: Little, Brown, 1976), 951.

38. Nixon, *RN*, 518.

39. Poll data quoted in Barone, *Our Country*, 490.

40. Rowen, *Self-Inflicted Wounds*, 58–61.

41. The set of Nixon White House tape recordings that includes July 28, 1971, was finally released by the National Archives in February 2003; excerpts quoted here were transcribed by the author.

42. "Galbraith Urges Wage-Price Curb," *The New York Times*, July 21, 1971, 45.

43. Nixon, *RN*, 518.

44. See Rowen, *Self-Inflicted Wounds*, 61–62.

45. Connally quoted in Nixon, *RN*, 518; for a summary of meeting and policies, see Matusow, *Nixon's Economy*, 135–37; Haldeman quote is from Haldeman, *Diaries*, 335–36.

46. On Burns's views at Camp David and his general role in the Nixon administration, see Wyatt Wells, *Economist in an Uncertain World: Arthur F. Burns and the Federal Reserve, 1970–78* (New York: Columbia University Press, 1994). For a detailed overview of events prior to Camp David, see Neil de Marchi, "The First Nixon Administration: Prelude to Controls," in Crawford Goodwin, *Exhortation and Controls: The Search for a Wage-Price Policy, 1945–1971* (Washington, D.C.: Brookings Institution Press, 1975)

47. Stein, *Presidential Economics*, 176–77.

48. Haldeman, *Diaries*, 348.

49. *Public Papers of the Presidents of the United States: Richard Nixon 1971* (Washington, D.C.: GPO, 1972), 886–90.

50. Gallup poll cited in Barone, *Our Country*, 493.

51. Matusow, *Nixon's Economy*, 156–58.

52. Christopher Lydon, "Reaction Is Mixed to Nixon Address," *The New York Times*, August 16, 1971, 1.

53. Hobart Rowen, "Nixon Muted Economy Issues," *The Washington Post*, November 5, 1972, 22.

54. "Galbraith Gives Nixon an A-minus," *BusinessWeek*, October 16, 1971, 74–76.

55. Galbraith, *A Journey Through Economic Time* (Boston: Houghton Mifflin, 1994), 192.

CHAPTER 21: THE PRICE OF HYPOCRISY

1. On Nixon's pre-election economic policy, see Stein, *Presidential Economics*, 176–90. For a detailed charge that the White House's manipulation of the economy was for political ends that year, see Edward Tufte, *Political Control of the Economy* (Princeton: Princeton University Press, 1978).

2. Galbraith, interview with author.

3. Lamson, *Speaking of Galbraith*, 201–2.

4. Galbraith, *A Life*, 523.

5. Galbraith, *A China Passage* (Boston: Houghton Mifflin, 1973).

6. "Galbraith May Run for Brooke's Seat," *The New York Times*, May 17, 1972, 30.

7. "Americans Abroad Also Waging Campaign," *The New York Times*, October 14, 1972, 16.

8. Philip Shabecoff, "Meany Criticizes 'Elite' Democrats," *The New York Times*, September 19, 1972, 38.

9. George Lardner, Jr., "Nixon Defends Envoy's Groping; 1972 Tapes Also Reveal Talk of a Justice Dept 'Full of Jews,'" *The Washington Post*, March 1, 2002, A2.

10. Kissinger quoted in Stephen Ambrose, *Nixon: The Triumph of a Politician 1962–1972* (New York: Simon & Schuster, 1989), 651.

11. Kissinger quoted in A. J. Langguth, *Our Vietnam*, 611.

12. John Kenneth Galbraith, "Power and the Useful Economist," *American Economic Review*, March 1973, 10.

13. Ibid., 11.

14. See Patricia Carbine, "Women, with New Consciousness, Strive to Advance," *The New York Times*, December 31, 1972, 21.

15. See, for example, Leonard Silk, "A Disappearing Way," *The New York Times*, January 1, 1973, 22; "Harvard Fires Two 'Radicals' in Economics," *New York Daily News*, January 3, 1973, 12; Richard Weintraub, "Political Motives Charged in Dismissal of Two Marxist Professors at Harvard," *The Washington Post*, January 2, 1973, 17; "Economists Split by Two Theories," *Boston Globe*, January 2, 1973, 17.

16. Samuel Bowles, "Hardly a Surprise," *The Harvard Crimson*, February 27, 1973. One radical economist, Stephen Marglin, did get tenure, but did so by carefully concealing his political views and polishing his substantial mathematical abilities during the tenure process.

17. See Zygmund Dobbs, *Keynes at Harvard* (New York: Veritas Foundation, 1962); Roosevelt's letters to Hoover and Hoover's replies are in Galbraith's FBI files.

18. See Robert Church, "The Economists Study Society," in Paul Buck, ed., *Social Sciences at Harvard, 1860–1920* (Cambridge, Mass.: Harvard University Press, 1965), 18–90.

19. The Bowles-Galbraith correspondence is scattered in various boxes, 1960s General Correspondence, Galbraith Papers, JFK Library. See especially Bowles to Galbraith, March 15, 1965, June 16, 1966, July 9, 1969; and Galbraith to Bowles, June 28, 1966, December 5, 1967, July 11, 1969.

20. "Letter to Entering Graduate Students," Summer 1973 (mimeograph), Harvard Graduate Economics Club, Harvard 1973, box 4, Galbraith Papers, JFK Library. See also "Dissension Divides the Department," *The Harvard Crimson*, March 26, 1971, 1, and "Faculty Says No Room for Bowles," *The Harvard Crimson*, December 16, 1972, 1.

21. U. Mass. Dean Alfange to Galbraith, February 2, 1973, and Galbraith's reply, February 13, Harvard 1973, box 3, Galbraith Papers, JFK Library.

22. Galbraith to Dunlop, December 29, 1966, Harvard 1966, box 2, Galbraith Papers, JFK Library.

23. "Economics Dept. Reports on Faculty's Outside Ties," *The Harvard Crimson*, March 20, 1973.

24. Derek Bok, interview with author. Two months after the 1969 student strike, Galbraith and other full professors were notified that they would be receiving substantial salary increases, though in 1968 the administration had insisted on a faculty pay freeze, citing "hard times." Galbraith immediately wrote Dean Franklin Ford: "When you wrote a year earlier to tell me of the partial freeze on senior faculty pay raises last year, I indicated that it would be quite satisfactory were mine stabilized for the rest of my Harvard tenure. And as you are perhaps aware, I have started refunding its equivalent, more or less, to the Department of Economics for the use of the Department. I have a notice dated June 30 according me an increase . . . Needless to say I am grateful for the compliment but it leads me to say again that I would be most content if this were made the ceiling" (Galbraith to Dean Ford, July 7, 1969, Harvard 1969, box 2, Galbraith Papers, JFK Library).

25. "Economics Dept. Reports."

26. "Dept. Will Eye Plan to Divide Ec Curriculum," *The Harvard Crimson*, February 8, 1974.

27. Galbraith memo to Bok and Rosovsky, June 18, 1973, Harvard 1973, box 3, Galbraith Papers, JFK Library. He notes that his first-year graduate students "are squeezed . . . into a narrow model-building, problem-solving, quasi-mathematical routine that they find boring and unrelated to the world in which they live."

28. "Postponing the Arrow Report," *The Harvard Crimson*, March 23, 1974, 1.

29. Rosovsky, interview with author.

30. John Kenneth Galbraith, *Economics and the Public Purpose* (Boston: Houghton Mifflin, 1973).

31. William Doerner, " 'Cryptic Servants' and Socialism," *Time*, October 8, 1973, 109; Richard Barnet, "Economics and the Public Purpose," *The New York Times Book Review*, September 16, 1973, 1; Leonard Silk, "Galbraith's New Socialism," *The New York Times*, September 18, 1973.

32. Bernard Nossiter, "Economics and the Public Purpose," *Washington Post Book World*, October 7, 1973, 1.

33. Arthur Cooper, "The Public Interest," *Newsweek*, October 1, 1973, 94.

34. Murray Weidenbaum, "How Galbraith Would Reform the Economy," *Business-Week*, September 22, 1973, 10–11.

35. Barbara Bergmann, "Economics and the Public Purpose," *Journal of Economic Literature*, September 1974, 899–901. Fullest attention to the book was paid by the *Journal of Economic Issues*, which published a quartet of reviews in March 1975, 87–100.

36. See Herbert Stein, "Galbraith on Economics," *The Wall Street Journal*, October 15, 1973, 22; James Tobin, "Galbraith Redux," *Yale Law Review*, May 1974, 1291–1303. Tobin, anticipating Galbraith's likely displeasure, sent him an advance copy of his review with a note emphasizing that although he disagreed with many points in the book, "I think your work is so important and influential that it deserves serious and candid discussion." *The Wall Street Journal's* editor Robert Bartley, far less sympathetic, brusquely refused to publish a carefully documented article by two well-regarded empirical economists, Harold Vatter and John Walker, which rebutted, point-by-point, Stein's misuse of data in "refuting" Galbraith on defense spending, the economic status of women, and the enduring extent of poverty in the United States. See Tobin to Galbraith, May 6, 1974, General Correspondence 1974, box 2, Galbraith Papers, JFK Library; Vatter to Galbraith, December 17, 1973, *Economics and the Public Purpose* Reviews, Galbraith Papers, JFK Library.

37. Arthur Schlesinger, interview with author.

38. Myron Sharpe, *John Kenneth Galbraith and the Lower Economics*, 2nd ed. (White Plains, N.Y.: International Arts and Science Press, 1974), 101.

39. Galbraith had already discussed this strategy in somewhat greater detail in "The Big Defense Firms Are Really Public Firms and Should Be Nationalized," *The New York Times Magazine*, November 16, 1969, 50ff.

40. Galbraith, *Economics and the Public Purpose*, ch. 25.

41. Ibid., 251.

42. Ibid., ch. 4 (Friedan quote); ch. 23 (Lenin quote).

43. Ibid., ch. 23. A decade later, Galbraith had come to a more nuanced evaluation

of the way culture and emotional conditioning affected women's identities, and of the prospects of feminism's swiftly overturning dominant social customs and economic relations. See Galbraith, *The Anatomy of Power* (Boston: Houghton Mifflin, 1983).

44. Galbraith, *Economics and the Public Purpose*, 231.

45. Galbraith, *Affluent Society*, 355.

46. Galbraith, *The Liberal Hour* (Boston: Houghton Mifflin, 1960), ch. 1.

47. Reprinted in Galbraith, *Economics, Peace and Laughter*, 282–87.

48. Galbraith, *Economics and the Public Purpose*, ch. 28 ("The Environment"); see also the index, "environment," for the breadth of comment he offers.

49. Ibid., ch. 28.

50. *Economics and the Public Purpose* reached the best-seller list, but did not do as well as *The Affluent Society* or *The New Industrial State*, especially in the American market. No doubt Galbraith's use of the word "socialism" hurt sales, just as Schlesinger had warned. Overall, according to Houghton Mifflin, it sold more than 165,000 copies (roughly a quarter of *The New Industrial State*'s sales and a sixth of *The Affluent Society*'s).

51. On his intended slow-motion plans for retirement, see Galbraith to Bok, October 26, 1973, Harvard 1973, box 4, Galbraith Papers, JFK Library; and Galbraith to Derek Bok, June 18, 1974, and Bok to Galbraith, July 19, 1974, both in Harvard 1974, box 4, Galbraith Papers, JFK Library.

52. See Catherine Galbraith, "The Professor as TV Star," *American Film*, February 1977, 6–11.

53. Galbraith, interview with author.

54. Henry Rosovsky, "The Most Famous Professor at Harvard," in Bowles et al., *Unconventional Wisdom*, 327.

55. "Goodbye to Galbraith," *Time*, June 23, 1975, 60.

56. Harvard Crimson, *Confidential Guides*, years as cited, Archives, Pusey Library, Harvard University.

57. Rosovsky, interview with author.

58. Griliches to Galbraith, December 19, 1973, Harvard 1973, box 5, Galbraith Papers, JFK Library.

59. Galbraith, "Recessional," in Galbraith, *A View from the Stands* (Boston: Houghton Mifflin, 1986), 129–36.

CHAPTER 22: THE GREAT UNRAVELING

1. Ernest Holsendolph, "Reuss Opposes Stronger I.M.F.," *The New York Times*, August 24, 1974, 38.

2. Raymond Price, *With Nixon* (New York: Viking Press, 1977), 369.

3. Barone, *Our Country*, 536.

4. *Weekly Compilation of Presidential Documents* (Washington, D.C.: GPO, 1975), v. 10, 1247. Ford's views quoted in Collins, *MORE*, 153; public survey cited in Rowen, *Self-Inflicted Wounds*, 114.

5. See John Kenneth Galbraith, "Inflation: A Presidential Catechism," *The New York Times Magazine*, September 15, 1974, 14–32.

6. Samuelson quoted in Collins, *MORE*, 154. For a sophisticated view of stagflation in the 1970s, see Otto Eckstein, *The Great Recession* (New York: North-Holland, 1978).

7. Burns quoted in Rowen, *Self-Inflicted Wounds*, 110.

8. See Alan Blinder, *Hard Heads, Soft Hearts: Tough-Minded Economics for a Just Society* (Reading, Mass.: Addison-Wesley, 1987).

9. Connally quoted in Howard Wachtel, *The Money Mandarins* (New York: Pantheon Books, 1986), 85.

10. See Matusow, *Nixon's Economy,* ch. 8, esp. 228–32.

11. John Kenneth Galbraith, "Reply to Secretary Schultz," *The New York Times,* March 29, 1974, 34.

12. Galbraith quoted in "A September Sampler," *Harvard Magazine,* September 1973, 12.

13. See Joseph Pechman, "Making Economic Policy: The Role of the Economists," in Fred Greenstein and Nelson Polsby, eds., *Handbook of Political Science* (Reading, Mass.: Addison Wesley, 1975), v. 6, 23–78.

14. See Alice O'Connor, *Poverty Knowledge,* 173–82 (on the flawed adoption of Defense Department budgeting methods by OEO planners).

15. Galbraith, *Theory of Price Control,* 9–10.

16. For technical details, see Robert Lanzillotti et al., *Phase II in Review: The Price Commission Experience* (Washington, D.C.: Brookings Institution Press, 1975); the blithe admission of abysmal ignorance of economics is in C. Jackson Grayson, *Confessions of a Price Controller* (Homewood, Ill.: Dow Jones-Irwin, 1974), 9.

17. See election data in Barone, *Our Country,* 508.

18. Simon on "freedom and socialism" quoted in Rowen, *Self-Inflicted Wounds,* 123; on liberalism as "hash," see William Simon, *A Time for Truth* (New York: Berkeley Books, 1979), 79.

19. Stein, *Presidential Economics,* 211. As "energy tsar" under Nixon, Simon passionately and brashly established government controls over oil after the OPEC price hikes—to strikingly bad effect.

20. Ibid., 210 ("old-time religion").

21. Rowen, *Self-Inflicted Wounds,* 104.

22. Greenspan quoted in ibid., 115.

23. Ibid., 116.

24. Robert Lucas, Jr., "Tobin and Monetarism: A Review Article," *Journal of Economic Literature,* June 1981, 559. The origins of Rational Expectations can be traced to the Kennedy era and an article by John Muth, but the theory remained undeveloped until the larger political and policy crises of the 1970s engendered a search for new paradigms. Robert Heilbroner, taking the idea from Schumpeter, has noted that often certain theories emerge as a response to real-world economic crises after having lain about ignored for years. The failure in the 1980s of Rational Expectationists and monetarists to resolve the problems they'd blamed on the Neoclassical Synthesis left a void in theory and policy, although Alan Blinder and Paul Krugman claimed to see an updated Keynesianism on the rise in the early 1990s. See Heilbroner and Milberg, *The Crisis of Vision in Modern Economic Thought* (New York: Cambridge University Press, 1995); Krugman, *Peddling Prosperity;* and Blinder, *Hard Heads, Soft Hearts.*

25. Mark Willes, " 'Rational Expectations' as a Counterrevolution," in Bell and Kristol, eds., *The Crisis in Economic Theory,* 87, 90. For a more cautious assessment, see Thomas Sargent, "Rational Expectations," *The New Palgrave,* v. 4, 76–79.

26. See McCloskey's sympathetic yet subversive analysis of John Muth's 1961 article (from which Rational Expectations came), in Donald McCloskey, *The Rhetoric of Economics*, ch. 6. McCloskey helps to explain why Muth's dense language and references, which dress up an otherwise easy-to-state (though wildly controversial) point, made it appear profound and original to conservative dissidents like Lucas who adopted its claims a decade later.

27. Lucas coined the term "free parameters" to describe Keynes's nonclassical microassumptions. See Roger Backhouse, *Interpreting Macroeconomics* (New York: Routledge, 1996), ch. 8.

28. See N. Gregory Mankiw, "A Quick Refresher Course in Macroeconomics," *Journal of Economic Literature*, December 1990, 1652.

29. Justin Fox, "What in the World Happened to Economics?" *Fortune*, March 15, 1999, 94.

30. Blinder, *Hard Heads, Soft Hearts*, 84.

31. Word search for "Rational Expectations" and "Lucas" in *The New York Times*, 1970–80, performed online at ProQuest by author.

32. During the 1960s, Galbraith's name appeared in *The New York Times* nearly 800 times; Friedman's, fewer than 200. In the 1970s Galbraith appeared almost as often (750 times) but Friedman's appearances more than doubled, to 500. Author's online search at ProQuest.

33. See Henry Simons, "Rules Versus Authorities in Monetary Policy," *Journal of Political Economy*, February 1936, 1–30, and James Angell, "Monetary Control and General Business Stabilization," in *Economic Essays in Honour of Gustav Cassel* (London: Allen & Unwin, 1933). Many economists consider the work of Allan Meltzer and Karl Brunner of importance, both in developing the theory of monetarism, and through creation of the Shadow Open Market Committee, which publicized monetarist claims in the business press.

34. Stein, *Presidential Economics*, 140. According to Stein, Nixon and McCracken "thought money mattered, but did not think that only money mattered."

35. See Alfred Malabre, Jr., *Lost Prophets: An Insider's History of the Modern Economists* (Boston: Harvard Business School Press, 1994), ch. 5. Malabre, the longtime economics editor of *The Wall Street Journal*, offers an informative (and critical) history of the business press's promotion of Friedman and monetarism.

36. Friedman's first exposition of the "natural rate" argument was in his 1967 AEA presidential address, "The Role of Monetary Policy." Edmund Phelps came independently to the same conclusions in "Phillips Curves, Expectations of Inflation, and Optimal Unemployment over Time."

37. Stated more formally, Friedman's version of monetarism advanced the following propositions: (1) past growth rates in the money stock are the only systematic, nonrandom determinants of nominal GDP growth; (2) fiscal policies can affect the composition of nominal GDP (and interest rates) in limited ways, but don't significantly affect nominal GDP; (3) the overall real-world effect of both fiscal and monetary policies on nominal GDP is in practical terms expressed in the movement of the money stock, and monetary policy should therefore focus on this, not interest rates, credit flows, free reserves, and so on; (4) nominal interest rates are geared to inflation expectations, and to actual inflation with an appropriate lag; (5) a central bank (such as the Fed) should increase the money

stock at a steady rate equal to the growth rate of potential GDP plus a "target rate of inflation"; (6) because a "natural rate" of unemployment exists, government fiscal or monetary policies should not seek a lower unemployment rate, in which case the "target rate of inflation" can be practically treated as zero.

38. Milton Friedman, "A Monetary and Fiscal Framework for Economic Stability," *American Economic Review*, June 1948, 256–64.

39. Friedman set out the framework of his "fixed-rule" doctrine in *A Program for Monetary Stability* (New York: Fordham University Press, 1960), then refined it in subsequent works.

40. See Niehans, *History of Economic Theory*, 500. Friedman's exposition can be found in Milton Friedman and Rose Friedman, *Free to Choose* (New York: Harcourt Brace Jovanovich, 1980).

41. Malabre, *Lost Prophets*, 144–45.

42. An early short history of the soaring confidence among monetarists and the weakening courage of mainstream Keynesians is in Harry Johnson, "The Keynesian Revolution and the Monetarist Counter-Revolution," Ely Lecture to the 1970 AEA convention, *American Economic Review*, May 1971, 1–14. A Chicago colleague of Friedman's, Johnson was the more intellectually elegant of the two, and he made two subtle but vital points. First, he cannily affirmed something that too many theoretical economists often don't understand: he asked his audience to ponder the question, what made it possible for the monetarist counterrevolution to make so much swift progress? "I would judge," he said, "that the key determinant of success or failure lies, not in the academic sphere, but in the realm of policy. New ideas win a public and professional hearing, not on their scientific merits, but on whether or not they promise a solution to important problems that the established theory has proved itself incapable of solving" (11–12). Johnson then, to Friedman's discomfort, asked a second question: Would the monetarist counterrevolution finally sweep the Keynesians completely away or itself gradually peter out? He thought the latter, mainly because he believed the Keynesians were right to find unemployment a more serious modern problem than inflation, and also because, as he put it, "monetarism is seriously inadequate as an approach to monetary theory" and would need to compromise on many fundamental conceptual points to gain real intellectual respectability (12).

43. James Tobin, *The New Economics One Decade Older* (Princeton, N.J.: Princeton University Press, 1974), 61, 63.

44. Ibid., 69–70.

45. Friedmans, *Free to Choose*, ch. 2.

46. Galbraith, "Market Structure and Stabilization Policy," *Review of Economics and Statistics*, May 1957, 124–33.

47. Milton Friedman, *From Galbraith to Economic Freedom* (London: Institute of Economic Affairs, 1977), occasional paper 49. On the IEA's contempt for Mrs. Thatcher's perceived lack of conservatism, see "The Old New Right," *The Economist*, July 2, 1984, 85.

48. Galbraith, *Economics and the Public Purpose*, 297.

49. Ibid., 298.

50. Barone, *Our Country*, 542.

51. Galbraith quoted in Israel Shenker, "Rhetoric of Democrats Leans Heavily on Unity and God," *The New York Times*, July 16, 1976, 15.

52. See Michael Herron, "Indifference, Voting and Abstention in the 1976 Presi-

dential Election," unpublished working paper, Northwestern University Political Science Department, 1998.

53. Schlesinger, interview with author.

54. "Shell Oil's Money Machine," *Forbes*, August 1, 1977, 43–45.

55. U.S. Department of Commerce, Bureau of Economic Analysis, National Income and Product Accounts, table 6.16B ("Corporate Profits by Industry Group"), 1970–79, at bea.doc.gov.

56. "Can Capitalism Survive?" *Time*, July 14, 1975, 52ff.

57. Sidney Blumenthal, *The Rise of the Counter-Establishment* (New York: Times Books, 1986), 55.

58. Ibid., 77. For an example of the Business Roundtable's influence on U.S. exchange-rate policies, see Jeffrey Frankel, "Exchange Rate Policy," in Martin Feldstein, ed., *American Economic Policy in the 1980s* (Chicago: University of Chicago Press, 1994), 321–23.

59. Quoted in Ann Crittenden, "The Economic Wind's Blowing Toward the Right— for Now," *The New York Times*, July 16, 1978, F1.

60. Thomas Edsall, *The New Politics of Inequality* (New York: Norton, 1984), 131–33.

61. Charles Lewis, director, Center for Public Integrity, interviewed on *Frontline*, at PBS.org/WGBH/pages/frontline/president.

62. Phillip Lawler, "Dismal, Yes; Science, No," *Policy Review*, Spring 1980, 162.

63. Kristol and Baroody quoted in Crittenden, "Economic Wind's Blowing," *The New York Times*.

64. Catherine Galbraith, "The Professor as TV Star," *American Film*, February 1977, 11.

65. Galbraith, interview with author.

66. Galbraith emphasizes the criticisms in *A Life* (534); favorable reviews are described in Bernard Nossiter, "Galbraith and the BBC," *The Washington Post*, January 8, 1977, C1; Plumb, "History's Bottom Line," *The Washington Post*, April 24, 1977, E3 (his review was not of the television series but of its companion volume).

67. Houghton Mifflin's records show total *Age of Uncertainty*'s sales as 860,000; this figure, however, includes only those foreign sales recorded after the book's hefty advances were paid and domestically excludes Book-of-the-Month Club sales. The sales of *Money*, the second by-product of the television series, sold another 160,000, with the same underestimate of total foreign sales. A reasonable estimated total sales for the two books is 1.4 million to 1.7 million copies.

68. See KCET File, box 92, Galbraith Papers, JFK Library.

69. James Condon, "Rebutting Galbraith on TV," *The New York Times*, June 12, 1977, sect. 3, 15; see also Galbraith, *A Life*, 528–35.

70. See Friedmans, *Free to Choose*, ix–xi.

71. Reagan's endorsement appears on the dust jacket of *Free to Choose*.

72. Robert Brustein, "Whither the National Arts and Humanities Endowments," *The New York Times*, December 18, 1977, 97, provides a melancholic look at the Carter administration's sensitivity to criticism from the right.

73. Arnold Meltsner, *Policy Analysis in the Bureaucracy* (Berkeley: University of California Press, 1976), 173–75.

74. Clark Abt, *Problems in American Social Policy Research* (Cambridge, Mass.: Abt Books, 1980), 4.

75. Henry Aaron, *Policy and the Professors* (Washington, D.C.: Brookings Institution Press, 1978), 159.

76. For an overview of the trust issue, see Joseph Nye et al., *Why People Don't Trust Government* (Cambridge, Mass.: Harvard University Press, 2002).

77. James Fallows, "The Passionless Presidency," *The Atlantic Monthly*, May 1979, 33–46.

78. Greenspan quoted in Hobart Rowen, "Carter Backed by Greenspan," *The Washington Post*, May 1, 1977.

79. "New Thunder from Economists on the Left," *BusinessWeek*, December 3, 1979, 131.

80. Crittenden, "Economic Wind's Blowing," *The New York Times*.

81. "Carter's Camp David Guest List," *Newsweek*, July 23, 1979, 25.

82. Mondale quoted in Collins, *More*, 162.

83. Arthur Okun, *Equality and Efficiency: The Big Trade-Off* (Washington, D.C.: Brookings Institution Press, 1975). Okun later insisted that the dichotomy was a false one.

84. William Julius Wilson, *The Truly Disadvantaged* (Chicago: University of Chicago Press, 1987).

85. Cooper's arguments are summarized in Robert Gilpin, *The Political Economy of International Relations* (Princeton, N.J.: Princeton University Press, 1987), 148. Not until the very end of the century did a consensus among economists slowly form that the reality of "free" exchange rates might be undesirable, especially for smaller and weaker economies such as those devastated by the Asian Financial Crisis and its reverberations in Latin America and Russia.

86. Galbraith, *The Age of Uncertainty* (Boston: Houghton Mifflin, 1977), 161.

87. Galbraith, *A Short History of Financial Euphoria* (New York: Whittle Books, 1990), 14.

88. See Rowen, *Self-Inflicted Wounds*, ch. 13.

89. The 1974 figures are from Joseph Nocera, *Piece of the Action: How the Middle Class Joined the Money Class* (New York: Simon & Schuster, 1994), 197. Later figures are from Federal Reserve flow-of-funds data.

90. See J. Bradford DeLong and Barry Eichengreen, "Between Meltdown and Moral Hazard," in Jeffrey Frankel and Peter Orszag, eds., *American Economic Policy in the 1990s* (Cambridge, Mass.: MIT Press, 2002), 193.

91. For an early official defense of the policy, with notes on the problems it was creating, see Thomas Enders, "The Role of Financial Mechanisms in the Overall Oil Strategy," *Department of State Bulletin*, March 10, 1975, 312ff.

92. See Susanne Mundschenk and Stefan Collignon, "Raw Material Quotation: Pricing in Euros or Keeping the U.S. Dollar?" ECU working paper (unpublished), 2000.

93. Calleo, *Imperious Economy*, 107.

94. Collins, *MORE*, ch. 5.

95. See a 4,000-word interview of Galbraith, "Why the Economy Is in a Mess—And What to Do About It," *U.S. News & World Report*, November 3, 1975, 41–49.

96. Bank of International Settlements data cited in Calleo, *Imperious Economy*, 208.

97. Galbraith, *Short History of Financial Euphoria*, 72.

98. Nocera, *A Piece of the Action*, 33, 190–93.

99. Yankelovich quoted in Collins, *MORE*, 162.

100. "Book Briefs," *BusinessWeek*, November 20, 1978, 17.

101. Galbraith, *The Nature of Mass Poverty* (Cambridge, Mass.: Harvard University Press, 1979).

102. "The Equilibrium of Poverty," *The Economist*, May 26, 1979, 125.

103. Donnie Radcliffe, "Homecoming in Harvard's Yard; Camelot in Cambridge," *The Washington Post*, October 22, 1979, B1.

104. Keynes quoted in "God and American Diplomacy," *The Economist*, February 8, 2003, 33.

105. Galbraith, *A Life*, 525.

106. Ibid., 537.

CHAPTER 23: THE ECONOMICS OF JOY

1. Paul Samuelson and William Nordhaus, *Economics*, 12th ed. (New York: McGraw-Hill, 1985), viii (on changes in economics, and authoritative statement); 765 (on Galbraith).

2. Mankiw quoted in Malabre, *Lost Prophets*, 220.

3. Blinder, *Hard Heads, Soft Hearts*, 68.

4. Solow quoted in Malabre, *Lost Prophets*, 203.

5. Galbraith, interview with author.

6. Galbraith, *Economics in Perspective* (Boston: Houghton Mifflin, 1987), 268.

7. Ibid., 269.

8. Ibid., 267.

9. John Kenneth Galbraith, "General Keynes," *New York Review of Books*, November 22, 1984, 10ff.

10. See George Nash, *The Conservative Intellectual Movement in America* (New York: Intercollegiate Studies Institute, 1998); Rick Perlstein, *Before the Storm: Barry Goldwater and the Unmaking of the American Consensus* (New York: Hill & Wang, 2001); and Jonathan Schoenwald, *A Time for Choosing: The Rise of Modern American Conservatism* (New York: Oxford University Press, 2001).

11. Stein, *Presidential Economics*, 261.

12. William Niskanen, *Reaganomics* (New York: Oxford University Press, 1988), 15.

13. Collins, *MORE*, 165–66.

14. Galbraith, interview with author.

15. Galbraith, *A Life*, 508.

16. In the six months after Reagan's inauguration, he wrote nearly two dozen articles for *The New York Times*, *The Washington Post*, the *Des Moines Register*, the *Los Angeles Herald Examiner*, as well as the *International Herald Tribune*, *The Times* (London), *Der Spiegel*, and *Asahi Shimbun*, all warning of the dangers he foresaw in Reaganomics and Reagan's policies. See Articles Oct. 1979 to June 1981, box 2, Galbraith Papers, JFK Library.

17. Galbraith, "The Conservative Onslaught," *New York Review of Books*, January 22, 1981, 30–36.

18. For a brief synopsis of post–World War II GOP tax-cutting efforts, and their consequences, Stein, *Presidential Economics*, 237–39; Paul Studenski and Herman Krooss, *Financial History of the United States* (New York: McGraw-Hill, 1963) covers the forty years before the war.

19. Stein, *Presidential Economics*, 236–37.

20. Kevin Phillips, interview with author.

21. Rowland Evans and Robert Novak, *The Reagan Revolution* (New York: Dutton, 1981), 63.

22. Jude Wanniski, "The Mundell-Laffer Hypothesis: A New View of the Way the World Works," *The Public Interest*, Spring 1975.

23. Paul Craig Roberts, *The Supply-Side Revolution* (Cambridge, Mass.: Harvard University Press, 1984), offers a true believer's case; William Niskanen, *Reaganomics* (New York: Oxford University Press, 1988) offers a somewhat less passionate defense.

24. The relevant OECD data on GDP growth, productivity, wage growth, and income distribution are summarized in Lawrence Mishel et al., *The State of Working America 2000/2001* (Armonk, N.Y.: M. E. Sharpe, 2001), ch. 7.

25. See Institute on Taxation and Economic Policy, "An Analysis of the Cato Institute's 'The Case Against a Tennessee Income Tax' " at ctj.org/itep/tncatoan.htm.

26. Two congressional staff economists, Paul Craig Roberts and Bruce Bartlett, independently developed the supply-side idea for fiscal policy. See Roberts, *Supply-Side Revolution*, 7–33.

27. I have here condensed elements of a more complicated, circuitous history and set of arguments. For greater—and often conflicting—detail, see Stein, *Presidential Economics*, 250–53; Roberts, *Supply-Side Revolution*; and Niskanen, *Reaganomics*. Laffer's "fifty-dollar bill" is quoted in Haynes Johnson, *Sleepwalking Through History: America in the Reagan Years* (New York: Norton, 1991), 107.

28. Ed Meese, *With Reagan: The Inside Story* (Washington, D.C.: Regnery Gateway, 1992), 121, 123. Stein, *Presidential Economics*, 254–61, insists Reagan came to supply-side policy more slowly.

29. John Kenneth Galbraith, "The Uses and Excuses for Affluence," *The New York Times Magazine*, May 31, 1981, 51–58.

30. Robert Nisbet, "The Quintessential Liberal," *Commentary*, September 1981, 61–64.

31. Galbraith, interview with author.

32. John Kenneth Galbraith, "All Quiet on the Conservative Front," *The Washington Post*, April 29, 1981, A25.

33. Allan Schick, "The Deficit That Didn't Just Happen," *Brookings Review*, Spring 2002, 45–48. Calculating total U.S. military spending under Reagan involves methodological, and political, judgments. Conservatives point out that that defense spending fell dramatically after the Vietnam War as a percentage of the federal budget, a fall which alone justified the Reagan Administration's sharp boost in military spending quite apart from its foreign policy goals. Federal budget data can be misleading. Defense Department outlays aren't the government's only "military expenditures," which also include nuclear weapons research by the Department of Energy, the budget of the Department of Veterans Affairs, and the three departments combined pro rata share of annual interest payments for past deficits. Using this measure, U.S. "military expenditures" totalled more than forty percent of federal discretionary spending in the Reagan years.

34. Galbraith, "The Stockman Episode," *New York Review of Books*, June 26, 1986, 3–4.

35. Galbraith, "Nothing Succeeds Like Excess," *The New York Times*, August 28, 1989, A17.

36. Galbraith, "Let's Be Plain About Politics and Money," *The New York Times*, November 28, 1985, A27.

37. Mentions of Galbraith's name in *The New York Times* during the 1980s are calculated by author using ProQuest, which provides the newspaper online.

38. Andrea Williams, interview with author.

39. See Speeches March 1982 to January 1983, box 19, and Speeches February 1980 to March 1982, box 36, Galbraith Papers, JFK Library.

40. Stockman quoted in William Greider, "The Education of David Stockman," *The Atlantic Monthly*, December 1981, 27–40.

41. Martin Feldstein, ed., *American Economic Policy in the 1980s* (Chicago: NBER/ University of Chicago Press, 1994), 36–37.

42. Niskanen, *Reaganomics*, 33.

43. The speech appears as "The Compleat Politics of Arms Control: The American Context," in Galbraith, *A View from the Stands* (Boston: Houghton Mifflin, 1987), 8–18.

44. ECAAR's mission statement, board of directors, and published papers are at ecaar.org. Robert Schwartz, an economist and Wall Street investment adviser, initially had the idea for the organization, and went to Galbraith first, seeking his backing and endorsement; this led to the recruitment of the others. See robertjschwartz.com for a brief history.

45. On total arms sales to the Third World, see "Re-arm the World," *Common Cause Magazine*, May–June 1991, 18; on covert arms sales, see "The Second Oldest Profession," *The Economist*, February 12, 1994, 21–23.

46. See William Greider, *Secrets of the Temple* (New York: Simon & Schuster, 1987). Volcker briefly summarized his own reflections in Feldstein, *American Economic Policy in the 1980s*, 145–51.

47. Galbraith, "Up from Monetarism and Other Wishful Thinking," *New York Review of Books*, August 13, 1981, 27ff.

48. See Michael Mussa, "U.S. Monetary Policy in the 1980s," in Feldstein, *American Economic Policy in the 1980s*, 104, 145ff.

49. See J. Bradford DeLong, "The Triumph of Monetarism?," *Journal of Economic Perspectives*, Winter 2000, 83–94, offers a balanced view on why "political monetarism" has been eclipsed, though he rightly notes that economists are more deeply attentive to monetary policy today than in the Keynesian days.

50. Michael Prowse, "Greenspan Upbeat on U.S. Economy," *Financial Times*, February 20, 1993, 3.

51. See Alan Blinder, "Comments," in Jeffrey Frankel and Peter Orszag, *American Economic Policy in the 1990s* (Cambridge, Mass.: MIT Press, 2002), 46. See also N. Gregory Mankiw, "U.S. Monetary Policy in the 1990s" in ibid. for a detailed look at Greenspan's performance.

52. See Bob Woodward, *Maestro: Greenspan's Fed and the American Boom* (New York: Simon & Schuster, 2000), on the adulation accorded Greenspan.

53. Galbraith, interview with author.

54. Friedman quoted in Frankel and Orszag, *American Economic Performance*, 19.

55. Galbraith, "Big Shots," *New York Review of Books*, May 12, 1988, 44–47.

56. Galbraith, "Nothing Succeeds like Excess."

57. See Steven Neil Kaplan, "The Evolution of U.S. Corporate Governance," *Capital Ideas*, Winter 1998.

58. Galbraith, "From Stupidity to Cupidity," *New York Review of Books*, November 24, 1988, 12ff.

59. Galbraith, interview with author.
60. Galbraith, interview with author. Author's JSTOR search of the twenty-five leading economic journals shows barely a dozen articles discussing the "arms race" in the text between 1945 and 1971; that number doubled by 1987.
61. Lamson, *Speaking of Galbraith*, xi–xiv, and Galbraith, interview with author.
62. Samuel Bowles, Richard Edwards, and William Shepherd, eds., *Unconventional Wisdom* (Boston: Houghton Mifflin, 1989).
63. For a comprehensive introduction to neo-Keynesian thought, see N. Gregory Mankiw and David Romer, eds., *New Keynesian Economics* (Cambridge, Mass.: MIT Press, 1993). Many of the contributors saw their work as a response to the New Classical paradigm that grew from Lucas's work on rational expectations; the absence of any discussion of its implications for public policy is striking. For example, after using elaborate econometric testing to show that concentrated industries enjoy substantially higher profits than competitive ones (a conclusion that Galbraith had made central to *The New Industrial State* twenty-five years earlier), the author blandly observes, "The most important implication of excess capacity and market power in many industries is that businesses have little or no incentive to expand to full capacity," and then concludes vaguely that unspecified "procompetitive government policies . . . would increase output and welfare" (v. 1, 412).
64. The remark was made during an interview of a group of Harvard economists, including the author, for a three-part series in *The Washington Post*, "Reality Check: The Economic Perception Gap," October 13–15, 1996; this remark was not, however, quoted.
65. Russell Jacoby, *The Last Intellectuals* (New York: Basic Books, 1987), 7.
66. Ibid., 162–64.
67. Ibid., 234.
68. Leonard Silk, "Less Than Physics, More Than Beanbag," *The New York Times Book Review*, October 25, 1987, 27.
69. Galbraith, "The Heartless Society," *The New York Times Magazine*, September 2, 1984, 44.
70. Ibid., 45.

CHAPTER 24: JOY FADES

1. Organization for Economic Cooperation and Development data cited in Derek Bok, *The State of the Nation* (Cambridge, Mass.: Harvard University Press, 1996), 25–26. As part of their defense of Reaganomics, conservatives have argued that Europe has "lagged behind" America because of its welfare policies and labor market rigidities. On whether Europe is in fact "behind" America, see John Schmitt and Lawrence Mishel, "The United States and Europe: Who's Really Behind?," in Jeffrey Madrick, ed., *Unconventional Wisdom: Alternative Perspectives on the New Economy* (New York: Century Foundation, 2000), 237–56.
2. See Claudia Goldin and Robert Margo, "The Great Compression: The U.S. Wage Structure at Mid-Century," *Quarterly Journal of Economics*, February 1992, 1–34. Wage differences between high and low earners were compressed in the 1940s, remained stable for over three decades, then spread back out to pre-1940s levels in the 1980s, and narrowed only slightly in the late 1990s.
3. Timothy Smeeding and Peter Gottschalk, "The International Evidence on Income Distribution in Modern Economies," paper presented at Population Asso-

ciation of America conference, New Orleans, May 1996; Galbraith, interview with author (on Russian inequality).

4. National surveys in the two decades after 1977 show the percentage of households with two income earners rose from 66 to 78 percent, and both husbands and wives reported longer work weeks. See Families and Work Institute, "The 1997 National Study of the Changing Workforce," at familiesandworkinst.org.

5. See Mishel et al., *The State of Working America 2001*, ch. 3 (especially table 3.4).

6. *The Downsizing of America: A New York Times Special Report* (New York: Times Books, 1996), ch. 11 (polling results).

7. Bok, *State of the Nation*, 207–9.

8. Galbraith, *A Journey Through Economic Time* (Boston: Houghton Mifflin, 1994), 211.

9. Galbraith, "The New Dialectic," *The American Prospect*, Summer 1994, 9–11, offers a succinct summary of his skepticism toward claims of great novelty regarding globalization or the information economy, while maintaining that older analytic structures offer still-powerful insights by measuring political interests, consequences for income distribution, changes in institutional power, and so forth.

10. For Wildavsky and Moynihan quotes, see Collins, *MORE*, 204. Galbraith's observations on both are from Galbraith, interview with author.

11. Reagan's domestic policy chief, Martin Anderson, claimed that the United States didn't have balanced budgets in the 1980s "because those with the real power to decide . . . consciously and deliberately decided to unbalance the federal budget . . . [T]he real culprit in federal spending is the Congress . . . The president may propose the . . . budget . . . but it is the Congress that disposes . . . Time and time again [the] president . . . sent budgets to the U.S. Congress to limit and control federal spending. Time and time again, the Congress has rebuffed those plans, and substituted levels of spending they, and they alone, considered appropriate." The economist Brad DeLong has noted that this is simply not true. "The overwhelming proportion of the deficits of [the 1980s] were already proposed in President Reagan's and President Bush's original budget submissions. There was no explosion of federal spending over and above what the presidents had asked for. More than four-fifths of the 1980s deficits were 'presidential.' Less than one-fifth were 'congressional.'" See "Ancient History: The Deficits of the 1980s," at j-bradford-delong.net. See also Blinder, *Hard Heads, Soft Hearts*, 101.

12. Blinder, *Hard Heads, Soft Hearts*, 103.

13. Top marginal tax rates on joint incomes were more than 80 percent in the Eisenhower years, and bottomed in the mid-20 percent range in the Reagan years, before being raised under Bush and Clinton to close the deficits. See Federal Reserve Bank of Cleveland, "A Brief History of Marginal Income Tax Rates," *Economic Trends*, January 2002, at clevelandfed.org.

14. James Poterba, "Federal Budget Policy in the 1980s," in Feldstein, *American Economic Policy in the 1980s*, 269.

15. James Crotty, "The Effects of Increased Product Market Competition and Changes in Financial Markets," working paper, University of Massachusetts, Political Economy Research Institute, 2002, 12–13.

16. The OECD's econometric evaluation of the period's real interest rates singles

out the explicit effect of government liberalization policies, rather than "market forces," in maintaining them. See Adrian Orr et al., "Real Long-term Interest Rates: The Evidence from Pooled Time-Series," OECD Economic Studies, no. 25 (Paris: OECD, 1995).

17. Real long-term interest rates in the G-7 countries averaged 2.6 percent in the 1960s, fell to 0.4 percent in the 1970s, and then remained above 5 percent into the early 1990s. Even in the Clinton years, they averaged 3.8 percent—well above modern historical levels. See IMF, *World Economic Outlook*, April 2002, 223, and David Felix, "Asia and the Crisis of Financial Globalization," in Dean Baker et al., eds., *Globalization and Progressive Economics* (New York: Cambridge University Press, 1998), 184.

18. Determining exactly how much money poured in from foreign countries in response to these high rates is difficult. See Dorothy Meadow Sobol, "Foreign Ownership of U.S. Treasury Securities: What the Data Show and Do Not Show," *Current Issues in Economics and Finance*, May 1998, at newyorkfed.org.

19. See Roger Lowenstein, *When Genius Failed* (New York: Random House, 2000).

20. See the Cato Institute's Daniel Griswold, "America's Record Trade Deficit—a Symbol of Economic Strength," at freetrade.org, or the National Center for Policy Analysis, "The Meaningless Trade Deficit," at ncpa.org.

21. *Economic Report of the President, 2001* (Washington, D.C.: GPO, 2001), 392.

22. Bennett Harrison and Barry Bluestone, *The Deindustrialization of America* (New York: Free Press, 1983), offer the classic progressive argument; while accepting that the decline of manufacturing as a share of GDP relative to services is "natural" as economies "mature," they argue that government policies heightened and accelerated the process. Richard McKenzie, *Fugitive Jobs* (Cambridge, Mass.: Ballinger, 1984), is one of the better "pro–free market" attempts to refute Harrison and Bluestone. Stephen Cohen and John Zysman, *Manufacturing Matters: The Myth of the Post-Industrial Economy* (New York: CFR/Basic Books, 1987), argued that the deindustrialization argument was "overstated." But two decades later these refutations seem overstated: manufacturing has kept declining as a share of GDP, and the number of jobs in bellwether industries like steel and auto continues to decline. The Rust Belt did see an economic recovery in the 1990s, with substantial new job creation and a return of regional population growth as exports strengthened. But the largest factor in the recovery was a significant increase in labor-force participation rates, meaning simply that more people went to work, a fairly primitive achievement. See Federal Reserve Bank of Chicago, "Assessing the Midwest Economy: Looking Back to the Future" (Chicago: Federal Reserve Bank, 1997). The 1990s improvement was temporary in any case; manufacturing lost over one million jobs in the first three years in the new century.

23. For farm data, see Anne Bridges, "Is Another Farm Crisis Inevitable?" unpublished research paper, University of Nebraska; on the costs of the 1990s Freedom to Farm Act, see Robert Scott, "Exported to Death," briefing paper (Washington, D.C., Economic Policy Institute, 2001). GOP confidence that U.S. farmers would prosper under the new "free market" system was fed by a surge of American farm exports to Asia in the early 1990s. Those exports were being encouraged by the interconnectedness of the yen's rise against the dollar after the Plaza Agreement, Japan's economic bubble, and Tokyo's investments in

what became the Asian bubble. When the Asian bust came, U.S. agriculture paid the price as Asia's export demand collapsed.

24. "Governors Warned of Revolt Against Costly Farm Subsidies," *Journal of Commerce*, July 28, 1987, 12A.

25. See Robert Litan, "Banks and Real Estate: Regulating the Unholy Alliance," in Litan, Lynn Brown, and Eric Rosengren, eds., *Real Estate and the Credit Crunch* (Boston: Federal Reserve Bank of Boston, 1992), 187–217, and Donald Hester, "Financial Institutions and the Collapse of the Real Estate Market," in ibid., 114–35. Conservative economists have responded by insisting that all the private sector actors behaved rationally, and that it was the failure to deregulate even faster and more extensively that explains the problem. See Raymond Owens, "Commercial Real Estate Overbuilding," Working Paper 94-06 (Richmond, Va.: Federal Reserve Bank of Richmond, 1994).

26. For an excellent summary history of the crisis and bibliography, see FDIC, "The S&L Crisis: A Chrono-Bibliography," at fdic.gov.

27. Galbraith, "Taking the Sting Out of Capitalism," *The New York Times*, May 26, 1985, F1.

28. Seidman's family had established the prestigious Seidman Award in Political Economy; Galbraith was its second recipient, in 1975.

29. See Hobart Rowen, *Self-Inflicted Wounds*, 215–17. Chapter 10 is a useful introduction to the political and policy origins of the banking and S&L crisis.

30. A Federal Reserve Bank survey of thirty-nine major studies of the 6,300 bank mergers, worth $1.2 trillion, that took place between 1980 and 1993, concludes that "findings of the operating performance studies are generally consistent. Almost all of these studies that find no gain in efficiency also find no improvement in profitability if they include both measures. In contrast, the six studies that show at least some indication of a performance improvement do not obtain consistent efficiency and profitability results, or they are unique in some respect, or both. In general, despite substantial diversity among the nineteen operating performance studies, the findings point strongly to a lack of improvement in efficiency or profitability as a result of bank mergers, and these findings are robust both within and across studies and over time" (Stephen Rhoades, "A Summary of Merger Performance Studies in Banking, 1980–93, and an Assessment of the 'Operating Performance' and 'Event Study' Methodologies," Federal Reserve Bank staff study no. 167 [Washington, D.C.: Federal Reserve Bank, July 1994]; see also Rhoades, "Bank Mergers and Industrywide Structure," Federal Reserve Bank staff study no. 169 [Washington, D.C.: FRB, January 1996]).

31. See Paul Joskow and Roger Noll, "Economic Regulation," in Feldstein, *American Economic Policy in the 1980s*, 367–437, for a clear—and surprisingly harsh—evaluation of deregulation efforts under Reagan and Bush. It concludes that the net regulation of markets by government, instead of declining, shifted from "economic" to "social" regulation.

32. Galbraith, interview with author.

33. After their embarrassed admission of the massive failures of "structural adjustment" in the 1990s, the World Bank and IMF focused on Poverty Reduction Strategy, which requires poor countries to show how support from the multilaterals will help reduce poverty. But the PRS itself has come under withering attack, most notably from Joseph Stiglitz, the World Bank's former chief econo-

mist (and a Nobel laureate) and from William Easterly, another highly regarded World Bank economist. See Joseph Stiglitz, *Globalization and Its Discontents* (New York: Norton, 2002); William Easterly, *The Elusive Quest for Growth* (Cambridge, Mass.: MIT Press, 2001).

34. Under the Dawes and Young plans, Germany paid roughly 86 billion marks in reparations to the Allies between 1924 and 1931. At the same time it borrowed the equivalent of 83 billion marks abroad, mainly in the United States, leaving a net German payment of only 3 billion marks. Reparations were thus effectively financed by foreign subscribers to German bonds issued by Wall Street financial houses—at significant profits for the houses. The bankers played the role of financial "statesmen" in formulating the Dawes and Young plans to solve the reparations "problem," and then as bankers floated the loans they'd identified as the "solution."

35. Peter Kilborn, "Gold Called Aid to New Economic Order," *The New York Times*, October 13, 1987, D1.

36. James Feron, "Galbraith Bids Third World Focus on Farming," *The New York Times*, October 21, 1984, 22.

37. See "Three to Visit Argentina," *The New York Times*, November 4, 1985, D1; Galbraith, interview with author.

38. Alan Riding, "Resignation Rejected in Brazil; Finance Chief's New Policies Are Under Fire," *The New York Times*, November 28, 1986, D1. Paul Craig Roberts denounced Galbraith in "The Voodoo in Brazil's 'Economic Miracle,'" *Business-Week*, December 22, 1986, 12. Roberts, who counted himself a chief apostle of supply-side economics, had been Assistant Secretary of the Treasury in Reagan's first term and helped to draft the 1981 supply-side tax cut.

39. Some economists and business writers argued that American workers lacked the discipline and commitment to match the productivity of their Japanese peers, while others focused on the "anti-competitiveness" of Japan's intimate business-government *keiretsu* networks, and the myriad yet elusive ways in which the country's exports seemed to be controlled by a handful of powerful old trading companies such as Mitsui, Sumitomo, and Mitsubishi, allied with a tight network of bankers and suppliers and supported (if not overtly directed) by key government agencies. (The Ministry of International Trade and Industry—MITI—was most often cited for carefully or perniciously, depending on one's view, coordinating the long-term investment and export strategies of the island nation's biggest business.) Chalmers Johnson, Clyde Prestowitz, James Fallows, and Karel von Wolferen were among the leading "revisionist" figures who argued broadly for emulation of the Japanese "industrial policy" model, though each had significant qualifications.

40. See Sheldon Richman, "Reagan's Record on Trade: Rhetoric vs. Reality," policy analysis no. 107 (Washington, D.C.: Cato Institute, 1988), for an especially blistering conservative review of trade policy under President Reagan.

41. The role of the Plaza Agreement, the Baker-Miyazawa Agreement, and the Louvre Accord in the development of the Japanese bubble economy of the 1980s is generally well known to trade economists, though not the general public. On Galbraith's views, see his foreword to Shigeto Tsuru, *Japan's Capitalism: Creative Defeat and Beyond* (New York: Cambridge University Press, 1996). Galbraith and Tsuru were close friends for more than half a century, and Galbraith was quick to credit Tsuru's influence on his ideas about Japanese capitalism.

See also Tsuru, *Institutional Economics Revisited* (New York: Cambridge University Press, 1992).

42. Carl-Johan Lindgren et al., *Bank Soundness and Macroeconomic Policy* (Washington, D.C.: International Monetary Fund, 1996). As the title suggests, the study examined banking system crises only, and thus understates the full number of "financial crises"—including stock market failures, currency crises, and so on—that occurred.

43. See International Monetary Fund, *World Economic Outlook* (Washington, D.C.: IMF, 1998).

44. Robert Litan, "Financial Regulation," in Feldstein, ed., *American Economic Policy in the 1980s*, 537 (table 8.10).

45. Ibid., 535–40.

46. Bryan Appleyard, "Spectrum: The Seer Who Saw It All," *The Times* (London), October 26, 1987, 12. The number of articles citing Galbraith that week was compiled by the author from Nexis, searching for "John Kenneth Galbraith," October 19–27, 1987.

47. Galbraith, "The Parallel to 1929," *The Atlantic Monthly*, January 1987, available at theatlantic.com, and Kenneth Sheets, "Is the Sky Really Falling In?," *U.S. News & World Report*, September 28, 1987, 83. Most conventional economists in the 1980s, in line with their heightened belief in the rationality of markets, were supporters of "random walk" theory and related "efficient market" models of financial markets. Robert Shiller, *Irrational Exuberance* (Princeton, N.J.: Princeton University Press, 2000), offers the richest refutation of the view, and needless to say, echoes Galbraith's views.

48. U.S. Department of Commerce, Bureau of Economic Analysis, at bea.gov, "Fixed Asset Tables," table 4.2, shows annual change rates in business investment in fixed assets (basically plant and equipment). See also "National Income and Product Accounts," table 1.16, for net fixed investment as percent of business gross product, and table 5.2, which shows that net business investment in equipment and software was no higher in 1990 than it had been in 1980.

49. Alan Friedman, "Financial Markets in Turmoil; Galbraith Discounts Depression," *Financial Times*, October 27, 1987, 2.

50. One of the most detailed rejoinders to *The New Industrial State*, by Harvard Business School professor Bruce Scott, drew on the work of Alfred Chandler, and ended up critical of the "technostructure" thesis—but in a more subtle and more qualified way than Solow had in 1967. Scott concluded that while Galbraith was generally historically accurate in his conclusions about what Scott called the "second stage" evolution of U.S. corporate structure and behavior running from the 1920s through the 1960s, most large companies were by the late 1960s in, or moving into, "stage three," in which neoclassical profit-maximization was once again powerful. But Scott then qualified this claim by admitting that major industries with heavy capital requirements—such as paper, steel, autos, oil, defense, and meat-packing—still clearly met Galbraith's "technostructure" description. See Bruce Scott, "The New Industrial State: Old Myths and New Realities," *Harvard Business Review*, March–April 1973, 133–48.

51. See James Surowiecki, "Company Man," *The New Yorker*, January 19, 1998, 72–81.

52. Crotty, "Effects of Increased Product Market Competition," 23.

53. Ibid., 24–26 (executive compensation); 27–29 (corporate debt).
54. *The Downsizing of America*, 280 (hours and pay); 311 (losses permanent); 307–8 (benefits cuts); 318 (working class).

CHAPTER 25: CENTURY'S END

1. Galbraith, "At the Age of 85, a New Cause: The Still Syndrome," *Boston Globe*, October 15, 1993, 23.
2. A colorful and accurate description of the Long Table is in Galbraith, *A Tenured Professor* (Boston: Houghton Mifflin, 1990), ch. 1.
3. Galbraith, interview with author.
4. Ibid.
5. Galbraith, *A Life*, 536. Galbraith has expressed his appreciation not only in words; since the sixties he has assigned at least 10 percent of his royalties to Mrs. Williams.
6. Reviews quoted from dust jacket of *A Tenured Professor* are in *Time*, February 26, 1990, and *New York Review of Books*, April 26, 1990. See also *Washington Post Book World*, February 11, 1990, 3 and *Boston Globe*, February 4, 1990, B44, *The New York Times Book Review*, February 11, 1990, 9, and *The New York Times*, February 21, 1990, 16.
7. Nearly a dozen papers reviewed the book; the *Times* reviews were by Christopher Lehmann-Haupt, June 14, 1993, C16, and Robert Krulwich four days later, in *The New York Times Book Review*, 8.
8. David Ottaway, "Reagan Urged to Seek Arms Breakthrough," *The Washington Post*, September 14, 1985, A23. Galbraith used the trip for a *Washington Post* editorial in which he admonished the United States about its own need to confront bureaucratic inertia and mismanagement in government and the private sector. See Galbraith, "Carrying Convergence Too Far," June 14, 1987, H7.
9. Galbraith and Stanislav Menshikov, *Capitalism, Communism and Coexistence: From the Bitter Past Toward a Better Prospect* (Boston: Houghton Mifflin, 1988). See William Diebold, Jr., "Recent Books on International Relations," *Foreign Affairs*, Summer 1988, 1119; Dimitri Simes, "The Economic Consequences of Coexistence," *Washington Post Book World*, August 7, 1988, 4.
10. See Joyce Carol Oates, "Intellectual Seduction," *The New York Times Magazine*, January 3, 1988, 18ff.
11. Galbraith, interview with author.
12. One curious Western proposal was made in late 1990, shortly before Yeltsin took power, a Henry George–style idea that called on the Soviet government to retain title to all land and use rents from it to finance its operations. The signatories included James Tobin, Robert Solow, Franco Modigliani, William Vickery, Zvi Griliches, Robert Dorfman, Carl Kaysen, and Richard Musgrave, among others. See taxreform.com.au/essays/russian.htm.
13. See Lawrence Klein and Marshall Pomer, eds., *The New Russia: A Transition Gone Awry* (Palo Alto: Stanford University Press, 2001), in which Galbraith is given explicit credit for his foresight in supporting a gradualist approach.
14. Stephen Kurkjian, "Gorbachev, in Boston, Asks Americans to Back Reform," *Boston Globe*, May 16, 1992, B1.
15. Galbraith, "The Decade," *The Guardian*, December 16, 1989, 22.
16. Galbraith, *Culture of Contentment* (Boston: Houghton Mifflin, 1992), 10.
17. See Jeffrey Stonecash et al., "Class and Party: Secular Realignment and the Sur-

vival of the Democrats Outside the South," *Political Research Quarterly*, December 2000, 731–52.

18. Galbraith, *Culture of Contentment*, 17.
19. See pollingreport.com/institut.htm.
20. Nolan McCarty et al., *Income Redistribution and the Realignment of American Politics* (Washington, D.C.: American Enterprise Institute, 1997), 1–2.
21. In ibid., ch. 5, the rich vs. poor (or, more accurately, the rich and upper-middle-class versus the middle-class and poor) divide among *voters* shows up clearly, especially in table 5-1. Between 1972 and 1992, the bottom 60 percent of *voters*, measured by income, remained Democratic rather than Republican in their party identification by roughly a two-to-one ratio. The top fifth of income-earners, however, shifted dramatically rightward, increasing their Republican identification by twelve percentage points; the second-highest fifth of income-earners (that is, roughly the upper-middle class) shifted rightward by sixteen percentage points.
22. On the asymetrical "clustering" of congressional legislators, including the virtual disappearance of Republican (but not Democratic) moderates, see ibid., figure 2–5; for the reduction of divisions within parties over "close votes" between 1947 and 1995, see figures 2–3 and 2–4; Galbraith, *Culture of Contentment*, 14.
23. Galbraith, *Culture of Contentment*, 18.
24. Ibid., 19.
25. On Gilder's own view of his influence on Reagan, see gildertech.com.
26. George Gilder, *Wealth and Poverty* (New York: Basic Books, 1981), quoted in Galbraith, *Culture of Contentment*, 101–2. Gilder was a Harvard graduate who'd been partly raised by David Rockefeller, after Gilder's father (who'd been Rockefeller's college roommate) died in World War II.

   Backed financially by the ultraconservative Smith Richardson Foundation (which also bankrolled Jude Wanniski's pioneering exposition of "supply-side" economics), Gilder was close to William Casey, Reagan's campaign manager and then buccaneer CIA director; William Simon, Nixon's former treasury secretary; and David Stockman, Reagan's first OMB director. Gilder was a consummately passionate conservative: he once proudly declared his allegiance to "the New Right because they're tough, and I think the threat of government at the moment is very serious. Moderate, compromising political figures don't have the backbone to resist the new absurdities . . . The New Right is the militant edge to the cause." (In the 1990s, Gilder shifted his passions, while retaining his conservatism, to high technology, and authors a newsletter as well as occasional books on its incandescent promise.)
27. Galbraith, *Culture of Contentment*, 103.
28. Ibid., 149.
29. Ibid., 182–83.
30. William F. Buckley, "It's a Wonderful Life, Professor," *National Review*, July 20, 1992, 39–40.
31. Robert Bartley, "The View from Galbraith's Eyrie," *Wall Street Journal*, April 8, 1992, A18.
32. Robert Bellah, "Status Quo Seekers," *The New York Times Book Review*, April 5, 1992, 10. See also Christopher Lehmann-Haupt, "Why No One Fixes What Doesn't Seem Broken," *The New York Times*, April 6, 1992, c15. Jonathan Yard-

ley, "What, Me Worry?," *The Washington Post*, April 19, 1992, 3. A Lexis-Nexis search shows twenty-six reviews, all but four quite positive. British and Canadian reviewers were especially affirmative. Sales data supplied by Houghton Mifflin to author.

33. For a sample of Clinton's 1992 campaign literature, see 4president.org/brochures/billclinton92.pdf.

34. "A Liberal Welcome," *Maclean's*, November 16, 1992, 41.

35. George McGovern, interview with author.

36. Galbraith, interview with author.

37. See Thomas Edsall, *The New Politics of Inequality* (New York: Norton, 1984), ch. 3, for an early account of the politicization of business and its electoral impact.

38. A detailed, generally sympathetic account of the Democratic Leadership Council, its overarching ideology and shifting strategies, and its relations with Bill Clinton is in Kenneth Baer, *Reinventing Democrats: The Politics of Liberalism from Reagan to Clinton* (Lawrence: University Press of Kansas, 2000).

39. David Nyhan, "Forget What I Said; Clinton's Talkfest Was Terrific," *Boston Globe*, December 17, 1992, 19. "Clinton's Bequest Reconsidered," *The American Prospect*, at prospect.org/print/v4/11/chait-j.html.

40. Time/CNN polls, "Influence in Government," August 31 to September 1, 1994.

41. For Galbraith's views of Clinton administration policies early on, see "The Return of Keynes," *New Perspectives Quarterly*, Fall 1992, 10–12. For a retrospective analysis of Clinton's tax policy, see Frankel and Orszag, *American Economic Policy in the 1990s*, ch. 3. The principal features of the 1993 bill were the modest increase in effective top income tax rates (the statutory rate increase to 39 percent, and inclusion of a new 36 percent rate overstate effective collection rates); removal of the cap on Medicare tax contributions; and the expansion of the earned income tax credit, which almost unnoticed became the country's largest means-tested income transfer program.

42. Galbraith, "Return of Keynes," 11.

43. See Frankel and Orszag, *American Economic Policy in the 1990s*, chs. 2, 3.

44. See Galbraith, "The Autonomous Military Power: An Economic View," International Conference of Dutch-Flemish Economists for Peace, The Hague, The Netherlands, May 22, 1992 (unpublished speech), and his introduction to Ruth Leger Sivard, *World Military and Social Expenditures 1992* (Washington, D.C.: World Priorities, 1992).

45. The declines noted here are in percent-of-GDP terms, not dollars. See Frankel and Orszag, *American Economic Policy in the 1990s*, 729.

46. Bill Clinton and Al Gore, *Putting People First* (New York: Times Books, 1992), 7.

47. Carville and Begala quoted in Collins, *MORE*, 218.

48. Clinton quoted in Bob Woodward, *The Agenda* (New York: Simon & Schuster, 1995), 84. See ibid., 80–146 (on formation of Clintonomics once in office, and role of bond markets).

49. Clinton quoted in Frankel and Orszag, *American Economic Policy in the 1990s*, 74.

50. See David Broder and Haynes Johnson, *The System* (Boston: Little, Brown, 1997), 38–40, 233–34. With the conservative strategist William Kristol, Gin-

grich worked consistently to kill, rather than amend or revise, any White House health-care initiative.

51. H. D. S. Greenway, "Old Lion of the Left," *Boston Globe*, July 3, 1993, B5.

52. Galbraith, interview with author (White House note). Broder and Johnson, *The System*, ch. 22, details the impact of Clinton's health-care proposals on the 1994 elections.

53. Gingrich also made clear that as far as he was concerned, "Politics and war are remarkably similar," and that when it came to financing the Republican Revolution, "the idea that a congressman would be tainted by accepting money from private industry or private sources is essentially a socialist argument." Gingrich remarks at brainyquote.com.

54. Joe Klein, personal communication with author.

55. See Baer, *Reinventing Democrats*, 237–43, and "Man of the Year," *Time*, December 25, 1995 (cover story on Gingrich).

56. John Kenneth Galbraith, "Blame History, Not the Liberals," *The New York Times*, September 19, 1995, A22.

57. Jonathan Yardley, "Galbraith, Sticking to His Guns," *The Washington Post*, April 24, 1996, C2.

58. Matthew Miller, "Big Government by Popular Demand," *The New York Times Book Review*, May 19, 1996, 19.

59. John Harris, "Among New Deal Believers, President Has His Skeptics," *The Washington Post*, April 13, 1995, A1, describes the Warm Springs event. R. W. Apple, Jr., "A Paean to Roosevelt," *The New York Times*, April 13, 1995, 1, does not mention Galbraith's or Schlesinger's remarks. See Anne Devroy, "Democratic Meeting of the Minds," *The Washington Post*, July 9, 1995, A10 (on the subsequent luncheon). Theodore Sorensen, Joseph Califano, and William vanden Heuvel joined Galbraith, Schlesinger, and the President at the luncheon.

60. See Mishel et al., *State of Working America*, chs. 1, 2, and 5.

61. For a representative introduction, see Daniel Yergin and Joseph Stanislaw, *The Commanding Heights* (New York: Simon & Schuster, 1998). On the government's aid in creating the New Economy, with special emphasis on the Federal Reserve and its chairman, Alan Greenspan, see Bob Woodward, *Maestro: Greenspan's Fed and the American Boom* (New York: Simon & Schuster, 2000). For a shrewdly skeptical view, see Jeffrey Madrick, *Why Economies Grow* (New York: Perseus, 2003).

62. The *Fortune* writer Joseph Nocera was among the first to resurrect this phrase, which had first appeared in the 1920s to describe that decade's stock market run-up.

63. Mishel et al., *State of Working America*, 141–43, 267–69.

64. Ibid., 55. See also Elizabeth Mehren, "John Kenneth Galbraith," *Los Angeles Times*, December 12, 1999, M3. For a comprehensive review of executive compensation that supports Galbraith's thesis about managerial independence from shareholders' and directors' oversight on issues of executive pay, see Lucian Bebchuk et al., "Managerial Power and Rent Extraction in the Design of Executive Compensation," NBER working paper 9068 (Cambridge, Mass.: National Bureau of Economic Research, July 2002).

65. See "49th Annual Executive Pay Survey," *BusinessWeek*, April 19, 1999. On how,

during the markets' fall thereafter, CEOs successfully sold stock even while encouraging others to buy, see Mark Gimien, "You Bought. They Sold.," *Fortune*,
September 2, 2002.

66. Mishel et al., *State of Working America*, 50 (share of income growth), and Kevin
    Phillips, *Wealth and Democracy* (New York: Broadway Books, 2002), 361–62.

67. Mishel et al., *State of Working America*, 286.

68. Ibid., 288 (table 5.1).

69. Clinton, Rubin, and Greenspan quoted in Collins, *MORE*, 223.

70. Joseph Stiglitz, *The Roaring Nineties* (New York: Norton, 2003), 90–91.

71. See Galbraith, *A Journey Through Economic Time*, 196. For discussion of
    "C block" losses, see Congressional Budget Office, *The Budget and Economic
    Outlook: Fiscal Years 2001–2010* (Washington, D.C.: GPO, 2001), section 9, ap-
    pendix B. The problem of spectrum auctions wasn't America's alone; Europe
    faced its own fiasco of problems after wild overbidding for telecommunications
    licenses. The history of rigged bidding for initial public offerings (IPOs) of new
    corporations' stock is itself illustrative: see Jeremy Bulow and Paul Klemperer,
    "Prices and the Winner's Curse," *Rand Journal of Economics*, Winter 2002,
    1–21, and Paul Klemperer, "What Really Matters in Auction Design," *Journal of
    Economic Perspectives*, Winter 2002, 169–89.

72. Stiglitz, *Roaring Nineties*, ch. 5, provides a lucid nontechnical introduction.

73. For a succinct account, see J. Bradford DeLong and Barry Eichengreen, "Be-
    tween Meltdown and Moral Hazard," and related comments and discussion, in
    Frankel and Orszag, *American Economic Policy in the 1990s*, ch. 4.

74. Stiglitz, *Globalization and Its Discontents*, 97 (figures cited). Stiglitz's book, with
    its harsh indictment of the IMF (and, to a lesser extent, the World Bank, where
    he'd worked as senior vice president and chief economist) helped catalyze the
    debate.

75. On numbers of wars and war-related deaths, see Sivard, *World Military and So-
    cial Expenditures 1992*, 20.

76. Galbraith quoted in Francine Cunningham, "Markets May Dip," *The Irish
    Times*, December 18, 1998, 54.

77. Galbraith, *Name-Dropping From F.D.R. On* (Boston: Houghton Mifflin, 1999);
    Geoffrey Hodgson, "It's the Economy, Sir," *The New York Times Book Review*,
    July 11, 1999, 11.

78. R. W. Apple, "Critic of War in Vietnam Is Now Praising Johnson," *The New York
    Times*, November 27, 1999, A11.

79. Dan Atkinson, "Underside," *The Guardian*, July 3, 1999, 26.

CONCLUSION: THE GALBRAITH LEGACY

1. Galbraith, interview with author; John Kenneth Galbraith, *The Culture of Contentment* (Boston: Houghton Mifflin, 1992), 57 (on Galbraith's critical views toward airline deregulation).

2. Jacqueline Salmon, "The President's Honor Roll; Clinton Awards Medal to 15,"
   The Washington Post, August 10, 2000, C1. (Nixon's resignation on August 8,
   1974, was one day and twenty-six, not twenty-five, years earlier.)

3. Virginia Postrel, "Presidential Medal of Ignorance," *Forbes*, September 18,
   2002, 108.

4. Galbraith, interview with author.

5. Salmon, "President's Honor Roll," *Washington Post*.

6. Frankel and Orszag, *American Economic Policy in the 1990s*, 1–2.

7. David Wessel, "What's Wrong?," *The Wall Street Journal*, June 20, 2002, 1.

8. Galbraith, *The Economics of Innocent Fraud* (Boston: Houghton Mifflin, 2004).

9. E. J. Dionne, "Learning from the Enron Moment," *The Washington Post*, January 18, 2002, A25. Although Galbraith wryly conceded that the *Post* made him sound more like James Madison than himself, he willingly accepted the compliment. "In moments such as these, it is better to keep the best company possible," he said with a smile (Galbraith, interview with author).

10. Clinton, in an interview in the spring of 2002, said he still hoped to persuade Galbraith to undertake the project. Asked to describe his own memoirs, Clinton replied, "I want this book to be accessible to people, but I also want it to contain the serious ideas that were at the core of my whole public life and especially my presidency. But I don't want it to be too policy wonky. I may even do a series of shorter books when I finish focused on the policies and the ideas and throwing them into the future a little bit. Then I'll take a look at writing a textbook on government with John Kenneth Galbraith, who [is in his nineties but] has great mental acuity" (Jonathan Alter, "Life Is Fleeting, Man," *Newsweek*, April 2, 2002, 42).

11. Galbraith, interview with author.

12. See Elisabeth Warren, *The Two-Income Trap* (New York: Basic Books, 2003).

13. Citizens for Tax Justice, "CTJ's Bush Tax Cuts Scorecard," April 13, 2004; ctj.org/paf.gwbpi.pdf.

14. Galbraith, "Challenges of the New Millenium," *Finance & Development*, December 1999, 2–6.

15. Joseph Stiglitz, "The Roaring Nineties," *The Atlantic Monthly*, October 2002, is a brief and easily read introduction, at theatlantic.com/issues/2002/10/stiglitz.htm.

16. Waligorski, *Liberal Economics and Democracy*, 5.

17. See Robert Fogel, "Remarks on the Role of Research Universities in Innovation, Social Mobility, and the Quality of Life," paper presented at American Association of Universities Centennial Meeting, April 17, 2000, at aau.edu/aau/Fogel.html.

18. See Anne Krueger et al., "Report on the Commission on Graduate Education in Economics," and W. Lee Hansen, "The Education and Training of Economics Doctorates," *Journal of Economic Literature*, Fall 1991, 1035–87. See also Richard Parker, "Can Economists Save Economics?," *American Prospect*, March 21, 1993, at prospect.org/print/V4/13/parker-r.html.

19. David Colander and Arjo Klamer, "The Making of an Economist," *Journal of Economic Perspectives*, Fall 1987, 95–111.

20. The Morgan Stanley economist Stephen Roache quoted in John Cassidy, "The Decline of Economics," *The New Yorker*, December 2, 1996, 50–60.

21. Lawrence Summers, "The Scientific Illusion in Empirical Economics," *Scandinavian Journal of Economics*, Spring 1991, 146.

22. Coase quoted in Edward Leamer, "Let's Take the Con Out of Econometrics," *American Economic Review*, March 1983, 37. Leamer, himself an econometrician is even harsher in this article than Summers and Coase. "After three decades of churning out estimates, the econometrics club finds itself under critical scrutiny and facing incredulity as never before . . . The haphazard way we individually and collectively study the fragility of inferences leaves most of us

unconvinced that any inference is believable . . . If it turns out [as I suspect it will] that almost all inferences from economic data are fragile, I suppose we shall have to revert to our old methods lest we lose our customers in government, business, and on the boardwalk at Atlantic City." Leamer, *Specification Search: Ad Hoc Inferences with Non-experimental Data* (New York: Wiley, 1978) is still an invaluable introduction to the ongoing problems of econometrics.

23. On the painfully common misuse of statistical inference, see Dierdre McCloskey and Stephen Ziliak, "The Standard Errors of Regression," *Journal of Economic Literature*, March 1996, 97–114; on economists' distrust of empirical results, see Thomas Mayer, "Data Mining: a Reconsideration," working paper no. 97-15, University of California, Davis, April 1997.

24. Justin Fox, "What in the World Happened to Economics?," *Fortune*, March 15, 1992, 92, 102.

25. *The Economist*, "Ten Modern Classics: A Special Report" (London: *The Economist*, 1993), 4.

26. See Simon London "Lunch with the FT: Milton Friedman," *Financial Times*, June 6, 2003, 16; and Robert Solow, "How Did Economics Get That Way, and What Way Did It Get?," *Daedalus*, Winter 1997, 39–58; Galbraith, interview with author.

27. For a nontechnical introduction to the issues and challenges raised by these innovators, see Robert Gilpin, *Global Political Economy* (Princeton: Princeton University Press, 2001), chs. 5, 8, 12 (on the theories); ch. 6 (on their political significance); and chs. 2–3 (on political economy versus neoclassical economics). Economists have a vast array of technical literature available; Allan Drazen, *Political Economy in Macroeconomics* (Princeton: Princeton University Press, 2000), usefully if somewhat cautiously summarizes some of this theory and its means of application.

28. Amartya Sen, "Global Doubts," Commencement Address, Harvard University, June 6, 2000, Harvard Archives, Harvard University.

29. Sen quoted in Jonathan Steele, "The Guardian Profile: John Kenneth Galbraith," *The Guardian*, April 6, 2002, 6.

ACKNOWLEDGMENTS

While researching and writing this book I benefited greatly from the help and kindness of many men and women. Several extraordinary figures long associated with Harvard University were generous in sharing their knowledge and experience: Derek Bok, Henry Rosovsky, John Dunlop, Wassily Leontief, Edward Mason, and Raymond Vernon all helped me better understand the modern history of Harvard, its Economics Department, and Galbraith's career there; Graham Allison and Jonathan Moore were especially helpful in describing the early days of the Kennedy School of Government and Galbraith's involvement in its founding.

Arthur Schlesinger, Jr., was unstintingly generous in sharing his recollections and judgments about Galbraith's life in politics from the New Deal on, including the many years when they worked together in Americans for Democratic Action, the Democratic Advisory Council, many Democratic presidential campaigns, and the Kennedy administration. Paul Sweezy gave me several key insights into the Walsh-Sweezy debates of the 1930s, Galbraith's subsequent relations with Paul Baran, and the attitudes of America's left and of Marxist economists toward Galbraith. On Galbraith's time at the State Department and on early postwar economics, Charles Kindleberger and Walt W. Rostow, who worked with him at the State Department, were invaluable guides, while Leon Keyserling gave me additional insights into the tenor of liberal economics in the 1950s and the impact of *The Affluent Society*. Theodore Sorensen was also very helpful, on both John F. Kennedy's friendship with Galbraith and Galbraith as a presidential adviser. On Kennedy's complex and subtle relations to the various Keynesian strands in the policies of the New Frontier—including the influence of Walter Heller and the Council of Economic Advisors and Galbraith's frequently conflicting advice—I benefited especially from discussion with Sorensen, Rostow, and James Tobin. Sorensen, Schlesinger, and Rostow were also, needless to say, invaluable on President Kennedy's views on and actions in Vietnam and Laos, and Galbraith's influence. On Galbraith's ambassadorship to India, Harry Rositzke, who was CIA Station Chief when Galbraith was in India, offered especially useful reflections; Graham Allison advised on the specifics of the Sino-Indian conflict and its overlap with the Cuban Missile Crisis.

Galbraith's sister, Catherine Denholm, was a rich source of biographical insight into her brother and their family, and life in rural Ontario, and his niece Lynda Galbraith generously shared genealogical research, family letters, newspaper clippings, and photos. Peggy Lamson, who wrote a personal biography of Galbraith, kindly shared her notes and insights at an early stage of my work, helping me immeasurably thereby.

Andrea Williams, who has worked as Galbraith's principal assistant and editor since the late 1950s, was unfailingly generous in guiding me through the enormous files that have accumulated over the years, in sharing invaluable anecdotal insights, and in meticulously correcting errors and omissions in the manuscript.

In a more general way, I am indebted to a number of Cambridge friends and colleagues who shared their ideas and their reactions to mine with great generosity. When Robert Reich returned from Washington to Cambridge in 1996, he and I began a small monthly convocation of scholars, journalists, and political consultants, who over pizza and wine gave me a perfect forum for testing many of the ideas that found their way into this book. I am especially indebted to Reich, Susan Eaton, David Ellwood, Richard Freeman, Marshall Ganz, Lani Guinier, Jennifer Hochschild, Christopher Jencks, Larry Katz, Robert Kuttner, Lisa Lynch, Jane Mansbridge, John Martilla, Russ Muirhead, Katherine Newman, Michael Sandel, Theda Skocpol, and Ralph Whitehead for the lessons of intellect and commitment they so graciously shared.

At the Kennedy School, Robert Lawrence and Robert Stavins have been especially patient and informative in conversations about the modern state of economic theory and policy, and I have also gained much by listening and talking with Mary Jo Bane, Francis Bator, Dani Rodrik, Fred Schauer, William Julius Wilson, and Richard Zeckhauser. I am indebted to Marvin Kalb and Alex Jones, past and current director, respectively, of the Shorenstein Center; I can't thank them enough for their willingness to let me teach and write here. In the Economics Department, I learned much from participating in seminars led by Jeffrey Sachs, Brad DeLong, and Janos Kornai especially; farther away from Harvard I especially profited from a lengthy summertime conversation two years ago on the interplay of Keynes, Keynesianism, and modern economics with Amartya Sen and Joseph Stiglitz, which helped me better focus my explanation of some of the Keynesian elements in Galbraith's ideas.

I am also deeply indebted to several people who read early versions of this book, in whole or in part, and whose comments and criticisms significantly improved the drafts: Graham Allison, Derek Bok, Sissela Bok, James Carroll, James Galbraith, Charles Kindleberger, Robert Kuttner, Wassily Leontief, Stephen Marglin, Henry Rosovsky, Stanley Sheinbaum, and Robert Vipond all made this a better, more accurate book; they of course bear no responsibility for any errors that persist. I am no less indebted, with the same caveat, to Barbara Wallraff, who read the proofs for me.

There are innumerable libraries and librarians without whose help much of my research would have been impossible. Most important were the John F. Kennedy Presidential Library in Boston, where today most of Galbraith's papers now reside, and several Harvard libraries—especially Littauer, Lamont, Houghton, and the Pusey Archives—whose collections contain invaluable primary materials on Galbraith, the Department of Economics, and Harvard generally during Galbraith's career. In addition, the Johnson, Roosevelt, Truman and Nixon presidential libraries, the research library at the Wisconsin State Historical Society, and the libraries at the University of California, the University of Chicago, Columbia University, and Time, Inc., yielded crucial materials that enriched my work. The Library of Congress and the National Archives provided rich troves of information on Galbraith's several careers in Washington.

Needless to say, without the generous cooperation of Professor and Mrs. Galbraith, this would have been a much less complete biography. He sat for dozens of taped interviews with me over four years, while I worked through his writings, his files, and interviews with many of his colleagues, critics, and friends. His memory, even for events fifty or sixty years earlier, was remarkably durable and accurate, corroborated by written records and interviews with others. Mrs. Galbraith was no less generous in sharing with me family memories, photographs, letters, and news clippings, and her own impressions of their years together and of the people they have known. She was also consistently helpful in clarifying and, when necessary, correcting her husband's recollections.

Galbraith was an ideal biographical subject—obviously interested that I get the record straight, but meticulous in refusing to shape my judgments or conclusions. He opened literally all his files to me, including his tax returns (save for a few still-classified files related to his term as ambassador to India, of which portions were very recently declassified). That openness was a godsend in one sense and a challenge in another, since his prolific output and involvements meant that hundreds of archival boxes, dozens of file cabinets, and occasionally unsorted piles of material were all there for me to search through. (At one point in my research, I spent a sweltering July and August in the Galbraiths' basement, dressed in T-shirt and shorts, sitting on an aluminum folding chair beneath a hanging naked lightbulb, poring through papers that had not yet been turned over to the Kennedy Library.) Galbraith's only request, made at the start of this project, was that he be allowed to read the final proofs of this book before it was printed.

In carrying out my research, I was helped by Joshua Good, Parker Everett, and Christine Connare. Ms. Connare also patiently retyped various drafts of the manuscript, becoming uniquely adept at interpreting handwritten marginal notes and filling out partially complete citations.

Donald Cutler was the perfect guide, counsel, and collaborator as my agent. In the overall process of bringing this book to print, Elisabeth Sifton has been a singular editor—demanding, understanding, with a keen eye for arguments, facts, and stylistic infelicities. She single-handedly has made this a much finer book than it otherwise would have been. No author can hope for better treatment than I received in her brilliant hands.

A final, sad note: several of the men and women I have thanked here have passed away since they first gave so generously of themselves for this book: John Dunlop, James Tobin, Wassily Leontief, Ed Mason, Ray Vernon, Paul Sweezy, Charlie Kindleberger, Walt Rostow, Leon Keyserling, Harry Rositzke, and Catherine Denholm were all, like Galbraith, born early in the twentieth century. I attended funerals or memorial services for most of them, where I was reminded once again of how much each gave, and why their memories will live on.

Yet in those same years, and with great joy, I have become the father of two magnificent young sons. It is for Sam and Tom, and their generation, that ultimately this book is written—as a means to help keep alive and carry forward that enduring conversation about the purpose and direction of our common lives in which John Kenneth Galbraith has played such an important part.

INDEX